Beginnings of Interior Environments

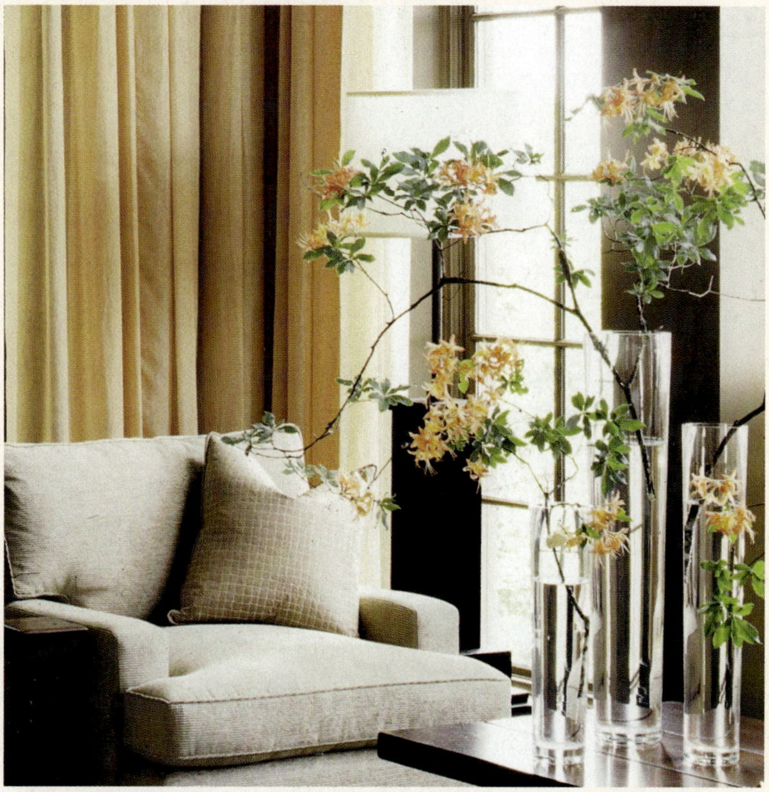

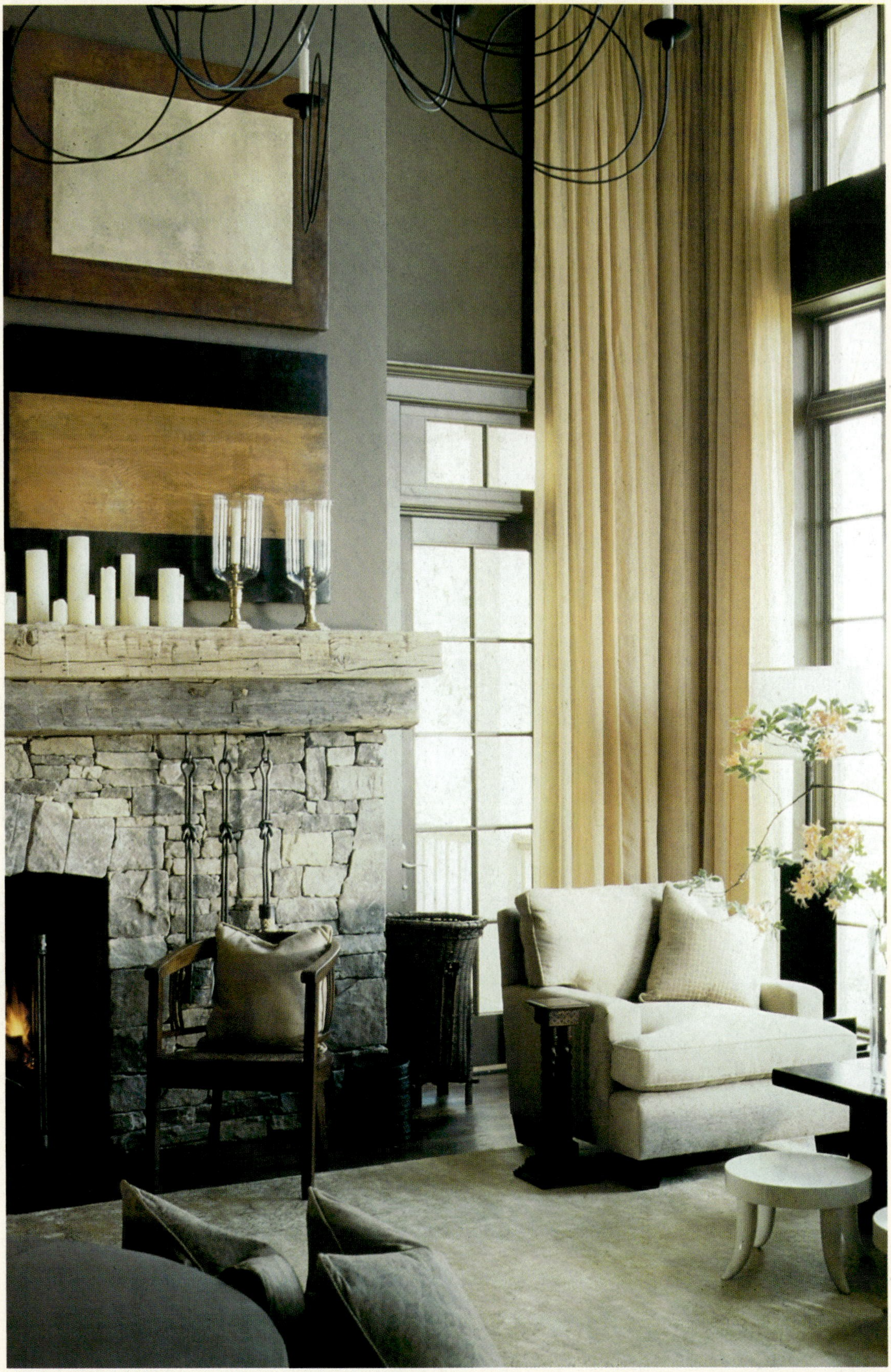

This stately living space speaks to the emotions of retreat and comfort. According to the designer, the interior "is traditional but with a contemporary edge. It's very clean, but very layered and rich. . . ." The play on flowing sheer apricot window treatments is juxtaposed to the rough ashlar stone fireplace. Natural woods and basketry mixed with highly polished stools and coffee tables add to the luxurious ambiance. (Architect: Harrison Design Associates. Designer: Phillip Sides Interior Design. Photograph by Tria Giovan. Courtesy of Southern Accents.*)*

Beginnings of Interior Environments

Ninth Edition

Phyllis Sloan Allen

Lynn M. Jones, ASID, IIDA, IDEC Brenau University

Miriam F. Stimpson Brigham Young University

PEARSON
Prentice Hall

Upper Saddle River, New Jersey 07458

Library of Congress Cataloging-in-Publication Data

Allen, Phyllis Sloan.
Beginnings of interior environments / Phyllis Sloan Allen, Lynn M. Jones, Miriam F. Stimpson.—9th ed.
p. cm.
Includes bibliographical references and index.
ISBN 0-13-045770-1 (alk. paper)
1. Interior decoration—Handbooks, manuals, etc. I. Title: Interior environments. II. Jones, Lynn M., III. Stimpson, Miriam F. IV. Title.
NK2115 .A59 2003
728—dc21 2003010740

Editor in Chief: *Stephen Helba*
Executive Editor: *Vernon Anthony*
Editorial Assistant: *Ann Brunner*
Prepress Production: *Chris and Monica Ohlinger, Ohlinger Publishing Services*
Managing Editor: *Mary Carnis*
Production Editor: *Emily Bush, Carlisle Publishers Services*
Production Liaison: *Janice Stangel*
Director of Manufacturing and Production: *Bruce Johnson*
Manufacturing Buyer: *Cathleen Petersen*
Creative Director: *Cheryl Asherman*
Photography Coordinator: *Philip A. Jones*
Copy Editor: *Sarah Greer Bush*
Senior Marketing Manager: *Ryan DeGrote*
Cover Design: *Mark A. Taylor*
Cover Illustration: Architect: *Harrison Design Associates* Designer: *Phillip Sides Interior Design. Photograph by Tria Giovan. Courtesy of* Southern Accents.

Pearson Education LTD.
Pearson Education Singapore, Pte. Ltd
Pearson Education, Canada, Ltd
Pearson Education–Japan
Pearson Education Australia PTY, Limited
Pearson Education North Asia Ltd
Pearson Educaçion de Mexico, S.A. de C.V.
Pearson Education Malaysia, Pte. Ltd

10 9 8 7 6

ISBN: 0-13-045770-1

Dedication

To all beginning interior designers who desire to enrich the quality of life through the respectful use of our earth's resources: May each of you come to appreciate the Earth's gifts and use them wisely in your future interiors.

Brief Contents

Contents

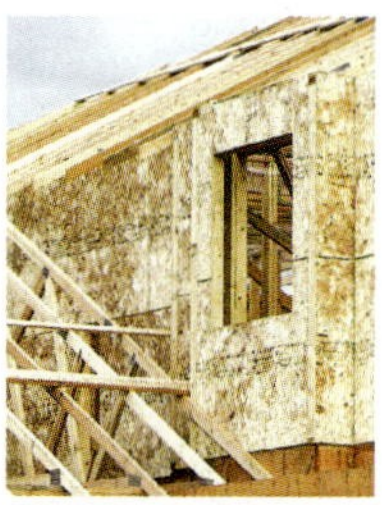

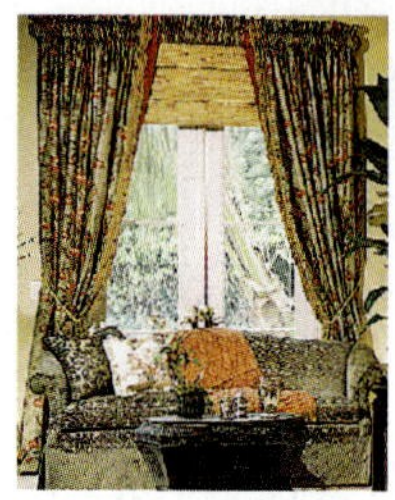

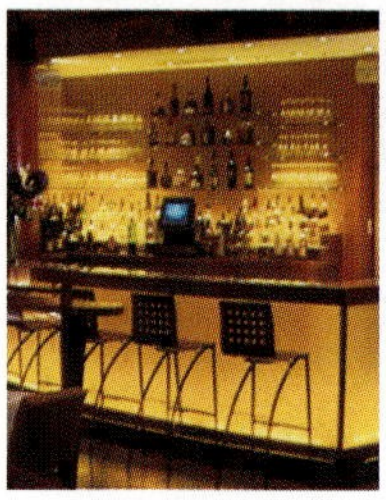

Preface

The field of interior design encompasses a unique blend of art and science. I have always told my students that successful designers construct a balance between their left and right brains. The designer's goal in any interior should be to analyze the needs and desires of the client, and then through the synthesis of this information to create a healthful and safe environment that enhances the client's quality of life. It is the mission of this text to assist beginning designers in achieving this goal.

Significant Changes in the Ninth Edition

The ninth edition of *Beginnings of Interior Environments* discusses foundation information that assists the reader in understanding the nature of interior design and the practice of the interior design profession. The text continues in the tradition of earlier editions as an introductory and practical approach to understanding interior design. Although early editions focused primarily on residential design, the more recent editions expand readers' awareness of commercial design as well. The ninth edition also includes new information on sustainable design, Internet resources, and on aspects of multicultural awareness.

The most significant change in the ninth edition is a discussion on visual literacy, including Gestalt psychology, patterning, and organization. This is followed by a discussion on *concept* and its application in the interior design process. Special features on sustainable design and actual design scenarios have been updated.

Much care has been taken to update images and ensure that illustrations and figures clearly enhance the text discussion. One of the greatest challenges of updating texts is as Don Schlizt once said is "knowing what to throw away and knowing what to keep." With almost 100 new images and plans from practicing professionals and over 150 updated and new illustrations, the text continues to be stimulating, intriguing, and current.

Text Overview

The following synopsis of each part of the text is repeated in the Introduction to ensure that students understand the broad knowledge base required of interior designers.

Part I, "Introduction to Interior Environments," discusses the history of the design profession and reviews in detail the process by which interior designers complete an interior space. Drawings and drafted plans demonstrate the use of visual communications. A pictorial essay on the history of style will familiarize students with significant eras of design that influence today's interiors.

Part II, "Design Fundamentals," establishes the basics for the study of design in all creative fields. Part II emphasizes visual literacy and the principles and elements of design that guide designers in technical and decorative design decisions. Color is given special attention because of its complexity.

Part III, "Building Systems," emphasizes the architectural, electrical, and mechanical aspects of design. This section assists future designers in understanding the visual communications needed to collaborate with electrical, mechanical, and structural engineers, the client, and the rest of the design team.

Part IV, "Space," addresses both the technical requirements and the creative dimensions of planning the layout of furniture and rooms. Designers learn to read floor plans by thinking and visualizing in three dimensions (3-D). These chapters encourage designers to recognize space as *volume* and to design from the *inside out*.

Part V, "Furnishings, Fabrics, and Background Elements," provides a foundation for understanding the multitude of selections available to designers.

Finally, **Part VI,** "The Profession of Interior Design," discusses the steps required to become a professional member of the interior design industry. It reviews basic business practices and the ethics and outlook of the profession.

Ancillaries and Supplements

As an additional education tool, the *Instructor's Manual* accompanying the text develops standard test questions and practical studio design problems. Also available is a Student Packet, which contains assignments and plates for students to execute in color paints.

Acknowledgments

Special appreciation is extended to the photographers, designers, architects, and manufacturers who contributed images and information for this text. Truly one of the most rewarding experiences of working on this text was opening the packages containing these wonderful images sent by so many talented professionals. The design community has been so very helpful sharing pertinent information and materials. I am particularly grateful to Karen Downs at *Southern Accents,* Kathryn Paige at Peter Paige Photography, Bob Shimer at Hedrich-Blessing, and Robert Thien of Atlanta for their extensive film contributions.

Many individuals have assisted in the effort of verifying information. Several practicing designers and educators (listed below, but who were anonymous to the author) reviewed chapters for accuracy and readability. I appreciate their candid and constructive comments and have altered much of the text based on these reviews. I am particularly grateful to whoever paid special attention to the material on design history. Reviewers included:

- Patricia G. Allen, Portland Community College
- Reed Benhamou, Indiana University
- Stephanie Clemons, Colorado State University
- Marcia Gonzales, Scottsdale Community College
- Janet Lacek, Brenau University
- Nancy Lickson, Kingwood College
- Jerry L. Nielson, University of Florida
- Joy K. Potthoff, Bowling Green State University
- Susan Reedy, Michigan State University
- Jane D. Reagor, Tennessee Tech University
- David L. Rodgers, Indiana University of Pennsylvania
- Suzanne Watkins, Chaminade University of Honolulu
- Andrea Birch, Brenau University

LuAnn Nissen was particularly insightful and I appreciated her words of wisdom as I started this project. The following individuals deserve special recognition for their assistance with their respective areas of expertise: Chris Strawbridge (UPS design scenario 3), Felicia Arfaoui and Deirdre O'Sullivan (Suntory), Tom Szumlic (concept), Chris Johnson (carpet in sustainable design), Andrea Birch (concept), Jason Haner (carpet), Shelly Hughes (IMS design scenario 1), Janet Morley (textiles), Michael Hinton (CRI), and Carol Platt (modern design history). Also, the accomplished freehand renderings of the space planning process visual literacy, furniture types and three-dimensional volume development are from the creative hand of Carol Platt. Mark A. Taylor assisted with the redesign of the text features and the development of the cover; I appreciate his expertise and enthusiasm. Paul Petrie, Marcia Davis, Charles Gandy, and Roger Godwin served as a constant source of encouragement, vision, and stability throughout my design career. I value their insights.

Chris and Monica Ohlinger at Ohlinger Publishing have been supportive throughout this process. Their staff (Dan, Kelly, Steve, and Wendy) has consistently proven to be gracious and punctual on all my requests. Emily Bush at Carlisle Publishers Services has been thorough, efficient, and a pleasure. Sarah Greer Bush is an awesome copy editor! All of Carlisle's staff has been efficient and encouraging.

Mary Carnis at Prentice Hall has guided me thoughtfully through the production process. I particularly appreciate her, Cheryl Asherman, and Janice Stangel for patiently working with me through the design changes. Vernon Anthony is a great editor; I would recommend him to all of my colleagues. Ann Brunner, his editorial assistant, is equally as vigilant and I appreciate her attention to detail. I am grateful to all the folks at Prentice Hall who helped make this text a reality.

To my colleagues in ASID, IIDA, IDEC, and at Brenau University, as well as to my students, I express my wholehearted appreciation for your support, motivation, and understanding. I particularly wish to express thanks to Helen Ray and Andrea Birch for allowing me a fall release to complete this project. My department, faculty, and staff have valiantly filled in the void during my leave.

To my dearest friends and family in Georgia, Indiana, and in the North Fork, I appreciate the space (both physical and psychological) all of you allowed for my husband and I to complete the text. Ray, Morgan, and Patty Hart graciously allowed us to use their office space during crunch times. The finely appointed surroundings, scrumptious dinners, and lively conversations created an exquisite environment so welcomed to a designer in the rustic North Fork. To Lee Secrest and Amy Edmonds, I am deeply moved by your generosity for the extended use of your cabin with its satellite Internet and solar power. Because the majority of this edition was written in a remote area, the use of your cabin allowed me access to the outside world, without which the research phase of this project would have been impossible. Lee and Amy, your cabin will always feel like home. To my parents, Verle and Nona Fiegle, I express an additional deepfelt gratitude for the tenacity and dedication that you instilled in me. These characteristics have helped immensely.

Finally, to my husband, Philip, I cannot adequately express my sincere appreciation for the hundreds of hours (taken from our personal time) that you spent wordsmithing, typing, calling, and generally assisting with the organization of this text and art manuscript. For your spirit and sustained encouragement, I am forever indebted.

Lynn M. Jones

Lynn M. Jones, ASID/IIDA/IDEC, knew she wanted to pursue interior architecture at an early age. In grade school she developed house plans on graph paper and raked leaves or shoveled snow into floor plan patterns; furniture in her room was always on the move. Lynn graduated from Purdue University magna cum laude with a Bachelor of Science in Environmental Design, and at age 23 became NCIDQ certified. She earned her Master's in Historic Preservation from the University of Georgia with a summa cum laude designation. Her thesis, The Design of National Park Visitor Centers: The Relationships Between Buildings and Their Sites, *took Lynn and her husband to more than 100 National Park locations.*

Lynn worked full time as a designer in Atlanta for several years, focusing on hospitality and commercial office design. She has served as an educator since 1984 and opened her own business, Jones Interiors, in 1989 to coincide with her educational endeavors. Her work has received awards from ASID, AIA, and IDEC. She was named outstanding faculty member at Brenau University in 1993, where she served as Interior Design Program Director from 1988 to 2000 and is presently Chair of Art and Design. Lynn spends her summers at a remote homestead in northwest Montana, where she finds inspiration and respite in the beauty and simplicity of nature.

Introduction to Interior Environments

PART 1

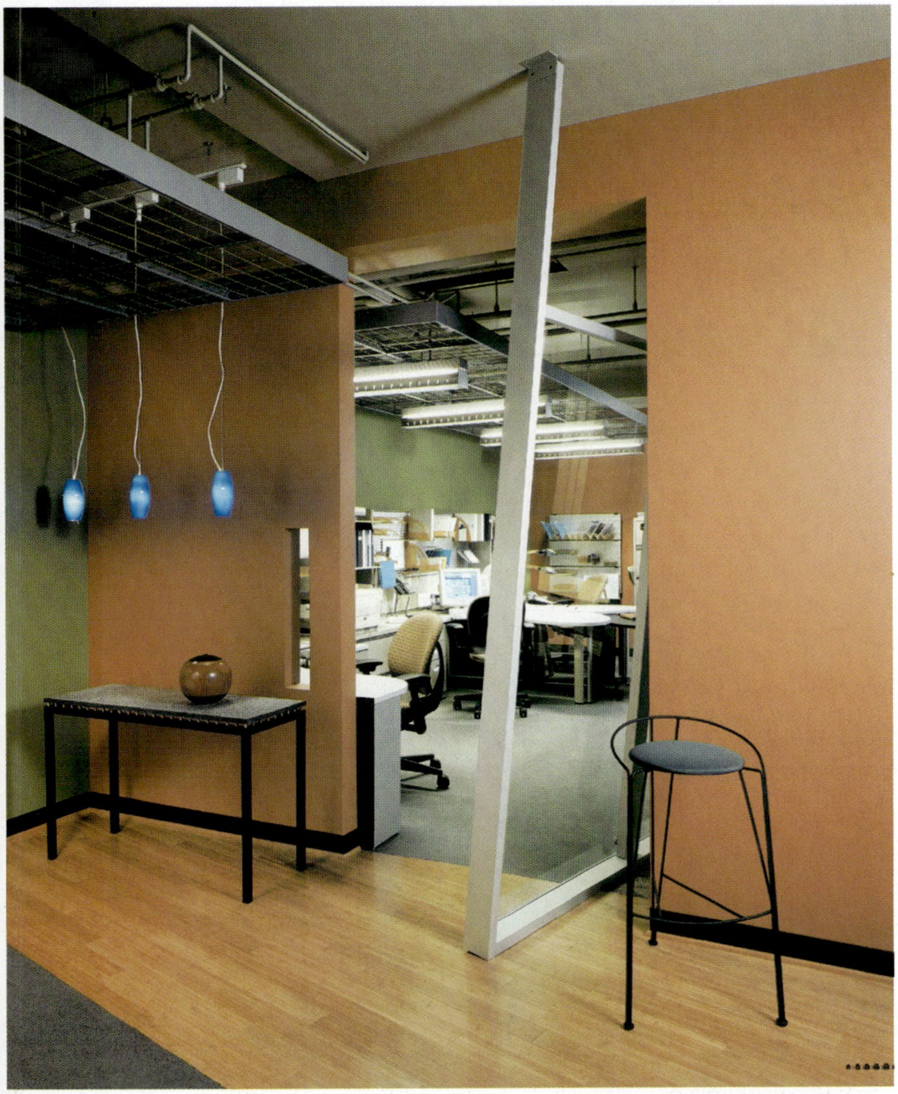

Figure I.1A *In the true blend of art and science, the FIDER office emulates the importance of interior design. The open office areas, collaborative spaces, and enclosed work areas meet the diverse needs of the client. Warm colors and bamboo flooring (a good sustainable product selection) provide a warm entry for visitors and employees. As seen on the floor plan on the next page, a strong angled axis leads the visitor into the workspace. (Designer: Progressive AE. Photograph by Kevin Beswick, People Places & Things.)*

Interior design unites the seemingly opposite disciplines of art and science by relying on the tools of science to craft the functional elements of three-dimensional space as well as the aesthetic ones.

—International Interior Design Association

Throughout history humans have organized and enhanced their surroundings to meet their physical and psychological needs. Tools and products were developed and refined to perform specific tasks. Furniture, fabrics, and finishes changed to meet people's needs. The physical arrangements of rooms, furnishings, and mechanical and electrical systems have relocated based on aesthetics and function. Today, the interior design profession incorporates a broad scope of services offered to a wide variety of clients (Figures I.1A, B).

Definition and Responsibilities of an Interior Designer

The following definition, developed by the National Council for Interior

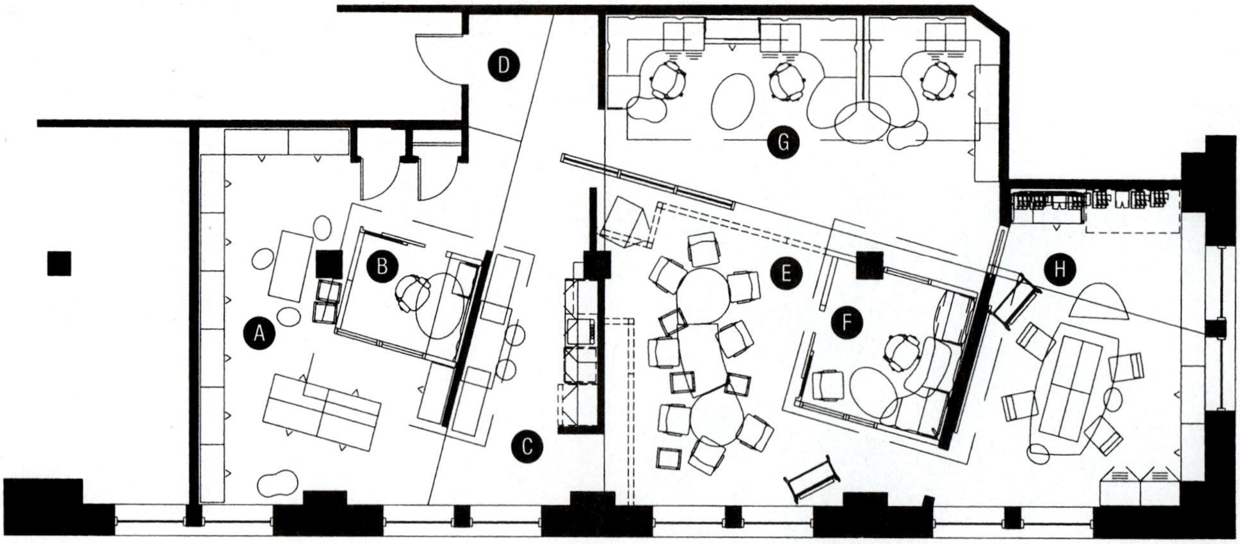

Floor Plan

A. Resource alley
B. Private enclave
C. Kitchen/cafe'
D. Entry
E. Collaborative space
F. Private office
G. Individual work space
H. Project workroom

Figure I.1B *The floor plan of the FIDER office illustrates the emphasis of interior design on concept, function, and aesthetics. The angled axis, as seen in the image on page 1 and in the computer-aided design plan above, draws the visitor into the space. Interior designers develop the ability to visualize interior environments by reading two-dimensional floor plans. These plans define the interior partitions, furniture locations, and traffic flow. (Designer: Progressive AE.)*

Design Qualification, demonstrates the scope of the interior design profession:

The professional interior designer is qualified by education, experience, and examination to enhance the function and quality of interior spaces for the purpose of improving the quality of life, increasing productivity, and protecting the health, safety, and welfare of the public. The professional interior designer:

- analyzes the client's needs, goals, and life and safety requirements
- integrates findings with knowledge of interior design
- formulates preliminary design concepts that are appropriate, functional, and aesthetic
- develops and presents final design recommendations through appropriate presentation media
- prepares working drawings and specifications for non-load-bearing interior construction, materials, finishes, space planning, furnishings, fixtures, and equipment
- collaborates with licensed practitioners who offer professional services in the technical areas of mechanical, electrical, and load-bearing design as required for regulatory approval
- prepares and administers bids and contract documents as the client's agent
- reviews and evaluates design solutions during implementation and upon completion.

Design for Special Population Environments

Interior designers are responsible for developing interior environments for people of all ages and abilities, including the elderly, children, and those who are temporarily or permanently disabled. According to Anita Rui Olds in *Child Care Design Guide,* one out of every three children under the age of five is enrolled in a part-time or full-time day care program. Conversely, by 2030, approximately 26 percent of the population will be over the age of sixty-five; many of these individuals will prefer to age at home, called *aging in place.* Designers must understand the complexities related to the diverse needs of these clients.

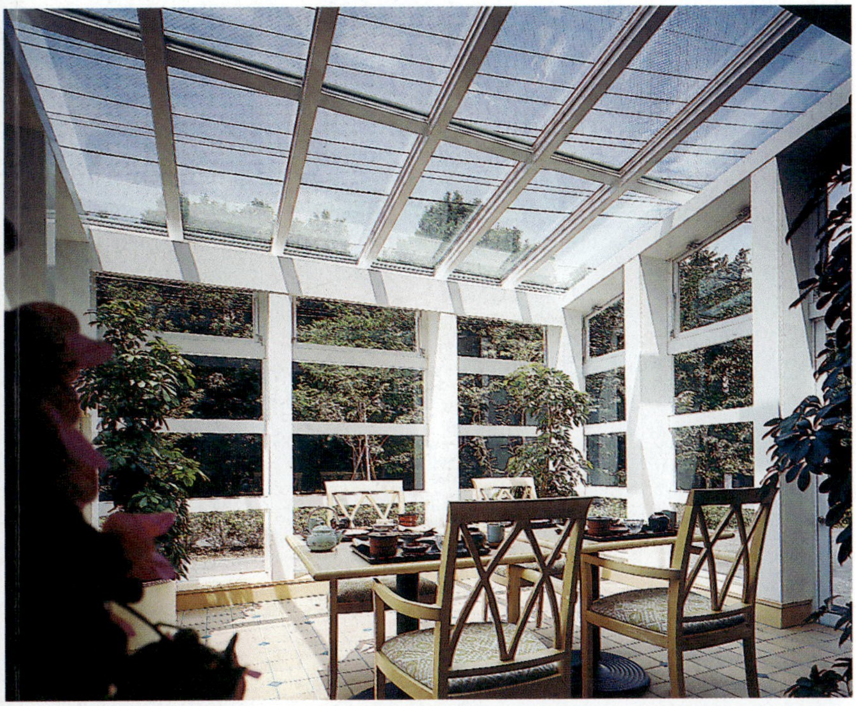

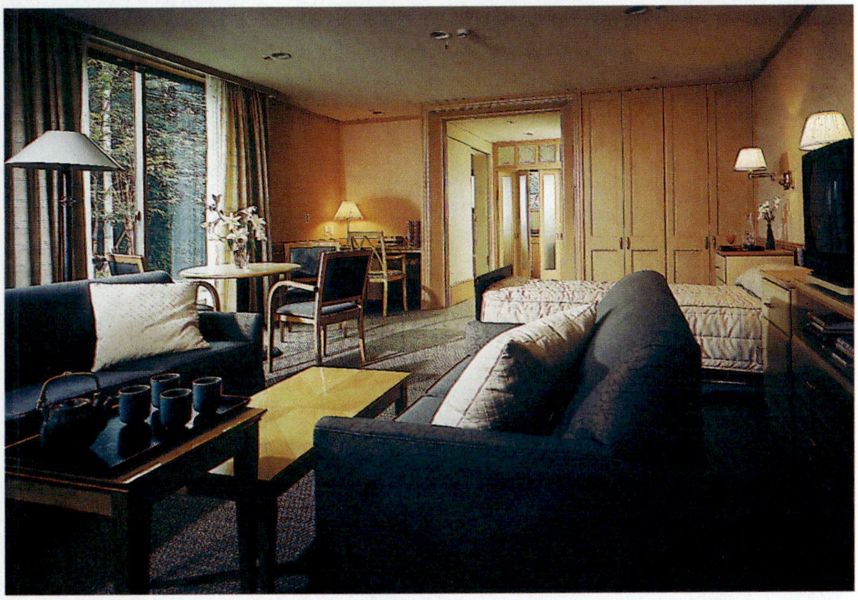

Figure I.2 *Designing for the elderly requires sensitivity to special needs. This continuing care retirement facility, located in Sun City Kanagawa, Japan, also required special research into multicultural awareness. (Architect/Designer: Hellmuth, Obata & Kassabaum, Tokyo and San Francisco. Photograph by Jaime Ardiles-Arce.)*

The concept of **universal design** focuses on creating spaces and furnishings to meet the needs of individuals regardless of age and ability. Interior designers must be able to integrate the needs of a wide variety of individuals into a particular space.

Design for Multicultural Environments

Designers are required to coordinate interiors that are welcoming to a multicultural community. Different cultures view color and space in a variety of ways. As global awareness increases and the Internet brings design communities closer together, designers commonly complete projects for overseas clients. Sensitivity to individuals' tastes and cultural preferences permits designers to suggest the appropriate design solutions for these clients (Figure I.2).

Design for Sustainable Environments

Interior designers also are responsible for protecting the environment by using sustainable resources whenever possible. Designers should develop design solutions that promote environmental considerations and should use and specify products that are recycled and can be recyclable. The use of sustainable products and the development of environmentally sensitive interiors is called **sustainable** or **green design** (Figure I.3).

Decorators and Designers

The terms *interior decorator* and *interior designer* have had various meanings. ***Interior design*** is the profession that embodies the above definition and responsibilities. (Some prefer to call it ***interior architecture.***) ***Interior decorating,*** or the embellishment of interior finishes and the selection and arrangement of fabrics and furnishings, is an important component of interior design. As defined earlier by NCIDQ, however, "the interior designer is qualified by education, experience, and examination to enhance the function and quality of interior spaces, and to insure the health, safety, and welfare of the public."

It is important to emphasize that although the designer may be responsible for the decorative design solutions for load-bearing walls, the

Figure I.3 *This house, called the Suncatcher, is constructed from used tires packed with dirt and stacked to form the walls. The walls are covered with stucco to create a Southwest adobe interior. Windows face south to aid in the solar design. (A) exterior; (B) entry hallway, looking back toward the front door; (C) living area. (Architect/Designer: Michael Reynolds. Photograph by Philip A. Jones.)*

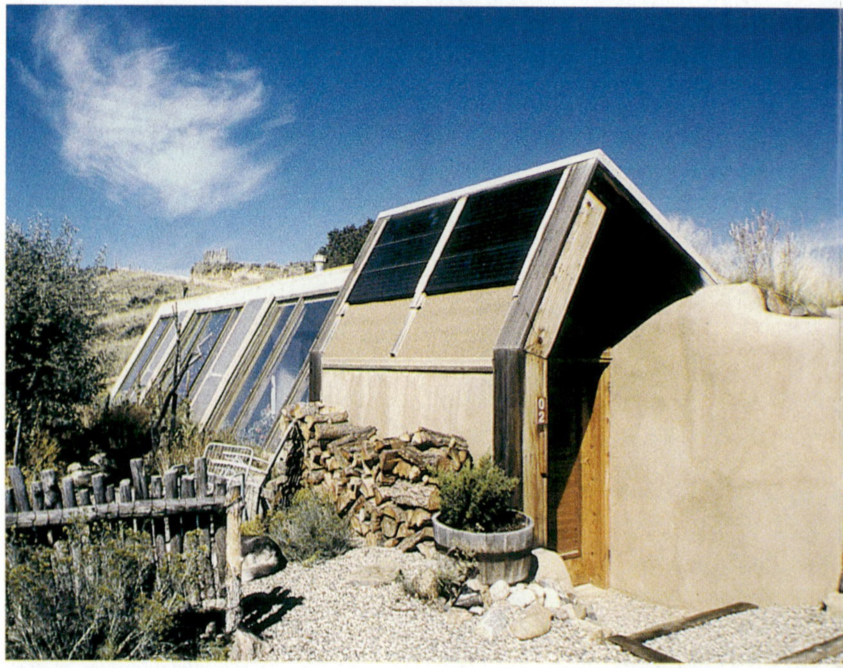

A

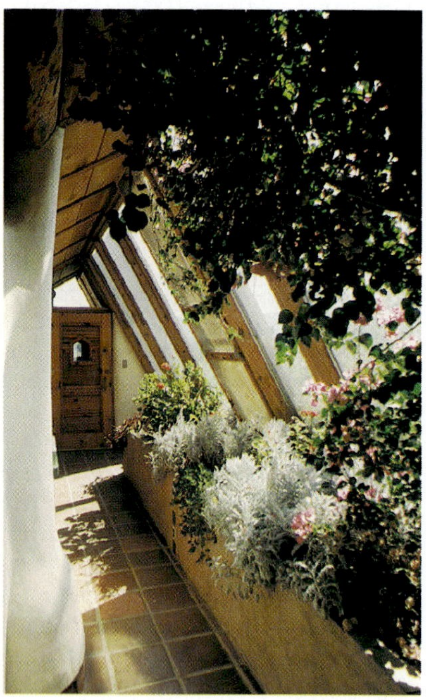

B

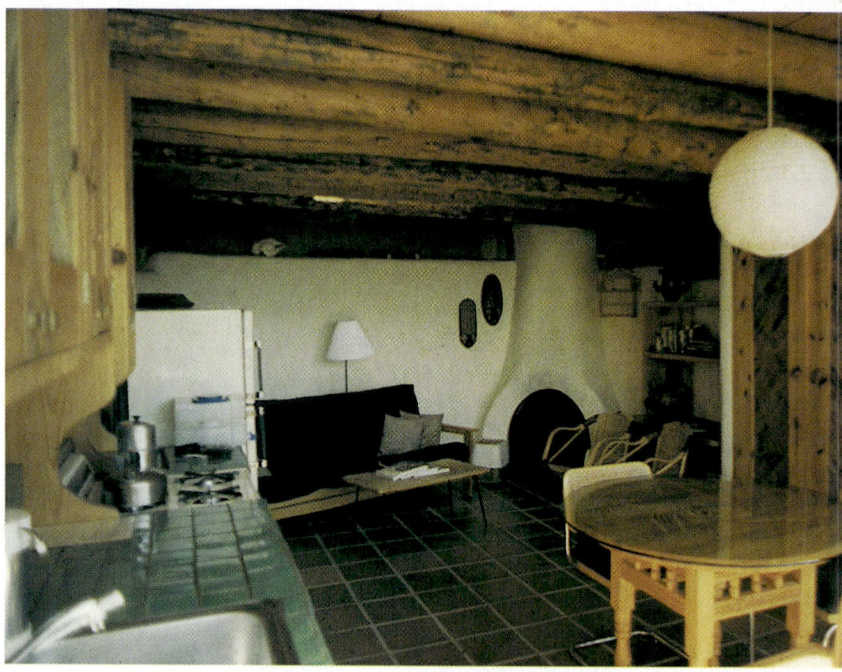

C

practice of interior design does not include the structural design of buildings. Designers collaborate with a team of allied professionals, especially when working with mechanical and electrical systems and construction components.

More info online @

http://www.fider.org Foundation for Interior Design Education Research

http://www.ncidq.org National Council for Interior Design Qualifications

Relationship With Allied Professions

While developing a new or renovated interior for a client, a designer works as a member of the design team. Interior designers may work

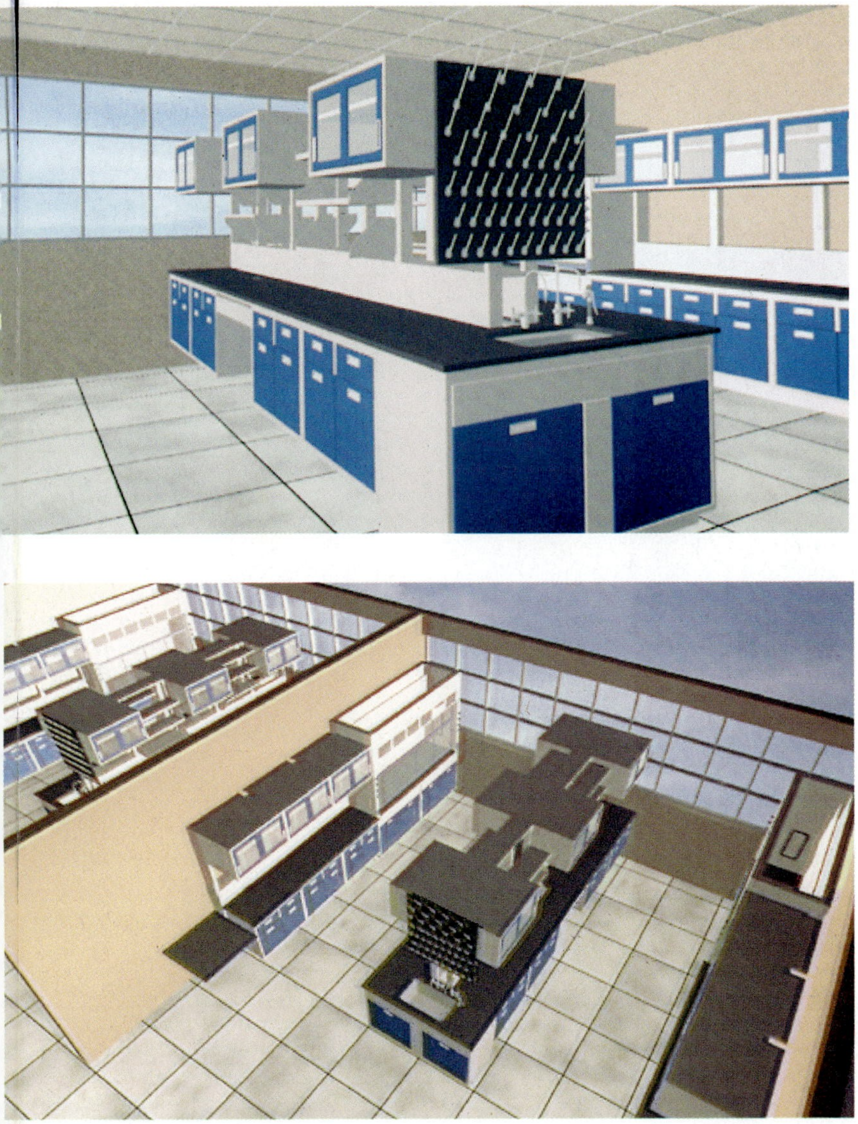

Figure I.4 *For this laboratory, a computer-aided design software program created interior views for preliminary presentation to the client. Visual interpretation is a critical skill required of designers. The computer allows the space to be viewed from various angles and helps clients (and designers) visualize the solution prior to construction. (Architect/Designer: Talka & Connor.)*

with architects, builders, decorators, landscape architects, mechanical, electrical, and structural engineers, and product and graphic designers. Designers are also likely to work with other professionals including lighting and sound specialists, historic preservationists, and a wide variety of other specialized contractors in interior finishes, fabrics, furniture, and products. The success of a job depends on communication and collaboration among these design professionals.

Knowledge Required by Interior Designers

In order to perform competently and communicate effectively with the allied professions, designers must acquire a broad foundation of technical and decorative knowledge.

Part I, "Introduction to Interior Environments," discusses the history of the design profession and reviews in detail the process by which interior designers complete an interior space. Drawings and drafted plans demonstrate the use of **visual communications** required of all design professions. Students using this text as a part of an introductory design course may be required to start drafting or to work with **computer-aided design (CAD)** software (Figure I.4). Also in Part I, a pictorial essay traces the history of style, showing how past eras influence interiors.

Part II, "Design Fundamentals," establishes the basics for the study of design in all creative fields, including the importance of **visual literacy** and the development of the **concept.** Part II emphasizes visual literacy and the principles and elements of design that guide designers in technical and decorative design decisions. Color is given special attention because of its complexity.

Part III, "Building Systems," emphasizes the architectural, electrical, and mechanical aspects of design. Lighting solutions are particularly important in interior spaces. This section assists future designers in understanding the visual communications needed to collaborate with electrical, mechanical, and structural engineers, the client, and the rest of the design team.

Part IV, "Space," addresses both the technical requirements and the creative dimensions of planning the layout of furniture and rooms. Designers learn to read floor plans by thinking and visualizing in three dimensions (3-D). These chapters encourage designers to recognize space as ***volume*** and to design space from the ***inside out.***

Part V, "Furnishings, Fabrics, and Background Elements," provides a foundation for understanding the multitude of selections available to designers. For example, designers need to know the advantages and disadvantages of selecting cut-pile carpet over level-loop carpet or flat latex paint over semigloss alkyd.

Finally, Part VI, "The Profession of Interior Design," discusses the steps required to become a professional member of the interior design industry and reviews basic business principles and ethics. The text concludes with an outlook for the profession.

Understanding Interior Design

1

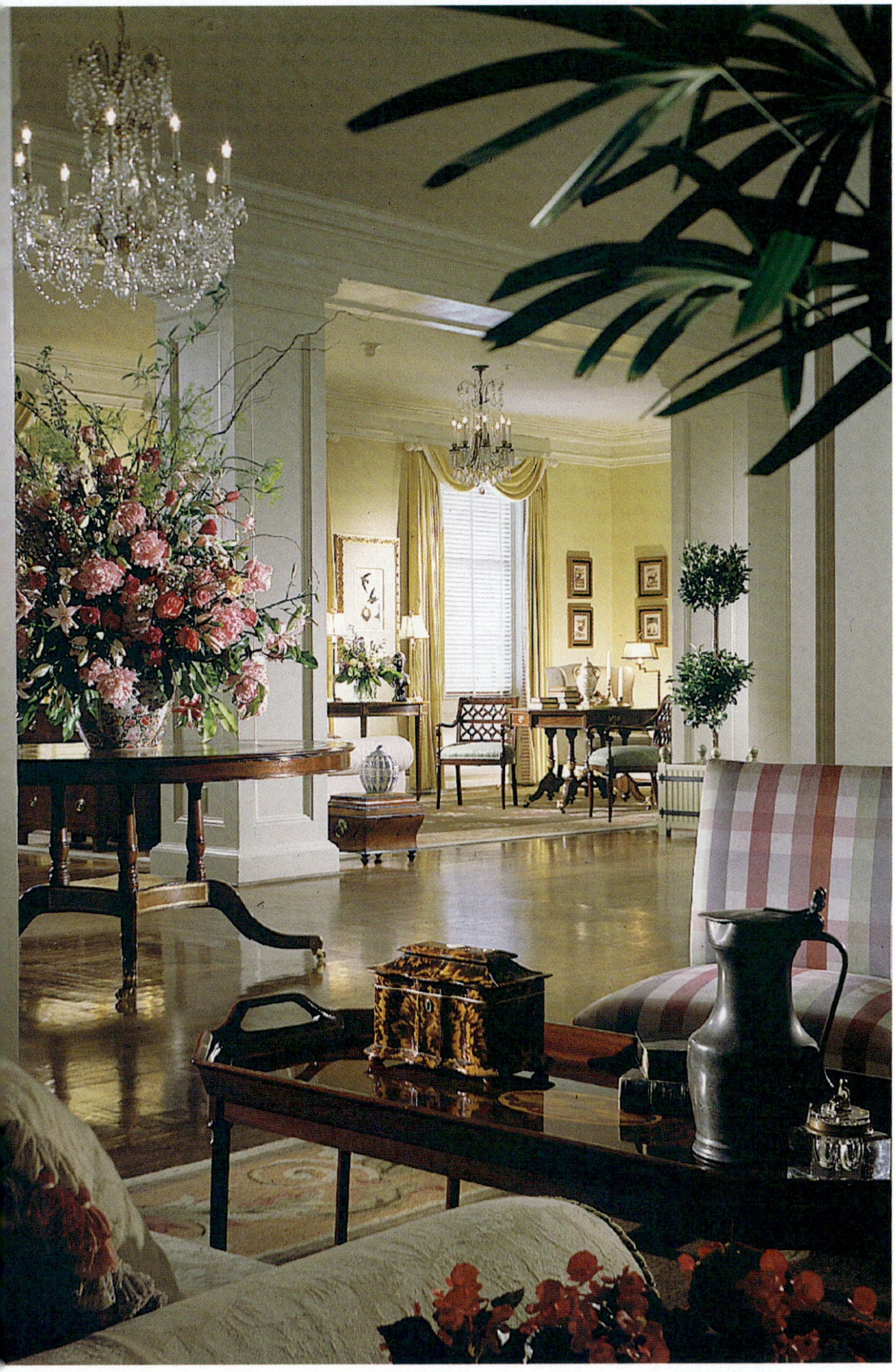

Figure 1.1 *This warm and inviting space welcomes guests into the Carolina Inn lobby and makes them feel pampered. Hospitality design requires designers to create interiors not only for their clients—the hotel owners—but also for the clients' client—the hotel guests. (Architect/Designer: The Glave Firm. Photograph by Robert Miller.)*

Interior design is as old as the Cro-Magnon culture, where walls were decorated to bring a *sense of place* to the interior environment. Ancient designs from the Egyptians, Greeks, and Romans form the basis of interior design. Middle Age and Renaissance designs are applied in many interiors, particularly in Europe. Dr. Henry Hildebrandt of the University of Cincinnati notes that during the 1700s the English designer Robert Adam and his family formed a business creating interior spaces by combining furniture design, interior architecture, and decoration—thus, integrating the entire interior environment. (See the "History of Style"—English Styles.) Adam and others like him, such as John Nash and John Soane, coordinated with cabinetmakers, painters, upholsterers, plasterers, and related artisans.

The *profession,* however, of interior design is relatively new. It evolved during the latter half of the nineteenth century and the early twentieth century, and then fully emerged following World War II. As with Robert Adam, interiors designed prior to the establishment of the profession as it is known today were executed primarily by furniture designers, cabinetmakers, architects, and others active in the decorative arts.

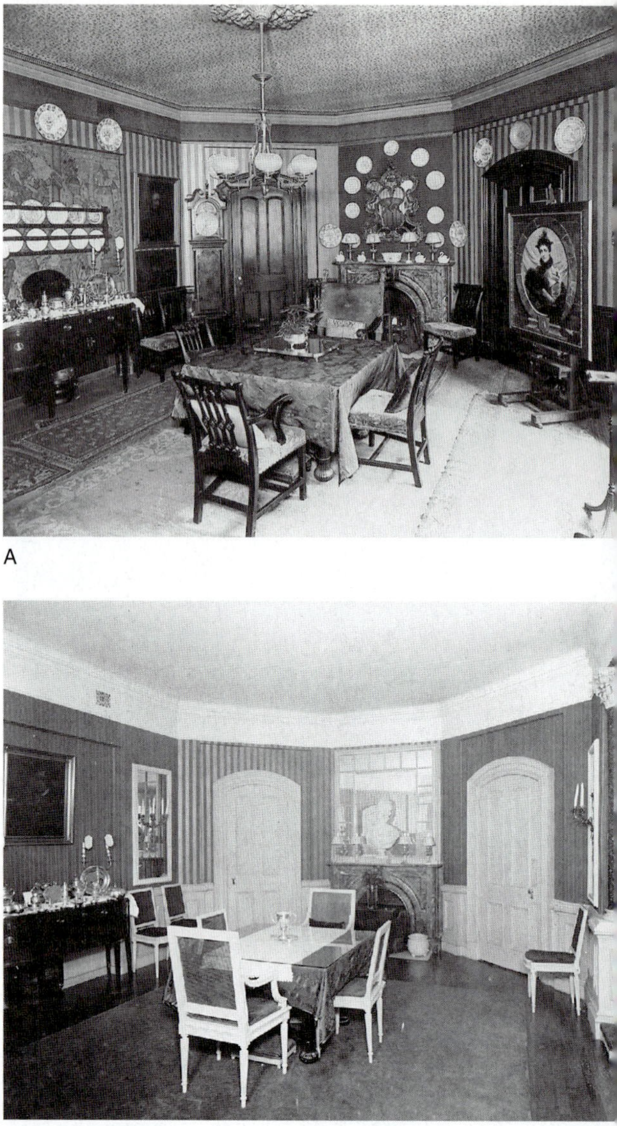

A

B

Figure 1.2 *A dining room designed by Elsie de Wolfe early i her career is shown in (A) The lighter, refreshing redesign (B) of the same room exemplifies de Wolfe's later design character. (Photographs from the Byron Collection, The Museum of the City of New York.)*

Development of the Interior Design Profession

In the 1850s, authors became deeply interested in how human comfort was affected by sound principles of design. At the time, the Industrial Revolution (particularly in Europe) was producing a variety of poor-quality household goods. Many individuals condemned the use of the machine to create inferior products and designs.

William Morris and the Arts and Crafts movement in 1860s England advocated "good design for everyone." English author and moralist Charles Eastlake wrote *Hints on Household Taste* in 1868, one of the first books on interior decoration. In the United States, American Arts and Crafts movement leader Gustav Stickley published *The Craftsman* at the turn of the century, featuring numerous articles on home design. In the late nineteenth century, various publications such as *Godey's Lady's Book, Harper's New Monthly, Harper's Bazaar,* and *Ladies' Home Journal* advocated more tasteful interiors. As early as 1890, Candace Wheeler published an article entitled "Interior Decoration as a Profession for Women." Later that decade, Edith Wharton and Ogden Codman wrote *The Decoration of Houses,* which was intended to show that the purpose of interior decoration was to bring out the proportions of a well-designed room. W. C. Gannet wrote a privately printed series of essays called "The House Beautiful," from which in 1896 a magazine of the same title derived its impetus and was first published. Soon, other home decorating periodicals appeared on the market.

Candace Wheeler and Elsie de Wolfe

Candace Wheeler, a textile designer, is also considered by many to be the first interior decorator. In the late 1870s, Wheeler established the Society of Decorative Arts. Louis Comfort Tiffany hired Wheeler to manage the textiles side his design firm. Wheeler's luxurious textiles with patterns flective of nature adorned the walls of the homes of Cc nelius Vanderbilt II and actress Lily Langtry. Wheeler al decorated Mark Twain's homes both in Hartford and l summer home in Onteora, New York (Susan Dominus, *Ne York Times Magazine,* Fall 2001).

One of the most famous individuals to offer interior de orating services to the public was New York actress Elsie Wolfe, who had expert knowledge of French furniture a antiques. Her decorating expertise could transform a roc with a somber, cluttered, Victorian feeling into one with light, airy, eclectic French design (Figure 1.2).

In 1901, Elsie de Wolfe began her business as "America's st professional interior decorator." Through her efforts, ong with the work of others during this period, including ındace Wheeler, Nancy McClelland, English decorator Syrie augham (known for her "white" interiors), Dorothy Draper vho wrote a decorating advice column), Rose Cummings, id later Billy Baldwin (who was known as the "Dean of ecorators"), the profession of interior decorating was esblished.

ank Lloyd Wright

hereas Elsie de Wolfe focused on the embellishment of surce decoration and the placement of furniture and accessories, Frank Lloyd Wright, an architect working in the early 1900s, brought to the profession an integration of structure and design. Wright was concerned with the planning of space, its function, and its relationship to the structure. He defined spaces based on furniture arrangements rather than enclosures. His integration of furnishings, light, construction materials, ornamental detail, and structural materials formed what he called **organic design.**

In the Robie House (Figure 1.3), as in all his prairie-styled homes, Wright emphasized the fireplace. Materials used on the exterior of the home were brought inside to become part of the hearth. The hearth became the heart or core of his homes, symbolizing the strength of the American household.

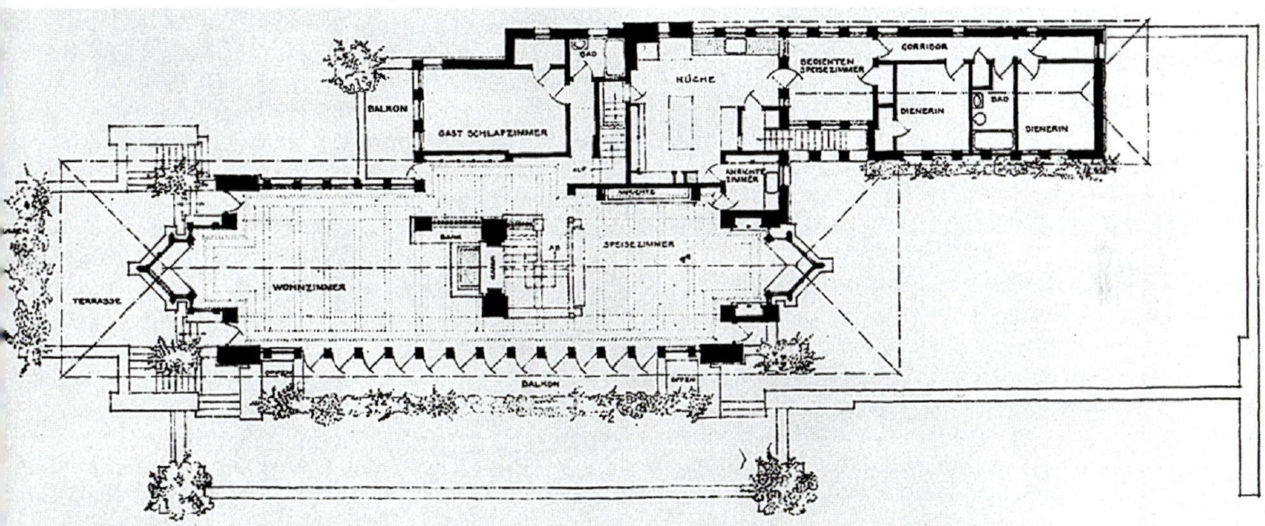

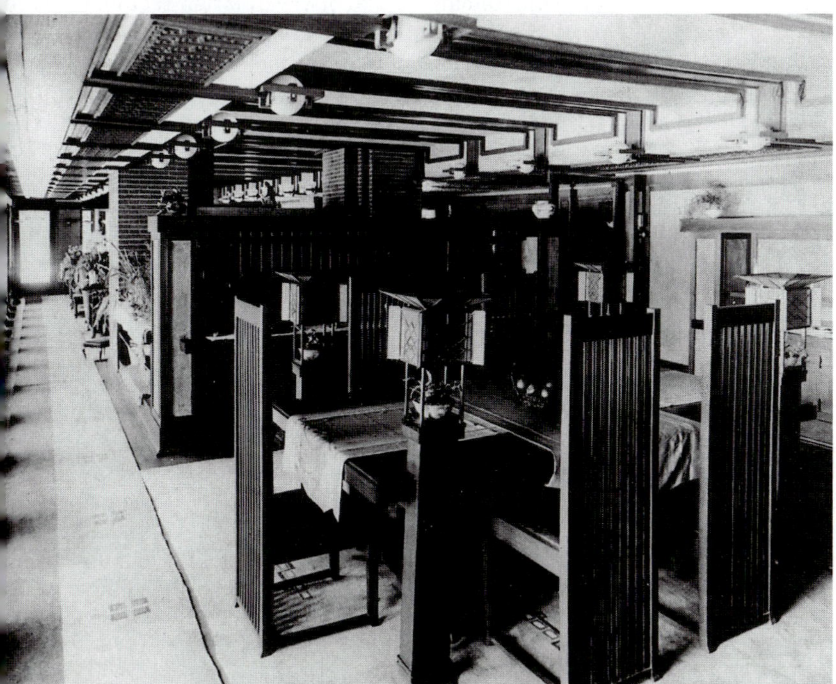

Figure 1.3 *In the plan of the 1909 Robie House (A) Frank Lloyd Wright's emphasis on the fireplace as the heart of the home is evidenced by its central location. (B) shows an interior view of the home from the dining room looking into the living room. The bank of windows to the left pulls the outdoors into the home. (Frank Lloyd Wright drawings copyright © 1998 The Frank Lloyd Wright Foundation, Scottsdale, AZ. Photo courtesy of The Frank Lloyd Wright Archives, Scottsdale, AZ.)*

Other progressive designers and architects, in both America and Europe, saw the need to integrate the exterior of a structure with the interior spaces and furnishings. Designers also began to integrate acoustical and lighting solutions into their designs during this era.

Following World War II, the explosive growth of commercial and residential development created a greater demand for interior design services. Americans wanted more efficient and aesthetically pleasing private and public environments—and were willing to support a new profession that would implement that desire.

More info online @

http://www.greatbuildings.com/architects/Robert_Adam.html Information on Robert Adam

http://www.britannica.com/women/articles/de_Wolfe_Elsie.html Information on Elsie de Wolfe

http://www.franklloydwright.org/ Frank Lloyd Wright Foundation

Professional Design Organizations

The establishment of professional interior design societies began in the 1930s with the development of the American Institute of Interior Decorators (AIID), which gave credibility to the new profession. In order to be a member of the organization, individuals were required to have a combination of education and experience. The society emphasized continuing education programs, a code of ethics, outreach to the community and students, and collaboration with related professions.

After World War II, the nonresidential or contract market developed. Decorators were designing hotels, offices, and retail establishments. Space planning became a focus of the decorating community. For many the term "decorator" no longer fit, and in 1957 the National Society of Interior Designers (NSID) was formed, the second professional design organization in the United States. In 1975 the two organizations merged to form the American Society of Interior Designers (ASID). Presently ASID has 20,000 professional members and 13,000 industry affiliates.

Various other professional organizations developed throughout the 1970s and '80s. In the 1980s and '90s, a movement called the "Unified Voice" was created to bring all competing professional interior design organizations under one umbrella. In 1994, three organizations (the Institute of Business Designers, the Council of Federal Interior Designers, and the International Society of Interior Designers) merged to form IIDA, the International Interior Design Association, with approximately 9000 members. Both ASID and IIDA require the passage of the National Council of Interior Design Qualification (NCIDQ) exam as one requirement for professional membership. In 2002, ASID and IIDA again joined forces to pursue merging into one interior design professional organization. Unfortunately, an agreement on critical issues was not met. Both organizations do, however, continue to collaborate, particularly at the local level. More information about these organizations is discussed in Part V "The Profession of Interior Design."

More info online @

http://www.asid.org American Society of Interior Designers

http://www.iida.org International Interior Design Association

http://www.ncidq.org National Council for Interior Design Qualification

Goals of Interior Design

Designers are aware of the impact of the physical interior e vironment on the occupants' lives. The need for adequa shelter is only the beginning. The environment must pr mote the comfort and convenience of the end users, bo physically and psychologically, while taking into accou economic realities. Meeting human needs in specific en ronments, whether residential or commercial, requires a b ance of technical knowledge and an appreciation of qual aesthetics.

The designer's ultimate goal when planning a residen or commercial structure should be the integration of the b sic requirements for an efficient and aesthetically pleasi space. If the interior space satisfies the *function* requested the client, meets the *aesthetic* criteria of the design, and completed within the client's *economic* directives, the pr ect is a success (Figure 1.1).

Function and the Human Factor

To be livable, an interior first should fulfill its intended fur tion of satisfying the needs of the people for whom it is c signed. Careful consideration of functional space begins the programming phase. Specific design requirements m be necessary for the special needs of users such as childre the elderly, or the physically challenged. The human fac is a primary concern when determining the function of t space (Figure 1.4). This is obvious when one considers t needs of a day care or elementary school in contrast to a ca center for the elderly or a university classroom building.

From a psychological viewpoint, humans must feel co fortable in relation to the scale and proportion of the arc tecture. The three-dimensional aspects of ceiling height, w length, and cubic feet should be considered, because if t space is too vast or too small, the occupants may feel u comfortable or out of place. Satisfying human psycholo entails many other design criteria as well, including selecti and arrangement of line, color, form, lighting, and texture create a sense of balance and harmony.

Interior spaces and fixtures need to be scaled to meet t proportions of the users, while also meeting their physi needs. Furniture should be suitably scaled and arranged purpose and efficiency. For example, a chair for relaxi should be comfortable and should fit the size of the occupa with a table at the appropriate height close by to accomn date a lamp that produces adequate lighting with no glare

The designer should create an environment that not o meets the client's needs, but is also a safe environment

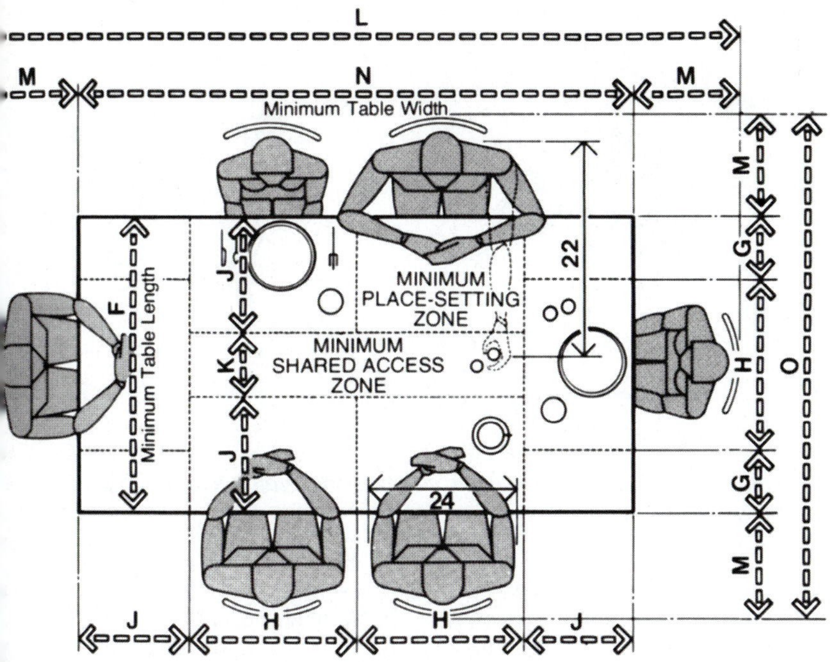

	in	cm
A	54	137.2
B	12	30.5
C	30	76.2
D	48	121.9
E	18	45.7
F	42	106.7
G	9	22.9
H	24	61.0
I	40	101.6
J	16	40.6
K	10	25.4
L	116–128	294.6–325.1
M	18–24	45.7–61.0
N	80	203.2
O	78–90	198.1–228.6

ure 1.4 *This drawing illustrates the minimum dimensions needed to seat six individuals around a table. (From* Human nension & Interior Space *by Panero and Zelnik © 1979 Whitney Library of Design.)*

ich to live. Life safety and building codes must be folved. No matter how wonderful an interior space looks, if users cannot efficiently complete the activities and funcns required in the space, the design has failed.

sthetics

e second goal of an interior space should be to create a asant and appealing environment. It is essential that stunts of design develop awareness and sensitivity to the aestics of all interior environments, including private ellings, financial or educational institutions, offices, retail d hospitality spaces, health care centers, and other nonidential interiors.

Anyone can express personal preference, but developing od aesthetic judgment requires a high level of *discernnt* that is acquired through years of experience and obvation. Good design has no absolute formula; however, successful use of aesthetic principles—scale and propor n, rhythm, balance, emphasis, and harmony—aids in deion making and enhances the designer's results. Integrity d simplicity are important ingredients in good design, ng with consideration for the design's function and its reonship to the environment and to people.

The following guidelines can help the beginning designer velop a discriminating eye for quality design:

- The elements and principles of design (discussed in Chapter 2) must be understood and applied.
- Objects in nature should be carefully observed. Their play of light and shadow, their shape, texture, pattern, and color are fine examples of design (Figure 1.5).
- Historical and contemporary eras of design serve as a foundation for current design solutions.
- Professional design periodicals provide valuable ideas. (A listing of selected periodicals appears at the end of the reference list.)
- Fashion is not a criterion of good design. Like fashion in clothes, fashion in home furnishings often becomes outdated. National trends, events, and celebrities can influence individual taste, but do not necessarily relate to good design.
- *Simplicity* is key to quality design. The famous architect Ludwig Mies van der Rohe coined the phrase, "Less is more."
- All design decisions and selections should possess *integrity.* Furnishings with integrity exhibit their true identity. For example, a plastic laminate surface should look like plastic, not like cheap wood grain.
- Quality design is not "cute."
- Quality design is timeless.

Knowledge of what constitutes good design enables designers to guide their clients toward wise design decisions. This may mean educating the client. Good design is a longterm investment, and although at times expensive, it is worth the cost.

Economics and Ecology

The third goal of interior design is to work within the proposed budget. Designers work to satisfy the client's needs and desires within a reasonable budget to which both parties agree. If during the planning stages it becomes apparent to the designer that the project is exceeding the cost of the original projection, the designer has an ethical obligation to inform the client. Changes in the project scope or budget need to be addressed immediately.

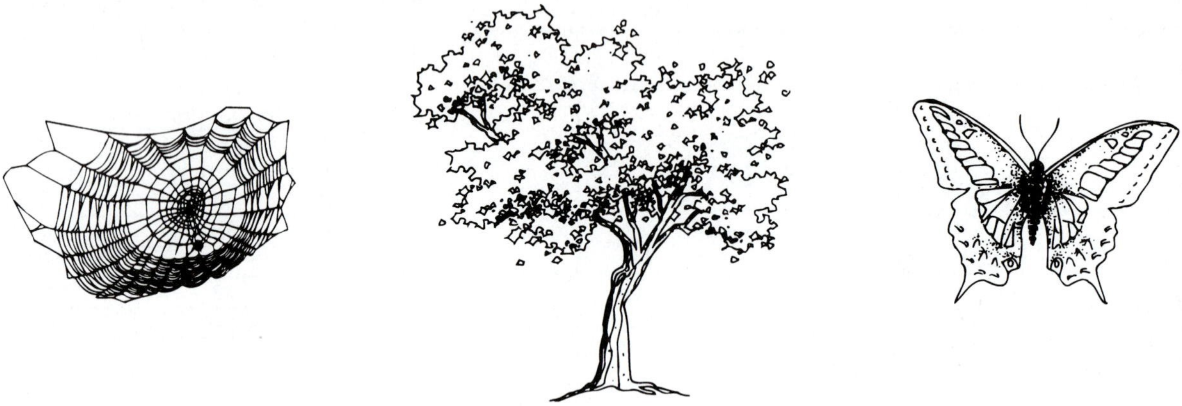

Radial balance Asymmetrical balance Symmetrical balance

Figure 1.5 *Objects in nature demonstrate the various types of balance. A spider's web indicates radial balance. This tree exhibits asymmetrical balance, whereas a butterfly is an example of symmetrical balance.*

Value becomes an important factor when designing and selecting interior components. Long-term upkeep and **life-cycle costing** (the total manufacturing and operating cost for the life of the product) are important factors when considering which items to recommend to a client. For instance, a desk chair for a client's office may be available at a local office supply store for around $100; however, if the casters easily fall off or the chair is not ergonomically designed to fit the client, the value of the chair is low. Conversely, a more expensive office chair with a five-star base, adjustable arms, back, and seat would prove to be the better long-term investment and therefore is a better value to the client.

Economic considerations also relate to ecological and environmental concerns, or sustainable design. Designers must not compromise their client's health by specifying potentially harmful materials to save on costs. For example, some inexpensive carpet padding may serve its intended purpose, but the gasses released from the padding could harm the building's inhabitants.

Similarly, designers should consider long-term environmental costs before specifying the use of any product that may be rare or endangered or that through its production may harm the environment. For instance, rare woods may look appealing, yet by specifying them the designer may be encouraging the harvesting of threatened forests. Effective environmental design decisions produce interiors that utilize materials and products that ensure environmental sustainability for future generations (Figure 1.6). Sustainable design solutions are discussed in various chapters throughout the text.

The Design Process/ Scope of Services

Knowing where to begin with a client, what information to obtain, and then how to proceed through the installation and evaluation of the completed space is a comprehensive task. Designers follow the **design process** to ensure creative and comprehensive design solutions that satisfy clients' needs and desires while meeting the goals of interior design (Table 1.1).

Designers may use a variety of terminologies to descri the design process or the methods of completing a proje All terminologies or methods center on the analysis and sy thesis of the design solution.

Analysis focuses on discovery. Analyzing a design proj requires gathering information, understanding goals and c jectives, researching related codes and other technical da comprehending the design problem, and defining the desi criteria. Once this information has been assimilated, desig ers begin to synthesize the solution.

Like the analysis phase, the *synthesis* phase also requi an immense amount of contemplative thought. Design stretch their imaginations and develop alternative solutic to the design problem. Only then does the designer return the analysis phase to select the best solution and refine it meet the client's needs. The designer creates, selects, a produces design presentations by way of visual communi tions for the client's review. Based on the client's feedba the designer will return to the analysis phase to rethink or tool the solution.

The design process is dynamic and cyclical, allowing t designer to create interiors that are responsive to particu situations. The analysis and synthesis of the design probl form the basis for all creative design solutions.

In some projects, phases of design may be combined condensed, and in other projects (particularly residential) t phases may occur simultaneously. The following discussi utilizes the terms frequently employed by the practicing p fessional.

Initial Client Contact

The initial client contact is an integral part of the desi process. It is through the initial meeting(s) that designers a clients evaluate their compatibility. Designers evalu whether the project fits their firm, time frame, and staff lo Clients evaluate previous projects related to their needs co pleted by the firm. Both the client and the designer shou interview each other to look for a cooperative blend. At t end of the initial client contact, the designer defines t

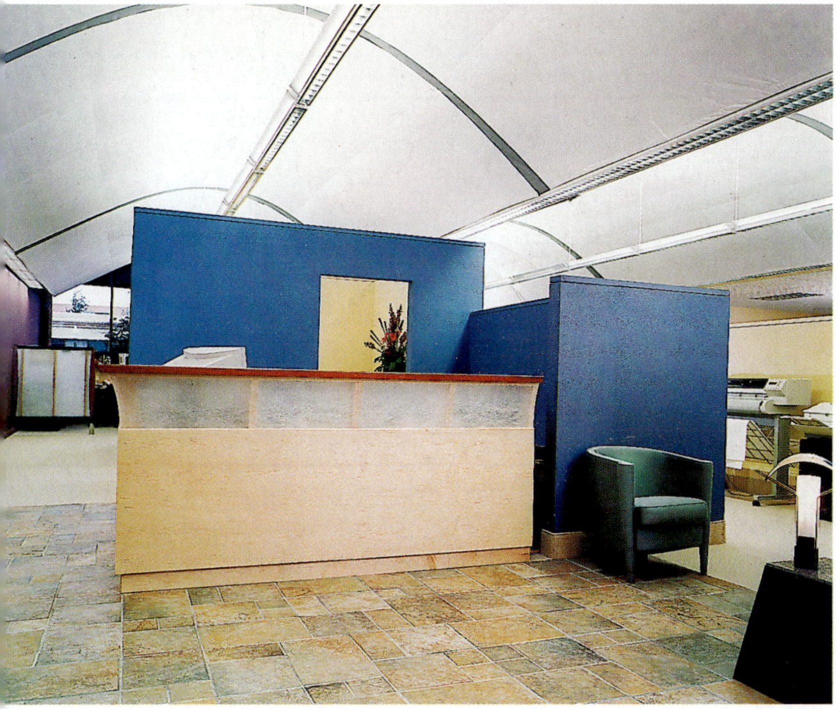

Figure 1.6 *This industrial and mechanical engineering firm's office is designed to bring the feeling of natural light into the building. With only one side of the building open to natural sunlight, a product called Tyvek (normally used in overnight express mail packages) was suspended from the ceiling. The translucent canopy allows light to filter into the room much like sunlight. (Architect/Designer: Lippert & Lippert Design, Palo Alto, CA. Photograph by Don Roper Photography.)*

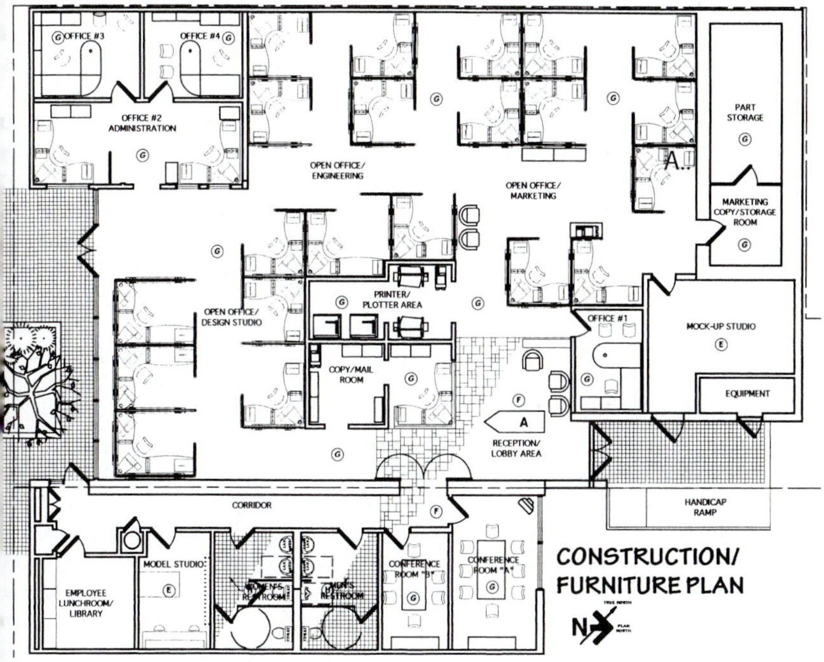

ope of services, establishes an estimated timeline and dget, and secures a contract with the client.

'ogramming

e **programming** phase is the information-gathering ase. Designers identify and analyze the needs and desires the client, usually through personal interviews. In a resintial project, the designer should meet with everyone in the household. A typical residential programming questionnaire or client profile can be found in Appendix A. In a commercial project, the president or facilities planner may serve as the client contact, or this person may appoint a committee or team to work with the designer. It is essential that designers understand the *corporate culture* of the commercial client. Typical questions relate to design preferences, space needs, and the interrelationships of spaces and departments. Information gathered in programming assists the

Table 1.1 *The Design Process*

		Scope of Services					
Designer's terminology	Initial client contact/ retainer	Programming	Conceptual/ schematic design	Design development	Contract documentation CDs	Contract administration	Post-occupancy evaluation
					Bidding	Bidding	
Design process steps	Commit to project	Define problem; gather information	Analyze facts; generate ideas & brainstorm	Select & refine	Implementation		Evaluate
	Analysis	Analysis	Analysis	Synthesis	Synthesis	Synthesis	Synthesis

designer in developing a concept for the project that is carried throughout the design process. More on concept development is discussed in Part II.

Designers also review existing conditions or items (furniture, artwork, etc.) that are to remain. Furniture and other artwork may be inventoried and photographed to help the designer assimilate all the information. An example of a furniture inventory sheet can be found in Appendix B. If the interior space already exists, the designer also develops a floor plan of the space. Sometimes clients have floor plans (a measured drawing produced by the architect or builder of the home or office), but frequently the designer will measure and draw a plan of the interior space. The floor plan is the first step in developing visual communications for the client.

During this programming phase the designer researches life safety codes (fire codes) and universal design requirements and begins coordinating with other specialists if necessary. As in all the phases of the design process, the designer will be reviewing the budget and schedule and making recommendations for changes.

By the end of the programming phase, the designer should fully understand the scope of the project and be able to produce a *design concept statement* outlining the broad-based requirements of the project. Depending on the scope of the design project, the programming phase may take one afternoon (if the client only needs a small bathroom remodeled, for example), or it could take months (for a commercial client with several hundred employees). In general, 5 to 15 percent of the time in a design project is spent in programming. As with all other design phases, the designer reviews the final programming information with the client and incorporates his or her feedback before proceeding to the next phase of design.

Conceptual or Schematic Design

During the **conceptual** or **schematic design** phase, designers formulate preliminary broad-based concepts. Design decisions regarding the character, function, and aesthetics of a project are presented to the client for approval.

When working with a client who is remodeling a hon the designer may show the client a preliminary floor plan dicating where new and existing furniture would be locat The designer would also present the client with a few fab and paint samples indicating the conceptual direction of t color palette and design scheme. The client can respond the plan and selections before the designer spends hours lecting the specific new sofa and exact fabric.

In a commercial project, or a residential project requir an entire custom home design, the designer may begin developing a **matrix** (sometimes called a *compatibility m trix*) indicating the relationship of particular individuals, partments, or spaces (Figure 1.7A). Another tool is t **bubble diagram** to help the designer and the client visu ize the requirements of the space (Figure 1.7B). The bub diagrams can lead to the **blocking diagram** that helps to tablish the flow and arrangement of rooms and the outli for the perimeter of the building (Figures 1.7C and D). A signer who is working with a multistory house or high-r office complex may develop a **stacking diagram** (see I sign Scenario) to help evaluate what departments or roo are located on each level. As with the smaller residential pr ect, the designer ultimately puts all this information or floor plan to illustrate the layout of the space. This proc is called **space planning.**

Also during conceptual design, the designer selects sa ple color chips for reference to the color palette, fabri and/or furniture for the design scheme. The designer m also prepare a preliminary three-dimensional drawing o perspective to help the client visualize the proposed n space. As with the floor plan and preliminary furniture pl all of these diagrams, drawings, and sketches add to t process of visual communication.

The designer prepares all of this conceptual design do mentation while considering the life safety and building cod universal accessibility codes, sustainable design options, a budget (all of which are discussed in later chapters). Only ter presenting these designs to the client *and* receiving cli approval will the designer move on to the next phase of t design process. The conceptual design phase consumes fr 15 to 20 percent of the time in the total design process.

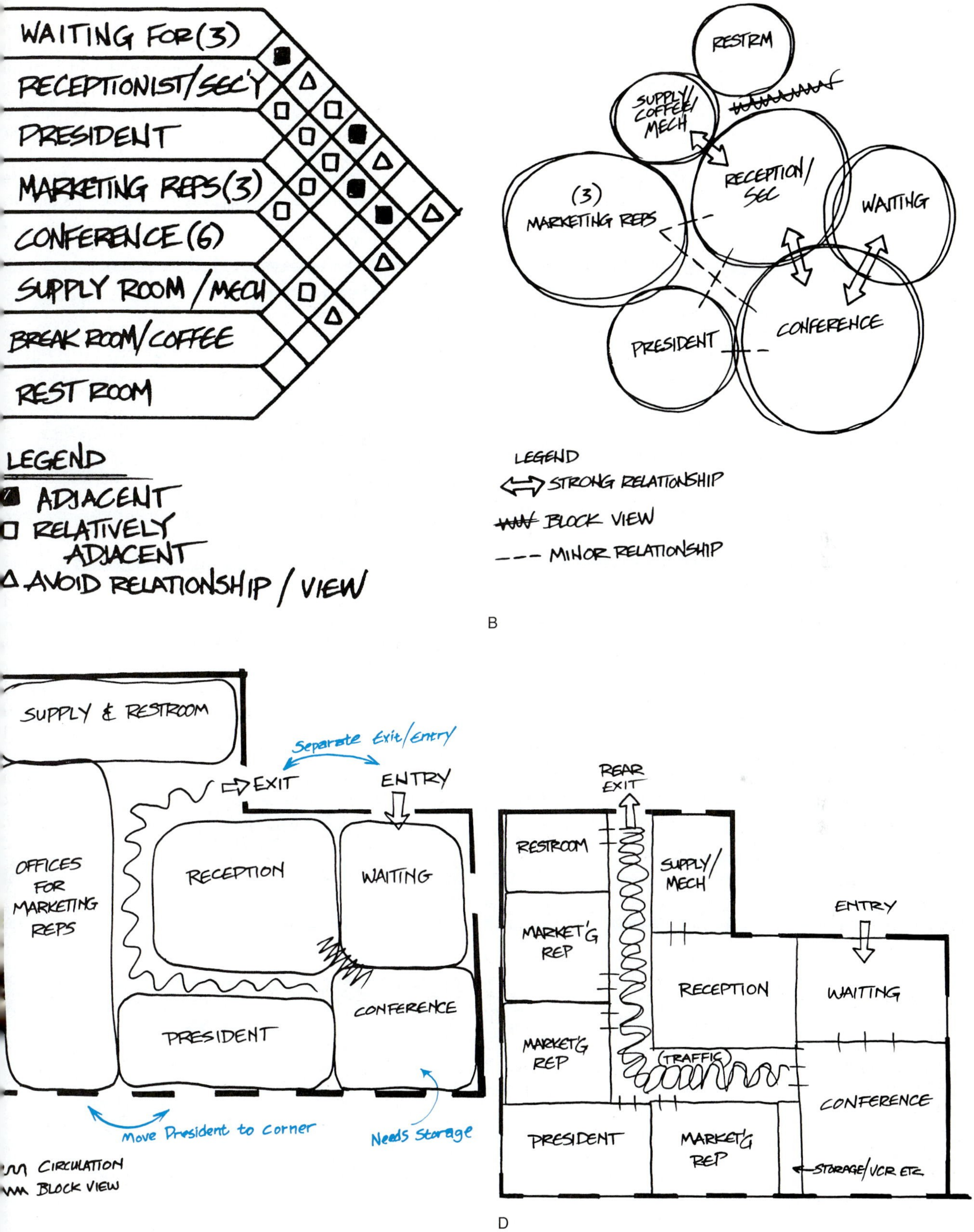

gure 1.7 *In this series of illustrations, a small commercial real estate office floor plan is developed through conceptual sign: (A) matrix; (B) bubble diagram; (C) blocking diagram—step 1; (D) blocking diagram—step 2.*

Design Development

The **design development** phase is also a creative phase. During this phase, all the furniture, fabrics, finishes, hardware, and lighting fixtures are selected for the client's review. Space planning of rooms and furniture arrangements is refined based on feedback from the client's review of the conceptual design. Designers may develop art, accessory, graphic, or signage programs. Walls, windows, doors, fireplaces, stairs, and ceiling designs are defined and detailed where necessary. This entire array of information is shown to the client via a presentation.

A small residential project presentation may include ph tographs of selected pieces of furniture and actual samp of fabrics, floor coverings, and wall treatments along with presentation floor plan. More likely, however, the client w be taken to a showroom or a decorative arts center to vie specific selections.

A more complex residential project or a commercial pr ect usually requires a series of presentation boards that ill trate the interior space (Figure 1.8). Visual communicatio

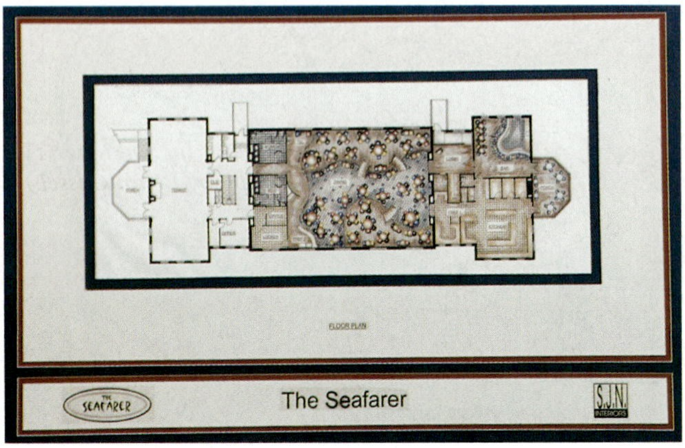

A

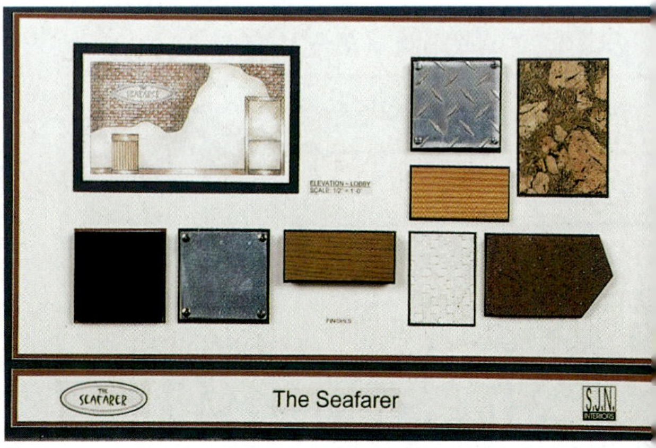

B

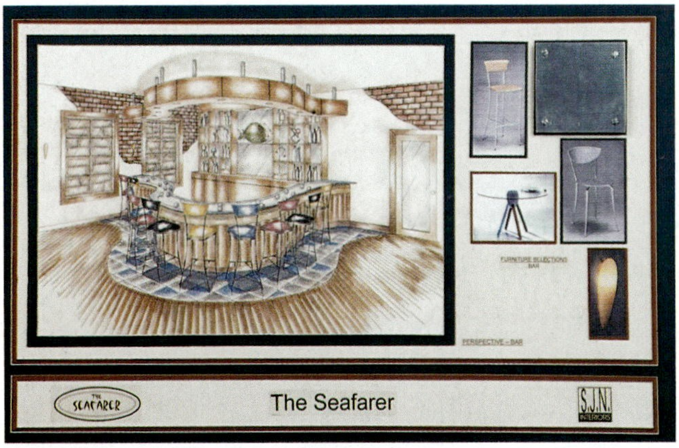

C

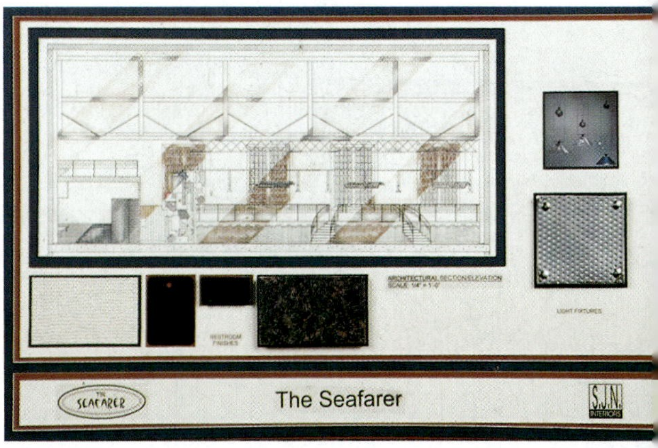

D

Figure 1.8 *In this design development presentation for a restaurant, the designer prepared a series of boards. The client requested an industrial style restaurant, based on shipyard elements. Figure 1.8A illustrates the proposed floor plan. Figure 1.8B illustrates an elevation of the concierge station and related finishes. A perspective of the bar and its finishes is shown in Figure 1.8C. Figure 1.8D illustrates the design of the restaurant through an elevation/cut section of the main room, as well as selected finishes. The final figure, 1.8E, reemphasizes the main restaurant area and furnishings, using a paraline drawing, sometimes referred to as an isometric. (Designer: Shoko Nishimura.)*

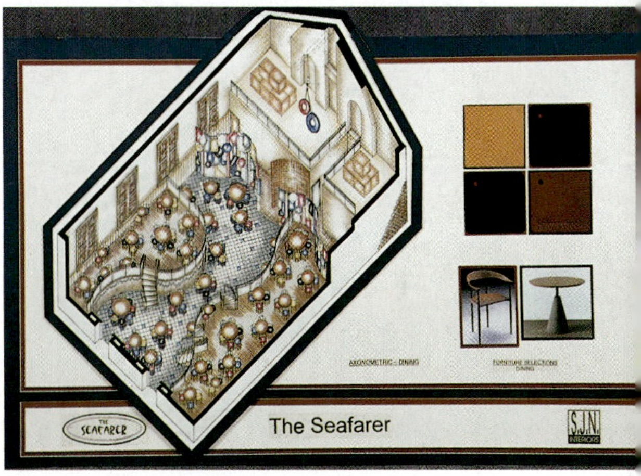

E

ıy include black and white or colored floor plans, **eleva-ns** (drawings of walls), or perspectives. The presentation ·ards include samples of fabrics and finishes, and photo-ıphs of furniture, art, and accessories. Models are some-ıes built to show unusual or dynamic spaces such as ›bies and entry halls or soaring ceiling designs. Current .D technology can visually walk clients through a virtual erior (Figure 1.9).

As in the previous design phases, the designer is always ·are of the budget, life safety, and universal design re-irements. None of the design recommendations are acted upon until the client has approved the design. This phase of design occupies 25 to 30 percent of the overall time in the design project.

Contract Documentation

The next phase of design, called **contract documentation,** allows the designer to document the design decisions made in the previous design phases. In collaboration with architects, designers prepare **construction** or **working drawings** (detailed plans, elevations, and sections).

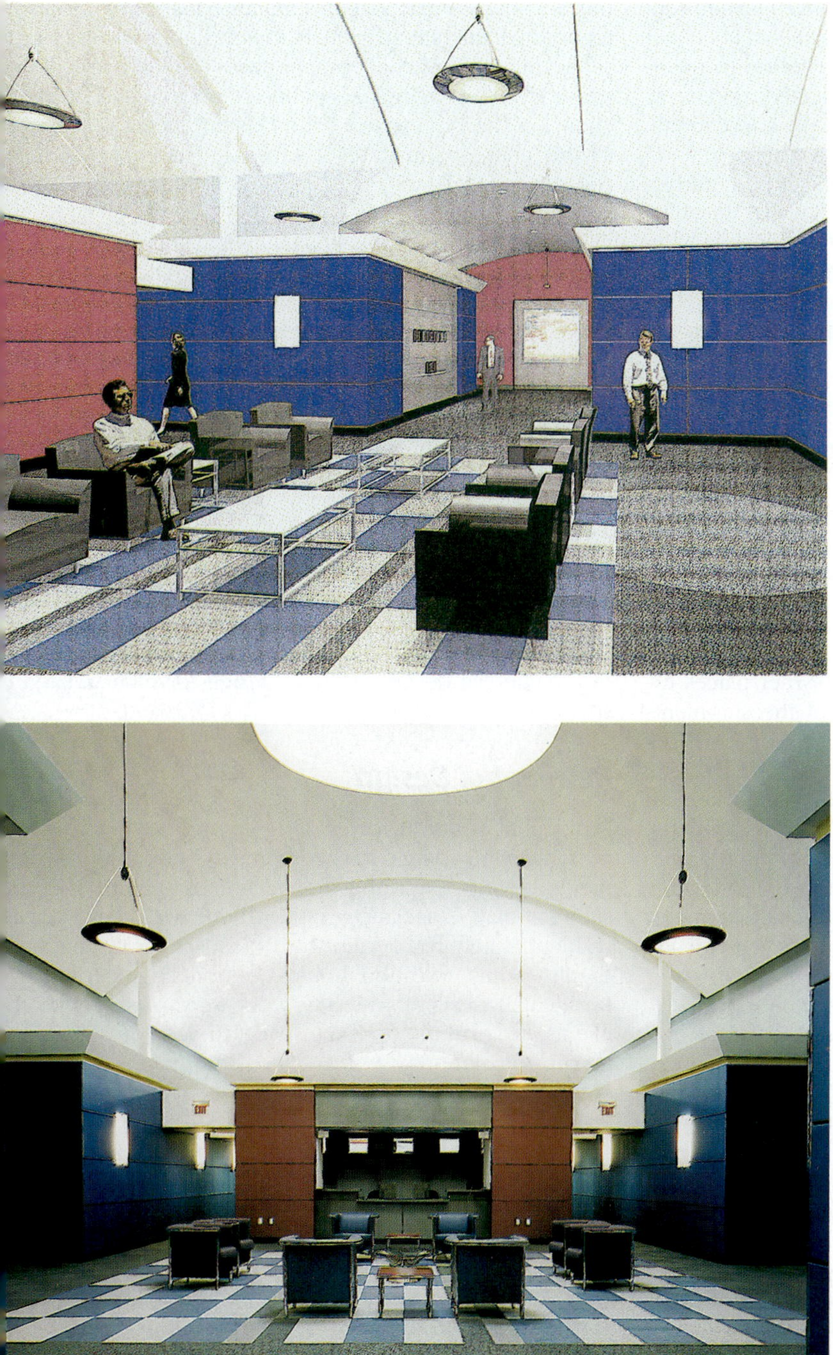

Figure 1.9 *A computer-generated view of the corporate office lobby is shown in (A), (B) is a photo of the completed interior. (Architect: Thompson, Ventulett, Stainback & Associates Inc. Designer: TVS Interiors. Photograph by Brian Gassel.)*

Designers also collaborate with allied professionals who determine architectural, mechanical, electrical, and structural requirements.

For a small residential project, the contract document (CD) phase may only include writing purchase orders for furniture, fabrics, and other items to be purchased for the client and installed by the vendors. For a large residential project or commercial project, the designer not only will be involved with the development of the working drawings but also may write **specifications.** The specification (or spec) book is a documentation of all the furniture and other items that are not attached to the building. The spec book or **furniture, furnishings, and equipment package (FF&E)** is then sent to several vendors for bidding.

The working drawings are also sent out to bid to qualified contractors. Once bids have been collected, reviewed, and awarded, the contract documents phase is complete. This tedious yet exacting phase of design may take 30 to 35 percent of the total design process time. If the budget preparation by the designer has proven effective, the bids meet the planned budget. Otherwise, the designer may need to select less expensive items, finishes, and alternative design solutions. Sometimes, however, the client may like the design enough to increase the budget to meet the higher cost.

Contract Administration

Contract administration is usually the most rewarding phase of the project. All of the design decisions become real as the walls are built, mechanical, lighting, and electrical systems are installed, finishes are applied, and the FF&E is placed according to the designer's plans. As the title implies, the designer is administering the contracts completed in contract documentation.

For a smaller residential project, the designer places orders, and continually monitors the status of the shipments and the installation of the items. For larger projects, the designer regularly visits the job site to verify that the working drawings are followed and the job is progressing as planned. The designer oversees the installation of the FF&E. At the end of this phase, which takes 5 to 15 percent of the design process time, the designer prepares a **punch list** indicating all the items not yet finished in the project. Final payments to vendors and contractors are withheld until the items are completed.

Evaluation

In this final phase of design, sometimes called **postoccupancy evaluation (POE),** the designer and client evaluate the effectiveness of the design decisions. The designer may interview selected individuals in the firm to determine their level of satisfaction with the new interior space. The designer may also photograph the space and visually analyze the design solutions.

According to NCIDQ's *Definition of Interior Design:* "The interior design process follows a systematic and coordinated methodology. Research, analysis, and integration of information into the creative process result in an appropriate interior environment." Utilizing these phases of the desi process helps ensure that designers' solutions will not o satisfy their clients' needs but will also result in successful terior spaces.

The design process is a continuous flow of informati through all phases. Certainly for billing and for educatio purposes it is simpler to establish separate categories, though in practice the phases tend to merge. For examp in residential design a client may accompany a designer a buying trip. On the trip, the selection, specification, a purchasing of goods (which correspond to the design c velopment, contract documentation, and contract admin tration phases) may occur simultaneously. It is importa to note in this situation that the designer completed t programming and conceptual phases (which correspond the analysis and initial synthesis) prior to escorting t client on the buying trip. The Design Scenario at the e of this chapter illustrates a successful commercial desi project.

More info online @

http://www.iida.org/DefinitionID.html Further explanation of the design process

Career Specializations in Interior Design

As the demand for quality housing, products, and comm cial facilities rises, interior designers are finding more a more opportunities for creative design positions. Wh searching for a career path, a designer may choose fron variety of possibilities including residential design, contr or commercial design, product design, or other related c sign industries.

Residential Design

Residential design involves designing private living quart or homes, including detached homes, condominiums, apa ments, townhouses, and mobile homes (Figure 1.10). D signers may specialize in kitchen and bath desig residential lighting, designs for the elderly or disabled, ch dren's rooms, vacation homes, remodeling, or additio Residential designers usually work very closely with th clients, the **end users** of the space, to develop specific p sonalized solutions.

Contract or Commercial Design

The opportunities in commercial design are broad. Tal 1.2 lists several of the options along with a brief explar tion of each area. Commercial or contract designers wc with a variety of clients who may or may not be the e user. For example, a designer working on a restaurant c sign may meet with the owner, the developer, and the cl to determine the desires of each for the new facility. U mately, however, the designer is designing for the clien

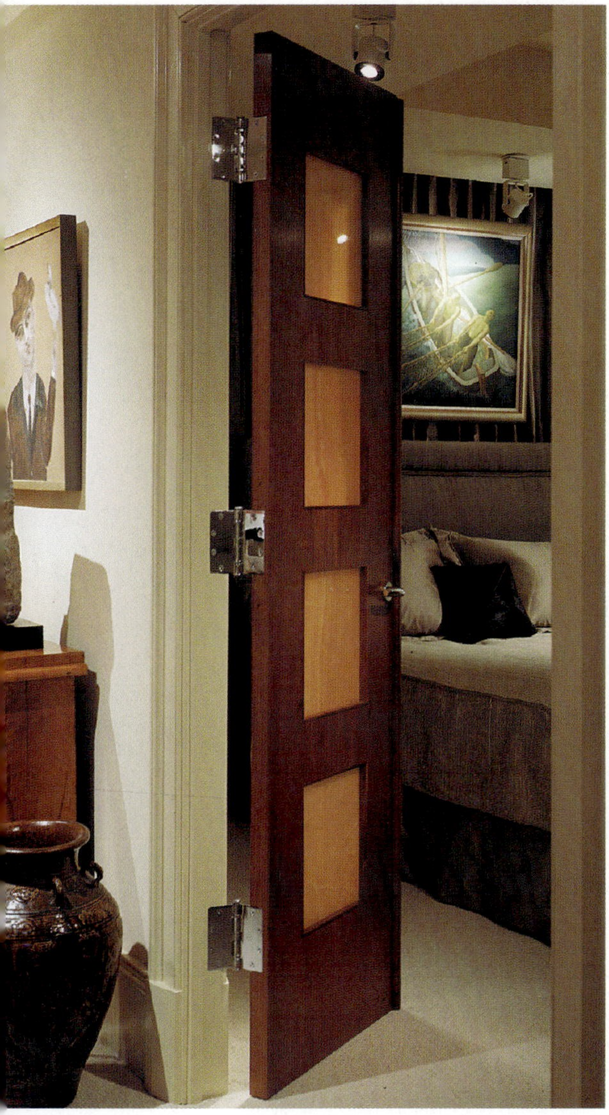

ȝure 1.10 *A custom-designed mahogany door with onyx* ›*ets adds character to this interior space. The designer* ›*ated an environment that accentuates the client's* '*lection of paintings and decorative arts. (Designer: BRITO* ›*sign Studio. Photograph by Brian Gassel. As seen in* Atlanta ›mes and Lifestyles.)

Table 1.2 *Opportunities in Contract (Commercial) Design*

Major Specialty Areas	
• Commercial office design	Involves extensive space planning and design of small to large corporate office environments.
• Health care design	Involves designs for hospitals, clinics, nursing homes, disabled and elderly care facilities, and doctors' offices. The current trend in elderly care facilities blends this specialty with hospitality design.
• Hospitality design	Involves the design of hotels, motels, restaurants, casinos, resorts, clubs, and inns. Blends many aspects of residential design with contract design (see Figures 1.1 and 1.8).
• Institutional design	Involves the design of government buildings, such as courthouses, city halls, libraries, and museums as well as educational facilities such as public and private universities, colleges, and schools.
• Retail design	Involves the design of shopping malls, stores, boutiques, strip malls, and showrooms. Designers must be sensitive to the products to be displayed in the various areas.
Minor Specialty Areas	
• Entertainment design	Involves the design of theaters, concert halls, auditoriums, and convention centers.
• Financial institutions	Involves the design of banks, stock exchanges, credit unions, and savings and loan facilities.
• Industrial design	Involves the design of warehouses, factories, laboratories, workshops, and manufacturing plants.
• Recreational design	Involves the design of health and spa centers, swimming pools, bowling alleys, and other sports facilities.
• Transportation design	Involves the design of airports, train stations, terminals, motor homes, boats and ships, and other transportation vehicles and facilities.

ent, the patrons who will be eating at the restaurant (Fig- ͤ 1.11). Commercial as well as residential designers must low strict fire and life safety codes and must also meet iversal design criteria. Surface materials, fabrics, and fin- ıes must not endanger the health, safety, or welfare of the blic.

›re info online @

ɒ://www.asid.org/design_basics/design_specialities/index.asp ɛcializations in interior design

ɒ://www.iida.org/organization/forums/ Specializations in interior ;ign

Related Design Professions

Designers may also choose to concentrate their efforts in one specific area or phase of design. Design specialty areas include communication (audio/video) design; exhibit design; model home design; solar design; and storage, cabinet, and closet design. Some designers may choose to specialize in selecting drapery and window treatment, or other finishes such as flooring or wall covering. Other designers may find that they have particularly strong selling skills and therefore may work as sales representatives.

Although many times overlooked, product design is an expansive field that requires creative minds. Product designers

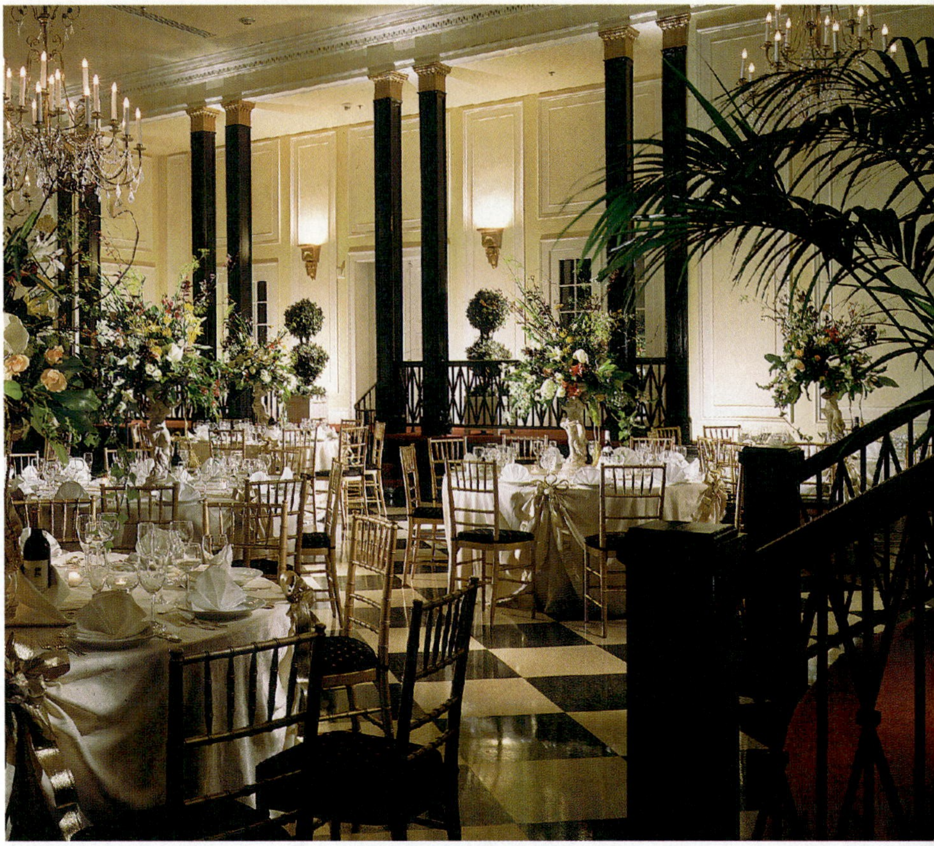

Figure 1.11 *The Old Well room in the Carolina Inn exhibits crisp cool colors, which create a comfortable environment for dining. The lobby (Figure 1.1) blends well with this dining room, creating a consistent flow of style. (Architect/Designer: The Glave Firm. Photograph by Robert Miller.)*

are responsible for the design of the furnishings, finishes, and fabrics in the interior environment. Textiles, wall and floor coverings, furniture, lighting, and hardware (to name but a few) are items product designers create to be placed in the interior space.

Other challenging specialty opportunities are available in industry, manufacturing, transportation, communications, recreation, and in state and federal governments, where the diverse skills of design professionals are considered essential to long-range planning and product development. Table 1.3 lists additional design specialties.

Allied Professions

Interior designers must develop strong working relationships with other professionals in the construction and design industries. Allied professionals work closely with designers to form design teams and partnerships. This collaboration and networking enhances the communication skills required of interior designers.

Architects

The architect generally designs the exterior of the building. In small remodeling projects an architect may be contracted to advise on structural or mechanical systems. On larger residential and commercial facilities the architect works directly with the client, designing the exterior as well as the structural components of the building. Architects and designers frequently collaborate on the building's interior construction non-load-bearing walls. The architect may also oversee t construction of the space.

More info online @

http://www.aia.org American Society of Architects

Engineers

Engineers work with architects and designers to produce t mechanical, electrical, plumbing, and structural drawings a building. Proper communication is particularly criti when working with engineers to ensure that the design co cept complies with engineering limitations. Designers shou examine drawings produced by engineers.

More info online @

http://www.asce.org/ American Society of Civil Engineers

http://www.ashrae.org/ American Society of Heating, Refrigeration and Air-Conditioning Engineers

General Contractor

The general contractor, or GC, administers the actual co struction process. Generally, the GC oversees the proce and subcontracts the work to others.

able 1.3 *Related Opportunities in the Design Industry*

• Adaptive use designer	Works on the restoration or remodeling of historic buildings for a new function.
• Buyer	Purchases merchandise for furniture or department stores and studios.
• Color consultant	Aids clients in both residential and nonresidential design, with regard to color.
• Design journalist	Completes work for newspapers, magazines, or publishers on a variety of timely aspects of interior design.
• Drafter or CAD operator	Prepares precise mechanical drawings, often on the computer, for architects, designers, builders, and furnishing manufacturers.
• Educator	After seeking advanced degrees the educator instructs at a college or university.
• Facilities manager	Works with companies to determine the best use of their space and equipment.
• Fine art or accessory designer	Selects and purchases personal and corporate art and accessories.
• Historic preservation designer	Restores and preserves a historic structure as it was in the past.
• Lighting specialist	Designs lighting plans essential in the design process.
• Purchasing agent	Orders, coordinates, and installs FF&E per designer's specifications.
• Renderer	Prepares realistic three-dimensional drawings and illustrations of a designer's concept for an interior.
• Set designer or stylist	Works on television, theater, and movie productions or creates complete room displays for department stores, furniture companies, and manufacturers for advertising.
• Sustainable design consultant	Aids in the design and product selection of materials that ensure environmental sustainability.
• Universal designer	Specializes in the design of spaces for the elderly and disabled.

ore info online @

p:/www.agc.org/ Association of General Contractors of America

p://www.nawic.org/ National Association of Women in onstruction

aphic Designers

commercial design, the graphic designer may assist in the velopment of appropriate signage for a building, brochure sign, menu design, or a corporate identification and marting package.

ore info online @

p://www.aiga.org/ American Institute of Graphic Designers

p://www.icograda.org/web/home/index.html International Council Graphic Designers

ndscape Architect

e landscape architect (LA) should be involved in theden process for the initial site selection. The LA can share ucial information with the architect and designer that may ect the shape and form of buildings. During contract docnentation the LA provides important grading plans to prent erosion and future water problems, and provides anting and vegetation plans allowing the building to relate its site.

More info online @

http://asla.org/ American Society of Landscape Architects

Summary

From its beginnings in the nineteenth and twentieth centuries, the profession of interior design has emerged into a multimillion-dollar industry. The profession has grown to encompass a broad scope of responsibilities, procedures, relationships, and opportunities, which NCIDQ synthesized into an established definition of the field of interior design. Professional design societies such as ASID and IIDA support NCIDQ by acknowledging the passage of the NCIDQ exam as one of their requirements for acceptance as a professional member.

Creating interiors based on the goals of function and the human factor, aesthetics, and economics and ecology allows the designer to address all aspects of a successful interior environment. In order to better analyze the abundance of information required in a design project and then synthesize that information into a cohesive design solution, the design process and scope of services were developed. Each phase of the process interlocks, ensuring creative design solutions that address the client's needs. These phases allow for the unique contributions of universal and sustainable design solutions. Finally, allied design professionals collaborate to create the accurate communications necessary for successful interior environments

Project Description

Godwin Associates has been retained by IMS Health Strategic Technologies, Inc. (formerly Sales Technologies, Inc.) to help facilitate the company's move into a new corporate office facility and a customer service center. The new three-floor corporate office space will utilize approximately 60,000 square feet. The customer service center will result from combining two separate groups in one central 60,000-square-foot facility.

Programming: Figures DS1.1 through DS1.3 indicate space quirements for different areas of the firm. Note the importa category called projected growth. Figure DS1.4 summarizes t square footage needs for the entire facility.

SALES TECHNOLOGIES CORPORATE FACILITIES PROGRAM 30-Jan-97	CURRENT - 1997				PROJECTED GROWTH		
DEPARTMENT/AREA	WORK AREA TYPE	QUANTITY	UNIT SQUARE FOOTAGE	TOTAL SQUARE FOOTAGE	QUANTITY	UNIT SQUARE FOOTAGE	TOTAL SQUARE FOOTAGE
RECEPTION/CONFERENCE							
Reception Area		1	600	600	0	600	0
Receptionist	WS	1	150	150	0	150	0
Conference		3	500	1500	0	500	0
A/V Storage		1	150	150	0	150	0
Subtotal:				2400			0
35% Circulation Factor:				840			0
DEPARTMENT TOTAL:				3240			0

NOTES:
1. All Conference Rooms to have the following: tackboards, whiteboards, recessed electric projection screens, variable lighting, and separate HVAC zone.
2. Conference Rooms to accommodate computer work area.
3. A/V Storage for slide/T.V. carts to be shared by all Conference Rooms.
4. Receptionist - 2 systems: Network PC with keyboard and Phone PC with keyboard
   - Would like to recess screens
   - Large Fax
   - Large Printer
   - Need wire management under desk
   - Currently no fax but will get one
   - Needs ticket drop-off areas
   - Transaction area needed for ticket pick-up

Figure DS1.1 *Programming requirements and estimated square footage needs for the reception/conference area. (Architect/Designer: Godwin Associates.)*

SALES TECHNOLOGIES CORPORATE FACILITIES PROGRAM 30-Jan-97	CURRENT - 1997				PROJECTED GROWTH		
DEPARTMENT/AREA	WORK AREA TYPE	QUANTITY	UNIT SQUARE FOOTAGE	TOTAL SQUARE FOOTAGE	QUANTITY	UNIT SQUARE FOOTAGE	TOTAL SQUARE FOOTAGE
PROFESSIONAL SERVICES/ IMPLEMENTATION							
Sr. Director	PO	1	150	150	0	150	0
Director	PO	2	150	300	0	150	0
Manager	PO	4	150	600	1	150	150
Customer Support Manager	WS	18	64	1152	4	64	256
Customer Support Specialists	WS	16	64	1024	3	64	192
Project Manager	WS	4	64	256	1	64	64
Intern	WS	1	64	64	0	64	0
Implementation Specialists	WS	8	64	512	2	64	128
Departmental Shared Areas							
File/Storage Room		1	120	120	0	120	0
Test Area		1	300	300	0	300	0
Subtotal:				4478			790
35% Circulation Factor:				1567			277
DEPARTMENT TOTAL:				6045			1067

NOTES:
1. Preferred department location is adjacent to Information Technology & Services, Customer Service and to Product Management/QA.
2. Implementation has total of (8) 36"W lateral files and (2) magazine racks.
3. Test area to be enclosed drywall area with glass sidelights and stereo/TV equipment.

Figure DS1.2 *Programming requirements and estimated square footage needs for the professional services area. (Architect/Designer: Godwin Associates.)*

SALES TECHNOLOGIES CORPORATE FACILITIES PROGRAM 30-Jan-97	CURRENT - 1997				PROJECTED GROWTH		
DEPARTMENT/AREA	WORK AREA TYPE	QUANTITY	UNIT SQUARE FOOTAGE	TOTAL SQUARE FOOTAGE	QUANTITY	UNIT SQUARE FOOTAGE	TOTAL SQUAR FOOTA
DEMO/TRAINING							
Manager of Customer Training	PO	1	150	150	0	150	0
Technical Training Coordinator	WS	1	64	64	0	64	0
Team Leader/Sr. Training Coordinator	WS	1	64	64	0	64	0
Sr. Training Coordinator	WS	2	64	128	0	64	0
Training Coordinator	WS	5	64	320	0	64	0
Team Leader Sr. Inst. Designer	WS	1	64	64	0	64	0
Sr. Instructional Designer	WS	1	64	64	0	64	0
Instructional Designer	WS	4	64	256	0	64	0
Departmental Shared Areas							
File/Storage and Demo Room		1	300	300	0	300	0
Test Area		1	300	300	0	300	0
Demo Room		1	800	800	0	800	0
Training Room		2	1200	2400	0	1200	0
Break Out Area		1	300	300	0	300	0
Telephone Area		4	25	100	0	25	0
Storage - Equipment		1	120	120	0	120	0
Subtotal:				5430			0
35% Circulation Factor:				1901			0
DEPARTMENT TOTAL:				7331			0

NOTES:
1. Test area to be enclosed drywall area not workstation area with sidelights and stereo/TV equipment.
2. Demo will require two entrances, one off of main reception area.
3. Training has total of (11) 36"W files and 40 L.F. of storage.
4. Training Room will have movable wall system to create (2) separate rooms.

Figure DS1.3 *Programming requirements and estimated square footage needs for the demo/training area. (Architect/Designer: Godwin Associates.)*

Godwin Associates' Project #96088 — January 30, 1997

PROGRAM SUMMARY FOR SALES TECHNOLOGIES
CORPORATE FACILITIES
REVISION #1

DEPARTMENT AREA	EMPLOYEE TOTAL	CURRENT - 1997 S.F. (INCLUDING CIRCULATION)	CURRENT PLUS GROWTH EMPLOYEE TOTAL (*)	CURRENT PLUS GROWTH S. F. (INCLUDING CIRCULATION)
RECEPTION/CONFERENCE	1	3240	1	3240
EXECUTIVE	9	3274	10	3578
LEGAL	3	694	3	694
DEVELOPMENT	61	9480	69	10403
PRODUCT MANAGEMENT QUALITY ASSURANCE	11	1655	13	1828
SALES AND MARKETING	5	818	5	818
INFORMATION TECHNOLOGY & SERVICES	4	462	4	462
PROFESSIONAL SERVICES IMPLEMENTATION	54	6045	65	7112
INFORMATION SERVICES	10	6743	11	6829
FINANCE	7	1418	9	1591
VENDOR	4	346	4	346
TRAVEL SERVICES	5	743	5	743
DEMO/TRAINING	16	7331	16	7331
MAILROOM/COPY CENTER	1	918	1	918
SHARED AREAS - FLOOR A	0	2403	0	2403
SHARED AREAS - FLOOR B	0	1053	0	1053
SHARED AREAS - FLOOR C	0	1526	0	1526
TOTAL:	191	48,149	216	50,875

Figure DS1.4 *Summary of square footage requirements. (Architect/Designer: Godwin Associates.)*

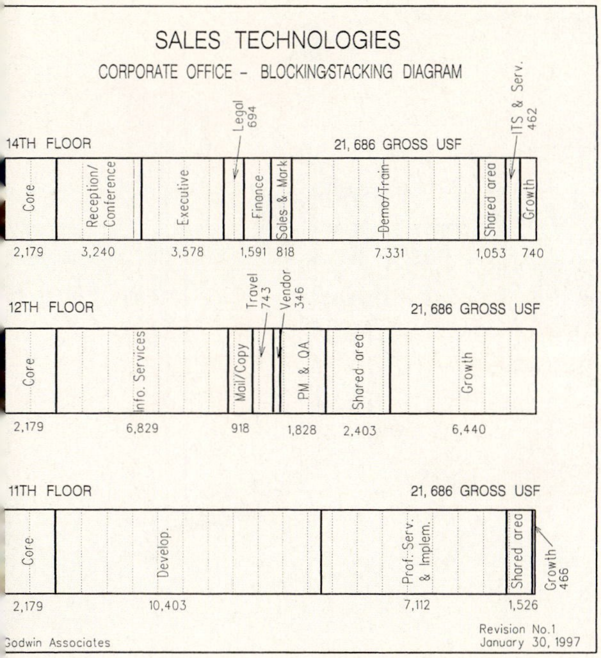

Conceptual/Schematic Design: After the programming information was analyzed, Godwin Associates developed a stacking diagram (Figure DS1.5). After generating bubble diagrams, blocking plans, and rough preliminary floor plans, the schematic furniture presentation plan was shown to the client (Figure DS1.6). Preliminary FF&E selections were also shared with the client.

Design Development: Based on the client's feedback and approval of the conceptual design, Godwin Associates continued to refine the design solution and select actual finishes and furnishings while defining custom details and elevations. The design development presentation had several components, including a computer-generated floor plan (Figure DS1.7) and several perspective renderings (Figures DS1.8 through DS1.10).

Figure DS1.5 *Stacking diagram. (Architect/Designer: Godwin Associates.)*

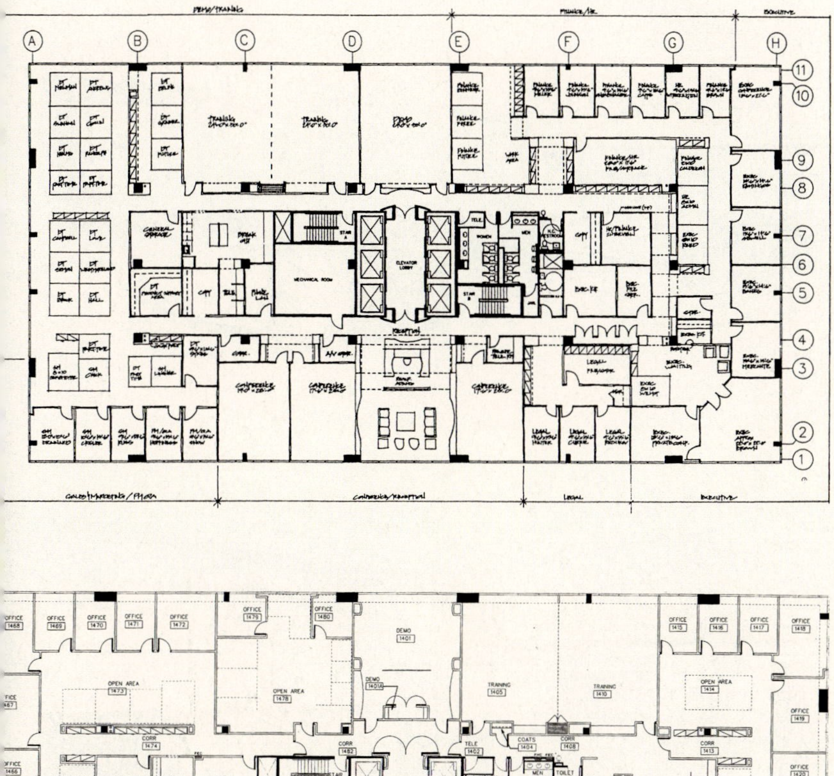

Figure DS1.6 *Schematic floor plan for the 14th floor. (Architect/Designer: Godwin Associates.)*

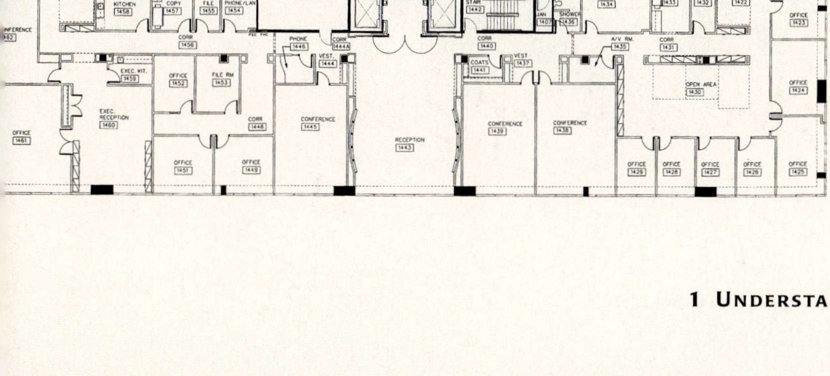

Figure DS1.7 *Design development—Computer-generated floor plan. (Architect/Designer: Godwin Associates.)*

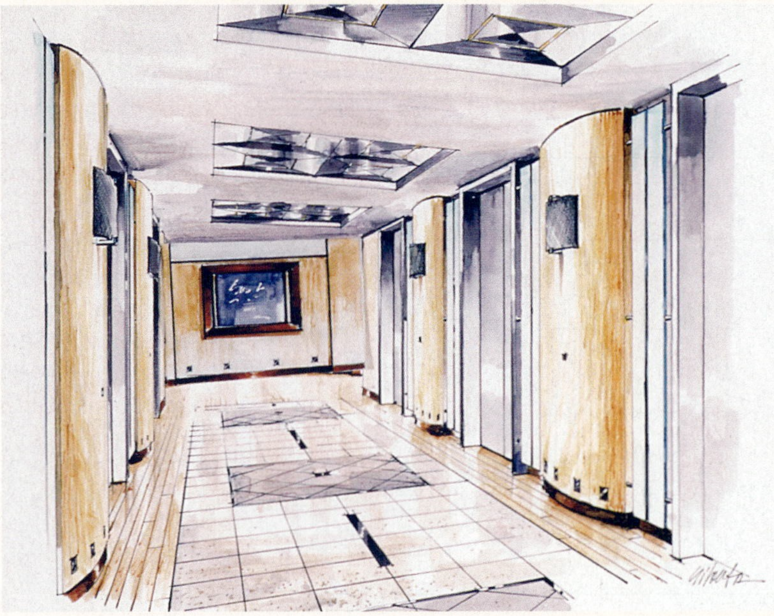

Figure DS1.8 *Design development—Presentation perspective of the elevator lobby. (Architect/Designer: Godwin Associates.)*

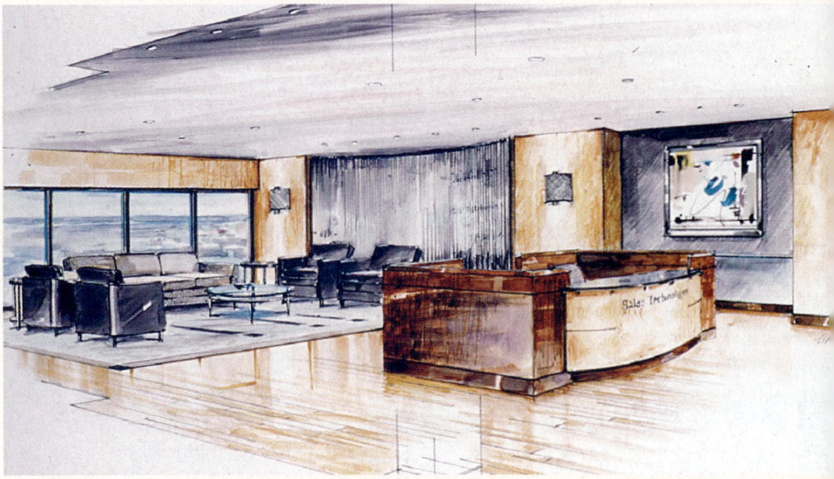

Figure DS1.9 *Design development—Presentation perspective of the reception area. (Architect/Designer: Godwin Associates.)*

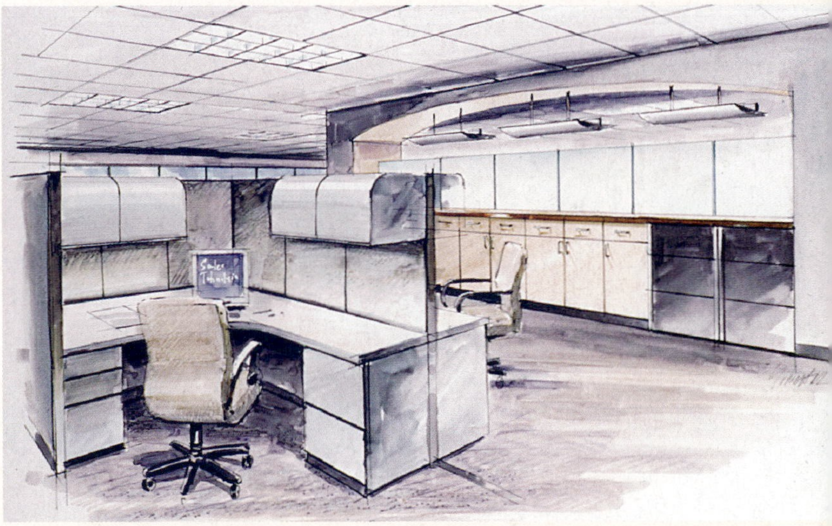

Figure DS1.10 *Design development—Presentation perspective of open office space. (Architect/Designer: Godwin Associates.)*

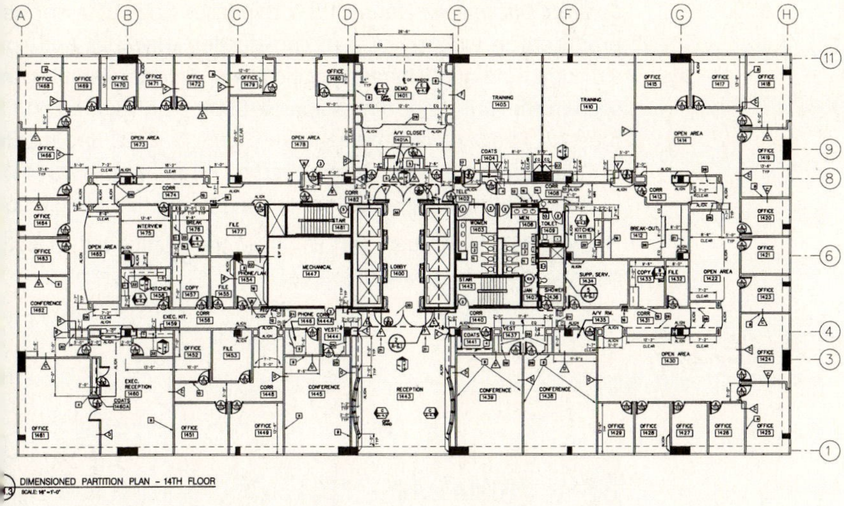

Figure DS1.11 *Construction drawing—Dimension partition plan for the 14th floor. (Architect/Designer: Godwin Associates.)*

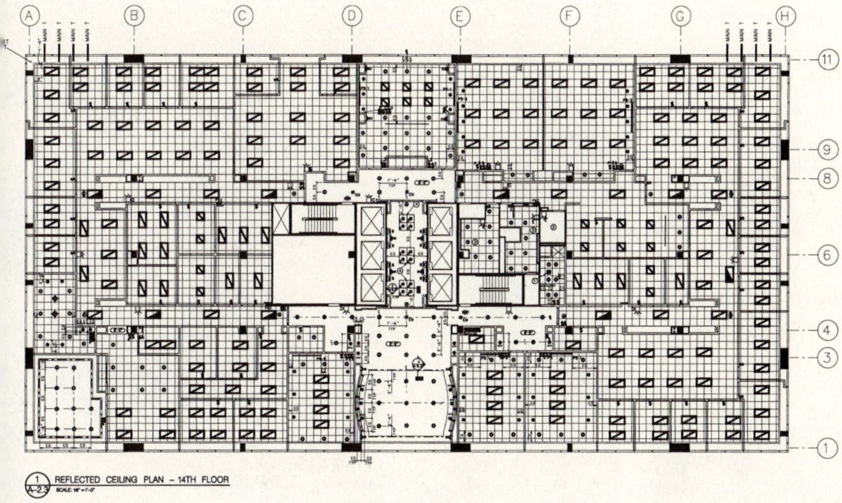

Figure DS1.12 *Construction drawing—Reflected ceiling plan for the 14th floor. (Architect/Designer: Godwin Associates.)*

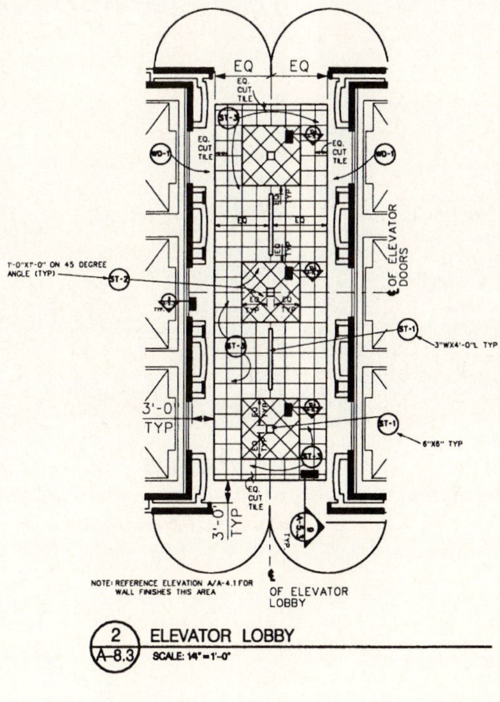

Figure DS1.13 *Construction drawing—Detail of the finish plan for the elevator lobby. (Architect/Designer: Godwin Associates.)*

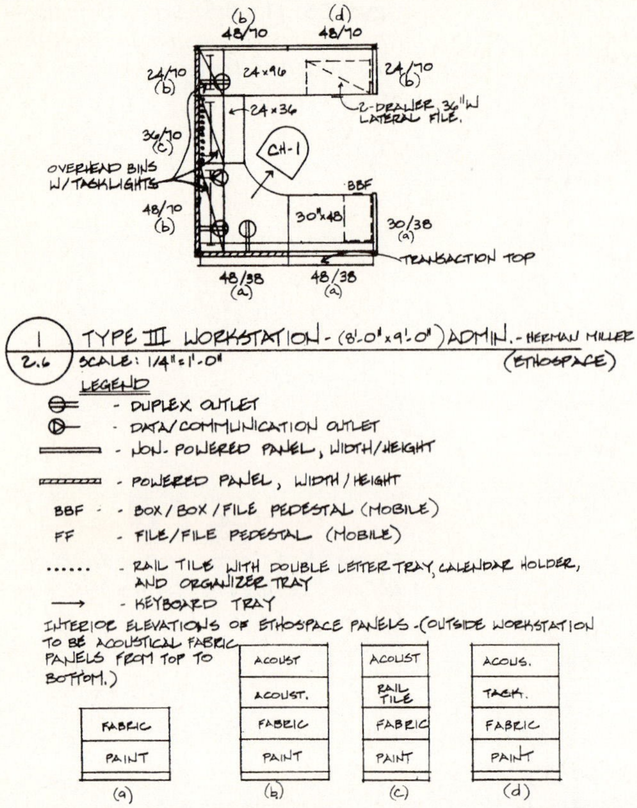

Figure DS1.14 *Construction drawing—Furniture design of a typical open office workstation. (Architect/Designer: Godwin Associates.)*

Contract Documents: During the CD phase, Godwin Associa produced an extensive set of construction drawings and co struction and furnishings specifications. Select examples seen in the 14th floor dimension partition plan (Figure DS1.1 the 14th floor reflected ceiling plan (Figure DS1.12), and the ish plan for the elevator lobby (Figure DS1.13). Figure DS1.14 lustrates a furniture specification for an open office workstati

Figures DS1.15 through DS1.17 show the completed eleva lobby and reception/waiting area.

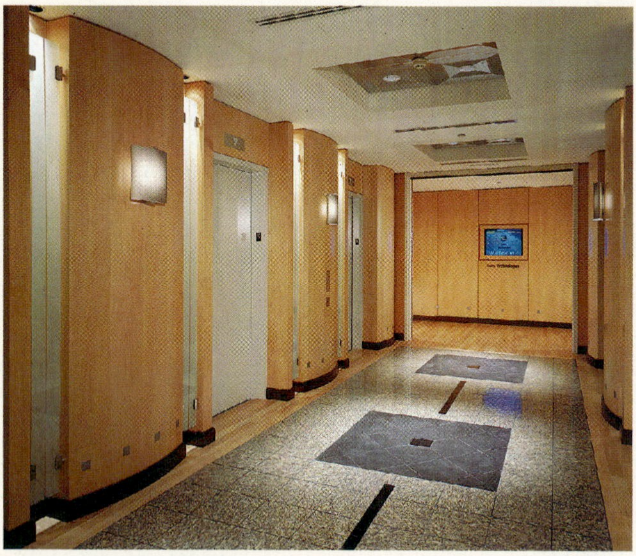

Figure DS1.15 *Completed space—Elevator lobby. (Architect/Designer: Godwin Associates. Photograph by Brian Robbins Photography.)*

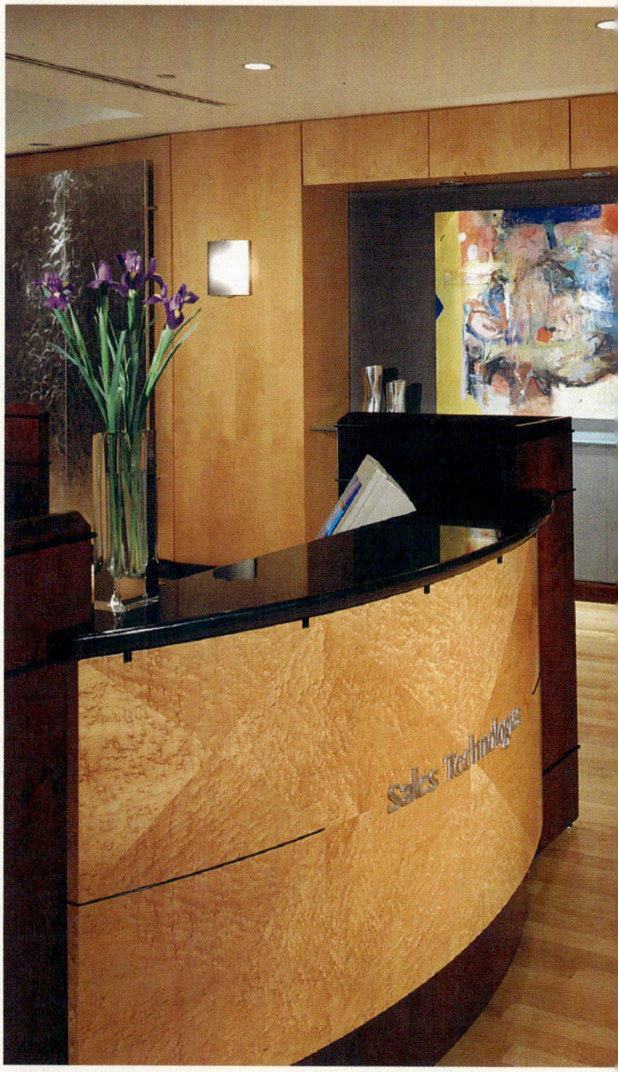

Figure DS1.16 *Completed space—Reception desk. (Architect/Designer: Godwin Associates. Photograph by Bria Robbins Photography.)*

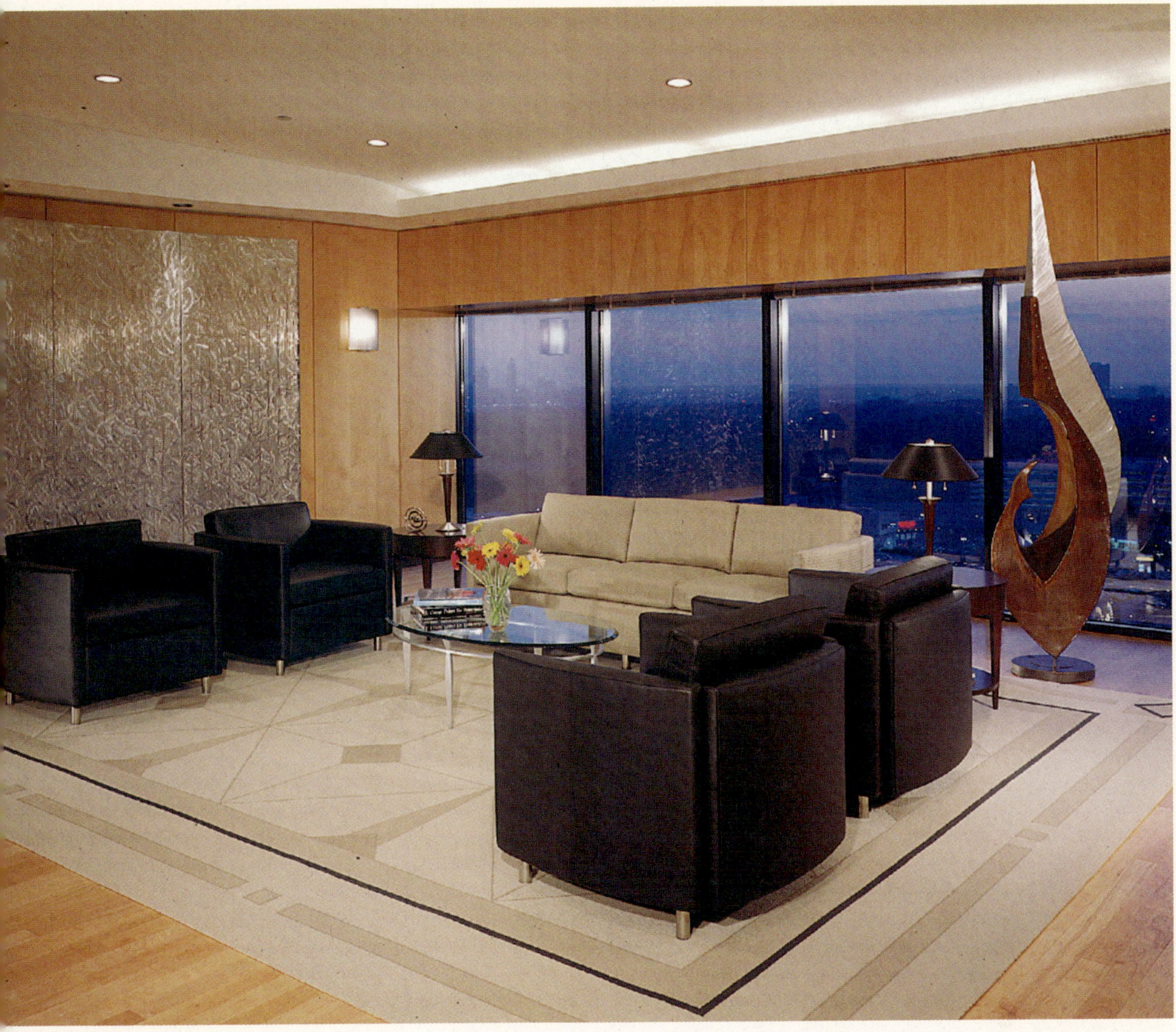

igure DS1.17 *Completed space—Reception area. (Architect/Designer: Godwin Associates. Photograph by Brian Robbins hotography.)*

History of Style

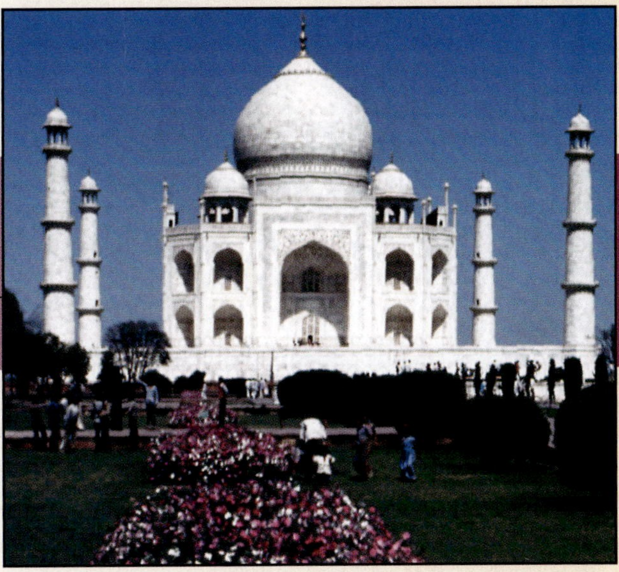

Built in 1631, the Taj Mahal is a memorial to Mumtaz Mahal, wife of Emperor Shah Jaham. The Dome is of white marble, and intricate tile patterns are used throughout the structure. Taj Mahal translates to "Crown Palace." (Photograph from Prentice Hall.)

ghout history, the diversity of cultures has found ssion in many directions, including the way people designed and furnished their built environment. n is shaped by many factors, including environmental, ous, and political circumstances. As these factors ge, design reflects these changes while building on ous design theories and philosophies. Styles of design, fore, reflect these social surroundings and their lations.

erm *style* generally refers to a segment of design history that is typical of an dual, a period, or a philosophy of design. Style may also refer to a particular culture gion. Style categories are developed by historians in an attempt to organize history. lity, however, styles do not necessarily have sharp starting and stopping points. ry is fluid. Designs from one region may influence others, and therefore styles mingle.

ng a working knowledge of these styles is essential. Such understanding deepens the or designer's aesthetic appreciation of design and serves as a basis to foster creative gies.

gners study styles of the past and present to enrich current interior environments. This rial essay briefly outlines the major styles that have had an impact on architecture nterior design. The first section, Historical Styles and Their Evolution, reviews classical n styles and how these styles have been adapted through history. The pages on ent, Middle Ages, Renaissance, and Baroque eras define universal design styles based me period classifications; the French, Chinese, Hispanic, African, Japanese, English, American pages define styles that are more typically associated with their respective ns. The second section, Evolution of Modern Design, looks at the development of ern design and how these styles and philosophies have been applied.

nfo online @

www.greatbuildings.com/ General website of world buildings

www.washington.edu/ark2/ University of Washington database of over 5000 buildings worldwide

www.dezignare.com/library.html Comprehensive site for all facets of design, this link specifically related to history

Historical Styles and THEIR EVOLUTION

Interior design and decoration dates back to the Upper Paleolithic era (30,000–10,000 B.C.). Drawings found in caves in Spain and France show evidence of wall decorations using grouping and spacing concepts as well as limited understanding of perspective. Sculptured figures of stone, ivory, and clay depicted the human form and often included enlarged reproductive organs, perhaps to influence fertility and thus the continuation of the species. These drawings and artifacts represent the following important concepts:

1. Creative expression is instinctive.
2. The art of interior design dates from early humankind and serves as an integral part of the human psyche.

Design evolved rapidly through the last several millenia. The Egyptians (circa 3000 B.C.), with their sophisticated art and architecture, made a lasting contribution to the interior design field.

Ancient

EGYPTIAN (4500–330 B.C.)

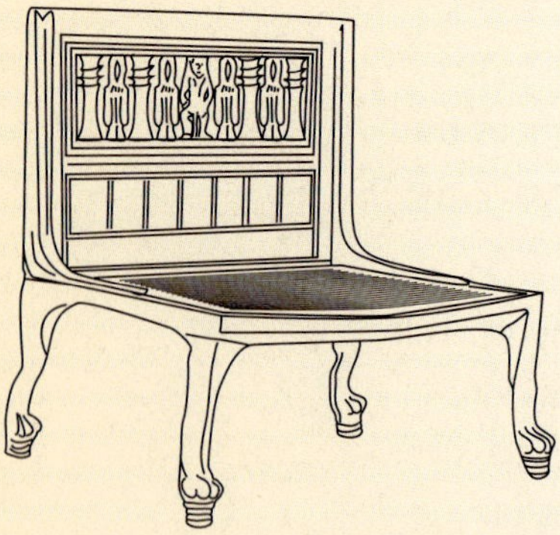

Egyptian chair with blocked feet

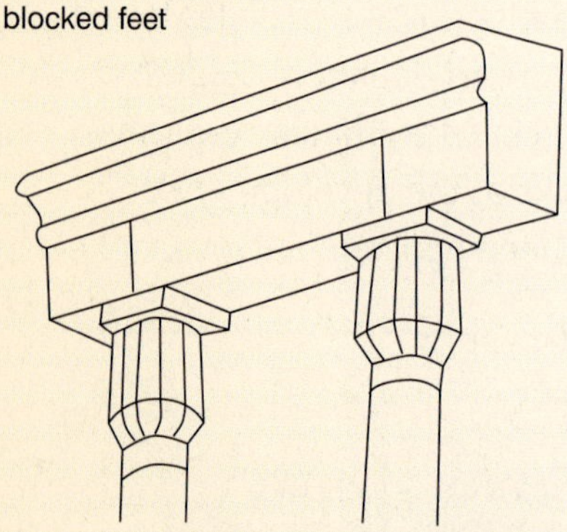

Trabeated construction

- Known for their pyramids built as tombs for kings and pharaohs
- Developed **trabeated** construction, in which vertical posts support a horizontal lintel
- Used **hieroglyphics** (a system of writing using pictorial symbols) inscribed on walls
- Columns, perhaps originally made from papyrus reeds lashed together, created vertical lines, which led to **fluting** on columns in later designs
- Utilized the mortise and tenon joint in their furniture
- Used straw for flooring, therefore furniture was raised on small blocks so animal-shaped legs could be seen
- Motifs included the lotus bud, reeds, papyrus, and lilies

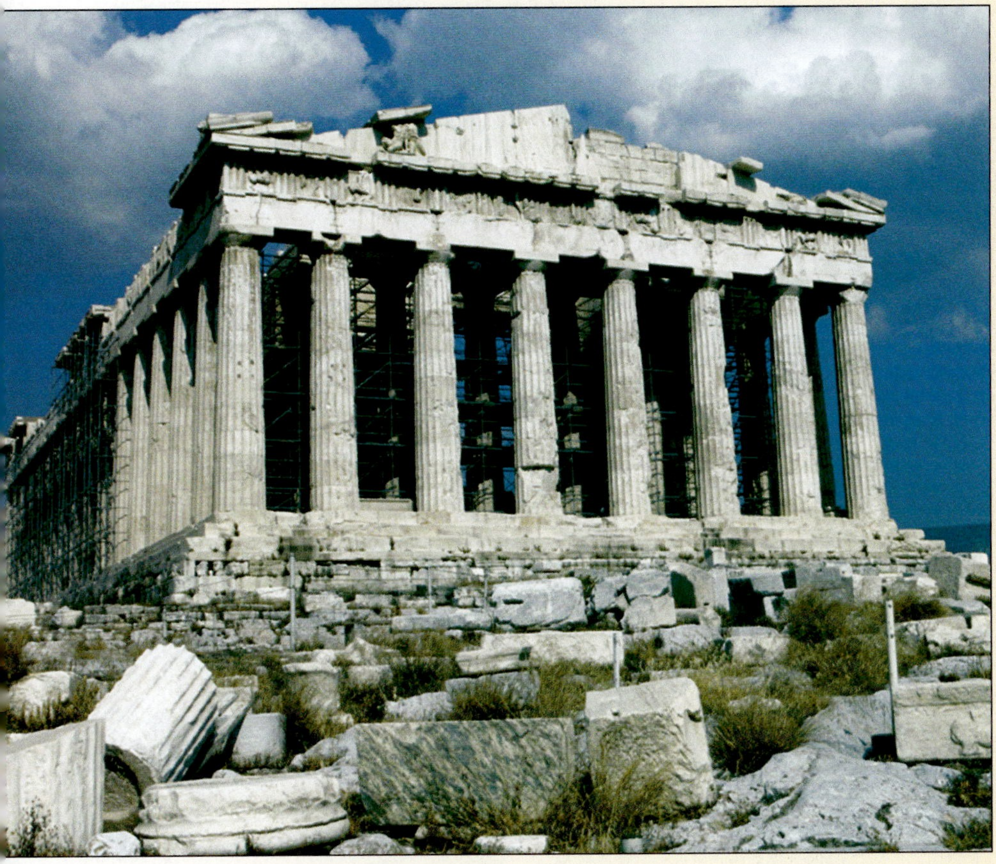

ırthenon is located on the Acropolis in Athens, Greece. ıeted in 438 B.C., the building was dedicated to the goddess ı. Doric columns form a portico around the building. graph by Adam Crowley from PhotoDisc.)

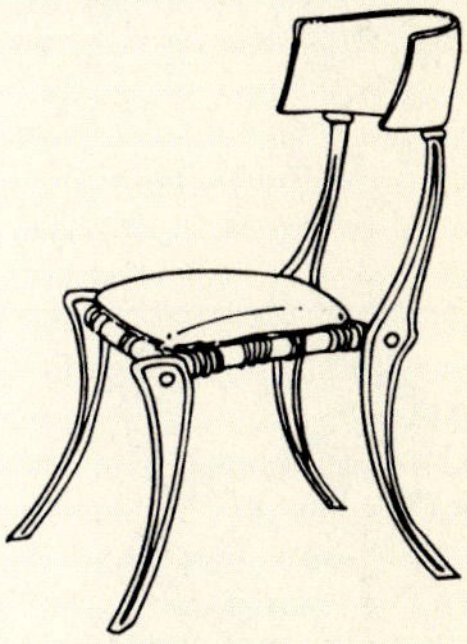
Klismos chair

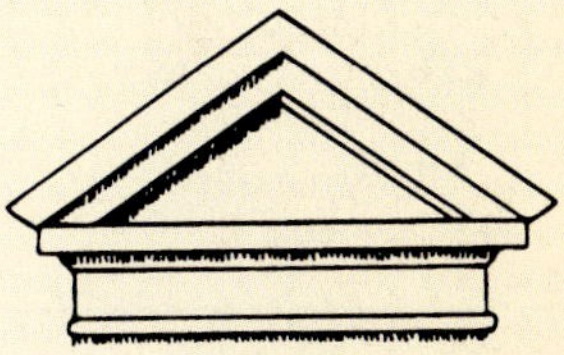
Pediment

wn for their order, proportion, and refinement of design

t temples to honor their gods, surrounded by open icos (porches) and columns

eloped the **truss** system, a triangulated load-bearing struction to allow for sloped roofs. The triangle formed ne truss is called a **pediment**

eloped a system of naming the design and details of ımns. These classical orders of architecture, still used ıy, include the Doric (plain square capital on top of ımn), Ionic (capital with spiral design called a volute), Corinthian (capital with two rows of acanthus leaves)

tered the art of carving marble into a human form. en used for support, the human form is called a **yatid**

eloped the klismos chair

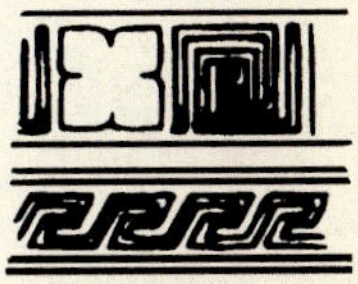
Fret

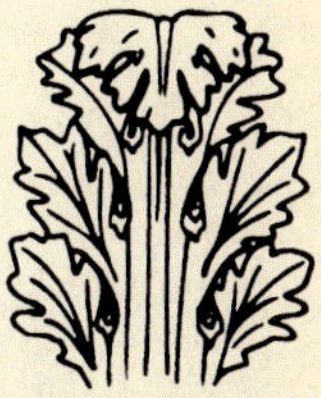
Acanthus leaf

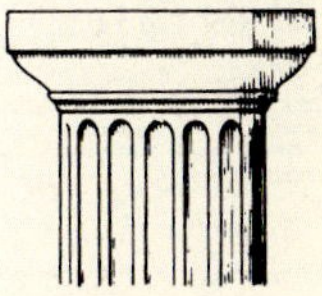
Doric

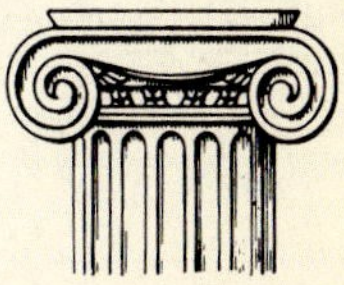
Ionic

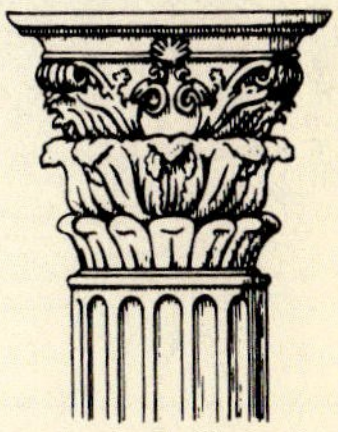
Corinthian

- Known for their engineering expertise, particularly the development of roads and aqueducts
- Adapted Greek designs
- Vitruvius, a Roman architect, developed standard sizes and dimensions for the architectural orders (columns)
- Added two classical orders, the Tuscan (similar to Doric but without column fluting) and Composite (capital combines acanthus leaves and volutes)
- Developed concrete arch, barrel vault, and dome
- Developed **pilasters** (columns partially embedded in the walls)
- Motifs included dolphins, eagles, ribbons, swans, and **grotesques** (fanciful human/animal forms)

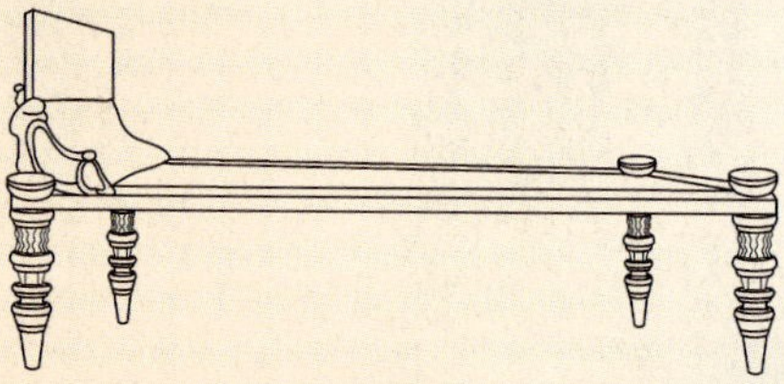

Roman bed

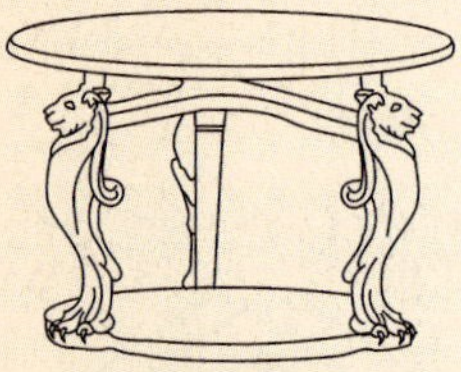

Roman marble table

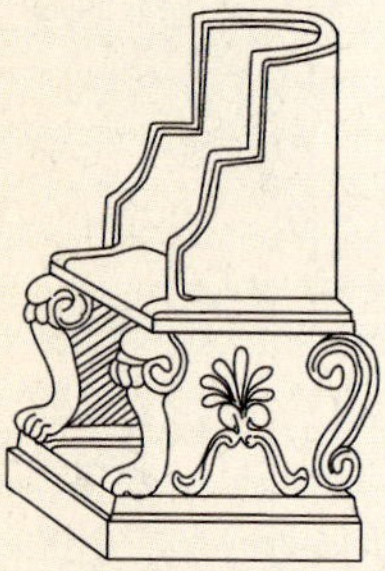

Roman chair

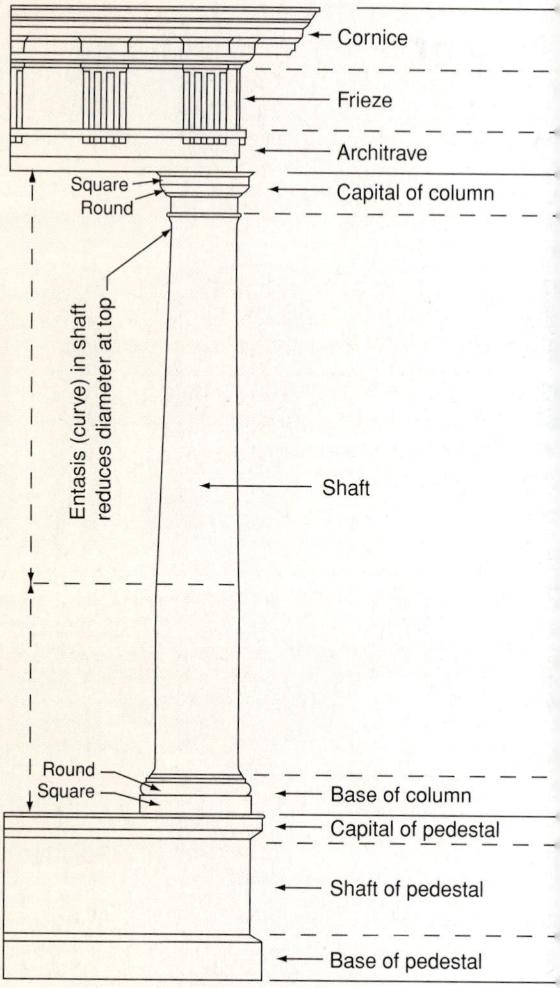

The parts of the Tuscan order as defined by Vitruvius.

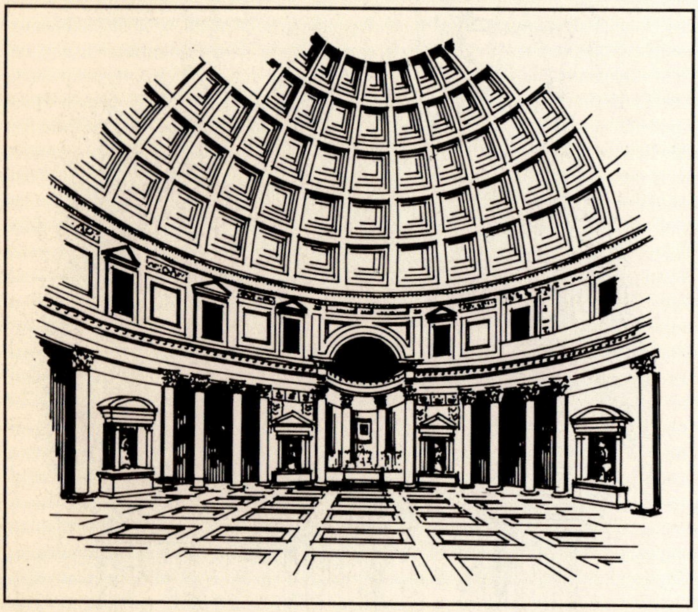

Interior of the Pantheon, Rome

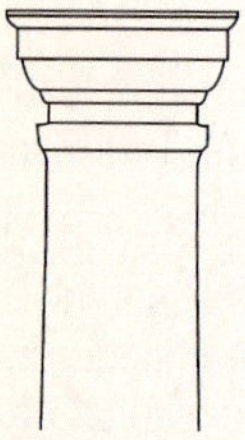

Tuscan

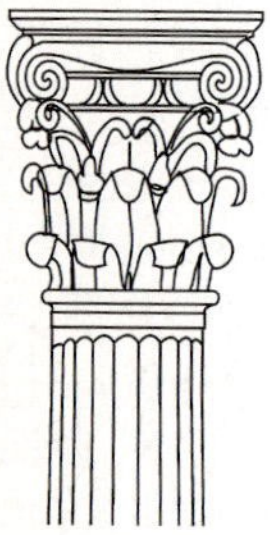

Composite

(325–1500)

Middle Ages

ɟns dominated by religion, particularly Christianity

general divisions:

- arly Christian era (325–800): characterized by the devel- ɔment of the basilica church plan, rectangular, with side sles and with **clerestory** windows lighting the central ɔace
- yzantine era (330–1450): church still the dominant build- g, with domed structures and elaborate mosaic designs
- omanesque era (Norman in the British Isles) (800–1150): assive stone structures, including churches, monaster- s, and castles, with round arches and heavy columns
- othic era (1150–1500): architectural features commonly ssociated with ecclesiastical design include the pointed ·ch and vault, tracery, slender columns in clusters, and ıttresses or flying buttresses

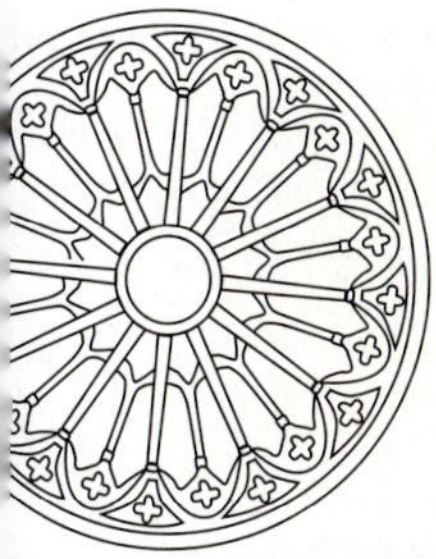

Early rose window

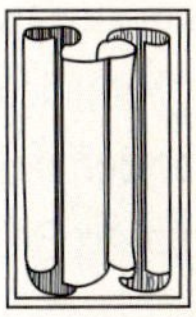

Linenfold motif

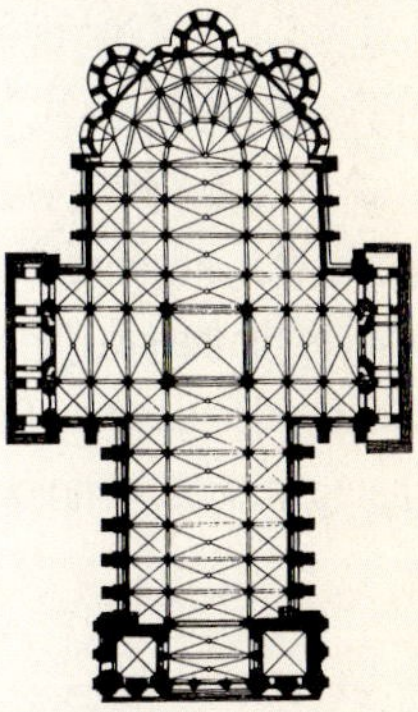

Gothic church plan

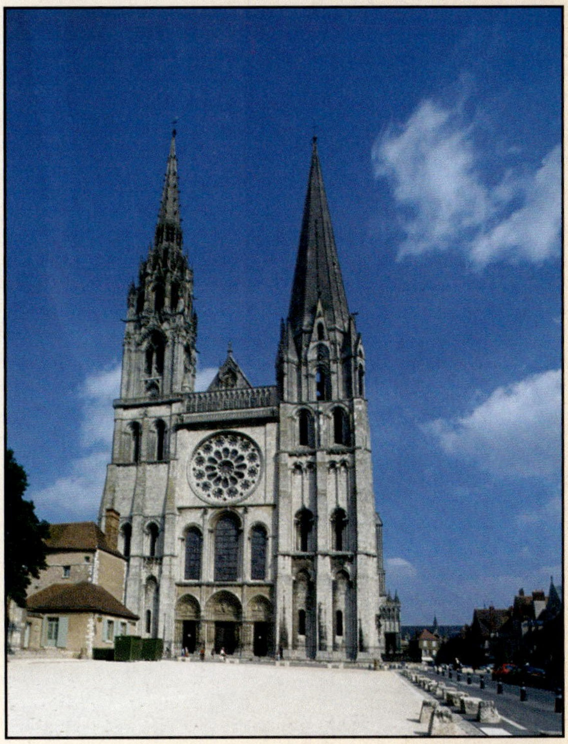

The cathedral in Chartres, France, with its large stained-glass windows and soaring interior space, is considered an outstanding example of Gothic architecture. (Photograph by Martial Colomb from PhotoDisc.)

(1400–1660)

Renaissance

- ns "rebirth"
- ɔr influence came from Italy (1400–1580), ɔugh it spread throughout Europe
- cted Middle Ages design and returned to sic design motifs
- ıded work by Andrea Palladio, Michelangelo, Leonardo da Vinci

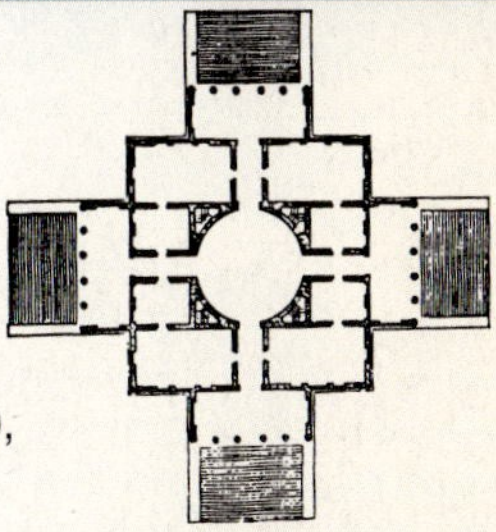

Plan, Villa Rotonda

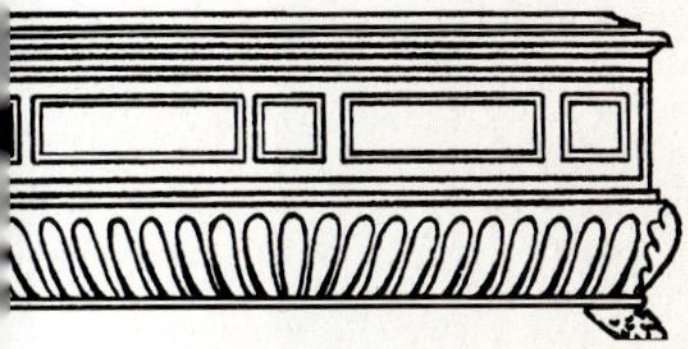

Cassone

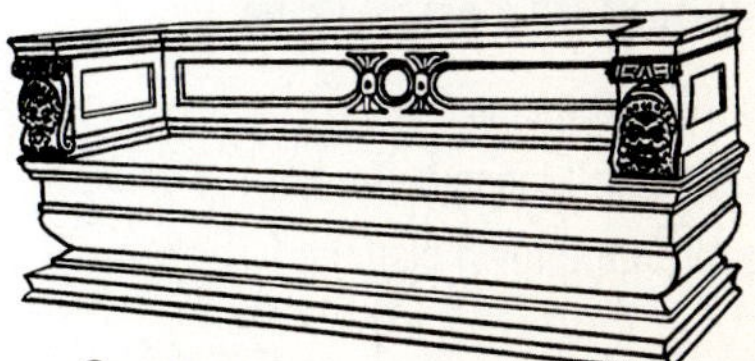

Cassapanca

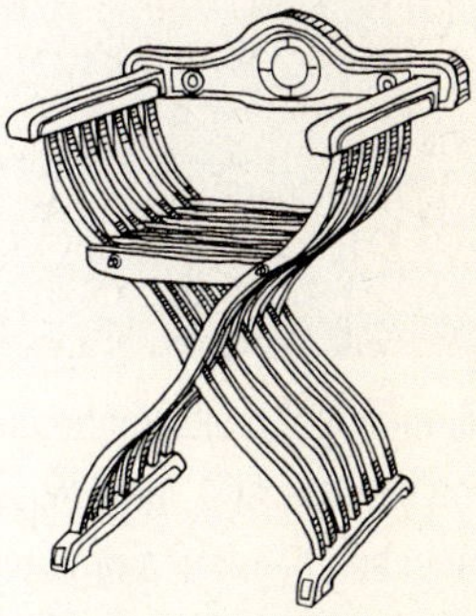

Savonarola chair

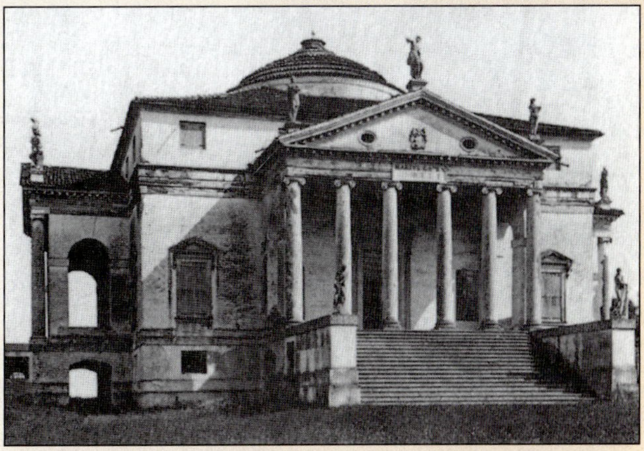

The Villa Rotonda (1550) was designed by Andrea Palladio, who helped promote the rebirth of classic style. (Photograph from Art Resource, NY.)

- Means “misshapen pearl”
- Major influence came from Italy and France
- Ornate, asymmetrical designs
- Flamboyant and heavy proportions

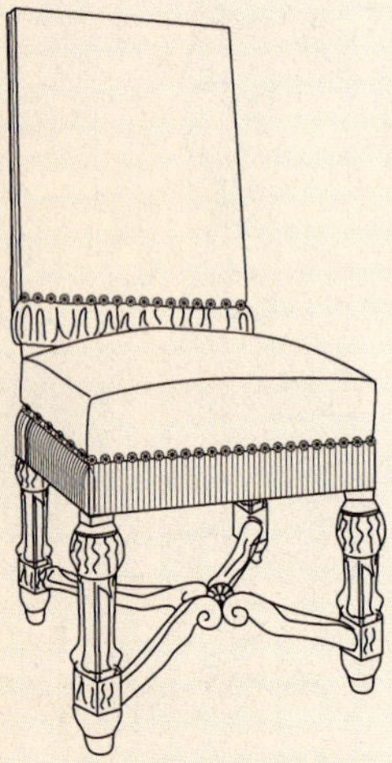

Baroque chair

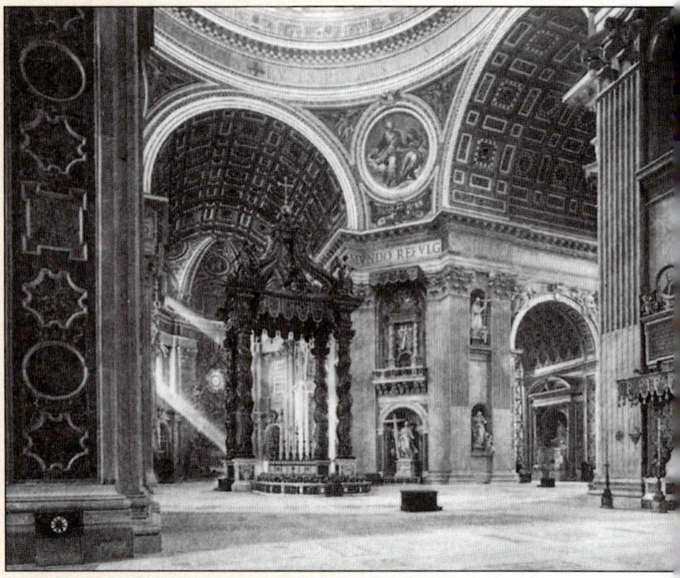

St. Peter’s in Rome was designed and built under the direction of a seri architects, including Donato Bramante and Michelangelo. The original d reflects the Italian Renaissance. In the interior, seen above, the immens canopy, designed by Gianlorenzo Bernini, incorporates Baroque characteristics. (Photograph from Art Resource, NY.)

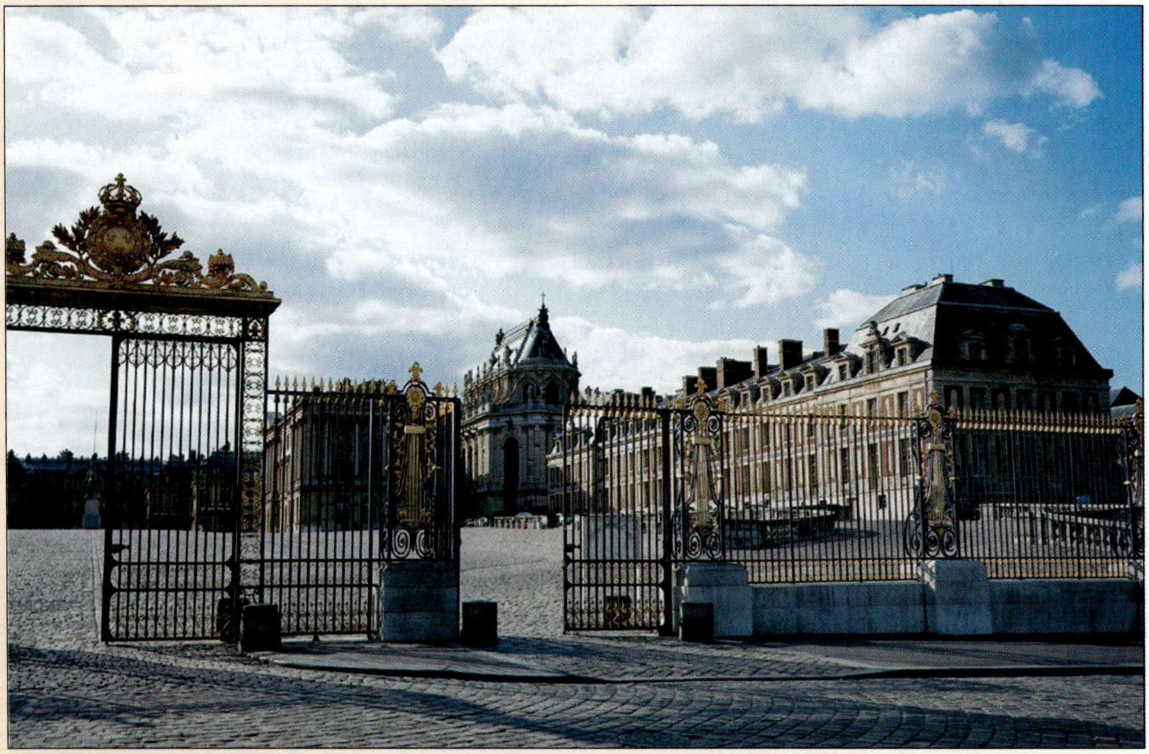

Built during the reign of Louis XIV, Versailles became an immense complex of buildings housing 10,000 people. The designers included the painter Charles LeBrun and the architects Louis LeVau and, later, Jules Hardouin-Mansart. Bernini was also consulted. André LeNôtre’s design for the surrounding landscape became a prototype for future town planning. (Photograph by Martial Colomb from PhotoDisc.)

OCOCO–LOUIS XV (1715–1774)

French Styles

- cides with reign of Louis XV
- ns "rock and shells"
- ted to interiors more than to architecture
- ing, feminine design with delicate decorative details free-form curves
- el colors
- ed, painted, or **chinoiserie** lacquered surfaces on iture (see Chinese styles)
- ese influence introduced by Madame de Pompadour
- fs included fret designs, and Chinese influences such xotic flowers, birds, pagodas, monkeys, and darins (officials at the royal court)

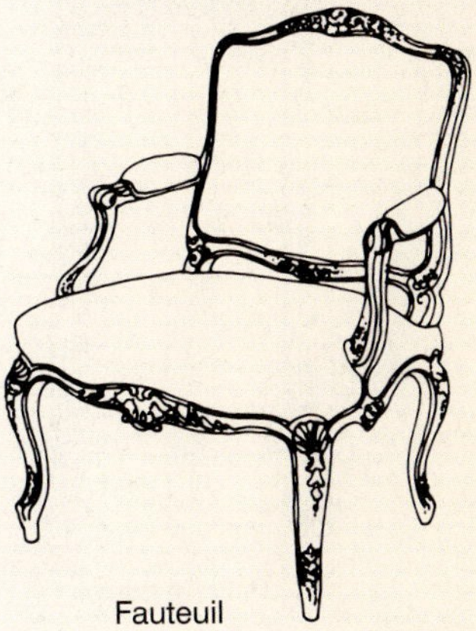
Fauteuil

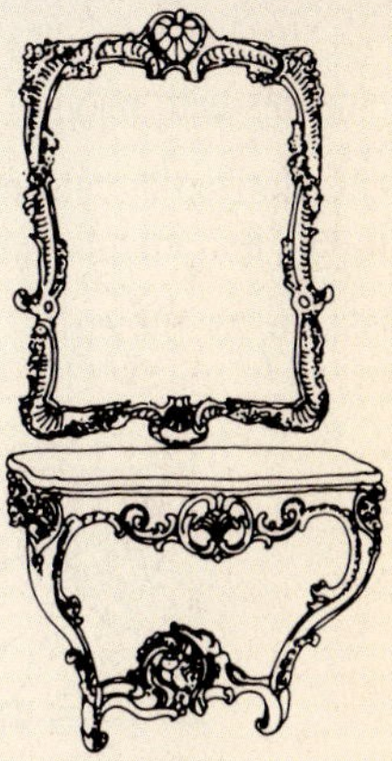
Console and mirror

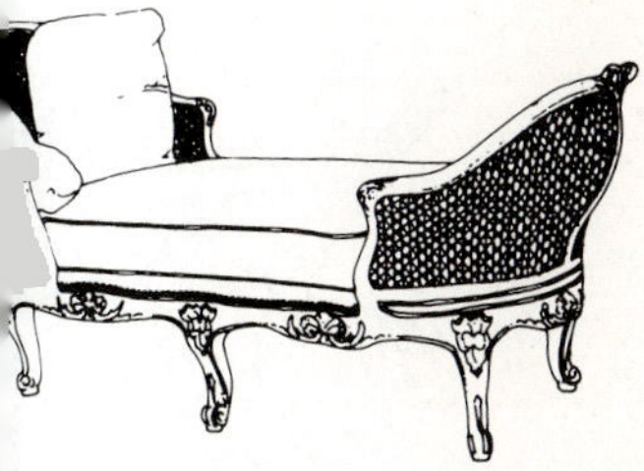
Tête-à-tête

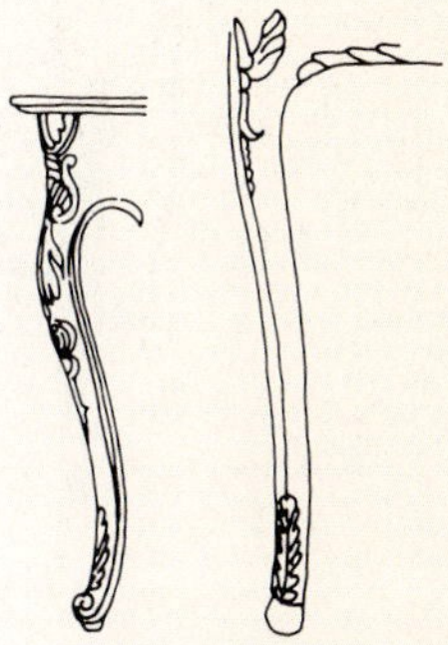
Cabriole legs

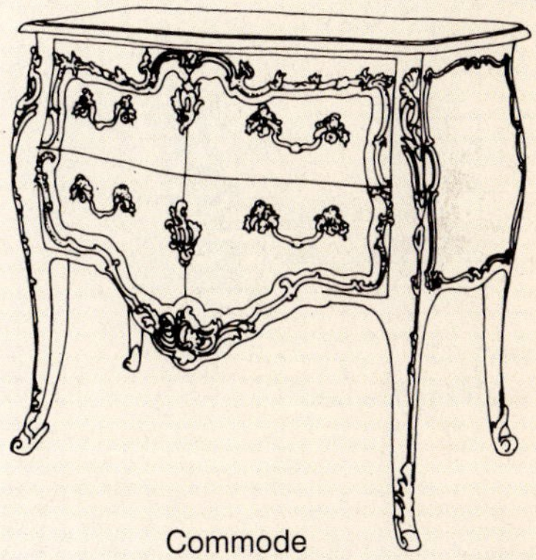
Commode

NEOCLASSIC–LOUIS XVI (1760–1789)

French Styles

- ncides with reign of Louis XVI and Marie Antoinette
- ilar to Rococo, but focused on straight lines, angular forms, and symmetrical balance
- tifs and designs influenced by the discovery of npeii, an ancient Greco-Roman resort city in southern y, which had been buried by the eruption of Mt. uvius in A.D. 79

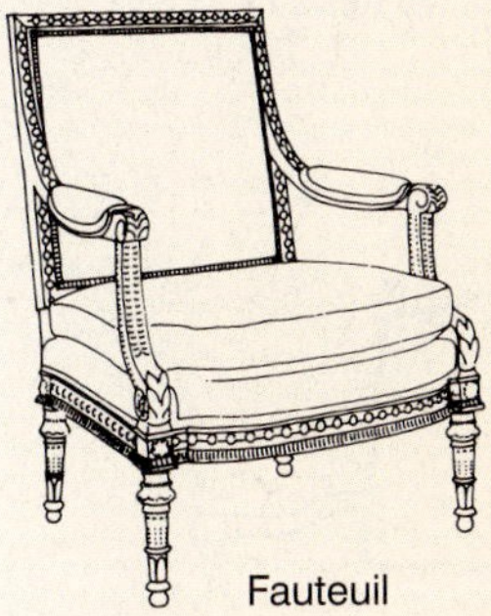
Fauteuil

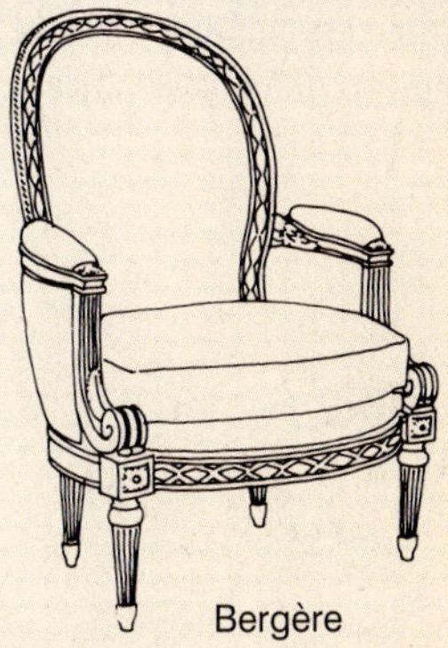
Bergère

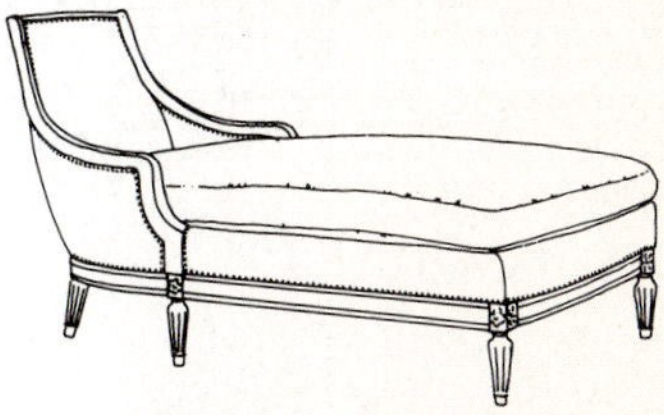
Chaise longue

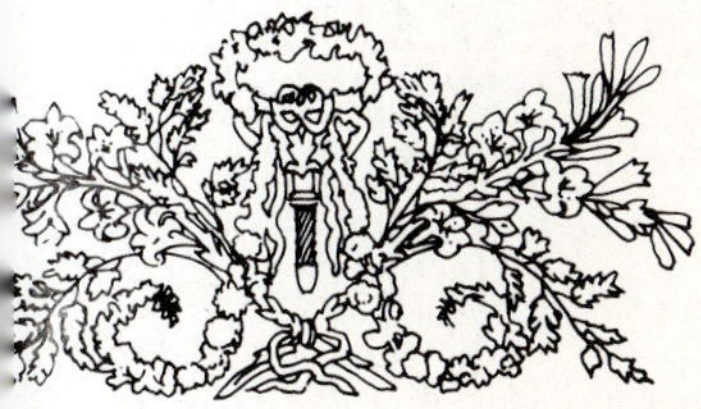
Ormolu

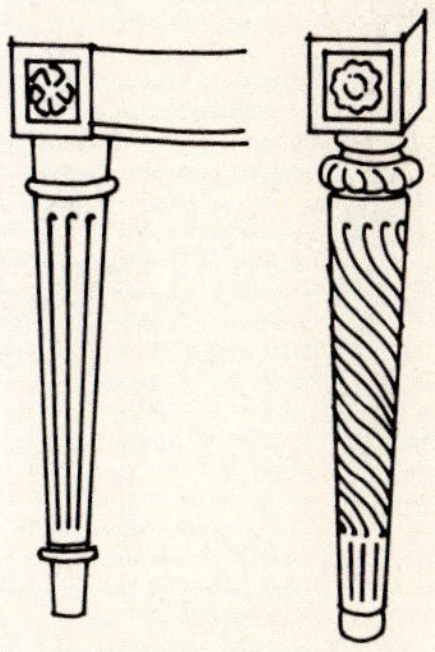
Reeded legs

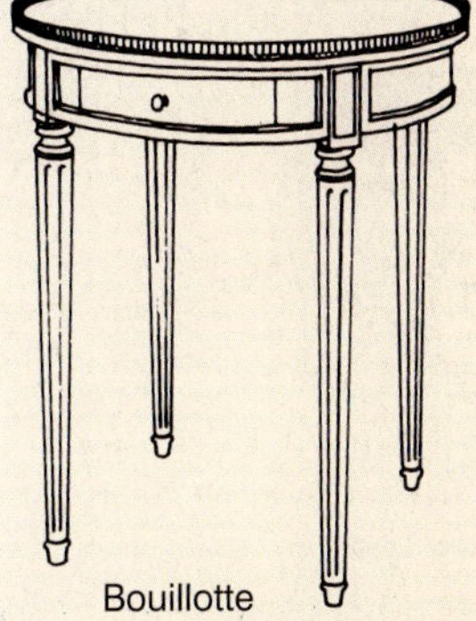
Bouillotte

French Styles

Empire (1804–1815)

- Coincides with reign of Napoleon
- Characterized by return of classic Greek, Roman, and Egyptian designs
- Massive, asymmetrical designs

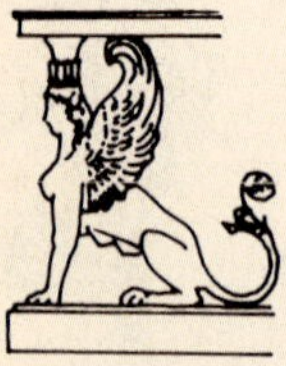

Table support

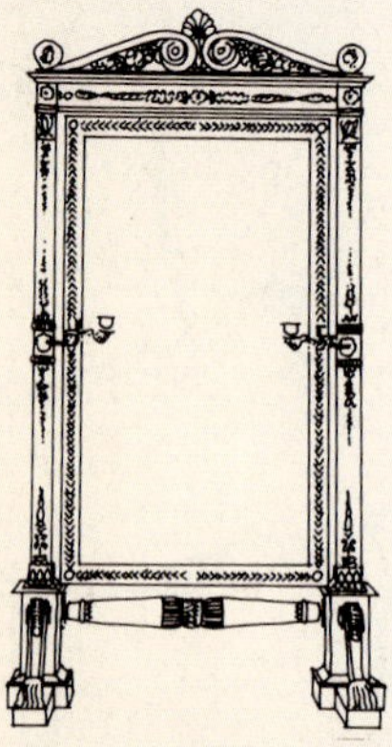

Psyche mirror

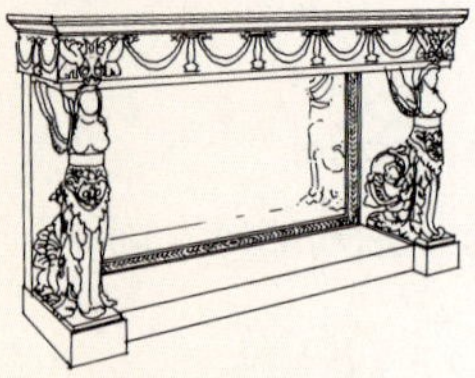

Console with Egyptian heads

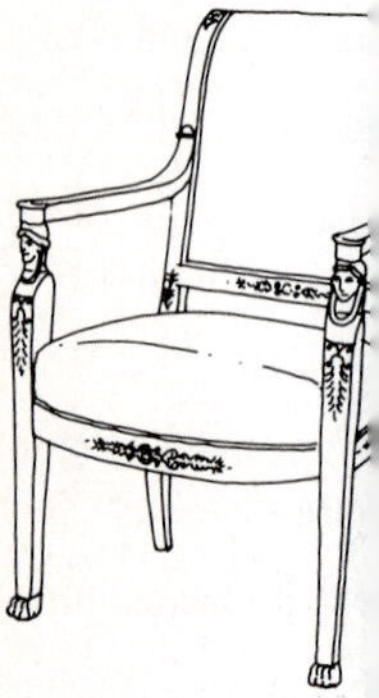

Fauteuil

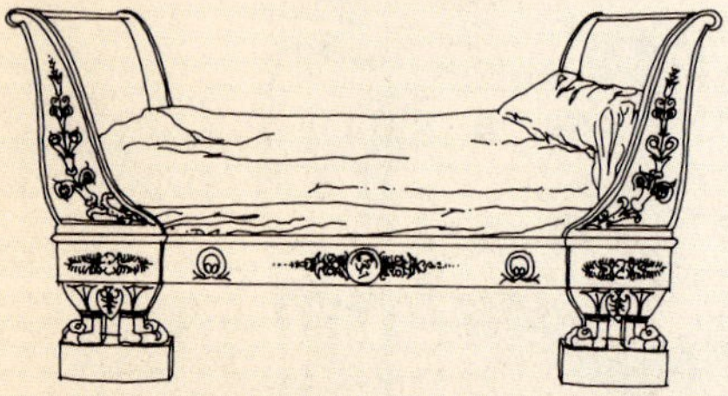

French Empire bed

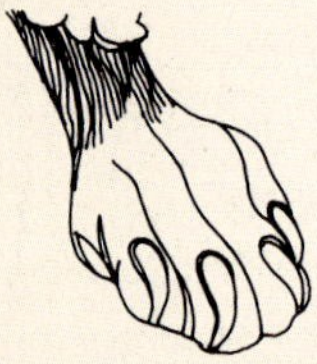

Lion's paw foot

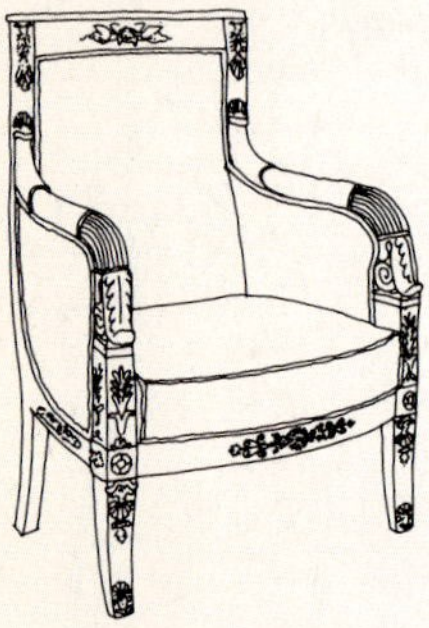

Bergère

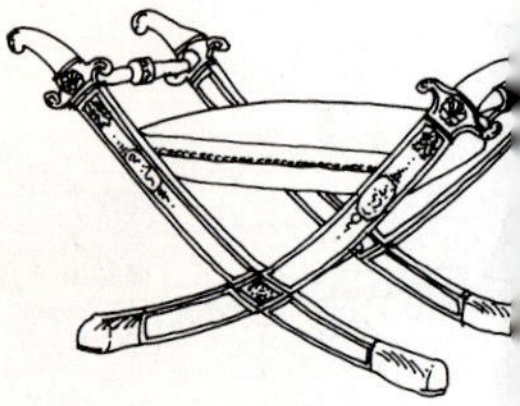

X-stool

French Styles

Provincia
(18th century–prese

- Designs for lesser nobility and merchants
- Copied or adapted Rococo and Neoclassic designs in simpler, unadorned styles

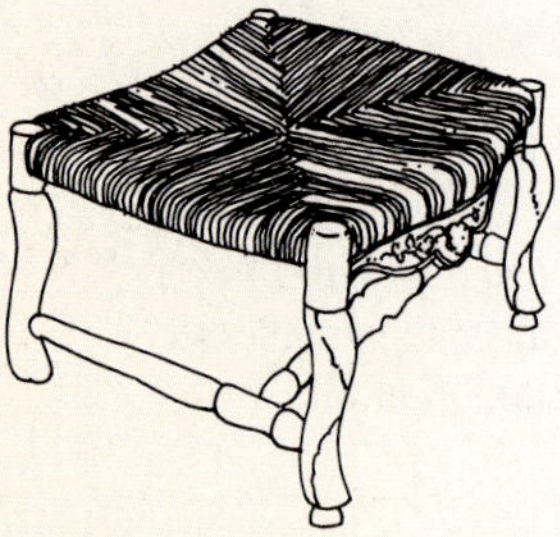

Stool

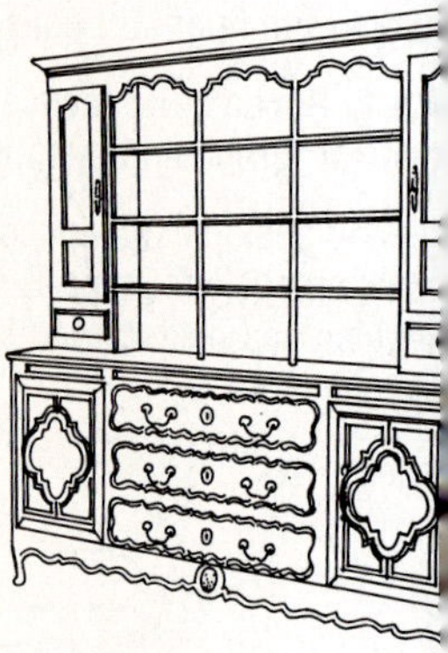

Hutch

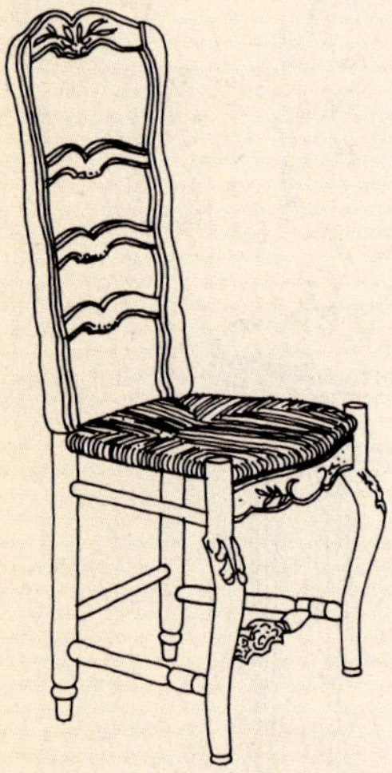

Salamander back

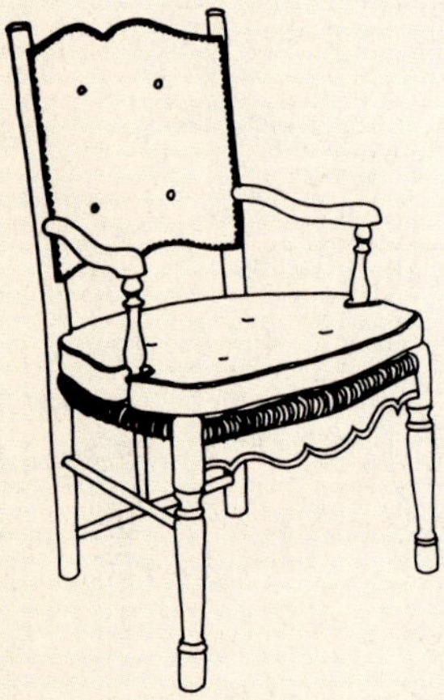

Open arm chair

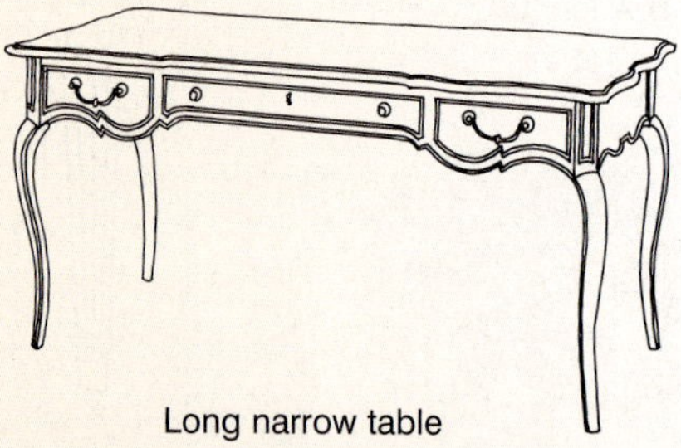

Long narrow table

ıcient to Present

Chinese Styles

- wung roof, distinguishing architectural re
- tly influenced French Rococo and lassical Styles
- ture characterized by **chinoiserie** surfaces
- fs of monkeys, pagodas, and mandarins cials at the royal court)

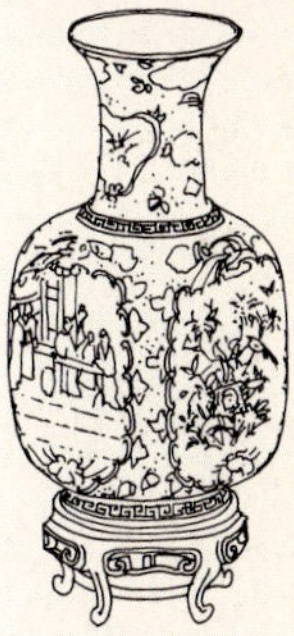
Porcelain vase on a stand

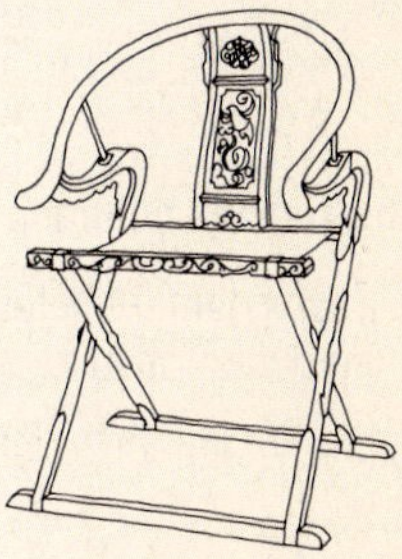
Lacquered Chinese chair

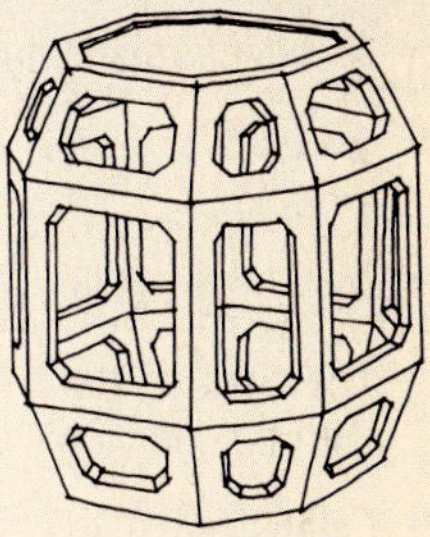
Chinese porcelain garden seat

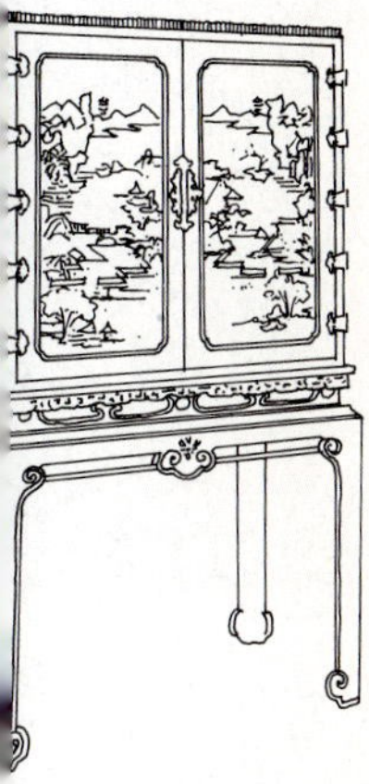
Chinese black lacquer and gilt cabinet on stand

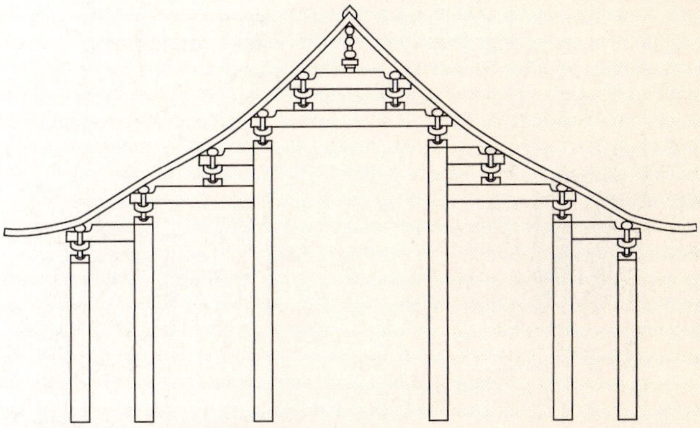
Chinese construction

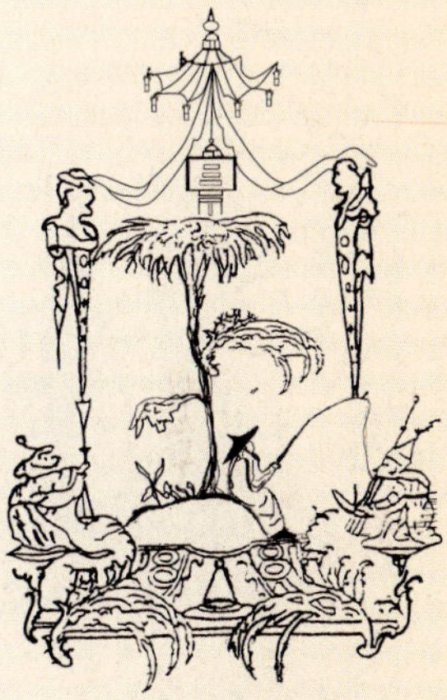
Chinoiserie motif

1200–Present

Hispanic Styles

- lar to Italian Renaissance but also included Moorish ence (1200–1600)
- rish interiors highly decorated and used the horseshoe
- red marbles, geometric patterns, tiled walls, and **ught iron** (worked iron)
- ed wood doors, window shutters, and ceilings called **sonado**
- ence in America called Colonial/Mission style

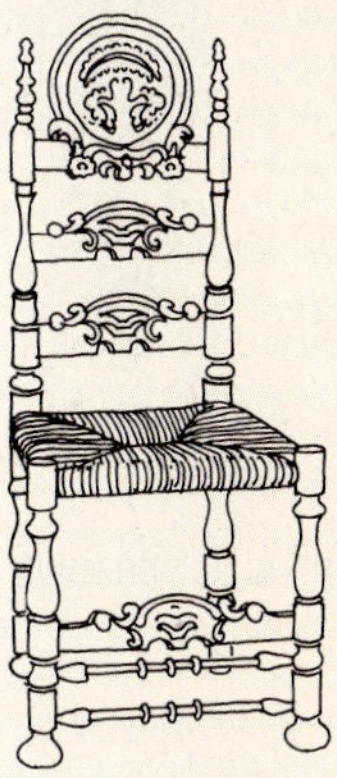
Ladderback

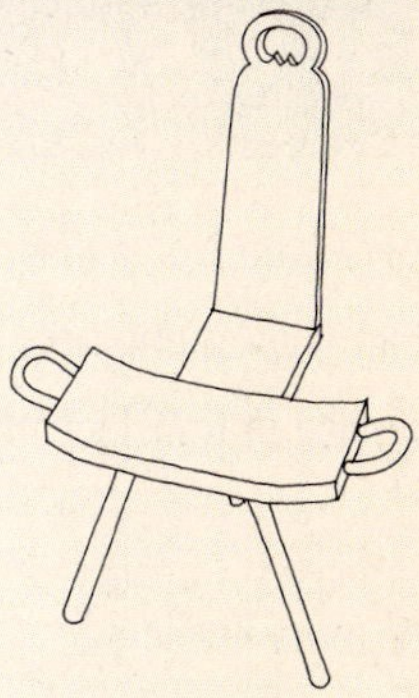
Shepherd's chair

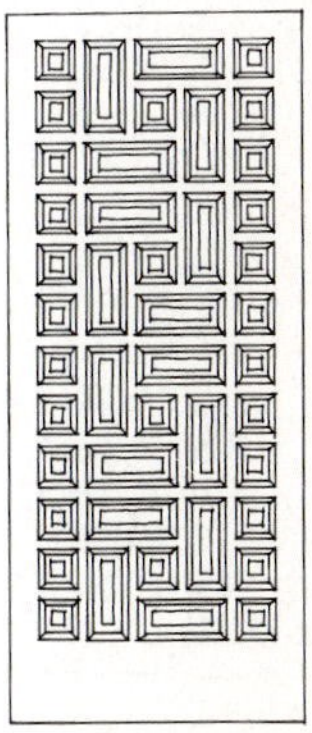
Paneled door

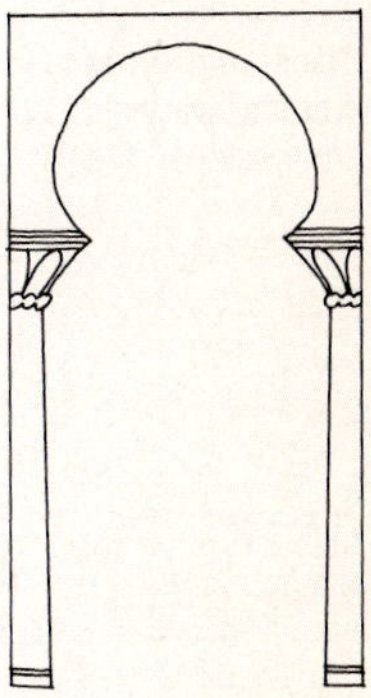
Moorish arch

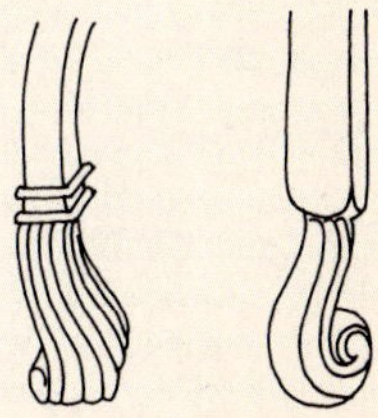
Spanish foot

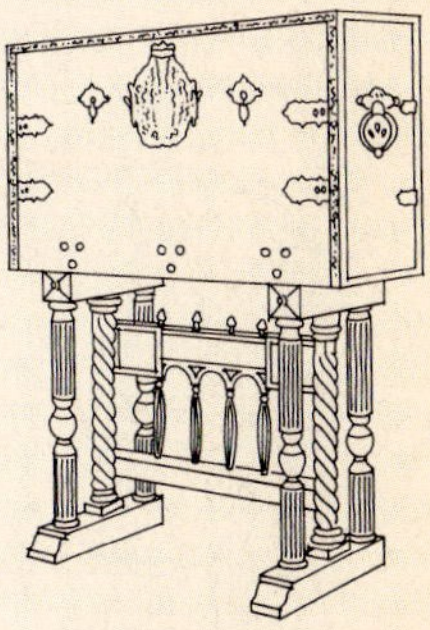
Vargueno

African Styles

1000–Present

- Architecture and design influenced by religion
- Art used to resolve conflicts, to educate, and to symbolize worship
- Rich in visual literacy. Patterns contain cultural meanings
- The chair or stool is a very personal item—historically carried with the individual and not shared with others.
- Extensive use of geometric patterns and inlays of ebony and ivory

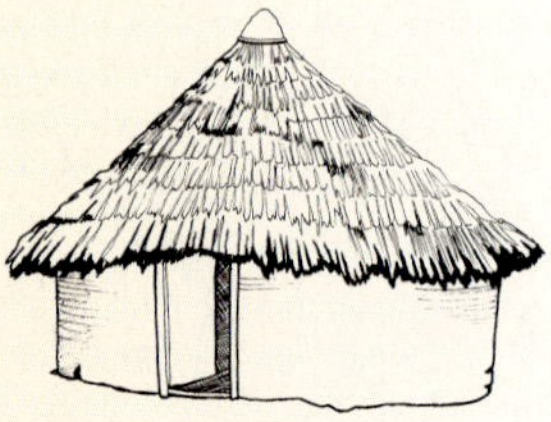

Zaire round home

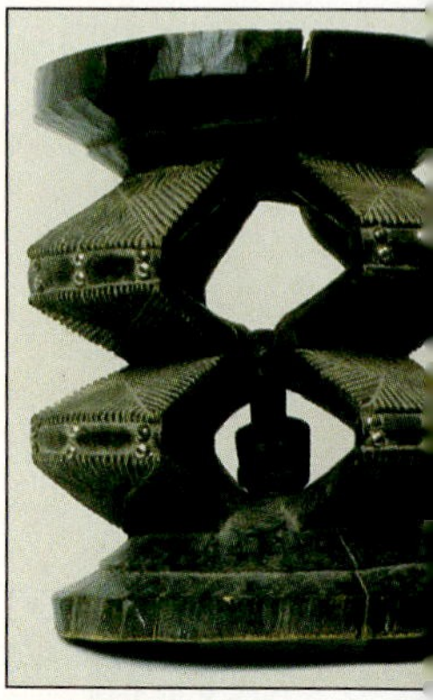

Zaire wood stool attribute Kusu tribe. (Courtesy of th Collection at the Tubman American Museum, Maco Georgia.)

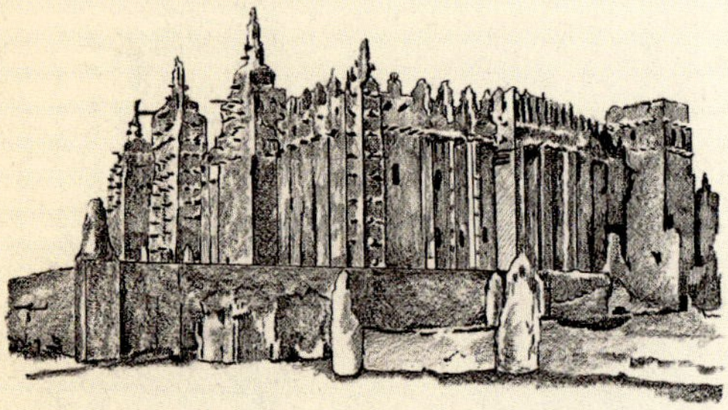

Great Mosque, Djenne (built 1906–1909)

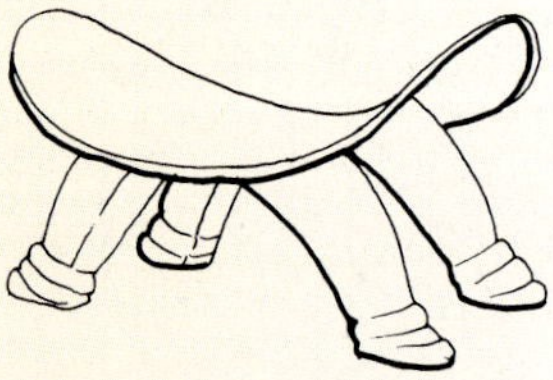

Dinka people's stool, Sudan

Japanese Styles

Ancient to Present

- Emphasized simplicity, horizontal line, and nonformal balance
- Rooms arranged around **tatami mats** measuring 3′ × 6′
- **Fusuma screens** made of translucent materials used to separate rooms
- **Shoji** doors or screens of translucent materials used at windows and sometimes as room dividers
- **Tokonoma** is an alcove containing a special item on display
- Architecture thought of as an art form, which influenced Wright, Mackintosh, the Greene brothers, and Godwin, among others in Modern Design

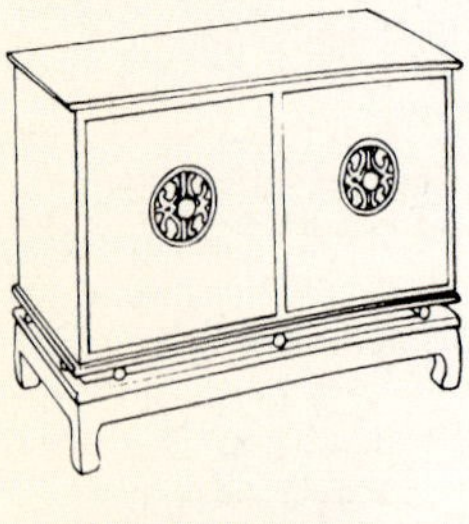

Chest with brass fret hardware and "monkey paw" leg

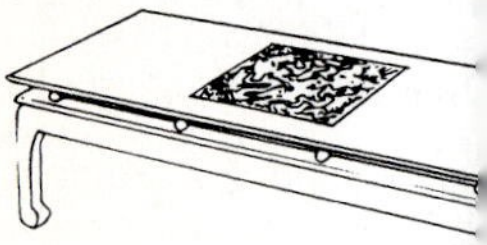

Cocktail table "monkey paw" leg

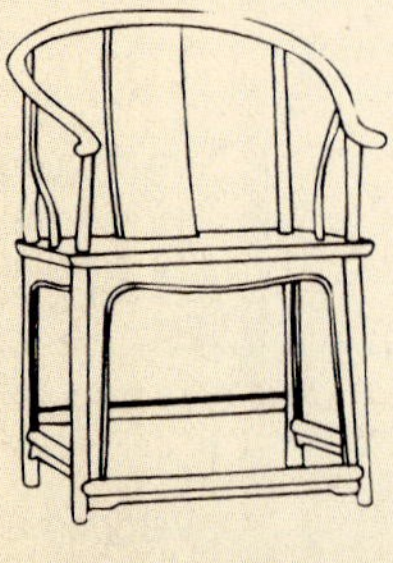

Wood armchair

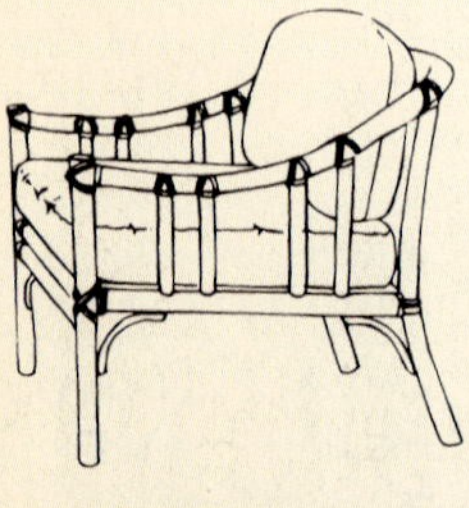

Rattan armchair

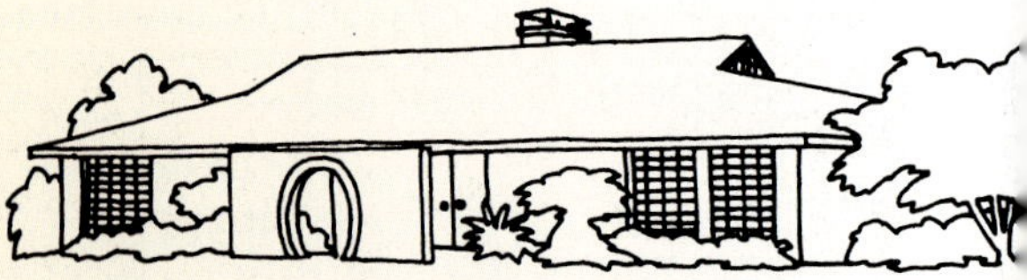

Japanese house

ɔor, Elizabethan, and Jacobean (circa 1440–1700s)

English Styles

- ıinated by heavy, masculine designs
- ıitecture characterized by **half-timbering** bers are visible on the outside of the building) oriel windows (projecting bay windows)
- ʼiors characterized by plain, plastered walls or ıtely carved panels
- ıiture frequently made of oak
- ıbethan furniture had bulbous (melonlike) legs
- ıbean furniture had turned legs

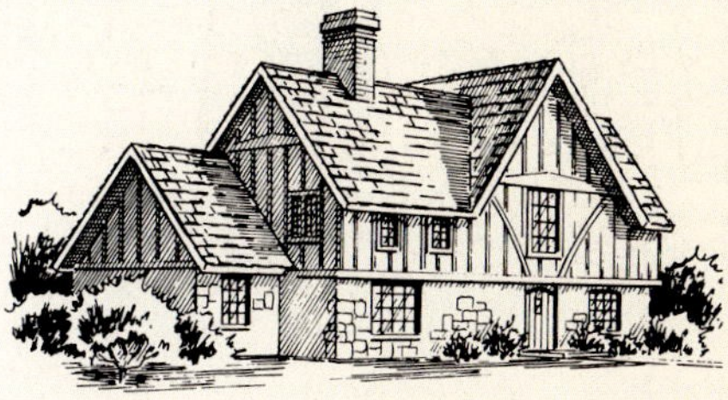

Tudor half-timber

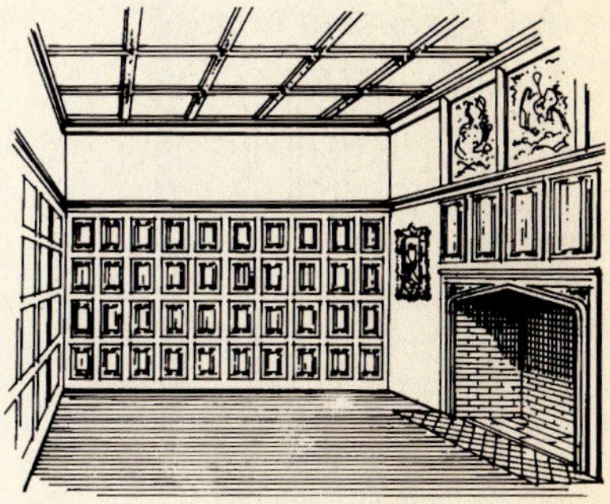

Paneled hall

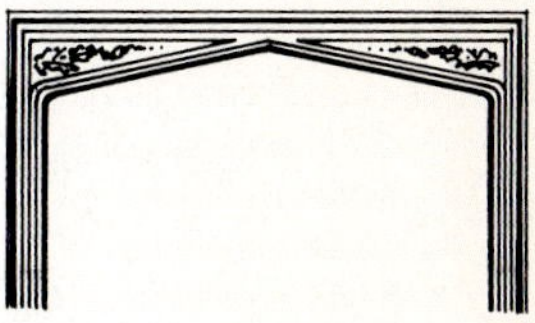

Tudor arch

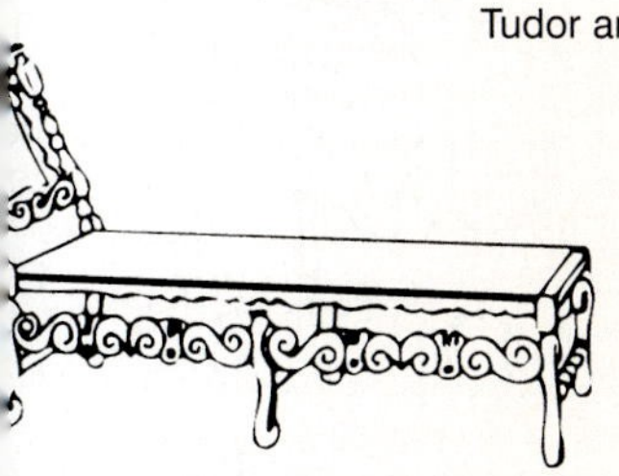

Jacobean daybed

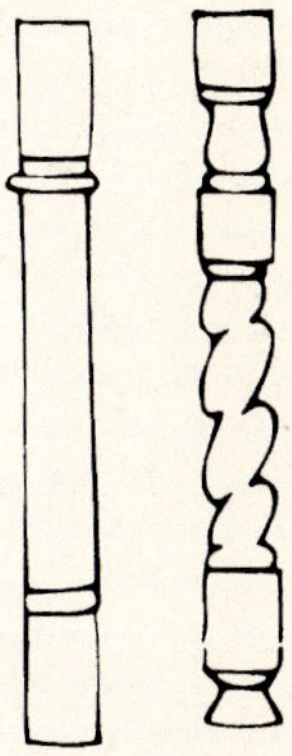

1612 1656
Chair legs

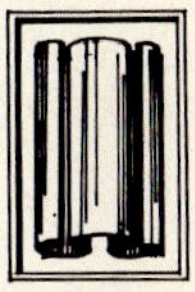

Linenfold motif

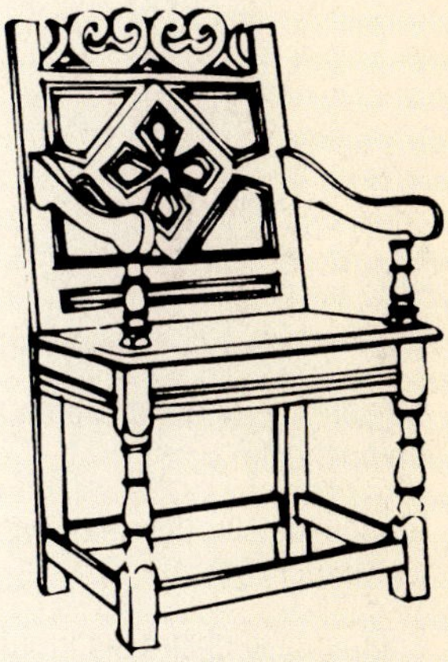

Jacobean wainscot chair

rly Georgian with Queen Anne Furniture (1700–1745)

English Styles

- ıinent architects included Inigo Jones and Sir stopher Wren
- ımetrical designs exhibited dignity and formality, cting classic Greek and Roman architecture
- en Anne furniture based on cyma ("S") curve
- ıt significant piece of furniture was splatback or ıeback chair with **cabriole** (animal-like) **leg** and or club foot. Later chairs had ball and claw foot

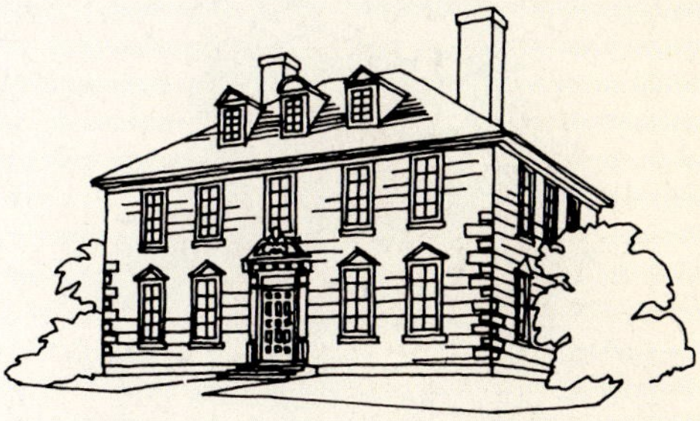

Wren Georgian

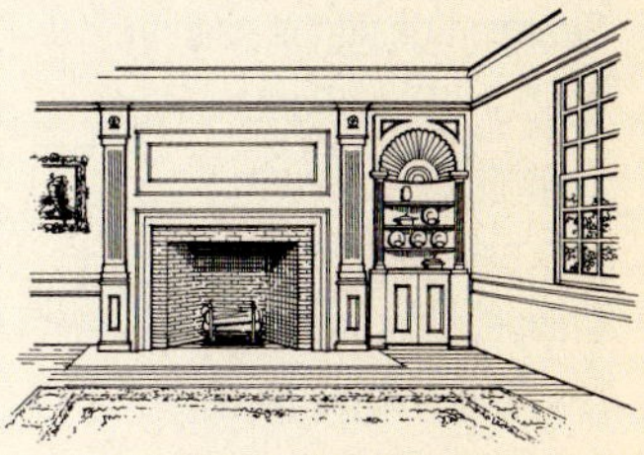

Shell cupboard

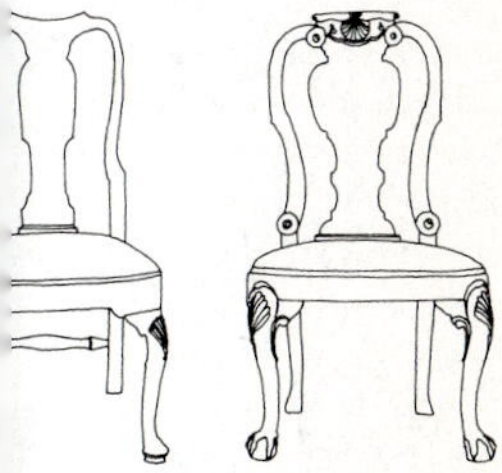

:.1705 c.1710
Fiddleback/Splatback side chairs

Finial

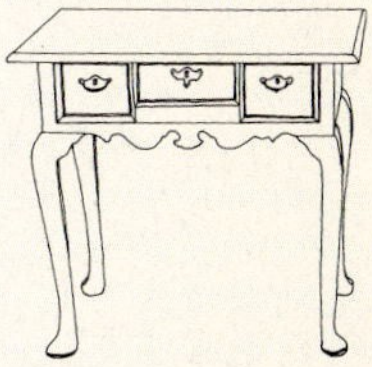

Lowboy

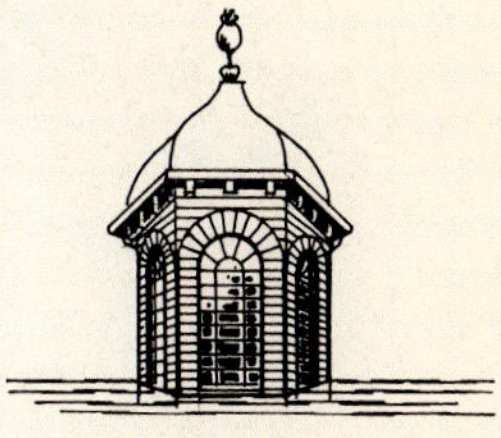

Cupola on roof

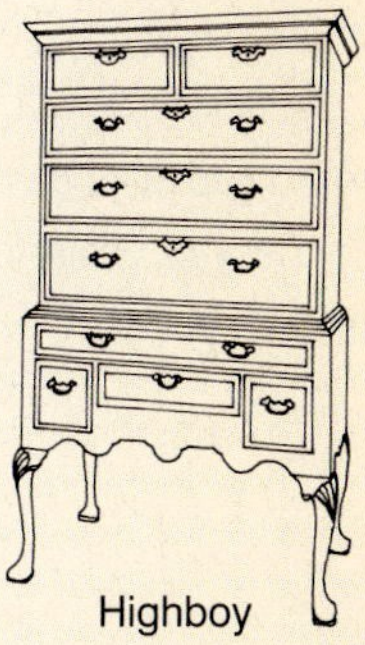

Highboy

English Styles

Middle Georgian with Chippendale Furniture (1745–1770)

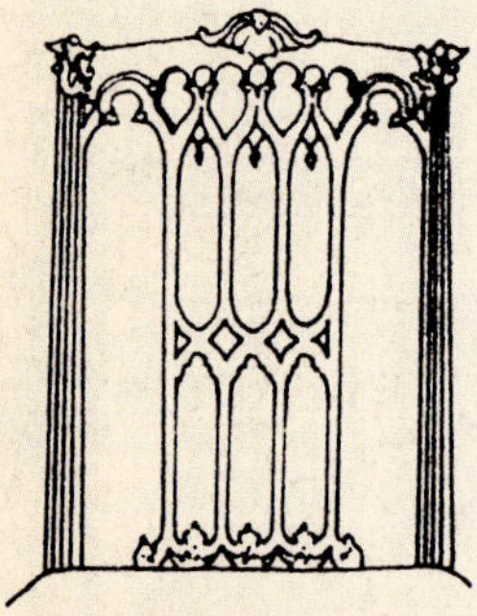

Gothic influence

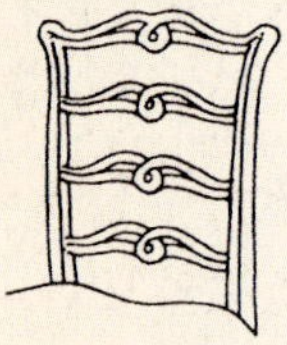

Ladderback

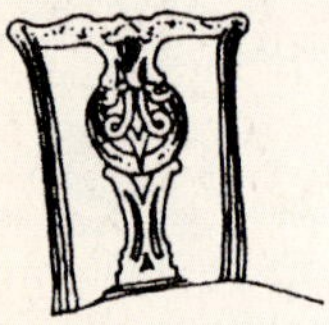

Ribband back

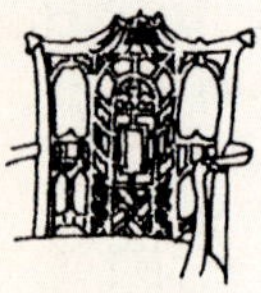

Chinese Chippendale

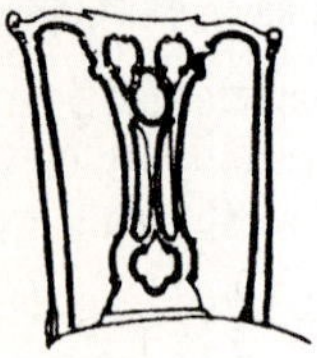

Gothic back

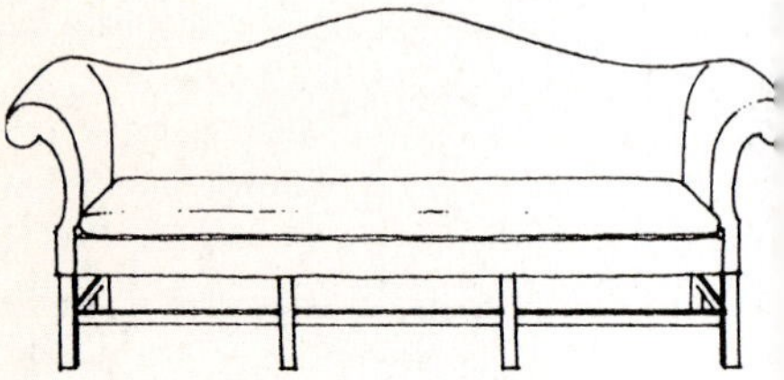

Camelback sofa

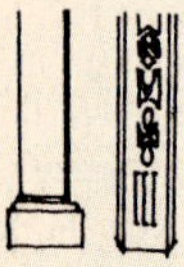

Marlborough (left)

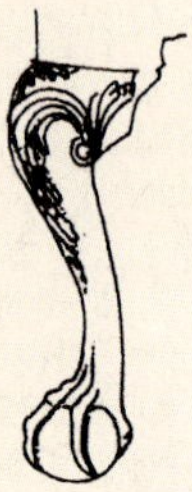

Claw and ball cabriole leg

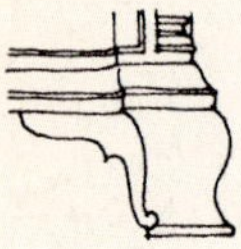

Goddard foot

- Architecture still influenced by Wren
- Golden Age of great cabinetmakers, including Thomas Chippendale
- Chippendale wrote *The Gentleman and Cabinet-Makers Director* (1754)
- Chippendale chairs distinguished by yokebacks with Chinese, Queen Anne, Gothic, French, and Neoclassic influences

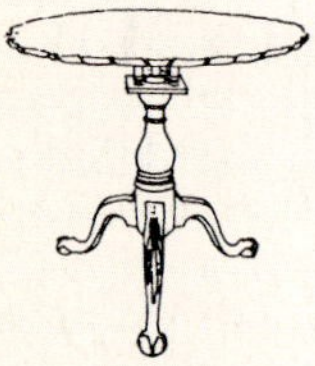

Pie-crust table

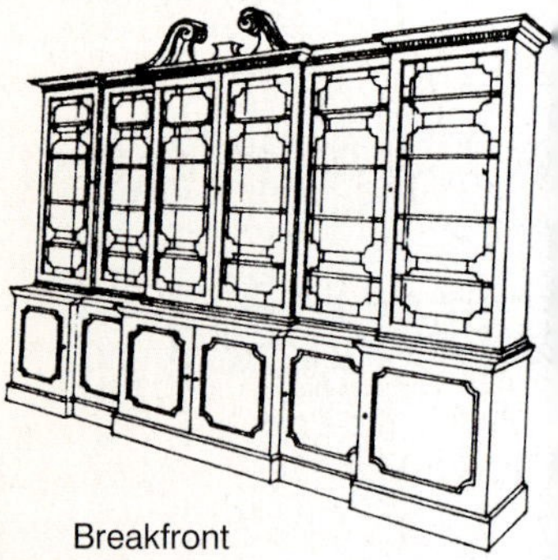

Breakfront

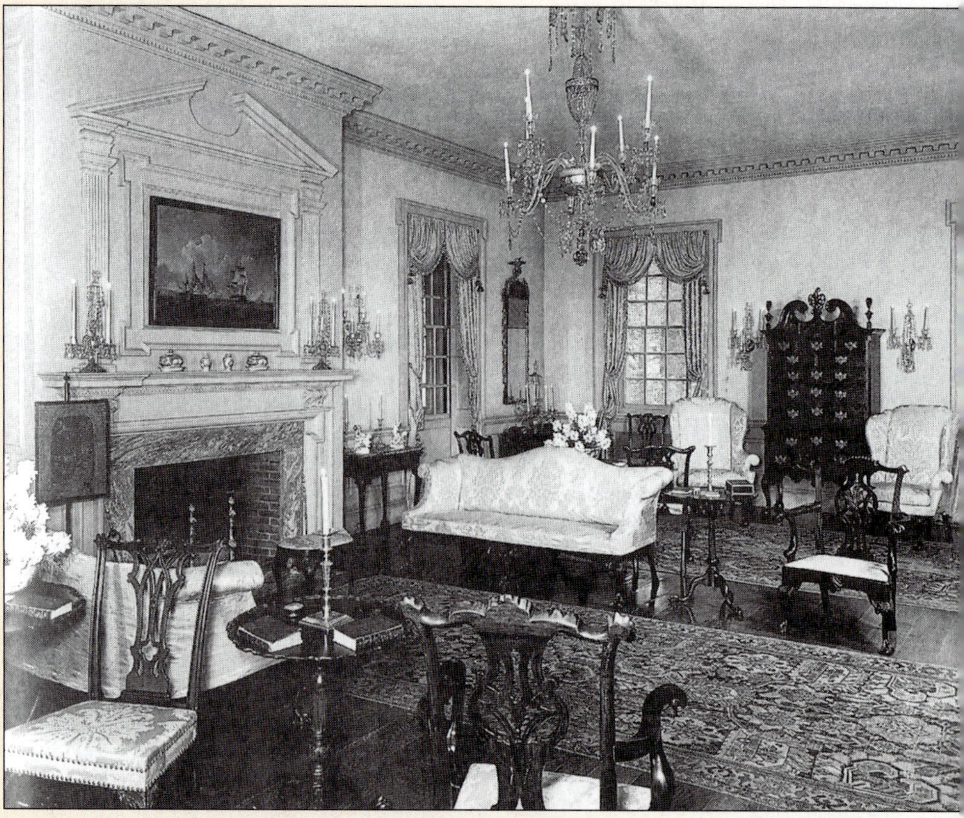

An American adaptation of Georgian design is seen in the Port Royal Parlor at the Winterthur Museum. Georgian features included Chippendale furniture with a few Queen Anne pieces, typical wood floors with Oriental rugs, dadoes, cornices with dentil trim, and a chimneypiece with the broken pediment design. (Courtesy of Winterthur Museum.)

itecture influenced by Roman
dian style; even more formal

cided with French Neoclassic style
the discovery of Pompeii

ert Adam and his four sons
gned classical interiors. Known for
sideboard designs. Utilized **paterae**
-shaped decorations)

ge Hepplewhite designed furniture
straight, square, tapered legs usually
inating with a spade foot. Known for
hield and heart-shaped chair backs

nas Sheraton designed furniture with
ght lines and classical motifs such as
, festoons, and scrolls

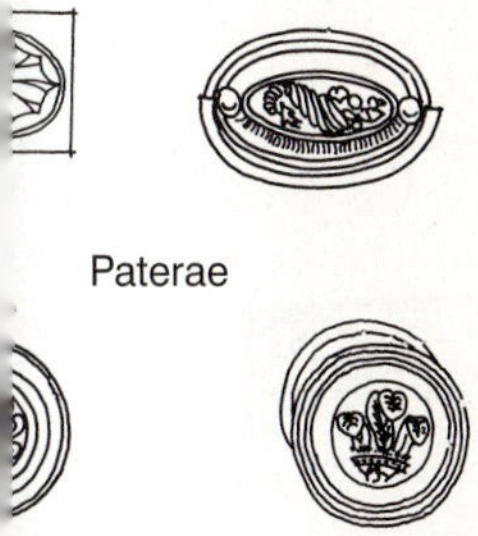

Paterae

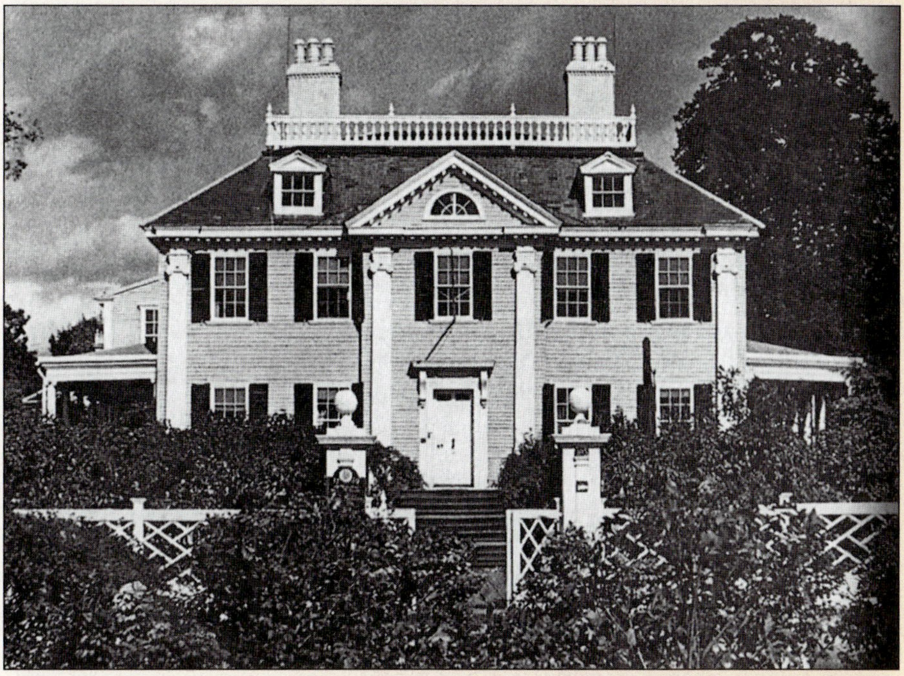

Longfellow House (1750), Cambridge, Massachusetts. Its classical detail with the triangular-topped pavilion reveals Gibbs's Palladianism. (Courtesy of National Park Service, Longfellow National Historic Site.)

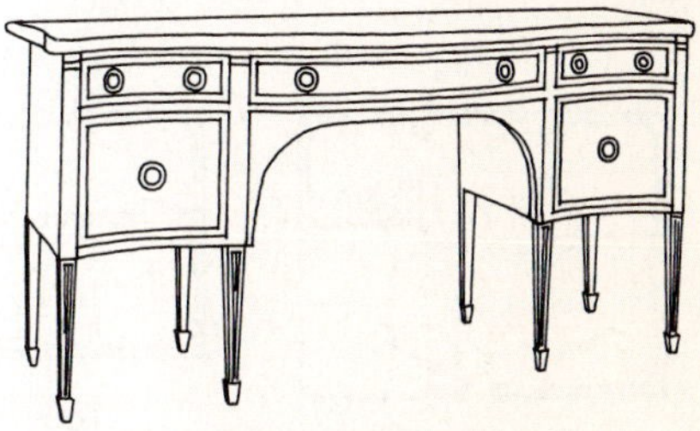

Hepplewhite sideboard

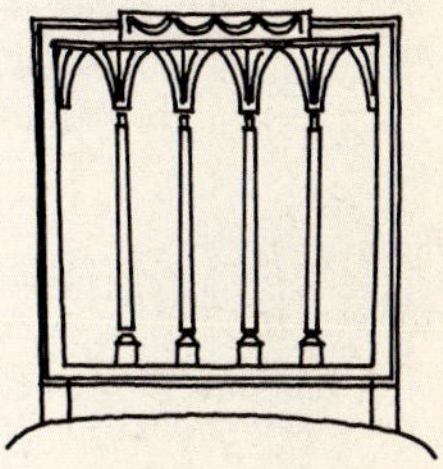

Sheraton chair back

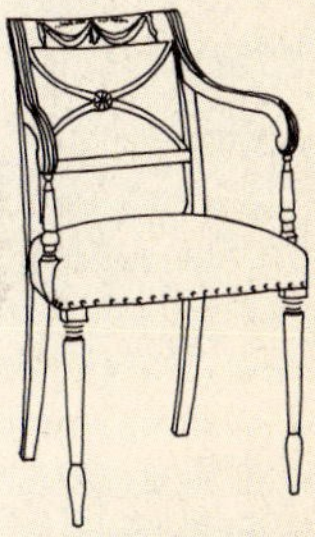

Sheraton armchair

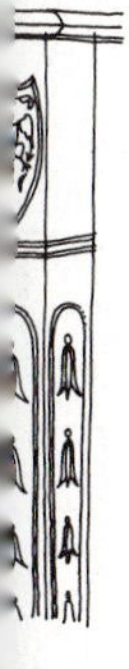

er & eagle
otifs

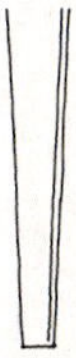

Tapered

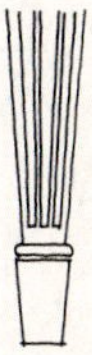

Hepplewhite fluted leg with thimble foot

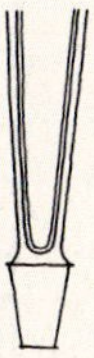

Tapered leg with thimble foot

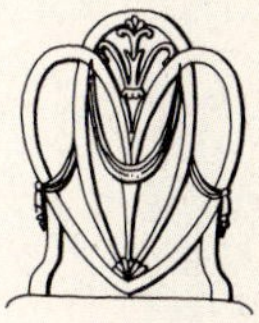

Heart back

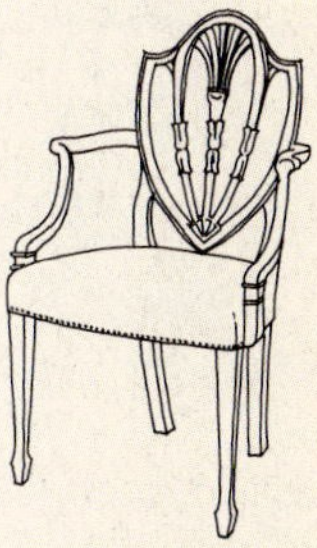

Shield back chair

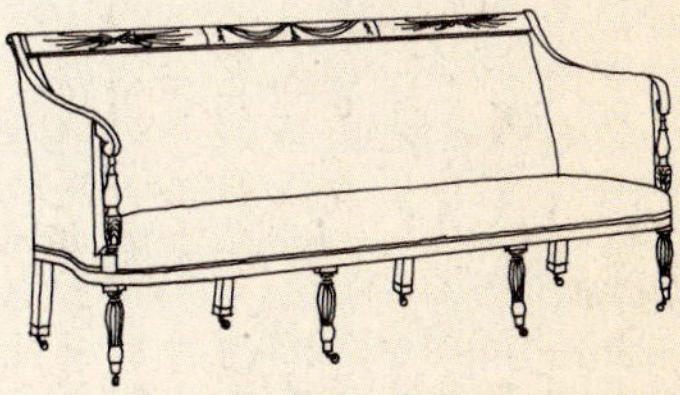

Sheraton sofa

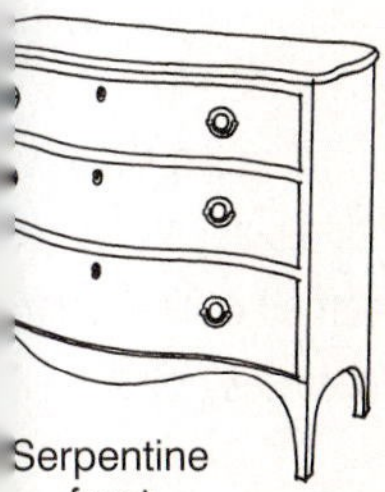

Serpentine front

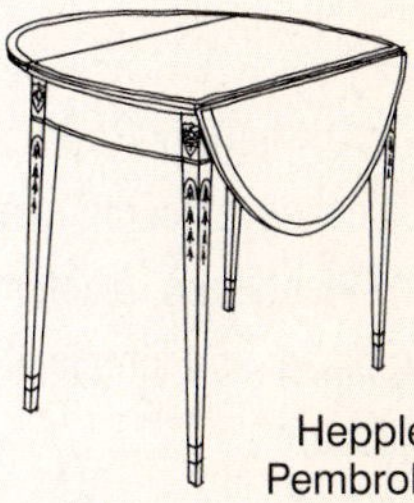

Hepplewhite Pembroke table

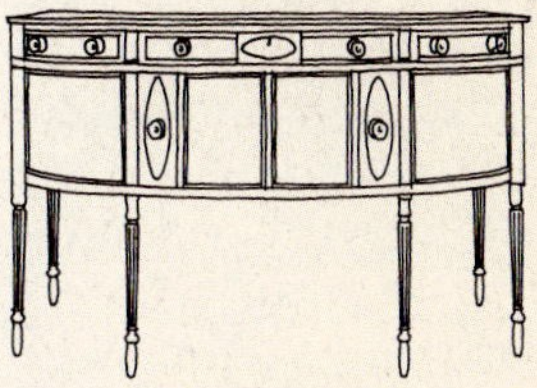

Sheraton sideboard

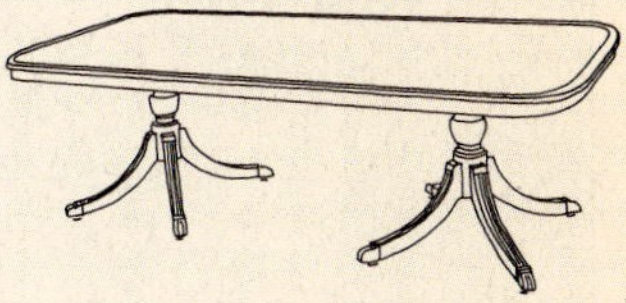

Sheraton extension table

- Influenced by Dutch, German, Swedish, English, French, and Hispanic styles
- Most common architectural styles true to American designs included the following:
  1. Saltbox: front rooms with a lean-to on the back
  2. Garrison (jetty): second floor extends over the first floor creating a **jetty**
  3. Gambrel: a house with a double-pitched roof creating more headroom in the attic
  4. Cape Cod: a house covered in wood with a sloped roof, central chimney, small paned windows, and plank door. Later features included dormers, Georgian details, and double-hung (sash) windows

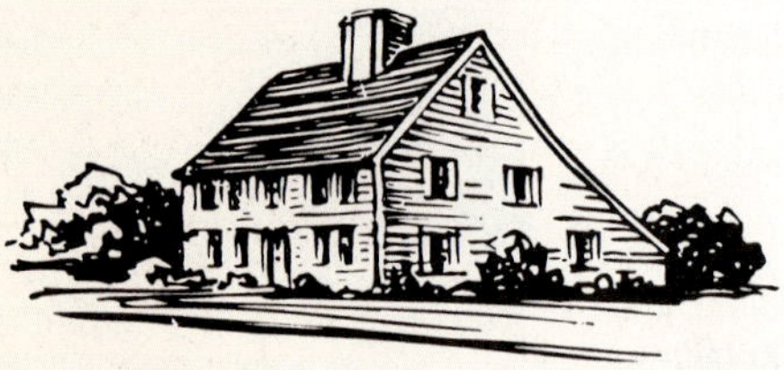

Saltbox

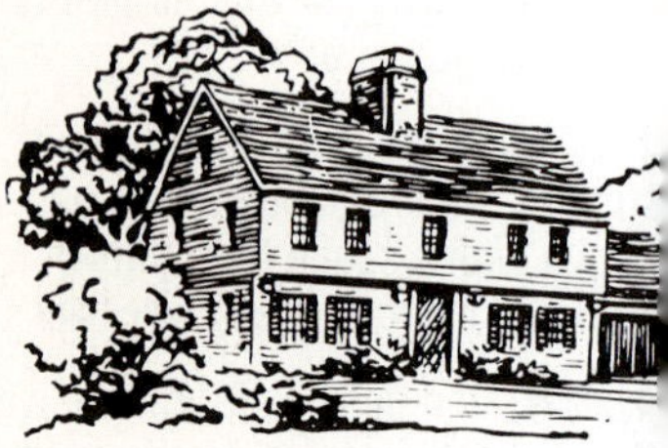

Garrison or Jetty

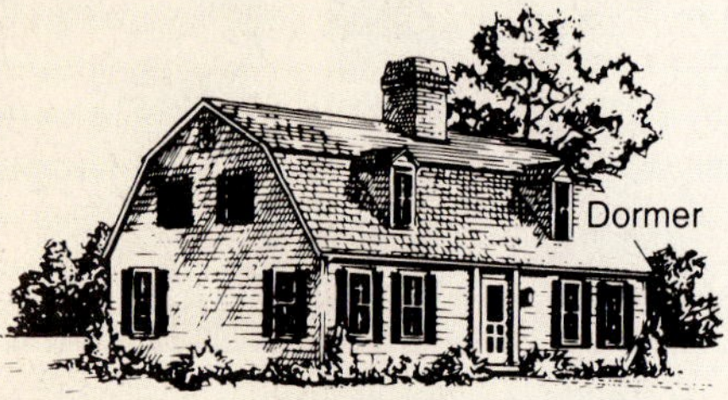

Gambrel

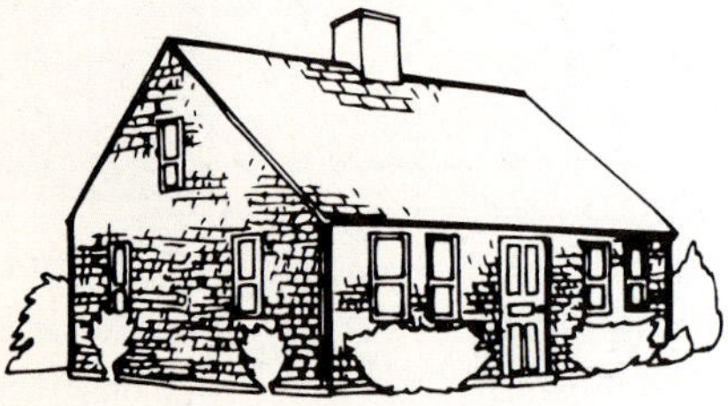

Cape Cod

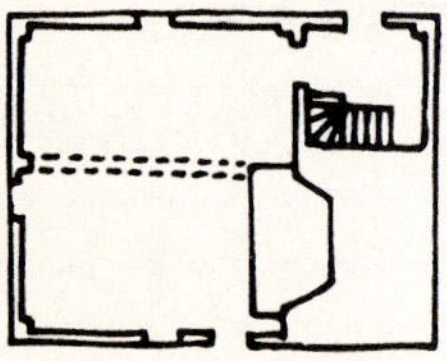

Half-house — 1650

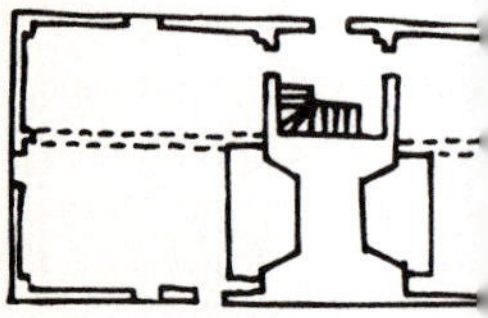

Two-room or doubl
house — 1675

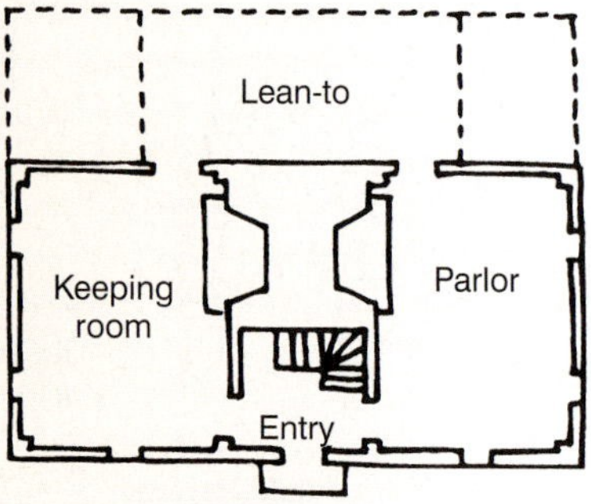

Lean-to or saltbox

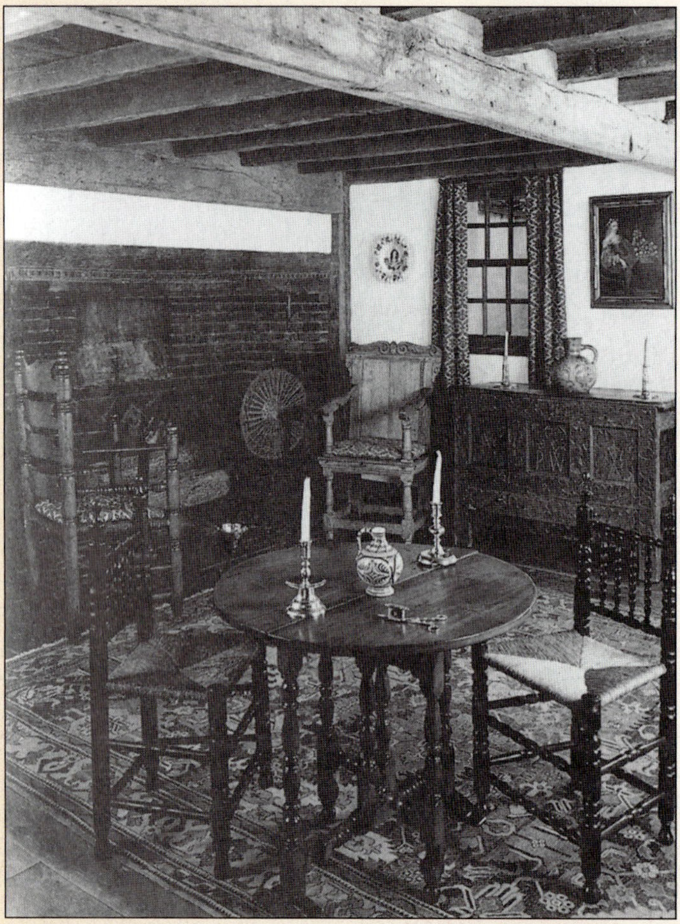

The Oyster Bay Room at the Winterthur Museum reflects typical seventeenth century interior: wood plank floors wi an Oriental rug, plaster walls, a low beamed ceiling, a lar fireplace, and simple wood furniture. (Courtesy of Winter Museum.)

common Early American interiors included Tudor, ɔethan, Jacobean, and Spanish Mission/Colonial style ɔnces

uthwest America, furniture designs were called the a Fe style and incorporated bold colors and geometric s

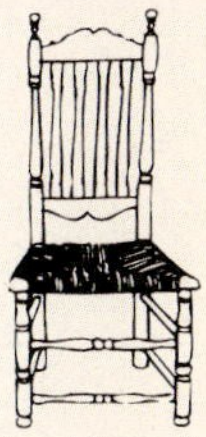
Bannister back

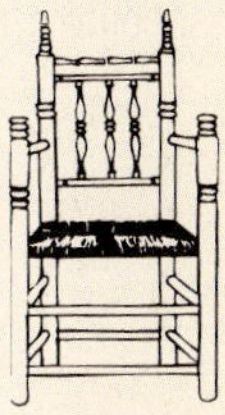
Carver

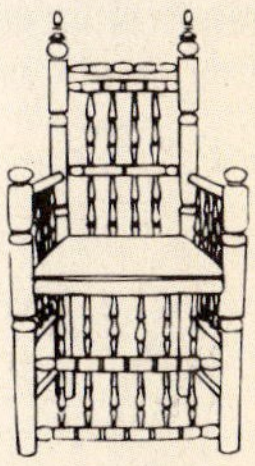
Brewster

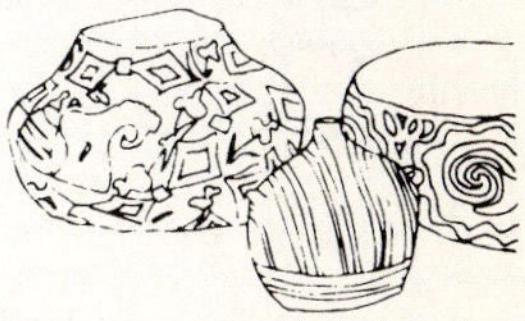
Indian pottery

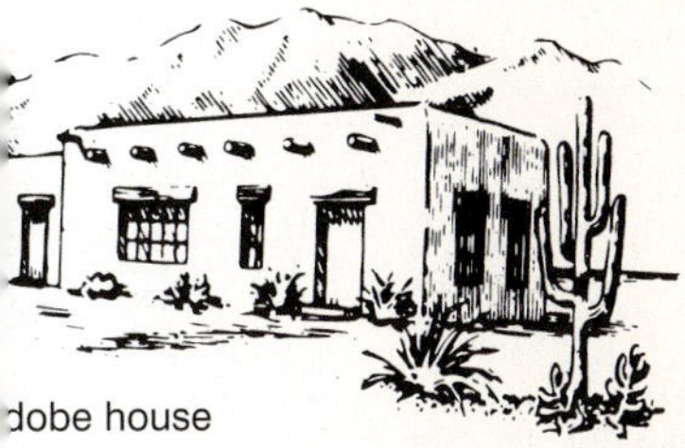
dobe house

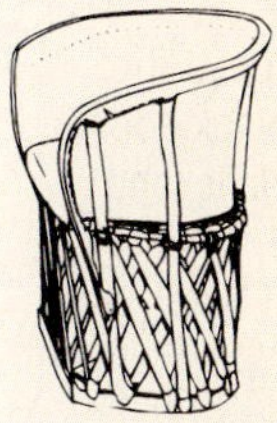
Equipale leather and wood chair

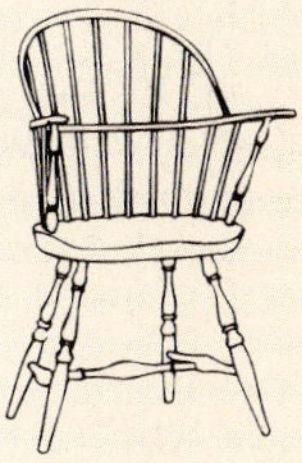
Windsor

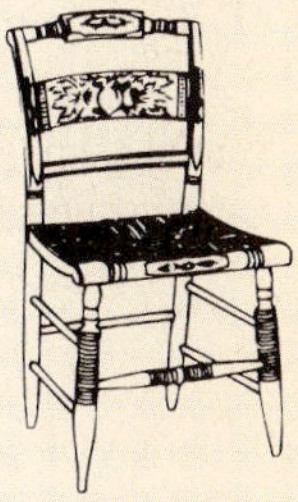
Hitchcock

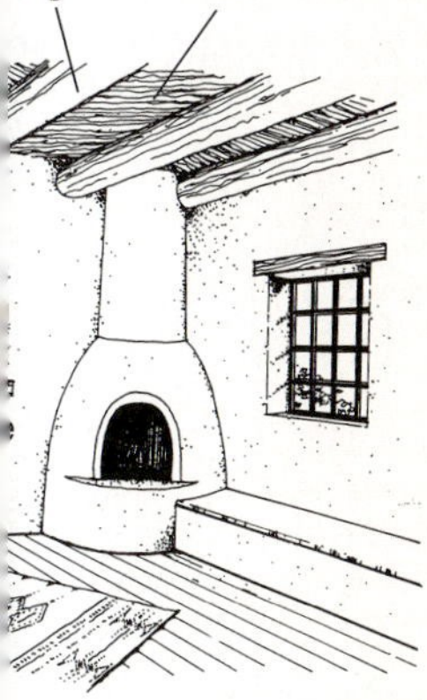

Adobe interior

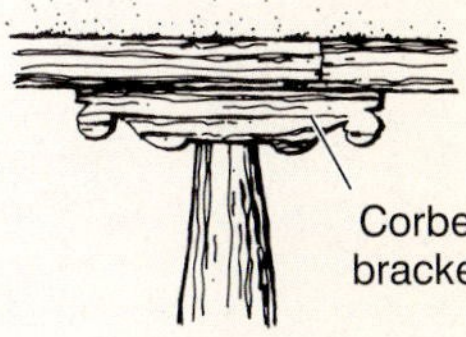

Zapata (double corbel bracket)

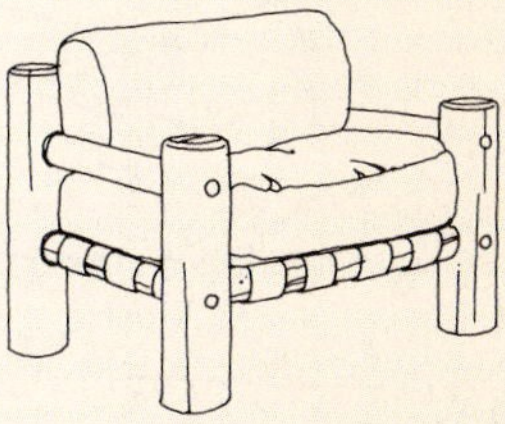
Lodge pole pine chair

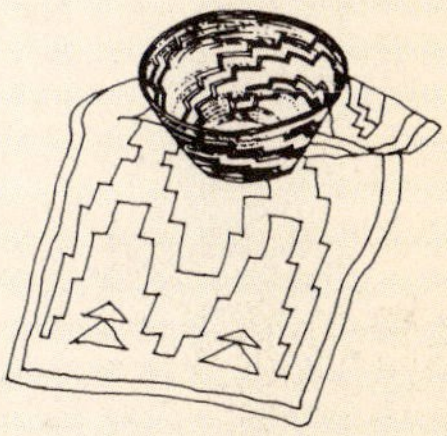
Indian basket and wool rug

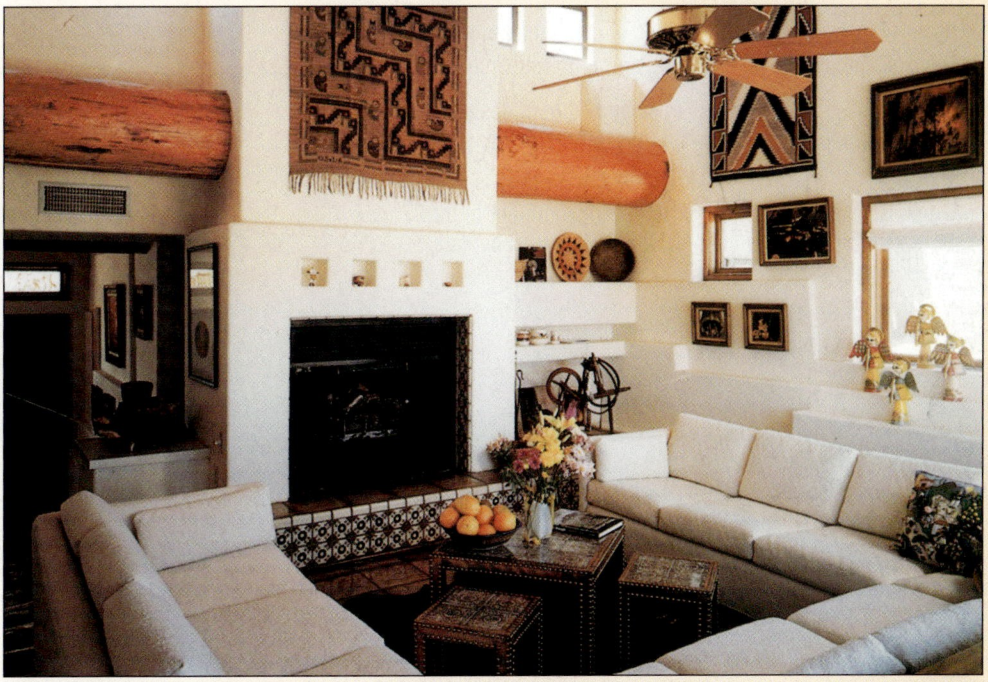

ior reflecting the Santa Fe atures an architectural ɔund of white plastered ɔcessed niches over the ɔ, Mexican tile, and c lodgepole beams. The further expressed by the Mexican, Native American, , and contemporary ngs and accessories. raph by Pam Singleton.)

Colonial Georg
(1700–1790)

- Greatly influenced by English Georgian styles with variations in wood usage, specific ornamentation, and proportions

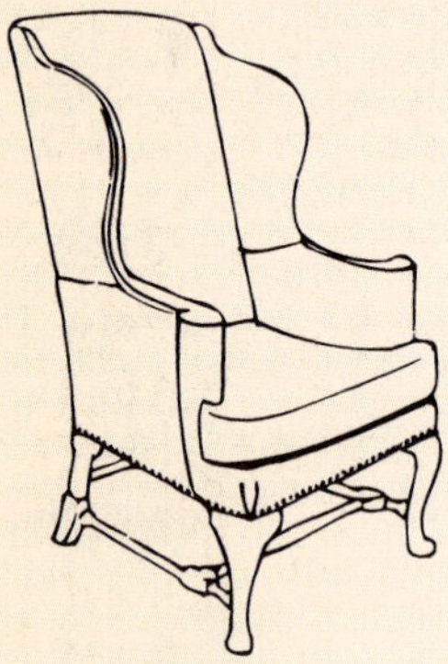

Wingback armchair

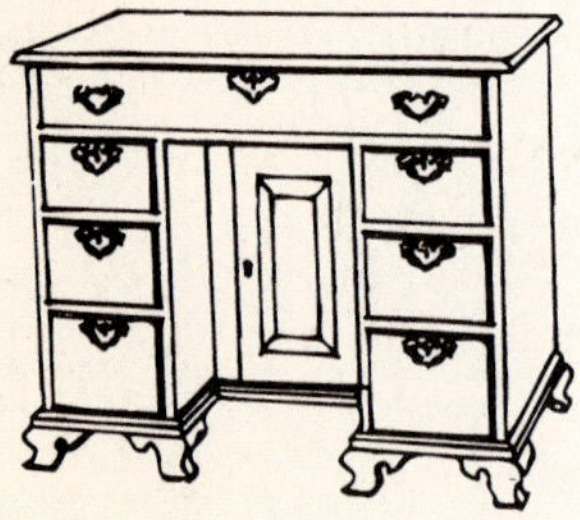

Desk

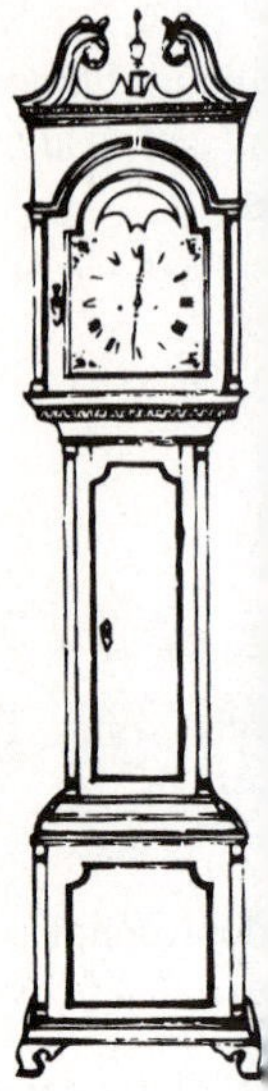

Grandfather clock

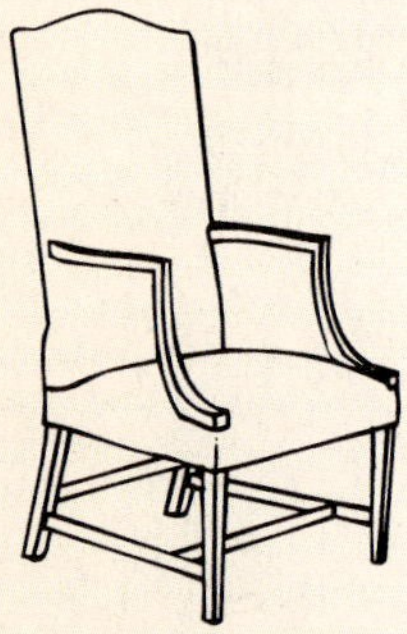

Martha Washington chair

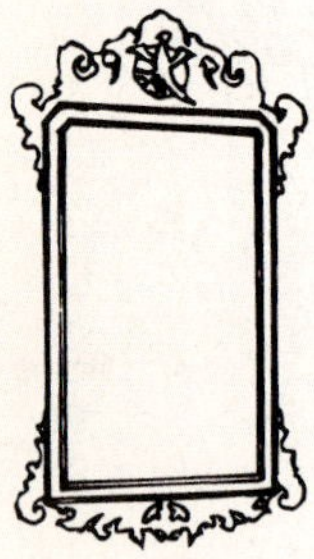

Mirror

Neoclassic
(1790–1845)

- Several distinctive designs including Federal, Greek Revival, Duncan Phyfe furniture, and Empire furniture
- Federal design emphasized Greek and Roman design, rejecting English influence. Thomas Jefferson was an advocate
- Greek Revival architecture particularly prominent in the South for plantation homes. Greatly influenced by early Greek designs

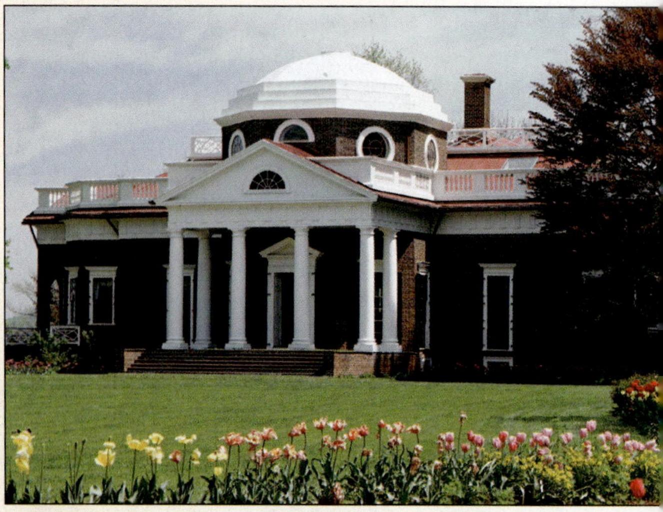

Monticello, home of Thomas Jefferson, was completed in 1809 in Charlottesville, Virginia. The Early Classic revival style was promoted as a "national" style by Jefferson. It reflects the Federal-Roman influence. (Photograph from PhotoDisc.)

- can Phyfe furniture characterized by fine proportions simple lines
- ire furniture was bold and monumental
- strial Revolution (circa 1830s–1900) brought about hine-made, mass-produced furnishings and a decline e fine art of furniture making

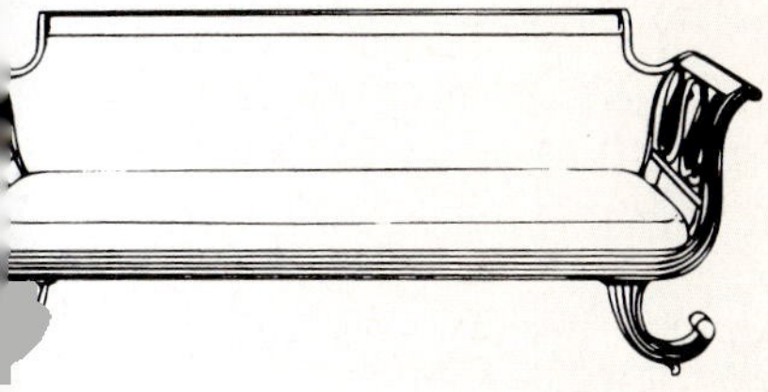
Duncan Phyfe sofa with cornucopia legs

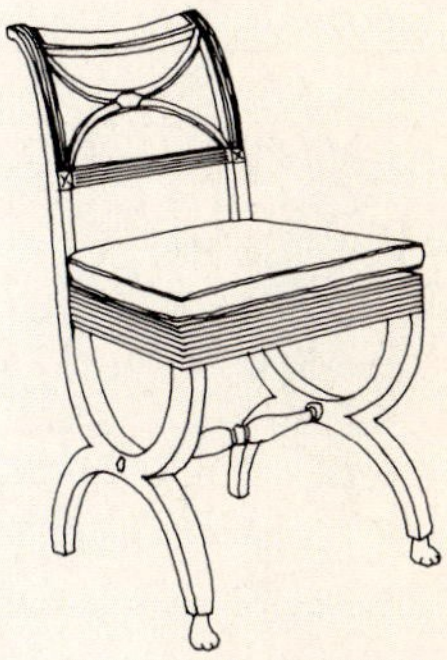
Curule form chair

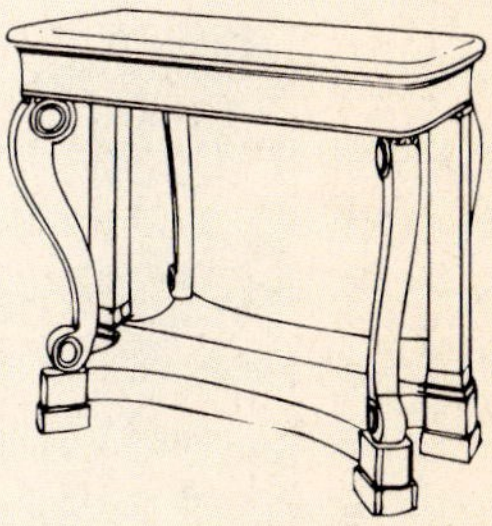
American Empire pier table

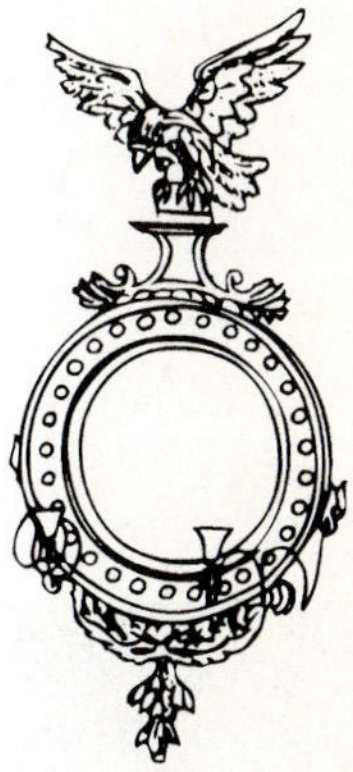
Girandole mirror (Bull's eye)

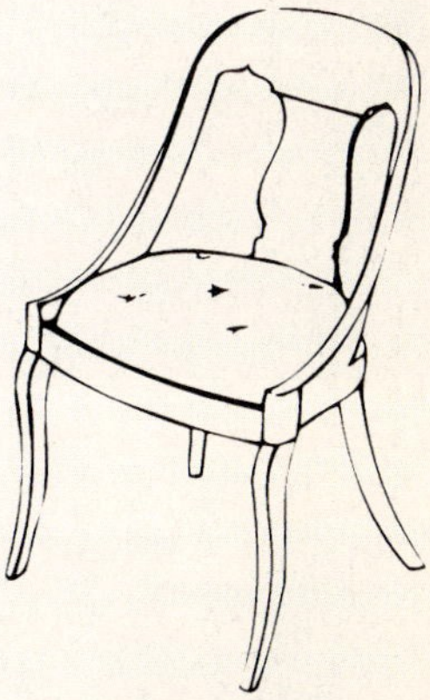
Greek Revival gondola chair

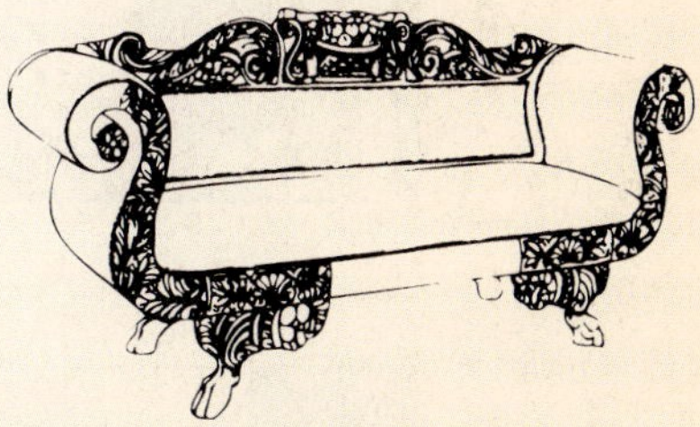
Greek Revival carved sofa

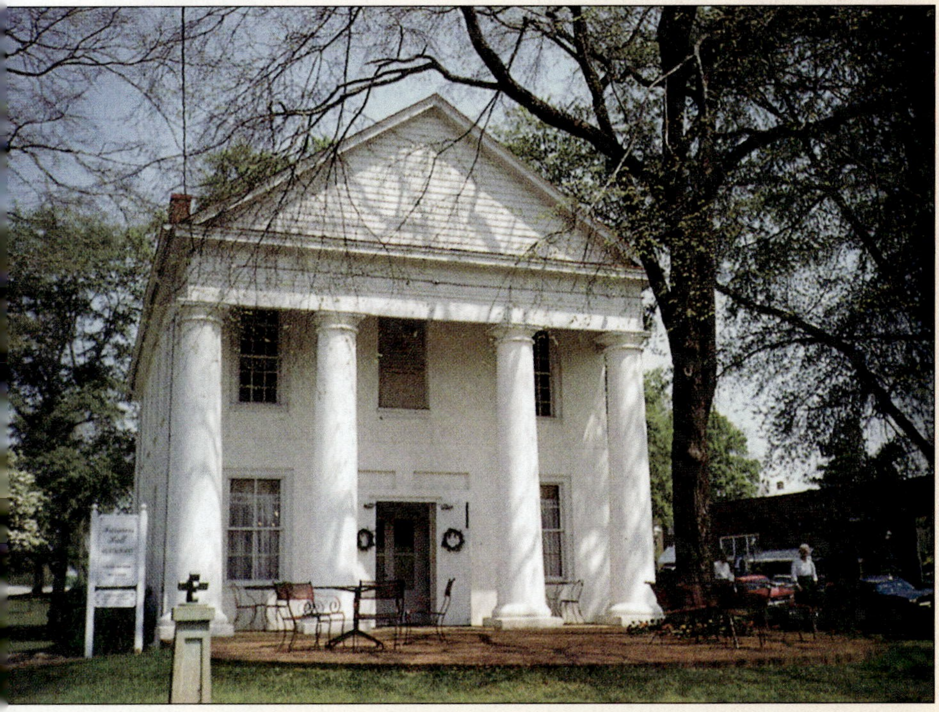
Farmers Hall, completed in 1826, in Pendleton, South Carolina, is an excellent example of Greek Revival architecture. (Courtesy of Lynn M. Jones.)

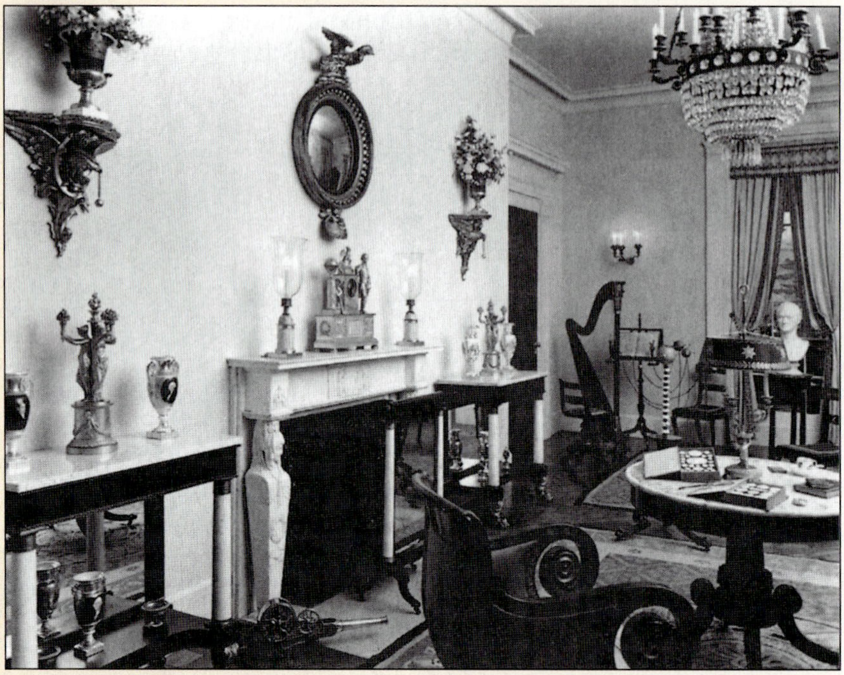

This parlor reflects the designs from the Greek Revival and Empire periods. (Courtesy of Winterthur Museum.)

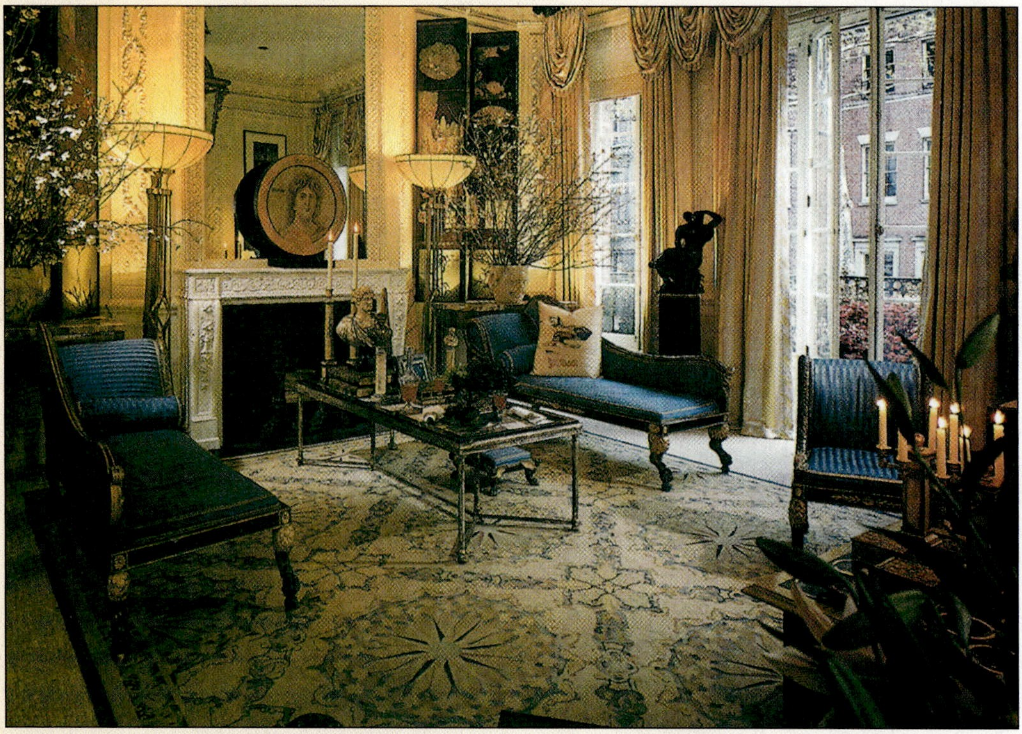

A contemporary Greek Revival interior designed by Robert Metzger is reminiscent of this early nineteenth-century style, including the use of gold and blue, a patterned rug, torchères, and asymmetrical couches with the distinctive lion's paw foot. (Antique architectural Aubusson courtesy of F. J. Hakimian, Inc., N.Y., and Robert Metzger Interiors. Photograph by Phillip Ennis.)

In the study of the history of design, a significant break in design occurs with the Industrial Revolution. The fine art of furniture making is overshadowed by the ease of mass-producing machine-made furniture. For this reason, the historical/classic eras end in the 1830s. It was also during this time that Americans first recognized the need to preserve our national heritage.

Sustainable Design AMERICAN CULTURAL HERITAGE

One of the finest examples of Sustainable Design is the preservation and reuse of historic structures. The need to preserve America's cultural heritage began as a grassroots movement in the 1800s and continues to have its most effective results at the community level. One of the first architectural buildings to be preserved was George Washington's home, Mount Vernon. The Mount Vernon Ladies Association was formed and raised the funds to purchase and restore the home in the 1880s. The Mount Vernon Ladies Association is still responsible for the home and the tours.

Before the turn of the twentieth century, America recognized the need to preserve its national treasures. Large areas of land were set aside as National Parks (a concept developed in America), National Monuments, and Historic Sites. In 1914 the National Park Service was formed to manage these and future acquisitions. Throughout the early 1900s many homes and buildings were preserved and restored to be used as museums to define America's heritage. Williamsburg, a reconstructed village, illustrates how an early American community lived and worked. The Historic American Buildings Survey, or HABS, was begun by the Park Service in 1933. The initial record produced 24,000 measured drawings of historic structures.

The National Trust for Historic Preservation in Washington, D.C., founded in 1949, is the largest organization in the country devoted to the preservation of historic buildings, districts, and neighborhoods. An organization sustained by both public and private contributions, the National Trust maintains the National Historic Register. The National Trust also administers historic buildings as museums, disseminates information about preservation to property owners and to the public at large, and assists in a variety of preservation, restoration, and rehabilitation efforts around the country. However, it is important to note that National Historic Register designation does not ensure the building's sustained preservation. The National Historic Register is a recognition status that requires only government-owned buildings to be subject to environmental review prior to proposed demolition. If a community is determined to maintain its local historic character, that community must invoke local ordinances and regulations to preserve its structures.

Through the 1950s, '60s, and '70s many national treasures were destroyed in the name of "progress." Of the structures surveyed by HABS in the 1930s, over half had been destroyed. Recognizing the need to reaffirm America's historical heritage, the grassroots movement lobbied Congress, and the national Historic Preservation Act was greatly enhanced in 1980. Tax relief and grants-in-aid (among other important legislative actions) were established to promote preservation. Downtown communities were granted funding through the Mainstreet Program to save their historic downtown character. Businesses that renovated historic homes, public buildings, and even factories helped to create the design specialty of adaptive use.

Through the grassroots efforts of many individuals and organizations, America's cultural heritage before and after European occupancy can be observed through buildings, historic sites, and communities, as well as in the open spaces of National Parks and Monuments. Americans have recognized the need to preserve a *sense of place*. They also recognize that natural resources, elaborate architecture, and unique details are costly to replace once destroyed. In fact, many are irreplaceable.

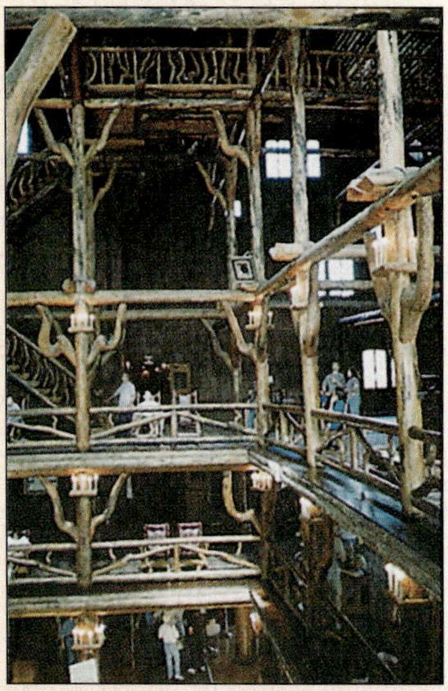

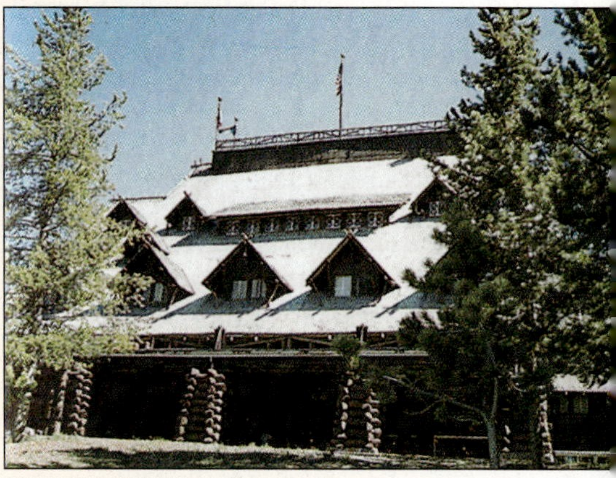

Old Faithful Inn (1901) in Yellowstone National Park, designed by architect Robert Reamer, is listed on the National Historic Register. Reamer created the rustic lodge to serve as a safe refuge from the wild. Victorian, Arts & Crafts, and Swedish details are prevalent. (Photographs courtesy of Lynn M. Jones.)

Historical Styles SUMMARY

The cyclical nature of design is seen in the shift from the clarity of the Egyptian and early Greek designs to the eventual heavy embellishment of the more ornate Roman designs. The cycle was repeated in the early simple English Queen Anne style that led to the Georgian and Federal styles, which eventually led to the heavy, ornate furniture of the Empire era. It is the nature of design to start with the purest and cleanest forms and then to embellish those forms again and again until the next generation must once more break free (or "rebirth") to new classics. The following section begins with yet another heavily decorated era, that of the Victorian period. From this ornately decorated state, designers once again rebelled against the elaborate motifs and designs; architecture and interior design evolved into the Modern Era.

Evolution of Modern Design

The roots of modernism are primarily traced to the Industrial Revolution, a period that continued from the early 1800s until the early twentieth century. This era introduced machines for manufacturing furniture and other modern conveniences, changing the way people lived. Advancements in technology and the development of new materials led to extraordinary architectural innovations. For example, iron grid construction allowed the architect to enclose vast spaces for railroad stations, exhibition halls, libraries, stock exchanges, theaters, and other public buildings.

The first World's Fair and Exhibition, held in London in 1851, is a fundamental starting point for modern designs. The Fair's Crystal Palace, designed by Joseph Paxton, was over 1600 feet long and resulted from technical advances in the use of glass and iron. The Exhibition serves as a transition between historic and modern design, for although the structure and modern machines housed within spoke to the twentieth century, the furnishings and architectural details produced by the machines were rooted in the past.

:irca 1840–1920) Victorian Era

cided with reign of Queen Victoria

algia for past styles prevailed with machinery ucing intricate designs, details, and carvings referred gingerbread

major architectural styles in America included the wing:

othic Revival: Andrew Jackson Downing main proponent

alianate: modified Italian villa

ansard or Second Empire: style delineated by sloping ansard roof defining the top floor

ueen Anne: most whimsical of all Victorian era eclectic yles (not related to Queen Anne furniture styles eviously discussed)

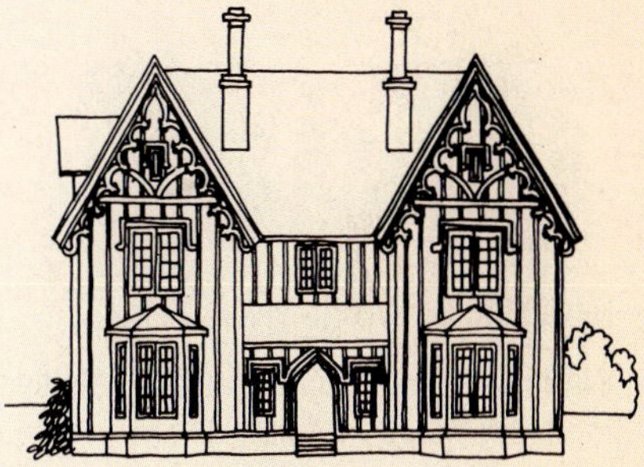

Carpenter Gothic

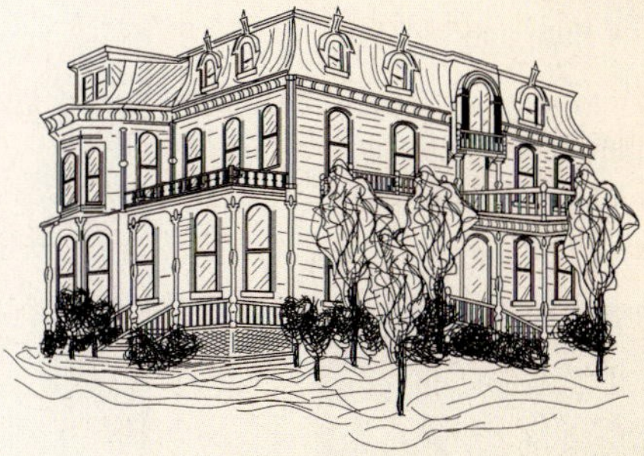

Mansard Victorian

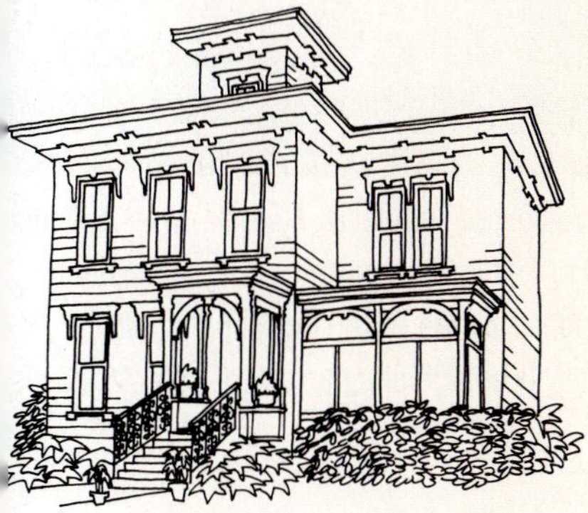

Italianate Victorian

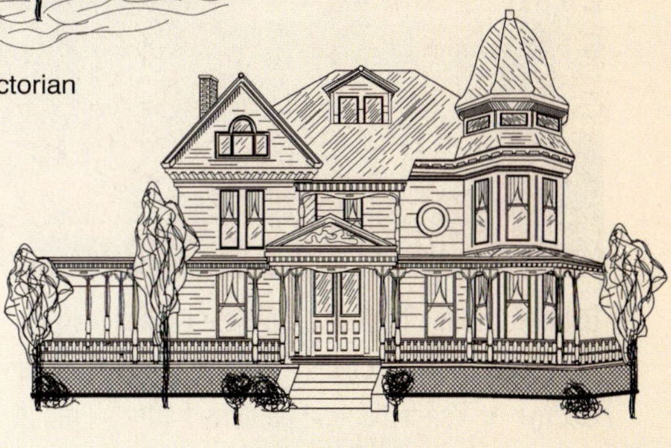

Queen Anne

Victorian Era

- Other Victorian styles included Exotic Revivals, Octagonal, Stick, Shingle, and Romanesque
- Interiors were profusely decorated with patterned wallpaper, fabrics, and rugs
- Elaborate furnishings were adapted from French Rococo, Neoclassic, Gothic, Renaissance, Oriental, and Elizabethan/Jacobean Eras
- Prominent designers included John Belter (who developed a wood laminating technique that allowed for ornate rosewood carvings) and Charles Eastlake

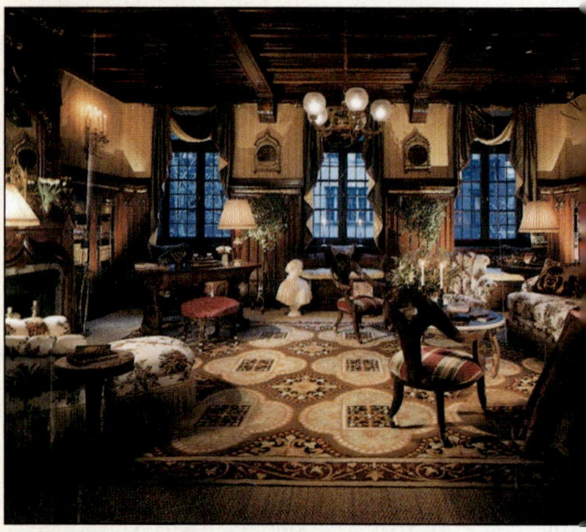

A contemporary Victorian interior, designed by Mich LaRocca, demonstrates the eclectic look. Tudor, Mo French, and Greek Revival are the principal styles employed. The patterned rug and numerous access further convey the Victorian feeling. (Antique French needlepoint courtesy of F. J. Hakimian, Inc., N.Y., an Michael R. LaRocca, Ltd. Photograph by Phillip Enni

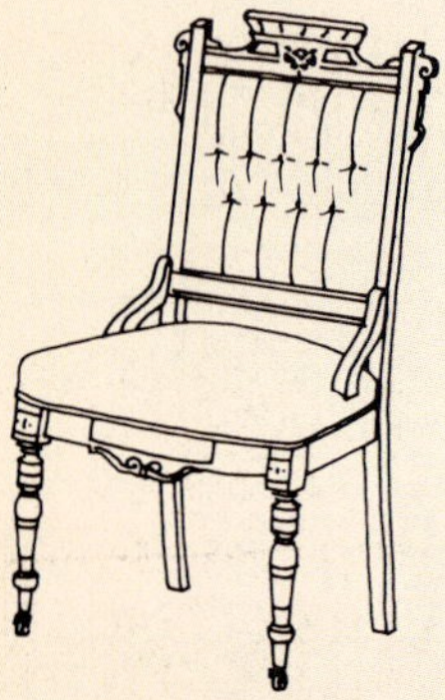

Eastlake chair

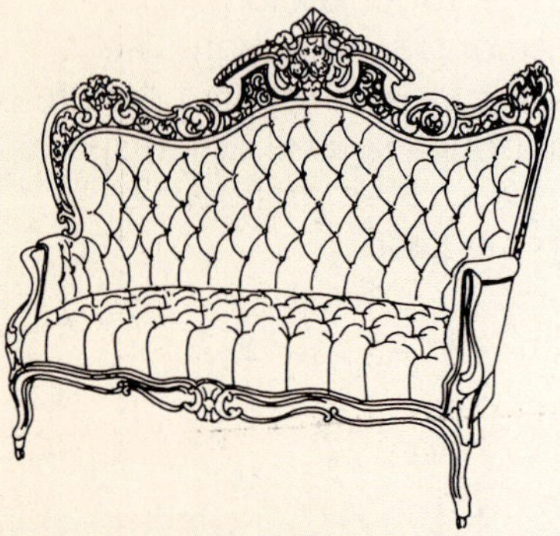

Belter carved rosewood sofa

Traditional Revivals

(circa 1880–192

- Revival of Old World styles
- World famous design school L'École des Beaux Arts in Paris promoted these styles
- Opulent designs by Richard Morris Hunt and McKim, Mead & White (architectural firm)
- Included Beaux Arts, Châteauesque, Georgian Revival, Spanish Colonial, Neoclassical, Tudor, Colonial Revival, French Eclectic, and Italian Renaissance

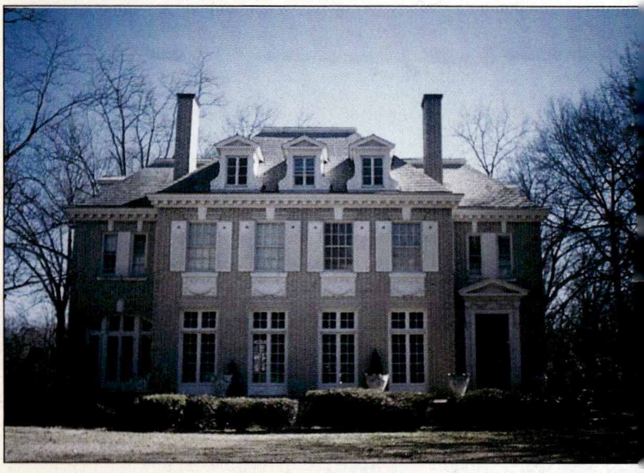

This Beaux Arts-style residence in Atlanta, Georgia, was designe by Neil Reed and built in 1911. The residence is in the historic Druid Hills district designed by the great landscape architect Frederick Law Olmstead. (Photograph courtesy of Lynn M. Jones

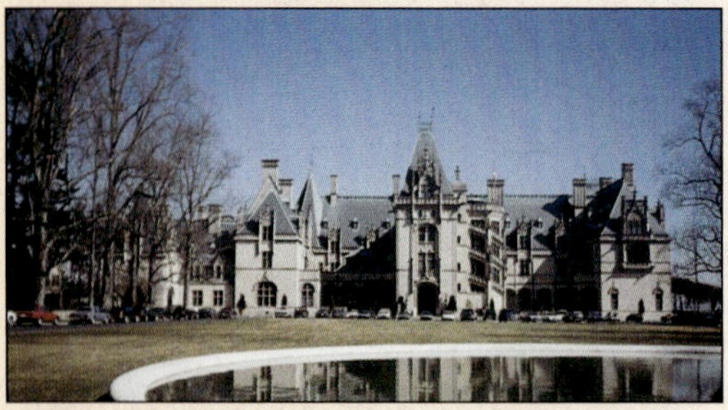

Biltmore House (1888–1895), the Châteauesque mansion built by architect Richard Morris Hunt for George W. Vanderbilt and patterned after a French Renaissance château. (Courtesy of Lynn M. Jones.)

- cided with Victorian Era and Traditional Revivals
- eering designers rebelled against historical eclecticism
- :ed technological advances in iron frame construction, nated wood, and plate glass windows
- ged art and technology
- est designs came from the Shakers, a religious order believed beauty resides in utility and simplicity
- rian designer Michael Thonet (1830–1870s) developed ess for bending wood into gentle curves
- et's designs still used today, including the famous wood rocker and café chair

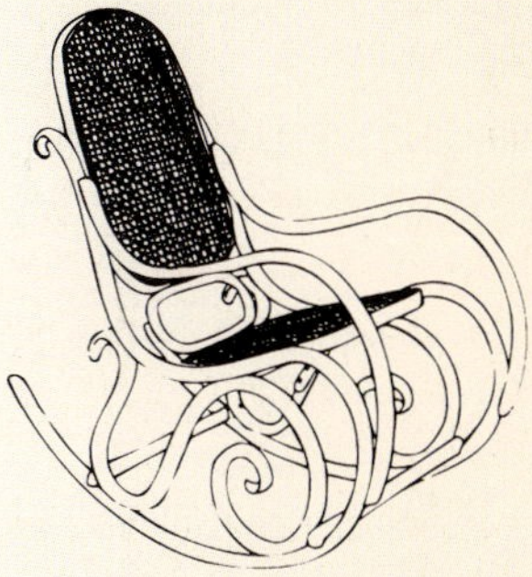

Bentwood rocker
Michael Thonet

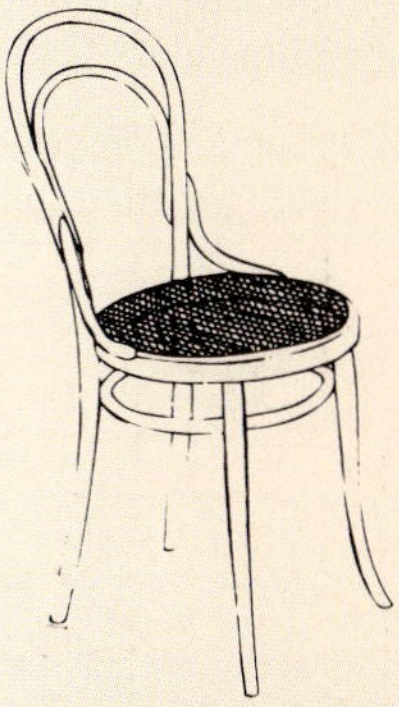

Vienna café chair
Michael Thonet

Arts and rafts Movement (1860s–1920s)

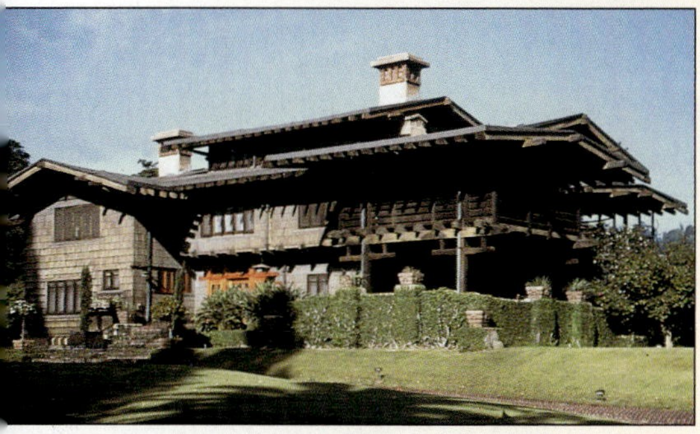

mble House designed by the Greene Brothers in na, California, remains the finest example of their ıan approach to architecture. (Courtesy of the Gamble Photograph by Alexander Vertikoff.)

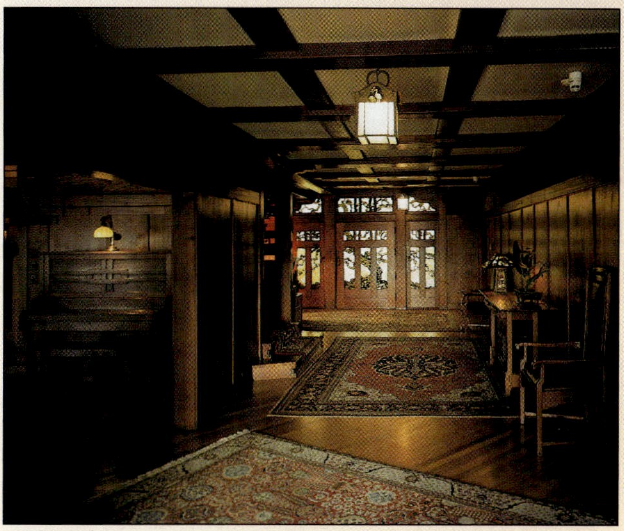

This interior view of the Gamble House reveals exquisitely handcrafted wooden architectural members and handcrafted furnishings. (Photograph by Tim Street-Porter.)

- lted against machine-made products
- cated handcrafted furnishings
- ninent English architects and designers included am Morris, Charles Eastlake, Edward W. Godwin, Webb, Ernest Gimson, and Charles F. A. Voysey
- ninent American architects and designers included av Stickley, Frank Lloyd Wright, Henry Hobson ardson, and Charles and Henry Greene
- ne brothers developed the bungalow

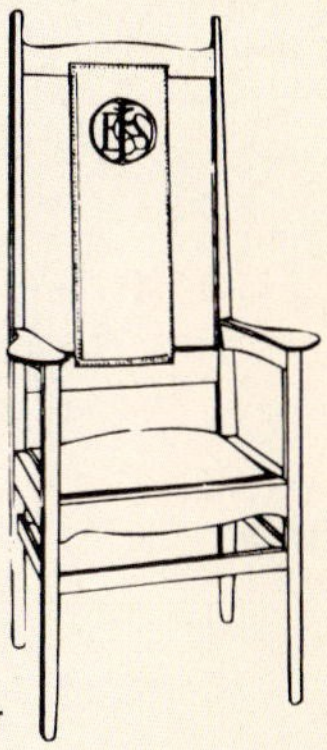

Voysey chair

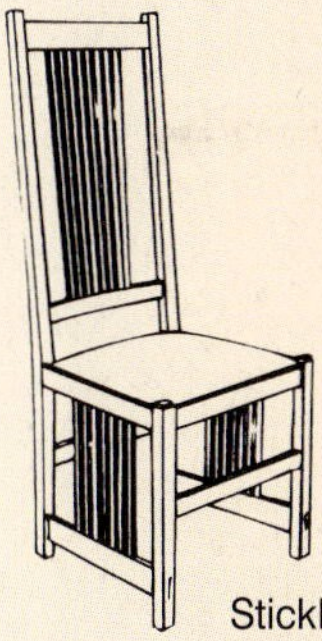

Stickley chair

Early Modernism

SKYSCRAPE (1880s–1920s)

- Although the first metal frame buildings were in New York, the skyscraper is credited to Chicago architects
- Louis Sullivan, father of the skyscraper, is credited with coining the phrase "Form follows function"
- Many skyscrapers reflect the three parts of a column: the base, the shaft, and the capital

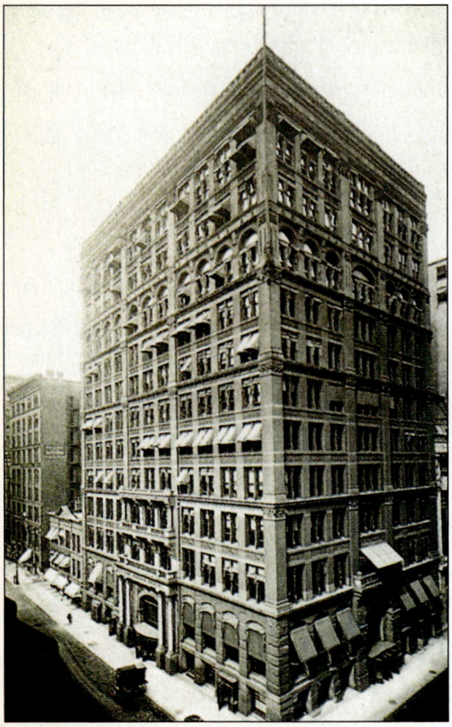

The Home Insurance Company Building (1883–1885), Chicago, by William LeBaron Jenney, was the first fully steel-frame building. Jenney studied in Paris at L'École Centrale des Arts et Manufactures. Unfortunately, the building was demolished in 1931. (Courtesy of Chicago Historical Society.)

ART NOUVE (circa 1890–191

- Style based on nature, employing organic flowing forms
- Prominent proponents included Victor Horta, Henri van de Velde, Hector Guimard, and Antonio Gaudi
- Called *Jugendstil* in Austria and Germany
- Charles Rennie Mackintosh combined aspects of Art Nouveau with strong geometric forms
- Louis Comfort Tiffany is best known for Art Nouveau stained-glass designs

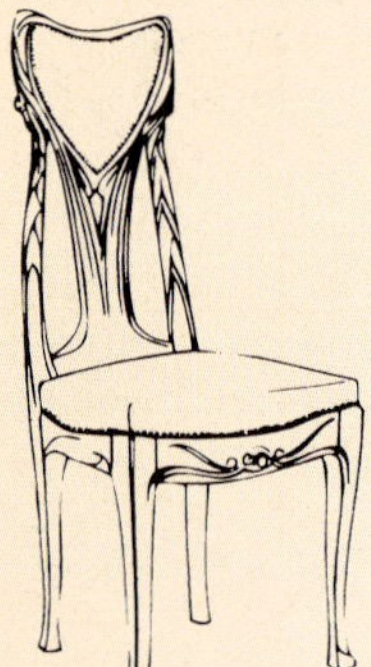

Art Nouveau chair
Hector Guimard

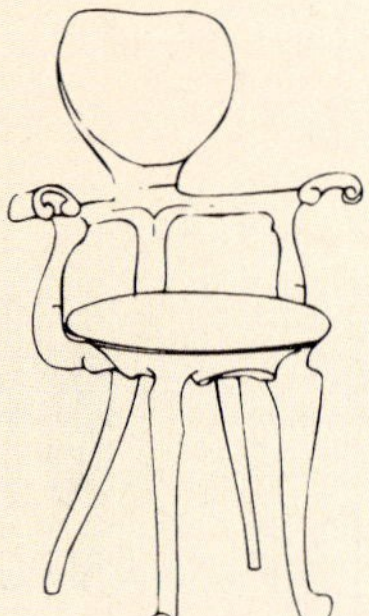

Art Nouveau chair
Antonio Gaudi

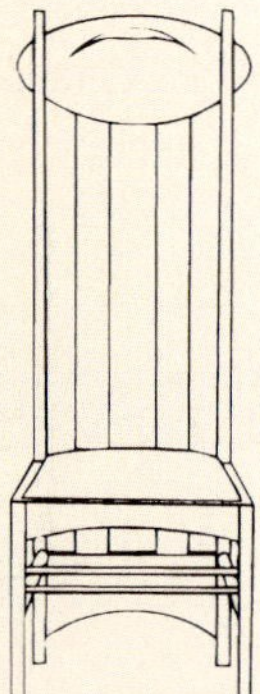

Argyle chair
C.R. Mackintosh

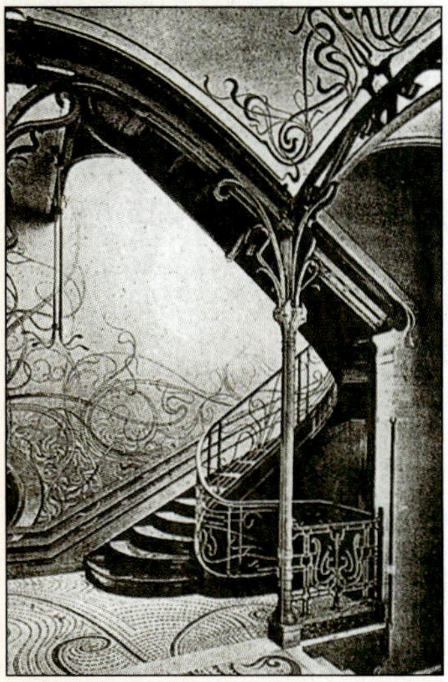

The Tassel House (1892–1893) in Brussels, Belgium, is on Victor Horta's best-known town houses and one of the earli private residences designed in the Art Nouveau style. Swirli organic forms decorate the entry. The graceful stair railings supports are fashioned in iron. (Photograph courtesy of the Museum of Modern Art, New York.)

ORGANIC ARCHITECTURE (circa 1894–Present)

- acterized by a building that appears to "grow out of ınd"
- est proponent was Frank Lloyd Wright
- ht developed *prairie style* house (see Figure 1.3)

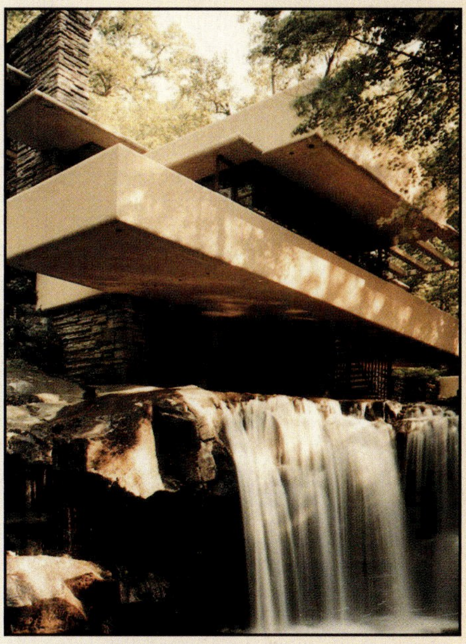

Frank Lloyd Wright's modern residential design, Falling Water (1936), in Mill Run, PA, was built over a waterfall. It demonstrates the architect's philosophy: "A house should grow out of the land." (Courtesy of Western Pennsylvania Conservancy.)

NTERNATIONAL STYLE (Turn of Century–1950)

- based on functionalism and purity of line
- coined by American architect Philip Johnson
- mon materials included reinforced concrete, stucco, , and glass
- white finishes
- floor plan and large expanses of glass
- national design movements leading to the fully loped style included the following:
  - he Secession—an artistic movement in Austria led / Otto Wagner, Adolf Loos, and Josef Hoffmann. offmann also led the Wiener Werkstätte (studio), more geometric offshoot
  - e Stijl—a movement in Holland that reduced design its basic elements, including the use of only red, ue, yellow, black, gray, and white. Most famous oponent was Gerrit Reitveld

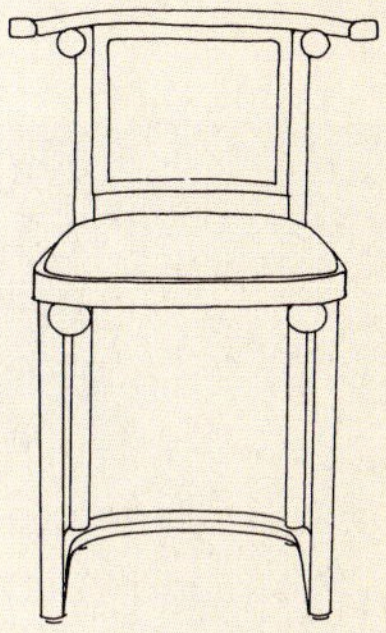

Fledermaus chair
Josef Hoffmann

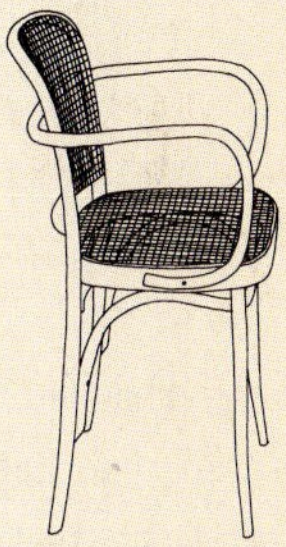

Prague chair
Josef Hoffmann

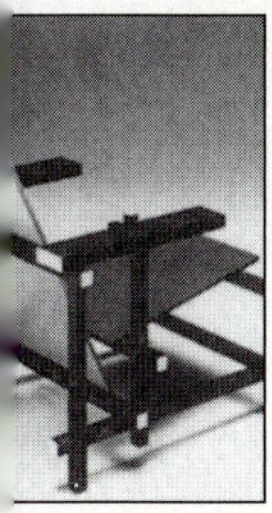

One of the finest examples of furniture from De Stijl is the Red/Blue chair (1918), designed in Holland by Gerrit Reitveld. It is constructed of wood in an abstract arrangement and painted red, blue, yellow, and black. (Courtesy of Cassina USA Inc.)

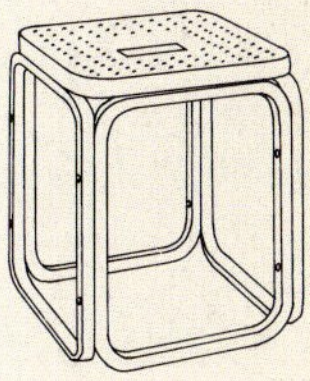

Secession stool
Otto Wagner

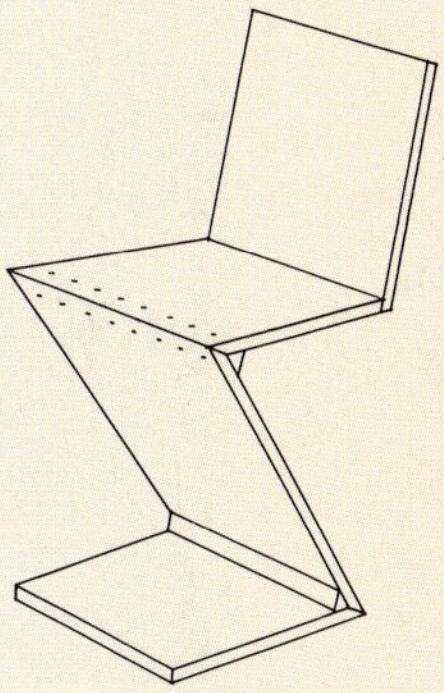

Zig-Zag chair
Gerrit Reitveld

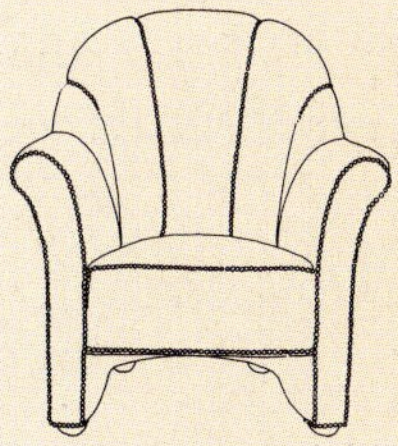

Haus Koller chair
Josef Hoffmann

3. Bauhaus–an experimental design school in Germany formed to simplify design to its purest state, incorporating machine-age manufacturing. School was closed by the Nazis in 1933, and designers fled to America. Most famous proponents included Walter Gropius, Marcel Breuer, and Ludwig Mies van der Rohe. Mies coined the phrase "Less is more."
4. Le Corbusier (Charles-Edouard Jeanneret-Gris)–a giant of modern architecture; studio was in Paris. Designed the Villa Savoye, the chapel at Ronchamp, and classic furniture pieces

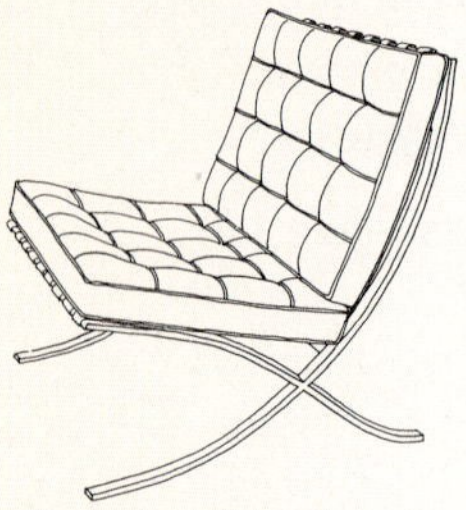

Barcelona chair
Mies van der Rohe

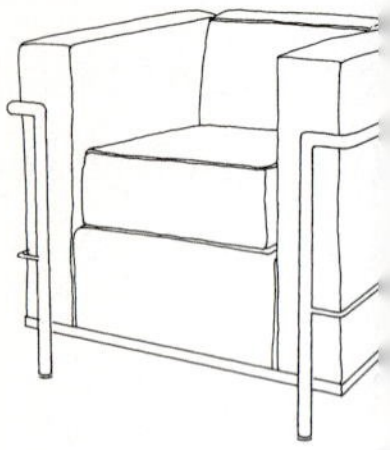

Grand Confort ch
Le Corbusier

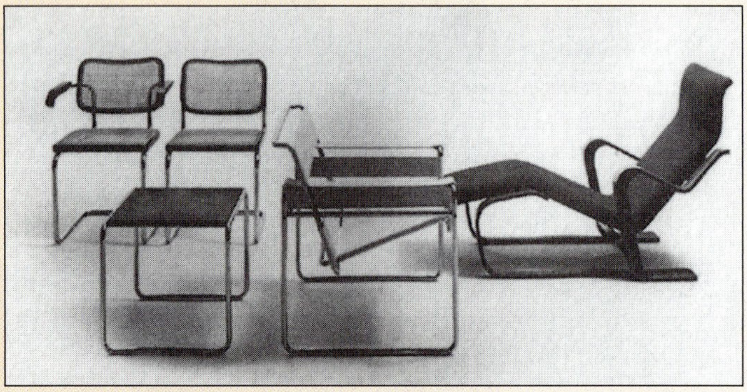

Classic Bauhaus furniture designed by master architect a furniture designer Marcel Breuer. From left to right, the Ce chairs, Laccio table and Wassily lounge, designed by Bre while he taught at the Bauhaus. The Isokon lounge, far rig designed in 1935 in England. (Courtesy of Knoll.)

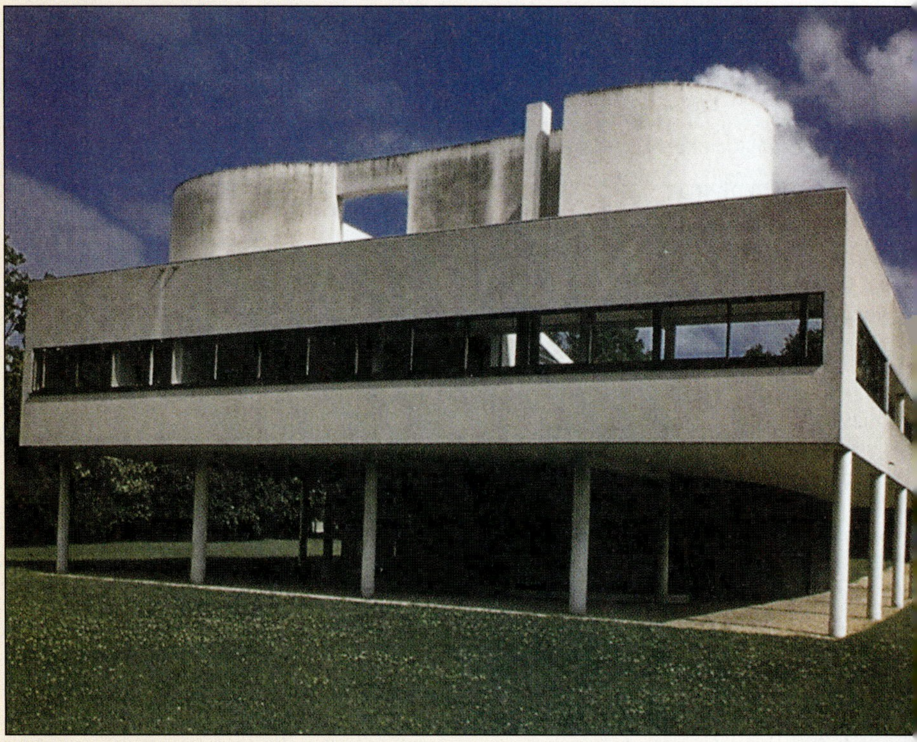

The Villa Savoye, designed by Le Corbusier, comprises three floors. The main living level is on the second floor, which opens to a terrace and the third-floor roof garden. Le Corbusier wrote, "The house is a machine to live in." (Photograph from Art Resource, NY. ©2000 Artists Rights Society (ARS), New York/ADAGP, Paris/FLC.)

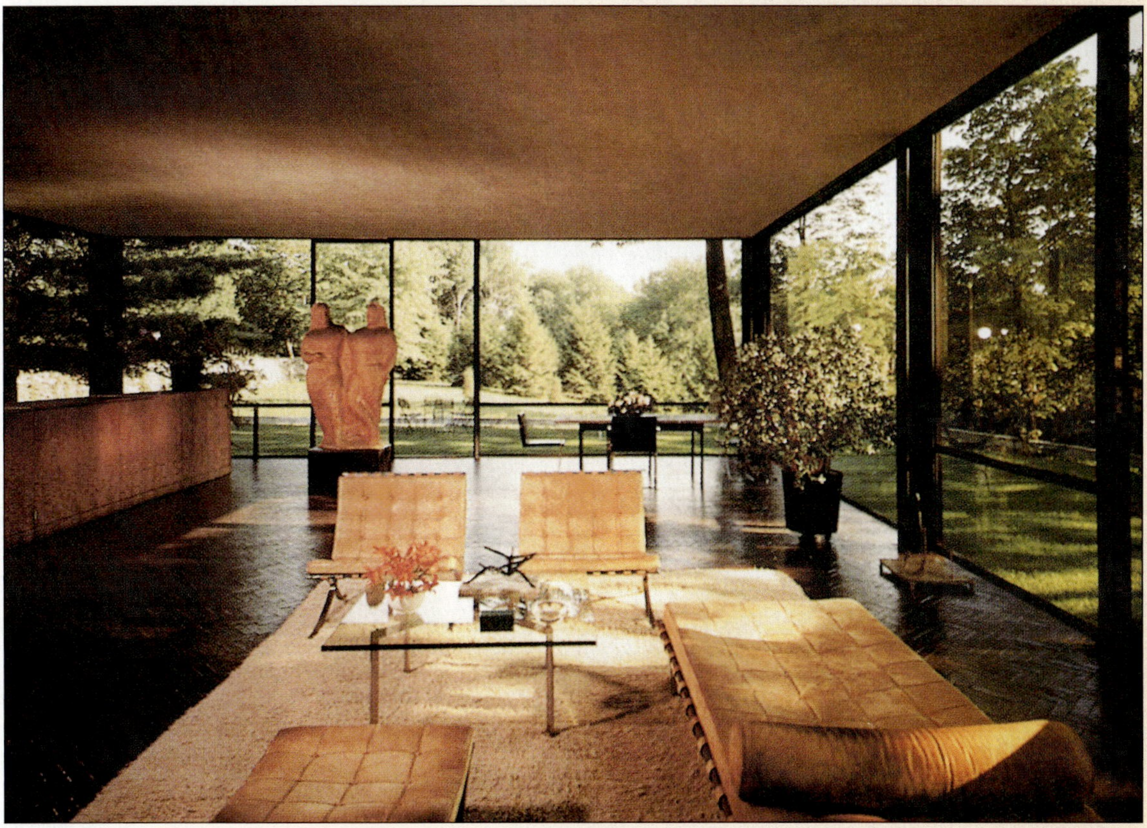

Architect Philip Johnson's "Glass House" in New Canaan, Connecticut (1949), with glass walls and Barcelona furniture by Ludwig Mies van der Rohe. Johnson was an early follower of Mies van der Rohe. (Photograph by Bill Maris, ©Esto.)

ART DECO
irca 1909–1940)

- orative style advocating strong geometric forms uding the pyramid, ziggurat (stepped pyramid), zigzag, sunburst
- ired by the glamour of movies and stage, jazz music, can art, and new technology
- ninent designers included Paul Frankl and Donald key
- Saarinen, a Finnish-born designer, started the tigious Cranbrook Academy in Michigan

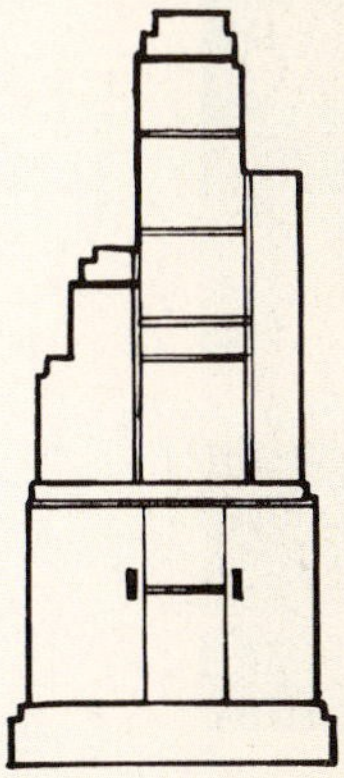

Paul Frankl helped promote modern American furniture during the 1920s and 1930s and was inspired in his own approach to furniture design by the uniquely American skyscraper—an Art Deco theme he employed for numerous pieces.

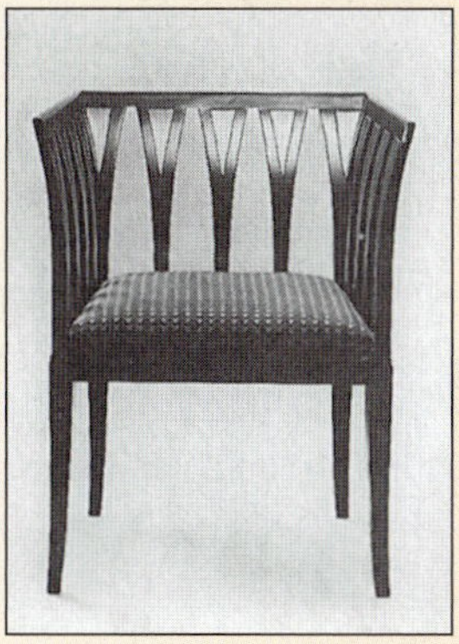

Eliel Saarinen designed the Blue Chair in 1929, at the Cranbrook Academy of Art. The Art Deco piece has a blue lacquered frame accented with gold leaf. (Courtesy of ICF.)

Modern Styles

POST-WORLD WAR (1950s–1970s)

- New architectural directions emerge
- New technologies included air-conditioning, suspended ceilings, synthetic fibers, and plastics
- Scandinavian designers included Alvar Aalto, Eero Aarnio, and Hans Wegner
- Italian designers in particular exploited the use of plastics; designers included Joe Columbo and Vico Magistretti
- American designers included the following:
  1. Charles and Ray Eames—pioneered chairs constructed of molded plywood and fiberglass
  2. Eero Saarinen—came to the U.S. with his father Eliel; known for his womb and tulip chairs
  3. Buckminster Fuller—known for his geodesic domes
- Brutalism develops as a reaction to the International style. Massive, sculptural structures of raw concrete were designed by noted architects such as Paul Rudolph and Louis Kahn

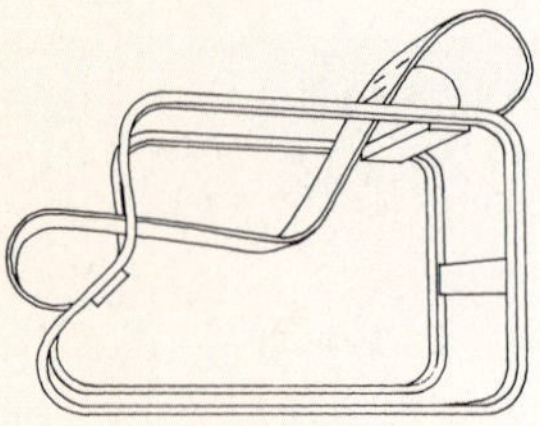

Palmio (Scroll) chair
Alvar Aalto

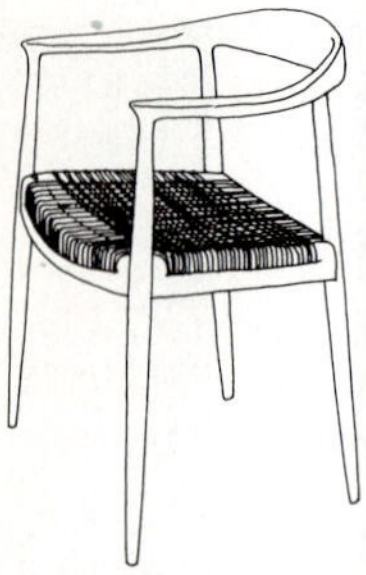

"The Chair"
Hans Wegner
Scandinavia

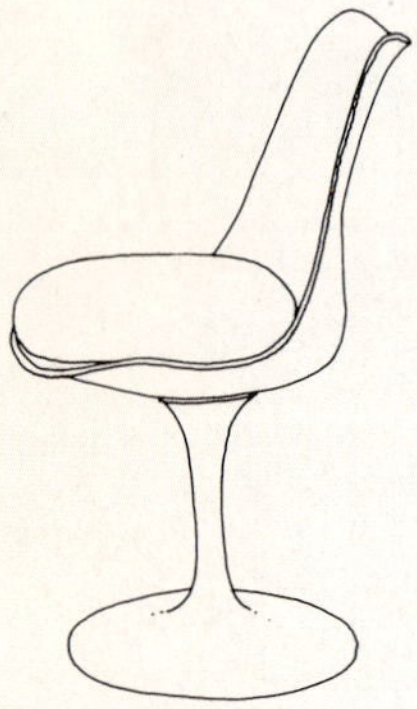

Tulip/pedestal chair
Eero Saarinen
U.S.A.

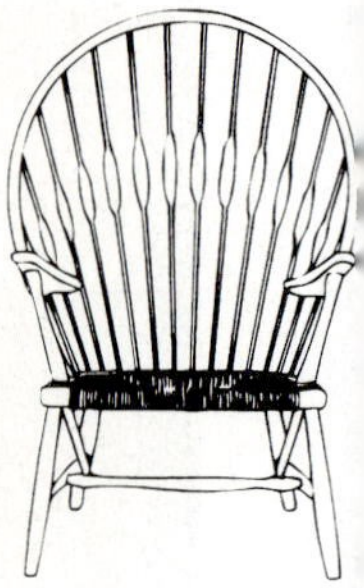

Peacock chair
Hans Wegner
Scandinavia

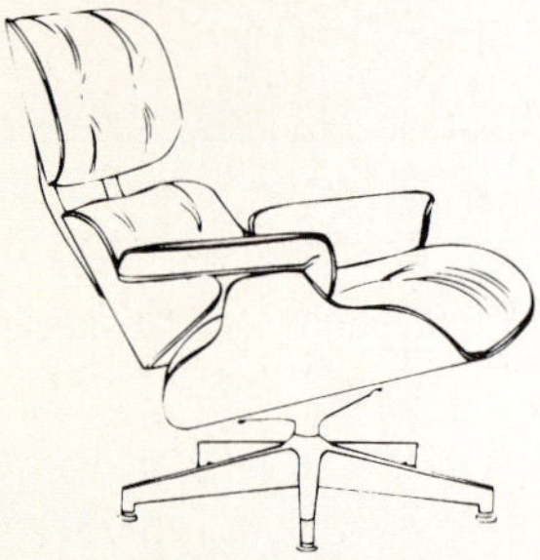

Eames lounge
Charles Eames, U.S.A.

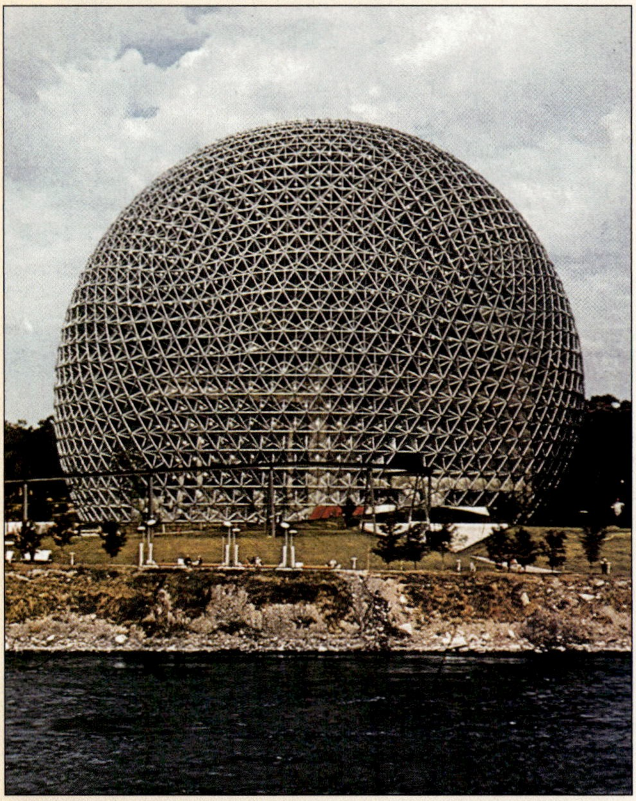

The spherelike U.S. Pavilion at the Montreal World's Fair Expo '67, designed by Buckminster Fuller, is a good example of the architect's patented method of construction known as the geodesic dome. (Courtesy of Miriam Stimpson.)

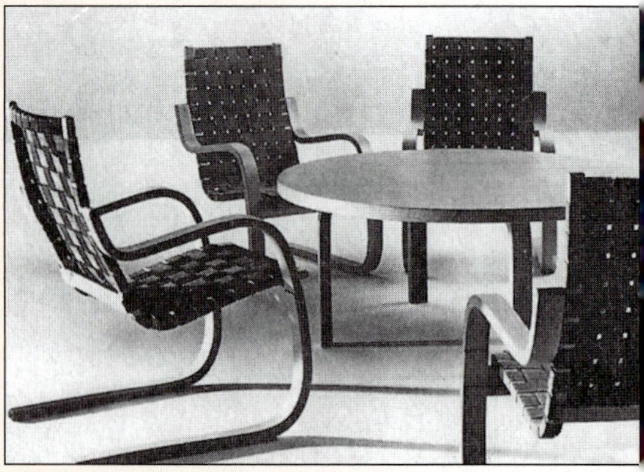

Finnish designer Alvar Aalto designed the cantilevered Pension chair in 1946 using laminated birch with a seat and back of webbing. The birch table is also by Aalto. They are excellent examples of Scandinavian modern furniture design. (Courtesy of ICF.)

- style borrows from the past but in extremely emporary terms
- or exponents include Michael Graves, Robert Venturi, ert Stern, and Philip Johnson
- iture styles include the Craft Revival, Art Furniture, nomic Furniture, and most recently furniture to meet needs of a mobile work force
- r design trends during the Post–Modern Era are rally divided into four categories:
  - High Tech Style—utilizes exposed industrial and onstruction elements; started by the Eames
  - Memphis Style—advocates freedom of expression in tyle, color, and form
  - Classic Modernism—advocates classical, simplified legance; influenced by ancient Greek designs
  - Deconstructivism—an extreme reaction to the negative spects of current society; leading proponent is Frank . Gehry

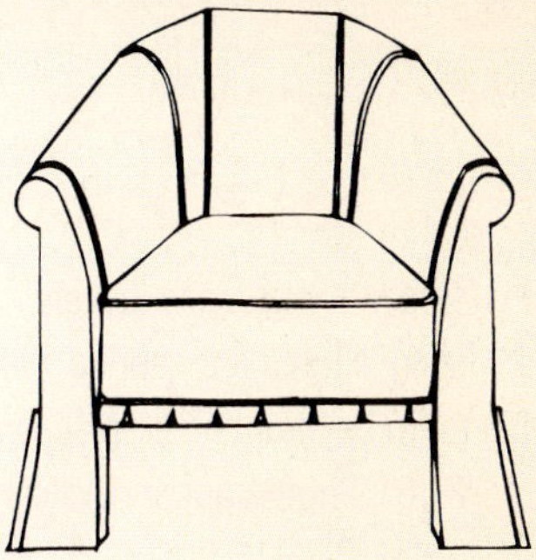

Graves chair
Post-Modern

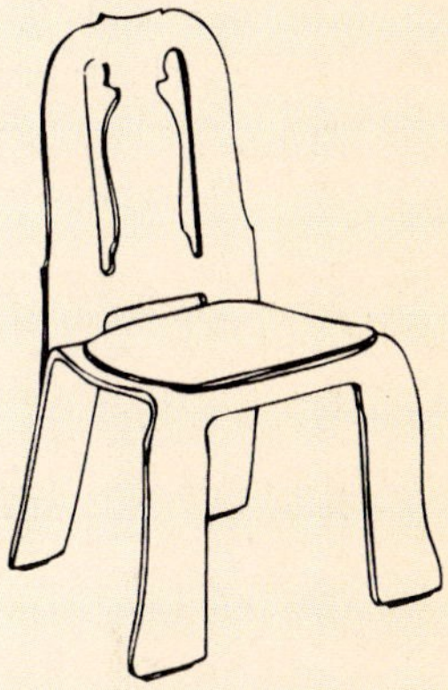

Venturi chair
Post-Modern

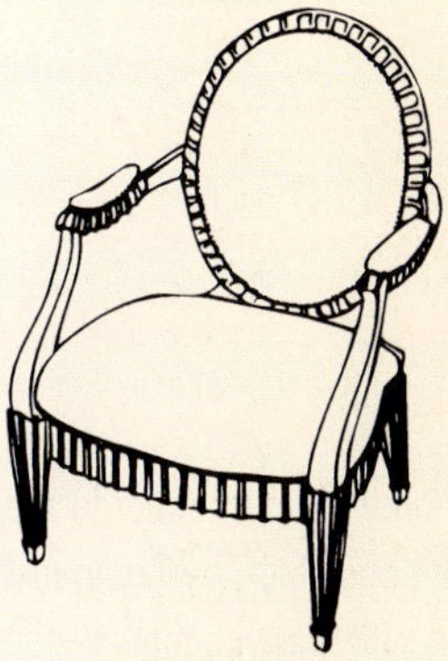

Grande Flute
Angelo Donghia
Classic Modern

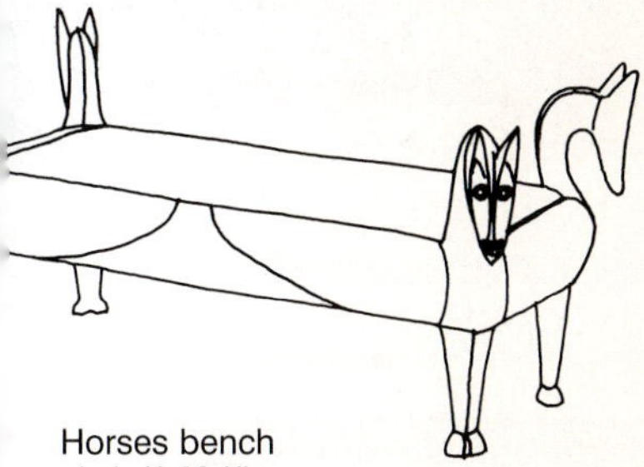

Horses bench
Judy K. McKie
Craft Revival

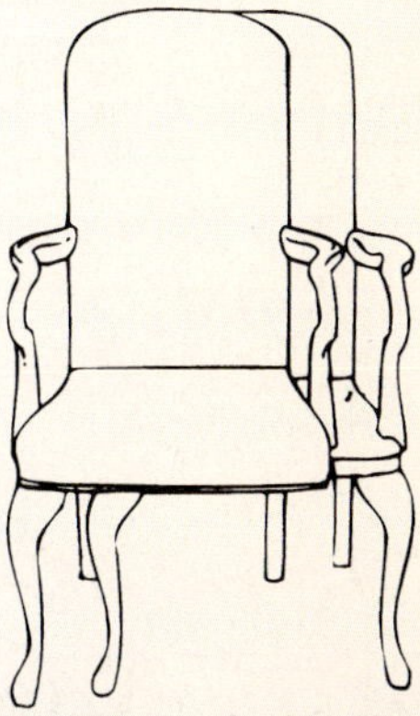

Queen Anne, Queen Anne
Terence & Laura Main
Art Furniture

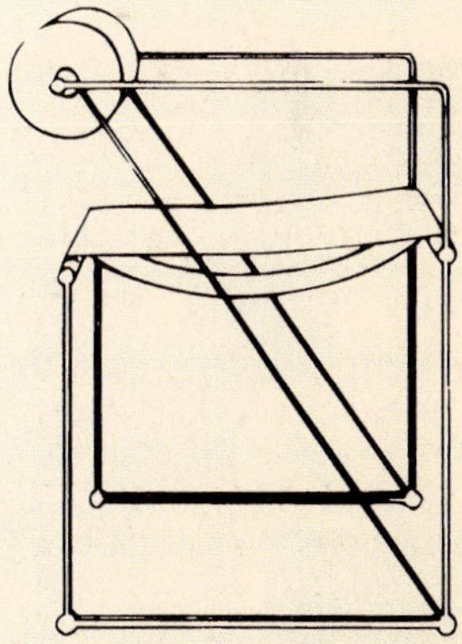

Seconda chair
Marlo Botta
Italy

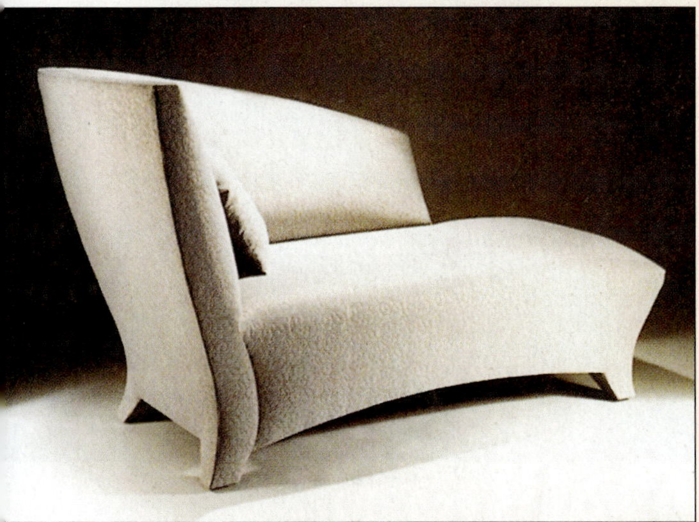

Dakota Jackson has designed many detailed functional pieces of furniture, including his Calliope Chaise (1995). (Also see Figure 8.21.) (Courtesy of and design by Dakota Jackson.)

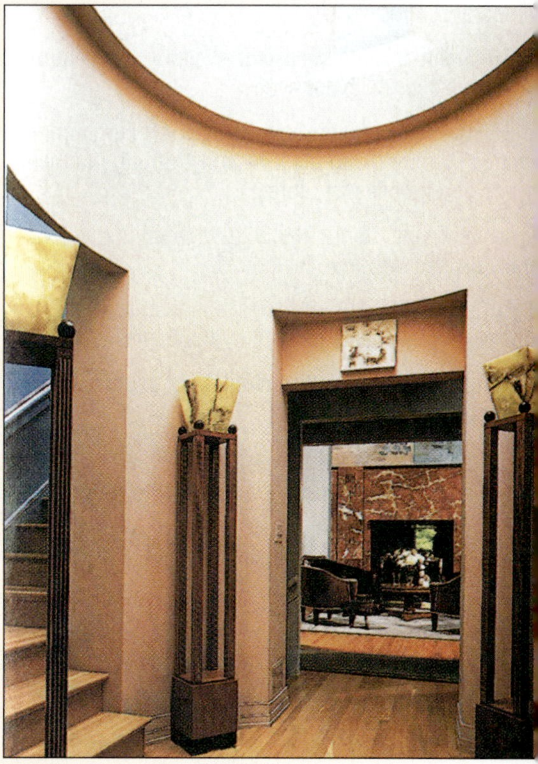

Michael Graves designed this Post–Modern residence in New Jersey in 1986. In the entry, tall lighting fixtures are capped with Egyptian-like capitals. In the living room beyond, the fireplace wall dominates the space. See Figure 12.36. (Photograph by William Taylor.)

This unique modern sofa upholstered in bright-colored fabrics reflects the Memphis style, a style originated by Austrian-born Italian designer Ettore Sottsass in 1981, advocating freedom of expression, especially when combining color and form. (Courtesy of Thayer Coggin, Inc. and designer Milo Baughman.)

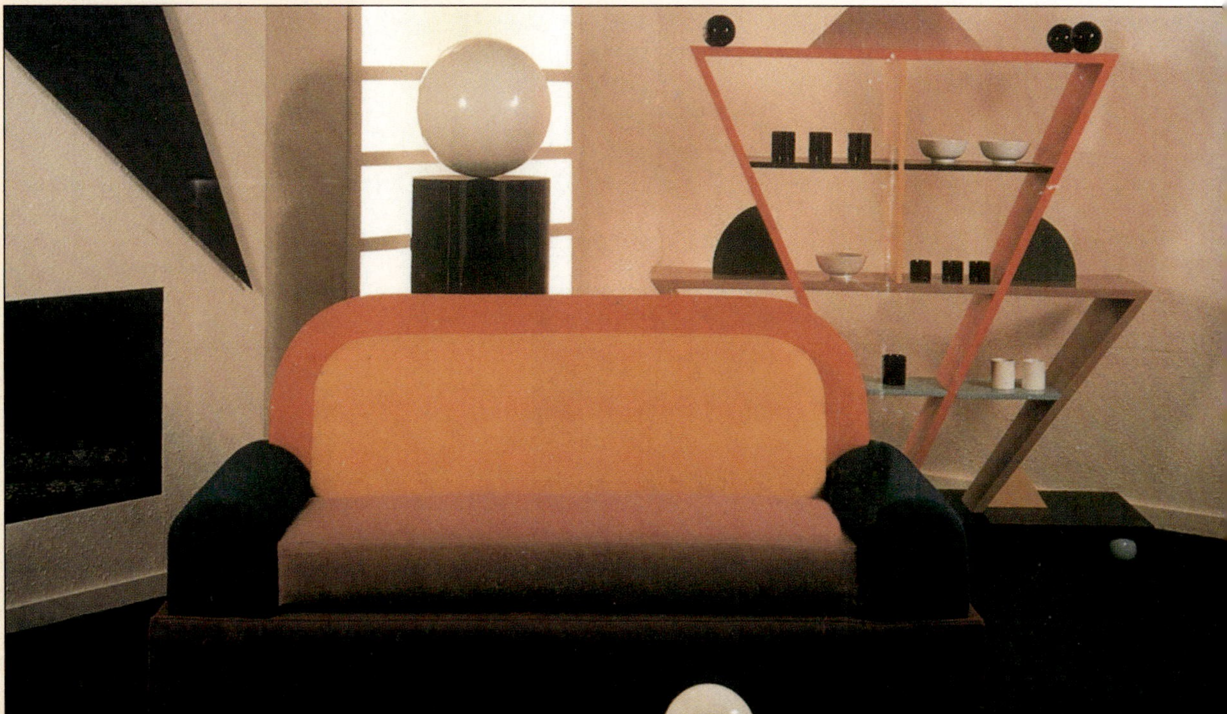

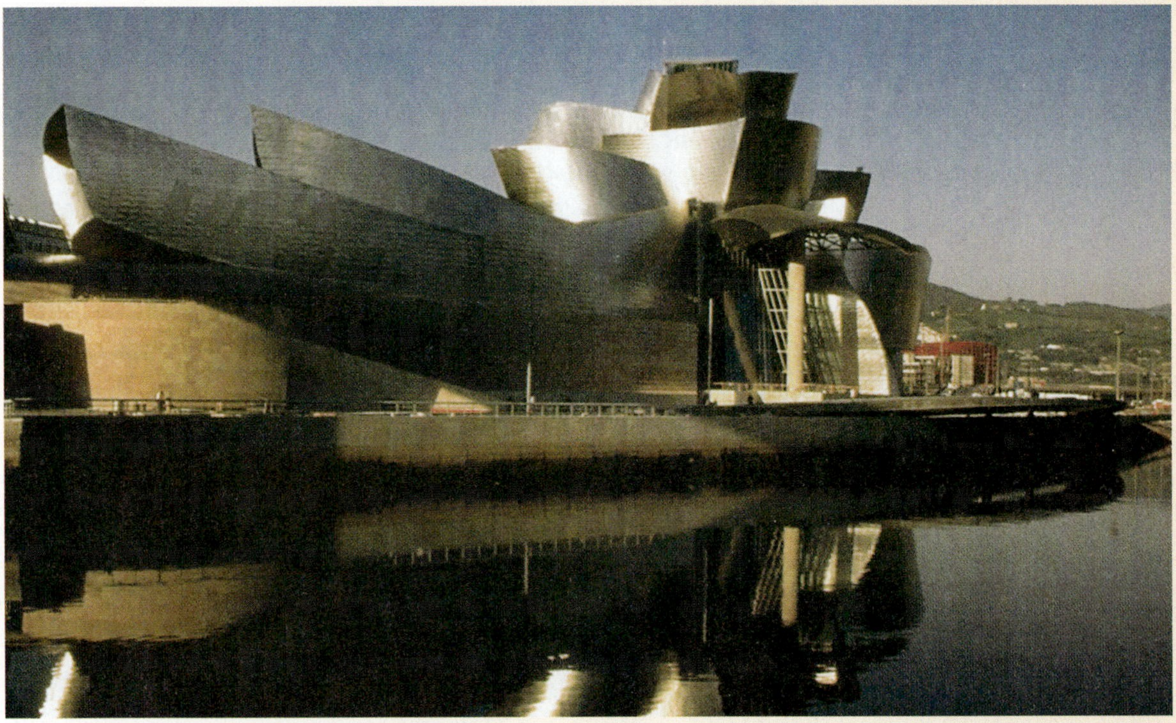

Completed in late 1997, the Guggenheim Bilbao in Spain was designed by Frank Gehry. The fragmented volumes and curved forms are covered with titanium. A central axis and curved interior forms reflect the influence of the Guggenheim Museum in New York by Frank Lloyd Wright. (Photograph by Eric Vandeville/Gamma.)

Modern Design SUMMARY

Historians find it difficult to define what will be considered classic 100 years from now. Current design trends may be remembered only as passing fads, or they may start a definitive movement in history. Note that once again design seems to have reached the end of a cycle. Whereas design was formerly clean, crisp, and uncomplicated (as promoted by organic architecture and the Bauhaus purism), the current images of the avant-garde Memphis-styled expression, the reinventing of the classic Queen Anne chair in style and color, and the radical nature of Deconstructivism suggest that the next movement may be to a new cycle of simplicity.

Style Selection

After studying these design styles, you should consider how these historical styles could be adapted and applied in current interiors. When selecting a style for a client, it is important to understand the overall feeling that the client desires. Generally, five basic style categories are used to help guide the client. They are formal traditional, formal modern, informal provincial, informal modern, and eclectic.

Formal Traditional

The term formal traditional refers to interior furnishings, finishes, and backgrounds from historical styles that are of the more refined or court types. Many of the traditional designs come from the eighteenth and early nineteenth centuries, an age of great prosperity during which the arts flourished in the Western world. French and English furniture styles of this period exemplify this warmth, grace, and elegance. Some of these styles have been adapted and scaled to meet present-day requirements without losing their character (see Figures VI.1 and VI.2). Styles appropriate for a formal traditional look include English designs (Queen Anne, Chippendale, Adam, Hepplewhite, and Sheraton), Court French (Louis XV, Louis XVI, Empire), and America's Federal.

Formal Modern

A formal modern environment can be created by employing modern furnishings, finishes, and backgrounds that are elegant and sophisticated. Art Nouveau, Art Deco, Classic Modern, and Post–Modern furniture are particularly well suited for a formal setting (see Figure VI.3). Italian, Secession, Wiener Werkstätte, De Stijl, Bauhaus, and International Style furniture may be very formal and sophisticated, depending on supportive elements. Modern Oriental is often used in a formal manner.

Informal Provincial

Historically, provincial furniture was produced in rural areas. Provincial furniture used native woods and techniques that imitated finer, more expensive furnishings. The provincial interior is generally handcrafted, simple, and casual, appearing unpretentious. The look is cloistered, comfortable, and rustic; it may incorporate furniture from a number of countries as long as designs are rooted in the past and have an aura of charm and informality (see Figure 13.6). Styles most commonly employed that provide this feeling are Colonial American, Medieval English (as well as simplified Georgian), French Provincial, and Spanish. Also appropriate are Dutch, Swedish, and German furnishings.

Informal Modern
Numerous types and styles of modern furniture are available on the market, drawing principally from European, Oriental, and American designers. When an informal modern setting is preferred, generally casual fabrics with a matte finish, simple materials, and unpretentious accessories are used (see Figure 13.1). Informal modern can also use fun, "funky" designs. Plastics and disposable furniture work in this style. Informal modern furniture styles particularly suitable for this direction include Scandinavian and modern furniture inspired by Japanese prototypes and the Craft Revival. Other modern styles including Secession, De Stijl, Bauhaus and International Style, Post–Modern, and Italian can generally be designed in either an informal or formal manner, depending on the supportive treatment.

Eclectic
The **eclectic** look—which is a mixing rather than a matching one—is common; however, eclectic does not mean hodgepodge. Furnishings should be related in scale and chosen with a final goal in mind. There should be a common theme—some element that ties the pieces together. For example, to achieve the provincial look, informality may be the key, and all country furniture, regardless of the source, is generally compatible. For a formal traditional look, dignity may be the key, and refined pieces of almost any style can be combined with pleasant results. The eclectic look often allows for more daring and imaginative interiors (see Figure 13.3).

Whatever the general theme of a room, it should not dominate and thereby create a feeling of monotony. Interest is aroused by the unexpected. For example, a pair of Victorian chairs placed in a modern setting brings something special to a room. A modern sofa gives a period room a fresh, updated look. The clean sweep of contemporary decor may serve as the most effective background for a highly prized antique.

PART II

Design Fundamentals

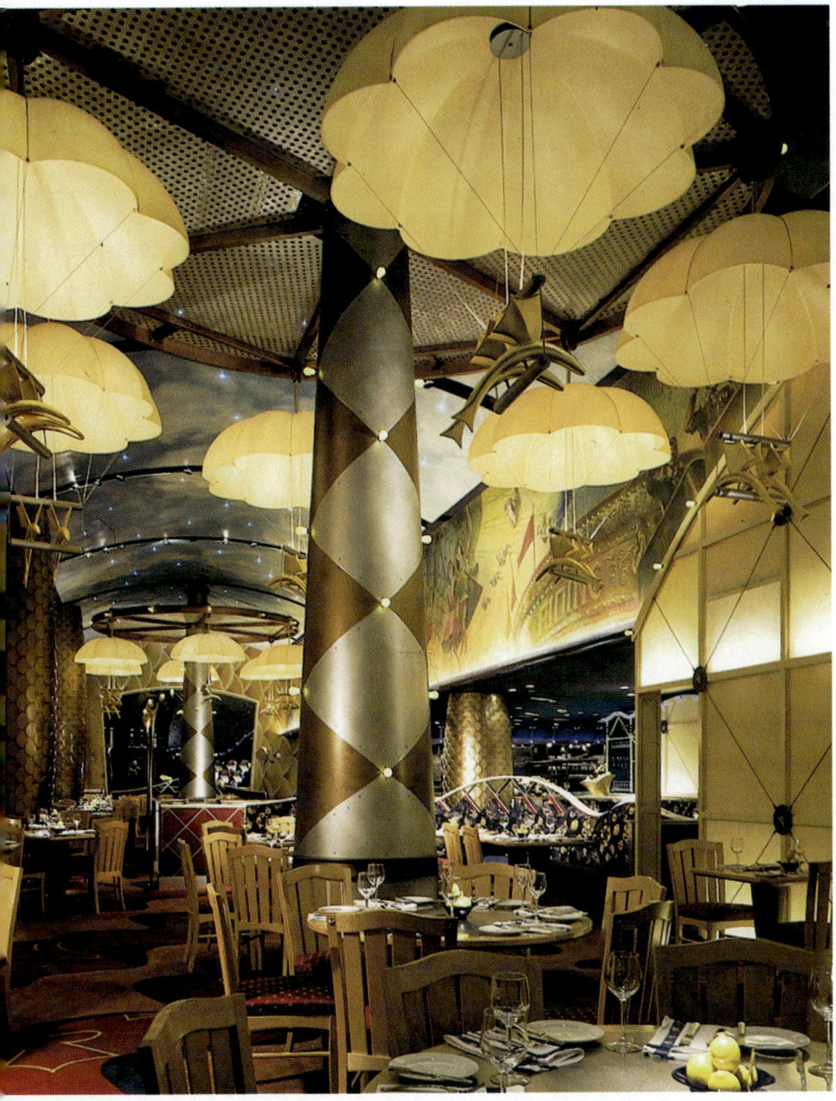

gure II.1 *In a wonderful application of concept, the Flying Fish restaurant, ·signed by Dorf Interiors for Walt Disney World Resort, brings the concept into all ·ements of design. The Flying Fish Café was undoubtedly inspired by Coney ·and—its heightened sense of reality, its sense of joy, its mystique, with grotesque ·apes, and rides that swallowed the visitor. This restaurant embodies the spirit of ·ney Island with abstract, dreamlike shapes and forms such as the roller coaster, ·rachute jumps, fish bodies and tails, fishbook lights, and fish scales of all shapes ·d sizes. More information about the restaurant and its concept is found on page ·. (Designer: Dorf Reber, Inc. [Formerly Dorf Associates Interior Design, Inc.] ·otograph by Peter Paige. © Disney Enterprises, Inc.)*

When planning a shelter, look to the fine arts. The goal is to create beauty and utility.

—Thomas Jefferson

The ability to read and write—to be literate—is learned within each culture. Children are taught the alphabet, spelling, appropriate grammar, and syntax throughout their formative years. Mastery of language is critical to the success of the individual. Once mastery is achieved, each phrase, essay, report, or book takes on the individual's creativity and becomes a unique work.

A similar progression occurs in the field of music. Based on twelve distinct pitches (seven white keys and five black keys when viewed on a piano), endless combinations, progressions, and rhythms create a variety of songs and styles. Likewise, the ability to effectively create an advertisement, lay out a web page, develop a floor plan, or design an entire interior environment requires **visual literacy.**

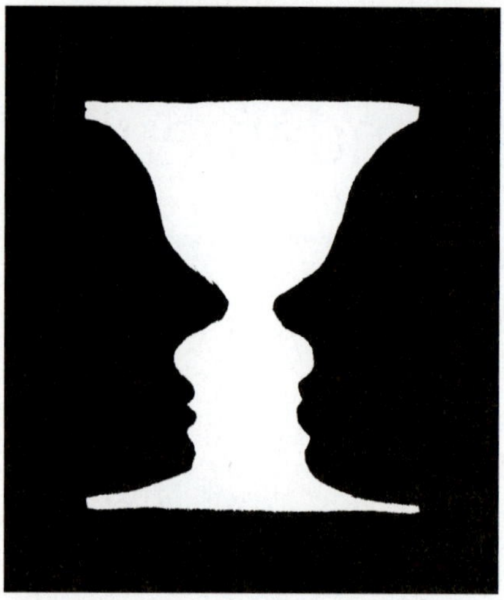

Figure II.2 *In this example, the eye attempts to find meaning in the shapes. The image can be read as profiles of faces looking at each other, or as a vase.*

Visual Literacy

Visual literacy requires the effective application of design elements and principles coupled with an understanding of pattern, ordering, and visual perception. There exists a natural tendency for individuals to organize and group information. The eye is automatically drawn to dominant elements; natural progressions lead the eye; the eye seeks to find closure in missing information, just as the ear seeks to resolve the final note of a song. The eye attempts to find meaning in that which it views. The classic example is the vase and profiles image (Figure II.2). In this example, the eye perceives either the vase (the white portion) or the profiles of faces (the black portion). Eyes work to find images or order in cloud formations or perhaps in cracks in a wall, ceiling, or pavement. The eye shifts from its focused vision to a broader wide-angled vision to perceive these changes.

Designers create environments that assist the occupants in these perceptual tendencies. Conflicting design comp nents, such as misplaced furnitu selection or poorly planned room la outs, create visual and physical am guity for the occupant.

More info online @

http://www.ivla.org/ International Visual Literacy Association

http://www.ivla.org/news/rdocs/vlbib/ International Visual Literacy Association Bibliography

Gestalt and Perceptual Theories

One theory of how humans percei what they see is called Gestalt psych ogy. In the early 1900s, German ps chologists studied how the brain ten to organize and group elements ir simpler patterns and how the bra closes a space with an approximate o line. Designers use these tendencies the brain and frequently group ite by their proximity, their similarity, through their perceived movement. A ditionally, designers may define a spa using closure.

For example, note Figure II.3. A though there are eleven distinct el ments, the eye naturally organiz them into three groups due to th proximity. The same could be said Figure II.4. Fourteen pieces of furn ture are represented, but the design has grouped them by proximity in three conversation areas.

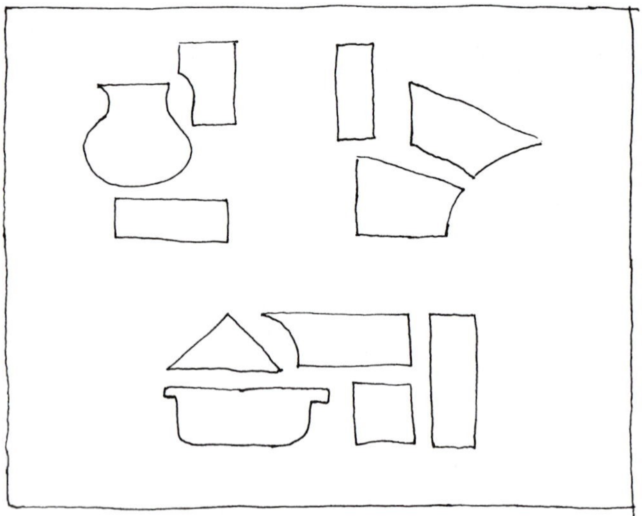

Figure II.3 *Organization of elements through the use of proximity.*

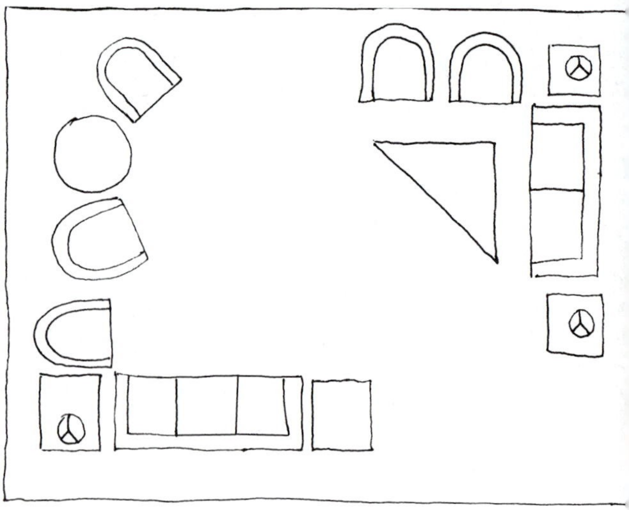

Figure II.4 *Organization of elements through the use of proximity applied to an interior floor plan.*

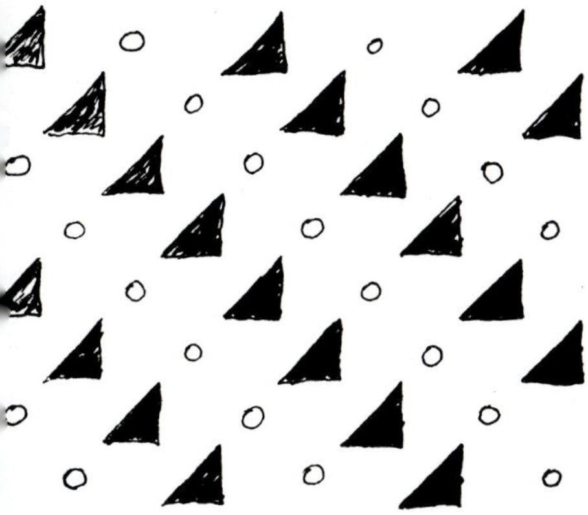

gure II.5 *Visual pattern perception using ·ouping tendencies of similarity and ovement.*

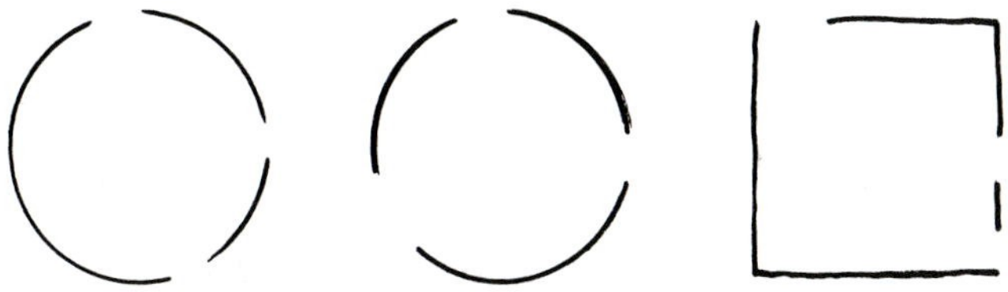

Figure II.6 *Visual perception through the use of closure.*

The eye also has a tendency to ·oup elements by similarity. In Figre II.5, the eye wants to order the triıgles and circles into diagonal rows. his type of organizing may be appliıble to designers as they arrange a ient's accessory collection or select multitude of chairs for a hotel banuet room. Figure II.5 also illustrates ow the arrangement of objects can :aw the eye in a desired direction, in ıis case, in a diagonal plane.

Another common tendency is for e eye to complete an image that is ·presented; this is referred to as cloıre. In Figure II.6, the eye recogizes a box and a circle instead of a ·ries of lines. This technique is used the development of universally unerstood symbols. Although there are ver 3000 different languages, symols transcend language differences ; a form of visual literacy (Figure .7). The eye completes the drawing of the male and female figures and understands the messages conveyed by the no smoking and handicap symbols.

Closure is frequently applied in space planning as designers create spaces that do not require four walls, a floor, and a ceiling. Note how the area rug in Philip Johnson's Glass House (see page 55) delineates the conversation area. The eye perceives the designated space through changes in ceiling heights, textures, surfaces, or even color.

More info online @

http://www.usask.ca/education/coursework/skaalid/theory/gestalt/similar.htm
Information on Gestalt

http://mitpress2.mit.edu/e-journals/Leonardo/isast/articles/behrens.html
Art, design, and Gestalt theory by Behrens

Alignment

Another theory that is applied in many areas of design involves the use of alignment. In the book *Form, Space, and Order,* Francis Ching discusses five forms of alignment or organization: clustered, radial, centralized, linear, and grided.

Clustered formations form groups of elements that are interconnected. The Design Scenario at the end of Part II (UPS Innoplex) was initially conceived based on clusters or, in the firm's words, "communities" (see page 119). Radial groupings are common in airport terminals where baggage processing and internal workings are centrally located and the concourses form the spokes of the wheel radiating from this central area. Elementary schools may also find their space planning based on a radial organization. Common-use facilities such as the cafeteria, gymnasium,

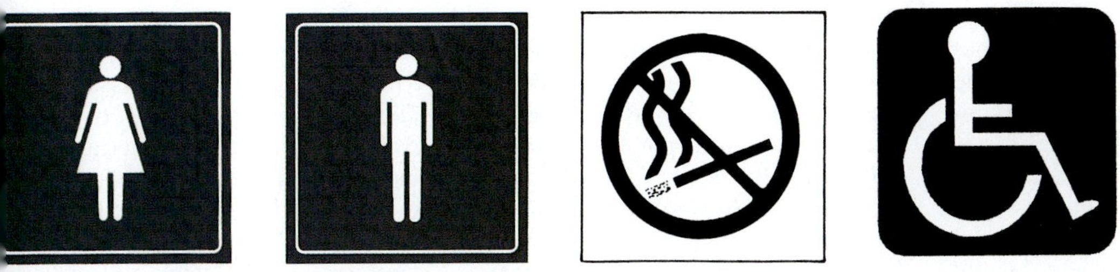

gure II.7 *Universal visual literacy used in symbols. Note how the symbols for men and women use ·oximity to create a form. Closure is used in the no smoking and handicap symbols, as the eye fills in e gaps and details to create the whole.*

art, and/or music rooms may be located in a central pod with various age/grade levels radiating from this central hub. Centralized plans focus on one area. The Villa Rotunda, as seen on page 33, is a Renaissance example of a centralized plan. Many designs and buildings are based on linear or grid organization. Open office planning, seen in the Suntory Water Group project (Figures II.9–II.13) or the reservations office (Figure 5.24), is based on strong linear and grid organization. It is important to note that both linear and grid organizations do not need to be rigid. As in the reservations environment, they may take on a diagonal form. Organic grids may even read as a contour map or as a flowing river or group of pebbles (Figure II.8).

Organizational systems create strong axes that naturally lead the eye to an appointed location. Designers develop their interiors to help lead an occupant through the space by carefully planning patterned organizations. Designers work with a variety of alternative schematic solutions, manipulating the spaces and elements to create the most effective solution, not necessarily the most predictable one. They seek out these patterns to solve design problems. The theories of visual perception and Gestalt psychology help designers define social and cultural solutions that are aesthetically pleasing while meeting the functional and economic requirements of the project. Visual literacy, the construction of components in an ordered and perceptive manner, is applied throughout the design process including the conceptual development of interior environments.

Concept

An important fundamental aspect of a design project is the *concept*. Concept refers to the underlying thought or motivator that defines the solution to the design problem. The concept may include the design and historical styles, but extends these concrete elements to include abstract characteristics. Tom Szumlic, a design instructor in Tampa, Florida, notes that "a concrete thought is a chair 20″ high by 30″ wide made of wood. An abstract thought is a place to sit, a place to read, talk to a friend" or look out the window.

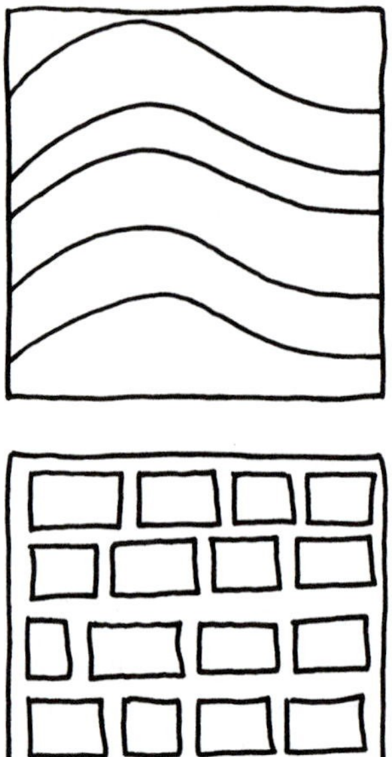

Figure II.8 *Alignment grids created in organic forms.*

In Figure II.1 (see page 63) the Flying Fish restaurant serves as a strong example of conceptual design. The restaurant received its name from the golden age of roller coasters in the 1920s when World War I had ended and the economy was booming. Coasters built during the time reflected a daredevilish attitude by designers adding tracks that twisted and turned in and out of dark tunnels and down drops from a 100-foot high lift. One of these new breed of roller coasters was called The Flying Turns, and one of the coaster cars carried the name The Flying Fish. Many components in the restaurant play off of this concept. The banquettes are shaped like the seats on a whip ride, and the perimeter wall draws its inspiration from fun-house attractions. The carpet is inspired by the Flying Fish icon that appears to be swimming upstream within the pattern of waves and sand. Its display of undulating movement creates not only visual interest but also a sense of the waves and currents of the ocean. The chairs are based on the simple vernacular prevalent in the 1930s and 1940s. The columns reflect the lighthouse desi[gn] seen on the capes.

Concepts give a project integri[ty] and character. They are used as [a] point of reference to help defi[ne] design decisions. Concepts may b[e] found in a company's business ph[i]losophy, professional image, or pro[d]uct. A concept may be found in [a] client's prized possession, favori[te] song, painting, or poem; it may ori[g]inate in a thumbnail sketch co[n]ceived by the designer or from a[n] abstract drawing or parti. The **par[ti]** is a sketch usually encompassin[g] geometric shapes or other series [of] lines and forms. The floor plan an[d] other elements of the design are d[e]veloped from the parti. Students u[s]ing this text may be required [to] design a room based on a particul[ar] fruit, vegetable, breed of dog, or ca[r]. The physical as well as the abstra[ct] traits associated with the selectio[n] should be brought forward in the d[e]sign characteristics of the space.

The Suntory Water Group proje[ct] (Figures II.9–II.13) illustrates again th[e] design process with added emphas[is] on concept. A commercial design fir[m], idealspan, was retained by Suntory [to] design a new call center that reflec[ts] the products it promotes and that e[n]courages customer service representa[ti]ves to familiarize themselves wi[th] these products. The majority of Su[n]tory's call center customers are res[i]dential and small businesses. The ca[ll] center representatives answer region[al] calls that focus on water products. Th[e] new one-story call center included ap[]proximately 20,000 square feet. R[e]view the following images and no[te] the emphasis on the concept and ho[w] it led to the formation of the design so[]lution.

Part II Design Fundamentals co[n]tinues with Chapter 2 and a revie[w] of the two basic design direction[s,] structural and decorative design, fo[l]lowed by a detailed discussion of th[e] elements and principles of desig[n.] Note how these elements and pri[n]ciples augment the theories of pe[r]ception and concept. Chapter 3 [is] dedicated to the study of color. Th[e] Design Scenario at the end of Part [II] discusses another project focused o[n] concept.

SUNTORY PROGRAMMING REQUIREMENTS

PRIVATE SPACES

Area and Description	Head Count	Square Footage	Extended Square Footage
Private Office	5	120	600
Supervisor	9	80	720
Customer Service Representative	135	36	4,860
Administrative	7	80	560
Subtotal	156		6,740
Circulation Factor (.50)			3,370
Total for Personnel	156		10,110

PUBLIC SPACES

Area and Description	Number of Rooms	Square Footage	Extended Square Footage
SERVICE FUNCTION REQUIREMENTS			
Privacy Rooms	5	100	500
Team Room (Seat 16)	1	400	400
Computer Training Room (Seat 24)	1	800	800
Conference Room (Seat 12)	1	400	400
Interview Room	1	64	64
Screening Room (Seat 2 – 3)	1	100	100
H. R. File Area	1	120	120
Receiving/Mail/Equipment	1	300	300
Equipment Areas	2	100	200
Central Break Room (Seat 50)	1	1,200	1,200
Reception Area (Seat 4 – 6)	1	500	500
Quiet Room	1	225	225
Sick Room	1	100	100
Coats	4	20	80
Storage	3	80	240
Subtotal			5,229
Circulation Factor (.45)			2,353
Total for Service Function Requirements			7,582
COMPUTER FUNCTION REQUIREMENTS			
MDF/UPS Room	1	800	800
Central Electrical Room	1	150	150
Wiring closets for tele/data	1	100	100
Restrooms	2	450	900
Janitor Closet	1	60	60
Subtotal			2,010
Circulation Factor (.45)			905
Total for Computer Function Requirements			2,915

SUMMARY	**Head Count**		**Square Footage**
Personnel			10,110
Service Function Requirements			7,852
Computer Function Requirements			2,915
TOTAL	**156**		**20,607**

Figure II.9 *As part of the programming, idea|span created the following analysis of the two major areas of the Suntory Water Group: Private and Public Spaces. (Designer: idea|span.)*

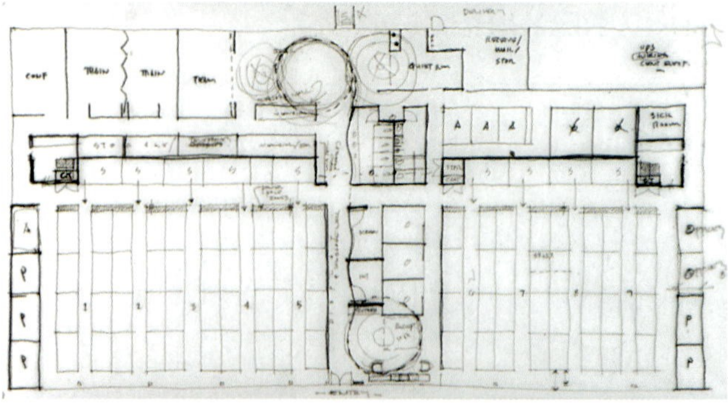

A

Figure II.10 *In the conceptual or schematic design phase, idea | span developed a space plan and a finishes and furniture palette based on three design concepts. Concept one (customer oriented) was to design a space that encourages customer service representatives to visualize the customer and to be familiar with all the products (water) in different regions. Concept two (product and branding) was to design a space that reflects the products the customer service representatives are promoting by using the environment as well as the products themselves. Concept three was to promote employee and potential customers' health. Note the rough schematic sketch Figure II.10A in the development of the plan. (Designer: idea | span.)*

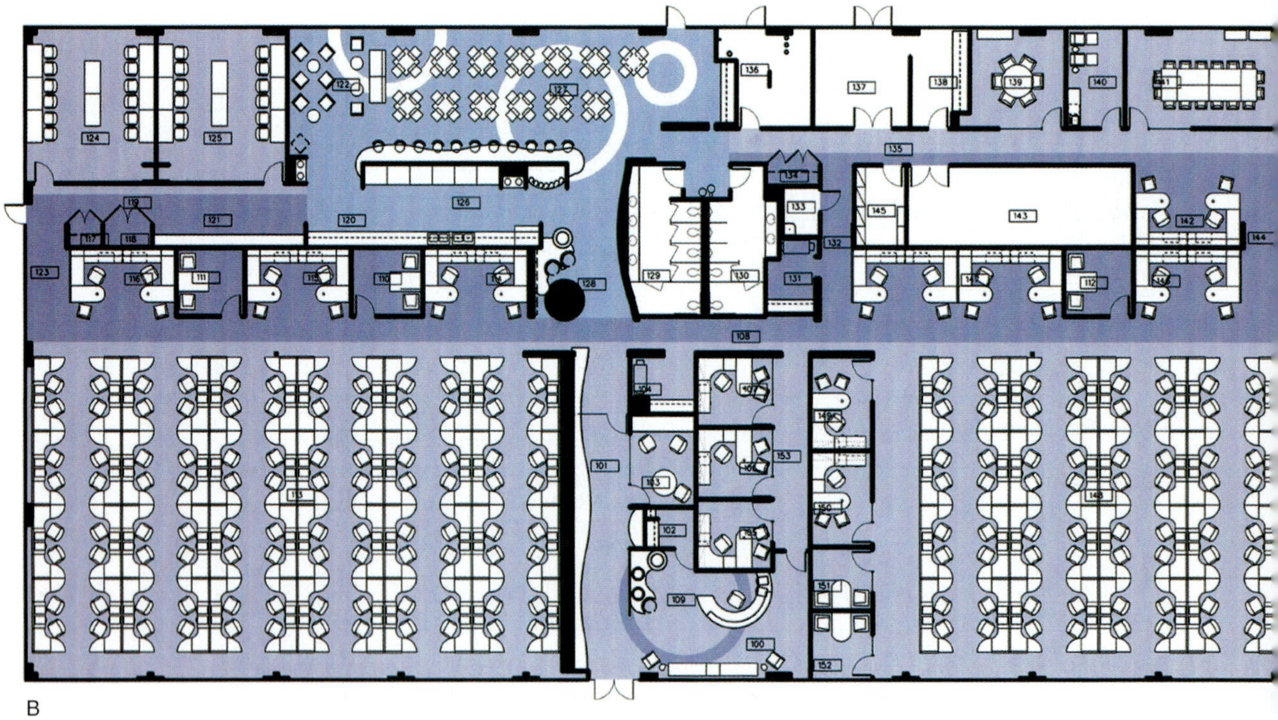

B

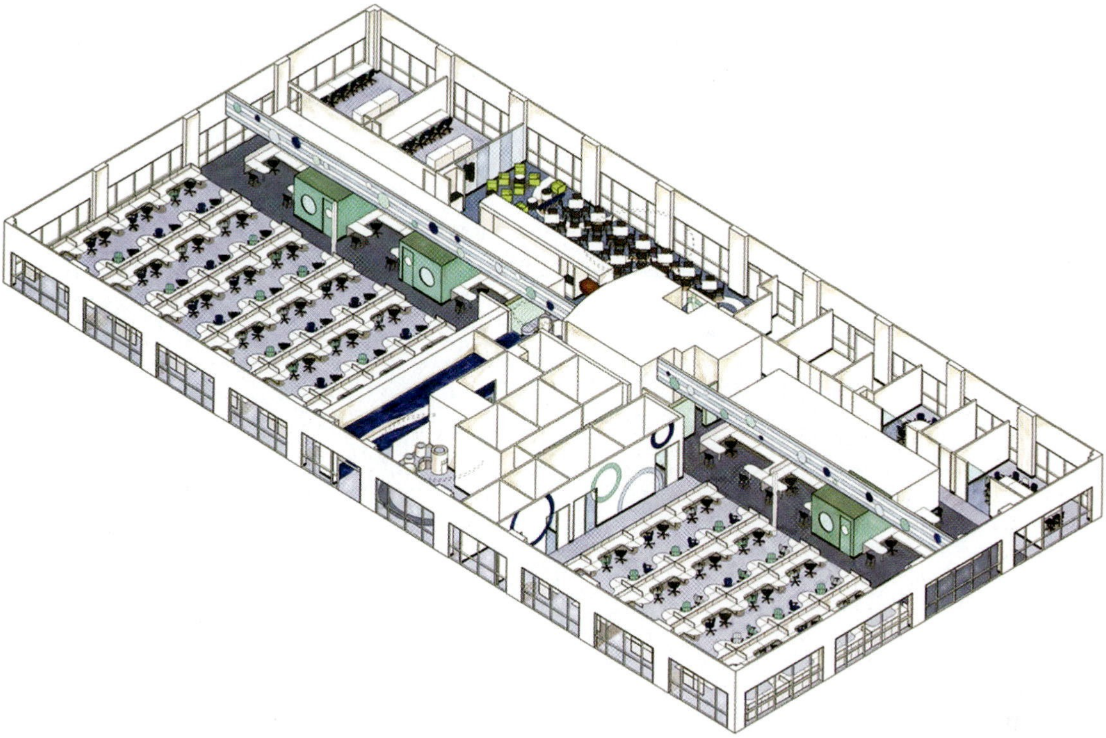

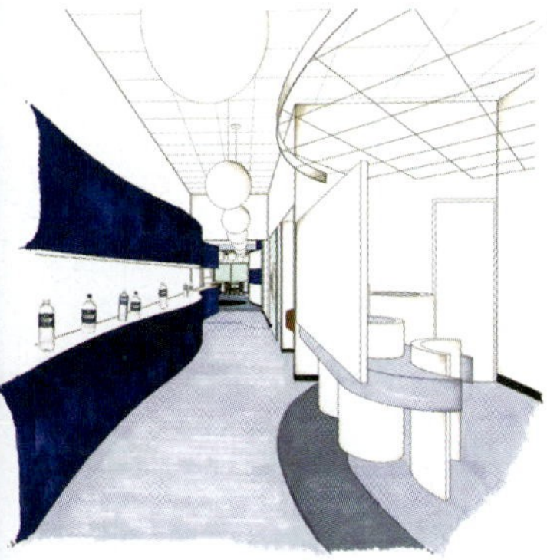

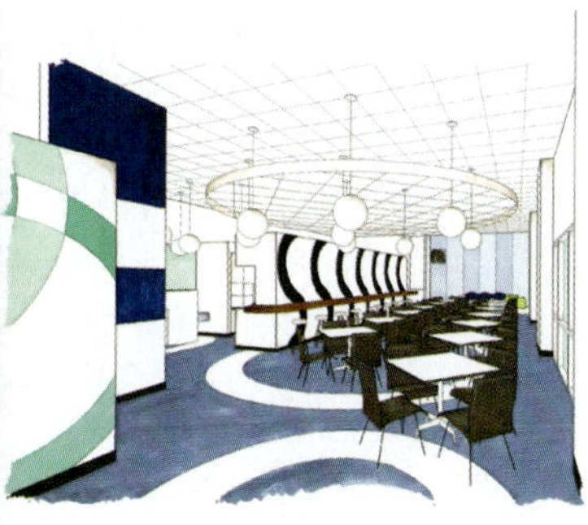

Figure II.11 *After client approval of the conceptual design, idea|span continued to develop and refine design solutions in the design development phase. Concept one was achieved by incorporating the products on a display wall as occupants enter the space. Concept two also utilizes the display wall for monthly specials to educate the customer service representatives about new products. Laminates with digital images of water are used throughout the space. Waves are incorporated in the carpet design and interior architecture. The breakroom is an "area of retreat" where employees can gather for a more social interaction at lunch. Ergonomics also played an important role in workstation configuration and task seating selections. These areas promote a healthy environment. (Designer: idea|span.)*

Figure II.12 *During the construction documents phase, idea|span produced a set of furniture specifications and construction drawings that also included mechanical and electrical drawings produced by a mechanical electrical, and plumbing (MEP) consultant. Examples from the set of drawings include a dimensioned partition plan (Figure II.12A), the reflected ceiling plan (Figure II.12B), the keyed furniture plan (Figure II.12C), and an elevation of the reception area (Figure II.12D). (Designer: idea|span.)*

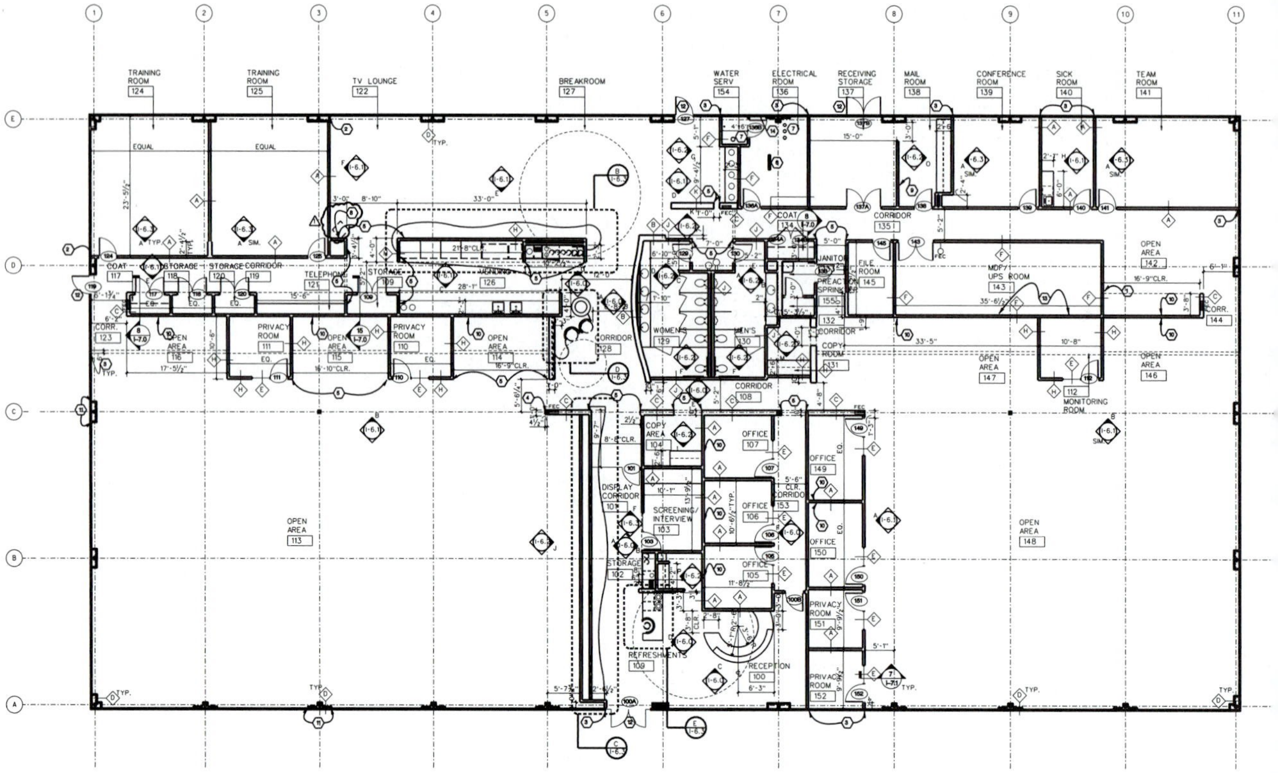

A

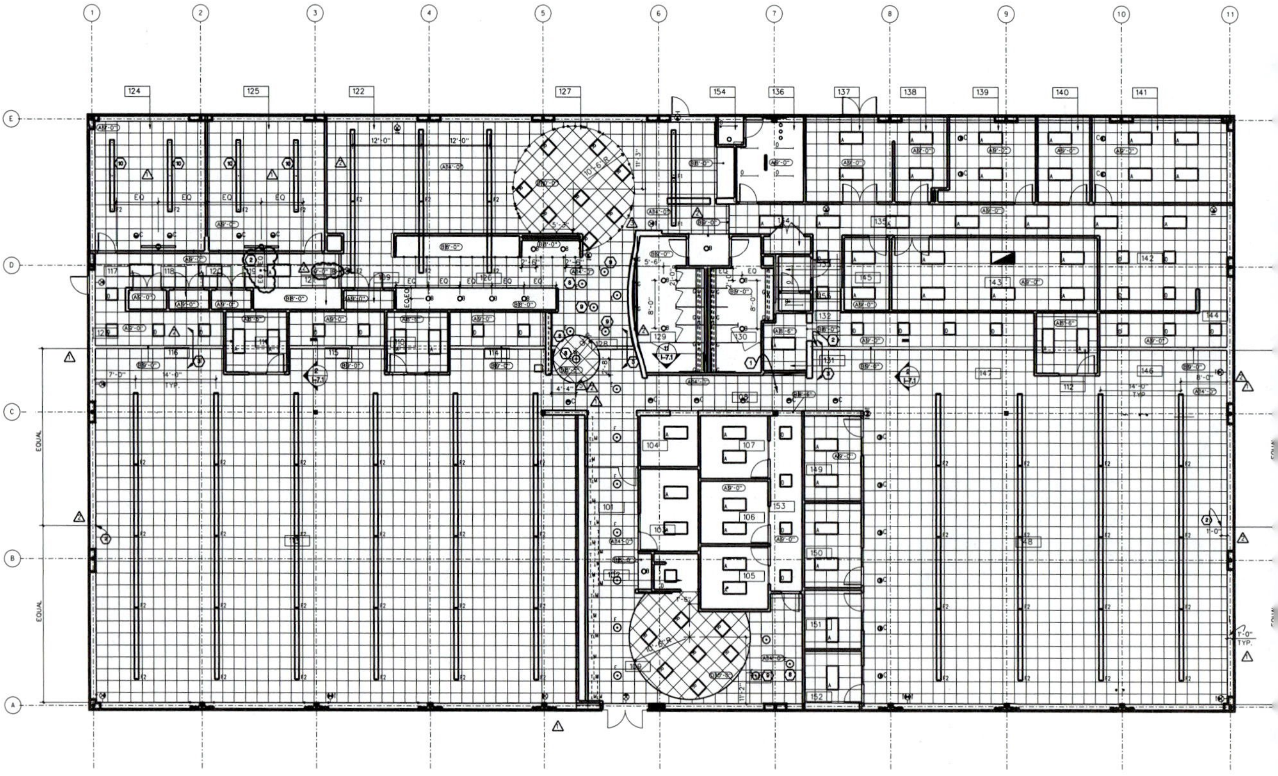

B

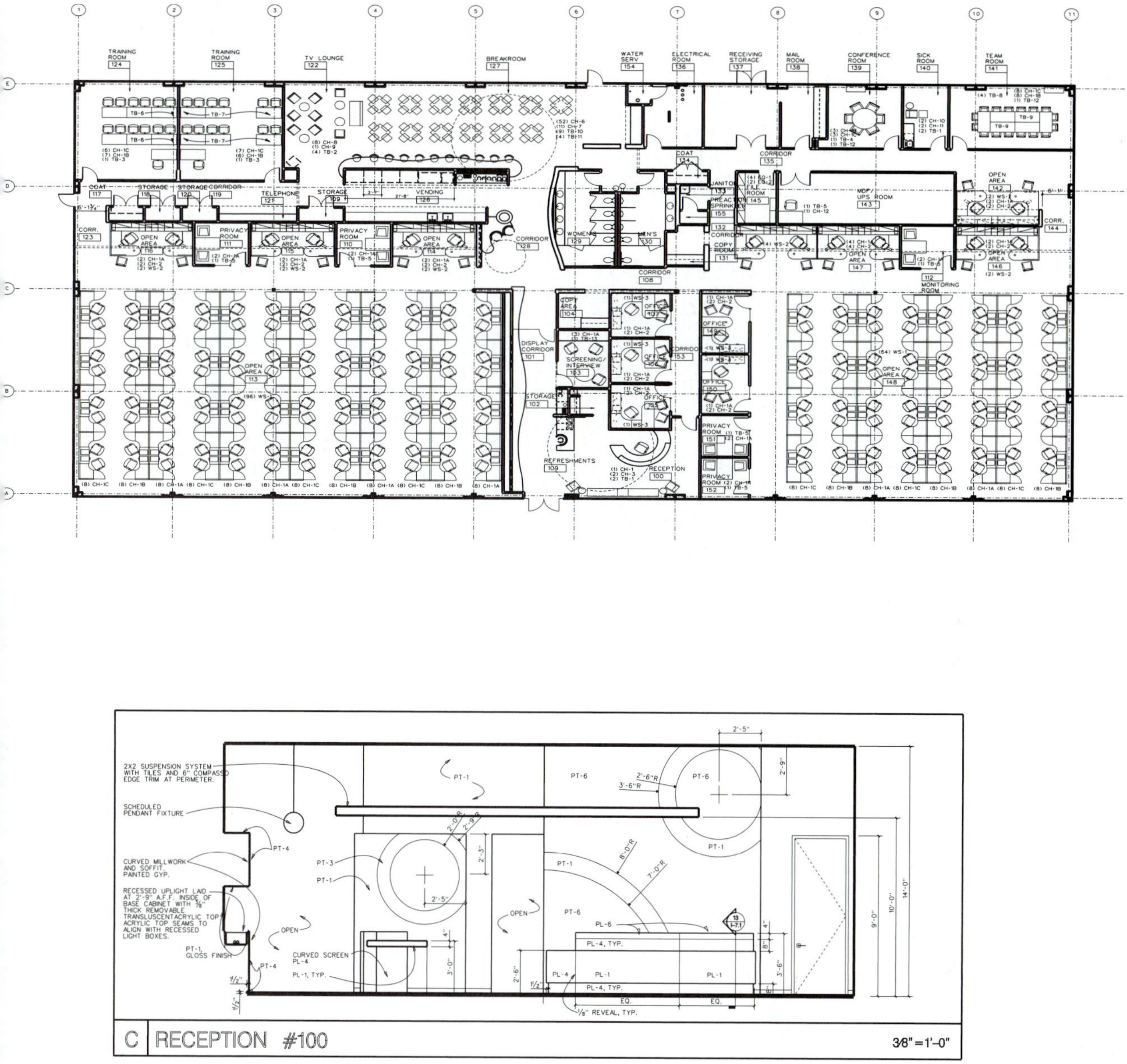

D

Figure II.12 *Continued*

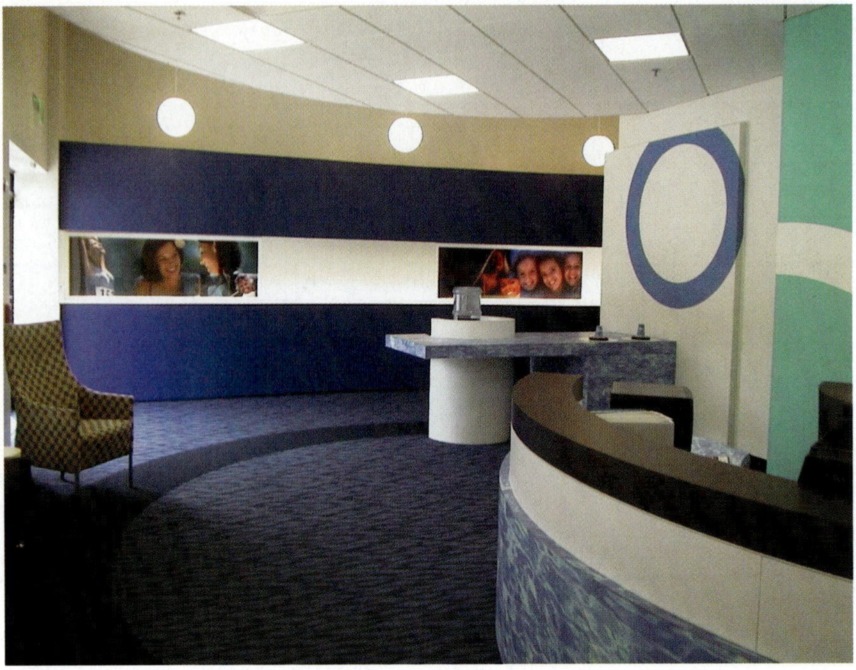

A

Figure II.13 *In the completed reception area (Figure II.13A), notice how the design concepts are illustrated in the forms, finishes, and space planning of the interior. After entering the reception area (labeled space 100 and 109 on the plans), occupants proceed through the display corridor (space 101) and arrive in a central congregating area (space 128, Figure II.13B). For this congregating area just outside of the breakroom, the designer focused attention on the product distributed by the company (water) as well as on the client who consumes the product (the end user). Ceiling height changes and color help the eye perceive the various spaces. Circles and wavelike forms emphasize the water concept. Beyond the congregating area is the employee breakroom (space 127, Figure II.13C). (Designer: idea|span.)*

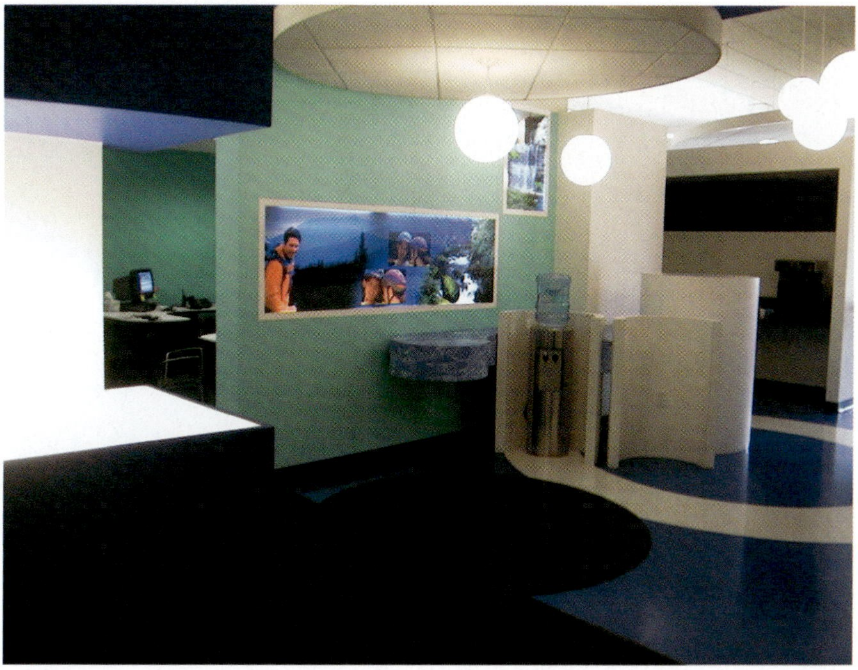

B

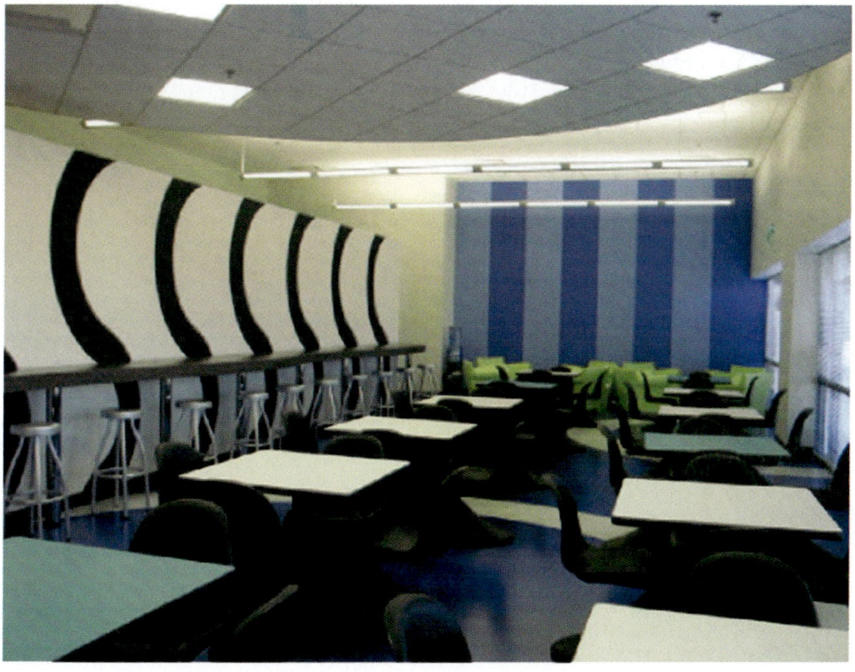

C

Elements and Principles of Design

2

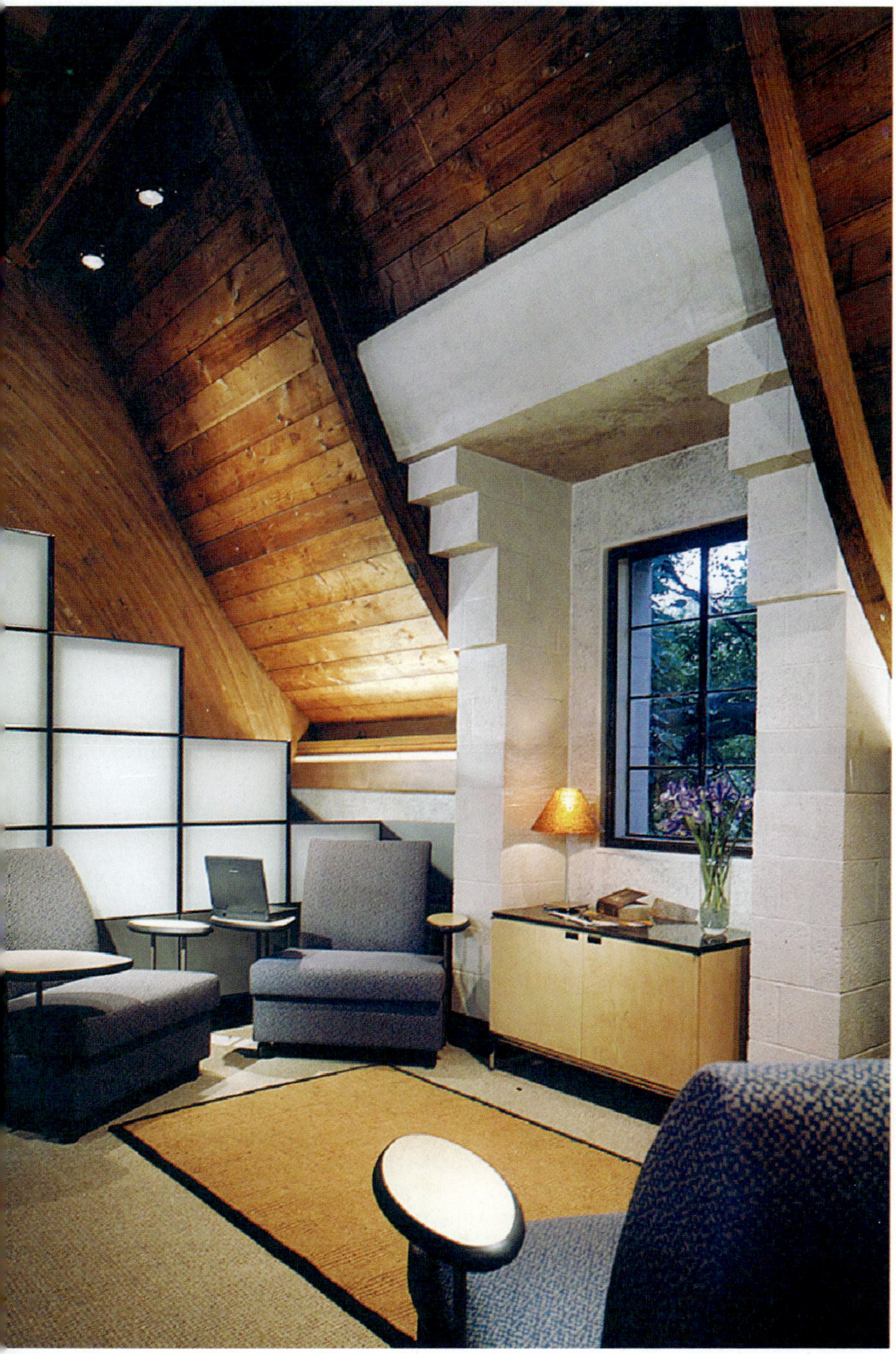

Figure 2.1 *A 5600 square-foot carriage house was converted into a development center. Using a combination of design characteristics, the designers meshed the old with the new. Rough limestone walls and sisal mats are complemented by sleek furniture and wall panels. (Architect/Designer: HOK. Photograph by Steve Hall/Hedrich-Blessing.)*

Design is the planned arrangement of basic elements and principles that work together to create an image, object, or environment (Figure 2.1). The creator of a well-planned and well-executed design—whether for a brass candlestick, a bedroom, or an entire office building—has carefully analyzed the use of space, line, shape and mass, texture, light, color, and pattern. The creator synthesizes these elements to ensure that the unity and variety of the design encompasses appropriate scale, proportion, balance, rhythm, and emphasis.

Two Basic Types of Design

Becoming familiar with the two basic types of design, *structural* and *decorative,* is a helpful introduction to the principles and elements of design (Figure 2.2).

Structural Design

Structural design relates to the size and shape of an object reflected in the materials. In other words, the design is an integral part of the structure itself. For example, the ancient pyramids of Egypt are structural designs because they expose the stone blocks from which they were made. Contemporary architecture, both inside and out, reveals the materials that make up the basic structure, such as wood or metal beams, brick, stone, and concrete (Figure 2.3). In modern furniture, the form itself (such as the metal frame of the Barcelona chair shown in Figure 2.15) is an integral part of the design statement. Successful structural design depends upon *simplicity* and *appropriateness of materials used.*

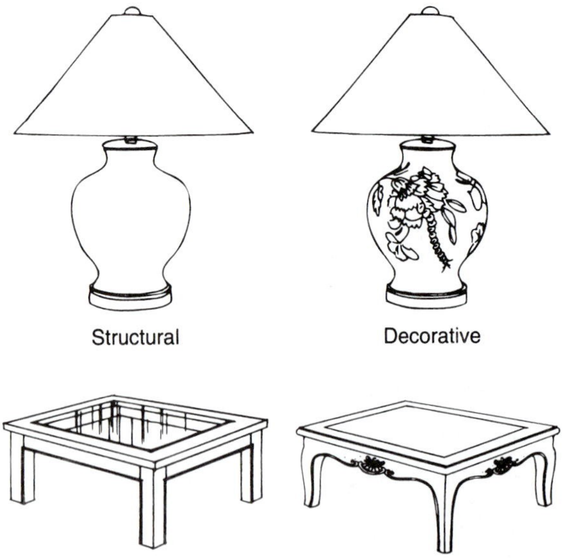

Figure 2.2 *Structural design and applied ornamentation or decorative design.*

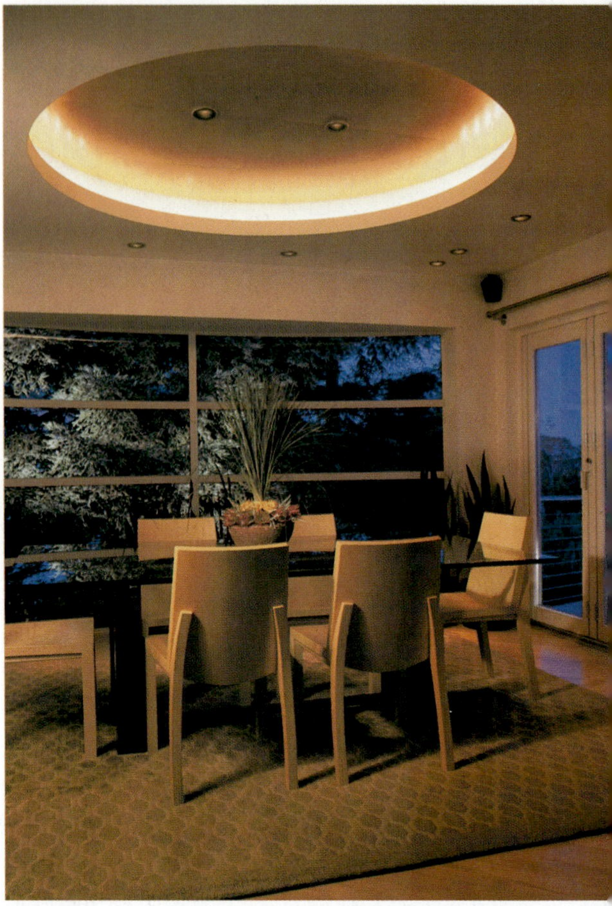

Figure 2.3 *In this ASID award-winning dining room, the basic type of design is structural. The simplicity of the desig belies the attention to detail. The geometric forms are highlighted by a cove lighting detail, recessed down lights, a accent lighting. The long horizontal windows are backlit to bring the exterior inside. (Designer: Bruce Benning, ASID/C Benning Design Associates. Photograph by David Duncan Livingston.)*

Simplicity

A structure, whether serving as the finished product itself as the supporting element of a design, should be kept si ple. For example, a room with too many or poorly plac openings, arches, and niches is seldom pleasing.

Appropriateness of Materials

Various objects use different materials and require differ methods of construction. Glass is blown and can be in cately decorated by skilled craftspeople; molded pla chairs may be turned out on an assembly line. Interchang procedures and materials when producing an object may be feasible or may not achieve the desired result. Materi selected for a structural design should be appropriate for intended purpose.

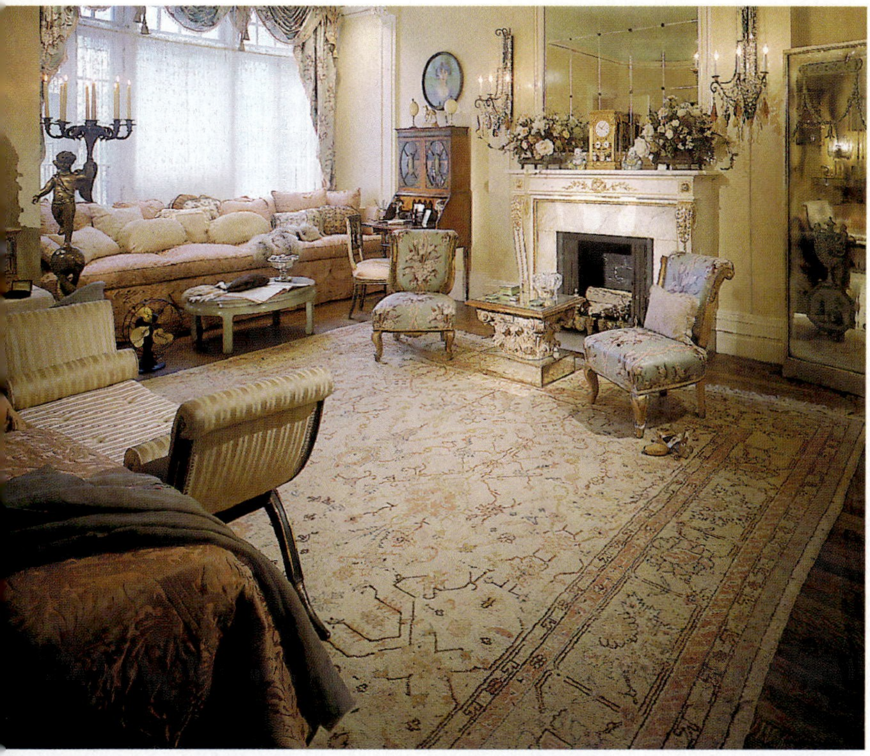

Figure 2.4 *Applied pattern, or ornamentation, is found on virtually every surface in this elegant bedroom, from the patterned rug and the brocade spread to the delicate carving on the chairs, paneled walls, and fireplace. (Antique Oushak courtesy of F.J. Hakimian, Inc., N.Y. Design by Ron Grimaldi for Rose Cumming, Inc. Photograph by Phillip Ennis.)*

›plied Ornamentation or Decorative Design

›corative design relates to the ornamentation of the basic ucture with color, line, texture, and pattern. For example, the erior surfaces of East Indian temples are completely covered :h embellishment in color, line, and texture. Victorian-style uses often couple fanciful decoration and bright color iemes with unique structural elements. Furniture may be ndsomely carved to add charm and dignity. Fabrics, wall- pers, rugs, accessories, and other furnishings can be attrac- ely enhanced with decorative design (Figure 2.4).

Four classifications (as seen in Figure 2.5) apply to ap- ed ornamentation or decorative design: *naturalistic, styl- ›d, abstract,* and *geometric.*

1. Naturalistic, realistic, or photographic design reproduces a motif from nature in its natural form. In naturalistic design, flowers look like flowers as they are seen in the garden or growing wild.
2. Stylized design creates a motif taken from nature but adapted to suit the shape or purpose of the object to be decorated. In this case, flowers are recognizable but are modified or slightly changed. This type of design is often used for interior furnishings.
3. Abstract design departs from nature. The elements, which may or may not be recognizable, are transformed into nonrepresentational design.
4. Geometric design is made up of geometric motifs such as stripes, plaids, chevron patterns, and zigzags.

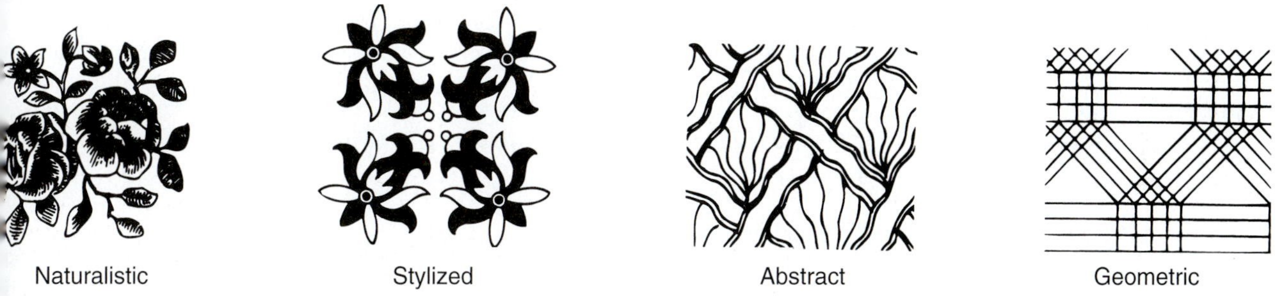

;ure 2.5 *Types of applied ornamentation.*

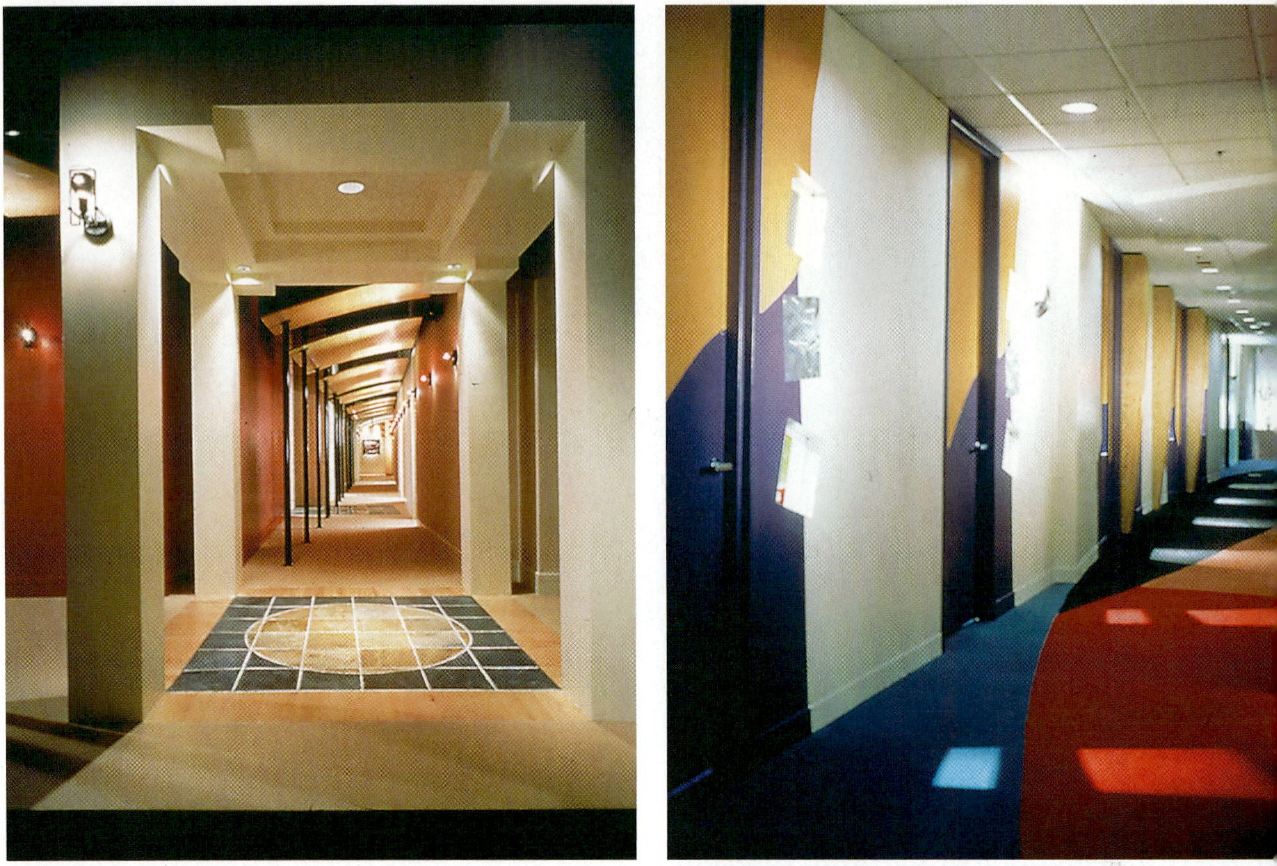

A B

Figure 2.6 *These successful corridor designs illustrate structural and decorative design solutions. Structural design is stressed in (A) Vertical and horizontal lines emphasize the angles of the building. Applied design is limited. (Resurgens Orthopedics, Atlanta, Georgia. Design Firm: Farrington Design Group. Hiro Isogai, Design Director. Photograph by Hedrich-Blessing.) (B) emphasizes decorative design. Applied ornamentation results in colorful walls and decorative carpet treatments. (MTV Network, Atlanta, Georgia. Design Firm: studio epic 5, Hiro Isogai, Principal. Photograph by Rion Rizzo.)*

Successful decorative design depends on *suitability and placement* and *appropriateness.*

Suitability and Placement

An item's purpose should be immediately recognizable. Additionally, the embellishment on any item should not interfere with the item's comfort or functionality. **Bas-relief** on a wall plaque is attractive and suitable, although such carving on the seat of a chair would be very uncomfortable to the occupant!

Appropriateness

Appropriate decoration should accent the shape and beauty of the object. For example, vertical fluting on a supporting column makes it seem higher, but crossbars appear to reduce its height and detract from its dignity. Classic figures on a Wedgwood vase emphasize its rounded contour, whereas harsh lines would destroy its beauty.

The amount and type of surface decoration should be chosen with great care, while keeping the basic structure in mind. Figure 2.6 illustrates contrasting examples of structu and decorative design.

Elements of Design

The **elements of design** are space, line, shape and ma texture, light, color, and pattern. These elements aid designer when creating a visual environment and are of referred to as *tools.* The organization and arrangement these elements or tools are closely allied to the principles design, which are explained later in this chapter.

Space

Space is best explained as the area found within an enc sure. As introduced in Part II, Gestalt psychology, th may be real or perceived. This may include one's perso space, the walls and ceilings of a room, a fence aroun yard, or even the boundary lines that define nations. Sp is the area in which people live. Line, shape or mass, t ture, and so on, are elements working together in space

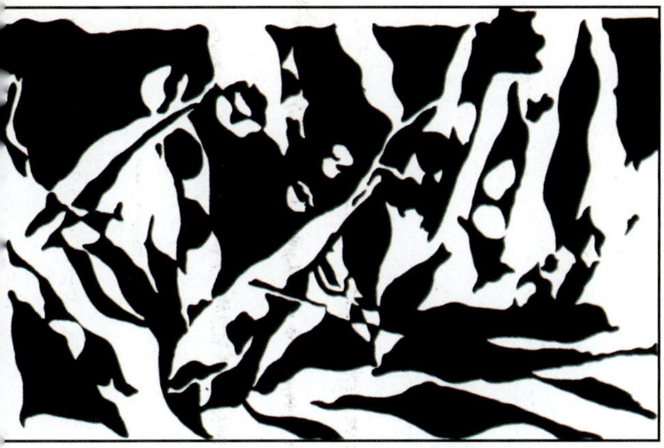

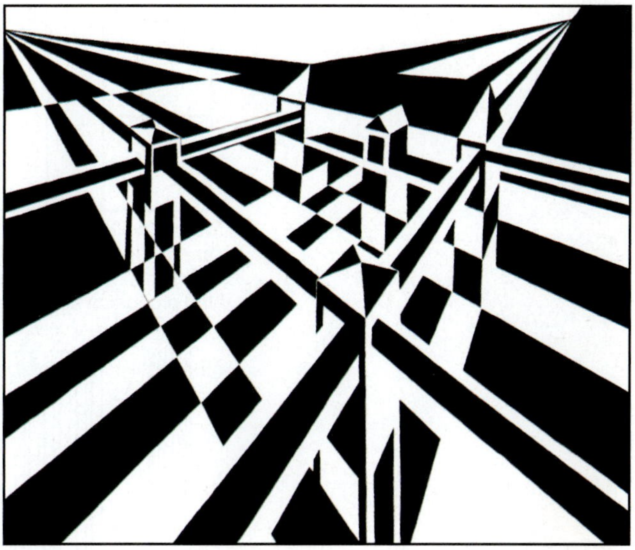

B

gure 2.7 *In these two studies, the artists illustrate the use of gative and positive space. Drawing (A) is more naturalistic d decorative; (B) is more geometric and structural. (Artists: awing A—Kimberly Dorsey; Drawing B—Antonina Grib.)*

rm dynamic negative-positive interactions (Figure 2.7). In sign, walkways or **traffic lanes** define some of the neg- ve space; furnishings define the positive. Well-planned d well-organized space produces a functional and com- rtable interior.

The challenge of many residential interiors is that they ay simply lack the adequate space required to complete cessary tasks. Many individuals have acquired more "stuff" an is needed; in some situations, in order to provide ough space, the designer must gently persuade the client remove some of his or her "precious cargo." In design, less more. On the other hand, an accumulation of memorabilia ay be important for the elderly; Louis Sullivan was quoted, ess is a bore." As always, designers must be sensitive to eir client's needs.

In commercial environments, the quantity of space is ually as important, especially when clients are leasing the erior and paying for it based on the quantity of square feet. designer who understands how to utilize the premium mmodity of space cleverly and efficiently will be rehired future projects. Part IV, "Space," reviews layout and space quirements for furniture arranging as well as space plan- ng for a variety of rooms.

ne

ne forms the direction or feeling of a design and is partic- arly dominant in contemporary art and interiors. The com- sition of a room is established by the lines that give it otion or repose. Skillful use of line is therefore of utmost portance (Figure 2.8).

Line can seemingly alter the proportion of an object or entire room. For example, in Figure 2.9, two identical ctangles are divided, one vertically and the other hori- ntally. As the eye travels upward along the vertical line, e rectangle seems higher. Along the horizontally divided ea, the eye is directed across, making the rectangle ap- ar wider. Each kind of line has a particular psychological

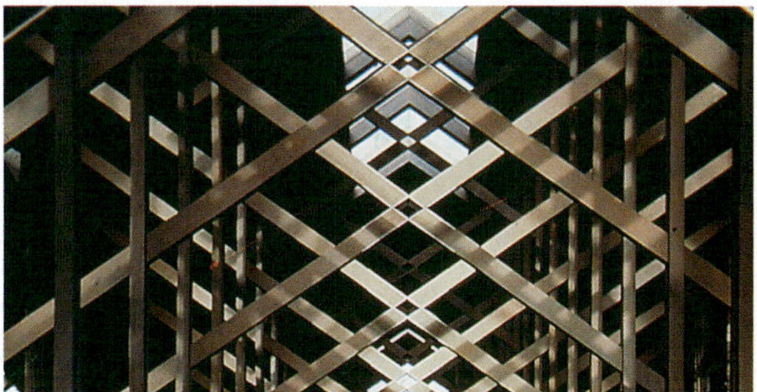

Figure 2.8 *Soaring verticals and intersecting diagonals silhouetted against the sky carry the eyes, and spirit, upward in the Thorncrown Wayfarer's chapel in Arkansas, designed by E. Fay Jones. (Courtesy of E. Fay Jones, FAIA, Maurice J. Jennings, AIA, and David W. McKee, AIA.)*

Figure 2.9 *The use of line.*

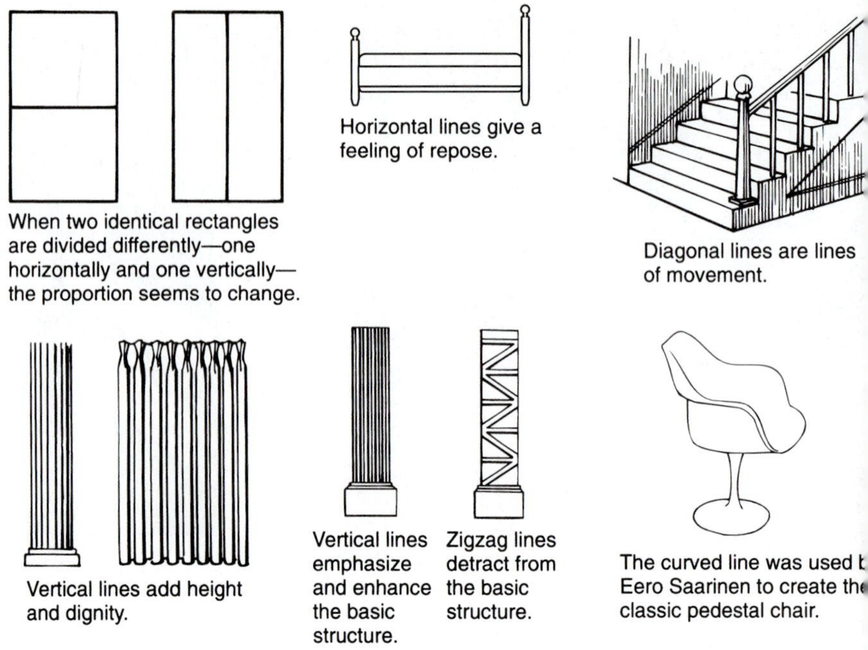

effect on a room. To achieve the desired result, the interior designer should keep in mind the distinct effects of each line.

Vertical lines tend to provide a feeling of height, strength, and dignity. These lines are particularly evident on the exterior of a building where columns are used, in the interior where upright architectural members are conspicuous, in tall pieces of furniture, and in the long straight lines of vertical louvers or folds of drapery.

Horizontal lines create a feeling of repose and solidity, and like vertical lines also provide strength. These lines are often seen in **cornices, dadoes,** bookshelves, and long, low pieces of straight-lined furniture. Falling Water, a famous Frank Lloyd Wright house, is an excellent example of horizontal architecture (see page 53).

Diagonal lines give a room a feeling of action and movement. They are evident in slanting ceilings, staircases, Gothic arches, and sloping furniture. Too many diagonals in a room, however, may create a feeling of unrest.

Curved lines have a graceful and delicate effect on a room. They are found in arches and other curved architectural treatments, drapery **swags,** rounded and curved furniture, and rounded accessories. Curved features may also be employed in interior architectural elements, such as counters and fixtures.

Curved lines fall into the following four general categories:

1. Large convex (upward) curves tend to provide an uplifting feeling, such as a curved staircase opening from a foyer.
2. Large concave (downward) curves often give a feeling of solidity, and in art, even sadness. (Artists have used this line to evoke a feeling of mourning or unhappiness.) Downward curves such as a domed ceiling or series of arches may also be very dramatic.
3. Long, flowing horizontal curves (like those seen on a shoreline or gently curving mountain road) can imply restfulness.
4. Small curves such as those commonly found in patterned carpets, rugs, and fabrics often express lightness and merriment. They add life and character to a space.

Too much line movement in a room may evoke a feeling instability. A careful balance of line is essential to the feeli of comfort and harmony in a room. A designer can use li to create a mood or feeling, give direction to a room, crea an optical illusion, achieve a feeling of balance and rhyth support a room's focal point by directing the eye toward th feature, and give variety and unity to a room through t skillful blending of the various line types.

Shape and Mass

The terms form, shape, and mass are frequently used int changeably in the profession. Technically, however, *form* d fines the essential nature of the design that distinguishes it piano looks like a piano because of its form. The contour an object is represented by its *shape,* which is made up lines. When a two-dimensional shape takes on a third mension, it becomes a *mass* made up of a volume outlin by the shape. In the planning of interiors, mass is perceiv as objects (e.g., furniture) that require space and may moved to various locations. The arrangement of mass with a room—furniture arrangement—is discussed in Chapter Basic masses (or forms as used below) or shapes fall into t following three categories:

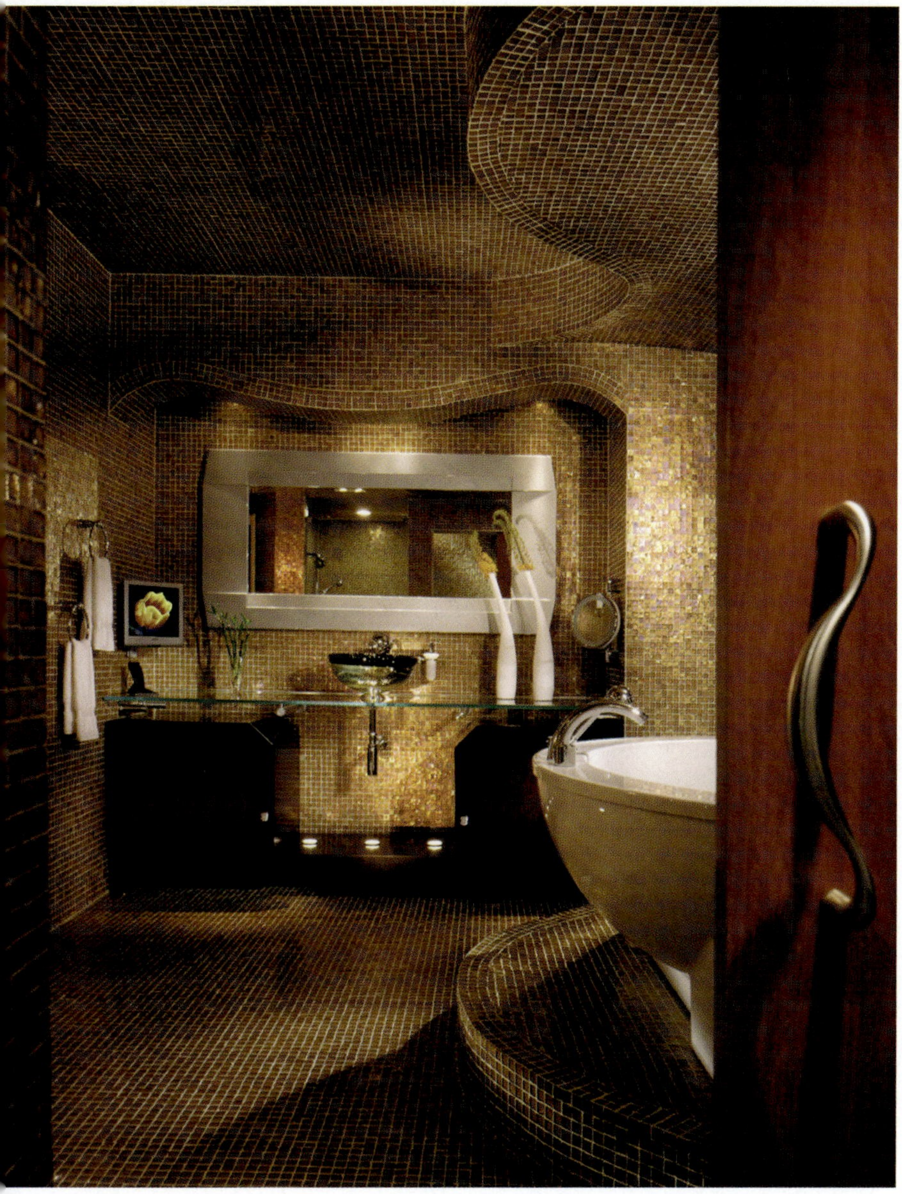

Figure 2.10 *In this custom-designed bathroom, emphasis has been placed on the curved line. Intricate tile patterns, a floating glass countertop, and amorphously styled hardware enhance the fine details. (Designer: Charles Greenwood, IIDA, of Greenwood Design Group, Inc. Photograph © Robert Thien.)*

Rectangles and squares are the most dominant shapes used in architecture and interior design. They provide a sense of unity and stability, are easy to work with, and may be arranged to conserve space. Too many rectangular and square forms may produce monotony; however, introducing circular and angular forms into the space alters this effect.

Diagonal forms frequently begin with triangle shapes. The diamond shape results when triangles are arranged base to base. A variety of other shapes using the diagonal line may be created. These forms are often seen in sloping ceilings and motifs applied to fabrics and wallpapers. Triangular, diamond, and other diagonal shapes may be used for flooring materials, furniture, and accessories, providing a dynamic effect.

Curved forms include spheres, circles, cones, and cylinders. Curved forms are found everywhere in nature. (The shape of the human body is curved.) Curved forms are constant, unifying, and pleasing. When used in the interior environment, curved forms may be dramatic, like a sweeping staircase or domed ceiling; curved forms are also used for accessories like pieces of pottery, plates, lamps, round tables, or sculptures (Figure 2.10). Curves may give relief and variety to a room with a predominance of angular and rectilinear forms.

Very few interiors employ only one shape or form. The environment is most often enhanced by skillfully combining the three basic forms for architecture and furnishings. However, too much variety of form and shape may produce a room with a feeling of confusion. The visual transition from one object to another should be easy and pleasurable. The emphasis created when a curved form is placed against a rectangular panel may provide unexpected and agreeable relief

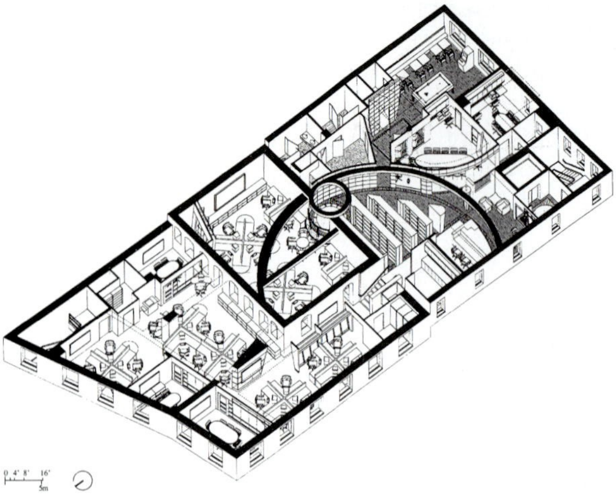

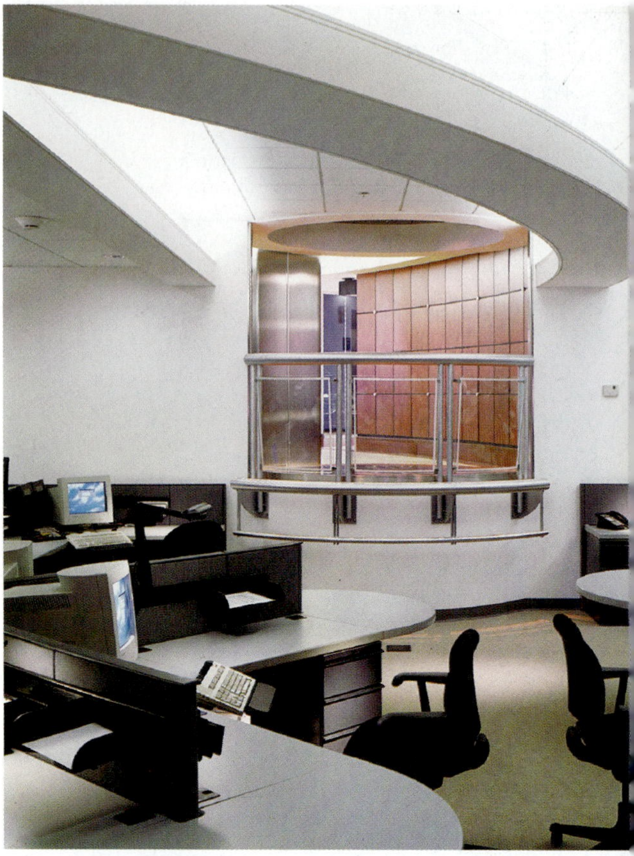

Figure 2.11 *In this curved office environment, the designers created a sweeping curve opposite the library. The circular balcony pierces the rectangularly shaped trade floor. The ceiling and furniture also employ the familiar curves. (Architect/Designer: Alan J. Feltoon & Associates, Inc. Photograph © Peter Aaron/Esto.)*

to a room's otherwise severe lines. For example, a curved floor plan, when used with rectangular rooms, as seen in Figure 2.11, creates such an effect. The sophisticated combination of forms is evident today in both modern and traditional styles.

Texture

Texture refers to the surface quality of objects—the quality that can be not only touched but also sensed in memory. In art and design fundamentals, texture is frequently discussed as an element paired with pattern. In interior design, these two are more distinctive due to the sense of touch inherent in interior design. The roughness of sandstone, the softness of a deep-pile rug, the smoothness of glass, and the shininess of growing leaves all produce a particular sensation because of previous associations with these textures.

Basically, textures fall into the following categories: soft or hard, smooth or rough, and shiny or dull. Throughout history, smooth, highly polished surfaces, lustrous metals, and fabrics of satin, silk, and fine linen have been symbolic of wealth and high status, whereas rough, handhewn textures and homespun fabrics have characterized lower economic classes. This is no longer the case. Many wealthy individuals prefer a handcrafted look, which may cost as much as the most refined look. Additionally, smooth and shiny surfaces have been reserved for formal interiors, whereas dull and rough textures have been associated with informal tre ments. Regardless of style, a knowledgeable use of texture a means to bring character to a room. Textures in the in rior environment often combine several characteristics. I example, a wool carpet can have a soft and dull textu Properties and considerations regarding texture are c cussed below.

Visual Interest, Beauty, and Character

Texture adds much visual interest in the environment. T early Greeks delighted in the smoothness and beauty of m ble floors. The people of Iran take pride in the fine text of their hand-knotted rugs, and the Japanese enjoy the w ven texture and look of grass mats called **tatami.** Modern teriors depend on the physical impression of texture create variety and interest. The texture of a surface reflect particular character and unique beauty that makes a lasti physical or psychological impression.

Light Reflection

Each texture has a surface quality that affects light refl tion. Smooth, shiny surfaces like glass, mirrors, sat porcelain, and highly polished wood reflect more li than rough and dull textures like brick, concrete, sto and coarse wood.

intenance

: choice of a particular texture determines the amount of intenance a surface requires. Smooth textures may show gerprints. Shiny textures may scratch easily. Rough tex-es, while more durable, may collect dirt in crevices. A ny, glossy paint will hold up longer but will highlight im-fections in the wall. A matte finish paint may not wash as ll, but it hides imperfections in the wall.

ustics

tures can absorb or reflect sound. Smooth and hard sur-es tend to magnify sound, whereas soft and rough tex-es have a tendency to absorb sound. Walking through an urnished room with a hard floor produces a high level of nd. When the same room is furnished with rugs, fabrics, peries, and furniture, the sound is greatly muffled. De-ners can control the acoustics of a particular space with e textural combinations.

ombination of Textures

mal textures like satin and polished marble and informal tures like burlap and stone generally are not mixed in the ne environment unless a specific effect is desired. The ninant texture of a room is often established by the ar-tectural background. For example, a room paneled in -grained and polished wood or papered in a traditional mal wallcovering generally requires furniture woods and rics with a smoother and shinier texture than that required room paneled with natural course-grained wood or constructed of masonry. Contemporary use of texture may break these traditional rules, providing an element of surprise. A combination of textures, whether employed for an avant-garde or conservative environment, enhances the total visual experience (Figure 2.12).

Light

The element of *light* combines the creativity of the arts and the technology of science. Light affects the physical as well as the emotional comfort of the user. A room must have sufficient light; however, too much light or the inappropriate use of light can cause headaches and inhibit productivity.

The mood and appearance of a room can be greatly altered through the use of light. Uniform light (light lacking in contrast) can lead to boredom and a lack of energy. The quantity as well as the quality of light is critical in a well-designed room. Light variations create interest in a room, but can also affect the perceived color of the interior. Without light, no visual elements can be experienced. Light, its effect on the user, and its proper placement and selection are discussed briefly in Chapter 3 and in detail in Chapter 4.

Color

Color is dependent on light. Color can alter the perceived shape, size, and location of an object. It can create the illusion of texture, stimulate interest, or calm a busy environment. Color has a strong psychological effect on the user. Because of its central role in design, color is discussed in greater detail in Chapter 3.

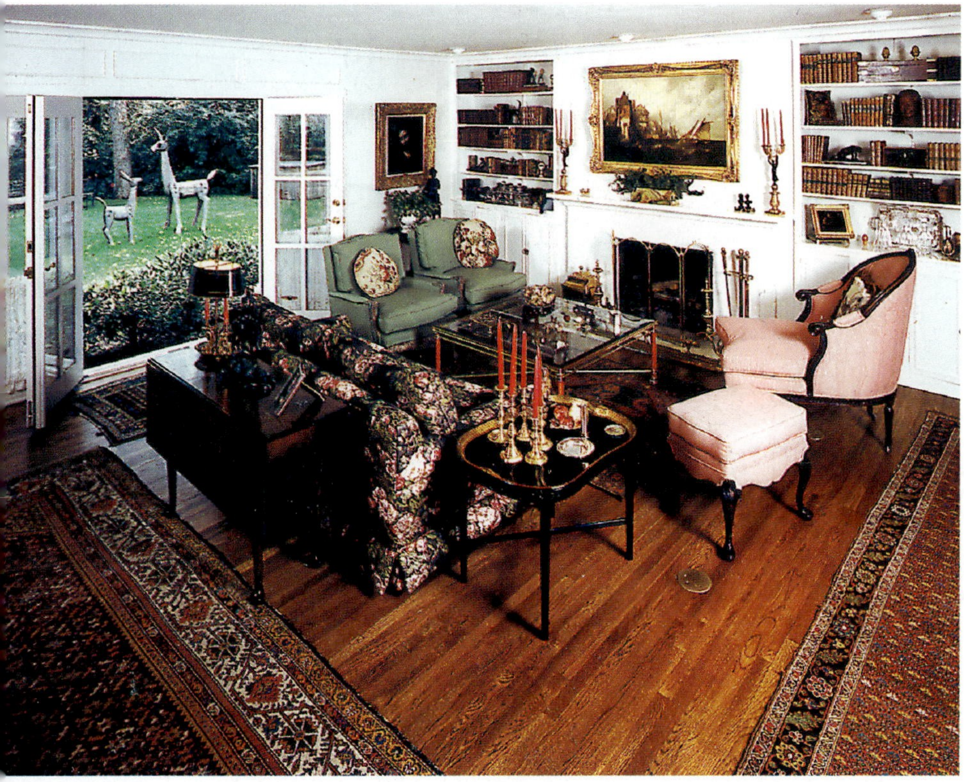

Figure 2.12 *To accentuate the formality of this room, textures are refined, subtle, and sleek. Plush oriental rugs and a quilted sofa fabric add depth and luxury to the interior. (Photograph by Alex Groves.)*

Pattern

Pattern as an element of design interacts and combines with other elements, including space, line, texture, and light. Color can also be incorporated into the patterned arrangement, adding character and focus. The ordering of elements creates pattern. Like the alignments and grid systems discussed in Part II, patterns are created and applied in the horizontal space plan and the vertical elevation, as well as the volume of space. For example, in Figure II.10B, note how the open office layouts in spaces 113 and 148 form a pattern, or visual literacy. Jonathan Hale in *The Old Way of Seeing* illustrates the pattern development of the façade reflected in the design of the windows (Figure 2.13) in Frank Lloyd Wright's Robie House. The proportions of these patterns are frequently based on the golden section discussed later in this chapter. The eye perceives the pattern and finds order in the arrangement.

Pattern is also used as a decorative design element. Japanese designs are known for their embellishment of pattern in the smallest detail. From a distance, the material or finish appears to be solid. It is only on closer observation that the playful pattern is revealed.

Pattern can be effectively employed to create interest (see Figure 2.4), although too much pattern can make a room too "busy" and uncomfortable. In contrast, a room devoid of pattern may be stark and uninviting. The total arrangement of the components of a room creates an overall pattern, but more obvious patterns are seen in fabric and wallpaper. The application of pattern and pattern combinations is more thoroughly covered in Chapter 9, "Textiles."

Principles of Design

Through the centuries, **principles of design** have evol through careful observation of both nature and art. W these principles of design (scale and proportion, balar rhythm, emphasis, and harmony) are thoughtfully con ered and sensitively applied, they contribute to achieving goals of design. The elements of design discussed in the part of this chapter (space, line, shape and mass, text light, color, and pattern) can be manipulated to achieve desired principles of design.

Although there are no absolute rules when creating a sign project, most interiors are enhanced by adhering these basic guidelines. Although some successful contem rary designs violate these time-tested principles, understa ing them is central to the interior designer's creativity an essential to the beginning designer.

Scale and Proportion

The elements of *scale* and *proportion* are both dependen size and the relationships between objects. Scale comp an item or space to *something of a known size*. For instar in order to understand the meaning of a small-scale sized) living room, one must know the standard scale or of a living room. Children's rooms or furniture in elemen schools are *scaled down* or reduced in scale to fit the ne of the occupants.

In interior design, human scale is the most comn source of a known reference. Interior design deals with relationships geared to human scale (Figures 2.14 and 2. The dimensions used in the classic styles of the Ancient, N

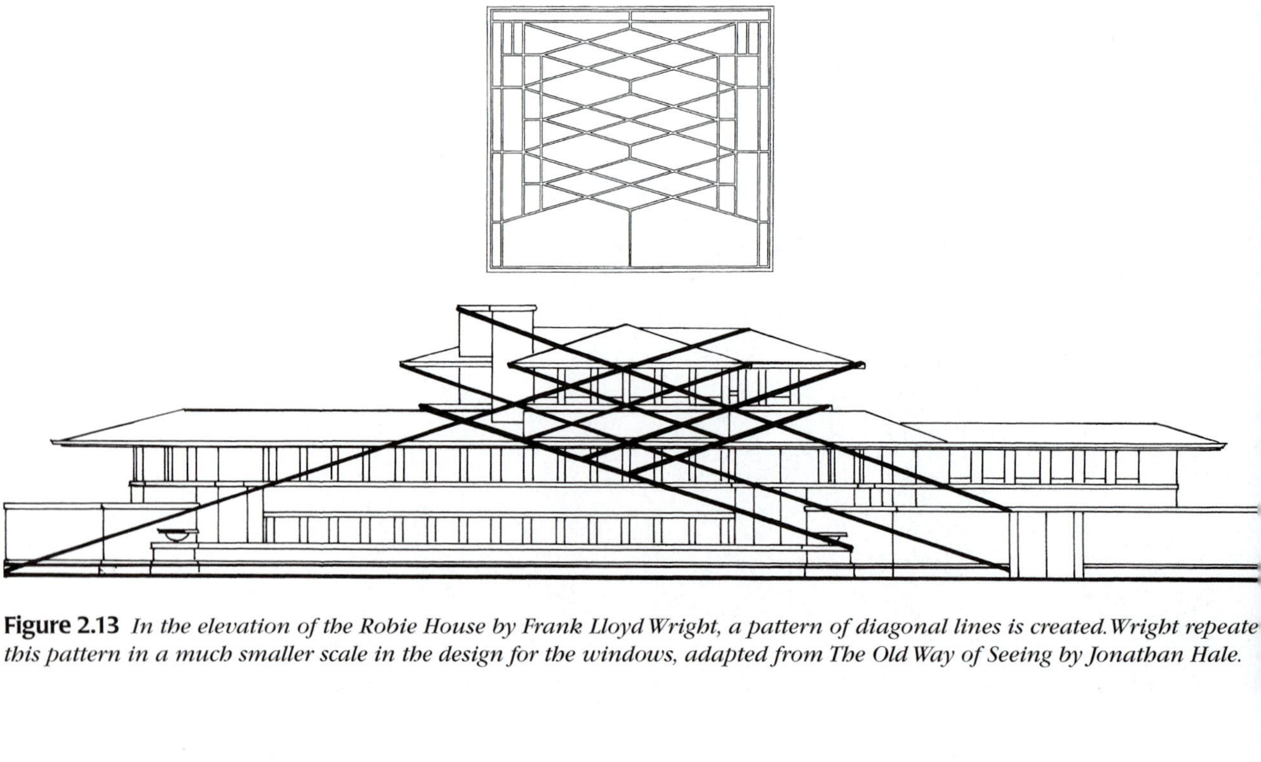

Figure 2.13 *In the elevation of the Robie House by Frank Lloyd Wright, a pattern of diagonal lines is created. Wright repeate this pattern in a much smaller scale in the design for the windows, adapted from The Old Way of Seeing by Jonathan Hale.*

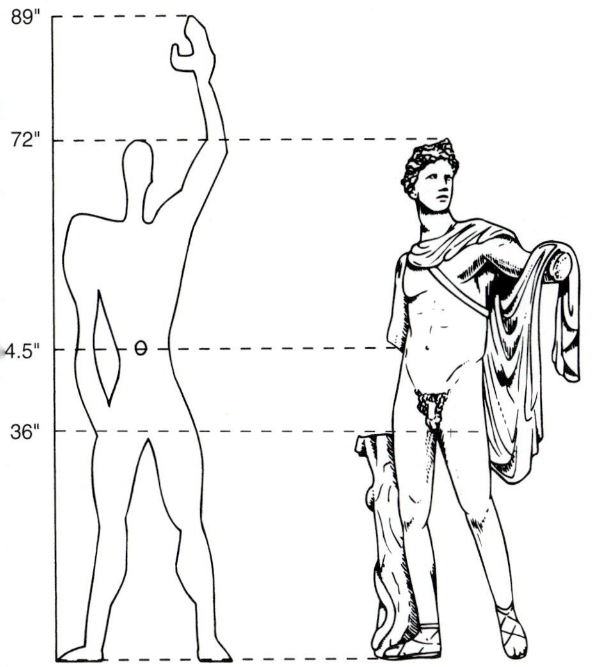

ure 2.14 *Le Corbusier planned his architectural projects to consistent with the proportions of this human Modular ft). The same ideal proportions can be applied to the nous statue of the Apollo Belvedere (right), probably a first ntury* B.C. *Roman copy in marble of a fourth-century* B.C. *eek original.*

Age, and Renaissance eras are based on the human scale. e foot measurement was based on the size of a human ɔt and contained 12 inches. Each inch is approximately ual to the length of the thumb from the tip to the first joint. s important to note, as Jonathan Hale does, that the meas- ement of 1 foot is equal to 1/360,000 of 1/360 (one degree) the circumference of the Earth, accurate to 99 percent. In eindustrialized Japan, the version of the foot was called the *aku*. It measured 11.93 inches. The Egyptian's version asured 12.25 inches.

Additionally, the length from the elbow to the tip of the ddle finger is 18 inches, or a cubit. The midpoint of a 6- ɔt person (usually at the top of the leg) is 3 feet or 1 yard. e Japanese frequently use the tatami mat for measurement. s 3 feet by 6 feet. The importance of human scale is ap- rent in all successful design solutions.

Scale is also based on perception. As per the theories of sign discussed in Part II, objects appear to change size sed on other objects around them. Note in Figure 2.16 the rceived differences in the sizes of the middle circles. Sim- ly, furniture should be sized to fit the scale of the room area that surrounds it.

Furniture that is too large crowds a small room and makes ppear even smaller, whereas furniture that is too small ems even smaller in an oversized room. Large, overstuffed niture should not be placed in a small living room (Figure 7). When surrounded by small-scaled furniture, a large

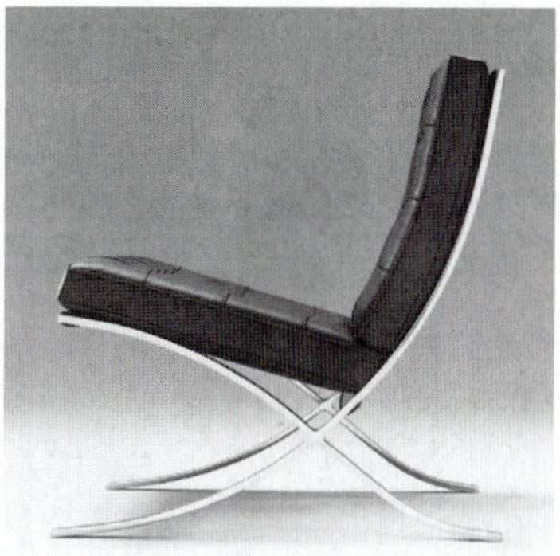

Figure 2.15 *The beautiful lines and scale of the highly acclaimed Barcelona chair, designed by Ludwig Mies van der Rohe in 1929 for the Barcelona Exhibition, have made it a timeless classic. (Courtesy of Knoll.)*

piece of furniture appears larger than when surrounded by large-scaled pieces. A small table with spindly legs placed at the end of a heavy sofa or chair looks out of place, and a large-scaled table placed near a dainty chair is not enhanced.

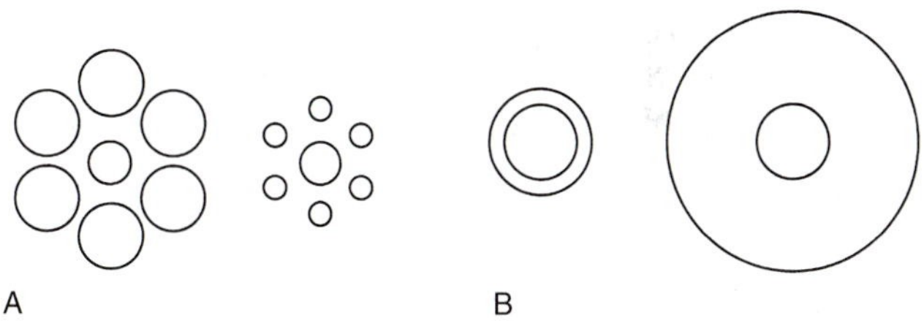

Figure 2.16 *Perception: The center circles in each of the diagrams are identical. The apparent change in size is due to the difference in size of the surrounding circles.*

Accessories such as mirrors, pictures, and lamps need to be scaled for the items with which they are to be used. A lamp generally must not overpower a table, nor should it be so small that it looks ridiculous. Both the lampshade and base must be suitably scaled.

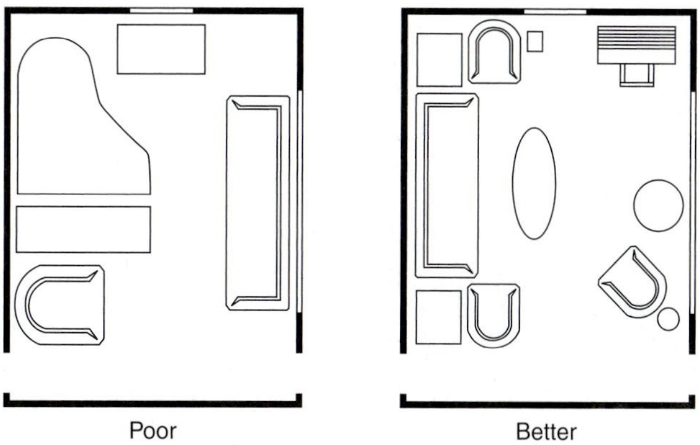

Figure 2.17 *These plan views indicate inappropriate and appropriately scaled furniture.*

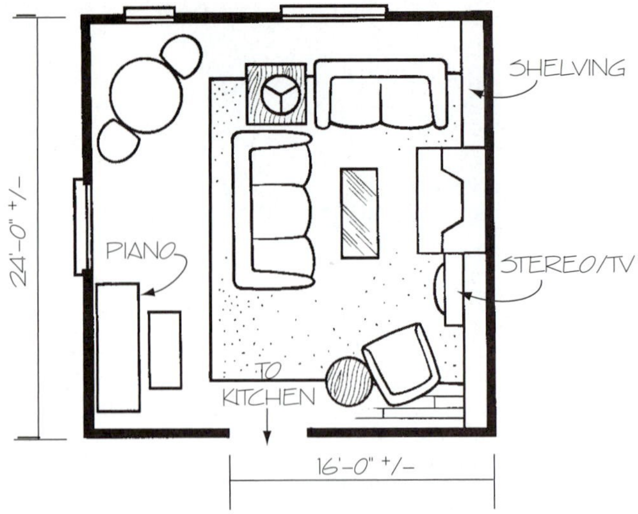

Figure 2.18 *In this presentation floor plan of a garage conversion, the designer arranged the furniture and floor coverings to allow the seating arrangement to more closely reflect the proportions of the golden rectangle.*

Scale is a relative issue, dependent on the known size of another object. *Proportion* is also a relative issue, but it does not depend on a known size. Proportion encompasses both the relationship of one part of an object to its other parts or to the whole, as well as the relationship of one object to another.

Proportion has been a major concern of creative minds through the ages. Although no absolute formula for good proportion works in all design projects, the Greeks discovered some secrets of good proportion over 2000 years ago and set down rules that have been incorporated into compositions for centuries. For instance, a square room has been considered the most difficult room to design and is also the least pleasing to the eye. Recognizing this, the Greeks developed the **golden rectangle,** which is a rectangle whose proportion of width to length is 2:3. This proportion is considered the most pleasing. A common use of the golden rectangle is in the residential conversion of a 24 ft by 24 ft garage. Designers must artfully place furniture and interior components to give the square room the illusion a rectangular space (Figure 2.18).

The **golden section,** also developed by the Greeks, volves the division of a line or form in such a way that t ratio of the smaller portion to the larger is the same as th of the larger portion to the whole (Figure 2.19). The p gression 2, 3, 5, 8, 13, 21, 34, and so on, in which each nu ber is the sum of the two preceding numbers, provides close approximation to this relationship. For example, 2:3 roughly the same as 3:5, and 5:8 is roughly the same as 8: and so forth. Another pleasing ratio is 4:7. These ratios c help designers decide room sizes and shapes, as well as t most pleasing proportions for windows and fireplace mo ings and openings.

Perhaps the most important application of these prop tions in planning and furnishing lies in the relationship sizes or areas. For example, if the length of a room me ures 25 ft, a desirable width would be 15 ft. This measu ment is determined by the following process. Because t length of the living room (25 ft) is divisible by 5, the 3:5 tio may be used.

$$\frac{3}{5} = \frac{x}{25}$$

To solve for x, cross multiple 3×25 to get 75. Now div 75 by 5 to get 15.

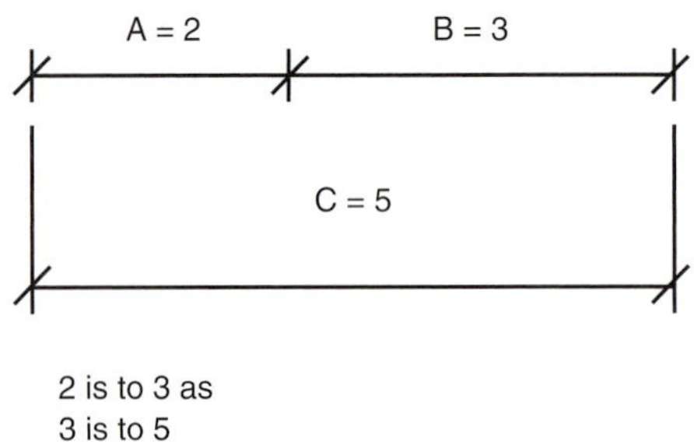

Figure 2.19 *In the golden section the ratio of A to B is the same as the ratio of B to C. In other words, 2/3 is approximately equal to 3/5. The precise ratio is 1:1.618.*

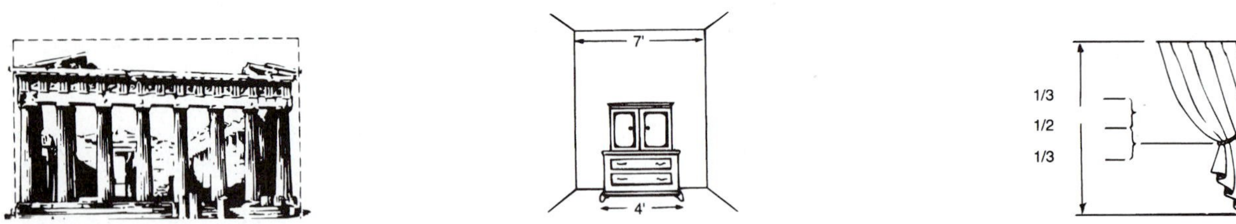

The Parthenon at Athens—based on a mathematical ratio of 1:1.6—fits almost precisely into a golden rectangle. Because of the frequency with which it occurs in the arts, the golden rectangle has fascinated experts for centuries.

4:7 is a pleasing proportion.

The golden mean. The divis of a line somewhere betwee one-half and one-third is th most pleasing.

Figure 2.20 *The use of Greek proportions.*

In another example, a piece of furniture 4 ft long would : a good size to place against a 7-ft wall space. These di- ensions have the desirable ratios of 4:7 (Figure 2.20). Even e human body contains the golden section. The ratio from e feet to the navel in comparison to the entire body height approximately 1:1.618, the precise ratio for the golden ction.

Another Greek discovery was that the division of a line mewhere between one-half and one-third its length is the ost desirable. This division, called the **golden mean,** can applied when planning any wall composition, such as de- rmining the height for a mantel, tying back drapery, or nging pictures, mirrors, or wall sconces.

The Greeks also observed that odd numbers are prefer- le to even ones. A group of three objects is more pleasing an two or four. These guidelines might be applied, for ex- nple, when selecting the quantity of pillows for a sofa or hen arranging pictures on a wall.

In addition to form, the elements of color, texture, and ttern are also important in the consideration of scale d proportion. Whatever attracts the eye seems larger. arse textures, large patterns, and bold colors cause the ject on which they are used to appear larger than an ob- ct with smooth textures, small patterns, and soft, light lors. Through the skillful use of these principles, the ap- rent size and proportion of rooms and objects may be tered.

ore info online @

tp://www.mcs.surrey.ac.uk/Personal/R.Knott/Fibonacci/fibInArt.html d

tp://www.math.vt.edu/people/gao/math/godensection/index.html ormation on the golden section and Fibonacci numbers

tp://www.digitalarchitectures.com/gmean.htm Digital Architectures, :. golden section information

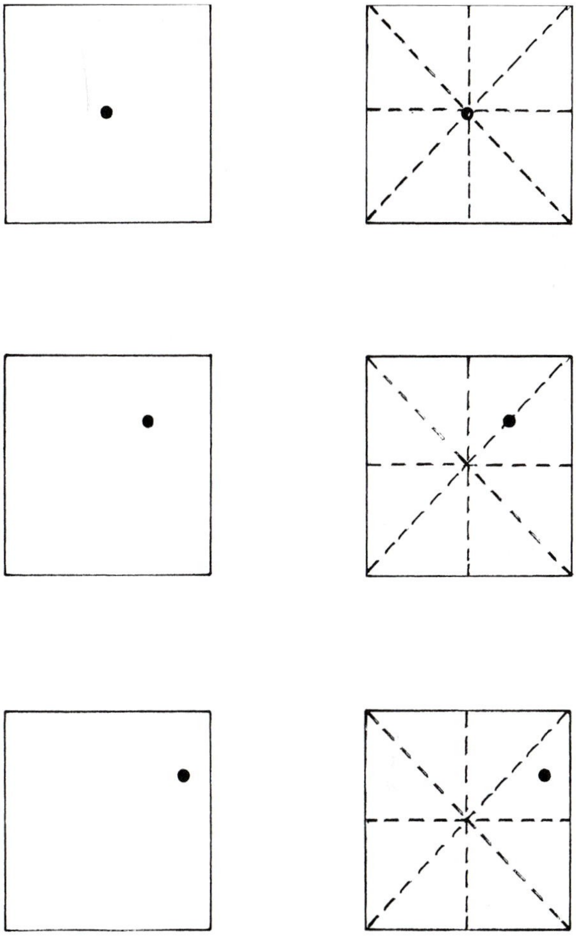

Figure 2.22 *In boxes (A) and (B), the dot is located on an imaginary vertical or diagonal axis. This brings a perceived visual order to the image. In box (C), however, the dot is haphazardly located, causing unrest to the viewer.*

alance

alance is that quality in a room that establishes a sense of uilibrium and repose. It is a sense of weight as the eye per- ives it. Generally, humans have a need for balance in many pects of their lives (review Figure I.5). In the interior envi- nment, balance is necessary to achieve a comfortable at- osphere.

Balance is based substantially on visual perception. Donis ondis in *A Primer of Visual Literacy* notes the importance of balance on movement. In Figure 2.21, the first circle appears balanced or stable; the second circle appears to be rolling to the right.

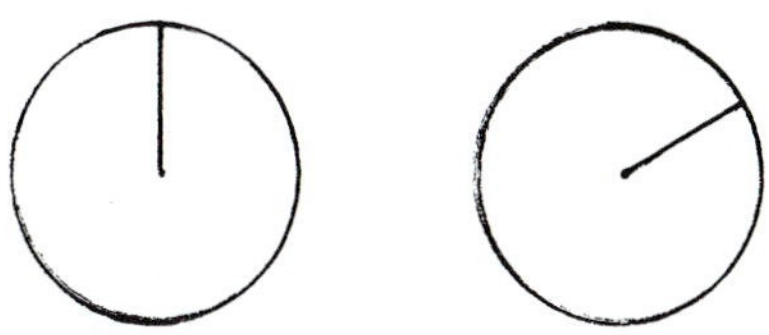

gure 2.21 *Note how the vertical line appears to balance the cle; however, in the second circle, the diagonal line adds ovement to the circle.*

Balance brings a sense of order. For instance, in Figure 2.22, box A appears to be balanced; the dot is centered. The dot in box B, although not centered, has been placed on a diagonal axis that allows for more visual comfort. In box C, however, the dot is placed in such a location to cause visual unrest or ambiguity.

The architectural background of rooms including doors, windows, paneling, and fireplaces, along with accompanying furnishings, can be effectively arranged to provide a feeling of equilibrium. Some considerations include the following:

- Opposite walls and interior spaces and objects should have a comfortable feeling of balance through the distribution of high and low, as well as large and small objects.
- When furnishings are positioned above eye level, they appear heavier than items positioned below.

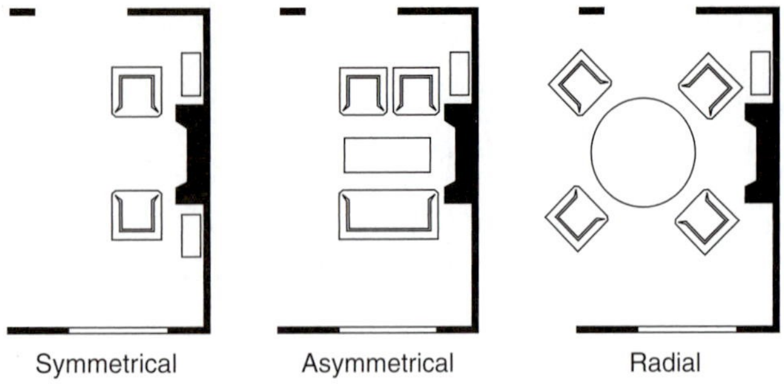

Figure 2.23 *Three types of balance.*

- Bright colors, heavy textures, unusual shapes, bold patterns, and strong lighting readily attract attention and can be manipulated to achieve balance within a space.
- Large furnishings in a space can be complemented by placing them next to groups of small items, and vice versa, creating a refreshing contrast.

The three types of balance used to provide this equilibrium are symmetrical, asymmetrical, and radial (Figure 2.23).

Symmetrical, or Formal, Balance

In **symmetrical balance** identical objects are arranged equally on each side of an imaginary line. This type of balance is often employed in traditional and formal environments and adds a feeling of dignity to the interior. Formal balance usually conveys a restful and peaceful sensation, because this type of balance is easily perceived and appreciated; however, too much symmetry can create a dull interior.

Asymmetrical Balance

Asymmetrical balance is more subtle than symmetri balance. It requires more thought and imagination, b once achieved, remains interesting for a longer time (F ure 2.24). In this type of balance objects of different siz shapes, and colors may be used in an infinite number ways. Two small objects may balance one large item, small shiny object may balance a larger dull one, a spot bright color may balance a large area of neutral color, a a large object moved closer to a central point may balan a smaller one pushed farther away (Figure 2.25). No me urement indicates at what point these different items m

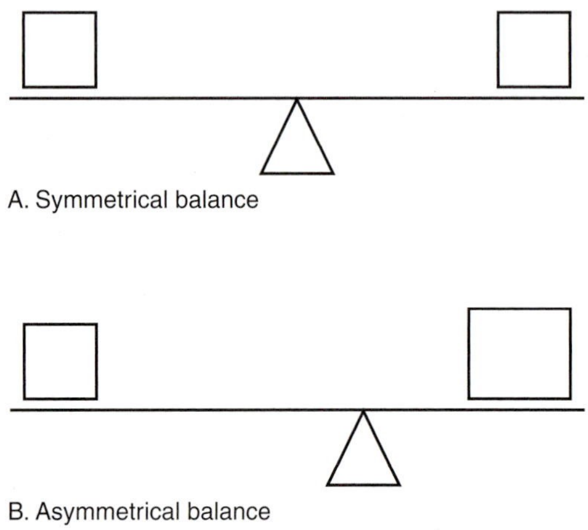

Figure 2.25 *In asymmetrical balance, the triangular balan point must be moved to the right in order to keep the seesa level.*

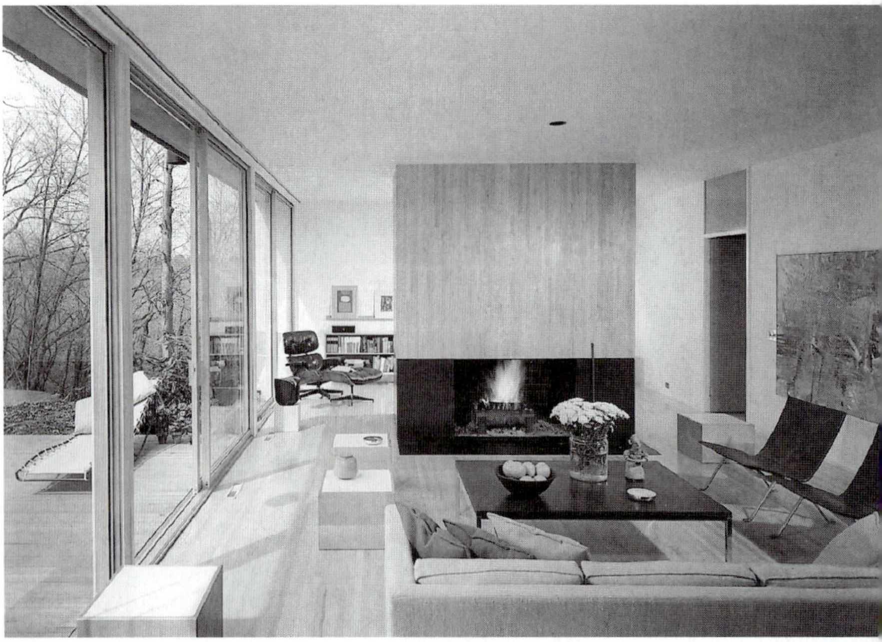

Figure 2.24 *The Scandinavian influence in the American home shows a congenial combination of the Organic and International styles. Clean white walls with wood detailing are typical. The classic modern Scandinavian chairs on the right were designed by Poul Kjaerholm of Denmark in 1956. The expanse of windows is balanced by the artwork. (Photograph by Ezra Stoller © Esto.)*

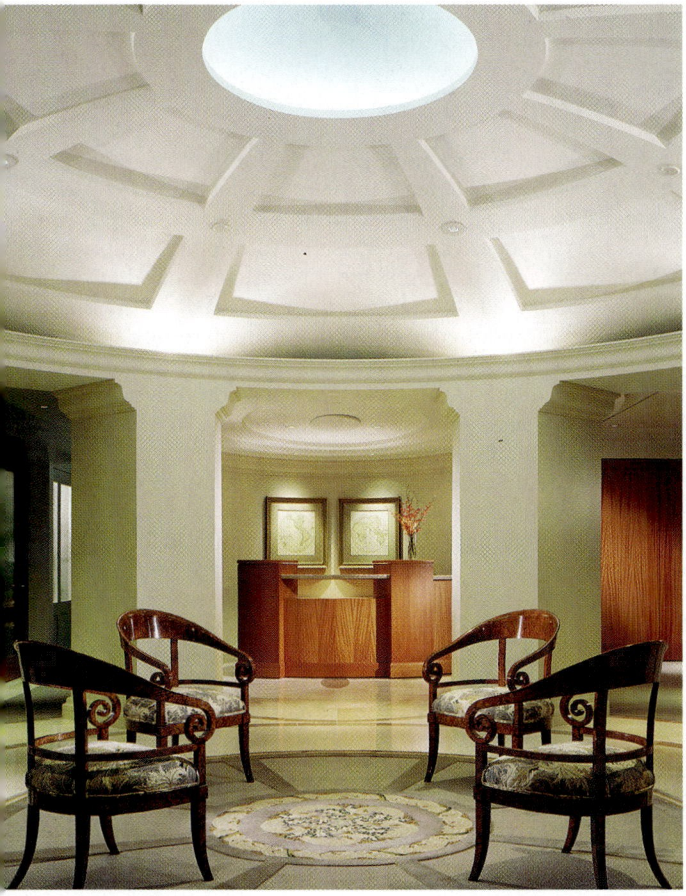

Figure 2.26 *The domed ceiling, floor pattern, and furniture arrangement in this investment office lobby indicate the use of radial design. (Architect/Designer: VOA Associates, Inc. Photograph by Steven Hall/Hedrich-Blessing.)*

e placed; the point at which balance is achieved must be ensed. Asymmetrical balance:

- Tends to shift the focus from the center and achieves balance by visual tension created between dissimilar objects
- Is predominant in contemporary interiors
- Tends to be informal
- Is generally more active than symmetrical balance
- Provides a more spacious appearance

adial Balance

ı **radial balance** all elements of the design radiate from a entral point like the spokes of a wheel radiating out from e hub. This balance can be seen in a room where chairs ırround a round table, in flower arrangements, and in chaneliers. Radial balance is often used in large congregating aras such as hotel and office lobbies (Figure 2.26) and central areas in shopping malls. Radial balance is often a visually pleasing alternative and combines effectively with the other two types of balance.

All rooms require balance, and most rooms combine symmetrical, asymmetrical, and radial balance in different proportions. The combination of all three will create a pleasing effect that will remain interesting over time.

Rhythm

Rhythm assists the eye in moving easily about a room from one area to another, creating a flowing quality. Rhythm can be achieved through repetition, transition, and gradation or progression (Figure 2.27). The effective application of rhythm creates continuity and interest.

Repetition is rhythm established by repeating color, pattern, texture, line, light, or form. For example, a color in the

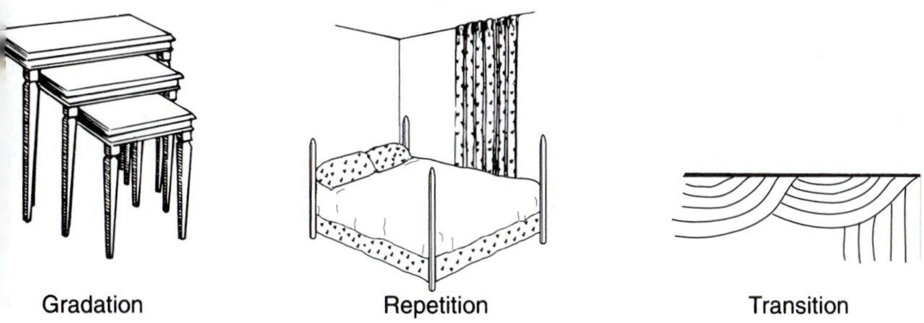

Figure 2.27 *Types of rhythm: Gradation, repetition, and transition.*

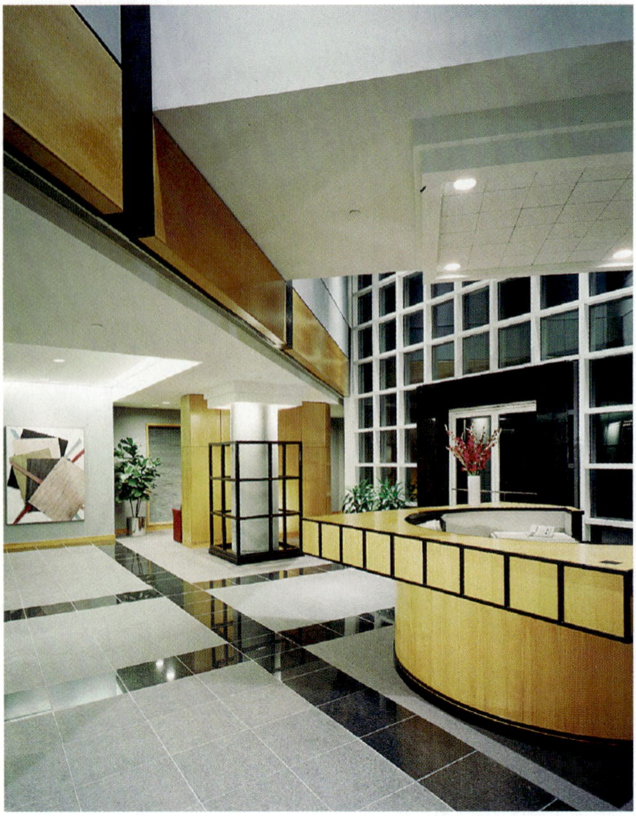

Figure 2.28 *In this commercial interior, the designer repeated a square motif from the architecture into the interior lobby. Grids demarcate columns and floor tiles, and are repeated through the use of contrasting woods on the desk. (Designer: Godwin Associates. Photograph by Gabe Benzur.)*

upholstery fabric of a sofa can be repeated on a chair, the drapery, and a pillow, thus introducing rhythm. The repetition may also include alternating an object or pattern in a sequence (Figure 2.28). Repetition is a common means of achieving rhythm in a room because it is a relatively easy approach, although too much repetition can produce confusion, monotony, or lack of stability.

Transition, another type of repetition, is rhythm found in a curved line that carries the eye easily over an architectural element, such as an arched window, or around items of furnishings, like drapery swags. A curved chair placed in the corner of a room beside a round table will soften the sharp angle of the merging wall planes, allowing the eye to flow through the space. In Figure 2.29, the curved window softens the corner of the room, thereby providing a transition.

Gradation or *progression* is rhythm produced by the succession of the size of an object from large to small or of a color from dark to light. Radiating lines are not only a form of balance (as previously discussed), but may also be a form of gradation (note the ceiling recesses in Figure 2.26). Other examples include the progression of one step up to another step, the gradation of a small salt container to a medium-sized sugar container up to a large flour container, and a rug that might have a dark border, a lighter inner border, and very light interior area.

Emphasis

Emphasis in a room refers to the focal point and supporti furnishings that create the center of attention. In every we planned room, it is effective to have one feature repeated draw the eye. This emphasis or focal point can bring a fee ing of order and unity into a room, with all other grouping subordinated to it. When there is a lack of emphasis in room, boredom due to a visually uninteresting space can re sult. Too much emphasis (i.e., more than one or several ce ters of interest) can produce chaos and unrest.

Emphasis is greatly affected by visual perception. O eyes naturally scan a room and seek out the focal point provide a sense of repose. When scanning an image, o eyes are first drawn to the lower left-hand corner. In adve tising, a company's logo is frequently located in this are Natural axes (as part of an alignment or grid) also are cr ated through focal points, drawing a person to an appoint location. Analyzing a room and determining what comp nents to emphasize and subordinate can be a challengi task. A general approach includes viewing the room on fo basic levels of emphasis and then determining what comp nents will be featured.

1. *Emphatic.* These features may include a dramatic view, fireplace, or architectural feature. For example, if a fireplace is prominently placed and designed, it naturally becomes a focal point; in addition, a burning fire radiates warmth, movement, color, and hospitality—a natural site for a main seating arrangement. Many rooms, however, may not have a emphatic feature.
2. *Dominant.* In many instances this is the level where most designers begin. In the absence of dramatic features in a room, a dominant focal point may exist or be created. A fireplace in this case may not be an architecturally dramatic feature, but it certainly can be played up and designed to dominate a room. Other dominant features might include a wall of books, a composition of paintings, a beautiful piece of furniture, or a garden view.
3. *Subdominant.* This category includes the level of furnishings that support the focal point and may include large pieces of furniture or the window, ceiling, and floor treatments. This might include the arrangement of furniture in front of a fireplace supporting the dominant focal point of the fireplace (see Figure 2.29).
4. *Subordinate.* This level most often includes accessories like lamps, plants, art objects, and small furnishings.

This method of analyzing a room and breaking it down in various levels of importance can aid the designer. Furnishin and architectural features can be rearranged within th framework depending on the desired outcome. The emph sis of the room may be planned or manipulated by the use the elements and principles of design, such as the followin

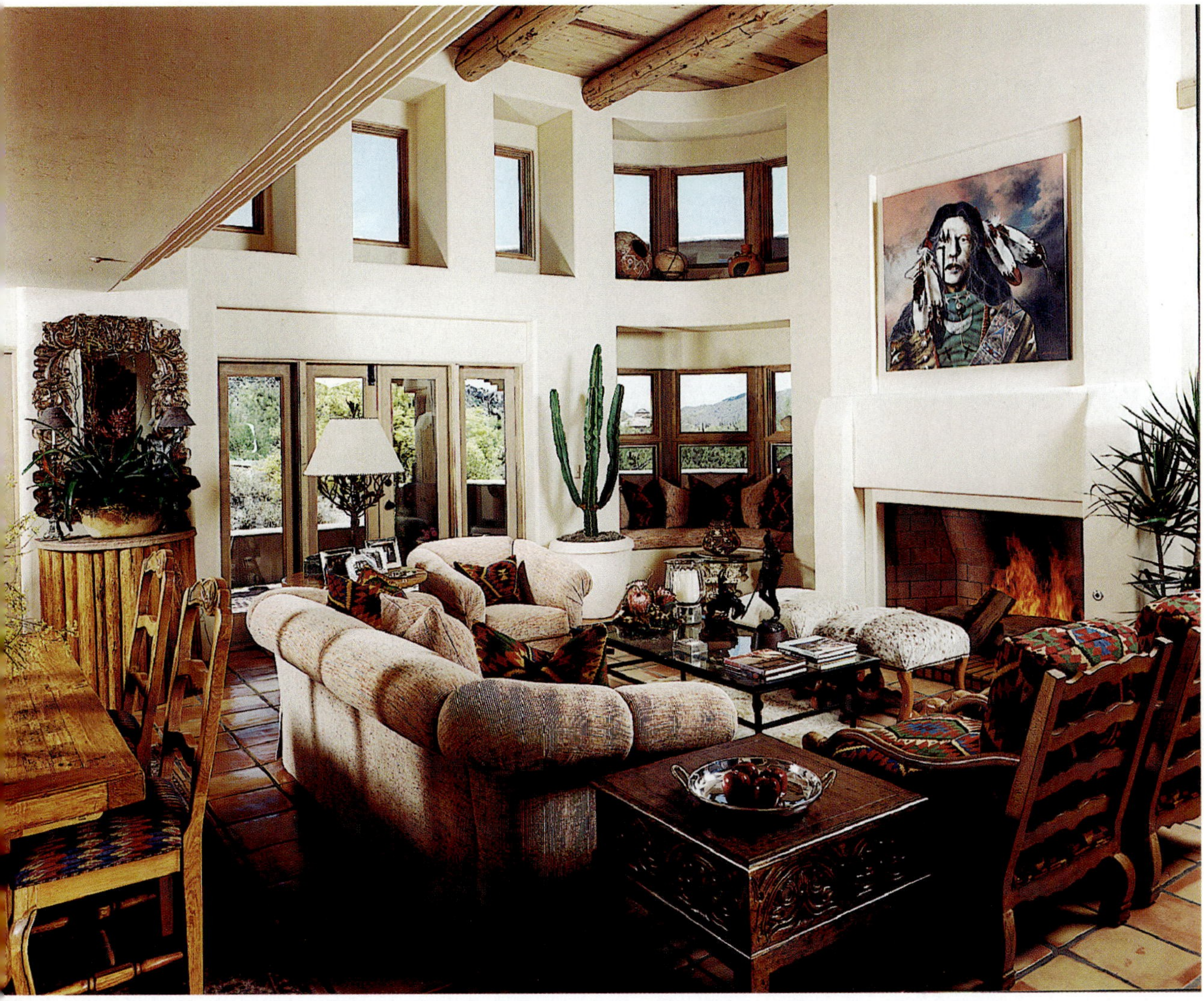

igure 2.29 *In this large room, the curved window bay and large sofa soften the edges of the converging architectural planes. he focal point of the architecture is the fireplace wall. The stunning painting by J. D. Challenger commands attention as a sult of its location and the elements of design used to draw the eye to this feature from any area in the room. (Photograph by ark Boisclair. Interior Designer: Carol Conway. Architect: Kevin Bain.)*

Color is probably the most important element by which a grouping may be brought into immediate focus. Color can be used artfully to achieve the desired amount of emphasis.

Form usually involves arranging furniture within the space—placing furnishings so they focus on the point of emphasis. Unusual or strong form used for furnishings or architectural background can be dominant or even dramatic.

Texture, whether rough, smooth, shiny, or dull, can help draw the eye to a particular item. The designer can use this tool to create dominance or to allow a component in the room to blend into the background.

Lighting can be used creatively to tie the group together, dramatize, attract attention, or create a focal point.

- *Pattern,* especially a distinctive design with strong color or value contrast, can attract the eye to a desired focal point.

Because emphasis in a room is planned and even manipulated through the use of the elements of design, it is essential that all parts relate to and support each other (Figure 2.30).

Harmony

All the other elements and principles work together to promote *harmony*. Harmony is the unique blend of *unity* and *variety*. A unifying theme or common denominator should run through all component parts and blend them together.

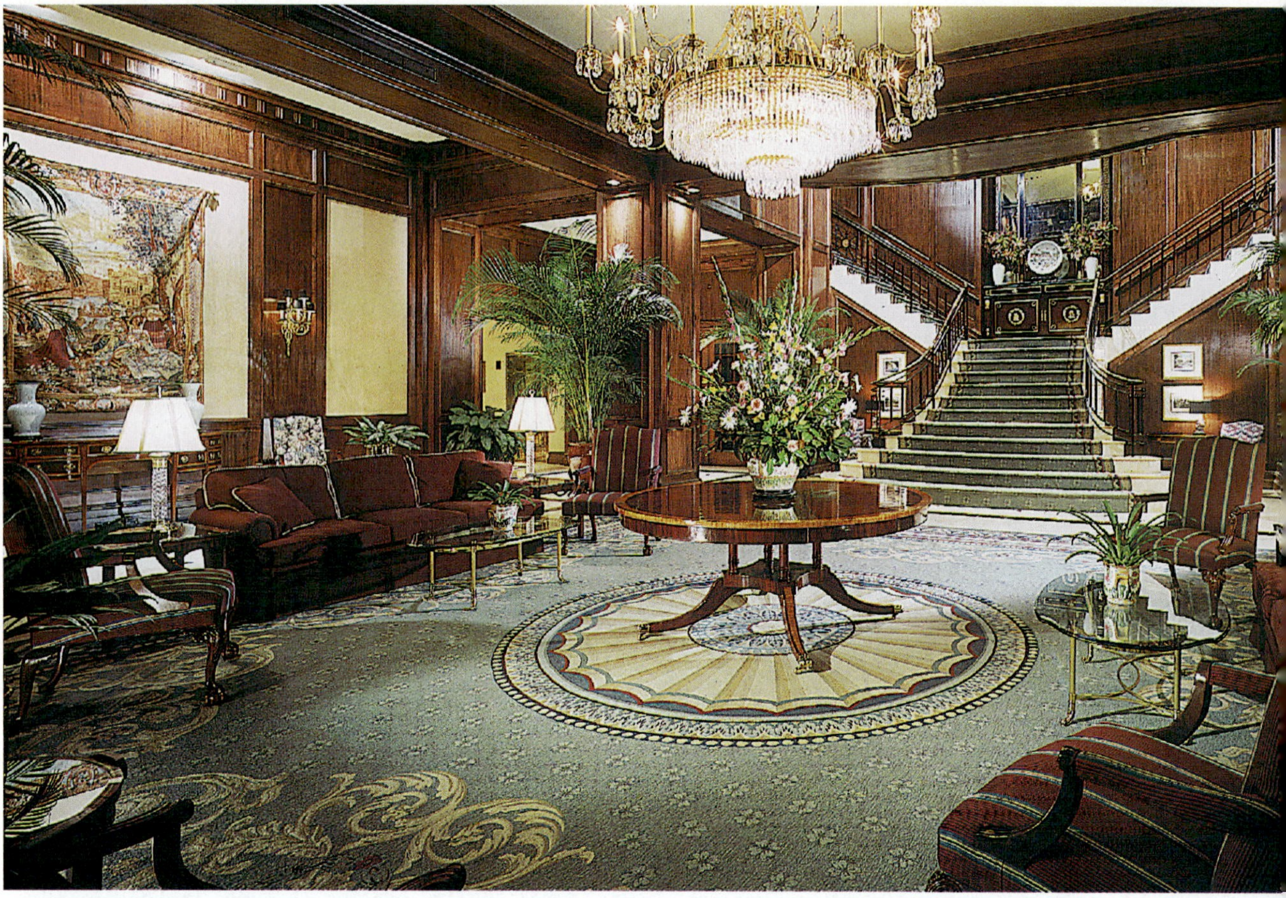

Figure 2.30 *In this hotel lobby, color, form, texture, light, and pattern all creatively support the central focus. Plants soften architectural edges and a custom carpet defines the seating area and grand staircase. (Designer: Marcia Davis & Associates, Inc. Photograph by Peter Paige. Courtesy: Lacey-Champion, Inc.)*

Exteriors and interiors are attractive when there is a pleasant relationship that provides unity, yet the aspect of variety is essential to provide interest. Variety can create the focal point or add the spark that enlivens the room. Following are some of the most common and important considerations when seeking a harmonious living environment:

- In every room, the *interior architecture* is a determining factor. Just as the exterior and interior architecture should be consistent, the furnishings of a room must also be in harmony with the background. For example, molded plastic chairs do not belong against formal eighteenth-century paneling, nor is a classic Louis XVI chair desirable against a heavy concrete block wall. A surprising juxtaposition of seemingly unrelated objects may occasionally add relief, but this practice requires sophisticated judgment.
- *Furniture* in the room should appear to belong there. Whether the room is large or small, furniture should be scaled accordingly. For example, if the architectural background is strong—perhaps with exposed beams and masonry construction—the furniture should reflect the same feeling.
- *Colors* appropriate to the style and scale of furnishings should be considered; however, today's interiors often show great flexibility in color usage. A sensitive approach to color harmonies in relationship to furnishings, background, and style is important in achieving an appealing result.
- The *textures* of surfaces (i.e., smooth, rough, shiny, or dull) help determine the success of a room's harmony. Textures should be compatible with the design and style of all furnishings. For instance, a heavy homespun fabric is generally not suitable on a formal Hepplewhite chair, nor is delicate silk damask usually at home on a rough-hewn ranch oak chair.
- A *window treatment* can contribute to the room's total harmony; planning a hard or soft line treatment suitable for the theme and style is essential. For example, ruffled cottage curtains are out of place in an Oriental-style house, and elegant damask swags are inappropriate for a country cottage.
- Carefully selected *floor coverings* help unify the scheme. Hard floor surfaces like wood, tile, and stone are extremely versatile and enhance most living areas. Area rugs, such as a Persian Oriental, are appropriate in any

decor, and wall-to-wall carpeting can tie an entire room together.

Accessories can enhance a room or completely destroy the desired effect. If an accessory is not beautiful, useful, or meaningful to the person using it, it does not belong. The final touches added to a room reveal individual personality more readily than any other items of furnishing and cannot be overlooked in creating rooms of beauty and interest (Figure 2.31). Items that are essentially attractive and well designed, however, can lose their charm when not well used. For example, a gracefully scrolled wrought-iron wall sconce can add much to a room of Spanish or Mediterranean styling but would look heavy and out of place in a pastel room with delicate furnishings. (Chapter 8 discusses accessorizing in greater detail.)

Consistency or harmony is achieved by carrying out a basic *style*. The style need not be followed slavishly, but a general feeling of unity should be maintained throughout (see the pictorial essay on "History of Style"). This allows the designer to combine good design from many periods with one dominating. Within this overall style, an occasional surprise to give variety and interest can provide charm and individuality. Consistency or harmony is also achieved when a *concept* has been established and followed. The concept may incorporate the basic style, but extends beyond the concrete elements to include abstract characteristics appropriate to the design solutions.

Summary

The elements of design (space, line, shape and mass, texture, light, color, and pattern) and the principles of design (scale and proportion, balance, rhythm, emphasis, and harmony) form the foundation for all designs. The ordering of these elements and principles creates a visual literacy, that when combined with the design process discussed in Chapter 1, helps to ensure a quality design that satisfies the needs and desires of the client. All of these elements and principles, including color and light (which are discussed in following chapters), help the designer create an interior that is physically and psychologically comfortable, as well as uniquely attractive.

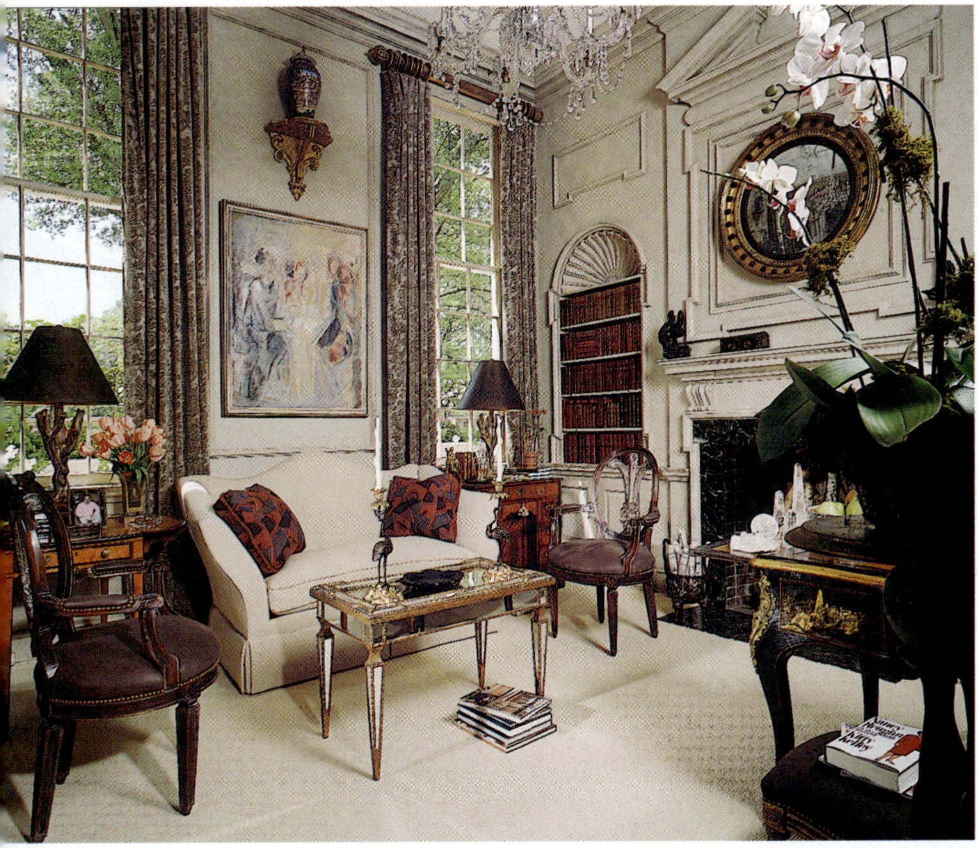

Figure 2.31 *All the elements and principles of design are effectively used in this exquisite private residence in Georgia, designed by C. Smith Grubbs. The eclectic room combines eighteenth-century English and French styles in a fresh contemporary interpretation. Final accessorizing touches add individuality and character. (Photograph by David Schilling/Atlanta.)*

Color 3

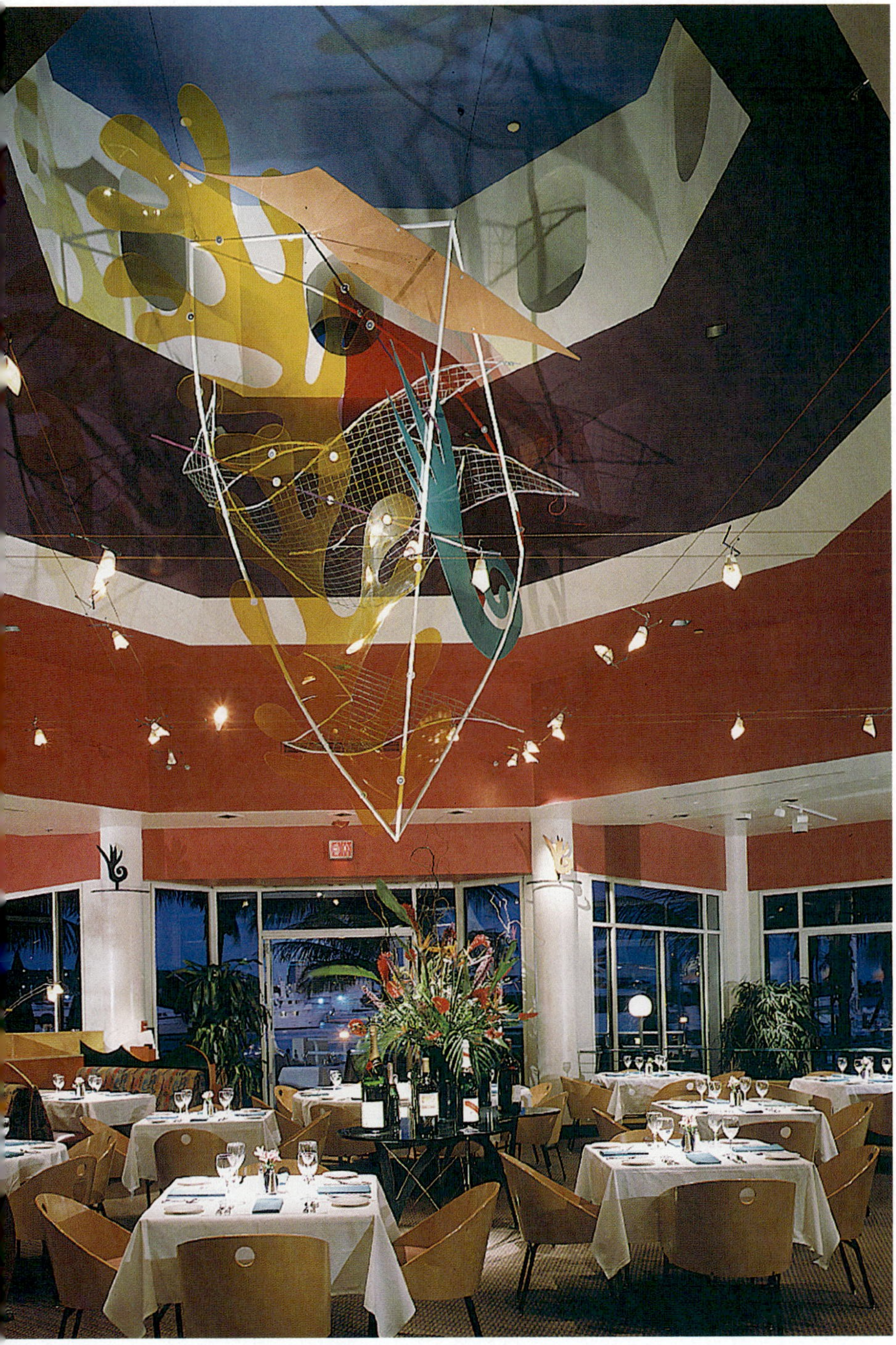

Figure 3.1 *This vibrant restaurant uses brilliant colors of intense chromas. Color defines this interior space. (Architect/Designer: Engstrom Design Group and To Design. Photograph by Dennis Anderson ©.)*

The great nineteenth-century writer and critic John Ruskin said, "Color is the most sacred element in all visual things." Designers agree that color is the most vital and expressive of the elements of design, as demonstrated in Figure 3.1. Therefore, it is essential that designers have a thorough knowledge of the properties and character of various colors, color theory, color schemes, color associations, and other considerations of color for use in planning both residential and commercial interiors.

Color can have psychological effects; it can enliven a room or create a subdued mood. Color's elemental partner—light—can do the same thing. Light affects the colors we see. In bright afternoon sun, colors are crisp and clear. In evening sunsets, red and orange tones cast a warm glow. In candlelight or moonlight, colors are muted and dulled. It is essential when studying about color to understand first that the source of color is light.

Light in Color

Light is a form of energy that is part of the electromagnetic spectrum. Daylight, or the light that humans are able to see in the *visible spectrum,* is a mixture of wavelengths in a narrow band of this field. Infrared waves, X-rays, and even radio waves are also forms of energy in this spectrum, but are not visible to the human eye. Color is light broken down into electromagnetic vibrations of varying wavelengths. The longest wavelengths form the reds, followed by oranges, yellows, greens, blues, and violets. This effect can be seen in a rainbow or when light is shown through a prism, which separates or splits the spectrum (Figure 3.2). Artificial lighting that is designed to mimic the sun's light is called white light. Other types of artificial lighting create different combinations of wavelengths that change the color or *look* of an object. Lighting is discussed in greater detail in Chapter 5; however, it is important to realize that without light, color would not exist.

The color that we actually see in an object is the color of light that is not absorbed by the object, but reflected into the eye from the object's surface. A particular surface absorbs or reflects a color of the spectrum depending on its composition. This is referred to as **subtractive color,** because the objects *subtract* all the wavelengths except those that are seen. For instance, a teal rug subtracts all the wavelengths except for some of the blue and green wavelengths, which it reflects back. A black tiled wall subtracts all the wavelengths.

Figure 3.2 *A ray of white light passed through a prism separates into distinct bands of color. The longest wavelength in the visible spectrum is red, followed by orange, yellow, green, blue, and violet, the shortest visible wavelength.*

SUSTAINABLE DESIGN

Natural Earth Colors

Natural earth colors are inorganic pigments found in minerals, principally iron oxides, from the soil. They are washed and ground, then mixed with other substances to create paints or dyes. Earth colors usually include ocher (yellow), sienna, red oxide (red), umber (brown), and terra verde (green).

Earth colors have been used for millennia. For example, these pigments were used by the ancient Egyptians to paint the walls of their tombs, and by the artists of the Middle Ages and Renaissance in their paintings.

Earth colors are still used today for many purposes, especially to help protect items from corrosion. Earth colors are the most permanent colors available, are usually nontoxic, and are not affected by atmospheric conditions.

The colors in objects are referred to as pigment colo Pigments are various substances that can be ground into fi powder and used for coloring dyes and paints. Pigments a combined to produce certain colors, such as when red ar yellow are mixed to obtain orange. Pigments may be nat rally occurring (as discussed in the feature on sustainable d sign), artificially created, or a combination of both.

Warm, Cool, and Neutral Colors

Colors are grouped into categories. The simplest division ca egorizes all colors as warm, cool, or neutral.

Warm Colors

The *warm colors* of the spectrum include red, red-orange, c ange, yellow-orange, and yellow. Generally, these war colors are considered engaging, active, positive, cheer

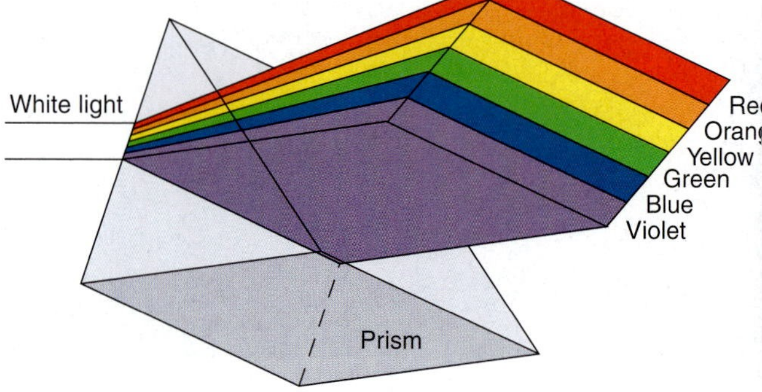

ᵣy, and stimulating. Warm colors tend to advance and can close space. If used in strong intensity in large areas, warm ors may cause individuals to feel irritable.

ol Colors

e *cool colors* are blue, blue-green, green, violet, and blue-let. Cool colors are generally felt to be relaxing, restful, l soothing. Cool colors recede and tend to expand space. ol-colored rooms may be perceived as cold and un-ndly, and may lack variety.

utral and Neutralized Colors

chnically, *neutral colors* are gray, white, and black be-use they are without an identifiable **hue** (another word for olor). These neutral colors are often called "achromatic," ich in Greek means "without color."

Colors falling midway between the warm and cool color oups, such as beige, brown, taupe, cream, ivory, off-black, l off-white (white with any small amount of a color led), are called *neutralized colors*. Neutralized colors are nerally important to every color scheme. They tend to be tful, tranquil, livable, unobtrusive, and supportive. How-er, if not used effectively, neutral and neutralized colors n produce feelings of boredom and weariness.

he Standard Color Wheel

rm and cool colors can be distinguished most easily using standard color wheel (Figure 3.3). This theory of color is own as the Palette theory, the Prang theory, or the Brew-r color theory; it is the simplest and best known of the or theories or systems. The standard color wheel system is sed on three *primary colors:* yellow, red, and blue (Figure). Primary means the colors cannot be mixed from other ments, nor can they be broken down into component col-. Theoretically, with five tubes of paint—the three primar- plus black and white—one could produce the entire range colors, although the degree of precision needed makes this nost impossible. By using the three primaries, however, the elve colors of the complete wheel can be derived.

Equal amounts of any two of the primary colors result in *econdary color* (Figure 3.5). The wheel has three such col-: green, which is produced by mixing yellow and blue; vi-t, by mixing blue and red; and orange, by mixing red and low. The secondary color lies midway between the pri-ry colors from which it is formed.

In similar fashion, a *tertiary color* or intermediary color is ated by mixing equal amounts of a primary color and a ondary color (Figure 3.6). These hues are also situated dway between the two hues that produced them and are ntified by hyphenated names such as blue-green, red-nge, and red-violet.

ore info online @

p://www.sherwin-williams.com/DIY/interior/colorselect/confidence/c4.asp Sherwin Williams Color Wheel with terminology

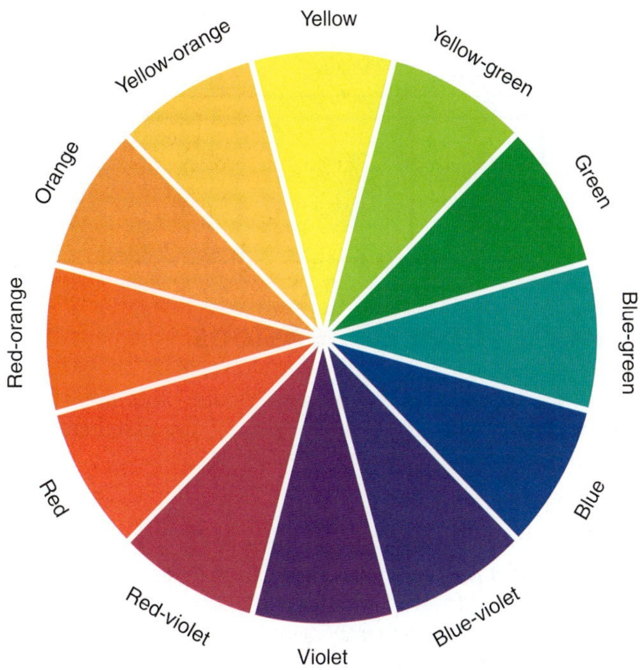

Figure 3.3 *The standard color wheel. It is often referred to as the Prang color wheel, but was originally developed by David Brewster for the Brewster color theory.*

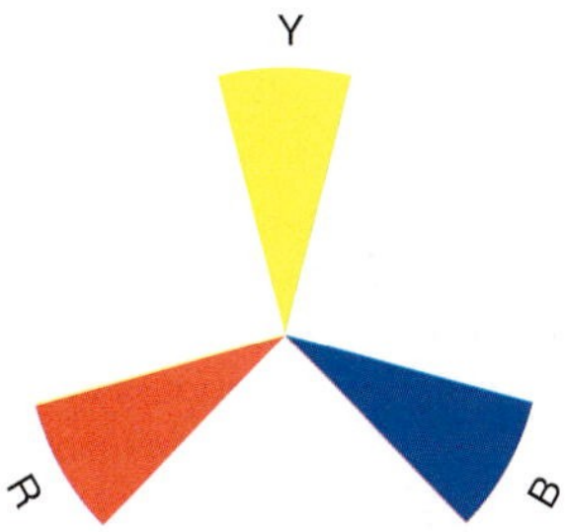

Figure 3.4 *Primary colors.*

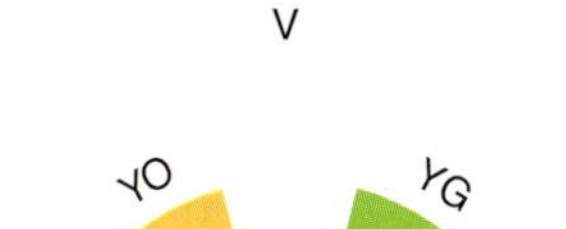

Figure 3.5 *Secondary colors.*

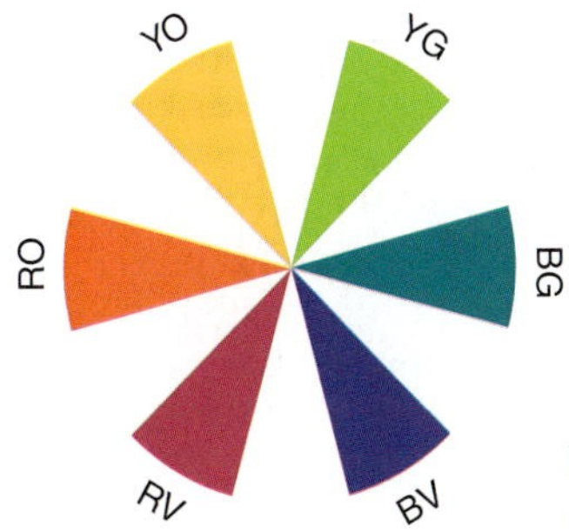

Figure 3.6 *Tertiary or intermediate colors.*

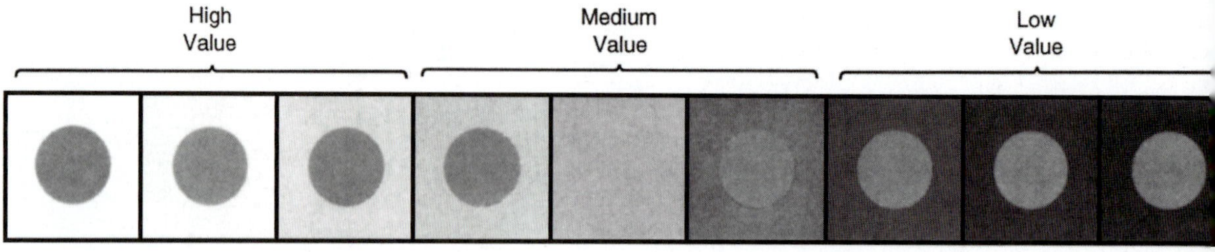

Figure 3.7 *In the nine gradations of value from white to black, the small circles are identical in shade, demonstrating that the eye perceives color not in itself but in relation to its environment.*

Color's Three Dimensions

The three dimensions of color (hue, value, and intensity or chroma) can be accurately measured and are essential in visualizing and describing any color.

Hue

Hue, or the color name, is a singular characteristic that sets each color apart from all the others. A color may be lightened or darkened, made more intense or less intense. If blue is the hue used, the result will be light blue, dark blue, bright blue, or gray-blue, but each will be of a blue hue. In all, about 150 variations of full chroma of hue exist, of which only 24 basic hues of full chroma have enough variation to be of practical use.

Value

Value is the degree of *luminosity,* or *lightness or darkness* of a hue in relation to black and white. Nine such gradations are easily visible to the eye (Figure 3.7). The value of any hue can be raised by adding white; this forms a **tint.** The value is lowered when black or another darkening agent is added; this is called a **shade.** For example, a tint of red is pink; a shade of red is burgundy.

In addition to shades and tints, a third classification is **tone.** A tone is formed by adding both black and white to the hue. These grayed hues are extremely useful in creating color schemes in which muted colors are necessary to tone down the brighter hues (Figure 3.8).

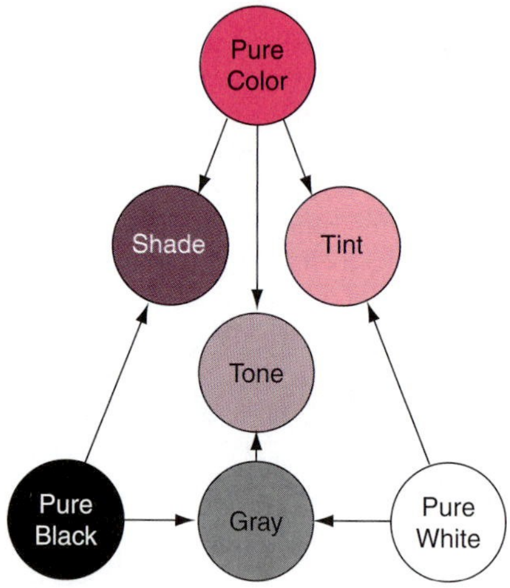

Figure 3.8 *Although black and white pigments are not considered true colors, their addition to colored pigments produces tints, shades, and tones. Adding black to a pigment color produces a shade; adding white produces a tint. Adding gray (a mixture of black and white pigments) to a color produces a tone.*

Intensity or Chroma

Intensity or **chroma** is the *degree of saturation* of pure color. It describes the brightness or dullness and strength or weakness of the pure color that a hue contains. Just as any color may be raised and lowered in value by the addition of white or black, its intensity may be strengthened by the addition of pure chroma or lessened by the addition of its complement (the color directly across from it on the standard color wheel). The more of the color's complement that is added, the less pure color the original hue contains. Two colors may have the same hue and the same value, yet may be markedly different because of the different color strength or intensity (Figure 3.9). Strong chroma visually enlarges objects.

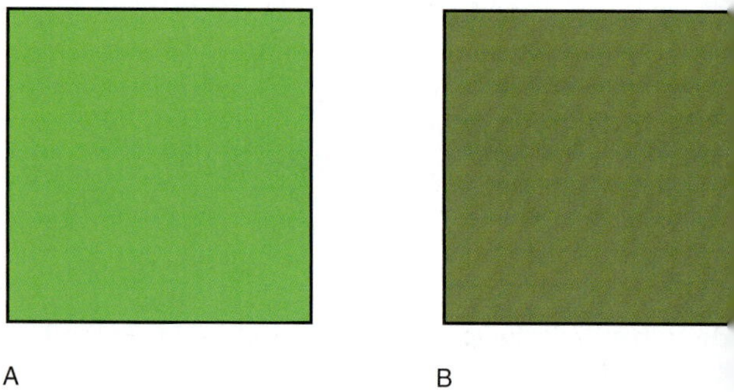

Figure 3.9 *In this example, the green on the left exhibits a high intensity, but when green's complementary color red is added, the intensity is lessened.*

The skillful application of color, value, and intensity can lay a vital role in creating exciting and livable interiors. ven when all the hues in a room work together, it may lack terest. Adding a contrasting value or intensity to the color armony can provide interest and variety.

olor Theorists and Color Theories

number of color theories, or color systems, have been deeloped and are used by interior designers. Some incorpote psychological as well as physical factors. Johannes Itten 889–1967) originated his ideas on color while a teacher at e Bauhaus in Germany during the 1920s. One of his theoes is the popular "Four Seasons—Personal Color Analysis" ased on color palettes associated with the four seasons of e year. Josef Albers (1888–1976) was a pioneer of modern esign and a teacher and color theorist at the Bauhaus in ermany and later at Yale University. He is particularly nown for his theories on color perception. Albers's series of aintings entitled *Homage to the Square* demonstrate how ne color reacts when placed next to another color. He ound that color changes greatly as a result of its environent.

A variety of color systems have been produced, each ased on a different group of basic colors. The three most ommon are:

The Brewster, Prang, or Palette system (which has already been discussed), based on the three primaries: yellow, red, and blue
The Ostwald system, based on four principal hues: yellow, red, blue, and green, plus black and white
The Munsell system, which begins with five hues: yellow, red, blue, green, and purple

The Ostwald System

The Ostwald system was named after its creator, German scientist Friedrich Wilhelm Ostwald (1853–1932). The Ostwald color wheel, which uses yellow, orange, red, purple, ultramarine blue, turquoise, sea green, and leaf green, is based on hue plus the white content and the black content of the hue. Theoretically, 24 hues can be derived from mixing these hues plus pure white and black. There are 28 variations of these 24 hues, resulting in a total of 672 hues and 8 neutrals. The cool group of hues is on one half of the circle and the warm group of hues on the other half of the circle. Ostwald arranged the hues in a conical configuration with a value and chroma scale similar to Munsell's system, discussed next (Figure 3.10).

The Munsell System

The Munsell system of color notation is essentially a scientific concept of describing and analyzing color in terms of three dimensions of hue, value, and chroma. The designation of each color is written as H v/c (Figure 3.11). Hue is indicated by the capital letter H, followed by a fraction in which the numerator represents the value and the denominator indicates the chroma. In the figure, hue is indicated by the circular band.

Value is indicated by the central axis, which shows nine visible steps from darkest value at the bottom to lightest value at the top, with 5/ for middle gray. Pure black would be designated as 0/ and pure white as 10/.

In the Munsell system, chroma, the Greek word for color, is used instead of intensity. The chroma notation is shown by the horizontal band extending outward from the value axis. It indicates the degree of departure of a given hue from a neutral gray of the same value.

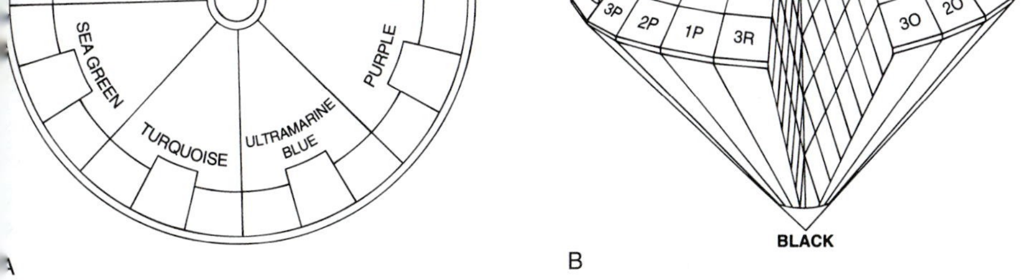

Figure 3.10 *The Ostwald color system. (A) The Ostwald color wheel is based on 24 hues that are either a pure hue or mixed with a pure hue plus white and black. The principal hues are yellow, orange, red, purple, ultramarine blue, turquoise, sea green, and leaf green. The other 16 hues are intermediate hues of these colors. (B) The hues and their ranges of value and chroma are arranged to form a three-dimensional double cone.*

Figure 3.11 *The Munsell color system, including hue, value, and chroma relationships. (A) The circular band represents the hues in their proper sequences. The upright, center axis is the scale of value. The paths pointing outward from the center show the steps of chroma increasing in strength, as indicated by the numerals. (B) Hue notations of the five principal and the five intermediate hue families are encircled. A breakdown into 100 hues is indicated by the outer circle of markings, and the breakdown of each hue family into four parts (2.5, 5, 7.5, and 10) indicates the 40 constant-hue charts appearing in the Munsell Book of Color. (C) Hue, value, and chroma are shown in relation to one another. The circular band represents the hues in their proper sequences. The upright center axis is the scale of value. The paths pointing outward from the center show the steps of chroma, increasing in strength as indicated by the numerals. (Courtesy of Munsell Color Company, Inc.)*

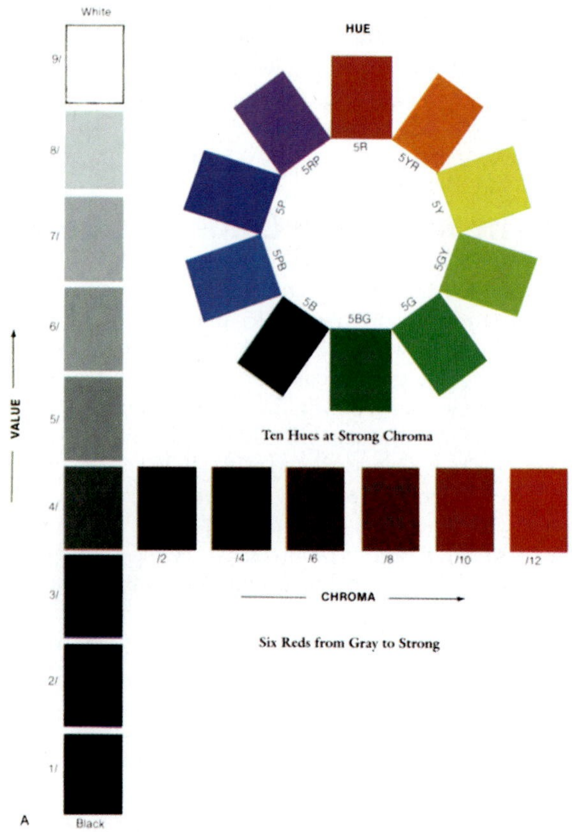

A

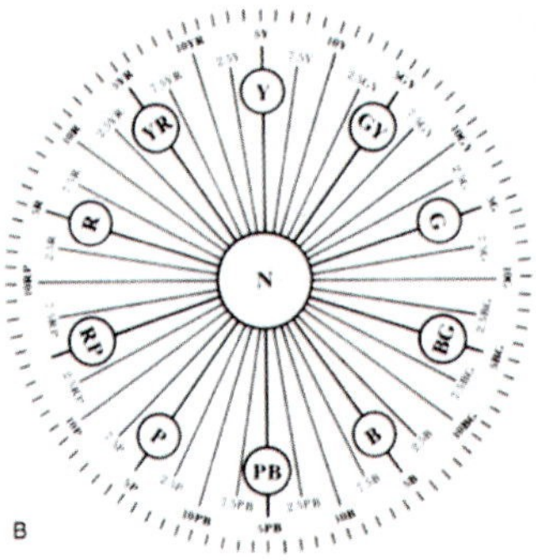

B

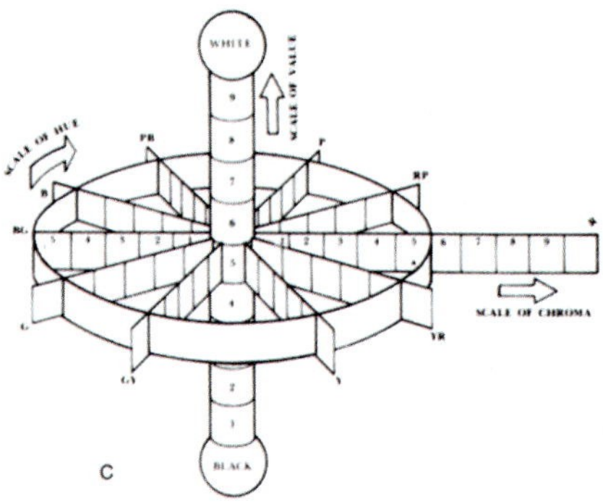

C

Related Color Systems

No one color system is universally accepted. Most industrial nations have their own systems of color classification and, regrettably, these systems are not interchangeable. Those working with color generally use the type of color system that best suits the needs of a particular project. In addition to the Brewster, Ostwald, and Munsell systems, other color systems are available to the designer. Two of the best known are the *Gerritsen color system,* based on color perception and six primary colors, and the *Kuppers color system,* based on six primary colors: blue, green, yellow, red, cyan (a blue-green), and magenta.

In addition, many major paint manufacturers have made available convenient color systems, color keys, and color codes that coordinate colors in particular ways with their products. The colors usually are coded according to cool, warm, and neutral harmonies.

Computer Applications

The computer is capable of performing many design-relate tasks including color analysis and color matching. Currentl a number of corporations offer designers and other clien color matching based on the latest computerized matchir technology. These systems contain thousands of color san ples for project specifications. Computerized colorant fo mulation systems can reproduce and record approximatel 16 million colors. Furthermore, they can accurately combin and reproduce these colors, showing such criteria as light r flection and textural effects, and can even deal wi **metamerism**—the tendency of samples that match und one light to appear mismatched under a different light. Prin outs can show how the specified colors will appear in a pa ticular setting—a valuable tool for the designer.

reating Color Schemes

nning and organizing color schemes can be a challenging d satisfying task. Endless color possibilities are available. lividual color preferences are naturally a consideration. rmonizing colors from the standard color wheel is a popr approach.

The basic color schemes are achromatic, monotone, monoromatic, analogous, and complementary. Color schemes y also emphasize international influences, as seen in the bui and feng shui color palettes. Although professional interiors seldom fit a specific scheme perfectly, most rooms can be classified into one of these categories.

Achromatic

An **achromatic** color scheme is created by utilizing black, white, or variations of gray. It contains no identifiable hue, only values (Figure 3.12). Accent colors in art or foliage may enhance these interiors, but do not affect the color scheme.

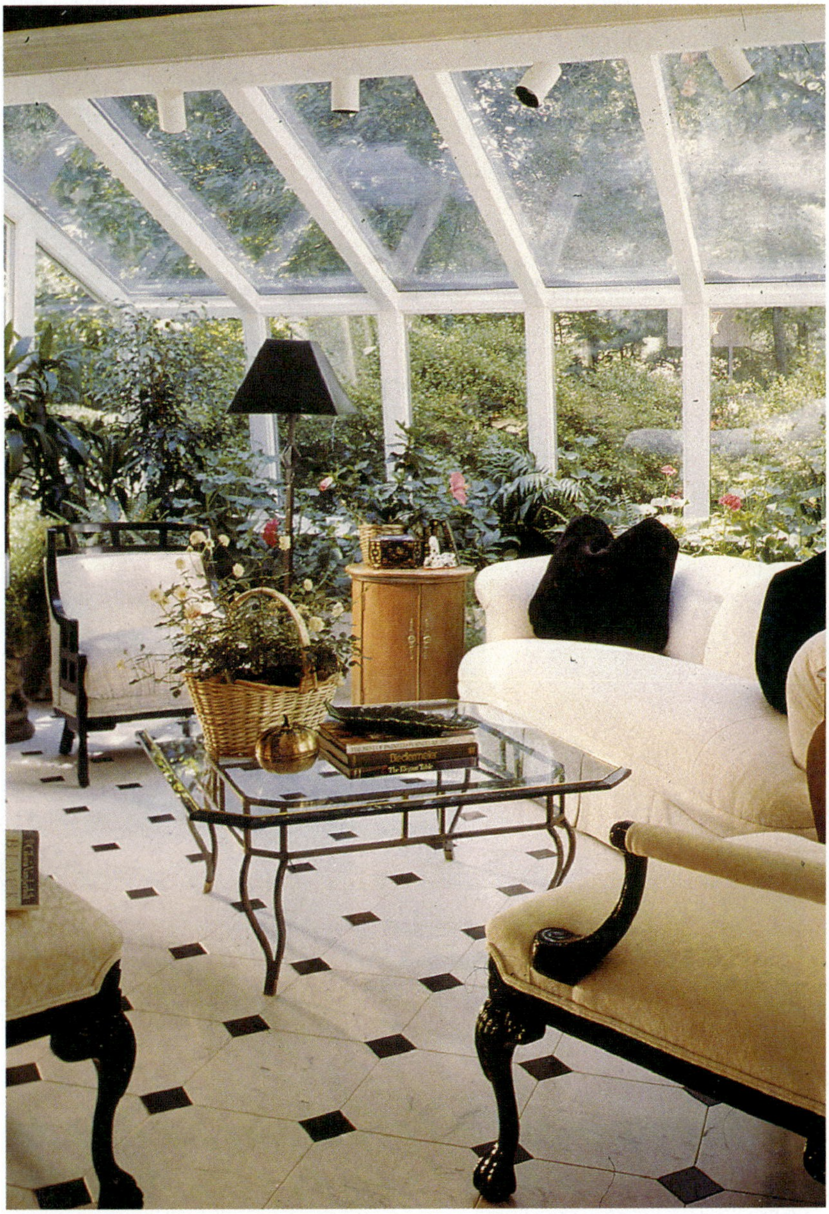

Figure 3.12 *The achromatic color scheme is an effective choice in this sunroom where brightly hued flowers change with the season. (Courtesy of Century Furniture Company.)*

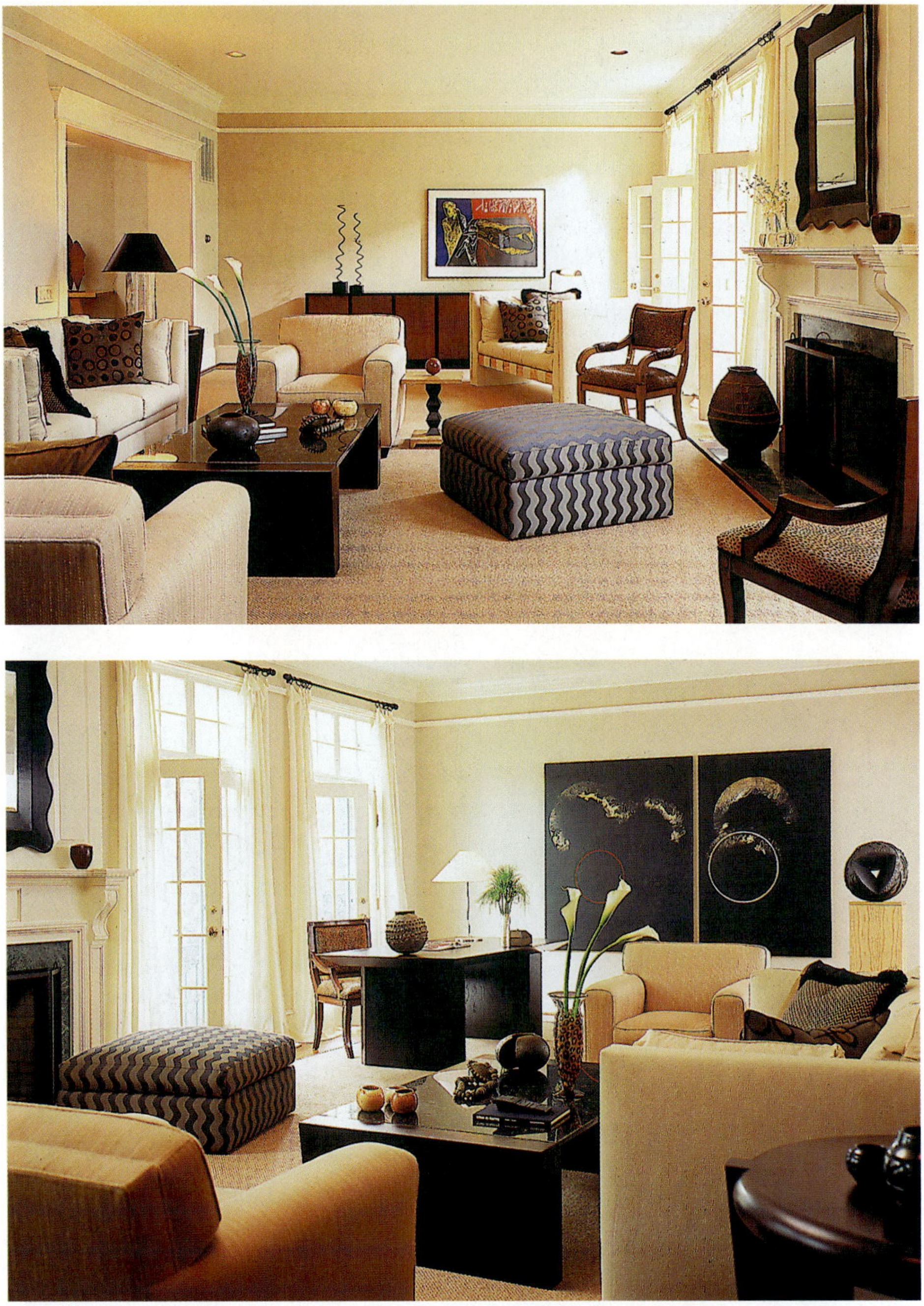

Figure 3.13 *Monotone colors have been applied in this sophisticated yet relaxed interior. A hint of yellow adds warmth to the contemporary living space. Strong art adds accent and interest. (Designer: David Mitchell. Photographs by Scott Frances. Courtesy of* Southern Accents.*)*

Monotone

Monotone color schemes are created from a color with low chroma. In other words, they contain some chroma as opposed to the achromatic or no-chroma scheme. Neutralized colors fall halfway between warm and cool colors and can be employed as tints, tones, or shades. The most typical neutralized or monotone colors include off-white (white with small amount of any hue), off-black (a rich brown-black beige, cream, tan, and brown (Figure 3.13). Accents stronger chroma may be used for smaller furnishings and a cessories without changing the neutral scheme and can ac visual interest.

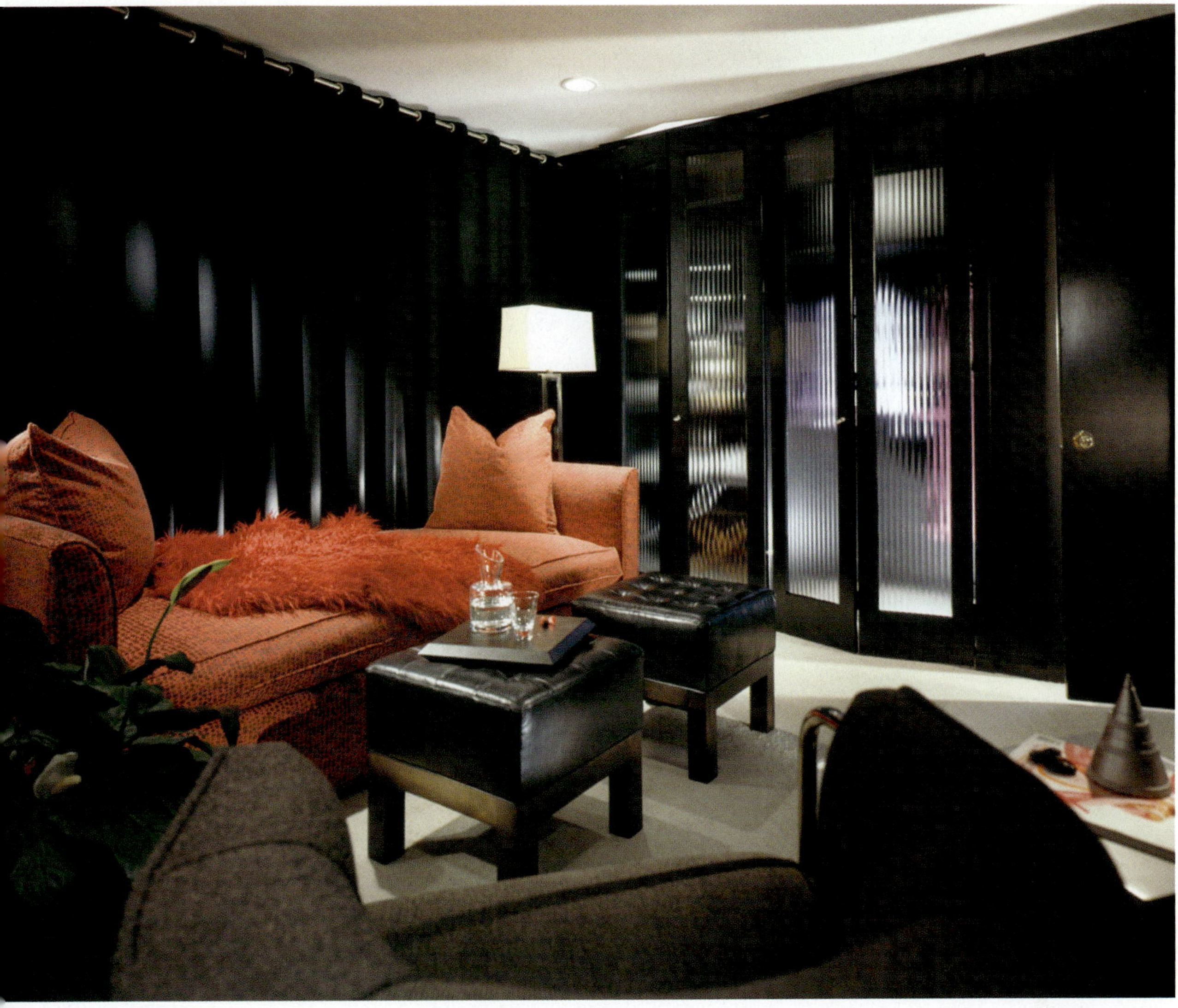

gure 3.14 *In this dramatic monochromatic room, the interior designer was presented with a plain vanilla interior ıd awkwardly placed clerestory windows. Floor-to-ceiling draperies provide window camouflage and the red fabric rves as the stimulus. A variety of textures adds to the room's ambience. (Designer: Jackie Naylor Interiors. Photograph Robert Thien.)*

lonochromatic

onochromatic color schemes are developed from a *ıgle hue,* but with a range of values and different deees of intensity. Unity is probably the most notable elıent in this type of scheme, and if light values edominate, space will appear to be expanded. A danr in the one-color scheme may be monotony; however, oking to nature, where monotony is never present, the idelines are clearly apparent. When examining the petals a rose, one may see shadings from soft, delicate pink to deep red. The variety of tones, tints, and chroma of the green leaf can be combined in a room using the subtle neutralized tones for large wall areas, slightly deeper tones for the carpet, medium tones for large furniture, and vivid chroma for accents.

Monochromatic schemes are often further enhanced by the use of textures such as fabric, wood, stone, metal, and glass (Figure 3.14). Pattern can also add variety and character to the one-color scheme. Black and white can be used without changing the character and, in fact, may sharpen the scheme and add interest.

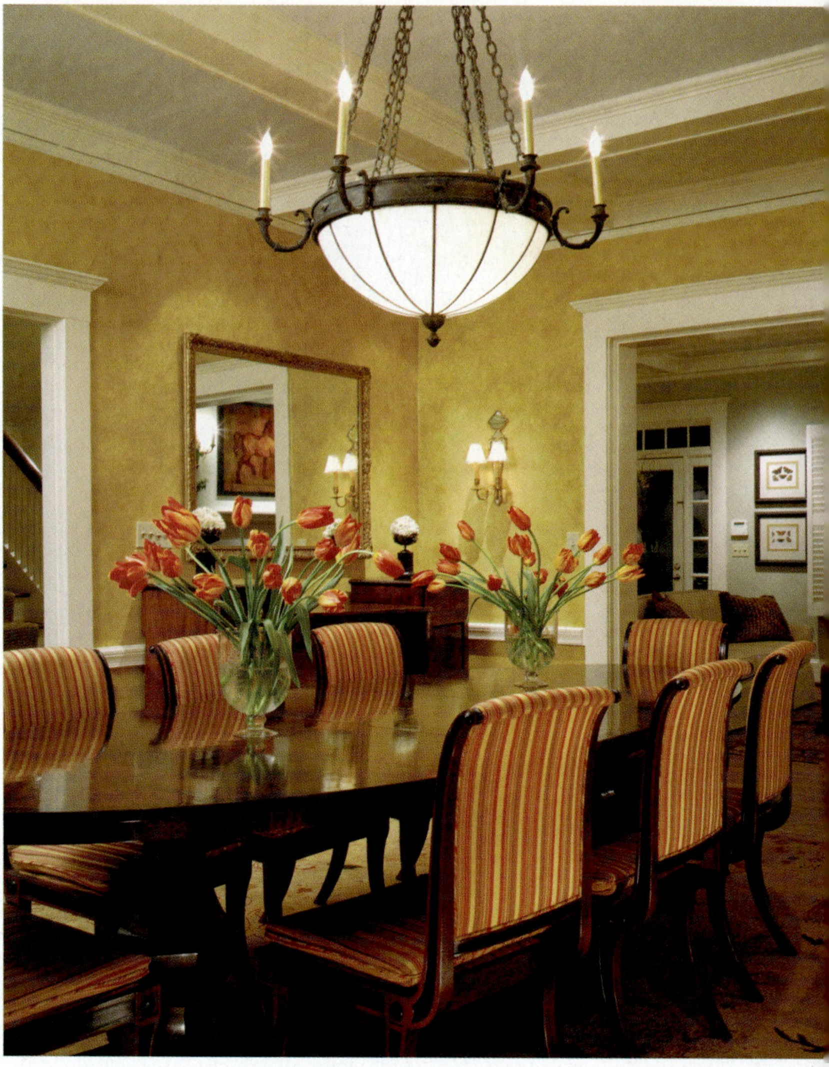

Figure 3.15 *This warm and inviting room is the result of conscientious design decisions. The table, for instance, is a custom height to fit the client's stature. Faux-finished walls add depth and texture. Antique and conventional lighting are combined to enhance the analogous color scheme. (Designer: Tory Winn, IIDA, RID, Agora Studio, Inc. Photograph by Brian Gassel.)*

Analogous

Analogous color schemes are produced from any segment of colors that are side by side but contain no more than half the colors on the standard color wheel, as seen in Figure 3.15. Harmony is easily established with analogous colors because generally one dominant color should be present. Yellow, for example, is the common factor in orange and green, and by using the intermediate colors of yellow-orange and yellow-green, an interior designer can achieve a close relationship with a great variety of values and intensities.

Complementary

Complementary or contrasting color schemes are also widely used because they offer variety. Values and intensities may vary depending on the use and the amount of area to be covered. All contrasting hues placed side by side enhance each other, and if they are of similar intensity, each makes the other seem more intense. Complementary schemes always contain warm and cool colo because they are opposite on the color wheel. In stro chroma they are lively and vigorous; in grayed tones th may be subtle and restful. One dominant hue usually se the mood.

Six types of complementary schemes are direct co plement, split complement, triad, double compleme alternate complement, and tetrad, as illustrated in Figu 3.16. The most commonly used ones are defined below

Direct Complement

The *direct complement,* the simplest of the contrasti color schemes, is formed by using any two colors that directly opposite each other on the color wheel. One of t hues should dominate. Used in equal amounts and strong intensity, complementary colors clash, thus creati an unpleasant element in a room. The secondary col therefore, works best when neutralized or used in small eas (Figure 3.17).

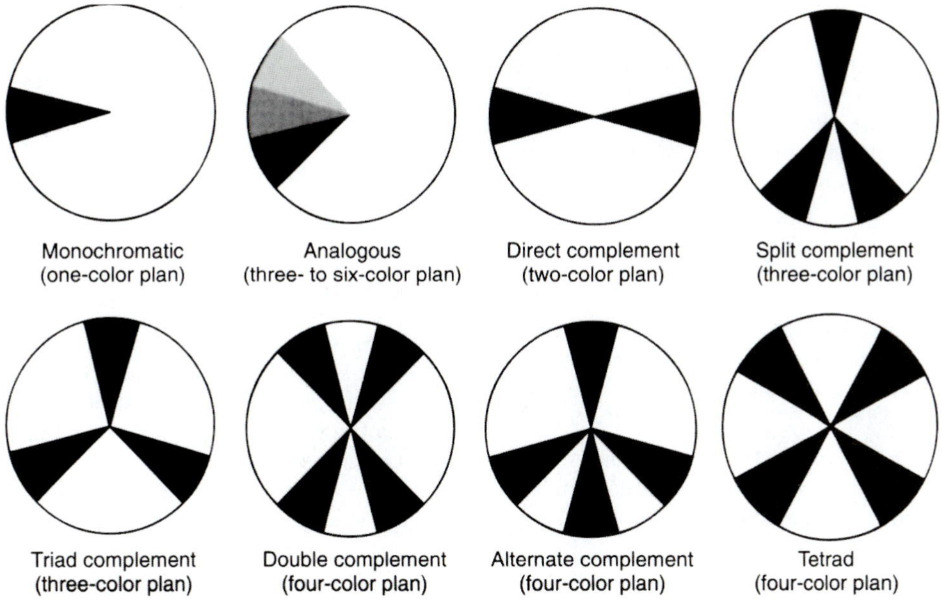

Figure 3.16 *Basic color schemes derived from the color wheel.*

lit Complement

: *split complement* is a three-color scheme composed of · hue plus the two hues next to its complement. For ex- ple, if yellow is selected as the dominant color, red-violet l blue-violet are the complementary colors. These colors ntrast less than the direct complement, which is violet. Red , been added to one and blue to the other, giving softness he scheme and at the same time adding variety.

Triad Complement

The *triad complement* is another three-color contrasting scheme. The triad is made up of any three colors that are equidistant on the color wheel. These colors may be sharp in contrast, using strong chroma such as the three primaries—red, yellow, and blue, or red-orange, yellow-green, and blue-violet—or they may be neutralized, raised, or lowered in value to produce a tranquil scheme.

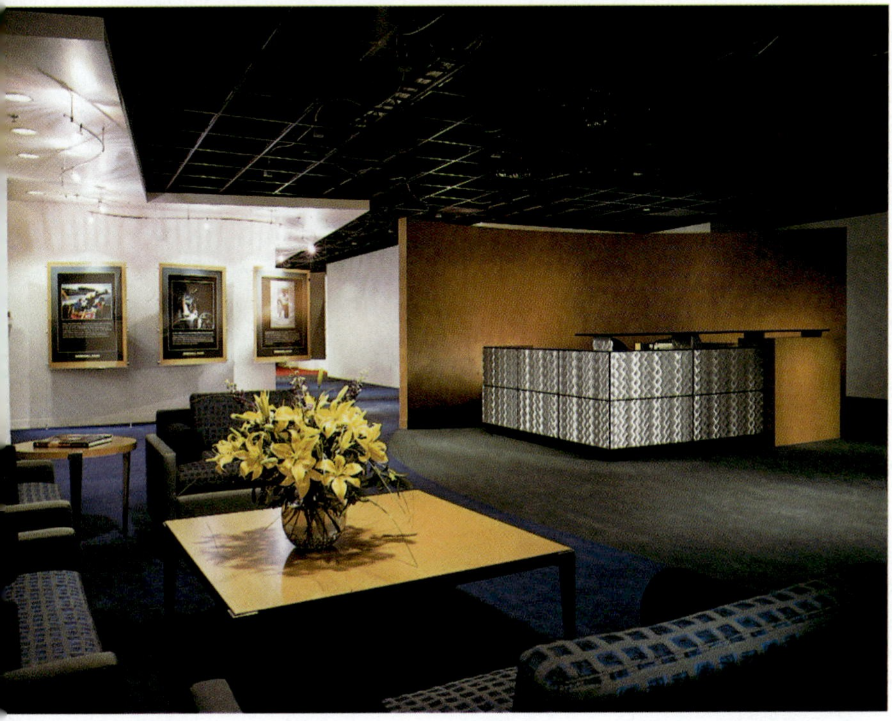

Figure 3.17 *The reception area for Ingersoll-Rand's Tool and Hoist Division utilizes a direct complement color scheme. The blue carpet helps to designate the waiting area, while the lower intensity orange walls demarcate the reception desk. A dropped ceiling and suspended track lighting system highlight the company's products. (Designer: Grad Associates, P.A., Architects & Interior Designers. Photograph © Peter Paige.)*

Shibui

Shibui (pronounced shih BOO ee) or shibusa expresses in one word the Japanese approach to beauty as well as the intrinsic nature of Japanese culture. No single word in the English language precisely describes shibui. It suggests an appreciation of *serenity* and a protest against ostentation. Belief in the power of the *understated and unobtrusive* dominates this sophisticated philosophy.

To produce a shibui effect, colors are brought together to enhance each other in a harmonious whole that will be deeply satisfying to live with for a long time. Schemes must have depth and complexity, or they will soon become tiresome. The following ideas are incorporated in achieving a shibui effect (Figure 3.18):

- The shibui concept of color is based on nature. Colors found in the largest areas are quiet and undemanding (neutralized). Bright, vibrant colors are found in a small proportion.
- Nature has thousands of colors, but none of them match or are uniform. In nature the darker, more solid colors occur underfoot. As one looks upward, colors become lighter and more delicate.
- Most of the natural landscape shows a matte finish with little shininess or glitter, such as the sun sparkling on a ripple in a stream.
- Pattern and texture in nature are everywhere, but they have to be discovered through close examination.
- No two patterns are identical, yet unity prevails. Although natural colors, textures, and patterns appear si ple, on close scrutiny they prove highly complex.

American architect Frank Lloyd Wright greatly admi the shibui design philosophy and incorporated its conce into many of his works.

Feng Shui

The feng shui (pronounced fung shway) color scheme based on several ancient Chinese philosophies and practic One such system, the compass mythology, is rooted in Pa Kua (pa gwa), an eight-sided symbol that corresponds the four compass directions and their subdirections.

Feng shui color schemes are interpreted differently each individual based on the birth year, which also relates the person's basic elements of earth, water, wood, fire, a metal. For instance, green represents wood; therefore, sor one born in the year of wood might use green as a cc scheme. The person would avoid red, which is associa with fire, because fire destroys wood.

In a feng shui color scheme, white is highly valued cause it is associated with light. Black is used selectively. cause it represents water and money, black is valuable, it is also the opposite of light and therefore should be plied carefully.

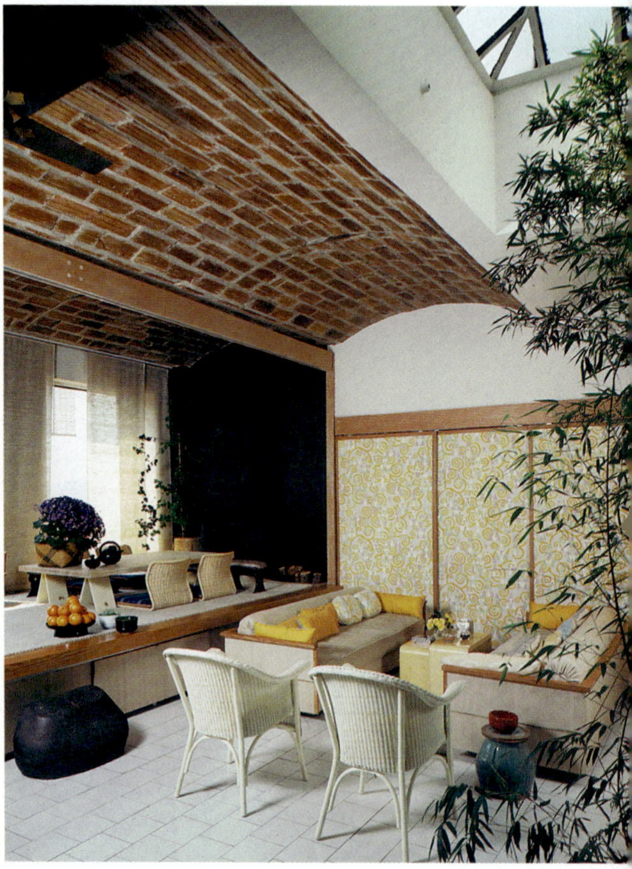

Figure 3.18 *The shibui concept of color scheming is translated into an American interior by Jack Lenor Larsen, with an emphasis on texture and simple colors. Foliage provides a connect to nature. The effect is subtle and unpretentious. (Photograph © Norman McGrath.)*

Another overlying principle of feng shui is the appropri- balance of the yin and the yang, which represent a bal- :e of complements or dualisms. Successful feng shui color iemes create a harmony of these balances.

ychological and Physiological ects of Individual Colors

lor creates powerful psychological and physiological (or ysical) effects. Psychological effects are sensed in the nd; physiological effects actually cause a change in the dy. It is important to note that people may react differently the same color, based on their previous experiences or rned behavior. Research studies have shown that:

- Color affects an individual's moods or feelings in regard to space. Light and cool colors seem to expand space; dark and warm colors seem to enclose space.
- Color affects the eye's perception of weight and size. Dark and bright colors seem heavier than light and cool colors. However, it is interesting that the opposite effect is true in fashion design. Dark colors tend to slim the figure, whereas light colors are usually thought to make one look heavier.
- Color affects a person's perception of temperature. Studies have indicated that body temperature actually fluctuates in response to various colors. For example, red, orange, and yellow can raise one's temperature; cool colors have the opposite reaction.
- Color can cause feelings of boredom and calmness, or stimulation and liveliness. Colors may cause the nervous system to become agitated, and the body reacts in negative ways to this stimulus.
- Colors can affect one's reaction to sounds, taste, odors, and time perception.
- Colors can improve the rate of recovery of sick patients.

elings and Reactions to Color

otional reactions associated with color are spontaneous. : reaction, often due to the perception of a color rather n to the color itself, may be positive or negative. The fol- ving section discusses typical feelings and reactions that y be created by colors; however, remember that clients y react differently to the same color.

d (Warm Group—Primary Color)

chological and physiological associations Courage, passion, :, excitement, danger, martyrdom, anger, fire, strength.

lication Red is conspicuous wherever it appears, and be- se it is lively and stimulating, it should be used with care. l mixes well and most rooms are enhanced by a touch of : of its tones. A variety of popular colors are derived from when it is lightened, darkened, brightened, or dulled. For mple, when red is darkened and muted it becomes ma- n, and when it is lightened it becomes pink. Pink, a del- e and flattering color, is often enhanced by a stronger contrasting color and blends especially well with grays, browns, greens, blues, and purples.

Yellow (Warm Group—Primary Color)

Psychological and physiological associations Cowardice, deceit, sunlight, optimism, warmth, enlightenment, and communication.

Application High-noon yellows are the most revealing and demanding and merit careful attention. Gray-yellows of early dawn are foils for more fragile colors—pinks, blues, and pale greens. Warm afternoon yellow is a foil for rich, warm woods. The burnished yellows of brass give a cast of copper gilt and bring life to a room. Gold provides an elegant and luxurious touch, especially for accents or accessories. All yellows are reflective, take on tones of other colors, and add flattering highlights.

Orange (Warm Group—Secondary Color)

Psychological and physiological associations Cheerfulness, stimulation, sunset, excitement. When lightened and muted, the peach tone may appear cool or refreshing.

Application Like red, orange has stimulating properties but is not as demanding. Peach tones enhance human skin tones. Peach also serves as a cross between a warm and cool color, partly due to the association with the fruit.

Blue (Cool Group—Primary Color)

Psychological and physiological associations Honesty, truth, loyalty, masculinity, formality, repose, tranquility, sobriety, sky, depth of sea.

Application Blue is cool and soothing, recalling sky, water, and ice. It is difficult to mix and varies greatly under different lighting. More than any other color, blue is affected by the different materials it colors. Lacquer and glass, for example, have a reflective quality that intensifies blue. In deep-pile carpet, blue has great depth. Nubby fabrics soften blue. Shiny materials make blue look frosted. Light blue can give a ceiling a cool and celestial appearance. Blue can be somber, cold, and even depressing if not used effectively.

Green (Cool Group—Secondary Color)

Psychological and physiological associations Nature, serenity, hope, envy, safety, peace, passivity, security.

Application Fresh and friendly, green is nature's color and is a good mixer, especially yellow-green and spruce or forest green. White brings out green's best qualities. When grayed, warmed, or cooled, green makes an excellent background. When lightened, it is retiring and restful. Green is particularly pleasing in food areas. Deep, dark green is a favorite color for floor coverings.

Violet (Cool Group–Secondary Color)

Psychological and physiological associations Royalty, nobility, snobbery, power, drama, opulence, mystery, worship, dignity.

Application Naturally a dark value, violet is a blend of blue and red. When pink is added, it becomes warm, and a touch of blue makes it cool. It combines well with both pink and blue. A light value of violet produces lavender. Other violet hues are plum, eggplant, and lilac. Often violet is used in small amounts as accents. It can be dramatic or even disturbing when used on large surfaces.

White (Neutral Color–Achromatic) and Off-White (Neutralized Color)

Psychological and physiological associations Purity, cleanliness, sterility, sophistication, freshness.

Application White and off-white have the quality of making all colors in a room look cleaner and livelier. Warm off-white is considered unequaled as a mellow background color and works wonders in blending furniture of different woods and styles. Changes of light from day to night are kind to off-white and give it quiet vitality. White and off-white can give a mood of sterility and emptiness if used alone.

Black (Neutral Color–Achromatic) and Off-Black (Black-Brown–Neutralized Color)

Psychological and physiological associations Mourning, sorrow, depression, sophistication, mystery, magic, night.

Application Black and off-black (a rich black-brown) in furniture finishes, small areas of fabric, or accessories add an important accent that makes other colors crisp and clear. When used for larger areas, black can be extremely dramatic but can also be oppressive and claustrophobic.

Gray (Neutral Color–Achromatic)

Psychological and physiological associations Penance, gloom, storm, fog, depression, wisdom, intelligence, business, high-tech, sophistication.

Application Gray is used when a neutral appearance is desired. It may be tiring or monotonous without colorful accents for other furnishings. Gray is a good mixer with other colors, especially pinks, purples, and blues. Dark gray on large areas may be depressing. Light gray provides a pleasant background color.

Brown (Neutralized Color)

Psychological and physiological associations Earth, wood, warmth, comfort, security, support, stability.

Application The homeyness of brown tones makes th universal favorites, especially for furnishings made of wo Ranging from pale cream beige to deeper chocolate brow these tones, tints, and shades can be used together in a ro to give infinite variety. Light browns, such as beige, make cellent supportive backgrounds.

Knowledge of the psychological and physiological eff of color is immensely valuable to the designer when pl ning both residential and nonresidential spaces. For exa ple, responding to the generally accepted notion that red excite one to action and blue will calm one's nerves, so athletic directors have painted their players' dressing roo in bright reds and oranges and visitors' dressing rooms pale blues. The directors claim that it works.

In another example, a *Los Angeles Times* article by Jo Dreyfuss reported that a meat market in Chicago lost b ness when the walls were painted a bright, cheerful yell A color consultant quickly informed the owner that the low walls caused a blue afterimage. It gave meat a purp cast, making it appear old and spoiled. The walls were painted bluish green, creating a red afterimage that hanced the appearance of meat, and sales zoomed.

Some color studies have found that:

- Workers function more efficiently in surroundings painted pleasant colors than they do in drab environments.
- Young people in detention homes responded more p tively when dull-colored walls were repainted in a bright color.
- Most people prefer to eat from a white dinner plate rather than a colored one.
- Doctors' offices painted in soft, calming colors, as opposed to stark white, make patients feel more comfortable.
- Fast-food restaurants tend to use bright warm colors f interior surfaces in order to stimulate the appetite and hurry patrons through their meals.
- Warm color tones are best in hospitals and nursing homes; cool, calming colors are more appropriate in i tensive care facilities.
- After factory workers complained how heavy their bl boxes were to carry, a color expert painted the boxes light blue. The workers then congratulated managem on making the boxes lighter.

The knowledge on which popular assumptions ab color are based is often superficial. But color and emot are closely related, people react differently to color, and dividuals have definite color preferences. Authorities do agree on the emotional effects of color, nor do they kn whether emotional reactions to colors are inherent learned.

Multiculturalism and Color

Color, like music, is an international language. Through the world, many objects are identified by their color ɔwever, colors may have different meanings. Green is uni- rsally accepted as sign of nature, freshness, or ecology. ·een Day in Japan is celebrated for the Emperor Hirohito ·cause he loved gardens. To Muslims green is a sacred lor, and to the Celtics green was associated with fertility.

According to *The Indian Tipi* by Reginald and Gladys ubin, to Native Americans, white used during one cere- ɔny may symbolize the north, yet in the next ceremony the ·rth may be represented by blue; the significance of color iginates in the visions of the individual.

In Western culture, white is associated with purity and ety; however, in many Asian cultures, white is the color of ɔurning. This is true in China, but white is also symbolic of ·ht and therefore very auspicious in that country. Red sym- ›lizes happiness and is used at weddings.

In ancient China, yellow had religious significance. In an- ·ent Greece and Rome, red was believed to have protective ·wers. Purple was the imperial color of the ancients and ıs restricted for the use of the nobility—hence the term ›yal purple." When the remains of Charlemagne (742–814) ·re disinterred in the middle of the twelfth century, the cof- · was found to contain robes of sumptuous purple velvet.

African cultures place much significance on color and ›w it is used in patterns. The palette is derived from the ·sert surroundings, such as savanna green, ivory, maze, and ight yellows. According to Rodemann in *Patterns in Inte- ›r Environments,* these colors represent strength and inde- ·ndence to the Africans.

Designers working with clients from different cultures ·ed to be sensitive to cultural color associations. Careful ob- ·rvation, thorough research, and comprehensive program- ·ing will help prevent cultural color mistakes.

eflecting Personality

›lor is a valuable design tool for reflecting personality. Ob- ɔusly, the problem of selecting colors that reflect person- ty is compounded when a number of individuals are to use · same interior space. The opinions of all occupants should considered before final color decisions are made. Current ·nds may be taken into account but need not be the de- ·mining factor. Regardless of what colors are in fashion, the ·rsonal preferences of the occupants should always be the ɪin consideration.

eflecting the Mood of the Room

ɔre than any other element, color is capable of setting the neral mood of a room. Strong chroma tends to create a ·ling of informality; soft neutralized hues are generally re- ·rved for a more formal atmosphere. Because rooms are ·ckgrounds for people, color is generally most pleasing ıen not too demanding. The psychological effect of large ·as of intense color can be irritating, so it may be wise to ·ect colors in softly neutralized tones for large background ·as in rooms where the occupants spend considerable ıe. General color moods can be evoked for specific areas the home or office.

The *entrance hall* introduces the home, the same way a *reception area* introduces an office space or hotel lobby (Figure 3.19). The entrance area can effectively set the tone for the space.

Living areas, boardrooms, or *conference rooms* used for more formal purposes generally have neutralized color schemes that tend to produce an atmosphere of tranquility.

Dining areas are at their best when the color schemes are unobtrusive, permitting a variety of table decorations as well as a serene dining atmosphere. In theme restaurants, color schemes vary greatly.

Informal living areas such as *family* and *recreation rooms* are often treated with stimulating color schemes that create a cheerful and casual environment. *Kitchens* and *break rooms* are usually more desirable when large areas of color are light, fresh, and clean looking.

Bedrooms are private areas, and personal preference should be the determining factor in the choice of colors. As a general rule, the master bedroom should be completed in restful tones pleasing to the occupants. Children can be given the opportunity to select colors for their own rooms (Figure 3.20).

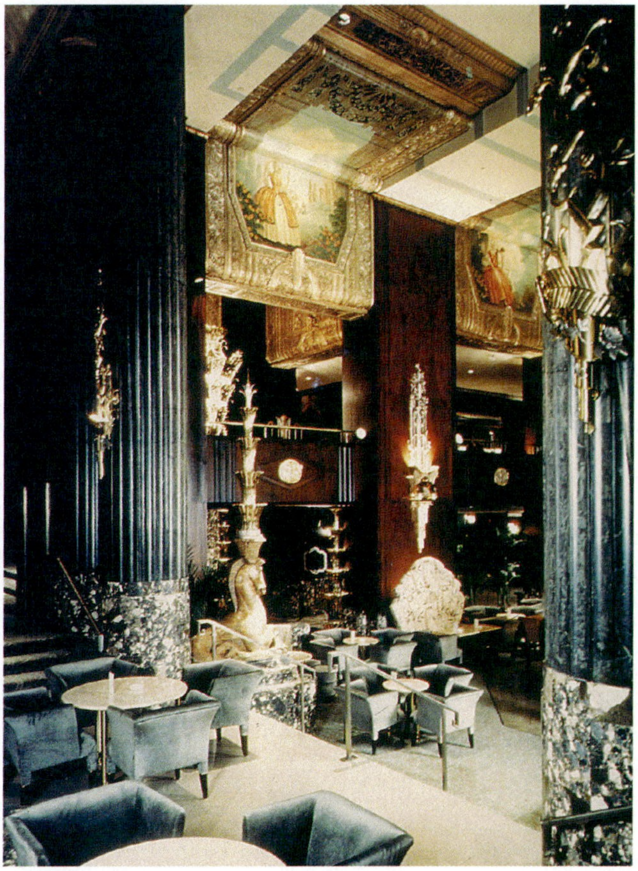

Figure 3.19 *The Palm Court establishes an art deco oppulent mood for the historic Omni Netherlands Plaza Hotel in Cincinnati. (Courtesy of White House Publishing Co., Cincinnati.)*

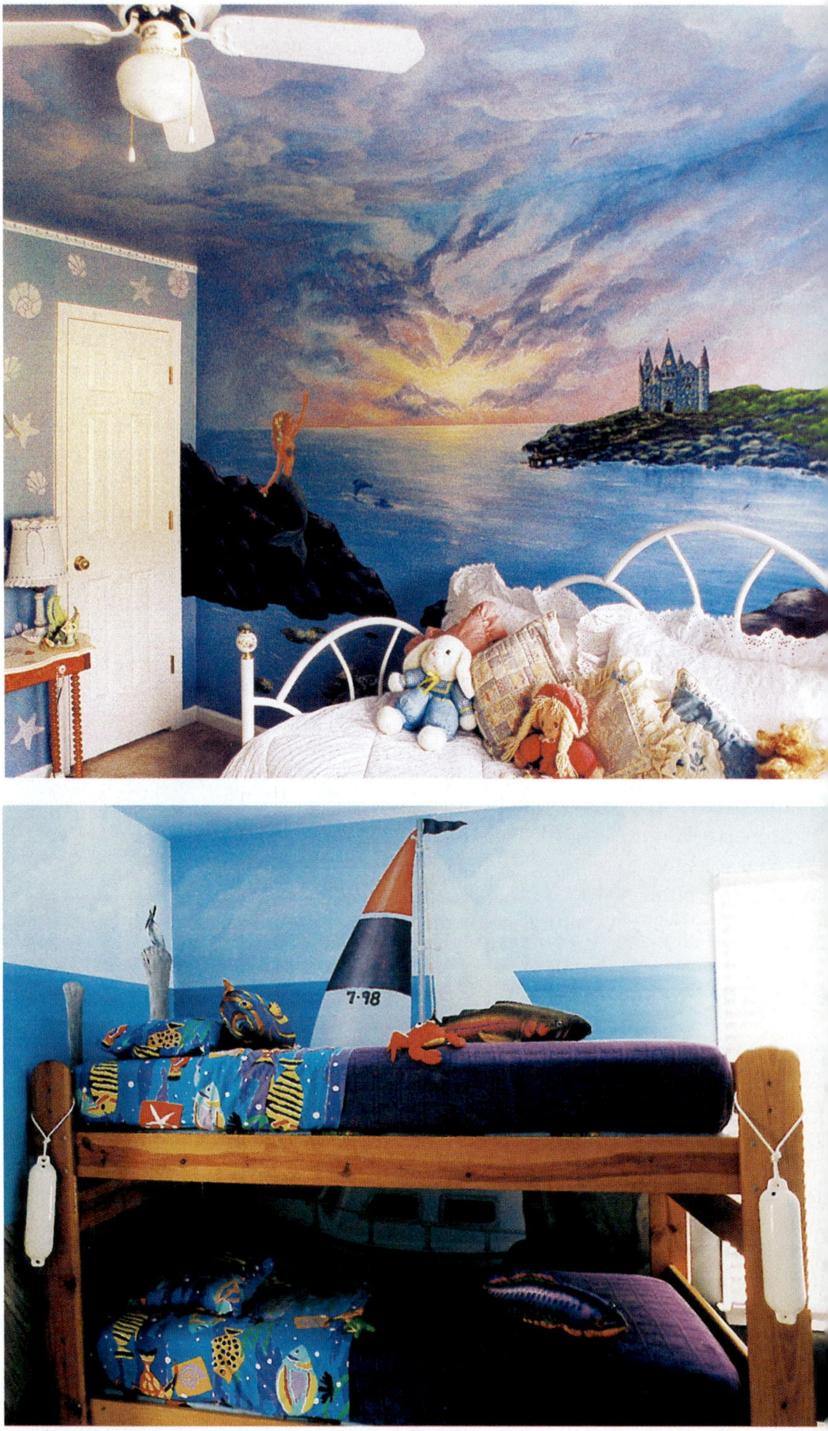

Figure 3.20 *In these children's rooms, a faux artist depicted scenes selected by the children. Furnishings remain neutral in order to grow with the child. Note the clever continuation of the mural onto the ceiling to increase the apparent room height. (Designer/Artist: Shannon Pable. Photographs by John Orth.)*

Private offices are like bedrooms, and personal preferences should be the deciding factor; however, bays or groups of offices should relate to one another. *Examination rooms* in doctors' offices should be comfortable. Colors should be warm and inviting.

Color schemes for *bathrooms* usually reflect the style and mood of adjoining rooms. Warm colors in muted tones enhance skin tones. Bathroom fixtures, sinks, toilets, bidets, and showers are difficult and costly to replace when trer in colors change, so select these fixtures in light neutra (Dark neutrals are difficult to maintain and require da cleaning.) Add the color in the walls, rugs, and other finish and decorative elements.

Color also interacts with the elements and principles design. The next section discusses the relationships betwe color and these design guidelines.

ıteractions Between Color and the ·lements and Principles of Design

·pace

›lors look different depending on space and distance. Near ·lors appear darker and more brilliant than the same colors a greater distance. Brighter and darker colors used in large oms therefore seem less demanding than the same colors ed in small rooms. Colors appear stronger in chroma when ›vering large areas. For example, a small color chip may be e exact color tone preferred for a room, but when that tone painted on four walls, it looks much darker and brighter ·cause the area of that color chip has been multiplied many ousands of times. When selecting a wall color from a small ›lor chip, it is best to choose a color several tints lighter an the color desired for the completed room. A good approach is to paint a sizable area of color on walls in oppo-e corners of the room and observe them at different times the day and night before completing the application.

·xture

›lor appears different when the texture is varied. Smooth rfaces reflect light. Fabrics with a deep, textured surface, ch as pile carpet, velvet, and all manner of nubby weaves, st tiny shadows. These materials appear darker than a ıooth fabric dyed with the same hue, in the same value and roma. A rough-textured wall may appear grayed or soiled ıder artificial light because of shadows cast from the un-en surface. A dull or matte surface absorbs color, and if it also dark, may absorb much of the light.

ze and Proportion

ı object that attracts the eye usually seems larger; therefore, rniture may appear larger if painted or upholstered with lors in strong chroma. A small room may seem even ıaller if demanding colors, which fill space, are used on ckgrounds and furniture. Light, cool colors expand a room d seem to create more space. Through the skillful appli-tion of color, a room's dimensions may be altered signifi-ntly and architectural features and furnishings can be ghlighted or minimized.

alance

·cause that which attracts the eye seems larger and there-re appears heavier, a small area of bright color balances a ge area of softly muted color, and a small area of dark lor balances a larger area of light color. For example, a ıall bouquet of bright flowers placed near one end of a ıg console table balances a large lamp of soft color placed ar the other end. A small bright blue chair balances a much ger gray-blue sofa. Entire areas of rooms may also be bal-ced through the use of color. A large end wall treated with ght or dark colors may be balanced on the other side of ː room with a dark, massive piece of furniture.

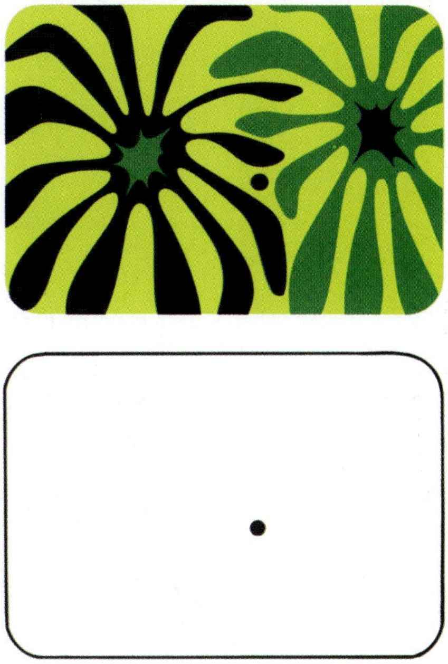

Figure 3.21 *Complementary afterimage. Stare at the black dot just below center in the image at top for 30 seconds, then look at the black dot in the white space below. Prolonged concentration on any color reduces eye sensitivity to it, and the reverse (complementary) color, remaining unaffected, dominates the afterimage for a brief period until balance is restored.*

The Juxtaposition of Colors

Color is not important in itself. What is important is what happens when different colors are brought together. The eye perceives color in relation to its environment. Physiologists have shown that people are not color blind to one color only but to two or four; the eye is sensitive to colors not singly but in pairs. The familiar afterimage effect demonstrates this perception. If a person looks at any one color for about 30 seconds, then looks at a white page, the complement of that color appears (Figure 3.21). Also, when the eye sees a colored object, it induces the color's complement in the environment. For example, when a green chair is placed against a light neutralized background, the eye sees a tinge of red in that background.

When two primary colors are placed side by side, they appear tinted with the omitted primary; for example, when placed near blue, red takes on a yellow tinge. When contrasting or complementary colors in strong chroma with the same value are used against each other, they clash, producing a vibration that is fatiguing (Figure 3.22). When contrasting colors with strong differences in value are used side by side or one against the other, the colors stand out but do not clash. For example, a painting with predominantly orange hues seems more orange if hung against a blue wall. Harmoniously blended colors of middle value used against each other tend to blend together, and at a distance the difference

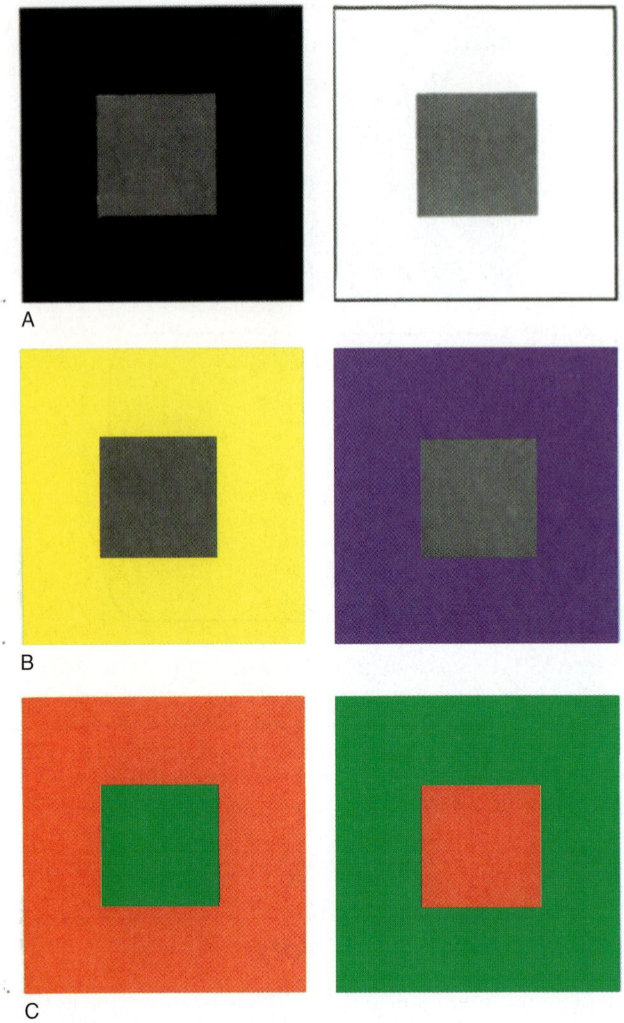

Figure 3.22 *These diagrams illustrate the effect of adjacent colors: (A) Gray looks much darker against white than it does against black; (B) A gray or neutral against a colored background appears to be tinted with the complement of the color; (C) When placed side by side, complements of equal intensity create visual conflict. Complements of varying intensities enhance each other. (Courtesy of Large Lamp Department, General Electric Company.)*

becomes almost indiscernible (Figure 3.23). The latter combination is the basis for most shibui color schemes.

Black and white have a strong visible effect on other colors when brought together. Black tends to make adjacent colors look richer. White reflects light into adjacent colors. Rooms that seem lifeless may be given sparkle and interest by the addition of black, white, or both.

The juxtaposition of colors affects not only hue but also value. The change of value may be seen when a gray circle is placed on a white background. As black is added to the background, which becomes progressively darker, the gray circle appears progressively lighter, showing that colors may be made to appear either lighter or darker according to the tonal value of the adjoining or background color. The use of sharp value contrast emphasizes an object. When black and white are placed side by side, the white looks whiter and the

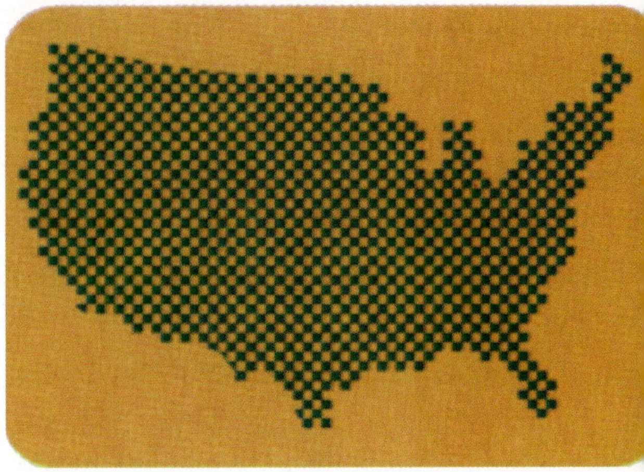

Figure 3.23 *Additive spatial fusion. The green dot pattern i the shape of the United States merges into solid gray when viewed from a distance of 6 to 8 ft. At that distance, the eye no longer distinguishes the individual colors. (Courtesy of Large Lamp Department, General Electric Company.)*

black looks blacker. For example, the fine lines of a da piece of furniture are accentuated if placed against a lig background. Colors closely blended conceal an object; cc trasting colors emphasize an object. A piece of furnitu seems unobtrusive if it is the same value as the backgrou (Figure 3.24).

Value may be applied in many ways when designing a furnishing a room. As an object is raised in value, its app ent size increases. A fabric colored in low value makes chair seem smaller than one in high value. Because light c ors recede and dark colors advance, one may, with skill, ter the apparent size and proportion of individual items or an entire room. In small rooms, light values expand wa and ceilings. In long narrow rooms, colors in darker val pull in end walls and make the room appear shorter.

The apparent size and proportion of a room or object m also be altered through the use of chroma. Color in stro chroma visually enlarges an object; walls in strong chron as with dark value, seem to advance and make a room a pear smaller.

Light

As previously discussed, without light, color does not ex Because light is so closely tied to color, a brief discussion light's interaction with color is in order. (Chapter 5 elabora on lighting.) A major consideration in planning the co scheme for a room is the study of the quantity and quality light and the method of lighting.

The level of illumination affects the appearance of col When the light is bright the color can be stimulating; lo light can produce a relaxing feeling. Color may become d lifeless, and dreary with insufficient light, however, and t much light can wash out a color. In general, as illuminati increases, color becomes more vibrant. A room with lo light levels is enhanced by light-reflecting colors. A roo

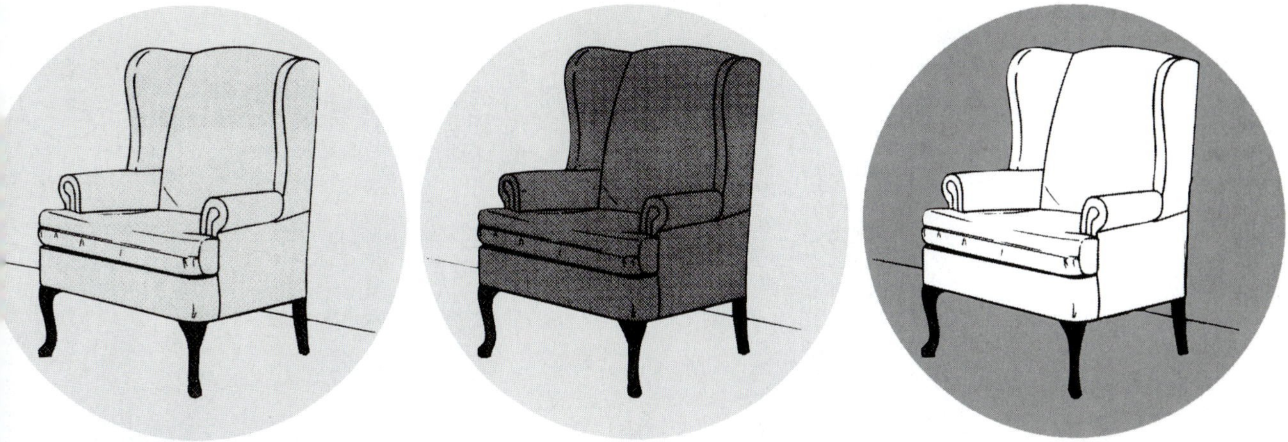

A chair in light value blends into a similar background.

A chair in dark value placed against a light background produces a contrast.

A chair in light value placed against a dark background creates a more pronounced contrast.

gure 3.24 *Value effects—three treatments.*

ith high light levels may be more pleasant with a predom-ance of darker light-absorbing colors.

One concern for the designer is how various qualities of tural and artificial light can change the visual perception a surface, the phenomenon known as metamerism. For ample, two fabrics that match in color during daylight may ot match under artificial light at night. All types of lighting atural lighting and artificial lighting such as incandescent, uorescent, halogen, etc.) produce unique effects. The qual- of natural light depends on the direction from which it omes and the time of day. The color of artificial light is de-rmined by the type of light and fixture used. Therefore, it important when selecting colors for backgrounds and fur-shings to view each surface under all types of lighting con-tions to ensure that the colors will match or be rmonious.

Review of the color wheel demonstrates that to gray or eutralize a color, some of its complement must be added; intensify a color, more of the basic hue must be added. ght produces the same effect. Warm light accentuates warm olors and neutralizes cool colors. Cool light intensifies cool olors and deadens warm colors. For example, a yellowish ght brings out the yellow in yellow-green and yellow-ange. A cool light brings out the blue in blue-green and ue-violet. Warm light is friendly and tends to unify objects. ool light expands space, produces a crisp atmosphere, and nds to make individual objects stand out.

Color is also affected by the method of lighting. Light rays at fall directly from the source onto a surface can create a arm glow over an area. An indirect light reflecting from a ove onto the ceiling produces an overall light resembling e light of midday.

When understood and used with skill, light may alter, sub-le, highlight, or dramatize the colors of a room in a way at no other decorative medium can. Because any situation s many variables, it is impractical to set down definite rules for the use of light and color. Therefore, before making a final choice, try each color in the environment in which it will be used and observe it during different hours of the day and after dark.

Application of Color to Interior Backgrounds

Applying color to a room's architectural backgrounds requires careful consideration. For instance, a common notion is that off-white in itself is a specific color and complements any decor. This concept needs refinement. Off-white is white tinted with a hue—any hue. To be compatible, however, off-whites must contain only the same or a similar hue as used in other areas of the room. Warm off-whites are more easily blended than cool off-whites, recalling a basic characteristic of warm and cool colors.

Ceilings

The ceiling is the largest unused area of a room, and its color is important to the general feeling. If the objective is to have the wall and ceiling look the same, the ceiling should be a tint of the wall, because the reflection from the walls and floor tends to make the ceiling look several shades darker than it actually is. If the walls are papered, the ceiling may be a tint of the background or the lightest color in the paper. Where walls are paneled in dark wood, the ceiling can be effective when painted white or a light tint of the wood color. If the wood trim is painted white, a white ceiling can work well. When the ceiling is too high, a darker shade or brighter hue makes it appear lower. For a low ceiling, the opposite treatment can help make it appear higher (Figure 3.25).

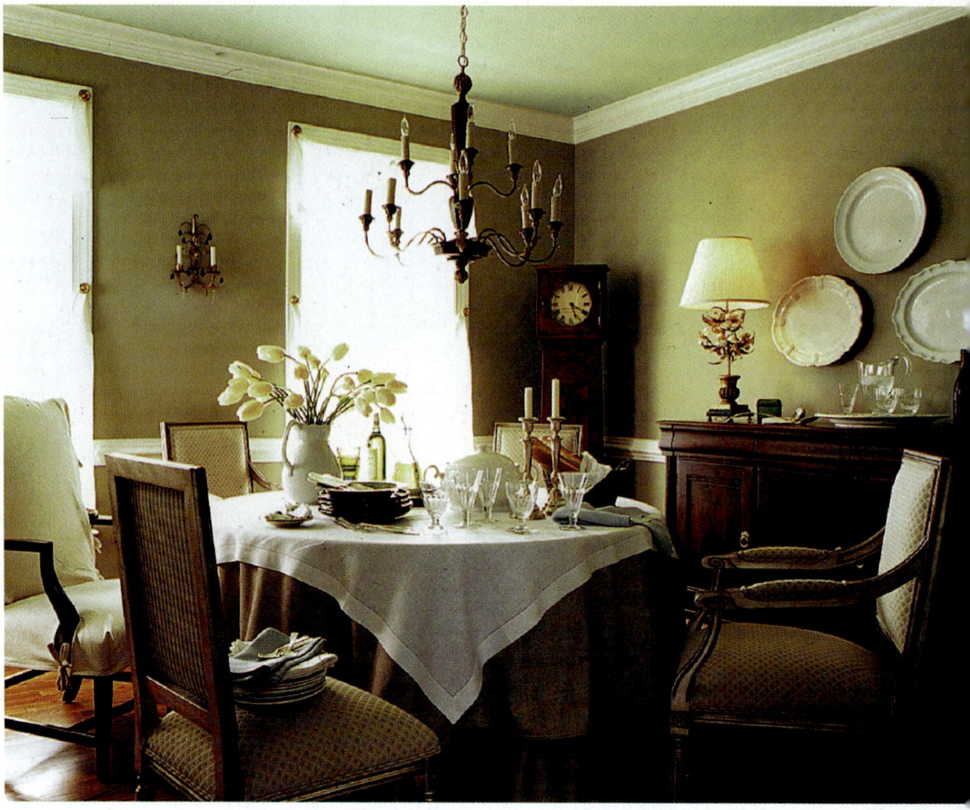

Figure 3.25 *In this dining room, the designer painted the ceiling a pale yellow-green (a tint of the wall color). The cool color helps make the ceiling recede. (Designer: Kimberly Latham Interior Design. Photograph by Dominique Vorillon. Courtesy of American Homestyle & Gardening.)*

Paneled Walls

In a room with dark wood paneling, colors of intense chroma can be used because deep wood tones tend to absorb color. If paneled wood walls are light and a blended effect is desired, colors may be light and less intense. More formal wood paneling calls for a more formal color scheme; if wood paneling is informal, colors should enhance that casual effect.

Window Treatments

The success of any room largely depends on the window treatment and the color used for draperies, curtains, blinds, screens, shades, shutters, or other window decor. If the objective is to have a completely blended background, the window treatment should be the same hue, value, and intensity as the wall. If a contrasting effect is desirable, a color that contrasts with the wall can be used, but it must relate well with other colors throughout the room. Remember to consider how the drapery lining or sheers will look from the outside. Sheers are usually more pleasing when white or off-white.

Wood Trim

The color of wood trim around doors, ceilings, floors, and other architectural features is important to the general color scheme of the room. When painted, trim may be: (1) the same hue, value, and intensity as the wall (which tends to cause molding to disappear into the wall); (2) a darker sha of the wall hue (which allows the molding to stand out); (3) a color that contrasts with the wall (which accentuates t molding). Many professional designers maintain the san wood trim color throughout the interior environment for effective color transition from room to room.

Color in Wood

Because wood has color and each type of wood has a pa ticular beauty, wood should not be overlooked when pla ning a color scheme. Heavily grained woods generally c for heavier textures and stronger colors than do fine-grain woods, as seen in Figure 3.26. Mixing woods can add inte est to a room, but it is wise to use woods in close proxim that are similar in feeling. For example, rough-grain golden oak and formal reddish-brown mahogany are n particularly good companions, but finely grained light-brov maple and brownish walnut usually combine well.

All of these items should be taken into consideratio when planning the colors for an interior environment. T next section should help the beginning designer start t process of choosing a color scheme.

The Selection of a Color Scheme

When deciding on a color scheme, designers must first co sider the needs and desires of the client. Many times clients s lect a specific color on which to base the interior environme

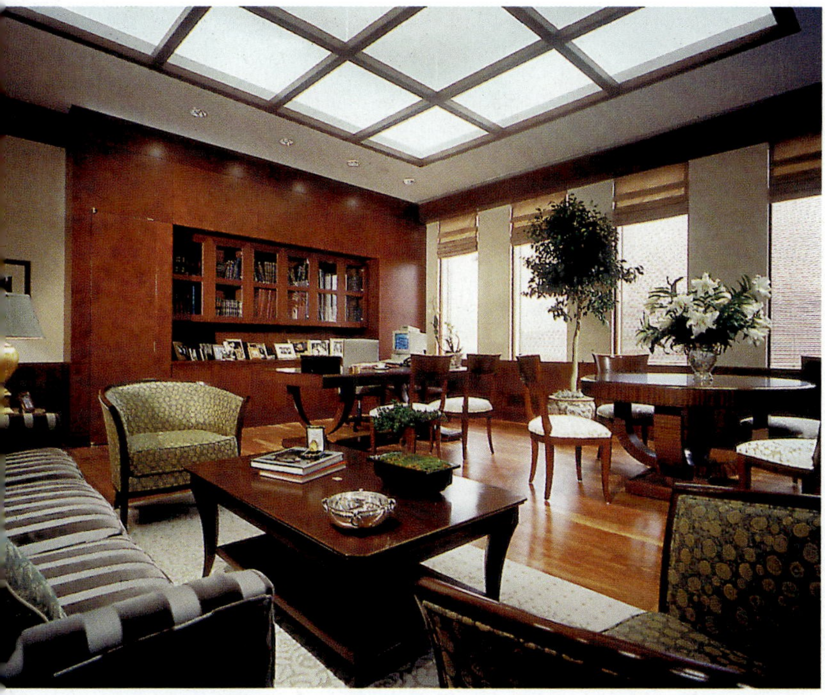

Figure 3.26 *Fine-grain woods, shown in this custom interior office space, blend with warm, refined fabrics creating an upscale interior. (Designer: Martha Burns. Photograph by Peter Paige.)*

her starting points for color schemes may include an attrac- e fabric or wallpaper, an area rug, or a prized painting or rk of art. Commercial office or hospitality environments y also begin color schemes based on a corporate logo or terned carpet. As discussed earlier, the color scheme may derived and should enhance the concept for the interior. matter where the designer begins, the color selections for room must also allow for the appropriate distribution of or and a transition from one room to another.

stribution of Color

lor is the most unifying element available to the interior signer, and its skillful distribution is essential to a feeling unity. Color distribution can be achieved in two major ys:

Planned value distribution is a necessary step. Each room can be enhanced with some light, some dark, and some medium values used in varying amounts according to the effect desired. In most cases the darkest values are used in the smallest amounts, and the less intense or more neutralized hues used in the large areas. The remaining areas are in medium values. This application of values is called the **law of chromatic distribution.** When applying the law of chromatic distribution to a room, backgrounds such as floors, walls, and ceilings will be in the most neutralized values, large pieces of furniture will have medium intensity, and accents such as small chairs and accessories will be in the strongest chroma.

Many successful rooms are planned around one dominant hue. This color need not be used on all major pieces of furniture, but it should be repeated at least once to give a feeling of unity. Unity may also be achieved by using colors containing one hue common to all. For example, hues on the color wheel going clockwise from red-orange to blue-green all contain yellow and combine well together. The color that is common to all—yellow—recedes and the other colors stand out.

Although the preceding guidelines describe the safest way to color scheme a room, deviating from them is possible and sometimes desirable (Figures 3.27 and 3.14). For example, dark walls can create a feeling of comfort, warmth, and security and unify the room's furnishings. A light floor visually expands space, and when adjacent to dark walls creates a dramatic effect. Under most conditions dark ceilings decrease the feeling of space and are oppressive. On the other hand, depending on the architecture, a ceiling may be painted in a dark value to give the illusion of viewing the infinity of the night sky. In commercial design, dark ceilings are frequently used in restaurants and retail establishments to conceal the network of **HVAC** (heating, ventilating, and air-conditioning), plumbing pipes, and electrical cables.

Color Transitions From One Room to Another

Whenever two rooms adjoin, their colors should relate. One or more colors carried from one room to the other—but not necessarily used in the same manner—will make a pleasing transition. For example, the accent color in the wallpaper of an entrance hall may be neutralized and used on the walls of the adjoining living room or may be emphasized in a piece of upholstery fabric.

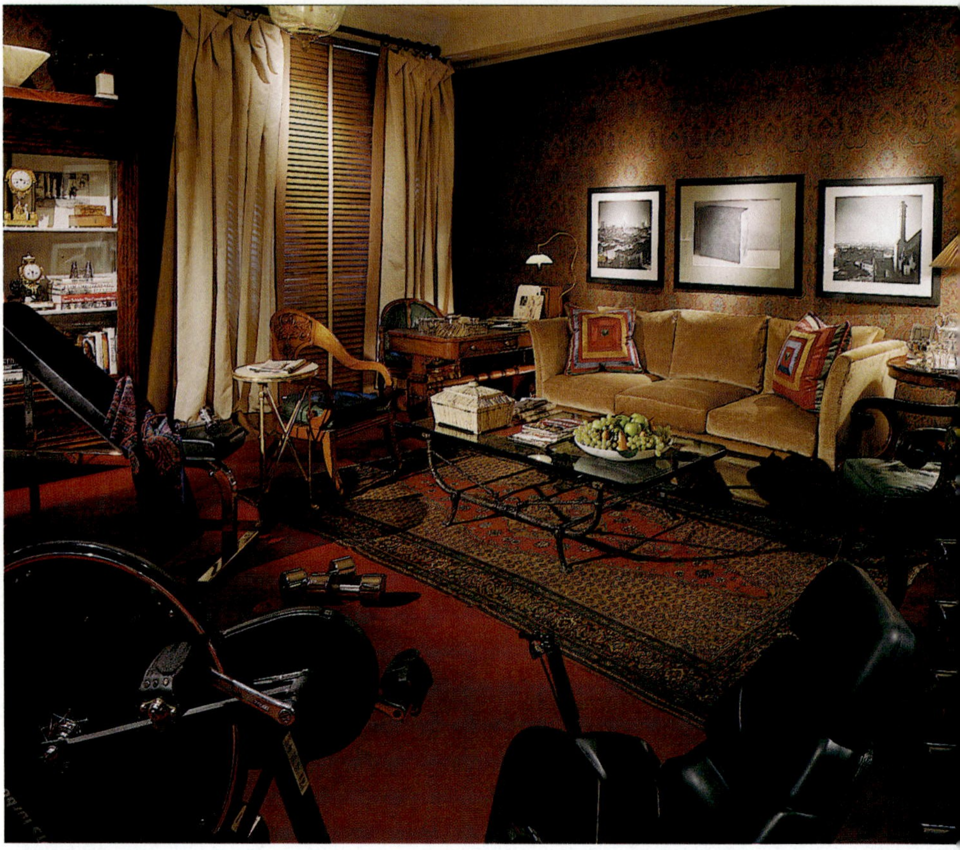

Figure 3.27
Predominantly dark and medium values have been used in this masculine retreat, establishing a cozy effect. Light values such as the pictures and coffee table accessories function as accents. The entire room is dramatized with pools of artificial light. (Antique sarouk faraghan courtesy of F.J. Hakimian, Inc. Design by Renny B. Saltzman, Inc. Photograph by Phillip Ennis.)

Where one room may be seen from another, as in conference rooms and reception areas, closely related colors establish color unity. Following are some of the most common and successful methods of achieving color transition.

- Many professional designers keep the floor covering consistent from room to room. For example, a gray carpet might be used for all rooms with the exception of hard floor surfaces for entries, conference rooms, or utility areas.
- Similar or matching wall and ceiling colors from room to room create a continuity of color transition.
- The consistent use of moldings and architectural trim throughout the home helps provide unity.
- Related colors employed on various pieces of furniture and for window treatments should be considered for effective color transition.
- Accessories carry colors from one interior space to another and aid in creating an effective flow of colors.

Developing the skills to bring a color scheme together while thoughtfully employing the law of chromatic distribution and considering the transitions required from room to room takes time and patience. The goal of all designers is to develop the skill to visualize the room before it is completed.

Visual Communication

Forming a mental picture of how colors appear when juxtaposed is not easy, and students and clients may need visual aids. Visual communication skills help the designer prep presentation boards, charts, and plans that help the client, well as the designer, visualize the completed space. Follc ing are three methods used for visual communication c color scheme. They are usually completed during the c ceptual design and design development phases discussed Chapter 1.

1. A chart using approximate proportions of various elements such as walls, floors, ceilings, furniture, and accents is developed. Fabric, paint, and hard material samples are attached to the chart. This method does n show exactly how the completed project will appear, but it is helpful.
2. A setup with actual samples of all items to be used, in approximate proportions, is assembled. This method more closely approximates the look of the completed room.
3. Many professional designers develop presentation boards that include rendered floor plans, elevations, a perspectives of the interior. The boards also include p tures of the furniture with samples of fabrics. Addition ally, finishes are shown for all walls, floors, and other surfaces (Figure 3.28).

Other color tools are also available to designers. Pa companies have interior and architectural sample kits, w paint samples that are 2″ × 5″ or larger. Pantone, a stand in commercial color identification, also produces color sa ple books that may assist designers in communicating col

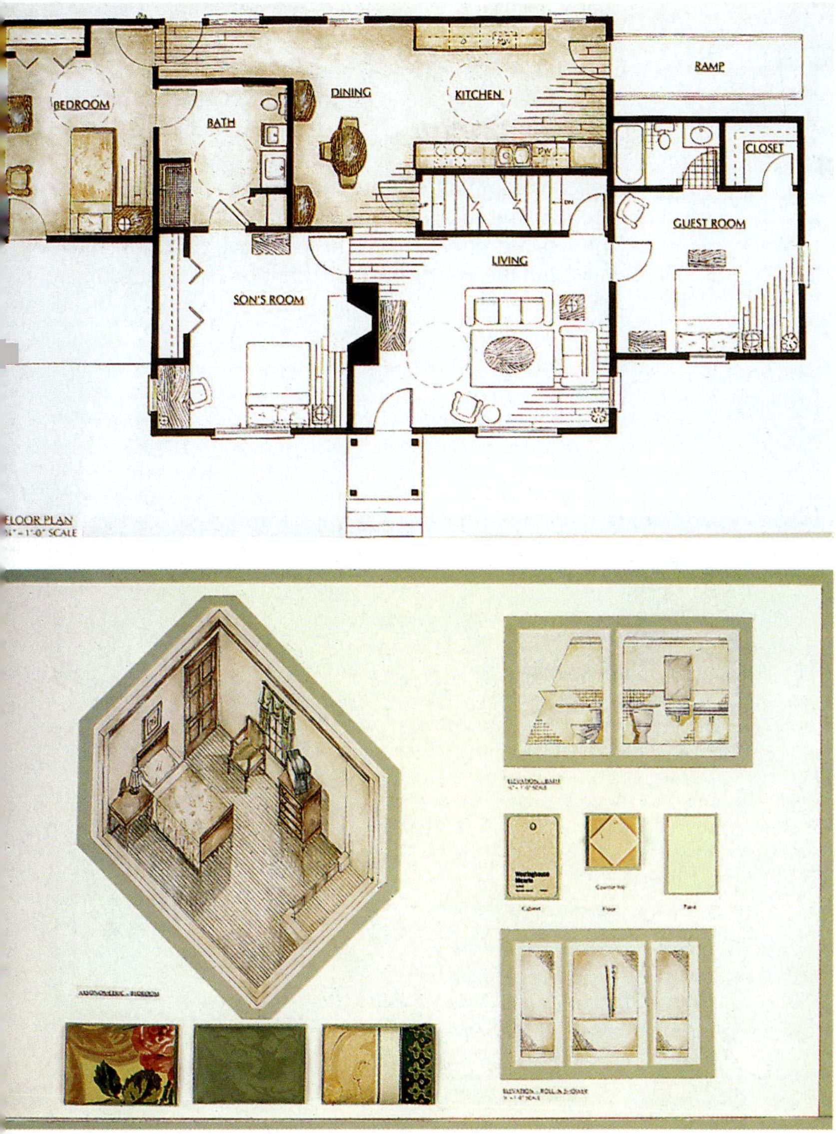

Figure 3.28 *The requirements for this residential design project for a woman with rheumatoid arthritis were developed by the IIDA Georgia chapter as a competition. Final presentation boards were necessary to visually communicate the design solution. In the presentation that won first place, the floor plan illustrates the layout of the furniture and rooms throughout the home. The designer added finish information to the plan, indicating hardwood floors, wood furniture, and tile. The second board in the presentation shows an axonometric drawing of the bedroom, which is very beneficial in helping the client visualize the space to be created. It also includes elevations (drawings of the vertical surfaces) of the bathroom. All drawings were color rendered to emphasize the color scheme. Actual fabric samples were added across the bottom of the board. (Design by Shoko Nishimura.)*

clients. Whatever method is used, it is important to re-ember that the goal is to visually explain to the client the ıal appearance of the color scheme.

olor Forecasting

·ganizations that help determine color preferences for nerican residential and nonresidential design include the ›lor Marketing Group, the Color Association of the United ıtes, the Home Fashions League, the International Colour ıthority, the National Decorating Products Association, and ›lorcast. Color forecasts are drawn from the latest research ›nducted by color stylists and authorities, and they provide ınual predictions that help consumers, professional de-;ners, and merchandising experts.

The Color Marketing Group is forecasting that colors will ›mbine with new technologies to produce colors with dimension and a sense of depth. Colors will include metallic, pearlescent, lacquered, and even sueded appearances. The Color Marketing Group researches color based on sociological, economic, and political effects.

Ken Charbonneau, Industry Partner of ASID, is a frequent speaker and presenter of color marketing forecasts. In *the GRID,* published by InPro Corporation, he notes the classic colors that will remain in style include "navy blues, hunter or forest greens, burgundy, terra cotta, black, and white. These great, reliable, dependable, and pleasing colors will always be there."

When reviewing color forecasts made by various professional sources, it is important to remember that there are no absolute color rules that can be applied at any particular time. It is good to be aware of color trends, but, ultimately, personal preferences for comfortable and pleasing colors are the most valuable consideration. The interior designer's responsibility is to help the client select colors that are right for a personal environment.

More info online @

http://www.colormarketing.org/ Color Marketing Group

http://www.colormatters.com This is a creative and fun hobby website

http://www.colorassociation.com/splash.html Color Association of the United States

http://www.internationalcolourauthority.com/ International Colour Authority

Summary

The interaction between light and color creates great opportunities for designers as well as unique challenges (Figure 3.29). Planning and accurate programming are required determine a client's personal tastes relating to a col scheme. Color schemes can be developed based on the mi ing or blending of colors from the color wheel, from natur or from another color source such as a work of art or a pa terned rug, but they should also support the concept. The nal development of the color scheme must also take in account the juxtaposition of different colors to each othe the desired effects from the elements and principles of d sign, and the appropriate distribution of color. Ultimately, t greatest challenge to any designer (and possibly the most sa isfying reward) is to achieve beautiful and livable schem that meet the client's needs.

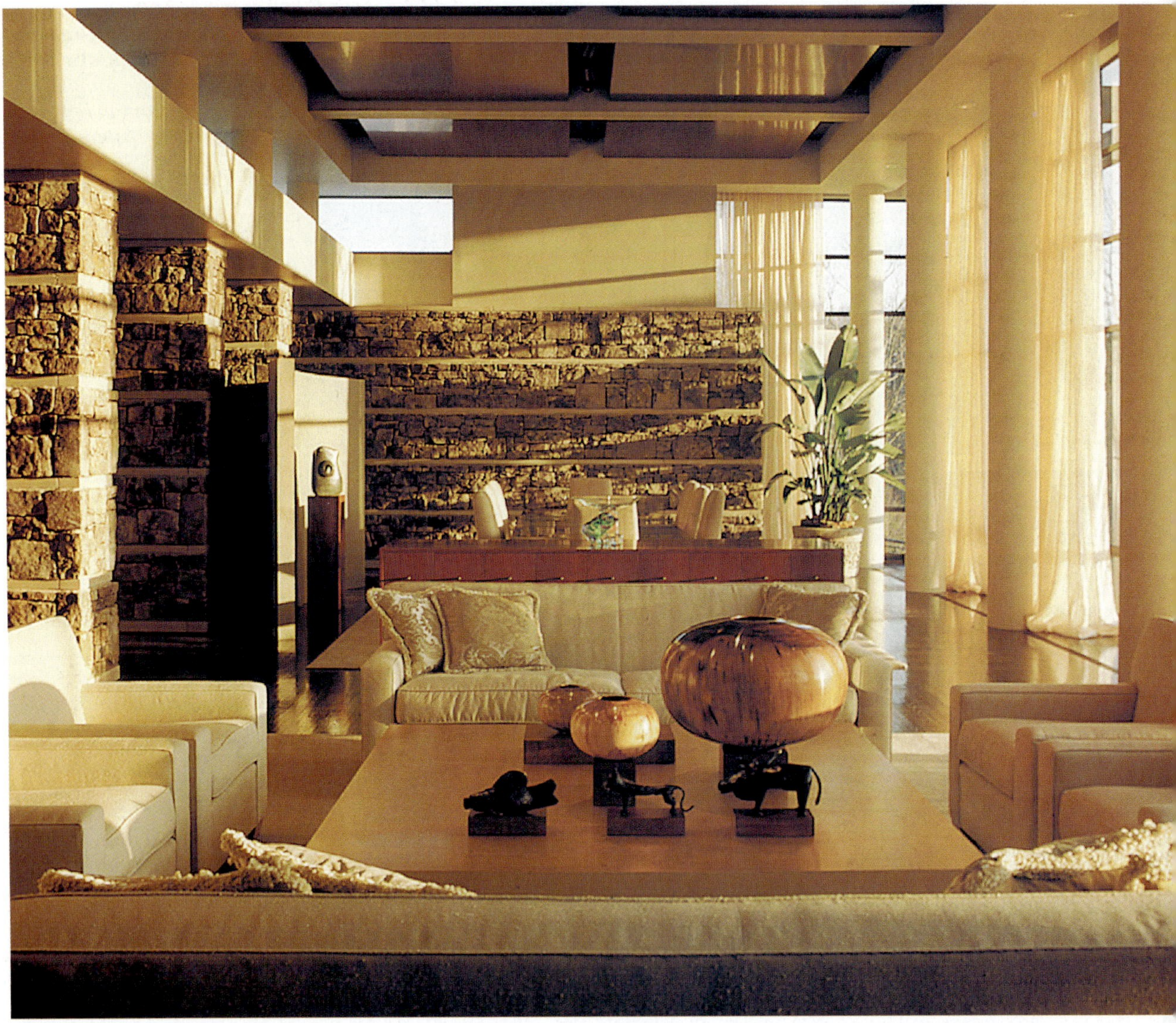

Figure 3.29 *Variations in texture and light play a significant role in the warmth and richness of this interior living environment. The designers were particularly observant of the effects of light as it changes throughout the day. Reflective surfaces on the floor and ceiling add to the character of the space and contrast with the rough stone walls. (Designer: Gandy/Peace, Inc. Photograph by Chris A. Little.)*

: following project illustrates the thorough development and ·cution of a concept. The Atlanta offices of Gensler (an inte- design and architectural firm) worked closely with their nt, United Parcel Service, to develop Innoplex.

ject Description

: existing 200,000 square-foot building had housed a furni- : manufacturing plant. The building renovation would ac- nmodate 650 employees in a new venture for UPS. The ployees include software developers, inventors, information nnology professionals, and investment advisors working to- her to help UPS become one of the top global e-commerce npanies. These individuals were brought together for one pose—to "get the product to market faster."

gramming: The design team worked in sessions with UPS em- yees, called the "e-Commerce Founders," to define the goals l clarify the direction for the new center. As a result of these gramming sessions, Gensler produced a bound volume de- bing the business goals based on actual quotes from the nders. Additionally, Gensler researched current and historical rature to help support and define goals. The document *UPS e- utions Facility: Building Program* was referred to throughout the ign process, thereby providing project direction.

Goals included the following:

- Maximizing real estate investment through effective long-term planning and development
- Providing an environment that would attract and maintain high-quality information technology professionals
- Providing an environment that fosters and nurtures creative thinking and promotes flexibility and excitement

ures DS3.1 through DS3.3 illustrate pages pulled from the *ding Program* document.

	Year end 2000	Year end 2001	Year end 2002	Hard Office Year end 2002	Type of work
Service Parts Logistics	70	75	80	4	Internet/other software development
Ups Capital	30	45	60	3	
PSI	30	50	50	5	
eVentures Core	30	30	30	12	Incubation
eVentures Team X	12	12	12		
eVentures Team Y	12	12	12		
Consumer Direct	115	120	150		
eLogistics	120	120	120		
Worldwide Logistics	60	80	100	5	IT Developers, WWL and transportation developers
eSolutions Development	131	300	450	23	
Interactive Communications	15	20	25	1	
Interactive Marketing	5	5	5	0	
EC Marketing					
Document Exchange					
CIM/eDeployment	10	15	18	1	
CIM/Functional Requirements	23	53	87	5	
CIM/Implementation & Support	25	30	33	1	
Human Resources	5	7	8	3	
Facilities	2	2	2	0	
Enterprise Support	3	4	6	0	
Total	698	980	1248	63	

ure DS3.1 *As part of the programming document, a ffing plan was developed indicating anticipated number of ployees per division. (Architect/Designer: Gensler.)*

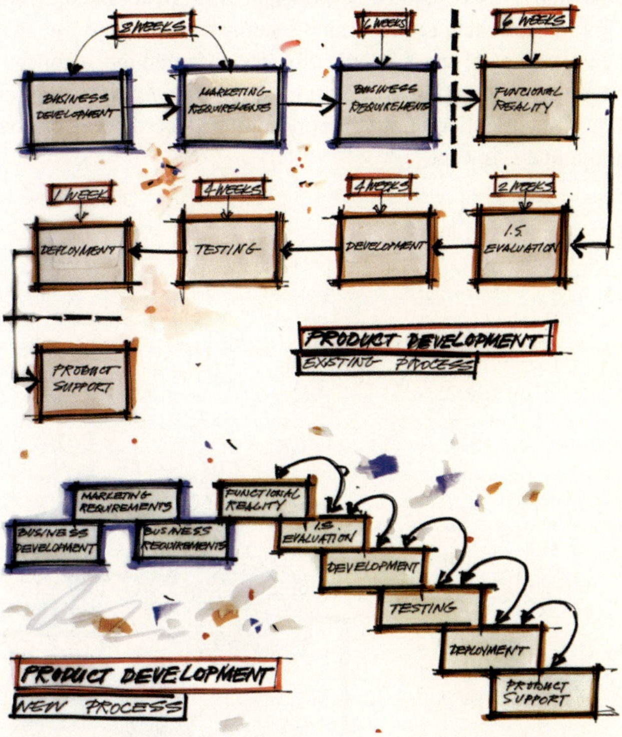

Figure DS3.2 *The programming document also graphically outlined the existing and new product development process. (Architect/Designer: Gensler.)*

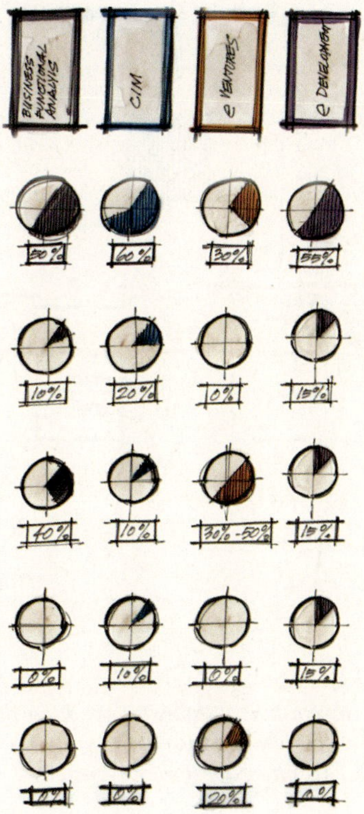

Figure DS3.3 *After observing work patterns of various employees, Gensler developed a timetable indicating a "Day in the Life" of each division employee. (Architect/Designer: Gensler.)*

Schematic or Conceptual Design: As the designer/client collaboration continued, design requirements emerged for the center. Specific requests included indirect and natural lighting, no fluorescent lighting, recreational and break areas, multipurpose collaboration areas to invite spontaneity and encourage "cross pollination," user changeable workspaces, a "green" building environment, quality acoustics and security systems, and the ability to have quiet space. As the discussions continued, a concept began to build. It circled around the word *community.* Figures DS3.4 and DS3.5 illustrate the conceptual plans centered on this community concept.

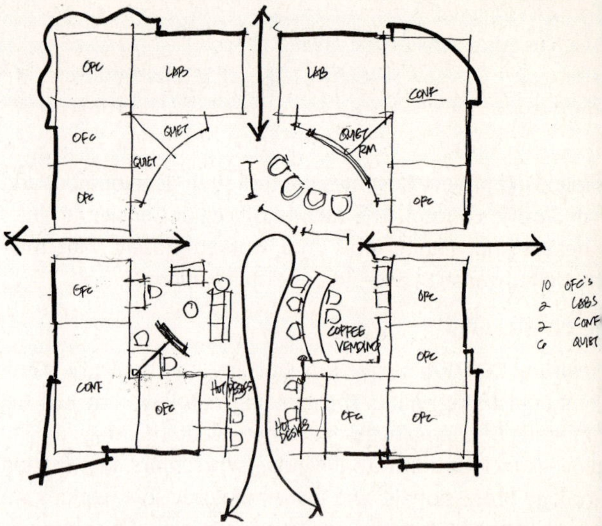

Figure DS3.5 *In a more specific conceptual plan, offices, la[bs,] conferencing areas, and quiet rooms create a framework f[or] the Common Centers. (Architect/Designer: Gensler.)*

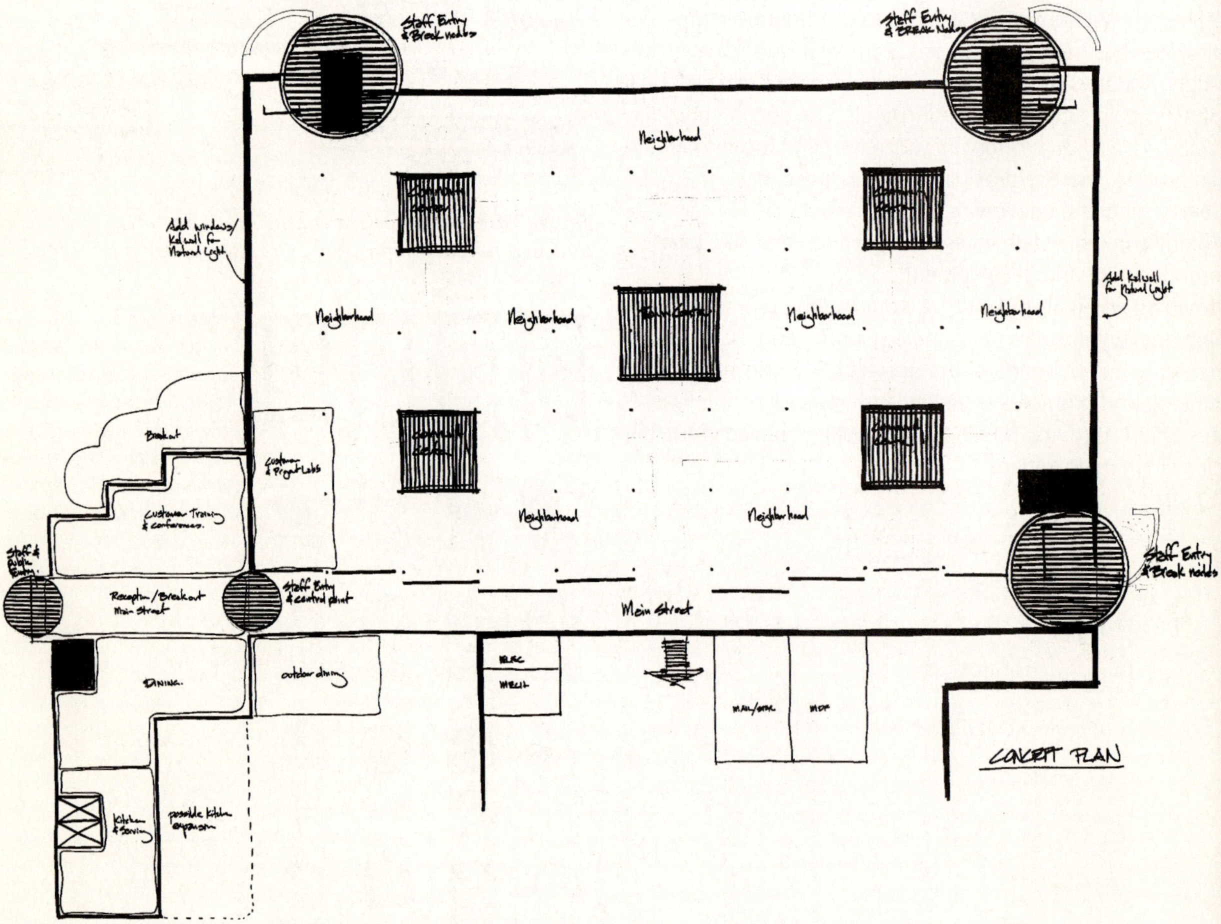

Figure DS3.4 *The attached concept plan illustrates the idea of community. The Town Center is surrounded by Neighborhoods (work areas) and Common Centers (collaboration areas). (Architect/Designer: Gensler.)*

sign Development: The design development phase for this oject continued seamlessly from the schematics. Figure DS3.6 strates a presentation furniture plan forming a strong netrk of office neighborhoods and community centers. Figure 3.7 depicts the community feel planned for the interior, inding the (A) Main Street Corridor the (B) Open Office Neighrhood and the (C) Community Break Area.

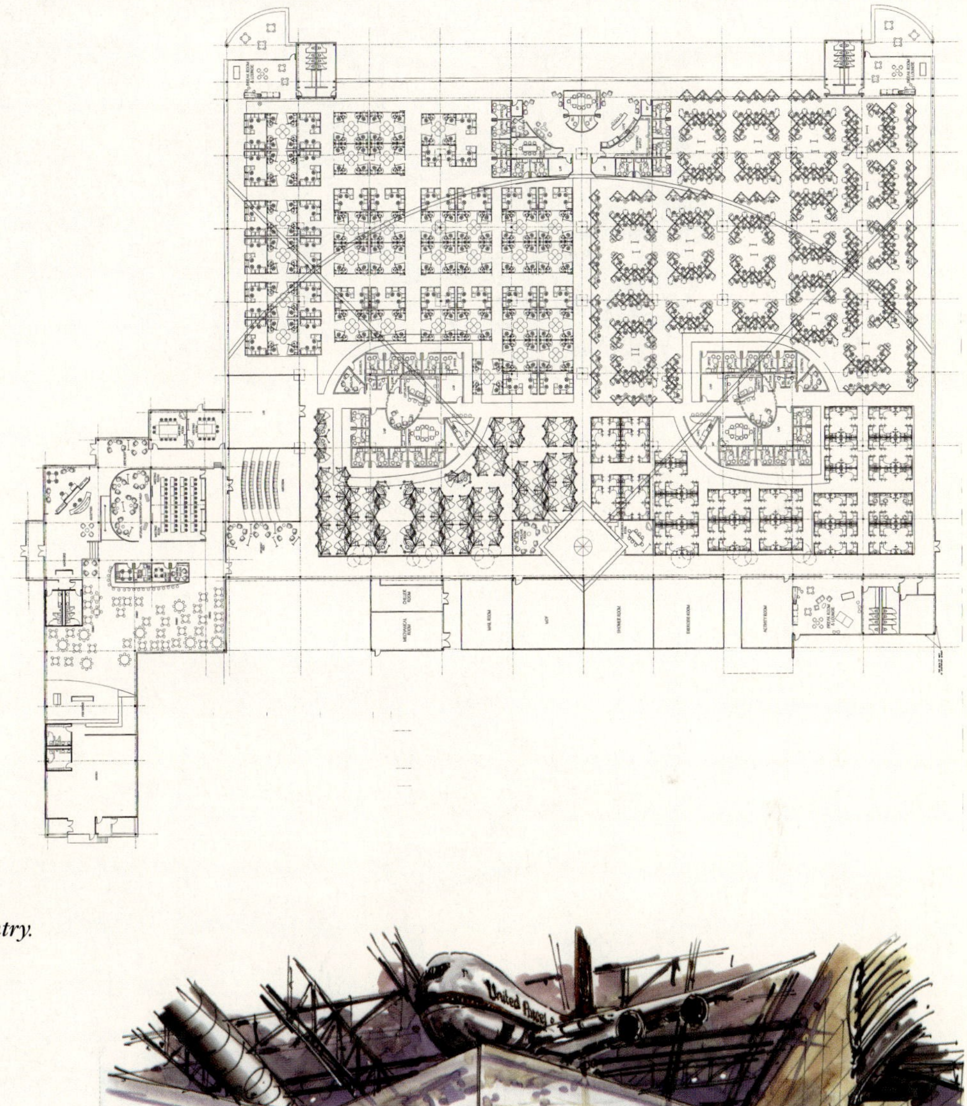

gure DS3.6 *Placing the nmunity concept into the cific building plan created resentation furniture plan strating potential walls, en office plans, and rridors. (Architect/Designer: nsler.)*

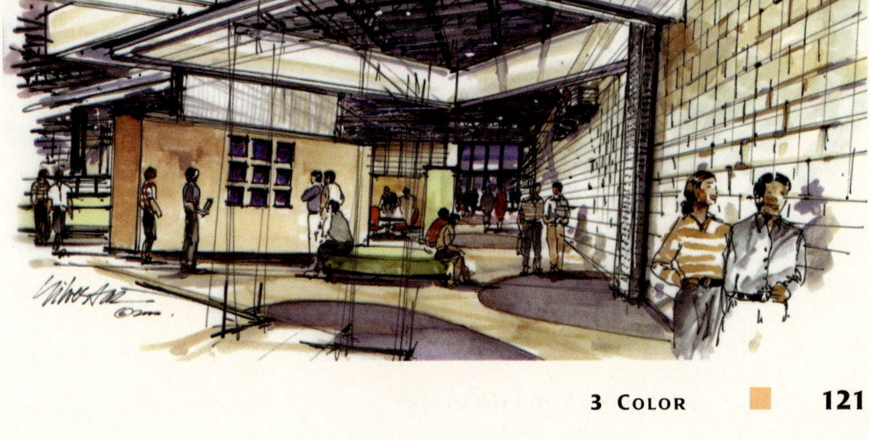

gure DS3.7A *Presentation rspective of the Main Street Entry. rchitect/Designer: Gensler.)*

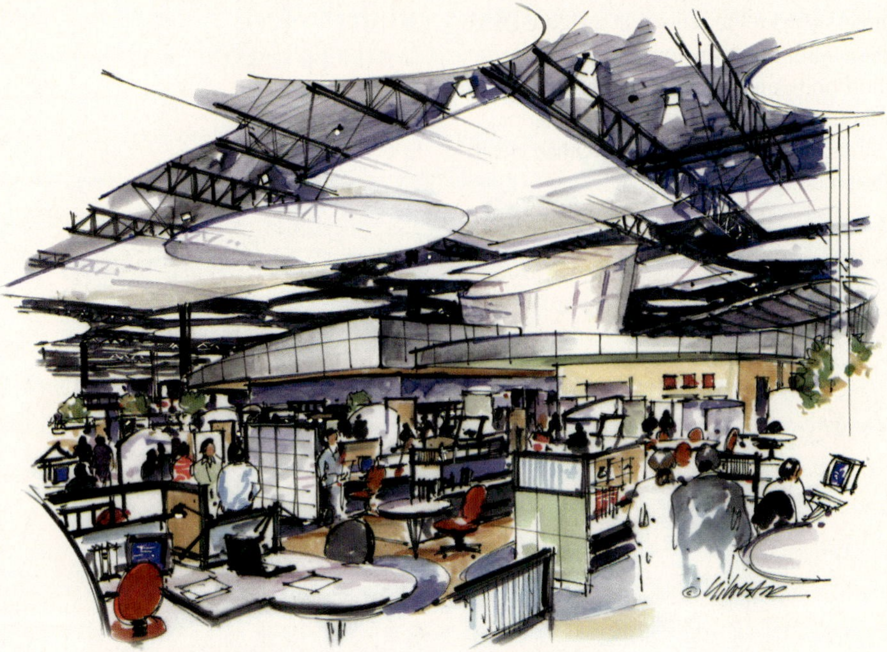

Figure DS3.7B *Presentation perspective of the Open Office Neighborhood. (Architect/Designer: Gensler.)*

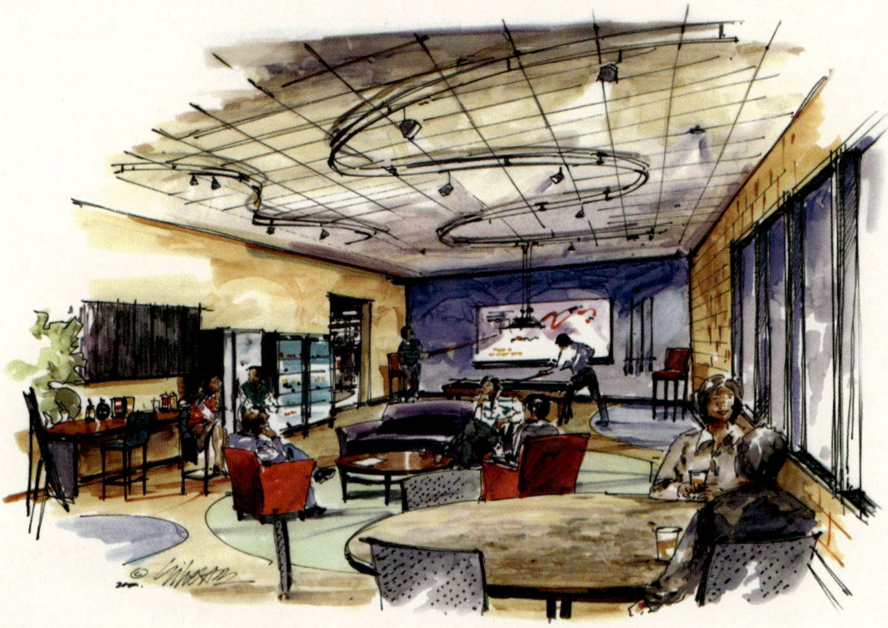

Figure DS3.7C *Presentation perspective of the Community Break Area. (Architect/Designer: Gensler.)*

ntract Documentation: Developing construction drawings for s project required a vigilance to community details and an ad-rence to the design requests identified in the programming d conceptual design phases. Figures DS3.8 through DS3.10 present a sample of the documents used in the process.

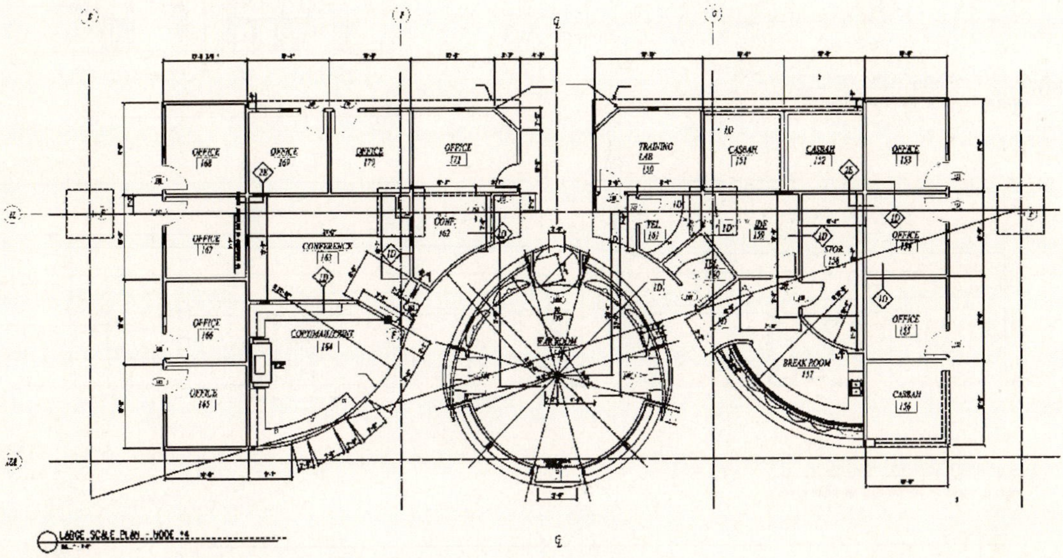

gure DS3.8 *Partition plan of the War Room. (Architect/ Designer: Gensler.)*

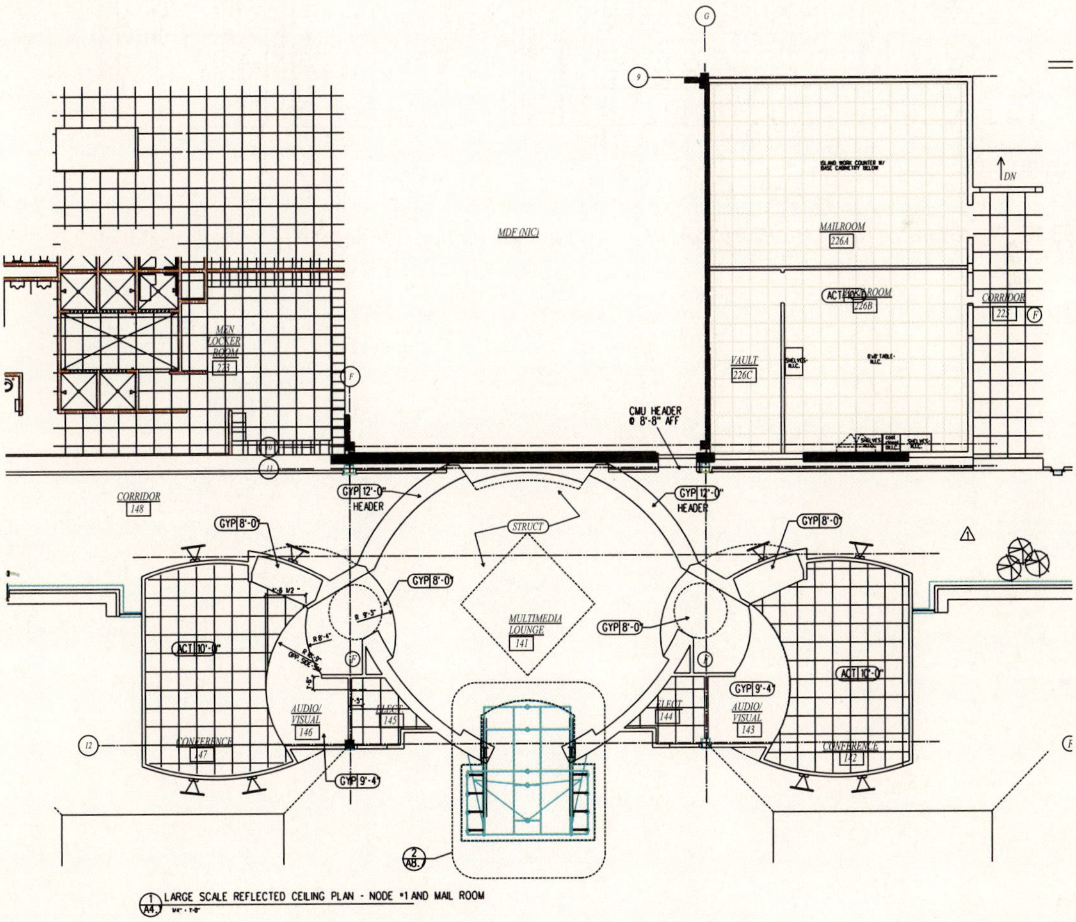

gure DS3.9 *Partition plan of the Multimedia Lounge. (Architect/Designer: Gensler.)*

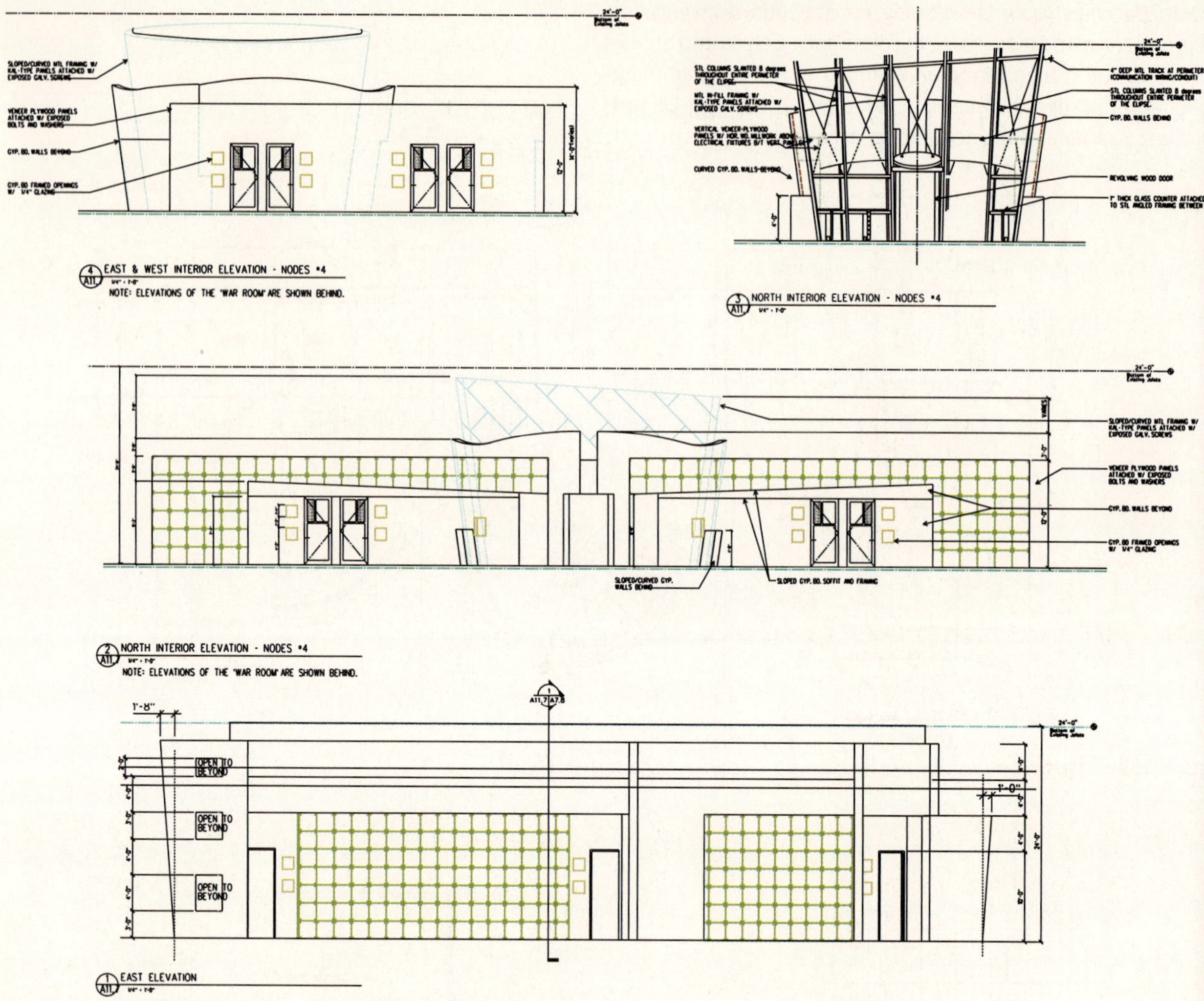

Figure DS3.10 *Elevations of the Main Entry Corridor. (Architect/Designer: Gensler.)*

Innoplex: Completed interior spaces are illustrated in Figures .11 through DS3.15.

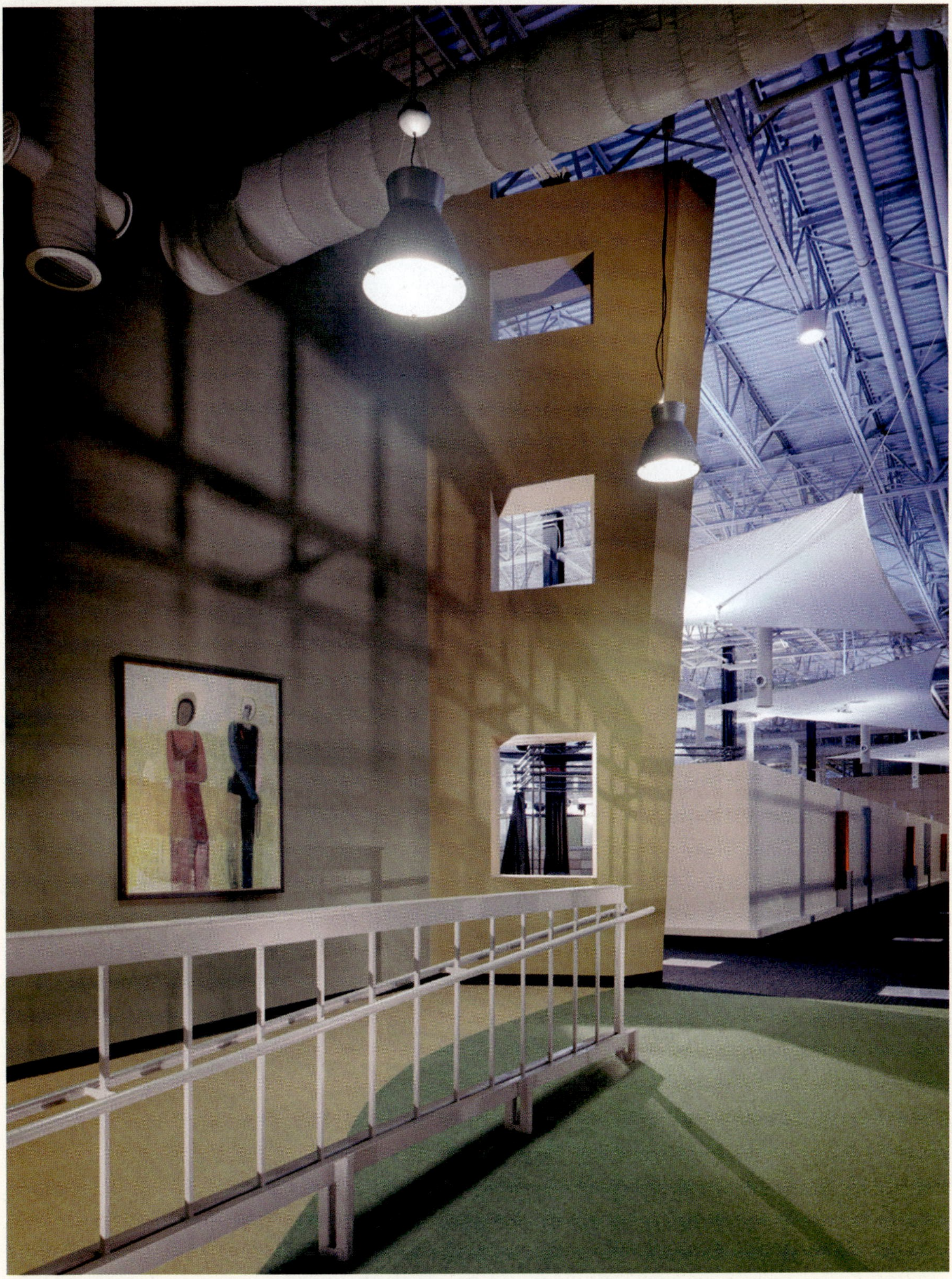

Figure DS3.11 *In the Main Street Corridor, bold colors, intersecting planes, and a strong axis set the tone for a fun and exciting interior environment. (Architect/Designer: Gensler. Photograph © Robert Thien.)*

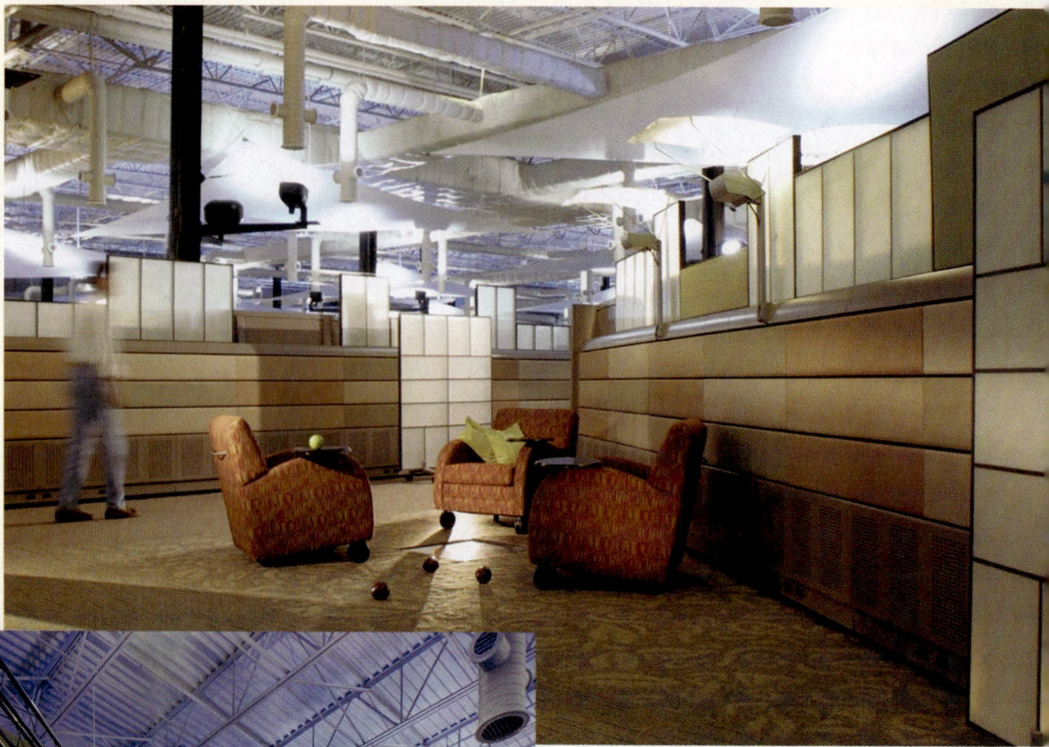

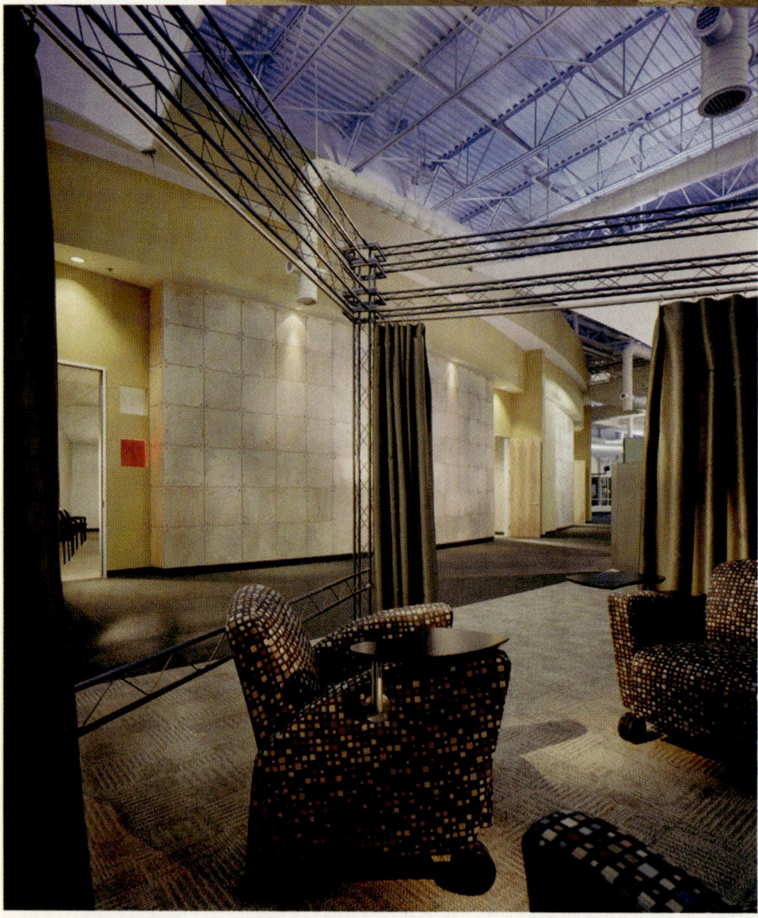

Figure DS3.12 and DS3.13 *Following the community concept and the request for "multipurpose collaboration areas," Gensler created streetside seating areas for spontaneo[us] conversations as well as planned meeting destinations. Flexibility was also essential in these areas to allow for growth and/or privac[y] for the participants. (Architect/Designer: Gensl[er]. Photograph © Robert Thien.)*

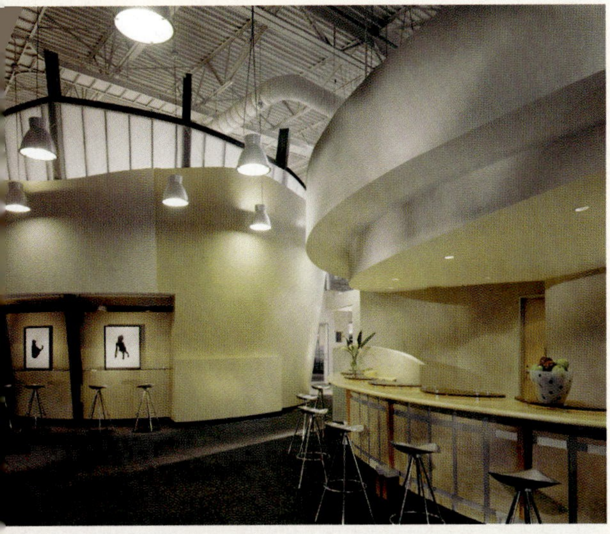

Figure DS3.14 *In another open community zone, employees are encouraged to gather at the "bar" for informal discussions. Strong chromas, curved walls, and playful art add to the enlivened interior space. (Architect/Designer: Gensler. Photograph © Robert Thien.)*

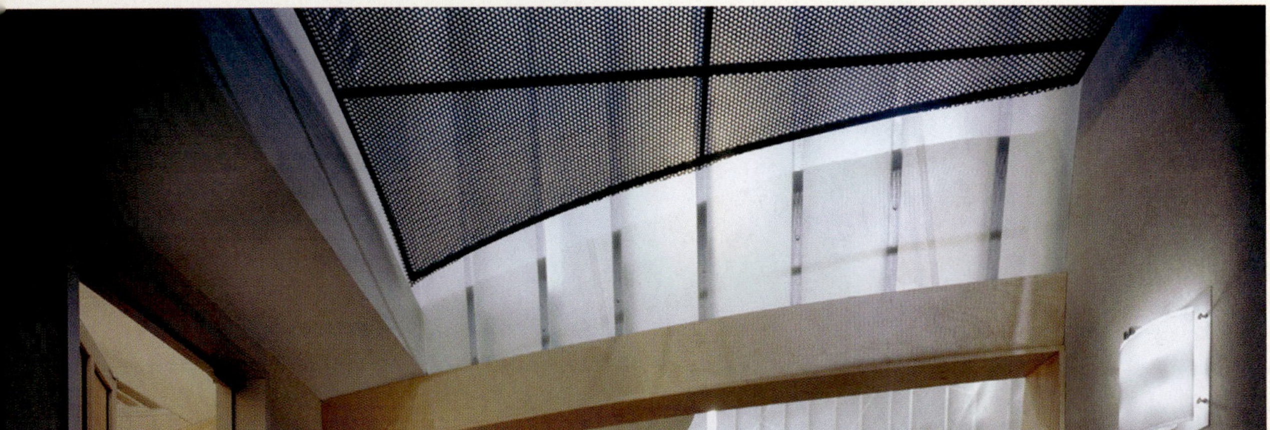

gure DS3.15 *Looking through a portal into one of the Common Centers, one can e that the environment continues to stimulate creativity. The intersecting planes ıd strong chromas continue, but the lowered ceilings and enhanced enclosures ctate more formality and a stronger sense of order. (Architect/Designer: Gensler. ɔotograph © Robert Thien.)*

Building Systems

PART III

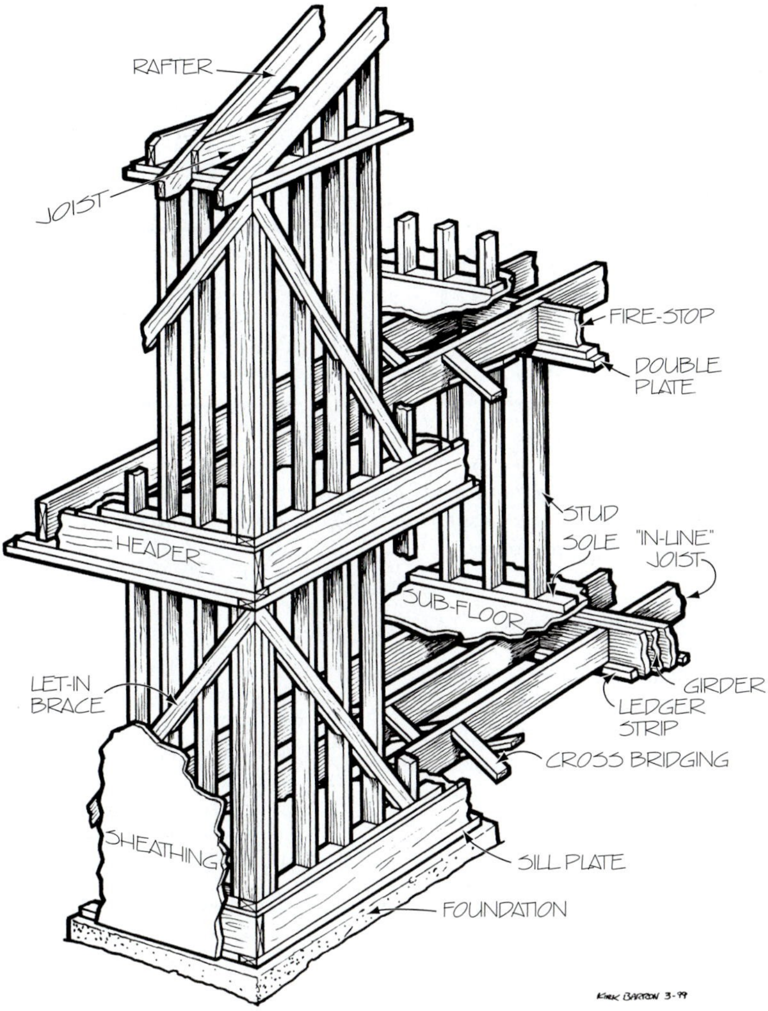

gure III.1 *This two-story framing diagram illustrates platform or western frame* ·*nstruction. Note the various terms for the different construction components.*

The play seems out for

an almost infinite run.

Don't mind a little thing

like the actors fighting.

The only thing I worry

about is the sun.

We'll be all right if

nothing goes wrong

with the lighting.

–Robert Frost

The building system components that are usually hidden in the alls, ceilings, or floors form the basis r human comfort in interior envi- nments. The heating, ventilating, and -conditioning (HVAC), electrical, light- g, communication, and plumbing sys- ms (to name a few) are integrated to the construction of a building. ιowledge of how these systems work gether and an understanding of when ey are installed during the construc- ɔn process allow the designer to accurately guide the client during construction or remodeling.

The interior designer is a member of a design team. Although the designer should be familiar with the construction process, he or she is actively working with (and in many cases relying on the expertise of) the allied design professionals (see Chapter 1). Communication, collaboration, and cooperation: These three C's are essential among design team members in order to create successful environments.

Understanding system terminology and recognizing standard architectural symbols enhance the designer's ability to communicate effectively with colleagues and clients.

The Construction Process

The process of building or remodeling a structure requires several steps. The **critical path** is a timetable (or schedule) that charts this process. For example, a small remodeling job may require only four or five weeks to complete, whereas a typical residence may take four or five months; a large commercial building may take one to three years to finish.

For almost all projects, the order of the steps is similar; steps that are not required are simply skipped. The scheduling of the project usually becomes the responsibility of the general contractor. The following explains the construction process for a residential project using wood frame construction. Refer to the figures for further understanding.

More info online @

http://www.b4ubuild.com/resources/schedule/6kproj.shtml A sample residential construction schedule

Site Selection and Development

Site selection is the first step in the construction process. The site frequently dictates the style of house to be built. Site work also contributes significantly to the flow of traffic and physical location of the building. Once a site has been selected and an appropriate house designed to fit it, the site must be prepared. Utility lines are buried (or strung) to meet local codes. Vegetation is removed or protected from large earth-moving machines and a hole is excavated for the footings, foundation walls, and basement or crawl space. Site work continues throughout the entire construction process and does not end until drains, lawns, shrubs, trees, driveways, sidewalks, decks, patios, and parking areas are installed.

More info online @

http://b4ubuild.com/resources/index.shtml#sitework Information on site work

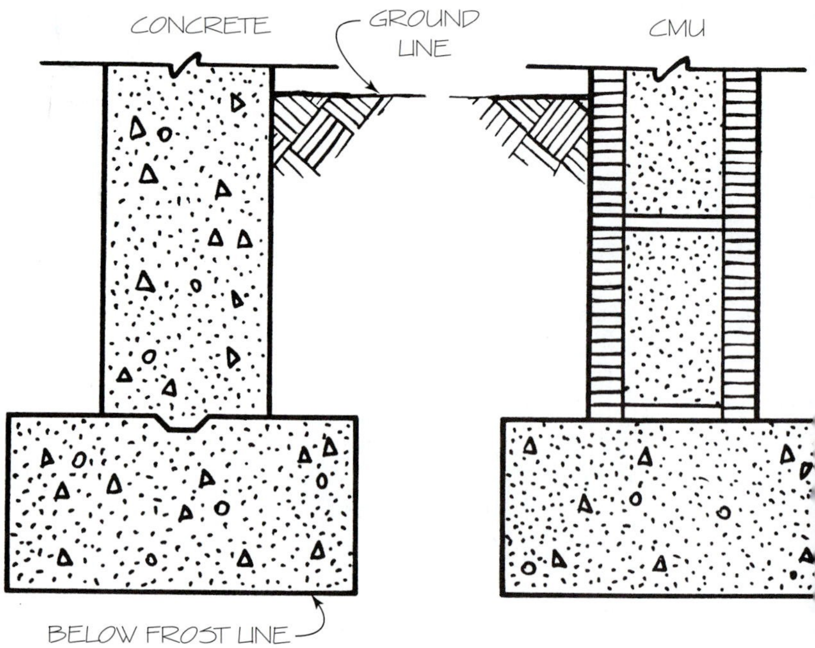

Figure III.2 *Left, a poured footing and foundation wall. Right, also a poured footing, but its foundation wall is formed using concrete masonry units (CMU), commonly called concrete blocks.*

Footings and Foundations

After the initial site work is complete and the initial hole is dug, careful measurements are made and forms are placed to hold the concrete that will be poured to form the footings. **Footings** are the structural foundation of the building. In colder climates, footings must be placed below the frost line.

Foundation walls are built on top of the footings. The walls may be poured concrete or concrete block (Figure III.2). (Note: *Cement* is a dry ingredient of concrete. Concrete is a mixture of cement, composed of lime, silica, and other materials, along with gravel and water.) Space must be allowed for basement windows (which must meet fire egress codes) or crawl space air vents in the foundation walls.

Some buildings have concrete slab floors. The floors are reinforced with rebar (strong steel rods) or wire mesh. In a building with a concrete slab, all plumbing, electrical, or mechanical ductwork that will penetrate the floor must be in place prior to pouring the concrete slab floor. It is wise for the architect or designer to make a site visit during this time to ensure that electrical and plumbing components are installed as noted on the blueprin Chiseling or coring a slab for ductwo after the concrete slab has set is pos ble, but costly. In remodeling jo however, this may be the only so tion.

Once the concrete has set and t forms are removed, the holes a backfilled with dirt and compacte The building is ready to be framed.

More info online @

http://www.b4ubuild.com/photos/footing/ot_p01.shtml Images of installing concrete footing

Framing

In wood frame construction, the fi item to be framed is the floor. **sillplate** secures the floor to the fou dation (Figure III.1). Horizontal wo members are attached to the sillpla and a subfloor is laid over the to The vertical load-bearing walls a added to support the weight of t roof, transferring the load to the fou dation walls, which transfer it to t footings. Not all walls are load bea ing. In a remodeling job, before spe ifying the removal of a wall, t

esigner must consult with an archi-
·ct or engineer to determine which
alls are load bearing. Load-bearing
alls can be moved after proper al-
rnative structural support is in place;
owever, the work must first be doc-
mented by the licensed architect, en-
neer, or builder.

The vertical walls are formed by 2″
4″ or 2″ × 6″ studs. Rough openings
the wall are made for doors and
indows (Figure III.3). A **header** is
laced over the opening to transfer the
ad to a supporting stud. Again, the
chitect or interior designer should
refully survey the construction as
alls are being built. Improperly lo-
ted doors, windows, and walls are
asier to move the sooner the mistake
noticed. Check the blueprints to
ake sure they are followed.

Next, the roof is framed and at-
ched to the vertical stud walls (Fig-
re III.4). The angular wood pieces
e called rafters. Many wood-framed
ofs are made from prefabricated
uss systems constructed off-site (Fig-
re III.5). Although more economical,
uss systems do not allow for attic
se.

ore info online @
tp://www.b4ubuild.com/photos/contents.s
ml#framing Images of framing

heathing, Roofing, and Interior uilding Systems

s the framing is completed, *sheath-
g* (rigid wallboard, plywood, or sim-
r material) is added around the
erimeter of the building and to the
of. The sheathing (sometimes called
ecking on the roof) adds structural
pport and insulating qualities. It also

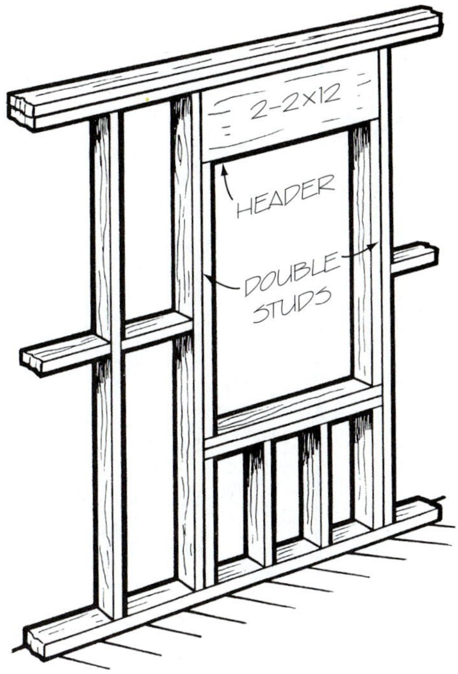

Figure III.3 *Additional support in the form of double studs and a header strengthen the rough opening that will eventually house a window.*

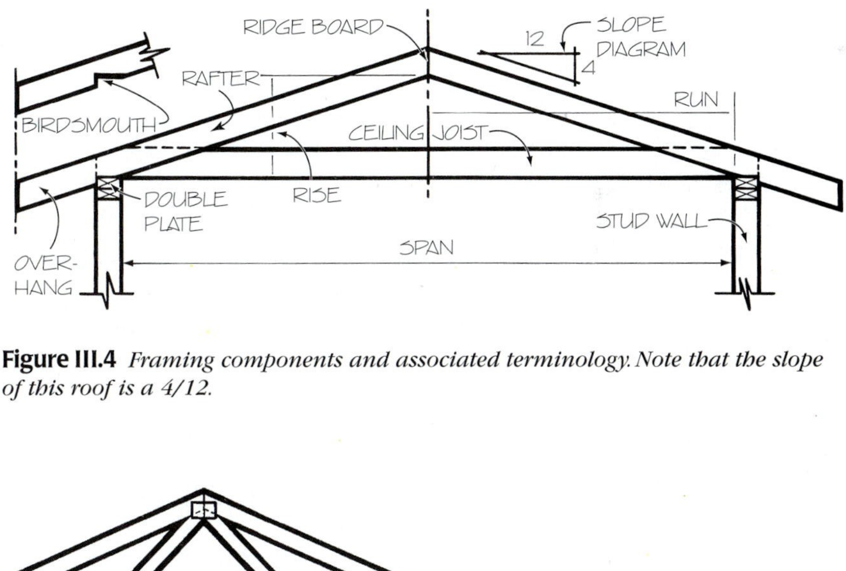

Figure III.4 *Framing components and associated terminology. Note that the slope of this roof is a 4/12.*

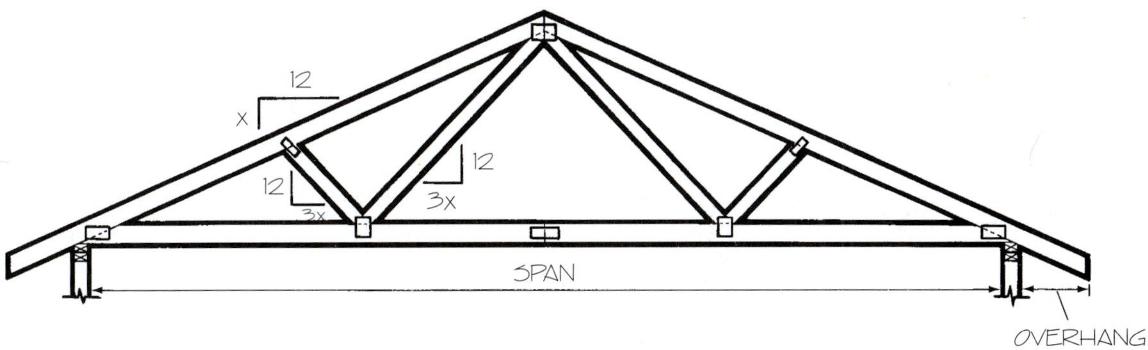

gure III.5 *A prefabricated truss system.*

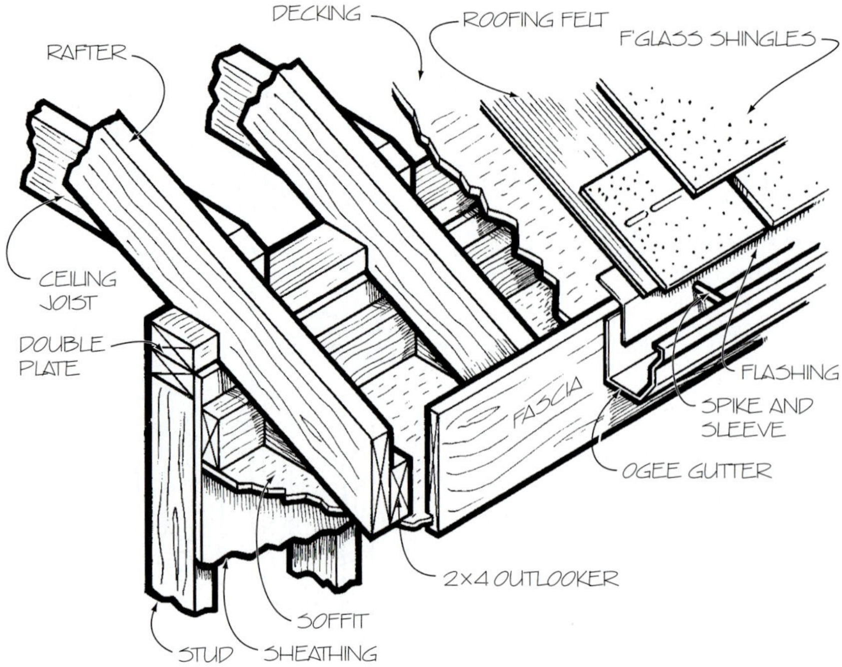

Figure III.6 *This cut-away section illustrates the construction components where the roof meets the walls. Finish materials such as shingles are applied over the roofing felt and decking.*

may serve as a nailer for the finish materials (see Figure III.6 and Figure 4.1).

As the roofing material is placed on the decking, windows and doors are installed and rough plumbing (sometimes called top-out plumbing), HVAC, and electrical lines are run in the walls and basement (if applicable). Shower stalls and tubs are installed so that interior finishes cover the seams. Central vacuum units, security systems, and intercom systems also are installed at this point. Once again the location of the outlets, switches, overhead lighting, HVAC vents, intercom systems, and other specified components should be carefully checked. After wall material is applied over the studs, it is more costly and difficult to make changes. Last, insulation is added to the walls and ceilings.

Finish Materials

The exterior of the building receives its final material, such as wood clapboard, brick, or siding, and it is finished appropriately. **Soffits** (the area below the eaves) and **fascia** (the front of the eaves) are completed (Figure III.6). Trim is installed around windows and doors. Concrete porches and walks, wood decks, and railings complete the site work. Exterior hardware is installed.

Interior finish materials are applied to the walls. (These options are discussed in Chapter 11.) Other construction components such as trim, bookshelves, closet systems, and doors are installed. Painting and staining are completed. Cabinets, countertops, tile floors, and backsplashes are installed. Wallcovering is hung and plumbing and lighting fixtures are placed. The interior door hardware, appliances, carpets, and window treatments are installed. Finally, the furniture is delivered. Artwork and accessories are arranged.

The last step is the final walk through, noting tasks yet to be completed on a punch list. Inevitably, the movers will dent a doorframe or the carpet installers will mar a wall. Electrical outlet covers and heater vents will be misplaced. Light bulbs will burn out or break. The architect or interior designer needs to ensure that all items are fixed prior to approving the final payment to the contractor.

The construction process is compl
and it is only through proper planni
that a building is completed in a giv
time frame. Attention to detail and
collaborative effort by all allied profe
sionals ensure a space that meets t
needs and desires of the client.

The following two chapters provi
more detailed information on buildi
systems. Recognition of building sy
bols and an understanding of ea
system's components and requir
ments will assist designers in worki
with clients and communicating w
construction professionals.

More info online @

http://www.homebuildingmanual.com/Glossary.htm Glossary of building construction terms

http://www.b4ubuild.com/ General residential building site

http://www.nahb.com/ National Association of Homebuilders

http://www.nahbrc.org National Association of Homebuilders Research Center

http://www.sweets.com/ Construction resources guide from Sweets Catalog

Construction, Systems, and Codes

4

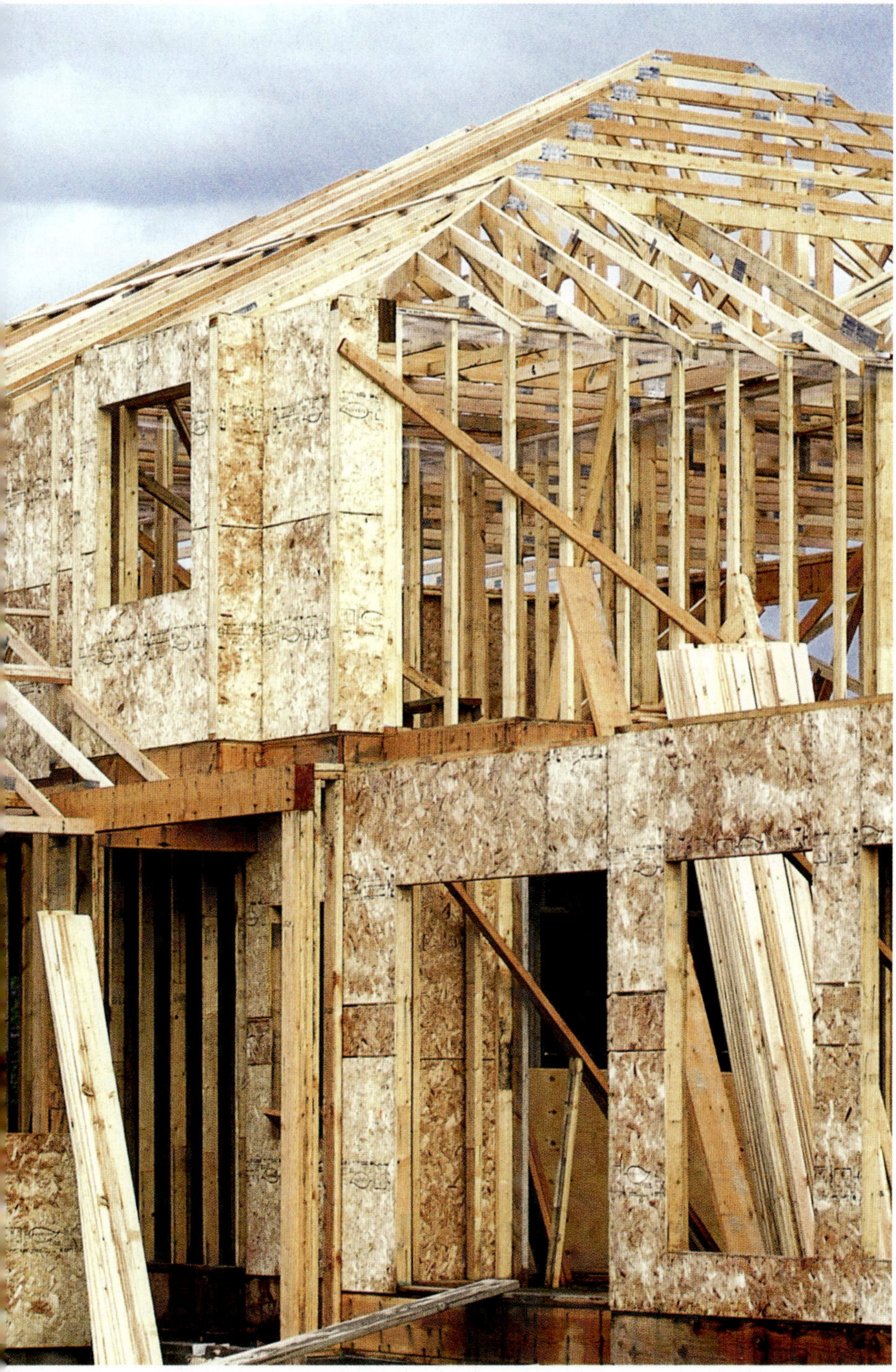

Figure 4.1 *Construction site. (Photograph from PhotoDisc.)*

The technical aspects of interiors help to define design possibilities. Understanding how construction systems fit together and developing a working knowledge of how these systems are visually communicated help the designer achieve the desired outcome (Figure 4.1). This chapter reviews the visual components in a set of construction drawings, defines and illustrates various systems in the built environments, and outlines the various codes and federal regulations relating to interior design.

Contract Documents

Contract documents consist of construction drawings and a set of written specifications defining the quality of materials and craftsmanship. Construction drawings (which are explained throughout this chapter) generally include the following information:

- Cover sheet, used as a table of contents
- Site and grading plans
- Landscape plans
- Foundation plans
- Floor plans, generally starting with the lowest floor and rising
- Lighting location plans
- Electrical and communication location plans
- Finish plans
- Exterior elevations
- Interior elevations
- Sections
- Schedules
- Details and custom cabinetry
- Roofing plans
- Engineering drawings, including lighting, electrical and communications, plumbing, HVAC, fire protection, and security

Drawings are deleted or inserted as required for the specific project. The written specifications (developed into a complex booklet) include requirements for each area listed above. For example, the specifications may list the acceptable tolerances (or gaps) between parts in wood construction.

Furniture, finish, and equipment specifications also may be developed and are considered part of the contract documents (see Chapter 1). The following section describes these various drawings. Appendix C illustrates a small set of construction drawings.

Plans

Plan drawings show the layout of a site or building when viewed from above, looking into the various floors of the building. Plans are generally drawn to 1/8″ = 1′-0″ scale or 1/4″ = 1′-0″. (This means that 1/8″ or 1/4″ respectively on the drawing is equal to 1′-0″ in real-life dimensions.) Designers need to be able to interpret the standard symbols used in plan drawings. Figures 4.2 through 4.4 indicate typical architectural symbols. (Chapter 12 also illustrates standard symbols for doors and windows.)

More info online @

http://www.constructionworknews.com/field-manual/index2.html Site containing construction symbols and terminology

http://www.hometime.com/projects/conbasic.htm Basic residential construction website with glossary and terms

Site, Grading, Landscape, and Foundation Plans

Site and grading plans and landscape plans, although rar used by the designer, are helpful in orienting the design the landscape and the direction of the sun. Foundation pla show the location of HVAC and plumbing lines.

Floor Plans

Floor plans are critical to the designer. These plans define cations of walls, doors, windows, and other built-in comp nents such as bathroom fixtures, cabinets, and stairways.

Stairways can be bold and dramatic or simply function Often the stairway functions as a focal point and can be a thetically stimulating as well as serviceable, as demonstrat in Figure 4.5.

The stairway consists of the horizontal portion, called t **tread,** and the vertical portion, called the **riser.** The dep of a tread should accommodate the entire length of the fo (11 in. is generally used).

In a residence, the tread is often carpeted for additio safety. The riser should be no more than 7 in. high. Trea and risers should be consistent in size. A person expects a needs each step to be the same height and depth (Figu 4.6). Headroom clearance should be planned for the top a bottom of the staircase; 6 ft. 8 in. is considered a minimu clearance.

A handrail (or **banister**) is usually mounted at 34″ abo the steps. The upright supports for the handrail are call **balusters;** they must be spaced close enough to prevent to dlers from falling through the supports. A **balustrade** is t handrail together with its balusters.

Designers may produce the floor plan on their own, b must collaborate with an architect or builder on structu components. Furniture plans, although not part of the form construction drawings, are generated from the floor plans

Lighting Plans

Lighting plans may be produced by designers in collabo tion with engineers. Lighting plans are slightly different fro the other plans because they are drawn as if looking up the ceiling instead of down at the floor. In residential desig lighting plans are commonly combined with electrical a communication (telephone) plans. In commercial desig lighting plans may be called **reflected ceiling plans** a may include HVAC and sprinkler information. Chapter 5 c cusses lighting fixtures and design, along with electrical a communication systems.

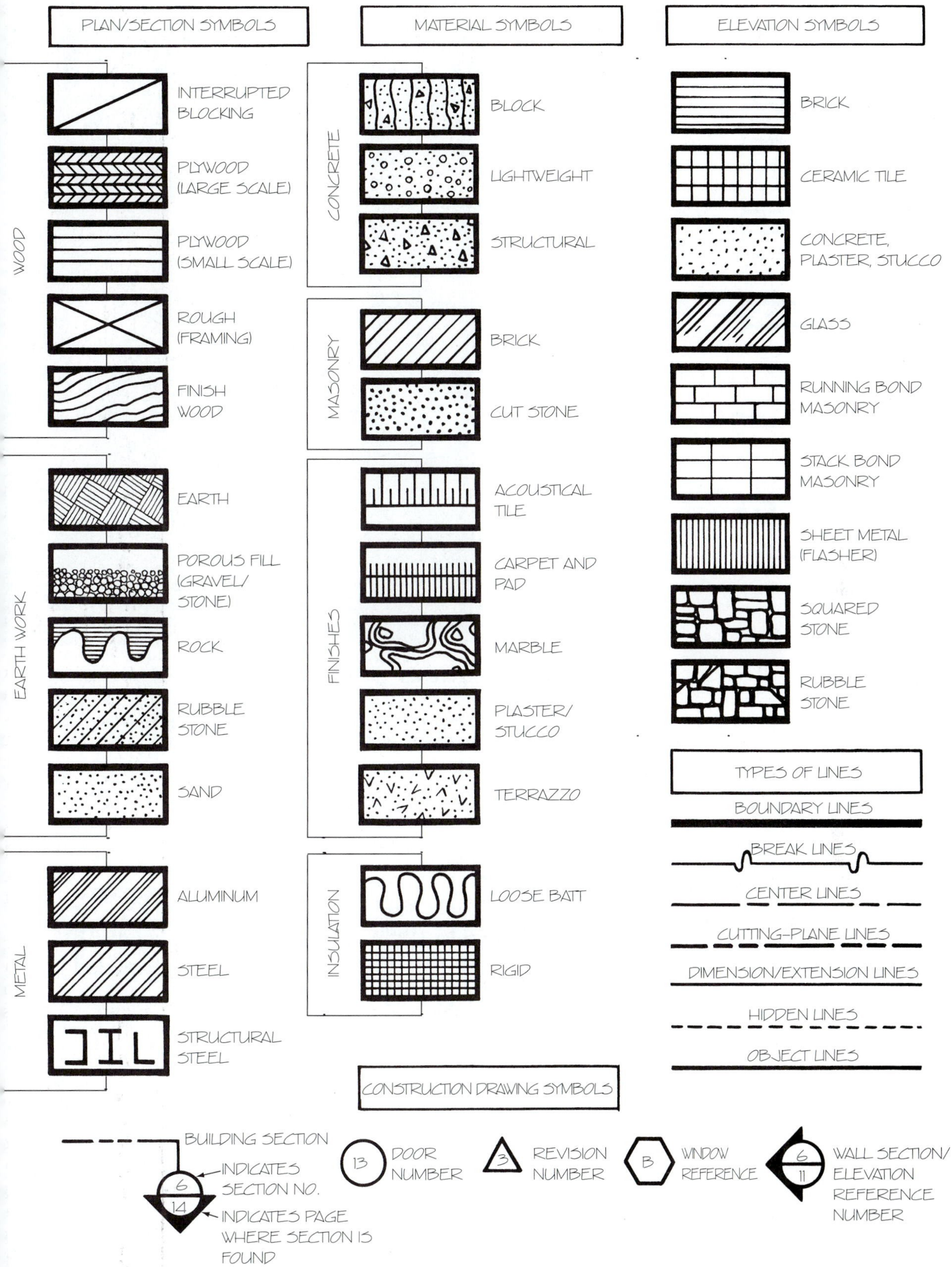

gure 4.2 *Material symbols in plan/section/elevation, and line and graphic symbols.*

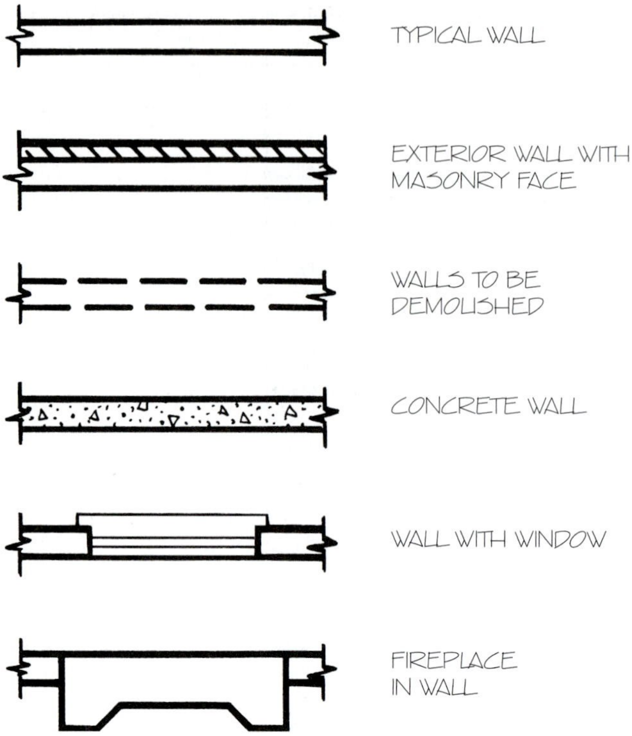

Figure 4.3 *Wall symbols.*

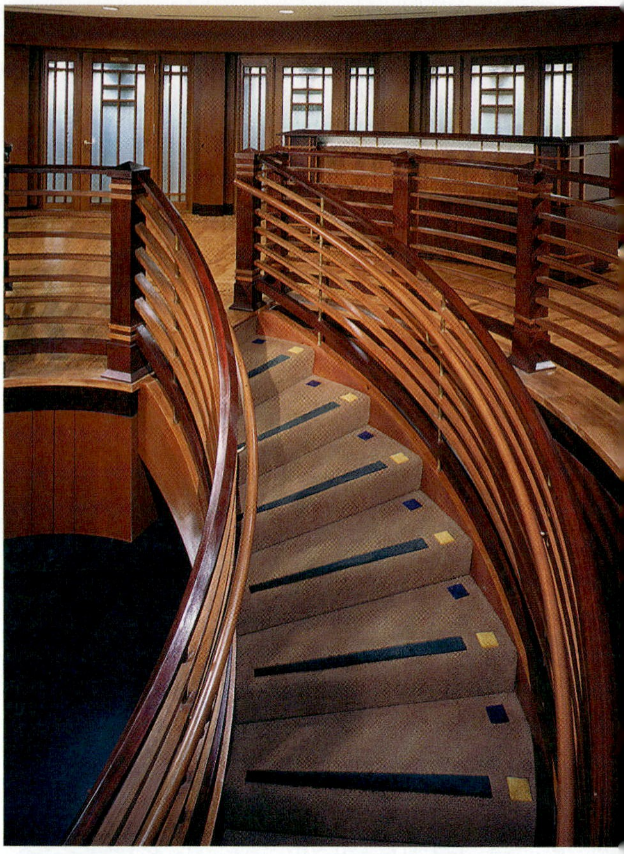

Figure 4.5 *The Arts and Crafts movement (see page 51) inspired this spiral staircase designed for the American Fores & Paper Association. (Architect/Designer: Greenwell Goetz Architects. Photograph by David Patterson.)*

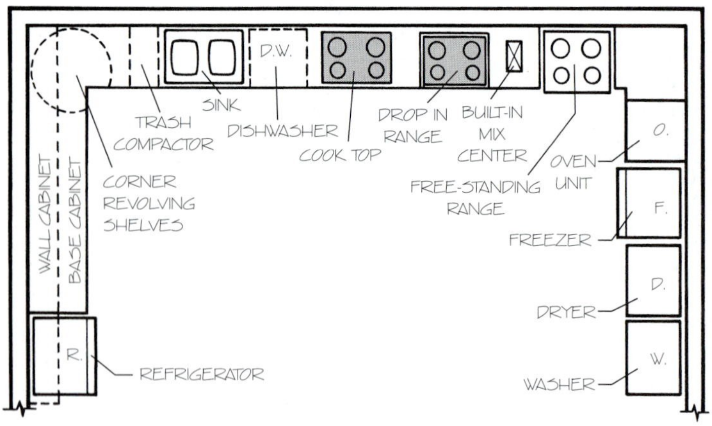

Figure 4.4 *Kitchen symbols.*

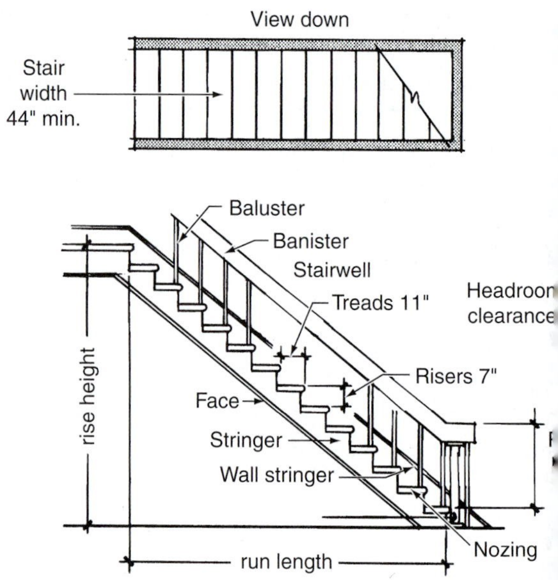

Figure 4.6 *Stairway terminology.*

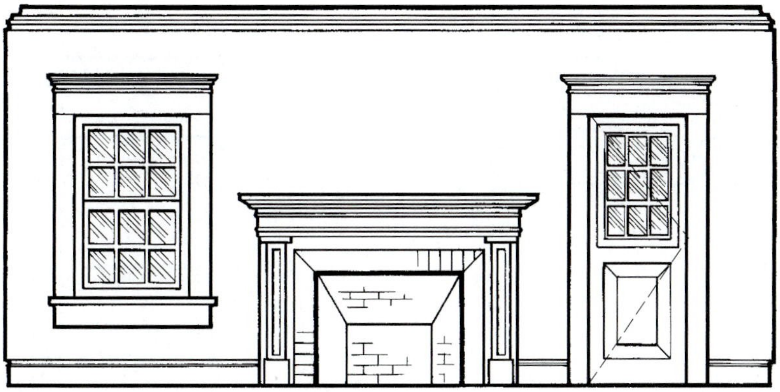

gure 4.7 *Typical elevation of a fireplace wall.*

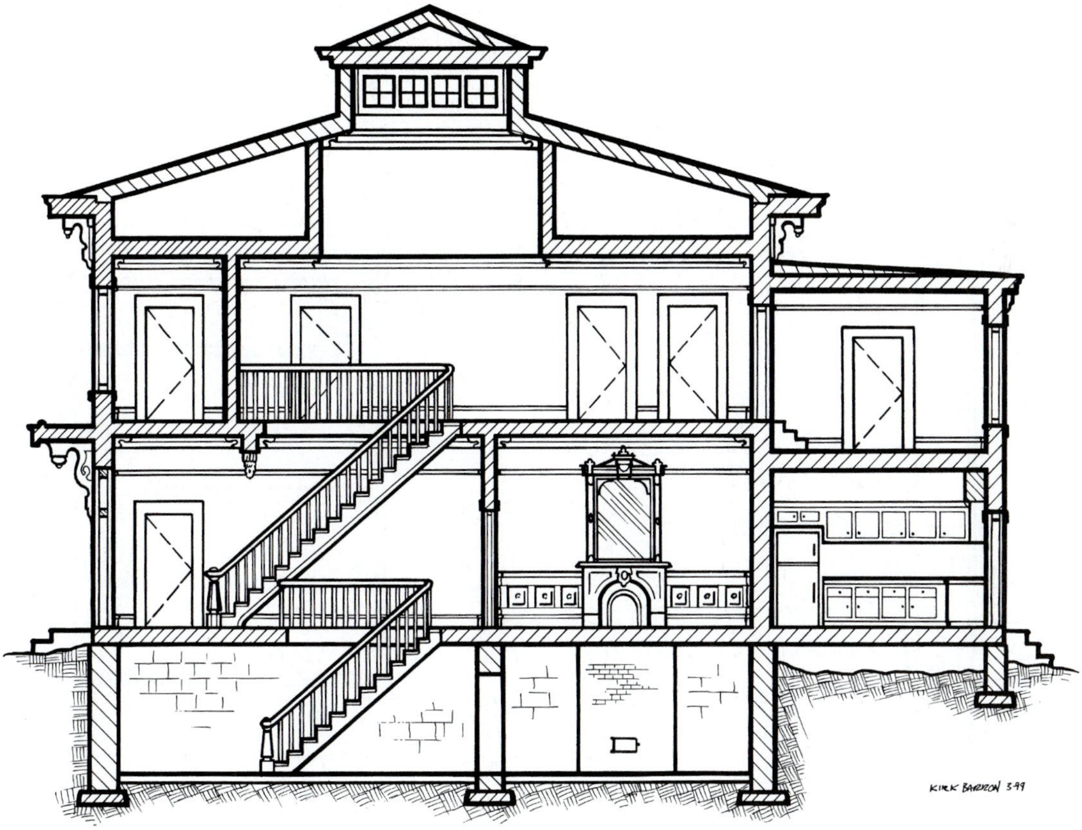

gure 4.8 *Transverse section of a three-story building.*

nish Plans

nish plans, drawn by designers, define what as well as here finishes are placed on floors, walls, and ceilings. Some signers use finish schedules instead of plans. The schedule a chart indicating the finish and its location on each surface.

evations

evations are drawings of the walls. Exterior elevations de- eate the outside of the building and define finish materials, as well as heights and locations of exterior components. Interior elevations are necessary to show custom cabinet or wall designs (Figure 4.7).

Sections

A **section** is a cut-through view of a building indicating appropriate framing and construction (Figure 4.8). Sections also may be cut-through interior walls or cabinets (Figures 4.9 and 4.10).

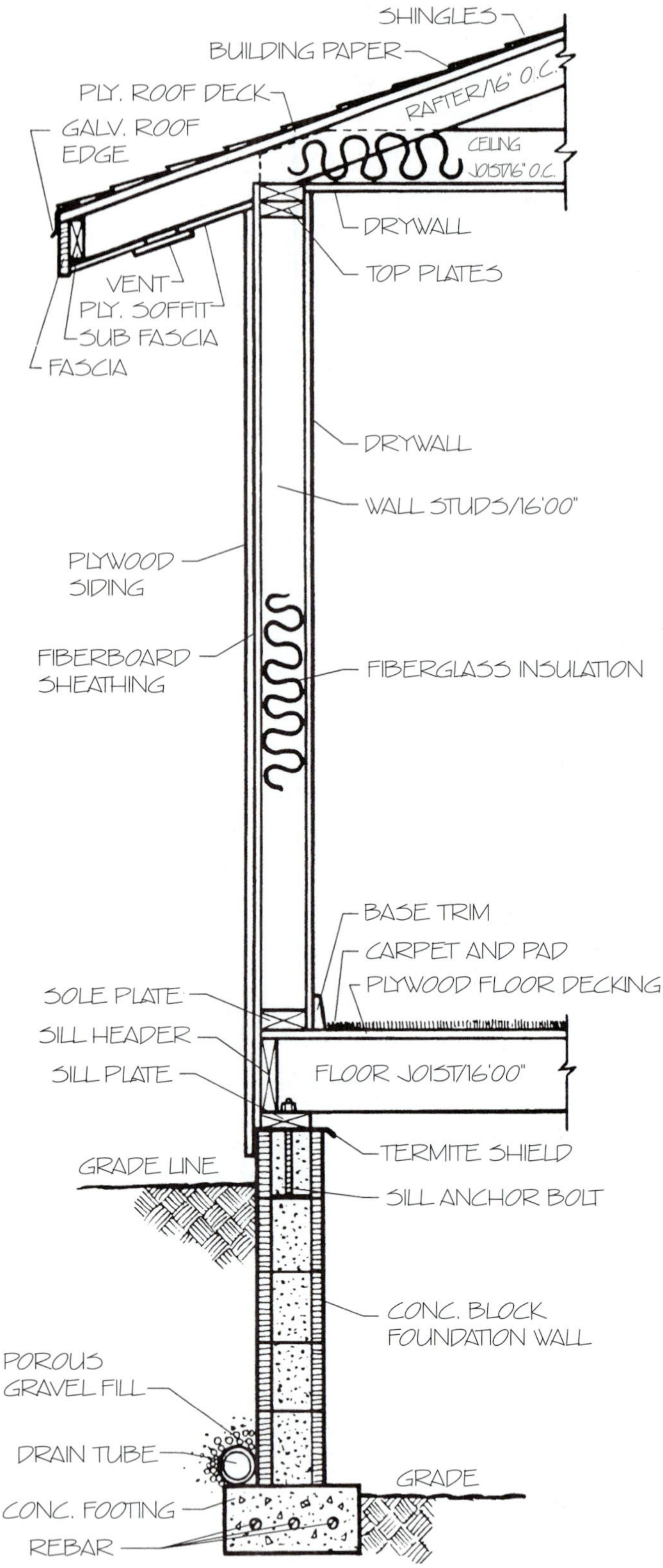

Figure 4.9 *Typical wall section. Note the terminology and use of construction symbols.*

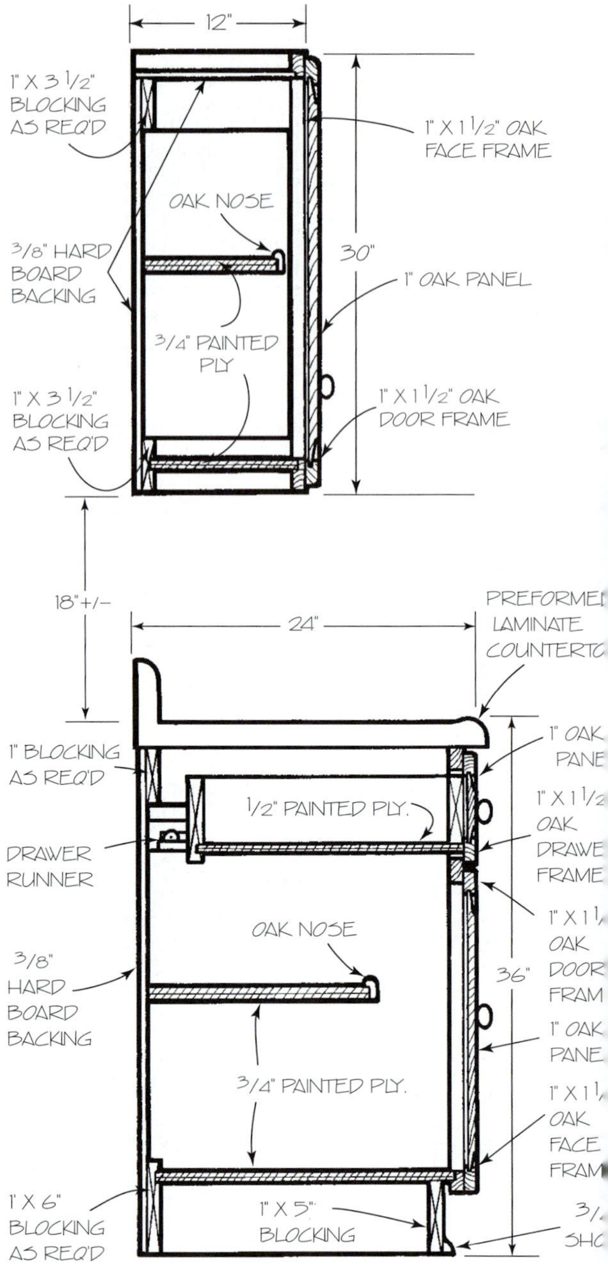

Figure 4.10 *Typical cabinet section. Designers frequently create custom cabinetry not only for kitchens, but also for media rooms, libraries, and family rooms.*

[Sc]hedules

[A] schedule is a table that indicates the material to be used in [a] specific building process, such as a chart indicating win[do]w and door information (Figure 4.11). Schedules also may [be] used to list hardware for windows and doors, as well as [fin]ish materials for floors, ceilings, and walls.

[D]etails

[De]tails are enlarged drawings indicating how components [ar]e to be constructed. Interior designers may design particu[lar] furniture pieces and wall moldings or trim. The most [co]mmon interior details relate to the design of custom cabi[ne]try such as bookshelves, media centers, built-in computer [de]sks, and custom storage and kitchen units.

One of the key design elements true to all cabinet con[str]uction involves construction style. The two broad divisions [ar]e *faceframe construction* and *frameless construction*.

Faceframe construction allows the doors and drawers of the cabinets to be flush (in the same plane). The frame of the cabinet is recessed forming a reveal, and may be made of the same or contrasting materials (Figures 4.12 and 4.13).

Frameless construction is a cleaner, contemporary style of construction. Only doors and drawer fronts are visible. Wood grains can be matched between door and drawer fronts. Plastic laminates are well suited for this style (Figures 4.14 and 4.15).

[Mo]re info online @

[htt]p://www.awinet.org/ American Woodworking Institute

[htt]p://www.kcma.org/ Kitchen Cabinet Manufacturers Association

[htt]p://www.kraftmaid.com/Main/DoorConstr.htm Images of cabinet [co]nstruction

[R]oofing Plans and Engineering Drawings

[Ro]ofing plans and engineering drawings provide designers [wi]th an insight into building systems. In general, designers [sh]ould check that electrical, lighting, communication, and emergency lighting systems are placed where specified by the engineers. Where possible, emergency lighting and alarms should be selected and placed to blend with the interior finishes.

Interior designers must be able to read, interpret, and in many instances assist in preparing construction drawings for non-load-bearing walls. Terminology and specific processes in building systems follow.

Heating, Ventilating, and Air-Conditioning (HVAC) Systems

HVAC systems are designed to maintain human comfort. In addition to controlling temperature, HVAC systems should also regulate the humidity, air quality, and air movement through a space. The most common heating systems are forced air heat, radiant heat, and solar energy. (Also see "Sustainable Design: Solar Energy.")

Forced Air Heat

Forced air heaters require a furnace and ductwork. The furnace heats air, which is then forced through the ductwork by a fan. Return vents draw cool air back into the furnace for recirculation (Figure 4.16). A heat pump works in conjunction with a furnace by extracting heat from the outside air.

Radiant Heat

Radiant heat is available through steam heating systems, electric baseboards, portable space heaters, and wood stoves.

In a steam heating system, water is heated in a furnace or boiler and then carried by a water pump through pipes. Thin metal fins surrounding the pipes radiate the heat into the room. Electric or gas baseboard heaters and portable heaters work in similar fashion by heating strips or coils, which in turn radiate the heat into the surrounding space. Wood stoves are discussed in Chapter 12.

Both forced air and radiant heating systems may require the use of a separate humidifier to control the level of humidity.

Key	Quan	Rough Opng.	Type	Mfg. No.	Mullion	Remarks
W-1	3	2'-11" × 2'-6"	SASH	3W 1748	NONE	Painted
W-2	8	3'-10" × 2'-6"	"	3W 1783B	1'-3 1/3"	Stained
W-3	7	3'-9" × 2'-6"	"	3W 1785	2'-3 1/3"	Stained
W-4	2	4'-11" × 3'-2"	CASEMENT	3W 1880	NONE	See Detail
W-5	4	4'-5" × 2'-3 7/8"	CASEMENT	AA6 1440	NONE	Stained

[Fig]ure 4.11 *Window schedule.*

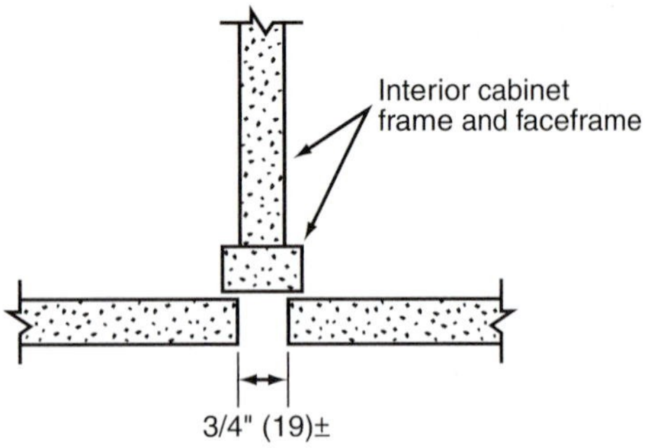

Figure 4.12 *Section looking down on two cabinet doors. Note recessed faceframe in construction.*

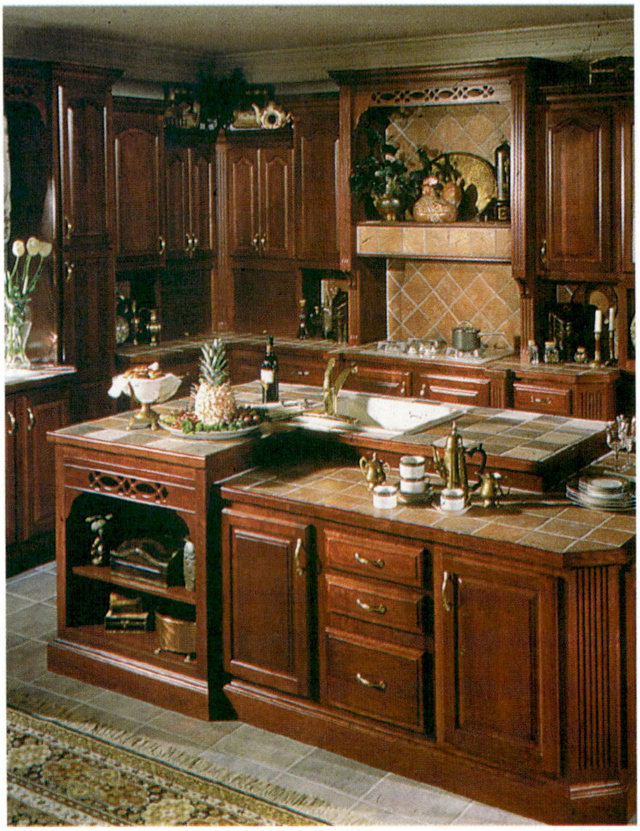

Figure 4.13 *In this interior, faceframe cabinet construction was used to give a warm traditional look. (Courtesy Quality Cabinets, Division of Texwood Industries Inc.)*

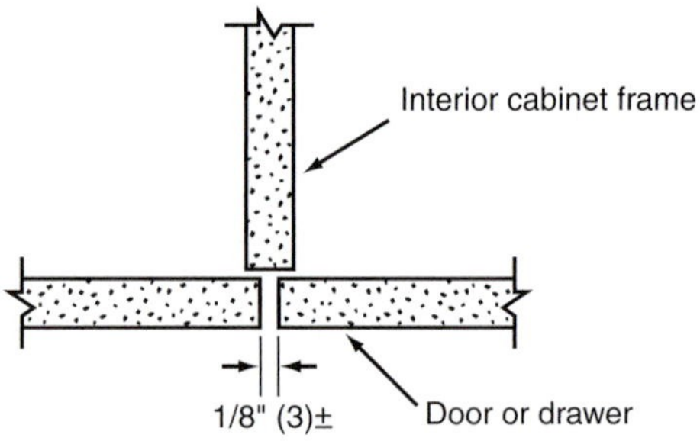

Figure 4.14 *Section looking down on two cabinet doors. No flush front appearance in frameless construction.*

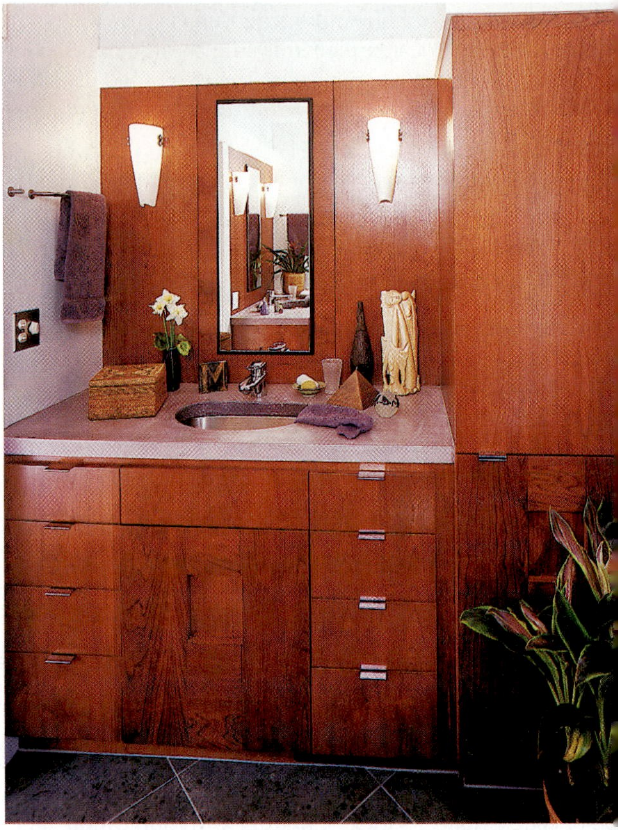

Figure 4.15 *This bathroom cabinet utilizes frameless construction to achieve its sleek, clean appearance. Cherry wood with chrome drawer pulls accentuates the image. (Architect/Designer: Lippert & Lippert Design, Palo Alto, CA. Photograph by Don Roper Photography.)*

Ventilation

Ventilation refers to the exchange of air inside a room. Natural ventilation occurs when windows and doors are left open to allow breezes to enter the building.

Hot, stale air rises in a room and should be vented via skylights, high windows, or exhaust fans. Ceiling fans also help to circulate air. Cooler, cleaner air is drawn in from windows and doors as hot air is eliminated. Cross-ventilation is also helpful wherever possible.

When fresh air is not brought into buildings, stale air a toxins emitted from plastics, chemical finishes, smoke, a other airborne pollutants can lead to **sick building sy drome.** (See "Sustainable Design: Indoor Air Quality.")

A ventilation standard has been set by the American S ciety of Heating, Refrigeration, and Air Conditioning En neers. The standard, called ASHRAE #62-1989, althou primarily applied by HVAC engineers, establishes airfl minimums for interiors.

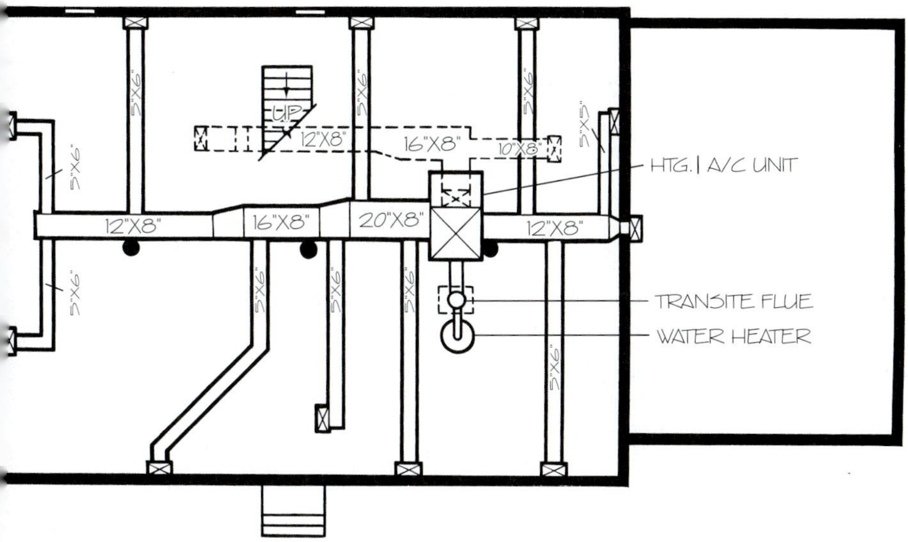

Figure 4.16 *In this HVAC plan, numbers indicate pipe sizes. Boxes with X's indicate registers. Dotted lines indicate the return air flow system.*

ir-Conditioning

r-conditioning refers to the cooling of a building. With cen- ıl air-conditioning, a forced air heating system's ductwork used in conjunction with a separate cooling unit. Individ- ıl units may be installed in the wall or window to cool sep- ate rooms or areas. In humid climates, a dehumidifier ould also be installed.

In dryer climates, evaporative coolers, called swamp olers, force air through moistened filters and pads, thereby moving heat and providing cooled air.

With all HVAC systems, designers must avoid blocking pply and return air vents; otherwise, the systems will not nction as designed. In new construction, designers should ork with engineers to place vents away from possible fur- ture arrangements and window treatments.

lumbing

umbing systems include the supply system for bringing ater to the building, the system for heating the water, the ctures involved in distributing the water, the removal of astewater (black water from commodes and gray water om all other sources), and the required venting of the sys- m. Plumbing also may include sprinkler systems in high- e buildings and public places. Typical plumbing symbols e shown in Figure 4.17.

upply Systems

ater may be supplied via a county or city water system, or may be received from a well. In remote arid regions, rain- l may be collected in a large reservoir and piped to a use. No matter what system is used, water must be pres- rized to flow from the faucet.

Water containing a high concentration of minerals may ed to be softened or purified to prevent laundry problems d accumulated deposits in pipes. Minerals also may add a rticular taste to water.

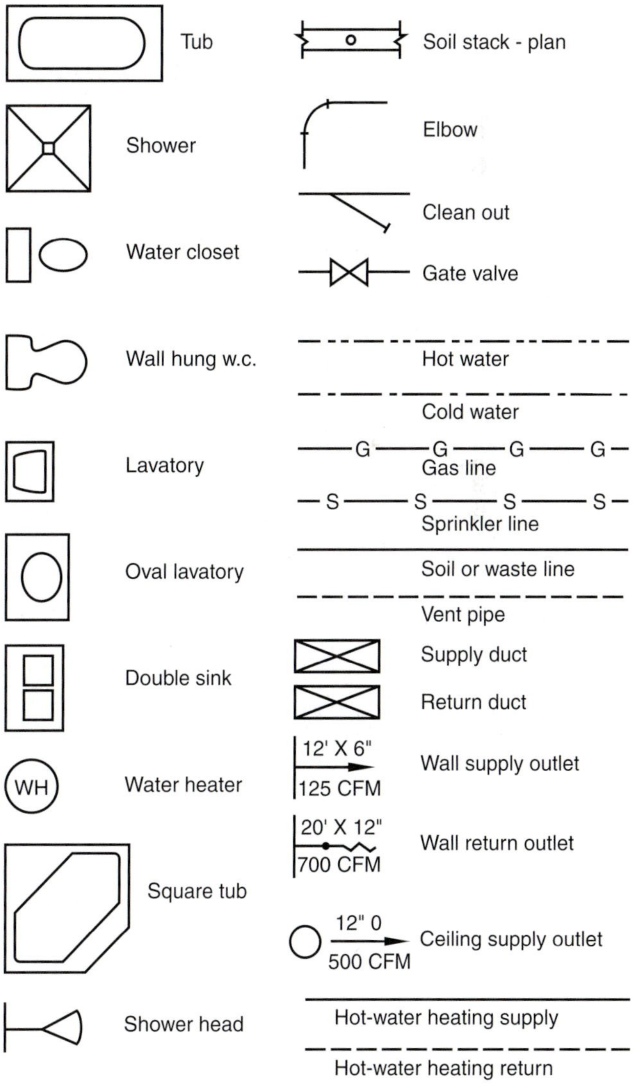

Figure 4.17 *Plumbing and heating symbols.*

SUSTAINABLE DESIGN

Solar Energy

Solar buildings are built to capture the sun's energy and conserve conventional fuel.

The passive solar system The **passive solar system** is a nonmechanical method relying on the building itself to absorb and store the sun's heat. (Note: All compass directions are given relative to the Northern hemisphere; for Southern hemisphere applications, substitute north for south.)

- Buildings are space planned so that frequently used spaces are on the south side.
- Windows are generally limited to the south wall, with occasional east and west wall use.
- The north side of the building is slightly **bermed,** or buried under dirt.
- Evergreen trees are planted to the northwest of the building to block cold winter winds.
- Deciduous trees (those that lose their leaves in winter) are placed to the south to block the hot summer sun, yet allow winter sun to reach the building.
- Overhanging eaves are designed in accordance with the angle of the sun to allow winter sun to enter a building, while blocking summer sun.
- Thermal storage units, such as masonry walls, fireplaces, stone floors, or large water containers (such as an indoor pool), are located to absorb solar energy during the day. At night, the stored heat is released into the building.
- Exterior doors enter into small passageways that serve as an air lock.
- Highly efficient stoves may function as auxiliary heating devices.
- In the summer, lower windows may be opened to draw in cooler air, while skylights, ceiling fans, and upper windows are used to draw the warmer air up and out of the building.
- Low-growing vines and shrubs are planted on the south side of the building to prevent glare.

The active solar system The **active solar system** relies on mechanical means—photovoltaic (or solar) panels, fans, and pumps—in addition to the principles of passive solar design to trap and use energy from the sun.

Active solar systems can also provide electricity for the building. Photovoltaic panels convert sunlight into DC electricity, which is stored in a series of batteries. An inverter changes the electricity from DC to AC, the type used in conventional building designs. Batteries are generally housed in a utility room with a small vent to the outside for gases to escape.

A solar batch water heater can be used in sunbelt areas. This type of water heater provides hot water by mid-morning on sunny days, and keeps it hot until well after sunset.

More info online @

http://www.ises.org/ises.nsf!Open International Solar Energy Society

http://www.seia.org/ Solar Energy Industries Association

Heating Systems

Water may be heated via gas, electric, wood, or solar water heater. (Gas and electric are the most common.) Water heaters should be reasonably close to their source of use. On-demand water heaters are placed immediately next to their source of use; they have no holding tank. These small units fit in walls or under sinks and heat water only as needed.

Plumbing Fixtures

Fixtures for commodes, bidets, and lavatories are availab from many manufacturers. Porcelain fixtures are the mo common and are available in many different colors. White neutral colors serve clients best, because black and oth dark-colored fixtures show soap rings easily. As color pre erences change, paint and wallcoverings can be adapted coordinate with white or neutral fixtures.

SUSTAINABLEDESIGN

Indoor Air Quality

Most people are familiar with the detrimental effects of outdoor air pollution, but indoor air pollution may be equally (if not more) hazardous to one's health. Indoor air quality, or **IAQ,** has come under close scrutiny because it is estimated that Americans spend 90 percent of their time indoors.

In general, indoor air pollution results in what has been termed *sick building syndrome* or SBS. SBS defines a building where inhabitants complain of health problems, such as respiratory, sinus, and digestive problems, irritability, and fatigue. The sources of indoor air pollution are complex but can be divided into three general types of pollutants:

1. Biological—organic toxins such as bacteria, molds, dust mites, and insects.
2. Earth elements—harmful naturally occurring materials such as sheetrock dust, asbestos, and radon.
3. Volatile organic chemicals (VOCs)—chemicals that are emitted into the air from building materials, furniture, fabrics or finishes, and other building processes. Typical VOCs include formaldehyde, styrene, and benzene.

According to the American Society of Interior Designers' *Indoor Air Quality Two-Part Program,* pollutants may stem from a variety of sources throughout a building, including the following:

- Construction products such as sealers, insulation, paint, caulks, and adhesives
- Fixtures and furnishings such as carpet, carpet pads and adhesives, furniture, finishes, and chipboard
- Waxes, polishes, solvents, and insect repellents
- Machines and electronics such as computer screens, printers, and lasers, which may emit electromagnetic fields
- Photographic processes, perfumes, and sprays
- Operational equipment, inadequate air filtering, poorly designed HVAC systems, or standing water

As a member of the construction team, a designer should be familiar with IAQ issues and products. For instance, the Carpet and Rug Institute (CRI) has developed a testing program for carpet, cushions, and adhesives. Products that meet low levels of emissions of VOCs are allowed to carry its label. CRI also makes the following installation recommendations.

- Carefully plan the carpet installation using the manufacturer's installation guidelines and/or the *CRI 104 Standard for Installation of Commercial Textile Floorcovering Materials.*
- Ensure adequate fresh air ventilation during the entire installation process and for 48–72 hours afterwards.
- Vacuum the old carpet prior to removal to minimize airborne dust.
- Vacuum the subfloors prior to carpet installation.
- Use low-VOC adhesive in glue-down installations.
- Use low-emitting carpet cushion.
- Vacuum the new carpet with a high-efficiency vacuum, using a high-efficiency particulate filter bag to minimize airborne particles. Make sure all moisture and cleaning agents are removed with each cleaning.

In addition to the proper selection of products, designers should remember the following:

- Avoid blocking air intakes and vents with window treatments or furnishings.
- Install exhaust fans in smoking areas, bathrooms, kitchens, and other areas where chemicals or sprays may be used.
- Provide humidity controls.
- Encourage proper maintenance.
- When installing open office systems, allow airflow at the base of the partition (1″–6″).*
- Arrange computer terminals so that users are seated 30″ away from the computer screen to avoid the electromagnetic fields.*

One part of an IAQ program is the installation of live plants, which act as air filters by absorbing indoor air pollutants. For example, the philodendron and the spider plant absorb formaldehyde, and the common peace lily absorbs benzene. Through the process of photosynthesis, plants trap airborne contaminants, as well as regenerate the air with oxygen. However, plants are not a quick fix for a sick building. They do require maintenance and proper light.

Finally, designers should monitor the market for advances in IAQ research and should maintain documents regarding IAQ design decisions.

*From Grazyna Pilatowicz, in *Eco-Interiors*.

More info online @

http://www.eeba.org/default.htm Energy and Environmental Building Association

http://www.sbicouncil.org/ Sustainable Buildings Industry Council

http://www.energybuilder.com/greenbld.htm Green Building Guide

http://www.epa.gov/iaq/atozindex.html EPA Indoor Air Quality Index

www.envirosense.org The Envirosense Consortium is a nonprofit organization that addresses IAQ

http://www.rmi.org/ Rocky Mountain Institute

http://www.carpet-rug.com/ Carpet and Rug Institute

http://www.healthhouse.org/ Information on how to build a healthy house sponsored by the American Lung Association

Contemporary bathrooms may also use the fixtures as sculptural forms (Figure 4.18 and Figure 2.10). Faucets that blend hot and cold water and do not require gripping are preferred. All lavatories, including freestanding pedestal sinks, need a surface nearby for the placement of toiletries.

Shower stalls and bathtubs are commonly made from fiberglass. These fixtures should have smooth corners and no crevices where dirt can collect. As with the commode and lavatory fixtures, white or light neutral colors are usually the wisest choice (Figure 4.19).

Waste Removal

The removal of wastewater involves three important concepts:

1. Wastewater from commodes (called black water) requires a minimum 4″ pipe, which will not fit in a standard 2″ × 4″ stud wall. Wastewater plumbing on upper floors must be routed through a wider 2″ × 6″ stud wall, or carried down a **chase** (a concealed column usually located in the corner of a room).
2. All waste lines (both black and gray water) must tie into air vents that allow fumes to escape through the roof of the building.
3. Wastewater relies on gravity to flow to the septic tank or municipal sewer system. Consequently, all wastewater pipes must have a downward slope of 1/4″ for every horizontal foot of length. In high-rise buildings and commercial spaces with poured concrete floors, commodes must be located near predetermined sanitary lines and wet columns (columns with hidden supply and sanitary water lines). If a drain is located in a basement that is below the level of the septic tank or mu-

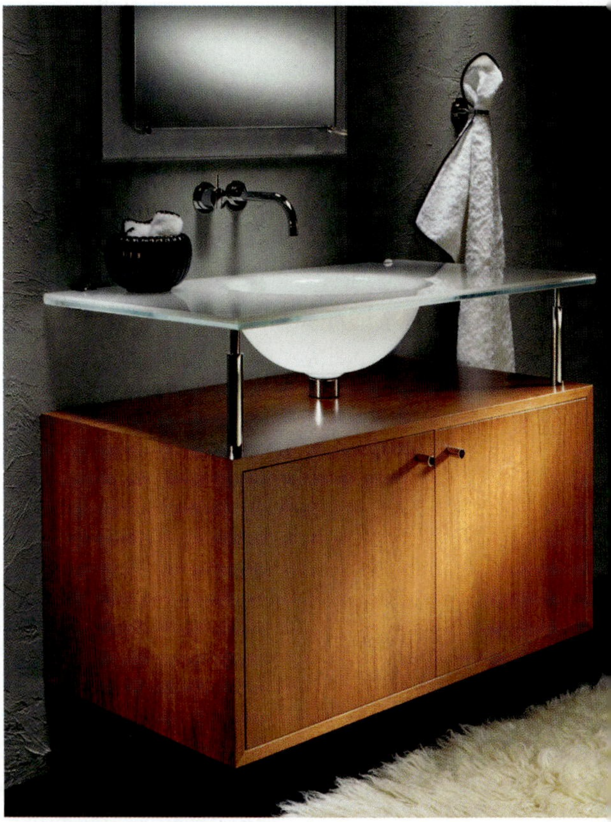

Figure 4.18 *This glass sink is artfully suspended from the wall and balanced on top of a flush front cabinet. Note the hardware recessed into the wall, combining a mix of hot an cold water. The level handle not only meets universal design criteria, but also is easily used even with soapy hands. (Courtesy of Vitraform.)*

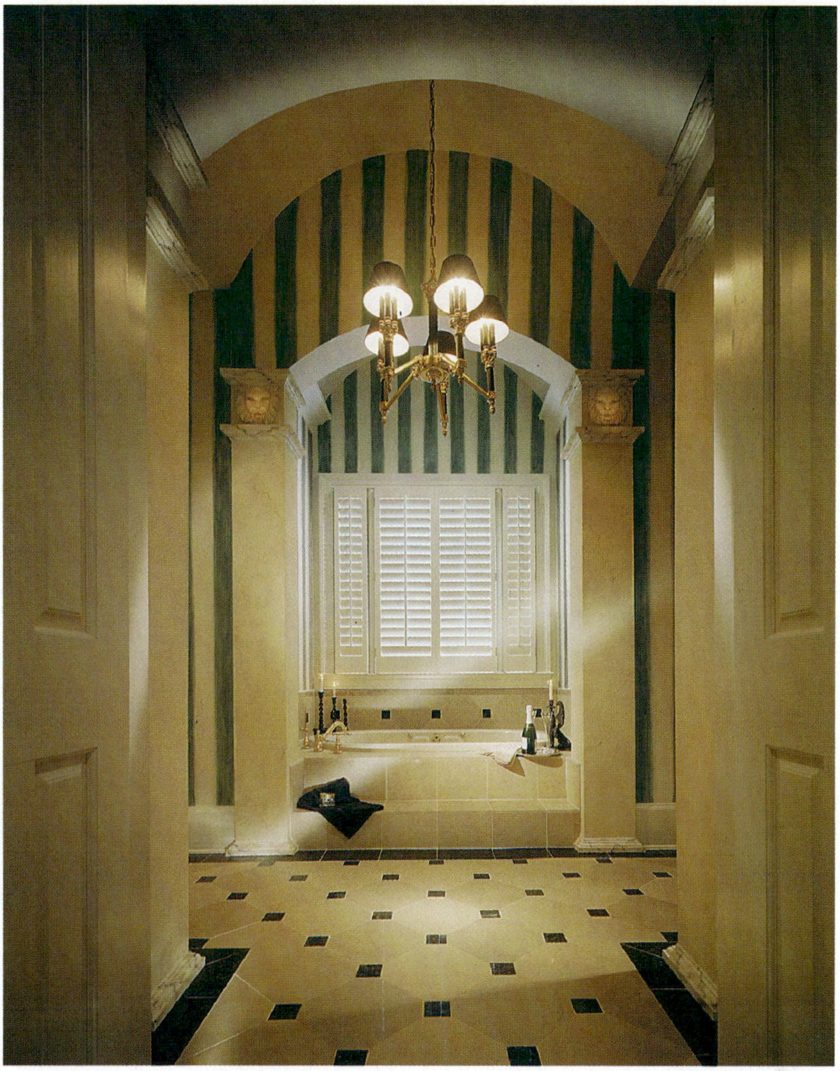

gure 4.19 *In this renovated bathroom, the designer provided a variety of lighting accents and classical details to create functional and elegant space. (Design by Jackie Naylor Interiors. Photograph ©Robert Thien. As seen in* Atlanta Homes & estyles.*)*

nicipal sewer system, a sump pump is installed in the floor of the basement to pump the wastewater up and out of the building.

gure 4.20 illustrates a typical residential drainage system.

coustics

und can travel directly through the air and also may be nsmitted through objects. Designers can assist in controlg sound through proper space planning and material age.

Sound is measured in **decibels** (dB). Zero dB is the ietest sound an average human can hear, and 130 dB is threshold of painfully loud sounds. A private office or home generally has noise levels at about 30 dB—the maximum level at which most individuals can concentrate on work.

Residential and commercial spaces are generally zoned so that noisy and quiet activities are separated. For instance, closets and bookshelves may buffer noisy areas (see Chapter 7). Walls may be constructed with additional layers of gypsumboard, dense insulation, alternating studs, or a combination of all three to prevent sound transmission.

Sound may also be controlled by using materials that absorb its energy. Hard surfaces such as concrete floors and tile are dense and although they are good at preventing the transmission of sound, their hardness causes sound waves to reflect back into the room. Carpeting, soft window treatments, upholstered furniture, and acoustical

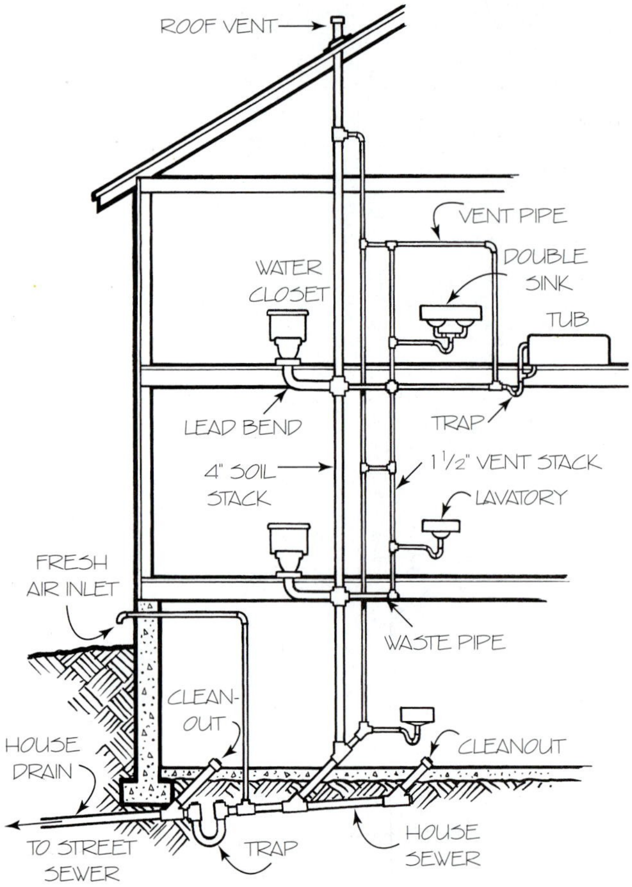

Figure 4.20 *Multistory residential wastewater system.*

ceiling tiles absorb sound waves and thereby help to quiet a room.

According to "Sound Solutions," published by ASID, the proper selection and installation of four important design elements help achieve an acceptable level of conversational background noise. These four elements are ceiling systems, systems furniture, sound masking systems, and carpeted floors.

Ceiling systems are best when they have an articulation class rating of 180–200. Articulation class rating measures a ceiling material's ability to absorb sound. Ceiling design should not include hard acrylic or small 1/2-inch cube lenses over light fixtures. The 3-inch to 8-inch cell fixtures function better to reduce noise.

System furniture (freestanding office furniture discussed in Chapter 8) also should meet criteria to be acoustically effective. For instance, panels are acoustically best when they are at least 65 inches high. They should have a Sound Transmission Class rating or STC of 18 or higher, and a Noise Reduction Coefficient or NRC of .60 or more. Additionally, designers of open office areas should avoid planning direct line of sight layouts between workers. Designs may incorporate smaller 60–80 square-foot enclosed spac that open into community areas. (See Design Scenario: U Innoplex at the end of Chapter 3.)

Sound masking systems provide an ambient backgrou sound that masks conversational noise. Systems are gen ally set at about 48 dB. Although this is louder than 30 d because the sound is consistent, it helps mask oth sounds.

The final primary design element to help reduce conv sational noise is the addition of a jute or polyurethane carp cushion. Both greatly enhance the acoustical privacy of interior environment.

Additional design solutions to conceal noise include va ations in wall angles to direct sounds to different are Avoiding the use of right angles and parallel surfaces will i prove sound attenuation. Acoustical engineers consult theatre, concert hall, and large auditorium designs to e hance and distribute reverberating sounds.

Other Concealed Systems

In residential interiors, *central vacuum systems* may routed through walls. These units are particularly helpful multistory residences so vacuum cleaners do not have to moved up and down stairs.

Security systems are another component concealed the walls of residential and nonresidential structur Sensing devices activate alarms, turn on lights, or m even dial the local authorities or security company. Ala systems are the least costly when installed prior to fi ished construction.

Fire alarms are required by codes in commercial bui ings and are integrated into the building structure. The smoke- and heat-sensing devices emit audible as well as sual alarms. Additionally, *sprinkler systems* are located commercial buildings to help stop or suppress the spread fire. The systems are usually concealed in the ceiling w only the head of the sprinkler exposed on or below the ce ing's surface. Most sprinkler systems spray water; however few emit fire-retarding foam.

In residential environments, homes are equipped w smoke detectors that alert occupants to potential fir Smoke detectors should be placed in kitchen, family, a bedroom areas.

Codes and Federal Regulations

Interior designers are legally responsible for being aware and implementing applicable local, state, or federal cod Federal regulations are mandated by law and required gardless of local codes. Codes can be divided into the f lowing general categories: model building codes; plumbi electrical, and mechanical codes; life safety (or fire) cod and residential codes.

The International Codes Council, ICC, was develop in 1994 to create a single set of national codes. The thr

Table 4.1 *Building Codes*

Type	Purpose	Common Codes
Model building codes	Define construction requirements and limit use of hazardous materials.	• National Building Code (NBC), published by Buildings Official Code Administration International (BOCA) • Standard Building Code (SBC), published by Southern Building Code Congress International (SBCCI) • Uniform Building Code (UBC), published by International Conference of Building Officials (ICBO) • International Building Code (IBC), published by International Code Council, a joint commission of BOCA, SBCCI, and ICBO
Plumbing, electrical, and mechanical codes	Define construction requirements for these specialties. Particularly helpful in determining the number of fixtures in a building.	• Plumbing and mechanical codes published by organizations that publish model building codes • National Electrical Code (NEC), published by National Fire Protection Association (NFPA)
Life safety or fire codes	Establish minimum requirements for fire safety.	• Life Safety Code (LSC, or NFPA 101®), published by NFPA
Residential codes	Define construction requirements in one- and two-family dwellings.	• One and Two Family Dwelling Code (OTFDC), published by Council of American Building Officials (CABO) • International Residential Code (IRC), published by International Code Council

evious code organizations serve as the founders of the C. Although the ICC has since established international ilding, plumbing, mechanical, and residential codes, t all states and jurisdictions have adopted the new des. Therefore, designers must check with local code ficials to determine which codes are used, and because des are usually updated every three years, from which ar.

The ICC includes prescriptive codes (codes that define act requirements) as well as performance-based codes. ese new performance-based codes allow for more xibility in design solutions, but require the designer to search information in order to convince code officials of e design solution's appropriate use. The ICC did t adopt a new electrical code, and it references the Nanal Electric Code. See Table 4.1 for more detailed scriptions.

ore info online @

p://www.intlcode.org/ International Code Council

p://www.bocai.org/ Building Official Code Administration ernational

p://www.icbo.org/ International Conference of Building Officials

p://www.sbcci.org Southern Building Code Congress International

p://www.nfpa.org/Home/index.asp National Fire Protection sociation

deral Requirements

e federal government has passed several laws that relate the design of interiors. The most common include the nericans with Disabilities Act (ADA), the Fair Housing Act HA), and the Occupational Safety and Health Act (OSHA).

The ADA, a civil rights act, was passed in 1990 and has greatly affected building design. Among other things, the ADA requires government buildings, contract design facilities (including all the specialty areas discussed in Chapter 1, Table 1.2), public accommodations (residential or otherwise), and public transportation systems to provide equal accessibility to all people regardless of disability. Many of the ADA's physical regulations are based on the 1986 American National Standards Institute (ANSI) codes (which have since been updated). Designers frequently reference the ADA. (A complete copy of the "Accessibility Guidelines for Buildings and Facilities" is available from the U.S. Architectural and Transportation Barriers Compliance Board at 1-800-USA-ABLE.) A sample of these regulations is shown in Figure 4.21. It is important to emphasize

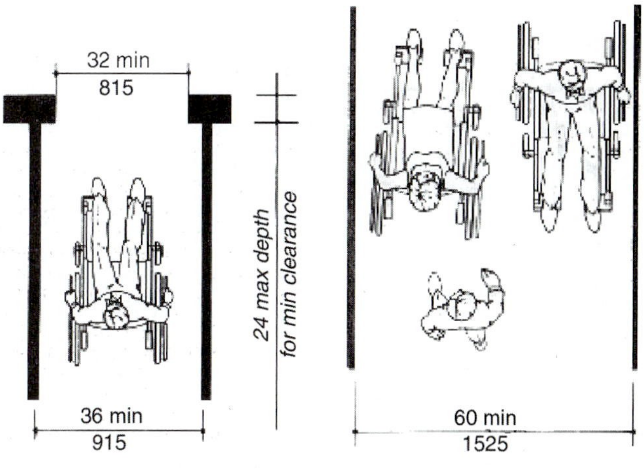

Figure 4.21 *Minimum clear width for wheelchairs, from the ADA guidelines. http://www.access-board.gov/bfdg.html*

that these regulations are laws, not codes or standards. The monitoring of these laws varies from state to state.

The FHA is similar to the ADA, but relates only to residential structures. The OSHA regulations mainly affect contractor and subcontractor work practices.

More info online @

http://www.ansi.org American National Standards Institute

http://www.hud.gov/offices/hsg/ Fair Housing Administration

http://www.osha.gov/ Occupational Safety and Health Administration

http://www.usdoj.gov/crt/ada/adahom1.htm ADA Homepage

http://www.access-board.gov/adaag/html/adaag.htm ADA Guide

http://www.ed.gov/offices/OSERS/NIDRR/About/ ADA assistance

Summary

This chapter has emphasized the designer's responsibility understand construction processes, building systems, and r lated codes. The symbols and terminology relating to the m chanical, plumbing, acoustic, and other concealed syster must be understood in order to communicate with allied pr fessionals and to share accurate information with the clier

Designers have an ethical responsibility to inform clier of alternative design solutions that may conserve energy lower utility costs. Additionally, designers must take into a count the effects furnishings and finishes may have on i door air quality. The application of low-emission produc helps to ensure a safer interior environment. Finally, it ca not be emphasized strongly enough that interior designe are legally responsible for complying with local and sta codes and federal regulations.

ighting, Electrical, and ommunications

5

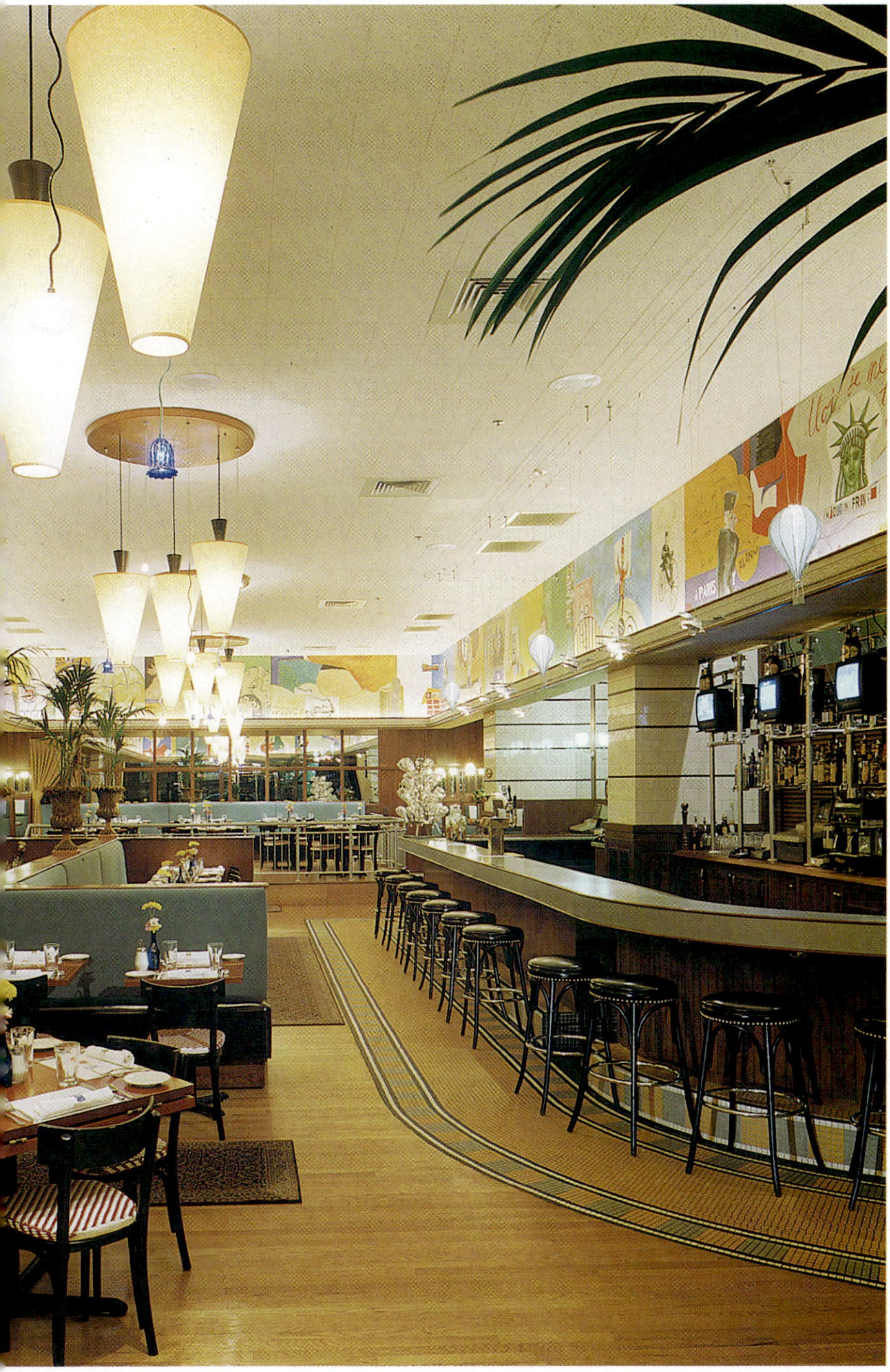

Figure 5.1 *In this vibrant French-styled brasserie, Voila!, the designers used perimeter lighting to visually widen the space and highlight the unique whimsical border. Other decorative pendant fixtures add to the carefree effect. (Architect/Designer: Knauer Inc. Photograph by Steinkamp/Ballogg.)*

Lighting, as discussed in relation to color in Chapter 3, is an essential element in all interiors. Lighting can be one of the most creative avenues in the field of interior design. Light, like color, can alter psychological and physiological reactions. Additionally, the fixtures that house the actual light source can be designed to serve as decorative art or sculpture, adding character and sometimes whimsy to the interior (Figure 5.1).

The quantity and quality of light affect the apparent size, shape, and character of an object. Interior designers can alter the perception of space in a room, focus attention, set moods, define texture, or create a specific atmosphere through the appropriate use of light. Understanding the scientific basis of light, applying this to an interior to create the desired effect, and communicating the plan to engineers and contractors are essential skills of interior designers. To begin to understand how to use light, designers must be familiar with the basic terminology and basic principles of the *quantity* and *quality* of the light source.

The professional terminology for light fixtures and lamps differs from everyday language. The light bulb itself is called the **lamp.** It is the source of light. The physical structure that holds the lamp and other necessary and decorative accouterments (such as the shade, reflector, or lens) is called the **fixture.** The lamp and the fixture form the **luminaire.**

The Quantity of Light

Light is measured in different ways (Figure 5.2), depending on where the measurement is taken:

- **Candela:** The unit of measure for the intensity of light in a given direction.
- **Lumen:** A measure of flow of light produced by one lamp. Lumens also determine the efficiency, called the **efficacy,** of a lamp. To determine the efficacy of a lamp, divide the lumens by the watts (the amount of energy consumed by the lamp). For example, suppose a new 75-watt incandescent lamp produces 1180 lumen 1180 lumens divided by 75 watts equals an efficacy ra ing of 15.7. The higher the efficacy rating, the more e cient the lamp. In practice, to select the most energy-efficient lamp, select the lamp with the lowest wattage and the highest lumen.
- **Footcandle:** The unit of measure for the amount of light falling on a surface. One footcandle is equal to t amount of light falling on one square foot of surface, one foot away from a candle. The farther the surface i from the light source, the lower the footcandle measu ment. The following are recommended footcandles fo specific tasks:

Theatre passage	1–2
Passage through a corridor	3–5
Passage though stairwells	5–10
General office work	10–20
Restaurant dining	5–20
Reading	20–30
Intense reading, kitchen preparation, shaving	40–60
Detail work	50–100+
Surgery	500+

- **Footlambert:** The unit of measure for the amount o light reflected from a surface. Generally, this is the amount of light actually seen. For example, a light-colored shiny wall may reflect 80 percent or more of the footcandles; a dark-colored, rough-textured wall may reflect less than 2 percent of the footcandles. The following are reflectance values of common colc

White	89%
Ivory	87%
Light gray	65%
Sky blue	65%
Intense yellow	62%
Light green	56%
Forest green	22%
Coconut brown	16%
Black	2%

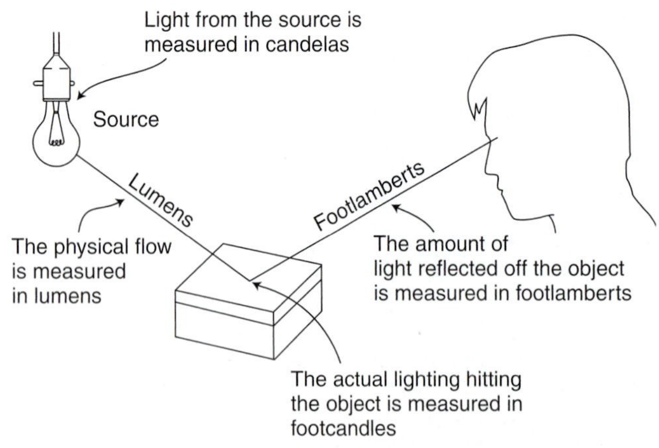

Figure 5.2 *The four measurements of the quantity of light are candelas (source), lumens (flow of light), footcandle (light falling on an object), and footlambert (reflected light).*

The Quality of Light

Light is created by wavelengths emitted from a light sou (such as the sun or a lamp). Long waves produce warm c ors; short waves produce cooler colors.

Natural daylight (the highest quality light) produces a ear color spectrum that evenly distributes the colors we (Figure 5.3). Artificial light sources do not exactly mimic r ural light's color spectrum, although some come close. instance, a typical incandescent light bulb's color spectr emphasizes the warmer red wavelengths.

As discussed in Chapter 3, the human eye sees the cc of an object when light of mixed wavelengths is reflec into the eye from the object's surface. For instance, if an ject is yellow, the surface reflects wavelengths found in yellow section of the spectrum and absorbs wavelengths the other colors.

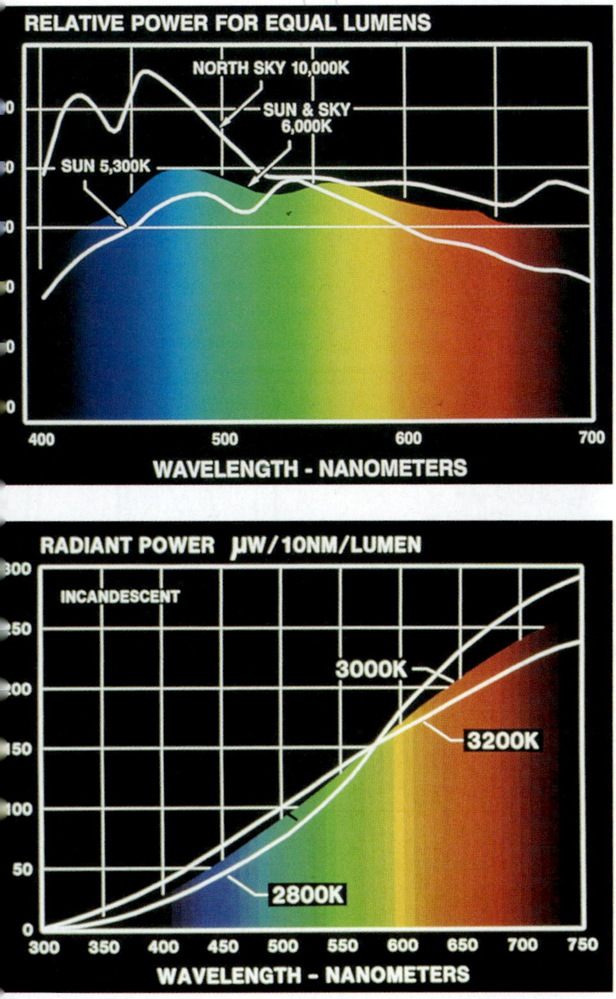

ure 5.3 *Top: The color spectrum of natural light. Bottom: e color spectrum of incandescent light. (Courtesy of GE hting.)*

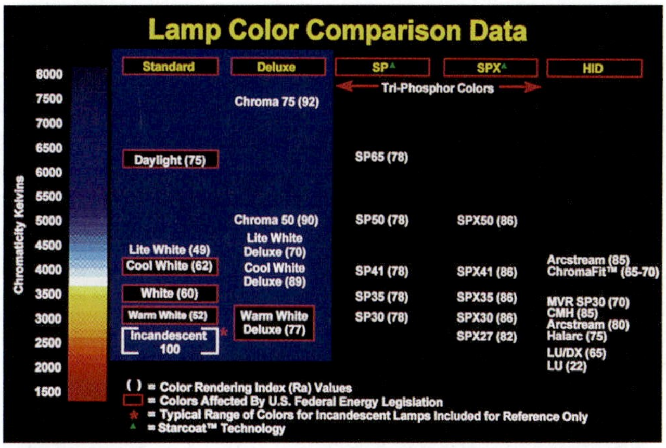

Figure 5.4 *Kelvin temperature lamp comparisons. (Courtesy of GE Lighting.)*

olor Rendering Index

e closer a lamp's color spectrum is to natural light, the gher the quality of light it produces. The measurement of s quality is called the **Color Rendering Index** (CRI). The I is based on a scale of 0–100. A CRI of 80 or better is nec- sary when color rendering is critical, such as inspecting nting proofs or selecting clothing. A CRI of 60–80 is aver- e; a CRI below 60 may be appropriate for street lighting or ner lighting when color selection is not important. Note it a higher CRI requires more energy to support the oader color spectrum.

elvin Temperature

other measurement of light quality is the light's tempera- e or **Kelvin** rating. This measurement places a candle me on the lower temperature range around 2000°K. A typ- l sunny day measures around 6000°K, and a northern night sky is said to be at about 8500°K. This concept seems backwards, but is best related to the heat of a gas fire or burner. Cooler flames burn red, warmer flames are yellow, and the hottest flame is blue. A Kelvin rating between 3000°K (typical of a quality fluorescent lamp) and 6000°K (a sunny day) is considered the natural benchmark (Figure 5.4).

Lighting Location

The quality of light also depends on the physical location of the light source. Designers must carefully locate the light source; otherwise, the resulting glare causes eye fatigue and general irritability (Figure 5.5). To prevent glare when using a portable light fixture, use a soft white bulb, a glass diffuser, and/or a lampshade.

More info online @

http://www.schorsch.com/ International website of lighting information. Includes a glossary

http://www.lrc.rpi.edu/ Lighting Research Center for universities published by Rensselaer Polytechnic Institute

http://www.lightforum.com/architecturallighting/about_us/site_map.jsp Lighting information published by *Architectural Lighting* magazine

http://www.lightsearch.com/resources/index.html Source for lighting specifiers and buyers. Includes a resource center

Natural Light Sources

Although light is regarded as a single form of energy, it is commonly divided into two categories: natural and artificial. The main source of natural light is the sun. Its properties, including ultraviolet light, warmth, and radiant energy, are important to people's health and well being. Sunlight emits all visible wavelengths of radiant energy, as well as invisible infrared wavelengths (long rays felt as heat) and ultraviolet wavelengths (short rays; see Figure 3.2).

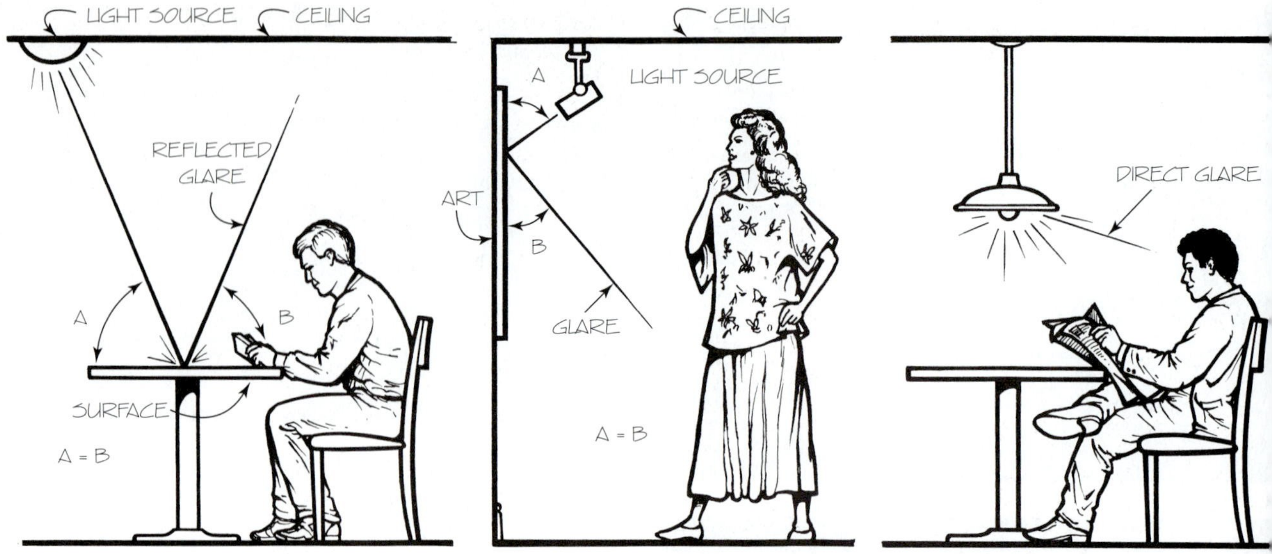

Figure 5.5 *Light is reflected off a surface at the same angle as it was received. In these diagrams, this means the angle of* A *equals the angle of* B. *Glare occurs when a viewer intercepts the reflected light or looks directly into a lamp.*

Often, the designer's challenge is to control natural light in a living space. Natural light changes from morning to evening. Therefore, a designer may treat a south- and west-facing room with muted, cooler, and darker colors to counter the sun's afternoon warmth and glaring rays. The designer can also determine the most suitable window treatment after considering the position on the site, geographic location, and climate. Natural light can be allowed to enter a space in a manner that enhances the environment and minimizes glare (see Figure 3.29).

The secondary source of natural light is combustion, pr duced by fire, oil lamps, candles, and gaslights. Until the c velopment of electric lighting, combustion was the or method of producing supplementary light.

Combustion lighting still deserves consideration as a dec rative element in residential design and for some commerc projects such as restaurants (Figure 5.6). Candles and a gas wood fire are frequently used as supplementary lighting heat. Their main value is in their soft glow that sheds a flatt ing light and creates an atmosphere of warmth and intimac

Figure 5.6 *The Canlis Restaurant, a dining landmark in Seattle, was updated from its 1950s origins. The designers used combustion lighting in the Penthouse dining room. (Architect: James Cutler Architects. Designer: Doug Raser. Photograph by Michael Jensen.)*

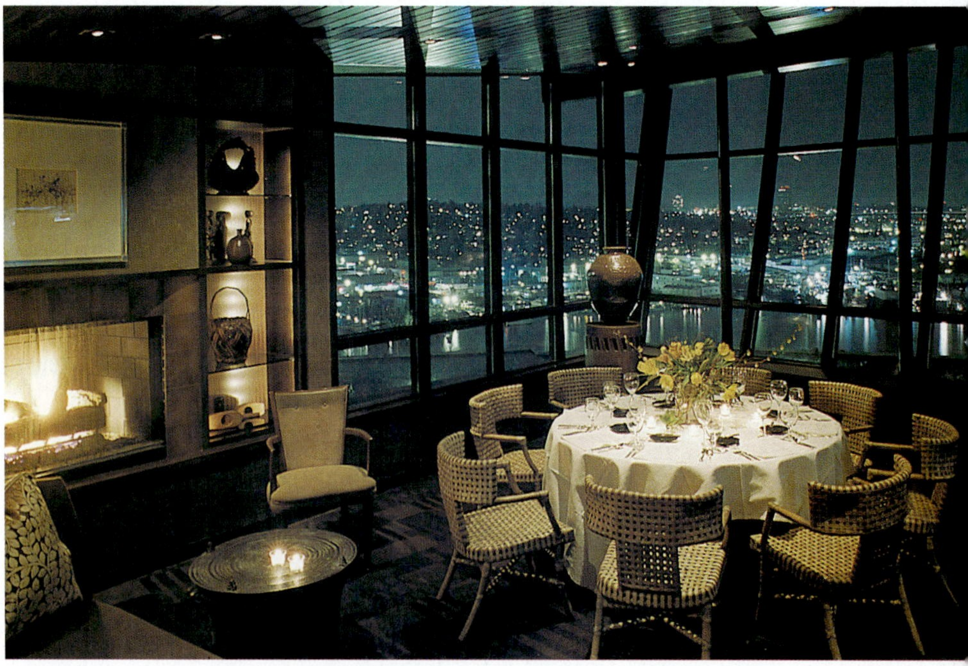

rtificial Light Sources

ificial lighting is a manufactured source of illumination de- ed from electricity. The electrical energy is transformed visible light and is identified by its wattage. The most fa- iar artificial light sources are incandescent and electric charge (which includes fluorescent) lamps. A new lamp the interiors market is the LED, or light emitting diode.

candescent Lamps

andescent lighting originated with the familiar light b invented by Thomas Edison in the latter half of the eteenth century. All **incandescent lamps** provide light heating an element (usually metal) to a Kelvin temper- re of approximately 2500–3000°K, at which point the ıp glows. Incandescent lamps include the typical gen- l service lamp, tungsten-halogen, reflector, low-voltage, l xenon lamps (Figure 5.7).

Lamps are designed by a letter identifying their style. The nber following the letter indicates the diameter of the lamp eighths of an inch. (For example, an MR16 is a lamp that ″ wide.) Lamps are usually clear or frosted (also called soft ite). The frosted lamp emits a more diffused light.

Incandescent lamps:

- Are available in a wide variety of sizes, shapes, colors, and types
- Are small and adaptable
- Produce white light that casts a slight red and yellow hue
- Are generally considered complimentary to most skin tones
- Effectively highlight textures and forms
- Can be easily dimmed
- Are relatively inexpensive to purchase, but are costly to run because of their low efficacy
- Produce heat, which can burden air-conditioning systems
- Permit precise optical control for effective accent and task lighting
- Can cause glare when exposed
- Can neutralize cool colors

A tungsten-halogen lamp is a type of incandescent lamp, but instead of a filament, the halogen lamp has a piece of hard quartz in a small enclosure. When heated it attains higher temperatures and therefore produces a more intense light and has a better performance output. Tungsten-halogen lamps also come in various styles (Figure 5.8). In addition to the above attributes, the tungsten-halogen lamps also:

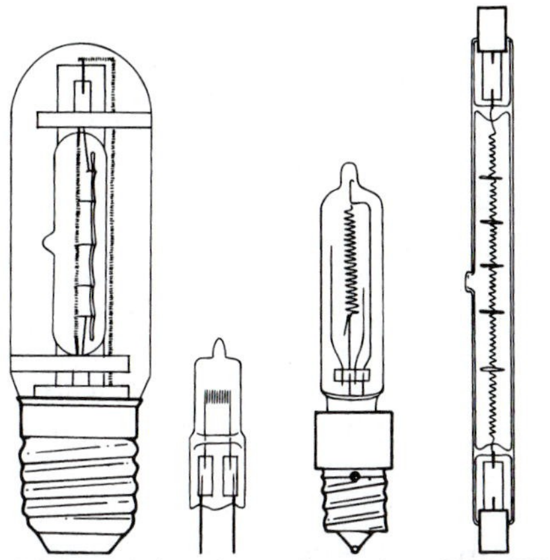

Figure 5.8 *Styles of tungsten-halogen lamps.*

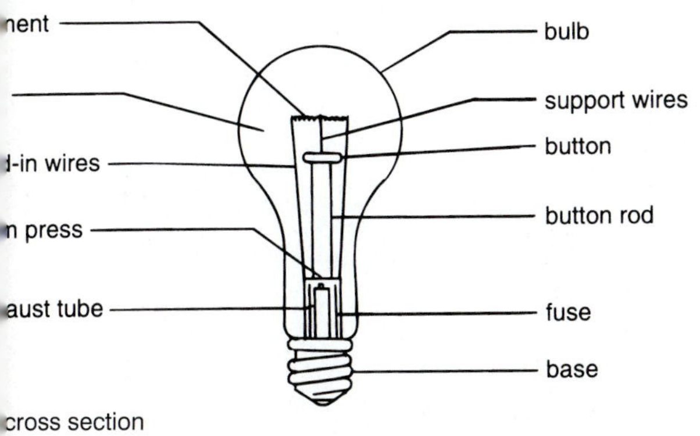

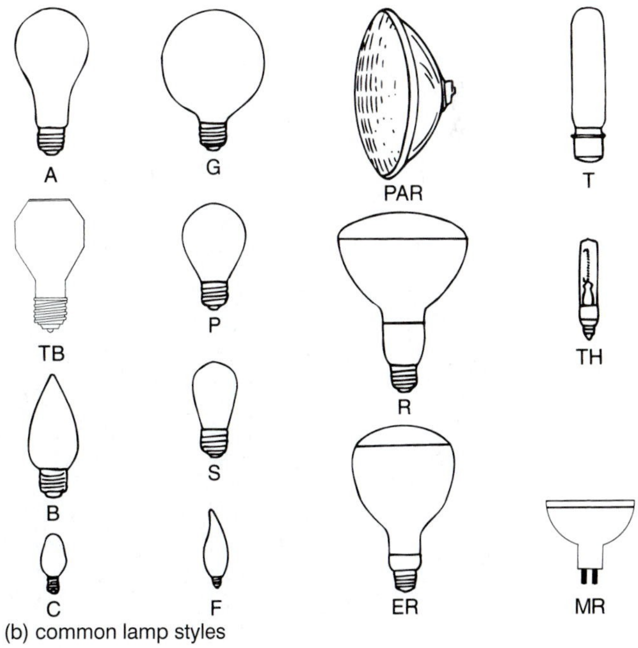

ure 5.7 *The incandescent filament lamp. (a) Cross section. (b) Common lamp styles. A: standard (arbitrary); TB: Teflon® b (used like an arbitrary); B: oval or ovoid; C: candelabra; G: globe; P: pear; S: straight side; F: flare; PAR: parabolic reflector; R: ector; ER: elliptical reflector; T: tubular; TH: tungsten-halogen; MR: multifaceted reflector (low voltage).*

- Run warmer (approximately 3000°K), producing a more intense light
- Last two to four times longer than a general service incandescent
- Are more expensive to purchase
- Must not come in contact with the oils on skin; gloves must be worn when changing a lamp
- Emit high levels of heat and therefore should not be placed near flammable objects
- Must be shielded and therefore cannot be used as a direct light source

Reflector lamps or parabolics have a hard-pressed glass covering and as the name implies, a built-in reflector to enhance light distribution. Reflector lamps are generally 3 1/2″ to 6″ wide. The typical residential exterior flood lamp is an example of a common reflector lamp.

Low-voltage lamps are basically miniature tungsten-halogen lamps commonly used to enhance retail displays. The lamps run on 12 volt or 24 volt electricity and therefore require a separate transformer concealed in the ceiling or walls. (Transformers reduce the standard 120 volt electricity into 12 or 24 volt electricity for use in these lamps.) The transformer must be accessible for maintenance.

Xenon is another type of incandescent lamp. The lamp produces a brilliant white light, like the tungsten-halogen, and is used because of its high output of lumens in low-voltage and low-wattage applications. It is frequently appl as accent lighting around countertops or in curves (Fig 5.9). The World Trade Center "Towers of Light" were p duced by xenon lamps.

Discharge Lamps

Discharge lamps produce light by passing electricity throu a gaseous tube. The most common discharge lamps are orescent, HID, and cold cathode.

Fluorescent Lighting

Fluorescent lighting, in wide use since World War II, produced in a glass tube lined with a fluorescent coati filled with mercury vapor and argon, and sealed at the en When gases are activated by an electric current, ultravic rays stimulate the phosphorous lamp coating, which en visible light. Fluorescent lamps are made in a variety shapes and sizes (Figure 5.10). The most familiar type is T12 tubular lamp that is about 1 1/2″ in diameter and con in lengths from two to eight feet.

- Fluorescent lamps emit less heat than incandescent lamps.
- Although the fixtures are expensive, they have a much higher efficacy rate (Figure 5.11). The tubes last up to

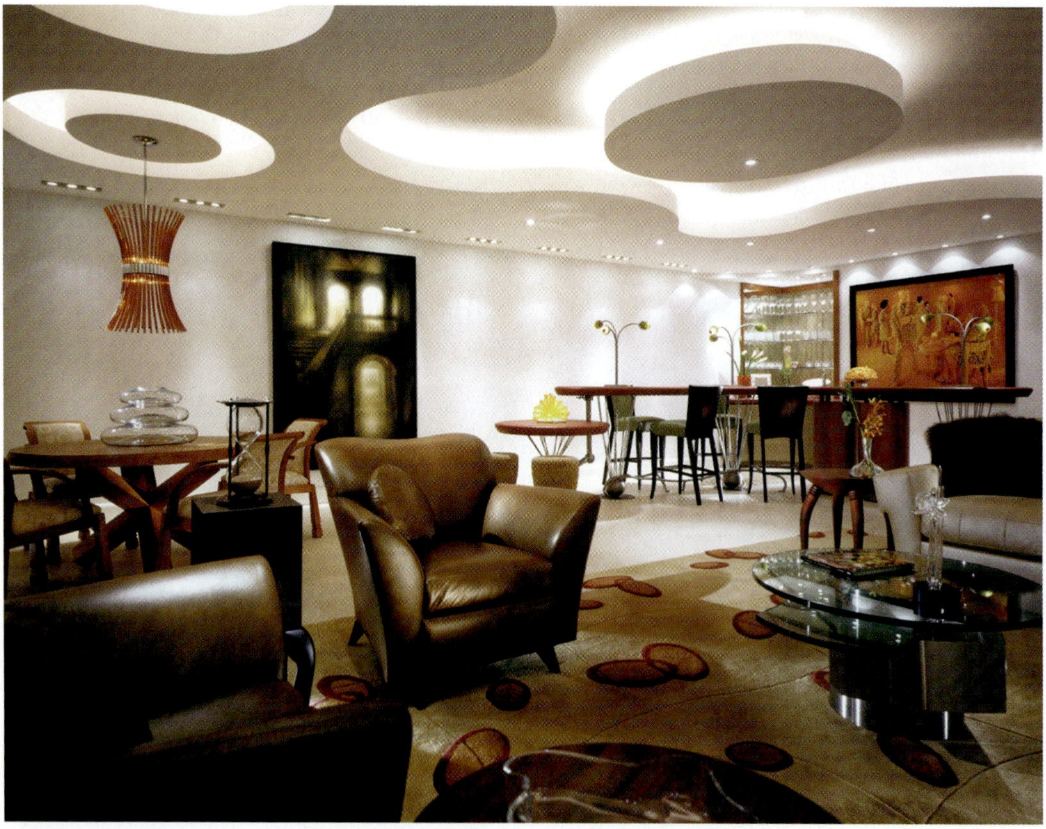

Figure 5.9 *In this contemporary residence, emphasis has been placed on the curve. Areas are defined by changes in flooring materials and ceiling design. The glow of light is produced by xenon lamps. The custom-built light fixtures on the bar are handblown to resemble olives. (Designer: Charles Greenwood, IIDA, of Greenwood Design Group, Inc. Photograph by Robert Thien © 2001.)*

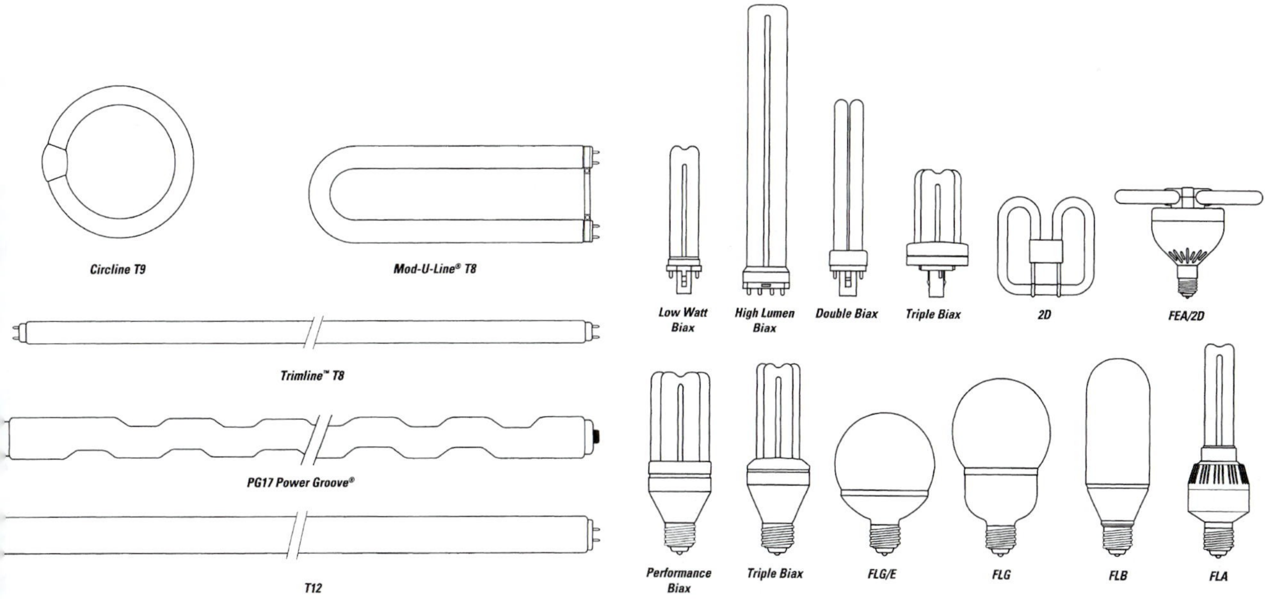

ure 5.10 *Fluorescent lamp styles, regular and compact (not to scale). urtesy of GE Lighting.)*

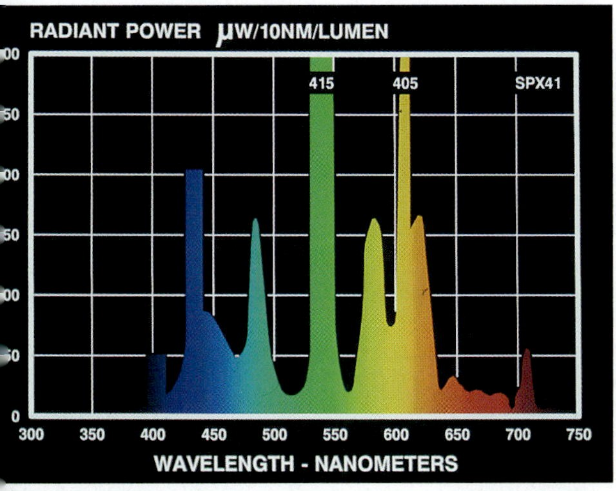

ure 5.11 *The SPX41 fluorescent lamp has a good efficacy d a good CRI rating. Its Kelvin temperature is about 00°K. (Courtesy of GE Lighting.)*

15 times longer than incandescent lamps and require about one-third as much energy.

Small fluorescent lamps may be used in many applications where incandescent lamps were formerly used.

Fluorescent sources are larger and create broader areas of light than incandescent lights.

They provide diffused, shadowless light.

Fluorescent lights are particularly efficient for commercial uses, especially in hospitals, schools, offices, stores, factories, and other large public spaces.

Fluorescent light can distort colors and details if not color corrected.

Fluorescent light is not as flexible and as easy to control as incandescent light.

Historically, fluorescent lamps produced a low CRI, but this has improved. Designers need to specify "color corrected" lamps to obtain the best color distribution.

HID Lamp

Another source of discharge lighting is the **HID** (high-intensity discharge) lamp, which incorporates some of the desirable qualities of both incandescent and fluorescent lighting. The discharge lamp is similar to the fluorescent in operational design, but in appearance it resembles an incandescent, only slightly larger (Figure 5.12). Three types of HID lamps include mercury (which tends to produce bluish light), high-pressure sodium (which tends to produce orange light and is the most efficient of the three types), and metal halide (which renders colors most accurately).

Characteristically, HID lamps

- Last from 16,000 to 24,000 hours
- Are highly efficient with about ten times the output of incandescent lighting
- Are suitable for commercial and institutional demands for energy-saving lighting

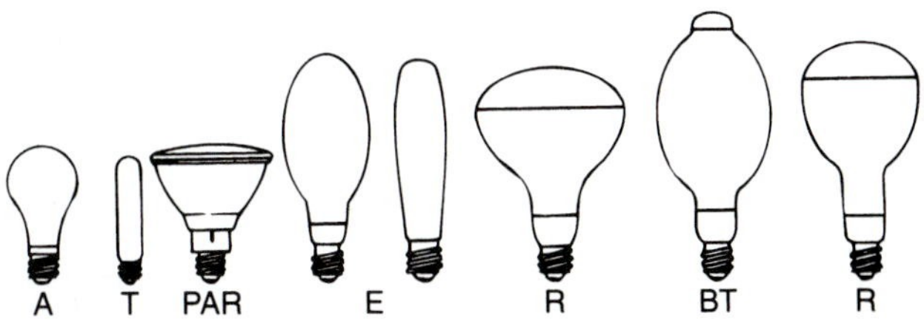

Figure 5.12 *Common HID lamp styles. A: standard (arbitrary); T: tubular; PAR: parabolic aluminized reflector; E: elliptical (conical or dimpled); BT: bulbous tubular; R: reflector.*

- May show color poorly
- Are noisy and therefore have limited use in small commercial and residential spaces
- Require up to nine minutes to reach full light capacity from startup

Because of their intense light, strong glare can occur if HID lamps are not shielded properly. These lamps are commonly used in very high ceilings to distance their intense glare from the occupants.

Cold Cathode

The well-known neon lamp or cold cathode is a low-pressure discharge lamp. It runs even cooler than a fluorescent, but requires a high voltage transformer that can be noisy. Cold cathodes have a high efficacy rating, but because of the transformer noise and heat, require thoughtful wiring plans. Tubes can be shaped into many decorative forms including curves (Figure 5.13).

Tubes are filled with various gases that produce different colors. Neon gas produces a reddish glow, and argon gas produces a blue-green glow. Tubes can also be coated with phosphors that allow the lamp to produce a variety of colors from blue to pink to a warm white. Cold cathode lamps useful where long stretches of low-level continuous light required.

LED Lamps

Light emitting diode lamps are a new form of interior sign lighting. The indicator lights on a VCR or car dashbo are usually LEDs. They typically are rated to over 100,(hours and run without a heated filament. Each lamp is v small (about one-eighth inch long) and produces a relativ low light output. For interior applications, lamps are ger ally grouped together inside a larger bulb.

The light produced can be colored and includes aml blue, green, red, and a cool white. Various colors may grouped to create a wash of color on a background of li value; a digital lighting control is used to make the walls pear to change colors (Figure 5.14). LEDs are also used decorative lighting or to accent a change in plane (as o step) or to highlight the edge of a counter or fixture.

More info online @

http://corp.colorkinetics.com/index.htm LED information

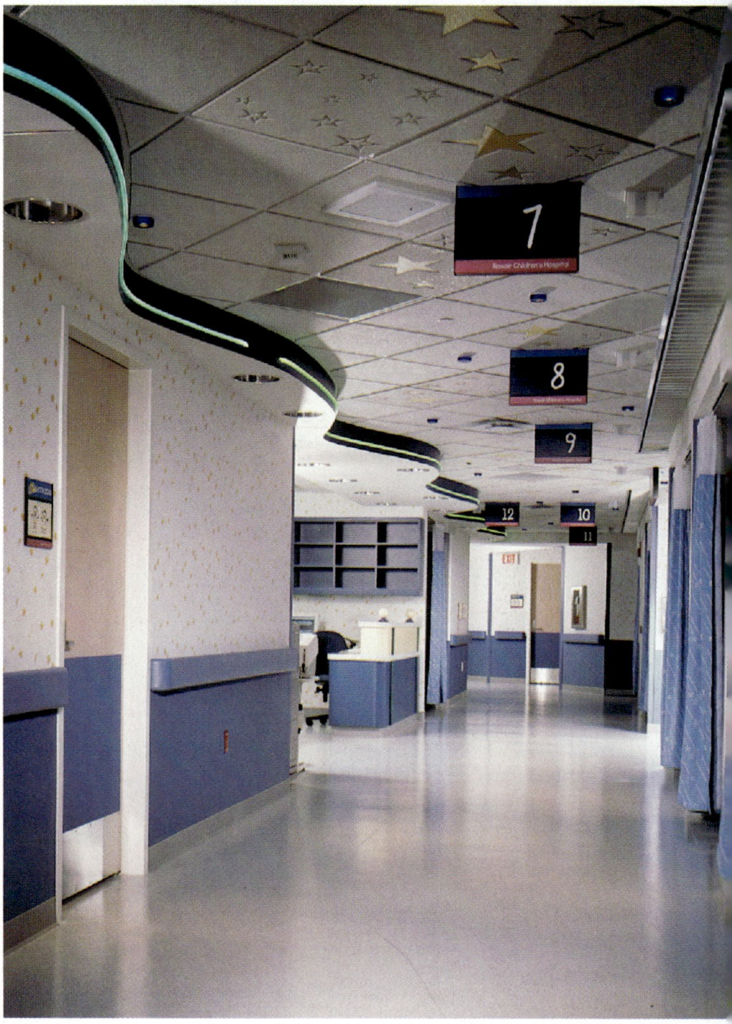

Figure 5.13 *Cold cathode lighting adds a playful quality to this pediatric surgery center. Curved ceiling forms and stars enhance its lighthearted atmosphere. (Designer: Kathy Helm & Associates Inc. Photograph by Quandrant.)*

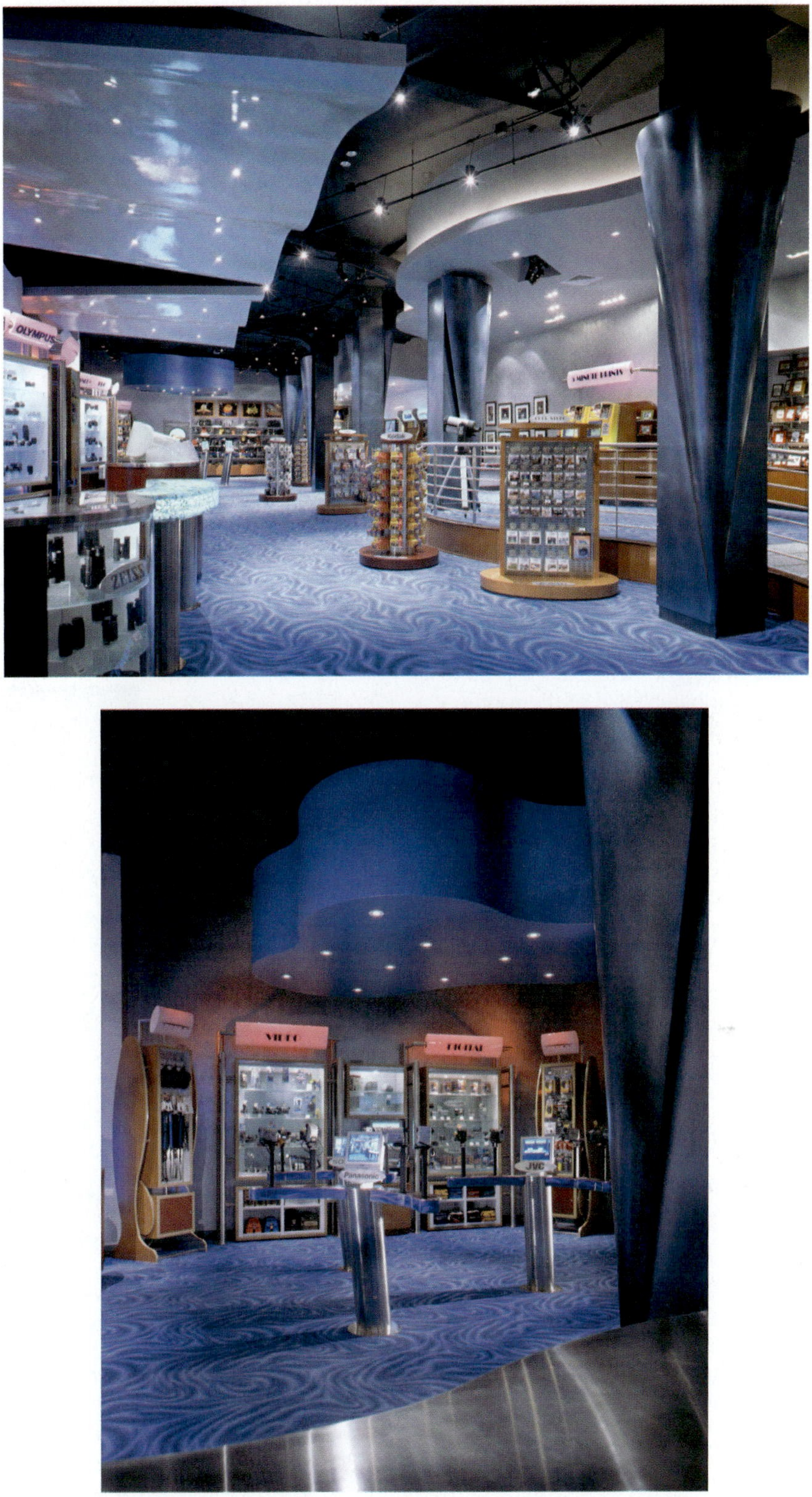

Figure 5.14 *A variety of lighting solutions have been applied in this retail setting. Through an electronically controlled system, LED lamps produce a variety of colors on plain vanilla walls and ceilings. Columns covered in a metallic finish add to the brilliance of movement in the interior. (Designer: Charles Greenwood, IIDA, of Greenwood Design Group, Inc. Photograph by Robert Thien © 2001.)*

Lighting Fixtures

Fixtures house the light source. All fixtures cast the light either *down* (onto an object or into a room) or *up* (onto the ceiling). **Downlighting** also may be called **direct lighting; uplighting** also may be referred to as **indirect lighting** or reflective lighting. The fixtures or luminaires for artificial lighting sources are either architectural (built in) or portable.

Architectural Lighting

Architectural lighting, which includes wall-mounted, ceiling-mounted, and custom-designed fixtures, is closely correlated with the structure of the room. This type of lighting is included in the lighting and electrical plans of the building as an integral part of the complete design.

Wall-Mounted Fixtures

Several types of wall-mounted fixtures are shown in Figure 5.15. A *canopy* overhead provides general illumination. This lighting is used mostly in baths and kitchens.

Cove lighting is placed near the ceiling, directing light upward and giving a feeling of height. When used around a perimeter it can increase the apparent size of the room.

Sconces are decorative lighting fixtures permanently attached to the wall. They may be modern or traditional in style and can be positioned to provide direct or indirect lighting. Commercial sconces must be designed and located to meet ADA requirements.

Valance lighting is positioned over a window. A lamp is placed behind a valance board and the light shines on the drapery. If the valance is open above the lamp, the light produces both indirect (reflected) and direct (downlight) lighting.

Ceiling-Mounted Fixtures

Ceiling-mounted fixtures are attached to the ceiling by one of three methods:

1. Recessed fixtures are hidden in the ceiling. The lamp (or a lens over the lamp) is the only visible component.
2. Surface-mounted fixtures are attached flush to the ceiling, but the fixture itself is exposed below the ceiling.
3. Suspended fixtures hang from the ceiling.

Figure 5.16 illustrates several kinds of ceiling-mounted fixtures.

Can lights (as they are commonly referred to in the industry) house lamps in cylindrical cans. Can lighting may be recessed or surface mounted depending on the design of the fixture. Can lights may be called downlights, wall-washers, or eyeballs. Downlights may focus on a definite object or produce general lighting when used in sufficient numbers. Figure 5.13 shows can lights combined with neon lighting. A **wall-washer** is an adjustable unit that can be directed at any angle to "wash" the wall with light. An **eyeball** is similar to a wall-washer but can swivel, allowing light to be focused where desired.

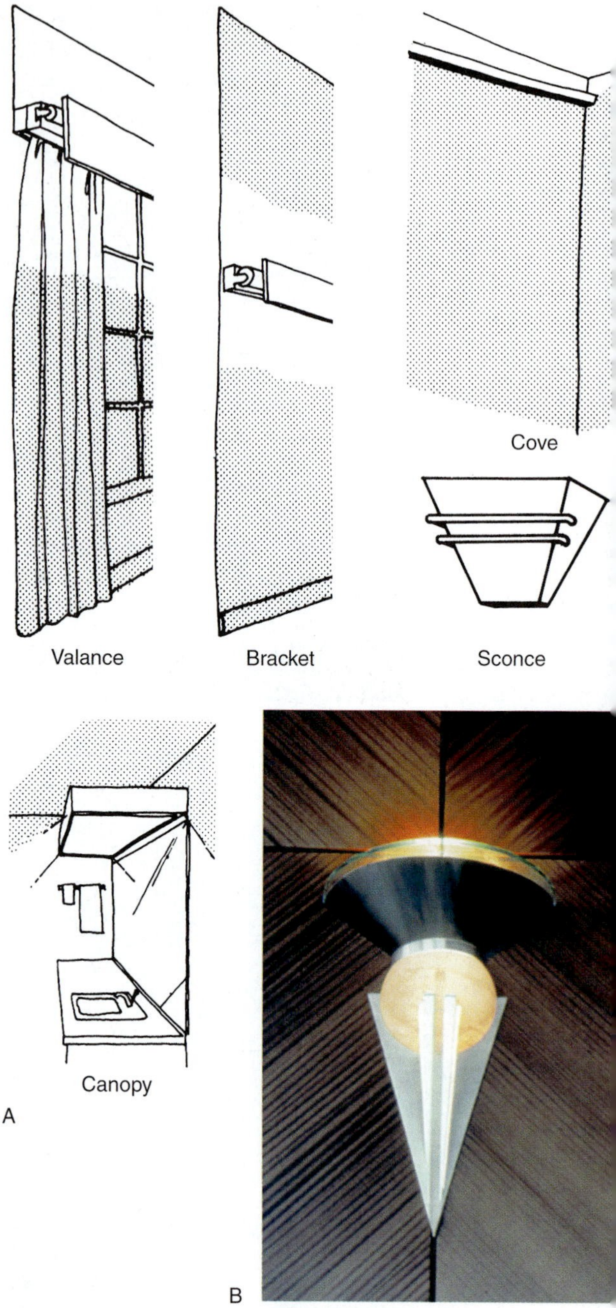

Figure 5.15 *(A) Common types of wall-mounted fixtures. (B This decorative sconce was custom designed to meet the nee of the space. Etched glass and metal are combined in this Starfire Select™ fixture. (Courtesy of Starfire Lighting.)*

A *cornice* is usually built on the ceiling to direct the lig downward. Cornices are fairly similar to valances. The d ference is the physical location of the mounted lamp. Wh used over a window it can aid in eliminating the black m ror or glare effect produced at night.

Fluorescent panels may be recessed, surface mounted, suspended. Fluorescent panels are frequently used in 2′ × squares or 2′ × 4′ rectangles because they are economic

gure 5.16 *(A) Common)es of ceiling-mounted 'tures. (B) This custom nging pendant was signed and scaled for a ail mall. Colored neon centuates the contemporary 'umns. (Architect/Designer: tthony Bellucchi Architects d. Lighting design by Roeder esign, a subsidiary of Pacific ghtworks. Photograph by bt. Ames Cook.) (C) This spended fixture of cone- aped glass is available with e, three, eight, or twelve ndants to fit the scale of the ace. ("Fucsia" courtesy of)s USA.)*

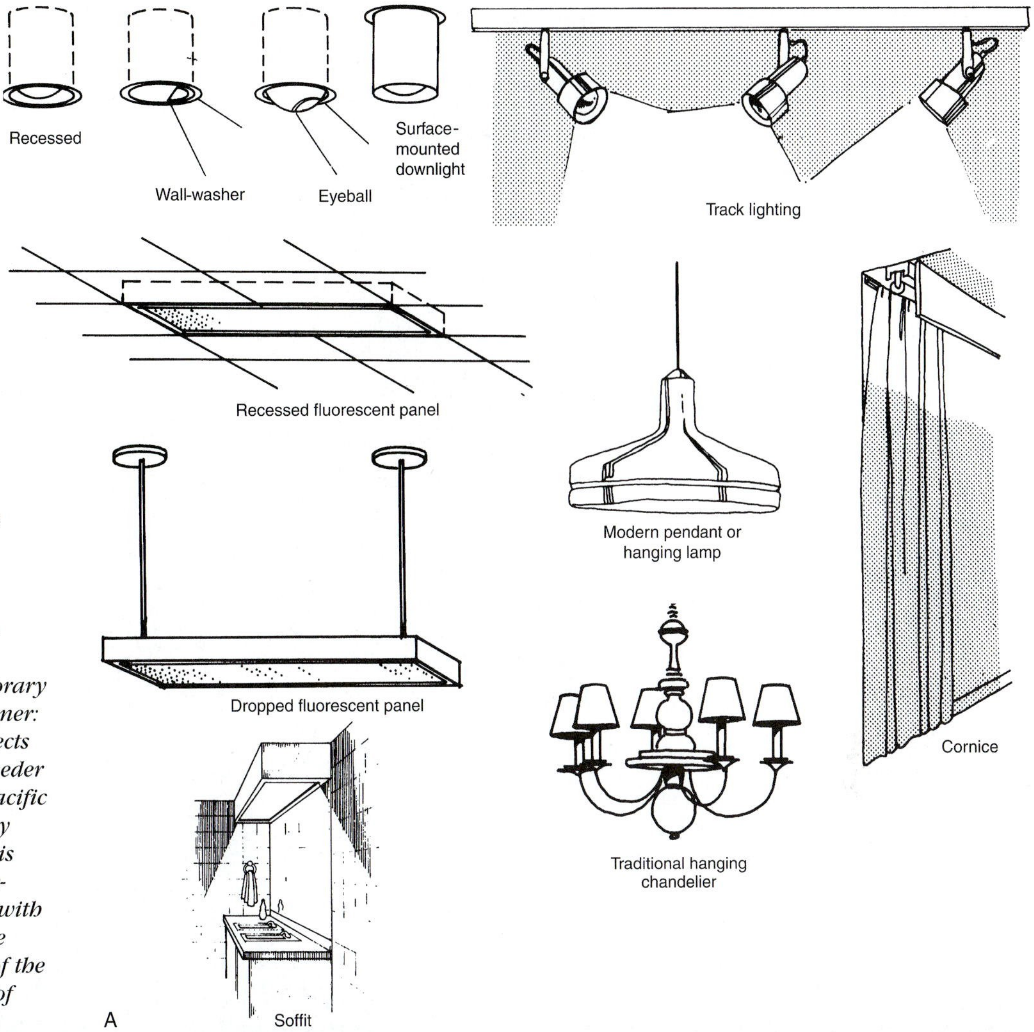

A

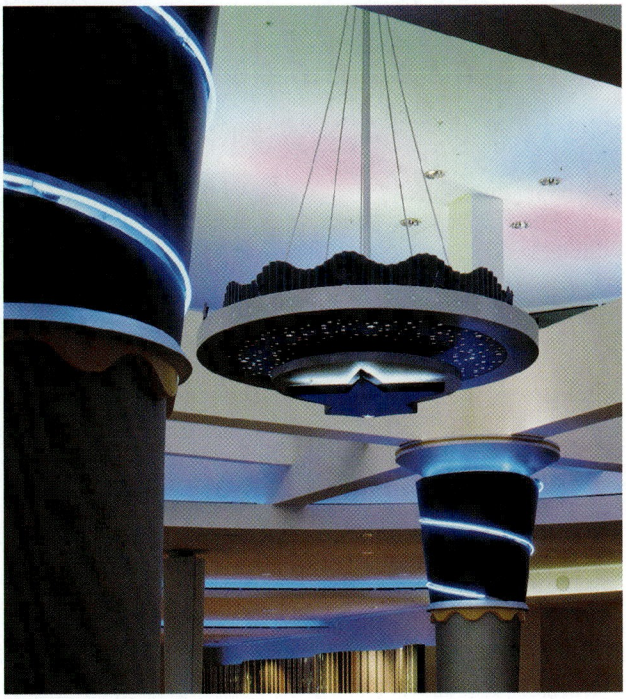

B

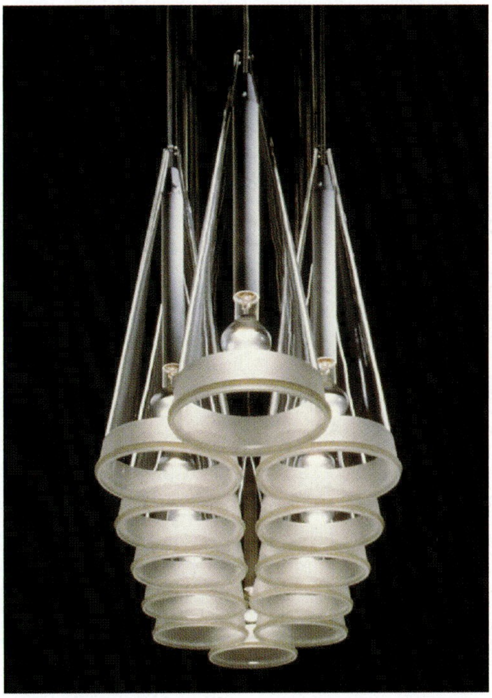

C

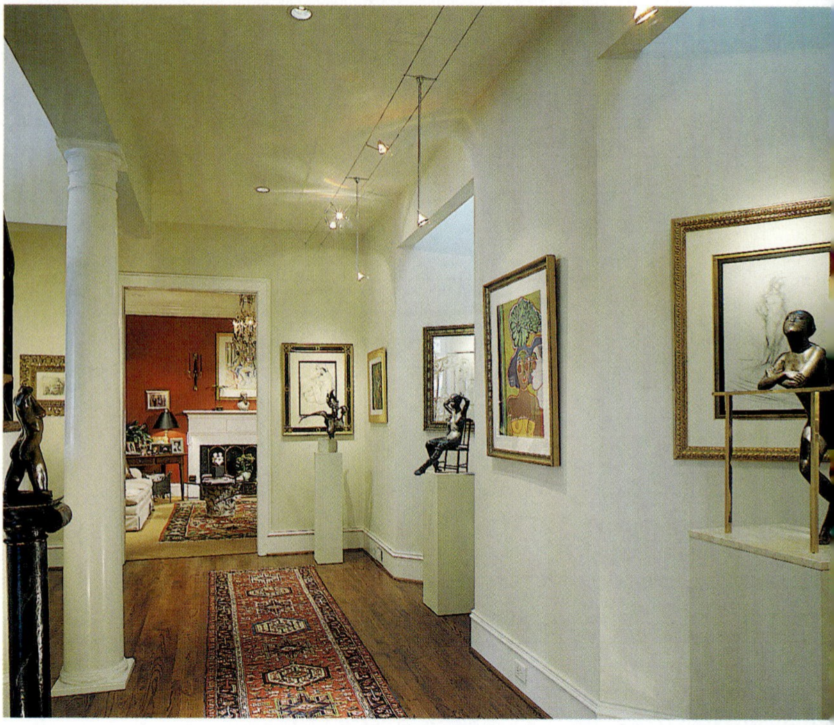

Figure 5.17 *In this gallery space, track lighting suspended from fine cables illuminates the sculpture and framed art. Incandescent halogen lamps pinpoint the selections. (Designer: Ambiance Interiors. Photograph ©Robert Thien. As seen in* Atlanta Homes & Lifestyles.*)*

Lenses are available in a variety of options to diffuse the light and soften the glare. This is especially important in environments where computer screens or VDTs are used.

Pendants and *chandeliers* (pendants with arms) are hung from the ceiling. Styles and lamp options are limitless (and sometimes custom designed). Pendants and chandeliers, when used over dining surfaces, should be suspended approximately 30 inches above the table in an eight-foot-high room, and raised three inches for each additional foot of ceiling height.

A *soffit* consists of an enclosed light attached to the ceiling and is designed to provide a high level of light directly below. This light is effective in bathrooms, niches, and over built-in desks.

Track lighting consists of a track surface mounted to or suspended from the ceiling. It comes in a broad array of sizes, shapes, and finishes. Fixtures clip or slide along the track or wire frame to create a precisely designed optical system with a vast range of lighting effects. Layout configurations are practically infinite (Figure 5.17).

Custom Fixtures

Custom-designed architectural lighting may be created to highlight steps or handrails, or for other design effects. Recessed floor lighting may be used in airplanes, theatres, or at the base of steps as a safety device.

Fiber-optic fixtures are a type of decorative lighting that often meets custom needs (Figure 5.18). Fiber optics are not in themselves a light source, but rather a style of distributing light. A fiber-optic light fixture is composed of a bundle of thin cylindrical fibers. A ray of light passed through the fibers produces an intense pinpoint of light at the opposite end. Fiber optics can be concealed in handrails and retail display

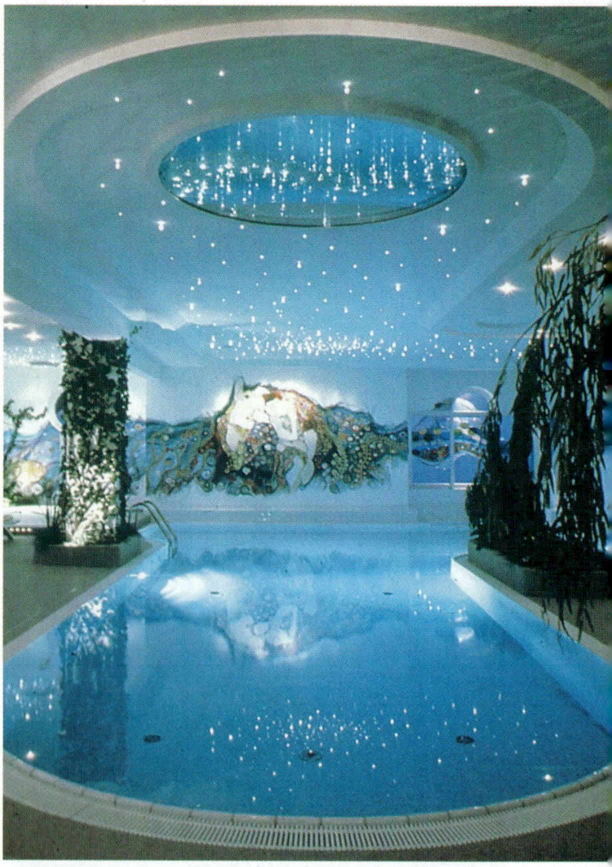

Figure 5.18 *Fiber-optic decorative lighting was used in this interior to create a starry sky effect. Strass® Crystal fiber optics from Swaro® Lite Crystal Architecture defines the delicate appearance. (Courtesy of Starfire Lighting.)*

ıbinets, or used for spot or downlighting. Fiber optics can e used to produce a curved glow similar to the cold cath- de lighting effect.

ore info online @

tp://www.americanlightingassoc.com/ American Lighting Association ʀetail Association)

ystems Furniture Lighting

urniture systems (as discussed in Chapter 8) can be pur- ɪased with attached lighting systems. The electrical and ghting systems are concealed within the panels of the fur- ɪture system. Light may be directed below the upper cabi- ets onto the desk surface, similar to canopy or soffit ghting. Pendant fixtures may be suspended from the furni- ıre system's walls to provide direct lighting. Lighting may so be directed upward. The area on top of the upper cabinets may conceal a light source that directs light onto the ceiling, similar to the lighting concept of a torchère.

Portable Lighting

A portable luminaire is a fixture that may be transported from one location to another. Portable fixtures (both table and floor models) are the oldest forms of electrical interior lighting. They provide flexible lighting in residential or public environments and may be purely functional, decorative, or both (Figure 5.19).

Fixture Selection and Placement

All light fixtures in an interior must be selected based on their intended function and the human factor, their aesthetic qualities, and their economic and ecological factors. These same goals were introduced in Chapter 1.

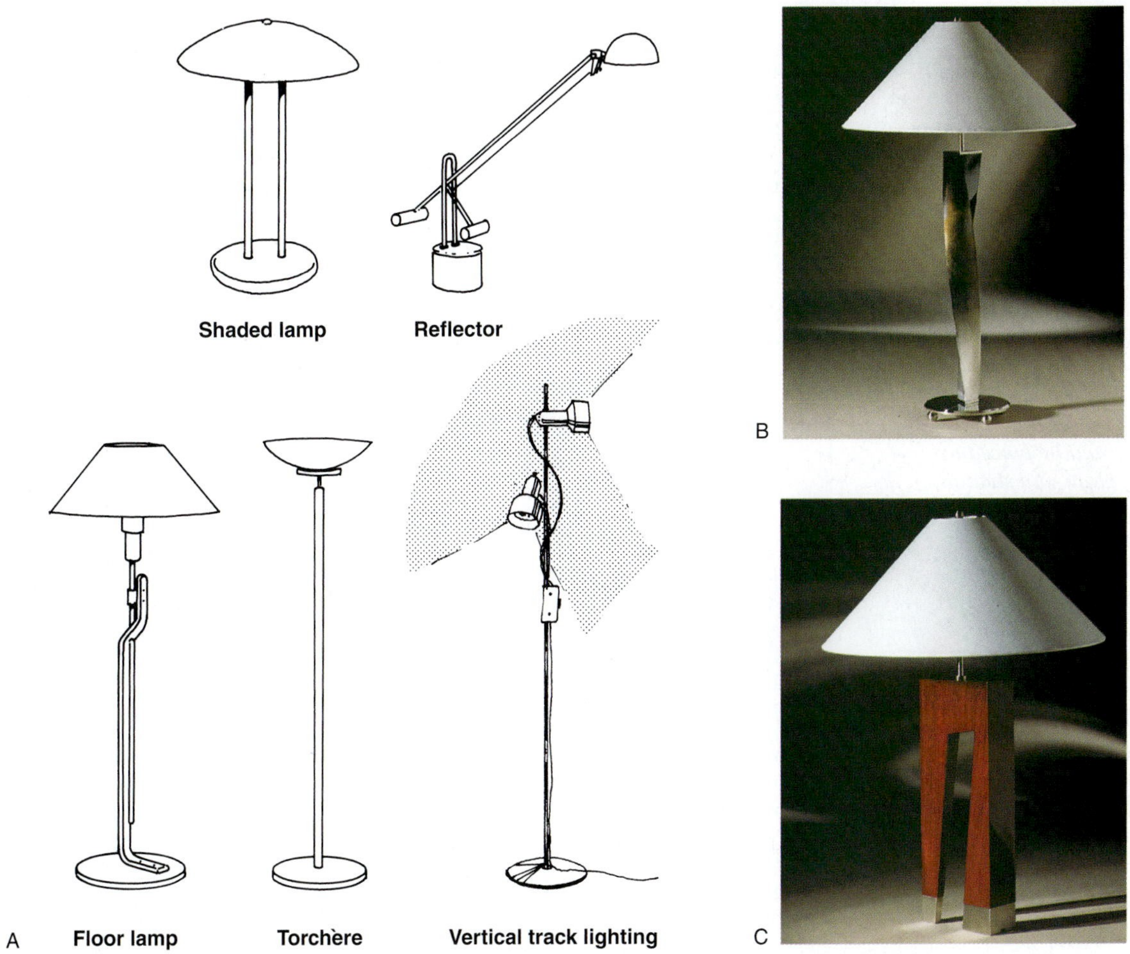

ıgure 5.19 *(A) Typical portable lamp fixtures. (B) "New Twist" table lamp. (Courtesy f HRS Design, Inc.) (C) "Derby" table lamp. (Courtesy of HRS Design, Inc.)*

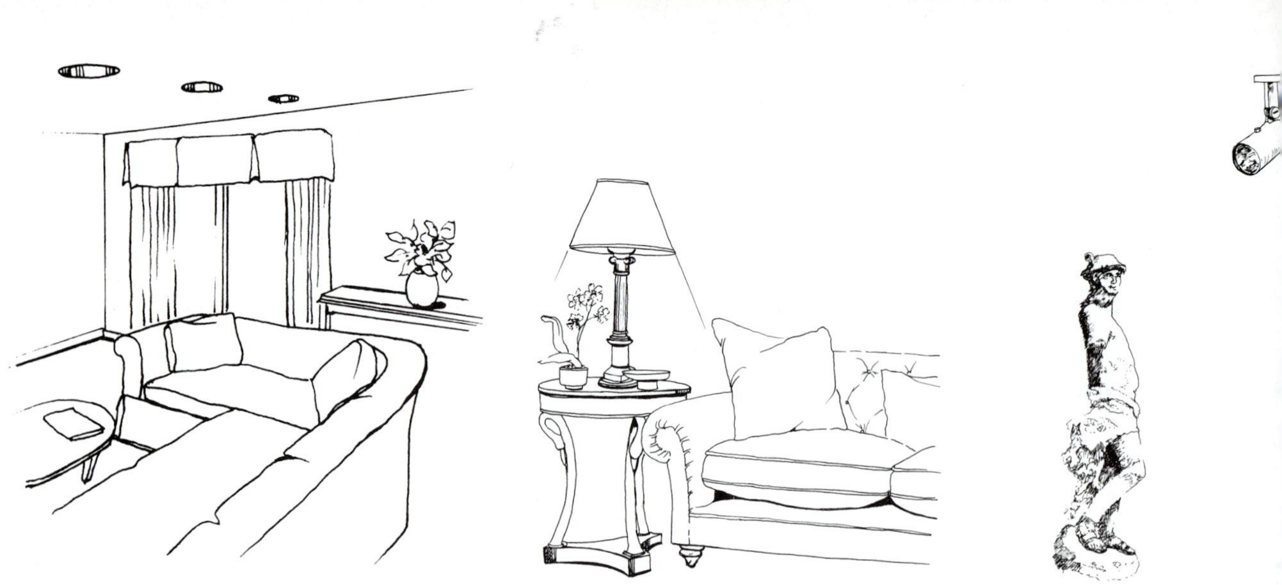

Figure 5.20 *Three major functions of artificial lighting.*

The Functions of Light

Light sources can serve three functions to meet human needs (Figure 5.20):

1. General or **ambient lighting** is background or fill light that spreads an even, overall luminosity and reduces harsh contrasts between pools of concentrated light.
2. **Task lighting** is functional and localized for a particular activity such as office work, reading, writing, preparing food, or grooming. Task lighting is placed near the activity but is aimed to avoid glare and minimize shadows (Figure 5.21).
3. **Accent lighting** employs a concentrated beam of light focusing on a particular object or area.

Interiors should include a combination of these lightir types in each room.

The size and shape of the lamp, along with the fixtu style, produce a typical light distribution pattern. To help d termine the correct fixture for a particular function, light di tribution charts (or photometric charts) are usually include in manufacturers' catalogs (Figure 5.22). These charts also i dicate the approximate quantity of footcandles, dependi on the height of the light. By reading the charts, designe can determine the appropriate fixture and lamp.

Because vision tends to diminish with age, older peop and those with visual impairments may require higher leve of light. Designers should provide higher light levels portable task lighting for individuals with special needs.

Figure 5.21 *Luminaires for task lighting should be placed to minimize glare and shadows.*

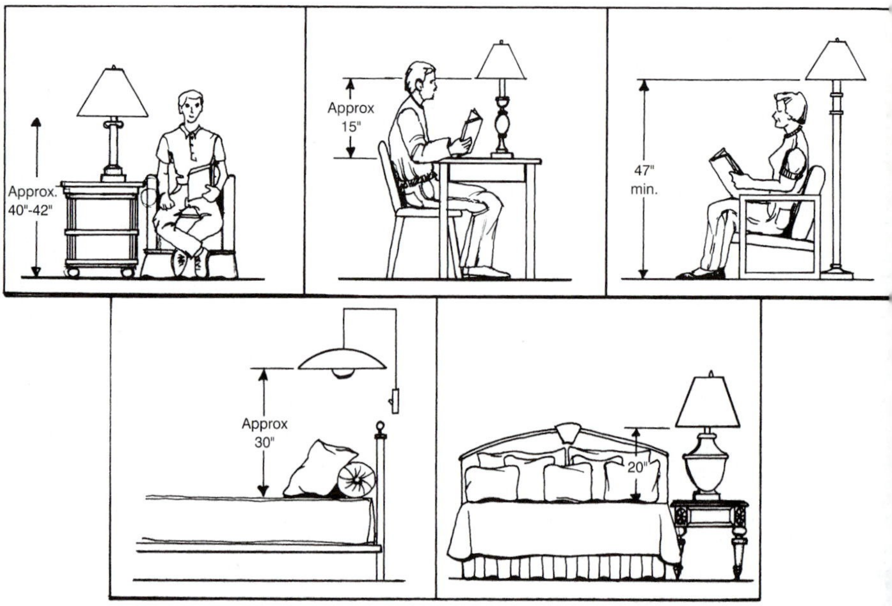

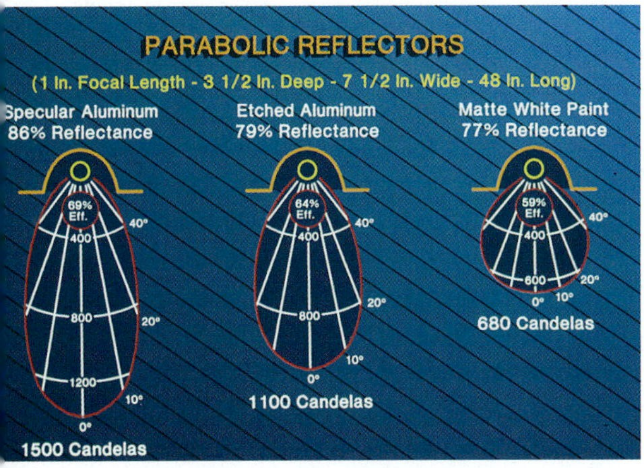

ure 5.22 *Typical photometric guides. Many nufacturers, including GE, offer these guides on computer c. (Courtesy of GE Lighting.)*

Lighting also affects people's emotions. Successful light-; provides a sense of well being. With respect to human ychological needs, light has the following attributes:

- Light is associated with the exuberance of life itself and with human well being.
- It can convey a sense of security, warmth, and comfort.
- It can evoke a mood. For example, low-level lighting can be intimate, cozy, and relaxing; bright light can be stimulating and active.
- Lack of light or insufficient light may provoke feelings of depression, gloom, or even fear. Seasonal affective disorder (SAD) is a medical condition that occurs in some people when they are deprived of natural sunlight.
- Too much light or glaring light can be agitating, uncomfortable, and annoying, even resulting in physical ailments and an inability to function adequately.

It is essential, therefore, when planning light requirements for either residential or commercial interiors to take into account the physical as well as the psychological impact of light on human needs.

Additionally, lighting must be durable. For example, fragile neon fixtures would be inappropriate in a childcare center. Lighting also figures in safety. Emergency light fixtures, operated by batteries, are particularly important during power outages or fires and are required in contract design.

Aesthetics

Aesthetically, lighting should reflect and enhance the style of the interior. The scale and proportion of a fixture should be considered in relation to other furnishings and to the size of the room. Decorative fixtures generally work best when their design is simple, unobtrusive, and suitable to the room's design. Some lighting fixtures serve as a focal point (Figure 5.23).

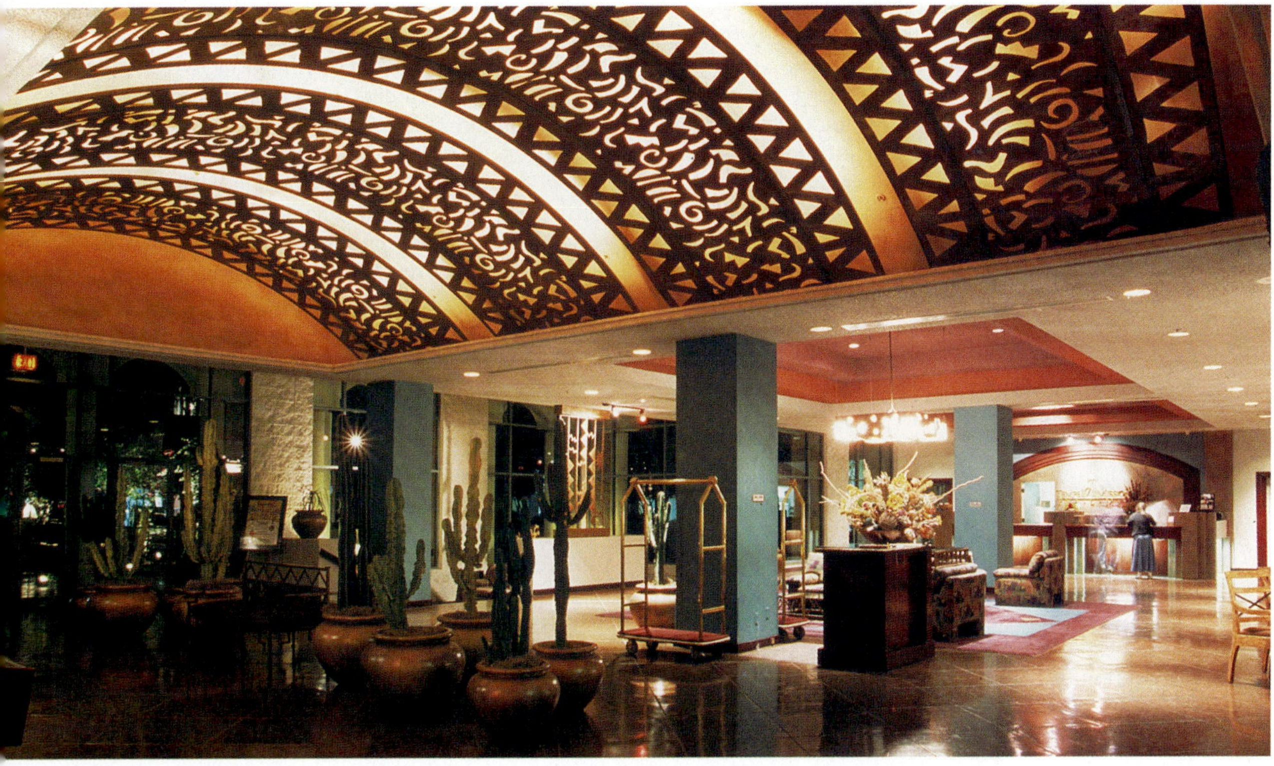

ure 5.23 *The combination of decorative iron screens and back-lit ceiling panels defines the entry into this hotel lobby. (Iron oducts manufactured by Design Lighting Products Co., Mesa, Arizona.)*

Designers can create many decorative effects when lighting is properly selected and placed:

- *Spotlighting* accentuates a particular object or point.
- A *pool of light* also focuses attention on a particular area, but a much larger one than that produced by spotlighting.
- A *wash of light,* in between a spotlight and a pool of light, generally covers a particular piece of art or other objects on a wall. An entire wall could be washed with light.
- *Grazing* is similar to a wash of light but the light barely skims the wall. This is usually applied to bring out a wall texture or pattern.
- *Perimeter lighting* is frequently used to expand a space, as seen in Figure 5.1.
- *Silhouette lighting* creates a decorative outline of an object. Sometimes plants or decorative ironwork are silhouetted to produce an interesting shadow effect on a nearby surface.

Economics

The designer's selection of lighting fixtures must not exceed the client's budget. In addition to the initial cost of purchasing and installing the fixtures, light also has continuous costs due to the use of electricity and the maintenance of lamps. Knowledgeable planning and purchasing can give a space sufficient lighting and still save watts and dollars. The following guidelines can help conserve energy in lighting.

- Lighting should fit specific needs. Task areas such as kitchen counters or desks require more light than nonworking areas such as circulation space.
- Dimmers are useful in adjusting light levels, increasing lamp life, and saving energy.
- Installing multiple switches and switches at every exit makes it convenient to use only the amount of light required in a specific area. Three-way incandescent lamps also allow selectivity in the amount of light used.
- Fixtures that can be adjusted and placed where light is needed are a wise choice. For instance, track lighting has great flexibility and permits the light to be directed where it is desired.
- A reflector lamp is good for accent or task lighting. Low-voltage spotlights are especially effective where a tightly controlled beam is required.
- Light sources should be efficient. Light output varies in efficiency according to wattage and color. For example, fluorescent lamps use as much as 80 percent less energy, produce 5 to 30 times as much light, and last 20 times longer than incandescent lamps. For this reason they are often used in commercial spaces, as seen in Figure 5.24.
- Where appearance is not a consideration, as in garages and some basements, industrial reflectors are an economical option.
- Ceilings, walls, floors, and furniture that have light-colored finishes reflect more light. Rooms designed in dark colors absorb light and require more lighting.
- Keeping reflectors, diffusers, and lamps clean helps to maintain lighting equipment.

Lighting for Areas and Activities

The selection and placement of the appropriate fixture i complex process. This section is a general guide to lighti goals for particular areas or uses.

In the lobby or entrance area, which is the keynote of interior, lighting plays an important role. During the day entry or lobby should be bright enough to allow a reas able transition from the bright outdoors to the darker in rior. Illumination needs to be at a lower level at night to eyes in focusing, but strong enough to enable visitors to and be seen. The entrance is an ideal place to try a drama lighting effect such as an accented art object. Often the ception desk is more brightly lit to draw visitors.

Waiting rooms and living rooms need soft general ba ground lighting supplemented by special area lighting, shown in Figure 5.25. Both direct and indirect lighting sour are desirable, although an excess of indirect lighting may sult in a washed-out appearance. Well-chosen portable f tures at necessary locations add a feeling of comfort a accent a room's focal point.

Conference rooms and dining areas deserve versa lighting around the table area that can be adjusted for a riety of functions. General lighting can provide a low-le background. Dimmer controls allow for a change of mood for an audiovisual presentation. In residential or restaur settings, candles give a flattering glow to skin tones. Creat use of accent light helps to avoid flat downlighting and ac interest (Figure 5.26).

Offices, libraries, and studies require general lighti Where computers are used, overhead lighting should be w diffused to prevent glare. Parabolic louvers that cover flu rescent fixtures function particularly well. Task lighting also essential for reading and studying. Refer to Figure 5 for a review.

Family and recreation rooms accommodate a variety activities and thus require particularly flexible lighting. Ge eral lighting is essential, with task lighting supplied for sp cific activities. Television viewing is most comfortable wh general lighting is at a low level with no strong contrasts glare. The television or computer screen itself reflects lig and contributes to the total lighting effect.

Workrooms, kitchens, classrooms, and utility rooms fu tion best when generous overall lighting for safety and e ciency is planned. Ceiling- or surface-mounted fixtures su as recessed downlights or track lighting can give adequ general light and eliminate shadows. It is also important provide recessed or shielded lights over work areas a

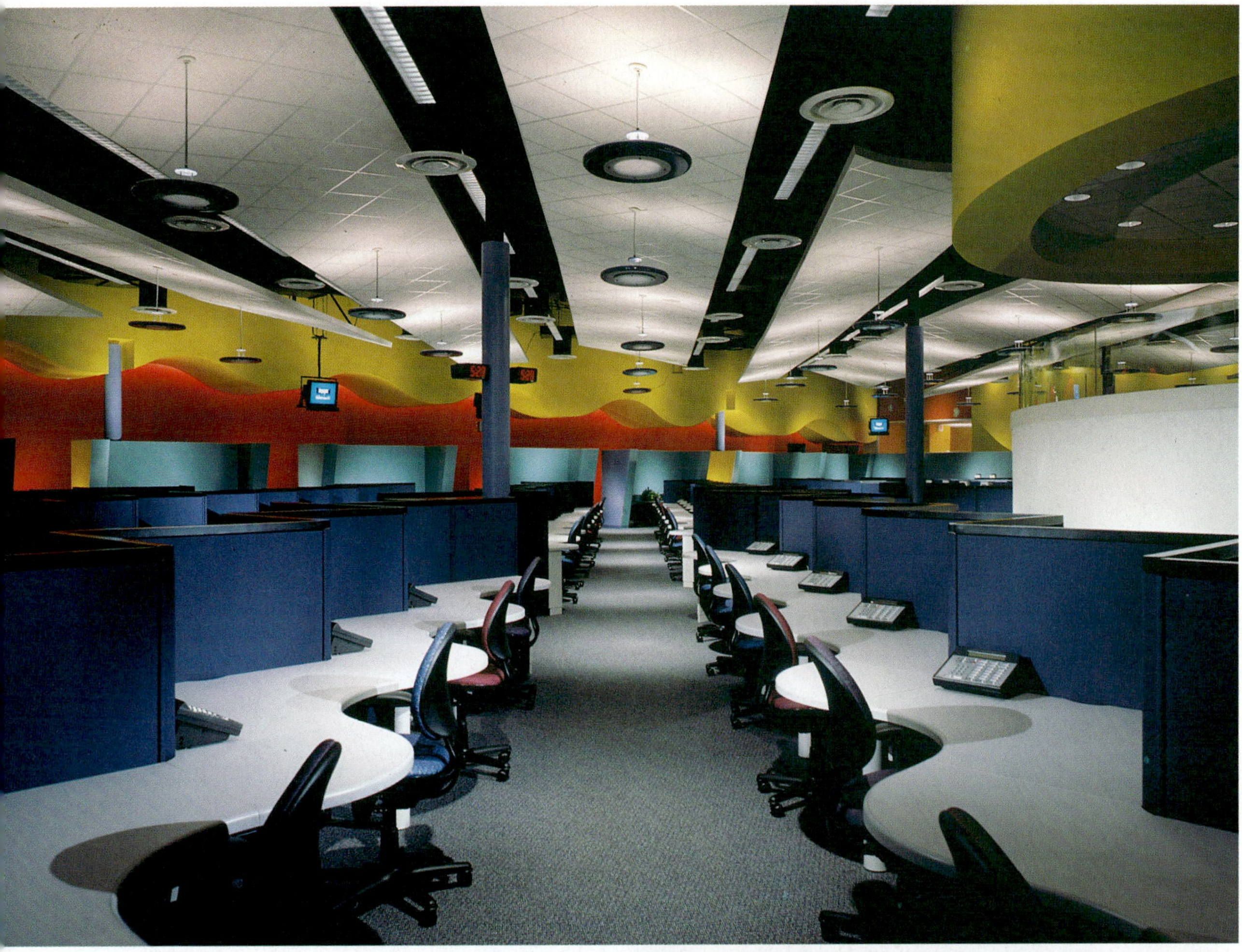

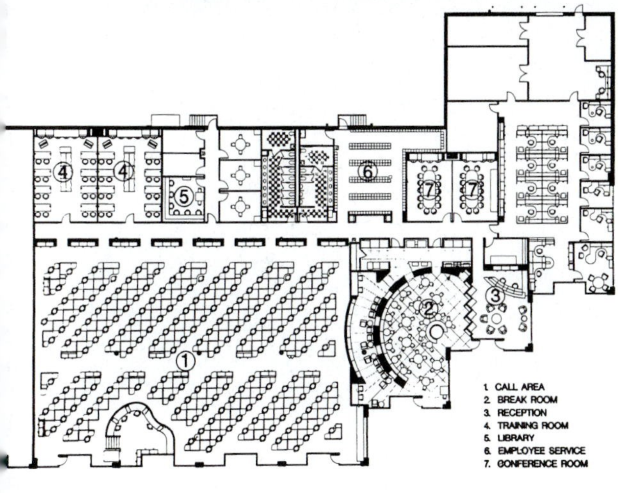

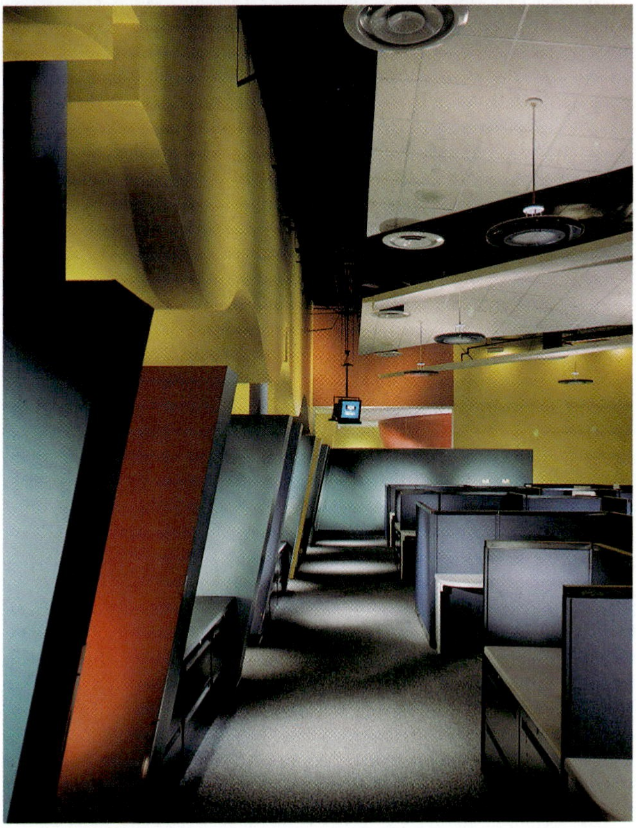

igure 5.24 *A combination of uplighting and downlighting ot only meets the needs of this reservations environment, ut also adds visual interest to the 2′ × 2′ lay-in ceiling. The ghting designer selected pendants, fluorescent troffers with igh-performance parabolic louvers, and can lights. rchitect/Designer: Hnedak Bobo Group, Inc. Lighting esigner: Benya Lighting Design. Photographs © 1997 Jeffrey cobs/Architectural Photography Inc.)*

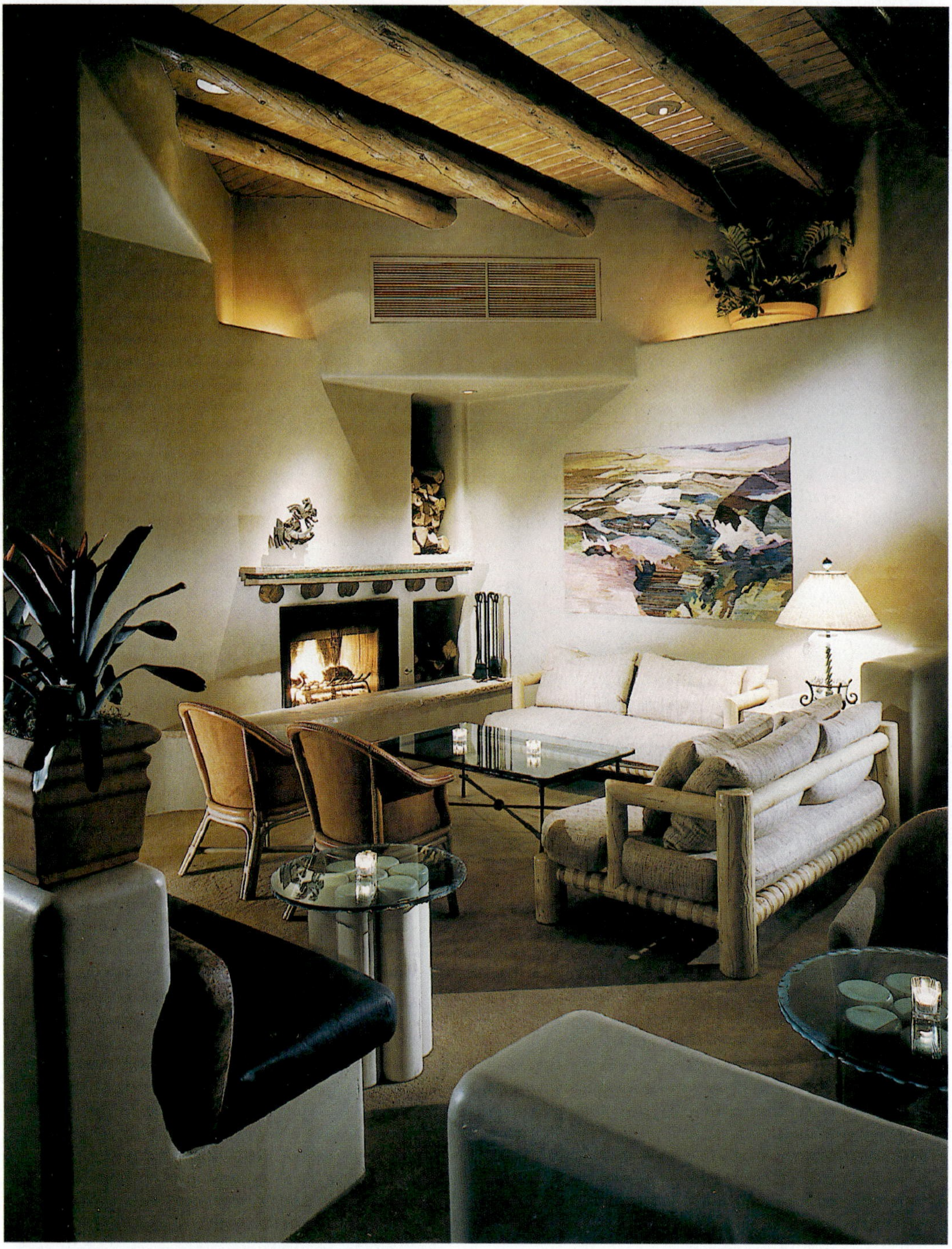

Figure 5.25 *Recessed ceiling lights, cove lighting placed high in wall niches, portable lamps, and firelight contribute to the cozy, warm atmosphere of this Santa Fe-style living room. (Photograph by Mark Boisclair.)*

mounted under wall cabinets to illuminate counters (Figure 5.27). Classrooms, like conference areas, also require a low light level option, suitable for slide or video presentation.

Bedrooms need comfortable general lighting with appropriate task lights for reading, grooming, deskwork, and other activities. Direct lighting is also helpful when placed over chests of drawers, in closets, close to seating, and over beds. Dim circulation lighting for safety at night is a basic requirement. Accent lighting can be effectively used to focus on painting or wall unit.

Bathrooms require shadowless lighting for shaving ar grooming, which can be supplied by light from overhead ar from both sides of a mirror, and by light reflected upward fro a light-colored basin or countertop. Mirror lighting is usual sufficient to illuminate an average-sized powder room; ho ever, general lighting is necessary with the addition of a tub

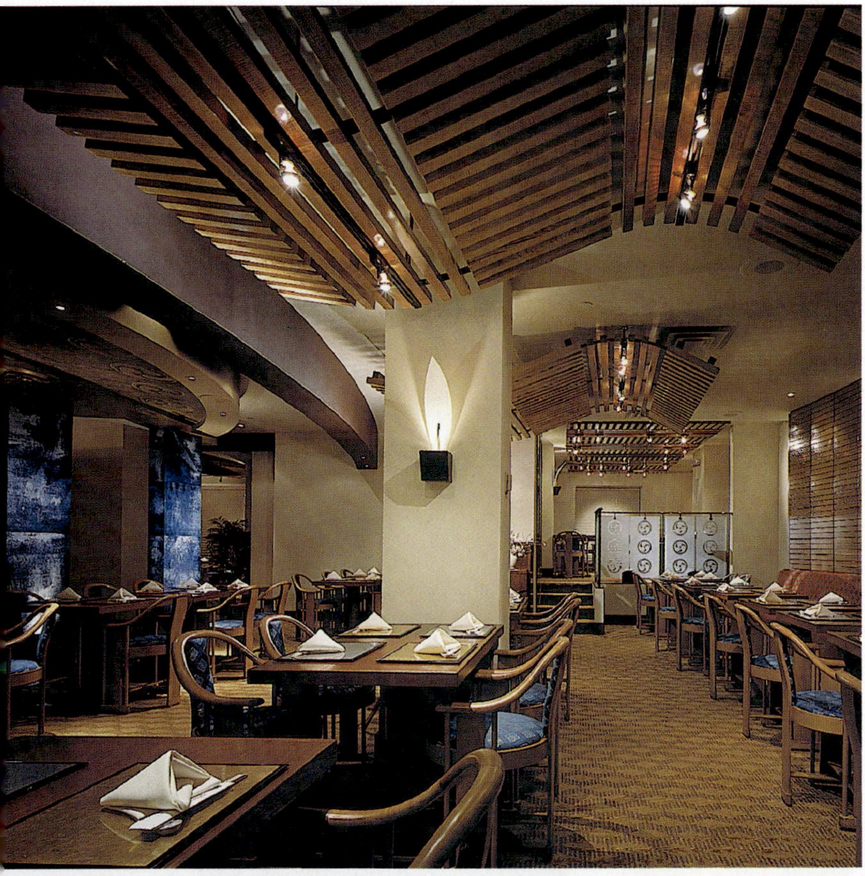

Figure 5.26 *In this Japanese restaurant located in New York City, a variety of lighting techniques have been incorporated. Track lighting is concealed in the wood slat ceiling. Decorative sconces, chandeliers, cove lighting, downlighting, and uplighting define this elaborate use of the stylized yin-yang symbol. Frosted panels diffuse the downlighting over the bar. (Custom lighting by Adam D. Tihany. Architect/Designer: Adam D. Tihany International, Ltd. Photographs by Peter Paige.)*

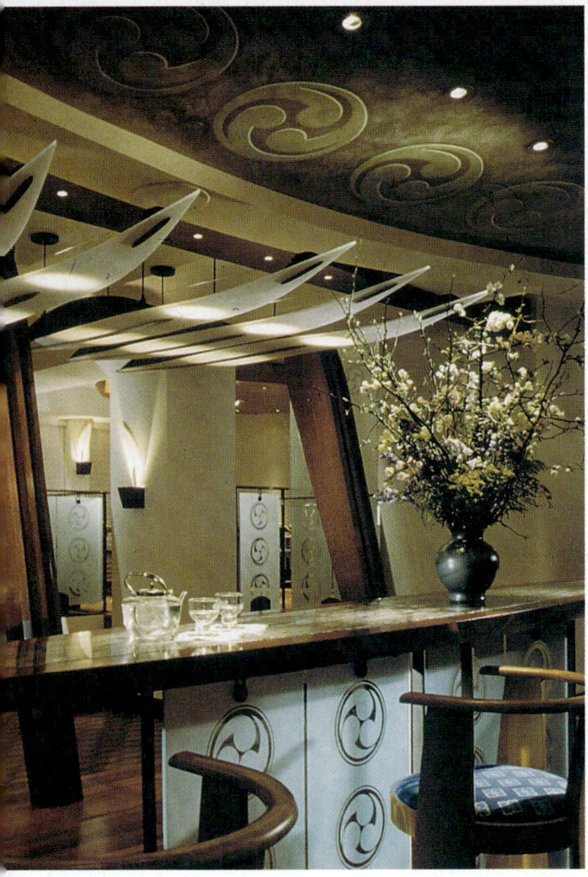

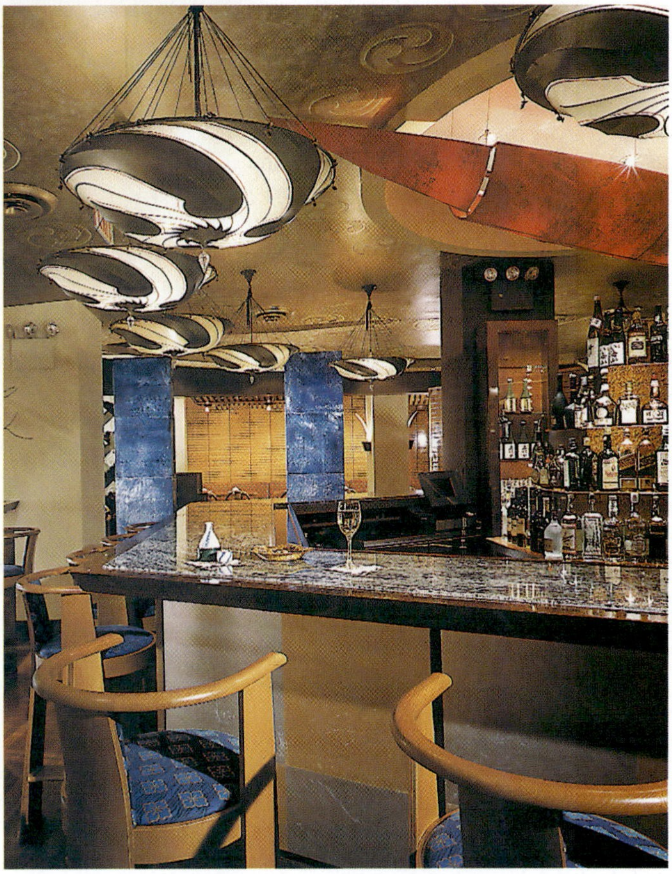

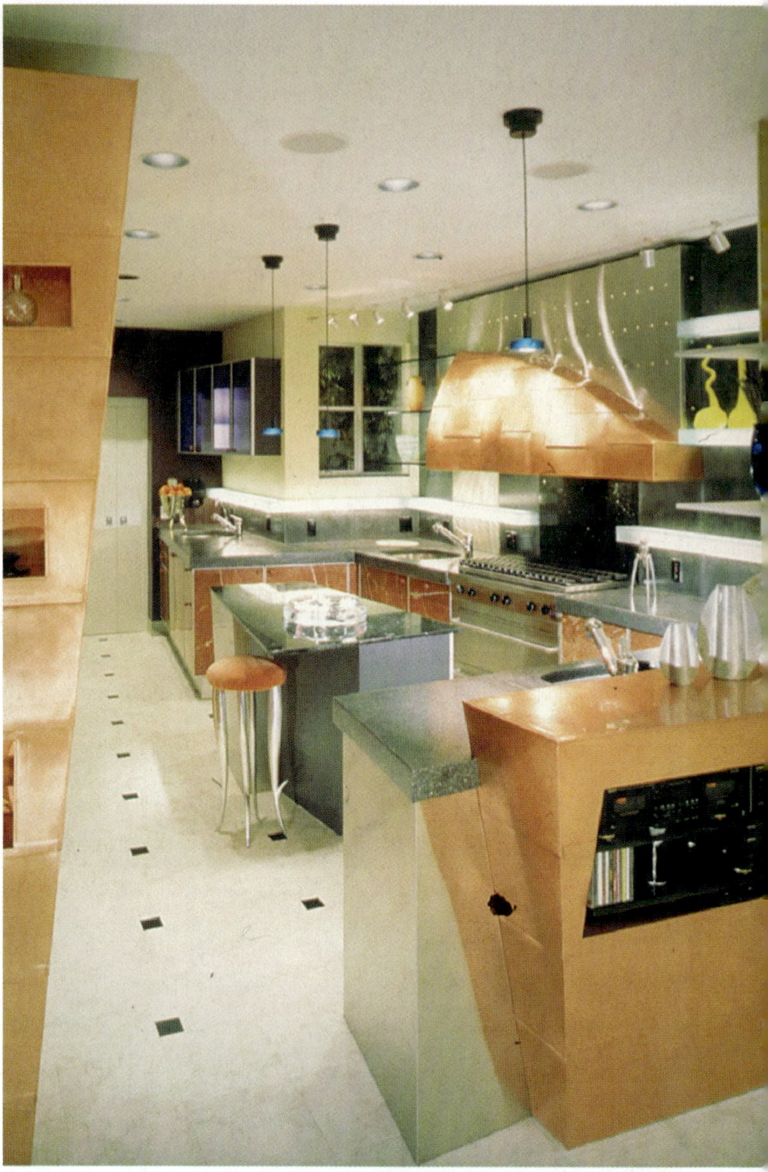

Figure 5.27 *In this contemporary kitchen, lighting has been designed to create interest while serving the importance of function. The 3″-thick glass shelves, lined with low-voltage incandescent lamps, provide task lighting. (Designer: Steven J. Livingston, owner, Studio Snaidero San Francisco. Photograph by Ellen Perlson.)*

shower stall. Lighting in the shower needs to be enclosed and certified for use in a wet environment.

Stairways require overall illumination for safe passage. Stairways should be well lit with treads and risers clearly defined. Well-shielded light fixtures that avoid blinding glare at the top and bottom of stairs are another safety factor.

Corridors require minimum lighting for passage. Art and other objects can be accented to create dramatic effects.

Outdoor lighting at night enhances exterior architecture, gardens, decks, patios, walkways, and other outdoor living areas and provides visual pleasure. This is true in residential, commercial, and institutional settings. Additionally, outdoor lighting helps alleviate the black glass look seen from inside by balancing and extending the lighting to the outside (Figure 5.28).

Weatherproof luminaires for outside use can be attached under the eaves and on exterior walls. Custom lighting often includes exposed and concealed fixtures placed at various important areas of the garden that throw light upwa[r] downward, or in both directions on trees, plantings, a g[ar]den sculpture or fountain, a gazebo, and other garden fe[a]tures to create a visually exciting experience. Front entr[ies] commonly serve as focal points (Figure 5.29).

Organizations and Regulations

Lighting is a complicated component of the interior en[vi]ronment. Design professionals must be aware of lig[ht] safety requirements related to the egress of a building du[r]ing emergencies. Lighting also affects the health of inha[b]itants. Additionally, new products and products that a[re] more energy-efficient are frequently introduced into t[he] market. Professional organizations exist to help designe[rs].

The Illuminating Engineers Society of North Ameri[ca] (IESNA) is a technical organization whose goal is to advan[ce]

nowledge and disseminate information for the improve-
ıent of the lighted environment to the benefit of society. he International Association of Lighting Designers (IALD) is professional organization for independent lighting consult-nts. The International Commission of Illumination (CIE) is ıe global organization for technical lighting concerns.

As a certification measure for industry professionals, the ational Council on Qualifications for the Lighting Profes-ons (NCQLP) was developed in the 1990s. Through expe-ence, practice, and testing, design professionals can (but re not required to) receive certification.

As with other building systems, lighting systems are regu-ted by codes. Lighting applications must comply with the Na-onal Electric Code (NEC), and all selections must meet the nderwriters Laboratory (UL) standards. Codes, such as the NSI code, also relate to lighting for emergencies. Battery- or enerator-operated fixtures must route people safely through orridors, stairways, and fire exits. Some codes set minimum ght levels for interiors. The Energy Policy Act of 1992 required ıat all states adopt standards to limit energy consumption. hese codes, working to conserve energy, actually limit the onsumption of watts per square foot in a building.

ore info online @

tp://www.iald.org/index.htm International Association of Lighting esigners

ttp://www.iesna.org/ Illuminating Engineers Society of North America

tp://www.ncqlp.org/ International Council of Qualifications for ghting Professions

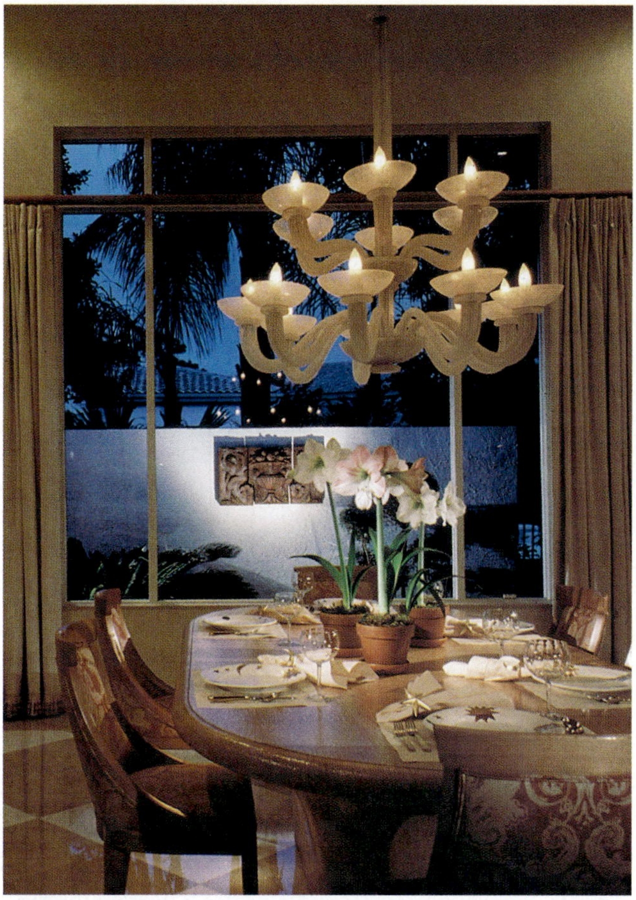

Figure 5.28 *In this elegant dining room of a private residence in Florida, the gently curving shapes of the chandelier and furniture are an effective contrast to the straight-line geometry of the interior architecture. The outdoor area becomes part of the indoor space by the artful lighting of a hanging architectural fragment on the existing privacy wall. (Courtesy of Michael de Santis, ASID, Michael de Santis, Inc. Photograph by Phillip Ennis.)*

witches and Outlets

losely related to the selection and placement of the light fix-ıres is the selection and placement of light switches and ectrical and communication (telephone) outlets.

All rooms require at least one light switch to operate an verhead light or to provide electricity to a portable luminaire.

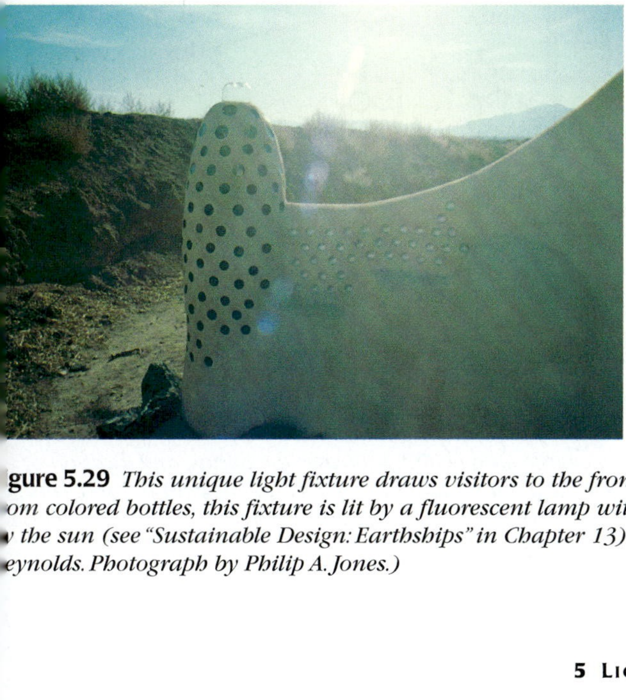

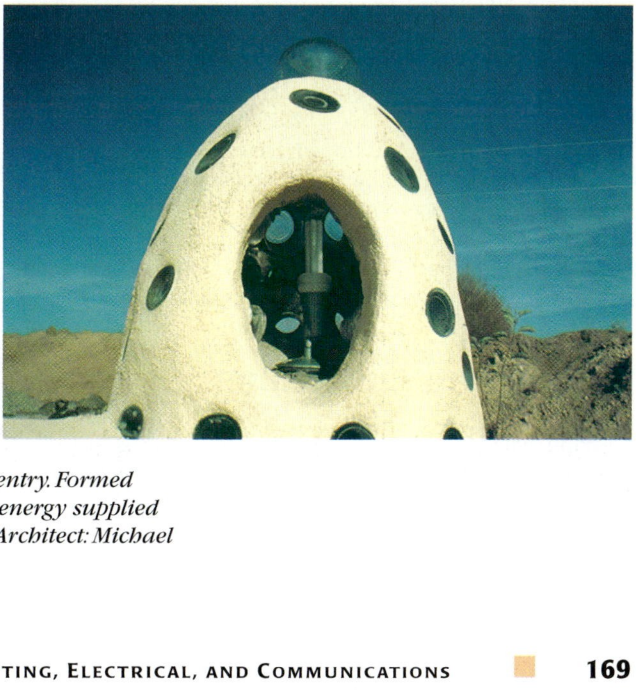

gure 5.29 *This unique light fixture draws visitors to the front entry. Formed om colored bottles, this fixture is lit by a fluorescent lamp with energy supplied the sun (see "Sustainable Design: Earthships" in Chapter 13). (Architect: Michael eynolds. Photograph by Philip A. Jones.)*

Switches are most commonly placed on the latch side of the door approximately 44″ above the finished floor (**A.F.F.**). Switches are also necessary at both ends of hallways and at the top and bottom of stairways. Lights may be switched at one, two, or three locations to meet the needs of the space. Where task lighting is necessary, switches should be placed within easy reach of the task and not at the entry to the room. Dimmers on switches are effective for incandescent lights but do affect the color of the light as they are dimmed. (Fluorescent dimmers are limited.) Dimmers allow great flexibility for various levels of lighting; they are ideal for creating a mood and also for conserving energy and the life of the lamp.

Typical electrical outlets are technically referred to as duplex outlets (because they have two receptors). Duplex outlets are used for 120 volt appliances. Some high-powered equipment, such as copy machines, require dedicated outlets or must have their own circuit.

Indoor outlets located near water sources (such as the bathroom or the kitchen sink) and all exterior outlets are required to be protected with a ground fault interrupt or GFI. Waterproof outlet covers are also required on exterior outlets. Electric ranges, clothes dryers, and other 220 volt equipment require a 220 volt outlet.

Throughout interior spaces, outlets should be plentiful and located for specific tasks. Outlets should be easily accessible for computer and desk accessories and for appliances in kitchens, utility areas, and bathrooms. When a room's function is determined, outlets can be conveniently located in accordance with local building codes. Outlets placed at regular intervals (approximately 6 ft. apart between doorways and floor-length windows) decrease the need for hazardous extension cords. Outlets are usually mounted 15 in. A.F.F. in barrier-free environments, but can be placed at other heights as needed.

Telephone outlets should be located wherever a telephone may be placed. Because Internet access presently requires connection to a telephone line, two lines should be placed close together in offices, studies, and libraries, or wherever a computer may be located. Like electrical outlets, telephone outlets are placed approximately 15 in. A.F.F. in barrier-free environments, but may be placed at other heights to meet the client's needs.

Other communication lines, such as television, stereo, or computer networking cables, should be located wherever they may be needed. Additionally, telephone and other communication lines should be located away from electrical lines to avoid interference with communication service. In general, it is more cost effective to install additional outlets and communication lines during construction or renovation. Adding one when a space is complete can be very costly.

Visual Communications

Lighting, electrical, and communication systems are documented in construction drawings in the following ways:

1. Lighting location plans indicate where and what kinds of fixtures are used and switch locations.
2. Power and communication location plans indicate where telephone, electrical, and computer outlets are located.
3. Reflected ceiling plans, which are similar to lighting plans, are used mainly in commercial design. They also indicate HVAC and emergency lighting locations and ceiling materials and heights.

Some projects are small enough or simple enough to combir items 1 and 2 above (Figure 5.30). Figure 5.31 indicates com mon symbols for lighting, electrical, and communication plan

No matter how lighting, power, and communication info mation is communicated, designers must understand the important points:

1. Engineers determine the number of circuits required fo the fixtures and outlets. The designer specifies only the style, location, and quantity of fixtures and outlets.
2. Designers need to be vigilant that the HVAC and plumbing systems do not interfere with critical lighting and outlet locations; sometimes a compromise may be required for practical or economic purposes.
3. Lighting design is a collaborative effort among allied professionals. Small residential projects may only requir minor assistance from an electrical engineer; larger commercial projects frequently employ a lighting designer or consultant to assist with the proper quantity and quality lighting decisions.

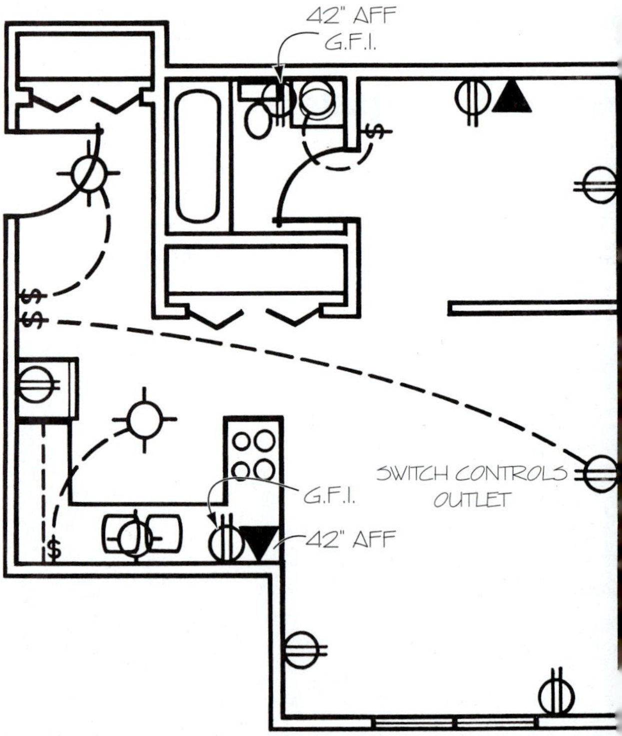

Figure 5.30 *A floor plan, called an electrical, lighting, and telephone plan or ELT, indicates the wiring and location of electrical outlets and switches as well as light fixtures. This information aids the designer in determining a functional furniture arrangement.*

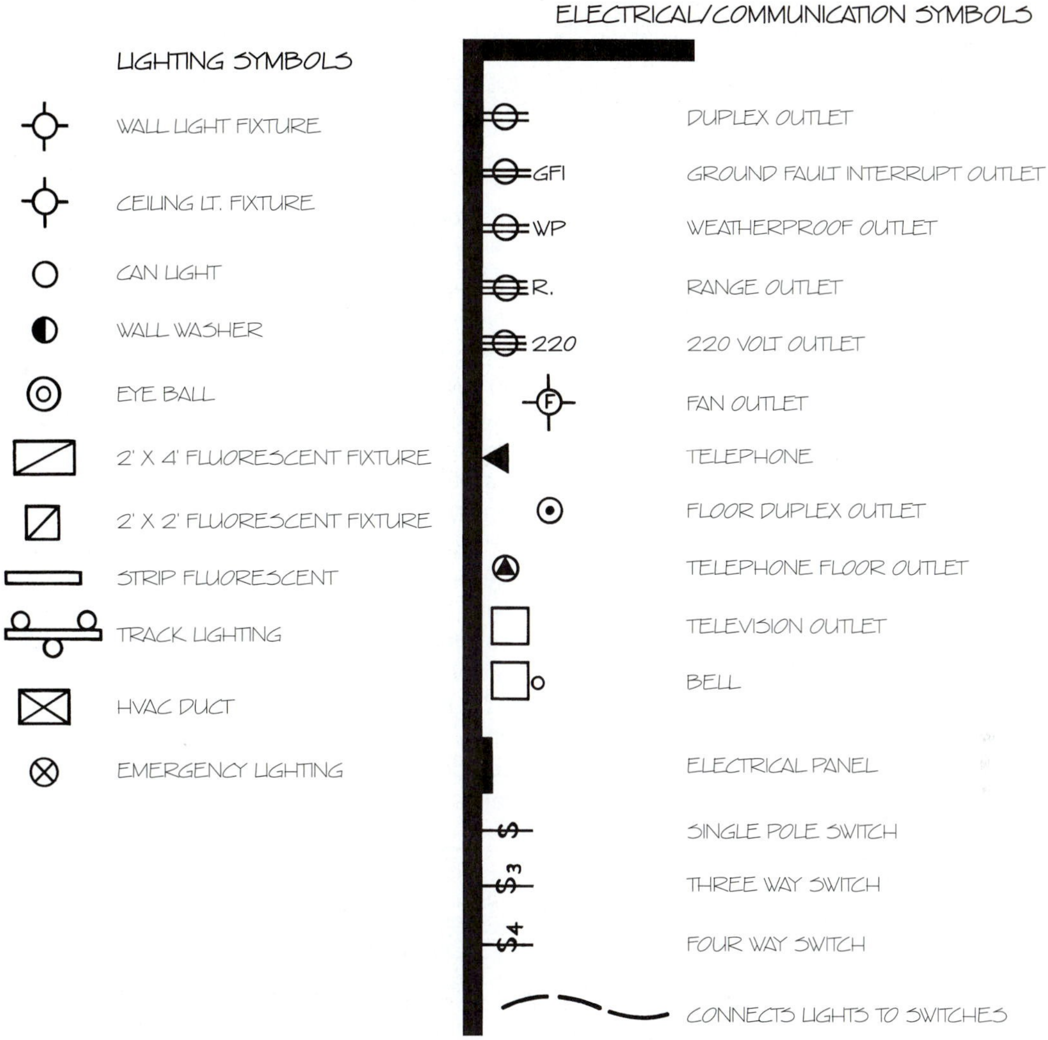

gure 5.31 *Lighting, electrical, and communication symbols.*

All electrical components must meet local, state, and national codes.

Lighting design software is available to assist designers with quantity and quality lighting requirements.

Creative solutions to lighting problems add depth and distinguish one space from another.

In the accompanying Design Scenario, a design for a fit-ess center is produced in a series of drawings and presen-tion boards. Designers are required to produce drawings ıch as these to communicate custom detailing and lighting ·quirements to engineers and builders.

ummary

ıterior designers must be familiar with many aspects of ;ht, including the quantity of light, the quality of light, the proper selection of the lamp, and the proper selection of the fixture. All of these aspects must work together to meet the function of the space in an aesthetically pleasing and economically efficient manner. To accomplish this, designers have many resources including recommendations for footcandles, reflectance values for various surfaces, CRI ratings, Kelvin temperatures, spectrum patterns, distribution charts, and so on.

Absorbing all this information and correctly applying it can be overwhelming. Many designers may delegate lighting design to a consultant. On larger projects, this may especially be appropriate; however, remember that the consultant is an assistant to the project and still needs direction as to the character and atmosphere desired in the space. Designers should be confident in completing the selection and placement of lighting, power, and communication needs on projects, and visually communicating these needs to engineers and builders.

Project Description

In this renovation of an existing health and fitness center, the client requested a "retro" look using wood and steel. The client also desired, however, a warm and inviting interior. The existing space used an exposed ductwork and ceiling construction system, which were to remain exposed. All new facilities were to meet universal design requirements.

Programming: During the programming phase, the following specific requirements were identified:

- Control desk with juice and smoothie bar

  To house a computer, printer, cash register, and telephone
  To contain a lowered surface to accommodate people with disabilities
  To include (2) blenders, undercounter refrigerator, storage for glassware, tableware, and a sink
  Accommodations for bar-styled seating

- Small open pro-shop adjacent to control desk
- Hardwood floors at entry and around control desk
- Childcare area
- Private office
- Storage facility
- Update of all other existing areas including cardiovascular and strength-training areas and the restrooms

Design Development Solution: In order to meet the client's reque the existing ceiling and ductwork remained exposed; howev to bring warmth to the interior, bright colors were added to tl walls and ceilings and were intermingled with stacked stor walls. Suspended light fixtures visually lowered the ceilin added sparkle, and helped to define specific areas (Figures DS5 and DS5.2).

Several design details were developed to illustrate the r quirements of the control desk and juice bar. Custom elemen such as the wavelike front of plastic laminate and changes countertop heights, met the functional and aesthetic design r quirements (Figure DS5.3).

A lowered ceiling and unique display rack define the pr shop. Attention to details, such as custom men's and womer restroom signs, adds uniqueness and a human element to th large, open environment (Figures DS 5.4 and DS 5.5).

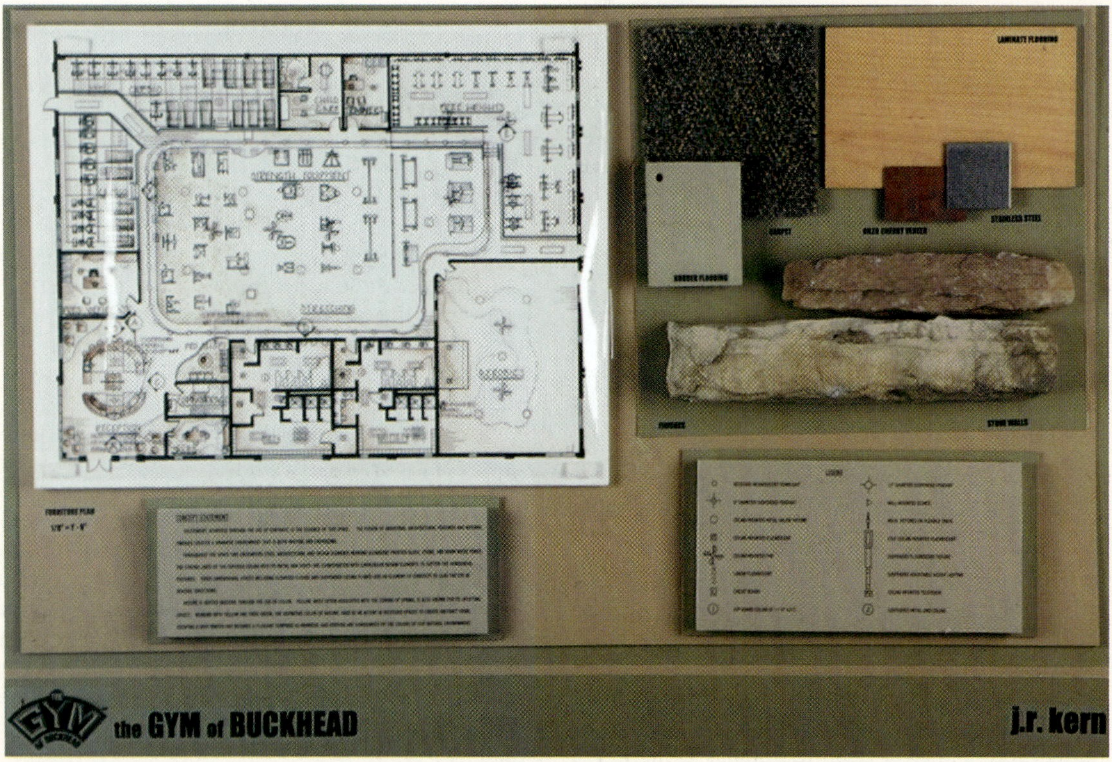

Figure DS5.1 *This presentation board illustrates the floor plan for the health and fitness center. Finishes used throughout the space are grouped together and include warm colors and stacked stone. (Designer: Jamie R. Kern. Photograph by Southern Lights Photography.)*

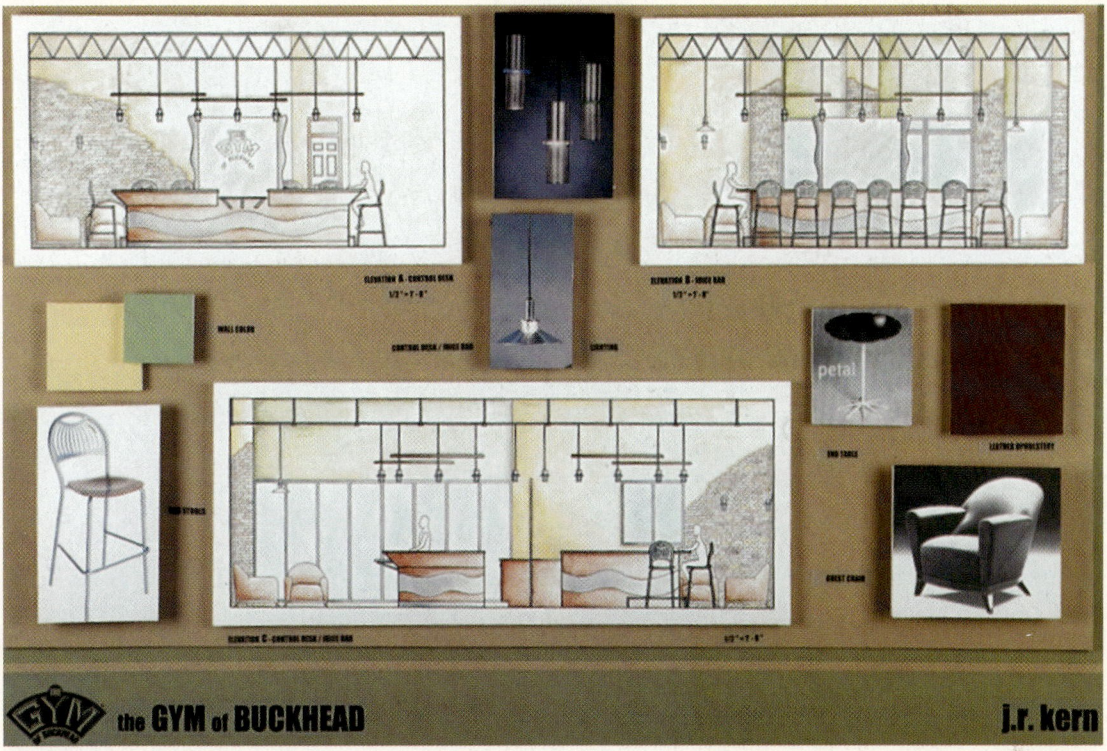

Figure DS5.2 *With these three elevations, the designer has effectively illustrated the control desk and juice bar. Furniture selections add warmth and invite the club members to sit down. (Designer: Jamie R. Kern. Photograph by Southern Lights Photography.)*

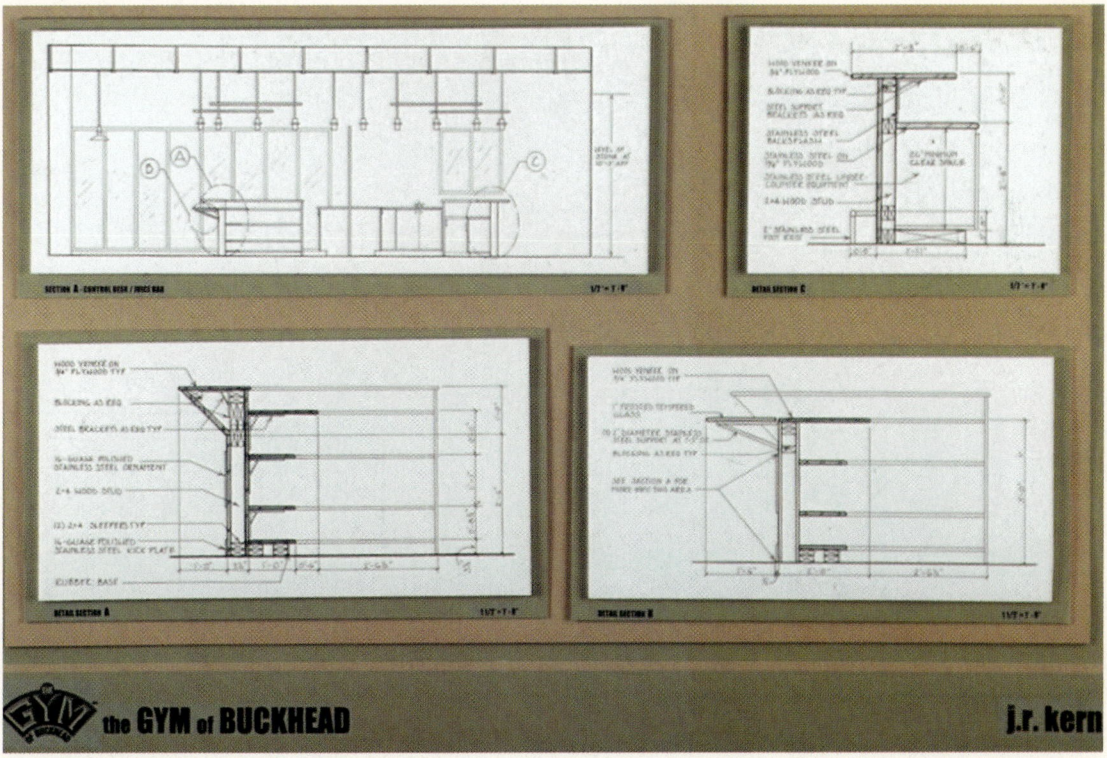

Figure DS5.3 *Because the control desk and juice bar were of vital concern to the client, the designer developed a series of details defining the specific requirements requested by the client. Custom details, such as these, add character and individuality to the design solution. (Designer: Jamie R. Kern. Photograph by Southern Lights Photography.)*

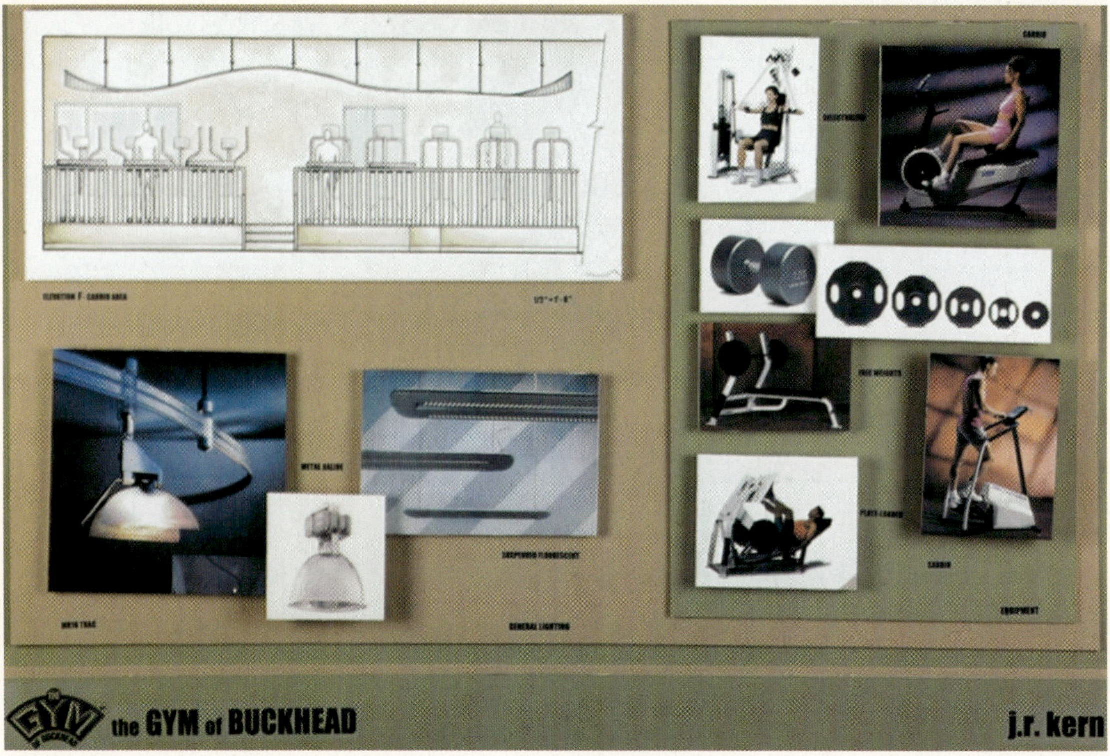

Figure DS5.4 *Lighting and equipment selection and placement were major design elements in this project. Specific selections are illustrated to visually explain the entire story to the owner. (Designer: Jamie R. Kern. Photograph by Southern Lights Photography.)*

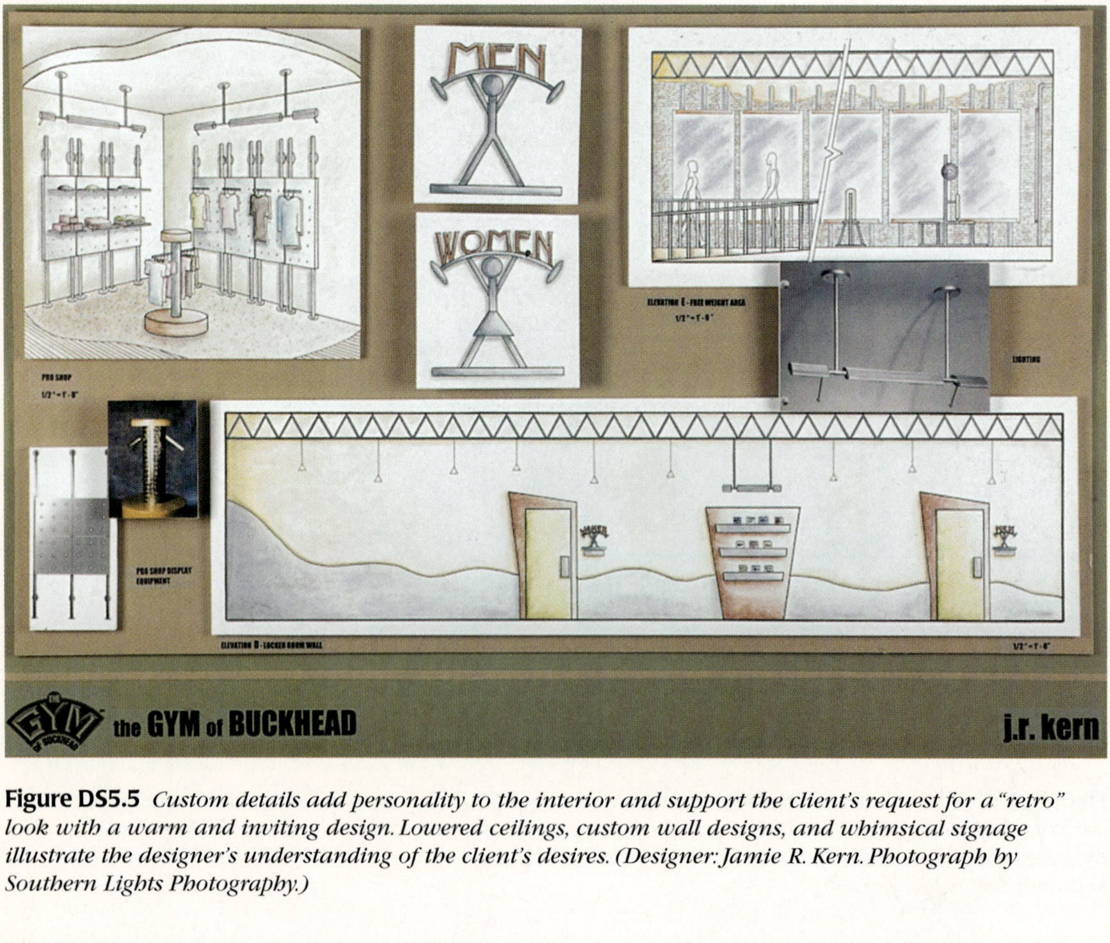

Figure DS5.5 *Custom details add personality to the interior and support the client's request for a "retro" look with a warm and inviting design. Lowered ceilings, custom wall designs, and whimsical signage illustrate the designer's understanding of the client's desires. (Designer: Jamie R. Kern. Photograph by Southern Lights Photography.)*

Space

PART IV

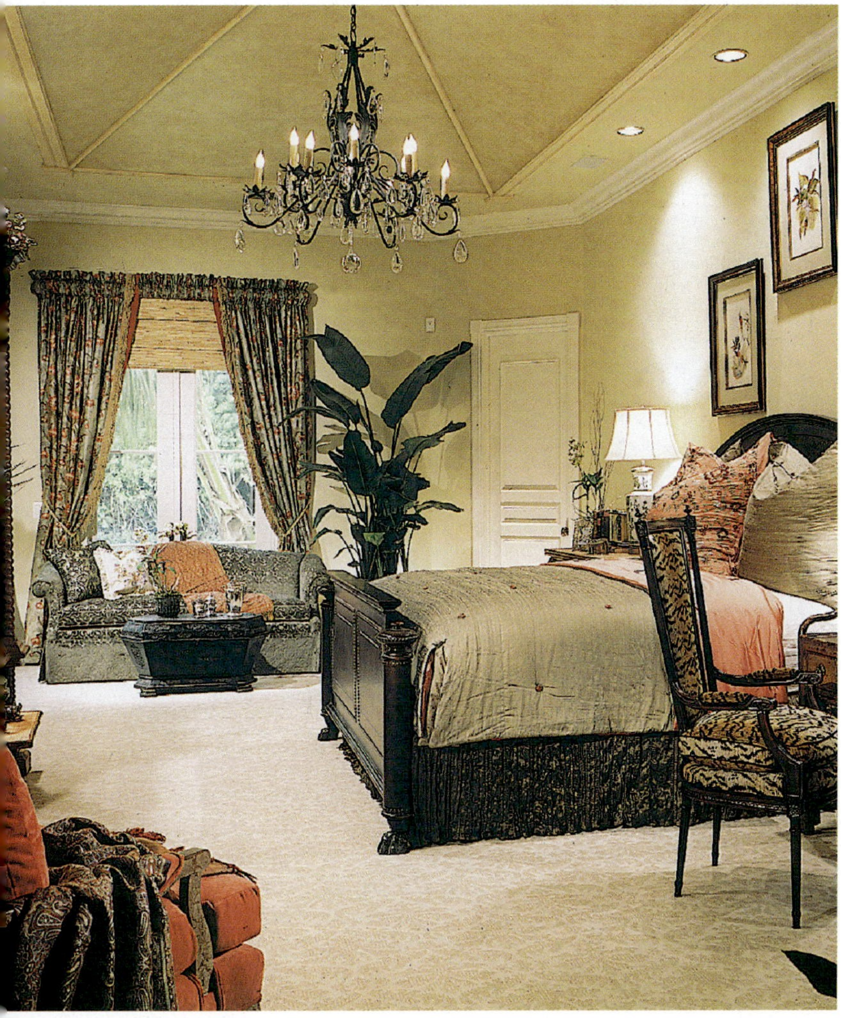

gure IV.1 *This opulent bedroom balances the use of vertical space by placing a ll narrow armoire opposite the larger, yet lower bed. Art over the bed also adds ight to the room. Figure IV.2 shows the design progression. (Designer: Marc- ichaels Interior Design. Photograph © Kim Sargent Architectural Photography. sidence: Private home, Phipps Estates, Palm Beach. Developer: Addison evelopment. Courtesy of* On Design.*)*

When arranging furnishings, I always seek the spaces in between. I am just as concerned about what I leave out of an interior as what I put into it.

–John Saladino

A s discussed in Chapter 2, space is one of the most important ele- ents of design; its appropriate use termines the success of an interior. ell-planned space should be given p priority to ensure an interior here human activity can be carried n with a minimum of frustration. n interior may have exquisite fab- s, brilliant colors, and comfortable ating, but if a person does not ve enough space to function (to work behind a desk, for example), the beauty of the furnishings is wasted.

Space is not limited to the area arranged on a floor plan. The designer must also arrange the space in elevation. Upper cabinets that protrude in front of windows, chair arms that will not fit under tables, or counter tops that are too low or high complicate the client's life. The creation of an environment that promotes comfort and

Figure IV.2 *These drawings show the progression of design from plan view and elevations into the drawing of volume. The photo in Figure IV.1 illustrates the finished room. (Interpretive design drawings by Carol Platt.)*

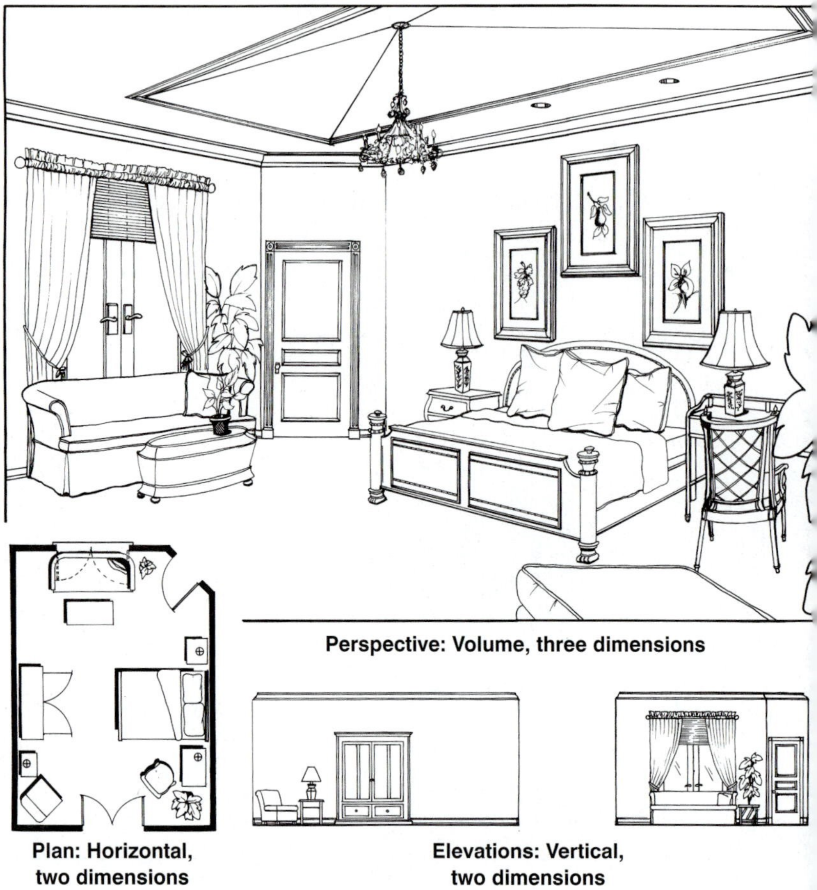

convenience requires the designer to analyze the use of all the planes. The horizontal, vertical, and in-between space is known as **volume.** Understanding and visualizing space in three dimensions are the keys to using space appropriately (Figures IV.1, IV.2, and IV.3).

In the field of design, the placement of furniture and the arrangement of rooms are part of space planning. As discussed in Chapter 1, in the commercial environment, space planning is a career track. Commercial interior designers may spend days, weeks, or even months working with a client to determine space needs and requirements. In the residential environment, a designer may work with the architect and builder to ensure that rooms are the correct shape and size to meet the client's needs. If the residence is already built, the designer must cleverly select and place furniture to utilize the space most efficiently; if necessary, some walls may need to be relocated. As always, the sooner the designer is involved with the design team on a project, the more successful the design solution.

Form and Space

Spaces that designers create form positive areas (the space occupied by the actual furniture pieces) and negative areas (the empty space between pieces). The negative spaces form the pathways or *traffic lanes* that allow people to move throughout a space (Figure IV.4). Hotel lobbies require an immense amount of negative space in order to accommodate the variety of activities and quantity of people moving about the space. Residential dining rooms require less negative space based on the decreased level of activity in the room.

Underfurnishing a room is often more attractive than overcrowding. Studies reveal that overcrowding space can actually have a negati psychological effect on the occ pants. Some empty spaces betwee groupings help give an unclutter effect. An occasional open space empty corner enhances a room a gives the occupants breathing spac On the other hand, a severely unde furnished room may be stark and u inviting. Avoid either extreme.

Space Planning

In many situations, particularly in re idential design, the clients may pu chase a home and then call upon t services of an interior designer make the existing space fit their need This approach, which may be d scribed as designing from the *outsi in,* is taken when the clients fall love with the look of a home witho having assessed its practical layo They may have utilized their enti budget for the purchase and may r

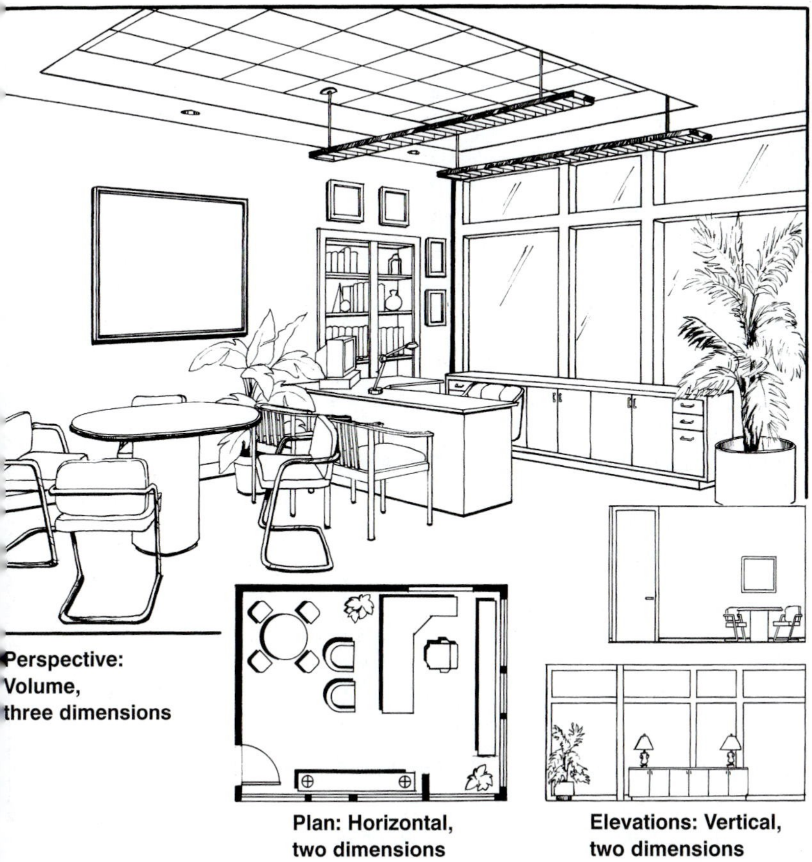

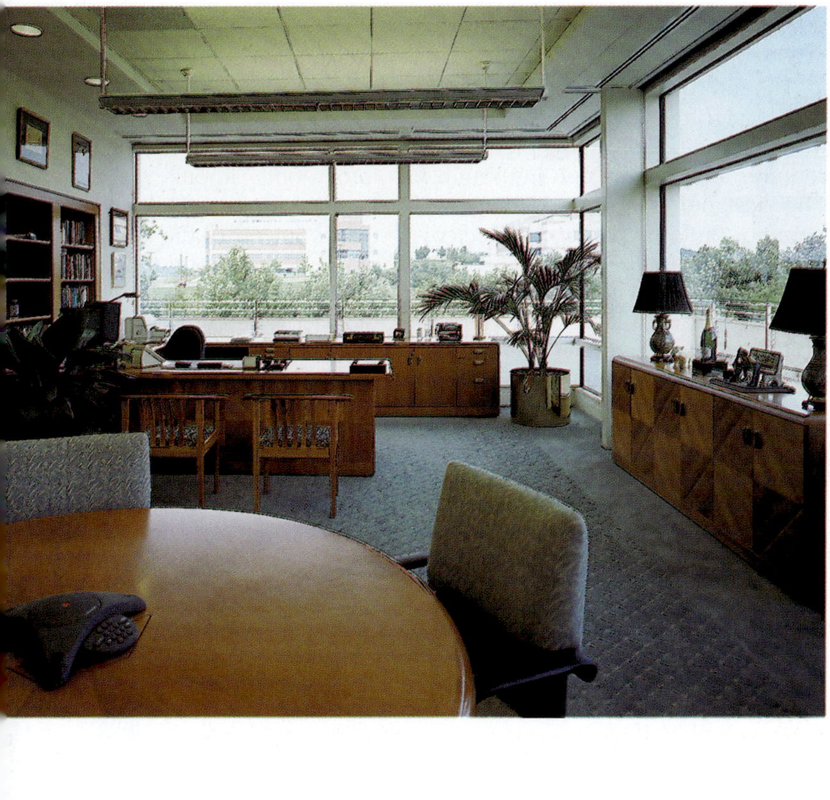

Figure IV.3 *Drawings show a progression from plan view and elevations to a drawing of volume. The photo illustrates the finished room. This custom design for a president's office included a flood of exterior window light balanced by a series of bookshelves. (Architect/Designer: Flad & Associates. Photograph © Norman McGrath. Interpretive design drawings by Carol Platt.)*

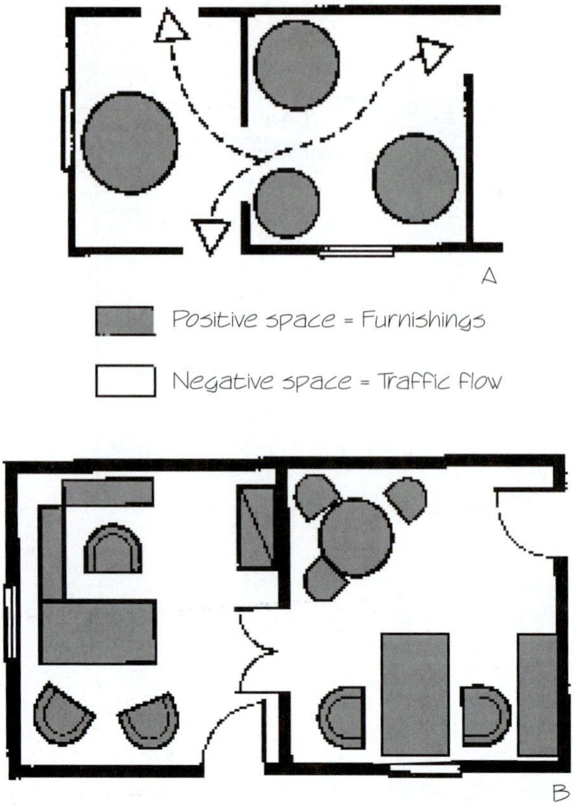

Figure IV.4 *In these drawings the negative space has been left open to allow for traffic flow. (A) use of a bubble diagram. (B) furnishings have been placed in the positive space.*

sort to substandard interior selections. Although the exterior of the home or building has aesthetic appeal, the interior, the space where people spend 90 percent of their lives, is left to awkward furniture arranging and mediocre design. The designer is required to alter apparent room sizes via clever furniture placement, finish and fabric selection, or portable lighting. In commercial situations, particularly in large spaces, the client often recognizes the need for professional help prior to the selection of the building and therefore avoids this mistake.

The alternative school of thought is to design the home or office from the *inside out*. For many clients this requires a paradigm shift in thought. The designer is contacted before a home or building has been selected, then works with the client to analyze spatial needs. The designer can assist the client in locating an appropriate building or home, or designing a new one that meets the client's needs *and* budget. The followi two chapters explore space planni from this inside-out method. F nishings are planned as part of act ity areas. Activity areas are group into rooms. Rooms are grouped interior zones, which then establ the perimeter of the interior envir ment. Throughout this process, tention is given to the vertical natu of space. Remember that interiors planned in volumes.

Space Planning: Furnishings to Rooms

6

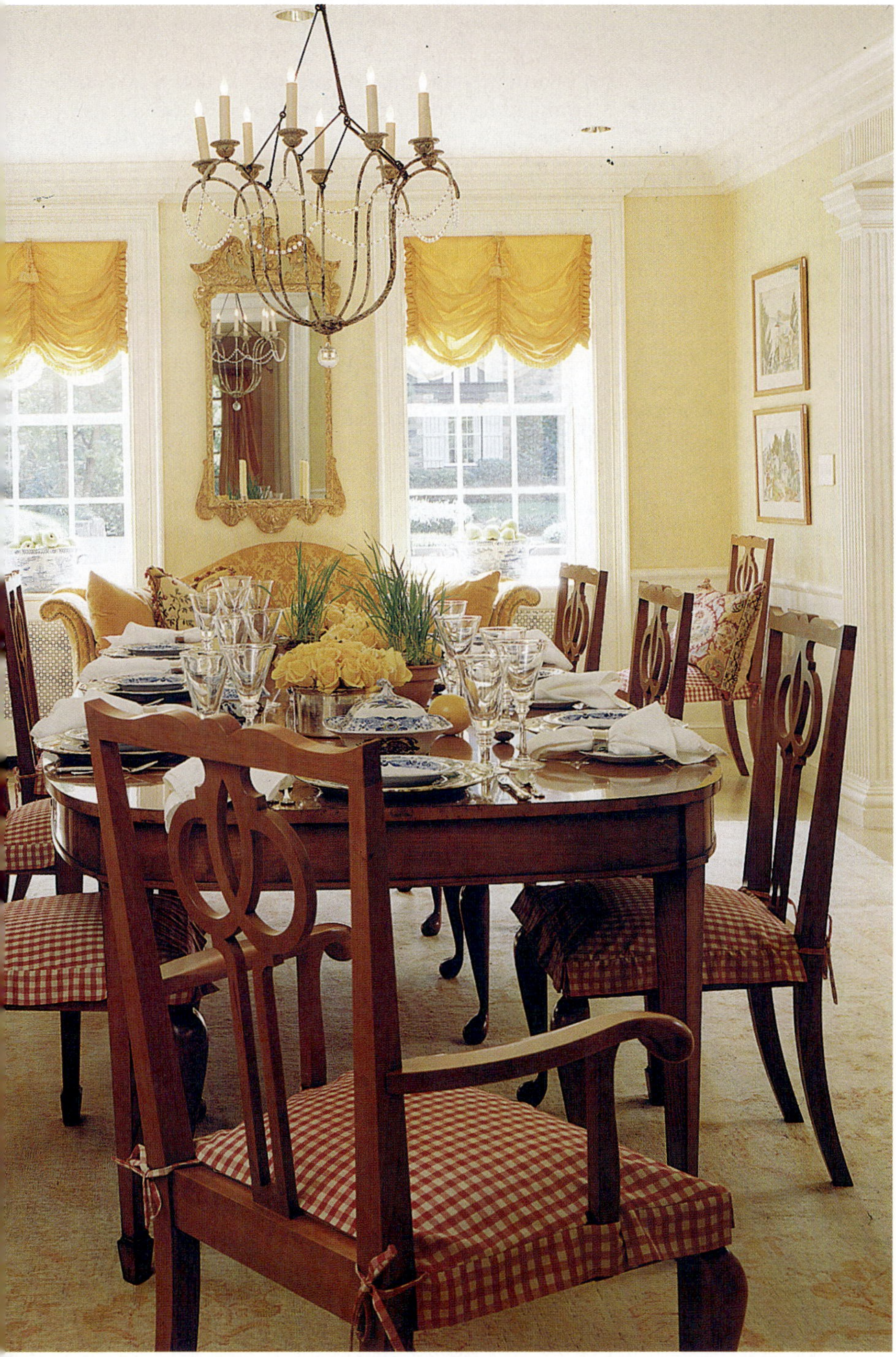

Figure 6.1 *This inviting dining room is based on function. The table allows ample room for each place setting. The sideboard functions as a serving and storage unit. Chairs were selected to promote upright body posture. (Designer: Drysdale Design Associates. Photograph by Antoine Bootz. Courtesy of* Southern Accents.*)*

To be livable, an interior must meet the needs of its occupants. The goals of interior design, as discussed in Chapter 1, include function, the human factor, aesthetics, and economics and ecology. These goals must be applied to space planning. Economics and function dictate spatial needs and are addressed before fabrics, furnishings, and finishes are specified (Figure 6.1).

Programming Information for Space Planning

Economic Concerns

Whether clients are searching for a new office space or a new home, the building and its furnishings are probably the most expensive investments they will make. They want the best value possible for every dollar spent. The designer should study costs and look carefully at such criteria as available budget, client needs, materials and components required, time limits, building requirements, and codes.

The cost of a structure varies depending on many factors: its size, structure, geographic location, materials specified, cubic footage or volume (the three-dimensional measurement of the height, depth, and width of the space), special construction features (such as raised ceilings, angled or curved spaces, custom windows and doors), and the cost of local labor. Average building costs per square foot, exclusive of the price of the land, depend on the region where the structure will be built. An excellent source for determining construction costs is the *Means Cost Estimation Index* by Robert S. Means.

Costs also relate to the selection of furnishings. A good-quality low-budget sofa could cost $1000, whereas the price of an elaborate custom-upholstered sofa could reach into the thousands of dollars. Designers must determine what level of furnishings will work within the client's budget. The deciding factor is the quality of the product, not necessarily its price. If a client cannot afford a quality product, it is better to wait until the product can be purchased. Placing inexpensive, low-quality furnishings in a space almost always results in an unhappy client and a poor design solution. It is better to have a few well-spaced quality pieces of furniture than a room full of cheap substitutes.

More info online @

http://www.jsc.nasa.gov/bu2/resources.html Cost estimating resources

Function

During the initial client contact and programming phase, the designer asks numerous questions to determine the function of an interior and the client's design preferences and space needs. The designer working with a residential client may complete a *personal profile* of each occupant and ask questions regarding the client's lifestyle. Nonresidential projects may require interviews with executives of the company ar some individual staff members. (Appendix A is an examp of a typical initial programming questionnaire.) In essenc the designer must understand the intricacies of the hous hold or the firm in order to carefully plan for spatial need

Human Factors

The physical and psychological comfort of the occupants an important aspect of the space planning process. Peop should be comfortable in relation to the scale and proportic of the architecture. The three-dimensional aspects of a spac must be considered, because if the space is too vast or tc small, people may feel out of place.

Furniture should be suitably scaled for comfort ar arranged for purpose and efficiency. It should also be ea to use and operate. For example, a desk and desk cha should be the appropriate height, and a storage cabin should have shelves the user can reach. *User-friendly* furn ture also should be easy to move or rearrange and clea Some terms related to design and human comfort are a thropometrics, ergonomics, and proxemics.

Anthropometrics studies the size and proportions of tl human body. Research in this area identifies typical huma heights, widths, and sizes in various postures, this inform tion can be used to determine optimum space needs and tl level of mobility and physical strength required of the er user (Figure 6.2).

Ergonomics is the study of human beings and their r sponses to various working conditions and environment Ergonomic data provide designers with information on suc

Adult Male and Female Miscellaneous Structural Body Dimensions in Inches and Centimeters by Age and Selected Percentiles

		A		B		C		D		E		F		G	
		in	cm	in	cm	in	cm	in	cm	in	cm	in	cm	in	cm
95	MEN	36.2	91.9	47.3	120.1	68.6	174.2	20.7	52.6	27.3	69.3	37.0	94.0	33.9	86.
	WOMEN	32.0	81.3	43.6	110.7	64.1	162.8	17.0	43.2	24.6	62.5	37.0	94.0	31.7	80.5
5	MEN	30.8	78.2	41.3	104.9	60.8	154.4	17.4	44.2	23.7	60.2	32.0	81.3	30.0	76.2
	WOMEN	26.8	68.1	38.6	98.0	56.3	143.0	14.9	37.8	21.2	53.8	27.0	68.6	28.1	71.4

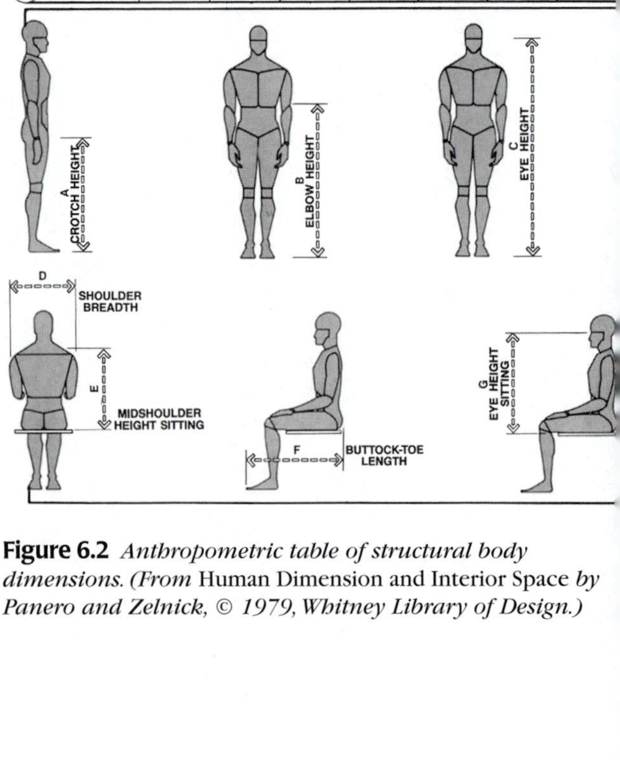

Figure 6.2 *Anthropometric table of structural body dimensions. (From* Human Dimension and Interior Space *by Panero and Zelnick, © 1979, Whitney Library of Design.)*

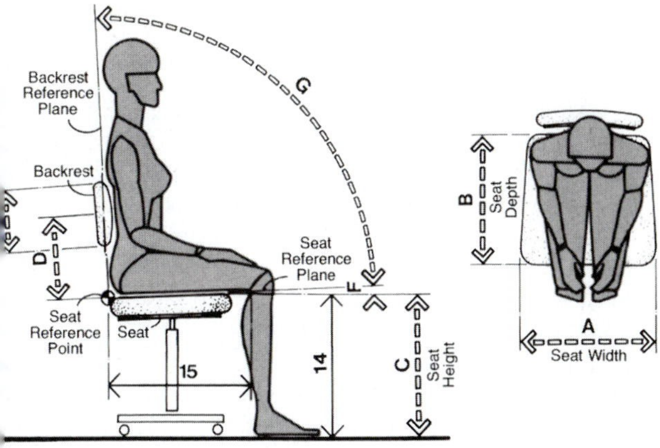

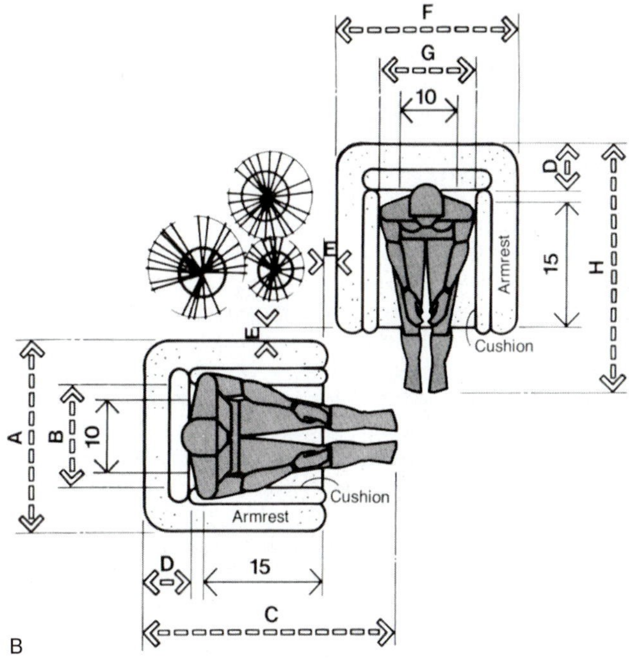

gure 6.3 *Anthropometric studies combined to form gonomic knowledge of (A) a work or secretarial chair and) a corner seating arrangement. (From* Human Dimension d Interior Space *by Panero and Zelnick, © 1979, Whitney brary of Design.)*

bjects as comfortable seating as well as visual and acousti-l issues. For example, a computer chair that provides max-um back, arm, and leg support may be said to be rgonomically" designed (Figure 6.3).

Proxemics studies the use of space by human beings in particular culture. Everyone has an invisible comfort zone area of surrounding space called a "space bubble" (Figure 4). Discomfort may result when a person with a smaller ace bubble gets too close to a person with a larger space ibble. Our individual comfort zones vary in relation to our lture and background experiences. The designer can use this information to create environments with furniture that will meet particular needs for comfort and space, especially in a nonresidential setting.

In all environments, most people want a space that belongs to them—like a bedroom, or a certain chair in the family room or breakroom. Observing children who share a bedroom often reveals this need for private space. For example, children may make it clear what side of the room is theirs, or what part of the closet is for their belongings only. This need for a personal space usually carries over into adult life, and a sensitive designer plans furnishings accordingly.

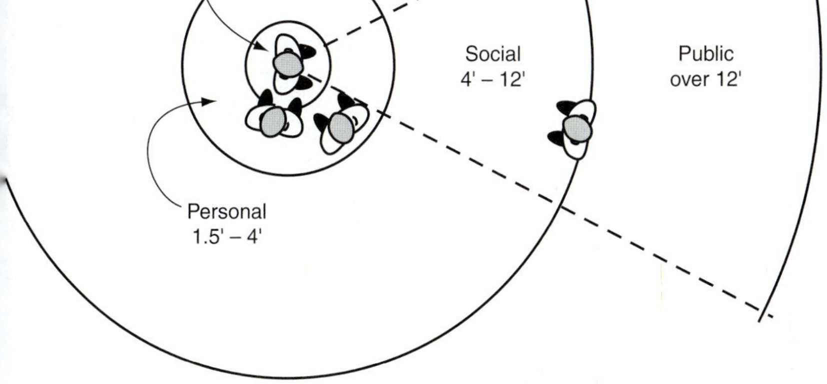

Figure 6.4 *Edward T. Hall, in his book* The Hidden Dimension, *discusses four distance zones: the intimate, the personal, the social, and the public.*

More info online @

http://www.design-technology.info/anthropometrics/
Teaching website on anthropometrics and ergonomics

Universal Design

The elderly, infants, and the physically challenged have special needs that designers must consider. In planning for both residential and nonresidential spaces, designers must adequately satisfy these special users' needs for safety, convenience, and comfort. In universal design, as discussed in Part I, environments are created to meet the needs of individuals regardless of age and ability. One aspect of universal design includes barrier-free environments. **Barrier-free designs** present no physical obstacles or barriers, allowing free movement for individuals with disabilities. Barrier-free access in a public space for users who are physically challenged is required by law. Designers need to be aware of these regulations and implement design solutions that conform to them (see Chapter 4). At a minimum, accessible planning should include the following:

- Parking spaces for individuals with disabilities must be conveniently placed, adequate in number, clearly marked, and not on a slope.
- The environment, both interior and exterior, should be free of architectural barriers so those who may be using a wheelchair, crutches, or a walker can easily circulate throughout various areas. In a commercial environment, doors must be a minimum of 36″ wide and must have lever handles. The pull side of the door should be free of any obstructions for a minimum of 18″ (preferably 24″). Though not required by law, this approach also works best in residential environments for people who are physically challenged (Figure 6.5).
- Traffic lanes or corridors must be kept free of clutter and be wide enough for easy movement in a wheelchair or walker (see Figure 4.21).
- Floor coverings that are hard, smooth, and slip-resistant work most efficiently for safe and easy movement. If carpet is used, a dense, short pile is best. Generally, area and throw rugs should be avoided. Thresholds should be flat, or not more than 1/2″ high.

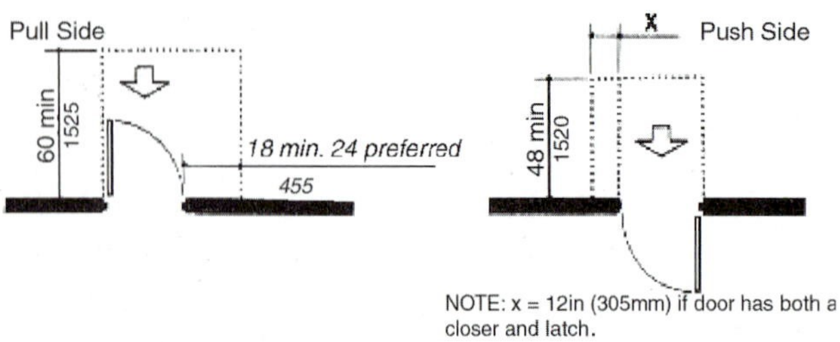

Figure 6.5 *The minimum clear requirements for an accessible swinging door. (Federal Register, Vol. 56, No. 144, Figure 25, Maneuvering Clearances at Doors, July 26, 1991.)*

- In the kitchen, where people are especially susceptibl to accidents, heights, clearances, and other measurements should be planned for convenience and safety. Working surfaces that pull out and storage areas with open and revolving shelves are an asset. A front-loadir dishwasher and washer/dryer, an upright refrigerator, and an oven with front controls are convenient. For those using wheelchairs, oven and dishwasher doors hinged at the side are better; however, controls on the front of the appliances may not be the best solution fo households with young children.
- Bathrooms and fixtures must be conveniently and safel located with ample room for manipulating a wheelcha Grab bars conveniently positioned by the tub and toile provide added safety (Figure 6.6).
- Signage, water fountains, sconces, telephones, and emergency alarms must also be easily used by people who have physical impairments.

More info online @

http://www.dezignare.com/newsletter/ergonomics.html
General information on Universal and Barrier-Free Design and Term

http://www.adaptiveenvironments.org/about/index.php
Nonprofit organization on adaptive environments

http://www.usdoj.gov/crt/ada/adahom1.htm
American with Disabilities Act site

http://www.arthritis.org/resources/Home_Life/design.asp
Arthritis Foundation information on barrier-free design

Guidelines for Furnishing Dimensions

Once the functions have been determined and the hum needs of each occupant evaluated, the designer determin how much space is required to meet the client's nee This is a component of programming. In order to acco

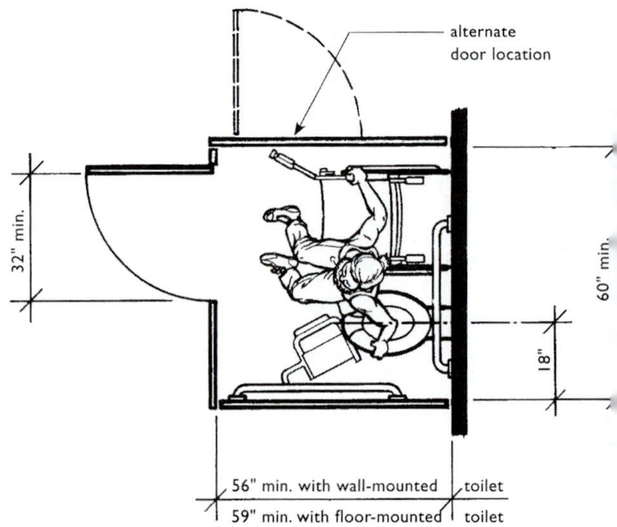

Figure 6.6 *A typical layout for an accessible commercial toilet area. (From U.S. Department of Housing and Urban Development.)*

ıble 6.1 *Typical Furnishing Sizes Drawn in Plan View*

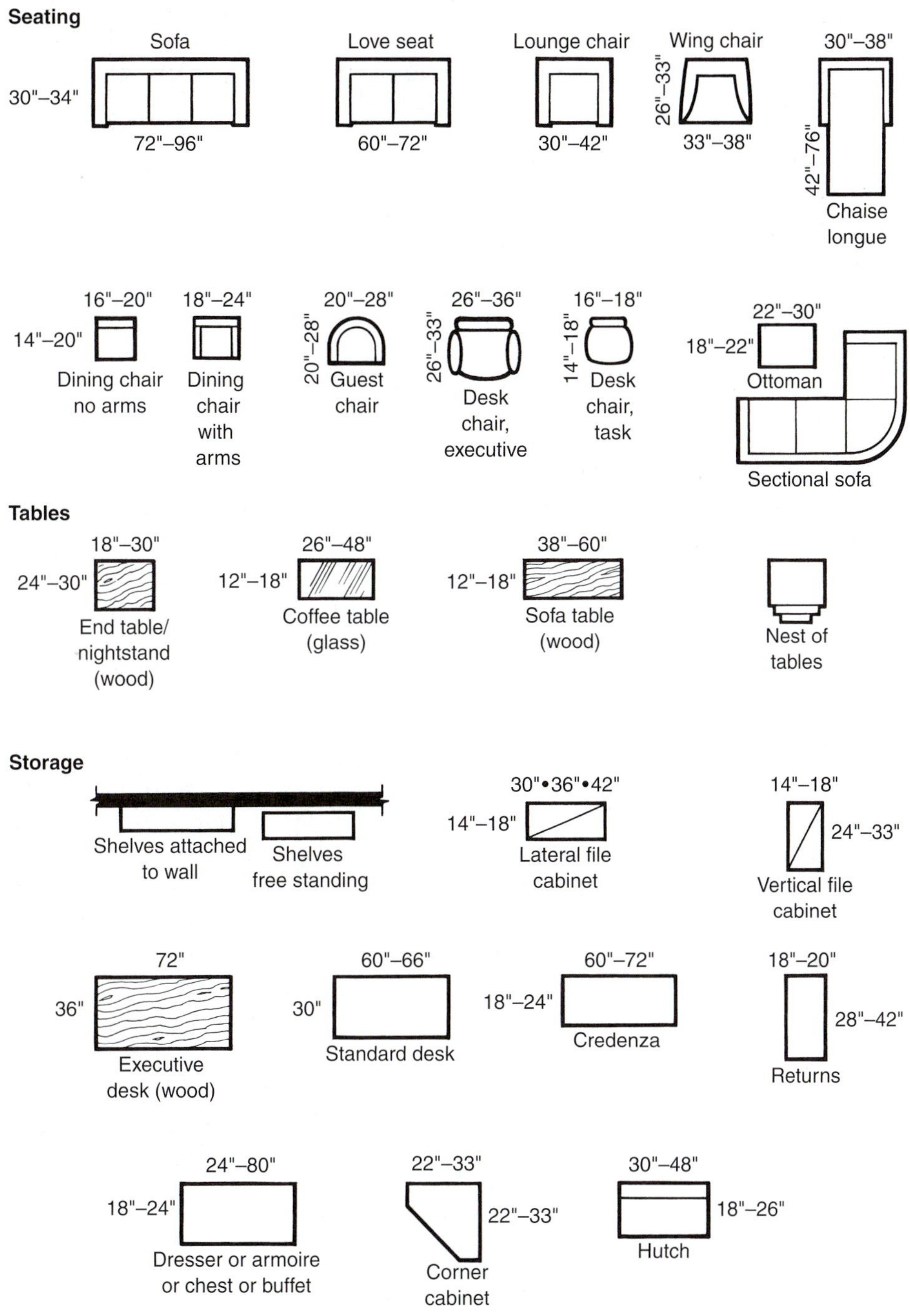

ɔh this, designers must have a working knowledge of · actual sizes of furniture pieces and the clearances nec- ary to move about the space. Study Tables 6.1 and 6.2; er to them often. In the design industry, furniture size is ːed in inches; architectural features are noted in feet and hes.

Traffic Patterns

Once the furniture (positive space) has been determined, the designer analyzes the clearances (negative space) required for major and minor traffic lanes. Study Table 6.3 on clearance requirements, and Figure 6.7.

Table 6.1 *Typical Furnishing Sizes Drawn in Plan View, Continued*

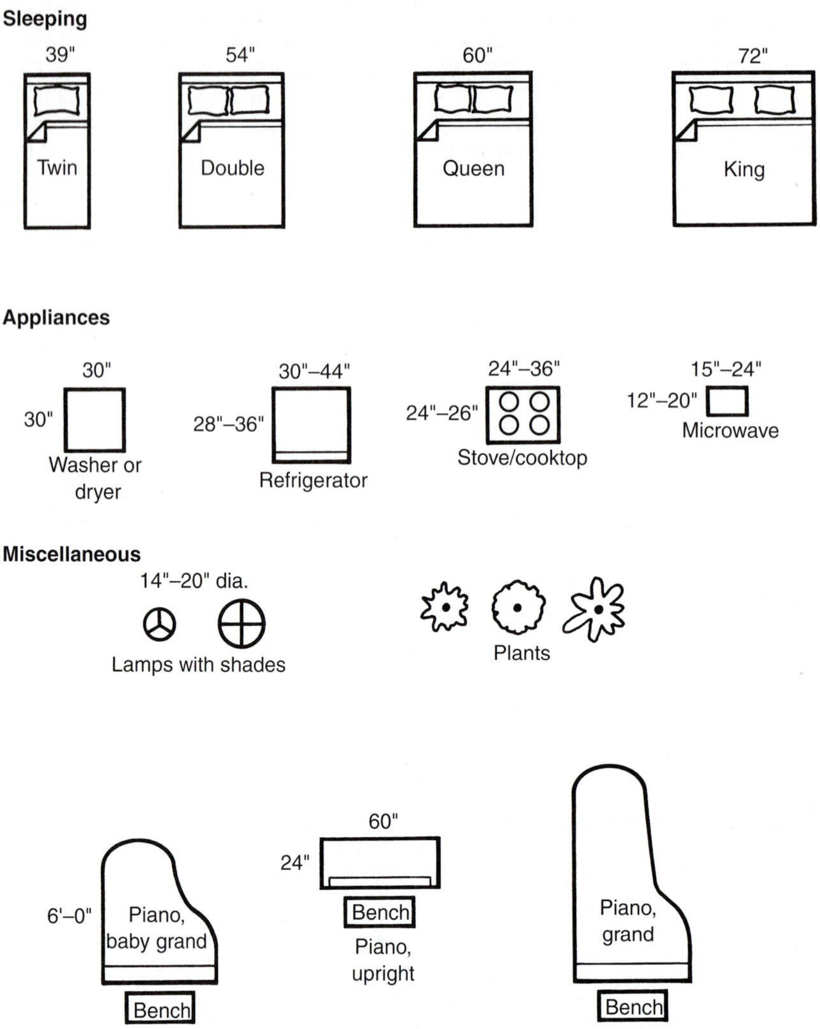

Table 6.2 *Critical Heights and Depths*

Heights

Chair seat:	18″
End table:	Matches arm of sofa
Sofa arm:	Varies with style
Desk:	29″–30″
Keyboard:	26″–27″ (Should be at user's elbow height when seated with arm bent)
Table:	29″–30″

Depths (and Heights if Critical)

Kitchen base cabinet/counter:	24″D × 36″H
Kitchen wall cabinet:	12″D × 24″–36″H
Space between counter and cabinet:	15″–18″
Bathroom counter:	22″D × 28″–36″H
Bookshelf:	8″–18″

able 6.3 *Clearance Requirements*

·affic Paths	
ajor commercial	60″ or more
ajor residential	48″–60″
inor commercial	36″–60″
inor residential	18″–48″
ıysically challenged	32″ minimum allowed, but only for a length of 24″
One-way passage	36″ minimum
Two-way passage	60″ minimum
Corner turn	42″ minimum
Wheelchair turnaround	5′-0″ diameter

onversation Areas	
oot room between sofa or chair and edge of coffee table top	12″–15″
oor space in front of chair for feet and legs	1′-6″ to 2′-6″
hair or bench space in front of desk or piano	3′

ining or Conferencing	
pace for occupied chair	1′-6″ to 1′-10″
pace to get into chairs	1′-10″ to 3′
pace for person to assist in seating	4′-6″
raffic path around table and occupied chairs	1′-6″ to 2′

Workspaces	
Space between desk and credenza	42″ to 48″
Space in front of files	30″ to 36″
Space for guest chairs in front of desk	42″ to 48″

Sleeping Areas	
Space for making bed	1′-6″ to 2′
Space between twin beds	1′-6″ to 2′-4″
Space in front of chest of drawers	3′
Space in front of dresser	3′ to 4″

Food Preparation	
Workspace in front of cabinets	3′ to 6′
Counter space between equipment	3′ to 5′
Ventilation for attachments in back of some appliances	3″ to 5″

Bathing Areas	
Space between front of tub and opposite wall	2′-6″ to 3′-6″
Space in front of toilet	18″ to 24″
Space at sides of toilet	12″ to 18″
Space between fronts of fixtures	2′-6″ to 3′

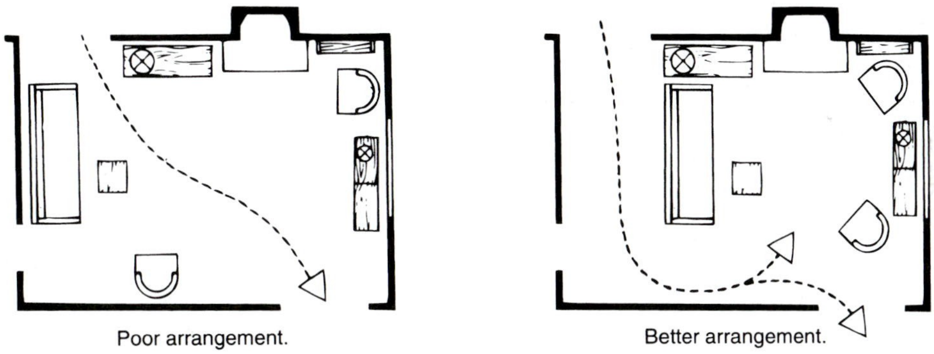

Poor arrangement. Better arrangement.

Figure 6.7 *Appropriate furniture layout to redirect traffic.*

Figuring Square Footage

An important aspect of space planning is the ability to figure square footage. Square footage is determined by multiplying the length of a room by the width. Therefore, $L \times W$ = square footage or □. For example, if a room were 10′-0″ × 12′ × 0″, it would contain 120 □.

The following charts may be helpful in figuring these problems.

Inches to Decimal Foot Conversion Chart

1″ = .08′	7″ = .58′
2″ = .16′	8″ = .67′
3″ = .25′	9″ = .75′
4″ = .33′	10″ = .83′
5″ = .42′	11″ = .92′
6″ = .50′	12″ = 1.0′

Conversion Chart

1 inch = 2.54 centimeters (multiply the number of inches by 2.54 to determine the number of centimeters)

1 centimeter = .3937 inches (multiply the number of centimeters by .3937 to determine the number of inches)

1 foot = 12 inches = .3048 meters (multiply the number of feet by .3048 to determine the number of meters)

1 meter = 3.2808 feet (multiply the number of meters by 3.2808 to determine the number of feet)

1 □ = 144 square inches = .0929 square meters (multiply the number of square feet by .0929 to determine the number of square meters)

1 square meter = 10.764 □ (multiply the number of square meters by 10.764 to determine the number of square feet)

1 square yard = 9 □ = .8361 square meters (multiply the number of square yards by .8361 to determine the number of square meters)

1 square meter = 1.196 square yards (multiply the number of square meters by 1.196 to determine the number of square yards)

Determining Square Footage in Feet and Inches (Does Not Apply to the Metric System)

If a room is 10′-3″ × 12′-9″, the process requires the following steps. (A calculator is useful here.) To figure the square footage:

- Using the inches to decimal conversion chart, change the inches to a decimal:
  10′-3″ becomes 10.25′ and
  12′-9″ becomes 12.75′
- Multiply the length by the width:
  10.25′ × 12.75′ = 130.6875 □
- Square footage or areas are usually figured in whole numbers. Simply round up or down to the nearest whole number, in this case, 131 □.

Determining Square Footage in Odd-Shaped Rooms

It is more complicated to figure square footage when the room has an odd shape. The room below is L-shaped. To figure the square footage complete the following steps:

- Divide the room into two separate rectangles.
- Figure the square footage of each space:
  The square footage of A = 10′-0″ × 20′-0″ = 200 □
  The square footage of B = 10′-0″ × 8′-0″ = 80 □
- Add the totals. The total square footage is 200 □ + 80 □ = 280 □.

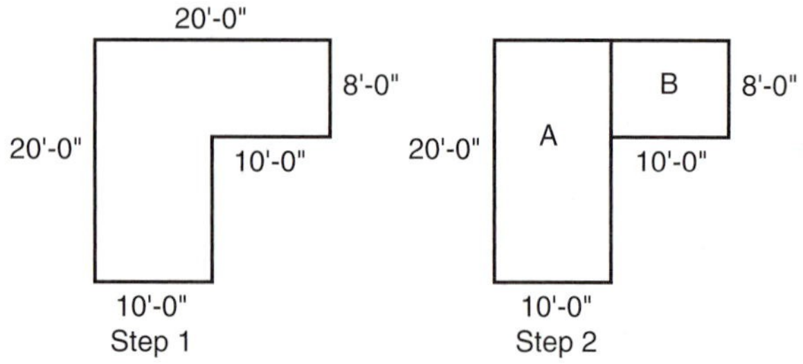

To figure the square footage of a room with an angle, such as in the following figure, more geometry must be used.

- Divide the room into as few rectangles and triangles as possible.
- Figure the square footage of the rectangular spaces:
  A = 16′-0″ × 14′-0″ = 224 □
  B = 6′-0″ × 8′-0″ = 48 □
  Hint: 20′-0″ − 14′-0″ = 6′-0″
- To figure the square footage of C, it is important to know that a triangle is simply a rectangle divided in half. Therefore, multiply the length by the width and divide the answer by 2:
  6′-0″ × 8′-0″ = 48 □ ÷ 2 = 24 □
- Add the totals of the spaces together to arrive at the total square footage:
  224 □ + 48 □ + 24 □ = 296 □

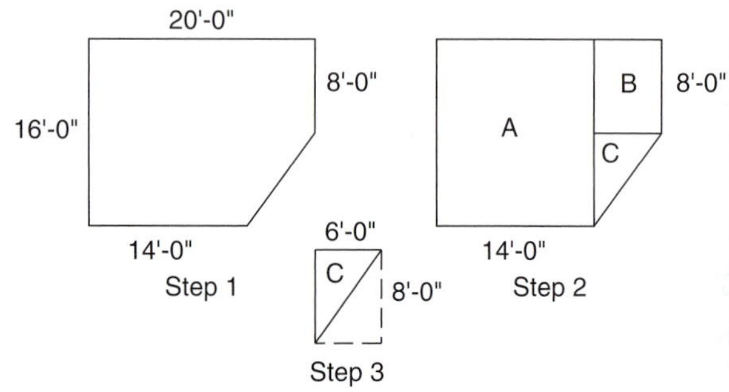

In all cases, convert the inches to a decimal before multiplying. Remember to round off the decimal to the nearest whole number when finished.

ıble 6.4 *Specific Activity Areas in Commercial and Residential Design*

ıecific Activity	Commercial Use	Residential Use
ɔnversation area	Hotel and health care lobby Waiting room Breakroom Reception room	Living room Family room Bedroom
ning/conferencing/lecturing	Restaurant Hotel ballroom Corporate office Presentation room Cafeteria Classroom	Dining room Breakfast room
deo/television viewing and presentation	Hotel and health care lobby Executive or typical office Classroom Waiting room Breakroom Hotel guest room Conference room Hospital room	Living room Family room Bedroom Media room
erical, studying, and computing	All areas of contract design	Home office Library Study Child's room
eeping	Hotel room Health care patient room Executive suite	Bedroom Guest room
'orage	All areas of contract design	All areas in a residence
ɔod preparation	Restaurant Hotel Hospital Cafeteria	Kitchen
athroom	All areas of contract design	Bathroom

ıace Planning r Specific Activities

ɜre are basically eight activity or functional areas required nterior settings. Table 6.4 illustrates their use in commer- and residential environments. Understanding the specific ce requirements for each of these areas allows a designer space plan an entire room.

Ideally, the designer works with the architect and builder determine room sizes. Specific functions and space re- rements are similar for commercial and residential envi- ments; however, commercial environments typically uire wider traffic lanes. The following groupings should considered when determining square footages. The in- mation in the box on page 186, "Figuring Square ɔtage," also may be helpful.

Conversation Area

In both residential and commercial environments, conversation groupings provide the critical backdrop for communication. Conversation groups should be designed out of the line of traffic and planned so that people can hear and be heard. There must be adequate space to access (or walk into) the grouping. The maximum conversation distance is 10′-0″, whereas six to eight feet is ideal. Figure 6.8 illustrates the six basic conversation groupings.

1. The *straight-line grouping,* although not conducive to intimate conversation, may work well for public places such as waiting rooms.
2. The *L-shaped grouping* is good for conversation and lends itself to both large and small areas.
3. The *U-shaped grouping* is comfortable and attractive but requires considerable space. Both the L- and U-shapes

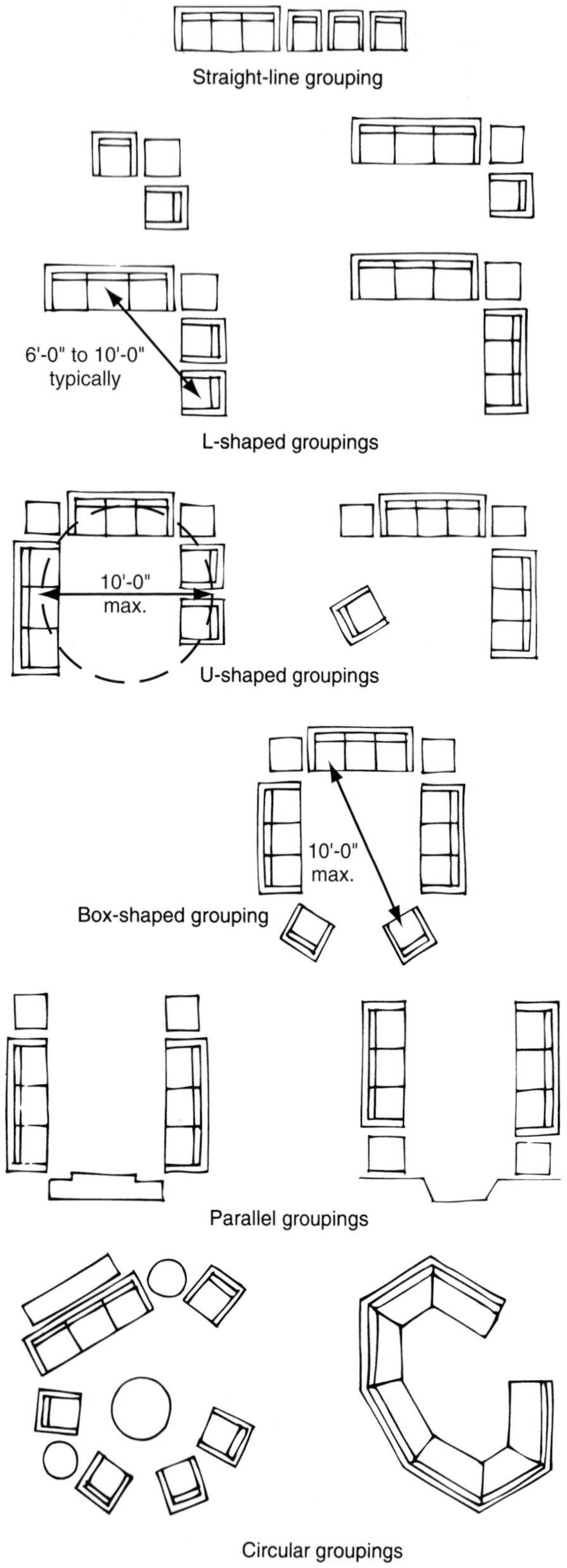

Figure 6.8 *Six basic conversation groupings.*

may be repeated several times in a large hotel, hospita
or office lobby.

4. The *box-shaped grouping* is popular where space is ample. Allow space for a sufficient opening to present an inviting entry.
5. The *parallel grouping* emphasizes an existing focal po such as a fireplace or a special wall feature and provic a pleasant arrangement for conversation.
6. The *circular grouping* may encompass an entire room an area of a large room. This arrangement can be inviting because it provides an enveloping seating element.

Once the furniture grouping is established, the desigr can determine the size of the room (Figure 6.9). If other fur tions are required in the room, or if special architectural artistic features are requested, these will be added to t square footage requirements.

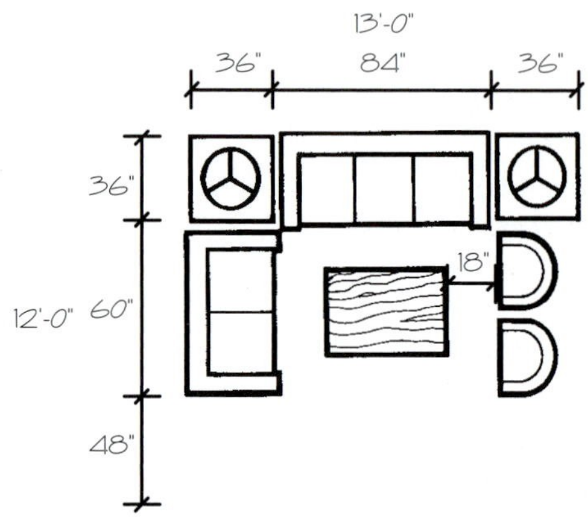

Figure 6.9 *If a U-shaped grouping to seat seven people is selected, the designer totals the perimeter dimensions to determine the size of the room. This space requires a minimum area of 12′-0″ × 13′-0″ or 156*☐.

Dining/Conferencing/Lecturing

Designers must know how many individuals are to be a commodated in a dining, conference, or lecture area. An ar planned for two to six guests is substantially different from area planned for two to six couples; an area planned for 2 people requires an even greater sensitivity to the human sca The goal is to plan a space that accommodates all the gues but does not feel austere when used by a lesser number.

Conference and dining tables may be round, square, re tangular, oval, or boat-shaped, and in very large conferen rooms may form a U-shape. Many conference tables are cu tom designed to fit a client's needs.

Each occupant requires approximately 2′-0″ to 2′-6″ space on the table in front of the chair as a work surface for dinnerware. Approximately 3′-6″ to 4′-0″ is required b tween the table and the wall. Typical arrangements a shown in Figure 6.10.

The process to determine the size of a conference or di ing room is the same as for the conversation area (Figure 6.1 When tables are grouped together, such as in a restaurant cafeteria, a minimum of 44″ is needed between them. Ad tional space is required for serving areas and storage, and conference rooms and classrooms for presentation areas.

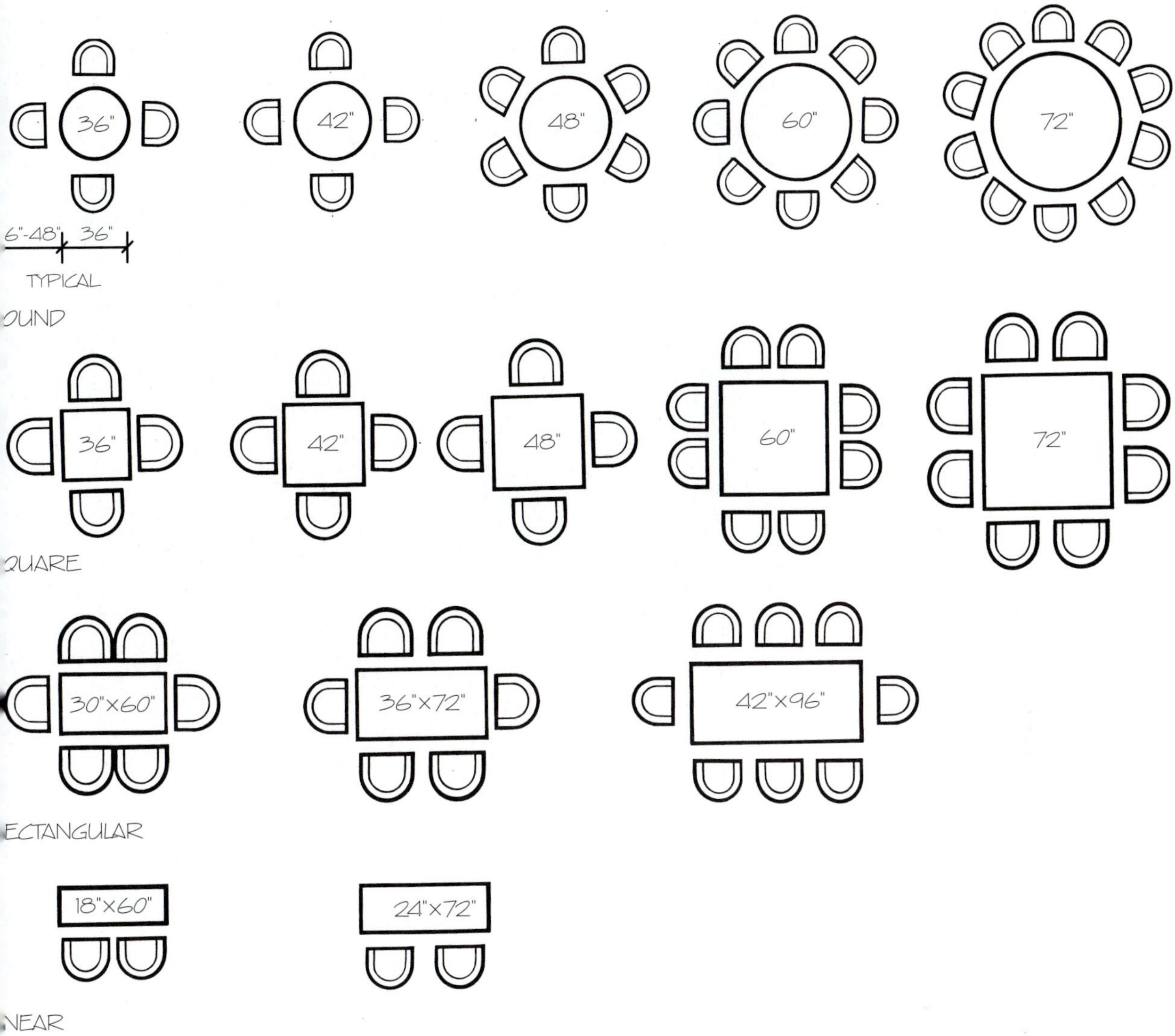

gure 6.10 *Typical table arrangements. Oval, boat-shaped, and U-shaped tables low similar requirements.*

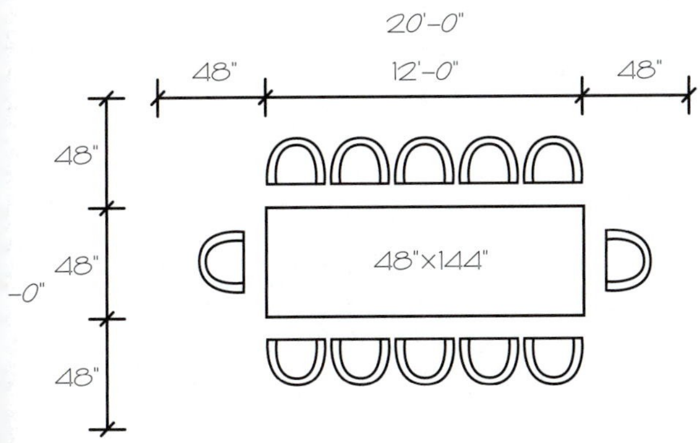

gure 6.11 *If the room must seat 12, the designer first ablishes the minimum table size: 2′-0″ to 2′-6″ is allowed each person (depending on the chair size desired), plus an ditional 12″ to 18″ on each end. Then distance is added for airs and traffic lanes. The smallest room possible would be ′-0″ × 20′-0″ or 240* ☐.

Video/Television Viewing and Presentation

Multimedia viewing has become an important aspect of daily work and home environments. Multimedia centers are custom designed to accommodate stereo equipment, VCRs, computers, and televisions, including HDTV.

Depending on the size of the screen, televisions are best viewed from a distance of 6′-0″ to 12′-0″. The viewer should be able to look directly at the screen. Straight line, L-, and U-shaped groupings allow for this arrangement. If a parallel grouping is selected and the media center is not the focal point, the media screen may have to be concealed (Figure 6.12).

In offices the systems may also be concealed. Classrooms may require custom mounting systems or portable carts. When televisions are used in lobbies, breakrooms, or waiting rooms, the video/television areas should be separated from conversation areas.

Figure 6.12 *In this informal breakfast room the television is neatly hidden in the cabinetry. (Designer: Lovick Design. Photograph by Martin Fine.)*

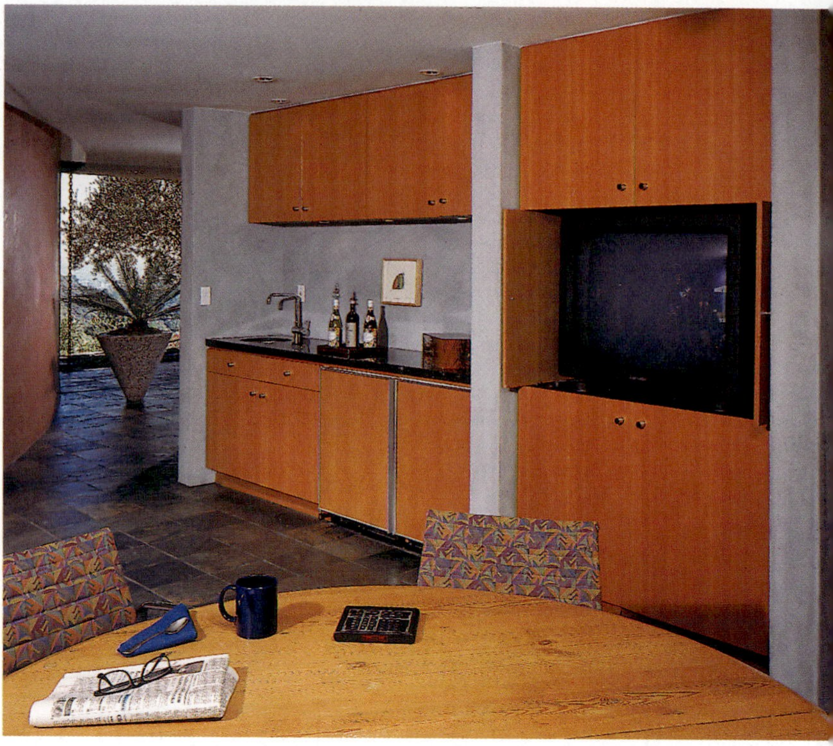

In a conference room, a projection screen should be placed on the narrow wall of the room. A projector for slide viewing or satellite receiving may be concealed in the ceiling or located in another room providing rear screen projection capabilities. Chairs should be on casters to allow ease of movement during presentations.

Clerical, Studying, and Computing

All areas of commercial design from health care to hospitality require workspaces to complete daily tasks. The home office is also becoming a standard. More than one-half of American households have a computer. Using the Internet is becoming as commonplace as making a telephone call. Hotels are also catering to these needs. Thus, both residential and commercial designers must have a working knowledge of office design.

The most efficient workspace is the combination of the desk, return, and credenza as shown in Figure 6.13. This allows a clear space on the desk for work. A monitor and keyboard can sit on the return or on the credenza. A printer and hard drive can sit on or in the credenza. Some clients prefer a pullout keyboard tray in the credenza, or may not want the return. In either case, the space requirements are the same. The office space may also need shelving, guest chairs, filing, storage, or a conferencing area. The designer adds square footage as necessary to meet these needs.

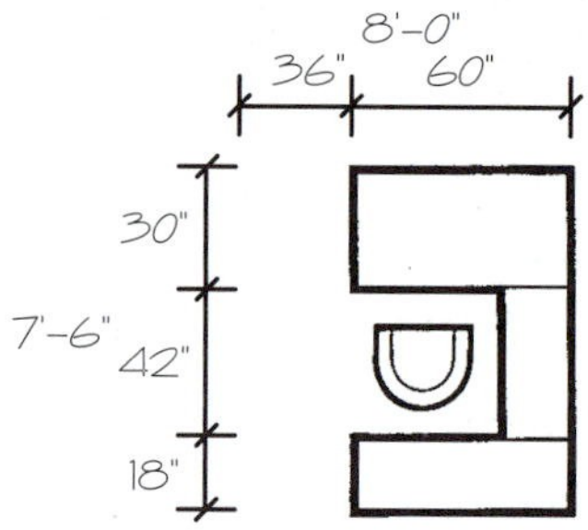

Figure 6.13 *To figure the space required for a typical office arrangement, draw the furniture, allow for a traffic lane, a total the dimensions. The overall minimum space required i 8'-0" × 7'-6" or 60□.*

Sleeping

Whether designing a master bedroom suite or a hotel room, designers must be knowledgeable about the space requirements for sleeping areas. Remember that although beds come in standard sizes, ample space must be allowed to move around the bed (Figure 6.14).

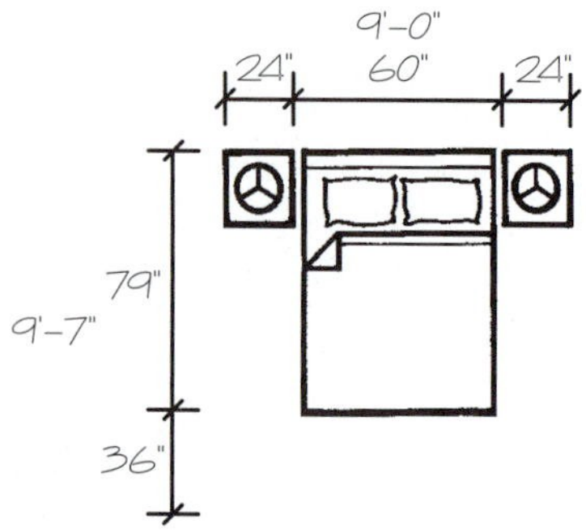

Figure 6.14 *In this plan for a queen bed, the minimum space needed would be 9'-0" × 9'-7" or 86.22□, or approximately 86□.*

Allowances need to be made for storage and seating ar-
ıs, and television viewing if requested by the client. In hos-
tal design, space should also be allocated to accommodate
edical equipment, patient personal care, visitors, and am-
e traffic areas for mobile equipment.

torage

ressers, armoires, chests, filing cabinets, and shelving units
ome in various sizes as noted in Table 6.1. In planning ar-
ıs for these spaces, always allow ample room in front of the
nit to open the drawers and doors. (A space 2′-6″ wide is
sually adequate.) Closets need to be at least 2′-1″ deep to
commodate hangers.

ood Preparation

ı residential design, food preparation areas encompass
any subactivity zones relating to the refrigerator, sink, and
ove or cooktop. Because most of the kitchen layout is
ased on built-in features, kitchen design is discussed in
hapter 7. Commercial kitchen design is a specialty area of
esign and requires advanced study.

athrooms

hapter 4 illustrated typical symbols for bathroom fixtures.
able 6.3 reviews minimum clearances and layouts. Appro-
riate bathroom layouts, like kitchen layouts, are based on
uilt-in features and are discussed in Chapter 7.

he Floor Plan

he floor plan is a communication tool that illustrates the space
lanning of furnishings and their relationships to the architec-
ıral features of walls, windows, doors, fireplaces, and so on.
o develop the floor plan, designers must synthesize an im-
ıense amount of detailed information, including the following:

- Principles and elements of design
- Functions of the space
- Needs and desires of the client
- Furnishing sizes
- Three-dimensional aspects of the space and furnishings
- Traffic lanes and clearance requirements
- Basic furniture groupings and space requirements

The floor plan allows the designer to synthesize all of this
ıformation into one drawing. A presentation floor plan, as
iscussed in Chapter 7, is shared with the client to explain the
esign. The presentation plan must relate to the elevations and
erspectives developed for the client. The next section illus-
ates several preliminary floor plans and perspective studies
ɔr various rooms.

pace Planning for Specific Rooms

ach room of a home or commercial space presents unique
hallenges. Because the activities in rooms vary greatly, each
ɔom is studied separately; however, throughout the home
r office, a sense of harmony must prevail.

Entry Hall or Foyer, Reception, and Lobby

The design of the home or building should be reflected in the details and furnishings of the entry. In a residential setting the entry serves as a passageway, and like all good design, should not be cluttered. An *easy flow of traffic* is essential. Ample storage areas need to be designed to accommodate coats, shoes, packages, and so on. Furnishings that may be appropriate in an entry include a console or narrow table, a mirror, a coat rack, and accessories. Many clients require a bench or small chair for sitting while changing shoes.

Where the front door opens directly into the living room, a desirable plan is to create an unobstructed entrance to redirect traffic and provide some privacy. One successful way to set off an entrance is with a built-in or freestanding storage wall. If space is available, a deeper storage wall may provide closet space for outer garments on one side, and open shelves for books or display on all or part of the opposite side. The storage divider may be a decorative as well as a functional element (Figure 6.15).

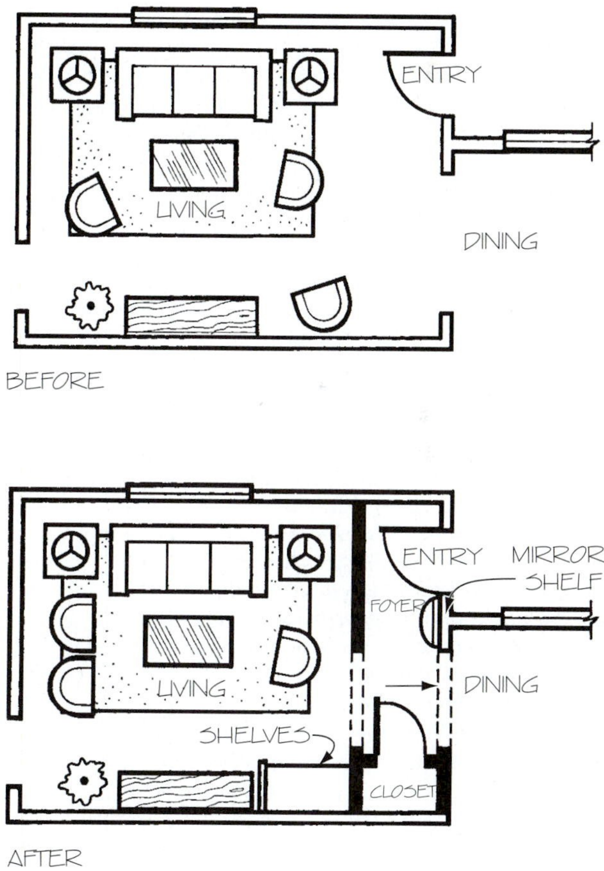

Figure 6.15 *Before, the front door opened directly into the living room. After, a wall was added, giving a more private entry. A closet provides necessary storage. A mirror and shelf were added for convenience. The furniture was slightly rearranged to pull the conversation group together. The rug works better in this plan because the chair legs all sit on the rug.*

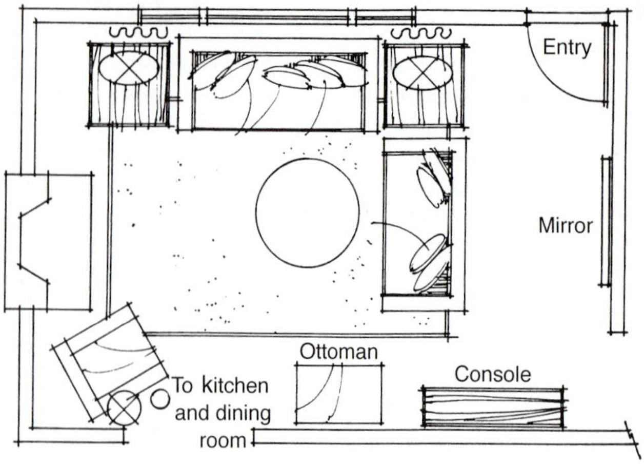

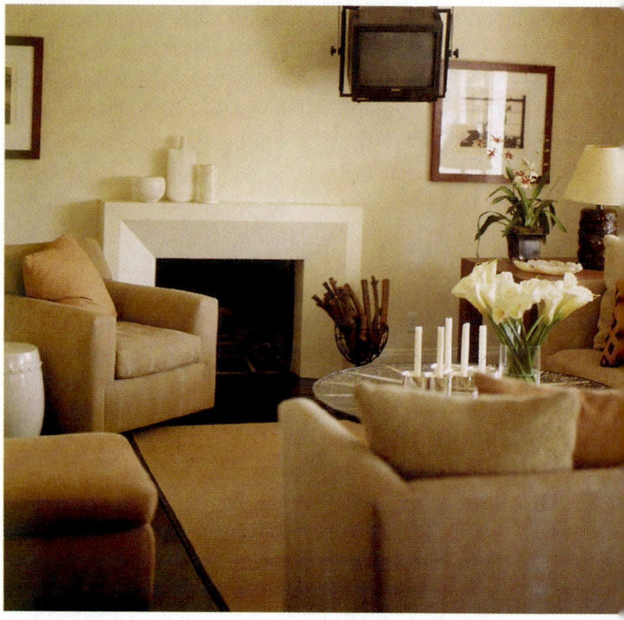

Figure 6.16 *The designer placed the furniture perpendicular to the front door and added a mirror and console to create the effect of a foyer in this ranch-style home. (Designer: Stephens Designs, Kurt Stephens. Photograph by Simon Watson.)*

Where space does not permit a heavy divider, a screen (either freestanding or attached) may serve as a partial divider. In a small room where any type of divider would cut needed space, the furniture may be arranged to redirect traffic by turning a sofa, desk, or chairs toward the room and at right angles to the door, leaving a passageway for traffic (Figure 6.16). Such devices provide limited privacy and create the feeling of an entranceway.

In a reception area, the client will usually request work space for a receptionist and a waiting area, which may need to accommodate only three or four guests. A waiting room for a doctor's office, however, may require seating for ten or more.

The receptionist may serve more than one function. He or she may operate the switchboard and serve as the office manager and secretary. In a doctor's office, the receptionist

Figure 6.17 *Programming needs: reception workspace for telephone, computer, keyboard, and printer; waiting room seating for four; access to conference room; privacy from offices.*

This plan offers many advantages: guests are immediately greeted by the receptionist; the waiting area easily accommodates four guests; there is a telephone for guest use; the company's name and logo are displayed behind the desk, balanced on the opposite wall by a piece of art over the love seat; the custom receptionist's desk has an ample work surface and file storage; a tall plant, door and sidelight, console table, and mirror help to balance the window wall opposite.

The conversation area requires approximately 96□'; the work area, approximately 60□'. The total area for the room is approximately 240□'. A room that is approximately 16′-0″ × 15′-0″ satisfies the needs of this client. The hard surface flooring area delineates the entry, provides durable flooring, and gives a pleasing proportion. The carpeted area is 10′-0″ × 16′-0″, meeting the approximate proportions for the golden rectangle.

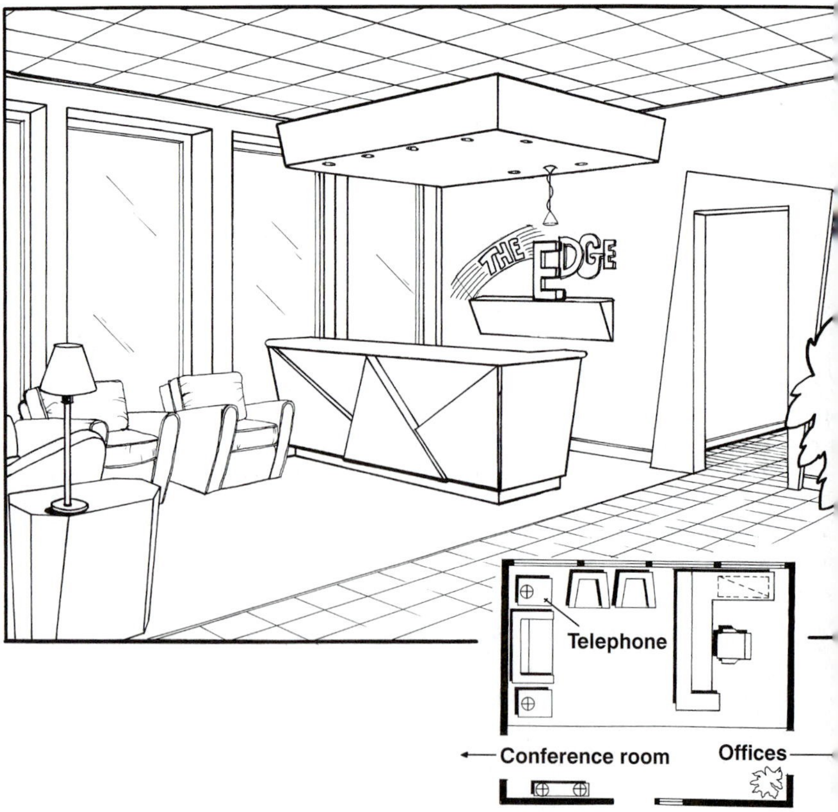

ay double as a nurse or a business accounting employee. is critical that accurate information be obtained before degning this important workspace. Many times a receptionist orks behind a desk that has a *transaction top*. This allows e receptionist a sense of privacy, keeps the paperwork on e desk from looking cluttered to the waiting guests, and erves as a shelf where guests can rest items while speaking ith the receptionist. The ledge is usually placed 12″ above e desk, or at 42″ above the floor.

A guest who enters a reception area should immediately e able to make eye contact with the receptionist. The waitg area should adjoin or be part of the reception area, yet ould be out of sight of the workings of the office. Figure .17 represents an acceptable reception area solution.

Lobby areas may serve many different functions. For inance, a hotel lobby needs adequate room for seating, lugage, bellhops, a reception desk, a concierge, and a directory; e hotel lobby also requires a focal point for ambience, such s a fountain or sculpture. On the other hand, an office lobby ay require only a conversation area. The intricacies of these youts are beyond the scope of this book, but the basics of pace needs remain the same.

iving Room and Conversation Areas

iving rooms may encompass many of the basic activity aras; conversation areas and video and television viewing are e most common. Other functions may include, but are not mited to, reading, listening to music, writing, and possibly asual dining. The conversation area, however, is usually the ost important group. It is designed to enhance or combine ith the focal point of the room.

Once the number of people who will regularly use the oom is determined, seating can be arranged or selected. *uilt-in seating* is usually not as comfortable or flexible as movable sofas and chairs, which may be regrouped for more intimate occasions or opened out to invite more participants. Rigidly placed chairs can make the guests believe that moving them would be a major calamity, so the best choice is to provide comfortable living room chairs of various types and sizes for flexibility.

Bringing furniture away from the walls in a room is more conducive to intimate conversation than placing it directly against the walls (see Figure 6.19). An angled or slightly curved sofa is more conducive to conversation than a long, straight sofa. The curve in a sectional sofa is invariably occupied first, just as the corner table in a restaurant is the most popular.

Another solution to providing a flexible seating arrangement is *modular furniture*. Two or three separate pieces that fit together may be purchased at once; others can be added later (although fabric matching may present problems). Modular furniture can be arranged in a variety of ways depending on space and the number of pieces.

Soft, low-level lighting adds a feeling of intimacy to a conversation area; however, the area should not be in semidarkness. People need to see the features of those with whom they are talking. A low-hanging light can pull a grouping together and allow light for reading.

Finding the right wall space for a piano is often a challenge. Direct sunlight and changes in climate can have a damaging effect on a piano, limiting possible placement within the room. An upright piano can be placed against an inside wall. A grand piano may be more difficult to place in the average room because of its size. The curved side should be toward the listeners, not facing a wall or corner, so that when the lid is raised the sound will be projected toward the audience. In addition, the pianist and the listeners should be able to see one another, as shown in Figure 6.18. A bay window furnishes a beautiful setting for a grand piano if temperature

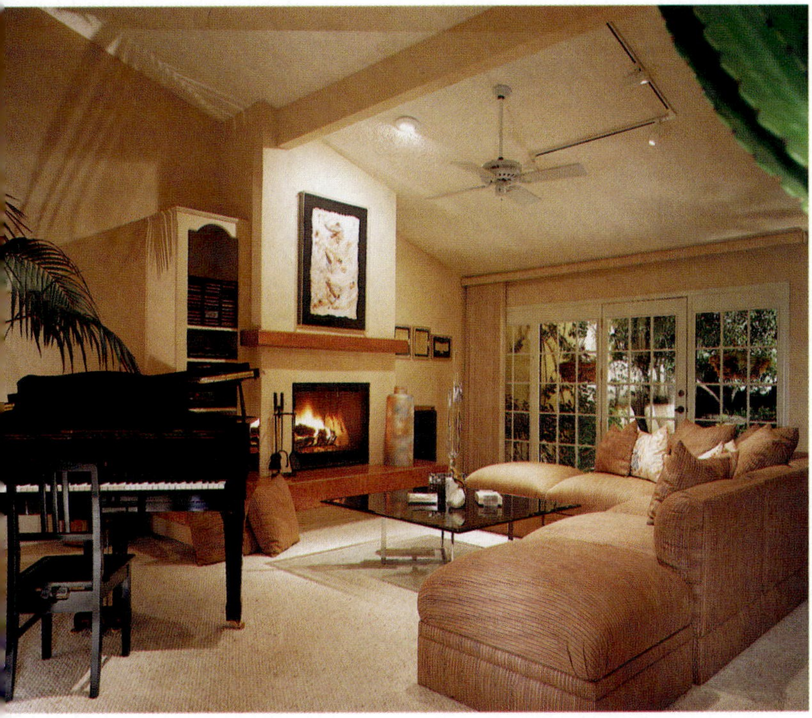

Figure 6.18 *Designer Lawrence Lake placed the grand piano on a diagonal with the room's architecture and in relation to the other furnishings in this living room, so the occupants can better hear the music and watch the pianist. (Photograph by Pam Singleton.)*

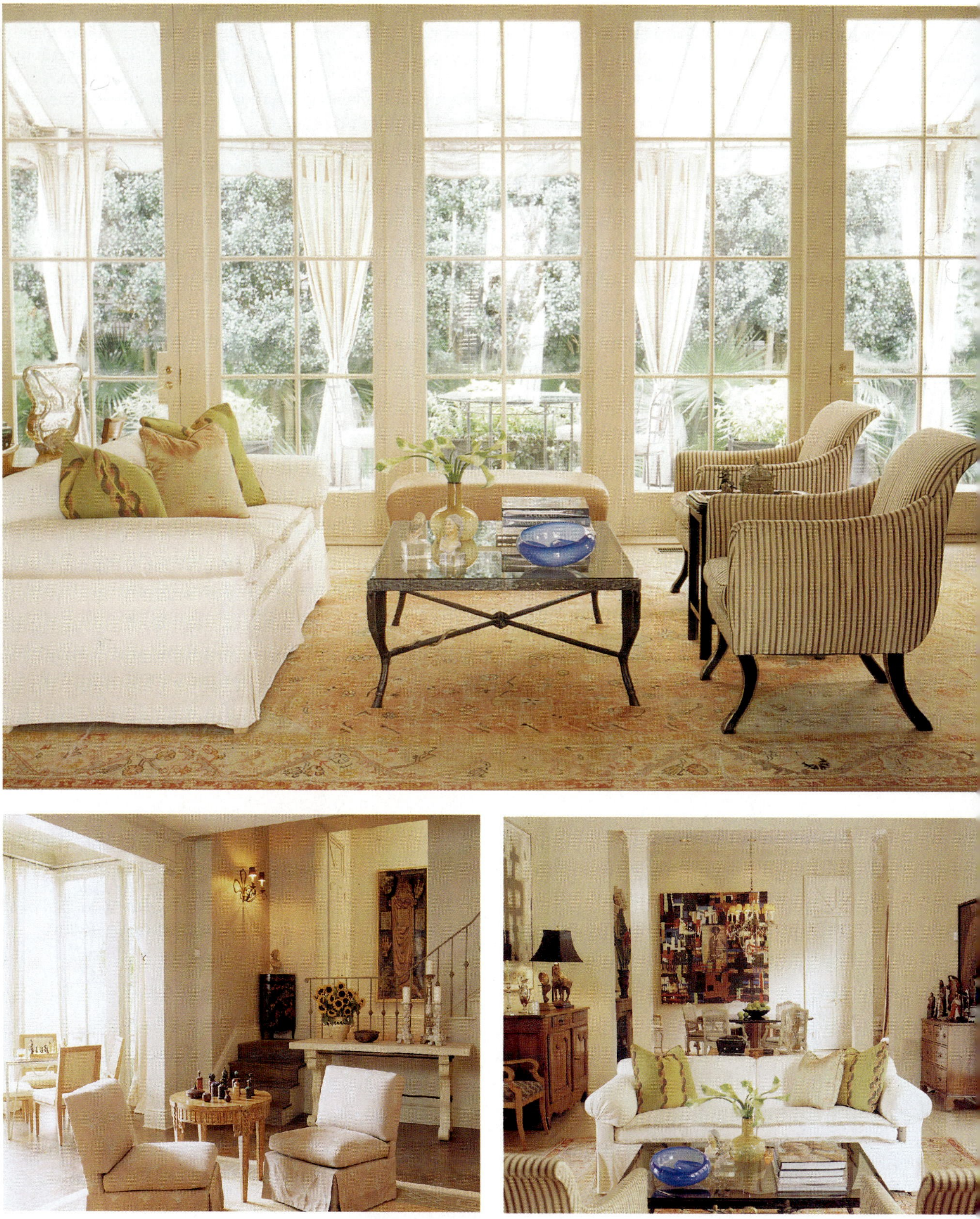

Figure 6.19 *In this nineteenth-century New Orleans cottage, furniture has been placed away from the walls to allow for optimum conversation groupings. (Designer: Chrestia & Staub, Inc. Photographs by Tria Giovan. Courtesy of* Southern Accents.*)*

light conditions permit. In a large room a grand piano ᐧ be placed to serve as a room divider.

n the living room, most tables are placed where a func- ,al need exists. Every seat in a room should have access . side table. The scale, shape, and height of each table ıld be right for the purpose and size of the chair or sofa :companies. A good height for a coffee table is gener- 16 inches. Tables placed next to sofa and chair arms ıld be the same height as the arm to help people avoid ›cking items off the table. *Console tables* can be decora- as well as functional, and when combined with a mir- or picture are assets to almost any room. *Writing tables* / be placed flush or with their short end against the wall. *:arge cases or wall pieces* are usually located to lend a ing of balance. If the area is small, careful planning is essary to place the large piece where it will be most func- ,al and will complement the wall space. A combination of ıiture heights in a room provides interest and helps balance architectural features such as columns, windows, doors, and fireplaces.

Pairs can enhance a living room in many ways. Identical items can be a unifying factor; they give balance and pull together unrelated furniture. A pair of chairs can create a conversation grouping in a number of ways: placed side by side to balance a sofa on the opposite side (see Figure 6.19 A and C), placed on either side of a fireplace, or angled about a table to give an intimate corner feeling (see Figure 6.19 B). Where space is adequate, a pair of love seats or sofas may be used in place of single chairs. A pair of tables may be placed in front of a sofa, creating a flexible substitute for a standard coffee table. Two similar chests placed on either side of a doorway or a fireplace enhance almost any room. Pairs of lamps, candelabras, or wall accessories can be pleasing. When carried to an extreme, however, the use of pairs can be boring. Figure 6.20 indicates a good solution for a living room.

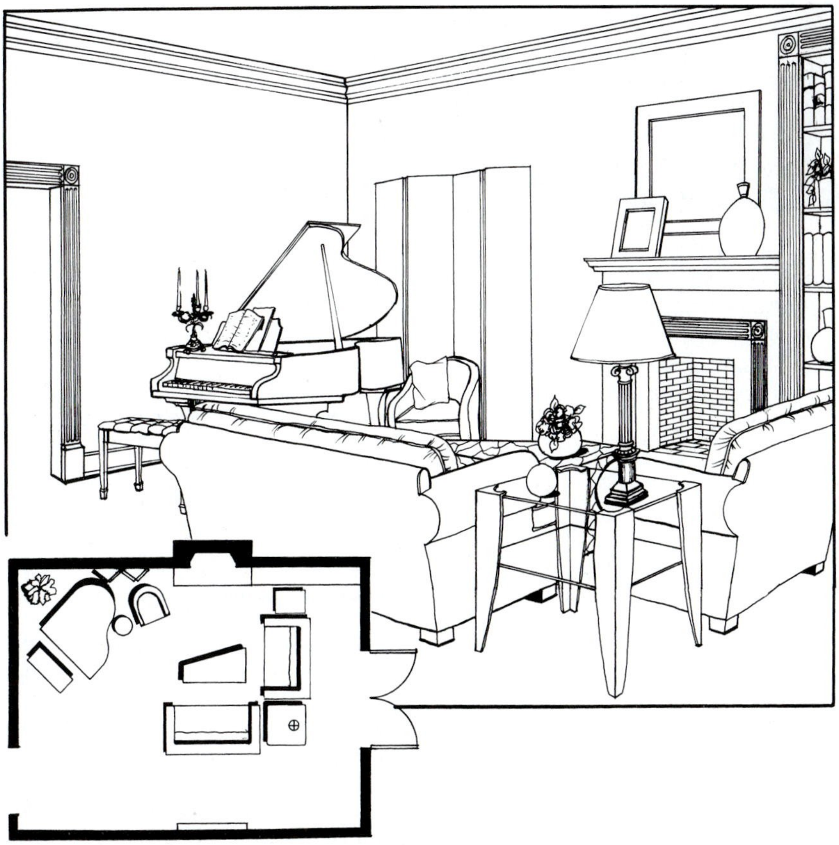

Figure 6.20 *Programming needs: conversation seating for six; grand piano; fireplace. This plan has these advantages: the conversation grouping complements the focal point of the fireplace; the piano faces into the room, balances the doors on the opposite wall, and is away from the windows; ample tables are placed for beverages and lighting; a console table and large piece of artwork balance the fireplace; a plant softens the corner of the room and provides height on the far left wall; furniture floats in the room, not aligned against the walls; there is a variety of furniture shapes and heights.*

The conversation area requires approximately 160□. the room is approximately 280□. A room that is approximately 14′-0″ × 20′-0″ works well for this client's needs. This size also meets the proportions of a golden rectangle.

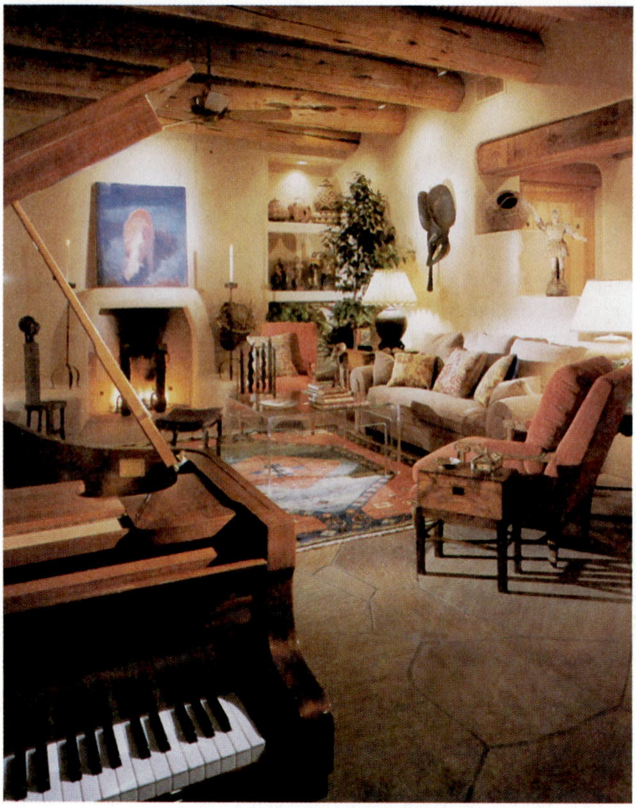

Figure 6.21 *The warm reds and rich blues of the area rug are picked up in the painting over the fireplace, the chair upholstery, and the accent pillows. A clear Plexiglas table allows the rug to be seen from all angles. A fascinating mix of African tribal pieces and objects from the American Southwest testifies to the personal interests of the owners. (Photograph by Mark Boisclair.)*

Family Room

The family room is probably the most used room of the house. Here, family members congregate around an entertainment center, read, converse, play games, and often entertain. More than in any other area of the house, the arrangement of furniture is of utmost importance to accommodate easy adjustment for various activities. Use, convenience, and practicality are guiding principles in arranging furnishings, as shown in Figure 6.21.

- *Seating* for conversation incorporates similar solutions discussed for the living room. When television viewing is an important activity, plan seating for easy viewing. Include additional flexible seating for various activities where space permits.
- A number of *tables* can add to the occupants' comfort, including a large coffee table to accommodate beverages and food and side tables for lighting and other necessary items.
- Convenient and adequate *lighting* is essential in a family room and must be comfortable and flexible enough to accommodate all activities (see Chapter 5).
- An *audiovisual entertainment system* is an important part of the family room. Special planning is necessary place a television set, movie screen, stereo, or comple entertainment center to take best advantage of the space.
- Family rooms may also serve as an area for quiet gam A *game table* can be incorporated into the space.

Family rooms are extremely difficult to design becaus their multiple uses. Figure 6.22 illustrates an example c well-designed family room.

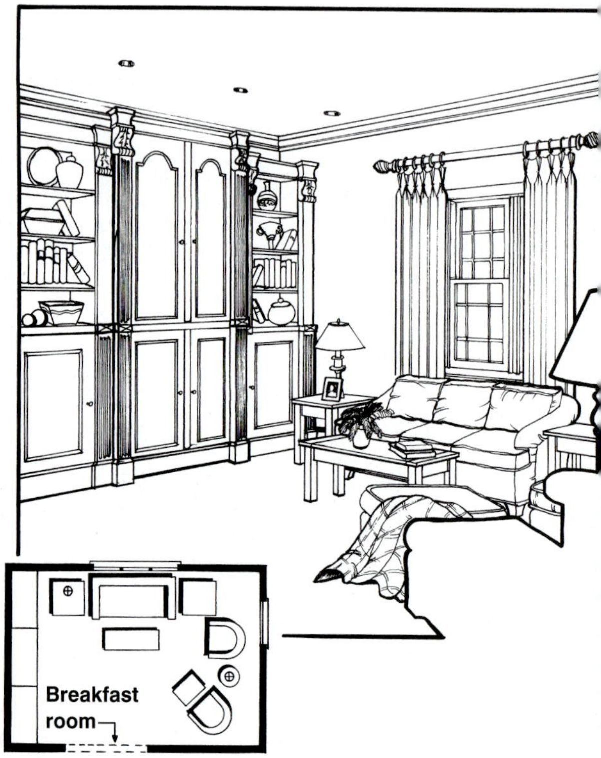

Figure 6.22 *Programming needs: comfortable seating for four to view the television; game area for four; storage and shelving; entertainment area; comfortable reading chair. Th advantages of this plan include the following: the adjoinin breakfast room is used as the game area to conserve space the family room; the television is opposite the windows to balance their height; the sofa placed beneath the window balances the archway leading into the breakfast room; the are four oversized seating areas for watching television; on of the seats is canted and has appropriate lighting to serve a reading chair; extra large pillows can serve as additional floor seating; shelving and cabinets flank the entertainmen system for storage.*

The conversation area requires approximately 100□. The room has approximately 150□. Therefore, a room that is approximately 10′-0″ × 15′-0″ is a good design solution, as long as the breakfast room doubles as the game area. The rectangular room also meets the dimensions required by th golden rectangle.

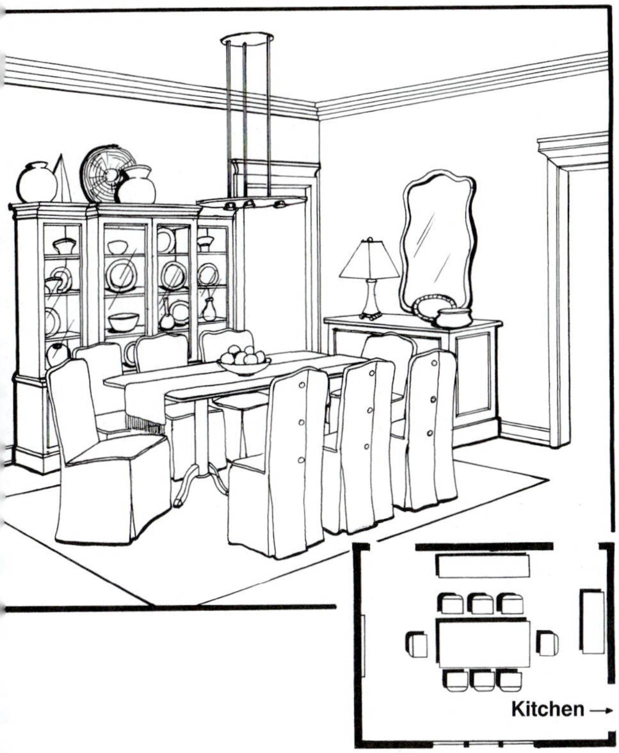

Figure 6.23 *Programming needs: seating for four to eight; storage and display for china and linens; surface for serving. The advantages of this layout include the following: the buffet is located near the kitchen door; a china cabinet for storage also balances the large windows and adds height and interest to the room; a large painting balances the buffet; there is comfortable seating for eight.*

The table area requires approximately 176□. The area of the entire room is approximately 234□. A room that measures 13′-0″ × 18′-0″ could accommodate this design solution.

ning and Conference Room

:ept for the selection of the actual furniture pieces, the ce requirements for dining and conference rooms are y similar. Dining chairs need to be relatively small in lth in order to fit around a table. Conference room chairs y be larger, but a larger table will also be required. Con- ence chairs should be on casters for ease in mobility. A ctical pedestal-base table gives maximum knee room, and nd and oval tables make it easier to squeeze in an extra rson.

A serving area is required in conference and dining ms. A *buffet* may be placed against a wall to be used for d service or the display of a client's product. Storage ces also may be needed. A high piece of furniture, such a *breakfront* or *china cabinet,* can provide space for dis- ys and adds dignity and vertical interest to the room. Cor- cupboards are appropriate storage and display items for esidence. Figure 6.23 indicates a design solution for a din- room.

Lighting is a key element in dining and conference rooms. nmed lights may be required for presentation purposes in conference room, and are usually desirable for setting a od in the dining room. Refer to Chapter 5 for further dis- ssions on lighting options.

Video conferencing, slide viewing, and presentation dis- y areas may be needed in conference rooms (Figure 6.24), ich may then require blackout draperies or shades. (Win- w treatments will be discussed further in Chapter 12.) ne conference rooms may include a conversation area for ormal discussions.

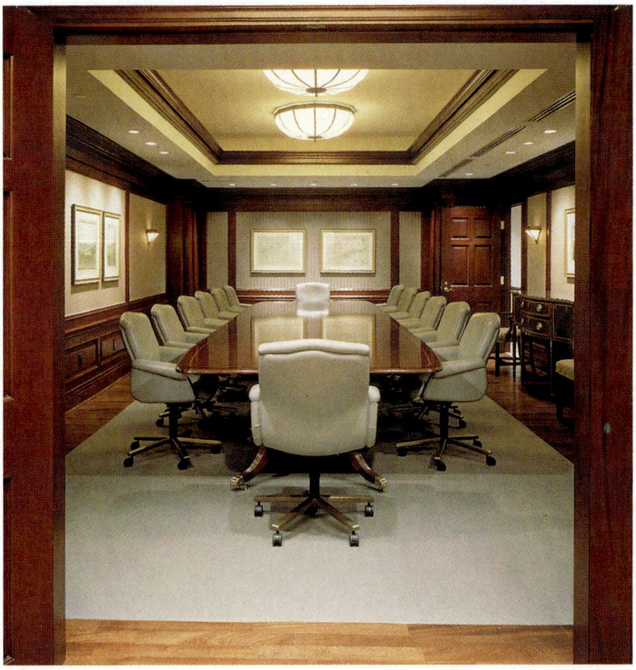

Figure 6.24 *At Balis & Co., Inc., in Philadelphia, this traditional conference room seats eighteen. The audiovisual equipment is concealed. Lighting is flexible to allow for a variety of presentation needs, and the sideboard functions well for additional service needs. (Designer: Daroff Design, Inc. Photograph by Elliott Kaufman.)*

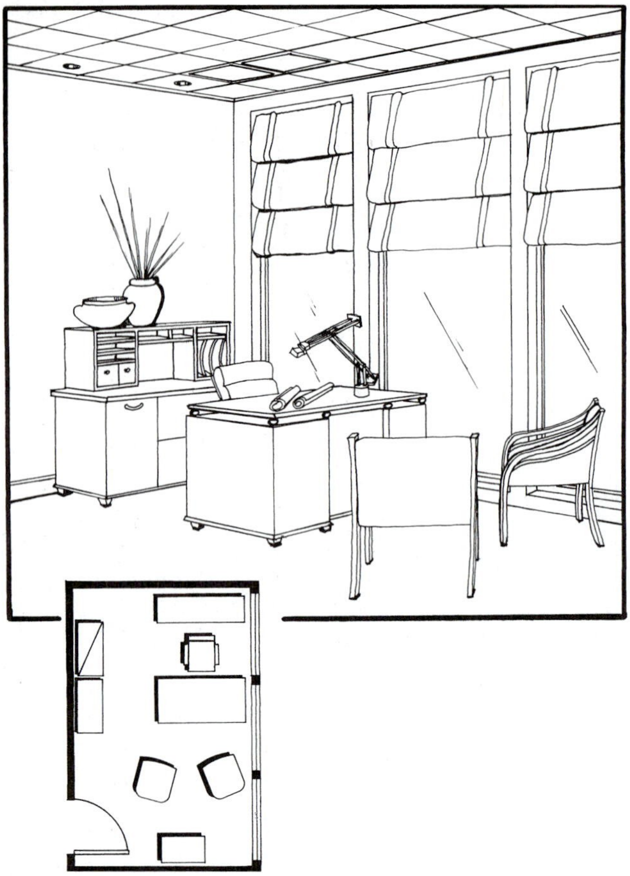

Figure 6.25 *Programming needs: desk and credenza; two guest chairs; filing and shelf storage. This layout provides these advantages: ample storage and shelving space; view to the door by employee; seating for two guests; ease in accessing file cabinets and shelving. These items, with the door, balance the long window wall. The computer can be placed on the credenza at a 90° angle to the windows. An accent furniture piece adds interest.*

The work area requires 68□. The entire room requires 120□. A room that is approximately 10′-0″ × 12′-0″ will accommodate this typical office.

Office

Home and commercial office spaces require much of the same equipment. Aside from the desk, credenza, and desk chair there needs to be ample shelving and filing storage. Commercial spaces require guest seating, usually for two. The designer needs to know if the client desires to sit across the desk from the guests or to have guests sit next to the desk. Executive offices may include a conferencing area or a conversation grouping (see Figure IV.3). It is not uncommon in a commercial space for furniture to be placed against a glass window wall.

When designing an office it is best to place the compu at a 90° angle to the window to avoid glare. If the compu is placed against the window, the bright contrast betw the sun and low-lit screen causes eye fatigue. When screen faces the window, an immense amount of glare is c ated. Also, the person sitting at the desk should be able easily see who is entering the office. It is disconcerting to seated facing away from the door.

Finally, consider the placement of electrical and teleph outlets. Cords should not be strung across the room or h den by the base molding. In a residence, a reading chai two may be requested, as well as substantial shelving for client's personal library. There should be a comfortable, gonomically designed desk chair to fit the occupant. In a idence, the chair may be used by different family memb and therefore should be easily adjusted. Figure 6.25 prese a scheme for a commercial office.

Bedroom

Whether in the home, hospital, or hotel, bedrooms ar place of retreat. Because of the size of the bed, it usually comes the focal point of the room. Traffic lanes are est lished around the bed with careful attention to nightti walking. Built-in units or nightstands placed beside the b are essential to accommodate necessary items. Like tab next to sofa arms, nightstands should be the same heigh the top of the mattress.

In residential settings, chests, dressers, storage chests, other case pieces are essential for storage. Built-in, unc the-bed drawers can convert unused space into storage cedar chest can serve as storage and also works well a bench for sitting. It is practical to have at least one chair seat in the room.

Hotel rooms require minimal storage facilities, but do quire a writing surface and seating area (Figure 6.26). Ca ful consideration is given to the location of the televis and a place to set luggage. Hospital rooms require an mense amount of attention to the location of medical equ ment. Although hospitality and health care design soluti are beyond the scope of this text, space requirements determined in a similar manner.

In a residential setting, a master bedroom may incor rate an intimate seating group for two, or possibly a *cha longue* (an elongated chair that supports the feet and le If a television is requested, the designer must know whet it is to be viewed from the bed, seating area, or both.

Children's and teenagers' bedrooms require special att tion. Work areas, play areas, and toy storage areas need be accommodated.

All bedrooms require a mirror. It can be freestandi mounted on the wall, or attached to a piece of furniture c closet door. Also, all bedrooms should have lighting con niently located next to the bed. Figure 6.27 shows an ceptable layout for a small master bedroom suite.

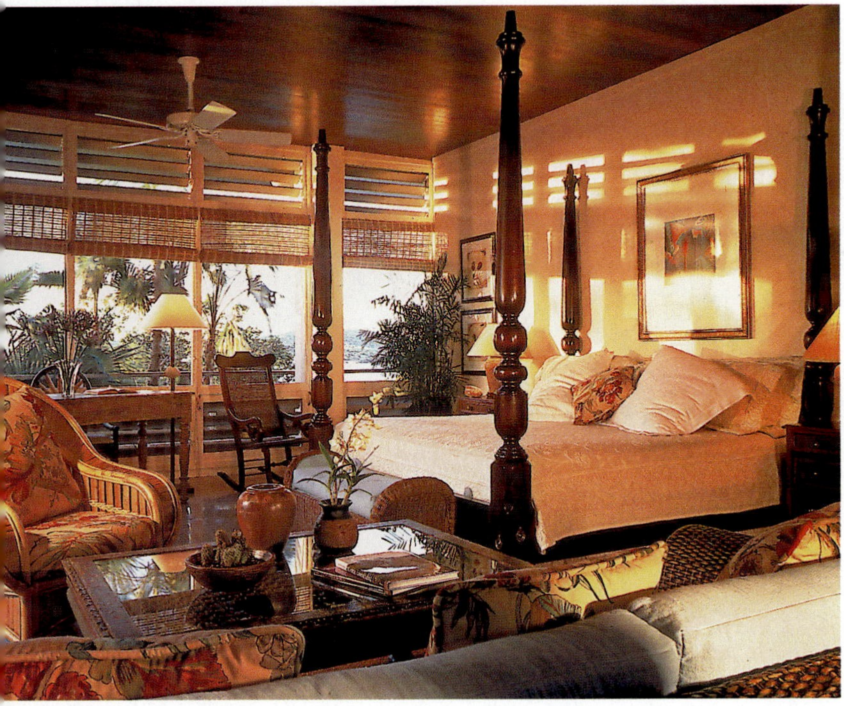

Figure 6.26 *Located on St. John, Virgin Islands, Caneel Bay Hotel boasts simple, elegant, and sophisticated rooms in the tropical style. (Designer: Vision Design Dallas. Photograph by Mike Wilson.)*

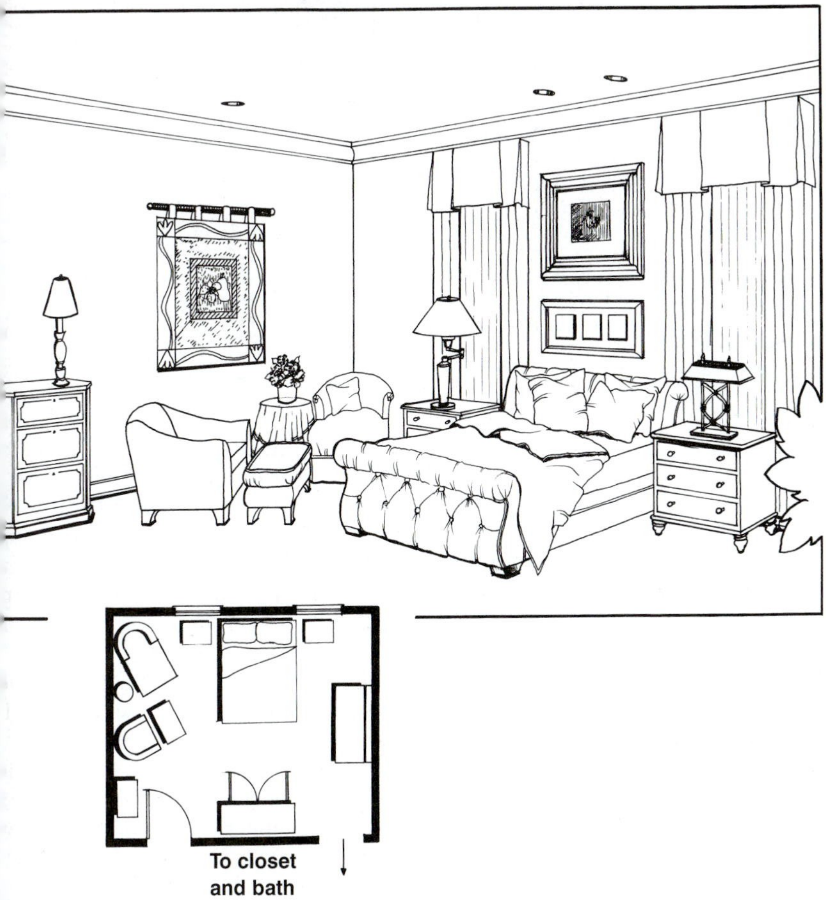

Figure 6.27 *Programming needs: queen-sized bed; triple dresser; seating area for two; television in armoire (viewed from bed). Advantages of this layout include the following: clothing storage near the closets and bath; the tall armoire, door, and cased opening into the closet and bath balance the bed and window wall; the triple dresser with mirror provides storage and balances the seating group on the opposite wall; ample walking space for making the bed and accessing drawers and storage units; lighting at the sitting area and on both sides of the bed.*

The sleeping area requires approximately 86□; the sitting area, 60□. The room requires 204□. A space approximately 12′-0″ × 17′-0″ would accommodate this master bedroom suite. This is close to the ideal size of the golden rectangle.

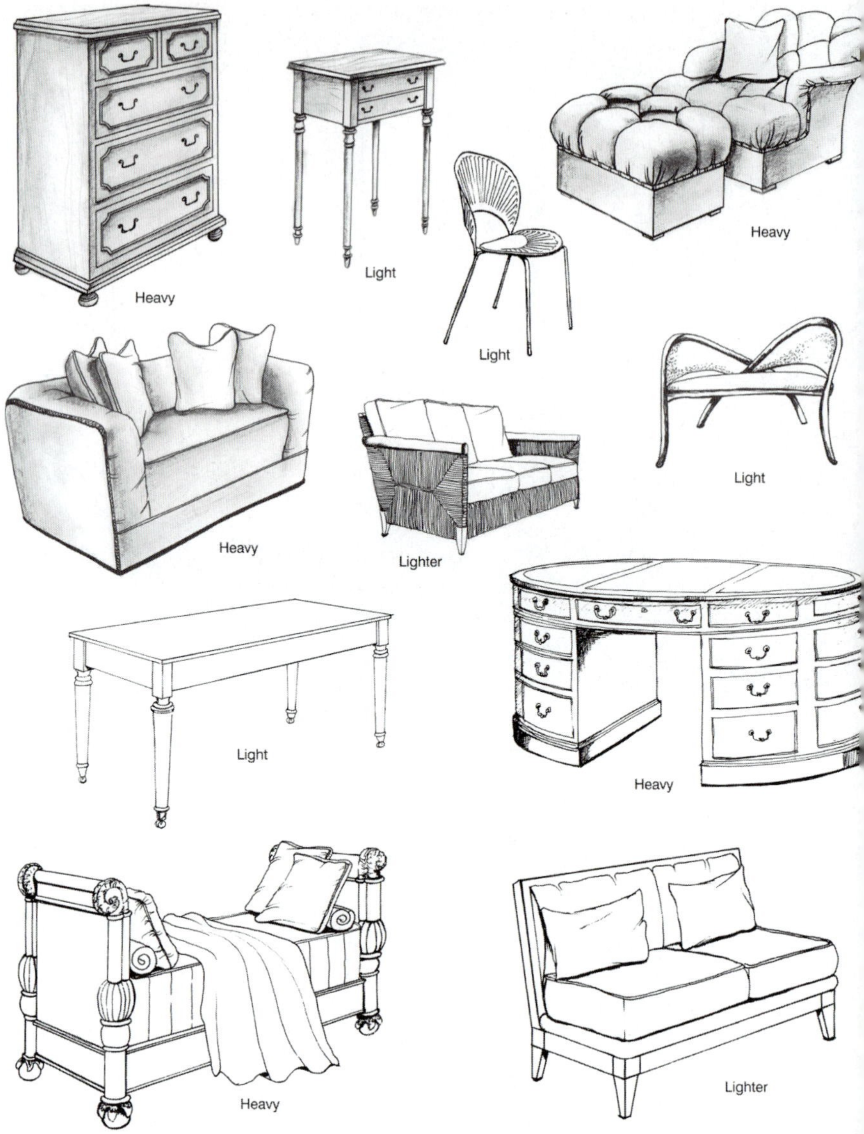

Figure 6.28 *These line drawings indicate heavily and lightly scaled furniture. Lightly scaled furniture creates the feeling of a more spacious room.*

Making the Most of Space With Furniture

In many instances, designers are required to work with an existing space and do not have the option of increasing or decreasing the actual room size. Therefore, through the clever use of the principles and elements of design, a small room can be made to appear much larger than it is, or a large room smaller than it is. The designer should first examine the room carefully and define the traffic lanes, then apply space planning principles to expand or contract the apparent size of the room.

Lightly scaled furniture can be accommodated more readily in a small space than heavily scaled pieces (Figure 6.28). Lightweight furniture is usually supported on legs rather than flush to the floor. It may have rounded corners and clear glass or plastic tops. Lightly scaled seating lacks arms and has backs and sides that are see-through or made of caning.

Upholstered pieces covered in a plain or small all-ov patterned fabric blended to the room's background provi visual space. Repeating the same fabric on other pieces hel unify furniture and has a space-making effect. Upholste that is neatly tailored and without skirts also gives an u cluttered look. Furniture aligned with walls leaves the cent of the room free.

Floor-to-ceiling shelves and high shallow storage un add visual height, and if terminated approximately one fo from the floor and two feet from the ceiling, allow t perimeter of the room to be seen, adding to the sense space. Smaller storage units such as serving tables, consol buffets, and desks can be wall hung, eliminating the need f space-using legs (Figure 6.29).

It may be possible to add a projecting window or a sk light. Space could also be arranged so the eye can eas travel through a room to outside areas like a garden, terrac or view. Finally, rooms should be free of clutter, with an o casional empty corner.

The challenge of making a big room livable is not a com-
on one, but it does occur. The most important considera-
on is *scale*. Massive furniture, overscaled patterns, and large
ctures can be chosen; all furnishings, however, need not
big. After large pieces have defined the grouping of the
om, lighter pieces can be used to complement the spaces.

Too little furniture in a big room can result in a cold, un-
viting interior. More important than quantity, however, is
rangement. The best technique is to plan separate areas of
fferent sizes. Utilize the architectural elements, such as floor-
g and ceiling changes, to create human-scaled spaces within
e big area. Some may be small and intimate; others, more
en (Figure 6.30). Occasional chairs may be moved from one
oup to another, forming a link between groupings.

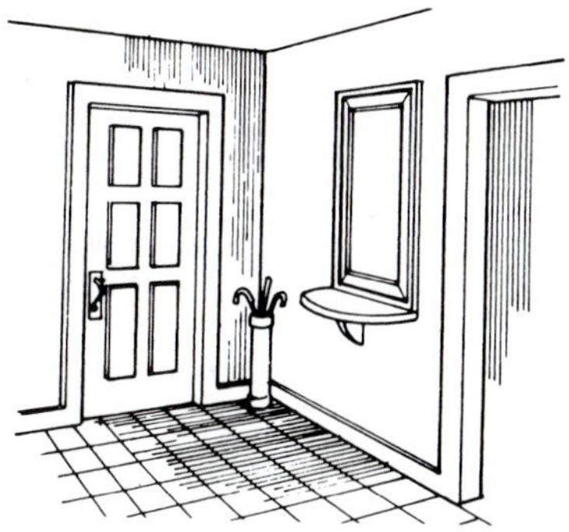

Figure 6.29 *A wall-hung shelf with rounded corners takes little space.*

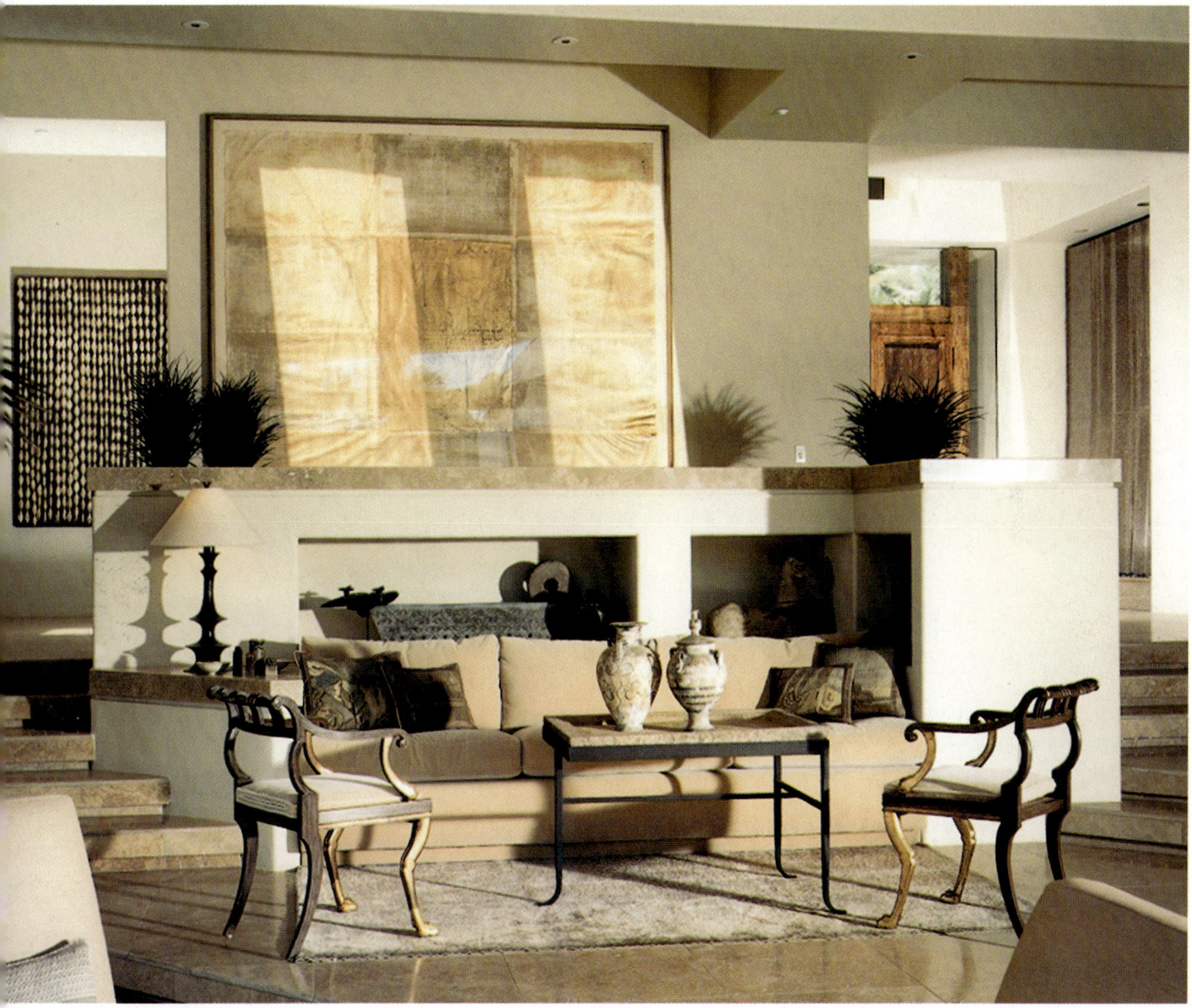

gure 6.30 *In this expansive living area designed by Michael Kreiss, vibrant art accents the interior. Built-in furnishings as ell as Egyptian chairs bring human scale to the grand room. Furnishings and fabrics from the Kreiss Collection add warmth d soften the powerful architectural edges. (Designer: Michael Kreiss of Kreiss Design.)*

Summary

When space planning furnishings for clients, successful designers remember the following key philosophies:

- Design to meet the function(s) of the space.
- Design for the client's needs and within the client's budget.
- Allow for ample traffic lanes and clearances.
- Follow the principles and elements of design as they relate to space and space planning.
- Scale the furniture to match the scale of the room or th desired feel of the room.

Whenever possible, design from the *inside out*. In ne construction, work with the architect or builder to establis the appropriate room sizes and shapes prior to constructio In existing construction, move walls (where possible) meet the needs for the function of the space, but be prepare to use space planning and design principles to make tl most of an existing space. And above all, *space plan furn ture in the third dimension*.

Space Planning: Rooms to Buildings

7

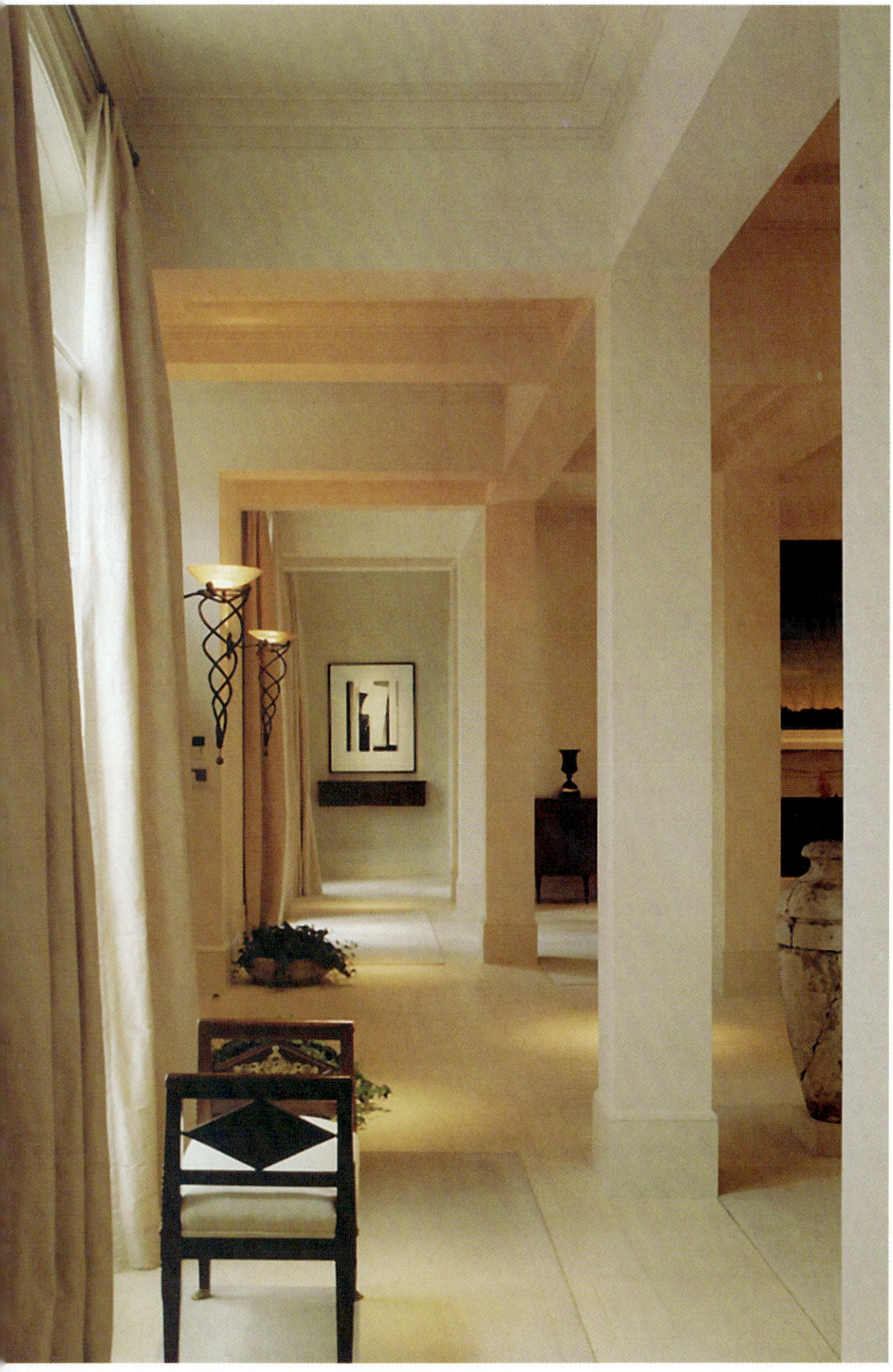

Figure 7.1 *In this warm contemporary environment, the foyer sets the tone. The simple, elegant lines and refined finishes are restful. (Designer: Gandy/Peace, Inc. Photograph by Chris A. Little. Courtesy of* Southern Accents.*)*

In the last chapter, furnishings were the smallest elements of the interior space planning puzzle that were grouped together to define activity areas. Activity areas were then grouped together based on the functional needs of specific rooms. This chapter explains how these rooms are grouped together into *interior zones* that are combined to form residences and commercial working environments.

When space planning rooms into buildings, a designer frequently serves in a support role to the architect, collaborating with the design team to establish appropriate zoning and massing of spaces. However, professional and/or legal guidelines may restrict the designer from developing the footprint of the building. Certainly a designer is not qualified to design the structural, electrical, or mechanical components of the building, jobs that are performed by the architects and appropriate engineers.

Defining basic areas in residential and nonresidential projects is helpful to the designer during the space planning process. Zoning interior spaces for a project depends on their intended functions. (Note that the term "interior zoning" is used in this chapter as it relates to spatial assessment; this should not be confused with zoning established by building codes and regulations.) Broad categories of zoning include divisions between public and private places. For instance, in a restaurant, the "back of house" is referred to as the kitchen and storage areas; the "front of house" is where the guests eat. In commercial office design, the public spaces include the reception area and conference rooms. Executive offices, accounting areas, copy rooms, and the like are considered the private spaces. In residential design, a similar division exists in private and public zones.

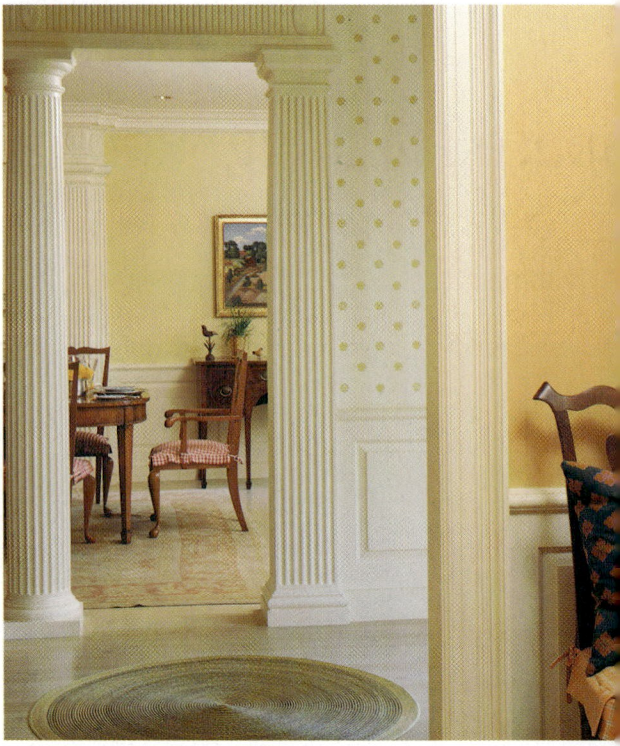

Figure 7.2 *The warm yellow hues in this foyer add casualne and give a fresh, informal look to a typical traditional settir The dining room glimpsed above is shown in detail in Figur 6.1. (Designer: Drysdale Design Associates. Photograph by Antoine Bootz. Courtesy of* Southern Accents.*)*

Residential Zones

The zones in residential design combine related activities. Public or social zones include formal areas such as the entry, living room, and dining room. Informal public areas include the kitchen, breakfast room, and family or recreation room. Private zones include bedrooms, dressing areas, bathrooms, studies, and laundry rooms. Offices may be considered part of the public zone if open to visitors; otherwise, they are part of the private zone. Zones should be viewed as a whole and should have compatible spatial organization. Analyzing and designing for individual differences, lifestyles, and activities that take place within the spaces contributes to the smooth functioning of the residence.

Public Zones

The public zone is where people meet for various activities. In years past, many of these areas, such as kitchens, may have been "off limits" to guests. However, kitchens and recreation rooms have now become common gathering places.

The Entry

The entry is usually placed to allow for access into the formal and informal areas of a residence. The entry may be open to the formal social zones, but it is best when it provides a visual block to informal rooms. Entries may include a large closet for occupants' and guests' coats, a mirror, and seat. A bathroom or powder room should be near (see Figures 7.1–7.3).

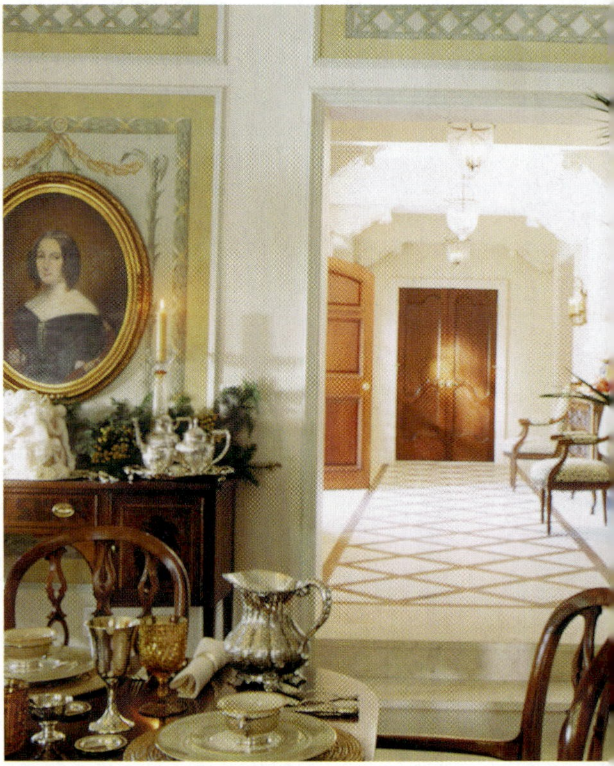

Figure 7.3 *In this formal traditional foyer, a limestone floor with oak inlays sets an elegant tone. (Designer: Ewing-Noble Interiors. Photograph by Tria Giovan. Courtesy of* Southern Accents.*)*

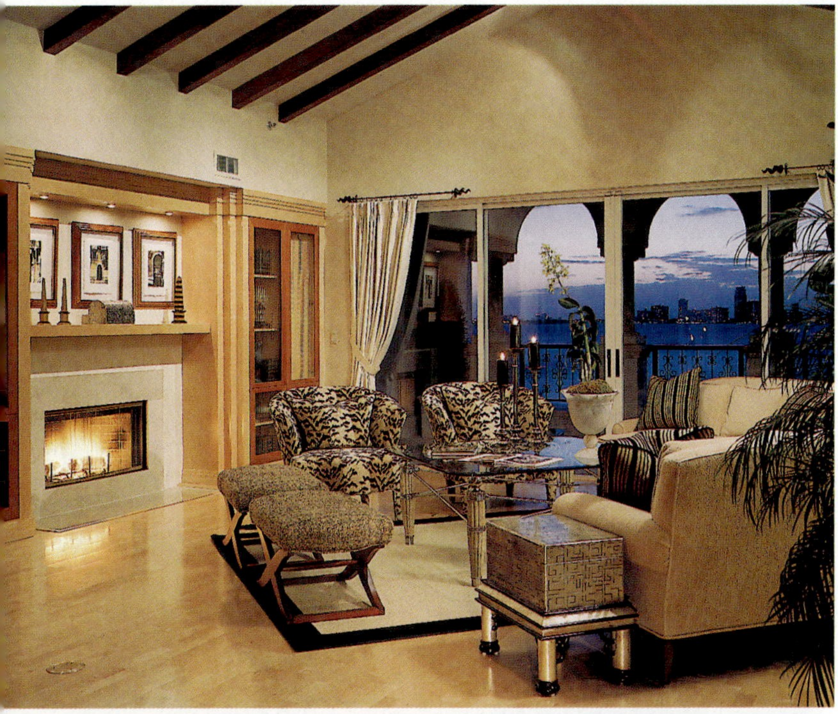

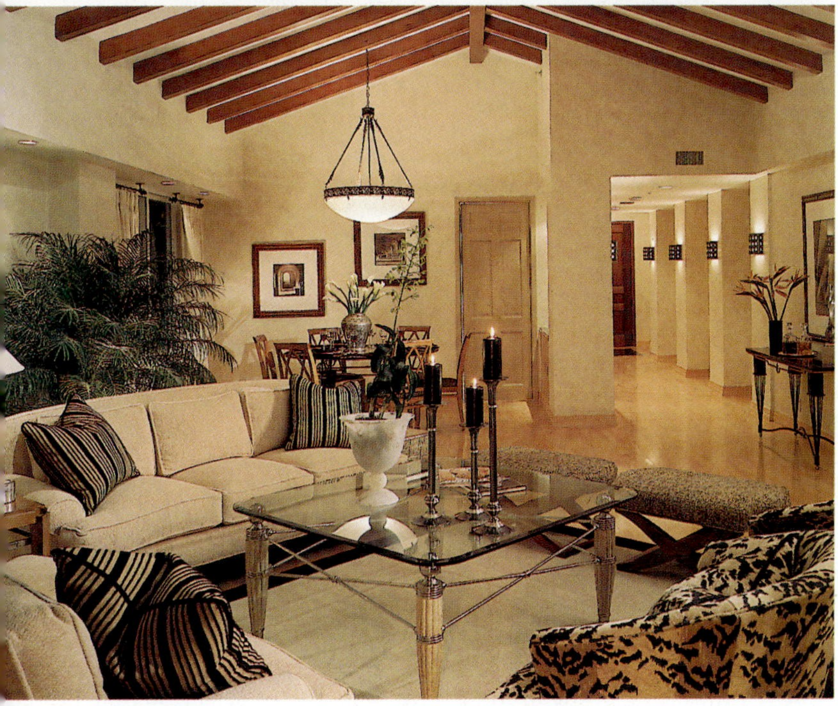

Figure 7.4 *This space shows a successful transition from the foyer to the dining area and the conversation area. Emphasis is on the conversation grouping; the fireplace serves as a backdrop. A soaring ceiling, warm lighting, and plants add to the comfortable yet sophisticated character of the space. (Interiors: Fine Decorators, Hallandale, FL/Ted Fine with Robert Perlberg. Photography by Brantley, Ocean Ridge, FL. Courtesy of* On Design.*)*

ving Room

e transition from the entry to the living room is important. e entrance area should flow easily into the living room th a smooth transition of design elements.

The formal living room works well when placed away om major traffic lanes. It may be planned for privacy as well various functions such as conversation, listening to music, ading, relaxing, and other activities (Figure 7.4).

A fireplace in the living room is often a natural focal point. It can be emphasized through such elements as texture, color, lighting, and the arrangement of other furnishings.

If the living room lives up to its name, it will provide for all household members and guests as well. The space may be relatively large or a cloistered parlor area, depending on requirements, preferences, and budget restrictions. In many homes, the formal living room or dining room may be

Figure 7.5 *In this renovated space, the dining area is distinguished by the use of an Oriental rug. Traditional French chairs are accented by the sleek lines of the glass-topped table. (Designer: Dana Maye. Photograph by Erica George Dines.)*

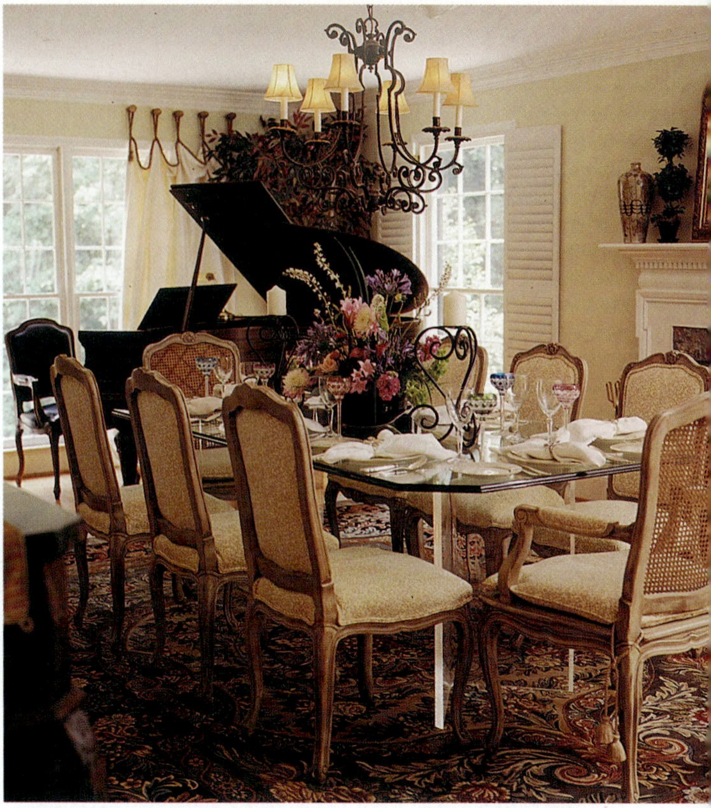

converted into a library, study, or music room. The room then functions as a quiet sanctuary where owners can relax.

Dining Room

An inviting formal dining area requires privacy from informal areas. It should be close to the food preparation area but shut off from the clutter of the kitchen. Keeping the dining room in the same basic theme and mood as the living room makes a pleasing transition (as seen in Figure 7.4).

If the dining room is an alcove or part of a living room, any number of treatments can set it apart. Walls may be papered or painted a different but coordinated color. Freestanding screens, a plant grouping, or an area rug can help define the space (Figure 7.5).

Kitchen

In many residences, the kitchen has become the hub of the home—an area where food preparation, serving, eating, and other socializing take place. The kitchen needs to be adjacent to the formal dining room, but also screened from its view. The kitchen also should be adjacent to the breakfast room, family room, and pantry. Additionally, the kitchen should be near the garage or the door where groceries are brought into the home; however, it is very important that the kitchen not be part of a major traffic lane. The location of the kitchen is obviously central to the residence.

The layout of the kitchen should be based on household needs, the physical limitations of the client, and the number of cooks working at the same time. The basic kitchen shap are U-shape, L-shape, island, parallel, and one-wall, as illu trated in Figure 7.6.

The kitchen is generally planned around three work ce ters, which may also include subcenters.

- The *refrigerator/storage area* is generally the first area used as items are removed for preparation. An 18″ wid counter adjacent to the handle side of the refrigerator i needed for holding items.
- The *sink area* (preparation and cleanup) is truly multipurpose and therefore is usually positioned between th other two centers. The sink center may include a dishwasher, a garbage disposal or trash bin, cabinet space, and a minimum of 18″ of counter space on both sides the sink. Lighting is particularly important over this are
- The *cooking area* (stovetop or range, oven, convection oven and/or microwave) receives particularly heavy us just before a meal. In a kitchen designed for two cooks the microwave or oven may be separated from the stovetop. Eighteen to 24″ of space should be included on either side of the cooktop. Ventilation should be pr vided for the range and oven. When the oven door is open, it should never obstruct a main walkway.

Subactivity zones include the *mixing area* (which is often l cated between the refrigerator and sink and includes an u interrupted counter space of 36″) and a *serving cent* (usually located near the eating space out of the gene work triangle). The serving center is particularly convenie when it is near the dishwasher and away from the cooki

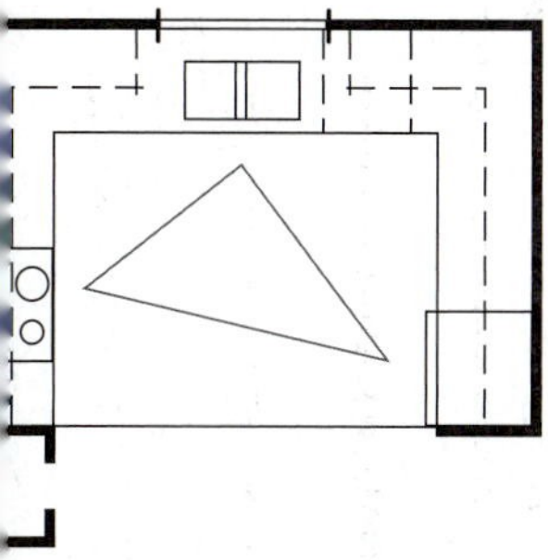

U-SHAPE KITCHEN
shape kitchens are generally
nsidered the most comfortable
d efficient. Work centers are
t of the way of traffic and
ore conveniently located.
ccommodates 1 person best.

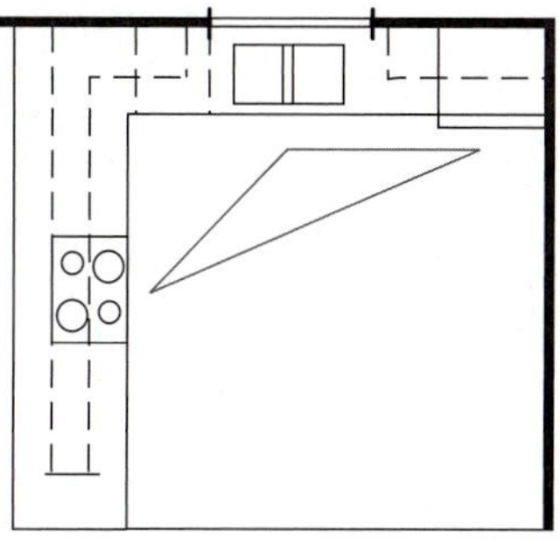

L-SHAPE KITCHEN
L-shape kitchens are a little more efficient than the parallel since traffic lanes do not intrude into the space. Work centers are conveniently located. Can accommodate 2 people.

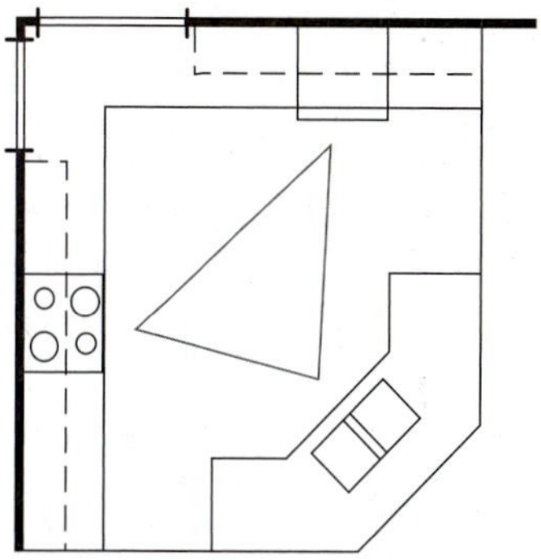

ISLAND KITCHEN
The island kitchen has similar qualities as the U-shape, but with the unwelcome addition of possible traffic through the space. Can accommodate 2 people.

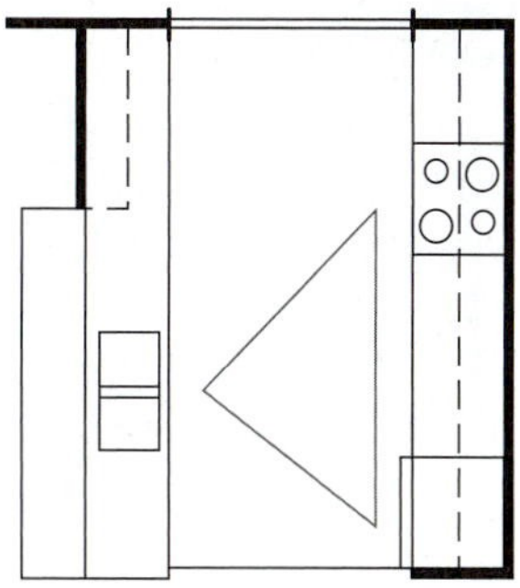

PARALLEL KITCHEN
Parallel kitchens provide undesirable traffic, especially when doors are located at each end. Work centers are more convenient than one-wall kitchens. Best with 1 person.

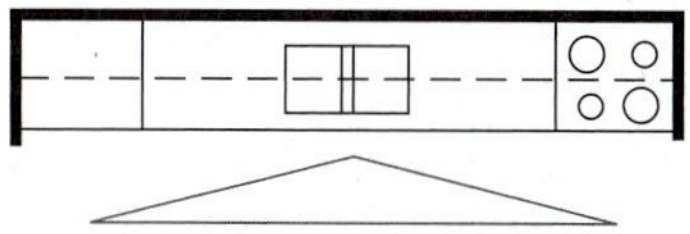

ONE-WALL KITCHEN
One-wall kitchens economically use one plumbing wall, can be concealed with folding doors, and do not take up much space. They are usually most suitable for apartments and small living spaces. They have very little counterspace and workspace pattern is long. Best with 1 person.

ure 7.6 *Basic kitchen arrangements.*

ı, because the table is frequently set while the final cook- is completed. Cabinets and counter space of at least 24″ important features.

fficient and adequate cabinet storage is necessary for a cessful kitchen plan. There must be storage for food (dry d, perishables, staples, and canned food), tableware (flat- e, dishes, tablecloths, napkins, etc.), cleaning supplies or cleaners, soaps, paper products, towels, etc.), and king utensils. Portable appliances such as blenders, food cessors, mixers, juicers, coffee grinders, and other task- ted appliances may be placed in lower cabinets, hung n upper cabinets, or concealed in appliance garages. table appliances should have a convenient and concealed ne and not be left to clutter countertops that are needed food preparation.

More info online @

http://www.nkba.org/ National Kitchen & Bath Association Site

http://www.kitchen-bath.com/kitchenandbath/ideas/index.jsp Kitchen and bath website published by *Kitchen and Bath Business Magazine.* Includes glossary and basic guidelines for design

Breakfast Room

Informal eating areas for quick snacks and everyday family meals are most conveniently located in or near the kitchen. The eating area close to the kitchen can vary depending on the space and shape allocated. Some kitchens have eating areas at a bar or counter, often with bar stools

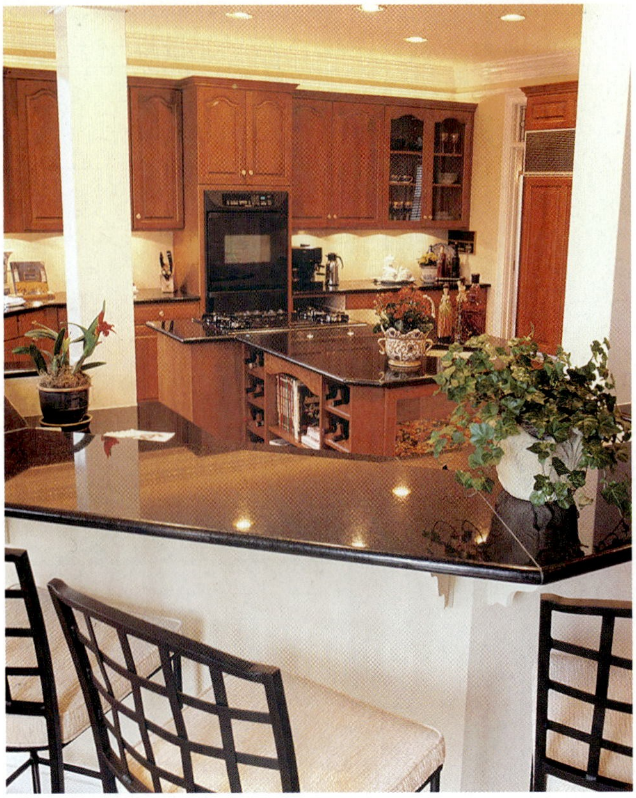

Figure 7.7 *This transitionally styled kitchen includes a breakfast bar for quick meals and snacks. Particular attention was given to the clean lines and contemporary finishes. (Designer: Burns Century Interiors. Photograph by Billy Howard. Courtesy of Brenau University.)*

or attached seats (Figure 7.7). Other kitchens may have the eating area in a bay window or alcove close by, as shown in Figure 7.8.

Family or Recreation Room

Family rooms should be located near the kitchen and away from quiet areas of the home, such as bedrooms, living rooms, and studies. Family rooms also should have immediate access to the outside. Of all the rooms in a house, the family room probably needs the most well-planned storage to take care of such items as a card table, folding chairs, games, CDs, videotapes, books, or even a screen and projector. Freestanding walls, built-ins, or wall systems may be set up to provide floor-to-ceiling banks of drawers, cabinets, and shelves.

The television and VCR are generally standard equipment in a family room. Locating the television in a central section of a wall of built-ins is an excellent way to incorporate this piece with other furnishings (Figure 7.9). Another good solution is to place the fireplace and television in an L-shape (Figure 7.10). With this arrangement, the television and fireplace are not in competition as the focal point. The television should always be placed so that several people can view it comfortably.

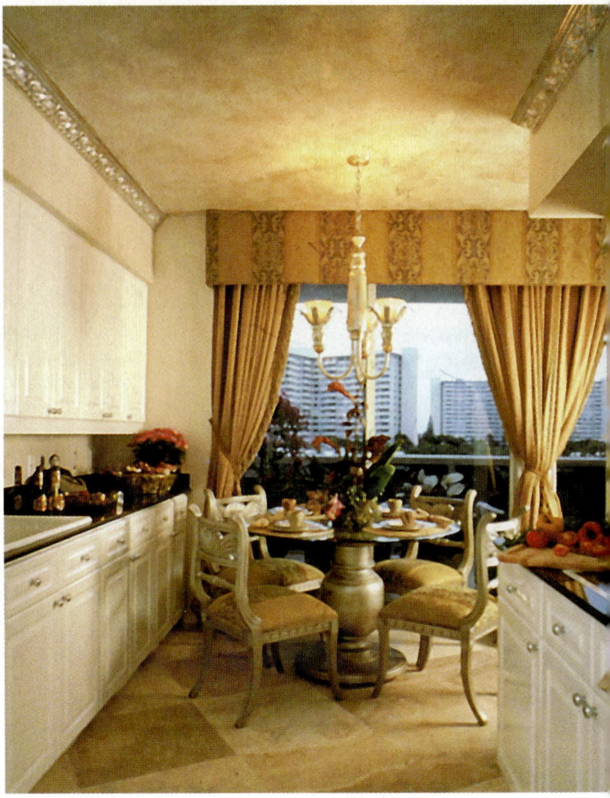

Figure 7.8 *This kitchen work zone is designed in a parallel arrangement with a traditional casual dining area at one end. The Mediterranean style of the residence was carried i the kitchen area. (Interiors: Perla Lichi, Perla Lichi Design, 1727, Tamarac, FL. Photograph by Barry Grossman. Residence: Condominium, private residence, Essex model a L'Hermitage, Ft. Lauderdale, FL. Courtesy of* On Design.*)*

As discussed in Chapter 6, family rooms may have dif ent activity areas for dining and game playing, televis viewing, and conversation. The designer's goal is to allow ample free-flowing and flexible space that can accommod a variety of activities.

Bathroom

A half-bath or powder room (one that includes a toilet sink) should be located in the public zone, so guests do have to enter the private zone to use the restroom. Typ bathroom layouts are discussed later in this chapter.

Laundry Rooms and Utility Rooms

Function and convenience are major considerations when cating laundry and utility areas. Laundry rooms are placed near the dressing and bathing area. Unfortunat laundry rooms are frequently relegated to a space clos the kitchen or garage, requiring occupants to haul clothes and down stairs or across the social areas of the home. Sc clients prefer to have the laundry area near the kitchen to

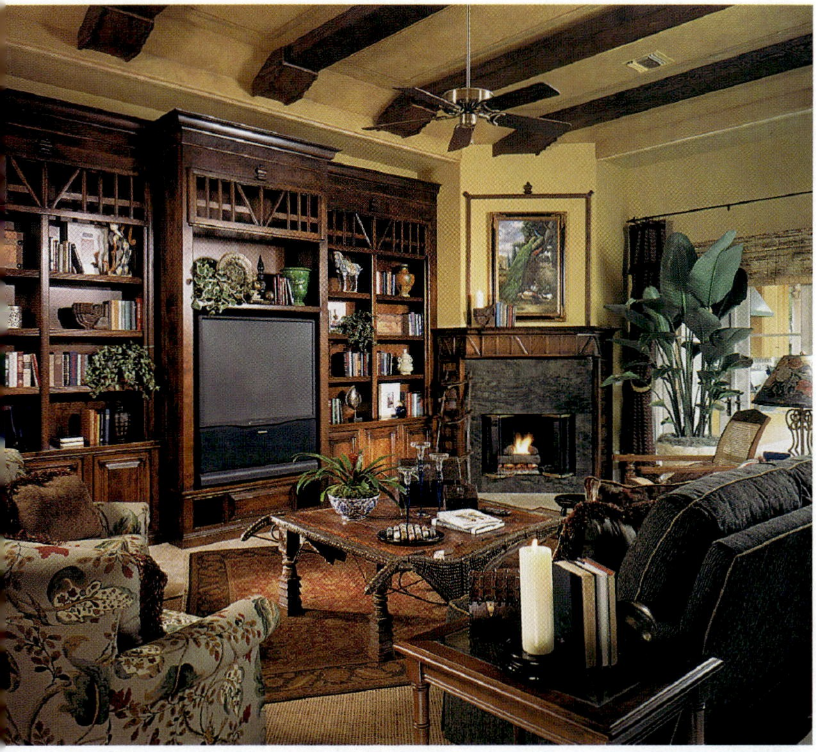

Figure 7.9 *Audiovisual equipment is tastefully displayed in a custom cabinet. The television and fireplace function together in this angled arrangement. (Interiors: Marc-Michaels Interior Design. Photograph ©Kim Sargent Architectural Photography. Residence: Private home, Phipps Estates, Palm Beach. Developer: Addison Development.)*

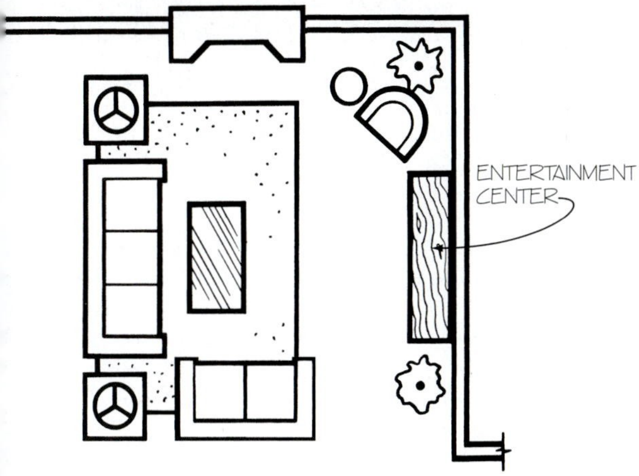

ıre 7.10 *This floor plan illustrates a quality solution in a ily room that has both a fireplace and a television.*

ate daily activities. Designers should check with clients to ɛrmine their preference. Placing the washer with easy ac- ; to water lines is also important. A laundry tub or sink, quate counter surfaces, space for the dryer and ironing rd, sufficient storage, hanging space, and good lighting also desirable.

ɜewing, workshop, office, garden, and other work areas ıld be conveniently located with well-arranged space for ıired storage, furnishings, equipment, and lighting.

Libraries, Studies, and Offices

These areas, when used by visitors, may be part of the public zone. As more people operate businesses from their homes, clients may be invited there. If this is the case, the office should be located near an entry that is easily accessible from the front of the house, away from noisy rooms, and screened from the formal social areas. If only the occupants use the office, library, or study, the room should be located in an area away from noisy areas such as family rooms, kitchens, and utility rooms (see Figure 13.3).

More and more households have computers, which are becoming central to daily household operations. In many families, children have their own computers and study spaces. Furthermore, the laptop computer has allowed virtually any surface to become an office. Although the study may be located in the private zone, additional computer stations may be located near the kitchen or family room and also in children's rooms.

Private Zones

For maximum quiet and privacy, sleeping, dressing, and hygiene areas function best when located away from the social zone of the residence. Guests, except for those in the guestroom, rarely visit this zone of the home.

Master Bedroom

The master bedroom has become a refuge from the pressures and stress of everyday living—a place for relaxation and sleeping. Often the master bedroom is a luxurious part of the home (Figure 7.11). There may be space for a fireplace, a

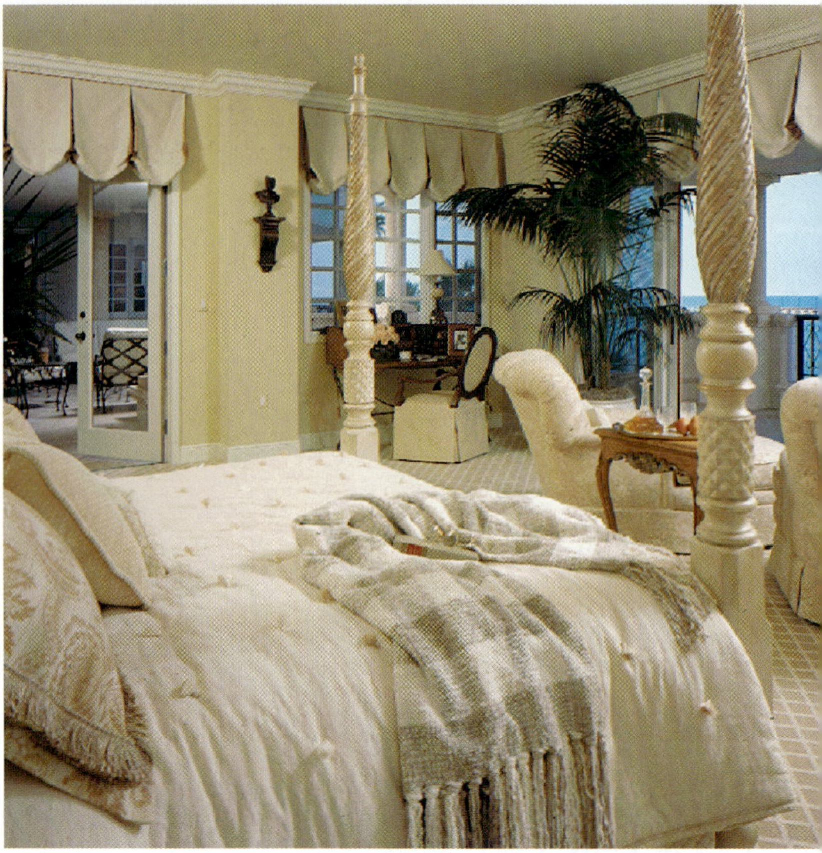

Figure 7.11 *In this seaside model home, the master bedroom faces the ocean. A writing area and a relaxed conversation area are included. (Interiors: Fine Decorators, Hallandale, FL/Ted Fine with Robert Perlberg. Photograph by Brantley, Ocean Ridge, FL. Courtesy of* On Design.*)*

bar, a television set, a study, a conversation arrangement, an office, and even a physical fitness area. The master bedroom is best located at a distance from all other rooms. It does not have to be adjacent to any other room except the master bath and, if appropriate, a nursery.

Bedrooms for Children and Young Adults

These rooms, like the master bedroom, should be located in quiet areas of the house. Children's rooms require ample storage, access to a bathroom, and perhaps a study or computer area. Designers should also be sensitive to the needs of children in blended families. When possible, the designer should talk directly with the children to determine their needs and desires in this specialty area of design.

Dressing and Clothes Storage

The dressing area may be in a separate space, in a closet, in the bedroom itself, or adjacent to or in the bathroom. Storage for clothing should be close to the dressing area and bathroom and planned for convenience. Closets should not protrude into the bedroom (Figure 7.12). A space for soiled clothing should be conveniently located. Storage for clothing, jewelry, and other dressing items is generally limited, so using space to an advantage is a challenge.

Guestrooms

Rooms set aside for guests are many times considere luxury; however, where space permits, a warm and i ing guestroom is a welcomed retreat for visitors. A other bedrooms, traffic lanes should be allocated arc the bed. A side chair for reading and a television are appreciated. Minimal storage is needed for clothing other personal items.

Guestrooms should be located away from noisy act areas and private zones and need to have access to a b room. Guests may desire access to public areas, such as kitchen or family room.

Bathrooms

Since the beginning of the twentieth century, the bathr has undergone many changes. Originally, it was one sh room at the end of the hall; then it became a personal junct to the bedroom, and became smaller and more uti ian. Today, utility and luxury are combined, and bathroom—once hidden behind closed doors—is freque exposed to sky, garden, terrace, and sometimes to c rooms of the house. What was once a small, sterile r with three basic plumbing fixtures (lavatory or sink, to and tub or shower) has become a powder room, dres room, and even sitting room, often with additional lu

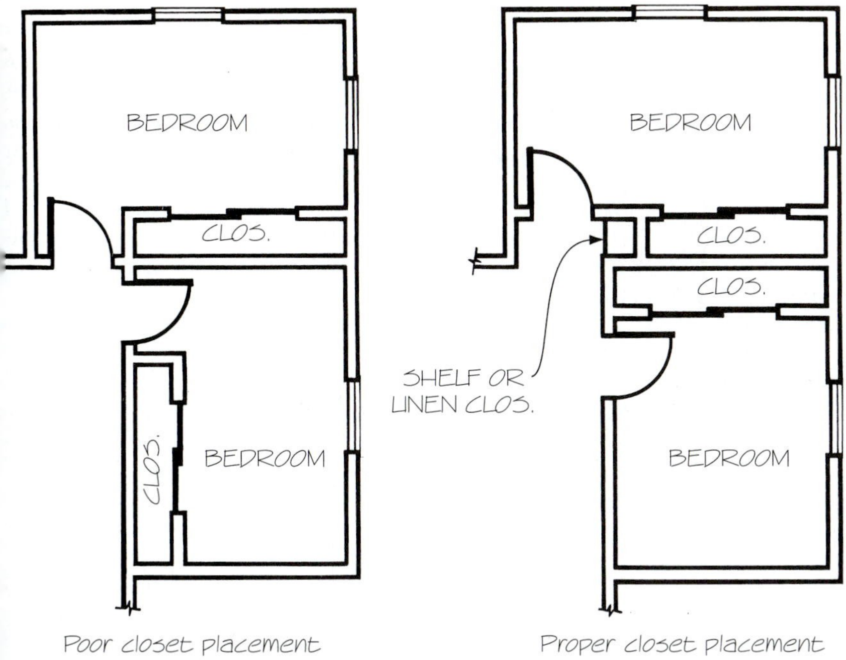

Figure 7.12 *Poor and proper placement for closets.*

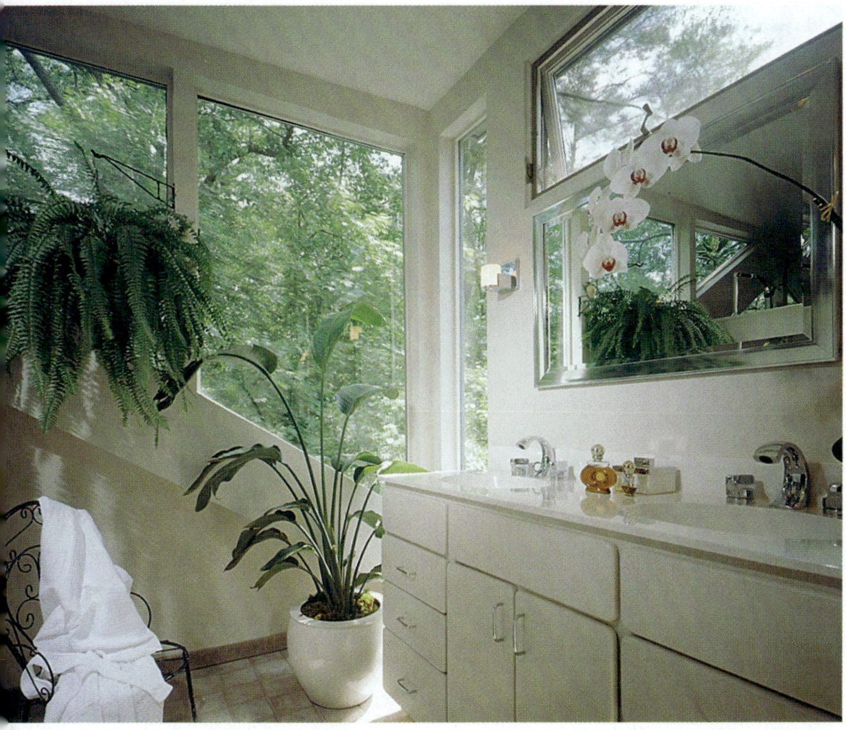

Figure 7.13 *In this contemporary remodeling project, the designer created a tree house effect for the master bath. (Designer: T. Duffy & Associates, Inc. Photograph © Robert Thien. As seen in* Atlanta Homes & Lifestyles.*)*

atures such as whirlpool, sauna, spa, hot tub, television, or eplace (see Figures 4.19 and 7.13).

Most homes have more than one bathroom. Some may ve half- or three-quarter baths (with a sink, toilet, and ower stall) as well. The designer must determine the ace available, the needs of the users, and the most effi- ent arrangement of plumbing fixtures and supportive fur- shings, storage, and lighting for each hygiene area in the sidence.

Bathroom design is still centered on the three basic fixtures—the tub, toilet, and sink. Ample storage for towels, medicines, and grooming and cleaning aids is essential. A place for soiled clothing is also desirable. Master bathrooms commonly contain two sinks, a separate area for the toilet, and a shower stall in addition to the tub. Tubs may be located almost anyplace, including the center of the room. They are available in all shapes, designs, colors, and sizes. Sometimes tubs are placed beside large windows to take

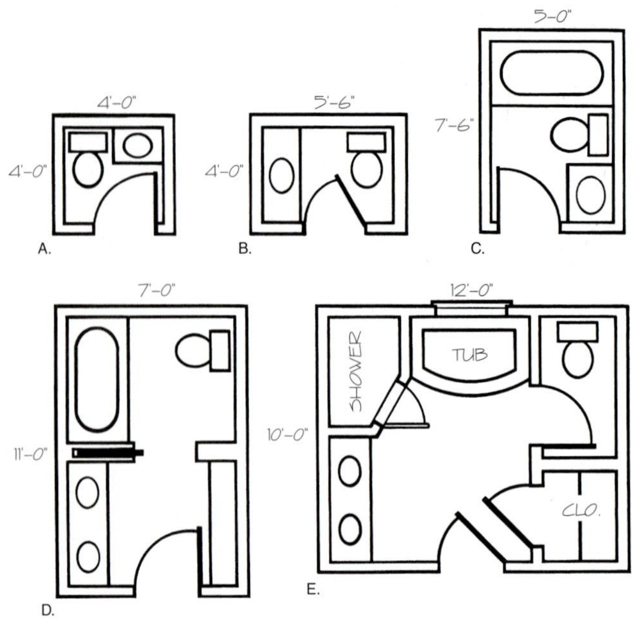

Figure 7.14 *Typical bathroom layouts. (A) and (B) are appropriate for half-bath layouts. A is extremely tight, but acceptable when a closet is converted to a bath; B is a better solution. (C) is the most compact three-fixture layout. (D) is a common inexpensive solution for a larger master bath. (E) illustrates one of an endless variety of solutions for an upgraded master bath.*

advantage of a view. It is safest for the user if the tub is sunken, because steps up to the tub can be treacherous when wet. Figure 7.14 illustrates some common bathroom layouts.

More info online @

http://www.nkba.org/ National Kitchen & Bath Association Site

http://www.abathroomguide.com/html/bathroom-design.htm General website with links on bathroom design

General Zoning Guidelines

Allowing enough space for each member of the household is an essential requirement in planning interiors. Space requirements vary for each individual, and in some cases may reflect clients' preferences rather than their needs. Generally, 1000 square feet of space meets the needs of one person; and an additional 500 square feet per person provides sufficient space. Designers must be able to guide clients and meet their essential needs while staying within financial boundaries.

Commercial Zones

Like residential zones, commercial zones also are divided into broad categories of private and public spaces. The myriad options for the specialty areas of design, such hospitality, health care, or institutional design, require se arate study well beyond the scope of this text. It is, ho ever, feasible to consider the space planning needs of typical commercial office. As was discussed in Chapter commercial buildings must also consider accessibility sta dards, from the entry to the snack bar at the rear of the fice complex. Space planning can be greatly affected these requirements. Figures 7.15 through 7.19 illustrate successful corporate office design and are used througho this section as examples.

Public Zones

The public zone consists of the area where clients, or gues arrive. Clients should feel welcome but should not be awa of activities in progress in the private spaces.

Reception Room

As illustrated in Chapter 6, the reception room includes tv activity areas—the conversation/waiting area and the offi workspace for the receptionist. The reception room needs be adjacent to the front door and therefore also serves as t entry or foyer. The reception room should be near the pu lic conference room and be easily accessible to other priva office areas (see Figures 2.23, 7.15, and 7.16). The recepti room needs access to a breakroom or coffee area so gue may be served refreshments while waiting. A storage area coats and umbrellas and a small private telephone room al may be required.

Conference or Presentation Room

This room also should welcome clients. Access should directly off the reception area (see Figure 7.16). In sor conference rooms, an adjacent audiovisual area conce equipment and doubles as a storage area for presentati materials.

Private Zones

In commercial spaces, private zones could more accurate be called semiprivate zones, because clients and guests m frequent almost all areas of a commercial office.

Offices

Offices are grouped together based on the company's di sion of departments. In large commercial establishments, e tire floors may be dedicated to a particular division. Offic may also require flexible spaces; for example, individu may share an office space, at other times working at hor or on the road. Offices should be in quiet zones of a buil ing away from breakrooms and near the support staff.

Executive offices may comprise a suite of rooms that cludes a private administrative assistant's office, private co ference room, office, bathroom, and storage clos Executive suites are generally located in private areas o building, frequently on the top floor (Figure 7.17).

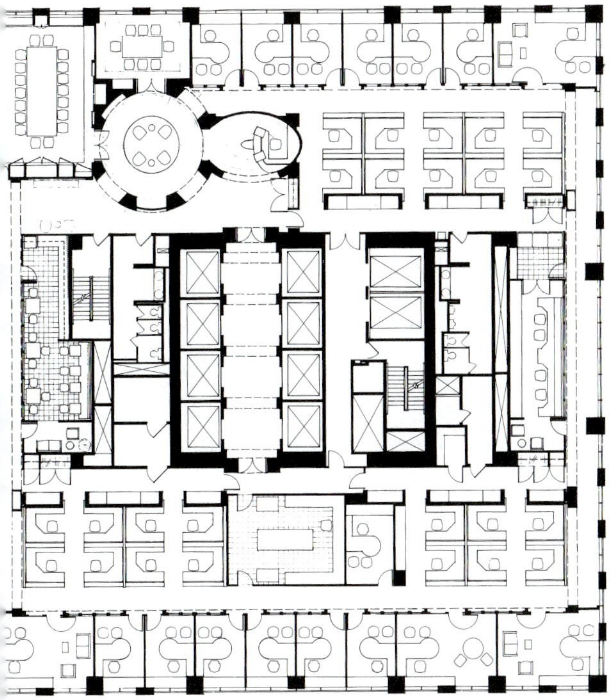

ure 7.15 *Figures 7.15–7.19 illustrate an excellent solution a commercial office space. The radial lobby (see Figure 3) defines the interior and sets the tone for the entire ice. (Architect/Designer: VOA Associates, Inc. Photograph by ve Hall/Hedrich-Blessing.)*

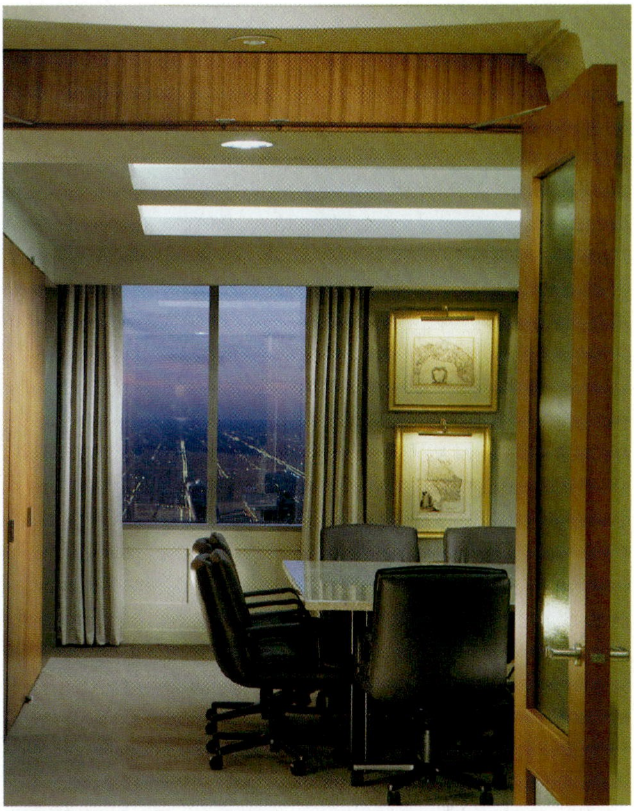

Figure 7.16 *Two conference rooms are located directly off the reception area. (Architect/Designer: VOA Associates, Inc. Photograph by Steve Hall/Hedrich-Blessing.)*

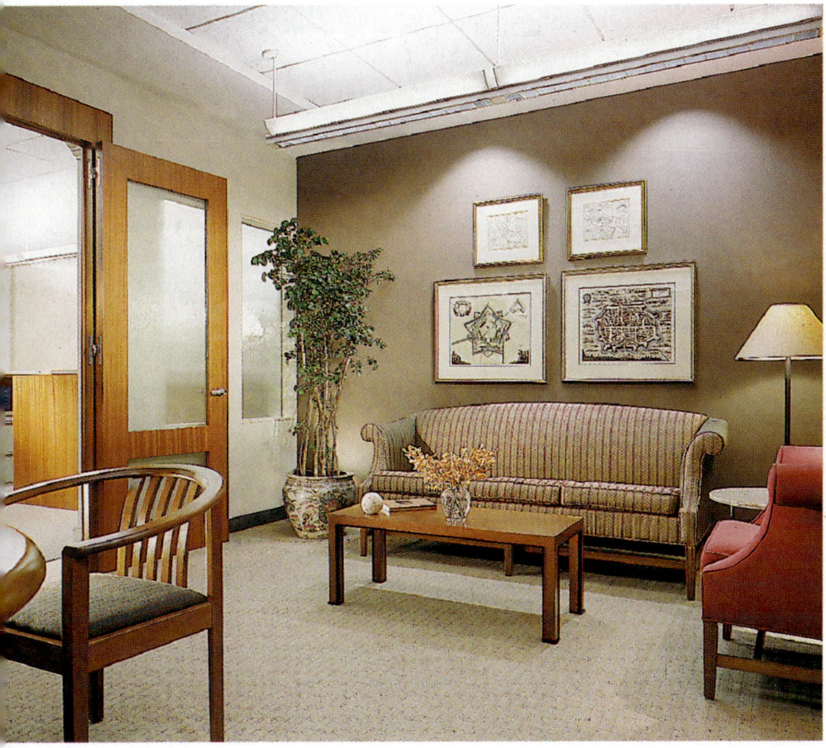

Figure 7.17 *Private offices are located out of sight from the main public areas. (Architect/Designer: VOA Associates, Inc. Photograph by Steve Hall/Hedrich-Blessing.)*

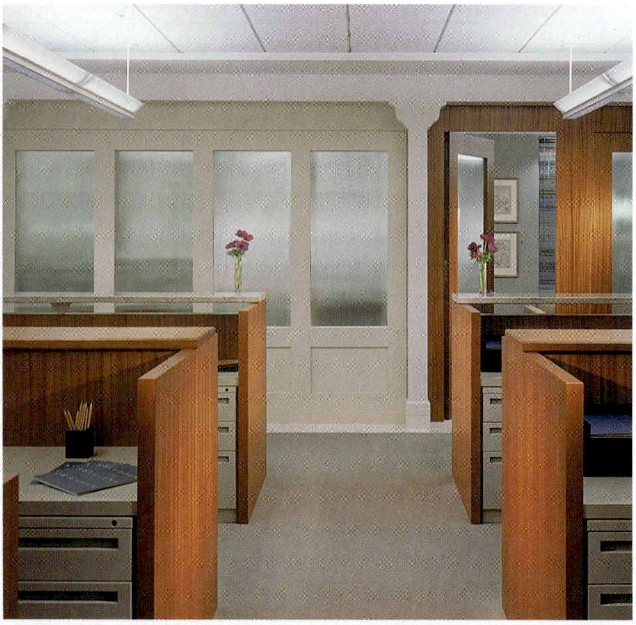

Figure 7.18 *Open office spaces and support staff areas maintain the formal design characteristics. Employees are provided ample lighting. (Architect/Designer: VOA Associates, Inc. Photograph by Steve Hall/Hedrich-Blessing.)*

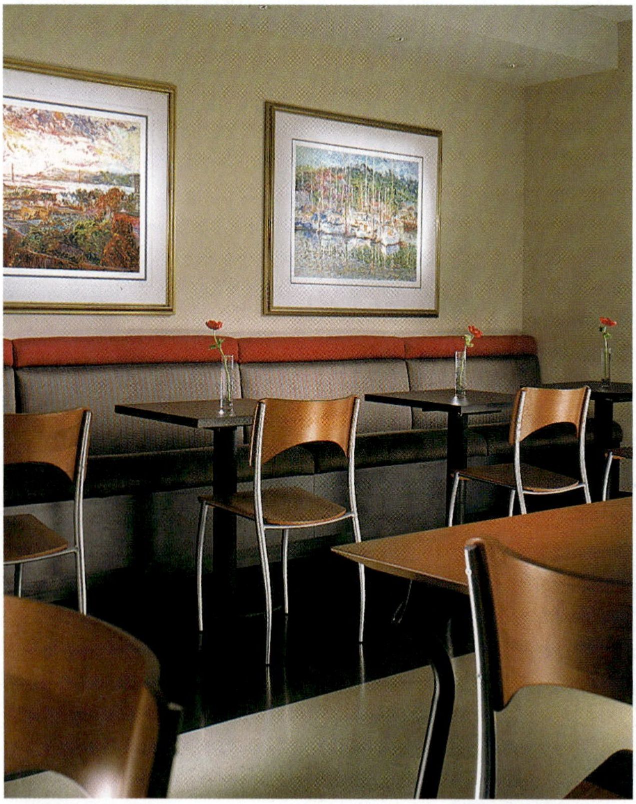

Figure 7.19 *Ancillary areas are centrally located and out of public view, yet even the lunchroom maintains the character and classical design details found throughout the office. (Architect/Designer: VOA Associates, Inc. Photograph by Steve Hall/Hedrich-Blessing.)*

Open Offices

In many commercial establishments, employees work open offices or systems furniture environments (see Chap 8). Open office areas should be grouped by departm away from noise and adjacent to support staff (Figure 7.1

Support Staff

In many firms, the support staff, secretaries, or administrat assistants serve more than one individual. Locating supp staff to meet the needs of those they serve can be diffic Support staff also must be near copy, file, and storage are In very small firms, the receptionist may be the support s for the entire firm. In larger corporations, support staff n be in an area of their own, sometimes referred to as a "s retarial bay."

Ancillary Areas

Ancillary areas include copy, mail, file, and other rela rooms necessary for processing various tasks. These ar are generally used only by the employees, but need to centrally located to expedite the flow of work. Noisy copi and printers should not interfere with the need for a qu office.

Breakrooms

Although the size of this room varies greatly depending the client's needs, the space planning remains the sa Breakrooms are potentially noisy areas that need pro sound attenuation. They also should be separated from public zone. Because most breakrooms require a sink, th must be located near plumbing lines (Figure 7.19).

Bathrooms

In commercial design, the location of the bathroom deper on the location of plumbing lines. In high-rise buildin bathrooms are located in a central core that serves the en floor. In smaller offices, the bathroom should be located tween the public and private zones to accommodate b employees and guests. Commercial bathrooms must m universal design requirements (see Chapter 6).

General Zoning Requirements

Whether designing for a residential or commercial client, designer should consider the principles of design, as wel various space and traffic flow guidelines.

The Principles of Design in Relation to Spac

Space, like all the elements of design, affects the princip of design. When arranging furniture or space plann rooms, designers should consider the following points.

- The *proportions* of a room can be altered through appropriate space planning. For instance, long, tall piece can divide a room into smaller areas. Dropped ceilings and area rugs can delineate an area needing a more intimate space (Figure 7.20). Furniture placed perpendicular to a wall can define a smaller area.

The *scale* of a room is greatly affected by the room's furnishings. As discussed in Chapter 3, the scale of the furniture must be in line with the scale of the room. If the furniture is too large, the room will appear cramped; too small, and the room will appear stark and uninviting (see Figure 2.16).

Furnishings should be arranged to give the room a sense of *balance*. Large architectural features, such as picture windows and fireplaces, require heavier furniture opposite them. In rooms with slanted ceilings, heavier furniture should be placed against the taller wall.

Balance also can be achieved through a mixture of high and low pieces of furniture and furnishings. Exclusive use of tall pieces makes a room appear heavy and overbearing, whereas a consistent use of low pieces makes a room look squatty, as if designed for children.

Achieving *rhythm* in an interior allows the eye to move easily about the room. The repetition of a side chair or end tables adds continuity. A person may be drawn from the living room to the dining room through a progression of steps. An architectural detail, combined with furniture and carpet placement, may form an axis drawing the person to an appointed location (Figure 7.21). In

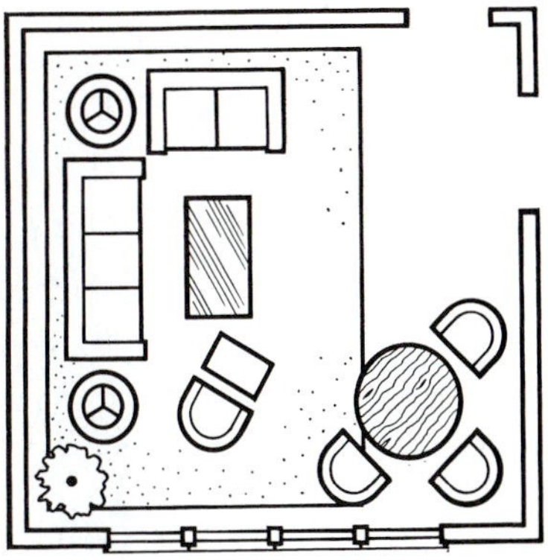

Figure 7.20 *In this square room, a rectangular rug was added to define the seating area and to control the proportions of the room.*

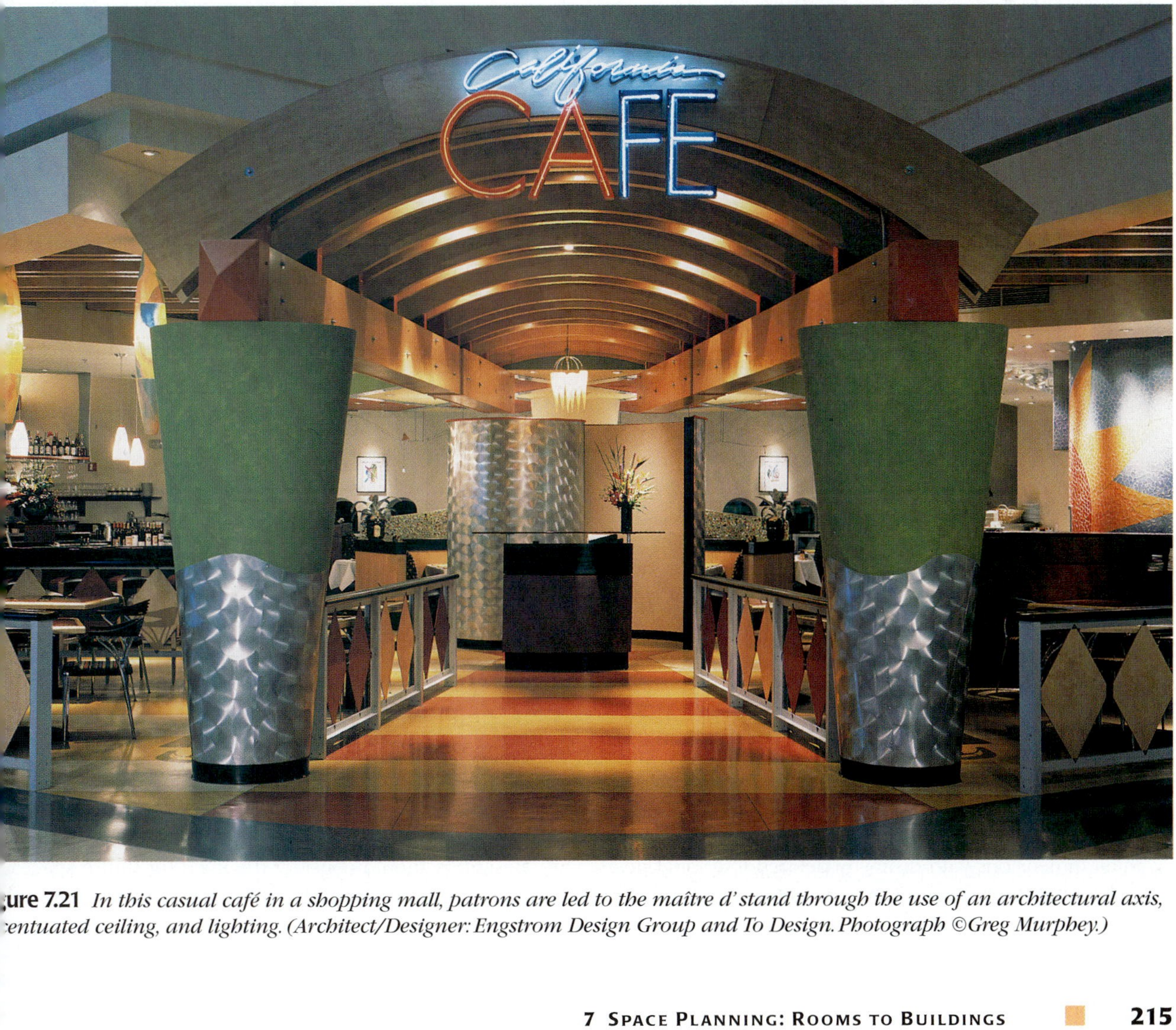

ure 7.21 *In this casual café in a shopping mall, patrons are led to the maître d' stand through the use of an architectural axis, entuated ceiling, and lighting. (Architect/Designer: Engstrom Design Group and To Design. Photograph ©Greg Murphey.)*

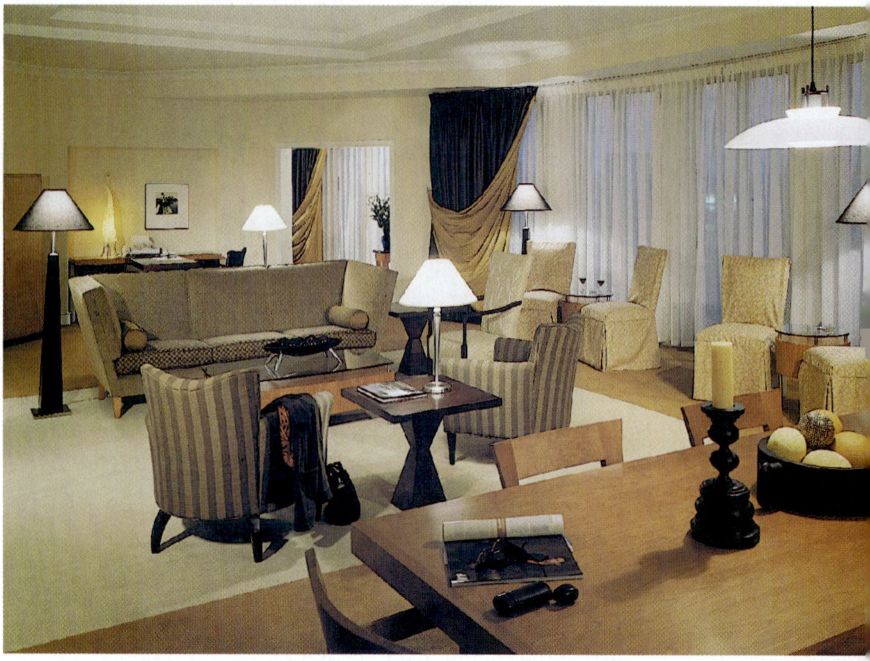

Figure 7.22 *This presidential suite located in the Westin Grand Hotel illustrates harmonious use of the principles and elements of design. Warm tones, soft lighting, and contemporary furnishings provide unity. Black accents and a sweeping window treatment create drama and variety. (Architect/Designer: NBBJ. Photograph by Assassi Productions.)*

large office buildings, hotels, and airports, corridors should be placed in systematic locations to aid visitors' directional sense. In retail design, this repetition is intentionally altered to encourage shoppers to wander through the store.

- All rooms or groups of rooms must have a *focal point.* The center of interest may be an information desk, painting, sculpture, coffee table, or panoramic view. In a group of rooms, the main conference room, reception area, living room, or great room may serve this purpose. Once the focal point of a room is decided, it should be supported by the arrangement of furnishings and corridors (see Figure 2.26).
- *Harmony* can be achieved only when space planning utilizes unity and variety. Offices need desks and chairs; living rooms require sofas and end tables. Bathrooms should be located near bedrooms and reception rooms near the front door. It is this typical placement of furnishings and rooms that allows the client to feel comfortable in a space; however, it is the unusual juxtaposition of a wall, chair, accessory, or architectural element that enhances a room and keeps the client's interest elevated (Figure 7.22).

Space and Traffic Flow Guidelines

Arranging space to meet clients' needs requires general guidelines that should be applied in all situations.

- The style of the home or office may guide the layout of the rooms. Some clients prefer a formal design balanced in all dimensions with distinctly defined interior zones. Other clients may prefer open planning and an informal approach to interior zoning.
- Floor and wall space must be adequate to support lar pieces of furniture, shelving, files, and art. Doorways, though convenient, cannot encompass every wall.
- Traffic patterns should not cross conversation groupin television viewing, workspaces, or the kitchen prepar tion area.
- A view to the outside should be accessible from every major room or workspace. Only storage rooms, closet baths, file rooms, movie theatres, and similar spaces should be without natural daylight.
- Windows should be located to preserve the function c the wall space. Properly placed windows allow for ea in operation and for placement of window treatment (Figure 7.23).
- Doorways should not be located at the end of corrido A corridor should end with a wall or other focal point
- Bathrooms, bedrooms, kitchens, breakrooms, copy rooms, and offices, along with any other private or ba of house function, should not be visible from an entry
- Sufficient storage should be located throughout a hou or office building.
- Rooms that require plumbing save costs when groupe near or on top of each other.
- Rooms should have the most pleasing proportions po ble. Ancillary areas such as closets, stairwells, or bathrooms should not protrude into a room (see Figure 7.12).
- Designers must adhere to federal, state, and local buil ing codes (see Chapter 4). Understanding these codes prior to initial space planning may prevent having to make changes later in the design process.
- Designers should consider the need for future space. good plan can effectively accommodate projected expansions.

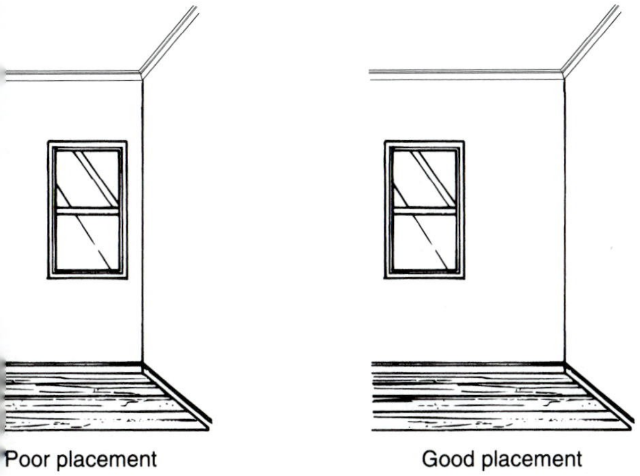

Figure 7.23 *Window placement.*

'e Orientation and Selection

: selection of the site must work in conjunction with the :ction of a floor plan. Although the physical placement of uilding is not the responsibility of the designer, on certain)jects the designer may have input into selecting the site. 'ore making a selection, the architect and designer should /e the general plan of the structure in mind. Not until the · has been analyzed should the plan be finalized. For ex- ple, when selecting a site for a residence, many factors)uld be considered including such criteria as location of ools, transportation, availability of police and fire protec- 1, quality of the neighborhood, availability of utilities (water, sewer, power, garbage collection), taxes, and building codes and restrictions. Depending on the building's intended function, criteria when selecting a site for a nonresidential structure might include public convenience, efficiency, accessibility, and aesthetic appeal.

A gently sloping lot that provides good natural drainage and allows sewer lines to be connected easily is desirable. A steep lot may cost less initially but may require expensive retaining walls and have other hidden costs; however, a view or a wooded site may be what the client wants. Effective positioning of the structure on the site and orienting it to take advantage of solar properties are also important. "Sustainable Design: The Economy of Space Planning" addresses additional space planning and site selection criteria.

SUSTAINABLEDESIGN

The Economy of Space Planning

One of the most important aspects of a sustainable environment is the physical layout of the building. Several design criteria assist in the conservative use of materials and energy.

- The more square the shape of the exterior walls, the less the cost per square foot. Cost does not increase in direct proportion to a structure's square footage—jogs and angles drive construction costs higher, as illustrated in Figure SD7.1. Two stories cost proportionally less than a low, rambling plan, because the roof and foundation can serve twice the space, and the second story provides extra insulation against summer heat and winter cold.

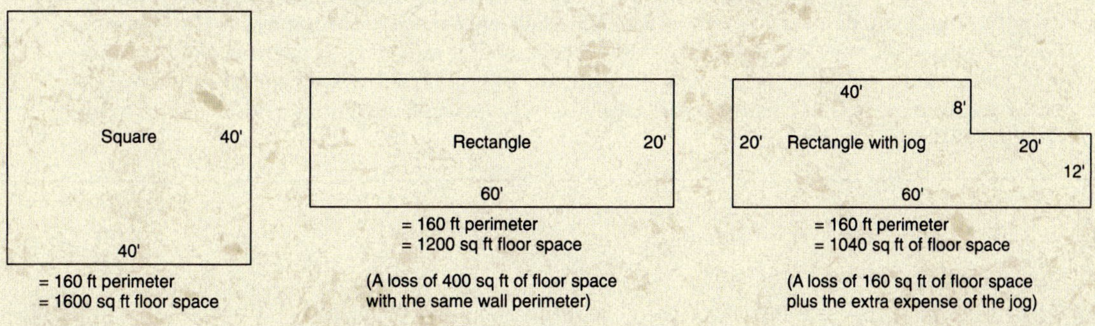

Figure SD7.1 *Price and square footage. The three enclosures, each requiring the same number of linear feet of exterior wall, illustrate how the price per square foot increases as the space deviates from the square.*

SUSTAINABLEDESIGN

The Economy of Space Planning—cont'd

- Adequate insulation reduces heating costs, as do wood- or coal-burning stoves that meet strict EPA requirements.
- Locating the structure to take the best advantage of the climate saves on heating and air-conditioning bills. The winter sun should strike long walls and large windows, but in the summer, large areas of glass should be screened from the afternoon sun (see Figure SD7.2). Positioning the house wisely also reduces the cost of connecting other utilities from the road to the house.

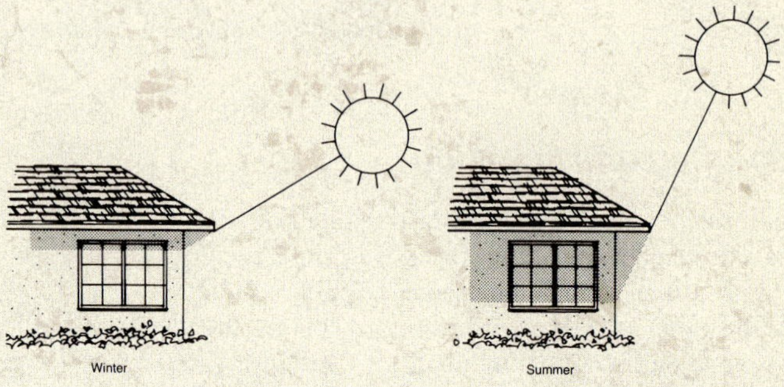

Figure SD7.2 *A well-designed roof can permit the warm winter sun to flood the interior spaces in December and block out the hot summer sun in July.*

- Centralized plumbing saves energy. Bathrooms can be placed back to back as seen in Figure SD7.3, or one above the other. Kitchen and utility room plumbing can be located to take advantage of the same major drains.
- Fireplaces can be planned to take advantage of a common chimney (Figure SD7.4).

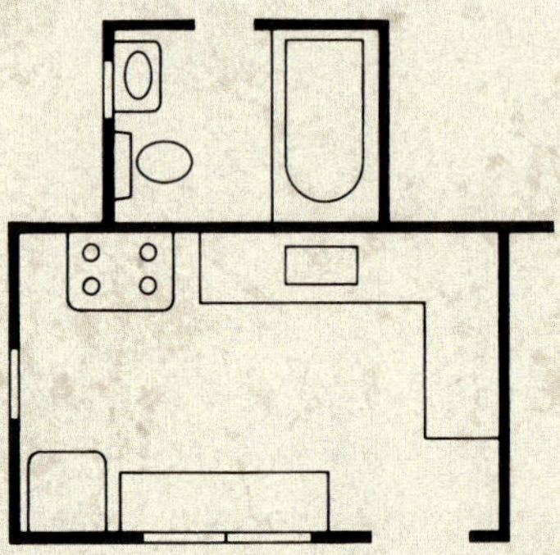

Figure SD7.3 *Back-to-back plumbing.*

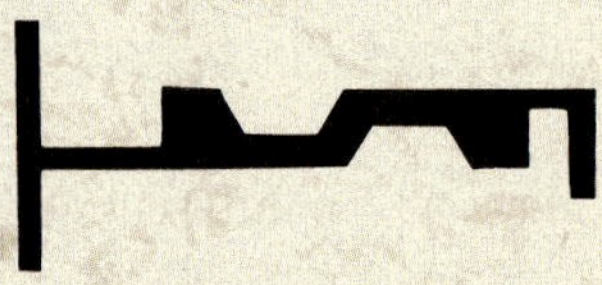

Figure SD7.4 *Two fireplaces can be combined to share the same chimney.*

- Materials found on-site in the construction area, called **indigenous materials,** offer great savings. Flawed materials may cost less, and character can be gained by making a feature out of a fault.
- Consider the cost of upkeep of building materials over a long period of time. This is called life-cycle costing. Some items that are more costly initially are the most economical in the long run. For example, brick may cost more than frame facades, but it never needs painting and the building's resale value is usually higher than for one made of wood. Hardwood balusters are more expensive than pine, but pine balusters are easily broken and replacement may soon add up to more than the cost of the hardwood.

More info online @

http://www.southface.org/ Southface Energy Institute

http://www.ases.org American Solar Energy Society

http://www.ises.org/ises.nsf!Open International Solar Energy Society

http://www.seia.org/ Solar Energy Industries Association

SUSTAINABLEDESIGN

A simple solution in sustainable design environments is to design spaces that meet the client's needs and are "not so big." The Not So Big residential concept has been popularized by architect Sarah Susanka. Many of the Not So Big design philosophies follow sustainable design principles as well. The overarching goal is to create interior spaces based on quality, not quantity (Figures SD7.5 and SD7.6). Other design principles include the following:

- Expression of the client's personality
- Attention to detail
- Combination of formal and informal living spaces
- All spaces used daily
- Custom tailoring
- Personal quiet spaces referred to as "Away Rooms"
- Diagonal views and axes to views
- Niches and window seats
- Access to daylight and exterior views
- Efficient use of space, similar to a sailboat or quality motor home
- Mail center near the main entry
- Welcoming family entry (not through the laundry room)

More info online @

http://www.notsobighouse.com/ Not So Big House website

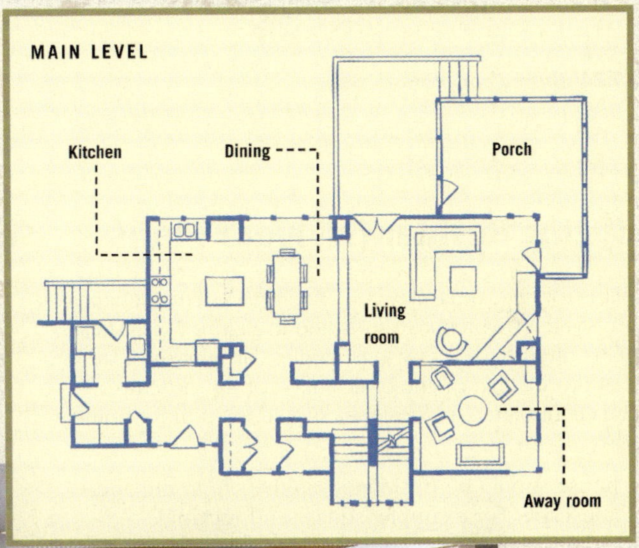

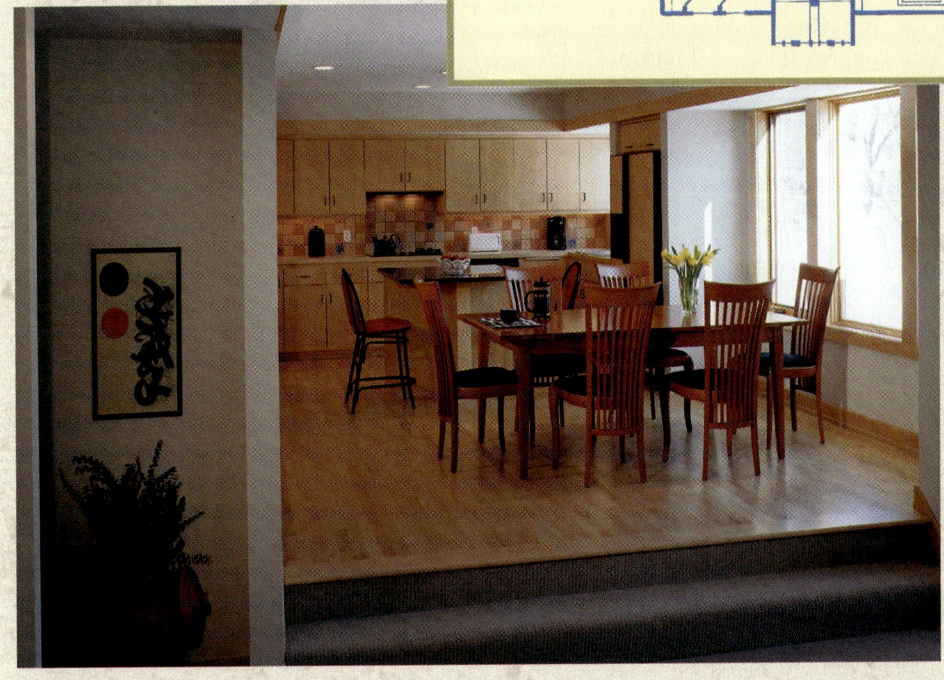

Figures SD7.5 and SD7.6 *In this residence, many of the Not So Big principles are evident. Note how the family entrance corresponds to the main front entrance. The Away Room provides for a quiet area, whereas the informal and formal public spaces are joined. A large expanse of windows ties the exterior to the interior. Niches, window seats, and custom cabinetry are tailored to meet the family's needs and provide for efficient space utilization. (Courtesy of Taunton Press.)*

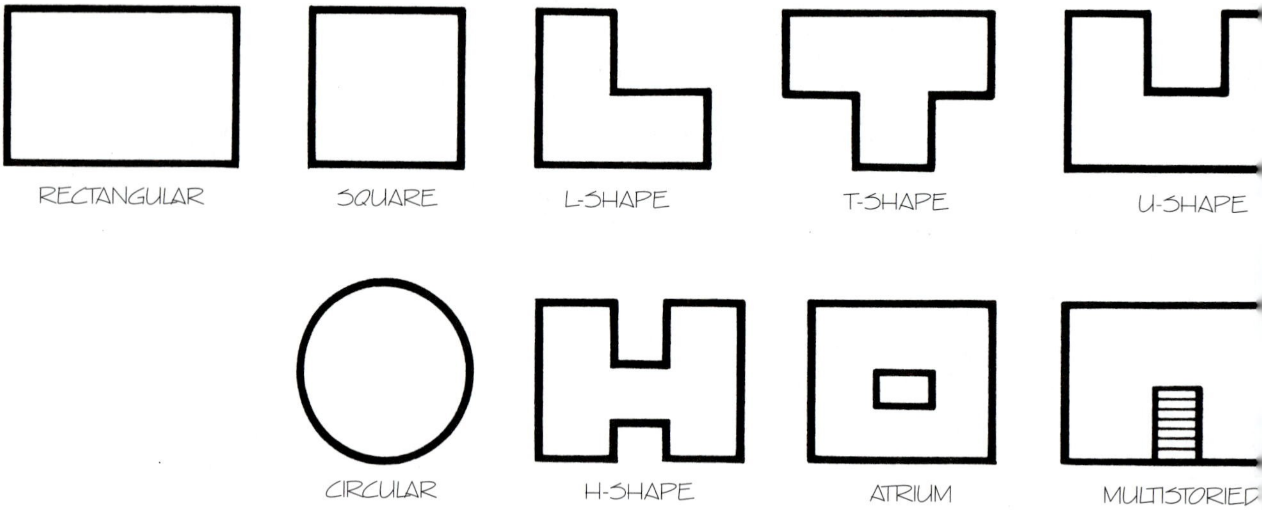

Figure 7.24 *Basic floor plan shapes.*

Analyzing Residential Floor Plans

Floor plans for residential design come in a variety of shapes or styles, some of which are illustrated in Figure 7.24. These floor plans often have a few jogs, angles, or window extensions that do not change the basic shape of the structure. To serve the client better, the designer should keep these points in mind:

- The house should be positioned on the site to enhance the landscape. For example, square and rectangle shapes can be more difficult to position and landscape attractively than shapes with more interesting angles.
- Each angle and jog of a floor plan shape adds to the expense of the structure.
- The shape of the residence may affect the interior arrangement of activities. For instance, it is more difficult to arrange various functions in a square because of the limited flexibility of the shape.
- Traffic patterns are usually more efficient in shapes with more angles than a square or rectangle offer.
- Heating and cooling costs are higher with added wings.
- Shapes with more wings or extensions allow additional light and ventilation in the residence.
- Some shapes offer more interesting ways to arrange furnishings, the T, U, H, and atrium shapes, for example.
- Private outdoor living space is possible with shapes like the T, U, H, and atrium, but very difficult with a square.
- Aesthetically, garage doors should open from the side of a home instead of the front; however, such an arrangement may require a larger lot and therefore is more expensive.

Square Plan

The square plan is a simple and inexpensive arrangemen space with distinct advantages and disadvantages, simila the rectangular plan. Most designers try to minimize or e change the boxy shape—both for interiors and exterior through creative manipulation of the elements of design (F ure 7.25). Some considerations when employing the squ plan include the following:

- The square plan is one of the least expensive to build because corners are limited to four. It requires only a simple roof and foundation—generally the most costly elements in house construction.
- Rooms should be arranged so traffic can flow freely. T placement of an entrance and hallways can be a challenge in the square plan.
- Good planning should provide adequate light and air circulation—often a problem with the square plan. Th center may be poorly lit. A centrally located skylight is one method of eliminating this condition.
- The square plan generally does not provide interesting and inviting outdoor living spaces; however, through skillful landscaping this problem can be eliminated. Sometimes the square plan is turned on an angle to th lot, providing a diagonal or diamond shape.
- Good separation of interior living spaces, such as the sleeping and activity areas, is more difficult to arrange the square plan.

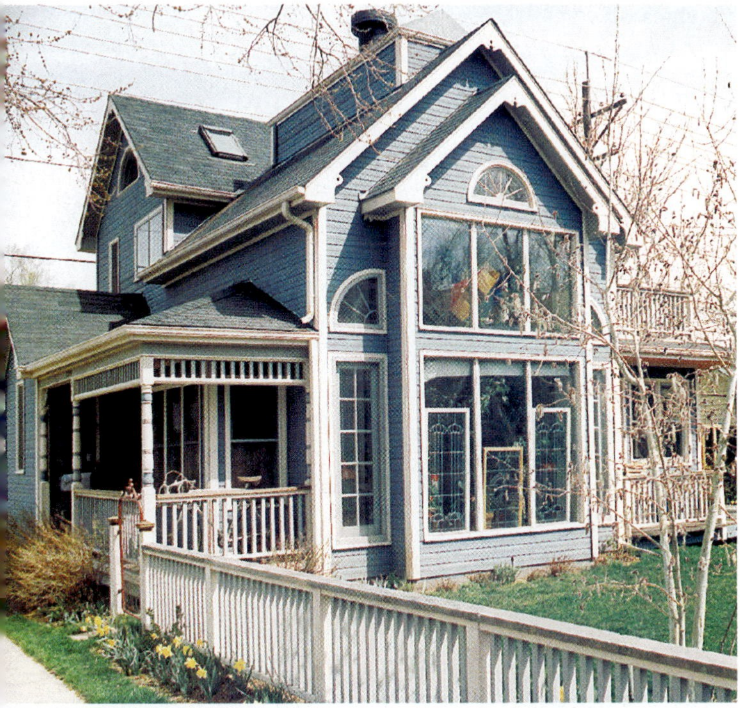

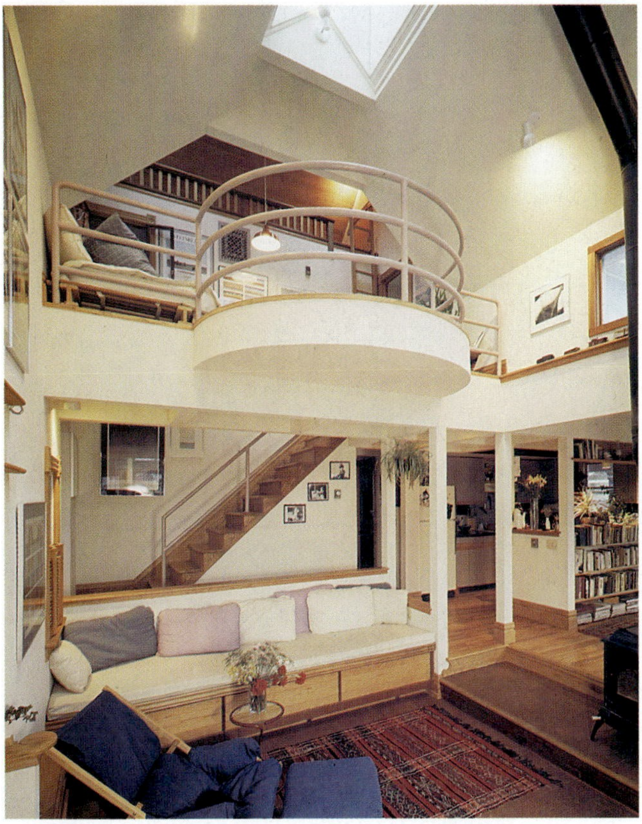

Figure 7.25 *This relatively small house plan, based on the square, efficiently utilizes less than 1300 square feet. The soaring living room ceiling adds the feeling of a grander space. (Designer: Wolff-Lyon Architects.)*

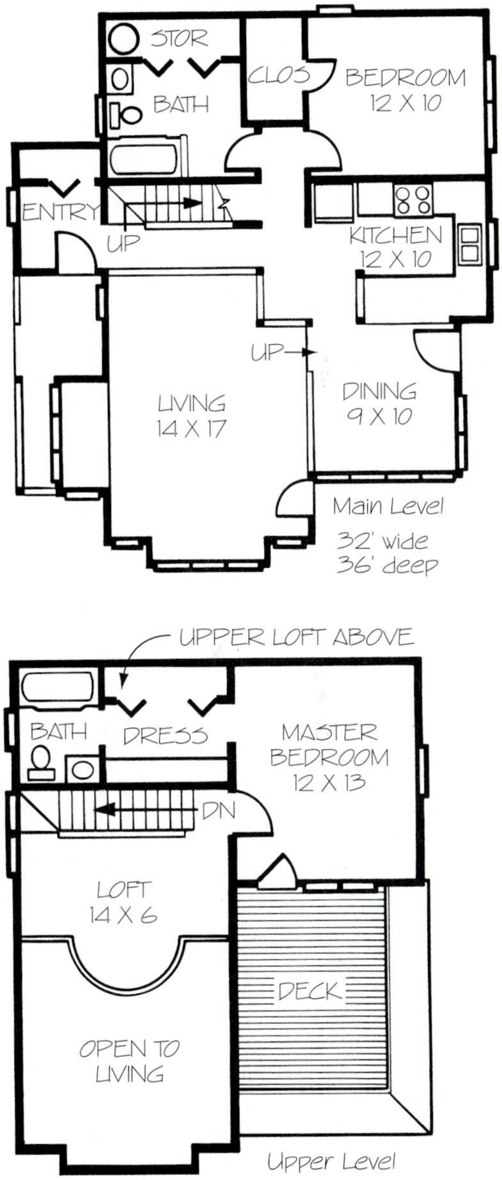

The basically square plan seen in Figure 7.26 incorporates many open planning concepts in its interior, including the following:

- The house was designed to fit its beachfront site. Upper floor windows provide an ocean view.
- The garage is enclosed and attached.
- Public and social zones are well defined.
- Closets and storage areas are incorporated into the plan.
- First and second floor bathrooms are stacked.
- Rear steps provide a secondary entry/exit to the second and third floors.

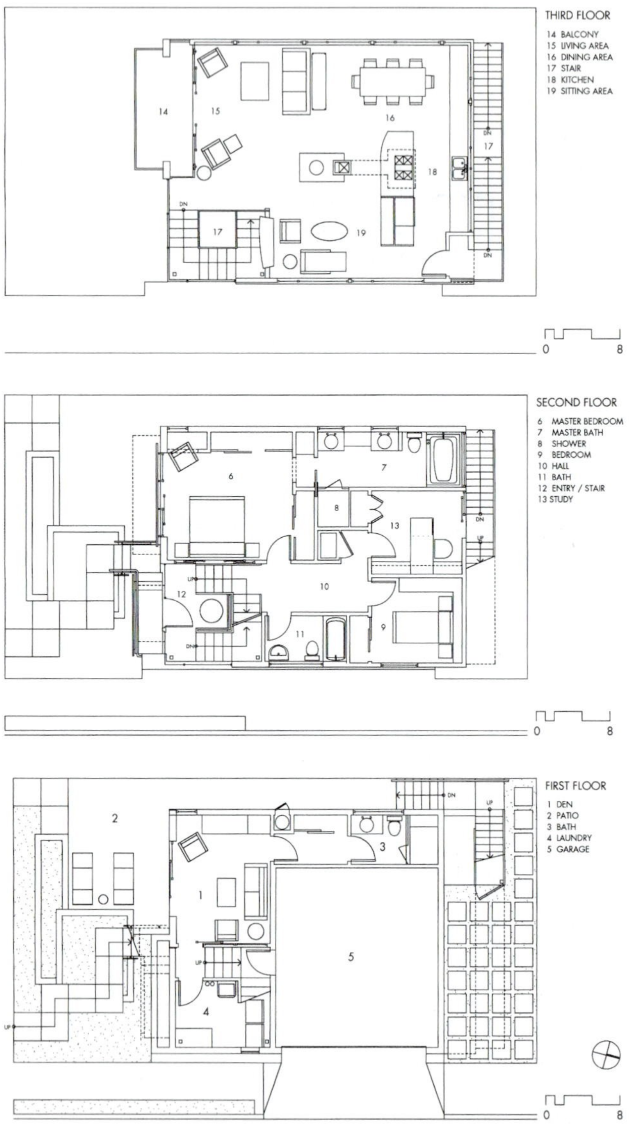

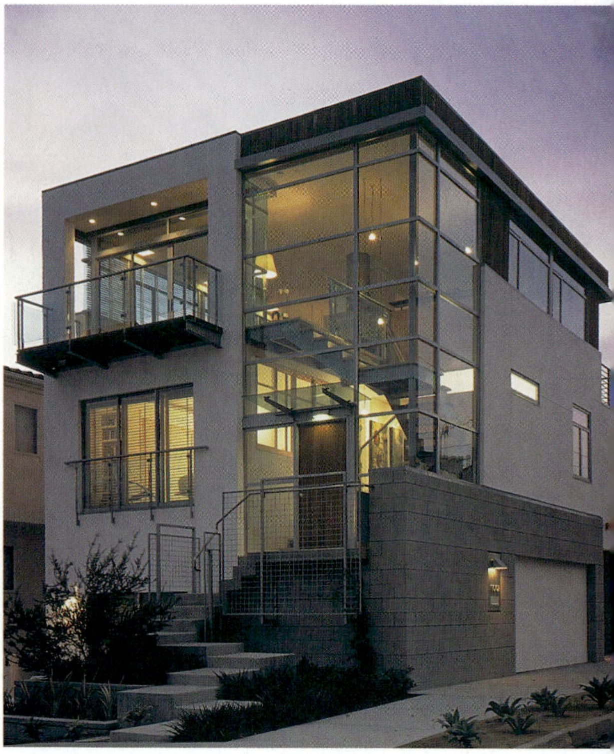

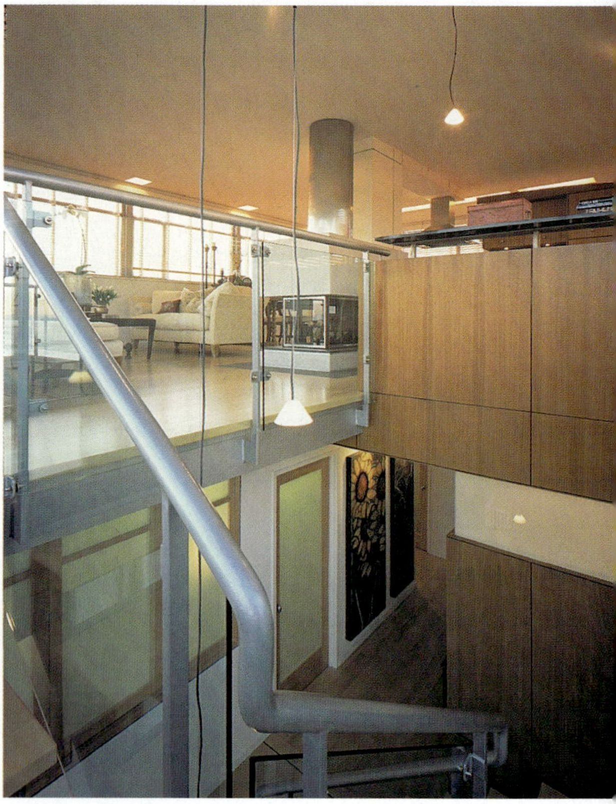

Figure 7.26 *This unique plan was developed to fit the site. Public areas are on upper floors for the best view of the ocean. An open stairway unites the floors. Closets, storage areas, and bathrooms do not infringe upon the space. (Architect/Designer: Rockefeller/Hricak Architects. Photograph by David Glomb.)*

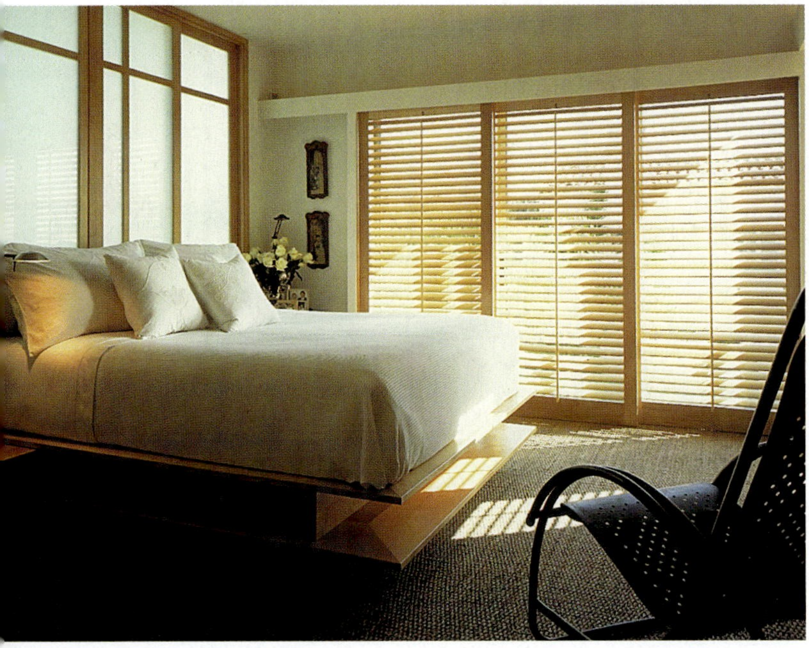

Figure 7.26 *Continued. In the master bedroom the custom bed sits in front of a set of shoji screened doors. The sliding doors can be opened to allow a full view into and through the stairwell. (Architect/Designer: Rockefeller/Hricak Architects. Photograph by David Glomb.)*

›ctangular Plan

e simplest floor plan is the rectangle. The more the plan parts from this shape, the more complicated and costly it comes. Each jog and additional roof angle mean added ex- nse, and thus more dollars per square foot of floor space. e rectangular plan is readily adapted to both traditional d contemporary exteriors. Figure 7.27 illustrates a rectan- lar plan with the following features:

- An entrance hall routes traffic to all areas of the house.
- Basic private and social zones are well defined and conveniently located.
- Plumbing is back to back in the private zone.
- Windows and openings are somewhat limited but allow adequate ventilation and light.
- The family room has easy access to the outside and is convenient to the kitchen. Although the fireplace is awkwardly placed off-center, there is room for an entertainment center on the same wall.
- Access from the kitchen and utility rooms to the outdoors and to the garage is convenient.
- An average amount of storage is provided.
- The garage door could be relocated to the side of the home. An access door to the garage could be added from the porch.

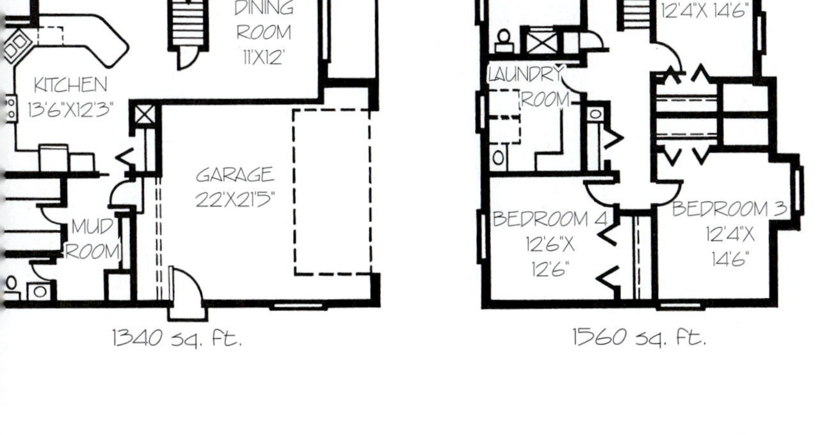

Figure 7.27 *This plan, basically rectangular in shape, has a few jogs and window extensions to provide additional interest. (Courtesy of Knight and West Construction.)*

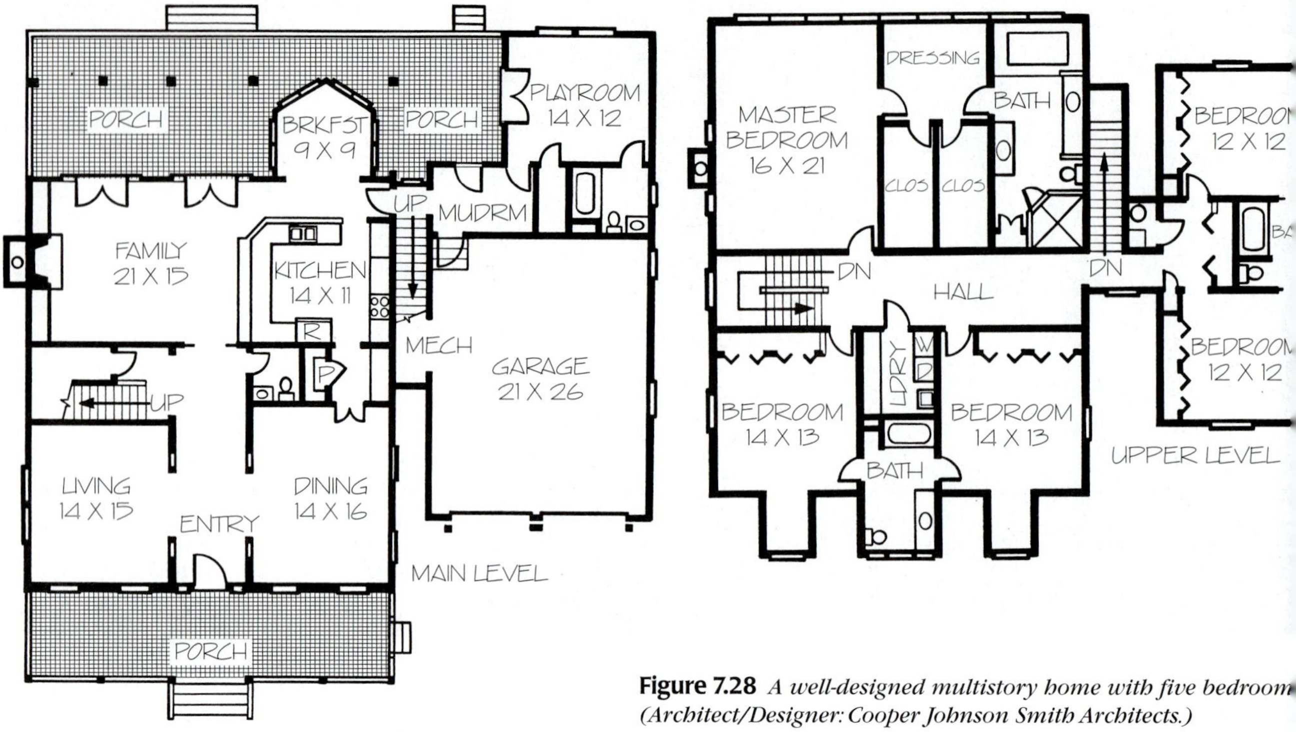

Figure 7.28 *A well-designed multistory home with five bedroom (Architect/Designer: Cooper Johnson Smith Architects.)*

Multistoried Plan

Multistoried plans provide living space on two or more levels, which allows versatile living. Features of the plan in Figure 7.28 include the following:

- The basically rectangular plan and the addition over the garage eliminate most unnecessary jogs.
- All zones are well defined on two levels.
- An entry hall channels traffic through the house.
- Doors and windows are well placed.
- Traffic lanes permit easy access. The rear stairway is pa ticularly important for a large family home.
- Closets and storage areas generally do not infringe on basic room shapes.
- The laundry room is well placed upstairs.
- As with the rectangular plan, the garage doors could b relocated to the side of the home if the lot permits.

T, U, and H Plans

The T, U, and H plans allow additional space extensions, wi advantages including more variety in room arrangement, ea separation of noisy and quiet areas, effective traffic lanes, o portunity for more efficient natural lighting and cross-venti tion, and more interesting landscaping possibiliti Disadvantages may include additional costs for heating a cooling; added expenses for foundation, roof, and jogs; a the need for a larger lot to accommodate these shapes. Figu 7.29 illustrates a U-shaped plan with the split bedroom desig

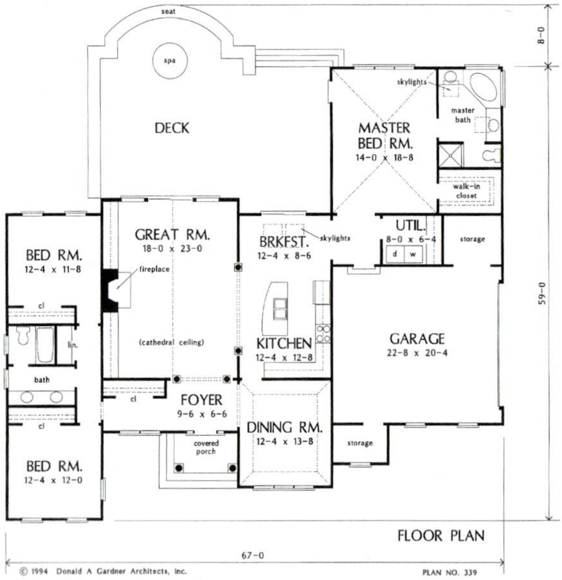

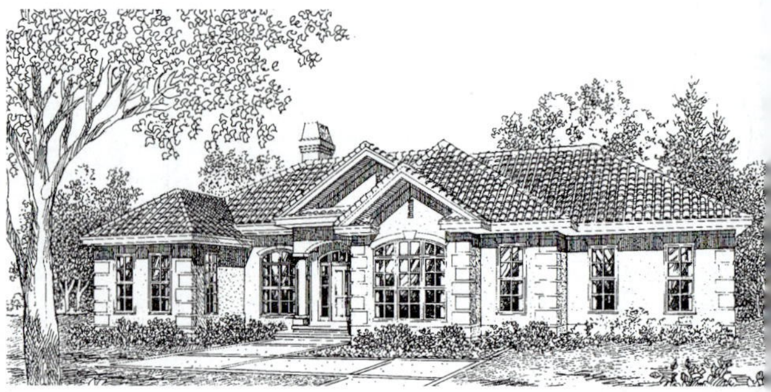

Figure 7.29 *A well-designed U-shaped plan with a split bedroom arrangement is similar to Figure 7.30, but has a more varie floor plan. (Plan #/339 ©1994, Donald A. Gardner Architects, Inc.)*

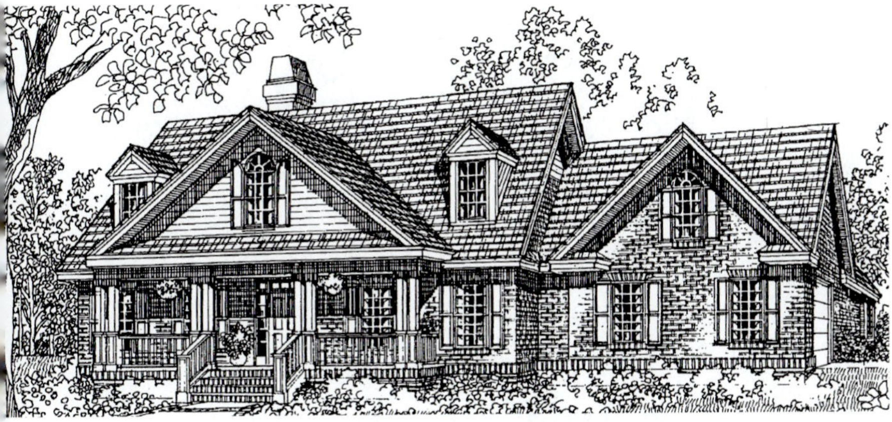

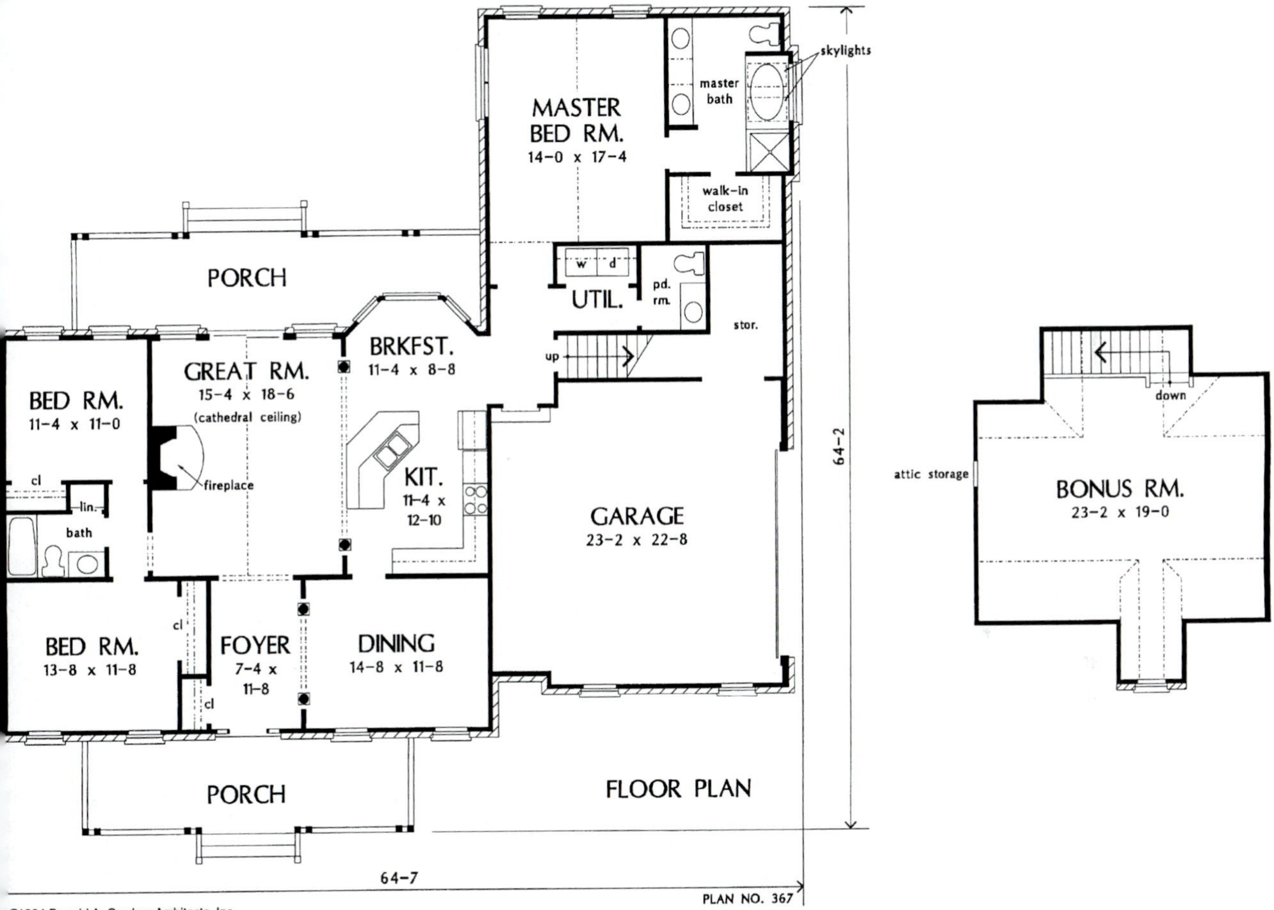

Figure 7.30 *A well-designed L-shaped plan gains character from a columned foyer. (Plan #/367 ©1994, Donald A. Gardner Architects, Inc.)*

-Shaped Plan

he L-shaped plan (Figure 7.30) allows variety in space plan-ing through an extension from the rectangular shape. Fea-ıres of this simple L-shaped plan are the following:

- The plan incorporates the basic requirements for functional space allocation.
- A central entrance hall welcomes visitors.
- The great (or family) room is combined with the kitchen for informal activities.
- The garage has a convenient access door to the kitchen. The garage door is located on the side of the home.
- The second bath is well situated between public and private zones. The third half-bath is well placed when access is needed from outside.
- The bedroom wing is away from the social areas. This split bedroom plan allows for a more private master suite.
- Closets are well placed.
- The bar in the great room is handy for quick snacks. The separate dining room invites more formal meals.
- The bonus room serves the needs of larger families or may double as an office.

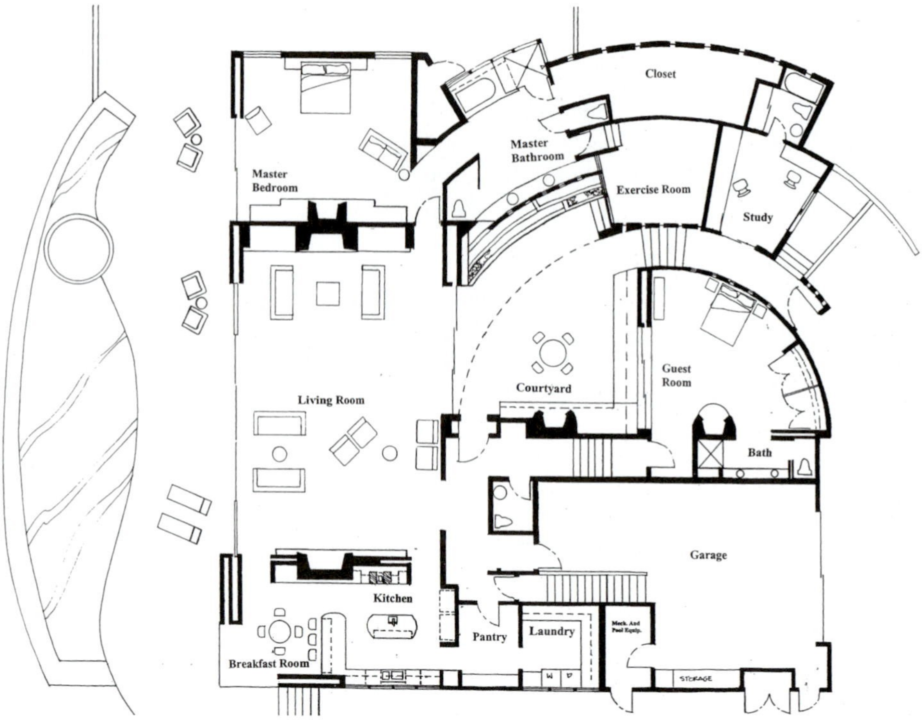

Figure 7.31 *In this atrium plan, the architect and interior designer created a unique floor plan that accentuates the ocean view. The open courtyard, used as a dining room, also allows a view to the ocean from the guest bedroom. Built-in fireplaces, curved walls, and a variety of ceiling height changes add clarity and crispness to the clean lines. The client's personal art collection has been highlighted through thoughtful placement and appropriate architectural lighting. (Designer: Mindy Meisel. Architect: Ken Ronchetti Designs. Photograph by Christopher Dow.)*

Atrium Plan

The atrium plan (Figure 7.31), with its inner courtyard, was used by the ancient Romans and is common in locations with a pleasant climate. This courtyard can be completely enclosed as the central focus of the entire house or built within a U-shape or to one side. The atrium can be open to the sky or topped with a skylight.

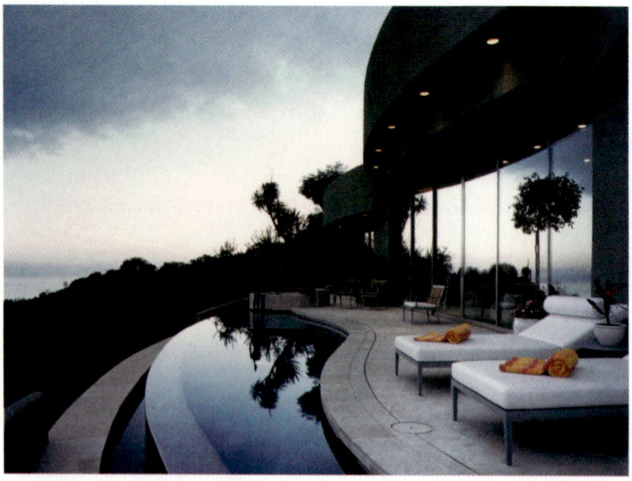

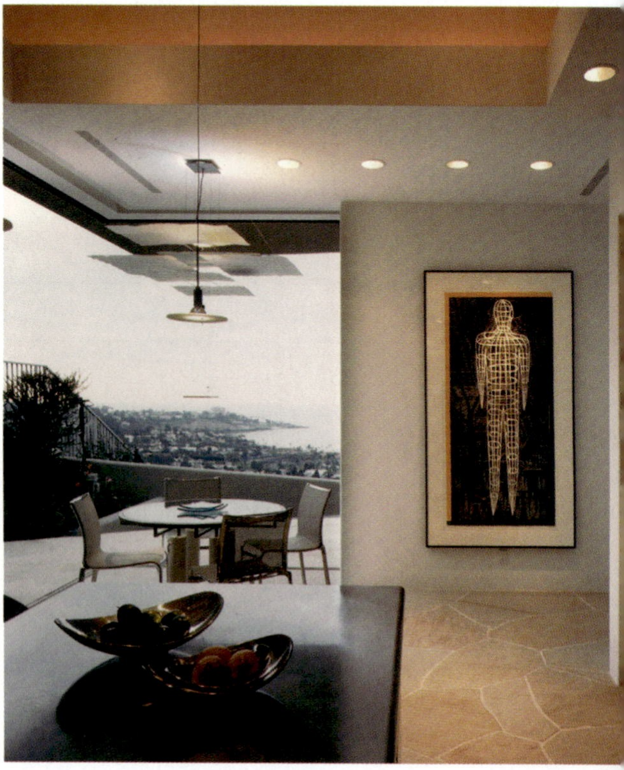

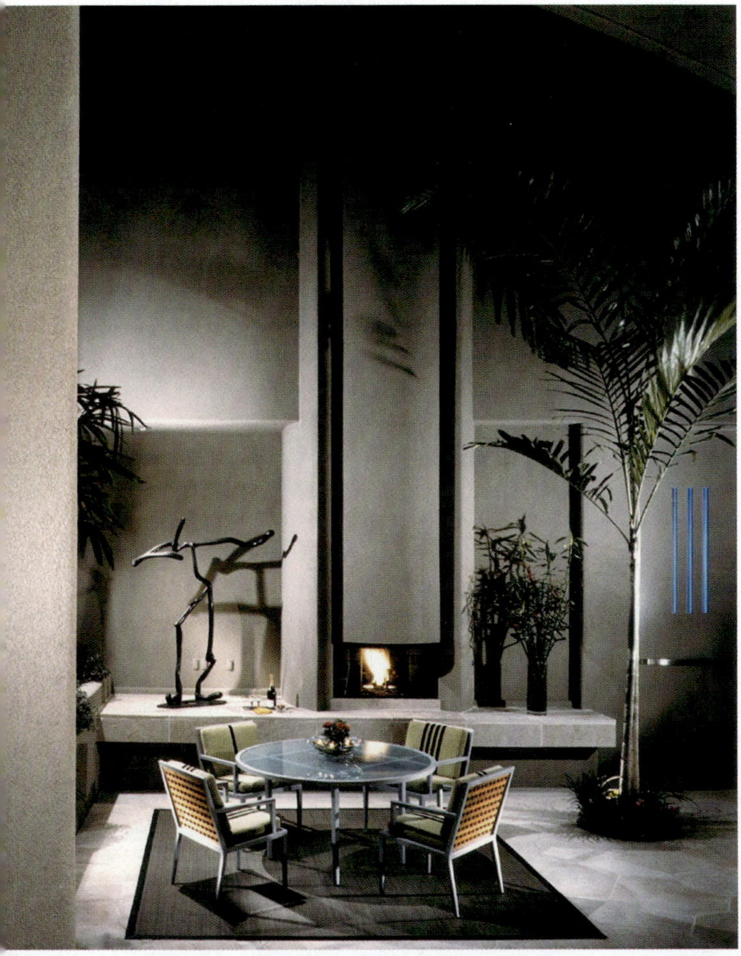

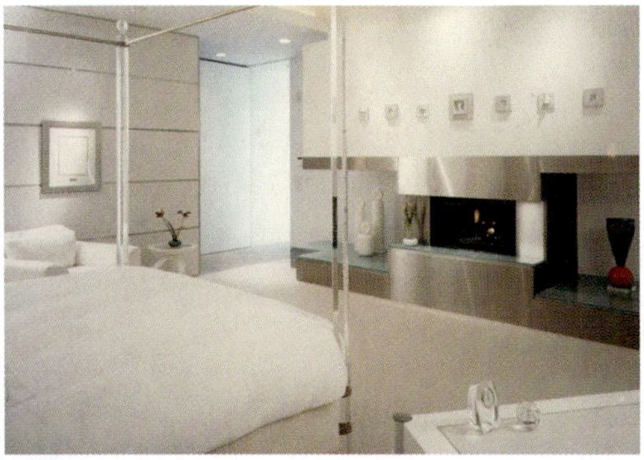

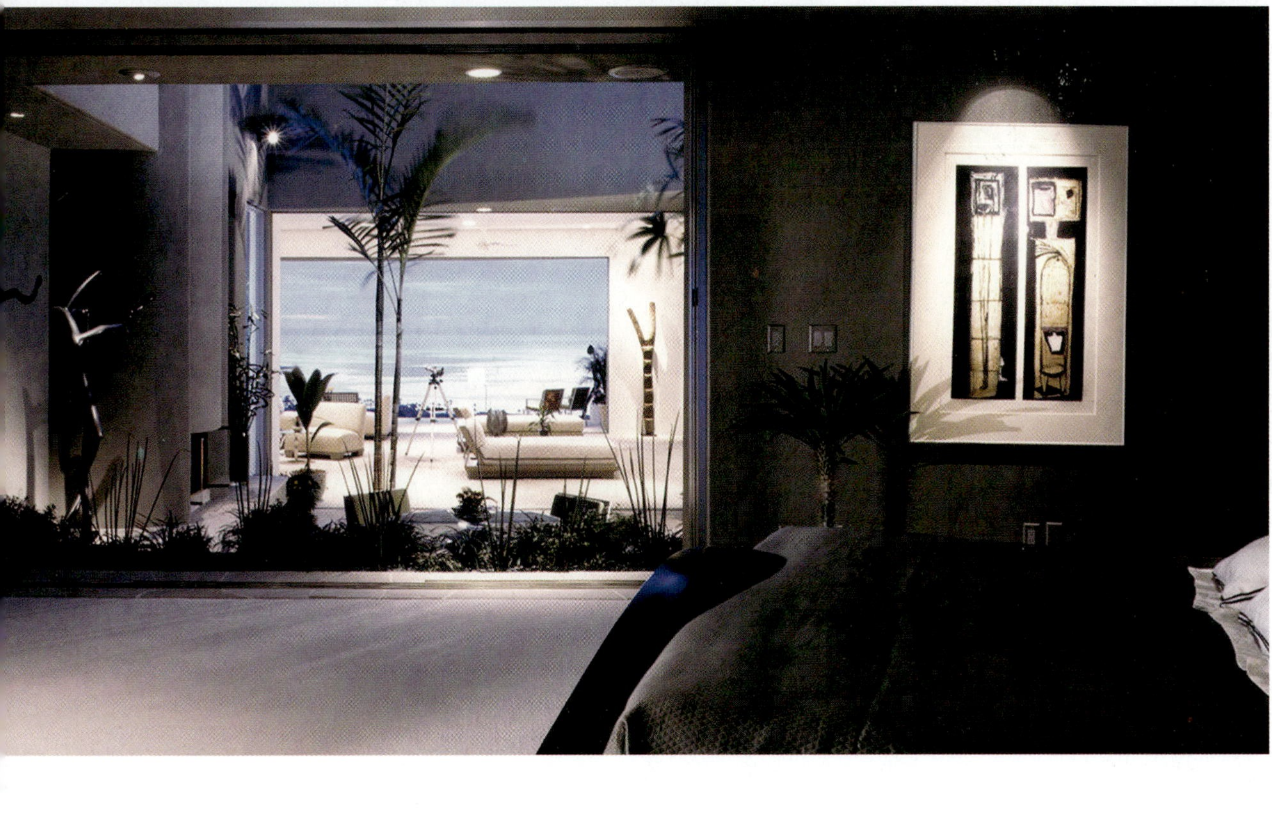

Figure 7.32 *The sweeping arrangement of these interior spaces gives fluidity and movement to the interior. Curvilinear design features are repeated in chair backs, bathroom cabinets, and ceiling details. (Architect: The Steinberg Group. Designer: Brukoff Design Associates. Photographs by Richard Barnes.)*

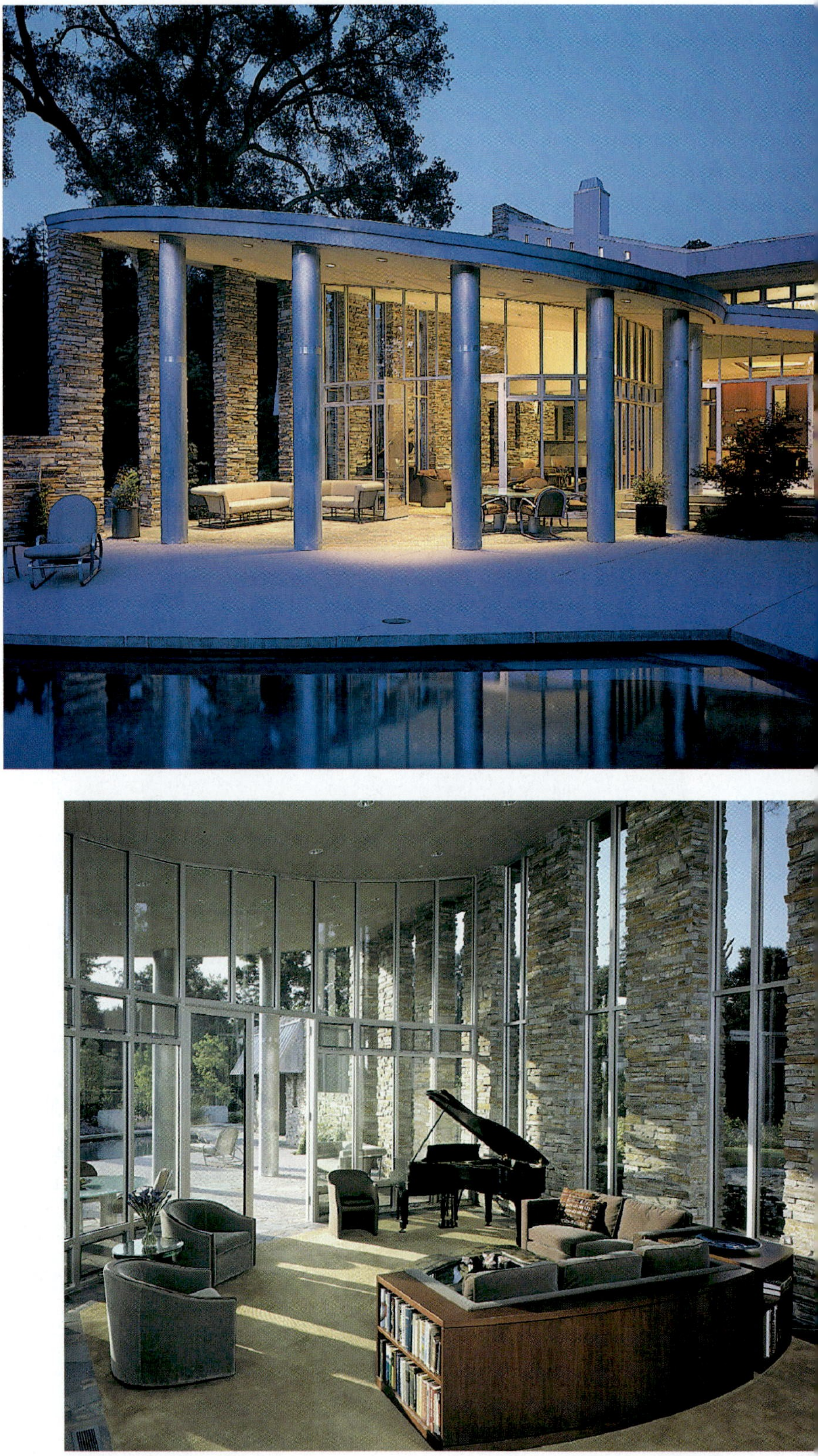

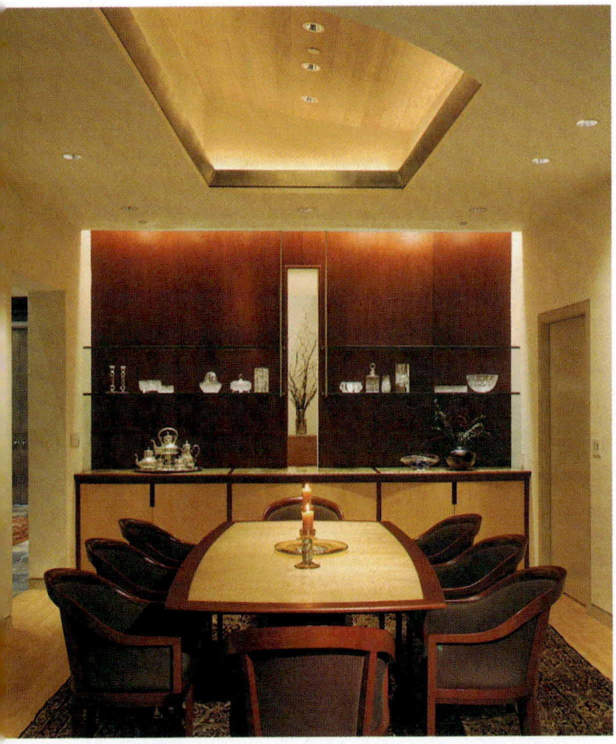

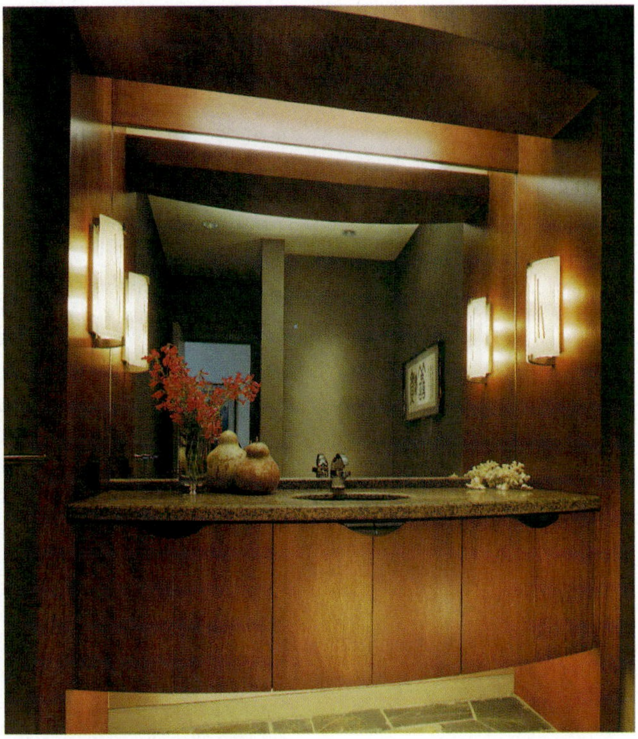

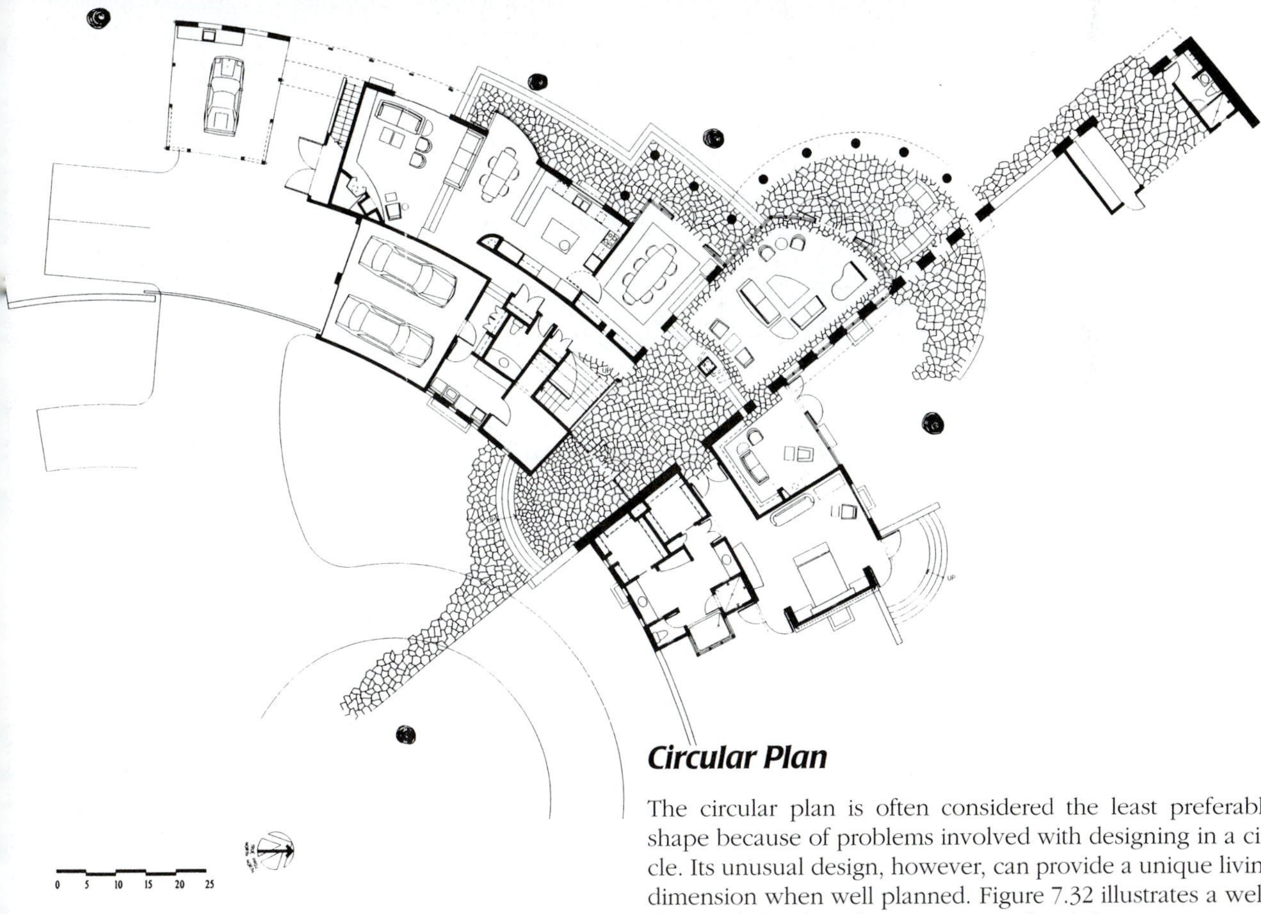

gure 7.32 *Continued. Including presentation floor plan.*

Circular Plan

The circular plan is often considered the least preferable shape because of problems involved with designing in a circle. Its unusual design, however, can provide a unique living dimension when well planned. Figure 7.32 illustrates a well-designed plan based on a portion of a circle.

Loft Plan

In urban and suburban communities, vacant warehouses, outdated factory buildings, and abandoned retail spaces are finding new life as renovated loft apartments and condominiums. A form of historic preservation (adaptive use), these renovations create unique residences. High ceilings, broad expanses, skylights, and exposed structural components characterize these spaces (Figure 7.33). These renovations also assist in urban renewal by bringing people back into downtown communities.

Figure 7.33 *In this loft renovation in New York, a substanti amount of demolition occurred before the designer began. Dropped ceilings, recessed lighting, and drywall covering brick walls were removed. The unique angular shape of the building and the 25-foot by 15-foot window formed an outstanding backdrop for the residence. Note the moveable translucent wall in the master bedroom, built-in cabinetry, and second floor retreat or guest bedroom. (Floor plan courtesy of Ike Kligerman Barkley Architects. Photograph © Durston Saylor.)*

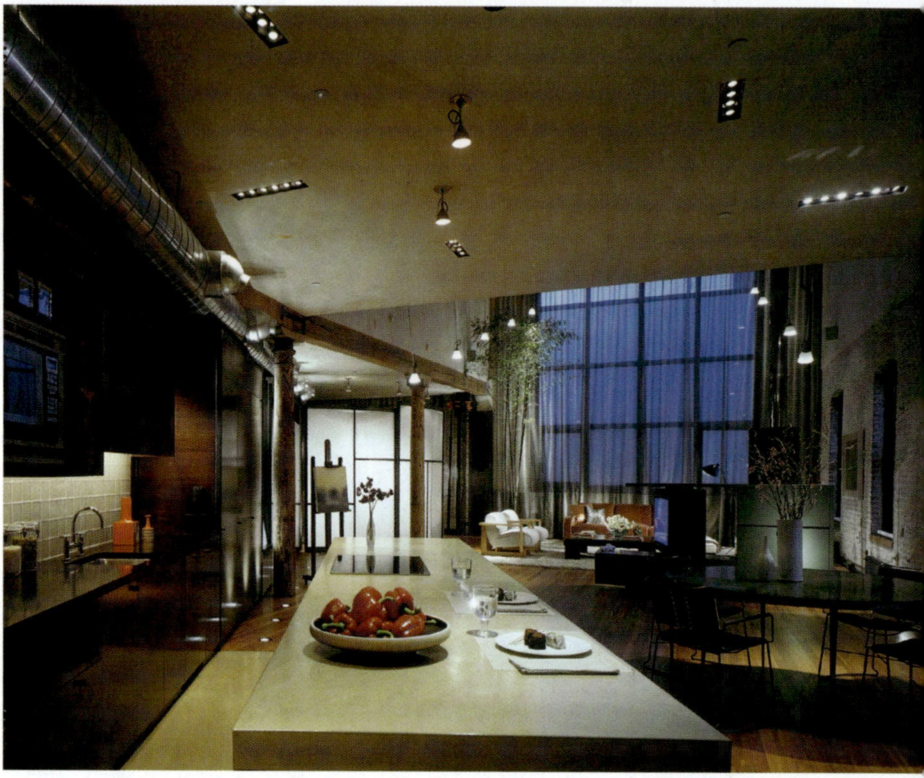

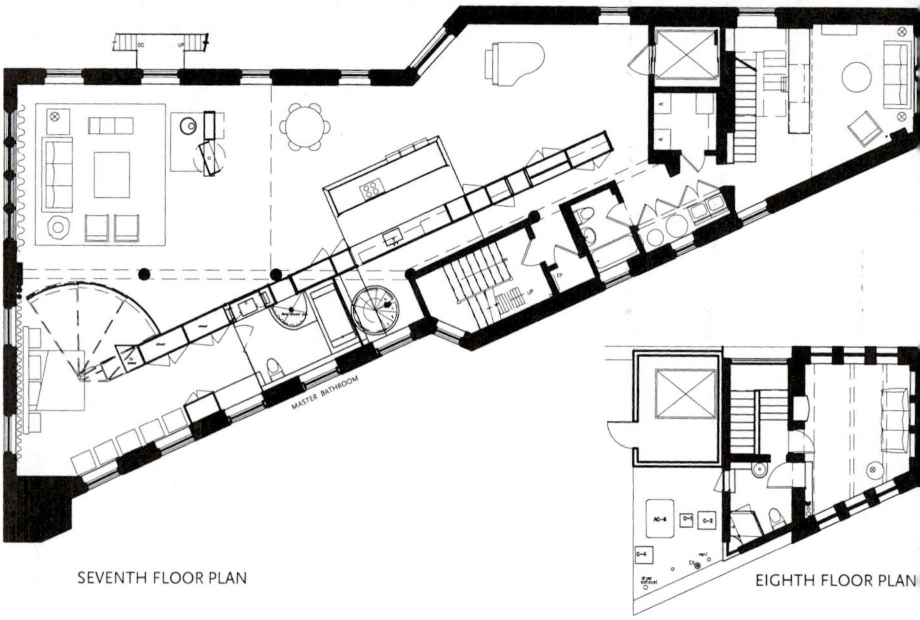

·tached and Multifamily Plans

:hitects are currently designing high-density housing units :commodating a variety of lifestyles and tastes. Main con·rns include efficient use of space, noise control, privacy, sy upkeep, security, and energy conservation. Apartment ·uses, duplexes, garden apartments, clustered condomini·ıs, and townhouses are planned inside much like single tached houses. Floor plans for attached and multifamily ·using may vary from large, two-level multiroom units to ·mpact one-room arrangements.

The one-bedroom unit in Figure 7.34 illustrates a well-·anged space that is convenient for a couple or for a sin-: person. In a *tandem arrangement,* the individual units ·n be placed side by side or one behind the other.

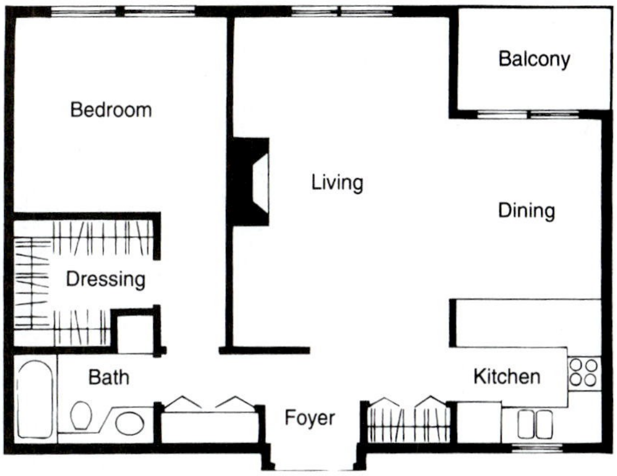

Figure 7.34 *One-bedroom unit.*

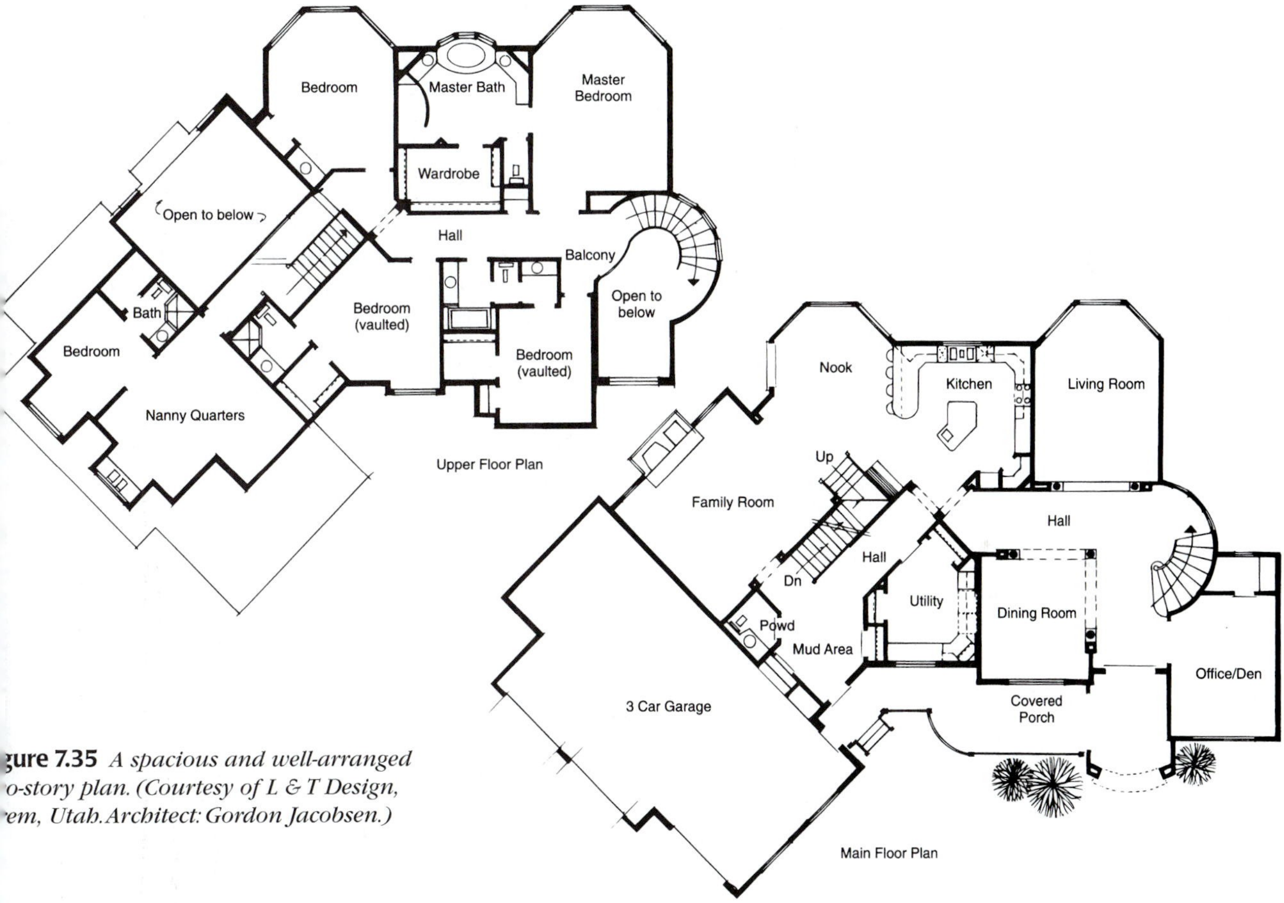

;ure 7.35 *A spacious and well-arranged ·o-story plan. (Courtesy of L & T Design, ·em, Utah. Architect: Gordon Jacobsen.)*

Well-Arranged Floor Plan

·e well-arranged plan in Figure 7.35, although expensive ·cause of numerous shapes, angles, and jogs, meets many :quirements for a successful and livable residential space. ·me positive advantages of this plan include the following:

- Well-defined and spacious public (both formal and informal) zones and private zones
- Creative and unusual arrangement of space to meet individual needs of occupants with the use of both open and closed planning
- Well-placed and convenient wall space and openings; adequate space for required furnishings
- Well-arranged traffic patterns; easy access to outdoors from social zones; spacious hallways throughout; large entry area
- Garage conveniently located to the kitchen; garage doors face away from the street side

A Poorly Arranged Floor Plan

Figure 7.36 illustrates a poorly arranged plan that includes the following undesirable features:

- Lack of an entranceway makes the living room a major traffic lane
- Poorly located front door causes traffic-pattern problems and prevents a private conversation area around the fireplace
- No privacy in eating areas
- Inconvenient placement of garage makes transporting groceries a chore
- Necessity of crossing through a bedroom to reach three-quarter bath from kitchen
- Uneconomical placement of plumbing
- Inconvenient location of washer and dryer in kitchen
- Window size and placement undesirable; window in small corner bedroom abutting the wall; windows in living room too small, providing inadequate light
- Noisy and quiet areas not adequately separated
- Private informal living space ignored; for example, television set would have to be placed in living room

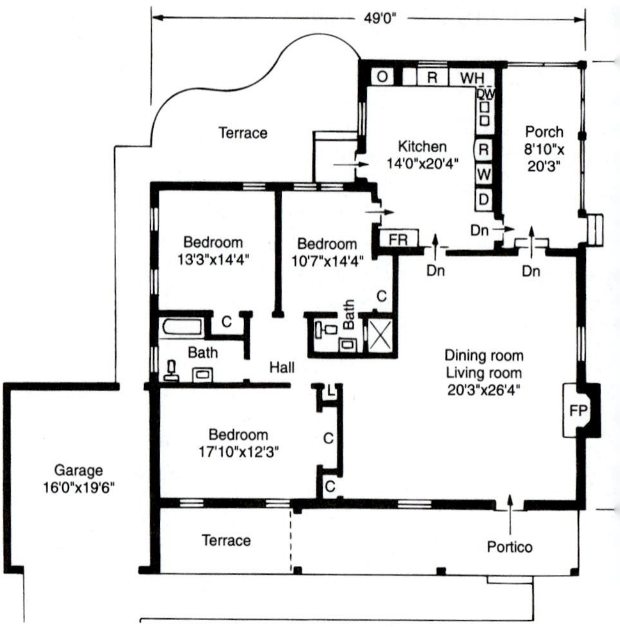

Figure 7.36 *A poorly arranged floor plan.*

Analyzing Commercial Floor Plans

Like residential floor plans, different styles of commercial office buildings meet clients' needs in varying ways. Although a detailed analysis of building styles is beyond the scope of this text, the beginning designer should be familiar with the following basic building options.

Stand-Alone Building

- Provides client with opportunity to design and own the building to meet a specific need.

Strip Shopping Center

- Spaces are leased from an owner who usually takes care of maintenance and utilities.
- Allows drop-by customers easy access.

Mall Location

- Benefits are the same as above, but encourages even more drop-by customers.
- Owner may find that the design and operating hours are restrictive.

Multistoried Building

- Clients may occupy a partial floor, an entire floor, or several floors within the building.
- Restroom facilities are centrally located and maintained by others.
- Cleaning services may be provided by the owner of the building.
- Exterior building design may add prestige to the firm. Buildings may have multifaceted walls that allow for many corner offices. Curved and angled walls add inte est and style to the interior.

In the accompanying design scenarios, pages 234–240, t clients are considering relocating to a multistory, histo building. In the first scenario, the client wants to use t space for a residence. In the second, the client wants to u the space for a commercial real estate office. Both clien floor plans will be developed from programming inform tion. As part of the design process, the information will gathered, the facts analyzed, and several ideas and plans w be generated from this information. Once a solution h been selected, a final plan will be developed.

Summary

Analyzing furnishing options, grouping them into areas, a synthesizing those areas into zones begins the space pla ning process. Sketching and resketching various options the essence of analyzing space usage that eventually leads the design of the *volume* of space. Figure 7.37 graphically lustrates this process.

Designers are fluent in the use of space and understa the relationship of space to volume. Space planning is sin lar to putting together a puzzle; however, there is no pred termined solution. Designers create the solution to fit t design parameters unique to each client.

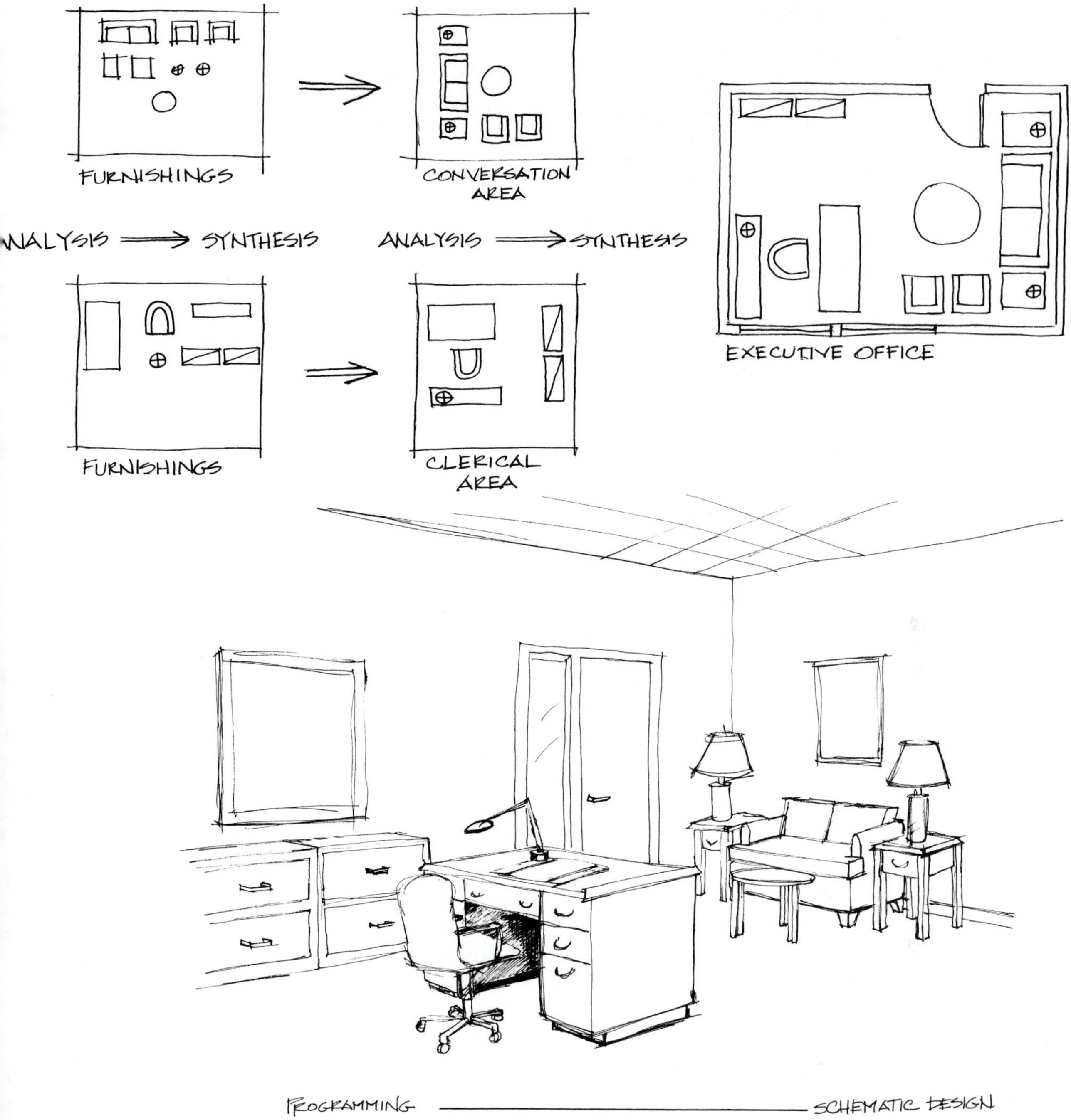

gure 7.37 *In the space planning process, furnishings are analyzed based on the ient's needs. The furnishings are grouped together in specific activity areas, lowing for ample passageways. Activity areas are then analyzed and grouped gether in rooms. Through the use of the design process and the elements and inciples of design the volume of space is composed.*

Design Scenario

RESIDENTIAL LOFT & COMMERCIAL REAL ESTATE OFFICE

In these two design scenarios, a space in a historic building will be converted into a residential loft and then into a commercial real estate office. The two projects illustrate how a designer analyzes and then synthesizes the client's spatial needs.

In the first scenario, a single woman is looking into purchasing space in a historic building that she could convert into a residential loft. She recognizes that she will not be allowed to move any windows, exterior walls, or infringe upon the corridor. She was also told by the listing agent that there were plumbing restrictions. Not wanting to sign the official papers until she knew whether her space needs could be met, she placed a deposit on the space and then hired a designer to analyze her residence's spatial needs and develop a floor plan for the residence. After meeting with the client, the designer determined the following programming requirements:

Entry

- Should feel like a foyer
- Needs closet

Living Area

- Minimum seating for four
- To be used as a guest bedroom
- Exterior view required
- View to television from all four seats
- Bar sink

Dining

- Can be open to kitchen and living room
- Seating for four
- Needs exterior view

Kitchen

- Major appliances, refrigerator, stove, and sink
- Needs dishwasher and microwave
- Needs pantry

Master Bedroom

- Minimum queen size bed
- Storage allowance for clothing
- Seating/reading chair
- Shelf for reading book—minimum 20 lineal feet
- Needs exterior view
- Closet for clothing and miscellaneous storage

Bath

- Needs to accommodate needs of guest and owner

Laundry Area

- Washer and dryer (could be stacked)

Office Area

- Room for computer, printer, fax, and files

Using the space planning guidelines for specific activity are[a] (as discussed in Chapters 6 and 7), the designer developed th[e] spatial needs assessment (Figure DS7.1). The designer allocate[d] 20 percent additional square footage for hallways and circula[-] tion areas.

The designer now needed a floor plan of the proposed ne[w] tenant space (Figure DS7.2). Because the total needed squa[re]

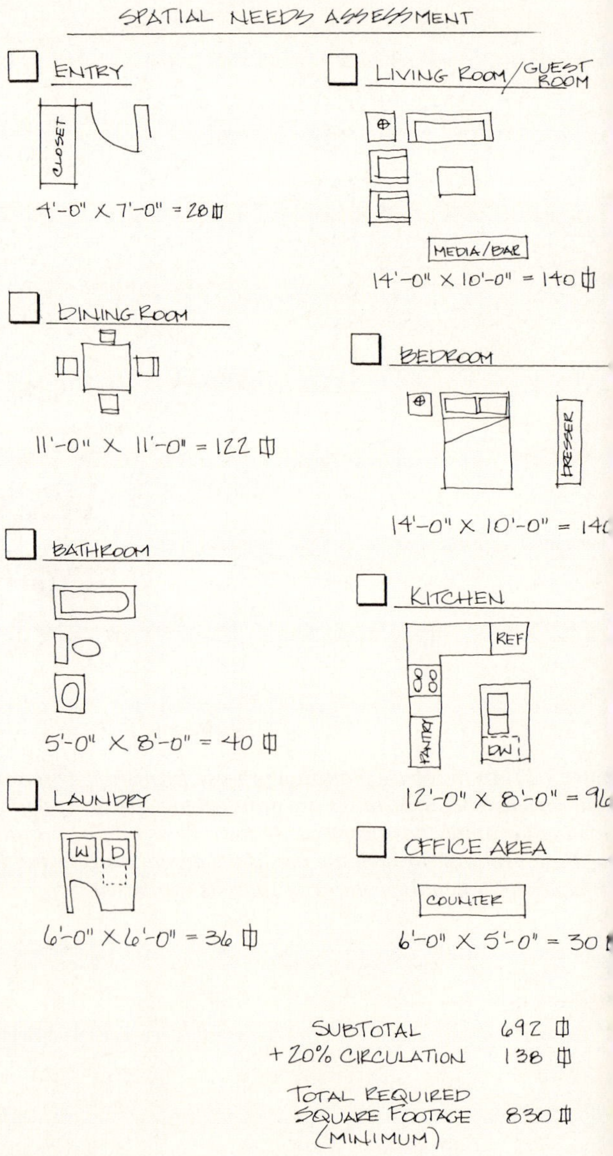

Figure DS7.1 *Residential spatial needs assessment.*

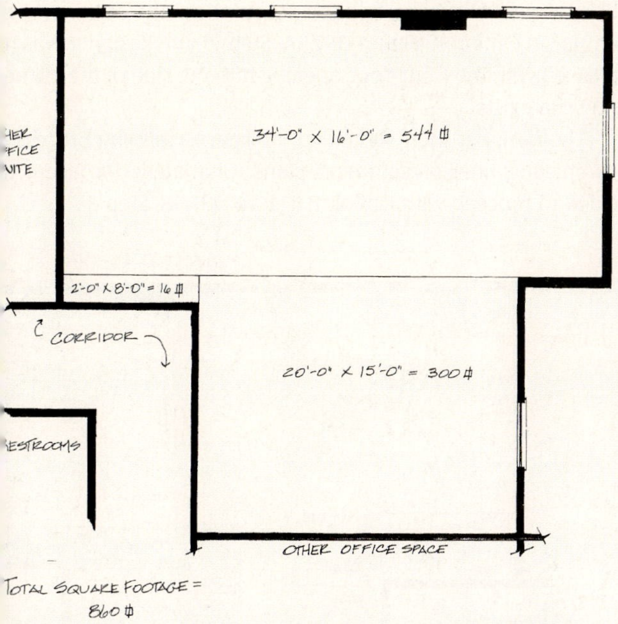

gure DS7.2 *Proposed tenant space. The designer determined at the space contained approximately 860′. Other offices or nants were located on either side of the proposed space. A ntral core area contained a public restroom and elevator.*

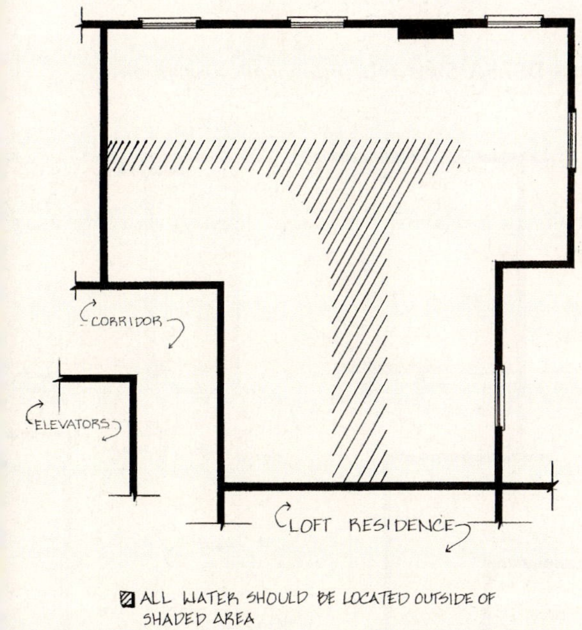

gure DS7.3 *In order to allow for appropriate slopes in ack water plumbing lines, all toilet fixtures needed to be cated outside of the shaded area.*

footage, 830′, was less than the existing 860′, the designer knew the client's request for the various activity areas could be accommodated in the space.

The designer also needed to know where black water plumbing lines could be located. The purchasing contract specified that all black water plumbing lines had to be located within 8′ of the corridor or an exterior wall. Figure DS7.3 was therefore created to indicate the appropriate plumbing locations.

Additionally, the designer needed to analyze the relationships between the various activity areas. For instance, because there is only one entry to the residence, the designer recognized this needed to be near the kitchen and the living room. Also, the bathroom needed to be visually screened from the living room. Figure DS7.4 illustrates the bubble diagram developed for this project.

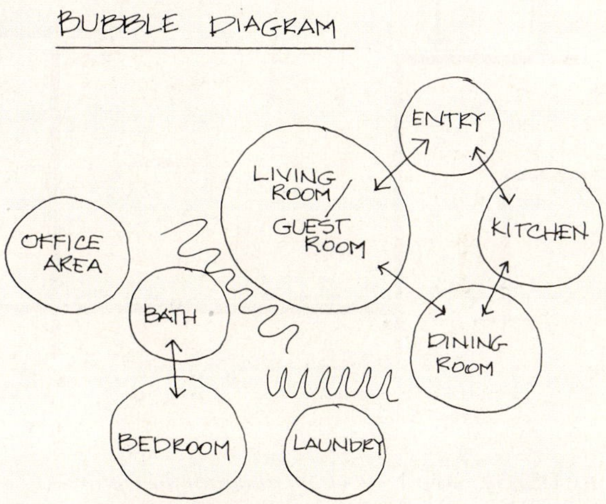

Figure DS7.4 *Residential bubble diagram. Relationships are indicated by proximity of the bubbles. Arrows indicate stronger, direct flow requirements. The wavy lines indicate areas that need privacy or screening.*

Once this preliminary information has been obtained, the designer is now prepared to begin the synthesis of this information. Beginning with blocking diagrams, the designer "blocks" in the various activity areas and decides to further develop both Option A (Figure DS7.5A, Step 1) and Option B (Figure DS7.5B, Step 1).

The next step (Figures DS7.5A and B, Step 2) illustrates the process of defining the walls. The designer indicated with notations areas of concern, or good points about the option. For e ample, in Option A (Figure DS7.5A, Step 2), the designer was n pleased with the front door opening into the side of the kitche no vista exists.

The designer then continued the space planning process completing final presentation plans. Ultimately, the client d cided to proceed with Option B (Figure DS7.5B, Step 3).

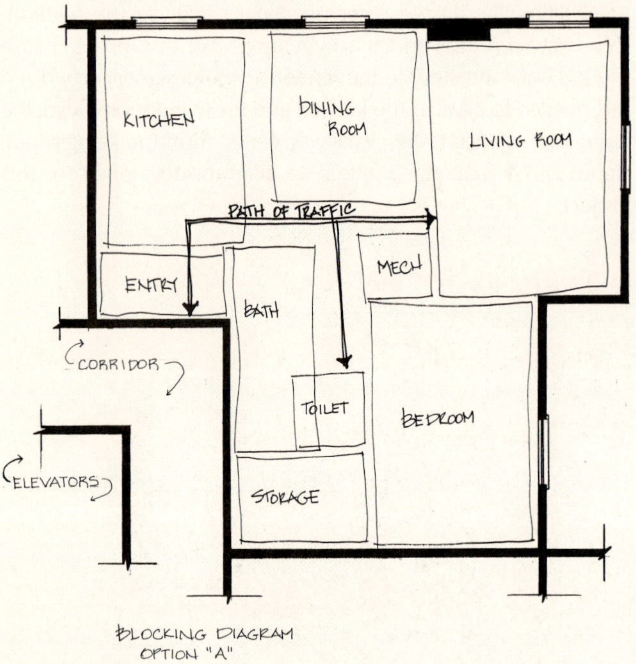

Figure DS7.5A, Step 1 *Blocking diagram for Option A.*

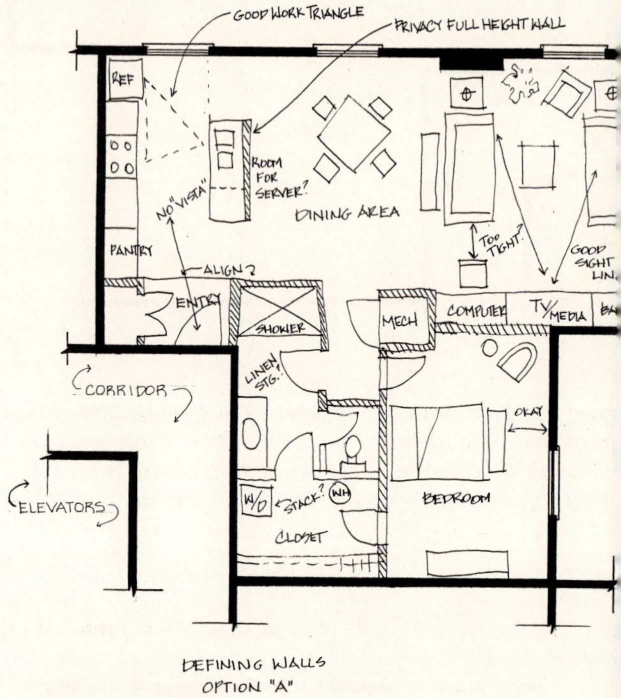

Figure DS7.5A, Step 2 *Defining walls for Option A.*

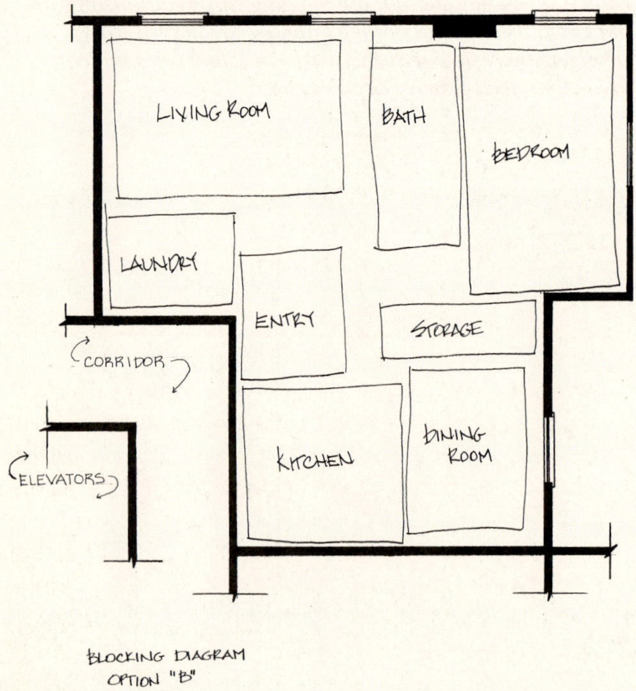

Figure DS7.5B, Step 1 *Blocking diagram for Option B.*

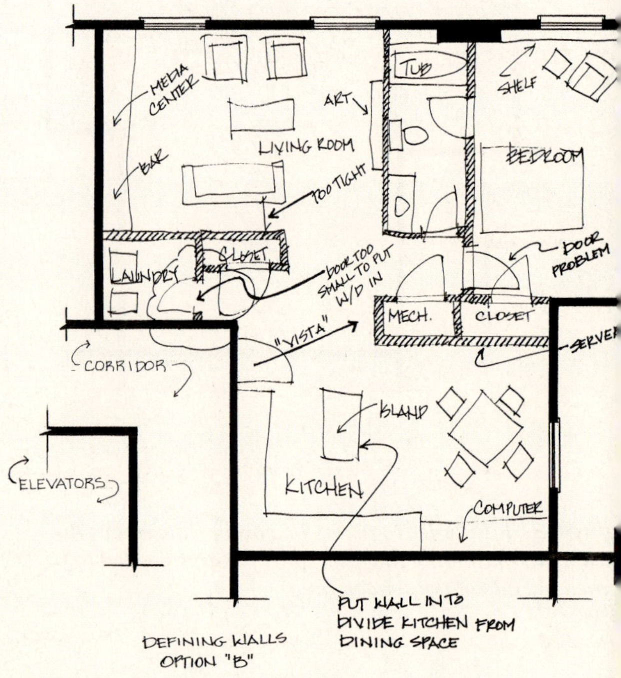

Figure DS7.5B, Step 2 *Defining walls for Option B.*

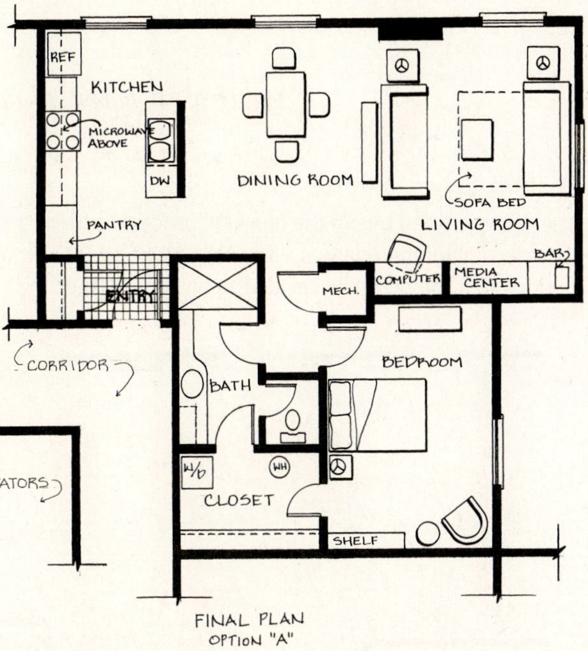

gure DS7.5A, Step 3 *Final plan for Option A as presented to e client.*

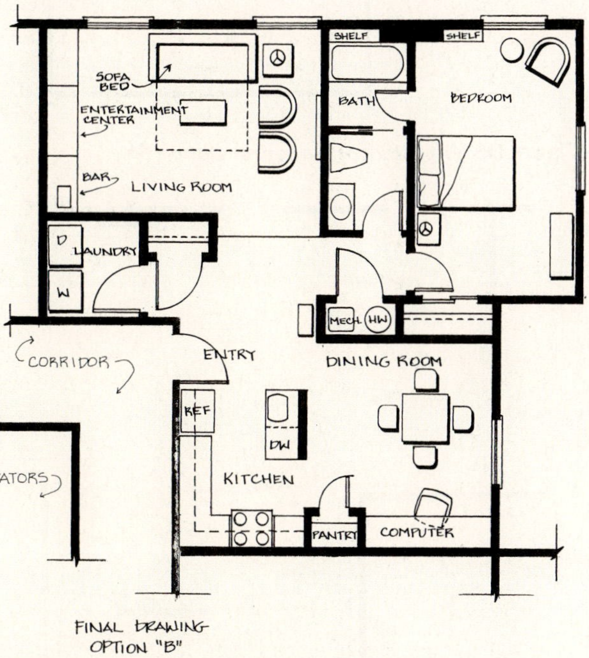

gure DS7.5B, Step 3 *Final plan for Option B as presented the client. This is the plan selected by the client.*

COMMERICAL REAL ESTATE OFFICE

In this second design scenario, a commercial real estate firm specializing in historic properties has found tenant space in a historic building (Figure DS7.2). A designer was hired to analyze whether the space would meet the firm's needs. As with the residential loft client, the designer first met with the real estate firm's employees and gathered the following programming requirements:

Reception Area

- Needs secretary/reception desk with room for computer/printer, typewriter, and 200 linear inches for filing/ telephone and typewriter
- Needs room for four guest chairs
- Receptionist must be able to receive guests, and guests should not see the workings of the office when seated
- Receptionist must work closely with president

President/Marketing Representative

- Needs desk, credenza, and two other chairs for seating
- Needs some bookshelves and wants a window

Three Assistant Marketing Representatives

- Need office space for desk, credenza, and two other chairs for seating
- Need some bookshelves and window exposure

Conference Room

- Needs comfortable seating for six
- Needs display area to show presentation boards and facility to show slides and videos of real estate

Supply Room/Breakroom

- Needs access to deliveries, copy machine, small refrigerator, counter for postage machine
- Needs cabinets for storage of paper and stationery supplies, coffee, etc.
- Needs to be close to receptionist

The designer then develops a spatial needs assessment based upon the client's requests (DS7.6).

After comparing the existing square footage, 860′, with the requested needs, 877′, the designer informed the client that the space would be a bit tight but that all requests could be accommodated.

Because the firm was new and presently had only three employees (but planned to add two more assistant marketing representatives in the next three to five years), the prospective owner requested that the designer proceed with the space planning analysis.

In order to better assimilate the client's needs and the relationships between activity areas, the designer developed a compatibility matrix (Figure DS7.7) and a bubble diagram (Figure DS7.8).

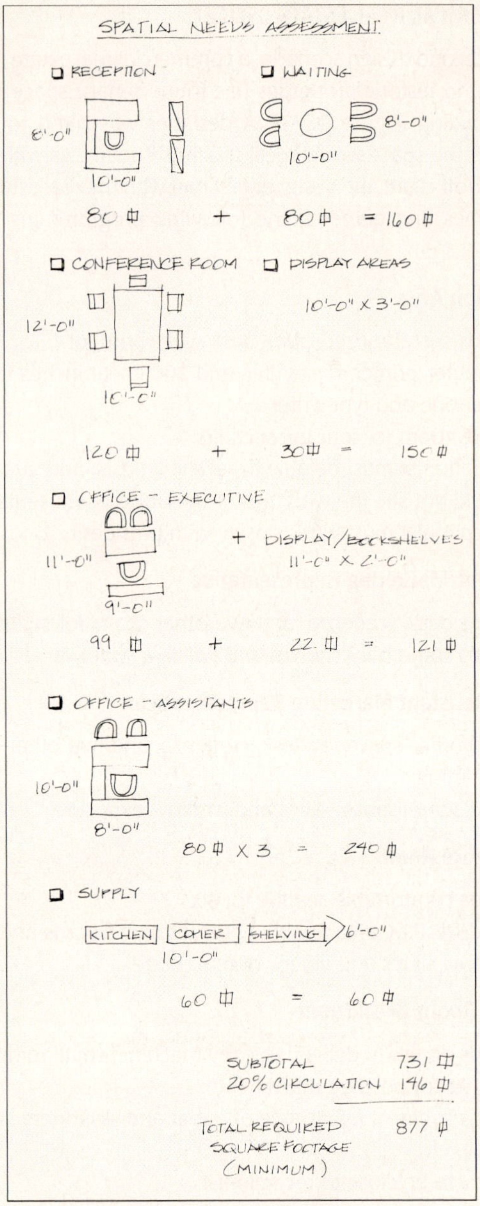

Figure DS7.6 *Spatial needs assessment.*

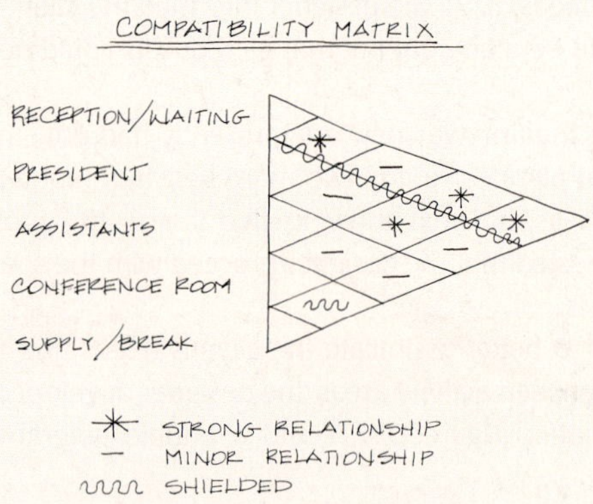

Figure DS7.7 *Compatibility matrix.*

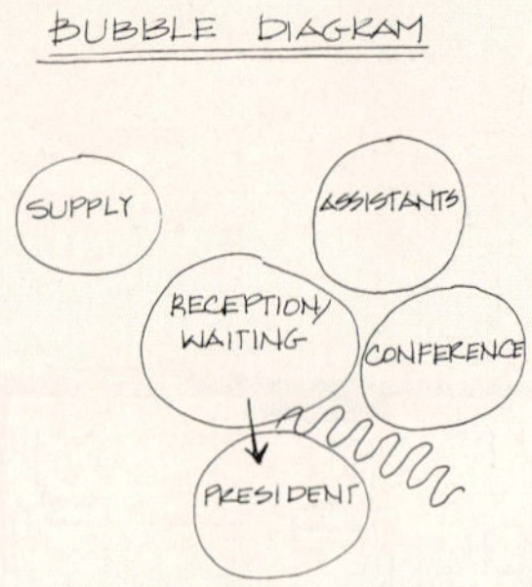

Figure DS7.8 *Bubble diagram.*

Blocking

The designer then began the blocking process as the first step the space planning analysis. Figures DS7.9A and B illustrate tw options that the designer decided to develop further.

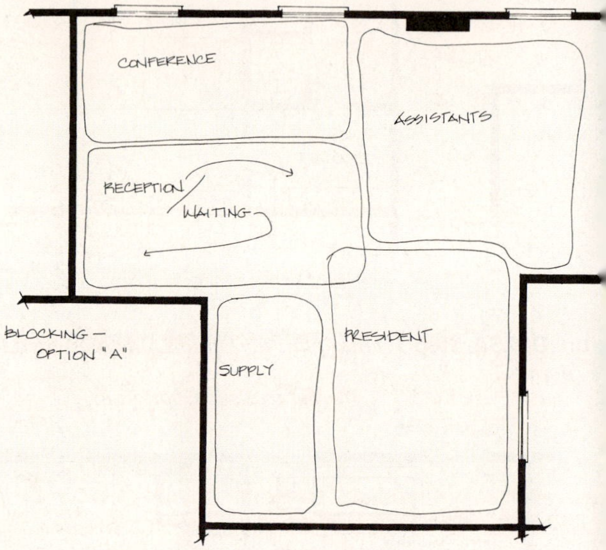

Figure DS7.9A *Blocking diagram Option A.*

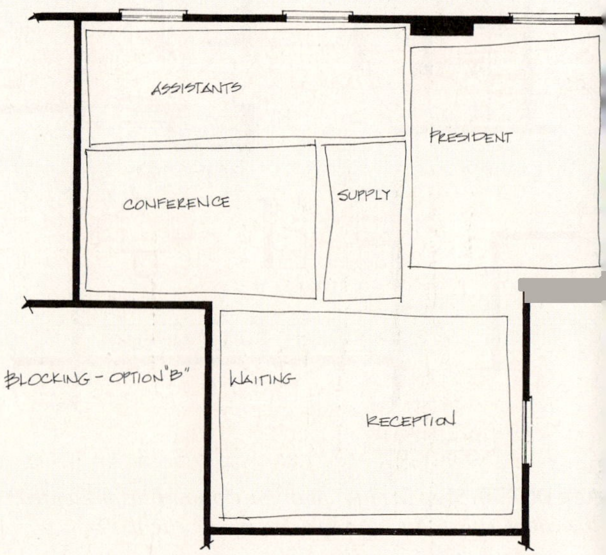

Figure DS7.9B *Blocking diagram Option B.*

tion A

fining walls in this commercial setting proved to be more of a allenge than it was for the residential loft. For Option A, the designer worked through three different defining wall stages before stopping at Step 4 (Figures DS7.10A, Steps 1–4). Throughout this process, the designer added notes to the plan indicating areas of concern.

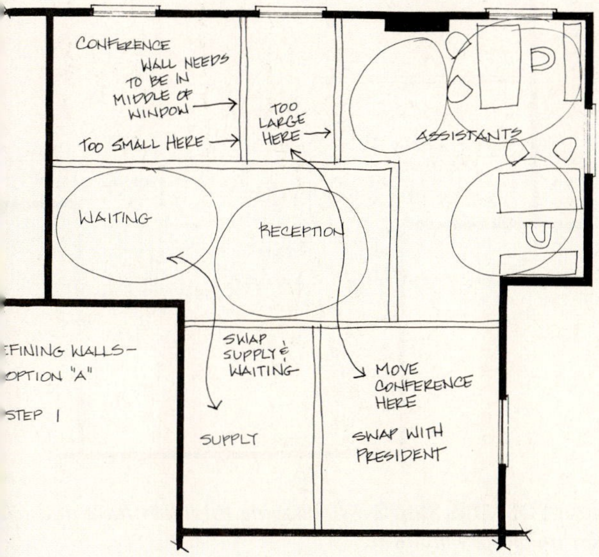

gure DS7.10A, Step 1 *Defining walls for Option A.*

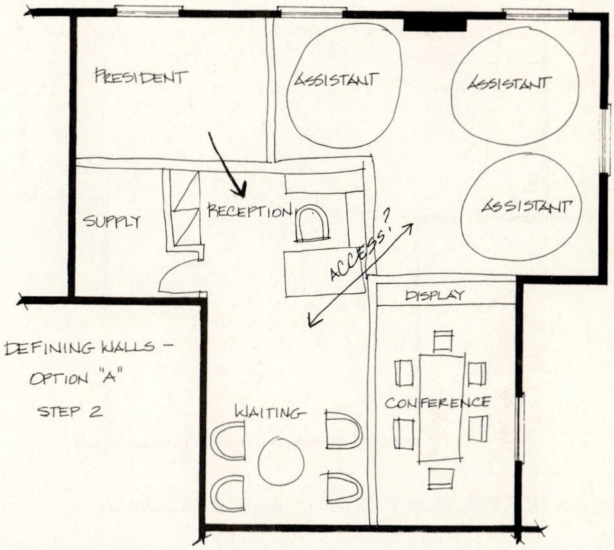

Figure DS7.10A, Step 2 *Analyzing wall placement for Option A.*

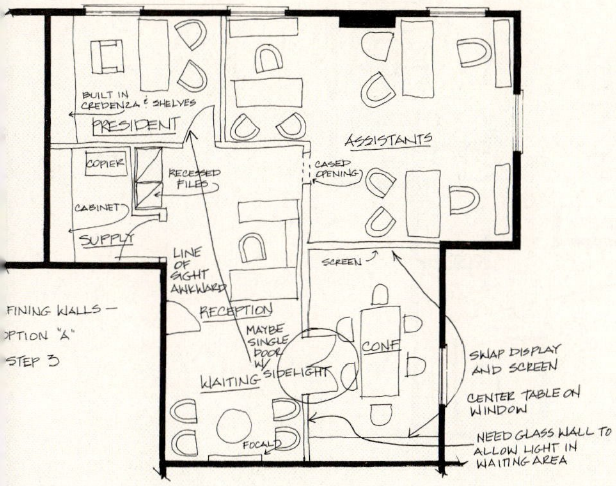

gure DS7.10A, Step 3 *Further analysis and refinement of tion A.*

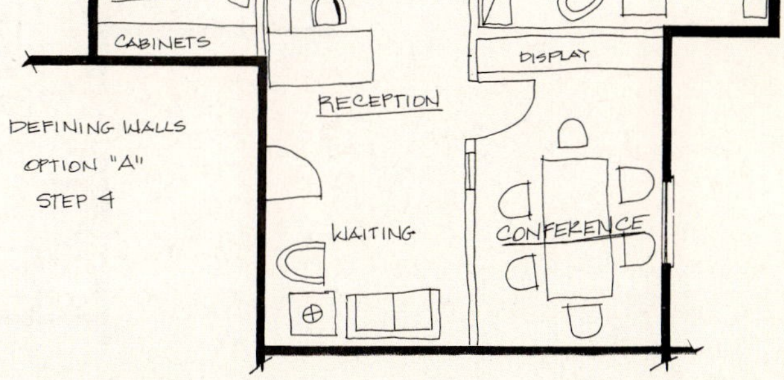

Figure DS7.10A, Step 4 *Establishing final furniture and wall placement for Option A.*

Option B

Defining walls for Option B proved to be less complicated. The designer developed Steps 1 and 2 (Figures DS7.10B, Steps 1 and 2) and decided to proceed with a presentation furniture plan, Figure DS7.11, to share with the client.

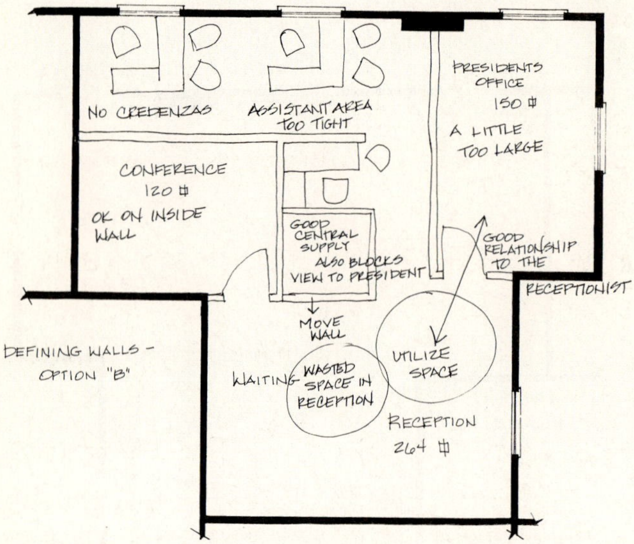

Figure DS7.10B, Step 1 *Defining walls for Option B.*

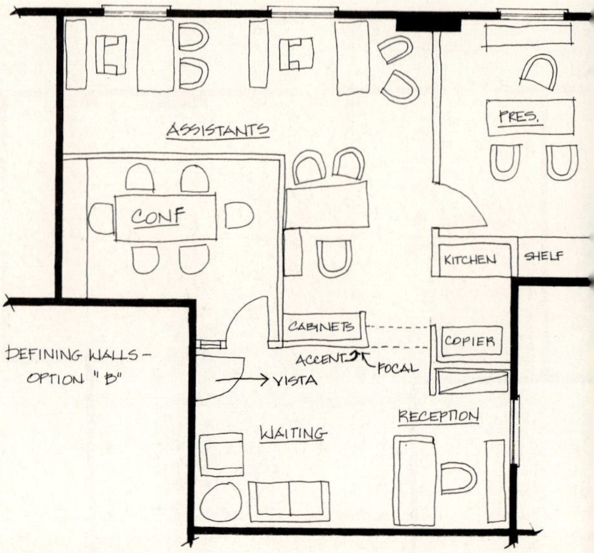

Figure DS7.10B, Step 2 *Establishing final furniture and wa placement for Option B.*

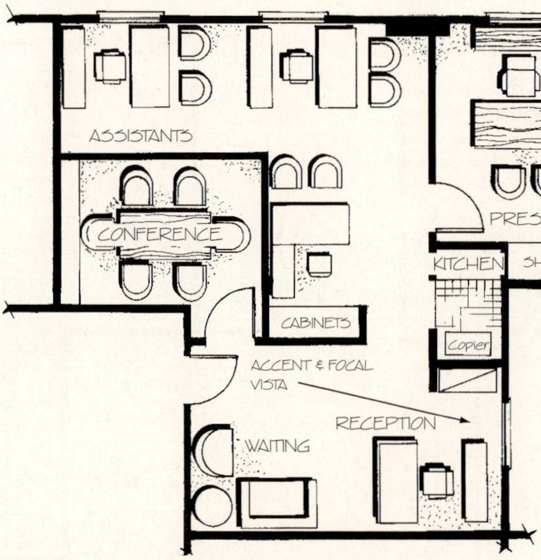

Figure DS7.11 *Final presentation drawing.*

Furnishings, Fabrics, and Background Elements

PART V

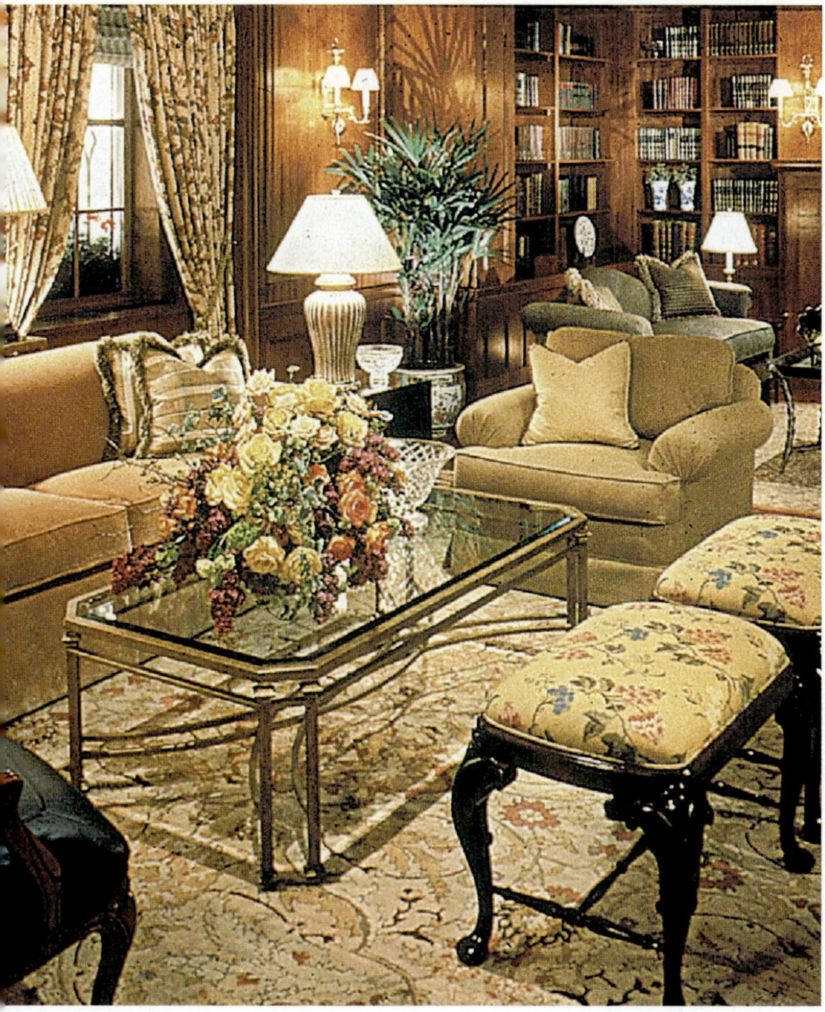

ure V.1 *Designers created an "18th-century, membership only" atmosphere in Sheraton Russell Hotel, Manhattan. The exquisite wood paneling, fringed ows, and fine rugs contribute to the living room's exclusive ambiance. (Interior Brennan Beer Gorman Monk/Interiors. Photograph by Jim Raycroft and hony P. Albarello.)*

Have nothing in your house that you do not know to be useful or believe to be beautiful.

—William Morris

art V encompasses five chapters that review the options available urniture, accessory, and textile se- ion as well as the material and sh options available for floors, ceil- s, and walls. The final chapter elab- tes on door, window, and fireplace ions. In all interiors, these varied nponents must work together to ate a harmonious, unified environ- nt and to set the mood for the room ure V.1).

As was discussed in Chapter 1, the goals of design include *function and the human factor, aesthetics,* and *economics and ecology.* Designers have the same goals when selecting furnishings, fabrics, and background elements.

Function

The interior materials and components in an environment must meet

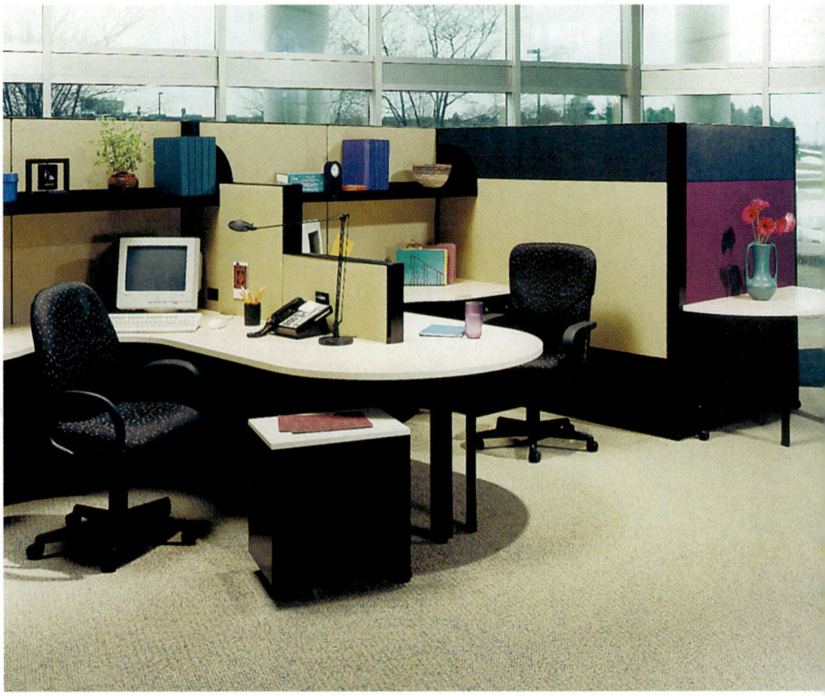

Figure V.2 *Quality Steelcase products were used to furnish this open office. Special attention was given to employees' ergonomic needs. (Designer: Steelcase, Inc. Courtesy of Steelcase, Inc.)*

the functional needs of the space. The functional needs of the space are intermingled with the *human factor, durability, safety,* and *acoustics.*

The Human Factor

In the selection of all interior materials, designers must be aware of the client's needs in order to meet the goal of the human factor. Different individuals require different furnishings to complete the same task. Meeting the needs of the specific individual is particularly important when selecting furniture. Like clothing, what fits one client does not necessarily work with the next. In furniture, one size does not fit all. Designers must pay special attention to the ergonomic needs of the client (see Part IV, "Space").

For example, in order to make it easy to get up, elderly clients may require chairs with high armrests and firm cushions. Younger clients may desire overstuffed sofas for lounging. Commercial office clients may require chairs that can be adjusted to suit various employees (Figure V.2). Suitable furniture may be required to meet the functional needs of users who are physically challenged.

Durability

Products selected must be durable; this is particularly important for flooring. White carpet may look great in a master bedroom suite, but would be a disaster in a reception area, for example.

Equally important is the durability of wall finishes and fabrics. Washable wallcoverings, for instance, are critically important in public corridors, but may not be as important in a library. Fabrics must also meet cleaning and durability requirements.

Furniture must withstand expected wear and tear. Residential dining room chairs may look good in a commercial conference room, but without proper bracing, they will quickly begin to fall apart. File cabinets that may be appropriate for occasional residential office filing will not withstand the rigors of an accounting office.

Safety

Products must also meet safety and fire regulations. Designers must consider regulations relating to flame resistance, slip resistance, and accessibility in order to meet functional requirements.

Acoustics

Textiles, wallcoverings, and floor c
erings greatly affect the acoustics
an interior environment. These ma
rials serve as a transition, soften
the edges (both physically and vi
ally) from the hard architectural e
ments. Proper selection is particula
relevant in restaurant design, wh
the noise from clattering dishes in
kitchen is not desirable in the din
room (Figure V.3). Other areas of c
cern include private offices, stud
libraries, classrooms, and confere
areas. Theatres and recital halls requ
a collaborative effort with acousti
engineers.

Aesthetics

The selection of the furnishings, f
rics, and background materials m
be in line with the basic princip
and elements of design; however,
client's personal preferences also m
be considered. Just as the function
the room conformed to the hun
factor, so must the aesthetics. Cli
preferences are particularly import
in residential design. The designer m
not only listen to the client's requ

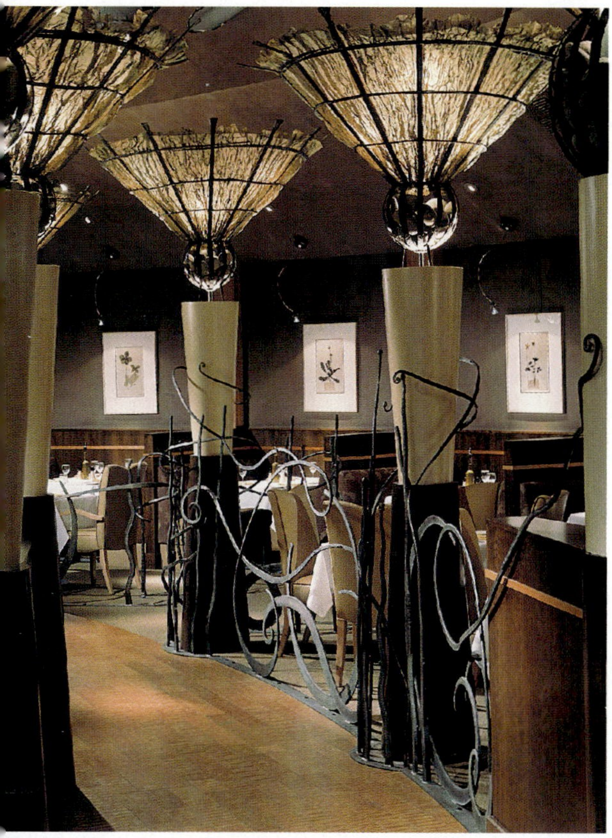

ure V.3 *Unique torchères and custom ironwork add rmth and vibrant character in this restaurant. Suspended ent lighting focuses on a series of botanicals. Control of wanted noise is critical in this upscale environment. chitect/Designer: Engstrom Design Group and To Design. otograph by Andrew Kramer AIA.)*

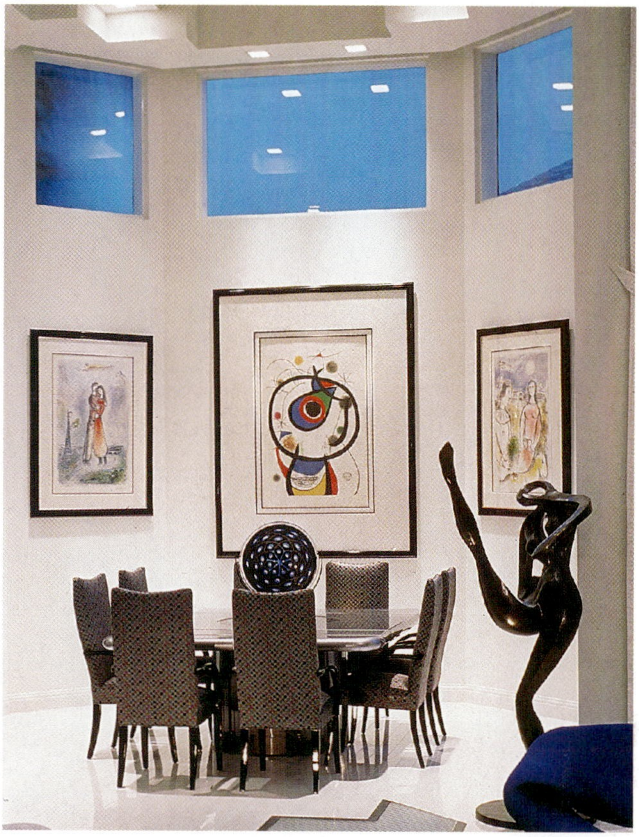

Figure V.4 *The designers worked very closely with the clients to create a dining space encircled by art. The custom glass inset flooring makes a visual delineation between the dining room and the living room (Figure 8.1 shows the adjoining living room). (Designer: Stevenson Design Group. Photograph by Robert Brantley.)*

: also observe the client, ideally his or her personal surroundings gure V.4).

The color, texture, and feel of the shes and materials help to define character of the space. Each comnent of the design needs to support overall theme and architectural kground of the space. As discussed Chapter 1, designers develop a disning eye through careful observan and experience.

onomics

e value of a particular furnishing, ric, or background element must considered in respect to the *quality, cost,* and *ecological nature* of the duct.

Quality

How a piece of furniture (or any other architectural component) is made and the quality of the materials used are of vital concern to both the designer and the end user. The quality of construction, materials, and finishes varies, and designers often depend on the integrity of the manufacturer and the word of a salesperson. A good manufacturer takes great pride in the skilled fabrication and detail that compose the product because the company's reputation depends on it.

Cost

The client's budget is a necessary consideration when planning and furnishing a space. The cost of the furnishings must be in line with the budget allocation. Almost all design projects have a spending limit that must be respected.

In addition to the initial cost, the costs over the life of the product (life-cycle costing) must be considered: the cost of maintenance, repairs, and replacement parts. Fine quality and good design are always wise investments and, if carefully selected, can be obtained at a reasonable cost.

Ecology

The designer is also responsible for encouraging the use of products and materials that do not harm the environment or create health hazards through the emission of toxic fumes. See the special sections on sustainable design in the following chapters on furniture and accessories, textiles, and backgrounds.

8

·urniture and Accessories

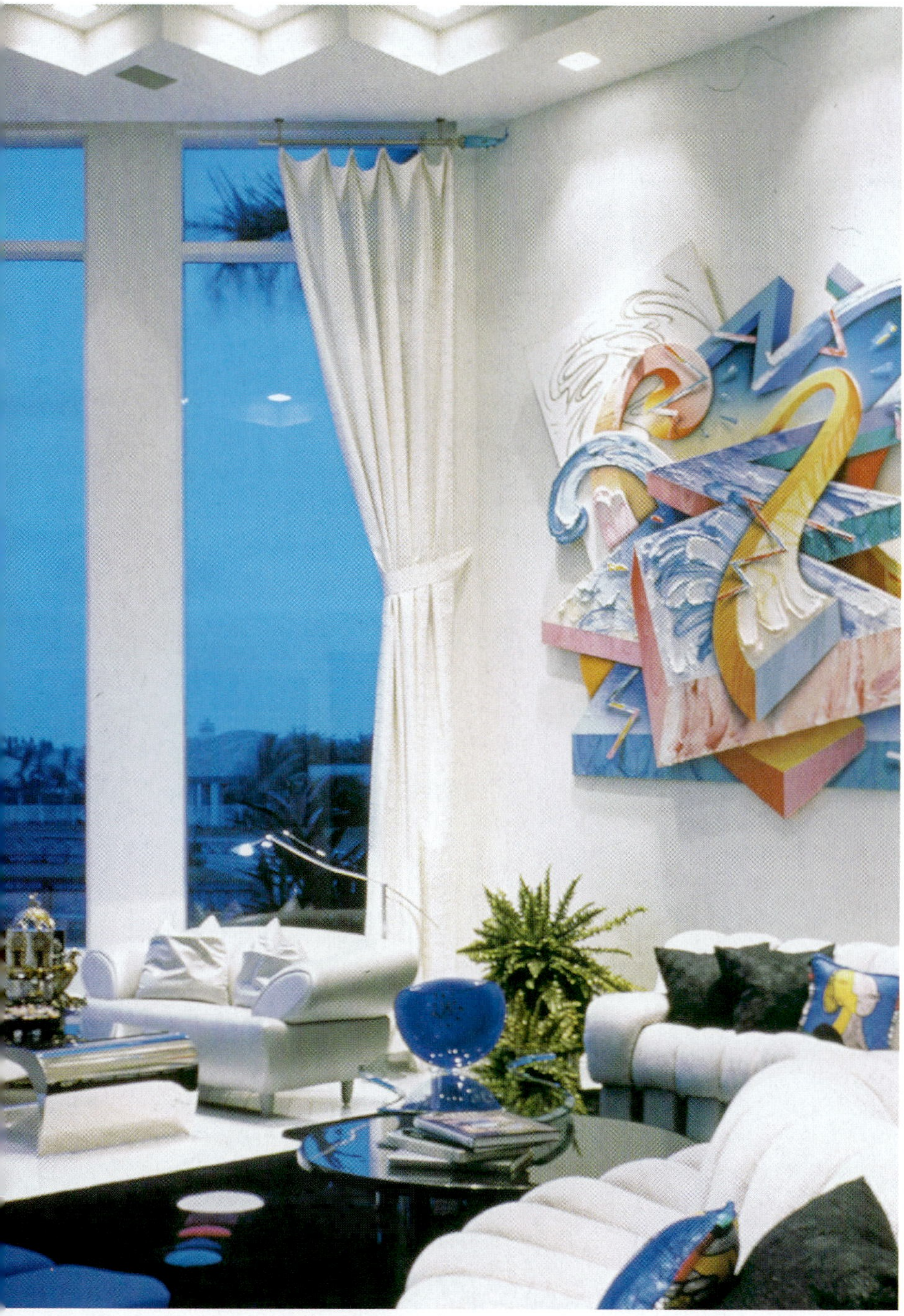

gure 8.1 *In this vibrant contemporary living room, the designers carefully placed the t to visually pull the room together. Note the accent pillows and custom rug design.)esigner: Stevenson Design Group. Photograph by Robert Brantley.)*

FURNITURE

Selecting furniture for residential and commercial projects is a major responsibility of the designer. Furniture is used to meet a range of human needs in a variety of spaces. Furniture can function as a simple utilitarian item (such as a barstool or bench) or it can serve as an artistic focal point in a room. Accessories and art placed on or around furniture can enhance and complement the furniture selection (Figure 8.1).

Furnishing a space can be a rewarding experience, and furniture can last a lifetime. Careful study and planning enable the designer and client to make wise purchases. This approach requires time and effort but pays long-term dividends. The ability to discriminate between long-lasting and faddish designs is a necessity. Different styles of furniture can be used together providing there is similarity of line, shape, proportion, and so on. Knowledge of the principles and elements of design and understanding of how a fine piece of furniture is made aid in the selection process. A well-designed piece of furniture will always be a quality piece.

Types of Furniture

Furniture has evolved from pure function to an important a form. By the time of the ancient civilizations of Egypt, Greec and Rome, furniture was elegantly formed and decorated, sa isfying the need for both function and beauty. In later period various styles have had lasting influence on following gene ations. English and French designs are particularly influenti in North America (Figure 8.2). Systems furniture, built-ins, an modular units emerged on a grand scale during the twentie century. Figure 8.3 illustrates many furniture types.

Chairs

People use chairs every day for a variety of functions; the are essential pieces of furniture. Materials generally incluc wood, metal, plastic, leather, and textiles. Sizes range fro simple and lightly scaled side chairs to oversized upholstere lounge chairs, with styles from all periods available to su any taste. Generally, a variety of chair sizes and designs a required within an interior environment. Figures 8.4 throug 8.10 show examples of different types of chairs.

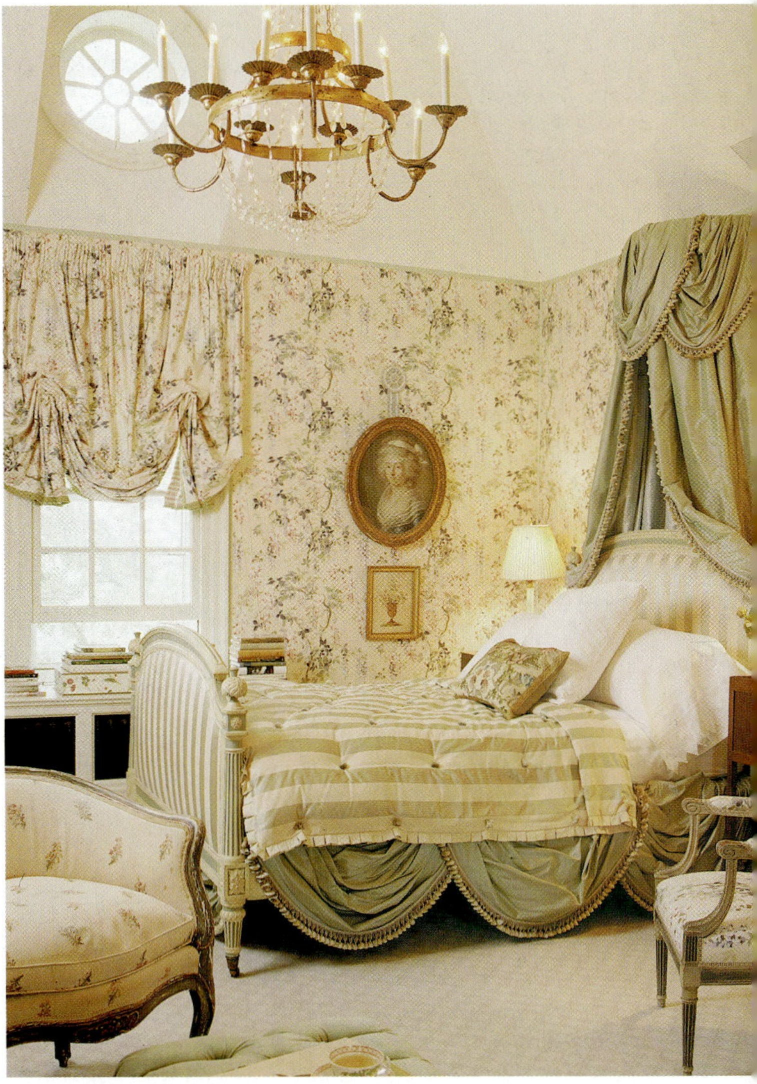

Figure 8.2 *This design is inspired by the French rococo and neoclassic styles. The original ceiling was removed to expose a circular attic window. Note the variety of patterns and textures working together. (Designer: Holly Hock Design, Suzanne Rheinstein. Photograph by Tria Giovan. Courtesy of* Southern Accents.*)*

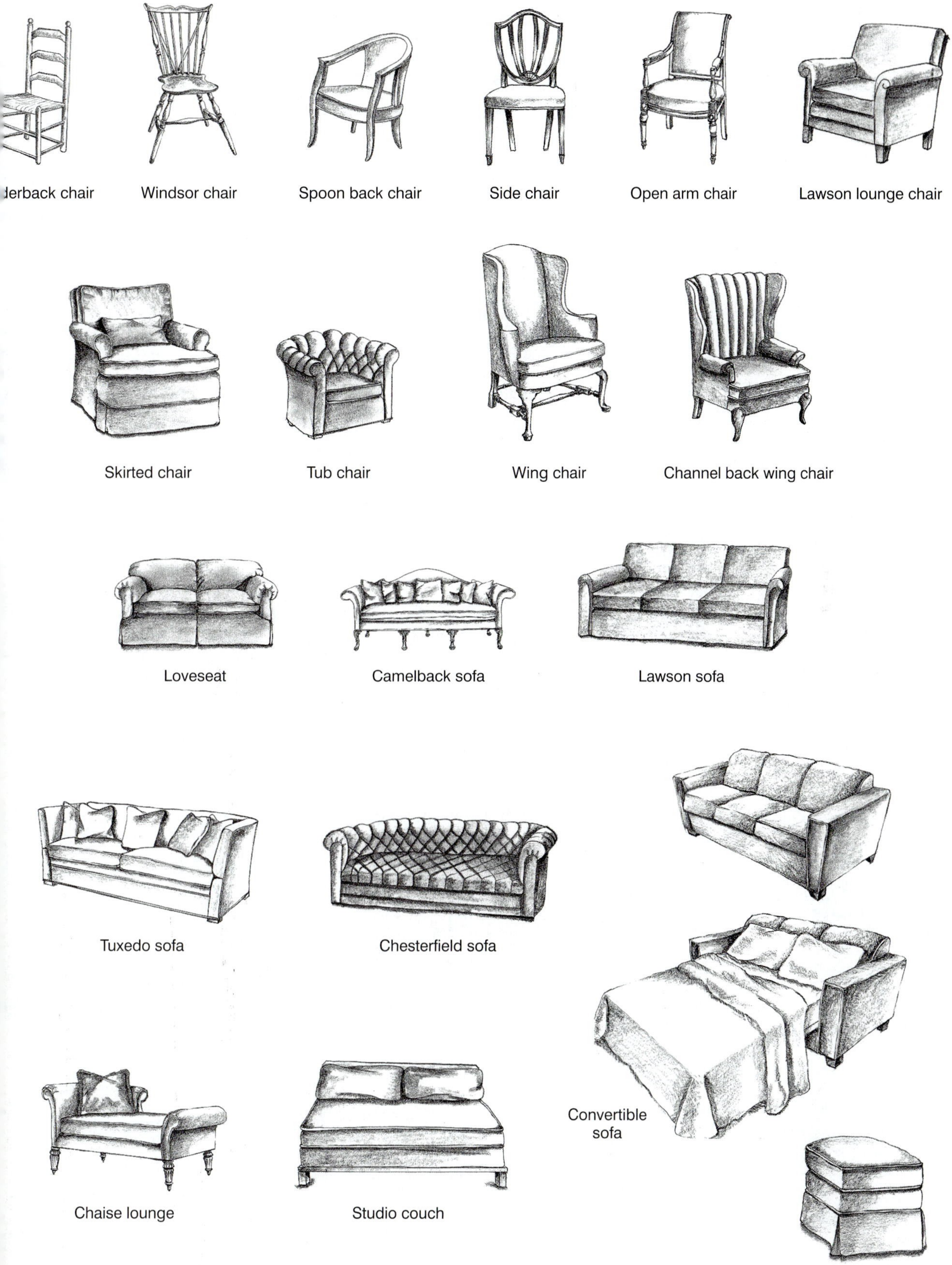

re 8.3 *Furniture types: Seating pieces and beds.*

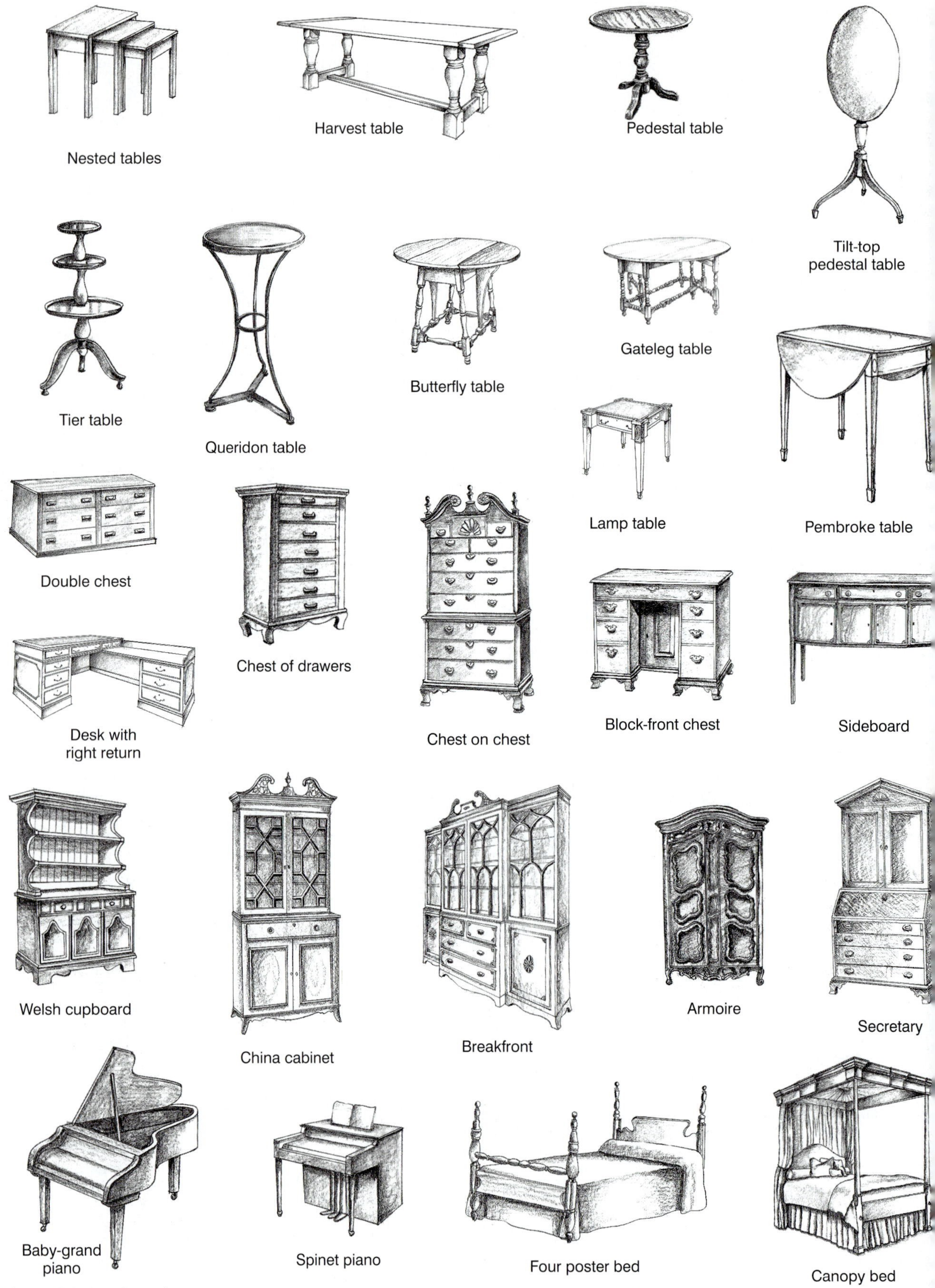

Figure 8.3 Continued. *Furniture types: Tables, case furniture, desks, pianos, and beds.*

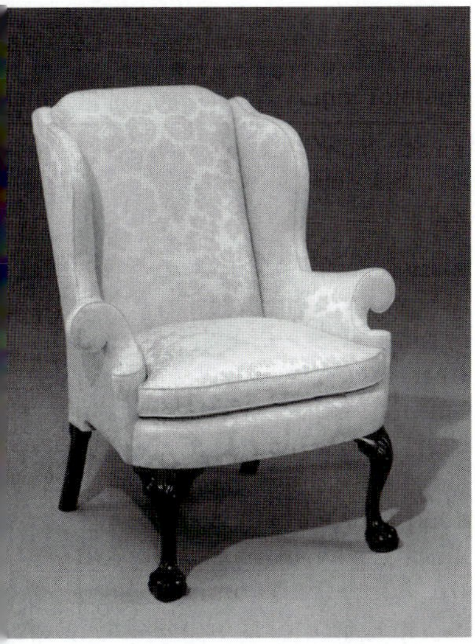

gure 8.4 *This Queen Anne "wing air," so named for the curved half-les that rise to the height of the high ck, originally offered protection from drafts and chills of poorly heated oms. The arms are made up of two olls, one vertical and one horizontal, hich meet to outline a graceful flat C-aped scroll. (Courtesy of Kindel.)*

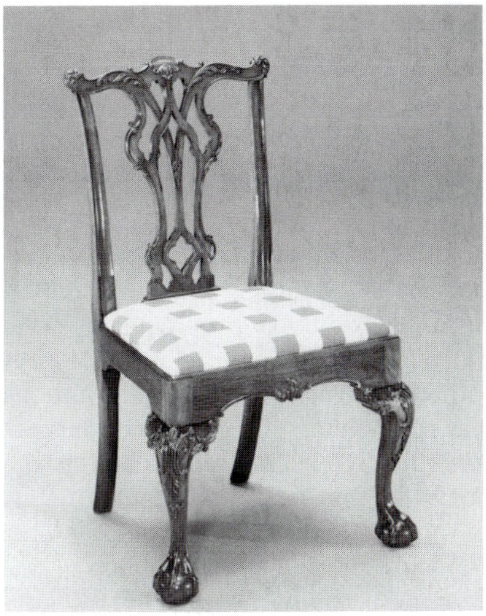

Figure 8.5 *This reproduction of a Philadelphia Chippendale side chair, originally made between 1760 and 1780, features heavily carved acanthus leaf clusters with cabriole front legs that terminate in claw-and-ball feet. (Courtesy of Kindel.)*

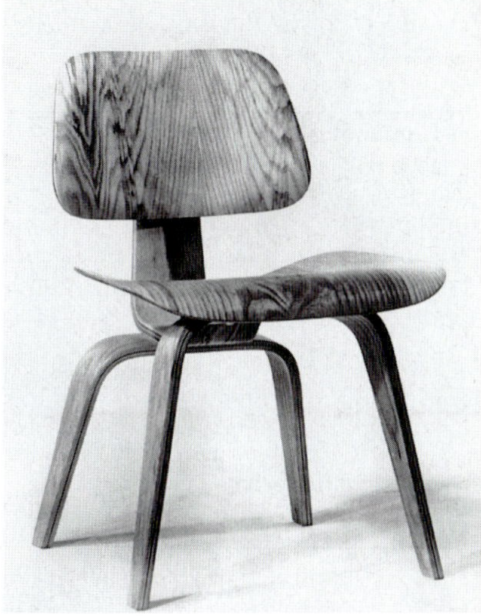

Figure 8.6 *Charles and Ray Eames experimented with various wood forms. The Eames® DCW chair (1943–1953) is an early example of a molded plywood chair design. (Courtesy of Herman Miller, Inc. archives.)*

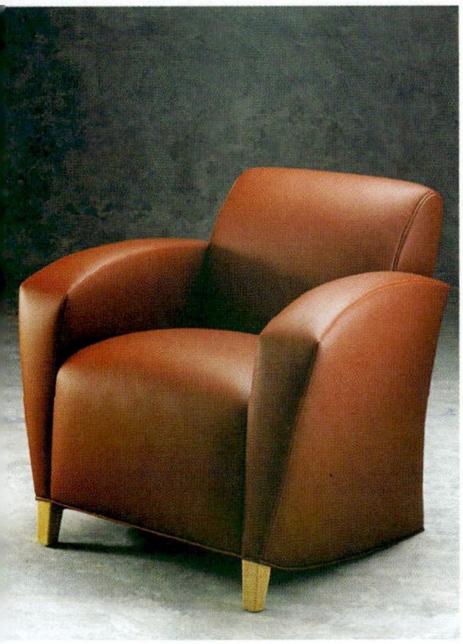

gure 8.7 *This lounge chair by ewenstein, called the "Royale," is holstered in fine, tight-fitting leather. e chair is appropriate in commercial fice lobbies, lounges, and ntemporary residences. (Courtesy of ewenstein.)*

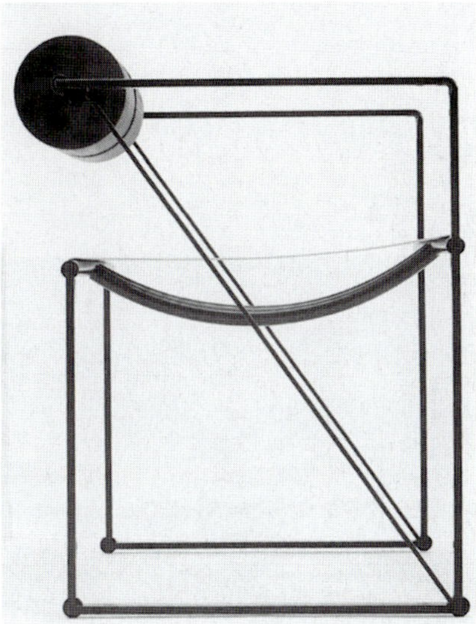

Figure 8.8 *The Seconda armchair (1982), designed by Swiss architect Mario Botta, is constructed of perforated sheet metal with a backrest of polyurethane. (Courtesy of ICF.)*

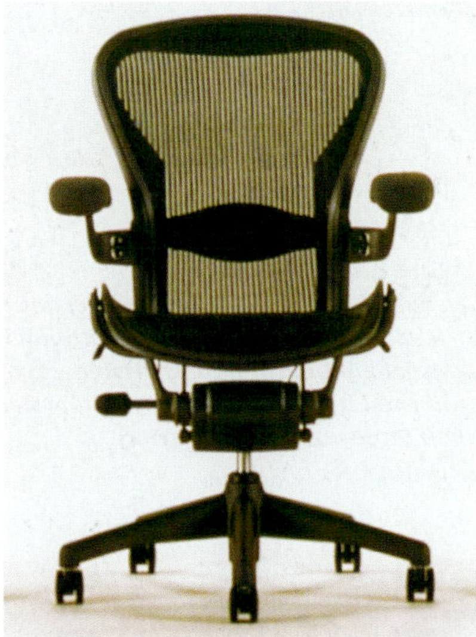

Figure 8.9 *This ergonomic desk chair, called Aeron, is designed to support the lower lumbar region of the user's back. Adjustable arms, seat, and back, along with a variety of sizes, provide personalized comfort for the user. (Photograph by Nick Merrick/Hedrich-Blessing. Courtesy of Herman Miller, Inc.)*

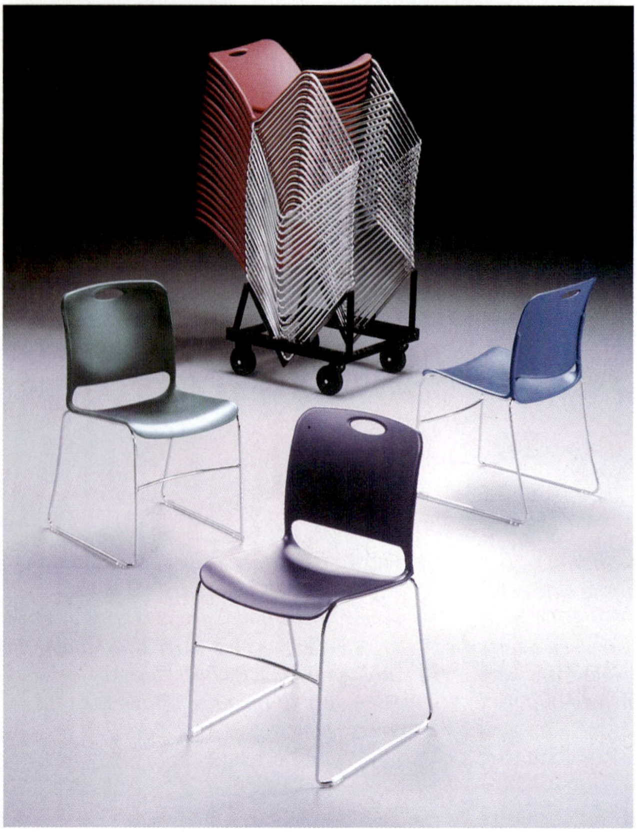

Figure 8.10 *The Maestro by KI is one of many styles of stacking chairs for corporate training areas, auditoriums, and offices. The chairs have polypropylene seats and chrome legs. The stackers allow for ease in storage and mobility. (Courtesy of KI.)*

When selecting chairs, consider the following:

- The height, depth, and width should comfortably accommodate the human form.
- An adjustable chair gives flexible service to a variety c users.
- Ergonomic designs, based on extensive anthropometr studies, provide maximum comfort.

Sofas

Sofas are upholstered seating units usually accommodat two or more persons (Figure 8.11). Through the ages pa ular terms have been associated with certain designs, though many times the terms are used interchangeably.

- The *Lawson* is a type with flat armrests lower than the back support (Figure 8.12).
- The *chaise lounge* accommodates one person and is a cross between a sofa and a chair plus ottoman.
- The *tuxedo* is a completely upholstered piece with arr rests the same height as the back (Figure 8.13).
- The *chesterfield* is a large, tufted, upholstered sofa wit upholstered ends and no exposed wood.
- The *divan,* a low sofa without arms or back, is derive from stacked rugs used in Turkey for seating. It is con monly placed against the wall and piled with cushion.
- The *love seat* is a smaller sofa for seating two persons.
- The *settee,* also generally for two people, is a lightly scaled piece, often with some upholstered sections (F ure 8.14).
- *Settles,* completely constructed of wood with very higl backs, originally were used in early American homes retain heat from fireplaces.

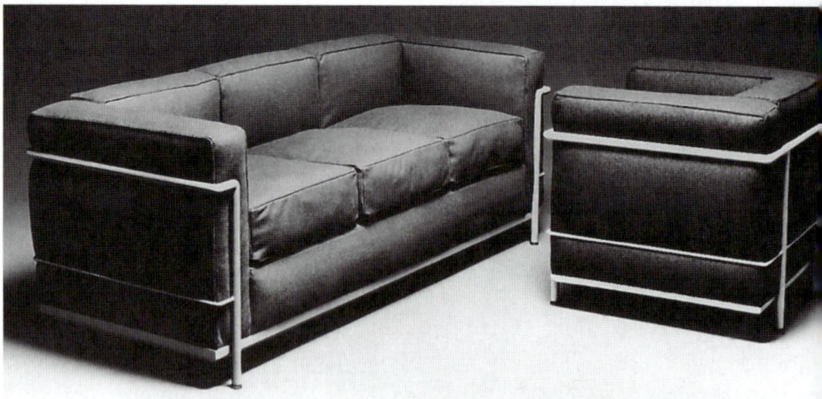

Figure 8.11 *When Le Corbusier designed the Grand Confort Collection in 1928, he eliminated the traditional construction of an upholstered piece and used a light support of tubular steel with loose cushions. (Courtesy of Cassina USA Inc.)*

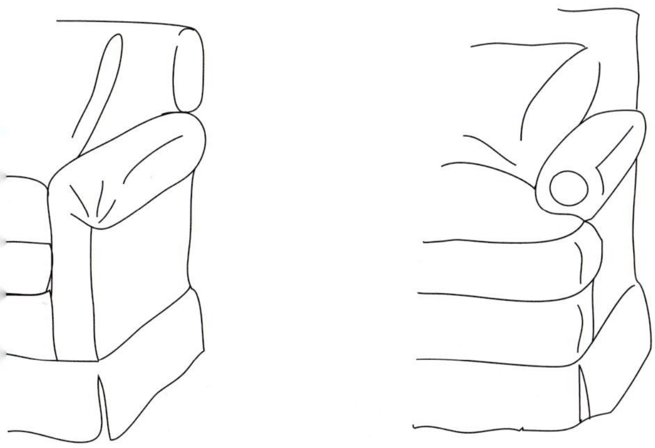

gure 8.12 *Lawson arm sofas.*

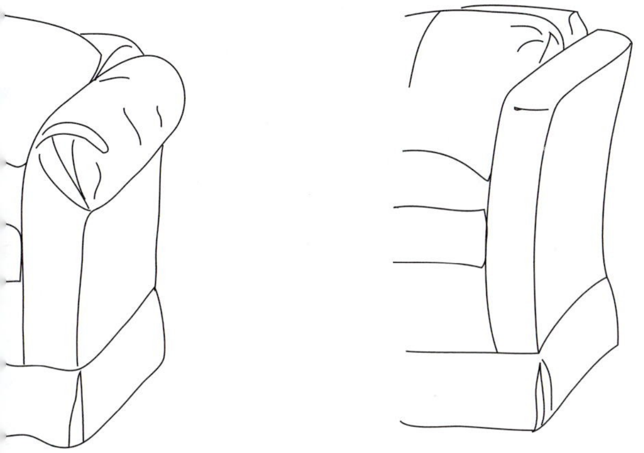

gure 8.13 *Tuxedo arm sofas.*

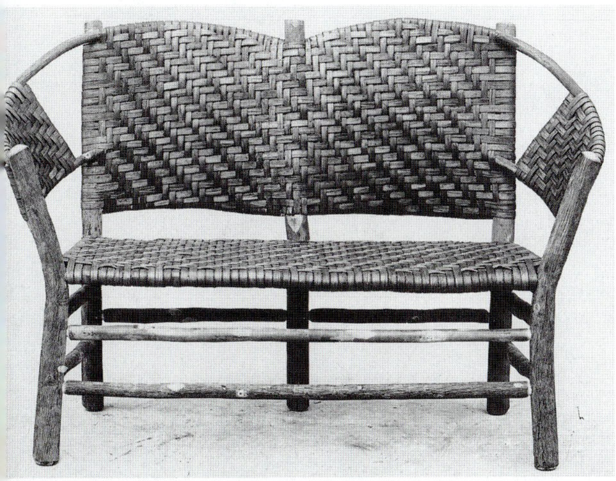

gure 8.14 *"Old Hickory" settee, used in historic lodges since e early 1900s. (Courtesy of Old Hickory Furniture Company. seen in* Fine Furniture International.*)*

- *Davenport* is an old term for a sofa that converts into a bed. It originally referred to a small writing desk named after its designer.
- *Modular* and *sectional* sofas consist of several units placed side by side to form one large sofa unit.

Sofas, like chairs, should be selected to comfortably accommodate the user. Care should be taken to ensure the stiffness of the seat is appropriate for the intended use. For example, an elder care center would require firm furniture seats with high arms to assist patients in standing up. An environment for individuals using wheelchairs might include a firm sofa without arms to allow a person to transfer easily from the wheelchair to the sofa.

Tables

Tables, like sofas, come in many forms, including dining and kitchen tables, coffee tables, end or occasional tables (Figure 8.15), game tables, and sofa tables. All tables should be sturdy and of appropriate size and height. Tables may also be attached to a chair for conferencing or educational purposes (Figure 8.16). Dining, kitchen, and game tables are usually 29″–30″H (Figure 8.17). End tables should match the height of the arm of the sofa as closely as possible (Figure 8.18). Sofa tables should match the height of the back of the sofa. Coffee tables are about the same height as the seat cushions on a sofa.

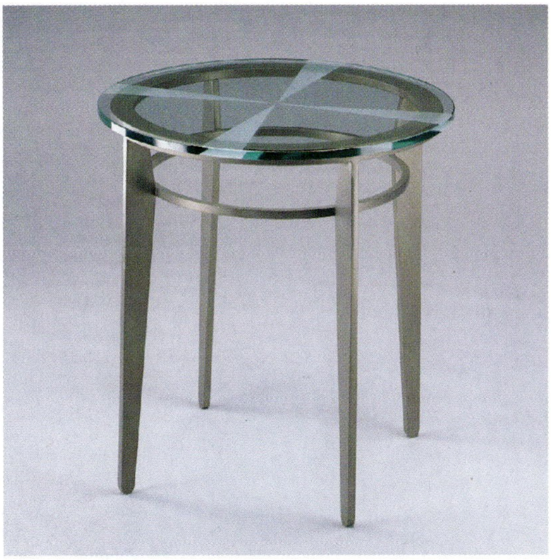

Figure 8.15 *This occasional table, the "Vector" from Carolina Business Furniture, is available in wood or metal. The pinwheel top defines its distinctive character. (Courtesy of Carolina Business Furniture.)*

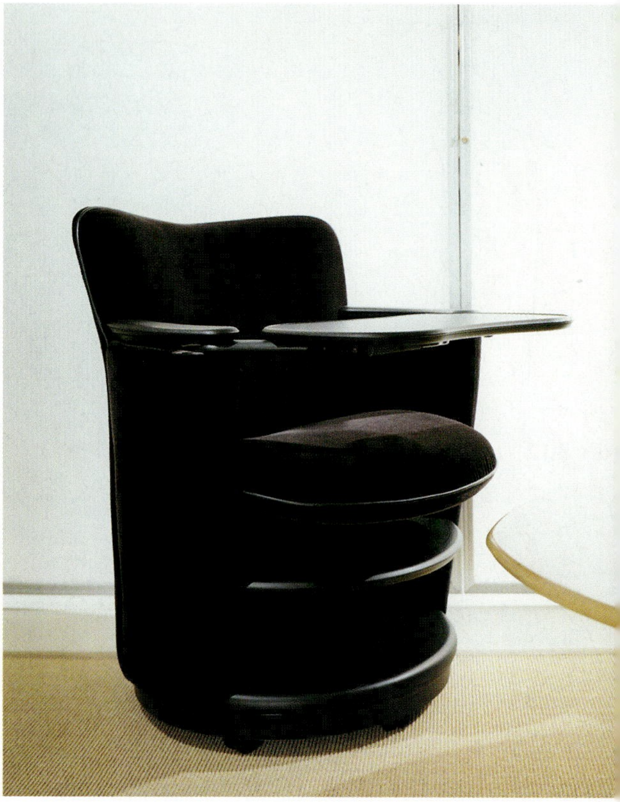

Figure 8.16 *This side table and chair combination functions as a conferencing table or for use in a lecture hall.* Migrations *is designed by Michael Shields. (Photograph courtesy of Brayton International.)*

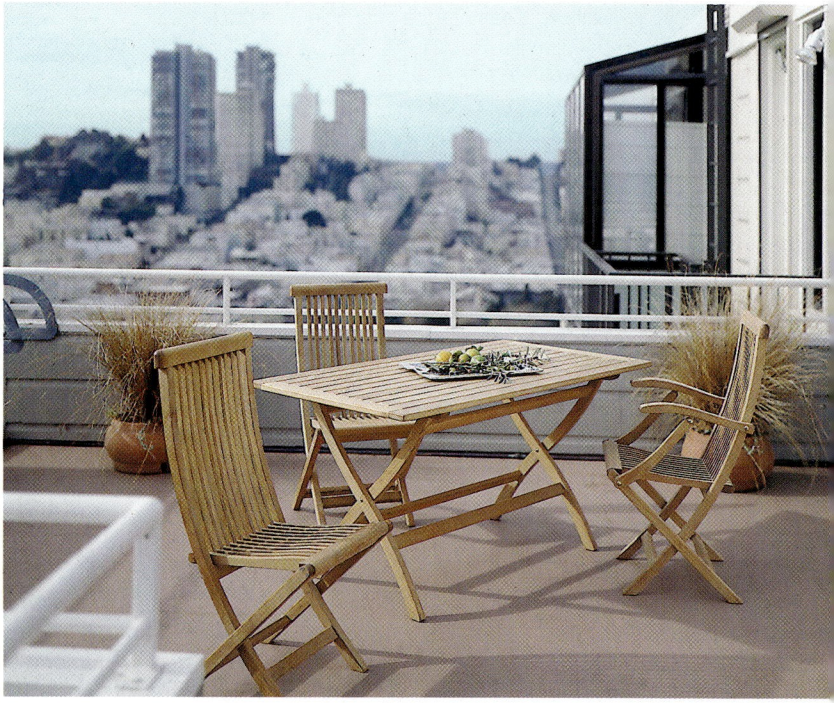

Figure 8.17 *This comfortable deck furniture is designed to endure harsh weather elements while folding to allow for portability. Tables are available in a variety of sizes. (Courtesy of Smith & Hawken.)*

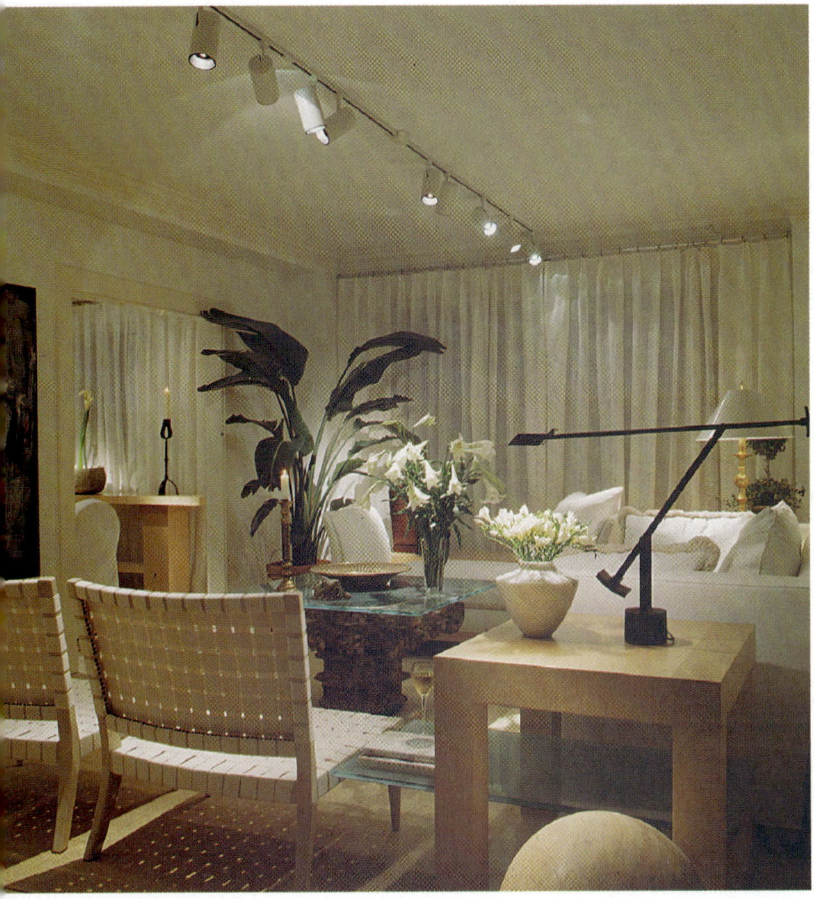

Figure 8.18 *This custom-designed endtable cleverly meets the needs of the high-armed sofa and the armless side chair. (Designer: Gandy/Peace Inc. Photograph by Chris A. Little.)*

sks and Credenzas

ks, credenzas, and associated computer furniture are par-larly important because of the surge in home offices and increased understanding of the importance of ergonomic iiture. A desk is a combination of a storage unit and a e. Typically desks are 29″–30″H. Desks (as discussed in pter 6) are available in a variety of sizes; however, the st common is 30″W × 60–66″L. Some desks are accompa-l by left- or right-hand returns. Returns are approximately D and 30″–42″L. Like credenzas, they commonly house nputer equipment. Credenzas are thinner than desks, but ally the same length, commonly 20″W × 60–66″L.

Desks and credenzas with articulating keyboard trays are ecially beneficial to the user's comfort (Figure 8.19). Ide-, the tray is at the same height as the bent elbow when person is seated at the computer. Keyboard trays, how-r, should be adjustable.

Desk drawers should vary in size. There should be a wer to accommodate hanging file folders; at least one llow drawer for pencils, paper clips, and other office sup-s; and a medium-depth drawer appropriate for storing ionery, computer disks, and CD-ROMs. Desks also may tain grommets that conceal channels for routing com-er cables, telephone wires, and electrical cords.

Desks used in reception areas should also contain a trans-on top. This top is usually 42″–48″H and serves two functions. It allows a person standing to rest materials on the ledge, and it conceals papers from view of visitors (as seen in Figure 8.23). To meet the needs of visitors in wheelchairs, transaction tops may have a lowered area not to exceed 36″H.

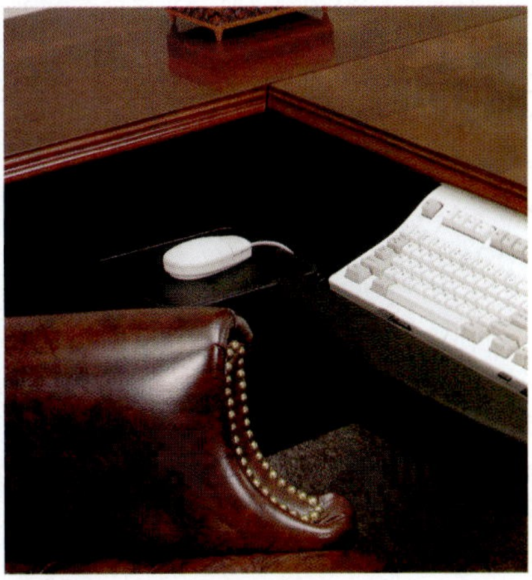

Figure 8.19 *This retractable keyboard tray is adjustable and provides a wristrest and an attached mousepad holder. All three features assist with healthful ergonomic designs. (Courtesy of Inwood Office Furniture.)*

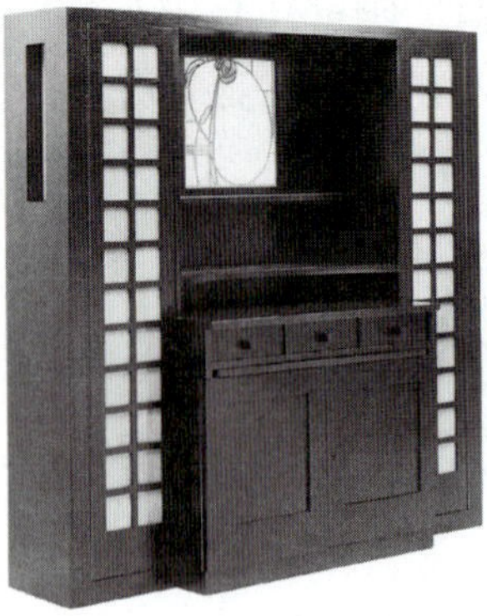

Figure 8.20 *A modern casepiece, Sideboard 2, designed by Charles Rennie Mackintosh at the beginning of the twentieth century, was put in production in 1974. The piece, made of ebonized wood and contrasted with pearlized and stained glass, can be used for a variety of functions. (Courtesy of Cassina USA Inc.)*

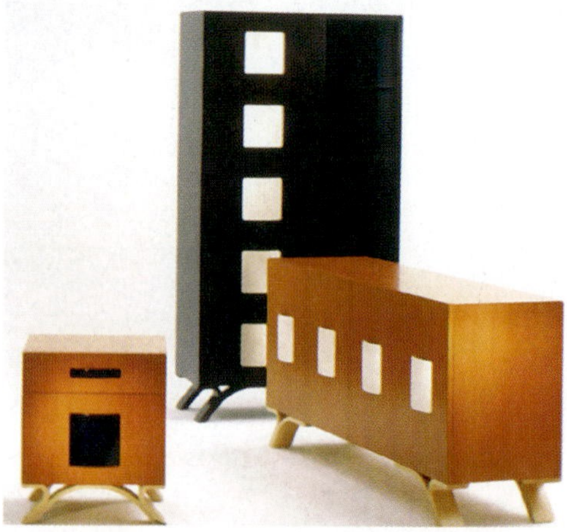

Figure 8.21 *Dakota Jackson, New York furniture designer, created these unique storage units called the Nuevo Tango Series. (Courtesy of and design by Dakota Jackson.)*

Storage

Many innovative pieces designed for functional storage are available. Built-in systems house stereos, televisions, and VCRs. Chests, cupboards, hutches, secretaries, china cabinets, shelves, armoires, and filing systems provide convenient and efficient storage (Figures 8.20 and 8.21).

Beds

A bed may be built-in or freestanding. It may serve dual purposes, such as a day bed or convertible sofa. Different styles include four-poster beds, Murphy beds (a type of bed that folds down from the wall), trundle beds (a bed that pulls from under another bed), bunk beds, and waterbeds. B may also be designed without the traditional mattress box springs (Figure 8.22).

Built-In Wall Units

Built-in furnishings may function as seating, tables, beds, storage space and are integrated with wall construct Built-in units have the advantage of providing architect unity and a more spacious feeling (Figure 8.23); a disadv tage is the inability to move the components.

Figure 8.22 *In this ASID award-winning bedroom, the designer created a Zen-inspired interior. The cool crisp walls, glass, and woods are balanced by the area rug's texture and the coarsely woven chair. (Designer: Bruce Benning, ASID/CID, Benning Design Associates. Photograph by David Duncan Livingston.)*

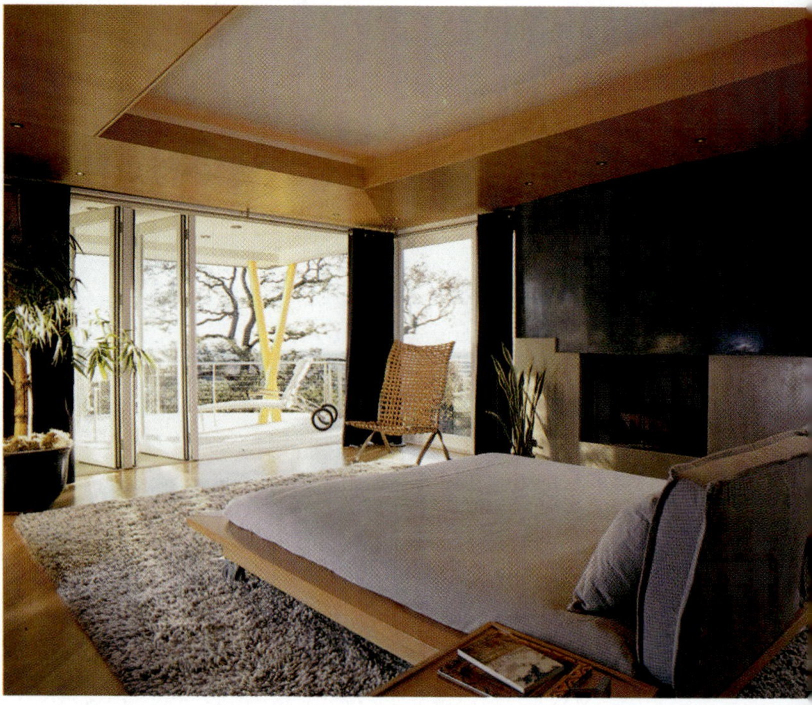

ystems Furniture

/stems furniture are modular pieces used for office design :ojects. They consist of work surfaces, storage units, and :rtical panels that make up a workstation (these may be pri- ıte, semiprivate, or a combination of the two). These flexi- e pieces can be set up in a variety of configurations to fit ıe space available. They serve the needs of executive, man- gement, secretarial, clerical, and word processing worksta- ons (Figures 8.24 and 9.14).

Aovable Furniture

s telecommuting becomes more prevalent and employ- es share office space, flexibility in design becomes more nportant in furniture design. Offices may be wheeled om one department to another based on current needs. iling cabinets may move from one department to an- ther as hardcopy forms are routed through an office. A udio apartment may also benefit from a mobile office igure 8.25).

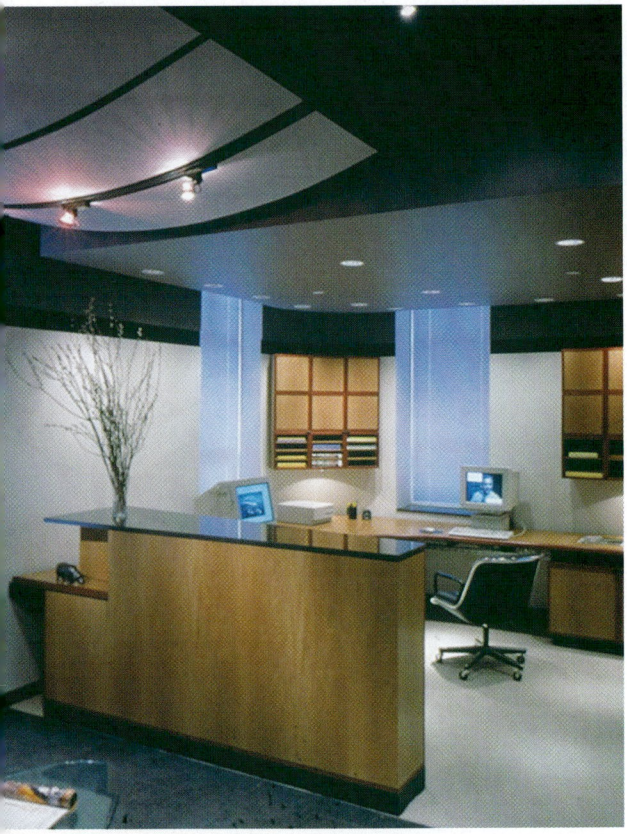

igure 8.23 *A built-in work counter was developed for this ffice suite. The maple and cherry woods are accented by rich lack stone. The black ledge functions as a transaction top. Notice that wires, paper, and files are concealed. Architect/Designer: Leers, Weinzapfel Associates. Photograph y Chuck Chói.)*

General Classifications of Furniture Styles

Furniture styles typically are referred to as traditional or contemporary; however, designers should be familiar with the following terms:

- **Antique**—A piece of furniture or work of art that, according to United States law, must be at least 100 years old.
- **Reproduction**—A copy of an original period piece. Some reproductions are made so meticulously that only the well-trained eye can detect the difference; other modern reproductions are far from exact copies.
- **Adaptation**—A piece in which some elements from the original have been adapted into a new design.
- **Period style**—A term used to designate a single item or a complete interior, including the architectural background, furniture, and decorative arts prevalent in a specific country or a particular time in history. This type is often referred to as traditional.
- **Contemporary style**—A term referring to designs that to some degree have been adapted from historical or modern influences. Usually considered a clean and elegant twentieth-century design.
- **Modern style**—Any time in history when a new art form emerges, breaking ties with previous design forms—whether in music, architecture, or furniture—it is referred to as modern.

Quality and Craftsmanship

The quality of construction and craftsmanship of a piece of furniture help to define the value of the item. Designers need to understand the nature of furniture construction in order to purchase wisely for clients. Construction features to consider include the following:

- Furniture should be well proportioned and comfortable. Sit on a chair or sofa to test its comfort. Check the depth of the seat and height of the back and arms. If a chair is being chosen for a particular person, have that person try it out.
- A fine-quality finish is smooth and evenly applied, with no spotting, sticky areas, running, or buildup of coats. Good wood furniture has the look of a fine **patina** (a mellow, refined appearance) resulting from much rubbing, a practice requiring time and effort and therefore adding to the cost.
- Back panels should be recessed and smoothly finished.
- Movable parts like drawers and door panels must be durable and easily operated (Figure 8.26). Drawer runners are best when made of metal, plastic, or durable hardwood. Well-made drawers have solid sides, three-ply nonwarp bottoms that are sanded and sealed against snags, and dovetail joints, and are separated by dust barriers. All drawers should have

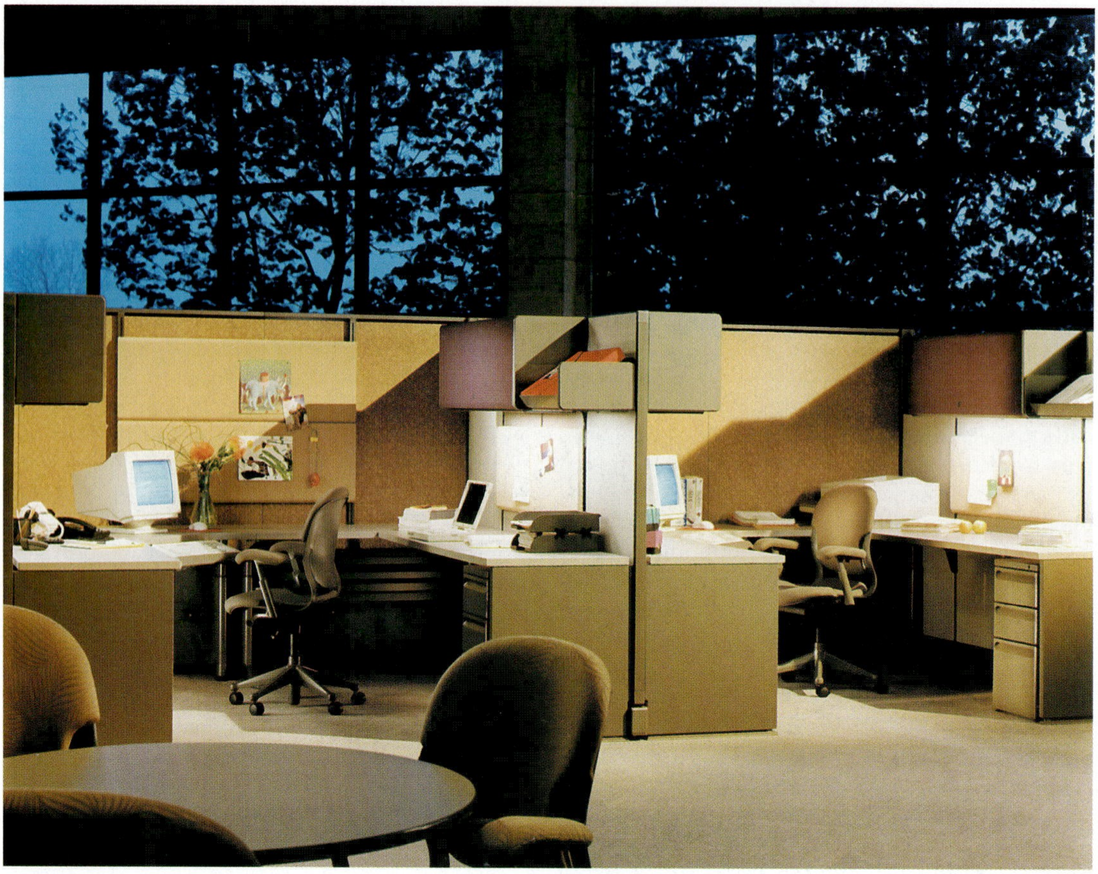

Figure 8.24 *This contemporary office space illustrates the use of open office systems furniture. Wires are concealed in the system's walls. Fabric-covered insulating wall panels are available in a variety of options. Task lighting is concealed below overhead storage bins. (Photograph by Nick Merrick/Hedrich-Blessing. Courtesy of Herman Miller, Inc.)*

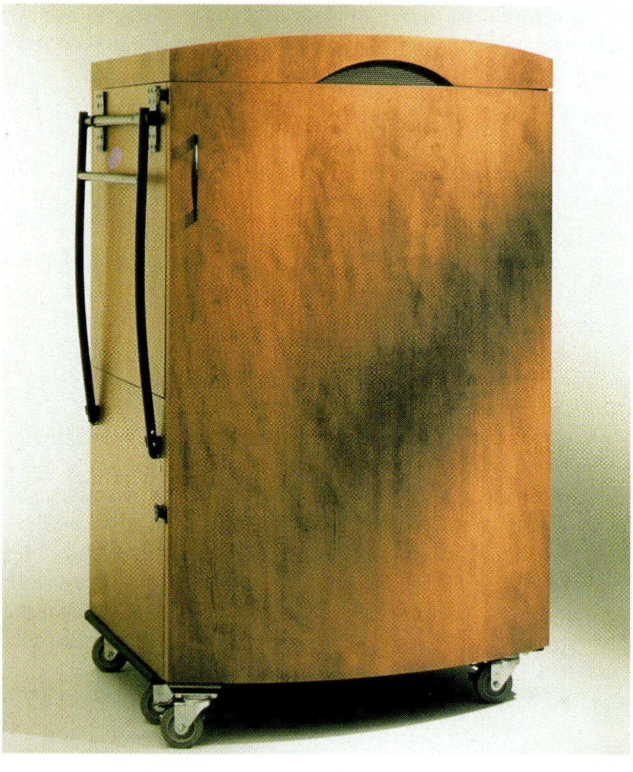

Figure 8.25 *With this self-contained portable office, a corner of any room can become an office space. When opened, this system provides 12′ of work surface, a keyboard tray, a markerboard, and a tackboard. (Photograph courtesy of Haworth.)*

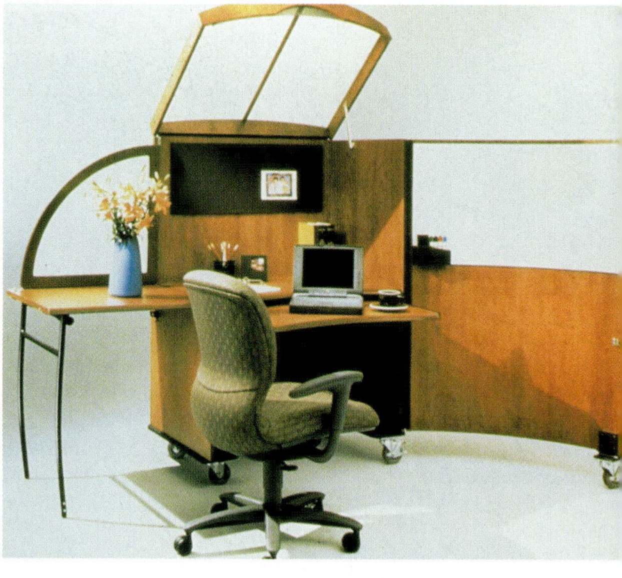

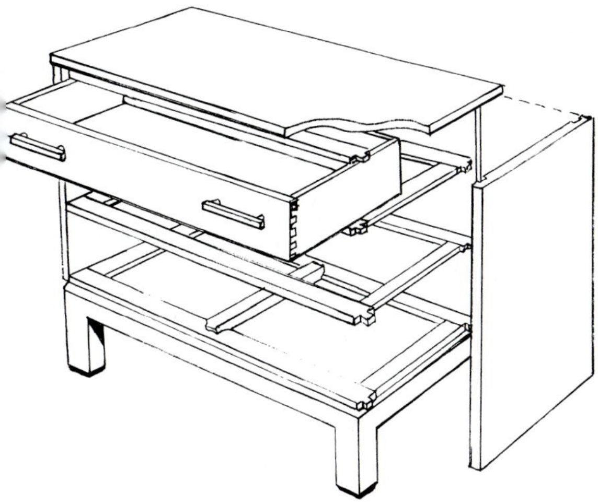

ure 8.26 *Inner characteristics of furniture determine* *ability: selected hardwoods; mortise and tenon joints;* *vy-duty center drawer guides; drawers dovetailed front* *d back; durable dust panels between drawers; durable* *wer bottoms held in grooves; strong casebacks recessed* *o ends; well-mounted top and sides; drawer interiors* *ded and sealed.*

drawer stops to prevent the drawer from being completely pulled out.

Hardware, such as drawer pulls and handles, should be securely fastened.

Furniture with flat areas like tables, cabinets, and desktops should be constructed of durable material to maintain function and appearance. Although some materials are practical, each may have a particular hazard; for example, marble may stain, glass may break, plastic may chip, and hardwood may scratch.

The edges of tables and other pieces are especially susceptible to damage and wear. Rounded edges, reinforced strips, and edges made of solid hardwood are more practical.

In general, all sections of furniture must be securely joined. The following pages discuss some of the specific materials and methods used in furniture construction.

Wood

Wood is the major material used for furniture construction. Furniture is made from both hard and soft woods. Hardwoods come from deciduous trees (those that drop their leaves), such as oak and maple. Hardwoods are more durable and dent-resistant than softwoods, but because they grow slowly they cost more. Hardwoods are preferred for fine furniture. Softwoods come from coniferous trees (those with needles that are mostly green year round), such as pine and spruce. Softwoods are used for less expensive furniture and in combination with hardwoods.

The woods most widely used in furniture construction are pine, birch, maple, oak, cherry, walnut, mahogany, beech, pecan, and teak. Labels describing the finish such as "fruit wood finish" or "walnut finish" refer to the color only, not to the species of wood used. Each wood has its own special properties. Wood selected for a particular furniture piece should be properly dried, well suited for its intended construction, purpose, finish, size and style, and resistant to warping, splitting, swelling, and shrinking. Table 8.1 lists the most common woods and their uses.

Solid Wood and Veneers

Solid wood refers to the parts of the piece of furniture made from one piece of wood, such as legs in chairs or tables, the frames, and trim. A **veneer** is a thin layer of finishing wood applied to the body of a less refined wood or a polymer (a material added to wood to strengthen it). Veneers may be cut in different methods that result in characteristic wood grains (Figure 8.27). With advanced methods of cutting and adhering veneers, a piece of veneered furniture can be stronger and more resistant to warping than a solid wood piece. The label *genuine* indicates that all the exposed solid pieces and the veneers are made from the same wood species.

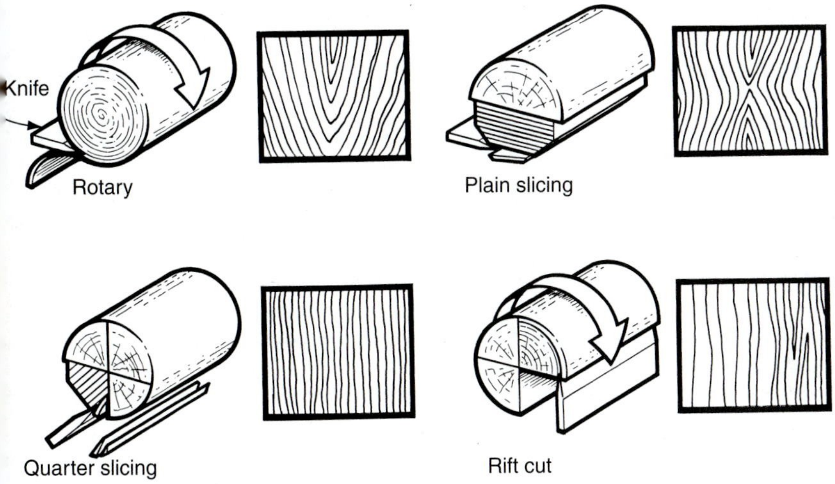

Figure 8.27 *Veneer cutting patterns.*

Table 8.1 *Most Common Wood Types*

Wood Type	Characteristics	Uses in Home
Acacia	Hardwood. Light brown.	Furniture. Woodwork. Often used for religious decorations.
Alder	A light, weak wood. White to light browns.	Furniture. Framing for construction.
Ash	A blond hardwood. Texture resembles oak. Relatively inexpensive.	Cabinetry and furniture. Furniture framing. Flooring.
Bamboo	A tropical tubular woody plant with a raised joint.	Asian-style furniture. Decorative accessories.
Beech	A blond hardwood. Fine-grain texture. Strong.	Informal furniture. Popular in Scandinavia. Flooring.
Birch	Subtle wavy grain. Hard and durable. Takes stain well, or beautiful in natural finish.	Furniture. Popular in Scandinavia. Flooring, doors, and cabinetry. Furniture framing.
Cedar*	Reddish-brown, often with yellow streaks. Soft. Lightweight. Strong odor. Moth repellent.	Closet lining, chests. Informal furniture. Shingles, siding, paneling.
Cherry	Reddish-brown hardwood. Resembles mahogany. Durable. Strong.	Used in small quantities. Inlay and marquetry work. Popular for early American furniture.
Cypress	Color varies from light yellow to darkish-brown. Soft. Warp resistant. Inexpensive. Weathers silver gray.	Particularly used as a finish wood. Outside finish work. Doors, shingles, and siding. Some informal furniture.
Ebony*	Exquisite dark hardwood with brownish-black streaks. Ebony, sometimes red or green. Hard and heavy.	Modern and Asian furniture. Inlay and marquetry designs.
Elm	Light brown with gray overtones. Takes stain well. Slight undulating grain. Hard and heavy.	Particularly used for veneers. Furniture. Interior finish work. Furniture framing.
Fir*	Strong and durable. Wavy grain. Takes stain well. Resembles pine.	Plywood and laminated sheets. Cabinetry. Trim pieces. Inexpensive furniture.
Gum	Reddish-brown. Medium hard. Resembles mahogany. Interesting grains.	Veneers. Doors. Interior trim. Furniture parts.
Mahogany*	Reddish or reddish-golden brown with fine grain. Can be beautifully finished.	Fine, expensive furniture. Especially popular for Queen Anne, Chippendale, and other 18th-century furniture. Paneling and cabinetwork.
Maple	White to pale yellowish-brown. Fine grain. Hard and heavy. Resembles birch. Relatively inexpensive.	Informal furniture. Popular for early American style. Flooring. Cabinetwork. Furniture framing.
Oak*	White oak is light to golden brown. Red oak has pinkish tones. Straight to strong wavy grain. Hard and durable.	Most important wood for furniture, trim, and cabinetwork. Quarter-sawn (straight grain) usually preferred for fine furniture and paneling.
Pecan	White to reddish-brown. Refined grain, often with darkish streaks. Hard, strong, and heavy.	Fine furniture. Furniture parts. Cabinetwork, paneling, and trim.
Pine	Off-white to pale yellow. Soft. Not strong. Lightweight. Inexpensive. Close grain with occasional wavy grain.	Flooring, doors, and trim. Early American or provincial furniture and paneling. Cabinetwork.
Poplar	Off-white to yellowish-brown. Softwood. Lightweight. Subtle straight grain. Inexpensive.	Informal furniture. Works well painted. Trim, cabinetwork, and exterior siding. Furniture framing.
Rattan	A jungle vine from Asia. Pale yellow to light brown. Soft and pliable.	Informal furniture with Asian feeling. Can be nicely painted and stained.
Redwood*	Uniform red color. Grays when exposed to weather. Available in large planks.	Exterior finishes. Beams, paneling, etc. Cabinetwork. Outdoor furniture.
Rosewood*	Fine-textured reddish-brown hardwood with black streaks. Beautiful when highly polished.	Popular for fine 18th-century furniture. Inlay designs. Danish modern furniture.
Satinwood*	Pale blond color with smooth satin finish. Unique grain. Expensive.	Fine furniture and finish work. Inlay and parquetry designs.
Teak*	Yellow to reddish-brown with fine black streaks. Strong and durable. Beautiful with oiled finish.	Popularly used for Asian- and Danish-designed furniture. Decorative and functional accessories.
Walnut	Light to dark golden brown. A variety of beautiful grains. Hard, strong, and durable. Expensive.	Used for fine furniture in many styles. Especially used during 18th-century Queen Anne period, called the "Age of Walnut." Paneling.
Yew*	Dark reddish-brown hardwood particularly found in England. Close grained.	Cabinetwork and some furniture.

*Make sure these woods are obtained from companies with sustainable forest practices before specifying.

More info online @

http://www.certifiedwood.org/ Certified Forest Products Council

http://www.isf-sw.org/ Institute for Sustainable Forestry

http://www.forestworld.com/ Sustainable Forest Products Resource

http://www.woodcom.com/woodcom/afpa/afpabp02.html Principles of Sustainable Forests by the American Forest and Paper Association

http://www.hardwoodcouncil.com/ The Hardwoods Council

:her Forms of Wood in Furniture

ywood, commonly used in building construction, is ıde by laminating together a number of thin layers of ɔod, with the grain of each layer turned 90°. In furniture sign plywood is sometimes used on the inner core of neers.

Particleboard (also known as fiberboard, chipboard, or mposite board) is made by combining chips of wood with sin and compressing the mixture to form a larger piece of ɔod. Because high-quality particleboard does not warp as sily as plywood, it is commonly used as a base in veneer rniture construction.

Hardboard, also made of compressed wood, is comɔnly used in the bottoms of drawers, dust panels, and on rniture backs. It is thinner than particleboard and gives the pearance of a thin sheet of solid wood.

Bentwood is made by placing thin strips of wood under essure and softening them with steam to fit around molds. chael Thonet's bentwood chairs, developed in the 1800s, main popular (see page 51).

Wheatboard, produced from surplus or waste straw, can stained and finished for use in custom-built cabinets, untertops, and shelving. Considered a "green" product, ıeatboard can also be used on interior furniture framing d is formaldehyde free.

ɔre info online @

:p://picturethis.pnl.gov/picturet.nsf/by+id/ 1AA-3XNRV2?opendocument Images and information on ıeatboard

---

Construction Methods

The quality and type of wood joining indicate the durability and aesthetic appeal of a piece of furniture. The most common construction methods for joining wood follow (also refer to Figure 8.28):

- **Mortise and tenon:** The mortise (hole) joins with a piece that has a projecting piece (tenon). This forms a strong joint used particularly where arms and legs join the frame.
- **Dowel:** Rounded dowels (pegs) are joined and glued into corresponding holes. The strength of this design relies on the strength of the dowel.
- **Miter:** Edges are cut at a 45° angle and must have a supportive strip straddling the joint to be strong.
- **Dovetail:** Semitriangular or fan-shaped protrusions fit into notches of the same size and shape. This type of joint secures drawer fronts and sides.
- **Tongue and groove:** The tongue-and-groove joint is similar to the mortise and tenon but runs the entire length of the joint.
- **Rabbeted or rebated:** One edge has a groove cut the entire width to accommodate a straight-edged piece.
- **Butt joint:** This type of joint is not used for fine furniture. The joints are merely glued or screwed together. It is sometimes found on inexpensive furniture, but it must have cross-supports or corner blocks to reinforce it.
- **Blocking:** Corner blocks or hidden blocks of wood help to reinforce joints such as those at table or chair legs.

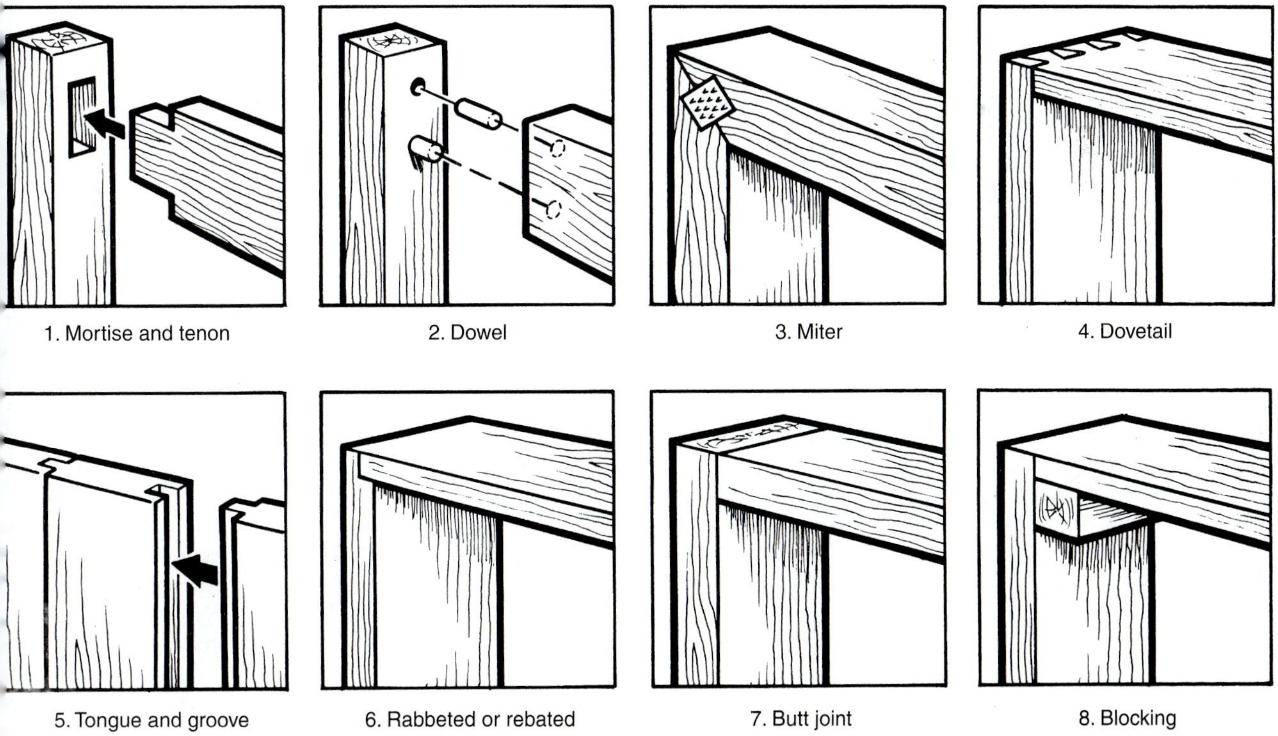

gure 8.28 *Types of wood joining.*

More info online @

http://www.taunton.com/finewoodworking/index.asp Taunton Press page on fine woodworking. Links to articles and site.

http://www.virginiagalleries.com/wood-recog.htm Images of types of wood

http://www.awinet.org/ Architectural Woodwork Institute

http://www.gocohens.com/hwtobuy/htbwod.html Guide to residential wood furniture construction

Types of Finishes

Principle types of finishes applied to wood furniture include stain, paint, oil, varnish, shellac, lacquer, and polyurethane (see Paints and Finishes in Chapter 11). Special or unusual finishes include stenciling, faux finishes (simulating other materials such as marble and granite), spattering, stippling, glazes, sponging, and hand-painted designs.

Metal

Metal is a common material in furniture construction and can be shaped in many forms. It can be riveted, bolted, or welded, providing great flexibility of design. The most common metals used for furniture construction are aluminum, chrome, iron, and steel.

Aluminum appears in tubes, cast leg frames, and sections of angles and channels. It requires a unique finishing process called anodizing to prevent corrosion. Aluminum is relatively weak in strength.

Chrome or *chromium* is used as a metal finish on furniture. It is characterized by its highly polished sheen, but is also available in a satin finish. Quality chrome plating is difficult to achieve and should be backed by a reputable manufacturer.

Iron, a black metal, is commonly used in outdoor furniture and on railings or grills. "Wrought" iron simply means "worked" iron.

Steel, a combination of iron and carbon, is the most commonly used metal in furniture construction. When formed into sheets, this metal is used in office furniture, cabinetry, shelving, and other products. The *gauge* or thickness of the steel determines its quality. Thin sheets are flimsy, easily dented, and when struck may produce a drumming noise. Quality metal furniture should be able to withstand normal dents and dings. Tubular steel furniture was perfected in the late 1920s through the works of several Bauhaus designers (Figure 8.29).

Steel rusts, and therefore must be finished with paint or be chrome plated. Stainless steel, a combination of steel and chromium, is used in hardware and trim. Other metals used in furniture, such as *brass, copper,* and *tin,* are primarily decorative elements.

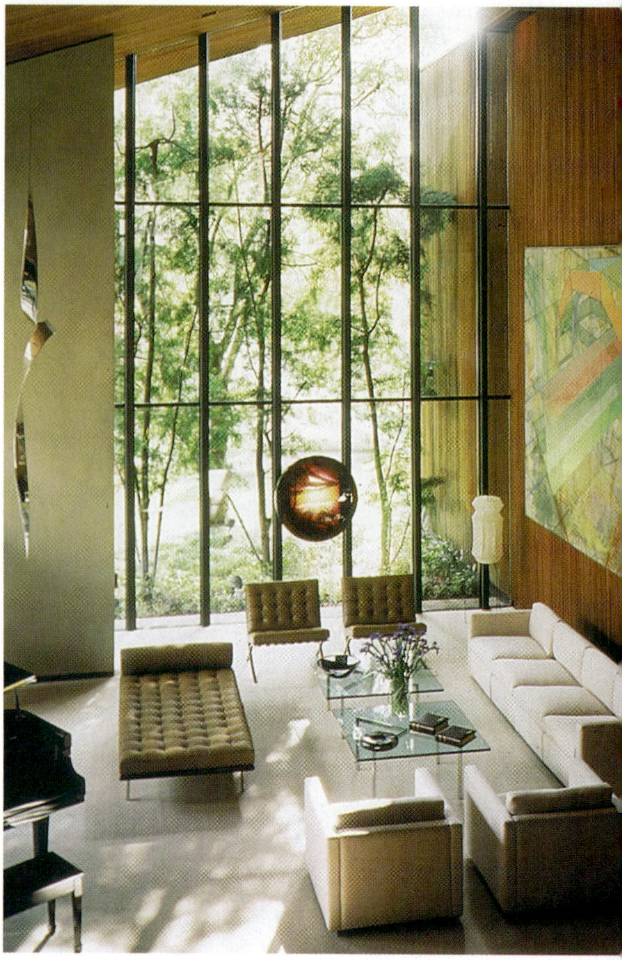

Figure 8.29 *The Barcelona chair, couch, and X table, designed by Mies van der Rohe, combine leather and steel. Th Barcelona chair has become a classic statement of contemporary design. (Courtesy of Knoll, Inc.)*

Synthetic Materials

Machine-made products for furniture construction have revolutionized the design field. Synthetic materials such as laminates, molded plastics, and acrylics are used for almost a furniture types. Plastic *laminates* are commonly used on cab inet surfaces and writing surfaces. Available in a wide var ety of colors, thicknesses, textures, and patterns, plast laminates are actually sheets of paper laminated togeth with resin. Glossy plastic laminates may be used on vertic surfaces, but will not maintain their glossy appearance used in the horizontal plane. Additionally, textured laminat are not appropriate on a horizontal plane where a smooth surface is desired.

Molded plastics such as nylon, vinyl, and polyethylene a only used in small parts in furniture construction (thoug they are often used in textile design). Fiberglass, a molde plastic mixed with glass fibers, is commonly made int chairs. These durable pieces of furniture can be molded int almost any shape (Figure 8.30). Other lightweight plastics ar widely used in institutional and outdoor furniture desig Plastic chairs should be tested for durability and stability b cause there are many grades of plastic on the market.

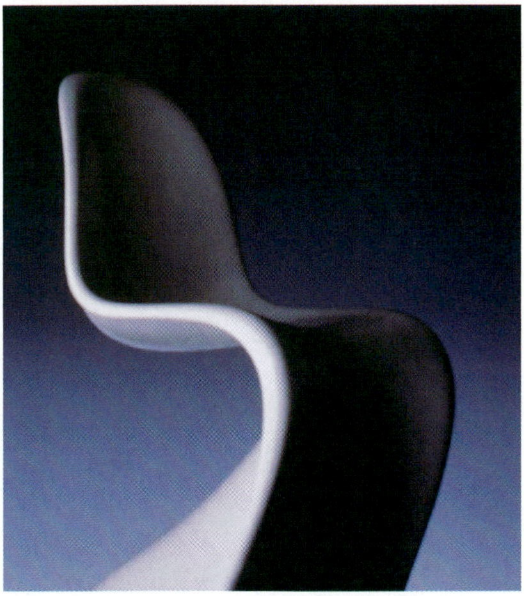

ure 8.30 *Danish designer Vernor Panton created his ısic stacking chair in the 1960s. Now made of yurethane, this graceful cantilever design is the first mple of a single-form molded fiberglass chair.*

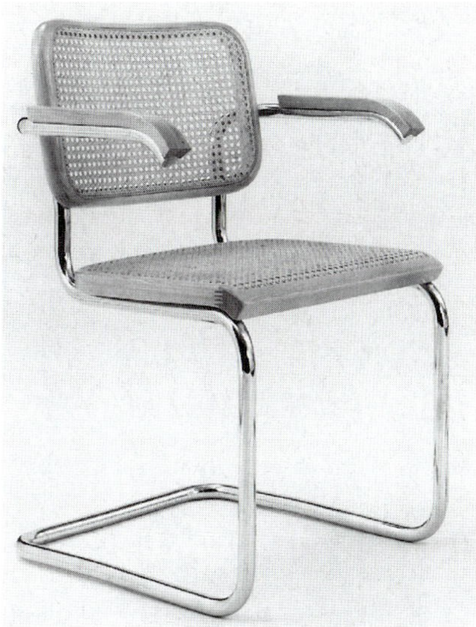

Figure 8.31 *Marcel Breuer combined cane with tubular steel for his famous Cesca chair while he was a faculty member at the Bauhaus design school during the 1920s. He was the first designer to use tubular steel for furniture construction. (Courtesy of Thonet Industries, Inc.)*

Acrylics such as Lucite and Plexiglas can be either trans-ent or translucent. They are commonly used for contem-ary furnishings or as a safe substitute for glass.

Synthetics are durable and easy to keep clean; however, ne synthetics may dull over time, break, or scratch. Some thetics are flammable and when damaged can rarely be aired. Because synthetics are mainly petroleum-based, y use up nonrenewable oil resources. Not all synthetics biodegradable; however, some can be recycled. Synthet-used as upholstery fillers are discussed in the section on ıolstered furniture.

ass

nufactured by combining sand, soda ash, limestone, omite, and a small amount of alumina, glass is a common ment in furniture design, particularly for tabletops. De-ıs can be etched or sandblasted into the glass (Figure 5), or the entire surface may appear slighted frosted (Fig-8.18) or opaque (Figure 8.20). A variety of beveled edges available; edges without a bevel should be avoided due the sharp nature of glass. Additionally, tabletop glass ould be at least 1/2″ thick and tempered to prevent sharp ges if broken.

Clear glass tops, as seen in Figure 8.29, are artful and help expand a space. Glass also brings an element of sparkle the interior, thereby adding contrast and interest to the ce. Glass can be cut to virtually any shape and is some-es used on the top of antiques or fine wood furniture to tect the finish. Glass is also used in the bathroom indus-to provide sculptural basins and countertops.

Palms and Grasses

Bamboo, rattan, cane, rush, and the materials used in wicker come from natural sources such as palms and grasses. Because of their nature, rattan, wicker, cane, and rush are compatible with an informal setting; in an eclectic formal room, they can add interest to the decor (see Figure 8.14). These materials can be used effectively in both inside and outside spaces.

Bamboo is a grass characterized by woody, hollow stems and ringed joints. It is used in lightweight furniture.

Rattan poles are cut from the rattan palm and can be bent to form a variety of designs. They are mainly used for chairs, tables, and beds.

Cane is split rattan or bamboo that is woven to form a mesh. Cane was introduced into England about 1660. It was used for chair seats and backs and some outdoor tabletops (Figure 8.31).

Rush is tightly twisted long grass (paper is often used as a substitute) made into a cord. The cord is then woven and mainly used for seats and backs of chairs.

Wicker (or basketwork) is a *method* of woven chair construction rather than a specific material. Used since ancient times, wicker chairs can be made of rushes, twigs, or reeds.

Upholstered Furniture

People in ancient civilizations first created "upholstered furniture" by stretching textiles, animal skins, or other natural materials over a sturdy frame. Chairs with fabric stretched

Figure 8.32 *Upholstery construction.*

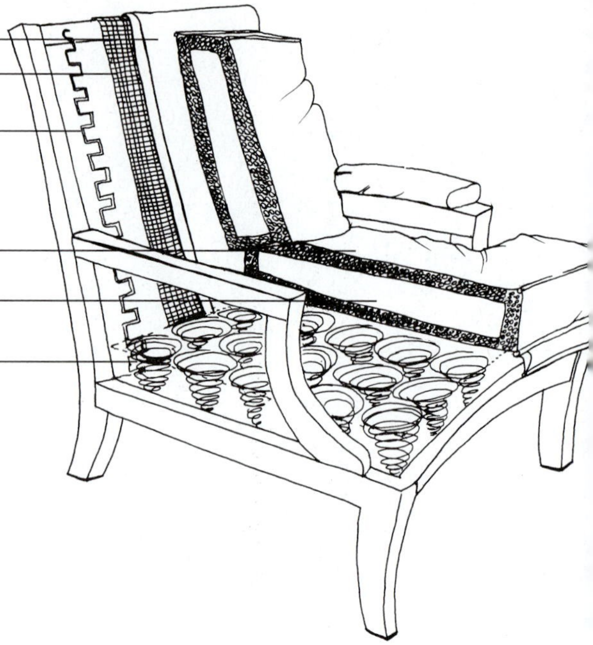

over seat and back frames are still used for lightweight pieces. During the Renaissance, simple cushions were placed on top of the stretched fabric. Later, fabrics were stretched over those cushions. By the sixteenth century, padding made of horsehair, feathers, wool, and down made cushions deeper and more comfortable. In the nineteenth century, springs were introduced and modern upholstered furniture had arrived. After that, little change occurred in upholstery construction until the introduction of synthetics during the 1930s, which had a tremendous impact on the furniture industry. There are two basic types of upholstered furniture: overstuffed (furniture that has padding or stuffing attached over the frame), and partially exposed (furniture that has some exposed frame pieces). The padding or stuffing is covered with a fabric or natural hide, which is referred to as upholstery.

Parts of Upholstered Furniture

Hidden beneath the upholstery are the components that should produce durability, comfort, and quality in upholstered furniture (Figure 8.32). Because these elements are hidden, the designer must rely on the manufacturer's written specifications.

Frame

A frame is constructed of metal, plastic, or kiln-dried hardwood such as maple, poplar, oak, ash, birch, or elm. (Softwoods tend to split.) The wood frame should be firmly assembled and usually joined by double dowels that are spiral grooved and then glued in place. Reinforcement braces of metal or wood should be glued and screwed to the corners. Nails are never used in the frames of good-quality furniture. Frames should be smooth to prevent the fabric from sagging.

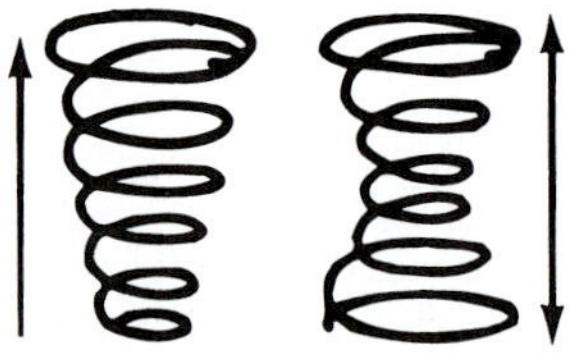

Figure 8.33 *Single- and double-cone coils.*

Webbing and Felt

Generally made of linen, jute, plastic, or rubber, the webb is arranged in a basketweave to provide support for springs and cushions. Good-quality webbing measures 3 4 inches in width and is tightly woven with little to no sp between the bands. Cotton felt may also be used to prot springs and other materials.

Springs

Springs are constructed of either sinuous wire or coils. T sinuous wire is simpler, and may be more desirable for sl line modern furniture and lightweight occasional chairs. T cone coil comes in both single and double cone (Fig 8.33). The single-cone coil is a prefabricated all-wire unit. create a spring cushion, single coils are tied to each ot and attached to top and bottom border wires. Double-co coils are affixed to a resilient base such as strips of webb or metal and are hand tied at the top to prevent slipping. T construction provides maximum comfort and is used in m expensive deep-seated upholstery. In fine-quality furnit individual coil springs are contained in muslin; however most furniture burlap is used to protect and cover spri and prevent the filling from working into the springs.

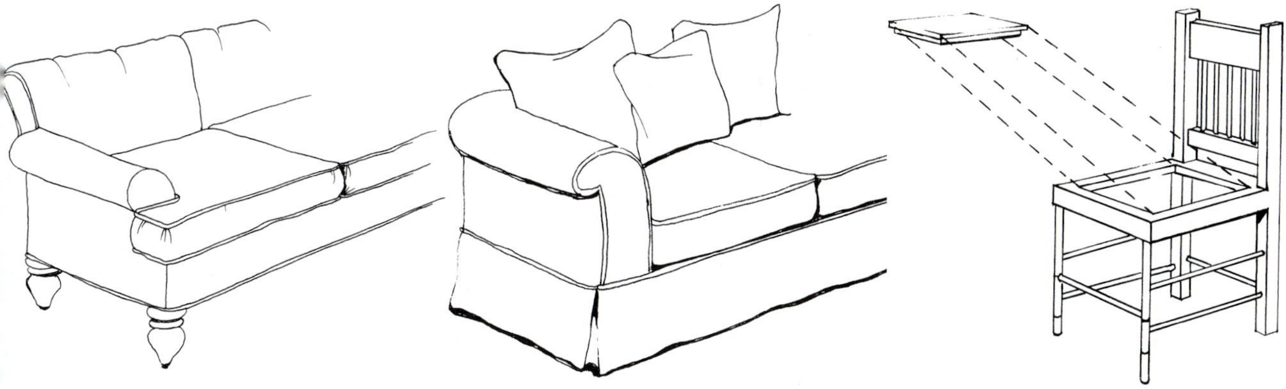

T-shaped cushion　Square cushion　Slip Seat

igure 8.34 *Types of cushions.*

illing, Stuffing, and Padding in Cushions

illing, stuffing, or padding materials of various types and ualities are used for cushioning, either alone or in combiation. These materials are listed on the label. The most comonly used fillings include the following:

. *Polyester* is lightweight, resilient, odorless, and resists mildew and moths. It may be used alone or combined with cores of foam, down, or innersprings. Polyester or fiberfill fillings should be wrapped with fabric (such as muslin) to retain their shape and prevent abrasion on the final covering.
. *Polyurethane foam* is commonly used and is available in a variety of densities. It is often wrapped with polyester fiberfill to add softness. Polyurethane resists liquids, moths, and mildew and is very resilient.
. *Down* or *feathers* are used in seat cushions, usually in combination with polyester and a thin foam core for shape. Although historically considered luxurious, 100 percent down is expensive and because it is not resilient, it requires frequent plumping.
. *Rubberized fibers* (which have less resiliency than the previously mentioned filling materials) are used in moderately priced furniture.
. *Shredded fibers* from natural sources (such as certain types of leaves) or synthetic felts are generally used in low-priced furniture.
. *Cotton* is occasionally used for small pieces.

pholstered cushions may be used on some or all of the contruction of the furniture piece. Seat and back cushions and illows are added to complement the furniture's style, and ushions may be fastened or loose, depending on the style nd preferred degree of flexibility. Cushions may also be ufted, a process in which the final covering is securely tied o the inner springs. Tufting is often accented with fabricovered buttons. Cushioning should be comfortable, reilient, durable, and should stay in place. Three types are hown in Figure 8.34.

Fabrics and Finishing Touches

Upholstery fabric is used to cover the cushions and other parts of the furniture frame as dictated by the style. Guidelines for selecting durable, stylish, and functional upholstery fabrics are discussed in Chapter 9. Finishing touches add character and detail to upholstery pieces. Welts (a cord around the edge of cushions and/or wood trim wrapped with fabric) can be applied in single or double rows in the same or contrasting fabrics. Cording, a wrapped decorative piece of rope, may also be added in these places. Nail heads (usually brass) give a masculine feel to a piece of furniture. Decorative trims and fringes create interest in a design.

Selecting Quality Upholstered Furniture

In selecting a piece of upholstered furniture, consider the following criteria:

- Precise tailoring is necessary for a well-finished appearance. Seams, welts, and cording should be smooth, straight, and firmly sewn with no loose threads. Hems and pleats should hang evenly.
- Large patterns should be carefully centered and matched on each cushion and skirt.
- All patterns, including those on the sides of the seat cushions, should run in the same direction.
- When fabrics are quilted, smaller stitches prevent snagging.
- Cushions should fit snugly.
- If zippers are used, they must be sewn straight with no puckering, and they must operate easily.
- If a nap is present, it should run in only one direction.
- Fabric should be smoothly stretched over the frame with no buckling.
- Back panels should be firmly and neatly tacked or stitched.
- Exposed wood parts should be of well-finished hardwood.

SUSTAINABLEDESIGN

Selecting "Green" Furniture

The process of furniture manufacturing, if not carefully undertaken, can harm the environment. When selecting "green" furniture, designers should look for products that utilize lumber from renewable wood resources or select furniture made from recycled materials.

Many furniture companies have strict policies regarding the use of wood from threatened or endangered species of trees, many of which are found in rain forests. In some cases federal and state laws restrict the use of certain woods for furniture construction. Some species, such as maple and oak, are easier to replenish than other rare woods, such as mahogany, teak, and rosewood. Wood species that are endangered but are grown specifically for furniture industries and replenished are often used only as fine thin veneers. These woods may be farmed as plantation-grown lumber or in a sustainable forest. More plentiful wood byproducts, such as particleboard, are used for the veneer backing.

According to *Design Solutions* magazine, the Tropical Forest Foundation is one organization that works to educate consumers and producers about the benefits of conservation and forest management. One of its primary goals is to educate individuals and companies on the benefits of low-impact logging.

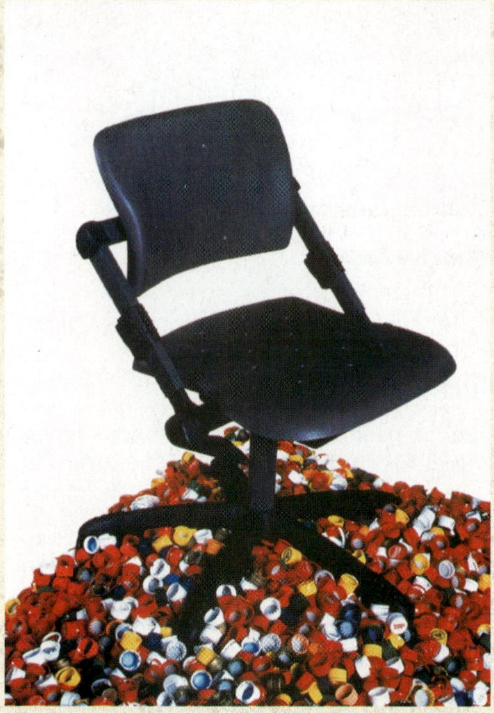

SD8.1 *The ergonomic Scio chair with seat and back made from recycled plastic bottle caps. (Courtesy of HAG, Inc.)*

Another alternative is to select furniture made from recycled products. For example, HAG, a furniture manufacturing company, has designed the adjustable Scio chair whose seat and back are made of recycled bottle caps (Figure SD8.1). Environmental Furniture Company produces chairs from used automobile tires utilizing fire-retardant padding processed without formaldehyde and dichloro-fluorocarbons.

Proper selection of green furniture also includes ensuring the items have safe, environmentally friendly finishes. The process of applying paint to furniture can cause the release of toxic volatile organic chemicals, or VOCs, into the air. These solvents are carried into the exhaust stacks and released directly into the atmosphere. VOCs contribute to smog and harm the ozone layer, allowing damaging ultraviolet rays to reach the earth.

The Clean Air Act passed by Congress in 1990 requires companies to reduce these harmful emissions. Some companies have developed alternative painting processes to reduce emissions. At an Interior Design Educators Council conference, Elizabeth Rylan and Gordon Kerby outlined several ways this can be accomplished. For example, paint can be applied to wood as it rides on a conveyor belt, reducing the VOCs emitted into the air; metal furniture can be given an electrical charge and coated with paint of the opposite charge, bonding the two together electrically. Additionally, substituting water-based stains and natural coatings for paint and using carbon filters can also lessen the release of VOCs.

In order to help protect the environment, designers should ask manufacturers for their policies and statistics on sustainable forestry and about their compliance with the Clean Air Act before specifying their products.

More info online @

http://www.tropicalforestfoundation.org/ Tropical Forest Foundation

http://www.epa.gov/oar/oaqps/peg_caa/pegcaain.html EPA's Clean Air Act in "Plain English"

http://www.certifiedwood.org/ Certified Forest Products Council

ɔre info online @

p://www.gocohens.com/hwtobuy/upholstery.html and
p://www.rosefurniture.com/yellowpage/upholsteryvalue.html
ides to residential upholstery furniture construction

p://www.upholsterysupply.com/yardage.htm Chart of approximate
dage quantities for upholstered goods

p://interiordec.about.com/cs/upholstery General information on
holstery furniture

beling

mentioned previously, federal and state laws require labels providing specific information about the piece to be attached to furnishings. Reputable manufacturers warranty the terials used, and guarantee that the furniture's performance will meet the specifications outlined on the label.

CCESSORIES

rniture and accessories work together in defining the style d feeling of a space. Because accessories can greatly ennce a space, the process of selecting and arranging accesries for both residential and commercial settings deserves oughtful consideration. Accessories add the finishing touches a room, reflecting the personal taste and individuality of the user more than any other element. Accessories may have sentimental value to the client and may incorporate personal collections. Accessories can also be a powerful tool in establishing the concept or expressing a cultural background. Interiors are enriched by the addition of both functional and decorative accessories.

Functional Accessories

Functional accessories serve a utilitarian purpose but may become an interesting display item as well. Some items, such as towel racks, drapery rods, door handles, or accent plumbing fixtures (Figure 8.35), may be attached to the architectural background. Other practical accessories such as a mirror, lamp, clock, or tray may be moved from one place to another within the space.

The purpose or use of the room should be the prime consideration when selecting functional accessories. For example, if lighting is required beside a lounge chair in a living room, choose an appropriate lamp that will meet the needs of the user. Making a list of accessories necessary in each room will help with the successful selection and placement of each item.

Lamps

Lamps, known in the industry as *portable luminaires,* are attractive accessories serving the purpose of providing light

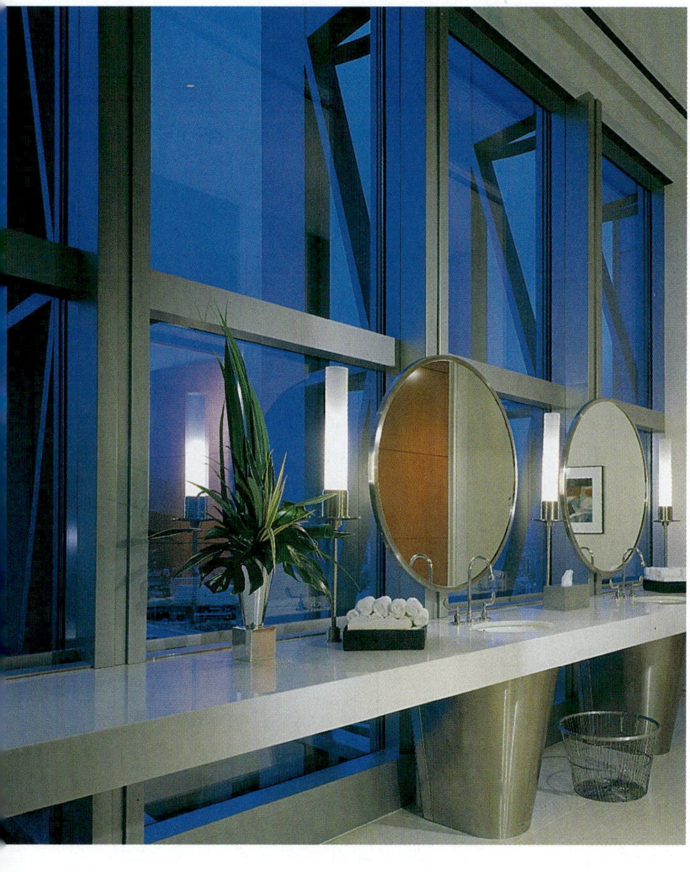

Figure 8.35 *In this bathroom with a 15′ceiling and a view of the Hawaiian mountains, the designers chose lighting and accessories to complement the clean, contemporary lines of the building. (Architect/Designer: Gensler. Photograph by Marco Lorenzetti/Hedrich-Blessing.)*

Figure 8.36 *Blending contemporary lines with historic elements, Michael Kreiss designed his residence to reflect his heritage while incorporating his line of furnishings. Note how the nightstand lamp is at an appropriate height to allow light to fall on the surface of reading materials for someone sitting in bed, but the light is shielded from the person's eyes. Also note the rich variety in textures. (Designer: Michael Kreiss of Kreiss Design. Furnishings from the Kreiss Collection.)*

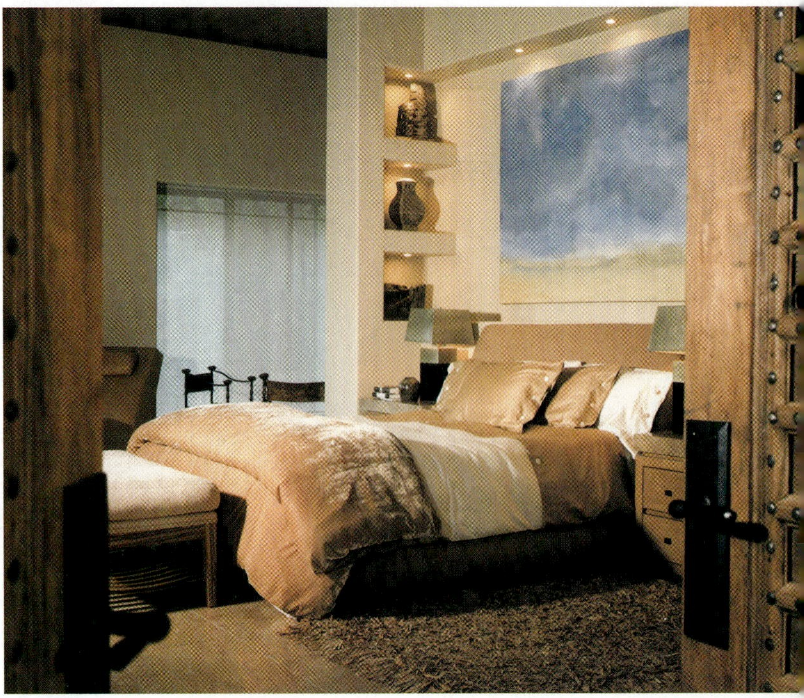

when and where needed. Common types of lamps include table lamps, floor lamps, sconces, torchères, and pendants (chandeliers). Lamps are available in a wide range of styles—traditional or modern, decorative or structural. A lighting fixture that is carefully chosen for a specific room, style, mood, location, or purpose can be an important contributing element, as shown in Figure 8.36. (Refer to Chapter 5 for further information on lamps and lighting considerations.)

Books

Cicero said, "A room without books is a body without a soul." Books add friendliness to a home. Usually no room has a mood that precludes their use, or a color scheme so complete it could not benefit from their warm tones and textures. Bookshelves can go in almost any room, require little space, and create a warm, friendly atmosphere, as illustrated in Figure V.1. Children need bookshelves in their rooms at a height they can easily reach. Other bedrooms can accommodate shelves where space permits—usually close to the bed for nighttime reading. Kitchens need handy shelves for reference books and cookbooks. Conference rooms benefit from shelves used to display company memorabilia, awards, and reference books. Bookshelves often can be fitted into unused spaces and odd corners. They can also work around or over doors and windows or as a space divider.

Additionally, books can add a decorative quality to a room with their textures, colors, and shapes. They also mix well with other accessories; for example, a few books flanked with interesting bookends, next to a plant and a small sculpture, or placed on a coffee table with other items add interest to a room (Figure 8.1).

Mirrors

Since the fourteenth century mirrors have been used as fur tional and decorative objects in homes and public plac Mirrors are available in almost any size and in frames to any decor. Mirrors are a helpful tool for the interior design they can add beauty, multiply space, conceal unattracti structural features, distribute and double light, brighten da areas, and bring life into an otherwise drab room. Becau of their myriad uses, mirrors have steadily increased in po ularity and now play an indispensable role in all styles of i teriors (Figure 8.37).

Clocks

Clocks have long been important accessories in the hor and office. From the handsome antique grandfather clo encased in an elegantly carved case to the high-tech cloc of the late twentieth century, timepieces not only serve necessary function but can also add a calming backgrou "tick-tock" sound to any room. Naturally a clock must placed where it can be seen easily. Outdoors, clocks f quently serve as landmarks in metropolitan settings. smaller communities the chime of a clock tower helps to c fine the "sense of place."

Screens

In addition to its decorative value, a screen may serve ma functional purposes. Screens can set off an entrance whe the front door opens directly into the living area, act as a vider between living and dining areas, close off a kitchen, set off a private area by making a room within a room. Th

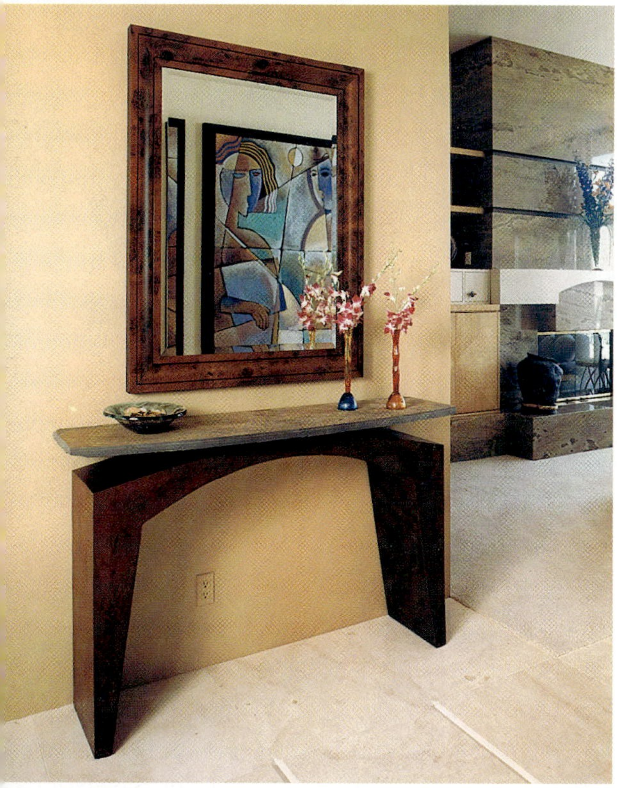

;ure 8.37 *This custom-designed table is accentuated by the e of a mirror and floral accessories. The table, designed by 'frey Jurasky, ASID, is fabricated from steel and slate. 'esigner: Jurasky & Associates. Photograph by Kaminsky oduction.)*

so can redirect traffic when strategically placed, extend the parent size of a room by replacing a door, control the flow air and the direction of light, camouflage an old-fashioned diator or air-conditioning unit, or conceal storage. A deco- ive screen can give an architectural quality to a room, en- nce the room's decor, provide a backdrop for a furniture ouping, substitute for side drapery, or serve as the room's cal point.

ardware

contemporary room can be made strikingly modern and a ditional room can take on an authentic feeling through the scriminating use of small accessories such as doorknock- s, doorknobs, switch plates, curtain rods, and tiebacks. awer pulls, **escutcheons** (the plate behind the pull), and nges can give a piece of furniture the feeling of a particu- period (see Figures 8.36, 8.38, and Chapter 12).

ecorative Accessories

ecorative accessories generally provide no other value than e pleasure derived from looking at them. Decorative items ound in furniture and antique stores, galleries, design stu- os, art and craft exhibitions or shows, and numerous other

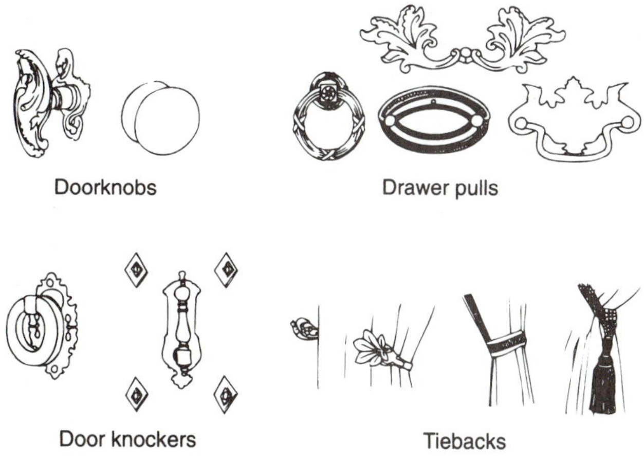

Figure 8.38 *Finishing touches.*

sources. Accessories are available in traditional or contemporary styles and may be handcrafted or machine-made, old or new.

Following is an outline of the basic accessories that complete a room and give it an attractive, desirable, lived-in feeling.

Art

In residential design paintings, drawings, original prints, photographs, sculpture, and other types of art are usually selected personally by the client. Corporate art collections are usually selected by a professional curator. Designers should be aware of the following types of art and related terms in order to assist clients with their personal selection or to work effectively with a curator.

Paintings, Drawings, Prints, and Photographs

Original *paintings* in oil, acrylic, watercolor, or tempera are usually the most expensive type of art. They range from the works of famous painters to those of local artists, as shown in Figure 8.39.

Original *drawings* are usually executed in ink, charcoal, pencil, pastels, or crayon.

Original *prints* such as etchings, lithographs, woodcuts, steel engravings, and drypoints are *not* photographic copies. They are designed by an artist and usually produced by her or under her supervision. Limited edition prints are numbered and signed by the artist. A piece numbered 27/100 for example, is the twenty-seventh of a total of 100 prints made. The fewer prints produced, the rarer the piece. Limited prints are usually less expensive than one-of-a-kind paintings and drawings.

Posters, originally called "poor man's art," are available at minimal cost. They are usually considered a low-budget accessory but are often seen framed in fine contemporary settings. Photographic reproductions of original paintings, drawings, or prints are also inexpensive and widely available. Some early posters are now collector's items.

Family or artistic *photographs* personalize a space.

Figure 8.39 *The series of paintings by artist Alice Nesbitts complements the fine fabric on the racket-arm sofa. Accessories add texture and sparkle to the room. (Designer: Gandy/Peace, Inc. Photograph by Chris A. Little. Courtesy of* Southern Accents.*)*

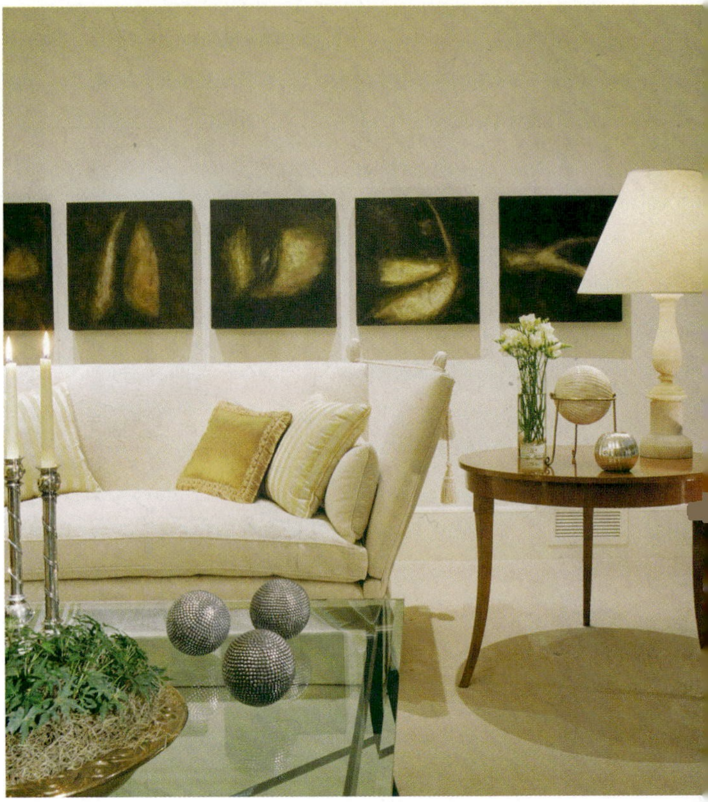

Frames and Mats

Frames and mats are most effective when they do not detract from the work but complement the medium, colors, and subject. The frame and mat should work with the style and architectural background elements. The size, line, and form of the frame should not overpower the art but enhance the overall composition. *Slip molds,* small gold inserts, are frequently used when a little sparkle is required between the frame and mat, or between mats.

A mat usually complements drawings, etchings, watercolors, and prints of all types. Oil paintings are seldom matted, but may have a liner made from linen, velvet, or leather. Mats protect original art from direct contact with the glass, where condensation can occur when the temperature changes. Quality mats are acid-free, protecting the displayed work from discoloration and serious damage.

Glass is usually used over prints, watercolors, and etchings but is almost never used over an oil painting. Regular glass, nonglare glass, and acrylic are available. Nonglare glass tends to give a clouded appearance but does cut down on reflections. Acrylic works well in environments where broken glass could be highly dangerous. Glass may also be purchased with built-in ultraviolet light protection to preserve colors in original and poster art.

Sculpture

Three-dimensional works of art can be treasured accessor in residential or commercial settings (Figure V.4). Sculptu is fashioned in many media, including metals, marble a other stone, wood, glass, and ceramics. Placement often d pends on the size of the piece. If small, the piece may be b displayed on a shelf, mantel, or tabletop. If the sculpture large, it can dominate an area or provide a focal point. pedestal may be used for either a small or large sculpture give it greater prominence. Lighting that spotlights the art does not wash it away adds visual interest.

Other Types of Art and Crafts

Ceramics are accessories made of clay and include scu ture, dishes, bowls, platters, pots, and tiles. Clay ranges fr coarse to fine and comes in a wide variety of colors. The tisan may create a unique ceramic piece by applying diff ent types of ornamentation, colors, textures, and sha (Figure 8.40). Ceramics fall into four basic categorie porcelain, china, earthenware, and stoneware.

A *mosaic* is made up of small, usually square pieces (cal tesserae) of ceramic, stone, or glass arranged in an artistic sign and set in cement. Used for floors and murals in anci

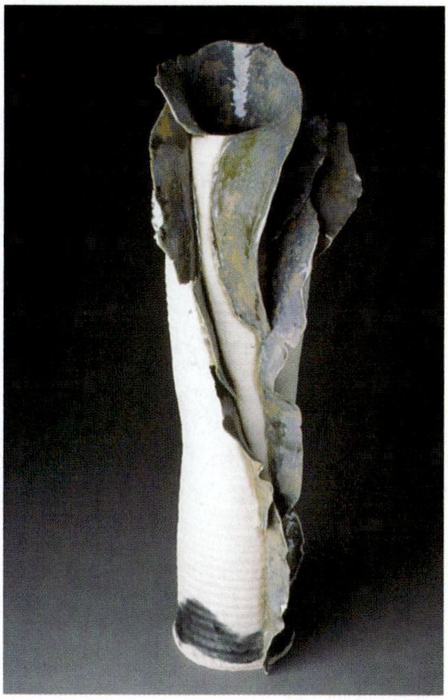

igure 8.40 *This ceramic sculptural vase, Perianth, was* *eated using the process called* raku. *Originally used in Japan* *ı the sixteenth century for ritualistic tea ceremonies, today* ıku *refers to clay pieces fired rapidly and cooled quickly,* *ften by immersion in cold water. The vessel stands 30″ high* *nd would serve as an excellent focal point or accent piece in* *n interior. (Artist: Mary Jane Taylor. Photograph by Light* *ources, Inc.)*

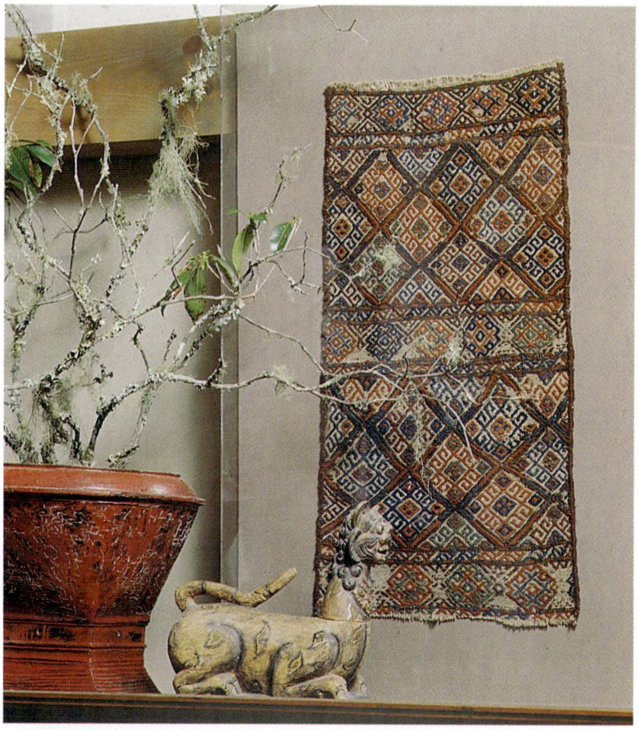

Figure 8.41 *This exquisite weaving protected by Plexiglas complements an antique dragon on a rustic glass cabinet. The textures and form enhance a Thai-influenced interior. (Designer: Jerry Pair. Photograph by Peter Vitale. Courtesy of Veranda.)*

ımes, mosaics currently are used for a variety of small decoıtive objects including trays, boxes, and small tables.

Glass art accessories include vases, dishes, bowls, and culpture. Glass can be etched, colored, enameled, pressed, ilded, cut, and engraved. Handblown glass has been a poplar art for centuries, and exquisite pieces from many counies, each with their own design approach, have been idely appreciated in America. Modern designs have been ioneered most notably by Italian and Scandinavian artists, ho fashion beautiful and unique pieces.

Stained glass, an artistic composition of small pieces of olored glass held together by lead, has also been known ırough the ages, particularly during the Medieval period hen stained glass was used to create extraordinary winows in Gothic cathedrals. Stained glass can be made into indow and door panels, hung at a window, or designed as freestanding piece of art.

Weaving and *textile art* have been known for centuries in most every country of the world, and each has developed istinctive cultural designs (Figure 8.41). Historically, most eavers have employed a simple handloom, wool yarns, and atural dyes. Tapestry is an intricate, usually pictorial, multiolored handwoven textile design with a ribbed surface. resently, most tapestries used as accessories are machinemade. Some copy patterns used in previous times, and some are more modern in design. Tapestries can be used as accessories in a similar manner as paintings.

Handcrafted and custom-designed rugs and blankets are often used as a focal point in a room or as the basis for a room's color scheme, as seen in Figure 10.15. Blankets such as those produced by the Navajo Indians and the Finnish add a pleasant decorative touch in a room. The traditional process of quilting involves arranging small pieces of colored, plain, or patterned fabrics into an overall design. Quilts are frequently employed in provincial design.

Animal hides may be hung as paintings, draped over furniture, or used as rugs in low-traffic areas. Before selecting a hide for use, the interior designer must be able to verify that the hide was legally obtained. Designers should be sensitive to ethical treatment and conservative use of all animal products. Endangered species should never be used.

Painted brain-tanned animal hides such as deer, elk, or bison are a popular art form in Western design. The art form, developed by Native Americans, requires the hide to be tanned using the animal's brain instead of harsh commercial chemicals. The designs painted onto the skin may be inspired by authentic pictographs, geometric designs, or original concepts of the artist (Figure 8.42).

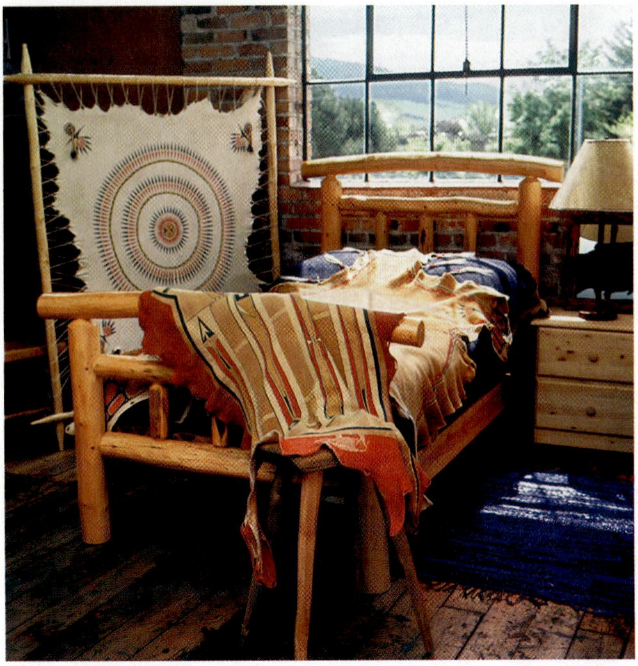

Figure 8.42 *These painted brain-tanned hides work well in a contemporary or rustic setting. Hung from custom-designed poles or draped over furnishings, they create an intriguing focal point. (Artist: Lee Secrest. Photograph by Laurie Lane.)*

Baskets and the art of basket weaving have changed little since ancient times. Artists have further developed this art by introducing new colors, forms, patterns, and styles. Traditional baskets created by particular cultures display distinctive characteristics and styles that are highly valued.

Handcrafted *candles,* originally used for purely functional purposes, are a highly intricate art form. Candles are created in many colors and in a wide range of textures and forms suitable for both traditional and modern settings. Candles are often used for decorative accents in the interior; when lit, they provide a warm, inviting element in the private or public environment.

Flowers, Foliage, and Plants

Of all accessories making up the final touches of a residence or commercial space, almost nothing can duplicate the effect of fresh flowers. Three popular flower arranging styles are Oriental (*ikebana*), traditional, and contemporary freestyle. *Ikebana* is asymmetrical with minimum foliage; traditional is more formal in balance and may contain numerous types and colors of foliage; contemporary may be asymmetrical or symmetrical and uses only a few varieties of foliage, sometimes only one species. The container contributes to the total success of the arrangement and generally works best when the texture, pattern, and size complement the surroundings. Glass, metal, porcelain, pottery, and baskets are often used because they can be effectively combined with traditional or modern furnishings.

Living plants placed around interior environments contribute to the total design scheme and help to bring something of the outdoors into the interior (Figure 8.18 shows th use of both living plants and fresh-cut flowers). Persona preference for texture, form, color, and size is a considera tion in selecting plants, as well as special care requirement for light, water, and temperature.

Dried flowers, branches, pods, and other foliage are ofte used as alternatives to fresh plants and flower arrangements They have the advantage of being permanent, and requir no upkeep other than dusting. Well-made artificial flowers foliage, and plants look amazingly natural. They may b manufactured from silk, polyethylene, or polypropylene (The latter two materials can be cleaned more easily tha silk.) Like dried arrangements, they are permanent and re quire only occasional dusting. Many commercial and institu tional organizations use artificial flowers and plants instea of fresh ones because of the easy upkeep and one-time in vestment.

More info online @

http://www.famsf.org/ Fine Arts Museum of San Francisco

http://www.louvre.fr/ The Louvre Museum

http://www.whitney.org/ Whitney Museum of Modern Art

http://www.metmuseum.org/ Metropolitan Museum of Art

http://www.artic.edu/ Art Institute of Chicago

Selecting Accessories

When determining what accessories are suitable for a partic ular space, consider a wide range of possibilities. Reviewin an outline of numerous items often sparks an idea of the ac cessory or accessories that tie an entire grouping togethe Table 8.2 lists commonly selected accessories for both resi dential and commercial settings.

The accessories may be utilitarian or displayed for aes thetic pleasure. The items may be incorporated into th scheme to enhance the background or they may function pr marily as a point of interest (Figure 8.43). The principles an elements of design must always be used. For example, th item must be suitable in texture, color, and form to the style background, and other accessories and furnishings in th room. The item should be in scale with the other furnishing and the space allocated. The accessory should help to brin balance and harmony to the room.

Accessories can either be authentic to a certain histori style or mixed to support a variety of styles. The latter ap proach is often considered more creative. Accessories ca also support the architectural background. For example, a informal arrangement of flowers in a basket enhances a rus tic wood wall, and an elegant porcelain vase enhances a fo mal French paneled wall.

Designers often play an important role in selecting acces sories for commercial and institutional spaces. The previou guidelines should be followed, but the art and accessorie should be placed so as not to interfere with the function o the facility. Usually, commercial spaces do not incorporat personal items except in private offices; however, acces sories in public areas do reflect the corporation's image an character.

ble 8.2 *Accessory Idea List*

- imal hides
- uariums and fish
- ms and armor
- t (two-dimensional)
- tificial flowers and foliage arrangements
- htrays
- skets
- th accessories (soap dish, toothbrush container, towel racks, towels, washcloths, scales, toilet-paper holder)
- rdcages
- ankets
- okends
- oks and magazines
- ttles
- wls
- xes
- assware
- lendars
- ndles
- ndlesticks
- nisters
- Ceramics
- Clocks
- Coat racks
- Collections (coins, guns, stamps, antique items, etc.)
- Cushions
- Desk accessories (pen and pencil holders, letter holders, desk pad, address book, small clock, etc.)
- Dishes
- Doll houses
- Dolls
- Figurines
- Fireplace tools and firescreen
- Flower and plant containers
- Flowers
- Foliage
- Frames (for art, photos, etc.)
- Games
- Glassware
- Hardware (door knobs, hinges, racks, pulls, tiebacks, hooks, escutcheons, rods, etc.)
- Kitchen and cooking utensils
- Kites
- Lamps
- Maps, charts, and documents
- Mirrors
- Models (airplanes, ships, etc.)
- Mosaics
- Music boxes
- Musical items (instruments, music stands, sheet music, etc.)
- Needlework
- Pedestals (for displays)
- Photo albums
- Pillows
- Pitchers
- Plants
- Plates and platters (decorative)
- Pottery
- Puzzles
- Quilts
- Rugs
- Screens
- Sculpture
- Serving carts
- Shells and rocks
- Shelves (a small, decorative, carved wood shelf, for example)
- Silverware
- Stools
- Tablecloths, mats, and napkins
- Tapestries
- Telephones
- Tools (antique spinning wheel, for example)
- Toy furniture
- Toys
- Trays
- Trophies
- Umbrella stands
- Vases
- Wastebaskets
- Weavings
- Wreaths

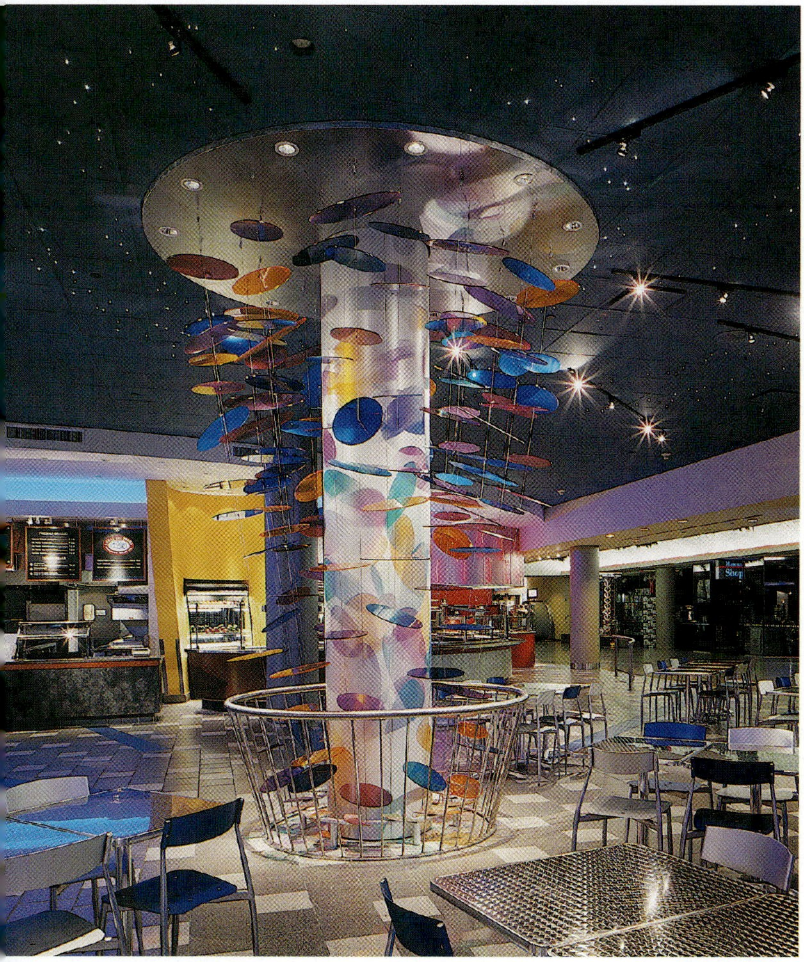

Figure 8.43 *This creative art piece establishes the whimsical feeling in the Galaxy Café. The restaurant, which can seat more than 500, draws 2500 visitors a day from Boston's Museum of Science. (Architect/Designer: Prellwitz/Chilinski Assoc. Photograph © 1996 Steve Rosenthal. Artist: David Tonneson.)*

Adding art and accessories to a commercial setting can give an inviting, warm character to an otherwise institutional setting. Often the designer is limited in purchasing fine-quality items for the commercial setting because of budget restrictions and the possibility of theft. Obtaining accessories that project an aesthetic appeal and that will last through the years are additional challenges. Such items as plants and artwork—usually large in scale—are often chosen for schools, offices, hospitals, libraries, hotels, retail stores, restaurants, and other public settings. Also, accessories that relate to the function of the facility itself can add character to the space; for example, prints in a restaurant might pertain to the history or theme of the establishment. All accessories selected for the commercial setting should enhance the environment and humanize the space.

More info online @

http://www.guild.com/ Excellent source for fine one-of-a-kind art and accessories

Grouping and Placing Accessories

The desire to display prized possessions is universal; the challenge for a designer is to arrange these treasured objects into an appealing composition. If the collected items are worth acquiring, they are worth displaying. Successful placement of accessories lies in training the eye to see beauty in color, texture, form, and spatial relationships. Applying the principles and elements of design is helpful when choosing the best location for each item.

Grouping items in an artistic arrangement can be an effective means of creating an interesting display in the room. By themselves, small things may be insignificant, but through skillful arrangement even the simplest items can take on special meaning. When grouping small objects, keep in mind that they are seen against a background of walls and furniture, which can be considered part of the arrangement. Be aware of the relationships of the items to each other. Perhaps a grouping of round objects of varying sizes is pleasing, but adding a rectangle can provide an interesting contrast. In an arrangement with three elements—a horizontal piece, a higher intermediate piece, and a tall vertical piece—the eye moves from the low horizontal to the high vertical, providing a sense of transition. This rhythm is seen in nature when the eye observes the earth, flowering plants, and tower trees. A common color subtly running through each elem can add unity to an arrangement; varying colors and textu can create a sense of interest and variety.

Two-Dimensional Art in Wall Composition

Pictures can be hung individually or in groupings, but t should always relate to the sofa, desks, chairs, tables, or ot furnishings constituting the wall composition. Usually a ture relates best to the composition when not "floating" al on the wall. A table, console, or other piece of furniture neath the picture can stabilize the artwork. Following are c siderations for selecting and arranging two-dimensional for a wall composition.

- Positive spaces are the areas filled with the two-dimensional artwork; negative spaces are the areas in between these pieces. Regardless of shape and size, each picture should have a pleasing space surroundin it (Figure 8.44).
- A single picture on a wall may work best when hung eye level.
- A picture hung above a chair or sofa should be place high enough so the head of the seated person does n touch the frame; if hung much higher, the picture lac continuity with the furniture arrangement. Approximately 6 to 8 inches above a sofa or chair back provi sufficient clearance. Additionally, pictures are best se and appreciated when not obstructed by lamps, flow arrangements, or other accessories.
- To assemble an arrangement, lay a large sheet of bro paper the size of the area to be covered on the floor. Arrange pictures and other objects on the paper until the final composition is created. Trace each object around the perimeter, and mark a point where it will hung on the wall. Then hold the paper up against the wall with marks made where nails or hooks will be placed. The pictures can then be hung easily in the planned arrangement.

Arranging Art in Storage Units

The arrangement of accessories on wall units, bookca secretaries, breakfronts, or even baker's racks require sensitive eye. The elements and principles of design are

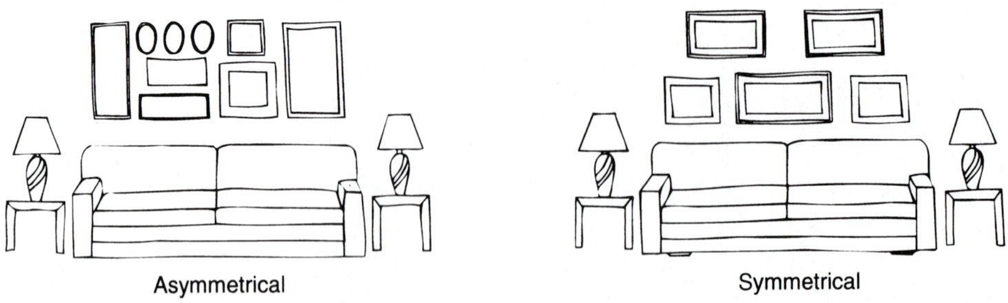

Figure 8.44 *Symmetrical and asymmetrical arrangements of art are hung with careful attention to the relationship of positive spaces (the art itself) and negative spaces (the spaces between the art pieces).*

·y to a successful design solution. The following ideas are ·lpful.

- Taller, heavier pieces look best on lower shelves.
- Books may fill an entire shelf, or be combined with accent plates, figurines, photographs, or small plants.
- Books also may be laid flat and stacked to serve as a bookend. Brass accessories or accent pieces may be placed on top of the books. It is common to group books in relationship to their height in ascending or descending order. Antique books with leather covers may be purchased if a client's collection requires additional character.
- Bookends can add a special character or accent to a row of books.
- Two-dimensional art may be placed on shelves at a slight angle.
- Accents from nature, such a geodes, shells, or driftwood, can add warmth and texture.
- Photographs and unusual frames can add interest.
- Clear, simple glass objects look best when grouped together and placed at or near eye level.

is important to remember that the composition of acces·ries is not a static element in the room. Collections of books and accessories will grow. (Landscape architects continually deal with this dimension of growth.) Designers must allow empty space for new prized objects. Conversely, some objects will be moved to other rooms where the client finds them more useful or appropriate.

Summary

Knowledge of the various furniture types and their proper construction will aid the designer in the development of a successful interior. Furnishings that withstand years of use will be remembered by the client and produce positive referrals; conversely, furniture that falls apart will also be remembered by the client, most likely in the form of negative referrals. Because of the financial investment, longevity is the expected outcome and designers must be able to specify and recognize quality construction.

Accessories work directly with the room's furniture and should complement the selections. Accessories should include items of personal value to the client or company. Items for functional or decorative use in all areas of the interior add visual pleasure, whether displayed alone or in groups (Figure 8.45).

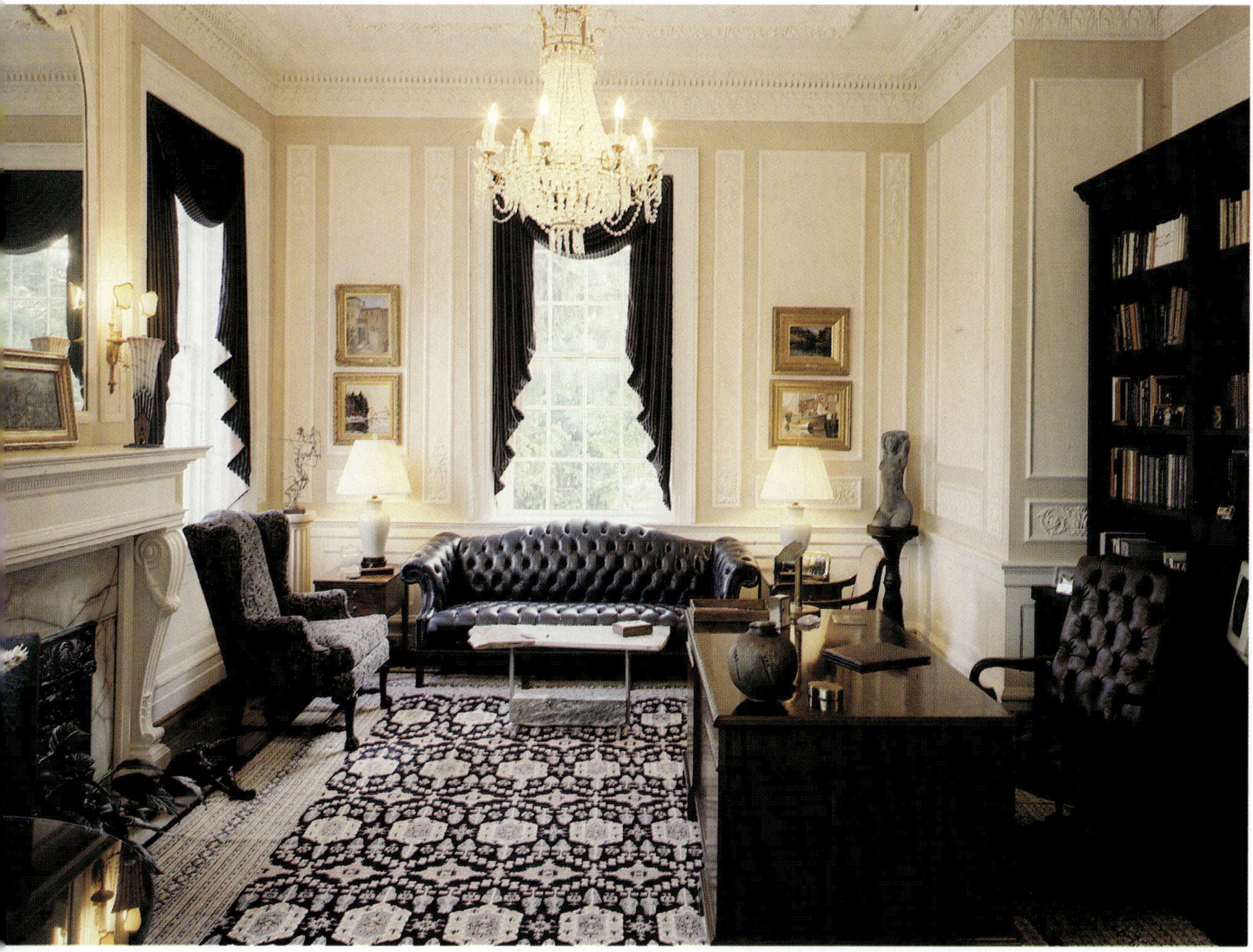

gure 8.45 *In this award-winning university president's office, art and accessories from the university's collection add ·armth and variety to the traditional setting. (Designer: Lynn M. Jones. Photograph by J. J. Williams.)*

extiles

9

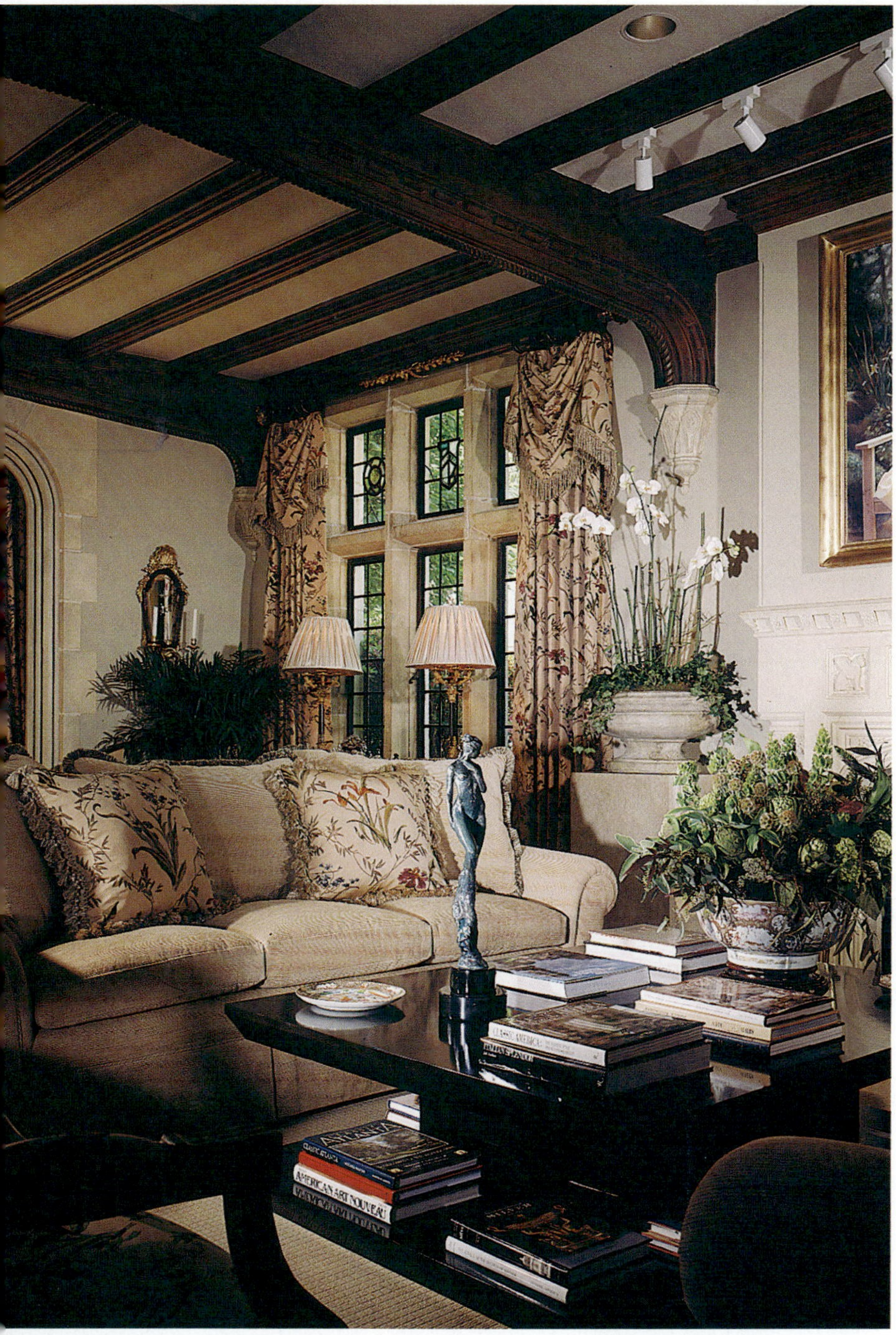

ure 9.1 *In this masculine Tudor home, warm tones were selected by the igner to humanize the interior. Note the addition of trims and fringes on peries and pillows. (Designer: James Essary & Associates. Photograph © Robert en. As seen in* Atlanta Homes & Lifestyles.*)*

Textiles enhance both residential and commercial interiors; they are probably more versatile than any other element used for interior design. Textiles are pliable; they can be sewn, draped, bent, folded, wrapped, pleated, gathered, and stretched. Textiles are used in every room for upholstery, window treatments, slipcovers, pillows and cushions, bedspreads, blankets and throws, towels, table linens, wall coverings, ceiling coverings, lamp shades, and trim.

As discussed in the introduction to Part V, there are several basic considerations in the selection of interior materials: function, aesthetics, and economics. One of the primary purposes of textiles, however, is to humanize living spaces. Textiles provide a transition between architecture and furniture, bringing comfort, warmth, and softness to homes and public places (see Figures 9.1 and 9.2).

Textile is an overall term used to describe a fiber, yarn, or fabric. The terms *fibers, yarns, fabrics,* and *textiles* are often used interchangeably in the profession, and are defined as follows:

- **Fibers** are the raw materials, either natural or synthetic, that produce yarns and fabrics.
- **Yarns** are fibers that are twisted or assembled together to form the strands that produce fabrics.
- **Fabrics** are the results of the weaving, knitting, twisting, felting, or lacing of fibers and yarns. Fabrics also may be formed from plastics.

Fibers

Fibers, such as raw cotton, silk, or polyester, are the most basic element of a fabric. A perfect fiber that will adequately serve every general design purpose does not exist. Each fiber has its own advantages and disadvantages. M ufacturers have found that by blending certain fibers, most desirable qualities of each can be incorporated int single fabric.

Yarns are made by spinning various lengths of fibers i strands used for fabric construction. A fabric's performa and appearance are affected by the method and the amo of twisting of the fibers. A high twist produces more stren and durability but takes away some of the luster. Long f ments with little twist generally maintain a high luster lose much of their stability. *Ply* is the result of twisting t or more single yarns together before weaving to give ad strength or to create a surface effect.

Natural Fibers

Fibers that come from nature fall into four classificatio protein, cellulose, metallic, and mineral.

Protein Fibers

Wool and silk are the most important protein, or anin fibers.

Wool is the fleece of sheep, Angora goats (known mohair), camels, and other animals. It has been used si the seventh or eighth century B.C. In early Egypt, Gree Asia, and the Middle East, it was used for clothing a some household articles. Wool has several advantages. resilient, flame retardant, resists abrasion, is a good insu tor, and can be woven in a variety of textures. It can dyed from the palest to the deepest colors, cleans well, sists dirt, and can absorb up to 20 percent of its weigh moisture without feeling damp. Its disadvantages includ

Figure 9.2 *In the renovation of this historic mansion in Buffalo, New York, the designer converted the residence into a hotel/bed and breakfast. Extensive care was taken to authentically recreate the original details and restore the molding. Contemporary furnishings and fabrics were selected to complement the historic interior. (Designer: Susan Dario, ASID. Photograph © Rion Rizzo/Creative Sources Photography.)*

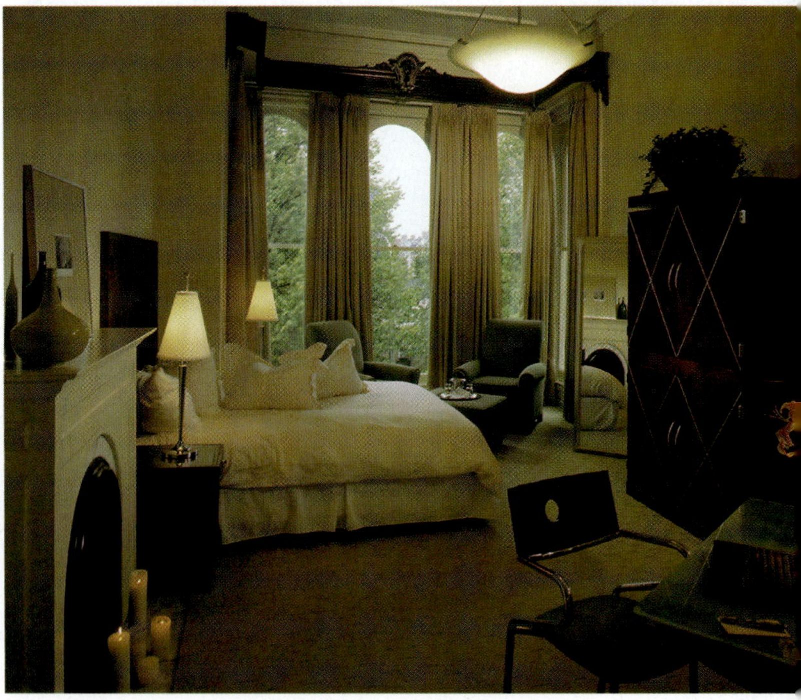

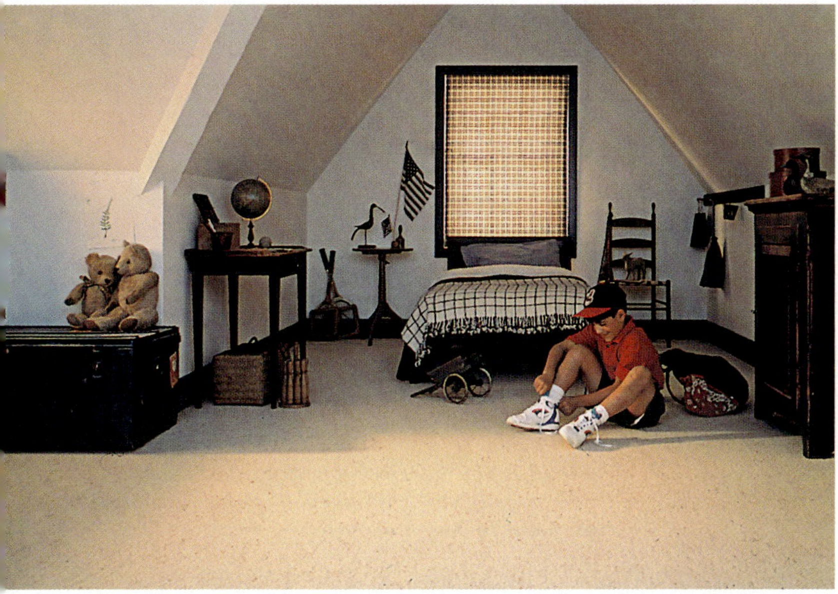

Figure 9.3 *In this child's room, a berber wool carpet adds warmth and durability. The short looped pile provides a soft flooring, as well as a masculine appeal appropriate in a boy's room. (Courtesy of Wools of New Zealand.)*

ndency to yellow with age (particularly when exposed to nlight), shrink, and be damaged by moths and other in-cts. Additionally, wool can be expensive and it requires ofessional cleaning. It may also cause allergies. Wool is ed for both residential and commercial applications in-uding upholstery, carpeting, draperies, and wall cover-gs (Figure 9.3).

Silk is an ancient fiber that, according to legend, was dis-vered in China about 2540 B.C. The process of producing from the larvae of silkworms, known as sericulture, was pt secret for many years but gradually became known in untries around the world. The advantages of silk are that is a beautiful, long fiber that is soft and luxurious, and rpassed in strength only by nylon (Figure 9.4). It takes d holds dye well and drapes beautifully. One disadvan-ge is that the sun's rays break down the fiber, requiring it be protected from direct sunlight. Silk also is susceptible deterioration by soil, beetles, and moisture. It is expen-ve as well.

Raw silk, or uncultivated silk, is a shorter and coarser fiber th less luster. Both types of silk fibers are used for aperies, some upholstery applications (when backed), wall verings, trim, and fabric art.

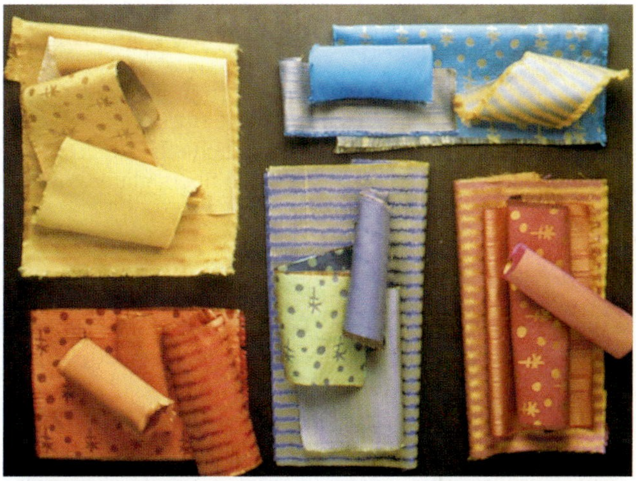

Figure 9.4 *Donghia's Sleight of Hand collection of four silk fabrics includes Abracadabra (a silk shantung), Hocus Pocus (a stripe), Shazam! (a zigzag design), and Presto! (a quilted matelassé). (Courtesy of Donghia Textiles. As seen in Fine Furniture International.)*

llulose Fibers

llulose (or vegetable) fibers include stems, leaves, and ed hairs found in plants. The two most common cellulose ers are cotton and linen (or flax).

Cotton is believed to have been grown in India during e fourth century B.C. and used in early Rome; it is the ost plentiful of the natural fibers. Its advantages are that takes and holds color well, washes easily, and can be oven to produce sheer or heavyweight fabrics. Its flexi-ility allows it to be adapted for such functions as uphol-ery, floor coverings, and window treatments (Figure 5). Its disadvantages are that it is not as durable as other fibers, and it wrinkles. It can mildew and fade. The cost of cotton varies according to the quality of the fiber, weave, and finish.

Linen, made from flax fibers, is the most ancient of all fibers. It was used for weaving in Egypt as early as 4000 B.C. Its advantages are that it is strong, pliable, lustrous, and washable, and it takes and holds color. It is absorbent. The disadvantages of linen are that it wrinkles readily unless chemically treated, which then reduces its wear potential; it fades; it is stiff; and it is difficult to clean. Linen is used for upholstery, drapery, table linens, and slipcovers.

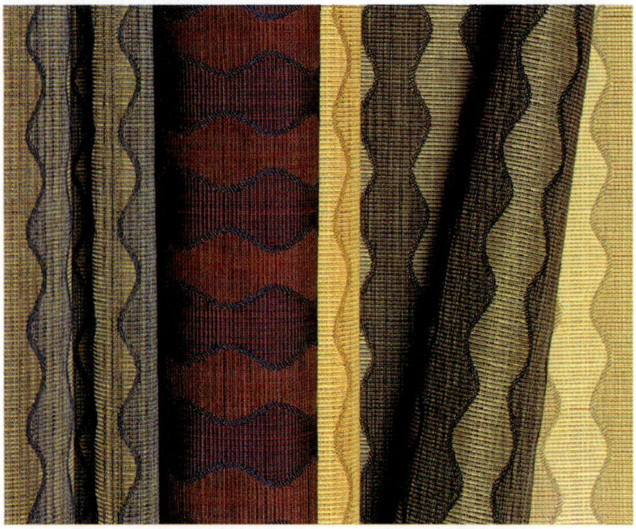

Figure 9.5 *Constructed of mercerized cotton, this fabric assures heavy-duty wear for contract use. (Courtesy of ICF Group/Unika Vaev.)*

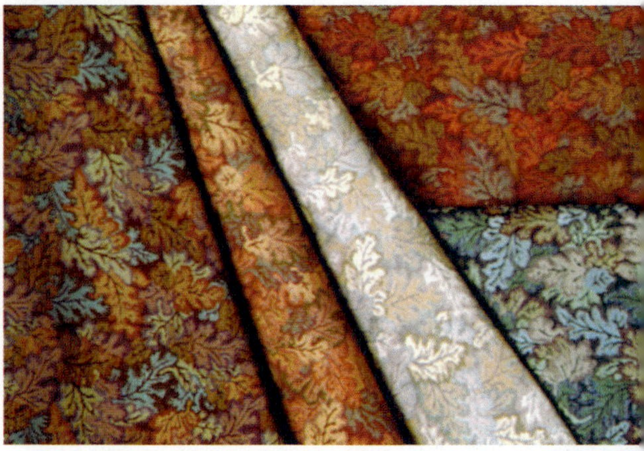

Figure 9.7 *This high-tech tapestry, called Lancelot, is woven of Trevira polyester. It is inherently flame-retardant, durable, and classic in design. (Courtesy of Anzea Textiles.)*

Mineral and Metallic Fibers

Mineral and metallic fibers are created from naturally occurring minerals, including metals. *Metallic fibers* include strips of gold, silver, or copper that are used chiefly as accents in decorative fabrics (Figure 9.6). Metallic fibers glitter without tarnishing and are washable.

Manufactured Fibers

Manufactured fibers are derived either from synthetic chemicals or natural solutions chemically treated. Manufactured fibers are designed to improve upon the qualit durability, and ease of care of natural fibers, as well as the resistance to soil, mildew, and insects. Although costs var manufactured fabrics tend to be less expensive than tho made from natural fibers. Manufactured fibers are mac by creating a liquid or viscose out of the original su stance, then forcing the liquid through holes in a showe head-like device called a **spinneret.** Varying the size ar shape of the holes in the spinneret changes the characte istics of the fiber. *Microfibers* are manufactured fibers th are finer than all natural fibers, including silk. They a used because they provide a luxurious drape, are ligh weight, and resist wrinkling and pilling. Manufacture fibers fall into two categories: regenerated cellulose ar synthetic fibers.

Regenerated cellulose fibers are produced by chan ing the physical and chemical properties of cellulo (plant and wood fibers). Some examples are rayon, a etate, and triacetate. *Synthetic fibers* are produced fro chemicals and carbon compounds. Some examples a nylon, acrylic, modacrylic polyester, olefin, and gla (Figure 9.7).

During the past six decades, the production and co sumption of manufactured fibers has steadily increased. 1940, manufactured fibers accounted for only 10 percent the fibers used. Today, over 80 percent of fibers used a manufactured fibers. Table 9.1 lists the most common ma ufactured fibers, their qualities, their most important dec rative uses, and recommendations for care to mainta appearance.

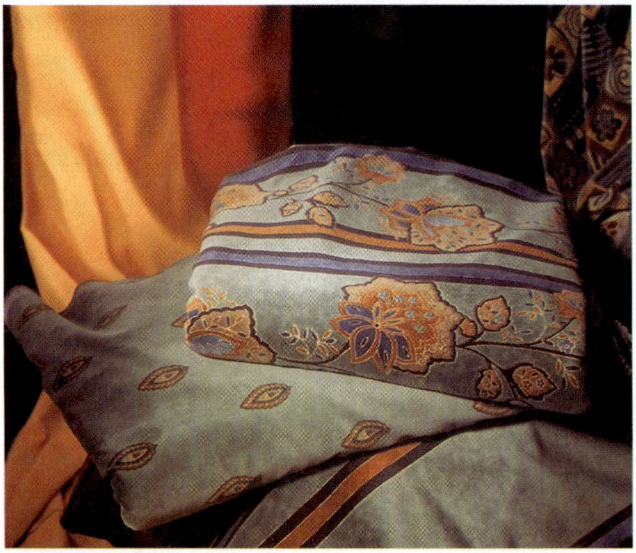

Figure 9.6 *Touches of metallic gold add opulence to this patterned fabric from Girmes, a German manufacturer. (Courtesy of Fine Furniture International.)*

More info online @

http://www.fibersource.com/ Educational link to fiber sources

http://www.nsf.gov/nstw/teach/nstw1996/nice/chart.htm Chart of fabric characteristics

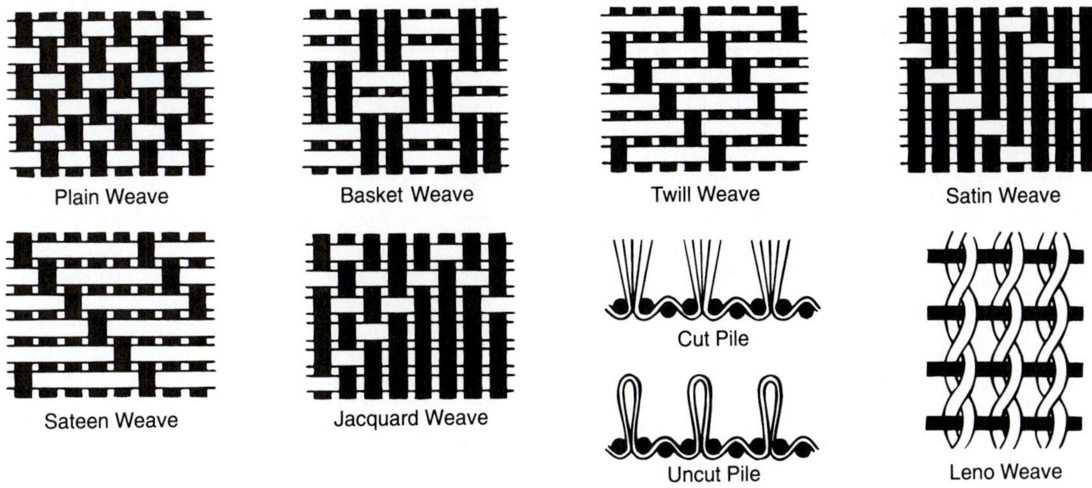

ure 9.8 *Common types of weaves.*

bric Construction

history of textile arts is almost as old as the history of ıanity. The exact origin of the loom is not certain, but lence suggests that it was used in Mesopotamia before 0 B.C. Although modern mechanization has brought ıt changes in textile production, weave structures are :h the same as they were at the beginning of the Re-ssance; these simple weaves are still standards in the in-try. More intricate weaves that originated in Asia, such as ıasks and brocades, are now produced on special **quard** looms. Invented in France in 1801 by Joseph-ie Jacquard (1752–1834), a Jacquard loom can create ticolored fabrics with intricate patterns.

ven Textiles

s section discusses the most common weaves (illustrated igure 9.8), as well as some more intricate ones used in orative fabrics.

in Weave

lain weave is made by the simple interlocking of **warp** tical or lengthwise) threads and **weft** or filling (horizon-ɔr crosswise) threads, and may be single or double, reg- or irregular. In the *plain single weave,* one weft thread ses over one warp thread and under the next. When the p and weft differ because of different weights or textures arn, the weave is called irregular or unbalanced. In the *ket weave,* two weft threads are interlaced with two warp ads. This weave may also be irregular from variations of ght or texture.

ill Weave

ll weaves are those in which two or more threads s over or under another set of threads, skipping at regu-ntervals to produce a diagonal effect. Twill weaves may be regular or irregular. Irregular twills are used for many decorative fabrics such as denim, gabardine, and herringbone.

Satin Weave

The satin weave floats one warp yarn over four or more weft yarns. This combination produces a fabric with luster, softness, and drapability, especially when the fiber is smooth, as with satin and sateen.

Jacquard Weave

The Jacquard weave requires an intricate series of hole-punched cards that tell the machine which threads to raise and which threads to drop. Some of the most common fabrics created on the loom include damask, tapestries, and brocades (Figure 9.9).

Pile Weave

Pile weaves are produced by additional threads in the weft or warp that form loops or tufts of yarn that stand out from the surface of the fabric. These loops may be cut, uncut, or a combination. Pile weaves are used in a wide variety of fabrics. The basic weave of the carpet industry is the raised-warp pile. Numerous fabrics are produced using pile weaves, including terry cloth, corduroy, and friezé. Velvets, originally woven by this method, are generally made today in a double cloth that is cut apart to produce the pile.

Double-Cloth Weave

Double-cloth weaves are woven in two attached layers, often resulting in a quilted appearance. These fabrics, known to the ancient Peruvians, are both durable and beautiful. The Jacquard loom is used to weave these fabrics for commercial applications.

Leno Weave

The leno weave is a loose, lacelike weave in which the warp threads are wound in half twists around each other,

Table 9.1 *Properties of Manufactured Fibers*

Generic Name	Appearance	Abrasion	Resilience	Heat Tolerance
Acetate (regenerated cellulose)	Smooth; silky; drapes well; holds shape well	Fair	Poor	Poor
Triacetate (a subdivision of the acetate group)	Crisp; smooth; silky; drapes well; strong colors	Fair	Good; resists wrinkling; retains pleats	Less sensitive than acetate
Acrylic	Wool-like; soft; bulky; warm; may squeak; rich colors; pilling depends on quality	Good; needs treatment for static	Good; holds heat-set pleats	Sticks at 450°F
Modacrylic (modified acrylic)	Similar to acrylic; good color retention	Good	Fair to good	Does not melt
Aramid	Stiff and smooth	High; exceptional strength	Excellent; low stretchability	Not affected
Fiberglass	Soapy; lustrous; silky; color range fair; Beta Fiberglas has remarkable sheerness	Strongest of all fibers	Excellent	Fireproof
Nylon (polyamide)	Squeaky; silky; cold; natural luster; good color range; drapes well	Excellent	Very good; resists wrinkling; can be heat set to hold shape	High resistance
Olefin (propylene and ethylene)	Waxy; wool-like; color range fair	Good to excellent	Good; resists wrinkling	Poor; heat sensitive
Polyester	Silky, cotton, or wool-like; drapes well; color range fair	Good to excellent	Excellent; resists wrinkles	Sticks at 400°F
Rayon (regenerated cellulose)	Soft; drapes well; excellent color range; bright	Fair to good	Low to medium; crease retention poor	Excellent; does not melt
Saran	Soft; drapes well	Tough	Crease retentive	Shrinks in intense heat
Vinyl (thermoplastic resins)	Smooth; variety of weights; expanded vinyl closely resembles leather	Good	Low	Shrinks at 212–230°F in dry heat, less in moist heat
Lyocell (cellulose derived from Eucalyptus trees)	Cross between rayon and cotton; luxurious hand and luster; drapes well	Fair, particularly if finished smooth or rubbed when wet	Fair, will wrinkle	Does not melt, but scorches

Notes: All manufactured fibers are resistant to moths and mildew. Insulation depends on construction and is primarily a function of thickness. Hollow polyester fibers provide particularly good insulation. Costs are variable, depending on construction.

able 9.1 *Continued*

lammability	Light Tolerance	Decorative Uses	Care
low	Long exposure weakens fiber; colors fade unless protected by special finish	Curtains, drapery, upholstery, rugs; for shower curtains in blends with other fibers	Soil resistant fair; wash in lukewarm water or dry-clean, depending on dyes, finishes, decorative designs; quick drying; iron at moderate heat
lowly combustible	More resistant than acetate	Same as acetate	Same as acetate
esists fire; burns ith yellow flame	Good	Rugs, carpets, blankets, curtains, drapery, upholstery	Keeps buoyancy when washed with warm water; machine dry; does not shrink, sag, or stretch; steam pressing reduces loft
elf-extinguishing	Excellent	Curtains, drapery, in carpet blends, furry rugs, blankets	Similar to acrylic; resists chemical stains; washable; use warm iron; shrinks unless stabilized; does not dry-clean well
ow flammability	Weakens with long exposure	Carpets	Not affected by moisture
onflammable	No loss	Curtains, drapery, bedspreads; Beta Fiberglas used for bedspreads	Impervious to moisture; hand wash; drip-dry; needs no ironing
lelts slowly	Poor	Upholstery, bedspreads, carpets	Washable; quick drying; use warm iron; resists soil; easy spot removal; static electricity unless treated
low to burn	Good	Rugs, blankets, upholstery, webbing, seat covers	Wash or dry-clean; iron at very low heat; good soil resistance
urns slowly	Loses strength in prolonged exposure	Curtains, drapery, upholstery, carpets and rugs, pillows, blankets	Soils easily; machine wash in warm water; dries quickly; use warm iron; resists stretching and shrinking
urns quickly	Fades when not solution dyed	Curtains, upholstery, drapery, table linen, rugs; probably most versatile fiber	Same as acetate; fair soil resistance
onflammable	Excellent	Outdoor furniture, upholstery, and screening; curtains, drapery, wall coverings	Excellent ease of care; resists wrinkling and stains; water-repellent
urns with difficulty	Weakens with long exposure	Shower curtains, wall coverings, upholstery when backed with fabric	Stain resistant; waterproof; wash and wipe clean
urns with a eathery ash	Good	Good green choice, is biodegradable and receylable; very stong when wet; household linens, sheets, and bedspreads	Varies based on manufacturing process; some shrinkage when washed; may require ironing to remove wrinkles

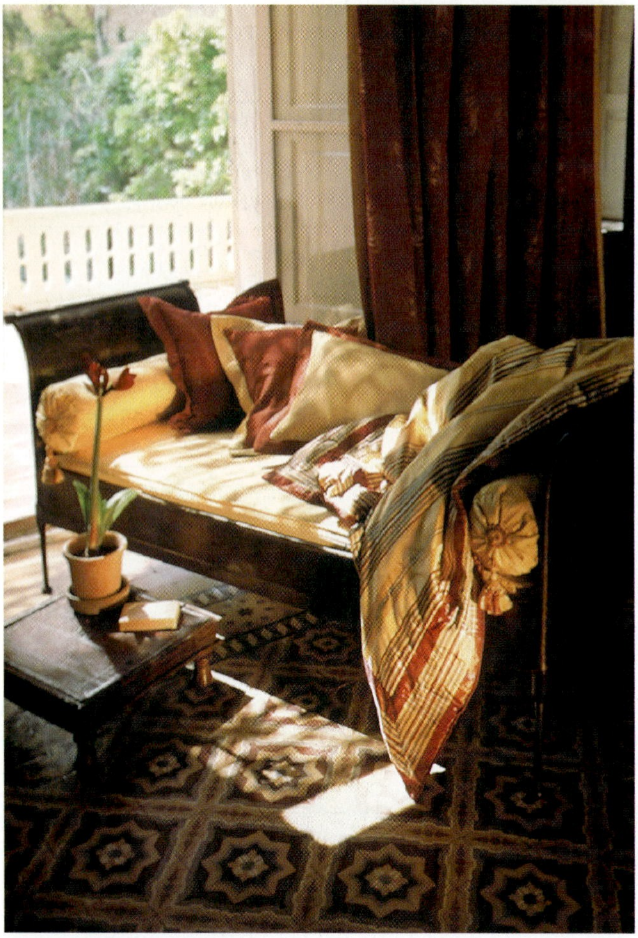

Figure 9.9 *This fabric selection includes a Jacquard drapery fabric of 74/24 viscose/acrylic, a cotton/silk bed cover, and pure silk decorative pillows from Zimmer & Rohde, Germany. (Courtesy of Fine Furniture International.)*

alternating positions on each row. Sheers, semisheers, and casements (coarsely woven sheers) use these weaves.

Nonwoven Textiles

Knitting

Knitting is a process of interlocking a series of yarn loops by means of blunt needles. Through a variation of stitches, patterns are formed. Knitted fabrics, either hand- or machine-made, range from loose, open construction to a close, fine mesh. Finely knit fabrics are used for many home furnishing needs because of their wrinkle resistance, tight fit, and ease of care. The tendency of knitted fabrics to stretch is being overcome by new methods of production.

Twisting

Twisting, interlocking, and knotting of yarns account for various types of mesh construction, such as nets, laces, and macramé. The intricacies of twisting are unlimited.

Felting

Felting is a process of subjecting a mass of fibers to moistu heat, and pressure, which produces a compact sheet tl does not fray, absorbs sound, and provides good insulati against heat and cold. Felt was formerly made from wool a hair fibers. Through modern technology, new fibers and f ing methods are employed to produce a variety of nonw ven materials.

Bonding

A bonded fabric results when two fabrics are adhered (bonded or laminated) together chemically or with heat. bonding a layer of fabric to the underside, the face fabric c be stabilized. If care is not taken, however, cleaning m cause separation of the layers. Bonded fabrics may be us as interfacing in upholstery to add stability.

More info online @

http://www.fabriclink.com/ Educational resource on fabrics

http://www.ntcresearch.org/ National Textile Research-Links to current articles

---

Textile Coloring/Dyeing

Fibers are dyed or colored throughout the various stages textile fabrication. In general, the most colorfast products dyed early in the manufacturing process; however, grea color variety (and therefore design options) occurs wh dyes are added later in the process. The various methods dyeing fibers, yarns, and fabrics include the following:

- **Solution dyeing**—the coloring agent is added to the viscous liquid of the synthetic before it is forced throu the spinneret to be formed into a fiber
- **Stock dyeing**—the dye is applied to the fibers before they are processed into yarns
- **Yarn dyeing**—the skeins or hanks of yarns are dyed before they are woven into fabrics
- **Piece dyeing**—fabrics are dyed after they are woven

Each time a new dye solution or dye bath is mixed, it m vary slightly in color from the previous one. Each solution called a *dye lot.* When using a fabric from more than one b for a certain project, it is important to make sure the bolts from the same dye lot or that the colors still match. A uniq alternative to dyeing is to select fibers in the desired colo to produce the fabrics (see "Sustainable Design: Color Fibers and Green Textiles").

Finishing

The finish is a treatment that may be applied to the fabric bef or after construction to change its appearance and performan When the unfinished fabric comes from the loom it is refer to as **gray goods** or **greige.** Before the cloth is ready for market it goes through a series of finishes: the preparation *prefinish,* the *functional finish,* and the *decorative finish.*

SUSTAINABLEDESIGN

Colored Fibers and "Green" Textiles

One of the purest means of ensuring environmentally safe interiors is to use natural, untreated, nondyed organic fibers. Designers developing green interiors need to consider the source of the fibers and their hidden environmental costs. For instance, according to Natural Cotton Colours, Inc., the process of dying fibers can be five times more expensive in the United States than in other countries. This is because government agencies in the U.S. require the residue from the dyeing process to be purified. Obviously, this should be required worldwide, but other countries do not apply these restrictions and thereby pollute the environment. Natural Cotton Colours found an answer to this problem—it grows cotton in different colors; dyes are not applied to the fibers. FoxFibre® has developed several lines of fabric from these fibers (Figure SD9.1).

Other textiles that are emerging as quality green products are Lyocell (Table 9.1) and Xorel. Xorel is a durable synthetic fabric that is used for commercial wallcoverings and upholstery. It creates no harmful by-products during its production, does not off-gas, and is no more toxic than wood when burned. Penny Bonda, FASID, a leader in environmentally sensitive design, has placed Xorel on her "Top 10" list according to *ISdesigNET.*

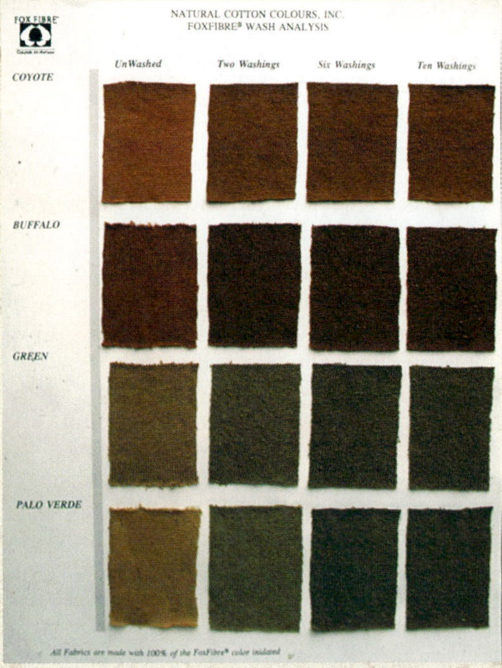

Figure SD9.1 FoxFibre® *color chart shows that after repeated washings the color of the natural fiber actually darkens. (Courtesy of Natural Cotton Colours, Inc. Photograph by Cary S. Wolinsky.)*

'efinishes

efinishes and preparation of the gray goods consist of a va-ty of treatments including the following:

- Beetling or pounding to give luster
- Bleaching to whiten
- Boiling to rid the fabric of grease or other unwanted substances
- Calendering to provide a smooth finish and tighten the weave
- Durable finishing to strengthen the textile
- Gigging or napping to produce a flannel-like texture
- Heat setting to add stability, especially for permanent pleating
- Preshrinking to shrink the textile and make it ready for finishing, and prevent fiber contraction when exposed to moisture
- Singeing to remove surface fuzz or lint

llowing the prefinishing, the cloth is ready for the func-nal and decorative finishes.

Functional Finishes

Functional finishes are applied to improve performance. These standard textile finishes include the following:

- Antibacterial finishes to help prevent mold and mildew
- Antistatic finishes to help guard against static
- Carefree finishes to help resist creasing or wrinkling
- Flame-retardant finishes to help retard burning
- Insulating finishes to improve insulation qualities; a coating of foam or other material is bonded to the fabric
- Mothproofing finishes to help prevent damage by insects
- Soil-repellent finishes to help resist soiling
- Water-repellent finishes to resist stains and moisture

Soil-resistant finishes are particularly important. Water-repellent, soil-resistant or soil-repellent, and soil-release finishes are all chemical finishes that increase a fabric's resistance to dirt and stains and help make cleaning easier. For example, Scotchgard™ is a trade name for a finish that makes the surface of the fabric stain resistant. It is best when this finish is applied to the fabric at the mill; however, it is possible to purchase the soil-resistant or water-repellent finish separately and apply it manually. Manufacturers' labels or instructions accompanying the fabric inform the consumer about what to look for, how often to clean, and how effective the finish is.

Decorative Finishes

Decorative finishes include printing by hand or machine, custom finishes, and needlework.

Printing (Hand Processes)

In general, printing is completed after the fabric is woven. Obviously, hand processes require human labor. Some popular hand processes are the following:

- *Batik printing:* Sections of the cloth that are not to be colored are blocked out with wax; then the cloth is immersed in a dye solution. The wax is then removed, revealing the pattern.
- *Hand block printing:* A carved wooden or linoleum block is inked and stamped onto a piece of fabric to create the design.
- *Tie-dye:* A resist process that employs strings or knots tied on the fabric. The fabric is then immersed in dye, creating abstract patterns.
- *Silk-screen:* A specially prepared fabric screen resists the color penetration except in desired areas. Dye in paste form is forced through the screen onto the fabric below. A separate screen is prepared for each color used in the design. Only the silk-screen process produces hand-printed textiles on a commercial scale.

Printing (Mechanical Processes)

Many prints are produced mechanically by the transfer of color from an engraved copper roller onto the fabric. This process is called *roller printing.* A separate copper roller must be engraved for each color of the design, but once prepared, the rollers can be used in a variety of color schemes on thousands of yards of fabric. Other types of roller printing include the following:

- *Embossing:* Engraved rollers produce a pressed high-low design into the fabric.
- *Moiré:* A type of embossing in which rollers press a watermark design into the fabric.
- *Warp printing:* Printing is completed on the warp yarns of a fabric before it is woven.

Printed fabrics come in designs of unlimited styles, including documentary prints (designs copied from patterns of a particular historical period). These designs help establish an authentic feeling in a room.

Custom Finishes

Some examples of custom finishes include the following:

- *Etching:* Acid burns out one fiber, resulting in a design on a sheerer fabric.
- *Flocking:* Small fibers are bonded to the fabric in a pa terned design.
- *Softening finishes:* Chemicals are added to a fabric to soften the feel.
- *Texturing:* Chemicals applied to the fabric create a puckered surface.

Needlework

Needlework, embellishing fabrics with intricate stitchery, an ancient art form. A wide variety of needlework, such embroidery, needlepoint, candlewicking, appliqué, a quilting, is utilized, usually in residential applications.

More info online @

http://www.surfacedesign.org/ Surface Design Association

Fabric Testing and Safety Codes

Fabrics, particularly those for commercial uses, must m standard tests for *durability, colorfastness,* and *flammabil*

Durability

Durability generally refers to the fabric's resistance to abrasic The Wyzenbeek test is commonly used to indicate the nu ber of double rubs, or revolutions, required before a fab is damaged. A typical commercial-grade fabric may sust 25,000 or more double rubs. Residential fabrics are also cod based on double rubs. Heavy Duty, HD, sustains 15,000 dc ble rubs; Medium Duty, MD, sustains 9000–15,000; Light Du LD, sustains 3000–9000; and Delicate Duty, DD, sustains few than 3000 double rubs. About 3000 double rubs represe one year of residential use.

Another way to test durability is to measure the fabri stability, its resistance to sagging or elongation, its flexibili and its resistance to tearing (its *tenacity*). Fabrics also shou be *resilient,* which means they return to their original sha after stretching or crushing.

Colorfastness

As previously discussed, the colorfastness of the fabric partially a function of the dyeing method. Colorfastne measures a fabric's resistance to fading from the sun's ra and from various cleaning methods. Fabrics also may tested for crocking (the color rubbing off onto another fa ric or the skin).

Flammability

The speed at which a fabric will ignite and spread flames, ability to extinguish itself, and the quality of the fumes em ted are all measurements of flammability. Fabrics used most commercial applications are subjected to two tests flammability: the Tunnel Test (ASTM 84) and the Vertic ne Test. Interior finishes are rated from Class A (the most ne resistant) to Class C (the least flame resistant).

beling

help consumers differentiate among the huge array of nufactured fibers, the Federal Trade Commission (FTC) ablished the Textile Products Identification Act. Under se regulations, each manufactured fiber is defined in spe- c terms and given a *generic name,* which along with the npany's trade name must appear on the label attached to fabric. The generic name is the term assigned to a chem- family of which all members exhibit certain traits. For ex- ple, all members of the nylon family are characterized by isual strength and resistance to abrasion, but they will not d up well under direct sunlight. The polyester family is own for its drip-dry quality and resistance to sun deterio- on. The *trade name* identifies the manufacturer. Because nufacturers need to give specific names to their products, re are hundreds of trade names for manufactured fibers, king it virtually impossible for the consumer to recognize m all. Familiarity with the general properties of each fiber nily, however, and checking the label to make sure of the ric content help when selecting the fabric that best serves cific needs. The label alone, however, does not ensure od performance if the construction, dyes, and finishes are properly handled.

Textiles used for most commercial applications should be eled to indicate their flammability and their fiber content th percentages of natural and manufactured fibers when olicable), and whether they have been treated with pro- tive finishes such as Scotchguard™.

The Association for Contract Textiles (A.C.T.), founded in 35, has established performance guidelines to make fabric cification easier. Figure 9.10 defines these specifications l accompanying symbols.

re info online @

.://www.contract-textiles.com/ Association for Contract Textiles

>://www.rosefurniture.com/howdo/fabric.htm Fabric Upholstery de for Residential Use

extile Care and Maintenance

hough not required, after a design project is complete, erior designers can offer the client a valuable service providing manufacturers' manuals, booklets, and other e instructions. Knowledge of the cleaning properties particular fabrics is essential for upkeep. For instance, ter-repellent and soil-repellent finishes must be reap- ed periodically, especially after a fabric has been aned.

The designer also may recommend added protection from sun for certain fabrics. Many fabrics are susceptible to damage, and glass can multiply the destructive element he sun's rays. Even the winter sun and its reflection from ow can be harmful. Lined and interlined draperies help protect fabrics from sunlight, especially when fragile materials are used. Blinds drawn during the day and exterior awnings are practical. Trees or shrubbery that shade windows can help prevent interiors from becoming damaged by the sun. Protective coatings can be applied to glass to prevent harmful UV rays from entering the interior.

Textile Uses in Interior Design

Interior designers have a wide choice of textiles with new fabrics always in production. The market abounds with fabrics suitable for every taste, style, and decorative purpose in every price range. Adding to the appeal of improved fibers is the seemingly unending variety of designs, ranging from folk patterns from around the world to traditional and contemporary designs. Following is a discussion of the principal decorative uses of fabrics.

Window Treatments

Styles of window treatments are discussed in Chapter 12. Typical fabrics used for these styles are covered here.

Drapery

Fabrics for drapery should have a light to medium weight, like silk, antique satin, chintz, and damask. Fabric should drape gracefully, clean without shrinkage, and meet the decorative needs of the room in which it is used (see Figure 9.1).

Sheers or Semisheers

Sheers filter the light, giving softness to the room and providing daytime privacy. The fabric should be sunproof but sheer enough to permit light, and should wash or clean well without shrinkage. Batiste, voile, ninon, and chiffon are four popular fabrics.

Casements

Casements are usually made of a coarser weave than a sheer, and are available in a variety of patterns. The fabric should be drapable, sun resistant, and should wash or clean well without shrinkage. Leno weaves especially help control sagging and are commonly used in commercial environments.

Linings

Drapery linings are necessary to protect the drapery from sunlight and provide a uniform exterior appearance. Acrylic and modacrylic fibers are particularly resistant to sunlight.

Curtains

Lightweight and decorative curtains are frequently made from cottons and cotton-polyester blends. Curtains used in kitchens and restaurants should be constructed of washable

Flame Resistance

APPLICATION	PASSES
Upholstery	California Bulletin 117 Section E
Direct Glue Wallcoverings	ASTM E 84 (adhered method)
Panels and Upholstered Walls	ASTM E 84 (unadhered method)
Drapery	NFPA 701 Small Scale

Flame resistance refers to a fabric's ability to resist burning.
The appropriate flammability test is dictated by the intended end use for the fabric.

The two testing methods most commonly used to measure flame resistance are the Tunnel Test (ASTM E-84) and the Vertical Flame Test (used by California Bulletin 117 and NFPA 701).

In the Tunnel Test, the fabric to be evaluated is clamped (unadhered method) or glued (adhered method) to a substrate. The substrate is placed on the ceiling of the test chamber and ignited by a flame from below. The fabric sample is then evaluated for the density of the smoke formed, the amount of fuel contributed, and the extent of the flame spread. Based on these factors, a rating is established.

In the Vertical Flame Test, the fabric to be evaluated is mounted in a vertical holder and exposed to an open flame for a specified amount of time. Once the flame is removed, the after flame and char length of the test sample are measured against various code standards to establish a classification.

The NFPA 701 utilizes the Vertical Test but unlike California Bulletin 117, the test is conducted in "oven dry" conditions, meaning the fabric to be tested is heated and thoroughly dried out prior to testing. The test then proceeds under the standards described above and a classification is established.

Colorfastness to Wet and Dry Crocking

APPLICATION	PASSES
Upholstery	AATCC 8 Dry Crocking, Class 4 minimum Wet Crocking, Class 3 minimum
Direct Glue Wallcoverings	AATCC 8, Class 3 minimum
Panels and Upholstered Walls	AATCC 8, Class 3 minimum
Drapery	AATCC 8 (solids) AATCC 116 (prints) Class 3 minimum

Colorfastness is a fabric's ability to retain color in various conditions. Crocking refers to the rubbing off of color from a fabric when subjected to abrasion.
To measure for colorfastness to crocking, the fabric to be tested is rubbed with squares of white cotton fabric (both wet and dry) under controlled pressure for a specified number of times. The amount of color transferred to the white test squares is matched to a control chart and a rating is established.

Class 5 = no color transfer

Class 1 = high degree of color transfer

Colorfastness to Light

APPLICATION	PASSES
Upholstery	AATCC 16A or AATCC 16E Class 4 minimum at 40 hours
Direct Glue Wallcoverings	AATCC 16A or AATCC 16E Class 4 minimum at 40 hours
Panels and Upholstered Walls	AATCC 16A or AATCC 16E Class 4 minimum at 40 hours
Drapery	AATCC 16A or AATCC 16E Class 4 minimum at 60 hours

Colorfastness to light refers to a fabric's ability to resist fading when exposed to light.
To measure for colorfastness to light, the fabric to be tested is exposed under specific conditions to a controlled light source which simulates the sun's rays. At timed intervals, the test swatch is compared to a gray scale and the degree of fading is rated.

Class 5 = no fading

Class 1 = high degree of fading

Physical Properties

APPLICATION	PASSES
Upholstery	Brush pill ASTM D3511, 3 minimum Breaking strength ASTM D3597-D1682-64 50 lbs. minimum is warp & weft Seam slippage ASTM D3597-D434 25 lbs. minimum in warp & weft
Panels and Upholstered Walls	Breaking strength D5034 Grab Method 35 lbs. minimum in warp & weft Seam slippage ASTM D3597-434 25 lbs. minimum in warp & weft
Drapery	Seam slippage ASTM D3597-434 for fabrics over 6 oz./sq. yard 25 lbs. minimum in warp & weft Seam slippage ASTM D3597-434 for fabrics under 6 oz./sq. yard 15 lbs. minimum in warp & weft

Pilling is the formation of fuzzy balls on the surface of a fabric. Pilling occurs when loose fibers in the fabric are worked to the surface after the fabric is subjected to abrasion.
The Brush Pill Test uses nylon bristles to rub the surface of the fabric to be tested for a specific amount of time. The number of balls or pills that form on the surface of the fabric are counted and the fabric is evaluated in a 1 to 5 rating system.

Class 5 = no pilling

Class 1 = severe pilling

Breaking strength measures a fabric's ability to resist tearing or breaking when subjected to tension.
To evaluate breaking strength, the fabric to be tested is gripped by clamps at one end while weight is applied to pull it from the other end. This test is performed in both the warp and the filling directions. The number of pounds required to cause the fabric to break or tear determines the rating.

50 pounds minimum = upholstery

35 pounds minimum = panel and vertical surface fabrics

15 pounds minimum = drapery

Seam slippage refers to the condition when fabrics pull apart at a sewn seam.
To measure a fabric's ability to resist seam slippage, a seam is sewn in the fabric to be tested. These sewn fabrics are then clamped at one end and pulled by weights at the other end. This test is performed in both the warp and filling directions. The weight is increased until the seam separates a specified distance. The number of pounds required to cause this separation determines the fabric's rating.

25 pounds minimum = upholstery

25 pounds minimum = panel and vertical surface fabrics

15 pounds minimum = drapery

Abrasion

APPLICATION	PASSES
General Contract Upholstery (a)	ASTM 3597 modified (#10 cotton duck) 15,000 double rubs Wyzenbeek method ASTM D4966 (21 oz. weight) 20,000 rubs Martindale method
Heavy Duty Upholstery (A)	ASTM 3597 modified (#10 cotton duck) 30,000 double rubs Wyzenbeek method ASTM D4966 (21 oz. weight) 40,000 rubs Martindale method

Abrasion resistance is the ability of a fabric to withstand surface wear from rubbing.
Two of the test methods used for measuring abrasion resistance are the *Wyzenbeek* and the *Martindale.*

Wyzenbeek Test Method (modified)
The fabric to be tested is pulled taut and rubbed in both the warp and filling directions, using a piece of cotton duck fabric as the abradant. The number of cycles, or double rubs endured before the fabric shows "noticeable wear" is counted. This number determines the fabric's abrasion rating.

15,000 = general contract upholstery

30,000 = heavy duty upholstery

Martindale Test Method
The fabric to be tested is mounted flat and rubbed in a figure eight-like motion using a piece of worsted wool cloth as the abradant. The number of cycles endured before the fabric shows an objectionable change in appearance is counted. This number determines the fabric's abrasion rating.

20,000 = general contract upholstery

40,000 = heavy duty upholstery

Figure 9.10 *Continued*

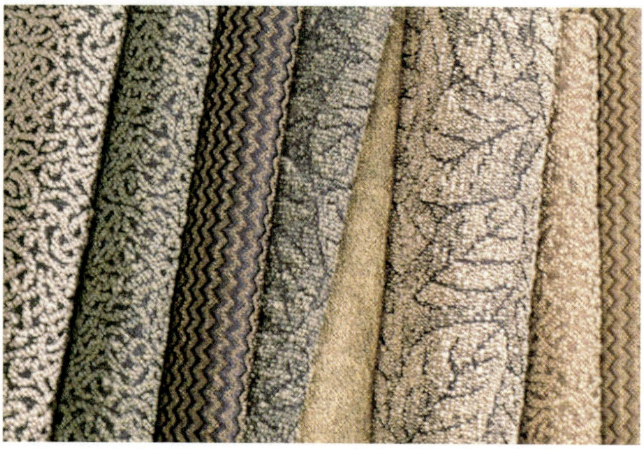

Figure 9.11 *Inspired from famous nineteenth- and twentieth-century archeological discoveries, these intricate woven patterns achieve luxurious lines by use of bouclé and chenille yarns and a unique weave structure from Pallas. (Courtesy of Pallas Textiles.)*

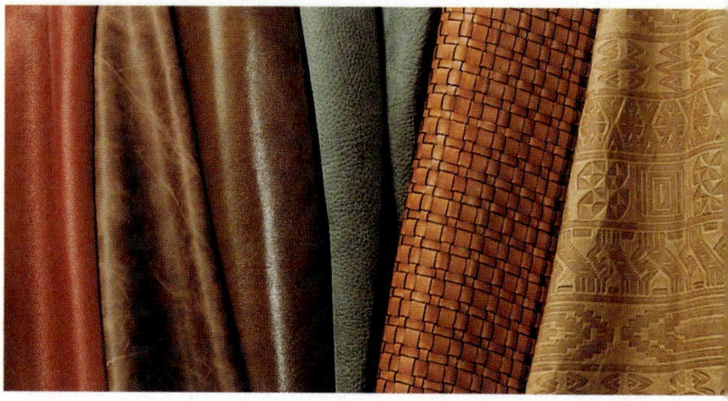

Figure 9.12 *A variety of finishes have been developed for these leathers. Some are treated to produce a weathered look others are given a high sheen appearance or made to look antique. The velvet-napped leather is shrink-retardant and wear-resistant. The leather second from the right is part of a group of leathers laced into patterns. (Courtesy of Cortina Leathers.)*

material. Curtains are a relatively inexpensive window treatment solution and will have a shorter useful life than a drapery treatment.

Upholstery

Upholstery is a fabric, animal skin, or other material that covers furniture permanently, adds beauty and comfort, conceals or emphasizes the furniture design, and adds to or sets the theme or mood of the room.

Upholstery Fabric

Fabric used for upholstery should have a tight weave, be durable, comfortable, and easy to clean. Common upholstery fabrics include heavyweight fabrics such as matelassé, tweed, tapestry, velvet, bouclé (Figure 9.11), and friezé; mediumweight fabrics such as damask, brocatelle, and canvas; and lightweight fabrics such as chintz, linen, homespun, and moiré. A relatively new category of upholstery fabric that is extremely durable, heat and stain resistant, and breathable is Crypton. It is used in commercial upholstery applications.

When purchasing upholstered furniture, fabric is a primary consideration because it is an expression of personality and individual taste. In selecting the fabric, use is generally the determining factor. Selecting suitable upholstery fabric involves answering questions such as the following:

1. What type of fiber and weave are employed? An upholstered fabric, for example, will last longer if the warp and fill are the same weight and tightly woven.
2. Is the fabric attractive and comfortable to the touch?
3. Is a patterned or plain fabric preferred? Fabrics with small overall patterns tend to show soil less than solid colors. If a pattern is chosen, is it in scale with the furniture and the room, and does it support the style?
4. Is the fabric suitable for its intended function? For example, will the upholstery be used by active children in a family room or by a single professional in a seldor visited area?
5. Is the fabric the best quality the budget will allow, considering long-term wear and maintenance? It is inadvisable to buy expensive fabric for cheap furniture and fabric of lesser quality for fine furniture.
6. What maintenance process is necessary? Does the particular upholstery fabric require a water- and soil-repellent finish like Scotchguard™ or Zepel?
7. Does the upholstery fabric fit the style, mood, and character of the room? Is the fabric formal or informal? Does it conform to the lifestyle of the occupants and complement its environment?

Upholstery Leather

Leather (tanned animal skin) is a product that has long bee used for aesthetic and utilitarian purposes (particularly tl hides of cattle and swine). Its advantages are that it is p able and durable, may be dyed or used in its natural colc and may be embossed or made into suede (Figure 9.12 Genuine leather can be expensive; simulated leather (viny is available, but needs to be carefully selected to ensu proper aesthetic qualities. The disadvantage of leather is th it is susceptible to marks, holes, and tears. Leather is al used for wallcoverings and floor tiles.

Slipcovers

Slipcovers may cover worn upholstered furniture, prote more expensive fabrics, and brighten or change a room's a mosphere. Usually, slipcovers are used only in residenti settings.

Slipcovers are made of light- to mediumweight fabrics th should be tightly woven. Some manufacturers offer furnitu upholstered in muslin or other plain fabrics that can be pu chased with several changes of slipcovers to help dress tl furniture for seasonal changes. Sailcloth, ticking, chint whipcord, and corduroy are all good choices for slipcover

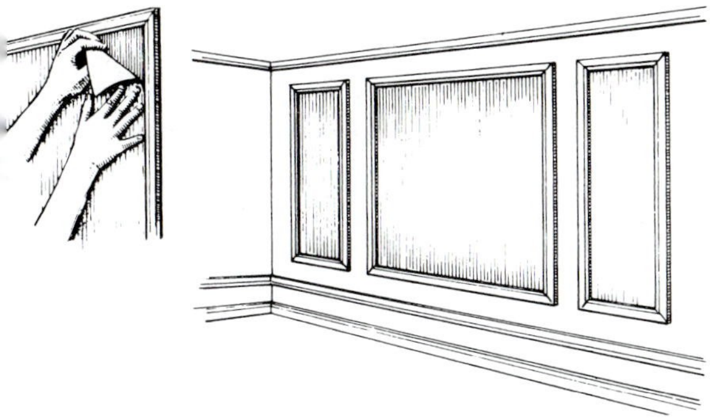

ure 9.13 *Framed fabric on a wall can add interest and* *le.*

alls

orics can be used on walls to add beauty (as illustrated in ure 9.13) or to solve a decorative problem. (See Chapter for uses of fabric wallcoverings.) The fabric should have ght weave with firm body. Canvas, burlap, moiré, ticking, avy cotton or linen, velveteen, crypton, and damask are en used for wallcoverings. In commercial environments, mmability codes for wallcoverings must be followed.

stem Furniture Panel Fabrics

commercial interiors, and particularly in commercial of- es, panel systems create office spaces. As discussed in apter 8, panel systems are an effective solution in offices where employees communicate frequently. One of the design challenges of the open office panel system is the redirection of noise. Covering the panel with fabric assists with noise reduction.

Fabrics on the panels must meet several criteria. First, they must be durable. Employees and visitors will lean their hands and bodies against the panel. Second, the fabric must be able to accommodate pushpins. Although tackboards are incorporated in panel systems, the experienced designer knows that, over time, notes, calendars, pictures, and so on are pinned up everywhere. Finally, the fabric must be cleanable; food and drink stains and marks from fingerprints will occur.

The fabric may be used as a subtle background color or it may be patterned to add interest to a space (Figure 9.14). Sometimes vinyl wallcovering is used below desktop level and fabric is used above. Fabrics may vary on different sides of the system or from panel to panel. Panel manufacturers supply many optional fabrics that have been tested for panel use. If a designer selects a custom fabric, the fabric may require testing to insure its appropriateness for use on the panel systems.

Accents

Textiles also may be used as accents in a room. Trims, fringes, and braids add character and distinction to an interior (see Figures 9.1 and 9.15). Originally intended to conceal seams and tacks, *passementerie* (decorative trims, cords, tassels, etc.) is used as ornamentation. Passementerie can be found in the tombs of pharaohs and on kings' clothing, but made its historical mark during the reign of Louis IX in

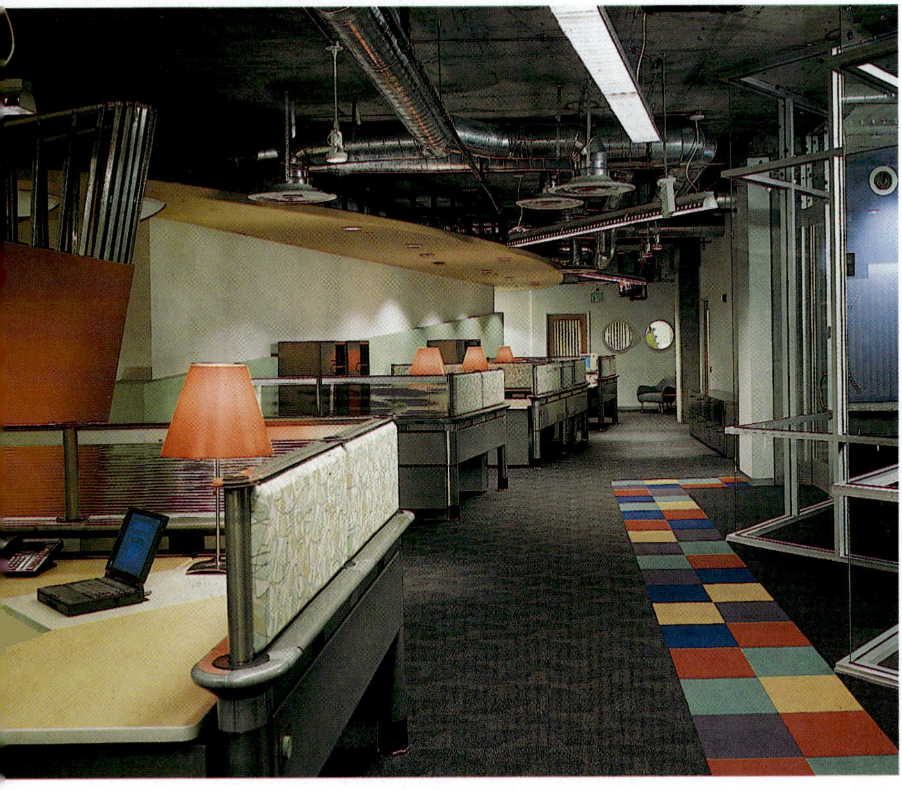

Figure 9.14 *The open office system designed for MTV employees incorporates a variety of textile choices. Upholstery fabrics add interest to the walls. Colored lampshades create a warm, friendly glow and contrast well with the crisp metals and geometric edges. (Designers: Felderman & Keatinge Design Associates.)*

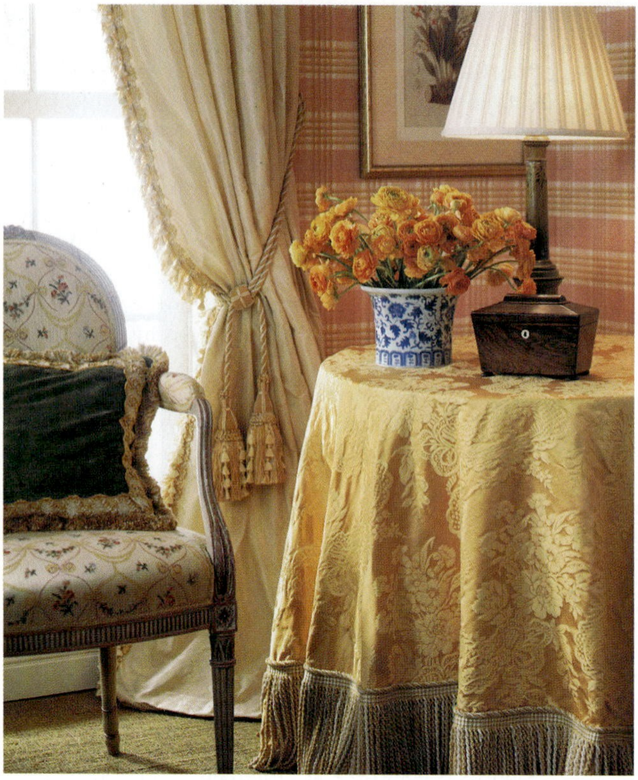

Figure 9.15 *Trims are available for drapery tiebacks, skirts on upholstery pieces, edges, and borders. (Photograph © Schumacher & Co. Permission has been granted by F. Schumacher & Co. to use copyrighted work.)*

France. Guilds of artisans were organized to create passementerie. The development of the machine during the Industrial Revolution brought passementerie to every corner of the Victorian interior. Currently, traditional interiors use many decorative trims, and even contemporary interiors use accent cording and the occasional tassel.

Chapter 10 discusses the use of textiles as accent floor coverings and Chapter 8 discusses fabrics as a form of art for wall accessories. Textiles also can be used for accent throw pillows, adding interest as well as comfort and continuity to a room. For instance, a particular silk fabric may not be suitable to cover an entire sofa, but may function well on accent pillows.

Selecting Textiles for Interiors

Perhaps the most common question clients ask professional interior designers is "What fabric goes with what?" This question has no absolute answer. Combining fabrics is a matter of training and skill. Some people seem to have an aptitude for this; others require much patient study and practice.

Combining Fabrics

Although an unexpected combination of materials may create a feeling of great interest and charm, some general principles will be helpful to the inexperienced designer when combining patterns, textures, and colors.

- The selection of any combination of textiles must coincide with the desired feeling or mood in the room. For example, a formal contemporary studio apartment wou have crisp shiny fabrics, possibly with leather accents; a woven flamestitch upholstery would appear out of plac
- Many designers coordinate textiles based on a pattern fabric or rug, called the *color source* (Figure 9.16). Thi method is fairly safe because the basic colors of the scheme are already coordinated; however, without car ful consideration this approach can become static or u interesting.
- Select a textile scheme appropriate for the chosen styl For example, a Victorian-style room would include de purples, mauves, greens, and reds in rich brocades, ve vets, and heavy tapestries.
- To be certain the colors and fabrics are harmonious, compare textiles under all the natural and artificial ligh to be utilized in the interior.
- Often, predictable color and fabric combinations and those that match exactly are not interesting or creative Trying out fabric combinations trains the eye and help develop a sense of what fabric selections are complementary and what groupings do not work well togeth Some manufacturers develop "mix and match patterns for wallcovering and fabrics; designers with a discerni eye generally select alternative textures and fabrics to enhance these predetermined schemes.

Pattern

Pattern indicates that the design has motifs sufficiently la in scale, or with enough contrast in color or tone, to be d tinguished clearly. The skillful use of pattern can camoufla defects, create beauty and glamour. As with color, no a solute do's or don'ts govern the successful use of pattern. few general guidelines, however, may be helpful:

- Patterns used within the same room should be related. Common elements such as color, texture, or motif tie them together and unify the design.
- The principal pattern need not be repeated in the roo so long as one or more of the colors in that pattern ar carried over into another area (as seen in Figure 9.16). The pattern, however, may be repeated on furnishings or used on windows or walls, depending on the overa effect desired. Odd pieces of furniture can be unified l covering them in the same fabric, and repetition of the fabric brings continuity to a room.
- Using no more than one bold pattern of the same type c design, such as a floral, is usually more effective. Once t dominant motif is established it can be interestingly supplemented with more subdued patterns, stripes, checks, plaids, with complementary plain textures added.
- When combining patterned fabrics, consider the scale size of the pattern. For example, if a bold floral print with a large scale is combined with a plaid, a stripe, o both, a smaller scale pattern in these complementary fabrics will be most effective (Figure 9.17). If an unobtrusive floral pattern is used, accompanying fabrics wit bolder characteristics may blend well.
- Success in combining patterns can be achieved with practice, experience, and consideration of basic guide-

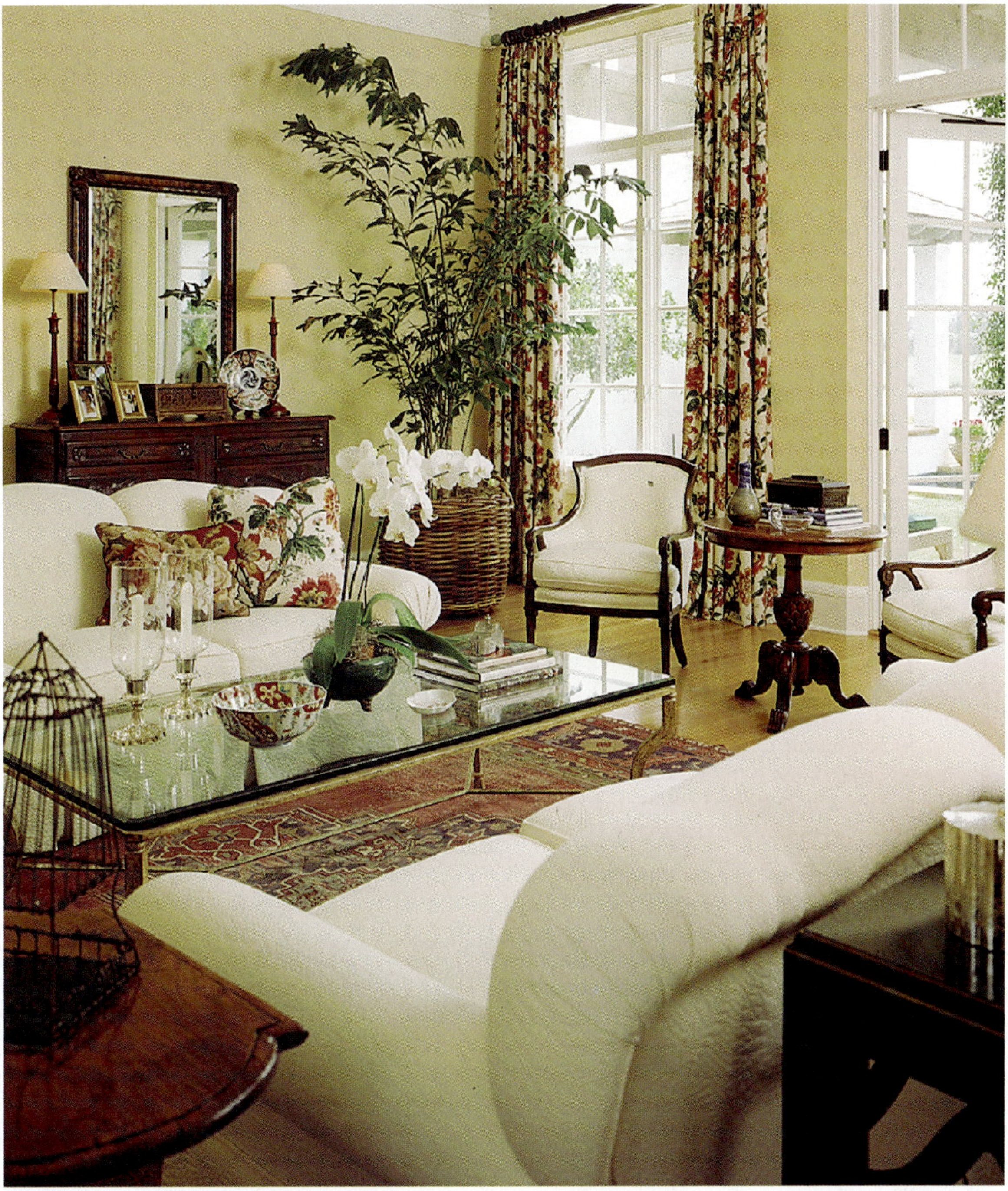

Figure 9.16 *Contemporary fabrics are mixed with traditional fabrics and furniture styles in this refreshing interior. The color source is found in the antique rug. Simple yellow walls with crisp white trim and floral fabrics contribute to the eclectic blend of old and new. (Designer: Spectrum Interior Design. Photograph © Kim Sargent.)*

lines. It is helpful to observe pattern combinations assembled by experienced professional designers in design periodicals, design studios, showrooms, and at home shows.

xture

e surface quality of a textile is also an important element consider when combining fabrics in a specific project. Knowledge of what makes a fabric formal or informal is essential for successfully combining textiles.

Formal fabrics are primarily those with smooth and often shiny textures, displaying elegant stylized and geometric patterns. Some examples of formal fabrics include velvet, damask, brocade, brocatelle, satin, shantung, and taffeta. Formal fabrics are often creatively used in both traditional and modern interiors in a wide range of colors and patterns.

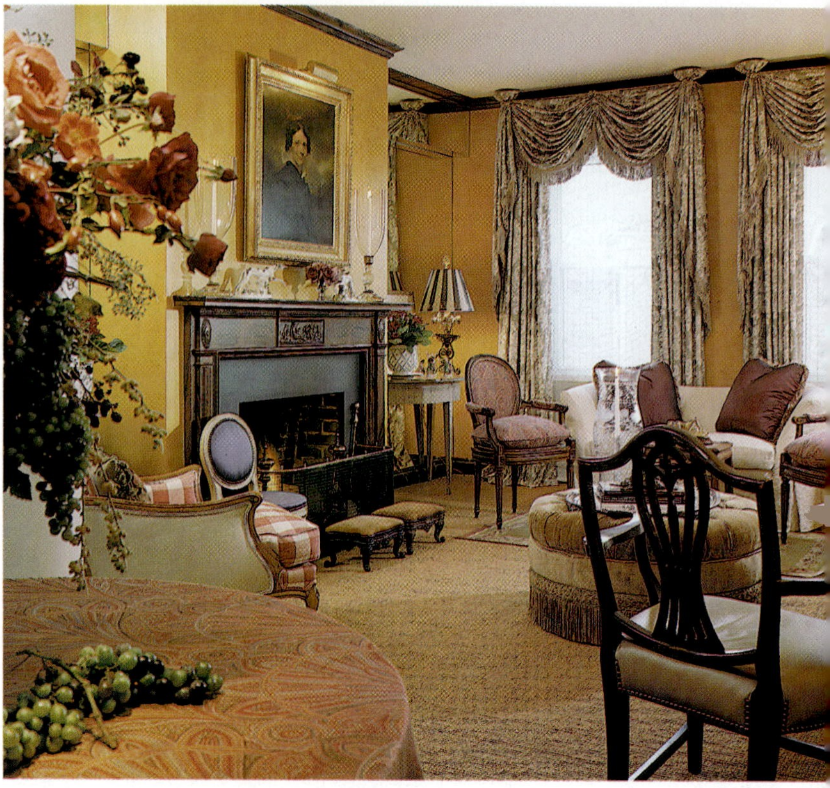

Figure 9.17 *In this room, the designer combined several patterns for an interesting interior. A pale paisley pattern on side chairs and the tablecloth contrasts with the strong plaid chair and formal swag and jabots draperies. Crushed velvet and a sisal rug add three-dimensional textural character. (Designer: Bill McGee. Photograph by Antoine Bootz. Courtesy of* Southern Accents.*)*

Informal fabrics are generally those with a rougher texture and matte finish, such as burlap, canvas, hopsacking, muslin, tweed, and bouclé (Figure 9.18). Fabrics with a handcrafted quality often fall into this category. If the informal fabric employs pattern, the design may be bold, naturalistic, abstract, or geometric.

Many fabrics can be used in either category. For instance, cottons and linens may have textures, colors, and patterns that fit into a formal setting or are at hor in an informal room. Leather also may be used in form and informal settings. When designing a room, keep mind that a combination of textile finishes is importa to add interest. Some fabrics should be glossy, where others should have a deeper nap or pile. For example, room of furnishings covered only in cotton chintz lac depth.

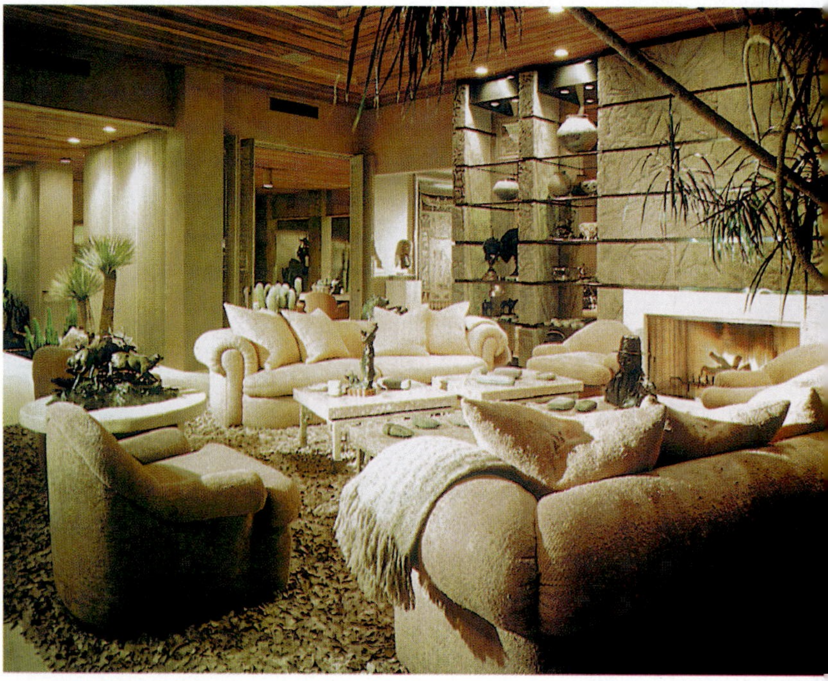

Figure 9.18 *Nubby wool textures and dull matte finishes on the upholstered furnishings, pillows, and throw enhance the effect of informality in this living space. The leaf-textured rug further supports the informal and artistic mood of the contemporary style. (Courtesy of Steve Chase & Associates. Photograph by Mary E. Nichols.)*

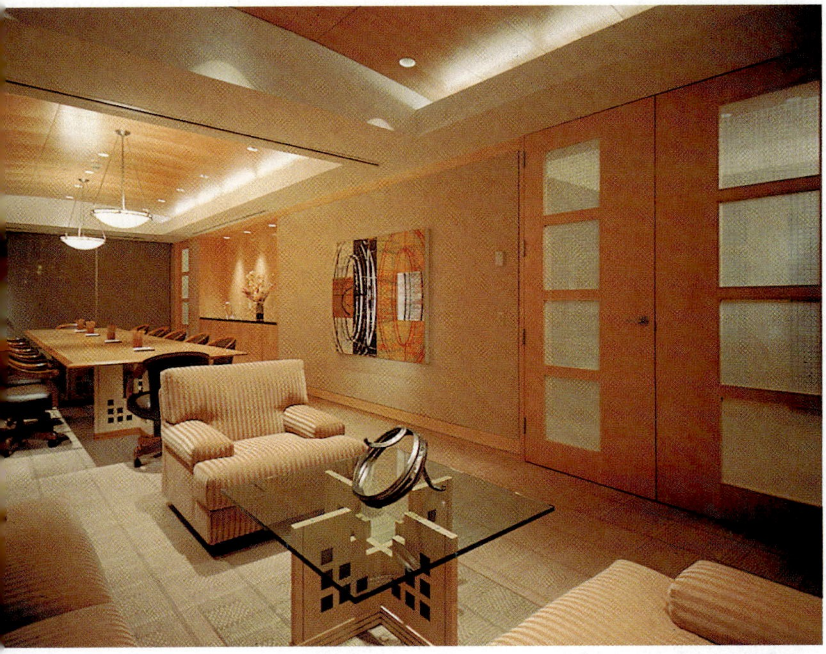

Figure 9.19 *In this sophisticated boardroom the predominant muted tones are accentuated with small amounts of black on chair seats and in furniture details. The bold artwork adds interest to the space. (Designer: Spector Group. Photograph by Peter Paige.)*

The unique surface quality or *hand* (rough, smooth, hard, t, shiny, or dull) of each fabric should be considered when ordinating them. The relationship should be appropriate the room's style and mood. For example, informal monk's th is not at home in an elegant eighteenth-century English om with smooth and shiny damasks and satins, but is com- ible with a wicker chair in a country style.

The character of the texture should be appropriate for its ended use. For example, for a comfortable chair in a fam- room, a smooth, soft leather would be preferred over a gh burlap.

lor

en coordinating fabrics, another goal is to select colors t are compatible and harmonious. When selecting colors fabrics, remember from Chapter 3 that color has three di- nsions: hue, value, and chroma.

Hues fall into warm or cool color classifications. One of se can be selected to dominate the scheme. The best hues l fit the needs and preferences of the occupants. Such cri- a as climate, positioning of the space in relationship to the , and lifestyle should be considered.

Fabrics are either light, medium, or dark in value. Most ric coordination is enhanced by including fabrics in all ee levels of luminosity. For example, if the major fabrics the room are light in value, the fabrics for smaller fur- hings or accessories might be medium and dark in value. ny designers use darker values below, medium values in middle areas, and lighter values on the upper portions of space; of course, this method can be reversed for a more usual effect. Using only dark and light values in a space ates drama, as in a color scheme using black and white.

Fabrics are either muted or bright in chroma. A color eme is usually successful when varying levels of chroma selected (Figure 9.19). For example, if the major fabrics for the room are muted in chroma, some accents of bright fabrics are visually interesting. A room with all muted colors can be dull and boring; a room with all intense colors can be tiring or even agitating.

Textiles for Period Rooms

Design in textiles was used in ancient times as a symbolic medium for religious purposes. With the passage of time, fabric became a significant medium for aesthetic expression. The design motifs used in the early rugs of East Turkistan are much the same as the designs used in the early rugs of the Inca and Navajo peoples halfway around the world. This similarity occurred because people represented natural phenomena in their early art forms. For example, the sun and stars were represented in identifiable form. The difference in early textile weaves is minimal because all were completed on simple looms, using natural fibers and dyes. Although each country developed different characteristic styles, a common quality in their early crafts blends them together harmoniously.

A close relationship often existed among the designs of European, Near Eastern, and Asian countries during the Middle Ages and the Renaissance. The conquerors brought artisans of all kinds to their newly acquired lands, where the artisans continued to carry on their trades. In time they were influenced by the designs of their new environment, eventually blending different methods and motifs. During the Renaissance and the seventeenth and eighteenth centuries, fabrics from Asian countries, with their unique motifs and colors, were in great demand in Europe and America.

Historic designs can establish an authentic feeling of a specific period or style. Documentary fabrics bearing designs from a wide range of historic periods are produced by manufacturers. Seldom, however, does a client wish to create an entirely authentic period room; this is usually reserved for restoration projects and museums.

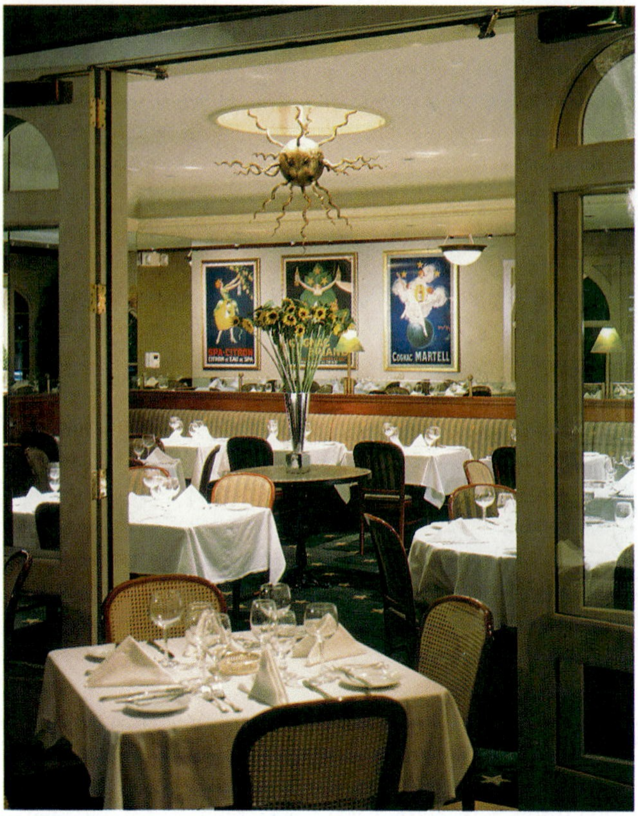

Figure 9.20 *In this restaurant, named Stars, the theme is carried through the clever design on the rug, in the fabric (repeated on chairs and booths), in the lighting, and even in the poster art. (Architect/Designer: DES Architects + Engineers. Photograph by Paul Bardagjy.)*

More info online @

http://info.cas.org/STNEWS/OCTOBER98/textiles.html Information on textile history

http://textilesociety.org/about_about.htm Textile Society of America

http://www.interlog.com/~gwhite/ttt/tttintro.html Information on textile history with links to many sites

Textiles for Commercial Interiors

Although the previous discussions on fabric testing and safety codes and on combining patterns, textures, and colors apply to commercial interiors, additional design criteria are important for commercial use as well.

In general, commercial interiors will not have as much variety in fabrics as residential interiors. Fabrics for restaurants, offices, and hospital or hotel rooms will be repeated to obtain unity and flow throughout the interior (Figure 9.20). Corridors or hallways must unite the spaces while allowing for high traffic flow, requiring durable textiles.

Commercial interiors in general contain more understated classic materials and colors. Bold colors are reserved for accent walls, children's areas (Figure 9.21), and for use in theme restaurants and hotels. Occasionally, however, a cl will request a strong, bold look.

All fabrics must be durable. Designers should select f rics from reputable commercial manufacturers who h tested their products to meet flammability and abrasion te

Fabrics used in commercial interiors should be treate resist stains. A lovely peach chair will not look so lovely ter coffee has sunk into its fibers. At home, the spill may cleaned within minutes; in a hotel lobby or office envir ment, it may remain for hours until housekeeping can cl it. Additionally, medical facilities such as hospitals and n ing homes require fabrics that are easily washable as wel highly resistant to blood and urine stains. To help clients, signers should supply maintenance procedures for clean all textile products. Some solution-dyed products can bleached; piece-dyed fabrics are more sensitive.

Finally, remember that in most commercial situations, design selections are not for the client, but for the clie client (the customer at the restaurant, for example). So times designers must select items in the end user's best terest and gently explain this to the client.

Textiles in Presentations

In order to communicate fabric and furniture selections t client, designers may prepare a series of presentation boa that incorporate images of the furnishings as well as ac samples of the fabrics and finishes (see Design Developm in Chapter 1). Frequently, these boards are combined w presentation furniture plans, elevations, and perspectiv thereby communicating the design to the client (Figure 9.

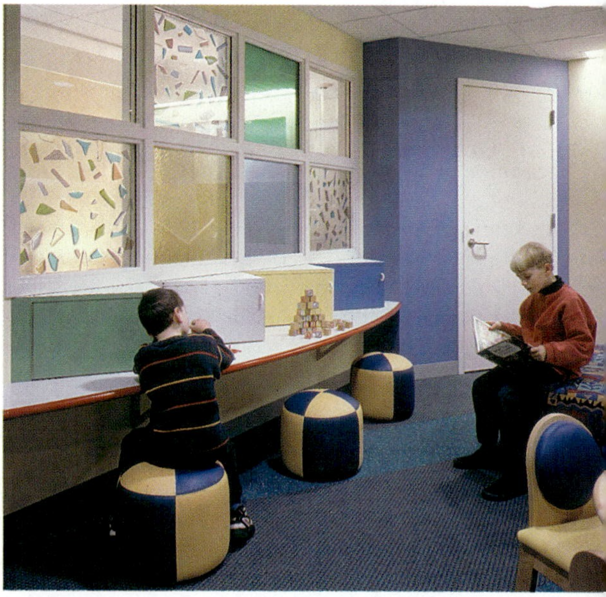

Figure 9.21 *In this Seattle medical facility, the children's p area utilizes bold colors and durable fabrics. Upholstered a built-in furniture is sized to meet the children's needs. (Architect/Designer: NBBJ. Photograph by Steve Keating.)*

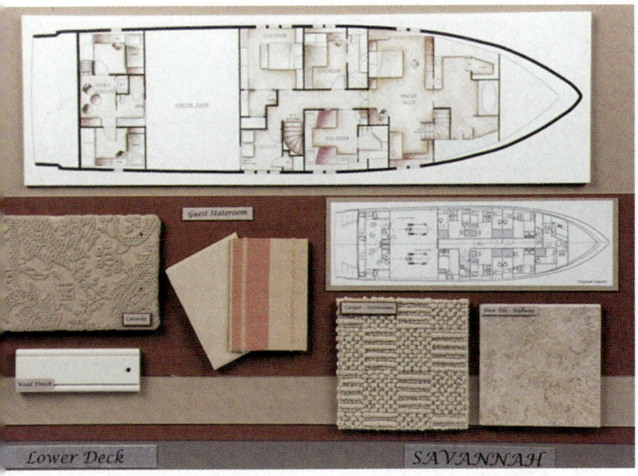

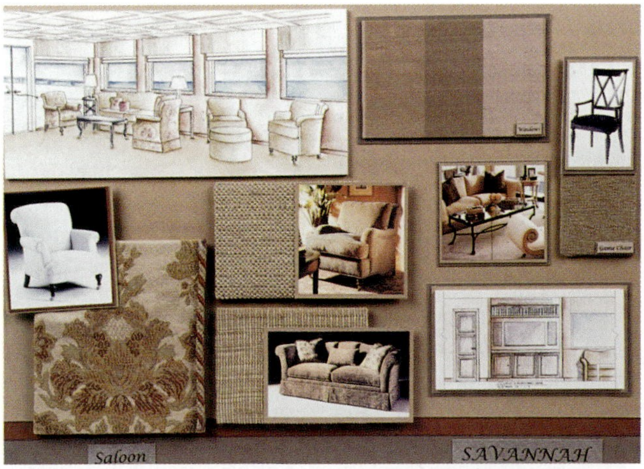

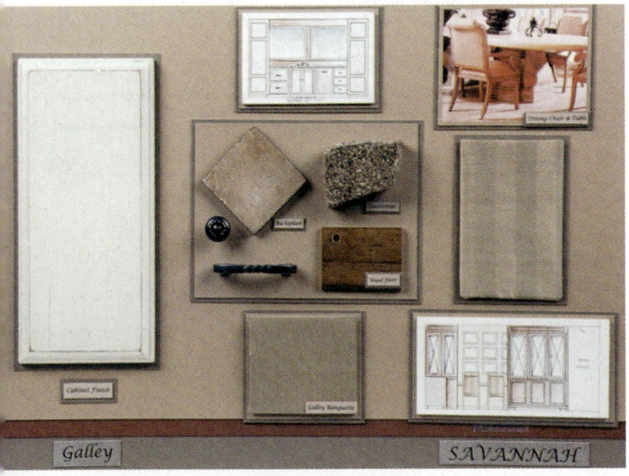

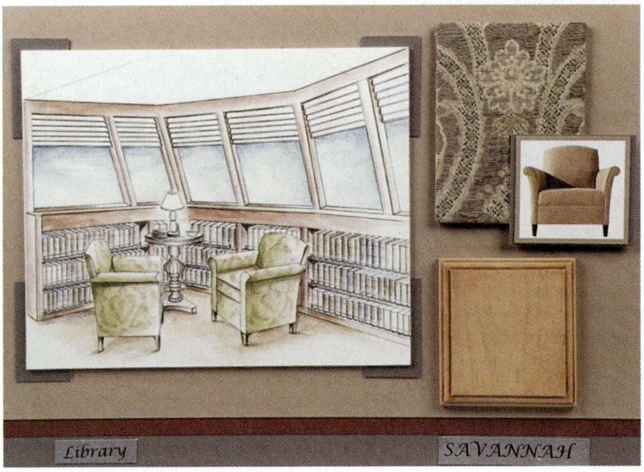

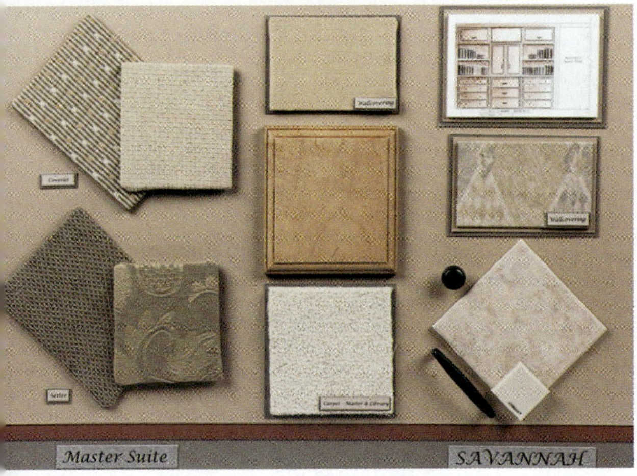

Figure 9.22 *In this extensive presentation, the designer was hired to convert a charter yacht into a private yacht. In Board #1, the smaller plan indicated the pre-existing layout. Boards #2 and #3 illustrate the main living area and dining area, including furniture, finish, and fabric selections. Board #4 illustrates the owner's library. Board #5 indicates the lower deck and master suite furnishings. (Designer: Susan E. Gillespie. Photographs by Southern Lights Photography.)*

The samples used by the designer are available through anufacturer representatives, as well as decorative arts cen-rs and the Internet. Design firms develop a Source Library f products (discussed in Chapter 13) that fit the needs of eir clients. These sources, or custom versions of them, are resented to clients for their review and approval before pro-eeding with ordering. While computer aided plans and ele-ations and computer generated images can help explain a project to a client, computer images of textiles lack the warmth of the true fabric. Clients should be given the opportunity to feel the hand of fabrics during presentations.

More info online @

http://www.tapestria.org/ and http://www.bluebolt.com to the trade websites for fabrics

---

Solving Design Problems With Textiles

Design problems often can be solved through the skillful use of fabric. A well-chosen fabric can:

- Lighten or darken a room. Fabrics in high values can work wonders to visually lighten the room. If the room has too much light, fabrics in low values help darken the room.
- Emphasize walls, windows, or furnishings to attract desired attention.
- Provide balance to a room. For example, a bold-patterned fabric at a window or on a small piece of furniture balances a larger piece of plain furniture at the other side of the room. A spot of bright color balances a larger area of muted color.
- Change the apparent size and proportion of a piece of furniture or an entire room. For example, a sofa covered in a large pattern or bold-colored fabric appears larger than the same sofa covered in a light, plain color, or a small unobtrusive pattern, as illustrated in Figure 9.23. A chair or love seat upholstered in a vertical stripe looks higher than the same piece covered in a plain fabric.

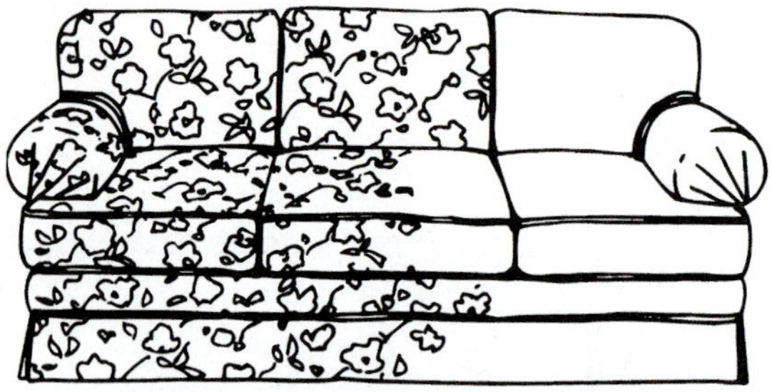

Large or conspicuous pattern tends to make furniture appear larger.

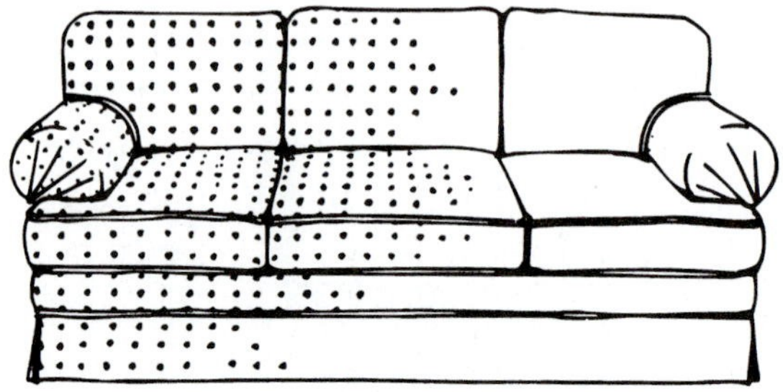

Small pattern diminishes size.

Figure 9.23 *The effect of pattern and size.*

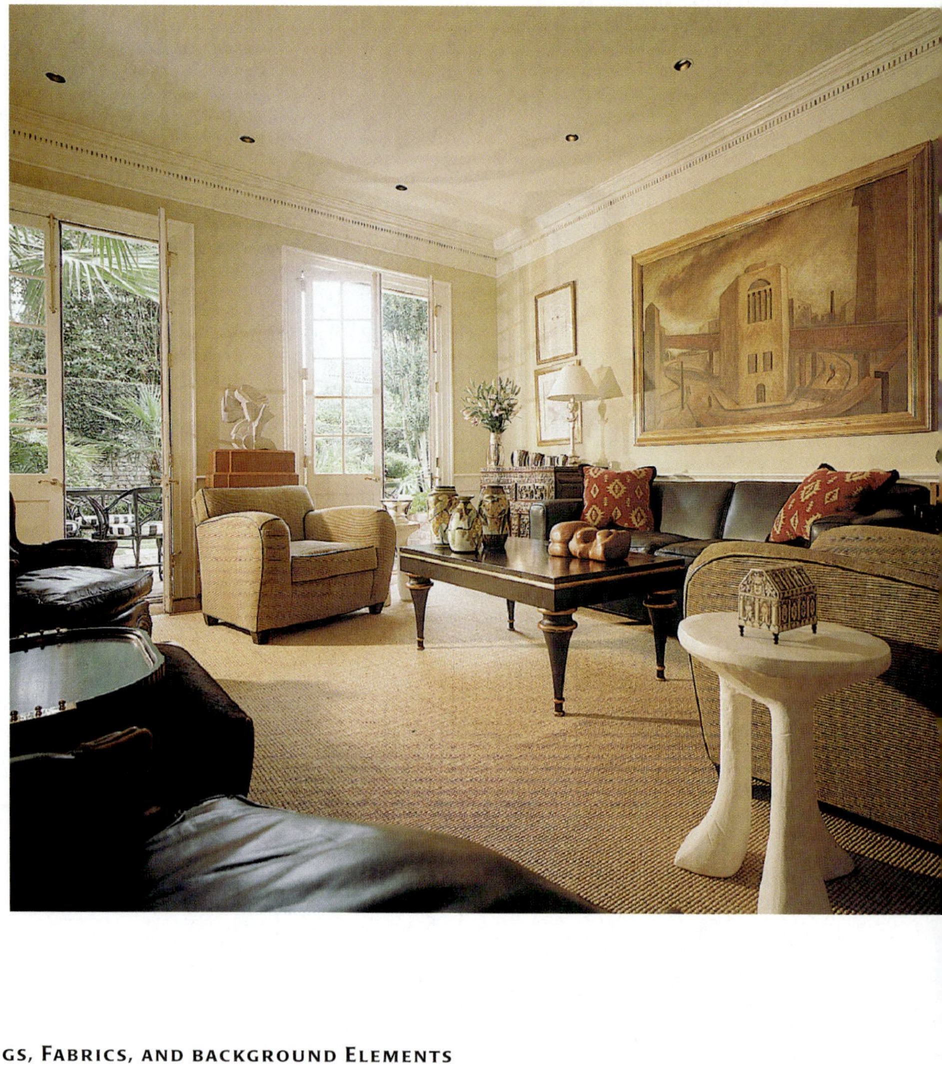

Figure 9.24 *This living area provides a secluded and comfortable retreat. The warm browns and rich-textured fabrics create a relaxing environment. (Designer: BRITO Design Studio. Photograph © Robert Thien. As seen in* Atlanta Homes & Lifestyles.*)*

Conceal walls, windows, or furnishings. A designer may want to draw attention away from or cover up a particular wall, window, or piece of furniture.
Bring harmony and unity to a room by repeated use of the same or complementary fabrics.
Establish the room's color scheme. A successful method by which to color scheme a room is to choose a favorite patterned fabric as a starting point.
Establish the historic or modern style of a room. If the room is based on a certain period, the fabric, more than any other item or furnishing, can set the desired feeling. Documentary fabrics can provide historically authentic styles.
Change the look of a room for different seasons. For example, a sofa and chairs in deep warm colors may be slipcovered in light-colored ticking for summer. Heavy winter drapery may be changed to light sheers in summer to create a cool atmosphere.

Summary

All fabrics supply softness and comfort to an interior. Fabrics also add character, absorb sound, and provide for textural enrichment in a space (Figure 9.24). Selecting the appropriate fabric requires knowledge of fibers, fabric construction, coloring or dyeing procedures, finish selections, and product testing and safety codes. Combining fabrics demands careful discernment and an appreciation for the human factor and the elements and principles of design. Careful fabric placement can solve unusual architectural or interior construction dilemmas.

According to Jack Lenor Larsen, "Fabric is one of the principal devices for introducing color, texture, and pattern into interiors and certainly the most easily manipulated one." The beginning designer will find great satisfaction in selecting fabrics that fit the unique needs of each client in each situation.

extile Terminology

e information in this section can assist the designer in getg maximum service from fabrics. The following are comon fabrics, their qualities and uses, as well as terms relating the textile industry. Fabrics are listed under their common corative name. Pronunciations of difficult terms follow in rentheses.

tique satin A satin weave fabric with textured horizontal striations that imitate antique silk. Antique satin is lightweight, usually a solid color. Draperies.

stiste A fine, soft, sheer fabric of plain weave made of various fibers. Sheers.

uclé French word meaning "curly." It indicates yarns are curled or looped in a flat or pile fabric. Heavyweight. Upholstery.

aid A band of lace, embroidery, or metallic thread used as trimming.

oadcloth A lightweight fabric in a plain or twill weave. Cotton, wool, or synthetic fibers popularly used. Draperies, bedspreads.

ocade A mediumweight fabric woven on a Jacquard loom. An embroidered multicolored pattern stands out in relief against a satin or ribbed background. Drapery and upholstery.

ocatelle A mediumweight Jacquard fabric with an extra set of wefts for backing, unevenly twisted, which results in a high-relief embossed appearance on the surface. Upholstery and draperies.

ckram Stiffened material sized with glue. Reinforcement for draperies and valances.

llion fringe A heavy strand of threads forming cords attached to a heading.

rlap A mediumweight coarse fabric woven of jute in a plain, loose weave. Drapery and lamp shades.

Calico A lightweight plain cotton weave with a small all-over print. Curtains.

Cambric Plain weave cotton or linen. Called "handkerchief linen." Originally made in Cambrai, France. Very sheer to coarse. Linings.

Canvas A mediumweight, closely woven cotton. A plain, diagonal weave in solids or prints. Upholstery, drapery, walls.

Casement A broad term covering a relatively coarse fabric used like a sheer. Usually light neutral colors in leno or open weaves. Commonly used in commercial settings.

Challis A lightweight wool, cotton, or synthetic soft fabric in a plain tight weave. Printed designs or plain. Drapery, upholstery.

Chenille A heavyweight fabric woven with chenille yarns. When woven in a fabric, can create a pile similar to velvet; if woven on a Jacquard loom can look similar to cut velvet. Upholstery.

Chiffon A translucent fabric. Tight weave, lightweight. Sheers.

Chintz A plain, tightly woven, lightweight cotton fabric with fine yarns. Sometimes processed with a glazed finish. Can be either a solid color or printed. Draperies, slipcovers, bedspreads.

Color flag The series of clippings attached to a purchased fabric sample to show the colorline.

Colorline The complete color range of a given fabric series.

Colorway The color of an individual fabric.

Cord Threads twisted to form larger diameter strands. Strands over 1″ wide are called ropes.

Corduroy A heavyweight cotton or synthetic pile fabric, ribbed or corded lengthwise. Drapery, slipcovers, upholstery, bedspreads, and other uses.

Crepe Crinkled or puckered fabrics of many types. Usually produced by twisting the yarn when weaving or by a chemical process. Cotton, silk, wool are typical. Plain weave.

Cretonne First made in Creton, France. Similar to chintz but heavier. A cotton fabric with a printed design. Plain or rep weave.

Crewel embroidery A heavyweight plain-woven fabric of cotton, linen, or wool embroidered with fine, loosely twisted, two-ply worsted yarns. Usually worked by hand in the Kashmir province of India. Drapery and upholstery.

Crocking The rubbing off of color from dyed or printed fabrics.

Crypton A patented upholstery formulation designed for commercial seating. Extremely strong and durable, resistant to moisture, stains, and bacterial growth. Breathable and quality hand.

Customer's own material or **COM** The "COM" designation is used when designers supply material to the furniture manufacturer. The fabric is purchased separately and shipped to the upholstery company to be used on a particular piece of furniture.

Cutting A sample of a fabric for presentation or design purposes.

Damask A Jacquard-woven mediumweight fabric with patterns providing unique weave effects. Can be woven self-tone, one-color warp, different-color filling, or multicolor in design. Distinguished from brocades because face of fabric is flatter. The color is reversed on the wrong side. Drapery and upholstery.

Denim A mediumweight, tightly woven cotton twill made of coarse yarns. Usually in a solid color, but can be patterned. Drapery, upholstery, bedspreads, walls, and numerous other uses.

Dotted swiss Sheer fabric woven with extra yarns forming dots when clipped. The effect may be produced by flocking. Curtains.

Duck Similar to canvas. Tightly woven and durable cotton textile. Often striped and used for awnings.

Embroidery Needle and thread art. Originally handwork designs. Can also be machine produced.

Faille (fīl) A lightweight, flat-ribbed fabric woven with fine yarns in the warp and heavier yarns in the filling using a plain weave. The ribbed effect is flatter than grosgrain and smaller than rep. Faille can be the base cloth for moiré. Drapery, upholstery.

Felt Wool or mixed fibers pressed into a compact sheet. A heavyweight fabric used for walls, table covers, and other uses.

Fiberglass Fibers and yarns produced from glass and woven into flexible lightweight fabrics. Noted for its fireproof qualities. Beta Fiberglas is a trademarked glass fiber. Curtains.

Film A lightweight thin or thick plastic sheet used for upholstery, shower curtains, or table coverings. Can be textured, patterned, or plain.

Flannel Twilled fabric made of wool or cotton. Soft yarns are brushed to produce a napped texture. Used for interlinings.

Friezé (frē-zā′) A strong heavyweight fabric with a fine, cut or uncut, low-loop surface woven on a wire loom to maintain loops of an even size. Upholstery.

Fringe Thin strands of threads or cords attached to heading.

Gabardine Twill fabric with a distinct diagonal design. Durable, lightweight or mediumweight, made with natural or manufactured fibers.

Gauze Sheer, thin textile constructed of leno or plain weave both. Originally silk, now also cotton, wool, linen, and sy thetic fibers. Used for sheers.

Gimp Ornamental braid used to cover upholstery tacks.

Gingham Mediumweight or lightweight cotton or cottonli fabric for informal use. Made of colored yarns formi checks, plaids, or stripes.

Grenadine A leno weave textile similar to marquisette, b thinner. Often woven with dots or patterns. Sheers.

Gros (grō) point Heavyweight needlepoint embroidery. U holstery.

Homespun Loosely woven lightweight fabric made to rese ble handwoven material. Curtains or drapery.

Hopsacking A rough-surfaced mediumweight fabric loose woven of various fibers in a plain basket weave. Mainly f drapery and slipcovers.

Insulating Fabrics processed with reflective metallic or foa plastic on one side to provide insulating qualities.

Jacquard Damasks, brocades, tapestries, and all fabrics requ ing the Jacquard loom.

Khaki A coarse lightweight to mediumweight cotton tw weave dyed an earthy green color.

Lace Open needlework fabric. Originally handmade, now pr duced by machine. Often has net background with floral a geometric designs. Curtains and tablecloths.

Lampas Fabric having narrow ribs with satinlike figures form of warp threads and contrasting figures formed of w thread. Drapery and upholstery.

Leather Animal skin, usually from cows. Upholstery.

Lining A term applied to plain cotton or sateen fabrics that li or back support draperies or other decorative textiles.

Marquisette (mär′-kĭ-zĕt) A sheer lightweight leno wov textile used for sheers. Made of natural or manufactur fibers. Looks like gauze.

Matelassé (măt-lä-sā′) A double-woven heavyweight fab with a quilted appearance. From the French *matelass* meaning "to cushion" or "to pad." Upholstery.

Memo sample A sample of a fabric that must be returned the fabric showroom.

Mohair Napped fabric from the hair of the Angora goat.

Moiré (mwä-rā′) A wavy, watery effect pressed into a ribb surface such as taffeta or faille. A lightweight fabric suital for drapery, upholstery, or bedspreads.

Monk's cloth A coarse mediumweight fabric in a loose wea of flax, jute, or hemp mixed with cotton, generally in neut colors. May have sagging problems.

Muslin Bleached or unbleached plain, lightweight cott weave. Has many uses in decorating, especially in Ea American and modern rooms. Walls, draperies, slipcove Solid colors or printed patterns.

Needlepoint A heavyweight handmade or Jacquard fab Fine and delicate effect is known as petit point; larger need point is known as gros point.

Net A sheer lacelike fabric with a consistent mesh texture av able in a variety of fibers. Suitable for sheers.

Ninon (nē′-nŏn) A plain tight weave. Has a smooth, cri gossamer appearance. Sheers.

Organdy A sheer crisp cotton fabric with good pleating qu ties. Available plain, embroidered, or printed. Sheers.

naburg A lightweight to mediumweight fabric similar to homespun. A loose, uneven, coarse cotton with solid color or printed motifs.

xford A plain-weave fabric. Large filling yarn goes over two warp yarns. An informal fabric with many uses.

isley A printed design inspired by original motifs from India and shawl motifs from Paisley, Scotland. Exaggerated curved raindrop or pear shape most typical design. Lightweight to mediumweight. Usually cotton.

ssamenterie Fringes, braids, gimps, tassels, and other decorative ornamentation added to upholstery and window coverings.

rcale A tightly woven and durable lightweight textile. Can be plain or printed. Most often used for bed sheets.

lling Formation of fiber fuzz balls on fabric surface caused by wear or friction; encountered in spun nylon, polyester, acrylic, cashmere, or soft woolen yarns.

qué (pĭ-kā′ or **pē-kā′)** A mediumweight to heavyweight cotton textile with raised cords or geometric designs running lengthwise. Often used for bedspreads and curtains. Many variations of this textile type.

ssé (plĭ-sā′) A lightweight fabric with a crinkled or puckered effect created by chemical treatment. Curtains.

ısh A heavyweight pile fabric with greater depth than velvet. Usually has a high sheen. Upholstery.

lished cotton A plain- or satin-weave cotton cloth characterized by a sheen ranging from dull to bright. Polish can be achieved either through the weave or by the addition of a resin finish.

ngee (pŏn-jē′) Term derived from Chinese words for "natural color." Made from wild silk and left in its natural tan color. Lightweight and durable. Used for curtains.

plin Lightweight. Similar to rep. Has a lightly corded surface running through the fabric. Made of natural or manufactured fibers. Often used for draperies.

ilted fabrics A pattern stitched through a printed or plain fabric and through a layer of batting. Outline quilting traces around the pattern of a printed fabric. Loom quilting is a small repetitive design made by the quilting alone. Ultrasonic quilting produces thermally bonded welds in place of stitching threads.

p Plain weave, lightweight fabric with narrow rounded ribs running the width or length of the fabric. Usually a fine warp with heavier filling yarns. Drapery, upholstery, slipcovers, bedspreads, and other informal uses.

sette Applied ornamentation fabricated by gathering materials in a circular manner.

ilcloth A mediumweight fabric in a plain weave similar to canvas. Popular for informal indoor or outdoor upholstery.

teen A highly lustrous fabric usually made of mercerized cotton with a satin weave. Drapery lining.

tin *Plain:* Fine yarns woven to give a more lustrous surface. May be lightweight or heavy enough for upholstery. Has many decorative uses when a formal style of decor is desired. *Antique:* A smooth satin face highlighted by slub (or twisted) yarn in a random pattern. An important fabric for drapery.

rge Twill weave with a hard clear finish. Made from rayon, silk, cotton, or wool.

antung A heavy pongee. Usually made of wild silk and has a textured, striated surface. Antique satin simulates shantung.

Sheer General term for thin, lightweight textiles.

Suede Leather with a napped surface. Polyester suede washes and wears well. Upholstery.

Swiss A fine, thin cotton textile originally made in Switzerland and often used for sheers. May be plain, but usually is embroidered or designed with dots (dotted swiss) or figures that have been chemically applied. Manufactured fibers also used.

Taffeta *Plain:* Tight, crisp smooth weave with slight horizontal ribbed effect. When woven of silk, it is a luxury fabric for drapery, bedspreads, and lampshades. *Antique* or *shantung:* A smooth, soft weave with random slub yarn creating a texture effect. A lustrous fabric with many decorative uses, especially drapery and lamp shades.

Tapestry A figured multicolored fabric woven on a Jacquard loom made up of two sets of warp and weft. The design is formed by varying weave effects brought to the surface in combination with colored yarns. The surface has a rough texture. A heavyweight upholstery fabric.

Tassels Suspended strands of cut or looped yarn or cord attached to a header.

Terry cloth A mediumweight cotton or linen pile fabric. May be cut or uncut. Loops may be on one side or both. Bedspreads, upholstery, and towels.

Ticking A mediumweight, tightly woven cotton or linen fabric. A strong, usually striped fabric in a satin or twill weave. Mattresses, pillows, wallcoverings, slipcovers, and drapery.

Toile de Jouy (twäl də zhwē′) A floral or scenic design usually printed on a plain cotton or linen ground. Originally printed in Jouy, France.

Trapunto (trəün′-tō) Quilting that raises an area design in one color on the surface of upholstery fabric.

Tweed Plain-weave, heavyweight upholstery fabric with a tweed texture because of flake (or knotted) yarn, in multicolors. Upholstery.

Union cloth Half linen and half cotton fabric that is plain or patterned. Coarse weave. A variety of uses.

Velour A French term loosely applied to all types of fabrics with a nap or cut pile on one side. Specifically, it is a cut-pile fabric similar to regular velvet but with a higher pile. Heavyweight upholstery fabric.

Velvet A heavyweight fabric having a short, thick warp pile. May be of any fiber. *Crushed:* Most often the fabric is pulled through a narrow cylinder to create the crushed effect. *Cut:* Jacquard design, usually cut and uncut pile on a plain ground. *Antique:* Velvet that has an old look. Upholstery.

Velveteen A heavyweight weft-pile fabric with short pile, usually of cotton. Drapery, upholstery, bedspreads, and innumerable other uses.

Vinyl A heavy nonwoven plastic fabric capable of being printed or embossed to produce any desired finish such as a leather, wood, floral, or textured design. Cloth backing prevents tearing. Walls and upholstery.

Voile (vôyl) A fine, soft, translucent fabric in a variety of textures, used for sheers.

Webbing Heavyweight jute, cotton, or synthetic strips, generally 1 to 4 in. wide. Interwoven and plain or printed. Particularly used for sofas and chairs. Can also be used to support springs for an upholstered piece.

10

Backgrounds: Floors

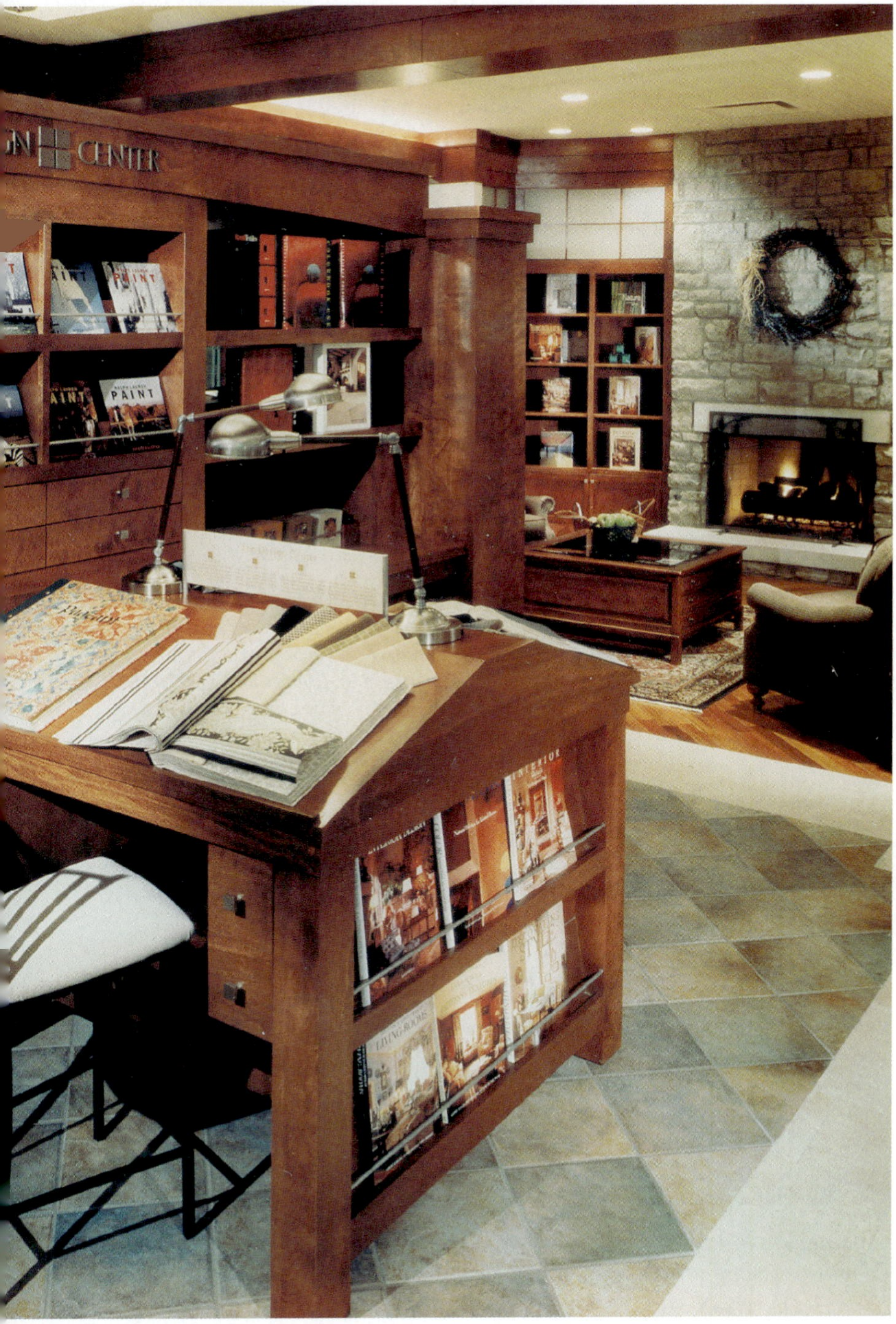

gure 10.1 *In this carpet showroom, the variety of flooring materials serve to owcase the flooring industry. The design center includes options for compatible allcoverings and fabrics, along with an abundance of layout space. (Architect: hite Associates. Designer: Chute Gerdeman. Photograph by Michael Houghton udio. Courtesy of Stanley Steemer International.)*

The general scheme of any room is established by the architectural background: floors, ceilings, walls, and other items such as trim, doors, windows, and fireplaces. The decorative treatments added to these backgrounds (as well as to the movable objects in the room) should be in keeping with the overall feeling to give the room harmony and unity (Figure 10.1). This chapter focuses on the material and finish options for floors.

Floors are designed primarily to be walked on and to provide a foundation for furnishings; therefore, floors must be made from or covered with durable, stain-resistant materials. Due to improved technology, developments in old and new materials, and methods of production, today's flooring materials are both beautiful and practical. The decision to select a specific type of flooring is based on the same criteria discussed in the introduction to Part V: *function and the human factor, aesthetics,* and *economics.*

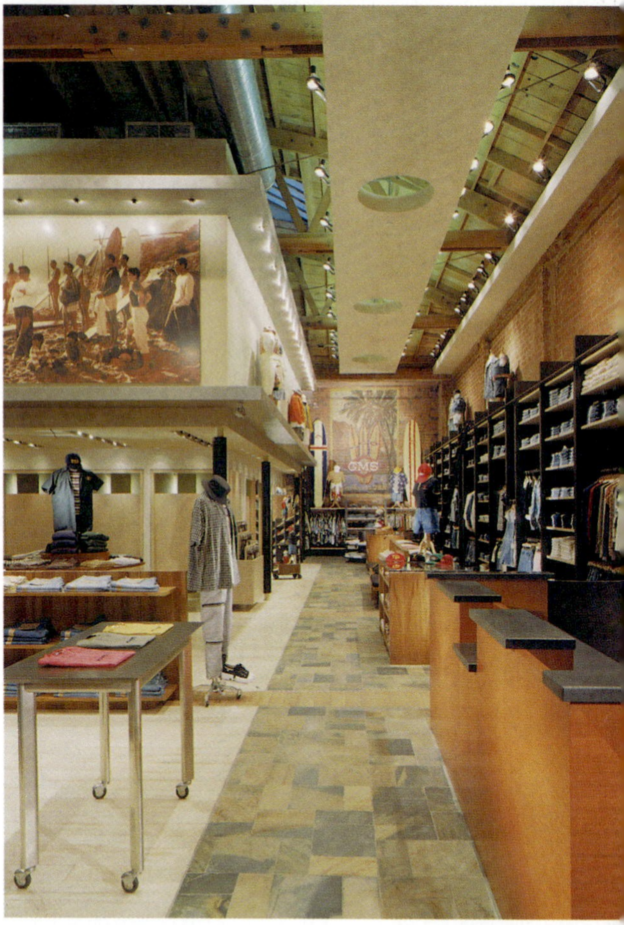

Figure 10.2 *Chinese slate and bleached pine flooring are combined in this retail store. Note how traffic is directed by the changes in flooring material. (Architect/Designer: Area Design, Inc. Photograph by Jon Miller/Hedrich-Blessing.)*

HARD FLOORING

Recent decades have witnessed a renaissance in hard-surface floor coverings, both nonresilient and resilient. The term *resilient* refers to a material's ability to spring back when pressed. In contrast, *nonresilient* materials lack flexibility.

Nonresilient Flooring

Masonry

The initial cost of nonresilient flooring is generally high; however, hard-surface **masonry** flooring such as brick, stone, and tile remain popular because of their extreme dura-

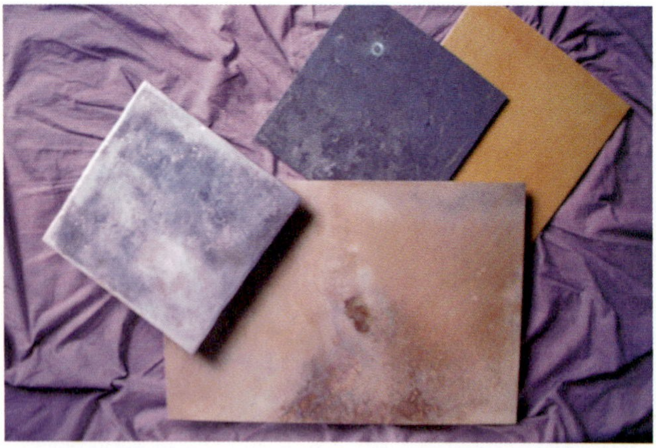

Figure 10.3 *Ceramic tile offers a broad range of finishes from aged and weathered stone to polished marble. The square on the left is Cerdomus Ceramiche, the rectangle is Graniti Fiandre, the bottom two squares are Emilceramic and Vives Azulejos y Gres. (Courtesy of* Interiors & Sources.*)*

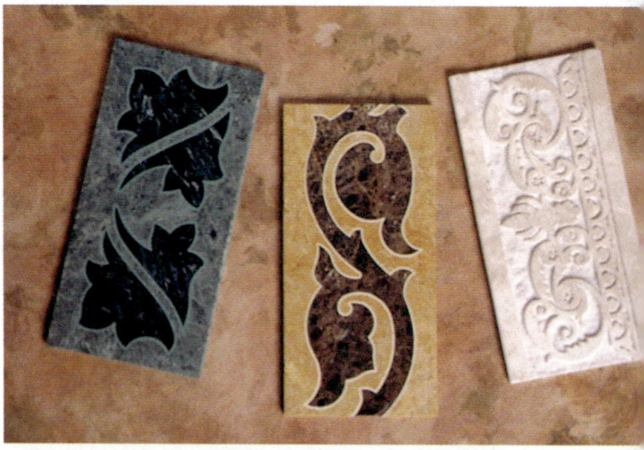

Figure 10.4 *Natural stone borders are available in intricate designs. Shown from left are waterjet-cut marble borders fro the Corolla and Victoria collections by Stoneworks, and the Wrought Iron border in carved St. Croix travertine by StoneArt. (Courtesy of* Interiors & Sources.*)*

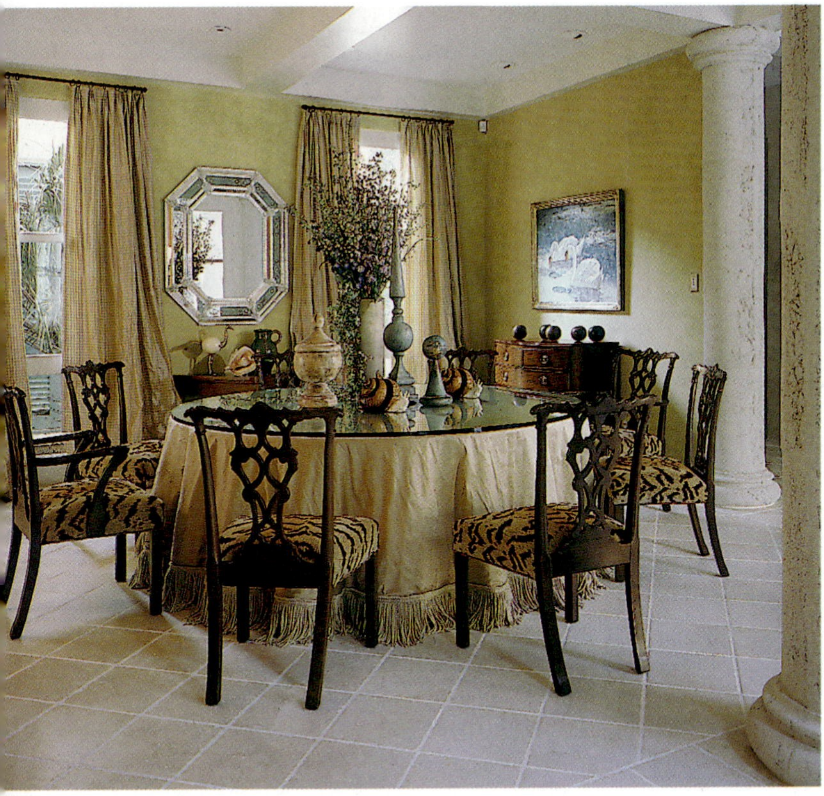

Figure 10.5 *A travertine floor and rusticated columns provide an interesting contrast to the fringed tablecloth, glass top, and faux animal print. (Design and Architecture: Wells Design. Photograph by Hickey-Robertson. As seen in* Southern Accents.*)*

ty, versatility, low maintenance requirements, and time-
s character. Masonry floors are installed in either thin or
:k mortar.

The durable qualities of tile, stone, and other masonry
ors allow these materials to be used throughout the home
l commercial environment. In the home, masonry floors
y flow from the entrance hall to the porch or patio, thus
viding unity and minimizing upkeep. Designers of restau-
ts, hotel lobbies, and shopping malls find masonry floor-
an extremely durable and creative solution (Figures 10.2
ough 10.7).

Table 10.1 contains information on the most commonly used nonresilient hard floor coverings, their characteristics and uses, and suggestions for treatment and care.

More info online @

http://www.tile-assn.com/ National Tile Contractors Association

http://www.ctdahome.org/ Ceramic Tile Distributors Association

http://www2.cr.nps.gov/tps/briefs/brief40.htm
National Park Service, Historic Preservation Brief
on Restoring Ceramic Tile

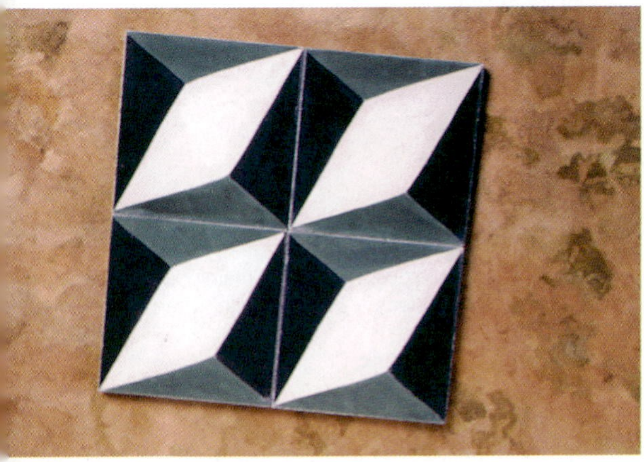

ure 10.6 *This tile creates a* ***trompe l'oeil*** *(three-
ensional) effect: Astra from Wholesale Tile & Accessories.
urtesy of* Interiors & Sources.*)*

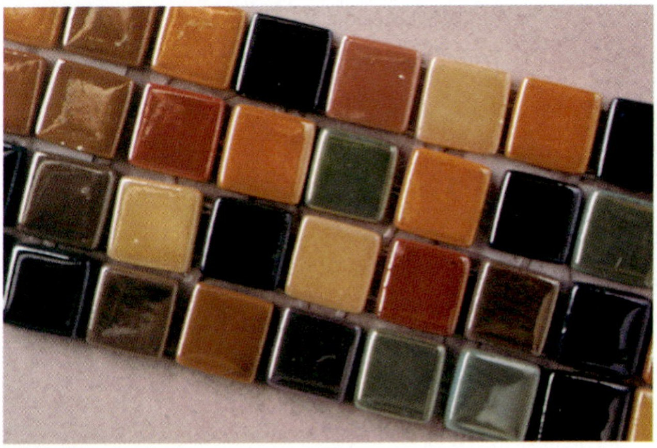

Figure 10.7 *This rich, vibrant color palette of ceramic tile is offered by Briare Tile. (Courtesy of* Interiors & Sources.*)*

Table 10.1 *Hard-Surface Flooring: Nonresilient*

Material	Characteristics	Uses	Treatment and Care
Brick	Durable, little upkeep needed Comes in many textures, sizes, and colors Transmits moisture and cold readily, and absorbs grease unless treated Absorbs and stores solar energy, but not sound Rough to touch	Walks, patios, foyers, greenhouses Adds a country look or historical appearance	Careful waxing softens rugged effect and produces soft patina Coating of vinyl protects from grease penetration Dust with dry mop, wash occasionally For stubborn stains, use trisodium phosphate
Ceramic tile (see Figures 10.3, 10.6, 10.7)	Has unique aesthetic quality One of the hardest and most durable floor and wall coverings Versatile Common type using small squares is called mosaic May be glazed or unglazed; comes in many colors, patterns, and textures Glossy surface squares usually 4 1/2 in. New developments producing handsome tiles 12 in. square with variety of designs, textures, and colors Pregrouted tile sheets up to 2 by 14 ft. now available Absorbs and stores solar energy, but not sound Expensive	Especially attractive for bathrooms, and may be suitable for any commercial interior	Unglazed: may be waxed to giv soft sheen Glazed: dust with dry mop, was when needed with soap and warm water
Concrete	May be solid or in squares, smooth or textured, polished or unpolished Color may be added before pouring or after Absorbs and stores solar energy, but not sound Easy upkeep Inexpensive Tends to give cold, industrial feeling when brought inside	Particularly desirable for some hard use areas and for support of heavy equipment Usually used commercially	Heavy waxed surface necessar for maintenance Do not use lacquer, varnish, or shellac Special finishes available Wet before cleaning and use detergent Easy to maintain
Exposed aggregate	Stones are laid in concrete and polished to smoothness, but surface remains uneven Absorbs and stores solar energy Can be too uneven and difficult to walk on	Especially appropriate for exterior walks	Dust, wash occasionally
Flagstone	Any flat stone; varies in size, thickness, quality, and color Versatile, durable, handsome Easy upkeep Colors range from soft grays through beiges and reddish-browns May be cut geometrically or laid in natural shapes Surface slightly uneven Absorbs solar energy, but not sound Expensive Difficult to repair if damaged Cold when not heated	Walks, patios, foyers, greenhouses, any heavy traffic area May be dressed up or down, making it appropriate for wide range of uses	Treatment and care same as fo brick
Granite	An igneous hard stone of cooled molten rock Has a fine- or coarse-grain (crystal or grain) texture Main colors are variations of gray, brown, black, pink, green, yellow, or combinations of these Has a coarse finish or can be polished until it shines Easy to cut for various uses Harder than marble Expensive Cold to touch Difficult to repair if damaged Does not absorb sound	Floors, walls, tabletops, countertops, and steps Highly durable and excellent for heavy traffic areas Especially popular for commercial use	Easy maintenance: sweep clea wipe with water when necessar

Table 10.1 *Continued*

Material	Characteristics	Uses	Treatment and Care
Marble (see Figure 10.4)	Extremely hard Available in many varieties, colors, and veining Gives feeling of elegance, luxury, and formality More expensive than most other flooring materials, but is permanent New stone-cutting techniques make it lighter and less expensive Tiles are reinforced by epoxy-fiberglass coating Cold to touch Difficult to repair if damaged Does not absorb sound Slippery when wet	Wherever elegant durability is needed Especially appropriate with classic styles of furnishings Not appropriate in settings where water may be prevalent	Wash with soap and warm water Easy maintenance
Mexican tile or terra-cotta	Crude base made of unrefined clay Hand shaped and sun dried Allows little control of color and shape Durable, informal, inexpensive Absorbs solar energy, but not sound Easy upkeep Difficult to repair if damaged Cold when not heated	Wherever a hard, cementlike surface is desired or wherever solar energy storage is desired	Dust with dry mop, wash occasionally with detergent Surface seldom waxed
Quarry tile	Type of ceramic tile One of the hardest and most durable tiles May be glazed or unglazed Heat and frost resistant, easy upkeep, durable Both ceramic and quarry tiles are practically impervious to grease and chemicals Absorbs and stores solar energy, but not sound Variety of shapes to select Inexpensive Difficult to repair if damaged Cold when not heated	Suitable for many period rooms, especially Italian, early English, and rooms with Mediterranean feeling Can be used wherever hard surface is appropriate Coolness makes it desirable in hot climates	Care same as for ceramic tile
Slate (specific type of stone)	More formal than flagstone Qualities similar to flagstone except for color, which runs from gray to blue-green to black Absorbs solar energy Easy upkeep if sealed Expensive Difficult to repair if damaged Cold when not heated Shows dust easily when polished	May be used in traffic areas in formal rooms Appropriate for some period rooms Particularly appropriate for sunrooms, foyers, and greenhouses	May be polished or unpolished, but more often waxed and highly polished
Terrazzo	Consists of cement mortar (matrix) into which marble chips (aggregate) are mixed Custom or precast; comes in large or small marble chips Larger chips give more formal appearance Available in limited range of colors Sanitary, durable, and easy to clean Cold to touch Difficult to repair if damaged Does not absorb sound Slippery when wet	Patios, foyers, halls, recreation rooms, bathrooms, or wherever traffic is heavy	Care same as for Mexican tile Some varieties need occasional waxing
Travertine (see Figures 10.4 and 10.5)	Porous limestone characterized by irregular cavities that should be filled with either clear or opaque epoxy resin Clear resin has three-dimensional appearance Cold to touch Difficult to repair if damaged Does not absorb sound Slippery when wet	Formal settings where durability is required	Wash with soap or detergent and warm water

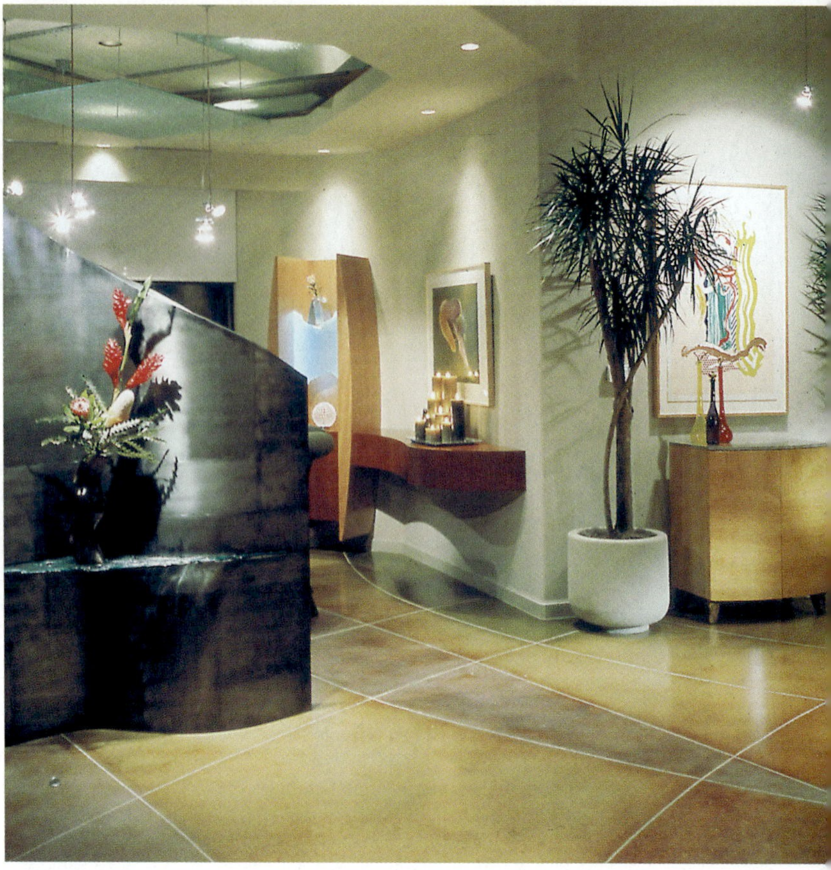

Figure 10.8 *The creative use of concrete has greatly evolved since its beginnings in Roman history. Concrete floors can be custom colored and patterned, as seen here, or they may also be textured. Patterned floors help to delineate space. Designs can be applied to existing or new floors, both inside and outside. (Courtesy of Bomanite Corp.)*

Concrete

Concrete floors or slabs are common base floors in commercial office structures. Left plain, the floors can give a harsh or institutional feel to the interior; however, concrete floors can be etched or scored into a variety of patterns. Concrete floors also can be faux painted and imprinted to resemble marble, brick, or other decorative motifs (see Figure 10.8). Bits of stone or gravel can be added to the cement mixture to create a rough surface; however, these surfaces can be difficult to negotiate.

Wood Flooring

Wood has both resilient and nonresilient properties; it is considered the most versatile of all flooring materials. Wood combines beauty, warmth, resistance to indentation, durability, and availability. It also has resistance to cold, which gives wood flooring the additional advantage of comfort over masonry floors. Wood floors can provide an attractive background for any style of furnishings, as seen in Figures 10.2 and 10.9. New methods of treatment have made wood a practical flooring choice for many environments.

More info online @

http://www.woodfloors.org/ National Wood Flooring Association

http://www.maplefloor.org/ Maple Flooring Manufactures Associatic

http://www.nofma.org/ National Oak Flooring Manufactures Association

http://www.hardwoodfloorsmag.com/ Magazine of the National Wood Flooring Association

Methods of Laying Wood Floors

The three basic methods of laying wood floors are in stri planks, and parquetry. In the *strip* method, pieces wood, usually about 2 in. wide with tongue-and-groo edges, are nailed in place. In the *plank* method, the plan may be uniform or random, varying in width from 3 in. 7 in. Some have square edges; others are tongue a groove. The *parquetry* method makes use of short lengt of boards, arranging them in various designs such checkerboard and herringbone (Figure 10.10). For eco omy and ease of installation, 9″ to 12″ squares are asse bled at the factory.

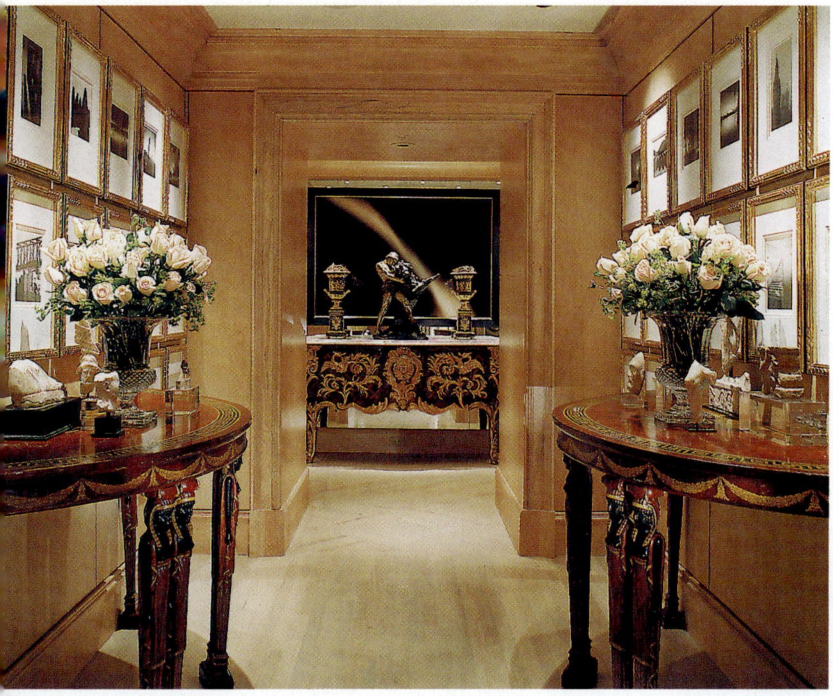

Figure 10.9 *The flooring in this entry foyer is bleached oak. The opulent, dramatic design complements the owner's collection of black and white photographs. (Designer: Dilger-Gibson. Photograph by Cheryl Dalton. As seen in* Southern Accents.*)*

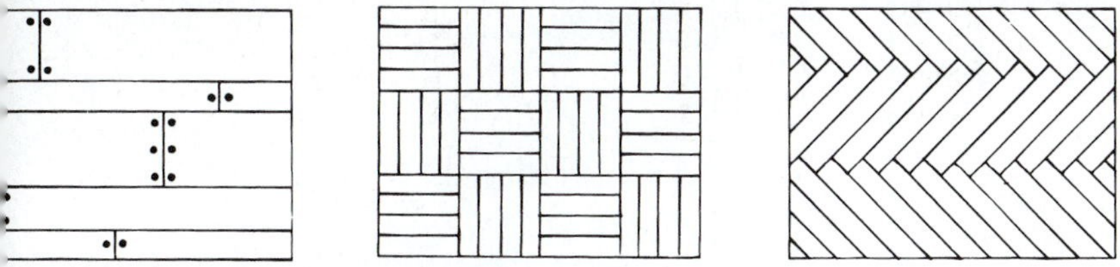

Figure 10.10 *Patterns of wood flooring.*

With the use of laser for cutting, floors can also be de-ned in a multitude of patterns. Medallions, starbursts, ettes, pinwheels, or even the Greek key can be produced wood and inlaid into wood floors. Frequently, exotic ods are used to create these patterns. It is imperative that signers confirm the source of the wood through the Certi-d Forest Products Council.

ained and Stenciled Wood Floors

od flooring is available in a variety of colors in addition the familiar tones of natural wood. Stain may be applied hout obliterating the natural grain of the wood. (Some in tones even emphasize the pattern in the wood.) A col-d wood finish can be achieved by a *stain and sealer thod,* in which the surface is stained and then sealed with yurethane, or the *stain wax method,* in which the stain netrates into the wood, leaving a wax residue on the sur-e. When the latter process is repeated and the wood is roughly rubbed, the surface has a soft, protective patina. Stained and sealed wood floors require vacuuming and asional damp mopping with a vinegar and water solution. Waxed floors must be protected from water and do require occasional rewaxing.

Stenciling, a process of applying paint through a stencil, was used historically as a substitute for expensive carpets. Today, stenciled floors are still an attractive alternative for residential environments.

Alternatives to Wood Flooring

Bamboo is an alternative to wood flooring. Bamboo, imported mainly from China's Hunan province, is technically a grass. The blades or grass canes are split long ways, planed, dried, and glued into strips under heat and pressure. Bamboo is harder than oak and does not absorb water as easily as most woods. It is considered a green product, but (as of this writing) must be imported from overseas.

Laminate flooring was introduced to the American market from Sweden. The flooring consists of a moisture-resistant particleboard core and a melamine top layer with a matte or glossy finish. Beneath the finish is a photographic layer that reproduces the pattern and color of wood (Figure 10.11). Laminate floors have many of the same warm characteristics

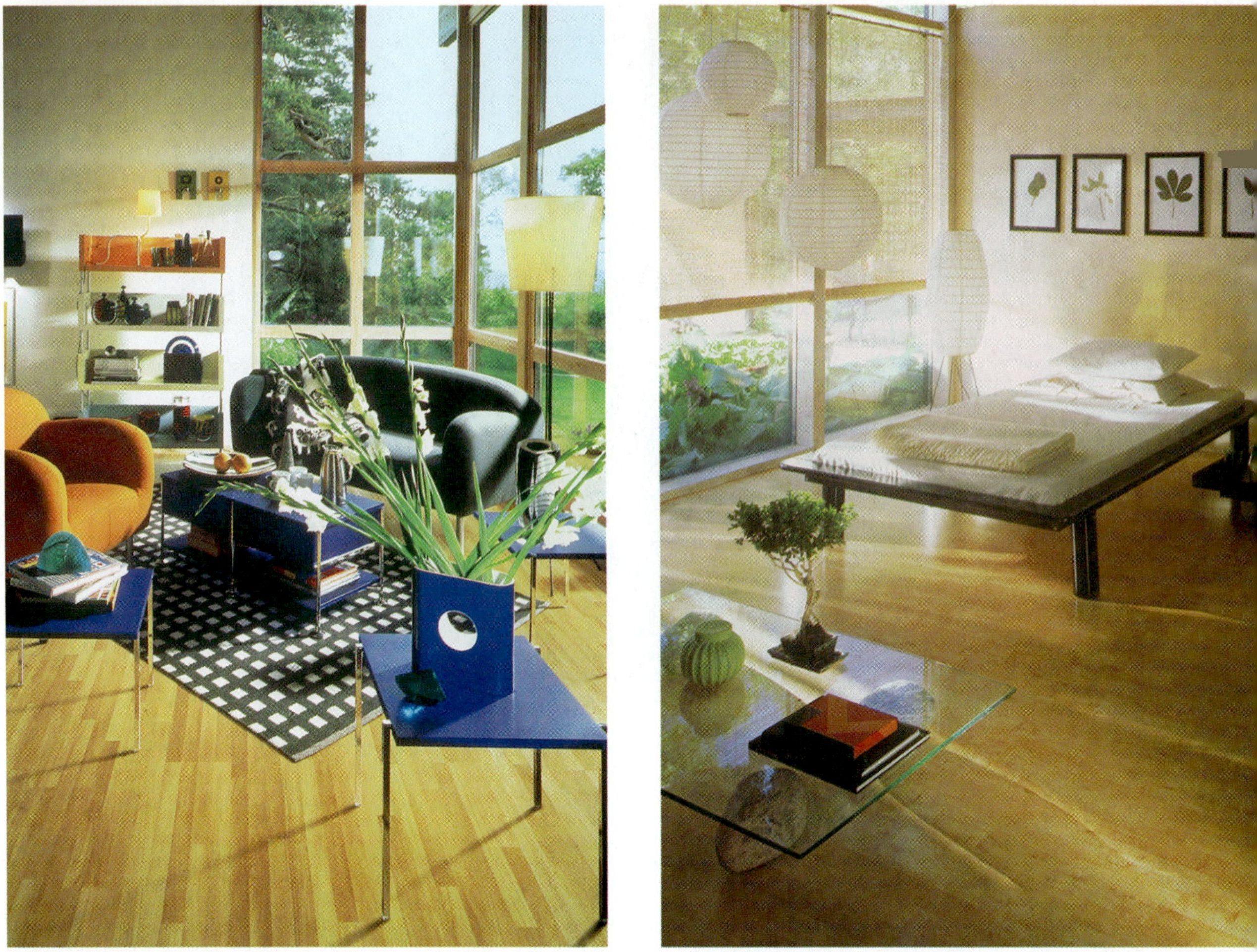

Figure 10.11 *A variety of design characteristics are now available in laminate floors. (Courtesy of Perstorp Flooring, Inc.)*

of wood, but have a greater resistance to water. Additionally, they may capture the appearance of rare woods, some of which may no longer be available. Laminate floors are a cross between nonresilient and resilient floors. Their properties are reviewed in Table 10.2.

Resilient Flooring

As previously mentioned, resilient hard-surface flooring has the ability to "spring back." The majority of resilient floors are made of vinyl and rubber; however, cork and leather are also used. Table 10.2 lists characteristics, uses, and methods of care for resilient hard-surface floors.

Vinyl and Linoleum

Sheet vinyl is one of the most common forms of vinyl flooring. The sheets are available in rolls 6′, 9′, and 12′ wide for installation with as few seams as possible. Sheet vinyl is available in various grades and qualities. Some high-grade varieties have antimicrobial finishes and resistance to urine and bloodstains, which makes them a good choice for m ical facilities.

Vinyl composition tiles, or *VCTs,* are a type of resili flooring commonly used in commercial environments. tiles are available in a variety of colors and textures. Lay the patterns on the tiles in the same direction gives a form appearance; a checkerboard effect appears when pattern tiles are alternately turned. Different colors and tures of tiles can create a pattern, define an area, or lea a destination.

Because tile floors have seams where bacteria can coll they are not recommended for health care areas. VCTs re water, but should not be used in pool areas where exten water damage could cause loose tiles. A type of vinyl called *conductive tile* is made especially for hospitals chemical and electronics laboratories to protect against st electricity.

New products are continuing to be developed by v manufacturers. Plynyl, by Chilewich, was recently in duced as a woven vinyl with a polyurethane cush Vinyls produce VOCs during their manufacturing proc Manufacturers are working to create safer methods

able 10.2 *Hard-Surface Flooring: Resilient*

aterial	Characteristics	Uses	Treatment and Care
ork tile	Provides maximum quiet and cushiony comfort underfoot Cork with vinyl or urethane surface highly resistant to moisture and stains, but natural cork not suited for abuse of kitchen traffic, water damage, etc. Colors range from light to dark brown Dented by furniture Rich color and texture Good insulation properties Shows dust easily Fairly expensive	Especially appropriate for studies and other rooms with little traffic Good green design alternative	Maintenance not easy Dirt hard to dislodge from porous surface Wash with soap and water, coat with wax Vinyl coating protects surface and eases maintenance
aminate	Available in a variety of patterns and finishes Offers the beauty of wood with greater durability Easy to install Very durable As much as 25 times tougher than laminate countertops	Appropriate in any environment except in areas with a lot of water, such as bathroom or poolside	Vacuum and damp mop
eather tile	Resilient but expensive Natural or dyed colors Quiet Luxurious look and feel Cleans well Rich colors, can be embossed	Studies and other limited areas with little traffic	Warm water and mild soap
inoleum	Natural linoleum made from linseed oil, tree resin, cork, wood flour, ground limestone, and pigments Jute backing provides good resiliency Available in a variety of patterns and colors First resilient flooring material (manufactured since the mid-19th century)	Can stain if liquids are allowed to soak in Good green design alternative	Warm water and mild soap
ubber tile	Tiles available 9 in. × 12 in., thickness $\frac{3}{16}$ in. and ½ in. Usually marble or dot pattern Sound absorbing, durable, nonskidding Safe when wet Raised surface knocks off dirt Relatively expensive	Kitchens, bathrooms, utility rooms Any commercial environment with heavy traffic	Easy to clean Wash with soap and water Avoid varnish or shellac
heet rubber	Available in 36 in. × ¾ in. untrimmed widths Plain or marbleized Durable, nonskidding Safe when wet Raised surface knocks off dirt Relatively expensive	Hard traffic areas Safe covering for stair treads	Same as for rubber tile
inyl omposition e or sheets	Excellent all-around, low-cost flooring Resists stains and wears well Hard and noisy Tiles may have self-adhesive backing	May be used in any interior environment	Exceptionally easy to maintain Wash with soap and water
inyl, cushion acked	Vinyl chips embedded in translucent vinyl base Has pebbly surface Shows no seams Has cushion backing, making it resilient May tear or dent	Wherever desired in residential setting	Same as for other vinyl
inyl, sheet	Lies flat with adhesive only on edges	Wherever vinyl flooring is desired in residential setting	Same as for other vinyl
inyl tile	Tough, nonporous, resistant to stains, durable Comes in clear colors or special effects, including translucent and three-dimensional effects The more vinyl content, the higher the price Comes in great variety of patterns and colors	Extremely versatile, may be used in any room depending on grade of vinyl	Easy care Some varieties have built-in luster and require no waxing

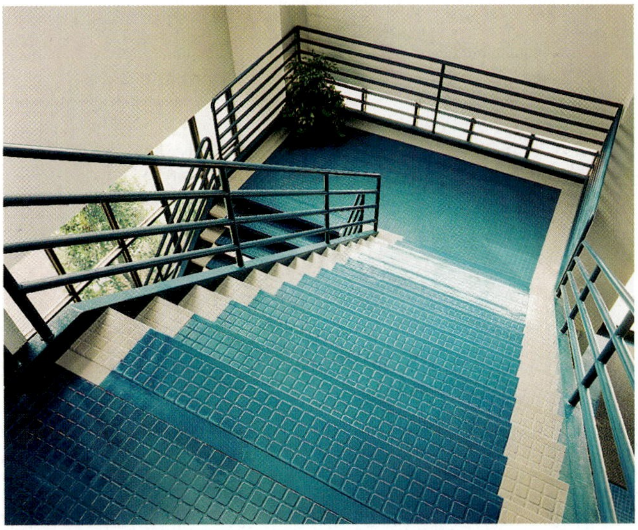

Figure 10.12 *In this interior, raised rubber flooring was used for its durability and resistance to water. (Courtesy of Roppe Corporation.)*

production. Some VCTs, for instance, are made with recycled vinyl content.

Linoleum, a natural flooring product manufactured since the 1850s, is receiving renewed interest due to its environmental friendliness. An updated version called LonEco by Lonseal is composed of 35 percent recycled materials and has the maintenance characteristics of vinyl. Linoleum is nontoxic, biodegradable, and durable.

More info online @
http://www.vinylinfo.org/index.html The Vinyl Institute

Rubber

Rubber tiles, with a raised dot or other dimensional surfa are designed for high traffic areas or areas around water. T raised areas allow dirt and water to settle below the walki surface. This surface is commonly used in airports and n pools (Figure 10.12).

SOFT FLOOR COVERINGS

Soft floor coverings are valued for their practicality, relativ low cost, and design characteristics. They insulate the flc muffle noise, and create a feeling of comfort. A well-anchor soft floor covering gives sure footing and helps prevent ac dents; it is also easy to maintain with regular vacuuming.

Essentially, there are two types of soft floor coverings: c pets and rugs. *Carpets* are sold by the yard from a roll (ge erally 12 ft. wide) and are called **broadloom.** (So broadlooms are available between 27 in. and 18 ft. wid Pieces of broadloom are taped or seamed together wh necessary and attached to the floor to form wall-to-wall c pet. Carpets may also be sold in tiles 12 in. to 24 in. squa

Rugs come in standard sizes or can be custom sized. Tl have edges finished with a binding thread, fringes, or ot materials and are generally not attached to the floor.

A room's décor may be based on the soft floor coveri as seen in Figure 10.13. It can bring furnishings into h

Figure 10.13 *The rug, a Tabriz from Iran (Persia) c. 1850, forms the color source for this room. (Designer: Francis □ Russell. Photograph by Peter Vitale. As seen in Veranda.)*

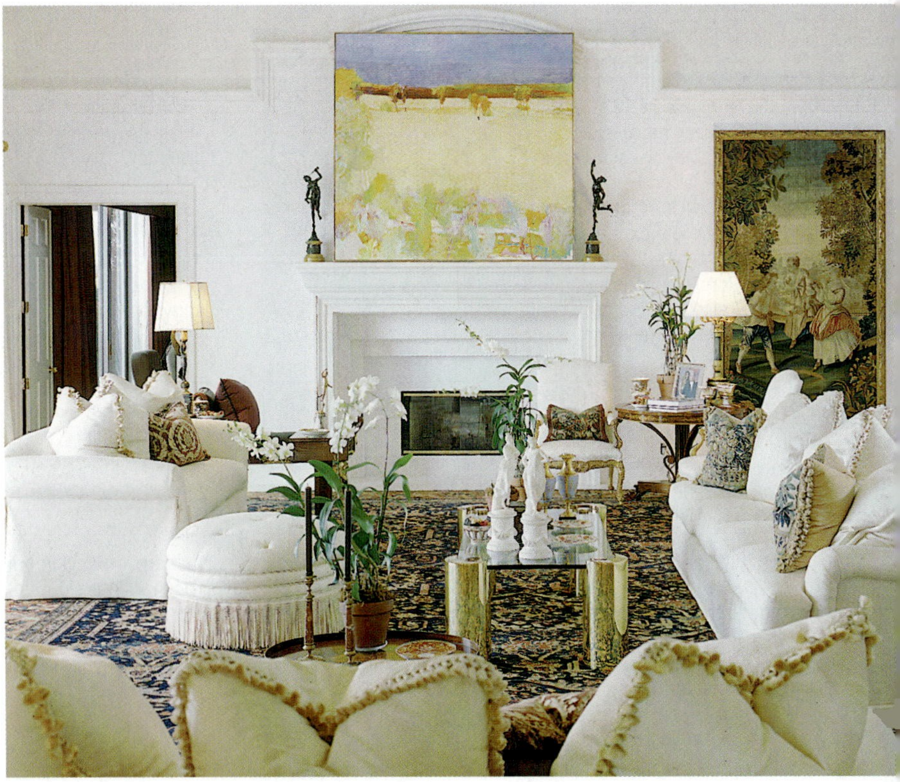

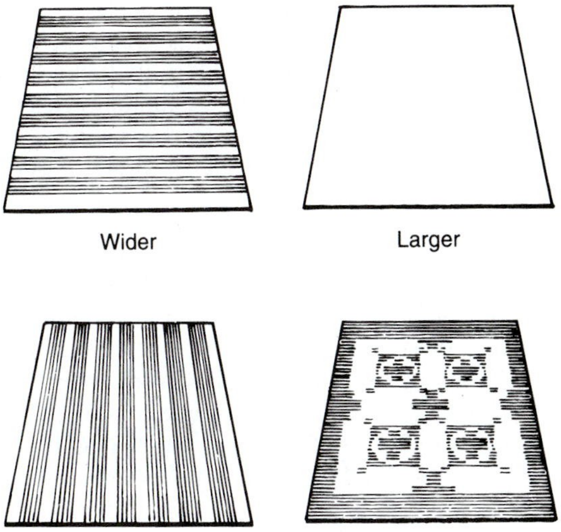

ure 10.14 *Carpet can change the apparent size and portion of a room.*

mony, create personality and a feeling of luxury, and alter the apparent size and proportion of a room (Figure 10.14). The same carpet carried throughout an interior can serve as a transition from room to room, providing a feeling of unity, whereas an art rug may be a room's focal point (Figure 10.15).

More info online @

http://www.carpet-rug.com Carpet and Rug Institute

http://www.carpetinfo.co.uk/pages/intro.htm Carpet information from the United Kingdom

History of Rugs and Carpets

Carpets were used in Egypt as early as 3000 B.C. Writers of the Bible and poets of early Greece and Rome allude to rugs, although walking on such floor coverings was usually the privilege of royalty. Colorful Oriental rugs have been produced in Persia (Iran), Turkey, China, and other Asiatic countries for centuries, where they were the principal item of

ure 10.15 *This art rug, influenced by the Art Deco style, forms the focal point for s Philadelphia penthouse living room. (Designer: Daroff Design, Inc. Photograph Mary E. Nichols. Project: Philadelphia penthouse.)*

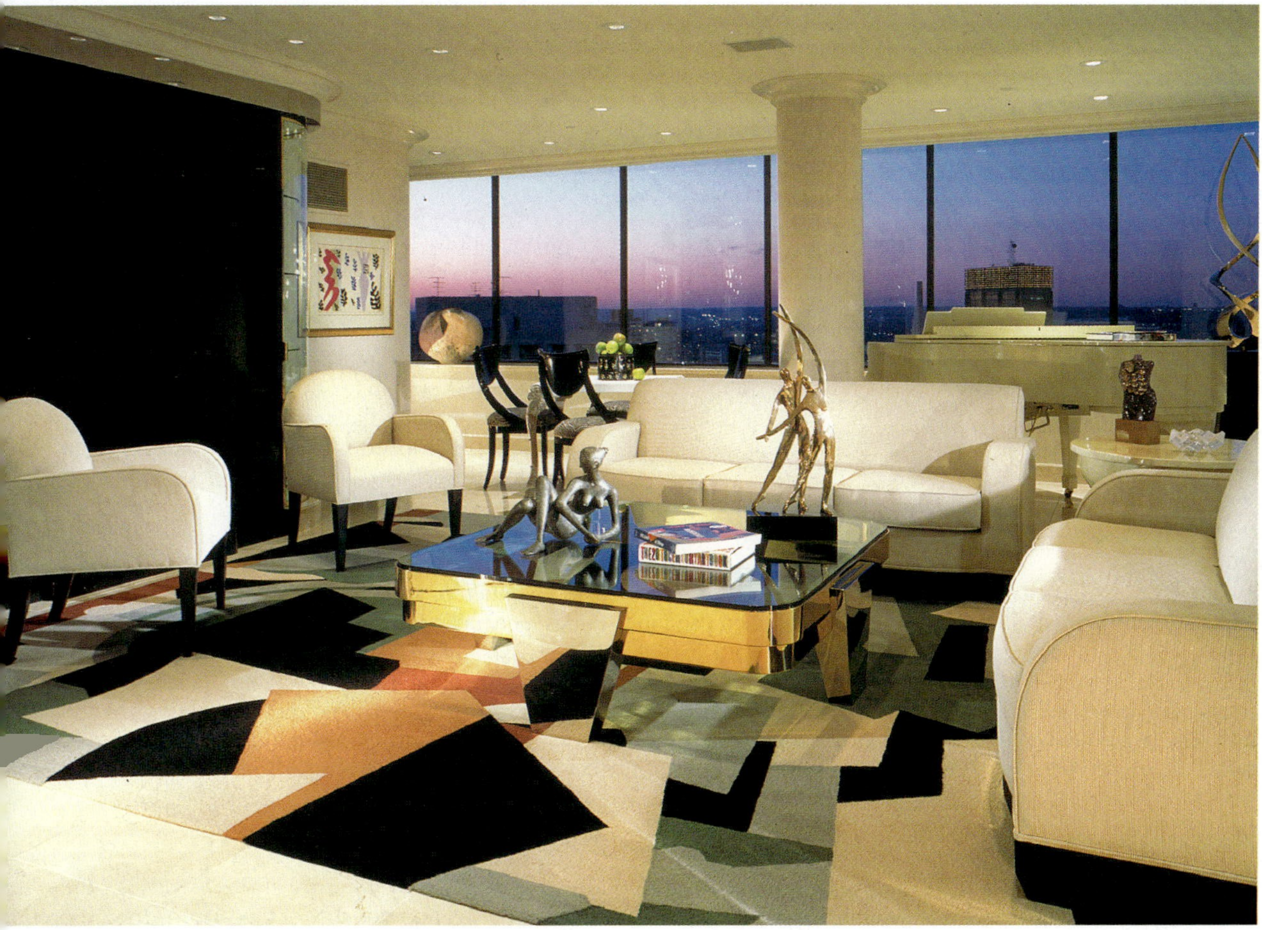

home furnishing. In the Middle Ages, the later Crusaders came into contact with Constantinople, Antioch, and other Eastern cities. They carried back many fine rugs, which created a great demand in the West. These floor coverings soon became a symbol of status in Europe and America. Since the time when the first rug looms were established in Aubusson, France, weaving fine floor coverings has been a continuously growing industry. In the twentieth century, the introduction of machine-made carpets revolutionized the floor covering industry.

More info online @

http://www.carpetinfo.co.uk/pages/aboutpp/history.htm
History of carpet-timeline from United Kingdom

http://www.carpetbiz.com/carpet-decorating/about-carpet.htm
A history on tufting

http://www.hobbypages.net/cpthist.html
A hobby site on carpet history

Design Characteristics

The selection of carpet and rugs is based on an understanding of carpet terminology and several design characteristics. Carpet quality is determined by the combination of several components including the *fiber, yarn, construction, backing,* and *surface characteristics.*

When evaluating the quality of carpet, designers should look for products that are resilient, resistant to abrasion, soil, and moisture, easily cleaned, and that do not produce static electricity. Soft floor coverings (particularly carpets and their padding) should also be environmentally friendly (see "Sustainable Design: Flooring Materials"). Overall, carpets and rugs should be durable and maintain their appearance.

More info online @

http://www.antron.dupont.com/ Antron/Dupont Website

http://www.carpetrecovery.org/ Carpet America Recovery Effort (CARE)

http://www.lafiber.com/ Carpet and Textile Recycling Plant

http://www.carpetbiz.com/carpet-buying-guide/carpet-construction/recycled-carpet.htm Information on recycled carpet

Fiber

Over the years, virtually every type of fiber has been used in carpets. Today, however, almost all carpeting sold in the United States is made of synthetic fibers, principally *nylon, acrylic, polyester,* and *olefin. Wool* is the most-used natural fiber. Fibers are often blended to bring out the best characteristics of each type.

Wool

Wool is the luxury fiber and has long been regarded as the top carpet fiber. Other fibers express their aesthetic qualities in relation to how nearly they resemble wool. Great silience accounts for the vital quality of wool in retaining appearance. Wool has warmth, a dull matte look, durabil and soil resistance. It takes colors beautifully, cleans w and when cared for, keeps its new look for years. Althou more expensive than synthetic fibers, natural wool is fiber of choice for many designers.

Nylon

Nylon is the single most important synthetic fiber, accou ing for about 90 percent of carpeting sold today. Nylon excellent abrasion resistance, resists crushing and matti and reduces static electricity, pilling, and fuzzing. When r ularly vacuumed it maintains its soil repellency. It is nor lergenic and is mold-, mildew-, and mothproof.

Acrylic

Acrylic's outstanding characteristic is its wool-like appe ance. Resistance to abrasion and soiling is good. It is a fairly resilient.

Polyester

Polyester is an exceptionally soft fiber offering good abras resistance, but lacks resiliency. Stain and soil resistance good, and it is easily cleaned.

Olefin

Olefin (or polypropylene) is predominant in needle-pur carpets, which are especially popular for indoor-outd use. Ease of care and a nonabsorbent nature are its c standing characteristics. Most stains lie on the surface, m ing it the easiest fiber to clean. However, olefin melts ea and when poorly constructed; lacks resilience.

Cotton

Although not as durable or resilient as wool and synth fibers, cotton is soft, takes dye well, and is less expensive is used most often for flat woven area rugs like *dhurries* fr India. Cotton fabric strips are braided into rugs and used informal settings.

Sisal, Jute, and Hemp

Sisal, jute, hemp, and other grasses are inexpensive floor c erings generally limited to area or room-size rugs (Fig 10.16). These fibers can be woven into simple or intricate signs, and are often made in sections and assembled. Althou they provide a natural look, they are not as comfortable derfoot. Japanese tatami mats are made from grasses; howe they are flammable and not particularly durable.

Yarn

The performance of a carpet also depends on the qua height, density, and quantity of the yarn. Yarns are produ

SUSTAINABLEDESIGN

Flooring Materials

A variety of options are available when specifying flooring materials that help protect the environment. Carpet can be one of the most costly finishes in an interior and creates a disposal problem when it must be replaced. The Partnership for Carpet Reclamation, created by DuPont, a manufacturer of carpet fiber, is one of the many solutions to this problem. The program reclaims used carpets and recycles them into new carpet fibers. Another interesting recycling program uses recycled polyethylene terephthalate (PET), also known as #1 plastic. Consumer products made of PET such as ketchup bottles and soda bottles are cleaned, ground up, melted down, and then extruded to form new fibers.

Collins & Aikman, a carpet manufacturer, incorporates an aggressive approach to environmentally friendly carpet. Its Powerbond RS® with ER 3® (Environmentally Redesigned, Restructured, Reused) uses reclaimed (old) carpet from existing buildings as its resource. Its credo, "Mining buildings for resources instead of the earth," has been adopted by many companies.

Solutia, another carpet manufacturer, has produced a product called Ultron® Renew. Renew uses 100 percent of its resources from Solutia's own nylon manufacturing processing. Solutia also is involved with the Carpet America Recovery Effort (CARE), in collaboration with the Carpet and Rug Institute. In a related environmental effort, Solutia is working on a reclamation program for carpet waste called Waste-To-Energy (W-T-E). Solid carpet waste can be combusted to provide electrical power, leaving inert, nonhazardous ash.

The Carpet and Rug Institute published a sustainability report for the industry. Specific improvements made by the industry include a 70 percent reduction in energy consumption, a 46 percent reduction in water usage, and a reduction of emissions from 3.5 million pounds in 1988 to .4 in 1999. The goal of the members is zero emissions and zero waste to landfills. (Carpet and Rug Institute, *Sustainability Report,* © 2001.)

As discussed in Chapter 4, another common problem with carpet and carpet pads is that they may emit volatile organic compounds, or VOCs, some of which are harmful to breathe. The Carpet and Rug Institute (CRI) has developed an Indoor Air Quality Testing Program, which evaluates carpet, carpet cushions, and floor covering adhesives, and labels products that have been tested and that meet stringent indoor air quality (IAQ) requirements. Carpet pads made of felt or a natural fiber such as jute are the best choice because they are low-emission products. Specifying low-emitting adhesives or selecting the strip method of installation also may limit the emission of VOCs (see "Sustainable Design: Indoor Air Quality" in Chapter 4).

Vinyl tiles and sheet vinyls can produce high levels of VOCs. Natural linoleum is a better choice. Cork flooring from renewable sources is also an appropriate environmental choice. Cork is taken from the bark of live trees that continue to grow after the cork is harvested. Although not appropriate for all situations, a cork floor is warm and resilient.

One of the best solutions to improve indoor air quality and to diffuse VOCs is to install the flooring materials three to four weeks before an interior is occupied. Recognizing that in many situations this is next to impossible, it is wise to consider installing flooring materials late in the week and then opening the building or home to the fresh air over the weekend. Many businesses are closed on weekends and residential clients possibly could relocate for a weekend. In general, designers should look for labels that mark the product as "low emission" and remember that natural products are generally a more renewable resource.

More info online @

http://www.antron.dupont.com/ Antron/Dupont Website

http://www.carpetrevoery.org/ Carpet America Recovery Effort (CARE)

http://www.lafiber.com/ Carpet and Textile Recycling Plant

http://www.carpetbiz.com/carpet-buying-guide/carpet-construction/recycled-carpet.htm Information on recycled carpet

· twisting fibers together into tufts. A tight twist helps the rn spring back, creating a resilient carpet. Proper heat setg of the yarn holds the twist in place.

The pile height is the length of the yarns; the pile density the number of tufts per square inch. Taller carpets with eater density contain a greater quantity of yarn. The combination produces a face weight measured in ounces per square yard. Face weights are commonly between 24 and 48 ounces.

A simple test to determine the quality of a piece of carpet is to fold the carpet back on itself. If there are wide spaces or gaps between rows and large amounts of backing show (called the "grin"), the carpet probably will not wear well. A

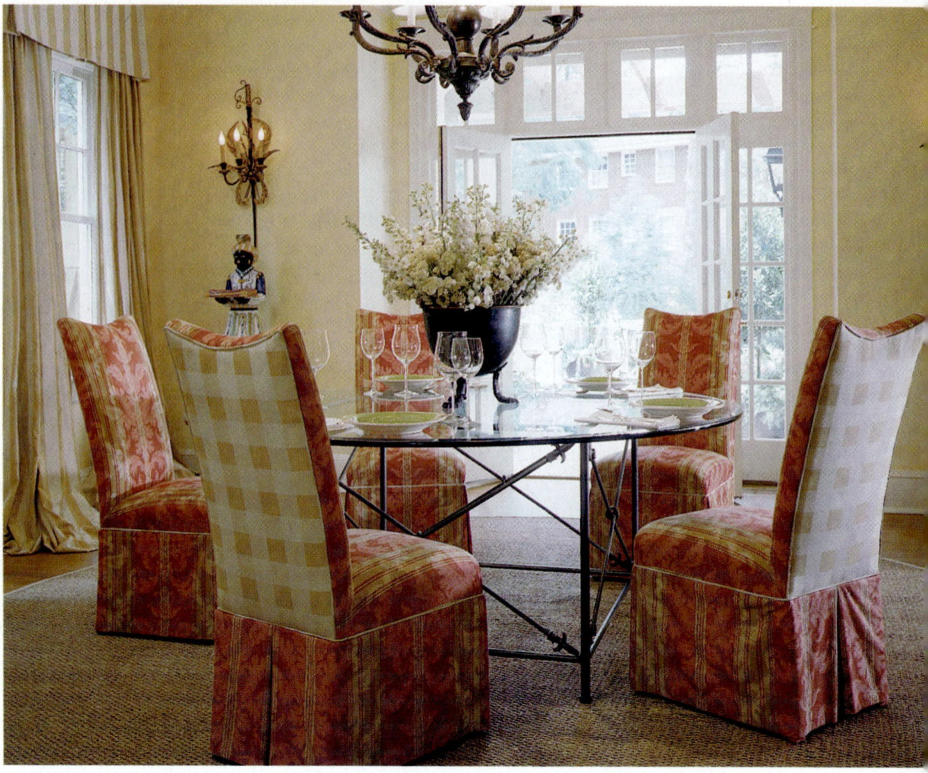

Figure 10.16 *A rug made from seagrass delineates the circular dining area. (Designer: Oetgen Designs. Photograph by Antoine Bootz.)*

short pile carpet will require a denser pile (more tufts per inch) than a taller pile carpet to pass this test.

In theory a tightly twisted yarn, properly heat set, with the appropriate combination of pile height and pile density produces the best carpet. In addition to fiber and yarn composition, other factors such as construction, backing, and surface characteristics also affect the outcome of these combinations.

Construction

Because of technological developments, the old carpet construction methods (weaving, needle-punching, flocking, and handmade construction) are not often used. Most carpets on the market today are tufted.

Tufting

Tufting accounts for approximately 90 percent of all carpet construction. Based on the principle of the sewing machine, this method involves inserting thousands of threaded needles into a backing material. Heavy latex coating is applied to the backing to permanently anchor the tufts. Some tufted carpets have a double backing for greater strength.

Weaving

The three types of woven carpets are Wilton, Axminster, and velvet, illustrated in Figure 10.17. The *Wilton* carpet takes its name from the town in England where it was first made in 1740. It is woven on a loom with a special Jacquard attachment. The yarns are carried along the background of the carpet until they are drawn to the surface to form loops. Af more than 200 years, the Wilton carpet is still regarded a standard of high quality.

The *Axminster* carpet also derives its name from the to in England where it was first manufactured in 1755. Ori nally a hand-knotted carpet, it is now made on a specializ American loom in which yarns are set in a crosswise ro permitting each tuft to be controlled individually. T process makes possible an almost unlimited combination colors and patterns. High-end residential clients and ma hotels may require or request the Axminster technique achieve the desired appearances and quality.

Velvet, the simplest form of carpet weaving, is traditic ally a smooth-surface pile, cut or uncut, in a solid color. T pile loops of velvet carpet are woven over long wires tending the full length of the carpet. Figure 10.18 illustra a custom-woven rug.

Needle-Punching

In the needle-punching process, an assembly of corded fil webs is compacted and held together by felting needles t mechanically interlock the fibers. The back of the carpe coated with latex or other weather-resistant materials. T method can produce a wide variety of textures and the c pet sells at a low cost.

Flocking

Flocked carpets have short clipped fibers providing the a pearance of velour. They may be produced by three ba methods: *beater bars, spraying,* or an *electrostatic meth*

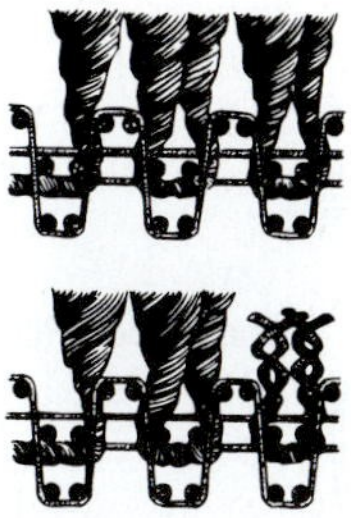

Axminster carpet. Top diagram shows different colored yarns. Bottom diagram shows use of curled down yarns for multilevel effect in face of carpet. (Courtesy of James Lees and Sons Company.)

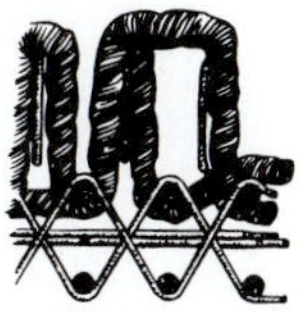

Wilton carpet (loop pile). Pile is woven over strips of metal, which are removed during weaving process.

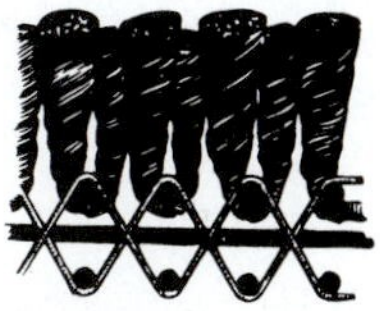

Velvet carpet (cut pile). Backing of jute and cotton holds pile yarn in place.

ure 10.17 *Three types of woven carpets.*

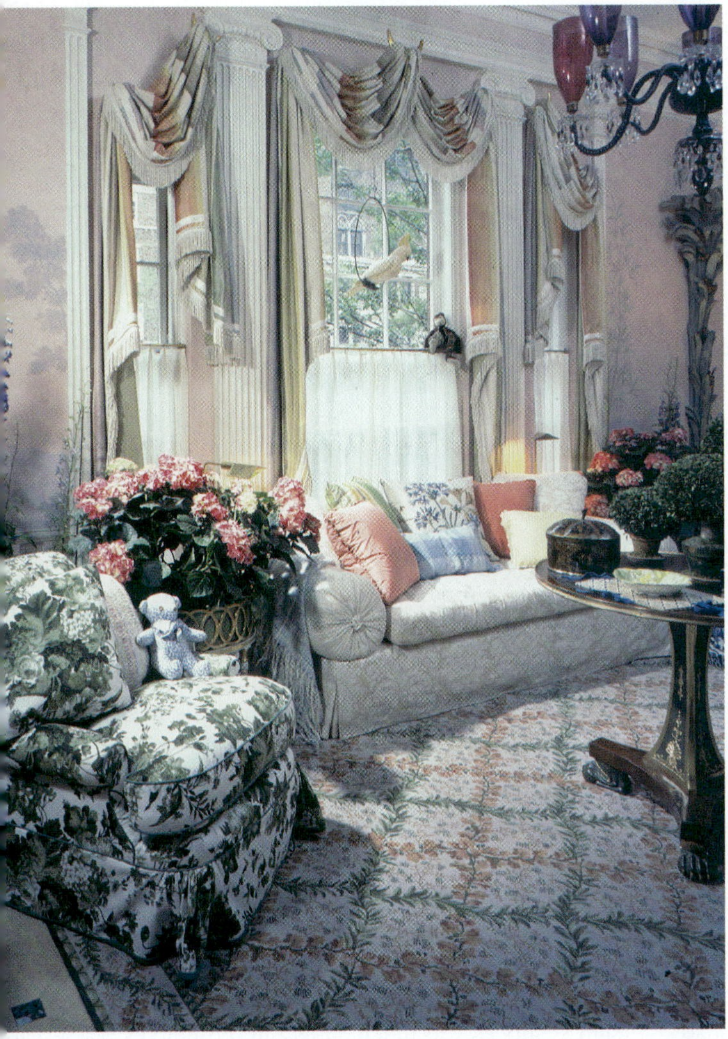

Figure 10.18 *This inviting feminine room, designed by Mario Buatta, features a custom-woven rug. (Room design by Mario Buatta. Carpets and fabrics courtesy of Stark Carpets.)*

(the latter accounts for most flocked carpets). In the electrostatic method, chopped fibers are introduced into an electrostatic field where they become charged. The charged fibers are then projected toward a backing fabric coated with adhesive, where they become vertically embedded. Flocked carpets have a low level of abrasion resistance.

Handmade Construction

Various types and styles of rugs are made by hand. These methods are discussed later in this chapter.

Backing

The unseen parts of a carpet—the backing and the glue that hold the backing—are important. Together they secure yarns to the foundation and prevent stretching, buckling, and shrinking. Polypropylene and jute are the most common backing materials. Jute is strong but may mildew and therefore is not suitable where floors may be damp. Polypropylene resists mildew and is also strong. Tufted carpets may have a secondary backing applied for extra strength. It may be jute, polypropylene, rubber latex, or vinyl.

Surface Characteristics

Carpets are described by their surface characteristics as either an uncut *level loop* or a *cut pile* (Figure 10.19). The length of the yarn and the texture or design created by the uncut or cut yarns produce these characteristics.

Level Loop

Level loop carpets are tufted or woven with looped tufts. Because the yarns are not cut, level loops wear extremely well when produced from durable fibers. Level loop carpets are available in solids, heathered solids, and a variety of geometric, stylized, and abstract patterns. Level loops are used in many commercial environments (Figure 10.20). When the heights of the loops are varied the carpet is called a multilevel loop.

Berber carpets, a type of level loop carpet, utilize thick, relatively untwisted yarns. Strong fibers must be used to compensate for the lack of twist. Berbers are found in neutral tones and occasionally soft pastels.

Cut Pile

Cut pile carpets are formed when the loops of yarn are cut or sheered. Various designs have the following characteristics:

- *Plush* or *velvet carpets,* the original style of cut piles, have a dense upright and evenly cut pile under 1″ in height. The carpet is enhanced by highlights and shadings, which provide an extra dimension. Plush carpets are generally more appropriate for formal areas with little traffic. Plush carpets are more resilient and appropriate in short pile heights, under 3/8″, for commercial wear. A short, fine, dense plush is called a velour.

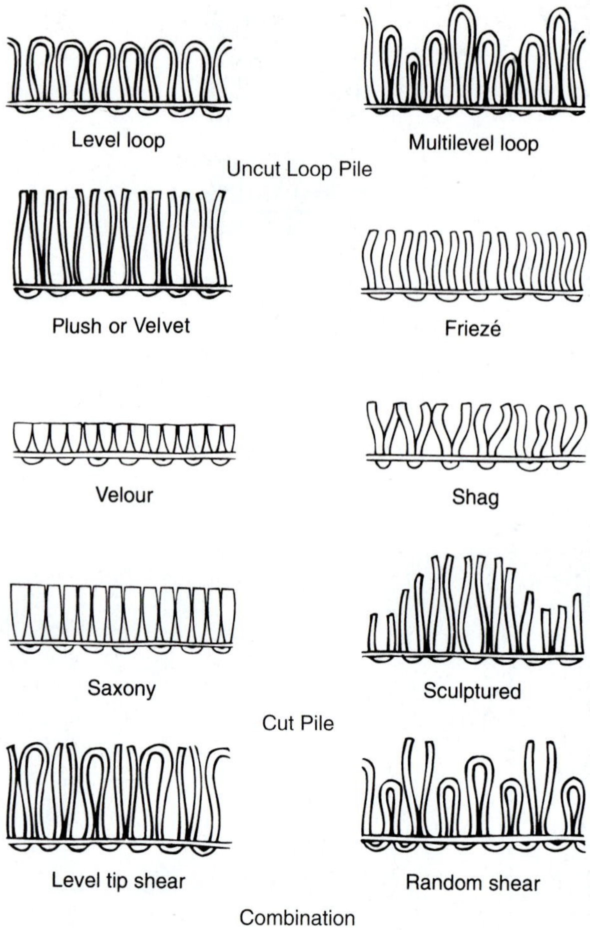

Figure 10.19 *Surface characteristics of carpet: Level loops: Level loop; multilevel loop. Cut piles: Cut or plush; velour; sha[g]; Saxony; friezé. Combinations: Sculptured; random shear; leve[l] tip shear.*

- A *friezé* carpet has a tightly twisted yarn, giving a roug[h] nubby appearance. Friezés are resilient and resist abrasion.
- *Shag carpets* have pile yarns that are more than 1 in. in height and low in density. The tufts are designed to lie flat giving a shaggy, informal appearance.
- A *Saxony carpet* is similar to a plush, but has more yarns twisted together. The surface of the Saxony appears rougher than that of the plush.

Combination Loops and Piles

Sculptured carpets combine various heights of cut pi[le] and/or level loops to create a design. Sculptured carpe[ts] such as the *random shear,* are most effective when the d[e]sign is subtle. Too much variety in the heights of the yar[n] can cause poor resiliency. Yarns that are left all the san[e] height and then selectively cut produce subtle patterns a[nd] are called *tip shear* carpets.

Custom-designed *hand-sculptured carpet* is one in whic[h] part of the surface has been cut away to form a pattern,

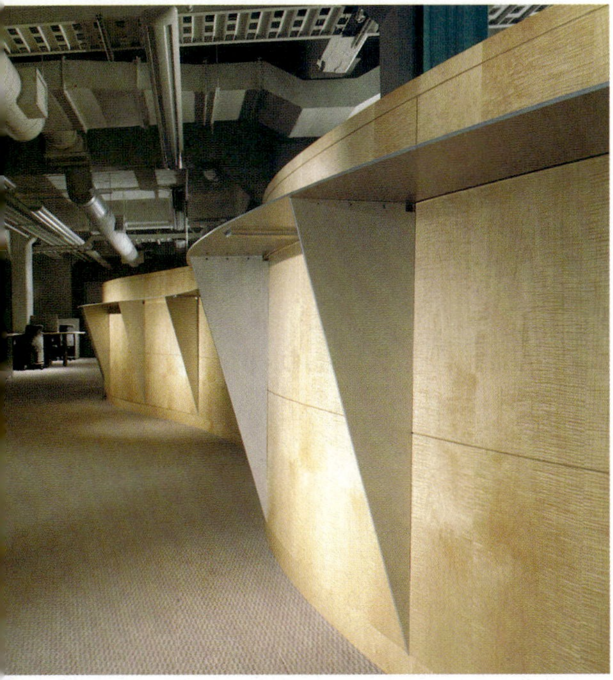

;ure 10.20 ***In this high-tech interior a multilevel loop ·pet adds warmth and tactile interest to the sleek wood and ·tal finishes. (Photograph courtesy of Holey Associates and ;ar Rubio Photography.)***

: pattern itself has been cut away from the background. is carpet style is often custom-made and expensive.

ıt Woven

ıt-woven cellulose fiber rugs are machine-made of coarse x fiber, paper pulp or "kraft" fiber, sisal, hemp, and other ısses and rushes. They come in full-sized rugs or in one-)t squares to be sewn together. Fiber rugs are usually in tural colors but are sometimes dyed. Popular in warm cli-ıtes, they also provide inexpensive year-round floor cov-ngs in many contemporary settings. Other flat-woven ·les include *dhurries* from India, *Navajo rugs* from Amer-, and *Rollikans* from Scandinavia.

ɔecial Features

ıditional design features may be necessary when selecting ·pets for specialty commercial uses. To control static elec-:ity, synthetic fibers can be altered during the viscose stage covered with a special coating after they are manufactured. .ow static electricity rating, usually less than 3.5 kilovolts, is ļuired in all areas where computers or electronic equip-:nt will be used. An antimicrobial treatment is necessary in alth care environments. Advanced soil-resistant treatments ıy prove beneficial in areas with extremely high traffic.

ɔre info online @

ɔ://www.carpet-rug.com/drill_down_2.cfm?page=3&sub=2
·rpet and Rug Institute's site on fiber and construction

http://www.ianr.unl.edu/pubs/homefurnish/g1316.htm and
http://www.ianr.unl.edu/pubs/homefurnish/g1222.htm
Articles on carpet construction, care, and selection adapted by Shirley M. Niemeyer, Extension Specialist, Interior Design/Home Furnishings

http://www.carpetinfo.co.uk/pages/aboutpp/construc.htm
Carpet construction information from the United Kingdom

http://www.carpetbiz.com/carpet-decorating/benefits.htm and
http://www.carpetguru.com/const.html General Information on the benefits of carpets

http://www.gocohens.com/hwtobuy/carpet.html and
http://www.carpet.org/retailer.htm Guides to residential carpet

http://www.carpetbuyershandbook.com/ Hobby site on carpet selection

Handmade Rugs

Oriental Rugs

The making of Oriental rugs is a great art, and these rugs have been coveted possessions for hundreds of years. During the eighteenth and nineteenth centuries, rugs from China and the Middle East were in great demand among wealthy Americans who wanted to adorn their Georgian- and Federal-period mansions.

With the advent of wall-to-wall carpeting, Oriental rugs were in less demand in America, but during the past few decades they have been rediscovered and are again desirable for contemporary use, regardless of style. To meet the current demand, American manufacturers are duplicating authentic Oriental designs in loom-woven rugs retailing at a fraction of the cost of the handmade ones. These rugs are called "Oriental design rugs" to distinguish them from the hand-loomed rugs made in the Orient called "Oriental rugs."

Oriental Rugs From Persia and Turkey

The great majority of Oriental rugs imported into America have come from Persia (Iran) and Turkey. These rugs are made by hand-tying a knot in each weft thread as it crosses the warp. The knot is either the *Ghiordes* (Turkish) or the *Sehna* (Persian) type, depending on the area in which it is made (Figure 10.21). Rugs are frequently made by members of a family who use the same pattern generation after generation. The name of the particular rug is usually that of the family or is taken from the name of the village or area in which the rug was made.

Given the myriad types with distinct design origins from different areas, towns, tribes, and families, the study of Oriental rugs can be a lifelong pursuit. A logical beginning is to become familiar with the three Oriental rugs from the Near East that are particularly pleasing to American tastes: the Kirman, Sarouk, and Tekke, commonly called Bokhara.

A top-grade *Kirman* is among the most costly of Oriental rugs. The most familiar type has a central medallion surrounded by a plain ground with a wide border of intricate design (Figure 10.22). Sometimes the entire ground is filled

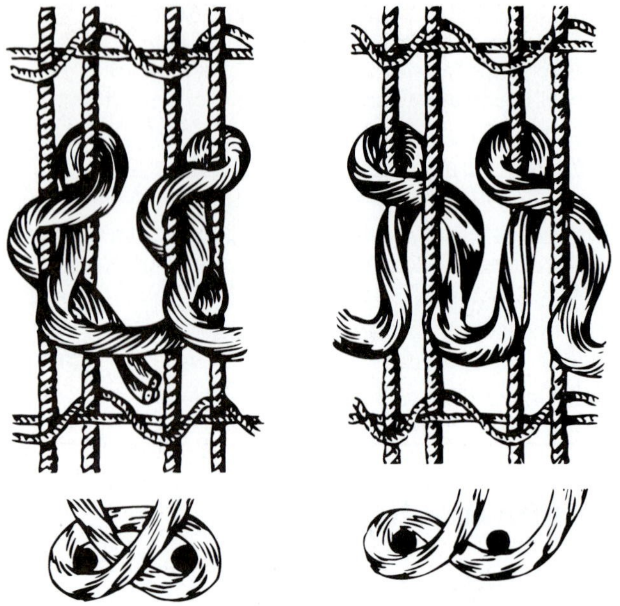

Ghiordes or Turkish knot, used in Turkey and elsewhere

Sehna or Perrsian knot, used in many parts of Iran

Figure 10.21 *Principal knots used in making Oriental rugs.*

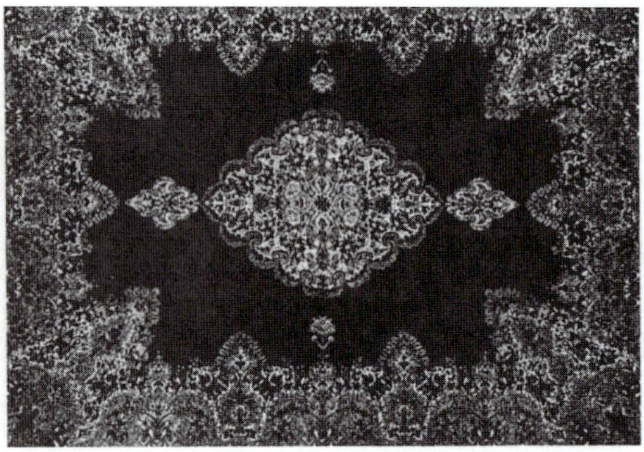

Figure 10.22 *The most familiar of the Kirman designs: an open ground, a wide, uneven border, and a medallion center. (Courtesy of Karastan Rug Mills.)*

with delicate blooms. This rug is one of the few Oriental rugs that are available with an ivory background.

The predominant colors in the *Sarouk* are exotic jewel tones of red, rose, and deep blue, with black and ivory as accent colors. Although the pattern is predominantly floral, it does feature some geometric devices. The Sarouk may also have a vibrant medallion outlined in dark colors. The pile is usually heavy (Figure 10.23).

The *Bokhara,* originally from Turkistan, is made in many Middle Eastern countries. The background of the Bokhara may be red, cream, or blue, but the predominant color is always red. The easily recognizable design is made up of octagons or polygons called *guls* (roses), which are repeated

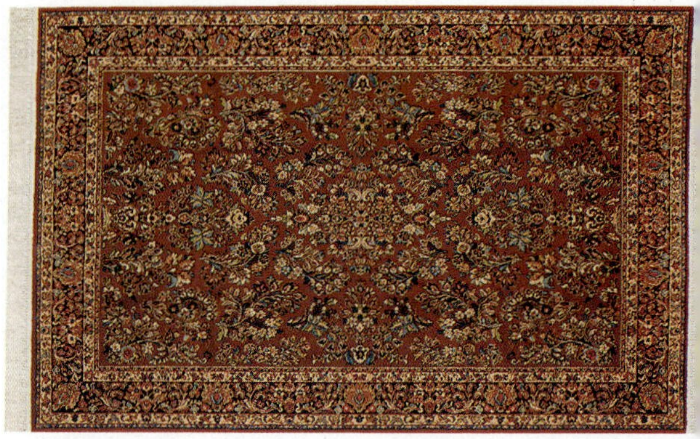

Figure 10.23 *The all-over floral with rose or red ground is typical of Sarouk rugs. (Courtesy of Karastan Rug Mills.)*

uniformly about the field. When the guls are quartered narrow lines running the length and width of the field, t design is popularly called *Royal Bokhara.*

Oriental Rugs From China

The art of rug making has been practiced in China for mo than twelve centuries. The oldest known rugs were from t T'ang dynasty (618–906). The oldest existing rug dates fro the Ming dynasty (1368–1644). Early designs were tak from ancient Chinese silk weaving and are symbolic of a cestor worship. Ancient symbols, of which there are ov 100, fall into a number of categories. Chinese rugs can recognized by the following characteristics:

- Colors of Chinese rugs are typically blue and white (of ten used for the field), with yellow-orange, red-orange gold, and cream also used in various combinations.
- Geometric designs are used primarily as border ornamentation. The Chinese "T," key, or fret designs are th most familiar. The circle with a square in the center an two curved cells within a circle, symbolizing male and female, are common motifs.
- Religious symbols are commonly used, including the dragon, which symbolizes God and emperor, and wav and closed bands (eternity). Among the mythological symbols are the lion (authority), horse (strength), fish (abundance), and stag and crane (longevity).
- Flowers most commonly used are the lotus (purity), pe ony (prosperity), and chrysanthemum (fidelity).

Chinese rugs are made from complete paper models, and t design is outlined on a cotton warp. The pile is higher th on rugs made in the Middle East, and designs are sculptur by clipping the yarns along the contour of the pattern.

Rugs made in eastern China usually have allover patter reflecting the Middle Eastern influence. The two most fam iar Chinese rugs are the *Mandarin,* which has no border, open ground, and a different asymmetrical floral spray each corner, and the *Peking,* which has a wide border, si ilar corner motifs, and a round central medallion. Peking c sign rugs made in India are called *Bengali* (Figure 10.24).

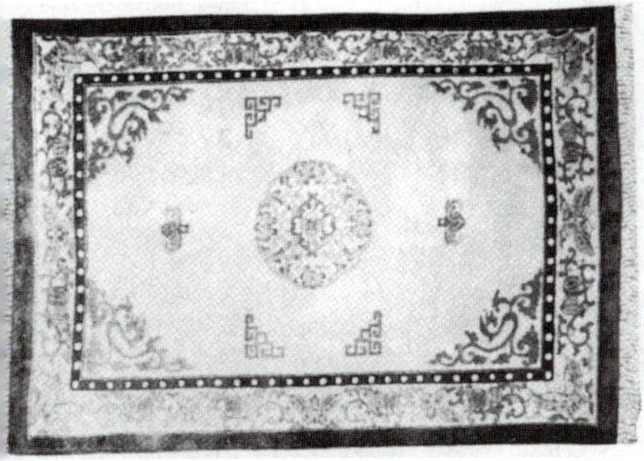

;ure 10.24 *A Bengali rug from India, made in the Chinese*
king design. (Courtesy of Stark Carpet Corporation.)

'iental Rugs From India

›day many rugs of excellent quality are handmade in India : export to Europe and America. Rugs employing old and ıthentic designs from China, Iran, Turkey, and France are ıde from top-quality wool (mostly from New Zealand) and ll at moderate prices.

Numdah rugs, used in India for centuries, have been im›rted into the United States for many years and recently ve revived in popularity (Figure 10.25). This rug is an in·rmal type made of felt. The wool surface is traditionally en·hed with bird and floral motifs worked with a long, open ıch.

Dhurries are flat-weave rugs hand-woven in India (Figure .26). They are tightly woven in wool or cotton and incor›rate both stylized and geometric designs. Colors are fre·ently pastels and medium tones on a natural field.

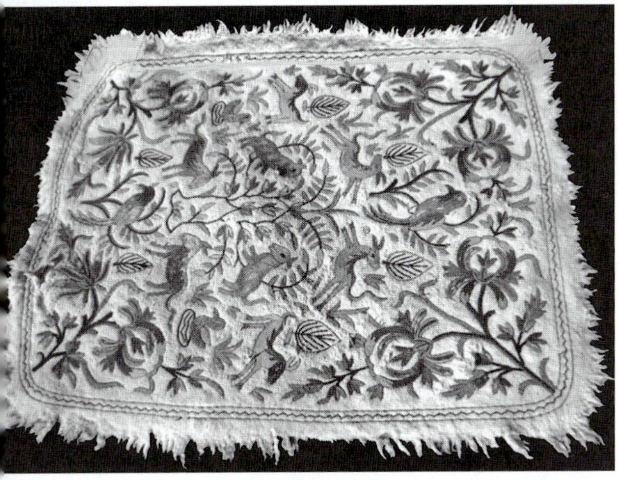

gure 10.25 *This Numdah rug is made of rough felt with*
ɔol embroidery in the "tree of life" design. (Photograph by
ark K. Allen.)

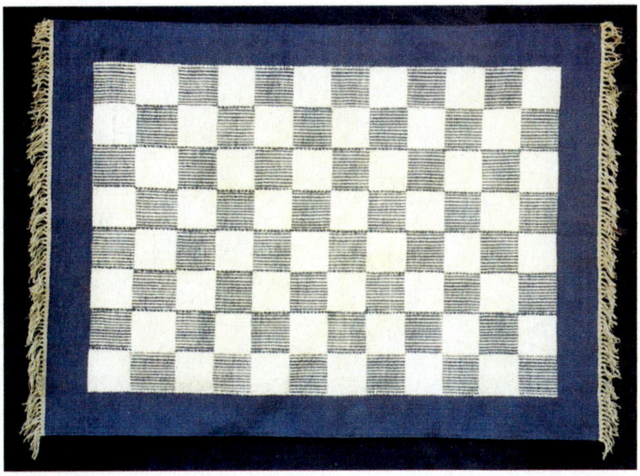

Figure 10.26 *The* dhurries *were used originally as sleeping bags for travelers. The thin wool or cotton rug could be rolled up and easily carried. (Courtesy of Designer Rugs Limited.)*

More info online @

http://www.mathforum.org/geometry/rugs/ Information and images on Oriental rugs

http://www.oria.org/ Oriental Rug Importers Association

French Rugs

Two French-style rugs have been produced with little interruption since the seventeenth century: the Savonnerie and the Aubusson.

The *Savonnerie* is a pile carpet made by hand with knotted stitches in the manner of Orientals but with French patterns (Figure 10.27). The Savonnerie factory, established in

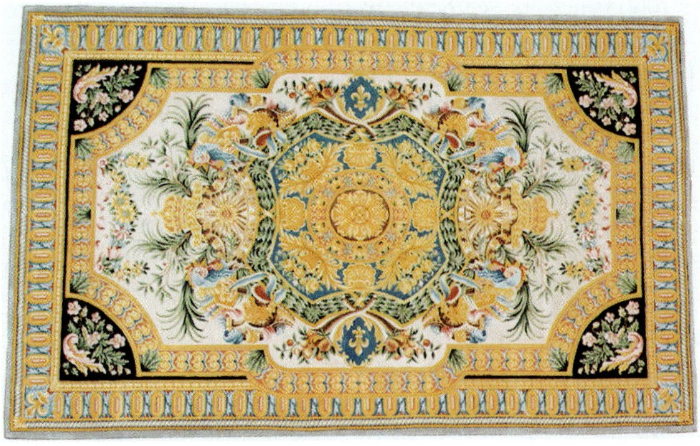

Figure 10.27 *The French Savonnerie is a velvety pile carpet, typically with intricate French designs. (Courtesy of Designer Rugs Limited.)*

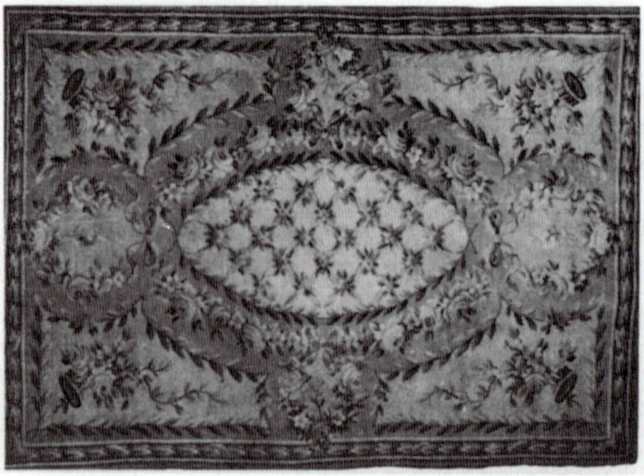

Figure 10.28 *Aubusson rugs are made of tapestry weave, usually with French designs in pastel colors. (Courtesy of Stark Carpet Corporation.)*

France in 1663 by Louis XIV, was an outgrowth of a workshop founded earlier in the Louvre. Although it was the first factory to produce tapestrylike rugs, it is best known for its velvety pile rugs, usually made in strong colors on a dark ground with elaborate designs sometimes take from formal French gardens.

Aubusson rugs are distinctive. During the late seventeenth century when the upper classes of France became interested in beautifying their homes, long-established, privately owned workshops at Aubusson strove to imitate the weaving completed at Savonnerie. Some of the oldest Aubusson rugs have an Oriental flavor, but later ones follow the French textile designs employing small-scaled, stylized floral themes. Colors are usually soft, muted pastels, giving a faded effect (Figure 10.28).

Other Types of Rugs

Moroccan Rugs

The Moroccan is a type of Oriental rug made primarily in Northwest Africa. The character of the rug has changed little in 1000 years. Its distinctive informality has made it a favorite in contemporary decor. The most common Moroccan rug is the Berber.

Berber rugs (the inspiration for American berber carpets) are traditional types made primarily by Berber tribes in the Atlas Mountains. The designs are abstract and geometric. Some are primitive, often of natural wool color with simple black or brown designs; others are vividly colored.

The Spanish Matrimonia

The Spanish matrimonia, the traditional bridal gift in Spain, is the fringed, bold-figured Manta rug. Woven on the Jacquard loom, these rugs have subtle shadings, a handcrafted-like texture, and a three-dimensional quality. Patterns are brightly colored and inspired by medieval motifs, classic Aubussons, Far East Orientals, mythical figures, and the tree of life (Figure 10.29).

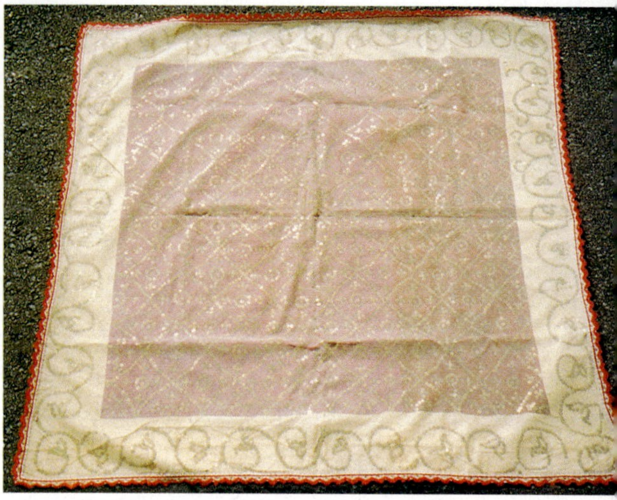

Figure 10.29 *The elaborately woven matrimonia rugs are created based on the bride's status. Handed down through generations, the fine rug is used in the marriage ceremony and may be made of linen, cotton, wool, silk, or gold and silver threads. (Courtesy of Designer Rugs Limited.)*

Navajo Rugs

The Navajo rug is a hand-woven rug or blanket made by t Navajo Indians in the American Southwest. Those of fin quality are made of wool and colored with vegetable dy Designs are usually geometric with frequent zigzag, chevr and diamond motifs combined with stripes (Figure 10.3 Stylized representations of birds, animals, and human figur are sometimes used.

Rya Rugs

Rya is a name derived from an old Norse word meani "rough." This hand-hooked rug is a traditional import fro Scandinavia, where it has been used for centuries. The rya a high-pile shag rug combining a blend of multicolored yar

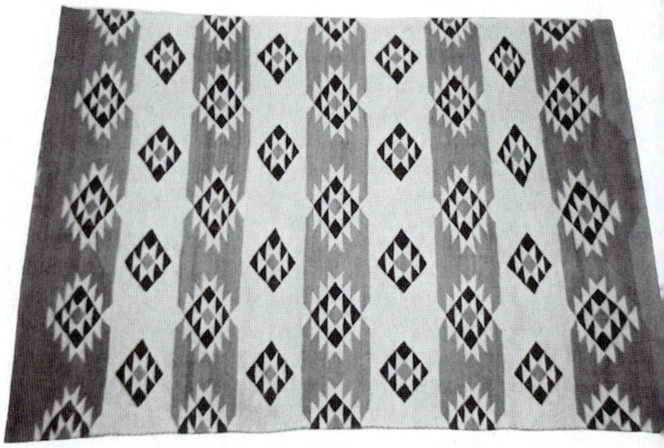

Figure 10.30 *This Navajo rug is characteristic of much of t art of the North American Indians and is similar to Peruvia rugs. (Photograph by Mark K. Allen.)*

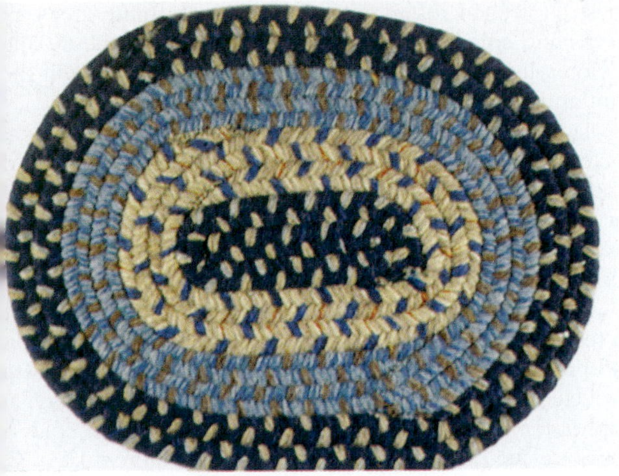

ure 10.31 *A braided rug can be used in any setting where ountry look is desired.*

ced into a wool backing with a rug hook. The yarns are t at an angle and at various heights, creating the "shaggy" pearance. Geometric designs of all types are often comied with stylized nature themes. Rya rugs are ideally suited use as area or art rugs in contemporary settings.

g Rugs

g rugs were one of the first floor coverings made by Amern colonists. Scraps of cotton, linen, or wool fabric were t in narrow strips and then sewn together to form long ands, then woven in a plain weave on a cotton or linen rp. The craft of making rag rugs is still practiced.

aided Rugs

aided rugs were originally made in the home from scraps clothing and blankets. They are still a favorite for rooms th a provincial atmosphere, especially in colonial Amerin and country French rooms. Strips of rags are stitched together (on the bias), then braided into long ropes, which are her sewn or woven together in rounded or oval shapes igure 10.31). Rugs of this type are also produced commerlly at reasonable cost.

oked Rugs

oked rugs are made by hooking colored rags or yarns rough a tightly stretched piece of burlap, canvas, or wool form a design. The foundation fabric and the type of maial used for filling determine the degree of durability.

edlepoint Rugs

edlepoint rugs were originally made by embroidering ol yarn on a heavy mesh canvas. Designs range from sim to highly complex floral motifs in a wide array of colors.

More info online @

http://www.hometime.com/projects/flooring.htm
General website on information on all types of flooring

http://www.dicknsons.com/glossary.htm
Glossary on floor covering terms

Padding

Most carpets and rugs require a quality pad or cushion, which provides tremendous value for the initial cost. Cushioning improves and helps to maintain the appearance of the carpet and enhances its resiliency. Carpet pads absorb noise, help to control the room's temperature, and create a feeling of luxury. Padding is particularly beneficial in areas where the subfloor is uneven because the pad assists in smoothing out the floor. There are three general categories of padding: fiber, rubber, and urethane foam.

- *Fiber cushions* can be made from natural products (such as animal hair or jute), synthetics (such as nylon or polyester), or recycled textile fibers. A fiber cushion creates a "firm" feel.
- *Rubber cushions* can be either flat or ribbed. The flat gives a firm feel and the ribbed a stiffer feel.
- *Urethane foam cushions* come in a variety of types. *Conventional* and *grafted prime urethane* foams are manufactured from a chemical mix and are available in a variety of densities. *Densified polyurethane* has undergone a further process to meet specific guidelines. *Bonded* foam is made by fusing shredded pieces of urethane foam together. *Mechanically frothed urethane* foam was originally developed as a cushion attached to the back of carpet. It typically has a higher density and firmer feel.

When selecting a pad for residential use, keep in mind the following recommendation from the Carpet Cushion Council (CCC): "The heavier the traffic, the thinner the cushion." For commercial use the CCC has developed a labeling system based on volume of traffic. Pads with a Class I rating are acceptable for moderate traffic, those with Class II for heavy traffic, and those with Class III for extra heavy traffic.

In some commercial office environments when level loop carpet is used, no padding is laid beneath the carpet. The carpet is said to be "direct glue," and is literally glued to the plywood or concrete subfloor. Thick padding is inappropriate in commercial environments because it gives the appearance of a luxury residence.

More info online @

http://www.carpetcushion.org/ Carpet Cushion Council

http://www.epa.gov/OSWRCRA/non-hw/procure/products/carpcush.htm EPA's guidelines on carpet cushions

http://www.afpf.com/carpetwhypoly.html Alliance for Polyurethane Foam Padding

Design Considerations

Aside from the performance characteristics of the carpet and pad, designers must also consider aesthetic factors. These factors include the *size and space, color and pattern,* and *texture.*

Size and Space

The size of the carpet or rug depends on the characteristics and intended use of the particular space. For instance, wall-to-wall carpets have distinct uses, but may also be bordered to give the appearance of an art or area rug.

Wall-to-wall broadloom carpet has some distinct advantages: It creates continuity within a room or from room to room, makes rooms look larger, adds warmth and a feeling of luxury, requires only one cleaning process, and provides maximum safety from accidents. This carpet treatment also has some disadvantages: It must be cleaned in place, and it cannot be turned for even wear.

Carpet tiles have many of the same benefits as wall-to-wall carpet with the additional advantage that a tile can be replaced should it become soiled or damaged. Carpet tiles are glued directly to the floor. They allow for greater flexibility in design and access beneath the floor (see Figure 9.14).

A *room-sized rug* is one that comes within a foot or so of the walls, leaving a marginal strip of floor exposed. The room-sized rug has most of the advantages of wall-to-wall carpeting, plus some extra benefits. It can be turned for even distribution of wear and removed for cleaning. Two processes, however, are necessary for complete cleaning—one for the rug and the other for the exposed flooring material around it.

An *area rug* does not cover the entire floor but is used to define an area of a room according to its function. The area rug should be large enough to accommodate all the furniture used in the area grouping. This type of rug is versatile and may easily be changed for different grouping arrangements.

An *art rug,* which is usually smaller than an area rug, is generally handcrafted and used as an accent or treated as a focal point. This rug is often placed so that furniture does not encroach on it, enabling it to be admired like a piece of art on the floor. Sometimes an art rug functions as an area rug (see Figure 10.15).

Scatter or *throw rugs* are smaller rugs often used as accents or as protection for a spot that receives hard wear.

Color and Pattern

Color is a critical factor in the selection of a carpet. As with textiles, dyeing processes vary and some fibers accept color better than others. As with fabrics, generally the earlier the color is added in the manufacturing process, the longer the color will remain.

Neutral color carpet allows for a variety of changes in other finishes. In apartments, tenant offices, and other places with frequent turnover rates, neutral colors are the best choice. In restaurants or other high traffic areas, pa terns and colors in middle values hide dirt the best. A lig color will easily show stains, whereas a dark color will sho lint and dust.

Lighting also affects the carpet's color. Fibers, style cha acteristics, and textures of carpet absorb and reflect light di ferently. A sunny room may call for a carpet in cool colo whereas a northern exposure or dark room may requi warm colors in lighter tones. Carpets should be tested f color in their final environment.

Wall-to-wall carpets in solid colors or overall texture gi a feeling of spaciousness. Large patterns tend to fill up spa and are usually best reserved for larger areas. If the carp selected has a pronounced pattern, then walls, drapery, a upholstery tend to be complemented when plain colors unobtrusive patterns are employed (see Figure 10.13). Ca pets with a plain overall effect permit a wider choice of fu nishings.

Texture

Each carpet or rug type has a unique texture, such smooth, shiny, dull, rough, and so on. The surface quality the carpet should be aesthetically compatible with other fu nishings. The same considerations discussed in Chapter 9 f selecting textures of textiles also hold true for the selectio of carpet textures. A carefully chosen carpet or rug can c ordinate all furnishings of the room and provide unity.

Codes and Regulations

Federal, state, and local laws or codes and regulations s particular standards (especially for flame resistance, flam spread, and smoke generation) regarding the performan and quality of a floor covering. There must be a label a tached to the floor covering indicating the name of the ma ufacturer, the Federal Trade Commission number, the fib content, the weight of the fiber, and flame-resistant qualitie Building codes vary in different areas; therefore, the design must be knowledgeable about local codes and regulatio before specifying a particular floor covering.

Measuring and Installation

Before purchasing the selected floor covering it is necessa to figure the amount of material needed to complete the jo To arrive at an estimate, determine the square footage of th space to be covered and divide by 9 (the number of squa feet in a yard). This will give the approximate square yarda needed; however, additional yardage is required for piecin the carpet and for matching pattern repeats. Many designe prepare a cut or seaming diagram for figuring the corre yardage (Figure 10.32). Try to avoid specifying carpet sean in major traffic areas. The *nap* of the pile (sometimes calle the *pile sweep*) must be laid in a uniform direction to preve light variation.

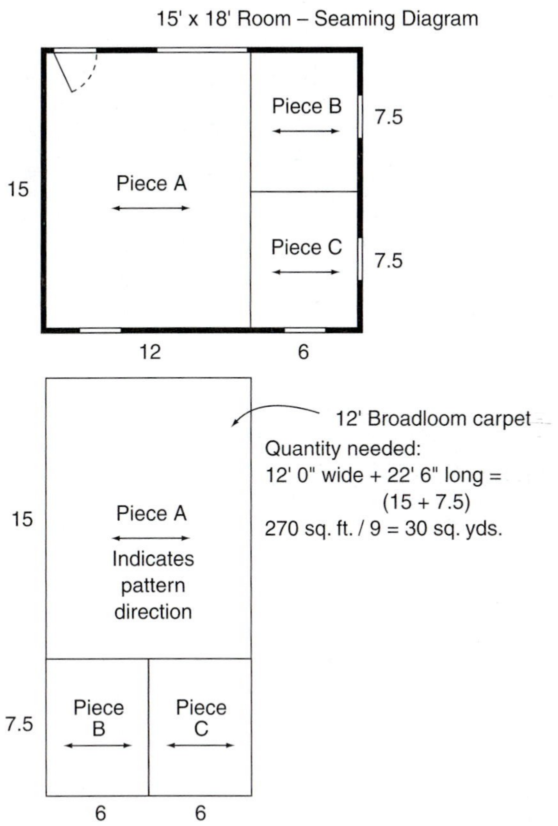

gure 10.32 *A seaming diagram for a 15′ × 18′ room vered with 12′ wide broadloom carpet and a cutting agram for the roll of broadloom carpet.*

When specifying carpet for a residential or commercial project the designer indicates installation methods and techniques. There are two basic installation methods: the stretch or tackless strip and pad method and the glue-down method. In the *stretch and pad method* a 1-inch-wide plywood strip with small projecting metal pins is nailed around the perimeter of the room and the pad is nailed, glued, or stapled inside the strip. The carpet is stretched over the pad and then attached over the pins of the strip. TACFAST™, by Karastan Bigelow, also offers a hook and loop technology that secures carpet to the floor through a system similar to Velcro™. In the *glue-down method,* glue or adhesive is applied to attach the carpet to the floor.

Summary

The decision to select a particular floor covering forms an important piece of the interior environment puzzle. Broad design decisions must first address the need for a hard or soft flooring material. The floor covering can create the interest or focal point, or serve as the neutral element unifying a room or series of rooms (Figure 10.33). Carpet selection requires close attention to design characteristics and construction methods to ensure durability. Considerable time should be devoted to selecting the proper floor covering that not only looks great, but also maintains its appearance through years of foot traffic.

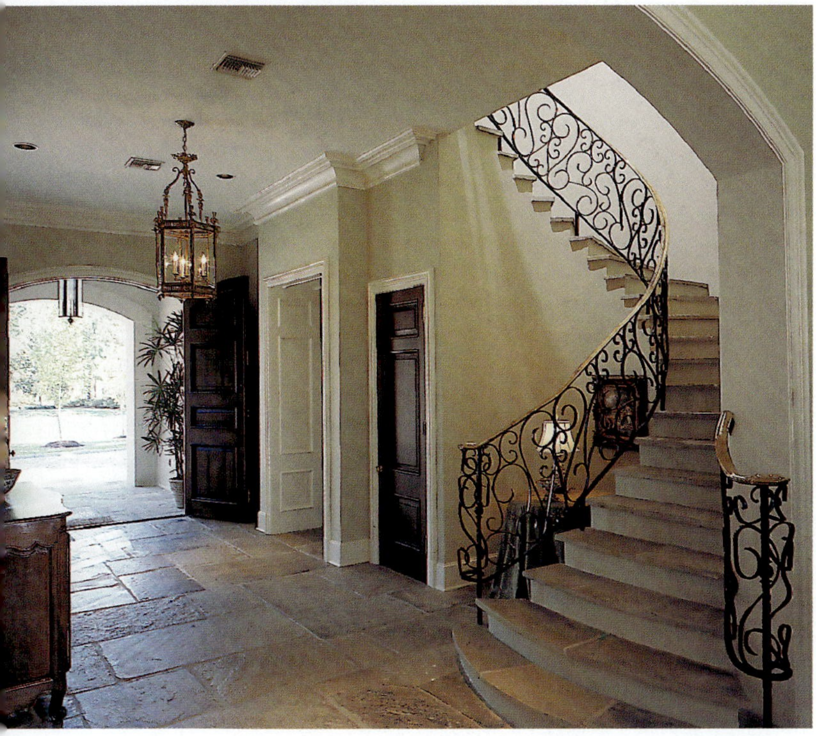

Figure 10.33 *This foyer sets a formal, masculine tone for the residence. The stone flooring unifies the interior and is an excellent selection for the high traffic area. (Courtesy of Renaissance Reclamation.)*

11

3ackgrounds: Ceilings and Walls

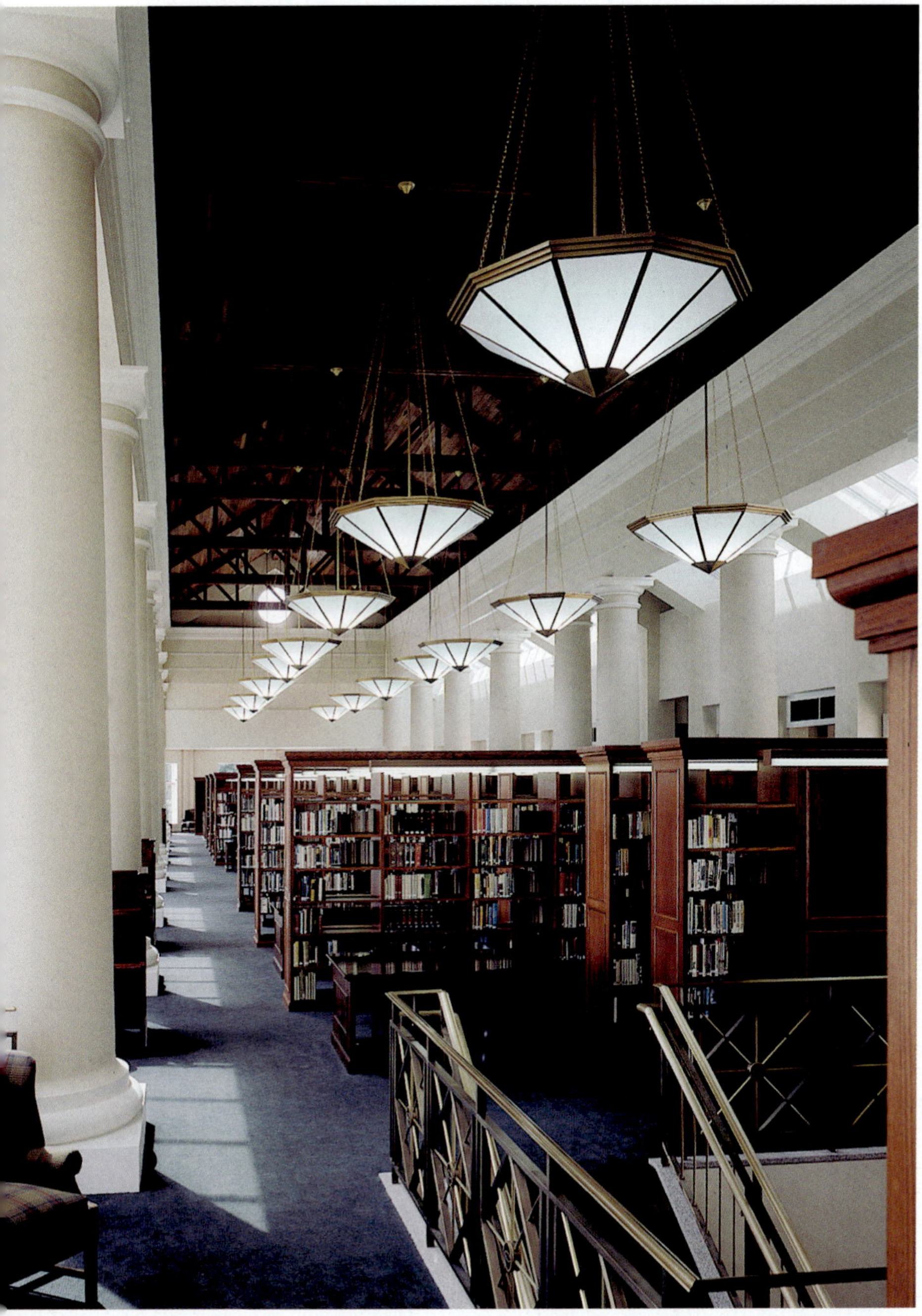

;ure 11.1 *In this library, located at Culver Academy in Culver, Indiana, the designers used ;abled and beamed ceiling to contrast with the refined traditional columns. rchitect/Designer: Hellmuth, Obata & Kassabaum. Photograph by Balthazar Korab Ltd.)*

CEILINGS

The ceiling—the largest unused area of a room—has been given special attention for hundreds of years. The ceilings of Renaissance palaces were magnificently sculpted and adorned with decorative plaster. Ceilings during the settlement period in America were usually low and plain with visible support beams. During the Georgian, Federal, Greek Revival, and Victorian periods, ceilings were generally not as ornately designed as in earlier periods in Europe, but did include some decorative treatment. Ceilings continue to receive special attention as illustrated in Figure 11.1.

The functions of the ceiling include providing (1) protection from the elements, (2) insulation for heating and cooling, (3) a source for artificial lighting (and natural lighting, when skylights are used), (4) an acoustic barrier for absorbing or reflecting sound, (5) a flame-resistant barrier that meets standard fire codes, and (6) an important element of the character and atmosphere of a room.

In many current interiors, the ceiling's potential to add character and atmosphere to a room has been neglected. It has been covered with gypsumboard (a type of wallboar and painted white. The following section discusses some the various types of ceilings that designers can use.

Types of Ceilings

Ceiling designs can be distinguished according to vario structural forms and their placement or direction.

- The *flat ceiling* is usually plastered, painted, or coverec with wood strips. The flat-beamed ceiling is one in which the structural beams are exposed or lightweight beams have been applied.
- The **shed** or *lean-to ceiling* rises diagonally to one sid in a single slope. The furnishings in a room with this ceiling must be arranged carefully to achieve a comfort able balance.
- The *gabled, double-pitched,* or **cathedral** *ceiling* expands vertical space, especially when beams extend u ward (Figure 11.1). Placing beams horizontally emphasizes the room's length.

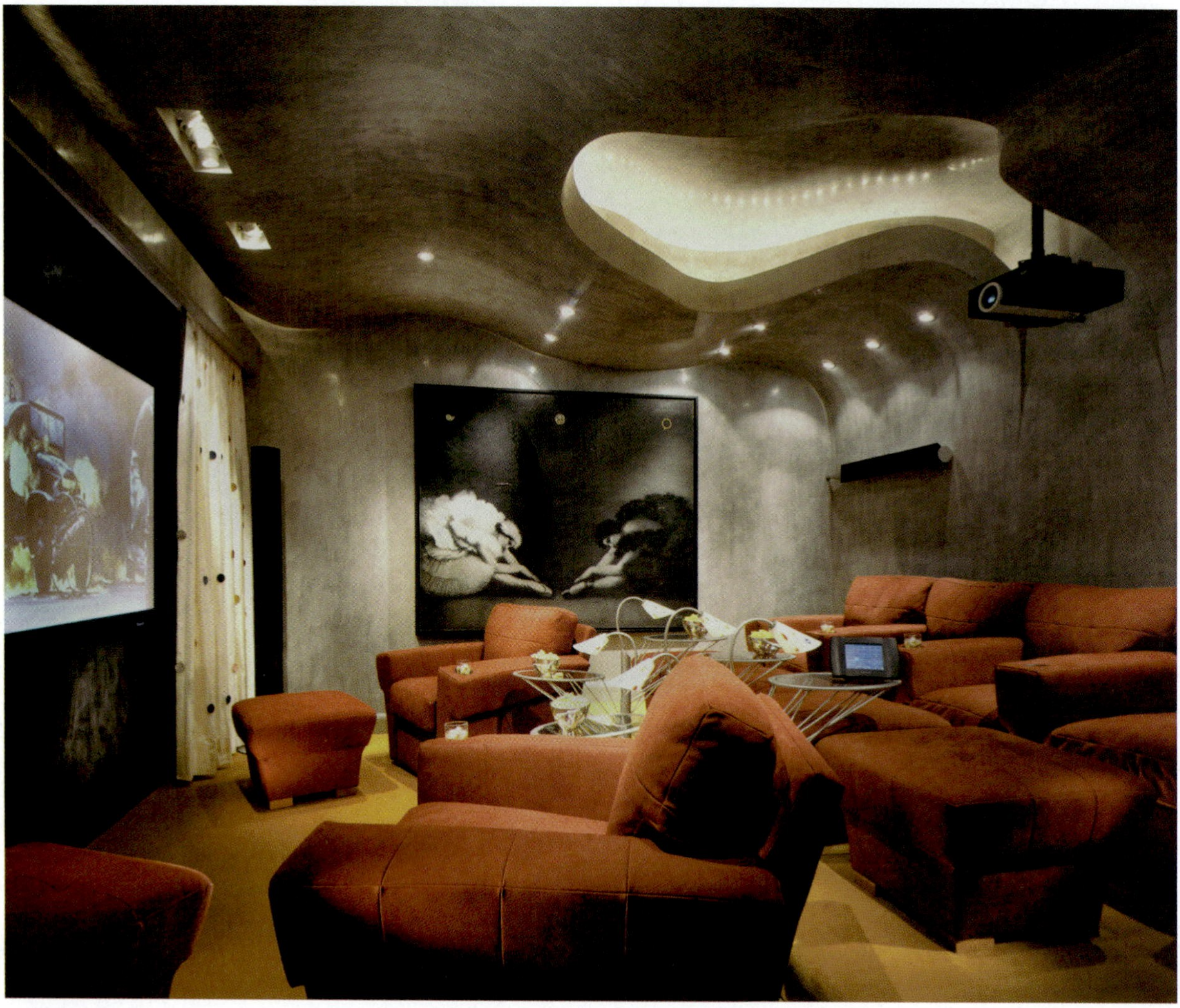

Figure 11.2 *In this home theater in Boca Raton, Florida, the designer created an amorphous ceiling recess to add interest an conceal the light source. Walls were designed to look like concrete and are complemented by overstuffed furniture and a plush fabric. (Designer: Charles Greenwood, IIDA, of Greenwood Design Group, Inc. Photograph © Robert Thien.)*

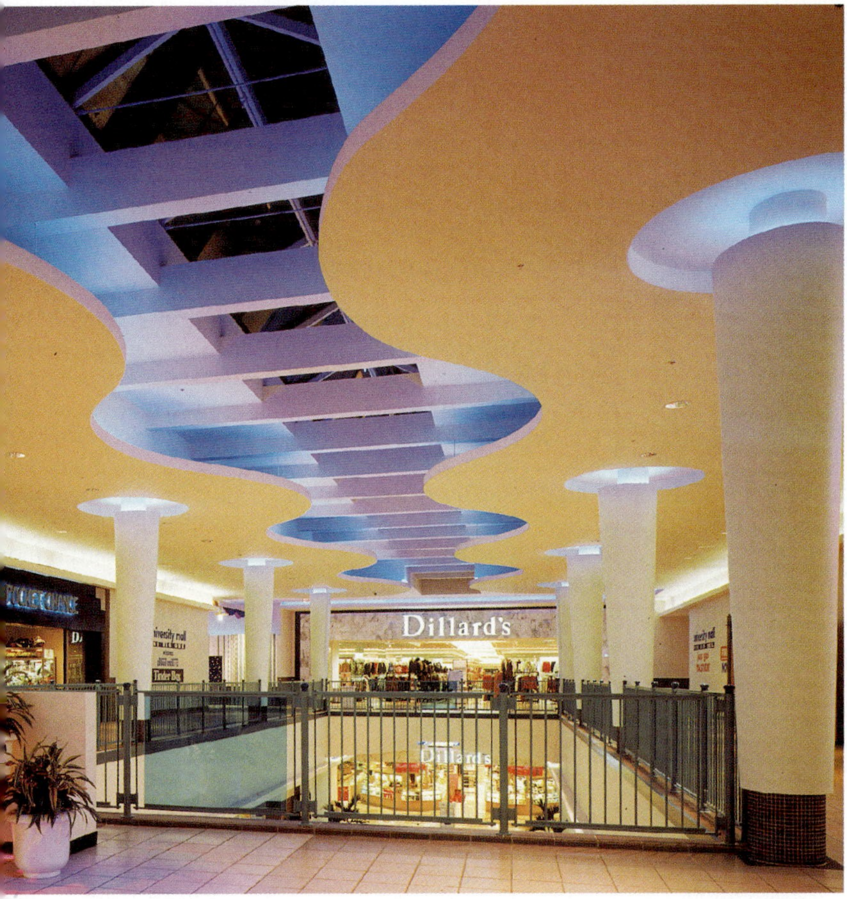

Figure 11.3 *The sculptured ceiling in this retail center not only adds interest and entertainment but also opens to skylights in the roof. (Architect/Designer: Anthony Belluschi Architects Ltd. Lighting Designer: Roeder Design, a subsidiary of Pacific Lightworks. Photograph by Robt. Ames Cook.)*

A ceiling whose middle portion extends vertically up about 6 in. to 18 in. is called a **tray** ceiling. Trays may be formed in many shapes and may conceal lighting around the perimeter (Figure 11.2).

The *sculptured, custom-designed ceiling* may call attention to itself as the room's focal point. Sometimes designed in highly dramatic ways, sculptured ceilings follow no set pattern and usually require ample space for construction and effect (Figure 11.3).

The **coved** *ceiling* meets the wall with a curve instead of a right angle, so the ceiling and wall flow into each other. Sometimes the perimeter is made to accommodate recessed lighting, allowing light to shine upward on the ceiling surface.

Vaulted and *domed ceilings* are arched structures as opposed to flat planes and can be considered a complete extension of the coved ceiling.

Coffered *ceilings,* popular in past centuries, are constructed of wooden members in a grid manner, often with moldings and sunken decorative panels.

A *dropped ceiling* has a portion or its entire area lowered below the main structure (Figure 11.4). This type of ceiling can define an area of a room (a dining area in a dual-purpose living room or a reception area in a lobby, for example), provide indirect lighting, and add interest to a living space.

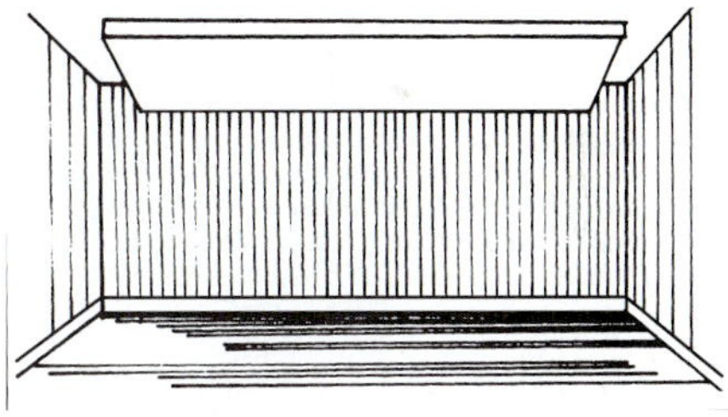

Figure 11.4 *Dropped ceiling.*

- In many commercial settings, the ceiling is actually nonexistent and is formed by the exposed structure above. This type of ceiling allows for extensive flexibility in lighting placement. Furniture showrooms and other retail establishments use this method of ceiling treatment to accommodate the great variety and abundant changes in the merchandise displayed. Restaurants may use this design to create an informal or high-tech feeling. In residential settings, this type of ceiling may be used to add drama (Figure 11.5).

More info online @

http://www.armstrong.com/commceilingsna/glossary.html
Armstrong commercial ceilings glossary

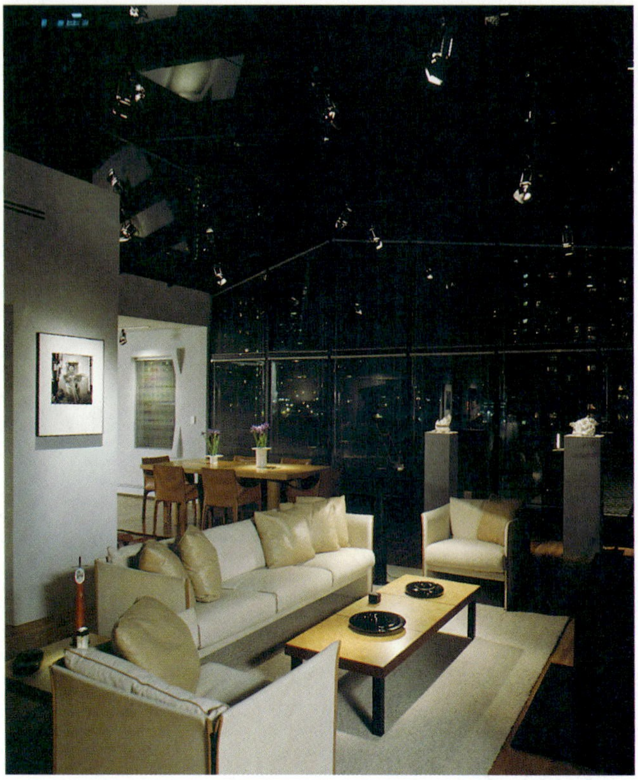

Figure 11.5 *To give the illusion of endless space, designer Harry Stein painted the beams and part of the ceiling black and strategically placed numerous lamps. Other sections of the ceiling are mirrored, adding to the effect of depth in this New York penthouse. (Photograph © Norman McGrath.)*

Ceiling Construction and Materials

Ceiling materials may be divided into two general categorie those that attach directly to the structure (such as plaste gypsumboard, glass and plastic panels, stamped metal, fal ric, and wood), and those that hang from the structure (suc as suspended ceiling tiles).

Plaster and Gypsumboard

Plaster is the most versatile of all ceiling treatments. Plast is a thick mixture of gypsum, water, lime, and sand. This mi ture is applied to a metal lattice, a special hardboard, or ar rough masonry surface. The finished surface may be smoot textured, wallpapered, or painted. Sometimes a plaster ce ing is stenciled or has applied decoration or moldings. Pla ter has been used for centuries, but currently the cost relatively high.

Because of the high cost of plaster, gypsumboard is mo commonly used. The 4 ft. × 8 ft. panels have a finished su face like plaster. Gypsumboard provides insulation and available in many thicknesses. When layered it is highly fi resistant. Gypsumboard also forms the main element fo unique sculptured designs (Figure 11.6).

Glass and Plastic

Glass or plastic panels, either translucent or transparent, a sometimes used in ceilings to provide overhead light—eith natural daylight or recessed artificial light. These panels ma provide overall illumination or striking lighting effects fro

Figure 11.6 *In this refined restaurant Adam D. Tihany utilized gypsumboard in a multilevel sculptured grid pattern to create a bold yet simple architectural statement. The texture of the materials provides warmth and adds depth to the interior. (Architect/Designer: Adam D. Tihany International, Ltd. Photograph by Peter Paige.)*

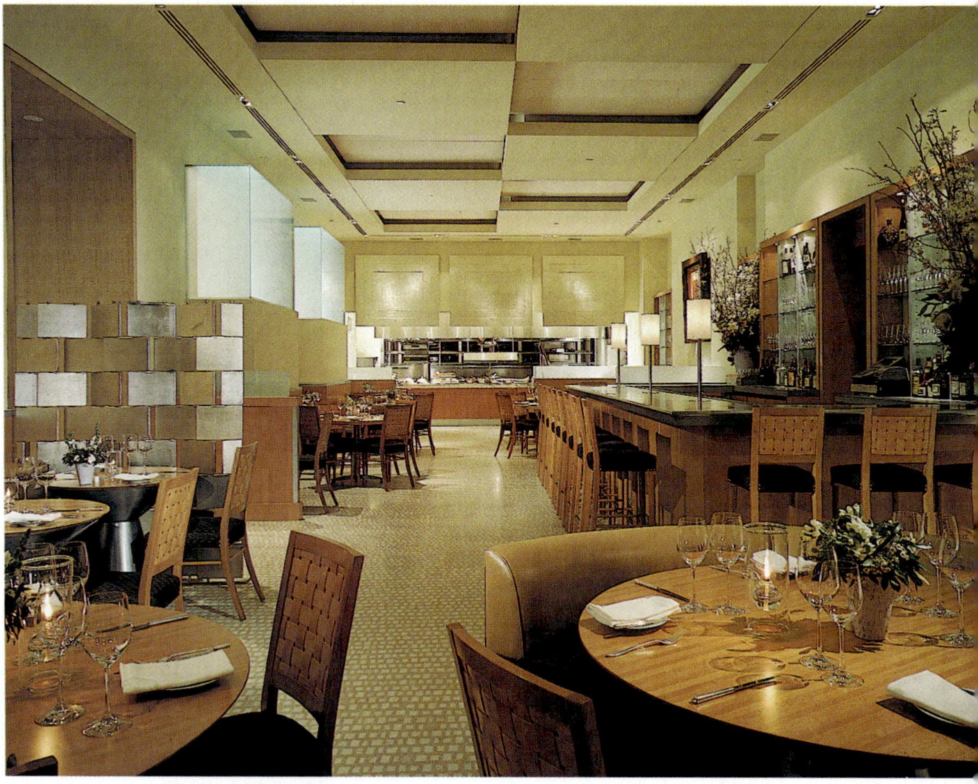

gh-up windows. Skylight views add a new dimension to y interior.

amped Metal

mped metal ceilings were popular during the nineteenth ntury and add a historical feel to interior environments. ese ceilings are used in the restoration and construction of torian buildings and are commonly seen in commercial eriors such as restaurants or retail spaces. This treatment volves stamping or pressing designs onto metal panels, oviding a unique embossed effect.

abric

bric, although not commonly used, can be stretched, irred, or pasted (like wallpaper) to the ceiling surface. Its ftness provides a comfortable, warm feeling, and when ed as a repeating fabric in the room can unify the interior. gure 11.4 illustrates an unusual treatment of a fabric ceiling.

'ood

ood, in strips, panels, beams, or planks, can provide a arm, inviting atmosphere. Because of its visual weight, ood tends to lower the ceiling and may create a feeling of aviness unless the ceiling is higher than average. Often ood is used in combination with plaster; for example, ood beams can stretch across a plaster ceiling. Wood can left natural, stained, or painted. Where natural beams are t feasible, ceiling beams of polyurethane (which simulate nd-carved wood to a remarkable degree) can be glued to e ceiling.

ispended Ceilings and Tiles

spended ceilings are common in commercial construction. etal tracks are suspended from the structure, forming a 2 ft. 2 ft. or 2 ft. × 4 ft. grid pattern, which is then filled with es. The tiles come in a wide variety of materials, colors, and tterns. Many have acoustical properties for absorbing ise. Others have a foil backing, which cuts down on air nditioning and heating costs. Some manufacturers wrap iling tiles in fabric to create a warm, plush look. Another oe of suspended ceiling system is the 1 ft. × 1 ft. concealed line. Although this ceiling is more difficult to install, it gives nore uniform appearance than the larger grids.

Suspended ceilings are versatile. Lighting and HVAC are ncealed above the grid system in the space called the **enum.** As interior furnishings are moved, the ceiling light- g may be moved to adjust to the new needs. Additionally, HVAC or plumbing systems need to be upgraded, repaired, moved, they are easily accessed.

iling Illusions

a ceiling is much above or below the average main-floor ight of eight to nine feet, it alters the general feeling of the om. A high ceiling emphasizes space and tends to create a feeling of dignity and formality. A low ceiling, which decreases space, can produce a warm, informal atmosphere. Designers should note the ceiling height with respect to the width and length of the room. A low ceiling in a very large room can be confining, whereas a high, tall ceiling in a small room can create the impression of living in a barrel. To accommodate the human factor, ceilings may be made to appear higher to suit an owner's preference for a more spacious feeling, or lower to provide a cozy, intimate atmosphere. To create the illusion of height, observe the following guidelines:

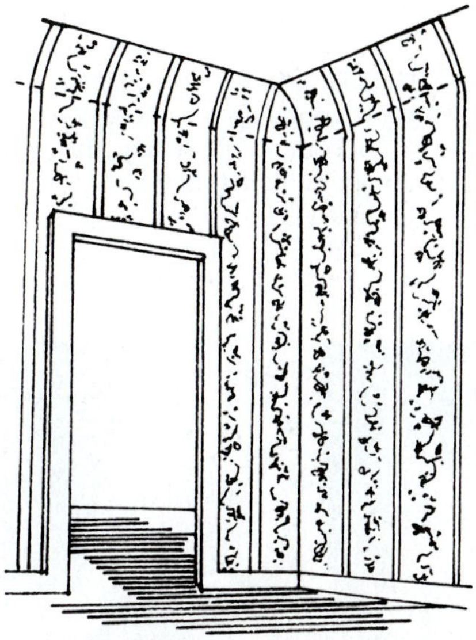

Figure 11.7 *Wallpaper extended beyond the walls and into coved ceilings gives the appearance of greater height.*

- Run the wall color or covering a short distance onto the ceiling, especially when the corners are coved. This treatment causes the eye to move upward and makes the ceiling appear higher (Figure 11.7). Use a light color on the ceiling.
- Use a predominance of vertical lines in the architecture of the room and in the decorative elements, like patterned wallpaper.
- Add a skylight to open up space.
- Use diagonal beams, which draw the eye upward, to make gabled ceilings appear even higher (see Figure 11.2).

To create a lowered ceiling effect:

- Paint the ceiling a darker color or use a patterned finish.
- Extend the color or covering down onto the wall a short distance and end it with a border or a small molding. As attention moves upward, it stops at the molding and the ceiling seems to begin at that point. In this way the ceiling can be psychologically lowered as much as three feet.
- Use a predominance of horizontal lines in the room's architecture and decorative elements.
- Use wood ceilings and horizontal beams, particularly in natural wood or a bold or dark color.

In recent years, changing interior styles have produced exhilarating ceiling designs, which add new dimensions to interior spaces. Through the use of creative materials and finishes, and by incorporating a variety of ceiling heights within a residence or commercial setting, the ceiling can become the focal point or an important backdrop for other interior elements (Figure 11.8).

WALLS

The vertical background elements of a room are importa factors in setting and maintaining the concept. Walls, wi dows, doors, and fireplaces are all part of the room's encl sure and provide the background elements for furniture a

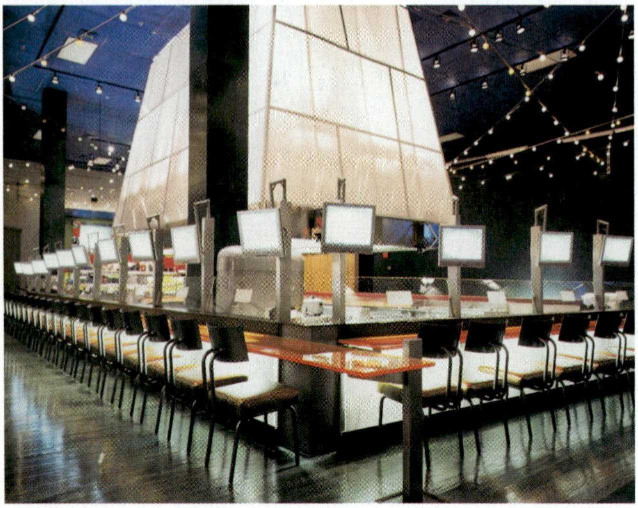

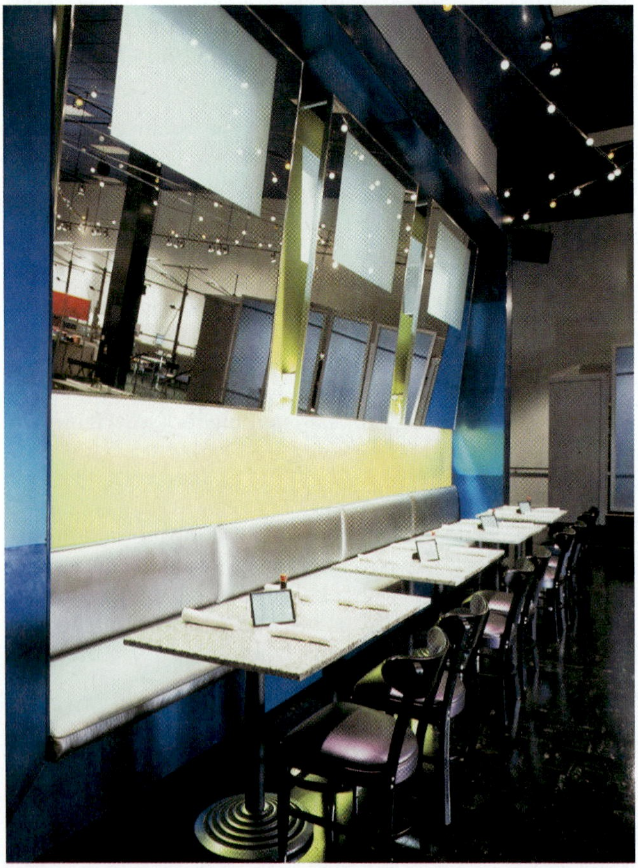

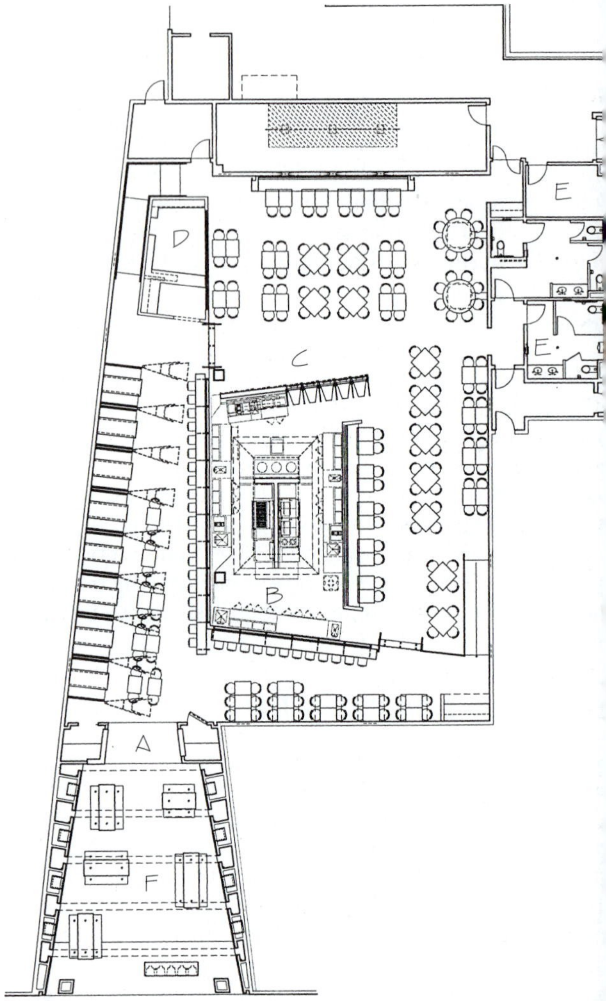

A: Entry/Maitre d'/Cashier
B: Exhibition Kitchen
C: Cart Loading
D: Service Station
E: Restrooms
F: Video Garden and Picnic Tables

Figure 11.8 *Patrons are treated to visual as well as gustator delight in this interactive restaurant. The designer altered th original cavelike appearance (caused by the 30′ ceiling and minimal windows) by creating a focal point with the translucent hood over the kitchen. The hood also conceals th HVAC and exhaust fan systems. LCD screens and mirrors distributed throughout the restaurant allow all patrons to view the chefs at work. The concept "restaurant as theater" creates drama and draws return customers. (Designer: Jeffre Beers International. Photograph by Troy Forrest.)*

brics; however, their most important function is to provide background for people.

Walls occupy the largest area of a room, define its size and ape, and serve purposes of both function and beauty. inctionally, walls provide protection and privacy from the terior surroundings and create interior areas of various apes and sizes for particular activities. Walls also provide ace for plumbing pipes, electrical and telephone wires, d HVAC, as well as insulation against heat, cold, and noise. sthetically, they contribute significantly not only to the ccess of a room but also to its general atmosphere and pernality.

Vall Construction

alls are generally defined as load-bearing or non-loadaring. Load-bearing walls support other parts of the structe such as the roof or upper-level floors. Non-load-bearing alls function as dividers and do not support the structure, it may support shelves, cabinets, or other interior elements. fore moving or cutting an opening in a load-bearing wall, designer must consult with a builder, engineer, or architect determine alternative structural requirements.

Some non-load-bearing walls are freestanding, stopping desk or counter height or just short of the ceiling. These alls provide some degree of privacy, but permit the flow of , light, and sound from one area to another.

onresilient (Rigid) Wallcoverings

iere are many materials available for wall treatments. Each pe has advantages and disadvantages with regard to aparance, cost, upkeep, noise, insulation, and longevity. me wall treatments are extremely versatile; others belong certain period styles or are used to evoke certain moods. hen selecting materials for wall backgrounds designers ould consider aesthetics, function and the human factor, onomics and ecology, as discussed in the introduction to rt V.

Table 11.1 lists the most frequently used nonresilient wallverings, plus information on their general characteristics, e ratings, insulation properties, and uses and care.

'aster and Wallboard

addition to its use as a ceiling material, plaster makes a rsatile but costly wallcovering. A less expensive alternative wallboard, which may be made of gypsum, pressed wood, plastic laminate. Gypsum wallboard—called drywall or by brand name of *Sheetrock*—is the most common and is ed extensively.

Drywall and pressed wood are inexpensive wallboard atments that come in 4 ft. × 8 ft. panels that are secured the wall's vertical stud supports. Wallboard provides insuion against heat, cold, and noise, and when painted proces a variety of effects from rough to smooth. Rough, isterlike walls are appropriate for informal rooms and for me period rooms (such as those in the Spanish style). Smooth surfaces can be used in any style room and with any style furniture.

Wood

Wood walls have been a favorite background treatment for centuries. Wood may be applied to walls in boards or panels. Boards can be of any wood type, cut in various widths, stained any color, and laid vertically, horizontally, or diagonally. They can be joined with tongue-in-groove, butted, or beveled edges. A wide variety of wood sheet panels (known as *paneling*), some with thin veneers, are also available with numerous finishes, colors, and styles, and is considerably less expensive than boards.

Masonry

Masonry used for walls includes brick, tile, concrete block, and stone. Brick, which has been used since the time of the ancient Babylonians and the pharaohs, has a timeless quality of warmth and adaptability. Its natural look is equally at home in traditional or modern settings and in residential or commercial spaces. Ceramic tile, available in many shapes, sizes, colors, patterns, and finishes, can be used for almost any style and room. It is especially popular for use in kitchens and bathrooms.

Marble, travertine, limestone, slate, fieldstone, flagstone, and quartzite, all types of stone, are available in a variety of textures and colors (Figure 11.9). Some stones, like marble, can provide a formal and elegant look, and some, like fieldstone, give an informal and casual feeling. Stone is popular for fireplaces, and in contemporary homes is widely used for walls. For additional stone characteristics, see Table 11.1.

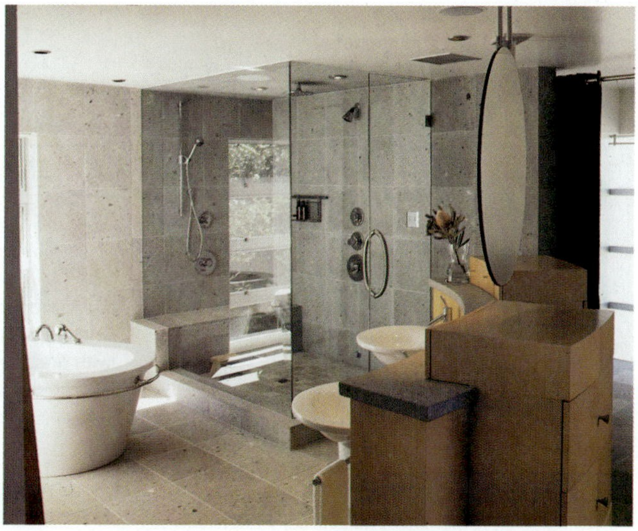

Figure 11.9 *Masonry tiles have been used throughout the space in this ASID award-winning bathroom. A glass wall insets into the masonry to define the shower. Note the curved island (including custom cabinetry) to house the pedestal sinks. A double-sided mirror is suspended over the island. (Designer: Bruce Benning, ASID/CID, Benning Design Associates. Photograph by David Duncan Livingston.)*

Table 11.1 *Nonresilient Wallcoverings*

Material	General Characteristics and Cost	Finishes	Fire Rating	Insulation Properties	Uses and Care
Brick (fired clay)	Solid and durable Variety of sizes, shapes, and colors Old, natural brick has feeling of warmth May be laid in regular or varied patterns Pleasant texture High cost	No finish necessary May be painted or waxed	Fireproof	Reflects noise Conducts heat and cold	Interior and exterior walls Appropriate for large- or small-scaled rooms, and for fireplace facings and hearths Little or no upkeep
Concrete blocks (lightweight aggregate)	Substantial, cold, regular shape, large scale, textured Moderate cost	No finish necessary May be painted Waterproofing necessary for exterior	Fireproof	Fair insulator	Interior or exterior walls, fireplace facings Best when used in large-scaled rooms Lacks domestic warmth Little or no maintenance
Ceramic tile (clay)	Comes in variety of shapes, sizes, colors, and patterns, and in pregrouted sheets Durable, resists water and stains, but may crack or break Moderately high cost	No finish necessary	Fireproof	Reflects noise Poor insulator	Bathrooms, kitchens, utility rooms, breakrooms Particularly appropriate for dadoes in Spanish- and Mexican-style rooms Minimum upkeep
Fiberglass (panels)	Translucent panels of reinforced fiberglass Most often ribbed or corrugated Also available in flat sheets and in several thicknesses Comes translucent, white, or colored Moderate cost	No finish necessary	Fireproof	Good insulator	Room dividers, folding screens, tub enclosures, translucent lighting panels for ceilings, built-ins, and sliding doors Easy upkeep
Glass (architectural)	Can be clear, rubbed, corrugated, pebbled, frosted, colored, or curved Metal mesh core will prevent breakage May be tempered Moderately high cost	No finish necessary	Fireproof	Poor insulator	Sliding doors, screens, room dividers, clinical purposes, numerous other uses Mirrors can usually expand space and add dramatic element to rooms One-way glass has many functional uses
Glass (block)	Excellent light transmission High-impact strength Moderately high cost	No finish necessary	Fireproof	Solid glass blocks conduct heat Blocks with hollow air centers are good insulators	Contemporary settings Suitable to lighten most dark areas Easy upkeep
Metal (panels and tiles)	Stainless steel: plain or grained (nonreflective finish) Serviceable, sturdy, not affected by acid, steam, or alkalies Solid copper; attractive May be plain, hammered, or antiqued Sealed to prevent tarnish or corrosion Aluminum glazes: solid aluminum Coated with permanent vitreous glaze of porcelain, enamel, or epoxy enamel Sturdy, easy to maintain Lightweight and strong, but subject to dents that are difficult to repair Tends to have commercial effect Moderate cost	Factory finished with grain, or enameled in variety of colors	Fire resistant	Reflects heat	Kitchens, bathrooms, utility rooms, and wherever sturdy wall is desired Unusual decorative uses residentially and commercially Easy maintenance

Table 11.1 *Continued*

Material	General Characteristics and Cost	Finishes	Fire Rating	Insulation Properties	Uses and Care
Plaster and stucco	Smooth or textured, no seams or joints Tends to chip and crack Moderately low cost	Paint, paper, or fabric	Fireproof	Special types have good insulation against noise	Most versatile of all wall treatments Appropriate for any room and any style Washable
Plastic (sheets)	Durable, resilient Comes in variety of colors, patterns, and textures Moderately high cost	No finish necessary	Poor Some do not burn but emit noxious gas	Poor insulator	Wherever durable, resilient walls are needed Resists stains and cuts Easy maintenance
Stone	Great beauty If covering too large an area, may appear cold, depending on color Natural colors and textures Feeling of strength and durability Improves with age High cost	Waterproofing sometimes required	Fireproof	Poor insulator Reflects sound	Fireplace surround or entire wall No upkeep
Wallboard (gypsum, drywall, or sheetrock)	Surface may be finished in attractive colors and patterns, or imprinted with woodgrain appearance Lowest cost	Same as plaster: paint, paper, or fabric	Fire resistant	Excellent insulator	Any room in which low cost is primary consideration Care depends on finish
Wallboard (hardboard, pressed wood)	Extremely durable, dent resistant, available in many woodgrains and colors Woodgrain applied via high-fidelity photo process Factory coated, virtually indestructible, easily installed Also available in embossed and textured surfaces simulating fabrics Moderate cost	May be stained, painted, or waxed	Surface melts Pressed wood burns	Reflects noise Insulation depends on thickness of pressed wood	Any area in which wood paneling of low cost and durability is required Wash with damp cloth
Wallboard (plastic laminate)	Extremely durable Surface of laminate similar to plastic countertop Photo process can produce textured appearance, woodgrains, colors, or patterns	Finished at factory Needs no additional finish	Smokes and melts	Reflects noise Fairly good insulator, depending on density and thickness	Hard-use areas of house (family rooms, children's rooms, basements) Resists stains and moisture Scratches are irreparable Wash with damp cloth
Wood (plywood)	Matte or shiny surface High cost Thin surface of wood veneer bonded to rugged and inexpensive panel backing Appears much like solid wood, but less expensive Comes in 4 ft. × 8 ft. sheets for easy installation May or may not have vertical grooves Moderately high cost	Same as solid wood—usually not considered a finished look	Susceptible to burning	Good insulator and noise reducer	Depending on type of wood and method of installation, will go in any room—period or modern Beauty improves with age and care Dust only
Wood (solid)	Natural grain throughout Comes in variety of natural grains from rough barn wood to rich grains for formal rooms Can be installed tongue and groove, plain edged, flush joint, or grooved Natural colors vary, but may be stained any color Subject to denting, but can be refinished indefinitely High cost	Needs protective finish to seal against stains and water	Susceptible to burning	Good insulator and noise reducer	Same as plywood

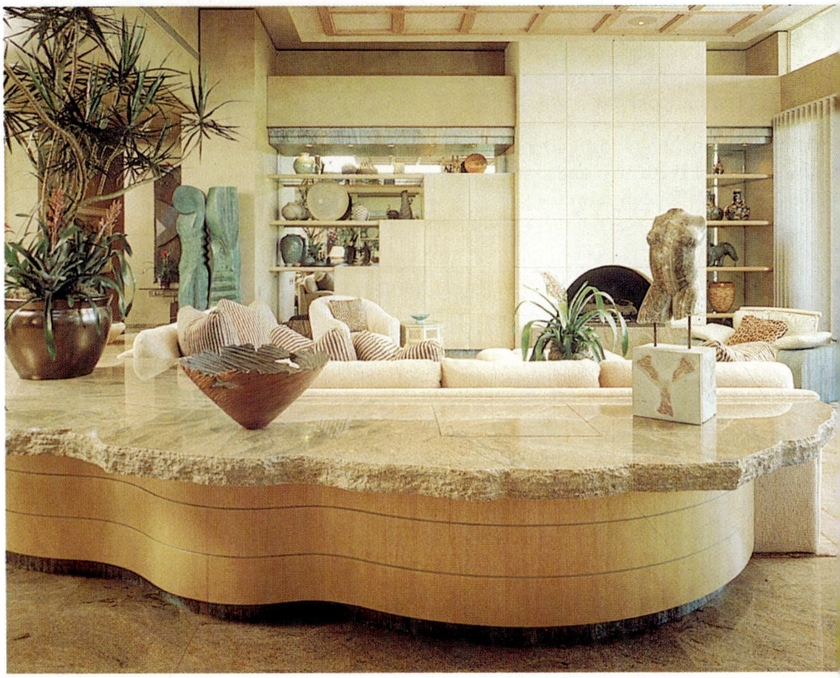

Figure 11.10 *This contemporary interior combines many hard-surface wall treatments. Mirrors and tiles are used on the fireplace wall. Stone and wood are used on the curved room divider. Gypsumboard walls cover the remainder of the room. The designer utilized curved and overstuffed furniture to add contrast to the angular surfaces. (Courtesy of Steve Chase Associates. Photograph by Arthur Coleman.)*

Other Wallcoverings

Mirrors

Mirrors can expand an area visually—an advantage in smaller living spaces. Mirrors are available in large sheets and precut panels ready to install. They can cover an entire wall or be spaced on a wall for function or aesthetic appeal. Mirrors also have great light-reflecting qualities and can be used to brighten a room (Figure 11.10).

Metal

Metals such as stainless steel, copper, and aluminum are available in sheets and tiles. Finishes may be smooth and shiny, or brushed. The latter has easier upkeep. Metal interior walls are contemporary in feel and provide a strong textural quality (see the wall design in Figure 11.6).

Plastics

Plastics are available in either sheets or tiles in a wide range of colors and styles. They are easy to clean and are completely waterproof. Plastic laminate wallboards are available in a wide range of colors and simulate a variety of textures. Although durable, plastics may appear inexpensive if used to simulate marble, wood, or other natural finishes.

Moldings

Moldings are used throughout the walls and on ceilings. Moldings are used most often where walls meet ceilings and floors. The molding hides the joinery at these corners and it also provides a transition from one surface to another. Moldings may also be used as a decorative treatment on wal Figure 11.11 illustrates typical molding terminology.

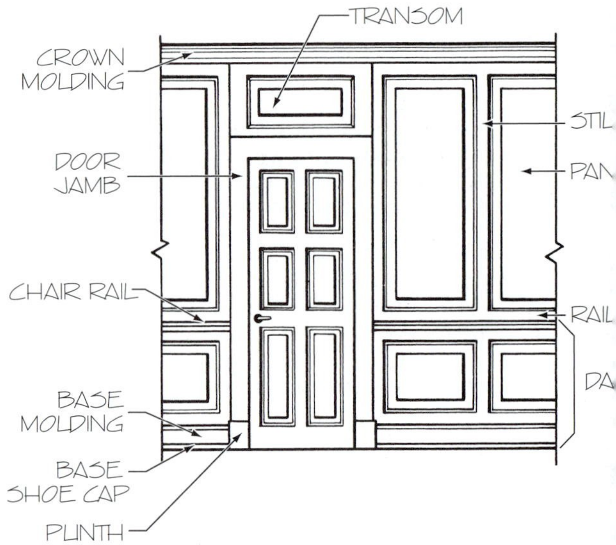

Figure 11.11 *Molding terminology.*

Wall Moldings

A *chair rail* divides the wall horizontally, usually about thr feet above the floor. The area between the chair rail and t base molding is called the **dado.** *Base moldings* usually cc sist of a *baseboard* (the taller portion) and a piece of quart round (usually called *shoe molding*).

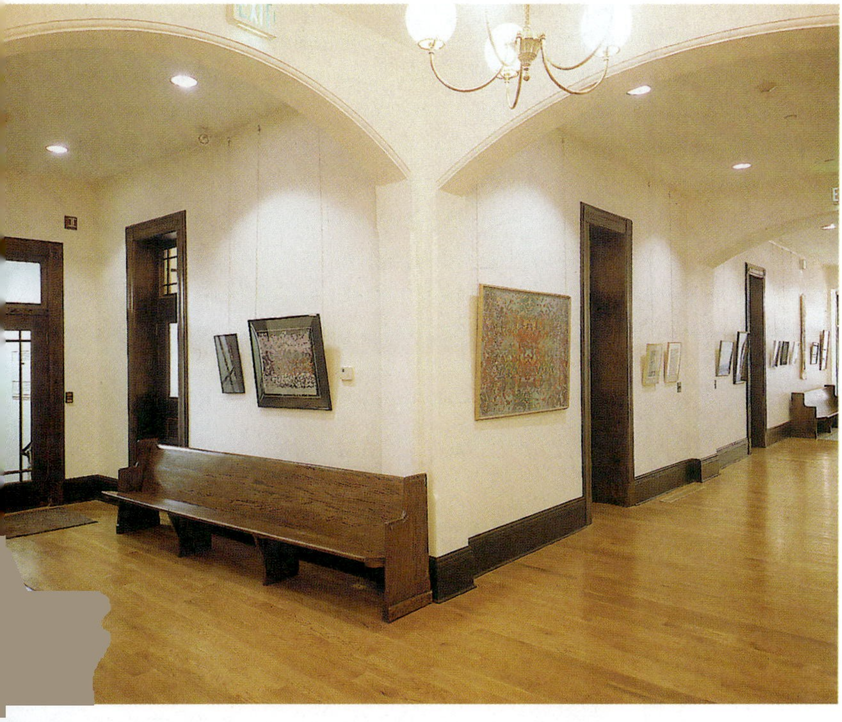

Figure 11.12 *In this historic courthouse, the designer recreated the custom picture rail and used it for its traditional function of holding pictures. (Architect: Office of Jack Pyburn, Architect, Inc. Designer: Lynn M. Jones. Photograph by J. J. Williams.)*

Wainscoting, a common practice in medieval interiors, is nately carved wood paneling that extends partway to the iling. A *picture rail* usually runs around the top of the wall, may extend one to two feet down the wall in a room with 10- to 14-foot ceiling. The picture rail traditionally was used suspend wires for hanging pictures. It also may be used a decorative element (Figure 11.12).

Panel moldings may be achieved in one of two ways. True nel molding is created by applying wood in various layers the wall and by applying strips of molding at the inter-ctions. A simpler form of panel molding consists of a flat aster or sheetrock wall with strips of moldings added to rm frames. A series of panel moldings is commonly used traditional dining rooms and conference rooms. **Boiserie** a French term describing ornately carved paneling.

rown Moldings

iling moldings are called **crown moldings.** Crown mold-gs may have three parts. The uppermost is called the **cor-ce,** the middle the **friezé,** and the lower the **architrave.** gether they are referred to as the **entablature** (see page 32). Moldings come in a variety of styles and shapes (see Fig-es 11.13 and 11.14). By combining these individual pieces,

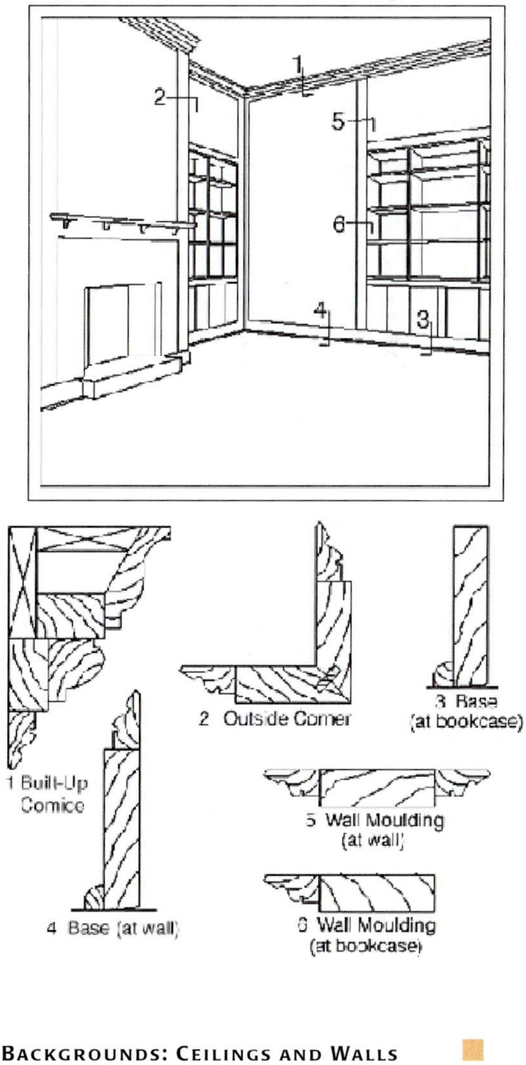

gure 11.13 *Moldings add warmth to this traditional library. e interior perspective (top) illustrates the room and dicates where the moldings are placed. The line drawing ottom) indicates the molding shapes used. (Reprinted with rmission from* Architectural Woodwork Quality Standards, *venth Edition, published by the Architectural Woodwork stitute, Reston, Virginia. All rights reserved.)*

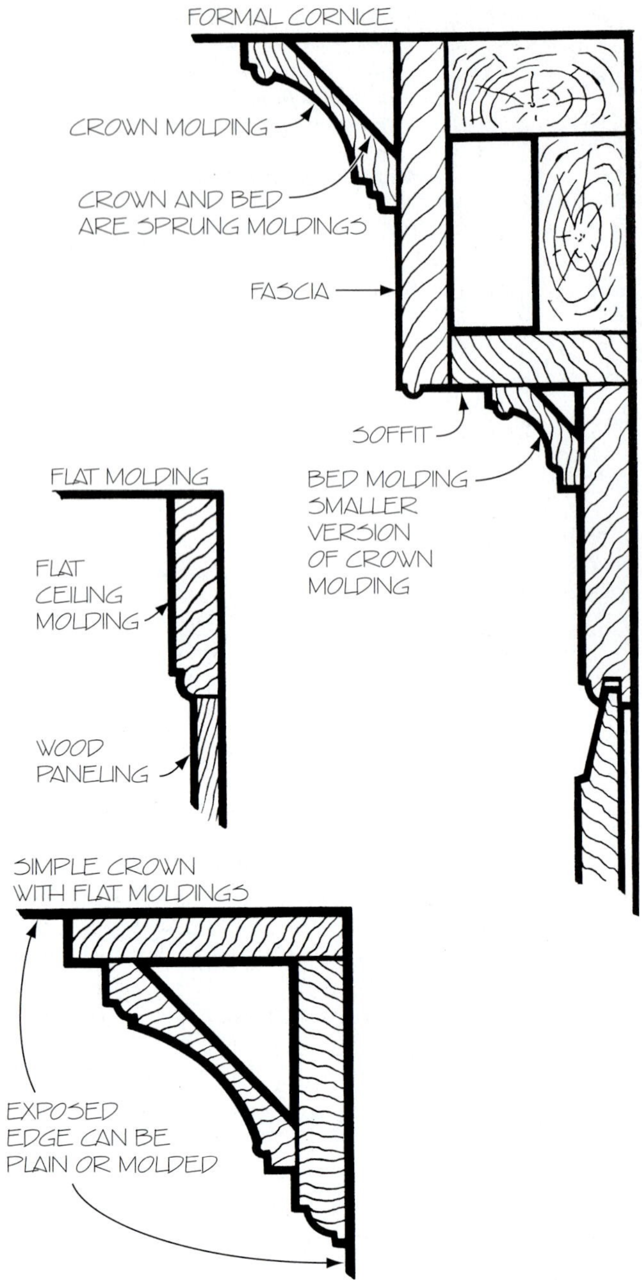

Figure 11.14 *Stock moldings add architectural interest.*

more ornate forms of moldings are developed. Higher ceilings (those above eight or nine feet) may accommodate a series of moldings. Ornate moldings add a feeling of dignity and grandeur, but if a ceiling is already low, a heavy crown molding may cause it to appear even lower. Chair rails and base moldings also may consist of one or more pieces of trim.

Trims are manufactured in wood, fiberglass, and foam. The latter are more versatile in design than wood and are lighter in weight (see Figures 11.15 and 11.16). When properly installed and painted, they are difficult to distinguish from their wood counterparts.

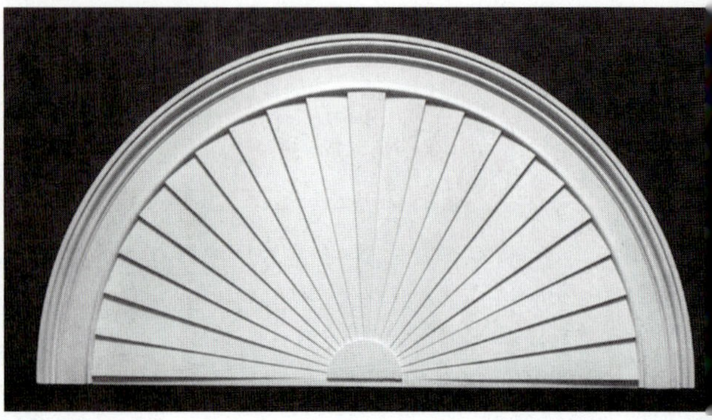

Figure 11.15 *This traditional sunburst design can add formality to a front door. It is sturdy, lightweight, and easily installed. (Courtesy of Focal Point.)*

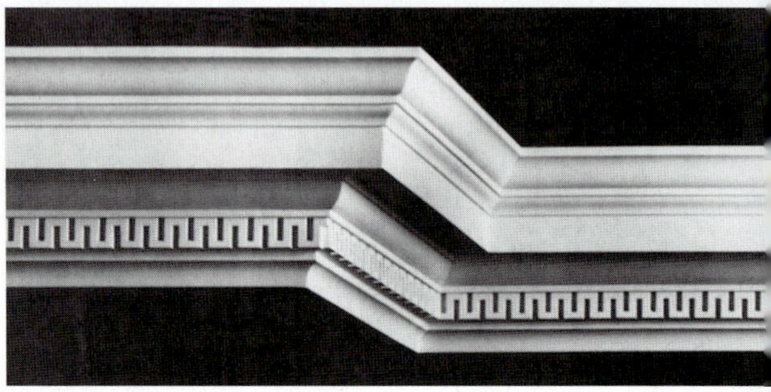

Figure 11.16 *This exquisite fretwork cornice, made of tough lightweight modern material, is molded directly from notab wood or plaster originals. (Courtesy of Focal Point.)*

More info online @

http://www.wmmpa.com/ Wood Moulding & Millwork Producers Association. Many links to other sites.

Paints and Finishes

To change the character of a room quickly with a minimu of expense, nothing works as well as paint. Of all wall tre ments, paint is the easiest to apply. It is made to adhere any surface and is appropriate for any room or any sty Some paints resist rust, fading, and fire. Paints come in r merous colors, producing unlimited shades, tones, and tin A painted wall surface can be smooth or given the illusion texture by use of a stiff brush, sponge, or special emboss roller. Paints are made from a vast array of synthetic and n ural materials.

Types of Paint

Alkyd Paint

Alkyd paint has virtually replaced oil paint. It is resin enan that is fast drying, resists yellowing, and cleans better than

x. Depending on the color, one coat is generally sufficient. kyd paints must be thinned with solvent. They are recom-ended for moldings, woodwork, trim, and anywhere mois-re, fingerprints, or scuff marks may be a problem. They are obably the best choice for painting metal.

:rylic Paint

:rylic paint is a water-based synthetic resin paint. The more rylic the paint contains, the higher the quality. Acrylic is tremely durable, odorless, easily applied, quick drying, d washable. Some acrylic paints resemble baked-on amel and are almost impervious to damage. Straight rylic paints are not commonly used on interior finishes.

tex Paint

tex is a type of acrylic and is frequently used on interior ishes. It is a water-based paint, so cleanup is easy during plication. Latex leaves no overlap marks, dries quickly, d the characteristic odor soon fades. Latex, however, does ow brush marks. A difference between indoor and outdoor ex is that outdoor latex "breathes," thus allowing moisture escape, which eliminates blistering. Latex paints are rec-nmended for plaster, gypsumboard, masonry, wood siding, oustical tile, and occasionally metal.

amel Paint

amel is a special type of paint similar to oil paint and is ade with varnish or lacquer. Its finish is exceptionally hard d durable.

oxy Paint

ere are two types of epoxy paint. The first type is ready-xed in a single can. The second type is a two-stage finish, catalyzed epoxy, which puts a tilelike coating on almost y surface. Once it hardens, this coating can be scratched, uck, or marked with crayon or pencil and still be washed ck to a high gloss. Epoxies can be used on such surfaces basement walls, shower stalls, and swimming pools.

/pes of Finishes

alers and Fillers

alers and fillers are special substances applied to new sur-:es as a base coat, ensuring a more professional finish.

int Finishes

›st paints are available in various finishes. Different man-ıcturers use different terms, but essentially there are three riations—*gloss, semigloss* or *eggshell,* and *matte* or *flat.* The ;her the gloss, the easier it is to clean; however, higher ›ss paint also shows the most imperfections in the wall.

Flat finishes tend to look richer than semigloss finishes; wever, a matte or flat finish is easily marred by furniture, gerprints, and spills. A semigloss or eggshell finish will prevent some scarring, and for an active family room or of-fice space it is the best solution.

Stain

Stain penetrates wood pores and contains various colorants that can enhance natural color or give a different color to wood. Stains should be tested on an inconspicuous area first, because different woods react differently to the same color stain. A varnish is generally required over the stain to seal it.

Varnish

Varnish is a word sometimes used as a generic name for all clear resinous finishes. A resin is a natural or synthetic sub-stance that, when dissolved in a suitable solvent, leaves a hard glossy film. Natural resins are the saps of certain trees or deposits of insects that feed on the sap. Synthetic resins are also available that duplicate natural ones. Varnish is made from natural resins with alcohol or a drying oil, and volatile thinners and dryers. A varnish is usually a transparent coat-ing and is commonly used on wood to protect the surface and allow the natural grain to show through. Some varnishes have a colorant added to darken the wood, but the result is usually less satisfactory than staining before applying clear varnish. Varnish comes in high gloss or matte finishes.

Shellac

Shellac is a protective coating similar to varnish. It is made of a resinous substance called lac, which is deposited on trees in India and Asia. Its solvent is alcohol. Shellac dries more quickly than varnish but is less durable and is subject to water spots. Clear shellac does not discolor when applied to a light-colored surface.

Lacquer

Lacquer is a superior, quick-drying, varnishlike finish made from resin from an Asiatic sumac (Chinese or Japanese lac-quer) or from a synthetic nitro-cellulose resin. The finish ranges from matte to high gloss and comes in white, black, brown, or beige. Commercially made furniture may be fin-ished with lacquer.

Polyurethane

Polyurethane is a varnishlike finish that provides an excep-tionally tough plastic surface coating. It comes in matte, medium-, or high-gloss finish. It is an excellent protective surface for hardwood floors in heavy traffic areas and walls where moisture is a problem. Polyurethane is also used to protect furniture surfaces and wood paneling.

Paint Textures

There are several methods of achieving unusual textures with paint. The following techniques involve applying one

Figure 11.17 *This warm, inviting interior (18′W × 24′L × 20′H) was originally a cold, vacant room. To give the room a more human scale, the designer created custom furniture scaled to fit the room. A subtle faux rag finish on the walls helps to envelop the occupants. (Designer: Pharr Design Group. Photograph © Robert Thien. As seen in* Atlanta Homes & Lifestyles.*)*

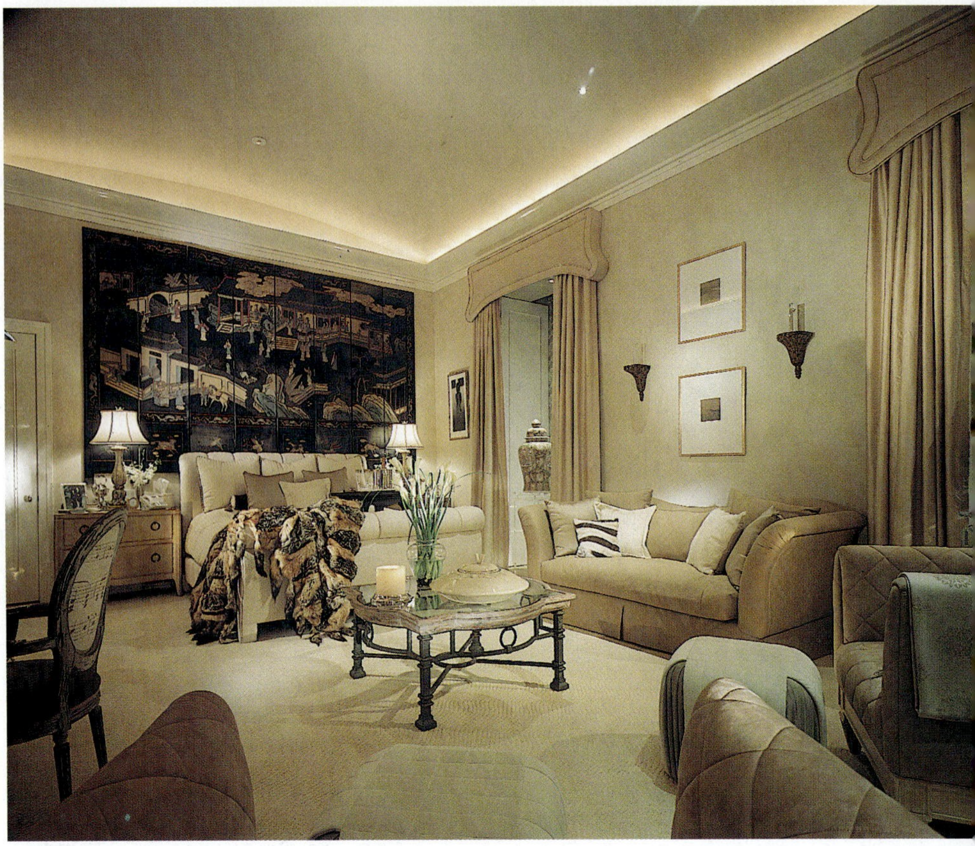

or more colors of wet (often thinned) paint over a dry base coat of another color:

- *Sponging*—Paint is applied with a sponge over a base coat, giving a mottled or blotchy texture.
- *Spattering*—Paint on a brush is flipped onto the base coat, giving a speckled appearance.
- *Stippling*—Similar to sponging, but a more delicate effect is achieved by using a stippling brush to apply a colored paint lightly over the base color.
- *Ragging*—One or more colors are applied over the base coat, then partly removed by blotting or rolling with a rag to achieve a marbleized effect (Figure 11.17).
- *Color washing*—A coat of thinned paint or glaze is lightly applied over a base coat of another color.
- *Glazing*—Layers of one or more transparent colors are applied on top of a base coat. The result gives the illusion of various depths on the wall.

Decorative Finishes

Faux is French for "false." Faux finishes simulate the look of another material, such as stone or wood, by using various techniques to apply paints to a surface. Among the more popular finishes are marble, granite, and woodgrains. More exotic faux finishes include tortoiseshell and malachite. In addition to being used on walls, faux finishes are used moldings, doors, mantelpieces, and furniture.

Trompe l'oeil is a delightful wall treatment, especia for those who desire an unusual effect or perhaps want inject a note of humor into their design. The French te literally means "to fool the eye." Trompe l'oeil is a han painted wall or wallcovering, in almost any subject matt giving a three-dimensional look. Very simple or extreme complicated designs can be used (see the ceiling in Figu 11.24).

Painted scenes, patterns, and borders that do not attem the illusionistic effects of trompe l'oeil can be created eith freehand (Figure 11.18) or with stencils. A stencil is a mas ing sheet with a pattern cut out so that the pattern can be peated. Stenciling is especially popular for rooms with informal or country look. Stenciling designs can be p chased or personally created.

More info online @

http://www.benjaminmoore.com/index.asp Benjamin Moore Home page.

http://www.sherwin-williams.com/diy/interior/ Sherwin Williams Do Yourself information

http://www.ppg.com/ppgaf/school.htm Pittsburgh Paint, online pain school

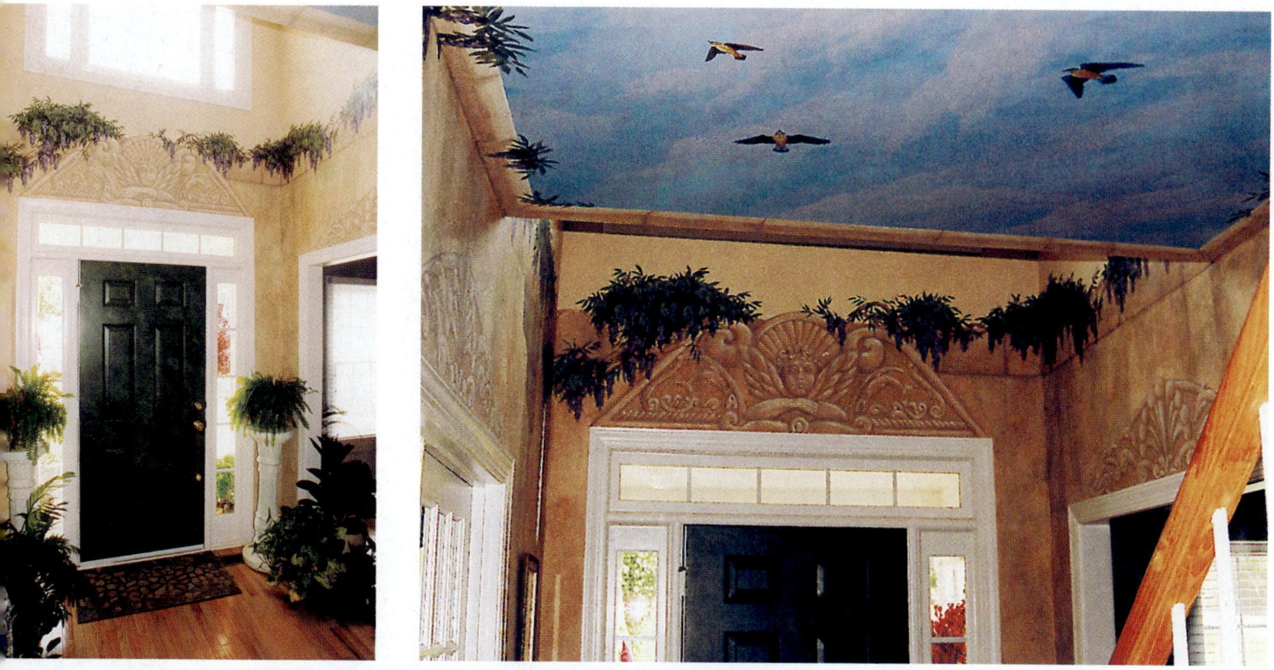

ure 11.18 *In this residential foyer, a painted faux finish creates a Renaissance ·rtyard illusion. Wisteria falls over the garden wall; bluebirds and robins gather in sky. (Designer/Artist: Shannon Pable. Photographs by John Orth.)*

silient (Flexible) Wallcoverings

allpaper

ng decorative paper as a wallcovering has been important enhancing interiors since the late sixteenth century in Eu- e and early colonial times in America. Although wallpa- s have been more fashionable during some periods than ers, they have always been esteemed as a valuable tool in nsforming the visual aspect of interior space.

tory of Wallpaper

nd-painted wallpapers were made as early as 200 B.C. in na, where they were used for decorating tombs. The first nufacture of wallpaper on an organized basis was in nce toward the close of the sixteenth century. The first pa- s were painted in a marbleized effect—a design copied n imported Persian papers—and made for facing book ers and lining boxes. These were called *domino papers*.

The introduction of flocked papers (wallpaper with a e-dimensional fuzzy texture) during the early seven- nth century made it possible for people to simulate the el- nt damasks used in the homes of the wealthy. In the latter of the seventeenth century a new printing method developed by Jean Papillon produced wallpaper that could be matched to make the pattern continuous around the room.

During the latter half of the eighteenth century, pictorial murals became popular through the works of Baptiste Reveillon in France and John Baptiste Jackson in England. During the eighteenth century in America, hand-painted papers from China were in vogue for the great Georgian mansions built along the Atlantic seacoast.

Copper printing rollers turned by a rotary machine were invented in northern England in the second quarter of the nineteenth century. Although wallpaper was frequently used during the nineteenth century, it was not until the Industrial Revolution that the wallpaper industry flourished in America. When the industry developed a new method of silk-screen printing in the mid-twentieth century that produced papers of high quality at affordable prices, the demand multiplied. *Documentary wallpapers* are used in replicating historic interiors (Figure 11.19).

More info online @

http://www.blonderwall.com/history.htm Timeline of wallpaper history

http://membres.lycos.fr/museedupapierpei/english/collections_uk.html Collections from the "Musee Du Papier Peint," wallpaper museum in Rixheim, France

Figure 11.19 *A documentary wallpaper establishes an authentic feeling of the period. (From the Winterthur Museum Collection. Courtesy of Van Luit and Company.)*

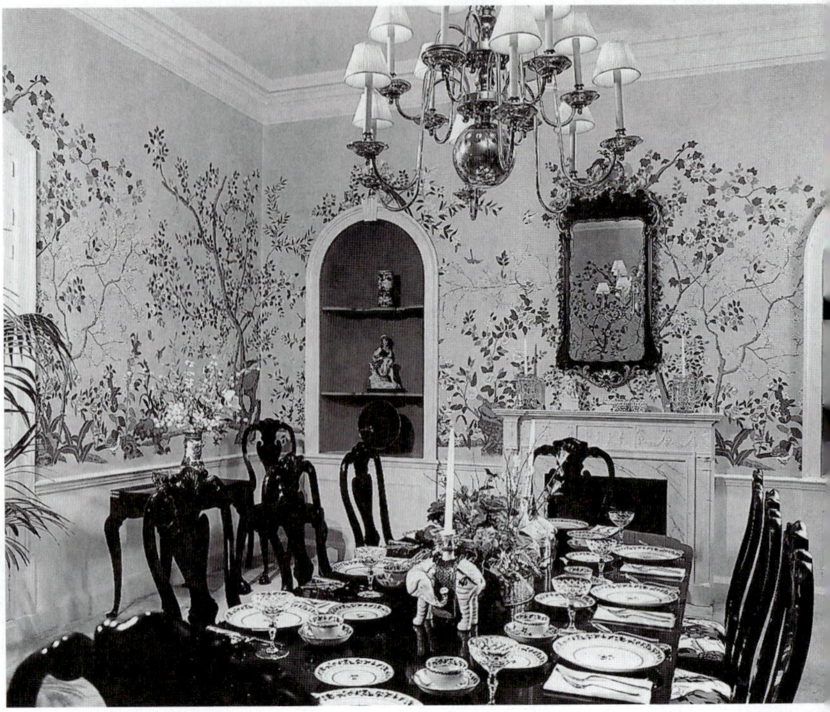

Methods of Producing Wallpaper

The three most common methods of producing wallcoverings are roller printing, hand blocking, and silk-screen printing. *Roller printing* is the most common process and the least expensive. It is a cylinder process in which each color is applied in rapid succession. In *hand blocking,* each color is applied separately after the preceding one is dry. This method is slower and more costly than the roller method. *Silk-screen printing* is a more complicated process in which a wooden or metal frame tightly stretches a silk, nylon, or metal screen made for each color of the pattern. Portions of the pattern not to be printed are heavily varnished or bleached out. Each repeat is made by applying pigment, which seeps through the screens as it is pushed across by a squeegee. Each color is allowed to dry before the next frame is printed. This method produces a high-quality wallcovering at reasonable cost.

Embossed and flocked wallcoverings have unique surface qualities. *Embossed* paper is made by a machine process producing high and low surfaces. This method is used where texture and three-dimensional effects are desired. *Flocked paper* is produced by a method in which the design motif is outlined and covered with glue or an adhesive material. Fine wool-like fuzz is then blown onto it, producing a surface resembling cut velvet.

Common Wallpaper Terms

Following are the most commonly used wallpaper terms:

- *Washable*—Usually refers to a wallcovering that may be washed with lukewarm mild suds, but not scrubbed excessively.
- *Scrubbable*—Refers to a wallcovering more resistant t rubbing than washable types. Stains such as crayon marks can generally be removed from scrubbable wal paper with cleaning agents recommended by the man facturer or with soap and water.
- *Pretrimmed*—Refers to rolls of wallpaper from which the selvage has been trimmed.
- *Semitrimmed*—The selvage has been trimmed from o one edge of the wallpaper.
- *Prepasted*—Paper that has had paste applied during t manufacturing process. Detailed instructions for hang are usually included. Generally, prepasted paper is soaked in water and applied to the wall while the pa is still wet.
- *Single roll*—Wallpaper is always priced by the single roll, but usually is sold by the double or triple roll. Regardless of width, a single roll usually contains 36 square feet. Eurorolls (wallcoverings produced in Europe and often used in the United States) typically co tain 28 square feet per single roll.
- *Double and triple roll*—Regardless of width, a double roll (two single rolls) contains approximately 72 squa feet, and a triple roll (three single rolls) contains 118 square feet. Generally, 18-inch and 20-inch-wide wal papers come in triple rolls. Double or triple rolls are used to minimize waste when cutting wallpaper into strips.
- *Dye lot*—Refers to the production schedule of a color colors. Each dye lot has a number. Because of color variations in different dye lots, all the wallcovering fo single space must come from the same dye lot. Desig ers should ensure that a sufficient quantity has been dered to meet the client's needs. Attempting to reord

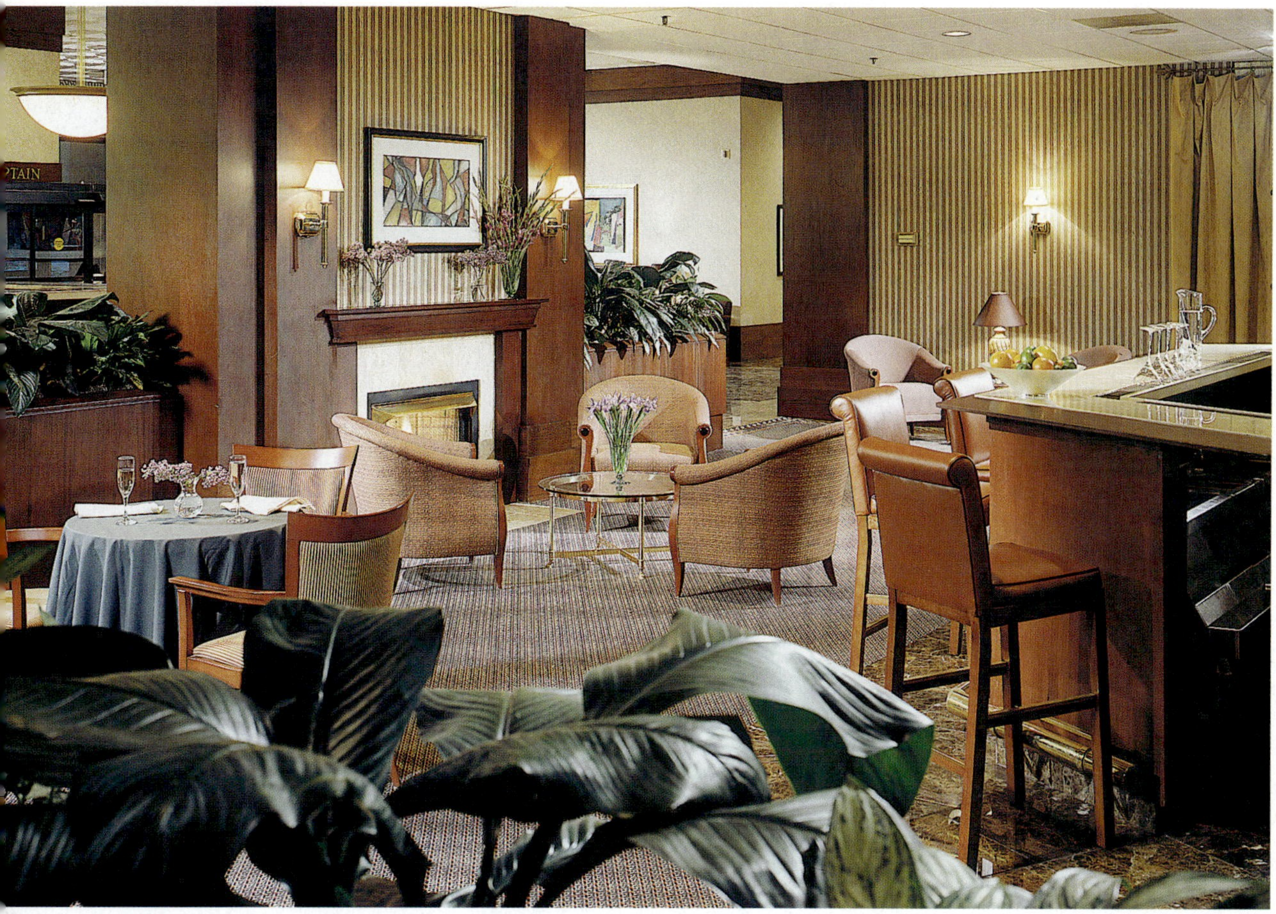

ure 11.20 ***A moiré print vinyl stripe wallcovering, in combination with a wood eer, adds warmth, beauty, and durability to this hotel lounge renovation. esigner: Gettys Group. Photograph by Bruce Van Inwegen.)***

during installation may be impossible because the particular dye lot may be sold out.

Pattern repeat—When a wallcovering has a pattern or motif, the pattern repeat is the distance from the beginning of the pattern to the point where it starts again. The patterns in the horizontal direction of the motif should match from the top to the bottom of the wall. The larger the pattern, the greater the wallcovering waste.

Sizing—A liquid that is painted on the wall before the wallpaper is applied. Sizing prevents the wallpaper from absorbing too much paste or adhesive and helps the wallpaper adhere better to the wall.

---

e info online @

://www.wallpaperinstaller.com/index.html Wallpaper installation rmation and terminology

---

nyl-Coated and Vinyl Wallcoverings

merous flexible wallcoverings are available that have n treated with varying thicknesses of vinyl. They are waterproof, highly durable, stain resistant, and may be washable or scrubbable. They can be used on nearly any type of wall and for any style. Vinyl-coated wallcoverings are applied using the same method appropriate for wallpaper (Figure 11.20).

Vinyl-Coated Wallcoverings

The following are the most common vinyl-coated wallcoverings:

- *Vinyl-protected wallcovering* is ordinary wallpaper with a coating of vinyl plastic to make it washable.
- *Vinyl-latex wallcovering* is a paper impregnated with vinyl, laminated to lightweight fabric or paper, then vinyl coated. The thickness of the vinyl may vary. This process produces a durable, scrubbable wallcovering.
- *Coated fabric* is a wallcovering with a woven cotton backing treated with an oil or plastic coating before the design is applied. This durable, tough, scrubbable material is ideal for kitchens and bathrooms.
- *Plastic foam* is a soft, flexible material available in rolls, squares, or rectangles. It absorbs sound, is soil and stain resistant, and insulates. It is easy to clean with soap and

water. Although more expensive than some wallcoverings, plastic foam is ideal for television rooms or apartments with thin walls, and is particularly useful in commercial and institutional settings.

Vinyl Wallcoverings

True vinyl wallcoverings are composed of a backing, a vinyl layer, and a finish layer. Vinyl wallcoverings are commonly applied in commercial environments where building codes dictate their use.

Vinyl wallcoverings are rated based on their total weight per ounce. Type I wallcoverings weigh from 7 to 13 ounces per square yard and are best used in light traffic areas. Type II wallcoverings weigh from 13 to 22 ounces per square yard and can be used in high traffic areas such as hotel and commercial office corridors. Type III wallcoverings weigh more than 22 ounces per square yard and are used in extremely high traffic areas such as cafeteria lines and elevator lobbies (Figure 11.21). Type II and Type III wallcoverings are usually 54″ wide to expedite installation.

More info online @

http://www.doityourself.com/wallpaper/commercialwallcovertypes.htm
Commercial wallcovering terminology

Fabric Wallcoverings

Many varieties of fabrics are used on walls (Figure 11.22). The best choice, except when using the shirred method of application (see p. 343), is a mediumweight, closely wov fabric. For an informal look use fabrics such as sailcloth, ti ing, Indian head, or glazed chintz; for a formal appearar use fabrics such as tapestry, brocade, or damask. Some fa rics come prepared for pasting on walls and are laminated a paper backing. Nondirectional patterns are easier to u because they require no matching. Like patterned wallpap a repeat pattern requires allowance for matching. Fabrics c be applied to walls in a number of ways.

The *shirring method* is the simplest way to cover a w with fabric. A lightweight fabric that drapes well is best. C to-fit rods are fastened just above the baseboard and near ceiling. The fabric is gathered, pleated, or folded and stalled on the rods.

The *double-face masking tape method* is not permane because masking tape will dry out in time; however, t method may be appropriate for temporary or seasonal plications. Fabric is prepared by sewing panels togeth Double-face tape is placed around the edges of the wall a the fabric is applied to the tape first at the top and botto and then at the sides.

The *Velcro™ method* is similar to the masking tape meth except that one side of the Velcro™ tape is stitched along edges of the fabric, then attached to the other side of the ta which has been secured around the edges of the wall.

In the *staple method* the fabric is prepared as in the ma ing tape method. The top is stapled first, then the botto and the sides last. Exposed staples may be concealed w braid or molding.

The *paste method* is the most professional looking a most permanent method, but it requires special care an set of wallpaper tools. The wall is prepared by applying

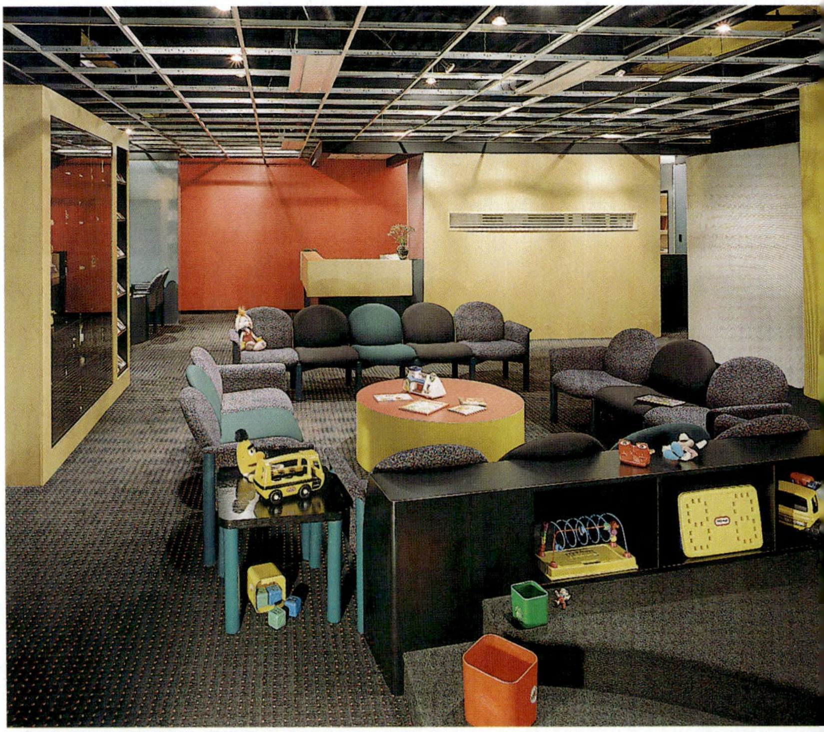

Figure 11.21 *In this children's ophthalmologist's office a ribbed vinyl wallcovering in strong colors creates nonstop movement and provides durability. (Architect/Designer: Stuart Narofsky Architecture. Photograph by Ron Solomon.)*

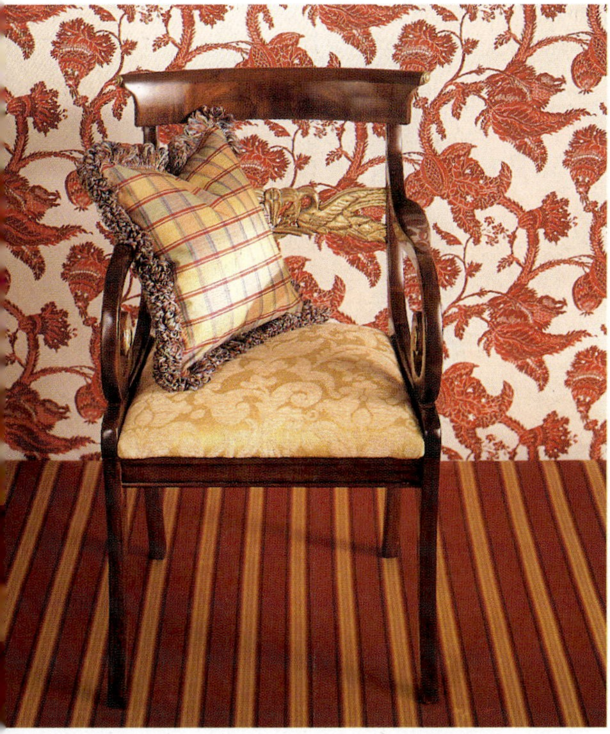

ure 11.22 *Boldly patterned fabric can be applied to walls :reate interest. Smaller scaled furnishings work best with a ge wall pattern. (Photograph © F. Schumacher & Co. mission has been granted by F. Schumacher & Co. to use yrighted work. Background fabric: Pomegranate Resist, a umacher ® design from Colonial Williamsburg.)*

it of liquid sealing or sizing to fill the pores in the wall sur-e. After the surface dries, a second coat of sealing is ap-ed to the wall, and the strips of fabric are positioned like llpaper. The fabric dries overnight and is then sprayed h a protective coating.

Fabric also can be applied to panels, which are then in-lled on the wall. Edges are often concealed with moldings.

her Resilient Wallcoverings

ass cloth or *hemp* wallcovering is flexible, long lasting, sy to care for, and provides suitable backgrounds for a va-y of styles. Colored grass cloth, however, fades over time. ner woven reeds such as *sisal* can provide handsome and ctical wallcoverings.

Wood veneer with fabric backing, another method of "pa-ing" walls, produces a true wood surface and, once ad-ed to the wall, is difficult to distinguish from solid wood. e advantage over wood paneling is that this material can around corners or curves. It is available in sheets up to 24 hes wide and 12 feet long. The cost, however, is high.

Leather tile, made of top-grain cowhide, provides a soft, rm, rich surface. It comes in a variety of fade-resistant col-to blend with traditional or modern decor. The leather is manently bonded to an aluminum tile base that has applied adhesive for easy installation. It is highly resistant scuffing, and the only maintenance required is an occasional washing with mild soap and water. Leather tile in suede is also available on a custom-ordered basis. The depth of the brushed nap provides an interesting texture, but its high cost limits extensive use.

Cork is a moderately priced textured material producing a warm atmosphere in natural colors of brown. It is particularly adaptable for studies or rooms in which sound insulation is important. Unless plastic-impregnated, cork is not suitable for bathrooms, kitchens, and other moisture-prone areas.

A historical wallcovering embossed with intricate designs dating from the Victorian era is marketed under the trade name of *Anaglypta*. This wallcovering is commonly used on dadoes. It is neutral in color and is intended to be painted (Figure 11.23).

Estimating Wallcovering Quantities

When working on a project, designers need to be able to estimate the quantity of wallcovering needed in order to calculate a budget. There are two generally accepted methods used to figure the quantity of wallcovering for a room.

The *general estimation method* is particularly helpful for quick "on the spot" estimates.

1. Total the wall area in the room. To do this multiply the height and width of each wall and then add the figures together.
2. Divide the total wall area by 30 square feet (slightly less than the average quantity per roll of wallcovering) to get the number of rolls of wallcovering necessary to cover the room.
3. Subtract 1 roll for every two openings such as doors and windows. Remember that wallcovering is usually packed in double rolls. Rolls cannot be split.

The *strip method* is more precise and should be used before making final purchases. It requires converting all dimensions into inches or centimeters. The designer will also need to know the *width, length,* and *pattern repeat length* of the selected paper. Once these dimensions are determined, proceed with the following steps:

1. Total the horizontal wall length for the entire room. To do this, measure the width of each wall in the room, add them together, and convert to inches.
2. Divide this amount by the width of the wallcovering. The answer indicates how many strips are needed to completely wrap the room in wallcovering. The next three steps will determine how long each strip should be to allow for a pattern repeat.
3. Determine the height of the room. Convert this to inches and divide by the pattern repeat. Round this number *up* to the nearest whole number.
4. Multiply the number of repeats (answer to Step 3) by the repeat length. This answer determines the cut length for each strip of wallpaper.
5. Divide the total roll length (single, double, or triple roll length) by the length required for each cut (answer to Step 4). Round this number *down* to the nearest whole number. This determines how many strips will be available from each roll of wallcovering.

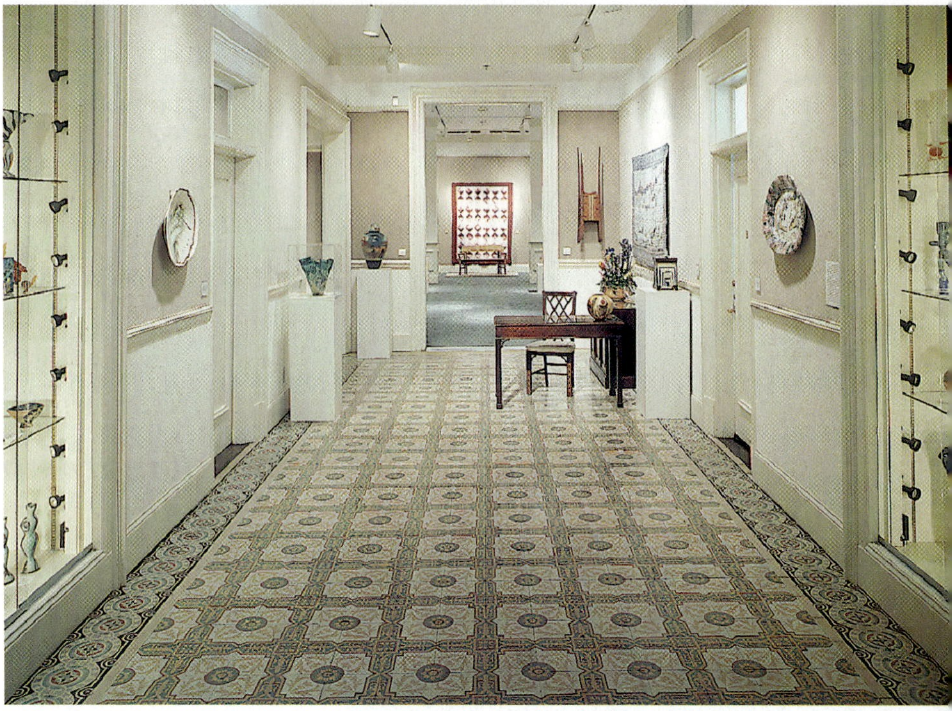

Figure 11.23 *This historic building was renovated into a fine arts gallery. Anaglypta was used on the dado and painted a pale peach. (Designer: Lynn M. Jones. Photograph by J. J. Williams.)*

6. Divide the total number of strips (the answer from Step 2) by the number of strips per roll (answer to Step 5). Round this number *up* to the nearest whole number. This final answer determines how many rolls (either single, double, or triple) will be needed.

More info online @

http://www.cheswall.com/global/HTML/howhang.htm#howmuch
Residential wallcovering estimation table

Selecting Wall Materials and Finishes

When selecting a finish for a wall, designers need an understanding of the functional, aesthetic, and economic requirements of the space. From a functional viewpoint, the amount of use or traffic in the area is a critical factor. For example, hospital, hotel, or other corridors frequented by large carts or wheelchairs require Type II or Type III wallcoverings. Chair rails made of molded plastics or metal also are appropriate in these areas.

Some rooms may require sound-absorbing wallcoverings. Libraries, studies, music rooms, and offices benefit from soft, absorbent wallcoverings. Large classrooms with hard surface flooring benefit from the use of cork walls or fabric panels, which also double as display areas.

In historic buildings, the designer may need to use materials that hide imperfections. Flat paint conceals flaws better than a semigloss. A vinyl wallcovering or product such as Anaglypta may also be appropriate.

Aesthetically, the architectural details of the room may rect the selection of the wall finish. An adobe fireplace wo allow for a more casual finish, as would the use of a nub material. A traditional fireplace may call for a more subdu wallcovering or paint. A traditional setting also may requ an elaborate pattern or trompe l'oeil print (Figure 11.24). strong contemporary structure may dictate the use of sle metals and poured concrete walls. Large expanses of glass glass block also may be appropriate.

Designers need to know whether the wall will serve a focal point or as a backdrop for other objects. A strong, b liant wallcovering may be appropriate for a kitchen; ho ever, in a gallery the wall material should be neutral so focus is on the art.

When selecting patterned wallpaper, it is important consider the scale of the room and select a pattern comp ible with it. A small pin dot or petite floral may function w in a bathroom, but would be out of scale for a dining ro or foyer. A wallcovering with a vertical stripe will incre the apparent height of a room, whereas a horizontal str will make the ceiling feel lower. Diagonal stripes on a w can create confusion and disorientation and are not reco mended unless vibrancy is the goal.

From an economic point of view, if the client is on a l ited budget, or if time is a major consideration, a new coat paint is probably the best solution. Paint is the least exp sive and easiest interior wall finish to change. A new coat paint will dramatically alter a room's presence. Accentua moldings or doors also will create a new energizing effec

Finally, designers concerned with environmental iss (or whose clients are) may wish to specify environment friendly products (see "Sustainable Design: LEED-CI").

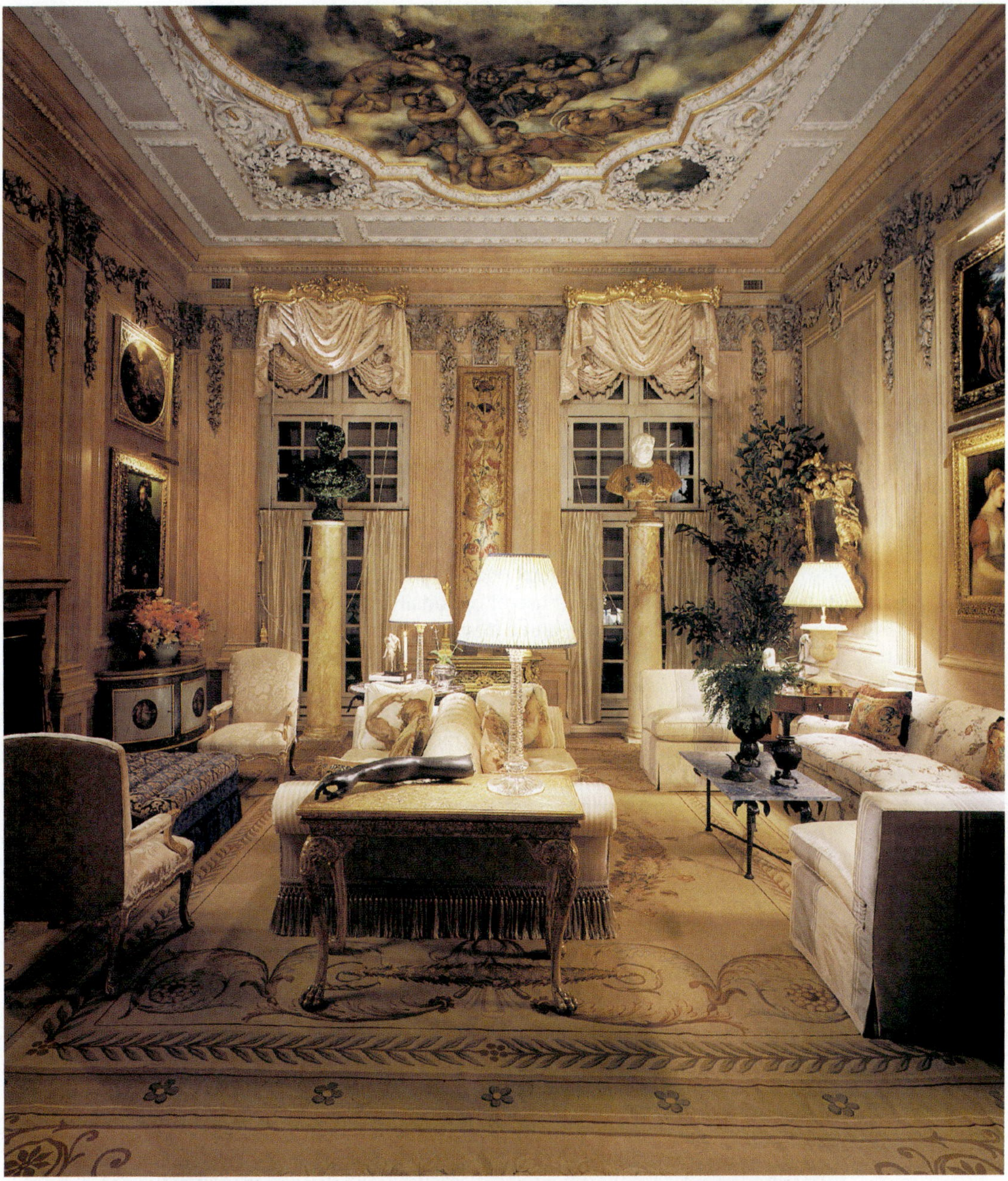

Figure 11.24 *This extravagant, opulent drawing room in the Kip's Bay Showhouse was designed by Juan Pablo Molyneux. The elegant backgrounds, including walls, ceiling, floors, windows, and fireplace, clearly establish a formal, eclectic French style and support the eighteenth- and nineteenth-century furnishings. (Antique Aubusson courtesy of F. J. Hakimian, Inc., NY, and Juan Pablo Molyneux. Photograph by Peter Vitale.)*

ummary

any interior environment, the ceilings and walls create a ckdrop for the inhabitants. These surfaces provide security, close the mechanical systems, and create a comfortable liv- g environment. Designers specify the materials and finishes that are applied to these surfaces. Care should be taken to ensure that the products used are durable, meet the functional needs of the space, and are sustainable. Designers must also utilize the principles and elements of design when selecting surface finishes so that they coordinate with the architectural components and enhance the human experience.

SUSTAINABLEDESIGN

LEED-CI

The United States Green Building Council, USGBC, developed the Leadership in Energy and Environmental Design, LEED, program. It is a voluntary, market-driven rating system quantifying a building's greenness. Through a self-certified point system, buildings can achieve bronze to platinum ratings. LEED's checklist evaluates several areas including the following:

- Sustainable sites
- Water efficiency
- Energy and atmosphere
- Indoor environment quality
- Materials and resources
- Innovation
- Design process

LEED is primarily focused on the architectural components of a building; however, in 2002 the USGBC launched its pilot phase LEED-CI for commercial interiors. The commercial interiors program is applicable to tenant spaces in new or existing buildings. The format complements the original LEED green building rating system, but is expanded to recognize the environmental impact of interior furnishings. Of particular interest to interior designers are ratings related to efficient lighting design, low VOC emissions, use of materials from recycled sources, and use of regionally manufactured goods.

According to Penny Bonda, FASID, a leader in green design and an advocate for LEED-CI, "The addition of the commercial interiors product is an important step in USGBC's goal of transforming the design and construction of buildings to one that encourages a collaborative and innovative process that optimizes environmental and economic factors. Its introduction reinforces the serious intent of the LEED program to help the built environment become a catalyst for the ultimate goal of regenerating the natural environment" (*Interiors & Sources,* July/August, 2002).

More info online @
http://www.isdesignet.com/Magazine/J_F'01/index.html

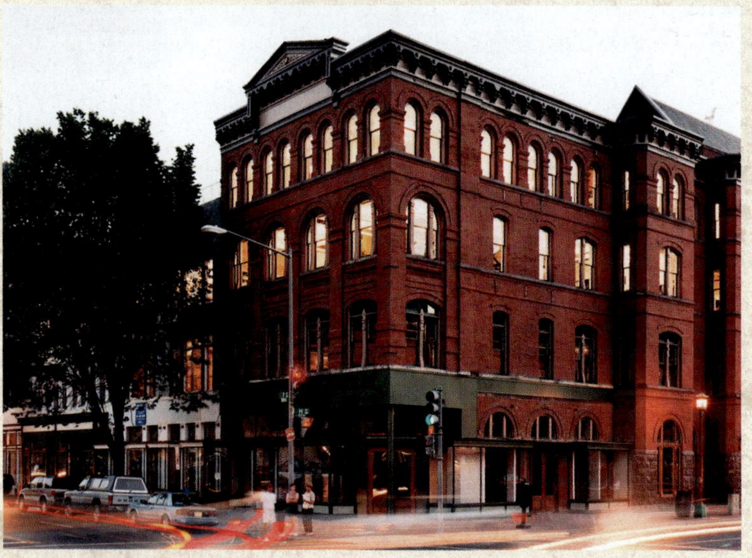

Figure SD11.1 *In this Romanesque turn-of-the-century building, Greenpeace relocated its USA headquarters to the upper floors. The 15,500′ project focused on sustainable design. Greenpeace's mission—to protect the environment—needed to be incorporated into the design solutions. The LEED Green Building Rating System served as a guideline. (Architect/Designer: Envision Design, PLLC. Photograph © Michael Moran.)*

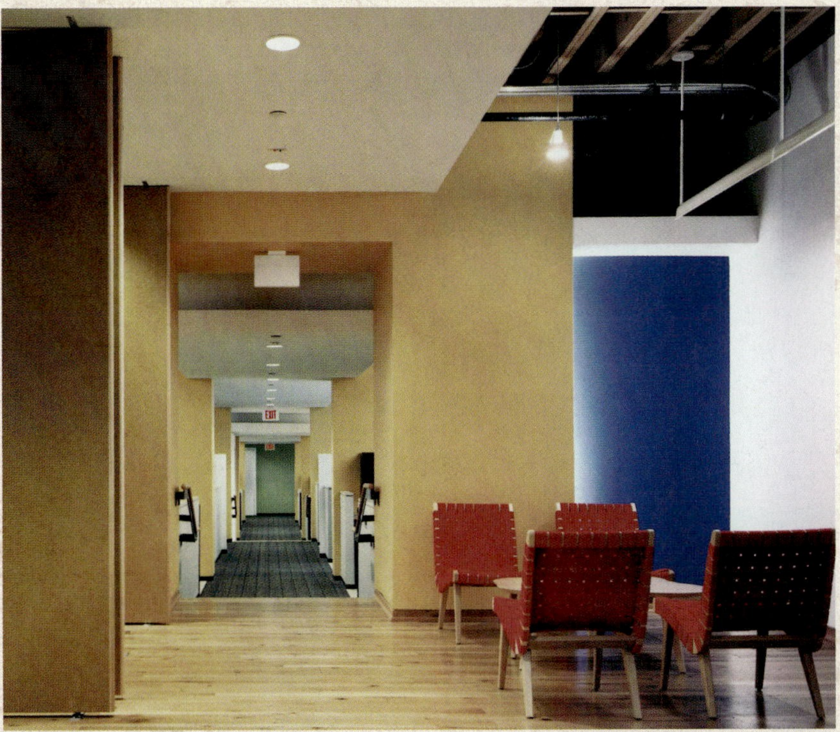

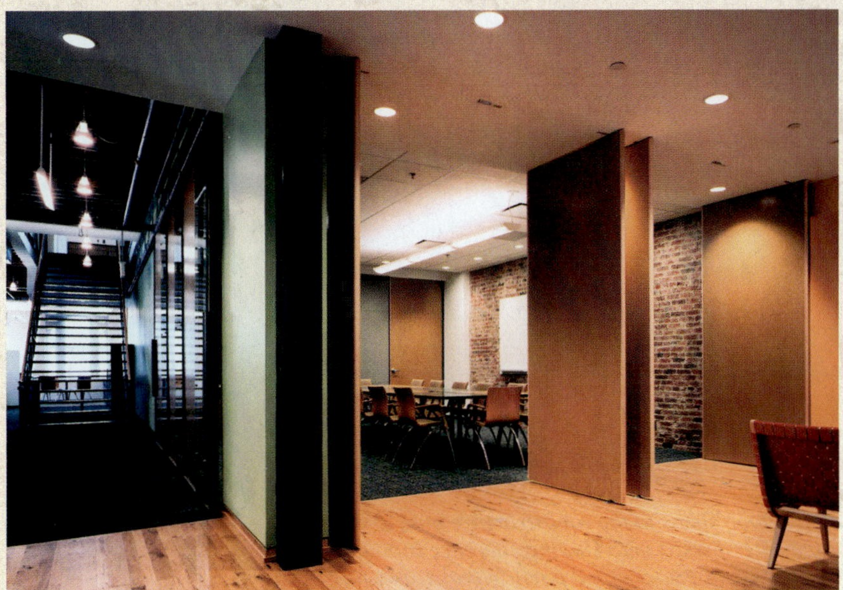

Figure SD11.2 and SD11.3
The main reception area on the third floor opens into the main conference room, allowing for flexible gathering space. Doors are made from wheatboard. The main corridor connects to the adjoining buildings. The stairway leads to the fourth floor. To allow more light to filter into the stairway, area risers are transparent. All woods used are certified by the Forest Stewardship Council (FSC), including the wood used in the Rison reception chairs, custom-made by Knoll for this project. Existing masonry walls were exposed where possible to avoid adding more building materials. Solid surface countertops, made from yogurt containers, were used in the pantry area, as was a refrigerator that runs on less butane than two cigarette lighters. (Architect/Designer: Envision Design, PLLC. Photograph © Michael Moran.)

SUSTAINABLEDESIGN

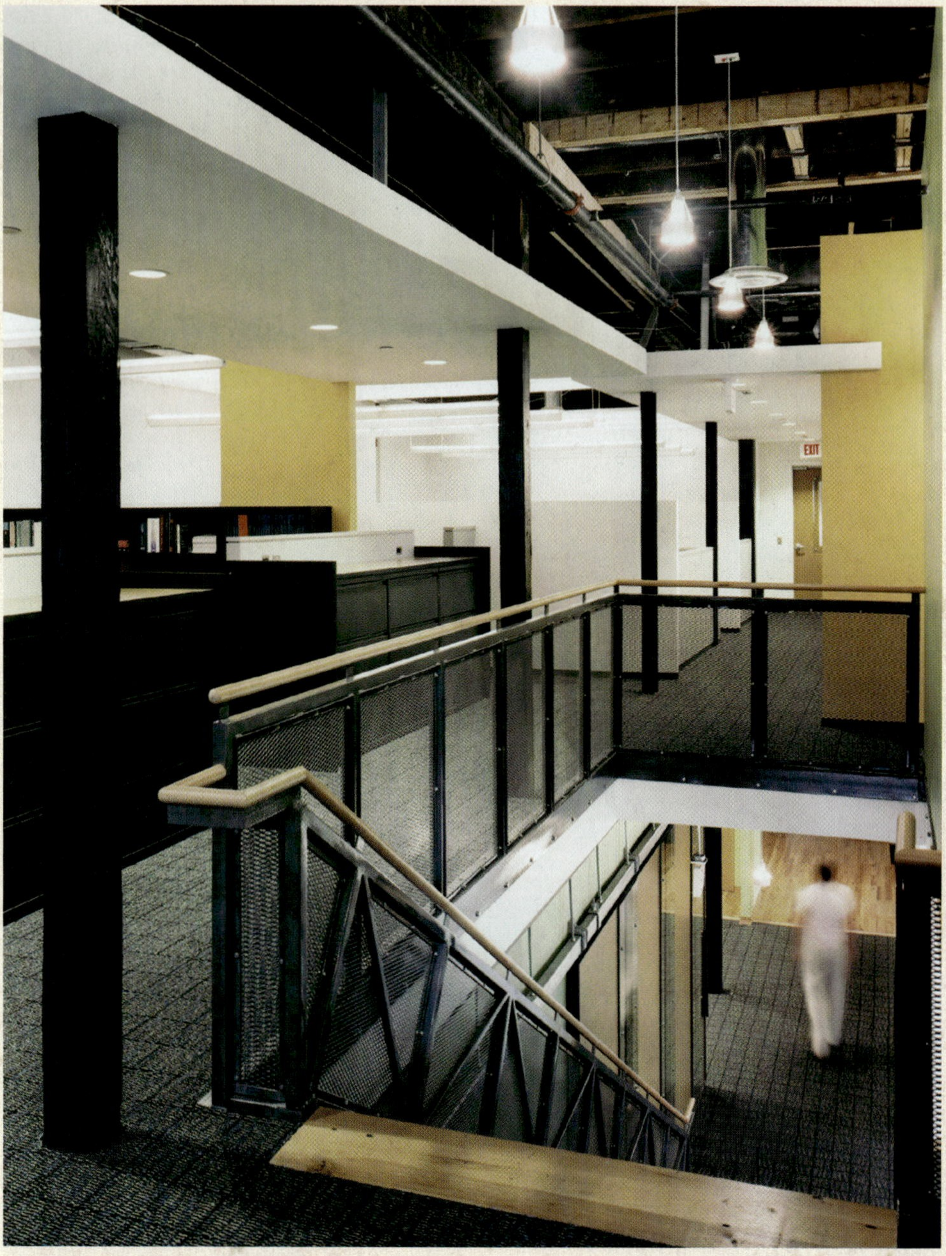

Figures SD11.4 *The fourth floor opens to the roof structure and, like the rest of the facility, uses an open plan concept interspersed with small conference rooms. Open office systems are built from wheatboard and an FSC-certified particleboard, and finished with VOC- and formaldehyde-free coatings. Natural cork is used for tack surfaces. Furnishings, such as filing cabinets, have been refurbished from previous uses. (Architect/Designer: Envision Design, PLLC. Photograph © Michael Moran.)*

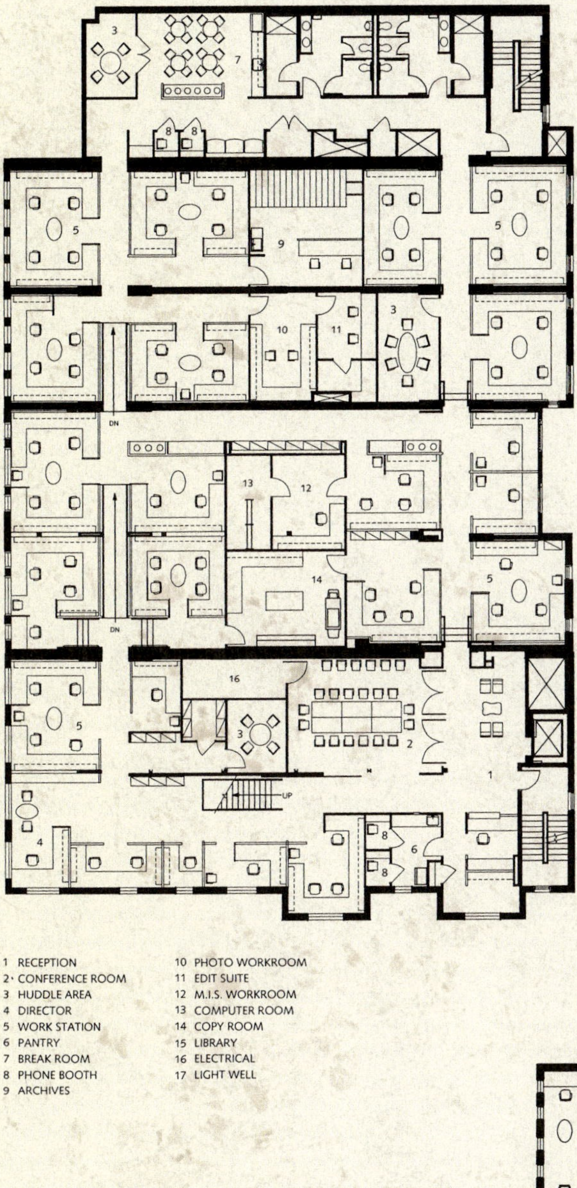

1 RECEPTION
2 CONFERENCE ROOM
3 HUDDLE AREA
4 DIRECTOR
5 WORK STATION
6 PANTRY
7 BREAK ROOM
8 PHONE BOOTH
9 ARCHIVES
10 PHOTO WORKROOM
11 EDIT SUITE
12 M.I.S. WORKROOM
13 COMPUTER ROOM
14 COPY ROOM
15 LIBRARY
16 ELECTRICAL
17 LIGHT WELL

Figures SD11.5 and 11.6 *These two floor plans indicate the complexity of joining buildings. Note that ramps have been installed to accommodate various floor levels and allow for accessibility. Ceiling heights varied greatly. To allow for uniformity and to conceal HVAC and electrical systems, dropped ceilings were set at 9′-6″ above work areas and 8′-0″ in the corridors.*

The design also incorporates solar panels on the roof for electricity and heating water, as well as light sensors and energy efficient lighting. The open office system allowed for 45 percent savings in unused drywall, 61 percent savings in unused doors, and 39 percent savings in lighting. The result is an aesthetically pleasing interior built of sustainable materials in an adaptive use historic building (Bonda, P. Treehuggers with Style. Interiors & Sources, *January-February 2001). (Architect/Designer: Envision Design, PLLC.)*

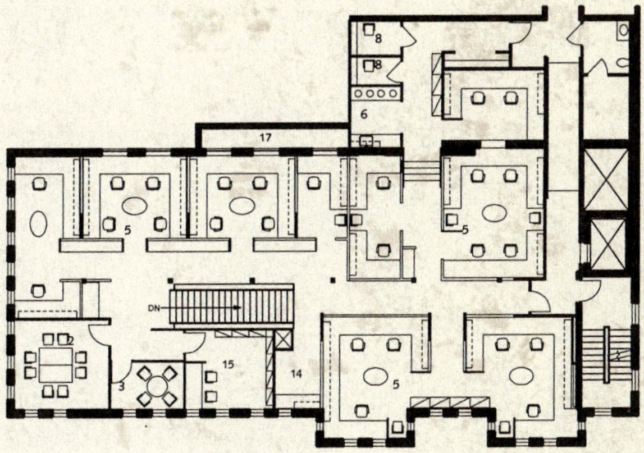

1 RECEPTION
2 CONFERENCE ROOM
3 HUDDLE AREA
4 DIRECTOR
5 WORK STATION
6 PANTRY
7 BREAK ROOM
8 PHONE BOOTH
9 ARCHIVES
10 PHOTO WORKROOM
11 EDIT SUITE
12 M.I.S. WORKROOM
13 COMPUTER ROOM
14 COPY ROOM
15 LIBRARY
16 ELECTRICAL
17 LIGHT WELL

10'-0"
4TH FLOOR

ackgrounds: Doors, Windows, nd Fireplaces

12

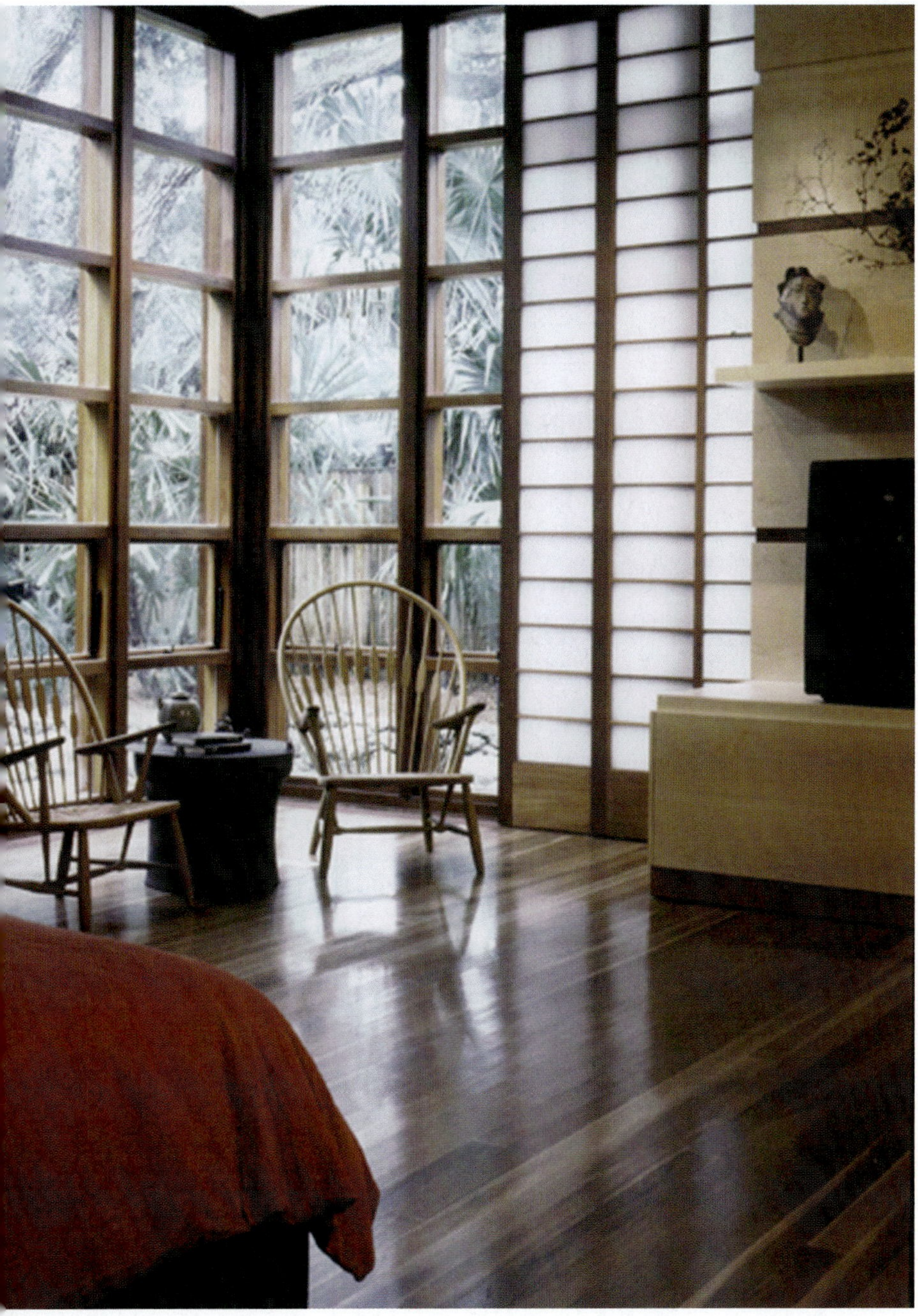

ure 12.1 *These custom floor-to-ceiling windows allow the residents to view their anese garden. Floor-to-ceiling shoji screens glide on tracks and can close off the ner window. The fireplace adds warmth and a focal point. The Peacock chairs, signed by Hans Wegner, complement the crisp, clean, and inviting interior. (Architect: rnard Zyscouich, AIA. Designer: Dennis Jenkins Associates, Inc. Photograph by Nancy binson Watson.)*

Chapter 11 discussed walls and wall trim in relation to materials and appropriate finishes. Another important element in the design of walls is the fenestration. **Fenestration** refers to the arrangement, type, and design of openings in a wall or building. For example, many traditional homes built in the 1980s were called "five over four with a door," which referred to the pattern of windows (plus front door) on the **facade** (the front elevation of a building or object) of a two-story house.

In the interior environment, doors, windows, and even fireplaces create fenestration within a room (Figure 12.1). This chapter reviews the material and design selections for these components. Many times these architectural features are already in place and designers must work around the existing conditions. In other situations, the designer may select the style of the doors and windows. Usually, the designer is responsible for the selection of the window treatment, and occasionally is fortunate enough to be involved in designing the fireplace facade.

DOORS

Doors are powerful design elements in any interior. By their location, doors control traffic flow, which in turn controls the furniture arrangement. Doors provide privacy and sound barriers. They allow for ventilation and temperature control. They provide a sense of safety and security.

The main entrance door is generally the most important element and focal point in the facade. Traditional paneled period doors and leaded glass panels continue to be popular. Many contemporary exterior and interior doors are plain and flush, sheathed on both sides with a veneer. Metal exterior doors with insulating cores are effective in saving energy.

Door Construction

Doors are composed of three basic parts—the *door* itself, t *frame,* and the *hardware.* These components work togetl to form the design of the door and all should be consider when selecting the door style and type. Figure 12.2 indica the various parts of the door.

Doors are available in a variety of styles, but are genera constructed of wood as hollow-core doors or solid-co doors. *Hollow-core doors* are composed of veneers laminat to a frame. *Solid-core doors,* also composed of veneers, ha a particleboard, solid wood, or mineral core, all of whi provide various degrees of fire resistance. Solid-core doo also provide better insulation and acoustical barriers.

Solid-core doors are the only acceptable solution for co mercial interiors and for exterior doors on residences. Me doors are also used in commercial (and occasionally re dential) interiors, particularly in high traffic areas or in sta wells where fire codes dictate their use.

More info online @

http://www.ballandball-us.com/commondoorconstructionterms.htm

Door construction terms

Door Frames

The doorframe supports the door and provides a *stop,* a s and a *jamb,* which allow the door to operate properly (F ure 12.3). Doorframes are made of wood or molded ste Wood frames are generally used for residential interiors; ste frames are more often used in commercial construction. T *stop* is the vertical portion that prevents the door from swi ing both ways. The *sill* is the horizontal member across t

Figure 12.2 *Door parts and terminology.*

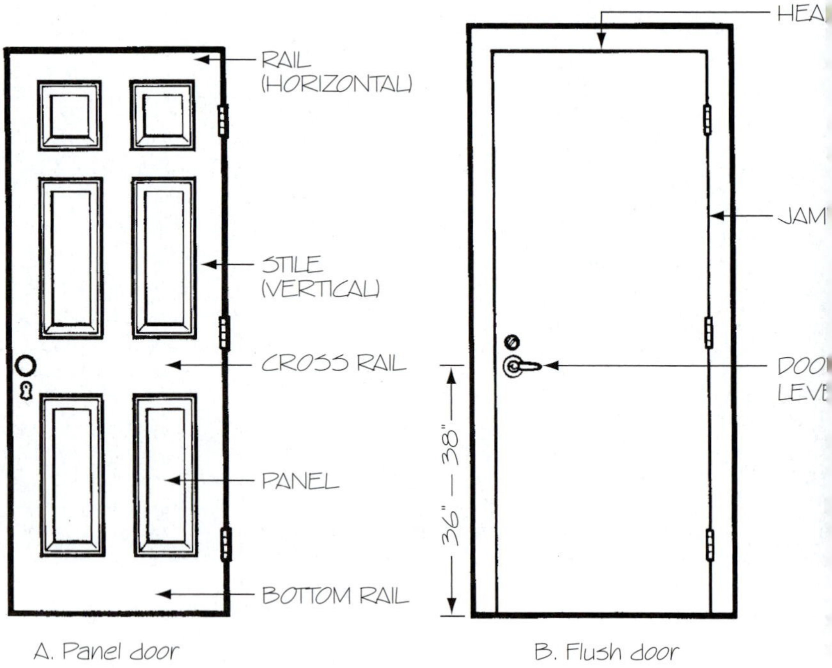

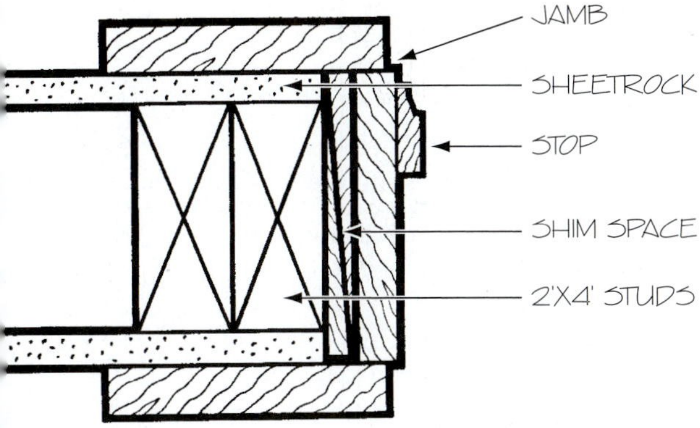

ure 12.3 *Detail of standard wood doorframe.*

ttom of the opening. The *jamb* refers to the vertical mem- :s of the frame that support the door. Some frames also in- de trim around the jamb. In steel construction, the jamb y actually serve as the trim.

oor Hardware

e selection of the appropriate hardware is often left to the ilder, who usually chooses the least expensive product ilable. This may not be the best design solution. Door dware includes *latchsets* or *locksets* (handles), *push plates pull bars, panic hardware, closers, hinges,* and *kickplates.*

nctional Hardware

tchsets and *locksets* are usually shaped in the form of a ob or lever. They include a mechanism to operate the door d to hold it closed, and in the case of a lockset, to lock the or. Knobs are common in most residential environments, t lever handles are much easier to operate. A lever does t require a person to grip and rotate a knob to open a or, but simply to push the lever up or down. Because of ir ease in manipulation, lever handles are required in nmercial spaces. Many high-end residential interiors in- porate lever handles. They also are beneficial in homes the elderly. These handles meet universal design stan- rds.

Push plates or *pull bars* serve the same function as a knob lever, allowing occupants to enter or exit a room. Push tes and pull bars, however, do not require the release of atching mechanism.

Panic hardware and *closers* are usually used in com- rcial environments. *Panic hardware* includes a push bar t extends across the width of the door. When pushed, it eases the latches at the top and bottom of the door, al- ving it to open. *Closers* automatically close a door and are uired by some building codes. Residential environments nmonly use a similar hydraulic device to close storm ors.

Hinges attach the door to the frame and permit the swing- movement of the door. *Kick plates* protect the lower por- n of the door and also can add a decorative touch.

Decorative Hardware

Hardware is obviously functional, but the selection of proper hardware also affects the character of the interior. Hardware can be finished in brass, antique brass, bright chrome, satin chrome, and a variety of other specialized finishes specific to each manufacturer. Flat-finished chrome hardware reflects a more contemporary interior, whereas a bright brass finish is more traditional. Hardware also can be highly decorative, sleek, or finely crafted. Because the same hardware is normally used throughout the interior spaces, it adds a unifying element.

Hardware should also "feel good to the touch." This is referred to as the hand of the object (as discussed in Chapter 9 on textiles). Sharp edges and rough corners are inappropriate; a firm smooth finish would welcome a visitor.

More info online @

http://www.bernards.co.uk/door_furniture_period_styles_faq.htm
Historic decorative door hardware

Types of Doors by Operation

As seen in Figure 12.4, the three basic types of doors are swinging, folding, and sliding. These doors and their components may be constructed of wood, steel, aluminum, plastic, glass, or a combination of these materials, depending on design, location, and function.

Swinging Doors

Swinging doors are easy to install and operate, and are available in standard sizes. Most doors are single-hinged and swing only one way; a double-hinged door swings both ways. The latter is convenient between kitchens and dining rooms. A swinging door placed near a corner, with the arc swinging toward the adjacent wall, preserves wall space and directs traffic along the side of the room. Pairs of **French doors** are glass-paned single-hinged swinging doors that open the same way, leading to an outside area or an adjoining room. The **Dutch door** is a single-hinged door divided horizontally, making it possible to have ventilation and visual communication from the upper half while the lower half is closed.

Swinging doors are considered right-handed or left-handed. To determine the swing, walk through the door so that you are pushing the door open. If the hinges are on the right, it is a right-hand door, and vice versa (Figure 12.5).

Folding Doors

Folding doors save space in a residential setting. They are available in sizes from a single door to a full wall divider, and they may be attached at both top and bottom or only at the top. Made in a wide variety of styles (such as louvered) and materials (including plastic and fiberglass), they are flexible and relatively inexpensive.

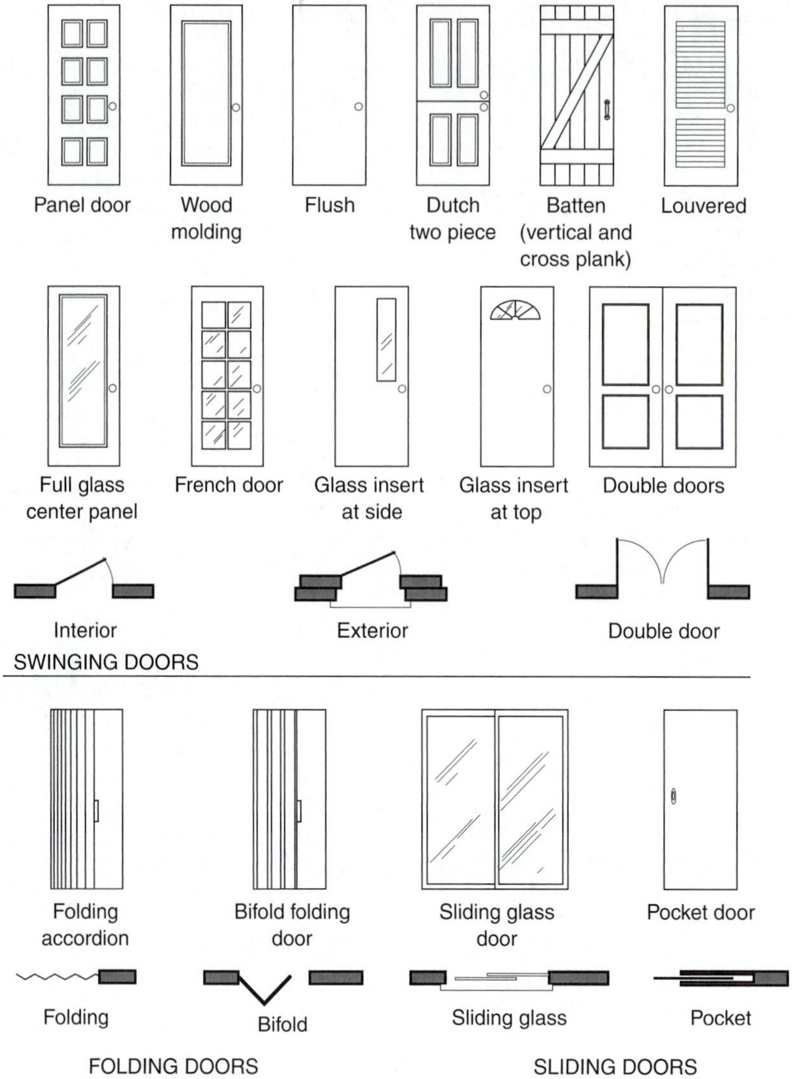

Figure 12.4 *Elevations and plan views of various types of doors.*

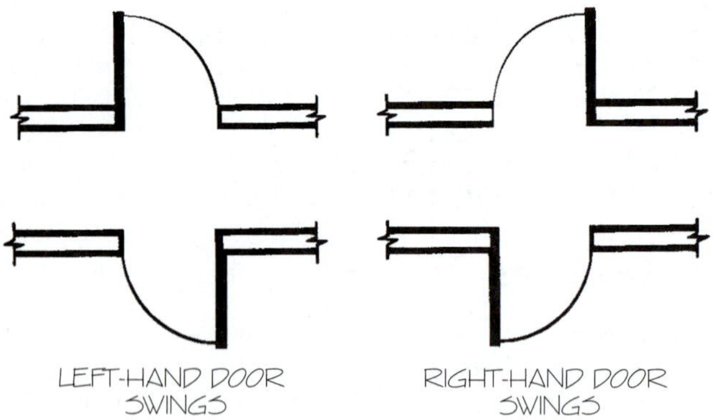

Figure 12.5 *Plan view of left-hand and right-hand door swings.*

Sliding Doors

Sliding doors used on the exterior may be part of a glass w or installed in pairs that slide one behind the other. They a popular in contemporary houses to make the patio or g den a visual part of the living area. Sliding glass doors shou be made of safety glass.

Interior sliding doors (known as *pocket doors*) slide int pocket in the wall, or when paired may slide behind ea other. Although not as flexible as folding doors, sliding do (like folding doors) are great space savers for residential u They can provide complete or partial privacy, depending their material, but they can be difficult to operate, especia for the physically challenged. The traditional Japanese sh sliding panel is appropriate in both traditional and mode interiors, serving multiple uses (Figure 12.6).

More info online @

http://www.selectmillwork.com/doors/ Images of door styles

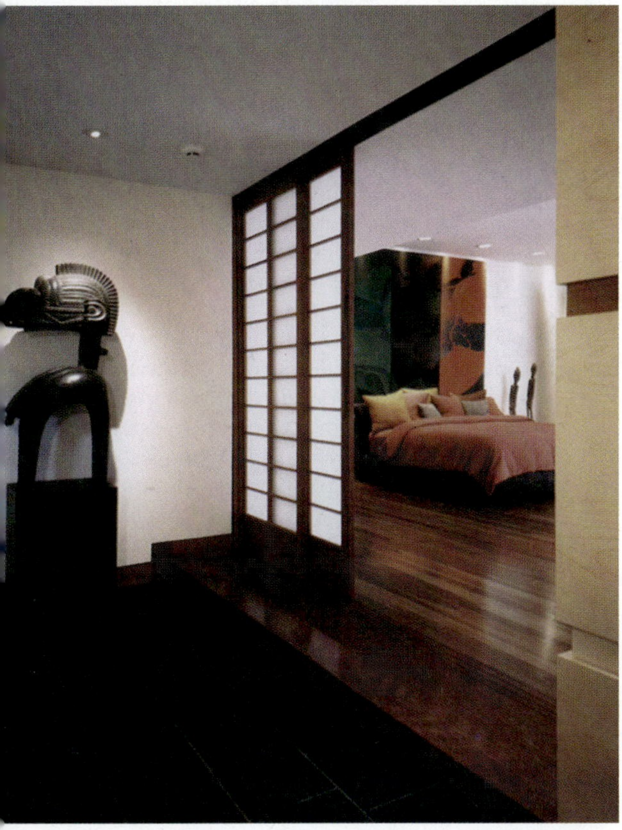

gure 12.6 *In this master suite addition, the client requested e serenity of a Japanese setting. Shoji screens, sliding along a 1/8″ slot recessed into the wood floor, were used in place a typical door. Woods, warm colors, and clean lines centuated the Zen-like retreat. Additional shots of the droom can be seen in Figure 12.1. (Architect: Bernard scouich, AIA. Designer: Dennis Jenkins Associates, Inc. otograph by Nancy Robinson Watson.)*

oor Design and Placement

doors are well placed to preserve wall space and direct affic efficiently, they present no problem. But if a room has surplus of doors, it may be necessary to camouflage them. ne option (if other passageways exist) is to remove the nges and fill the opening with shelves for books and small t objects. Relocating a door is also possible, and the result ay be worth the effort and expense.

Door treatment depends on the design and style of the om. Doors are often painted to blend with the walls; wood ors may be stained or left natural. If a door has a particu- rly good design, painting it a contrasting color may augment e room's decoration. When walls are paneled, doors may nform to the walls or be painted in a contrasting color.

Doors come in standard widths. The most common are 2′- ″, 2′-4″, 2′-6″, and 3′-0″. All exterior doors should be a min- num of 3′-0″ wide. Interior residential doors are commonly -6″. Standard door height is 6′-8″, but doors are available at are 7′-0″ and 8′-0″. Additionally, doors may be custom esigned to fit any space or shape.

As discussed in Chapter 6, barrier-free design requires doors to have a clear opening of 32″. To obtain this dimension, doors used in handicap-accessible areas must be 36″ wide. Additionally, the pull side of the door must have at least 18″ clear of any obstruction; the push side needs 12″ clear (see Figure 6.5).

WINDOWS

Although glass walls were known to the ancient Egyptians and Romans, historically, windows (or the "wind's eye") were merely small cutouts in the walls of a house. Over the years, many types of windows have been planned as an integral part of the structural design of a building. Although window treatments change with style trends, they are most attractive when attuned to the architectural spirit of the structure, both exterior and interior.

Windows perform three primary functions: They admit light, provide ventilation, and enhance visual communication. Even though light and airflow can now be mechanically controlled, and windows are not absolutely necessary, planning an interior without windows seems inconceivable. There are no substitutes for fresh air, natural light, and an outdoor view to create a psychological association with nature and provide a sense of well being.

The window is a conspicuous element in both the exterior and interior design of a house. As a source of interior light, the window is the first point to which the eye is drawn during the daytime, while at night, a lighted window is the first thing seen from the outside.

The window is an important architectural and decorative element in a room. Traditionally, windows with small panes were often symmetrically placed in the facade of the house. With the development of modern architecture and technology, new types of window openings were planned as integral parts of the basic design.

Window Construction

Window terminologies are identified in Figure 12.7. Windows are composed of panes of glass. A casement window has only one pane, whereas a sash window is composed of at least two panes, one at the top and one at the bottom. Some sash windows have several panes and may be referred to based on their number of panes, such as six over six (written "6/6"). Originally, these panes were separated by wood **mullions** and **muntins** (Figure 12.7). *Mullions* form the vertical divisions of the panes; *muntins* form the horizontal divisions. It is a common practice today to divide the panes with pop-in plastic mullions and muntins. Although the plastic versions are not as rich looking as the wood, they do make cleaning the panes easier.

Glass

Architectural glass is available in single, double, or triple panes and is technically termed *annealed glass*. When the window consists of double or triple panes of glass that are separated by a layer of gas (air) that serves as an insulator, the glass is

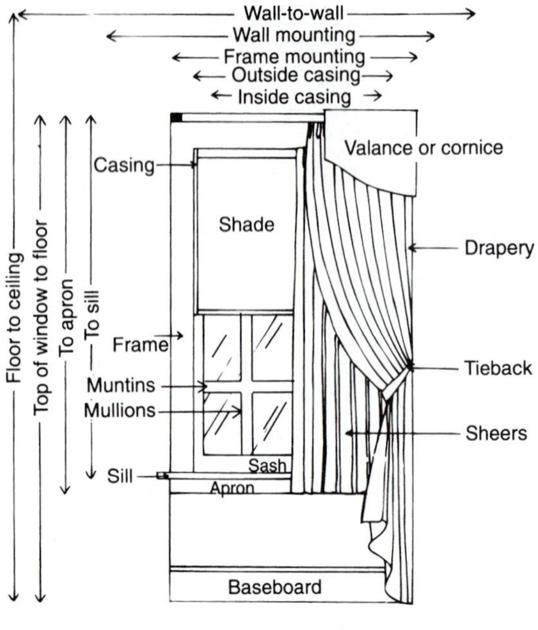

Figure 12.7 *Window parts and treatment placement.*

termed *insulated glass.* The air space also helps to prevent condensation on the glass. Insulated glass is sometimes called *thermopane glass.* For a further discussion of energy efficient glass, see "Sustainable Design: Low-E Glass."

Glass can also be *tempered,* meaning that if it were break, it would shatter into pebble-sized pieces instead large sharp-edged pieces. *Laminated glass* is actually put t gether with a thin film laminated between the layers of glas This is an excellent choice for overhead glazing.

In fire corridors or other hallways that are designed f fire egress, *wired glass* is used. Wired glass holds togeth when subjected to high temperatures or impacts.

Frames

Glass panes are supported by wood, metal, or plastic frame Each has particular advantages and disadvantages. *Woo* shrinks, swells, requires a protective finish, and is the mo expensive. It discourages moisture condensation, howev and emits less heat than does metal. Wood also has a rich appearance than metal or plastic. *Metal* is strong and do not shrink or swell perceptibly. Except for aluminum ar stainless steel, however, it requires protective paint ar causes moisture condensation in cold weather. Newer met windows are designed to eliminate excessive heat loss ar condensation. *Plastic* or *vinyl* is stable and resists heat ar cold, but may look inexpensive.

More info online @

http://www.onlinetools.com/cwd/vinylcut.html Cut section of a window and glossary of window terms

SUSTAINABLEDESIGN

Low-E Glass

Some windows can save energy without being bulky and heavy. Manufacturers are making glazed windows with a transparent, nonglare coating on the inside layers to help slow the transmission of heat energy through glass. Such windows are made with low-E (low-emissivity) coatings. They help interior environments stay more comfortable.

Low-E glass treats sunlight's different wavelengths in different ways. The sun's energy spectrum is divided into three ranges of wavelengths: ultraviolet, visible light, and infrared, which can be felt as heat. (These heat-generating infrared rays are further divided into long wavelengths and short wavelengths.) The challenge is to let in visible light and to control infrared transmittance.

Low-E glass, with its low-emissivity pyrolytic coating, lets in approximately 95 percent as much visible light as ordinary insulated glass, allowing the interior to look bright and the window to appear transparent. However, low-E glass reflects most of the long-wave infrared energy back toward its source, helping to keep summer heat out and winter heat in (Figure SD12.1).

Performance can be even better with the addition of argon gas (a superinsulator) between the layers of glass in the window unit. As a result of these new energy-efficient developments, windows can be practical as well as beautiful.

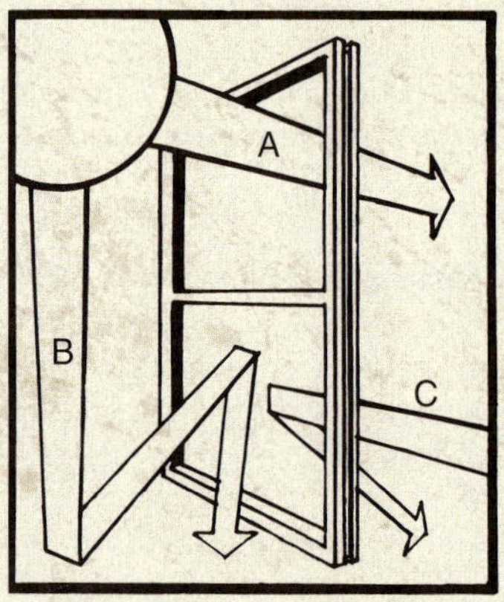

Figure SD12.1 *A: Low-E glass, coated on the inside layers, allows natural light and short-wave heat energy to enter freely. B: In summer, long-wave heat energy radiating from objects is reflected, lowering cooling costs. C: In winter, internal long-wave heat energy is reflected, lowering heating costs. (Courtesy of PPG Industries.)*

More info online @

http://www.efficientwindows.org/ Energy efficient window site

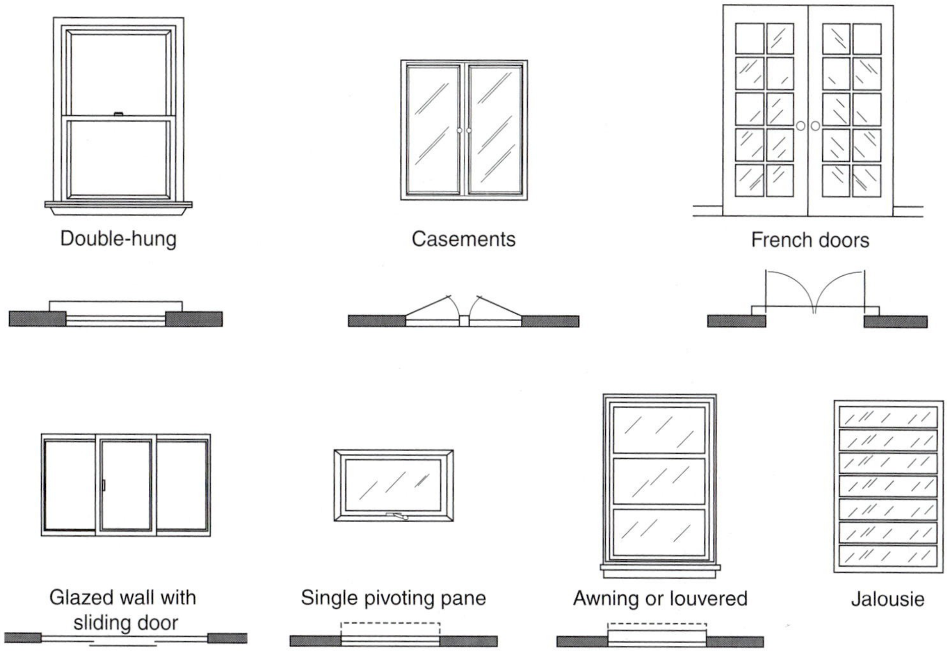

gure 12.8 *Various types of movable windows.*

ypes of Windows

indows are available in standard sizes and can be movable, ationary, or a combination of both.

lovable Windows

ovable windows open to permit ventilation. Some of the ost common movable window designs are illustrated in gure 12.8.

Double-hung windows are made up of two **sashes** that ay be raised or lowered to provide 50 percent ventilation. ney are simple and inexpensive. *Casements* may swing inward or outward and permit up to 100 percent ventilation. (In-swinging casements must have special window treatments designed not to interfere with the window's operation.) *Horizontal sliding windows* may use two sliding panes or a large stationary central pane with a sliding pane on either side or other combination. These windows work like a sliding glass door. *Awning* (or louvered) and *jalousie windows* consist of strips of glass, hinged at the top or bottom, that open outward or inward (Figure 12.9). Strips in jalousies are narrower than in the awning type. *Single-pivoting windows* are raised for ventilation by means of a hinged side. These windows are most often used as skylights or in light wells.

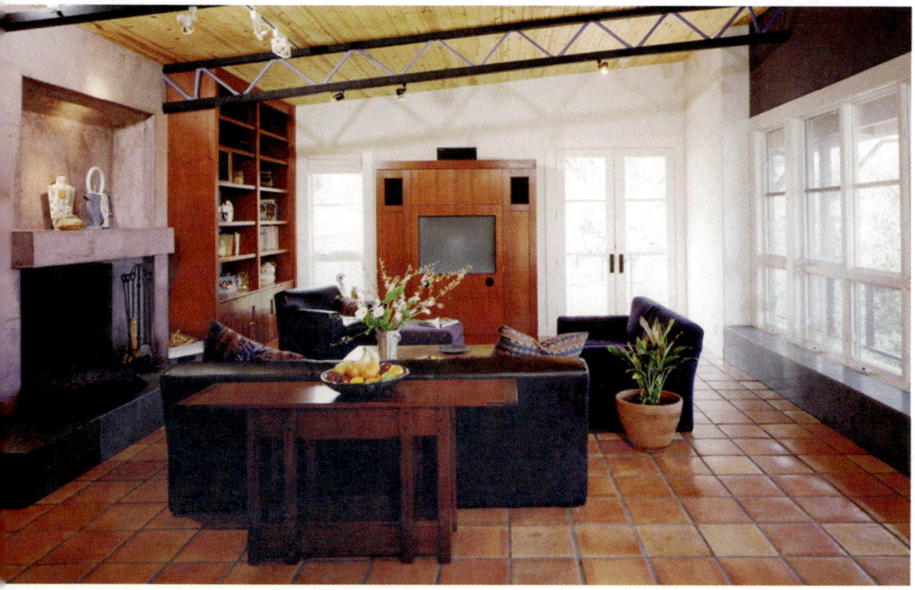

Figure 12.9 *This contemporary interior uses louvered windows on the lower portion of the windows for ventilation. Custom doors were designed to complement the window design. Note the concrete fireplace, shed roof, and custom multimedia unit. (Architect/Designer: Lippert & Lippert Design, Palo Alto, CA. Photograph by Quadra Focus.)*

Fixed glazing (another name for a flat window) is a common feature of today's contemporary homes and may extend from floor to ceiling or begin a short distance above the floor. Hexagons, circles, and other geometrically shaped windows are occasionally used to provide a point of interest and additional light, and are also considered fixed glazing. The *bow window* is a smooth, sweeping curve of multiple panes. In *arched windows* the upper part of a rectangular opening is topped by an arch.

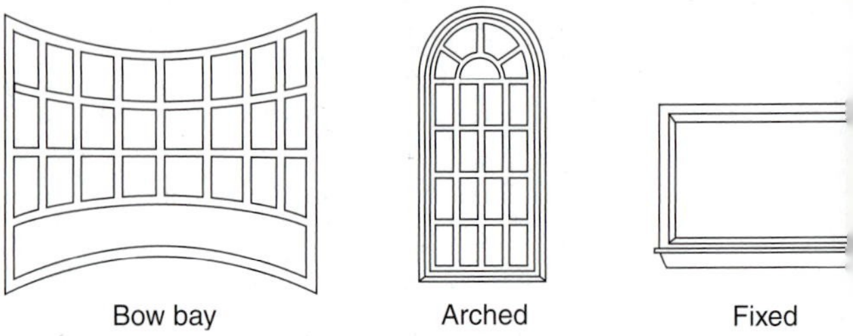

Figure 12.10 *Various types of stationary windows.*

Stationary Windows

Stationary windows are built as an integral part of the wall construction. They may be made of plain or nonglare glass. Common stationary windows include fixed glazing, bow, and arch (Figure 12.10).

Combination and Custom Windows

Many window types combine movable and stationary sections (Figure 12.11).

The *picture window* is composed of fixed glazing, usually with movable end sections. *Palladian windows* feature a central arched window flanked by two smaller windows, often with movable sections. This window type is associated with the Federal style and today is used in a wide variety of settings. The *angled bay window* is made up of three or more windows that angle out of the room. The central pane may be stationary with movable side panes.

Clerestory windows may be straight or slanting windows set at the ceiling or high in a wall. Operable windows at this level provide for excellent air circulation when combined with windows opened at lower levels. The *corner windo* consists of two windows of any style that meet or almc meet in a corner. A single corner window can be thought as a double window and treated accordingly. *Ranch* or *str windows* can be any style and are wide and shallow. Th are set far enough above the floor to allow furniture to be s against the wall, but they are not flush to the ceiling. *Dorm windows* are located in alcoves projecting out from the roc Any style of window may be located in the dormer.

Skylights (windows placed in the ceiling) may be single grouped panels of clear or translucent glass or plastic, either f or domed, and fixed or movable for ventilation. Skylights kitchens, laundries, and bathrooms have the special advanta of providing adequate daylight for inside rooms. In small area light from above can expand visual space and make the sky ar trees part of a room. The skylight window has a number of di advantages, however, including problems with water seepag insulation, and cleaning. Also, skylights present a security pro lem unless protected by safety-wired glass or other measures

Figure 12.11 *Combination window types.*

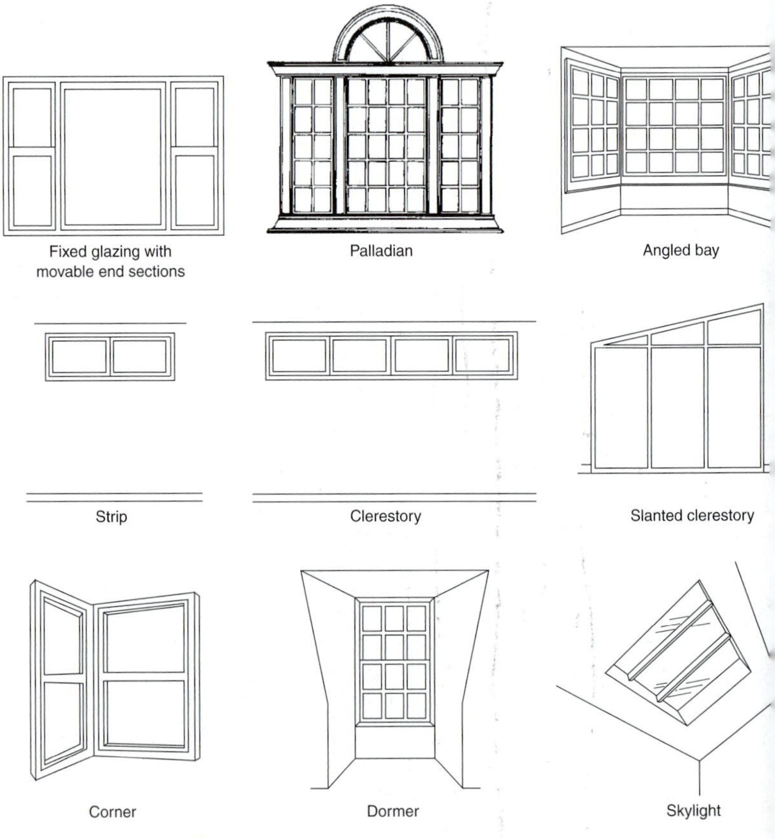

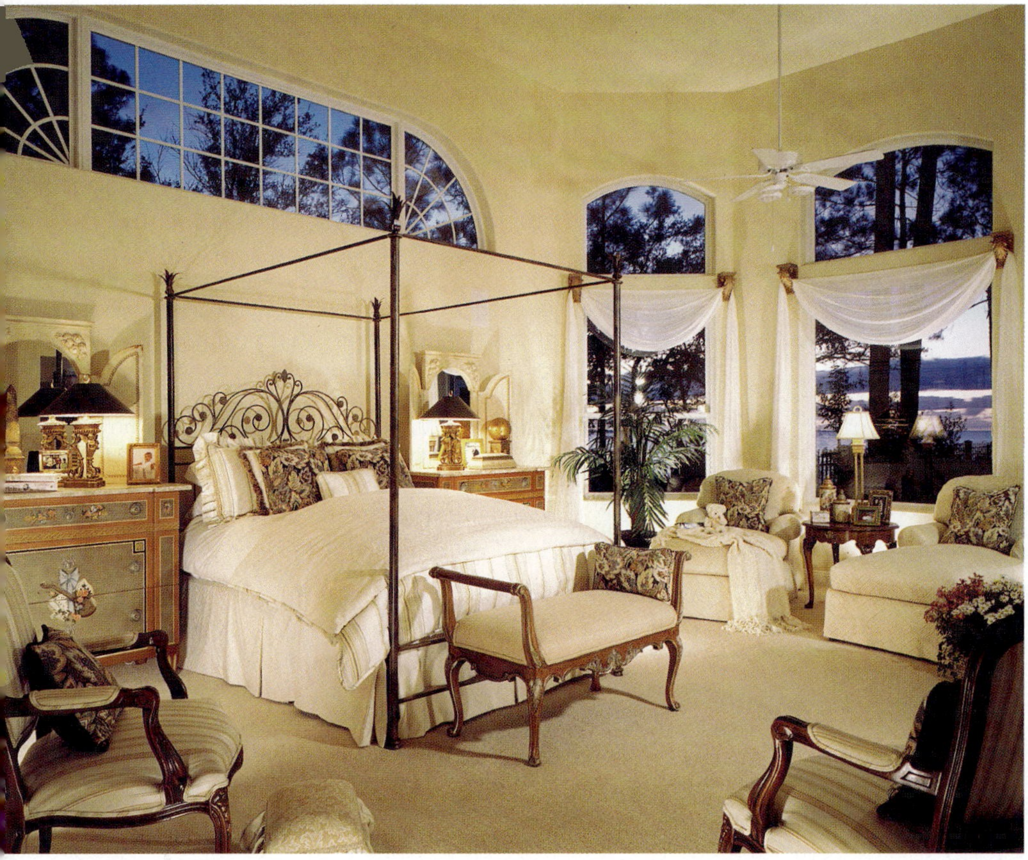

Figure 12.12 *Custom-designed fixed windows draw the outdoors into this eclectic French master bedroom. (Designer: Susan Lovelace, Lovelace Interiors. Photograph by Jack Gardner.)*

Architects and designers often create custom-designed indows for clients, as shown in Figure 12.12. They can be f various sizes and shapes and may be movable, stationary, r combinations of both types.

ore info online @

tp://www.pella.com/learn/glossary/ Pella's Glossary of terms for oors and windows

tp://www.hometime.com/projects/howto/windoor/pc3wdgl.htm esidential glossary of door and window terms

Hard Window Treatments

All window treatments fall into two broad categories: *hard* and *soft*. Deciding on an appropriate window treatment from the almost unlimited options available can be challenging.

Blinds

Figure 12.13 shows several types of blinds. *Venetian blinds* were popular in ancient times, in colonial America, and during the Art Deco period. Today, modern adaptations of the blind have again become popular window treatments in both traditional- and contemporary-style homes and commercial

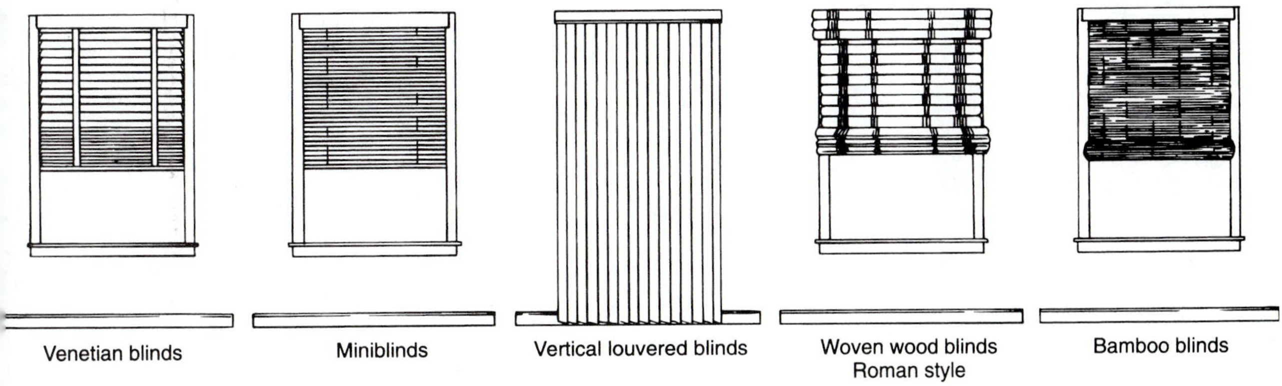

gure 12.13 *Types of blinds.*

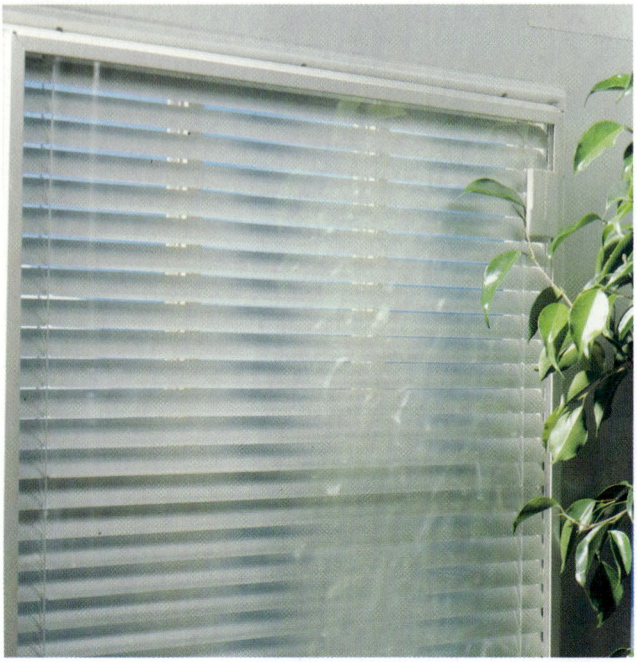

Figure 12.14 *These blinds are located between the pieces of glass within the window. This design is particularly beneficial for glass doors and anywhere dust is a problem. (Copyright: Permission has been granted by Hunter Douglas, Inc. to use copyrighted designs. Designs © Hunter Douglas, Inc. Photograph by Joe Stawdart.)*

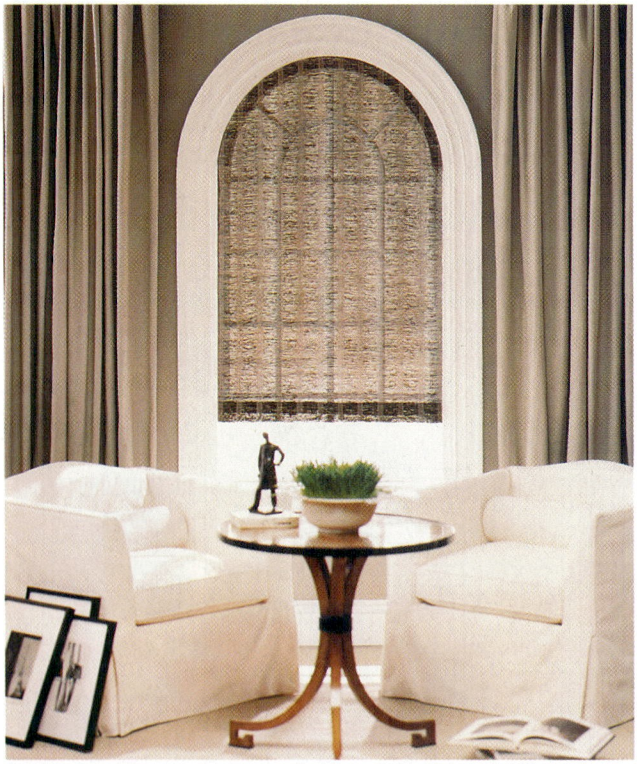

Figure 12.15 *These hand-woven shades conform to the arch-shaped window and provide contrast in texture to this formal interior. (Courtesy of Conrad Handwoven Window Coverings.)*

settings. In most cases, blinds are constructed of aluminur
stainless steel, plastic, or wood. (The wooden slat blin
have been so popular that they are generally known just
wooden blinds.) These horizontally or sometimes vertical
arranged strips can be adjusted precisely for light and p
vacy. Blinds can be mounted on the inside or outside of tl
window casing. They provide a clean, streamlined look ar
are available in a wide range of colors and sizes.

Miniblinds are narrow (about 1 inch wide) and create
sleek, trim look. Miniblinds are strong, lightweight, and con
complete, requiring no supplementary hardware. Used alor
they can add sophistication to a formal interior or be at hon
in a modest room. Miniblinds can be combined with a wic
range of draw and side draperies for a more traditional loc
These blinds are difficult to dust and clean; however, wi
dows are made with miniblinds enclosed between two pan
of glass to help eliminate dust problems (Figure 12.14). Th
style, although expensive, provides better insulation. *Micr
miniblinds* have slats that measure about 1/2 inch. They a
not as durable as miniblinds.

Vertical blinds are made of vertical strips that pivot at tl
top or at both the top and bottom. When drawn, the stri
overlap to provide maximum privacy and light control. Us
ally made of plastic or metal, vertical blinds may have a d
ferent color on each side or may be covered with wallpap
or fabric. They are also available in wood. Vertical blin
provide a uniform, tailored appearance, and work partic
larly well on sliding glass doors.

Woven split-wood and *bamboo blinds* are slats of wood i
terwoven with colored or plain yarn. Woven split-wood ar
bamboo blinds allow some light through, and their war
natural texture is appropriate for many rooms and vario
styles (Figure 12.15). They may be used alone or combin
with draperies and top treatments. This type of blind is rais
by rolling or pleating.

Shutters

Figure 12.16 illustrates several types of shutters. *Louver
wood shutters* have been used since ancient times and co
tinue to be used. They can substitute for drapery, be adjust
(by means of a vertical wooden support) for light and
(Figure 12.17), and are remarkably versatile. Shutters con
in standard sizes and can be custom made to fit any windo
Dark colors show dust more readily. Shutters can be used
tiers, have panels that are treated in the center with shirr
fabric, have raised panel designs, or have vertical louve
Plantation shutters have larger slats and are adaptable
many styles and window types. Although shutters can be e
pensive, they do provide good insulation.

Shoji Screens

The traditional Japanese shoji window or screen, with woo
mullions and muntins supporting rice-paper panes, can sli
or be stationary and may be used to establish an Asian or co
temporary theme. Like the shoji doors previously discusse
the translucent rice-paper panes do not allow a view but
provide daytime privacy. Shoji screens are often fitted on
track to slide in front of a glass window (see Figure 12.1).

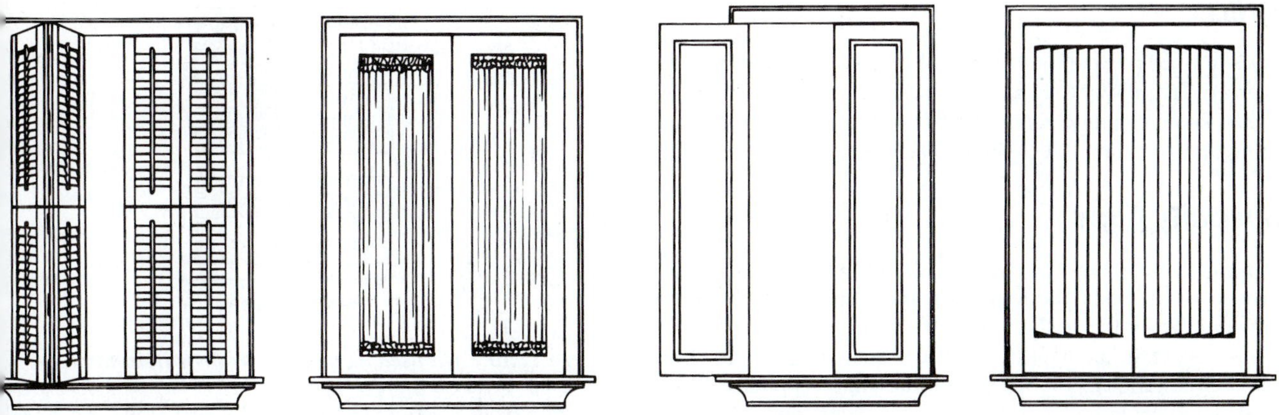

ure 12.16 *Types of shutters.*

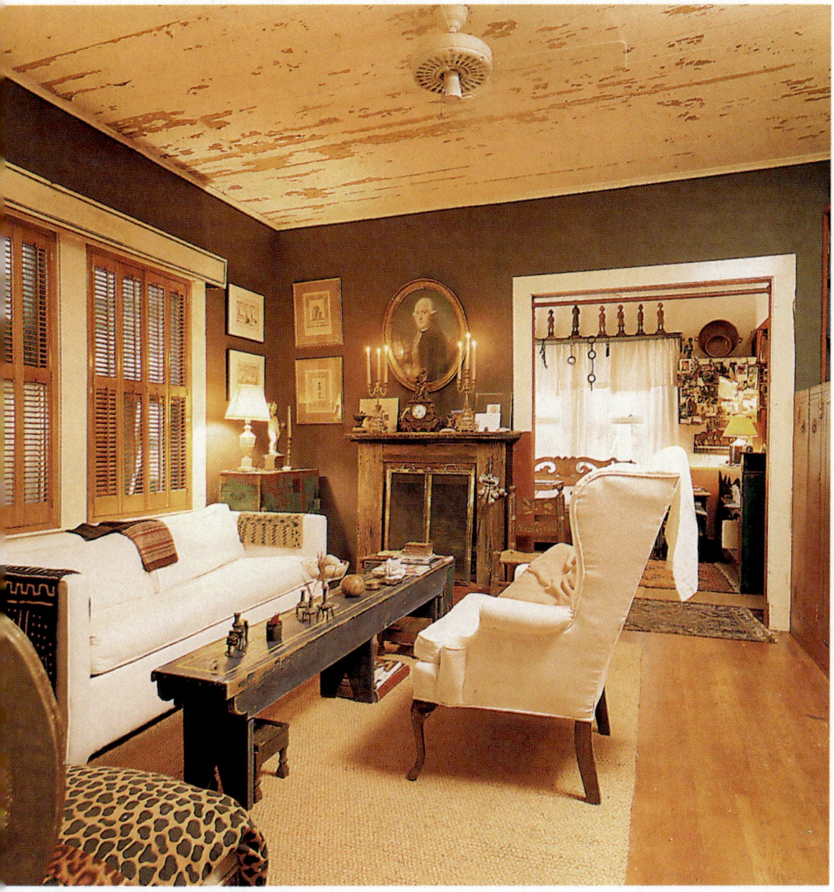

Figure 12.17 *This historical interior uses stained wood shutters to blend with the warm rich interior space. (Designer: Richard Warbolic. Photograph by Gross & Daley.)*

Grills

Widely used in Spain and the Middle East for centuries, the pierced or grillwork screen can be an exotic window treatment. Privacy can be secured while light filters through, creating an appealing effect (Figure 12.18).

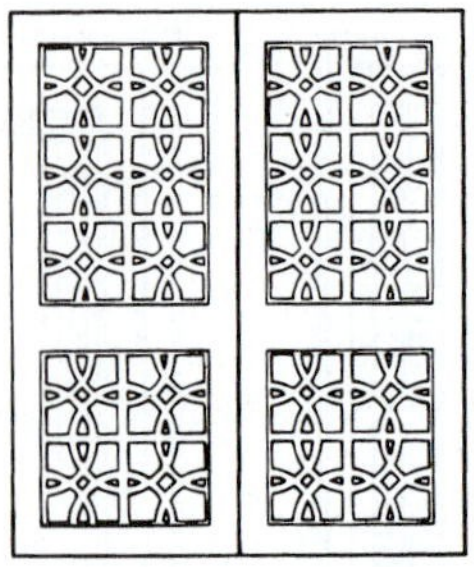

Figure 12.18 *Grill used as window or door treatment.*

Specialty Glass

Art glass, including *beveled* and *stained glass windows,* are common in both modern and traditional environments. *Beveled glass* refers to the angle ground into the edge of plate glass, reflecting the light in colorful ways. *Stained glass* is the art of arranging colorful pieces of glass into a pattern. Pieces of beveled or stained glass are joined by lead, zinc, or copper.

Beveled and stained glass panels are available for doors, windows, **sidelights** (windows beside doors), **transoms** (windows over doorways or above larger windows), and skylights. Used for the latter, they bring a brilliant glow into a room. Private craftworkers can provide custom designs (Figure 12.19).

Glass block (also used for wall construction) is a transl cent block of irregular glass, widely used during the perio of Art Deco and International Style in the 1920s and '3C Glass block is also appropriate in contemporary commerci and residential environments (Figure 12.20). The bloc come in a variety of sizes and shapes and are made of tw hollow half pieces joined together. The surface quality of tl

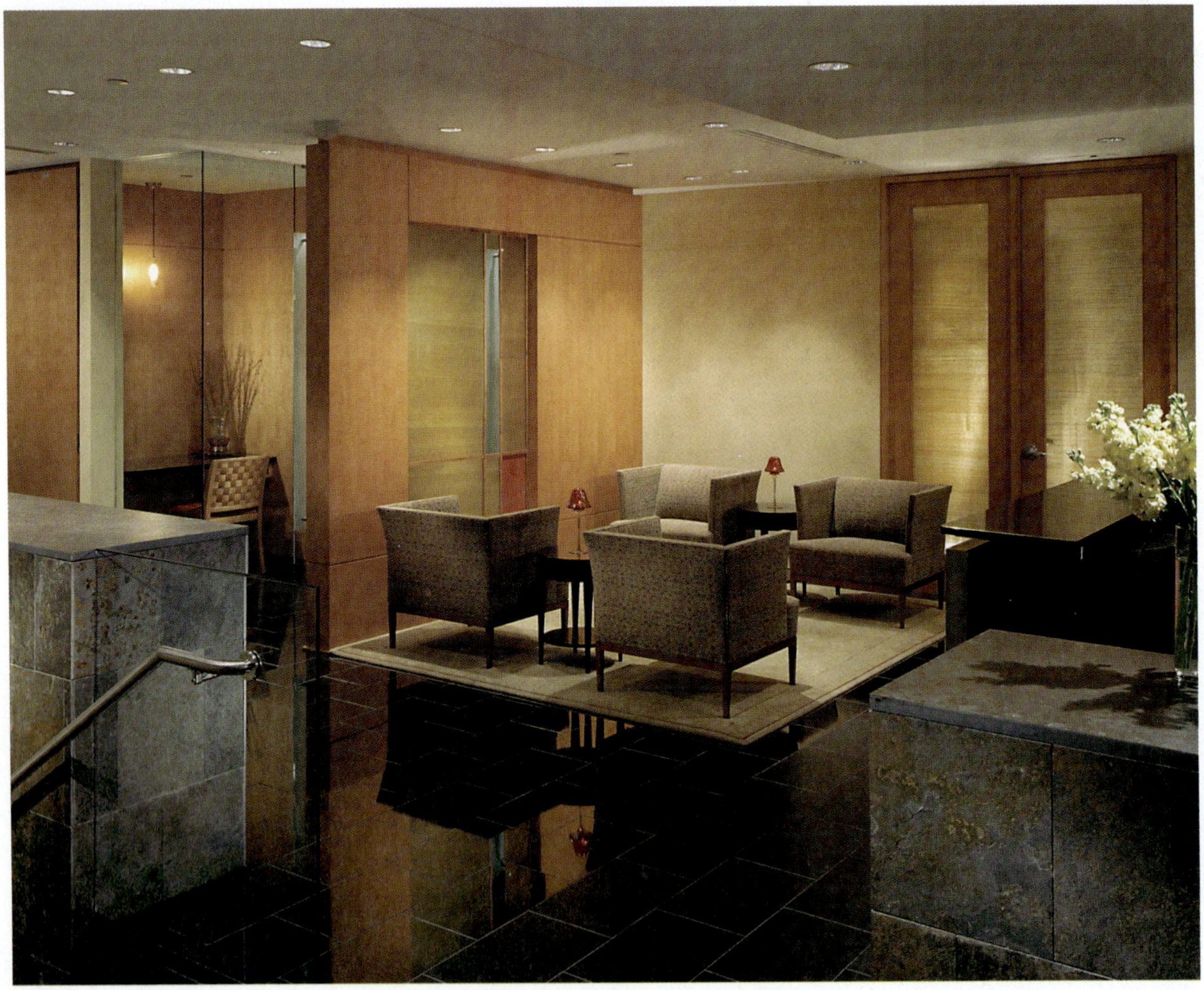

Figure 12.19 *In this lobby interior, emphasis was placed on creating an inviting environment. Glass doors and full height wood and glass doors provide clean, crisp lines that are softened by wood and warm colors. Details in stair railings, flooring, custom-colored glass, and masonry work add to the character of the interior. (Designer: Perkins & Will. Photograph © Rion Rizzo/Creative Sources Photography.)*

ıss can be plain, frosted, mottled, or textured. A few com-ınies produce glass block in triangular shapes to provide chitects and designers with more design options.

An alternative to glass block is *acrylic block*. It is up to 70 rcent lighter than glass block and is available in similar zes and shapes. Acrylic blocks are joined together with an ernal clip system and are sealed with a caulking compound at can include a mold inhibitor. Acrylic walls are assembled meet specifications before installation. The lighter weight d ease of assemblage is a great advantage over glass ocks; however, acrylic can be scratched and gouged.

Sandblasted and *etched glass* can create a variety of osted" designs. Such glass is often used as a design solu-n when a client specifies the need for privacy. Manufac-ers also supply films that can be placed on existing glass areas where sandblasting or chemical etching would be messy. The films are meticulously cut in a variety of de-ns (Figure 12.21).

Liquid crystal is a glass technology that can change ar-itectural glass from transparent to translucent and back ain at the flick of a switch. A thin film coated with liquid ystal droplets is laminated between panels of heat-engthened flat glass. When electricity is sent through the nel, the liquid crystals align to transmit light and the panel comes clear like a normal window. When the power is itched off, the liquid crystals scatter and the panel be-mes translucent. These glass panels are marketed for use corporate conference rooms, offices, and presentation fa-ities where the ability to see through glass normally is de-ed, but at certain times privacy is required. As the price of liquid crystal panels decreases, their use in residential ap-plications should increase.

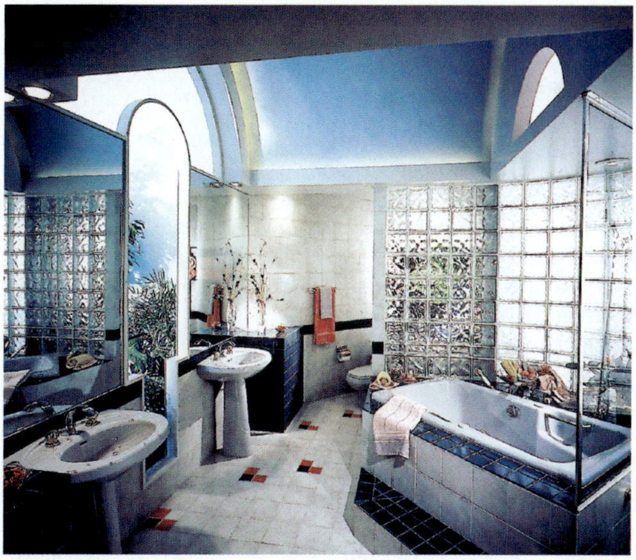

Figure 12.20 *Translucent glass blocks in this large contemporary bath area allow additional light into the space without sacrificing privacy. (Courtesy of Pittsburgh Corning Corporation.)*

Bare windows are sometimes beautiful in themselves and if privacy is not a problem, concealing them in layers of drapery can be a mistake. Triple glazing can help control en-ergy costs.

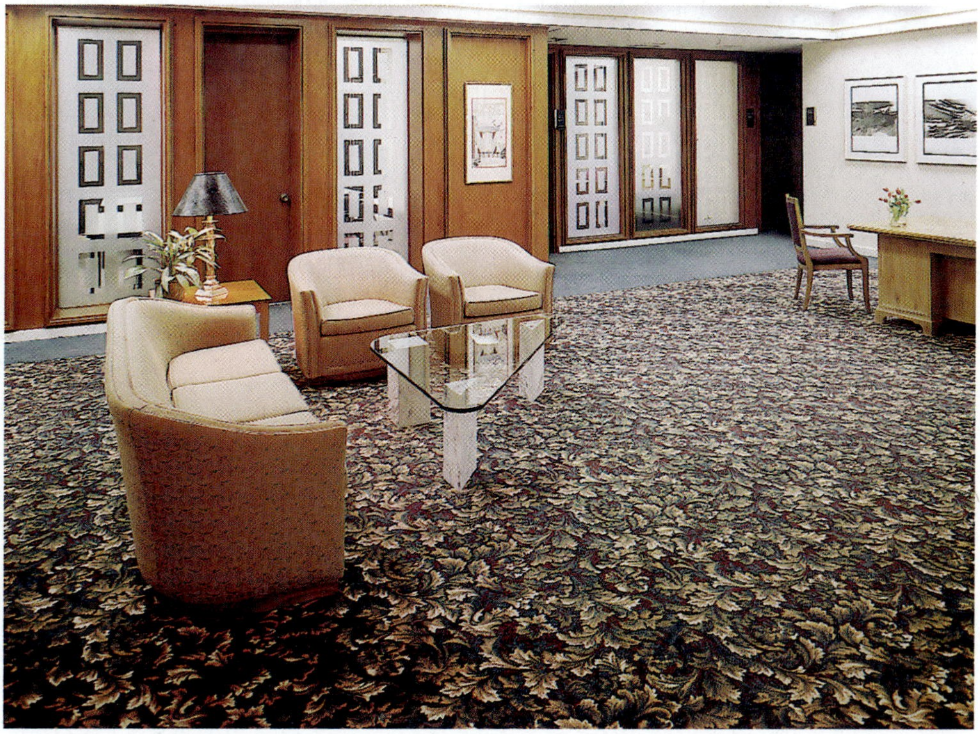

gure 12.21 *The nmons area in an ucational facility was novated from an isting bank. Large panses of glass window re softened by the dition of rectangular-aped film applied in a sign similar to existing ors. (Designer: Lynn M. nes. Photograph by J.J. lliams.)*

Soft Window Treatments

Draperies

Draperies are made of a heavier fabric than curtains; curtains are simple, lightweight decorative solutions. *Draw draperies* are made to draw over a window to control light, temperature, and privacy (Figure 12.22). Draperies terminate at one of three lengths: the windowsill, the bottom of the apron, or the floor; some draperies may be cut extra long to form a "puddle" effect on the floor (see Figures 12.23 and 13.11). They hang straight and may be used alone or combined with other blinds or shades. For example, with a combination of draw shee and draw draperies—the most common usage—the view ca be exposed, and light, sound, temperature, and privacy can b controlled. Draperies that draw closed from both the right ar left sides are called two-way traverse. Those that draw fro one side only are called one-way traverse.

Side draperies or *stationary panels* remain at the sides the window. Stationary panels may be hung straight or tie back. Their purpose is to bring beauty and style into th room. Because they are not designed to give privacy or pro vide insulation to a room, they may be combined with oth window treatments.

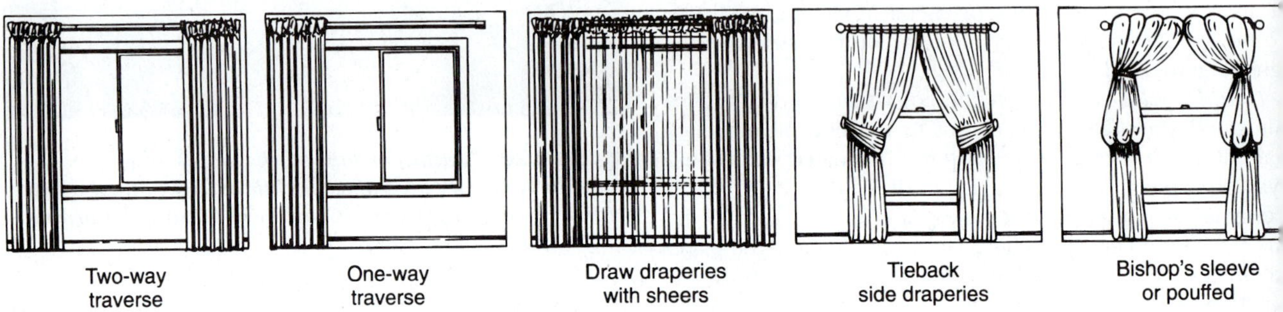

Figure 12.22 *Types of draperies.*

Figure 12.23 *Drapery lengths.*

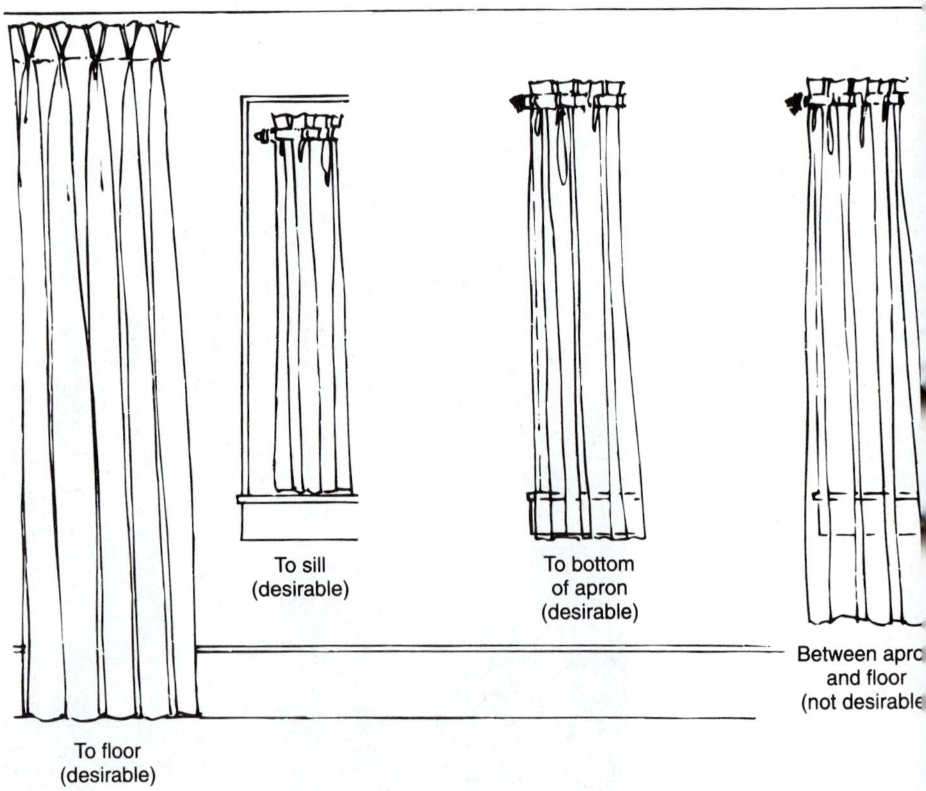

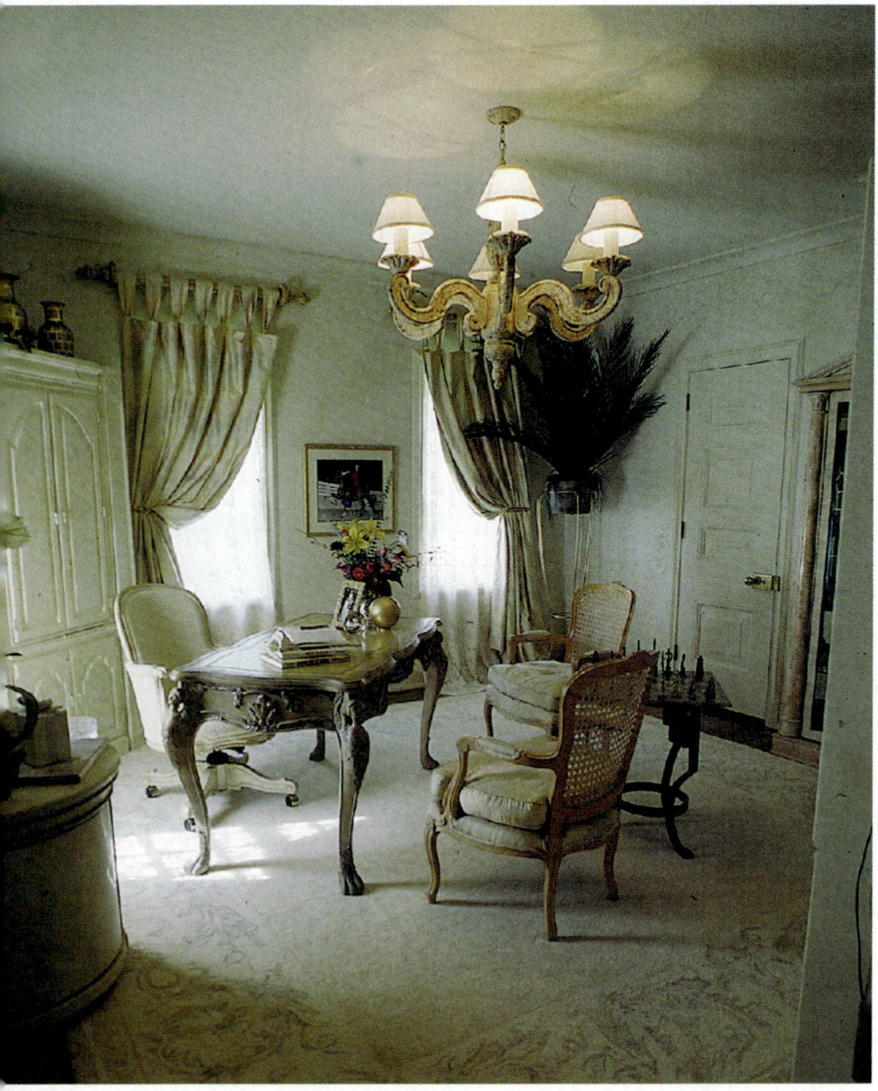

Figure 12.24 *This home office employs a custom-designed formal drapery with tab tops in front of a patterned sheer. (Designer: Pandy Agnew Interiors. Photograph by Lynn Barkley Photography.)*

Sheers or *semisheers* are used primarily to diffuse light and ovide daytime privacy. They may be hung permanently ;ainst the glass or drawn back (Figure 12.24). Much of their :auty and efficiency depends on their fullness, most often ree times the width of the window. When nighttime pricy is desired, sheers can be combined with draw draperies, inds, or underdraws.

Casements are generally made of a loosely woven fabric d are heavier than a sheer. They may be used in residences, it are most often used singly in commercial environments d drawn to control light.

Underdraws, more commonly called *blackout draperies* shades, are used in environments that require total dark-ss. Commercial office presentation and conference rooms ay employ blackout window treatments. Some are con-olled by mechanical devices. All underdraws should be ncealed and are not considered decorative.

Drapery lining serves several functions. Windows are ewed from two perspectives: outside and inside. Drapery lining provides a uniform and attractive view from the outside, covering patterns and colors seen more effectively from an interior perspective. When several windows face the street, it is best to coordinate their appearance through the use of drapery lining, especially for windows on the same level. Drapery lining also provides additional insulation from heat and cold, and protects the drapery from sunlight.

Ready-mades are draperies and curtains made to standard lengths and available in most drapery departments. Although often less full than custom-made draperies, ready-mades frequently give a satisfactory effect that belies their more modest cost.

Curtains

The most common types of curtains are illustrated in Figure 12.25. *Priscilla curtains* are ruffled tiebacks most often used in informal settings. They are usually made of light, sheer fabrics trimmed with a ruffle and shirred to a rod at the top

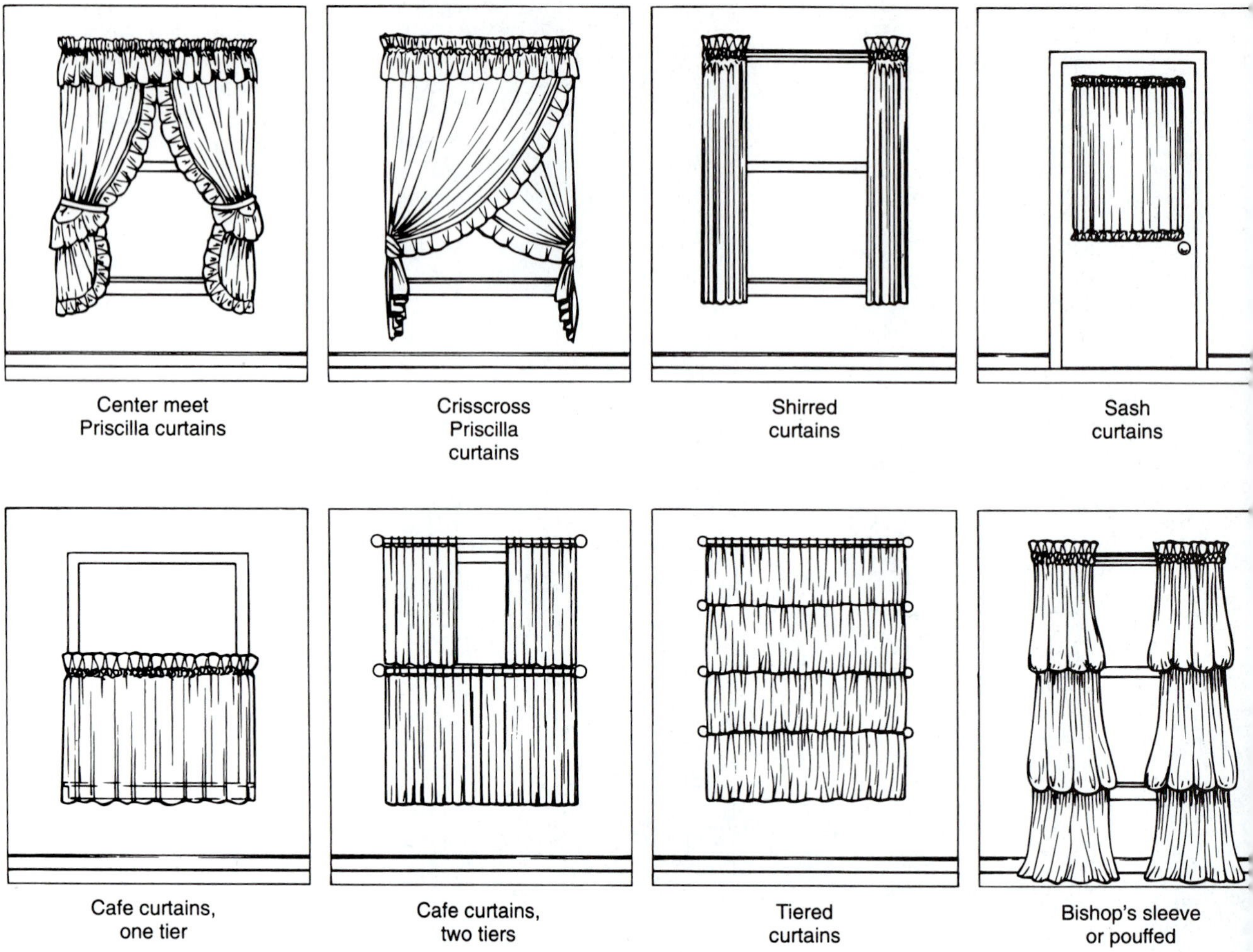

Figure 12.25 *Types of curtains.*

of the window. One type of Priscilla curtain has panels overlapped in a crisscross fashion, and another has a symmetrical arrangement.

Shirred curtains are gathered on a rod and hung at the top of the window, letting the fabric drape softly. The amount of fabric used determines how full the effect of the curtains is.

Sash curtains are usually hung close to the glass. They are shirred at the top and often the bottom on sash rods.

Cafe curtains are hung over the lower part of the window. Usually used for privacy, they may draw or be stationary. Two or more tiers may be hung to cover the entire window, in which case the rods are concealed. Cafe curtains may be teamed with draw or side draperies, shades, blinds, or shutters. Cafe curtains are often embellished with a window top treatment.

Bishop's sleeves or "pouffed" curtains are similar to the stationary drapery type illustrated in Figure 12.22, but employ a sheerer fabric.

Shades

Some of the most common types of fabric shades are ill trated in Figures 12.26 and 12.27. *Roman shades* have a f surface when extended down (Figure 12.28). When dra upward by a cord, the surface overlaps in horizontal fol made possible by a precreased rigid lining or by rings (ring tape) and cords attached to the back of the shades. R man shades come in a variety of styles, including shirr Roman, shirred balloon, flat Roman, soft-pleated Roman, b loon Roman, and accordion-pleated Roman.

Austrian shades consist of rows of lightweight fab seamed to fall into deep scallops. The shade is operated a draw cord and is similar in design to the shirred ballo Roman.

Pleated fabric shades are also called "accordion shad and "soft shades." Pleated shades are factory manufactur are available in a wide range of colors and finishes, and c be insulated. Fabrics vary from opaque to translucent a

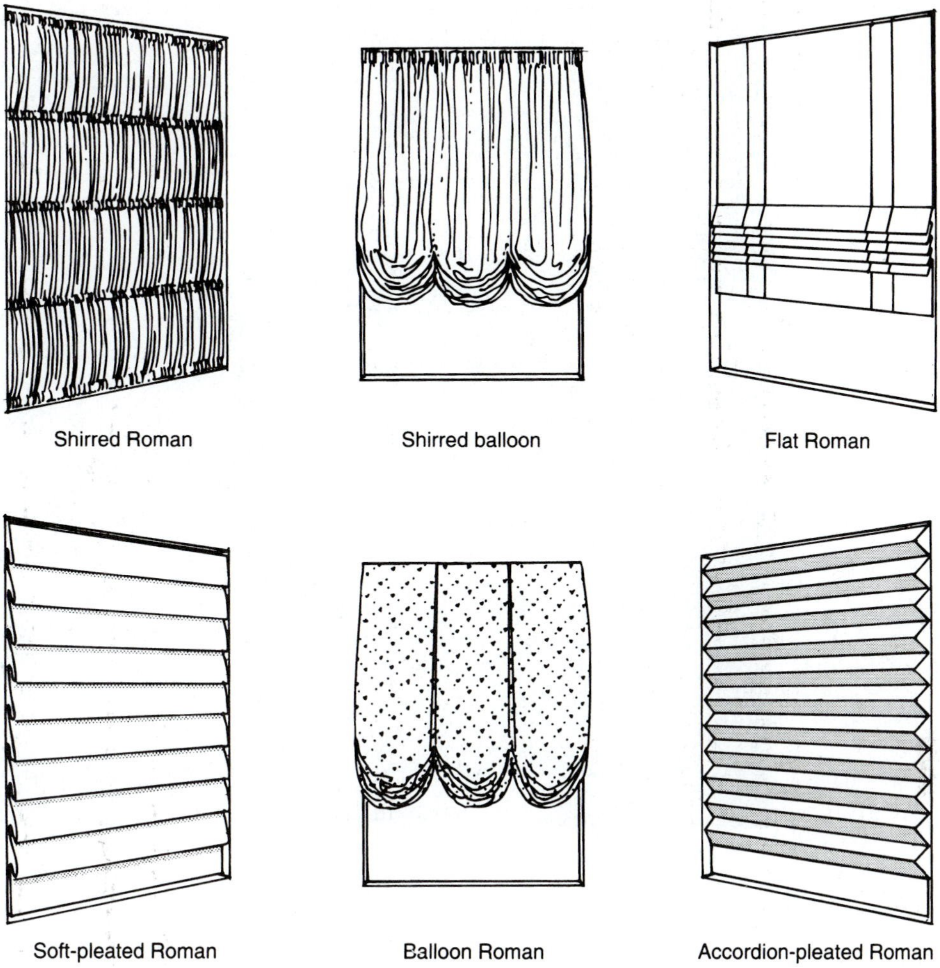

gure 12.26 *Types of Roman shades.*

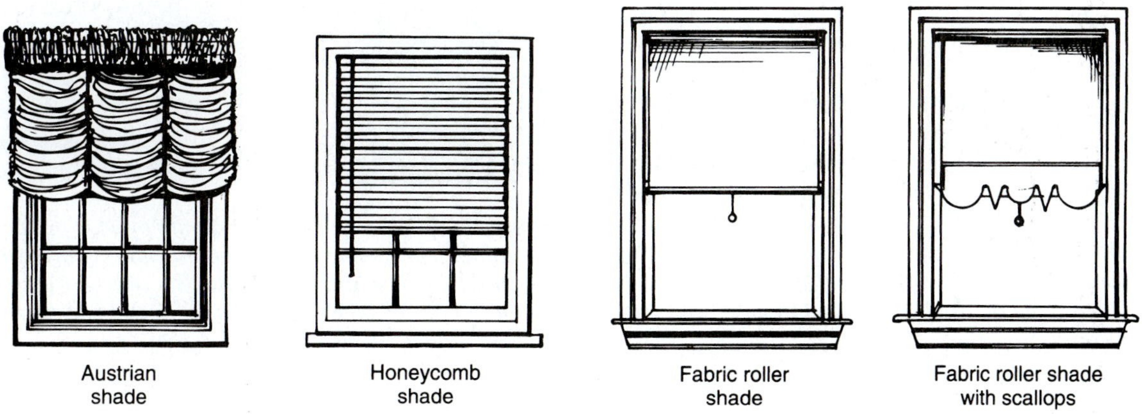

gure 12.27 *Other types of shades.*

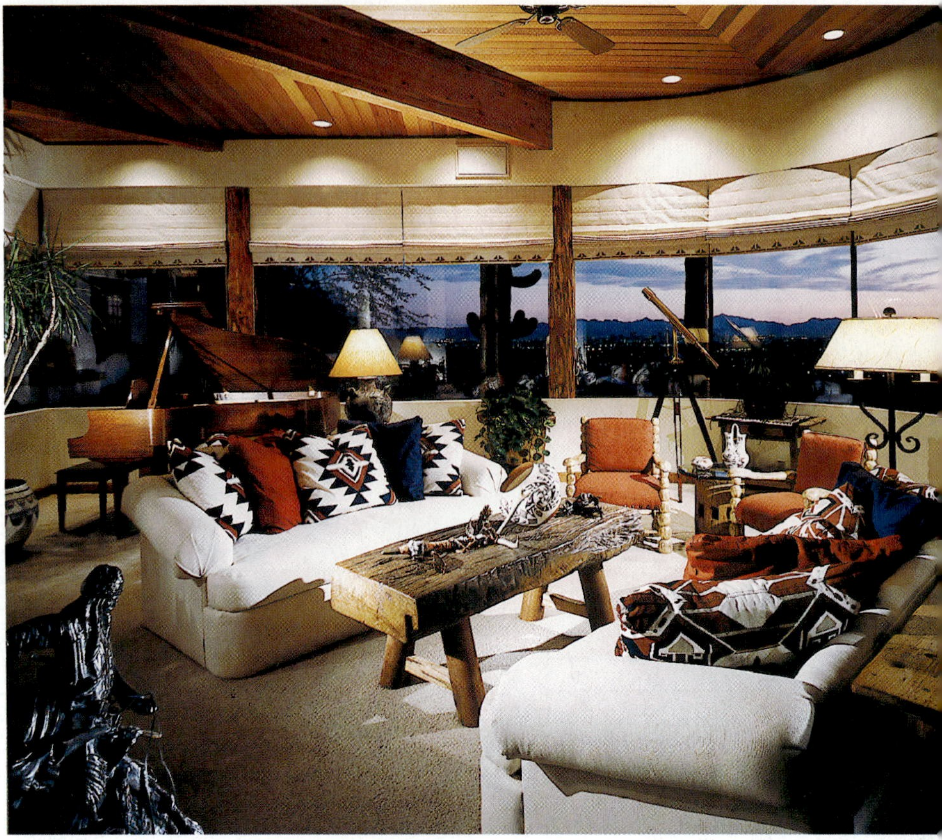

Figure 12.28 *Roman shades have been custom designed to fit the angles of this window, allowing a sweeping view of the city. The simple tailored effect complements the architecture and the room's Southwest decor. (Photograph by Mark Boisclair.)*

may be patterned or plain. *Honeycomb shades* have smaller pleats and are usually made of a heavy polyester fabric. They operate on the same principle as the single pleated shade except two pleated shades are bonded together, resulting in a "honeycomb" cross section (Figure 12.29). This construction provides an energy-efficient insulating air space. The exterior side of the shade is white to reflect the sun's rays and provide uniformity on the outside.

The *roller shade* is an inexpensive window treatment. It may be installed between window casings or on the outside of the frame. The most common material is vinyl, which is available in a variety of weights. Traditionally, roller shades were white or off-white, but they are now available in the full spectrum of colors; however, colors do affect the exterior facade. Originally thought of as purely functional, the simple roller shade can be laminated with fabric and trimmed in a variety of ways. When mounted at the bottom of the window and drawn up, it is especially effective for privacy. Roller shades may be light filtering or room darkening, depending on the thickness of the material. Shades are easy to maintain, and insulate against heat and cold. Window quilts or thermal shades are made of additional layers of fabric, often have a decorative stitched pattern, and provide extra insulation.

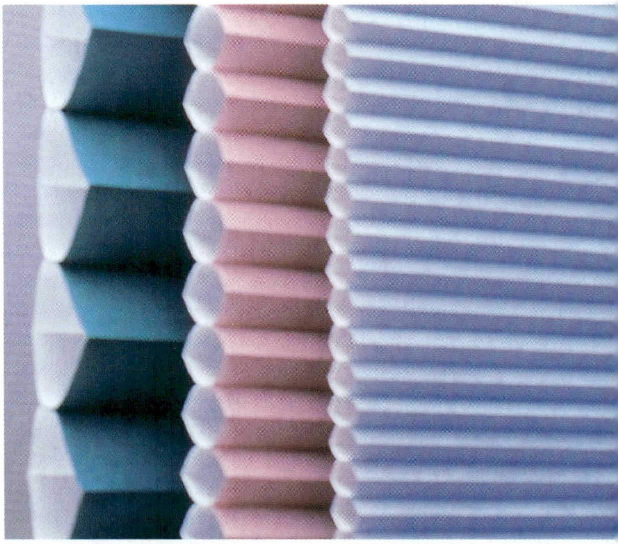

Figure 12.29 *These honeycomb shades provide privacy and insulation while allowing soft light to enter. A variety of ple[illegible] sizes, layers, and colors are available. (Copyright: Permission has been granted by Hunter Douglas, Inc. to use copyrighted designs. Designs © Hunter Douglas, Inc.)*

lants

ants can be used successfully in lieu of other window treat-ents. Hung at varying heights and placed on pedestals or e floor, plants can form a border of greenery that softens rd-edged architecture, filters the light, and affords privacy. built-out window in a sunny location can become a green-ouse. Greenhouse windows are often used in kitchens and n provide a focal point.

'indow Top Treatments

any windows are embellished with treatments at the top or the top and sides of the drapery or curtains. These treat-ents are of various designs and are made of soft or hard aterials (Figure 12.30).

Soft Materials

The **valance** is generally a shirred, pleated, or draped soft treatment across the window top. A valance screens hardware and gives the drapery a finished look. It is used solely for appearance; it does not change the function of the drapery. It can appear to extend the height and width of a window and unify windows of different sizes, thus altering the room's visual proportions. The valance may match the side or draw draperies and is often shaped by a stiff interlining. If the fabric is patterned, the shape of the valance looks best when it conforms to that pattern. The material in the valance should run the same direction as the drapery.

A *swag* is a type of valance treatment wherein fabric is draped over a rod at the top of the window. A *festoon* is a single draped member of a swag. A *cascade* drapes down from *under* the corners of the swag. The cascade has a vertical outside edge with an undulating edge closest to the

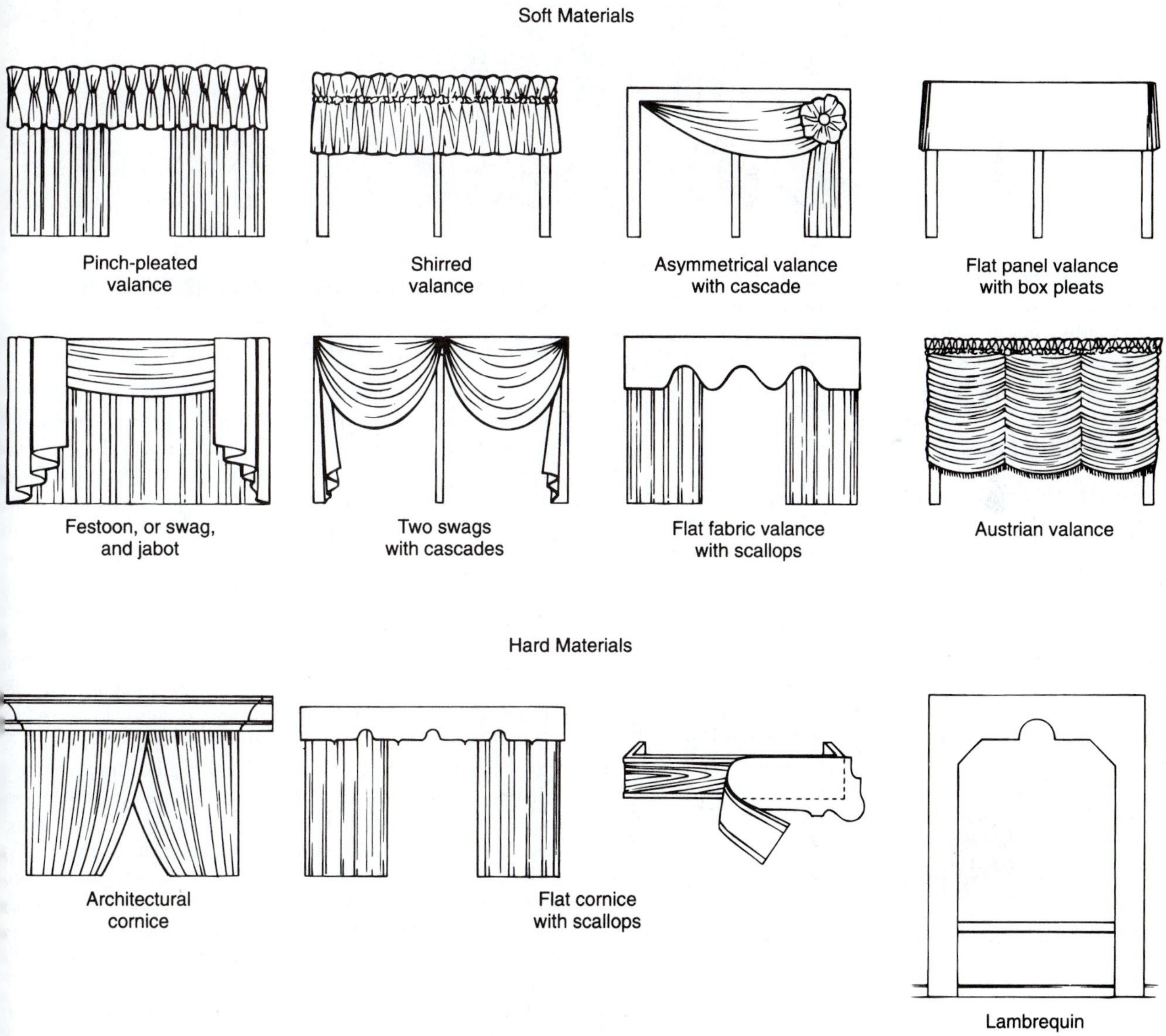

gure 12.30 *Types of top treatments for windows.*

Figure 12.31 *Fringed and tasseled valances swagged over gilded poles complement the traditional furnishings at Blair House, Washington, D.C. The warm, cheerful colors welcome visiting heads of state. (Designer: Mario Buatta. Courtesy of Mario Buatta, Inc.)*

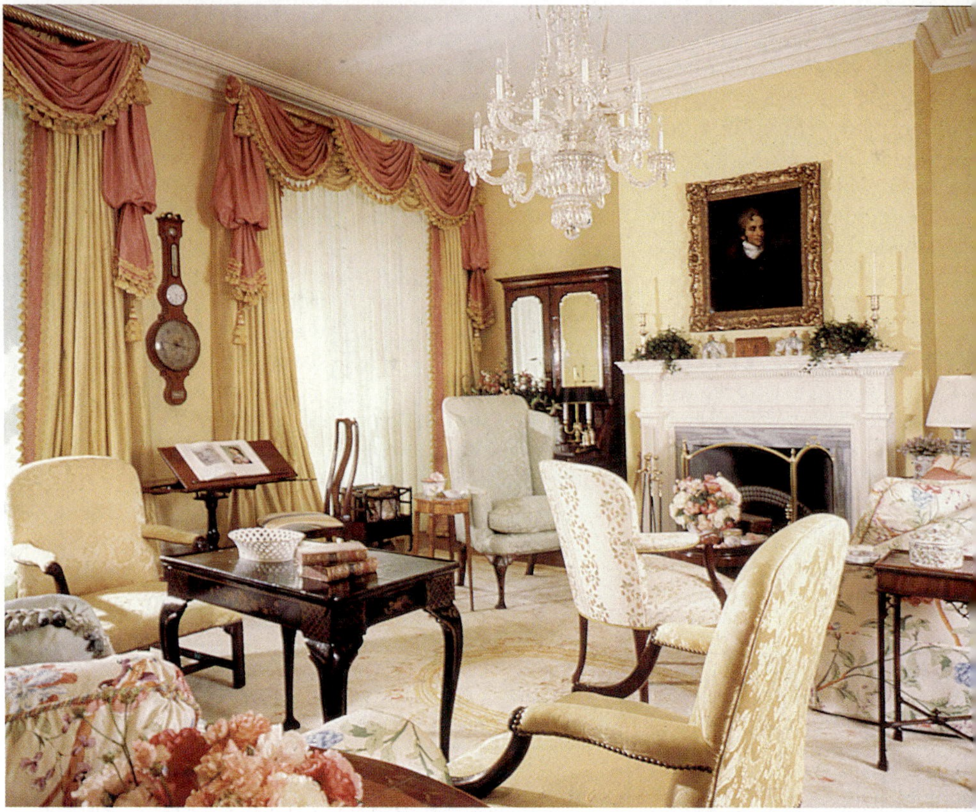

swags. A *jabot* is similar to a cascade, but drapes over the edges of the swag. It is usually pleated and may be of varying lengths. Swags, jabots, and cascades may be hung over sheers, drapery, blinds, shutters, or shades, or at the top of bare windows (Figure 12.31).

Hard Materials

Cornices are generally made of wood, metal, or another hard material and are placed at the top of the window treatment. Often cornices are a continuation of an architectural molding or cornice around the top perimeter of the wall extending outward to accommodate the window top. Cornices may be simple or decorative, such as a scalloped or pierced design. They may be stained, painted, or covered with fabric. A cornice with a fabric valance attached is an effective formal treatment.

Lambrequins are similar to cornices, but they also have a rigid treatment that extends vertically down both sides of the window. Lambrequins can be painted or covered with wallpaper or fabric, and used with or without draperies, curtains, blinds, or shades. They provide a tailored look and can alter the apparent size of the window.

More info online @

http://www.wcaa.org/ Window Coverings Association of America

http://www.dwcdesignet.com/DWC/ *Drapery and Window Coverings Magazine*

http://www.dwcinternational.com/ Drapery and Window Coverings International Directory

Window Treatment Hardware

Functional Hardware

Figure 12.32 illustrates types of functional and decorati window hardware. Purely functional hardware should inconspicuous. *Sash rods* are flat rods attached close to tl sash (often both top and bottom) on which curtains a shirred. *Extension rods* are used for stationary curtains a drapery. They extend to various lengths and are availab in single and double sets. *Traverse rods* operate on a pu ley system. Available as either one- or two-way traver types, they are used for drawing curtains and drape *Spring tension rods* fit inside the casing. *Swinging rods* a mounted on a mechanism that permits the rod to swi backward. These rods are suitable for in-swinging cas ments, dormers, and French doors. *Extender rods* exte outward to support stationary drapery beyond the sides the window. *Ceiling tracks* with concealed drawing mec anisms are especially popular in contemporary roon Small accessories such as hooks, rings, ring slides, bracke and draw cords are all part of the unseen draw-drapery sy tem. Rod placement on windows is illustrated in Figu 12.33. When drapery treatments are used in childre rooms, long dangling cords (such as those on blinds) pr ent a danger to children and should be secured out of th reach.

Like doors, windows also require security hardwa Locking and opening mechanisms need to be of a dural finish that blends with the room's style.

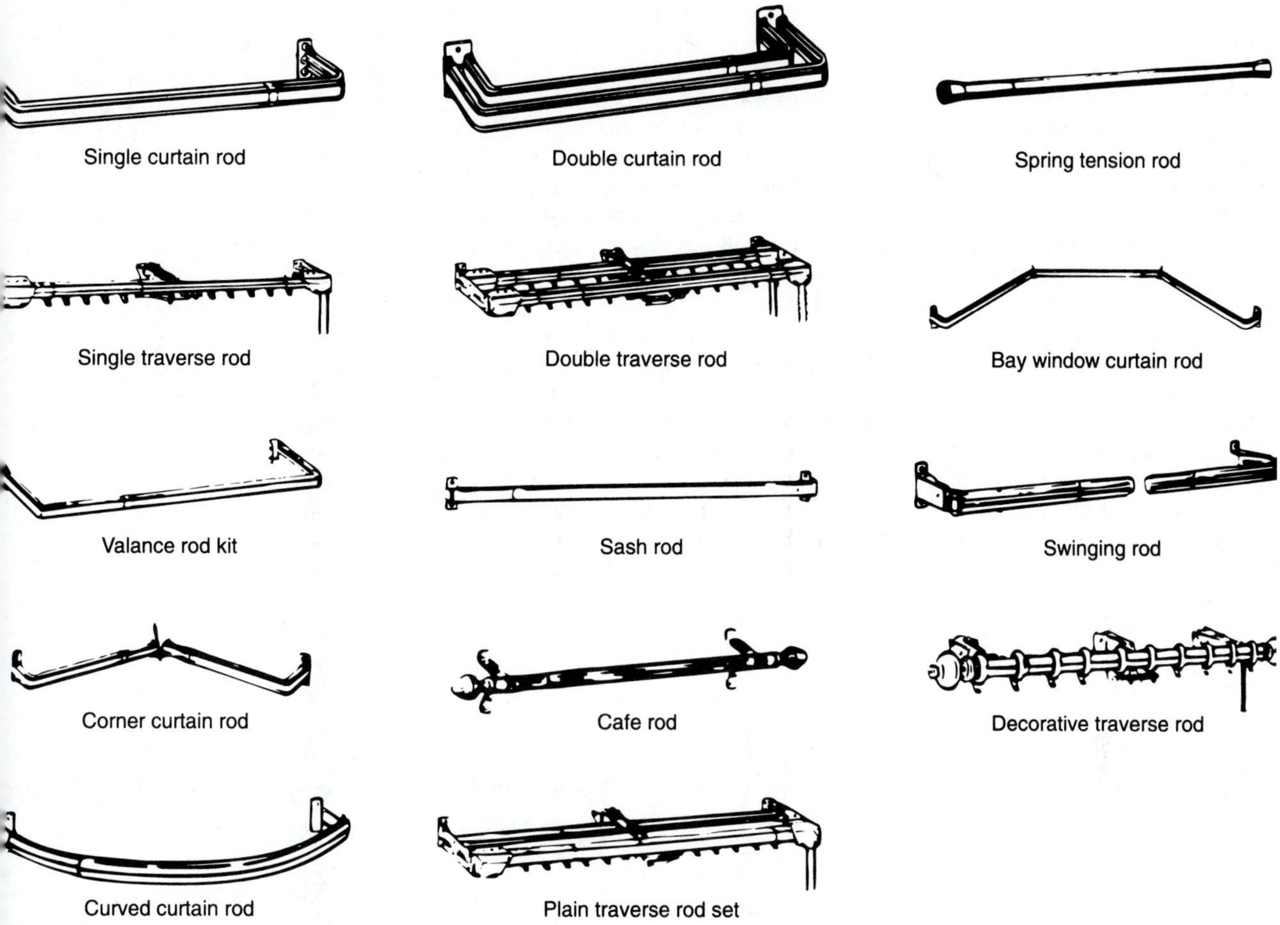

;ure 12.32 *Curtain and drapery rods.*

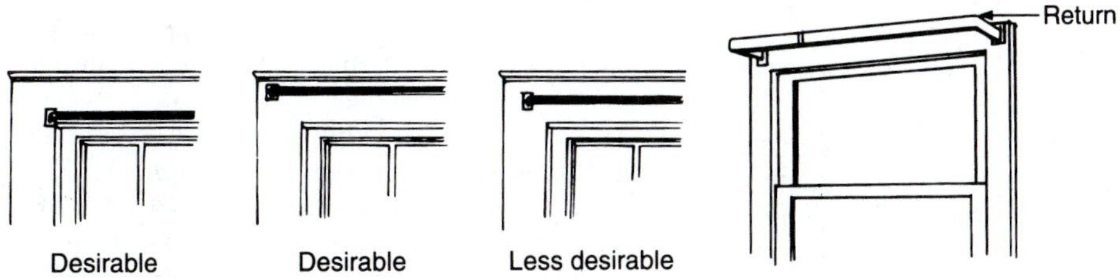

Figure 12.33 *Rod placement on window frame.*

ecorative Hardware

·corative hardware is functional but also adds to the room's le. Rods may be wood (with natural, stained, or painted fin- .es) or metal (such as pewter, shiny or antique-finish brass, rome, bronze, or wrought iron). Decorative hardware is uipped with a variety of **finials** (the decorative element at- ·hed to the end of a rod) to accommodate any style. aperies suspended on rings may be cord operated or hand wn. In the latter case, rings should be loose. Metal hold- cks that conform to the style of rods add a finishing touch.

Drapery and Curtain Headings

The *heading* is the pleating or gathering at the tops of curtains and draperies that forms the fold (providing the beauty of fullness for drawing). Headings are made in a number of ways. *French* or *pinch pleats* are made by stitching together three small pleats about 3 inches from the top. The pleats, which are spaced 3 to 4 inches apart, are held upright by an interlining. Ripplefold is a simple method of creating gentle, undulating folds by means of a compact track containing snap carriers. Folds are made from flat

SUSTAINABLEDESIGN

Energy-Efficient Window Treatments

A window's treatment may cut down on heating and cooling costs. Curtain and drapery manufacturers are producing a variety of insulators for windows to save energy, such as double-woven multilayered fabrics that trap warm air in the room and insulated shades, draperies, and linings that protect against heat and cold, thus cutting down on utility bills.

Generally, natural materials do the finest job of insulating. The more yarn used in the fabric, the tighter the weave, the bulkier the material, and the fuller the drapery, the more air it will trap. Layered window treatments are effective insulators. One efficient combination is wooden blinds placed near the glass, with drawn sheers and lined draw draperies. To trap cold or hot air, the sides of the drapery may be anchored to the window frame or wall by double-faced fabric tape. Other effective energy-saving window treatments are quilted blinds, lambrequins, and cornices sealed at the top and sides, and window shades (which can be operated by a mechanical device) equipped with side channels to seal the cracks. Edge sealing is the most critical point for effective energy saving in window treatments.

panels of fabric and are identical on both sides. *Accordion folds* are made by a combination of a compact track with snap carriers and a nylon heading tape. *Tailored pleats* form architectural-like folds. *Easy pleats* are made with a special tape attached to the inside top of the drapery. When pleater hooks are inserted in ready-made pockets, folds are automatically formed.

Shirred headings are made by stitching a pocket approximately 1 inch from the top, in which the rod is inserted. Tab top headings are similar to shirred headings, but the tabs are placed 2 to 4 inches apart so the decorative rod is exposed (see Figure 12.24).

Tiebacks hold back stationary draperies. They come in a wide variety of materials and styles and may be made of cords, tassels, metal, wood, or matching or contrasting fabric. Designers often tie back drapery somewhere between one-half and one-third from the bottom—employing the proportions of the golden mean (see Chapter 2). *Trimmings,* such as fringes, braids, edgings, cords, and tassels, can give a finished look to draperies, cornices, and valances.

More info online @

http://www.louishornick.com/measure/glossarywind.html

and

http://www.nobrainerblinds.com/info/a_b.asp

and

http://www.blindservice.com/glossary.html

and

http://www.home-decorating-made-easy.com/window-treatment-styles.html

Glossaries of window covering terms

Design and Placement of Windows and Window Treatments

The selection and placement of windows creates a po erful design statement. Poorly placed windows impe furniture arrangement and may allow for undesira views. Whenever possible, designers should work with chitects prior to construction. Furniture laid out in schematic design and design development stages can h the architect determine where to locate windows. Wind openings, however, are not always planned with ind function in mind. A clever designer must work arou these obstacles.

The following guidelines are important when selectin window and treatment design.

As with doors, consider the architectural backgrou of the room. Architectural features may be enhanced hidden.

- The exterior view also may need to be enhanced or h den.
- Privacy may need to be created either at night, during the day, or both.
- Light may need to be blocked to prevent glare or to p serve precious furnishings.
- The window design should complement the furniture style and placement.
- The treatment may need to conserve energy (see "Sustainable Design: Energy-Efficient Window Treat ments").

In many cases, to serve a variety of functions a combinat of treatments is required. These combinations should w together to become one design element.

re info online @

p://www.hunterdouglas.com/design/art_gettingStarted.asp

p://www.theblindman.net/select_treatment.htm

of questions and other ideas to consider when selecting window atments

p://www.golace.com/measure.html Guide on how to measure window treatments

REPLACES

e final form of fenestration discussed in this chapter is fireplace. Fireplaces have served important functional es through the centuries as a source of warmth and a ce to cook meals. In simple homes the fireplace was the us of the home and a place where the family congregated. In today's homes the fireplace may be a visual luxury, serving primarily as a room's focal point, or it may provide a source of heat.

Fireplaces can be expensive and hard to clean. They also require space for fuel storage. Gas fireplaces have become a common alternative, as have wood-burning heaters and stoves. A fireplace, however, is still considered a desirable asset; fireplaces in residential living spaces can add to a home's market value (Figure 12.34). Fireplaces in public settings like restaurants, hotels, and

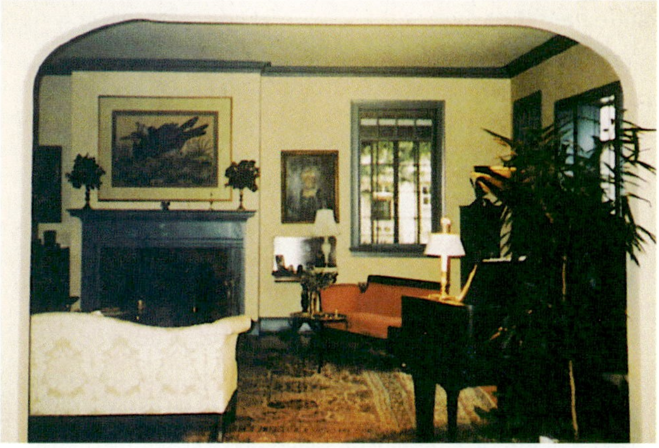

ure 12.34 *Before and after shots of this living room nonstrate the power of sensitive color usage and applied oration. In both shots, however, the fireplace is the focal nt. (Architect: Maresca & Assoc. Interiors: Louise Quinn. otographs by Cheryl Dalton.)*

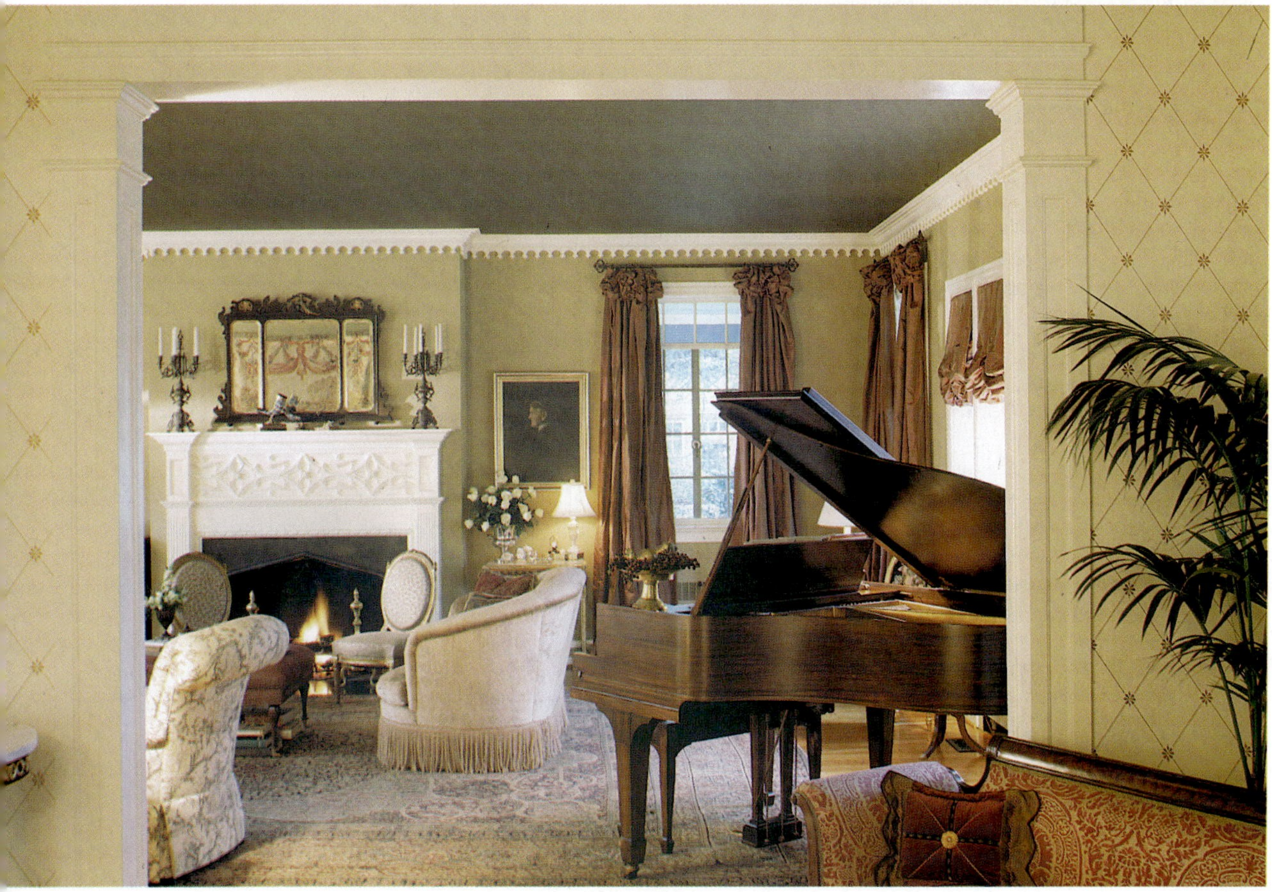

clubs can be particularly inviting, offering a friendly and intimate atmosphere.

Fireplace Construction

Fireplaces may be constructed of masonry or be prefabricated from metal. Masonry fireplaces require space away from combustible materials. Some prefabricated units require no space between the fireplace and combustible materials and can be installed within a regular stud wall. Models are available with openings on one, two, three, and even four sides.

The most common materials for fireplace surrounds include the following:

- *Brick,* available in many sizes, textures, and colors and laid in simple or intricate arrangements
- *Stone* of all types (marble, travertine, terrazzo, quartzite, fieldstone, granite, etc.)
- *Wood* of all varieties, either in strips (laid in numerous patterns and directions), panels, planks, or elaborately carved members, used on decorative surfaces
- *Facings* of plaster or stucco, painted or left plain
- *Concrete,* plain or with exposed aggregate accents
- *Tile* in a variety of colors, textures, and patterns

Fireplace design often includes combinations of these materials. For example, a stone fireplace may have a handsome wood mantel, or a plaster fireplace may be outlined around the opening with colorfully patterned tile.

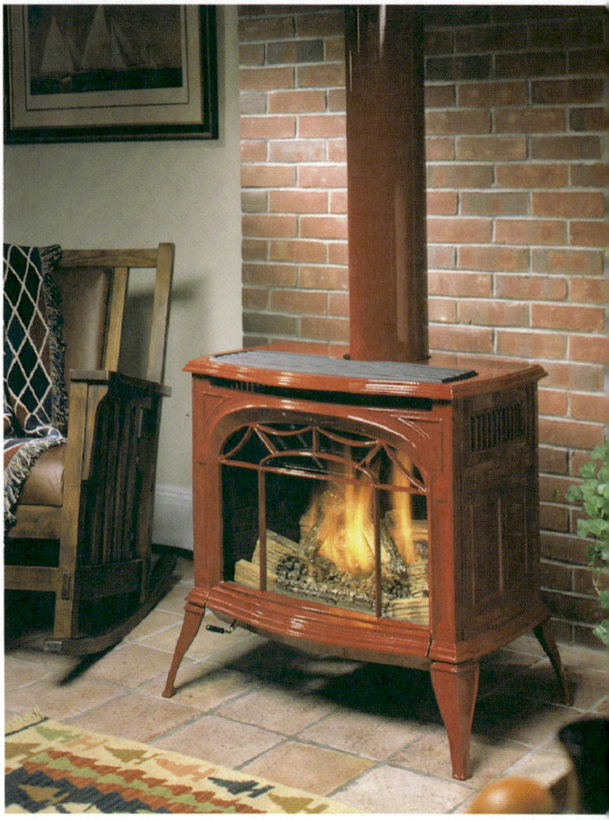

Figure 12.35 *In this contemporary setting, a wood stove enhances the interior architecture and provides a backup heating system. (Courtesy of Vermont Castings/Majestic Products Co.)*

Types of Fireplaces

The wood-burning fireplace is the most prevalent fireplace design. However, faced with deteriorating air quality as well as wood-burning restrictions, many designers and homeowners are choosing alternatives to the wood-burning fireplace, such as *wood-burning heaters* and *stoves*. The Environmental Protection Agency (EPA) establishes strict codes for wood-burning heaters and stoves: They may emit no more than eight grams of particulate per hour. (By comparison, an average wood-burning fireplace emits up to 1000 grams of particulate per hour.) Today, only certified wood heaters that meet the emission limits may be sold. Additionally, no person may install or operate a wood-burning heater or stove except in a manner consistent with the EPA's guidelines. Heating homes with these heaters and stoves instead of fireplaces can drastically cut down on air pollutants.

Wood-burning heaters and stoves are also much more energy efficient than wood-burning fireplaces. With the high cost of heating, wood-burning stoves and heaters have become popular and are available in a large range of styles (Figure 12.35).

Other alternatives to the traditional wood-burning fireplace are *natural gas fireplaces, fireplace inserts,* and *log sets*. These gas-burning devices provide the ambience of wood-burning fireplaces and stoves with none of the inconveniences. Compared with its wood-burning counterpart, natural gas fireplace equipment is cleaner burning, simp to start, easier to keep clean, and has lower fuel costs. though gas does not burn as hot as wood, a gas insert a a substantial amount of heat to a room. Flueless gas logs also available that require no venting to the outside.

Fireplace Design and Placement

The style of a fireplace is generally traditional or mode Traditional styles for fireplace design provide charm an feeling of authenticity. Modern fireplaces are often cust designed for a particular space. Modern fireplaces may s vertically, expand horizontally, or create a circular form. fireplace may or may not have a mantel, the hearth may on the floor or raised, and the fireplace may be set agai the wall or project outward. The style of a fireplace is g erally most successful when it complements the room's nishings and background.

The size of the fireplace within a living space is flexi Small fireplaces can have charm; an average- or mediu sized fireplace can be a focal point without overwhelmin room; and a very large fireplace can be a dramatic feat (Figure 12.36).

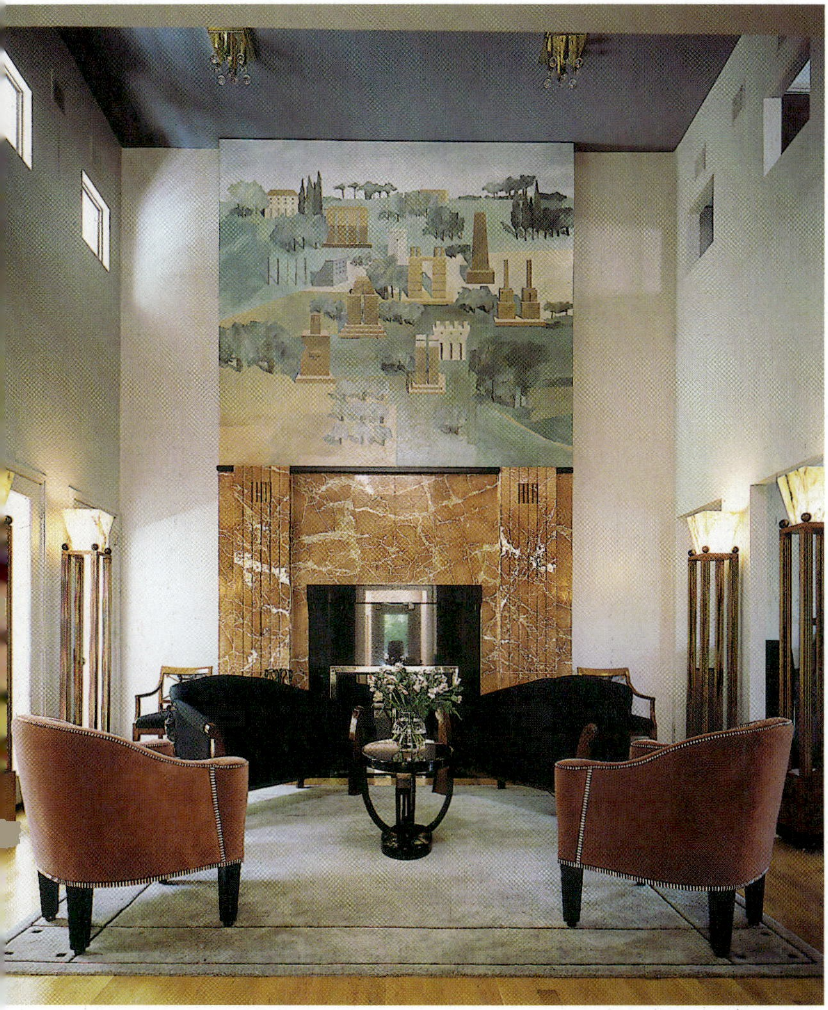

Figure 12.36 *Michael Graves designed this Post-Modern residence in New Jersey in 1986. In the living room, the fireplace wall dominates the space. The placement of classic Villa Gallia chairs, designed by Josef Hoffman at the turn of the century, complements the fireplace wall. (Photograph by William Taylor.)*

Designers may incorporate the fireplace as part of the to- wall composition by using shelves or built-in furnishings, ending the fireplace material the full length and height of wall. The fireplace may also be freestanding, independ- of any wall. As with doors and windows, consideration of scale and proportion of the room, the style, the materials be employed, and the effect and function desired help to ermine the most appropriate fireplace construction for a rticular space.

re info online @

p://www.maconline.org/tech/design/fireplace2.html
rgy-efficient fireplace design guide provided by the Masonry sign Council

p://www.sandkuhl.com/html/default_plan_design.html
sign and plans for masonry fireplace construction

p://www.solve-chimney-problems.co.uk/pages/section6.html
ssary of fireplace terms

p://www.hpba.org/consumer/2/Glossary/index.shtml
arth, Patio, and Barbecue Association, glossary of terms

p://www.hearthed.com/ Hearth Education Foundation

Summary

The fenestration of a room or building defines its style and creates natural divisions for interior zoning. Doors direct traffic and provide for privacy and security. Doors in combination with windows and fireplaces define furniture arrangements.

When given the opportunity, interior designers should work with architects and builders to determine the best furniture arrangements before the fenestration is established. However, in many cases this is not possible. Designers must cleverly apply the principles and elements of design, and where possible, design window treatments or fireplace surrounds that enable the room to function properly.

Part V focused on the various components applied to an interior to create a space that functions within the client's aesthetic and economic preferences. The integration of these varying components is key to the creation of a successful interior environment. On the following pages are two living rooms, both in a similar architectural setting. The discussion compares and contrasts the design solutions. Following the living room comparisons is a Design Scenario illustrating how one design firm visually communicated its design solution for these various components to its client.

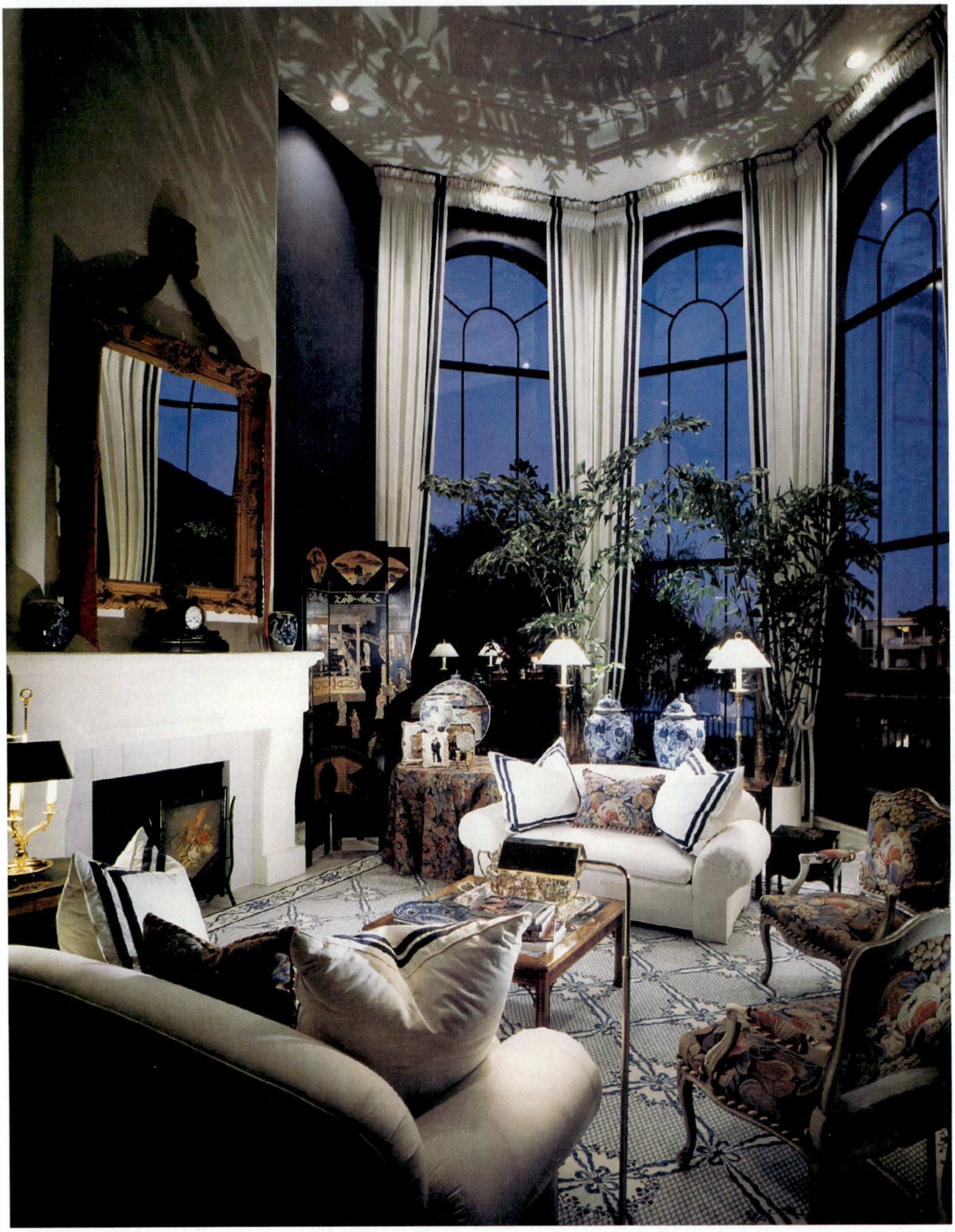

Figure 12.37A *Both of these living rooms are the result of understanding function, aesthetics, and economic requirements of the interior. Knowledge of the elements and principles of design were combined with an observance of visual literacy to define the interior spaces. (Photographs by Mark Boisclair.)*

Living Room Comparison

Carefully examine Figure 12.37A and B. An interior designer must learn to analyze interior spaces and look for possibilities and potential. Note the following similarities:

- Similar size, shape, and volume of space
- Large floor-to-ceiling accent windows with minimal window treatments
- Fireplace used to focus conversation area
- Combination of rug and hard surface flooring
- Abundance of personal items used for accessories, including plants
- Use of white sofas with accent pillows

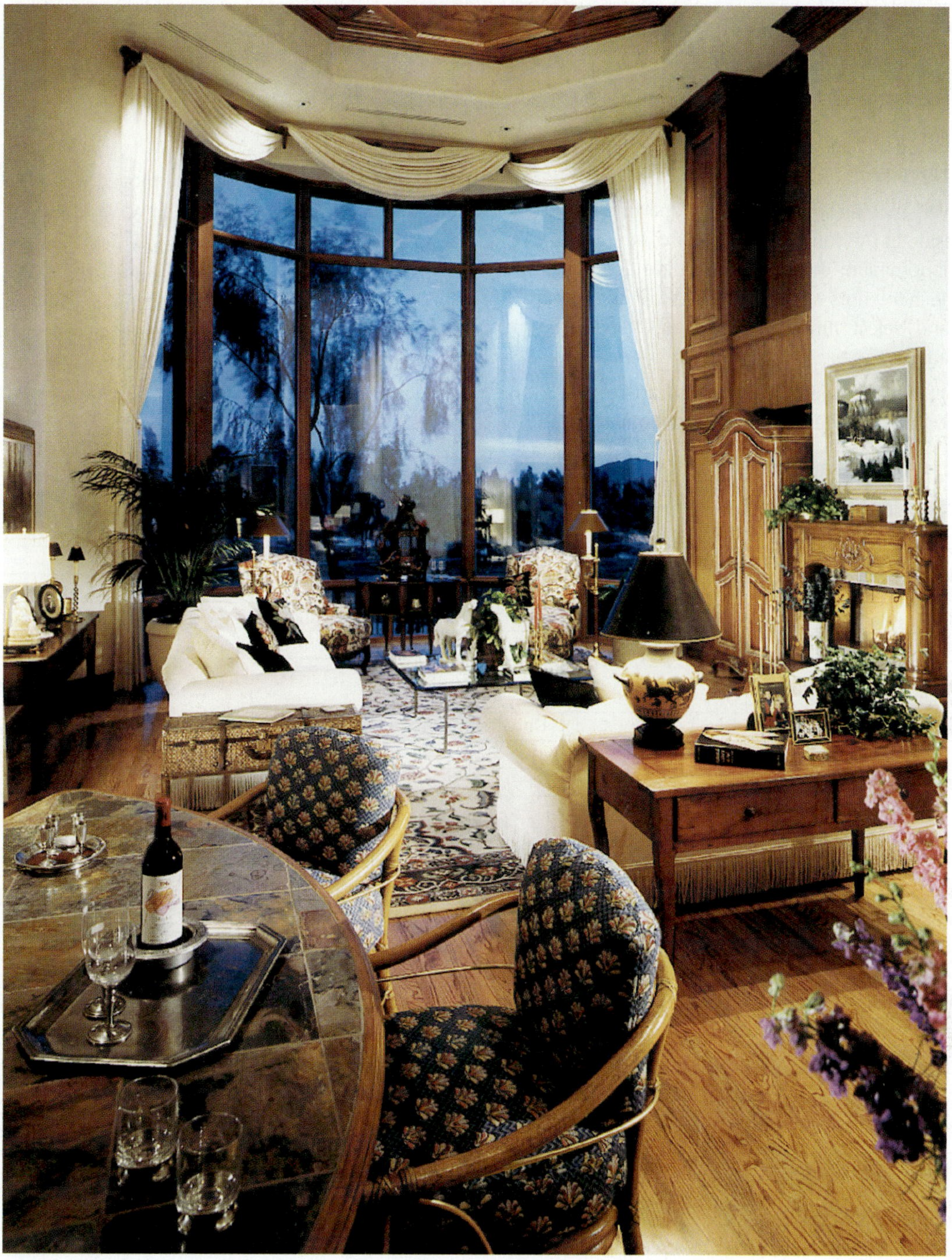

Figure 12.37B

›m a design perspective, the following differences affect › feeling, mood, and concept of this space:

- Room A utilizes silhouette lighting. Room B's lighting is more uniform.
- Room A focuses on the elaborate mantel and mirror. Room B focuses on the window and expansive view.
- Room A introduces deep values in wall colors. Room B uses a more neutral wall value, but places warm wood tones on the walls.

Consequently, the mood of Room A is more intimate and dramatic, the mood of Room B is set for a gathering of friends. Room A feels more contemporary, even with the traditional fabrics and furnishings; Room B feels more formal. Designers must be sensitive to subtleties that evoke these perceptions. Attention to detail is an essential element, as is perceptive visual awareness.

Design Scenario

RETIREMENT CONDOMINIUM

Project Description

Two sisters were moving into a retirement apartment. The sisters wished to reside in the same area of their community and had chosen a condominium that did not provide accessible apartment living. Rich Interiors was retained to adapt the physical environment and select furniture, furnishings, and equipment where needed.

Programming: The two-bedroom, one-bath apartment allowed for only minor wall changes in the bathroom and kitchen areas. Plumbing fixtures could only be moved within 5′-0″ of their isting location in order to be near water lines.

The sisters were very fond of their existing bedroom furnit and wished to reuse it. Zoa realized her room would be tight space because of the addition of the sewing table. Due to size of the new apartment and their diverse existing furnitu the sisters wanted new living and dining room furniture. The R idential Programming Questionnaire and Furniture Invent Sheet define other needs (Figures DS12.1 and DS12.2).

RESIDENTIAL PROGRAMMING QUESTIONNAIRE

I	**General Information**		**Date**
Client Name	ZOA SMITH & ZONA LEE JONES		
Address	100 ANY STREET		
Home Phone	555-1212	Work Phone	
Occupation(s)	RETIRED		

II Family Members

Name	Age	Universal Concerns
ZOA	65+	WHEEL CHAIR ACCESSIBILITY
ZONA LEE	65+	GOOD LIGHTING

III Family Members' Hobbies and Activities

Activity	Family Member(s)	Where does activity take place
Computer		
Television	BOTH	LIVING ROOM
Stereo	BOTH	NOTHING ELABORATE—LIVING ROOM
Sewing	ZOA	BEDROOM & LIVING
Crafts		
Instruments		
Model Building		
Reading	ZONA LEE	LIVING ROOM
Other	BOTH (GARDENING) FLOWERS	

IV Room Requirements

Living Room
Entertainment Yes ____ No X How Many? ____ How Often? ____

Dining Room
Formal/(Casual)/Both (circle one)
Number of people maximum 4
Comments

Breakfast Room
Number of people maximum ____
Comments ____

Living Room

Activities Shelves with doors to close off T.V. set/stereo. Straight firm chair for Zoa to sew in. Canister table to store sewing. Larger, softer, easy chair for Zona Lee. She requested this because this is what she is accustomed to.

Figure DS12.1 *The residential programming questionnaire (see Appendix A) was used to define the needs and desires of the two sisters. (Courtesy of Tammie Roper, Rich Interiors.)*

Bedrooms

#	Who	Requirements
1	ZONA LEE	MUST BE ACCESSIBLE FOR WHEELCHAIR. BRINGING EXISTING FURNITURE.
2	ZOA	BRINGING EXISTING FURNITURE (INCLUDING SEWING MACHINE) GOOD LIGHTING WITH CHAIR FOR SEWING.
3		
4		
5		

Baths

1		SHARED BATHROOM, REQUESTED MORE CONVENIENT TO ZONA LEE'S BEDROOM.
		ACCESSIBLE FOR WHEELCHAIR WITH ROLL IN SHOWER & BENCH.
2		GRAB BARS, LOWERED SINK WITH KNEE SPACE.
3		
4		

Other Rooms

Rooms	Requirements
Laundry	
Kitchen	LOWERED WORK SPACE; ZONA LIKES TO COOK. KNEE SPACE UNDER SINK, STOVE. SIDE-BY-SIDE FRIG.
Office	AND SIDE OPEN RANGE.
Workshop	
Garage	
Play Room	
Study	
Music Room	

V Design Preferences

Colors	THEY AGREE ON A SOFT, MELLOW GREEN THROUGHOUT	
Mood	CHEERFUL NOT DRAB	
Budget	MED.	
Time Frame	3 MONTHS	
Reuse items	BEDROOMS	(if yes, see furniture inventory sheet)
Other	DON'T WANT HEAVY TRADITIONAL-LIKE A TRANSITIONAL LOOK MAYBE WITH SOME COUNTRY FRENCH–	
	PREFER LIGHTER WOODS	

VI Other Information & Comments

ZONA LEE—RETIRED SCHOOL TEACHER. LOVES TO READ, COOK, AND LOVES FLOWERS.
MUST HAVE OPEN SPACE FOR WHEELCHAIR TRAVEL. HARDWOOD FLOORS WITH NO RUGS.
BUILD IN BOOKSHELVES FOR BOOK COLLECTION.
LIKES PLUM FOR ACCENTS.

ZOA—RETIRED HOUSEWIFE. LOVES TO SEW, COOK, & ALSO LOVES FLOWERS.

MUST HAVE ROOM FOR SEWING MACHINE. FLORAL PATTERN FOR BEDROOM WITH SOME WALLPAPER. LIKES PURPLES AND GOLDS FOR ACCENTS.
*BOTH REQUESTED NICE SEATING AND AREA FOR FLOWERS ON PATIO.

VII Business Information

Travel Directions

NORTH ON MAIN
RIGHT ON ANY STREET

Fee Basis

FLAT FEE & PERCENTAGE OF PURCHASES

ure DS12.1 *Continued*

FURNITURE INVENTORY SHEET

Item #	Description	Size W × D × H	Style	Comments
Zoa	Bedroom Furniture			
	Std Bed w/ head &	54" X 86" X 48"	Empire/ Sleigh Victorian	
	footboard			
	(2) Night stands	22" X 14" X 23"		
	Armoire	36" X 22" X 88"		Not for TV/ sewing storage
	Dresser	48" X 22" X 40"		
	Sewing table/ chair	28" X 24" X 30"		
	Side chair	28" X 30" X 44"	Slipperchair uph to floor	Needs re-upholstery
Zona	Bedroom Furniture			
	std Bed w/ headboard	54" X 82" X 46"	upholstery inset w/ wood trim	
	(2) Nightstands	22" X 20" X 22"	appears to have French Country influence	
	Dresser	48" X 20" X 40"		
	Chest	36" X 22" X 54"		
	Sidechair	30" X 32" X 48"	Armchair w/ legs	Needs re-upholstery

Figure DS12.2 *The furniture inventory sheet (see Appendix B) was used to document existing furnishings that were to be reused. (Courtesy of Tammie Roper, Rich Interiors.)*

Conceptual/Schematic Design: Rich Interiors worked with the clients in developing a floor plan with minor wall changes. Additionally, Rich Interiors noted the following:

- Additional bathroom space would shrink Zona's room to the point where not all of the bedroom furniture would fit.
- A sage green color scheme with gold and plum accents was agreed on by the women.
- A built-in unit would be designed for the living room instead of open shelving.
- Custom cabinetry would be used in the kitchen, incorporating the design of the built-in bookshelves in the living room.
- All flooring would be in an oak finish, except for the tile in the bathroom.

Design Development: To visually communicate the proposed de- sign, Rich Interiors developed three presentation boards. Figu DS12.3 shows the floor plan and furniture and finish selectio for the dining and kitchen area. Figure DS12.4 illustrates the f niture and finishes for the living room and bath. Figure DS1 truly warmed the clients' hearts—their individual bedrooms w clearly defined in a three-dimensional rendering. Care was tak to include clients' personal items such as family portraits, lam and favorite accessories.

Designer: Tammie Roper, Rich Interiors.

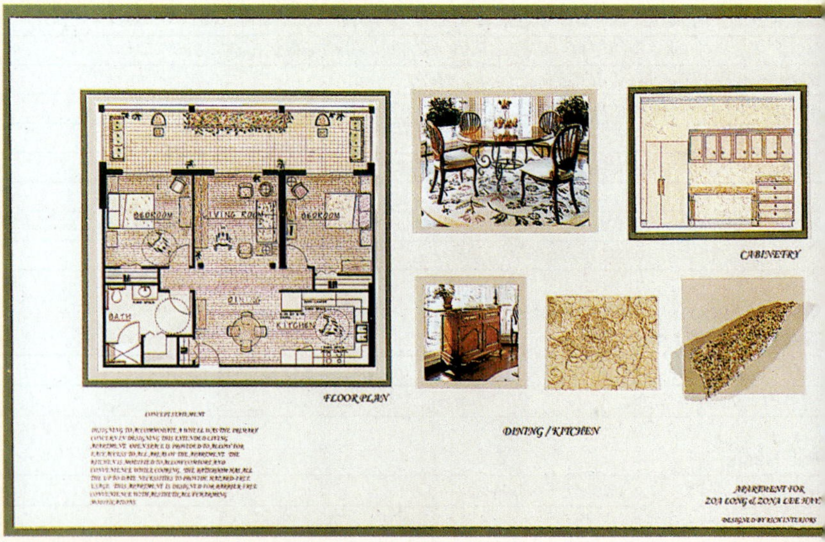

Figure DS12.3 *Presentation floor plan and furnishings for the dining and kitchen areas. (Designer: Tammie Roper, Rich Interiors.)*

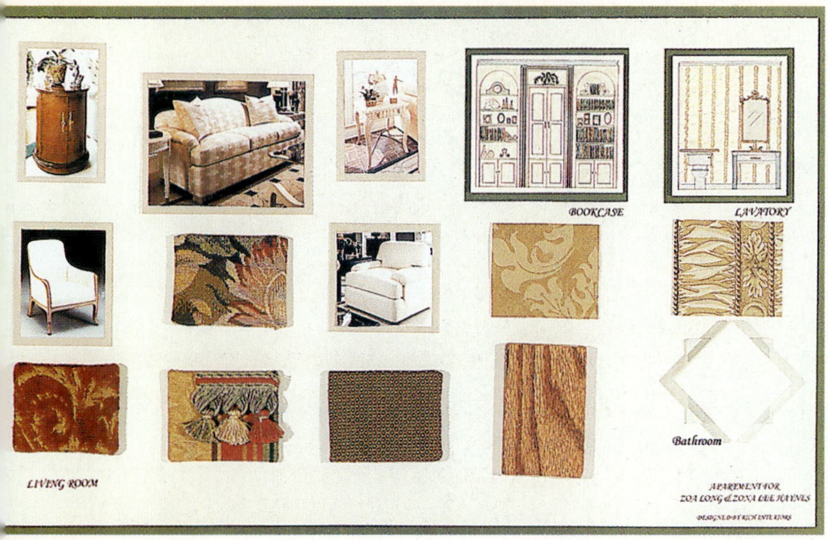

Figure DS12.4 *Presentation board for the living room and bath. (Designer: Tammie Roper, Rich Interiors.)*

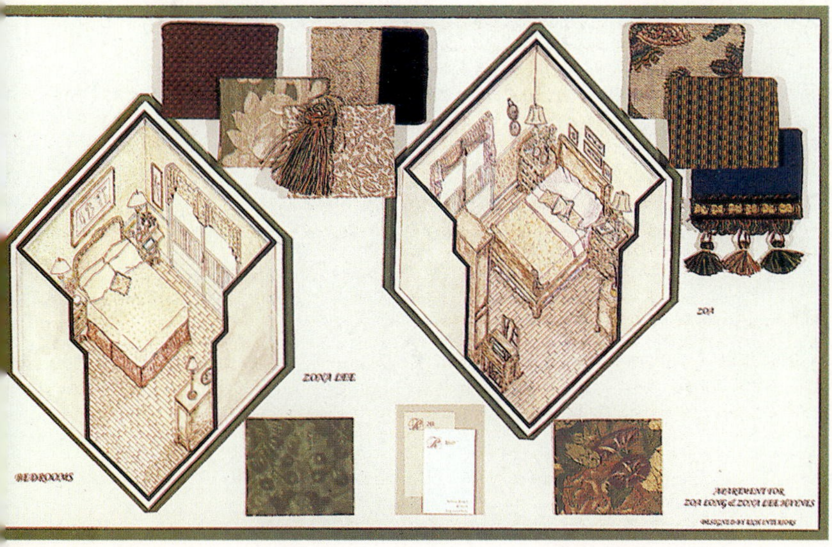

Figure DS12.5 *Presentation board with axonometric renderings of the bedrooms. (Designer: Tammie Roper, Rich Interiors.)*

The Profession of Interior Design

PART VI

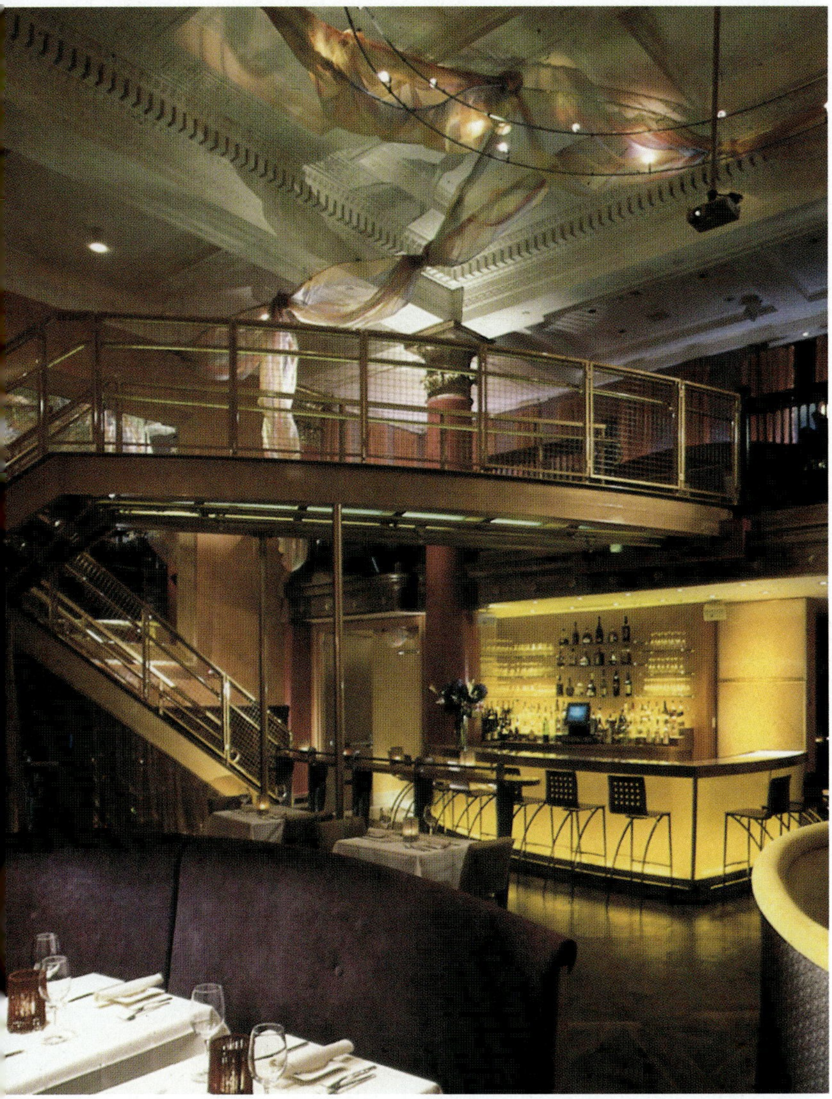

ure VI.1A *At Nyla's, guests are treated to a warm ambiance of colors and light lled from a "blooming flowers" concept and a Georgia O'Keeffe painting. The bar acklit with painted fluorescent lamps and yellow gels. Multicolored gels produce ethereal ambiance through the layers of chiffon. Architect/Designer: Haverson chitecture and Design. Photograph © Peter Paige.)*

> *The future belongs to those who understand that doing more with less is compassionate, prosperous, and enduring, and thus more intelligent, even competitive.*
>
> *Paul Hawken*

s discussed in Chapter 1, the interior design profession is a comex blend of technical design skills d creative artistic skills. Additiony, designers must possess strong siness skills in order to be accurate d competitive in the design market. erior designers must address the eds of their clients while balancing budget, environmental, aesthetic, and regulatory issues. Although many opportunities are open to the aspiring interior designer, a career should be based on a sound educational foundation that continues throughout the designer's career. Part VI addresses the path toward a career in interior design, professional involvement in

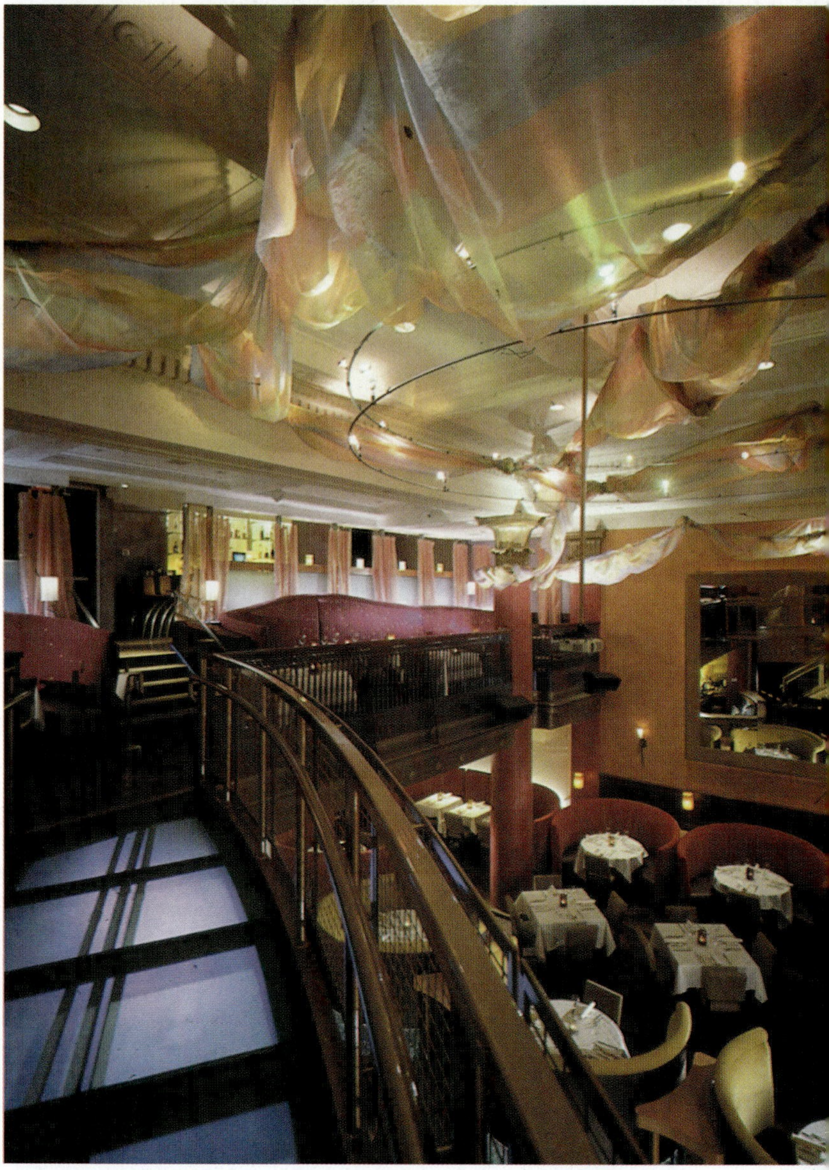

Figure VI.1B *The original grand hall was brought into human scale through the addition of a second floor catwalk. The fabric draped ceiling and colored gels are particularly poignant on this second level. Floor to ceiling mirrors on the opposite wall reflect the festive setting. (Architect/Designer: Haverson Architecture and Design. Photograph © Peter Paige.)*

design organizations, and specific issues relating to business practices, such as professional ethics.

Chapter 13 features outstanding interiors to inspire the beginning designer. These photographs were selected to represent a variety of specialty fields in residential and commercial design. Careful analysis of these interiors reveals professionals' accomplished use of visual literacy and the principles and elements of design. Figures VI.1, and VI.2 begin this process by reviewing two commercial design solutions.

Figures VI.1 and VI.2 represent two outstanding restaurant renovations, both located within a hotel. Figures VI.1A and VI.2A focus on creative solutions to bar design. Bars require an immense amount of preliminary planning to ensure the efficient use of space for the multitude pieces of equipment required in the "back bar." Figures VI.1B and VI.2B illustrate a broader view of the respective restaurants. Both designs accentuate the existing interior architecture; however, they also accentuate the distinct differences between decorative and structural design.

Figure VI.1 emphasizes a decorative feminine design creating a vivacious and warm interior. Existing masculine characteristics of plaster walls, wal patterned wood flooring, and 8′ wa scoting were softened by the use chiffon ceiling fabrics and colored uplights. A brass stairway, catwa and banquettes were added to cre a more intimate space and to all the restaurant to flow into the mez nine level.

Figure VI.2 emphasizes a m structural design allowing the expr sion of the architecture. Rigid diago and vertical columns are enhanced the organic movement created curved ceilings, undulating walls, a geometric patterns. The honesty of interior architecture has been expos

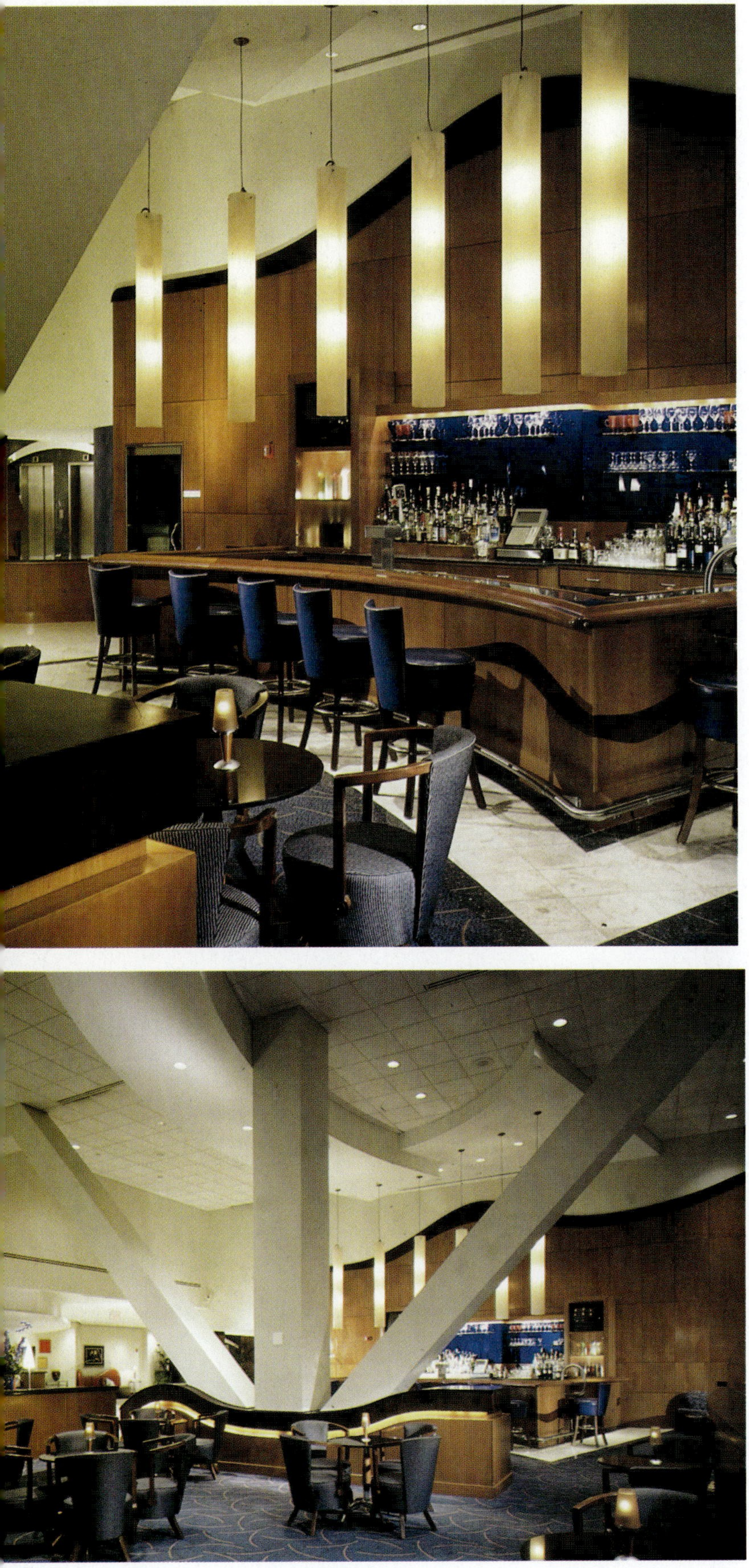

Figure VI.2 *Creating a welcoming interior in a building with unyielding architecture and a seven-story atrium requires vision. The strength of the architecture at Novatel was allowed to express itself throughout the restaurant. To add movement to the space and help direct the flow of traffic, curved forms were added to floor patterns, walls, and ceiling details. The custom bar accentuates the welcoming effect, while the deep, rich blue embraces the patrons. The organic forms and accent lighting enhance the inflexible architectural vocabulary of the building by creating a playful environment. (Designer: Elias Design Group. Photographs © Peter Paige.)*

nterior Design as a Career

13

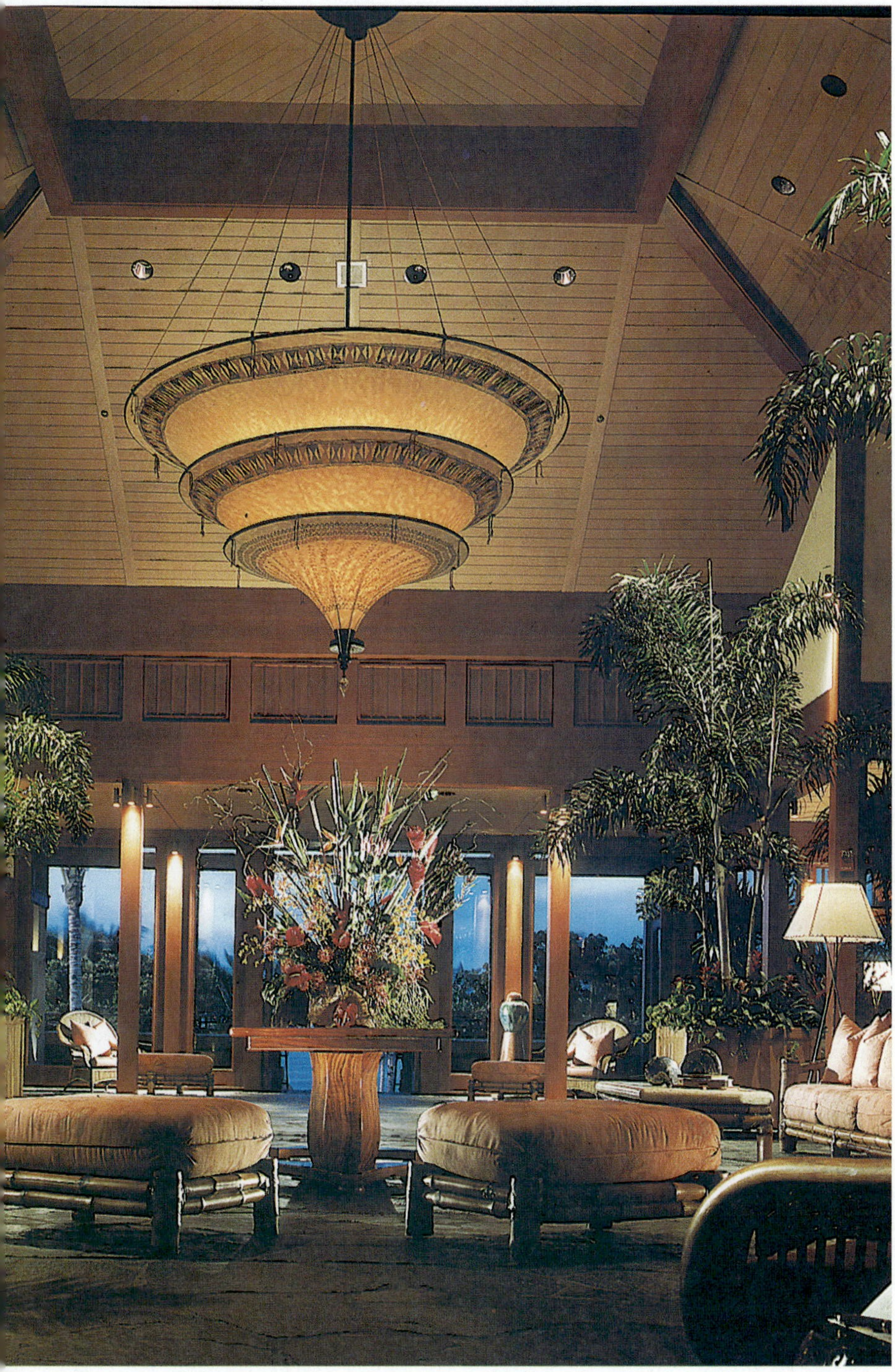

Figure 13.1 *Hospitality Design—Hotel. In this Hawaiian resort hotel, a custom silk and steel chandelier serves as the focal point. Furniture arrangements, floral designs, and architectural lighting add support to this locally inspired design. (Designer: James Northcutt/Wilson and Associates. Photograph by Robert Miller.)*

Career Progression

Deciding on a career is a search process that requires careful examination and evaluation of one's interests and capabilities as well as one's shortcomings. Creativity, sensitivity to the environment, and an interest in cultural heritage as well as contemporary design are all necessary traits for anyone who is seriously considering a career in interior design. Additionally, a designer is always concerned with improving the quality of the human environment.

As discussed in Part I, interior designers are qualified by education, experience, and examination. These three steps ensure the quality of the design professional and should be pursued *before* starting a business.

Education

One of the initial steps toward becoming a professional interior designer is to successfully complete an interior design program at a college, university, or design school. Programs are offered leading to an associate degree (usually two to three years) or a bachelor degree (four to five years). Advanced education is also possible. Master of science (M.S.) or master of art (M.A.) degrees require a minimum of one to two years of additional study. A master of fine art (M.F.A.) degree requires a minimum of two years of additional study, the acquisition of a fine arts skill, and a display of the resulting work. All master degrees in interior design may be considered terminal degrees. The M.F.A. is considered the equivalent of a doctor of philosophy degree (Ph.D.). Additionally, some universities are now offering a Ph.D. in interior design.

Curriculum

Bachelor-level programs teach a broad-based curriculum that prepares students for entry-level careers in the field of interior design. The Foundation for Interior Design Education Research (**FIDER**), founded in 1970, is a self-governing organization whose accreditation commission and teams of site visitors are composed of educators and practitioners who review educational programs in interior design. The standards developed by FIDER, with input from the practitioners and educators, form a common body of knowledge required by all interior designers, regardless of their specific career direction. These twelve standards include the following:

1. Curriculum Structure: Curriculum is structured to facilitate and advance student learning.
2. Professional Values: The program leads students to develop the attitudes, traits, and values of professional responsibility, accountability, and effectiveness.
3. Design Fundamentals: Students have a foundation in the fundamentals of art and design, theories of design and human behavior, and discipline-related history.
4. Interior Design: Students understand and apply the knowledge, skills, processes, and theories of interior design.
5. Communication: Students communicate effectively.
6. Building Systems and Interior Materials: Students desig within the context of building systems. Students use appropriate materials and products.
7. Regulations: Students apply the laws, codes, regulations, standards, and practices that protect the health, safety, and welfare of the public.
8. Business and Professional Practice: Students have a foundation in business and professional practice.

Standards nine through twelve relate to faculty, facilities, ar assessment mechanisms:

9. Faculty: Faculty members and other instructional personnel are qualified and adequate in number to implement program objectives.
10. Facilities: Program facilities and resources provide an environment to stimulate thought, motivate students, and promote the exchange of ideas.
11. Administration: The administration of the program is clearly defined, provides appropriate program leadership, and supports the program. The program demonstrates accountability to the public through its published documents.
12. Assessment: Systematic and comprehensive assessmen methods contribute to the program's ongoing develop ment and improvement.

All standards have indicators that further describe the r quired outcomes. Students are also required to be involv in team approaches to design solutions, and designs for mu ticultural and diverse populations, as well as adaptive u and historic preservation.

Of the approximately 200 bachelor-level interior desig programs throughout the United States, approximately (percent are accredited by FIDER at the Professional Lev Some institutions may meet or exceed FIDER's list of sta dards and guidelines, but for financial or pedagogical re sons elect not to apply. Some states, as part of the registration process, require students to attend a FIDE accredited school or its equivalent.

More info online @

http://www.fider.org/ Foundation for Interior Design Education Research

Internships

Most interior design programs require students to participa in an internship or work-study program as part of the r quirements for graduation. Internship programs vary, but a have the same objective: to enable the student to experien the professional business world firsthand prior to graduatic by combining classroom education with practice. Internsh experience is invaluable to the student. By becoming active involved in the professional world of interior design, studen

- Experience operational procedures, policies, and variou phases of design, such as client–designer relationships
- Learn about interactions of designers within a firm
- Observe and participate in design from concept to implementation

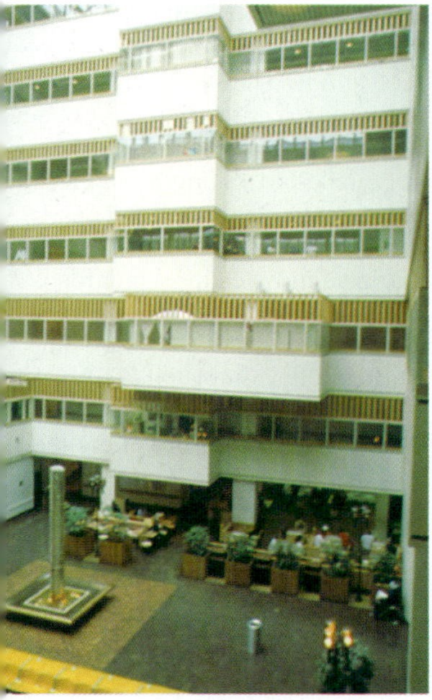

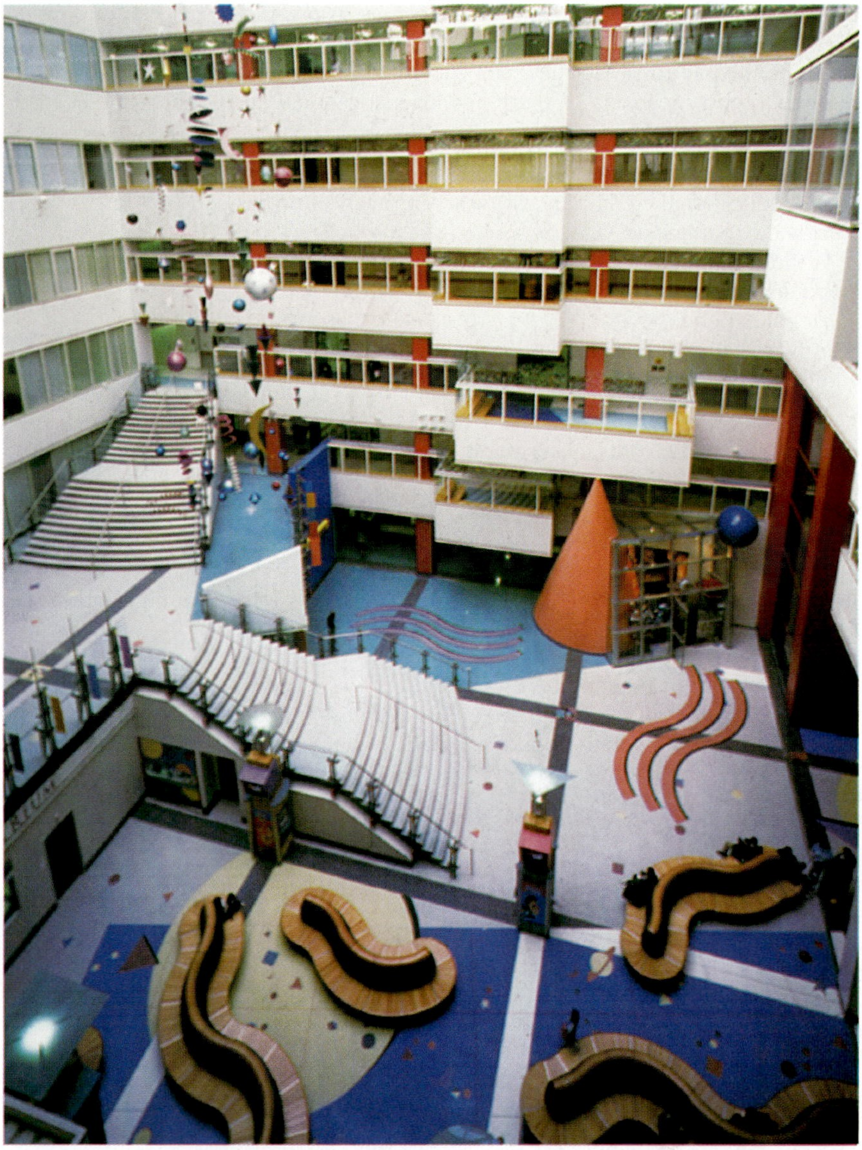

gure 13.2 *Health Care Design—ospital. Sensitivity to the quality of e is put to the greatest test in the sign of health care environments. tients may heal faster in vironments that are responsive to eir physical and psychological needs. ght, in this children's hospital, color, imation, and movement create a n, energizing atmosphere. Above, the rium before. (Courtesy of Karlsberger ompanies. "After" photograph by bert Benson.)*

- Learn to be open to new and different attitudes and perspectives in all aspects of design
- Learn more about themselves in terms of their goals as a professional interior designer
- Acquire valuable experience that can be entered on a job résumé for use after graduation

xperience

ere is no better teacher than experience. All designers, hether just out of college or pursuing a career change, need work with a licensed professional for a minimum of two ars prior to establishing their own firm. Experience offers any advantages that simply cannot be achieved in an edutional environment. Perhaps the most rewarding is the acal installation of one's design ideas.

In 1999, a structured work experience program called the terior Design Experience Program (IDEP) started a pilot program. This program, developed and researched by Buie Harwood and outlined in the *Journal of Interior Design,* links a graduate's internship experience to the FIDER and NCIDQ standards (discussed below). NCIDQ coordinates this program; candidates who successfully complete IDEP are eligible to take the NCIDQ exam for free.

More info online @

http://www.ncidq.com/fr_idep.htm Information on IDEP

Examination

The National Council for Interior Design Qualifications **(NCIDQ)** was formed in 1972 to establish a professional level of competence for interior designers. Level of competence is determined through an examination that is accepted as the standard in all of North America. NCIDQ is also investigating the advantages and disadvantages of pursuing legal registration or certification of the profession.

To be eligible to sit for the exam, potential professional designers must meet one of the following educational and practice combinations:

- A four- or five-year degree in interior design or equivalent educational credit plus two years of practical professional experience
- A three-year certificate in interior design or equivalent educational credits plus three years of practical professional experience
- A two-year certificate in interior design or equivalent educational credits plus four years of practical professional experience.

Additionally, participants must submit three letters of recommendation and official college transcripts.

The three-part exam is administered on a Friday and Saturday, lasting a total of thirteen hours. Section I, Principles and Practices of Interior Design, lasts three and one-half hours and includes 150 multiple-choice questions. Section I questions include the design process steps of programming, schematic or conceptual design, and design development. Section II, Contract Development and Administration, covers the final two areas of the design process. Section II contains 125 multiple-choice questions and lasts three hours. Sections I and II incorporate visual images, typical in the practice of interior design, requiring candidates to recall, apply, and a alyze information.

Section III, Schematics and Design Development, is practicum section divided into two parts. In a total of seve hours, candidates are required to create a floor plan, finis schedule, adjacency matrix, reflected ceiling plan, electrica data plan, section, and elevation to develop a total design s lution for a mixed use facility. All design solutions must me accessibility and health, safety, and welfare standards.

The test is administered twice a year, and participants m elect to take from one to three sections at any given time. three sections must be successfully completed within a fiv year period.

Passage of the NCIDQ exam provides designers the o portunity for professional membership in other design c ganizations. (NCIDQ does not offer membership individuals.) In fact, most of the professional design orgar zations *require* passage of the exam for professional mer bership. Additionally, passage of the NCIDQ exam mandatory in those states and provinces that have licensi or registration statutes.

More info online @

http://www.ncidq.com National Council for Interior Design Qualifications

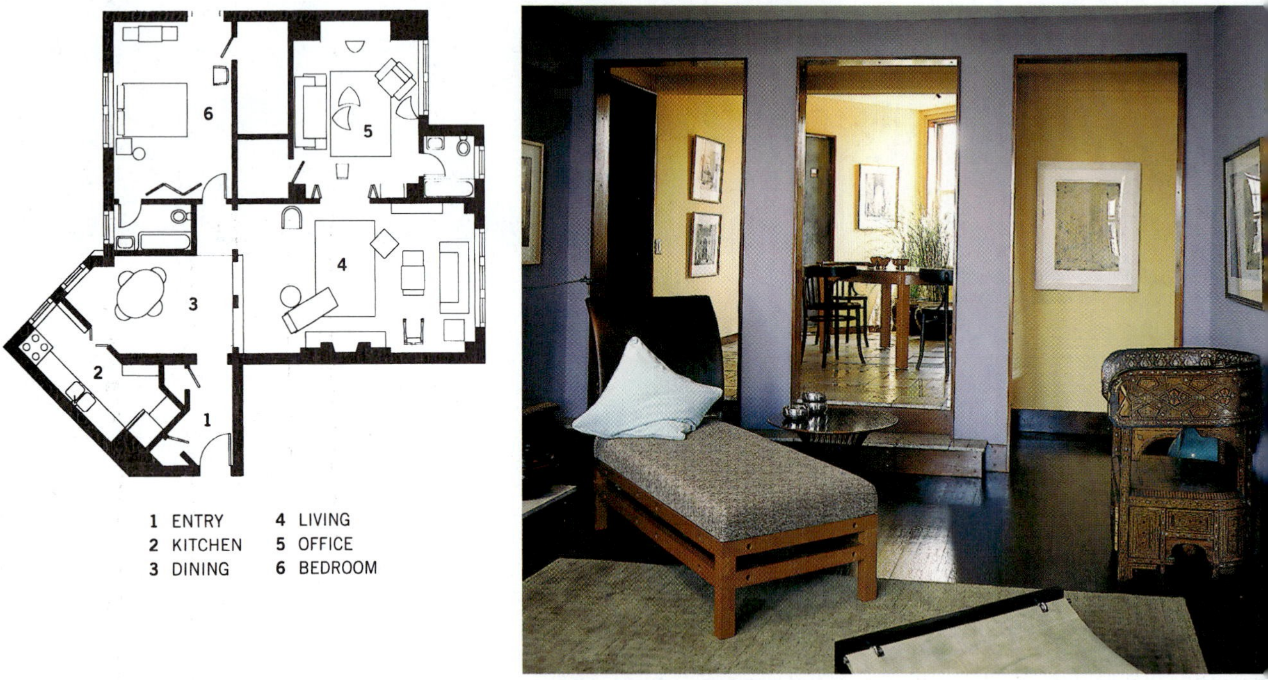

Figure 13.3 *Residential—City Apartment. This residence required many structural changes, including an expanded kitchen and visual division between the living and dining areas. Color and light are strong elements in this apartment, alternating the forms and adding an explosion of character. The floor plan illustrates the appropriate balance and clever use of relatively small space. (Designer: Hassan Abouseda. Photograph by John M. Hall.)*

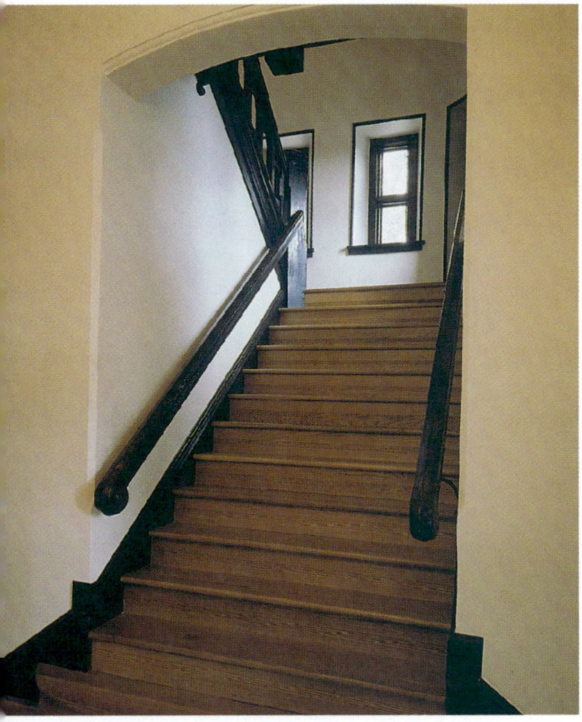

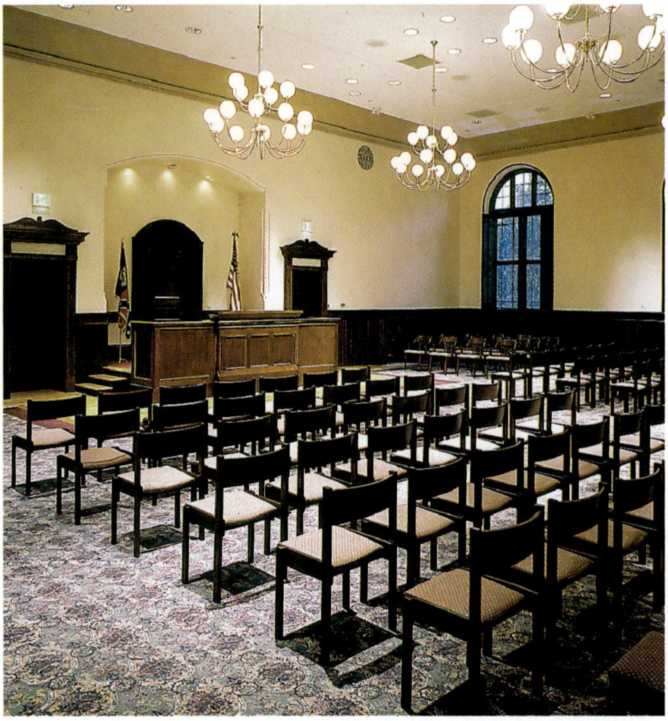

gures 13.4 and 13.5 *Historic Preservation/Adaptive Use, Institutional—Community Center. These two otos illustrate the attention to detail required in an historic preservation/adaptive use project. The urthouse was renovated to be used as a community center. Historical research uncovered the original int colors and the judge's bench design. Figure 13.4 shows the renovated steps and custom handrail. The asculine design was typical in public buildings during the era. To allow multiple use of the renovated urtroom, the judge's bench in Figure 13.5 dismantles into three sections. A custom carpet, designed in the ttern of the era, improves acoustics in the large room. Figure 11.12 illustrates the courthouse corridor. rchitect: Office of Jack Pyburn, Architect, Inc. Designer: Lynn M. Jones. Photographs by J. J. Williams.)*

icensing and Registration

veral states and provinces have passed some form of state gistration, usually in the form of a title act or practice act. *title act* protects those who are competent to use particu- "titles" such as "Certified" or "Registered" Interior De- gner. Because of the title act, clients can be assured that rsons using these titles are qualified professional interior signers.

A *practice act* requires those who qualify as professional terior designers and plan to practice this occupation to be ensed by a state board. The practice act is designed to gally recognize interior design as a profession, to ensure at designers work to protect the health, safety, and welfare their clients, and to ensure that interior designers are qual- ed by education and experience to practice. In addition to ssage of the NCIDQ exam, most of the acts require a com- nation of education and experience in order to qualify.

ore info online @

p://www.asid.org/legislation/grassroots/index.asp
ID legislation site

p://www.iida.org/legislation/ IIDA legislation site

Continuing Education

To maintain their registration, professionals are required in most states and provinces to acquire Continuing Education Units, or CEUs. CEUs are awarded for coursework completed at the professional development level and must be recorded by the state or province. NCIDQ serves as the repository for official transcripts of individuals completing approved CEU courses. CEUs must be approved by the Interior Design Continuing Educational Council to be applicable. Designers also voluntarily attend sessions on new products, designs, and procedures in order to remain current in the field.

Professional Interior Design Organizations

Many professional organizations assist professionals in sharing information, continuing their education, promoting the profession, and serving the public. Most organizations require a combination of education and experience in order to join, with professional membership also requiring passage of the NCIDQ exam. Names and addresses of many of these organizations are found in Table 13.1.

Table 13.1 *Professional Organizations*

American Institute of Architects, **AIA**
1735 New York Avenue NW
Washington, DC 20006
1-800 AIA-3837
www.aia.org

American Society of Interior Designers, **ASID**
608 Massachusetts Avenue NE
Washington, DC 20002-6006
(202) 546-3480
www.asid.org

Business & Institutional Furniture Manufacturers' Assoc., **BIFMA**
2680 Horizon Drive SE, Suite A-1
Grand Rapids, MI 49546-7500
(616) 285-3963
www.bifma.com

Color Association of the United States
315 West 39th Street
Studio 507
New York, NY 10018
(212) 947-7774
www.colorassociation.com

Color Marketing Group
5904 Richmond Hwy #408
Arlington, VA 22303
(703) 329-8500
www.colormarketing.org

Environmental Design Research Association, Inc., **EDRA**
P.O. Box 7146
Edmond, OK 73083-7146
(405) 330-4863
www.telepath.com/~edra/

Foundation for Interior Design Education Research, **FIDER**
146 Monroe Center NW, Suite 1318
Grand Rapids, MI 49503-2822
(616) 458-0400
www.fider.org

Illuminating Engineering Society of North America, **IES**
120 Wall Street, 17th Floor
New York, NY 10005
(212) 248-5000
www.iesna.org

Institute of Store Planners, **ISP**
25 North Broadway
Tarrytown, NY 10591
1-800 379-9912
www.ispo.org

Interior Design Educators Council, **IDEC**
9202 North Meridian, Suite 200
Indianapolis, IN 46260
(317) 816-6261
www.idec.org

The Interior Design Society, **IDS**
P.O. Box 2396
Highpoint, NC 27261
1-800 888-9590 ext. 6122
www.interiordesignsociety.org

Interior Designers of Canada, **IDC**
260 King Street East, #414
Toronto, Ontario, Canada M5A 1K3
(416) 594-9310
www.interiordesigncanada.org

International Association of Lighting Designers, **IALD**
Merchandise Mart, Suite 9-104
200 World Trade Center
Chicago, IL 60654
(312) 527-3677
www.iald.org

International Colour Authority
23 Bloonsbury Square
London WC1A 2PJ, England
(020) 7637 2211
www.internationalcolourauthority.com

International Facilities Management Association, **IFMA**
One East Greenway Plaza, Suite 1100
Houston, TX 77046-0194
(713) 623-4362
www.ifma.org

International Federation of Interior Designers, **IFI**
P.O. Box 91640
Auckland Park
Johannesburg 2006, South Africa
2711 888 8211
www.ifi.co.za

International Furnishings and Design Association, **IFDA**
191 Clarkville Rd
Princeton Junction, NJ 08550
(609) 799-3423
www.ifda.com

International Interior Design Association, **IIDA**
13-122 Merchandise Mart
Chicago, IL 60654-1104
(312) 467-1950
1-888 799-4432
www.iida.com

National Association of Home Builders, **NAHB**
1201 15th Street NW
Washington, DC 20005-2892
(202) 822-0200
1-800 368-5242
www.nahb.com

National Council for Interior Design Qualification, **NCIDQ**
1200 18th Street NW, Suite 1001
Washington, DC 20036-2506
(202) 721-0220
www.ncidq.org

National Kitchen and Bath Association, **NKBA**
687 Willow Grove Street
Hackettstown, NJ 07840
1-877 NKBA-PRO
www.nkba.org

National Lighting Bureau, **NLB**
8811 Colesville Rd, Suite G106
Silver Spring, MD 20910
(301) 587-9572
www.nib.org

ASID

The American Society of Interior Designers **(ASID)** is a professional international organization established to enact and maintain standards of excellence to enhance the growing recognition of interior design as a profession. ASID was formed in 1975 through the consolidation of the American Institute of Interior Designers and the National Society of I terior Designers, but its roots date back to the founding the American Institute of Decorators in 1931. ASID is t largest organization of interior designers in the world, repr senting over 30,000 members in the United States a abroad. It represents interior design as a profession de cated to serving people, and it provides a forum for its me

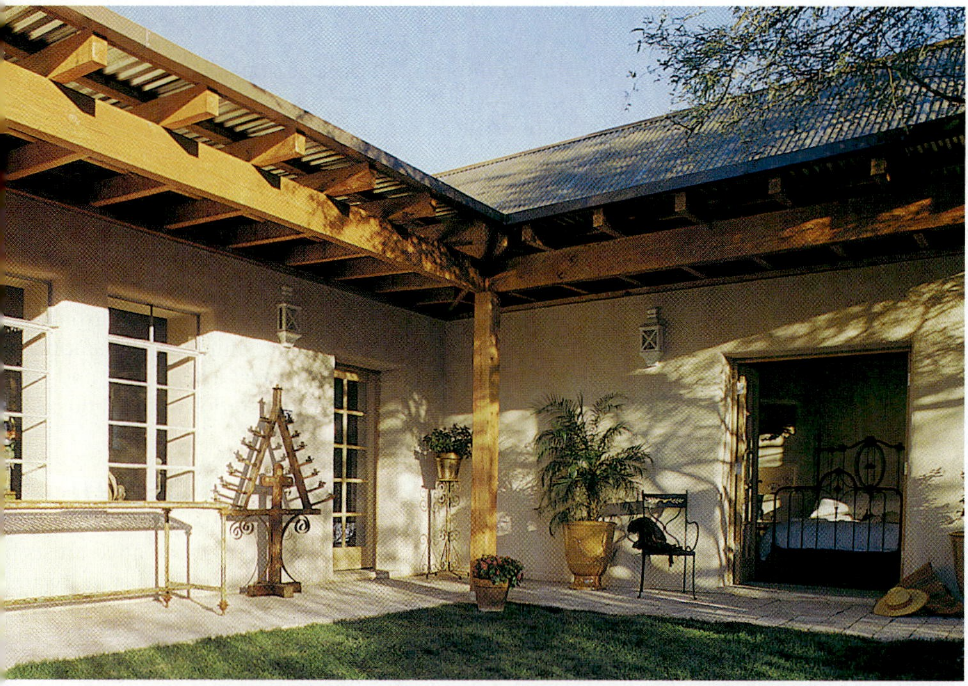

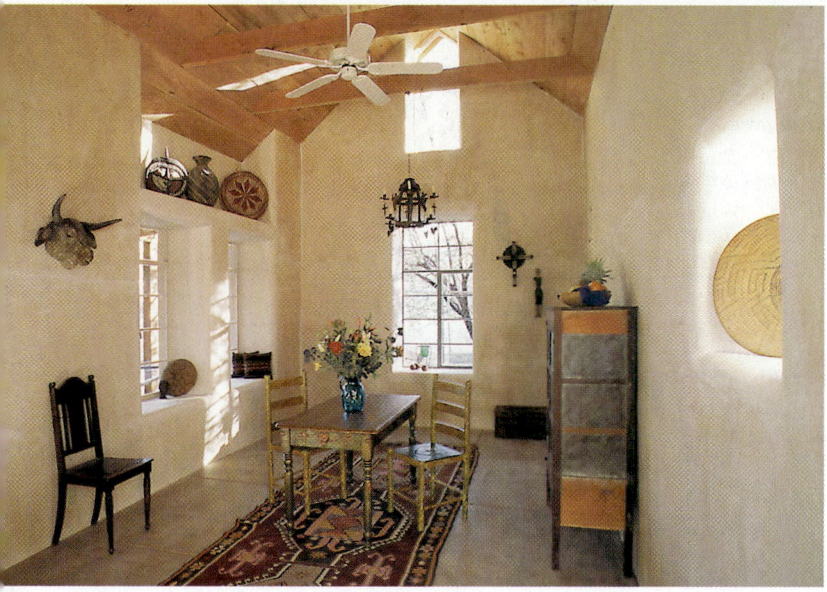

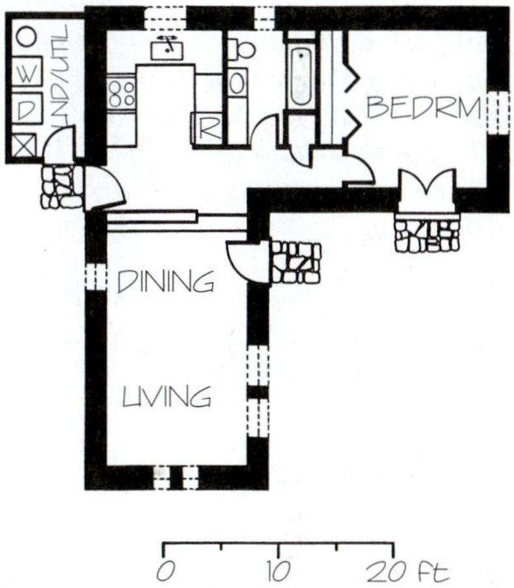

Figure 13.6
Environmental Design—Straw Bale House. Designed as a guest house, this 850-sq.-ft. straw bale home boasts 24″-thick walls with R values from R-40 to R-55. Custom niches, handmade tiles, and softly tinted plaster walls add to the cozy character. (Architect: Paul Weiner. Designer: Pam Tillman. Photographs by Bill Steen.)

rs to bring their differing points of view into harmony to omote unified action. ASID's mission statement is: "ASID is e definitive resource for knowledge sharing, advocacy of erior designers' right-to-practice, professional education, d expansion of interior design markets." ASID's vision as organization:

- Identifies interior designers by the results and benefits they bring to the built environment through their specialized design skills and sound business practices
- Is vital to the success of the interior design community, its partners, and customers through shared knowledge and collective action
- Gives interior designers the strategic tools to impact behavior and perform beyond customer expectations
- Is the catalyst for understanding and managing the changing working and living environments

IIDA

The International Interior Design Association **(IIDA)** is an internationally established design organization founded in 1994 as a merger of the Institute of Business Designers, the Council of Federal Interior Designers, and the International Society of Interior Designers. With over 10,000 members, the

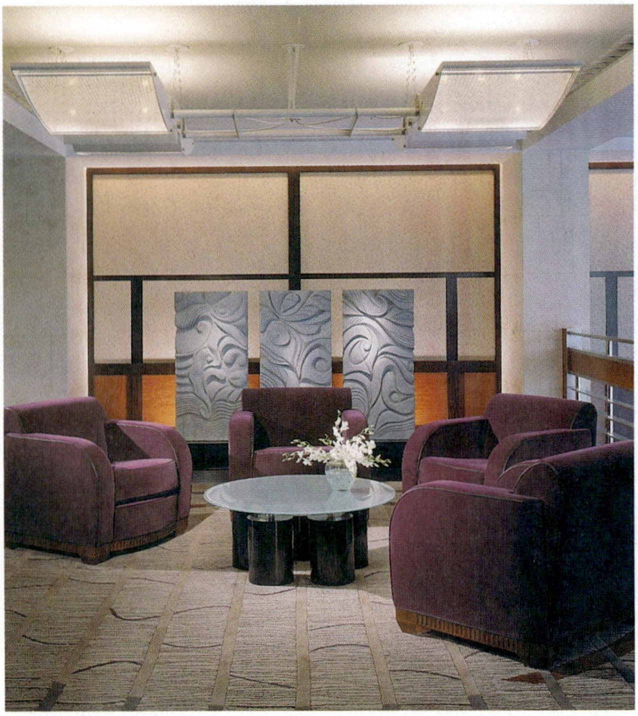

Figure 13.7 *Commercial Office Design—International Clients. At the Embassy of the Republic of Singapore in Washington, D.C., the designers were sensitive to the multicultural heritage of Singapore. The reception area is enhanced with naturalistic art and the adaptive grid pattern is accented by fine organic curved forms in the furniture and custom area rug. The floor plan, in the shape of a cross, reflects the typical residential floor plan in the "Garden City." (Architect/Designer: RTKL Associates. Photograph by Scott McDonald/Hedrich-Blessing.)*

organization serves a broad base of professionals, industry members, and students. IIDA's mission "is to enhance the quality of life through excellence in interior design and to advance interior design through knowledge." In order to enact this mission, IIDA:

- Advocates for design excellence
- Nurtures a global interior design community
- Maintains educational standards
- Responds to trends in business and design
- Provides superior information about interior design and related issues, using its own rapidly developing body of knowledge as a resource

IDC

Interior Designers of Canada is the national professional association. It works with the provincial associations to advance the interior design profession and to promote quality in education and practice. IDC has served the Canadian interior design industry since 1972, advancing the profession through high standards of education, professional development, professional responsibility, and communication. Full professional membership requires passage of the NCIDQ exam.

IDEC

The Interior Design Educators Council **(IDEC),** incorporate in 1967, is dedicated to the development of interior desig education. IDEC, according to Article 2 of its bylaws,

> is dedicated to the advancement of education and research in interior design. IDEC fosters exchange of info mation, improvement of educational standards, and development of the body of knowledge relative to the quality of life and human performance in the interior environment. IDEC concentrates on the establishment and strengthening of lines of communication among educators, practitioners, educational institutions, and othe organizations concerned with interior design education.

The Business of Interior Design

Successful interior designers are not only creative artists b also perceptive business people. Designers must be aware business practices, procedures, management, and marketi techniques in order to succeed in the profession. *Befo starting a business, a designer should consult with an atto ney, an accountant, an insurance agent, and a tax advis* The following section highlights the business issues involve in the practice of interior design.

The Business Plan

Most lending institutions require the submission of a bus ness plan in order to qualify for a business loan. The pla describes the business, its market, competition, locatio management, personnel, and projected revenue and e penses. The Small Business Administration can assist desig ers in developing this plan.

Business Structures

There are four basic ways to structure an interior design bus ness. The *sole proprietorship* is the simplest. The individu and the company are basically one. The owner personally r ceives all the benefits of the business, but also bears all t risks. Personal belongings, such as an owner's home, c and other valuables, may be garnished by a business los The *partnership* is similar to the sole proprietorship, exce the benefits and risks are shared by two or more individua

In an *association* an individual "associates" with an exis ing or established firm. The associate may bring clients to t firm, and the firm may offer the associate a working env ronment and limited liability. Other forms of associatio also exist.

The safest of all business types is the *corporation*. A c poration is a separate entity from its owners, who are t shareholders. Although more difficult to start, corporatio offer limited liability to their owners.

Insurance

Before starting a business, the designer must research and d cide upon necessary types of insurance. The two broad typ

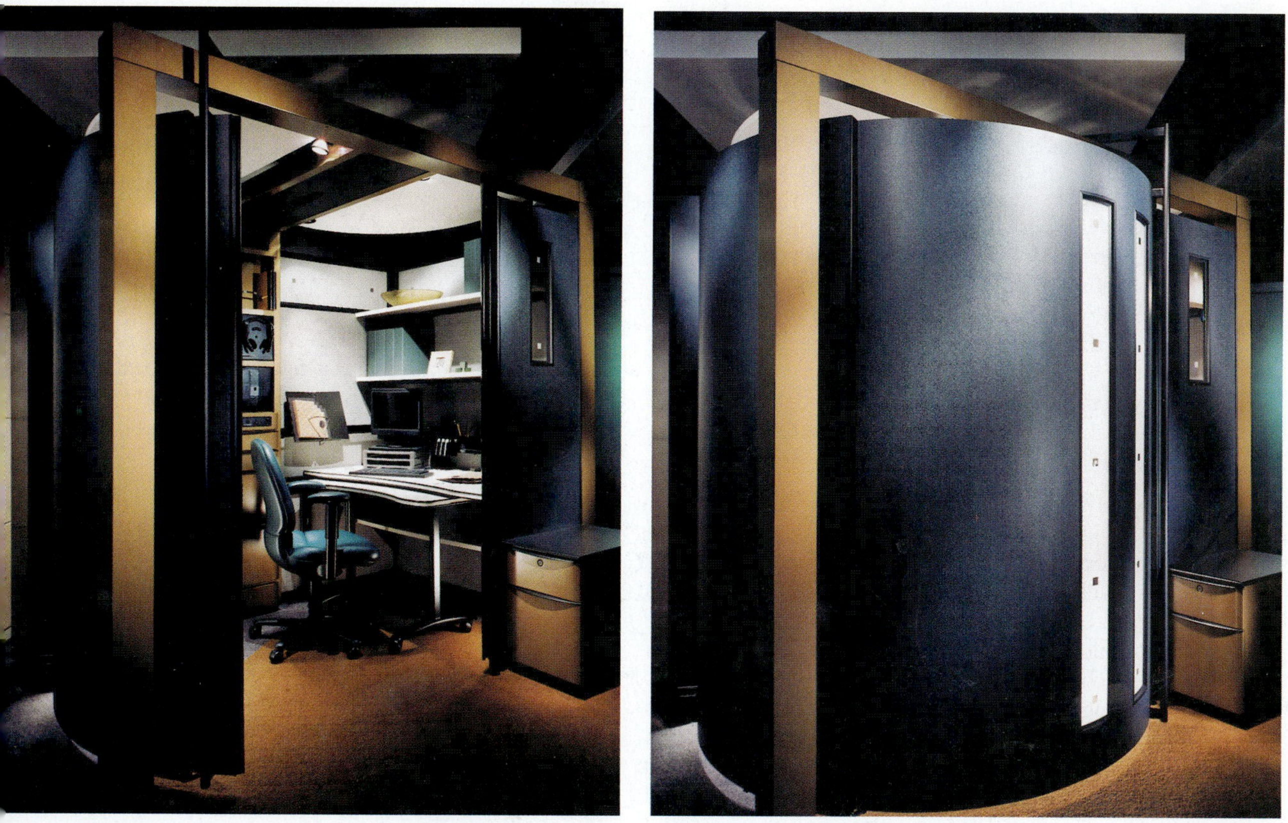

gure 13.8 *Furniture Design—Technology. The Personal Harbor is a 6′ circular office ace with a sliding door for total privacy. Designed for open office environments, the nservative space provides a quiet retreat. (Courtesy of Steelcase, Inc.)*

insurance include *property and liability insurance,* which otects the business, and *life and health insurance,* which otects the individuals. Another important type of business surance, called *errors and omissions,* protects designers hen errors are made in contract documents. Consulting with trustworthy insurance agent and attorney is important.

usiness Documents

esigners will find it necessary to acquire several business ocuments. Most municipalities require a *business license,* ailable from local city or county officials. A *resale certifi- ate* or *tax number,* required in some states, allows design- s to purchase products for clients; other states require ernative tax documentation.

Designers also will establish a separate business *checking count* to accurately track revenue and expenses. Other siness documents may include items such as purchase or- rs, invoices, timesheets, and telephone logs. An account- t can be very helpful in identifying and tracking income d expenses.

tting up a Design Studio

ere are generally three types of office arrangements when tting up a design studio: the home office, an office associ- ed with retail sales, and the business office. The decision should be based on the goals and financial viability of the firm. For any office arrangement, budgets need to be considered for furnishings and equipment. One significant consideration is the cost of computers for business and computer-aided design work.

Technology in the Studio

Computers and related technologies have become essential pieces of equipment in all design firms. Aside from their obvious assistance with word processing and general office tasks, advanced computer systems can help in performing the following functions:

- *Estimating costs*—With cost information stored in the computer's memory, the task of projecting plan proposals into cost estimates is simplified.
- *Preparing specifications*—The computer can store suppliers' catalog data, including prices and other valuable information, facilitating efficient preparation for project specifications. Manufacturers can supply electronic images of their products that can be introduced in plans and perspective drawings.
- *Ordering*—Orders for required furnishings can be placed directly through the computer to the manufacturer.
- *Drafting*—Computer-aided design (CAD) programs allow drafting on the computer. Although many firms

develop initial programming and conceptual designs by hand, construction documents are commonly completed on the computer.

- *Drawing perspectives*—CAD systems are also extremely beneficial in creating three-dimensional design drawings (see Figures I.4 and I.9 A and B). Some programs can render perspectives. Advanced computer systems perform immediate color changes, as well as changes in lighting design and location. Other advanced systems permit a client to visually walk through an interior by viewing the moving images on the computer screen.
- *Researching and communicating*—Because of the power of the Internet, manufacturers' data, new product information, current research data, and the ability to transfer mail and design files are all immediately available to the designer.

Design teams may consist of multiple firms located in different parts of the country or world. Designers and allied professionals frequently communicate via the computer. For instance, CAD files can be transferred via the Internet. Teleconferencing and digital cameras allow information to be quickly communicated on a global scale.

Obviously, technology is an essential tool in design firms. Before purchasing a particular software package, designers should thoroughly review the software marketplace. With prices ranging from $150 for basic software to over $15,000 for a complete system, a personalized hands-on class and demonstration are essential for understanding the possibilities and limitations of various programs.

The Source Library and Trade Relationships

A unique aspect of the design studio is the source room or resource library. The library contains catalogues of furnishings and furniture, along with actual samples of a variety of finishes and fabrics. The acquisition and organization of these materials require careful planning. A firm specializing in health care design will need to contact different sources than a firm specializing in residential design. A listing of manufacturers for specific sources is available through reputable design periodicals and their annual source guides. Various websites also display manufacturers' products.

Industry representatives also supply designers with these source materials. For a wider array of samples or to view actual furniture pieces, designers work with design centers or merchandise marts. Many of these centers are open only to members of the design trade. Clients are brought to these establishments as guests of the designer to view specific furnishings. Establishing a working rapport with these trade sources provides for efficient business transactions. It is said that "designers are only as good as their sources."

Interiors of design firms are seen in Figures 13.9 and 13.10.

Marketing

Before starting any business, the owners must decide who their prospective clients are, how to reach them, and who the competition is. Useful marketing tools include the followin among others:

- A creative yet professional name
- A proper business location based on the firm's needs
- Letterhead, business cards, résumé, and related marketing brochures
- A website
- A professional portfolio of previous projects
- Signage
- Advertisements in the telephone book and other strategically placed locations

Other places to advertise a firm include local chamber commerce gatherings, community clubs and organizatior and professional interior design society referral networks.

Business Contracts

Once the business has been established, designers must d velop contracts with clients. Contracts consist of two bas types: the letter of agreement and the professional contrac

The *letter of agreement,* a simple contract written in t form of a letter, is legally binding. It is typically used f smaller residential projects. *Professional contracts* more th oughly define the agreement between the owner and t client. Professional contracts are available to membe through professional organizations or can be developed conjunction with an attorney.

Both forms of contracts should contain as a minimum t following information:

- Date
- Identification of parties involved
- Location of work, including an address and descriptior
- Scope of services
- Cost of services and payment schedule
- Additional or reimbursed charges
- Arrangements for working with allied professionals
- Purchasing arrangements
- Expressed consent to photograph and publish project
- Time frame for completion
- Appropriate signatures with date
- Retainer due upon acceptance of contract

All contracts, regardless of their source, need to be review by an attorney.

Fee Structures

One of the most complicated tasks in writing the contract determining the cost of the services. Interior designers a compensated for their services in a number of ways. It is i portant that the designer and client agree on the terms payment. Following are the most common fee systems:

- A designer who receives a *flat or fixed fee* determines the time and expense involved for the particular proje and charges the client this specified amount.
- An *hourly fee* is a set rate for each hour of time spent on the project. This fee varies depending on many fac tors, including customary fees in a particular area, the

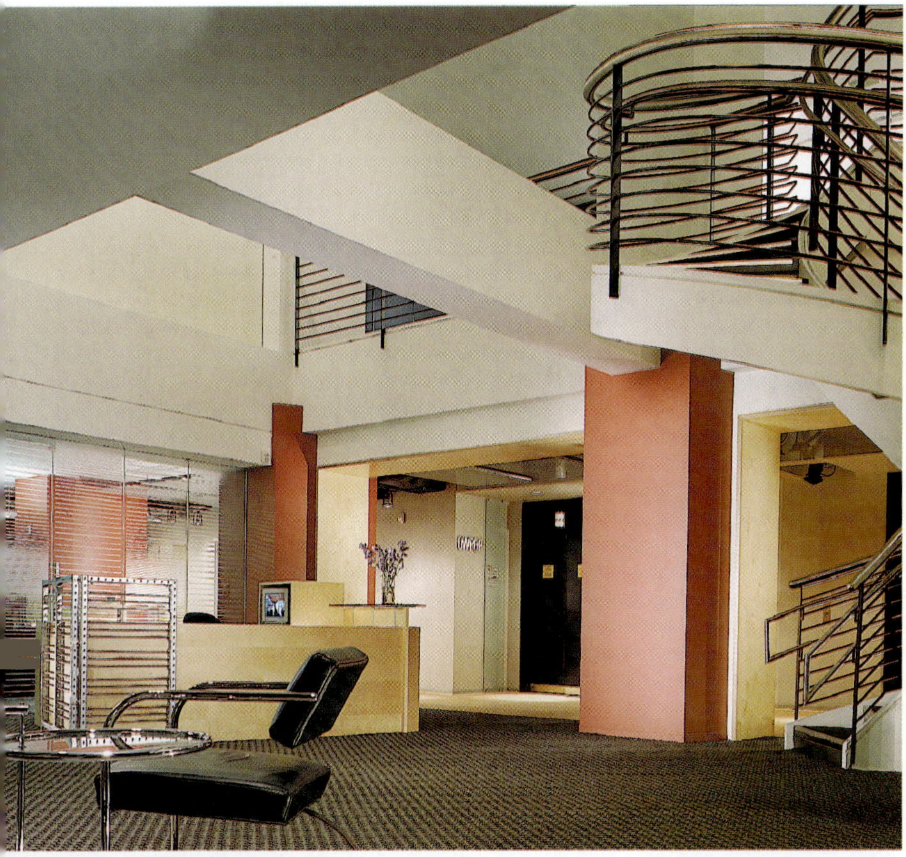

Figure 13.9 *Interior Design Studios. Designers frequently work in open office environments, as shown here and in Figure 13.10. Strong geometric forms and a keen sensitivity to natural light define the interiors of OWP & P in Chicago. (Architect/Designer: OWP & P. Photographs by Chris Barrett/Hedrich-Blessing.)*

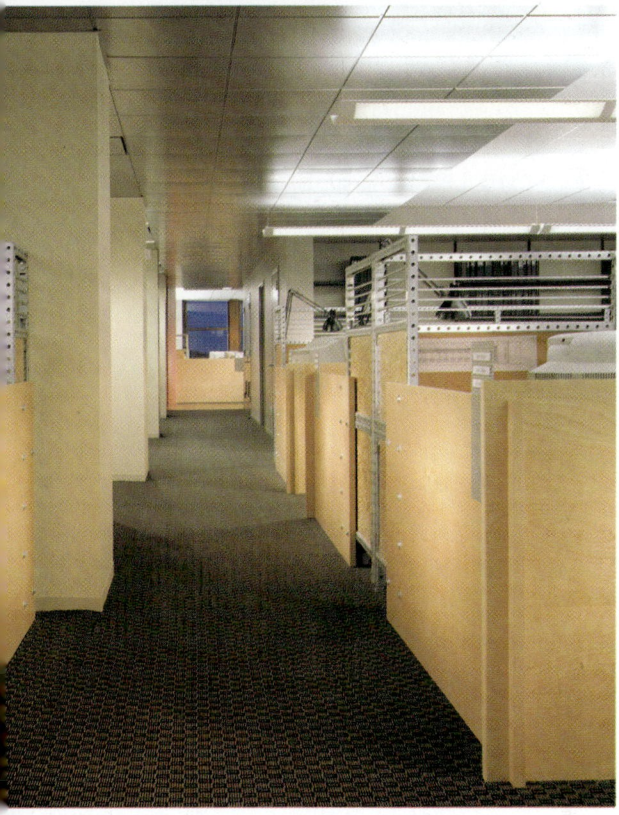

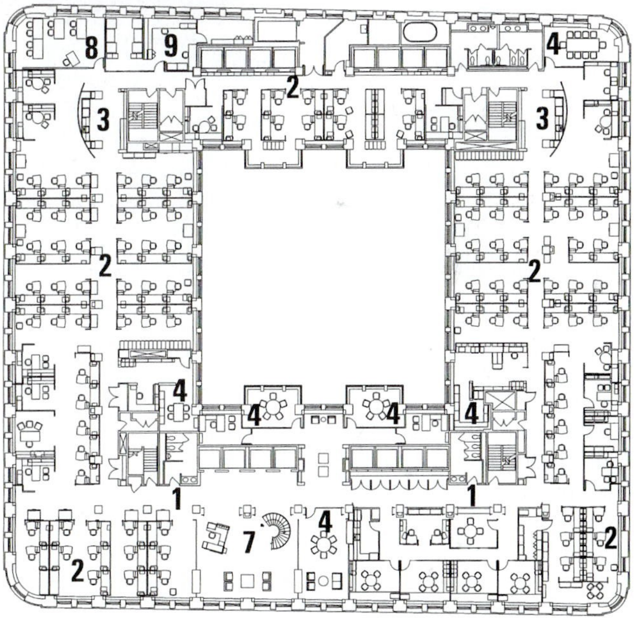

21st Floor

Legend
1. Main Street
2. Neighborhood
3. Town Square
4. Conference Room/Team Room
5. Central Resource Library
6. Office Services
7. Reception
8. Training Room
9. Information Technology

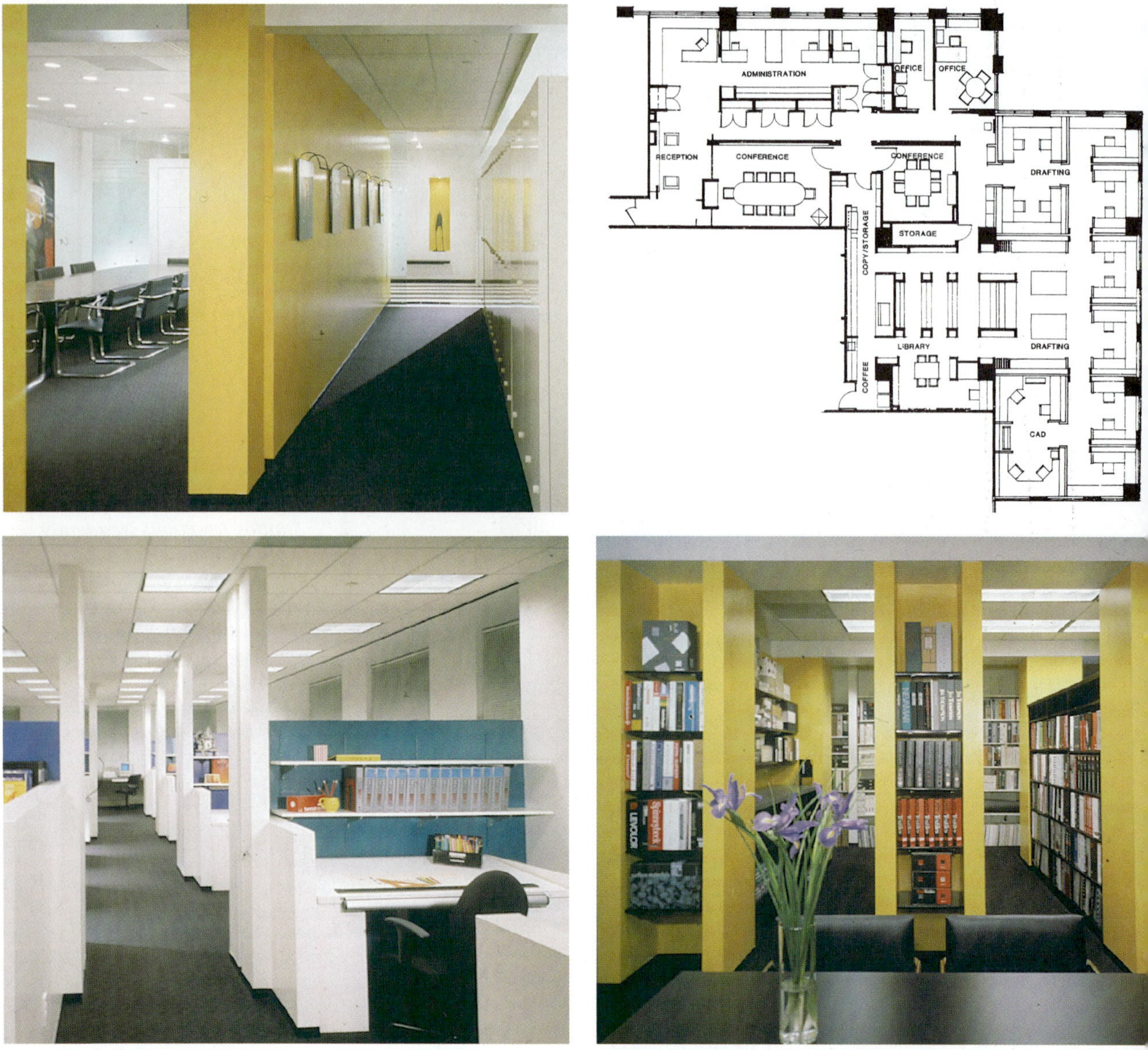

Figure 13.10 *Interior Design Studio. Intense colors and contrasting linear forms define the interiors of Quantrell Mullins & Associates in Atlanta. (Designers: Quantrell Mullins & Associates. Photographs by Brian Robbins Photography.)*

competence and status of the designer, and the demand for his or her services. Sometimes this fee has a cap on the total cost of the design services.

- A designer who charges a *cost plus fee* buys merchandise at wholesale prices and sells the goods to clients for an additional percentage charge. The reverse of this is the *retail cost less a percentage fee:* The designer purchases merchandise at wholesale cost, but sells it to the client at a percentage off retail.
- A *fee based on the total square feet of the project* is generally used by experienced designers who are fairly knowledgeable in estimating costs involved in completing a space. The fee is charged for each square foot based o the square footage required for the entire project.
- A designer may receive a *percentage of the total projec expenditure*. This system provides a guaranteed fee regardless of what the project may cost. If the completed project has additional costs, the designer is financially protected.

More info online @

http://www.asid.org/design_basics/working_with_designer/how_services.asp ASID article on how designers charge for their service

rofessional Ethics

ofessional interior designers must maintain the highest vel of integrity. Designers need a clear definition of right d wrong. Facts should not be muddied or glossed over to de the truth. Designers have a responsibility to maintain e highest of standards with the public, the client, other inrior design professionals, allied colleagues, and employers. SID's Code of Ethics preamble states, "Members of the nerican Society of Interior Designers are required to conict their professional practice in a manner that will inspire e respect of clients, suppliers of goods and services to the ofession, and fellow professional designers, as well as the neral public."

In regard to the public, designers must recognize that they e required to follow all building codes and regulations. Igrance of codes is not an acceptable reason to skirt reirements. Designers are responsible for researching codes r a project and then following those requirements.

When dealing with clients, the designer must clearly dee the scope of work and compensation received for the oject. Designers should not discuss one client's project with other client, and they should never accept a financial "kickck" from a vendor for specifying their product. Sources of venue should be clearly defined to the client. Furthermore, signers should always let the client know the status of a job. If a specified product has been discontinued, designers must verify the appropriate substitution with the client.

Designers also have a responsibility to their design and allied professional colleagues. Designers should never criticize other designers' work. Designers should not solicit other designers' business. If freelancing for another designer, the freelancer must honor the employer's design decisions. Designers should work as a collaborative team with allied professionals. When problems arise, shifting blame does not solve the problem; teamwork does.

Additionally, designers have a responsibility to the profession of interior design. They should encourage the exchange of information and remain current in design practices. Designers should become involved in community projects and always present the interior design profession in the best possible light. Problems should be addressed in professional society meetings where true grassroots change can take place.

Designers have a responsibility to their employers. Information completed at one firm should not be copied or taken to another firm or used in another freelance project without the consent of the employer. As designers leave a firm, every effort should be made to facilitate the exchange of information to the new employee.

Finally, designers have a responsibility to maintain a sustainable environment. Forty percent of all resources are

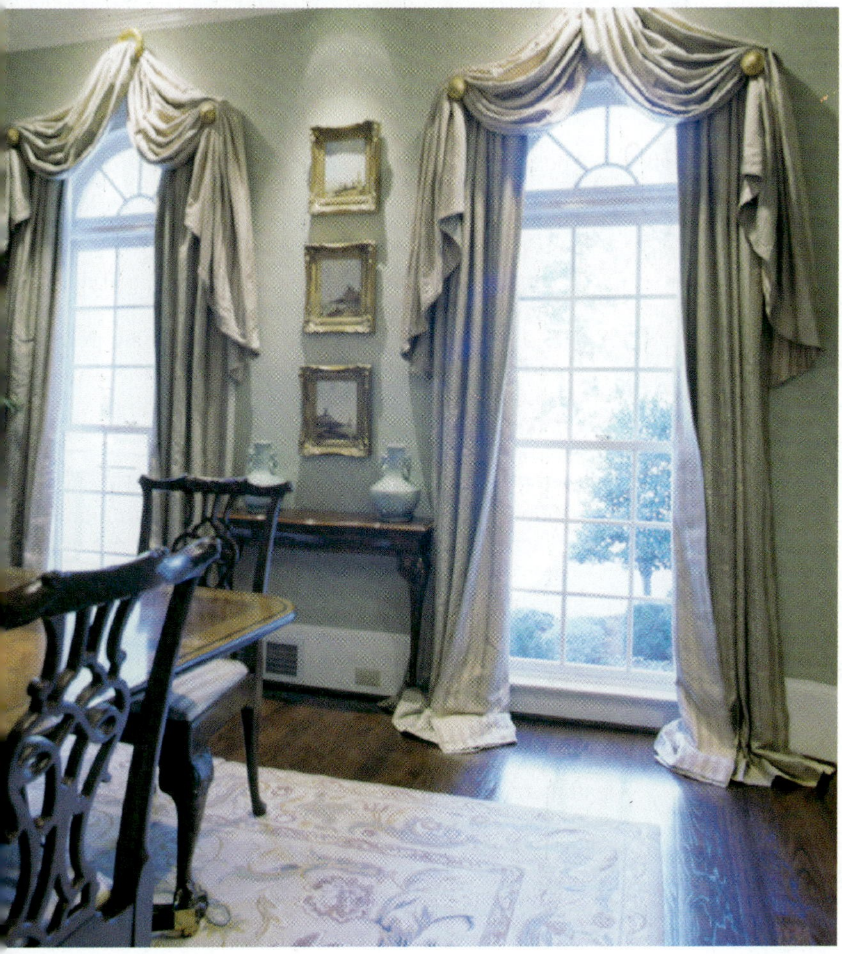

Figure 13.11 *Furnishings in Design, Attention to Detail—Window Treatment. Quality design requires attention to the finer points. In this formal dining room, the designer accents the window height through the use of a flowing window treatment. Custom lighting and carefully selected art and accessories add to the ambience. (Designer: Miner Details. Photograph by Deborah Whitlaw.)*

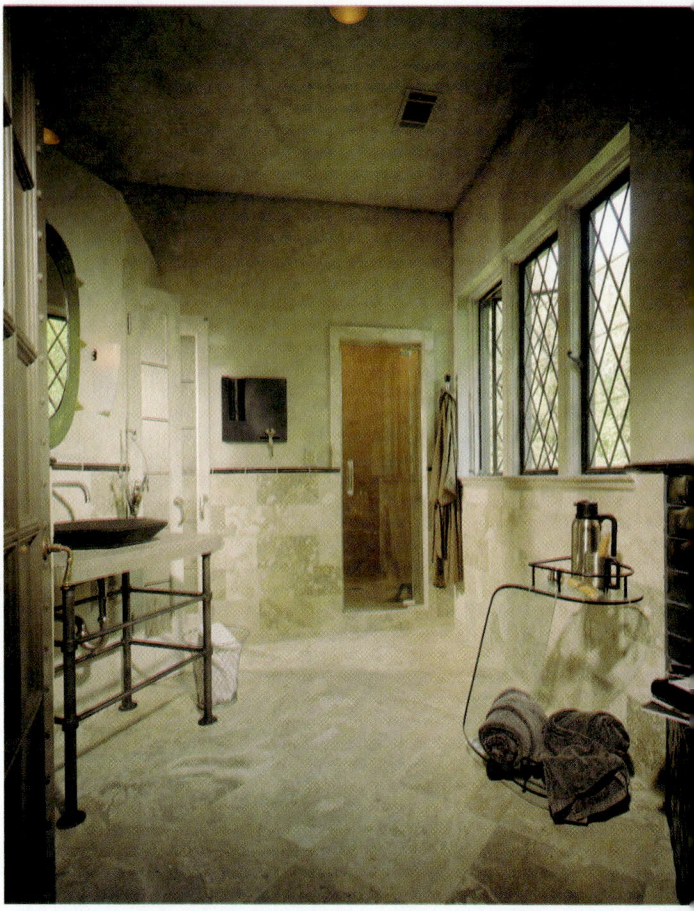

Figure 13.12 *Furnishings in Design, Attention to Detail—Bathroom Design. For this gentleman's bathroom, the original narrow room was gutted, and sleek, contemporary, moisture-resistant materials were used. (Designer: Jackie Naylor Interiors. Photograph ©Robert Thien.)*

consumed by the building industry, and 40 percent of all landfill waste comes from buildings (Lichtenwalter, R., *Green Eggs and Spam*). The protection of the "welfare of the public," as advocated in the definition of interior design, requires the respectful use of the Earth's resources. Designers must accurately research products and apply design solutions that do not harm occupants or result in wasteful or destructive harvesting or farming practices.

Interior Design Forecast

The profession of interior design is relatively young, since the field of interior design has emerged only in the last 100 years. Possibilities for career specialization and advancement in the profession are numerous.

Emerging Career Specializations

Because of the recognition of the health benefits of a comfortable environment, the aging population, technological advancements, the need for energy conservation, and a move toward a simpler and more meaningful lifestyle, significant changes in the design industry have occurred. For example,

- Clients are better educated than in the past and are asking more questions.
- The aging population is aware of the need for accessib housing and buildings.
- The medical profession has recognized the need for ae thetics in the health care industry.
- Because of the Internet and networking capabilities, more people are working at home.
- The private office is shrinking and becoming portable. Open office environments are interspersed with confer encing areas and personal spaces.
- Clients place a high priority on prestigious locations an security.
- People are interested in a sustainable environment. In residential design, owners want homes with high ener efficiency, low maintenance, labor-saving devices, and water-saving appliances, especially dishwashers, toilets and shower heads. In commercial design, clients are re questing sustainable products and building materials a attention to IAQ. Businesses recognize the significance of green design (see "Sustainable Design: LEED-CI" in Chapter 11).

These demands have created new career options that a leading to new and innovative design solutions in the hea care/elderly care industry, in design technology, and in su tainable green design. The similarity among these speci izations is the trend toward convenience in the work a home environment to improve the quality of life and t quality of the environment.

ealth Care Design and the Aging Population

vareness has evolved in the medical profession for the ›ed of quality aesthetics in the healing environment. Where)ssible, health care interiors are incorporating hospitality ıaracteristics. Fabrics and furnishings have taken on a armer and richer appearance. Hospital furnishings are now ›signed to conceal medical equipment and are losing their stitutional appearance.

The aging population has recognized the importance of cessibility in housing as well as in the commercial envi- nment. Because of the personal benefits of living at home ıd the high costs of institutional care, residences are lapted to allow the elderly to maintain independence (see gure 3.28). Retirement communities have also recognized e need for various levels of assistance to their occupants. dividual and community residences for the elderly are de- gned to accommodate wheelchairs; furnishings and cabi- ›try are readily available to meet universal needs.

esign Technology: The Virtual ffice in Homes and Hotels

ith the electronic developments of online networking, tele-)nferencing, and Internet access, going to work may no nger mean going to an office (Figure 13.13). The office fur- ture market has expanded to include ergonomically de- gned furniture available for home use. Designers should)ecify appropriate power and communication lines to all)tential computer locations including bedrooms and tchens.

The *virtual office* is a portable office. Furniture designed to be transported as luggage allows employees to take their office on the road. Consequently, the hospitality market is adapting to the electric and space needs of the virtual office in hotel rooms and restaurants. Conference centers are now equipped with teleconferencing and interactive video capabilities.

The airline industry has also recognized the needs of the commuting office and responded accordingly. Telephones are common amenities on airplanes, and airlines have begun to provide greater comfort via more first class and business seats and more gracious spacing in coach.

The portable office concept also affects the space requirements in commercial office designs. The private 12′ × 15′ office or personal open office cubicle may now be shared by various individuals (commonly called "hoteling"). Small conference rooms may be used when privacy is required (see Design Scenario: UPS Innoplex in Chapter 3).

Design Technology: The Smart House and the Home Theatre

A buzzword of the 1990s was the term "cocooning," and it has continued into the new millennium. Wishing to spend more time at home, people are investing substantial resources in home furnishings, accessories, entertainment, and other elements that contribute to a safer and more enjoyable environment. A continuing focus is the development of the "Smart House," a term that refers to an electronically controlled environment. For example, the amount of light for either nighttime or daytime illumination can be programmed to suit the occupants' particular needs. The custom-designed

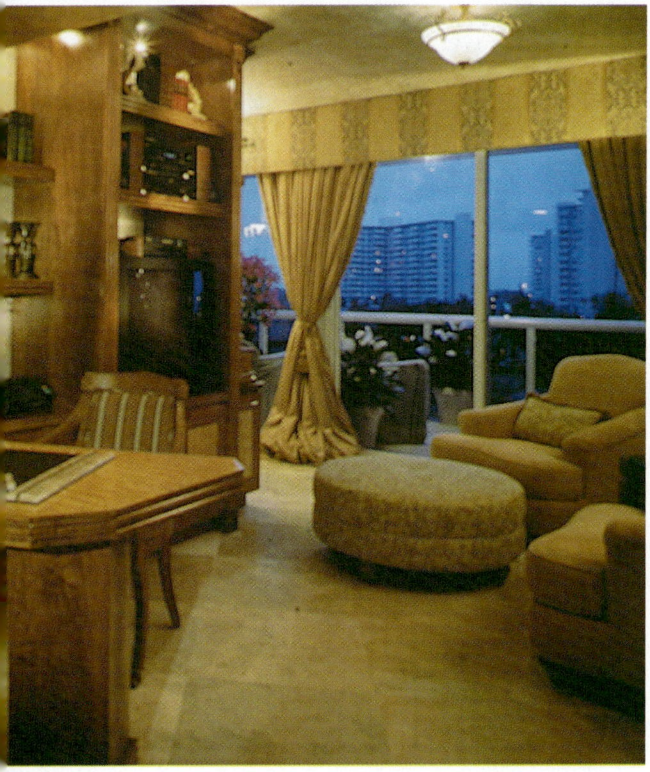

Figure 13.13 *Specialty Design, Home Office: This open office has been designed with sophistication and practicality in mind. Task lighting and concealed technology equipment allow the office to blend with the dining and living areas. Figure 7.8 shows the breakfast nook. (Interiors: Perla Lichi, Perla Lichi Design, ID 1727, Tamara, FL. Photograph by Barry Grossman. Residence: Condominium, private residence, Essex model at L'Hermitage, Ft. Lauderdale, FL. [Courtesy of* On Design.*])*

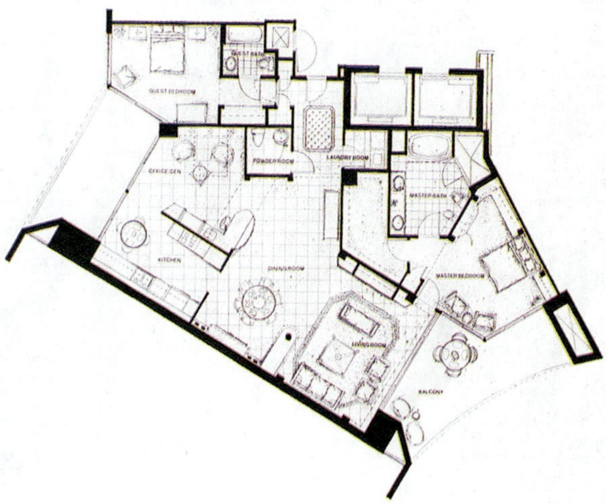

Smart House is planned to provide the latest developments in technology, including security systems, lighting, intercoms, central vacuums, entertainment systems, Internet access, and even equipment that can monitor children's activities within the home.

Because people desire to spend more time at home, the home theatre has become more prevalent in interior design. The theatre has evolved to include large-screen viewing, comfortable theatre seating, surround-sound, and accoutrements such as popcorn stands and soda dispensers (Figure 13.14).

Outlook for the Profession

The emerging career specializations just discussed result from the evolution of the profession of interior design. NCIDQ, FIDER, and the professional organizations often work together in analyzing the direction of this evolution. The Design Futures Council is one organization that works globally as a network of design professionals. Its mission is to explore trends, changes, and new opportunities in desi architecture, engineering, and building technology. newsletter, *DesignIntelligence,* is published monthly.

A prominent view of the future of the interior design p fession emerged through the efforts of FIDER. Having ceived funding from ASID, IIDA, and the Joel Polsky-Fixtu Furniture-FIDER Endowment, FIDER developed a resea project called *The Future of Interior Design*. The first ph of the project required the selection of fifteen to eighteen sionaries from design practice, industry, education, and search to form a focus group. Individuals were carefu selected based on their varied backgrounds, interests, a cultural and regional diversity. This group defined which ture trends, based on sociocultural, economic, political, vironmental, and technological changes, will most lik affect interior design practice, education, and research.

Phase two of the project was the assimilation of the sionaries' findings into a survey and its distribution to a r dom sample of over 2200 designers in the U.S. and Cana Twelve trends were identified as the basis for the surv

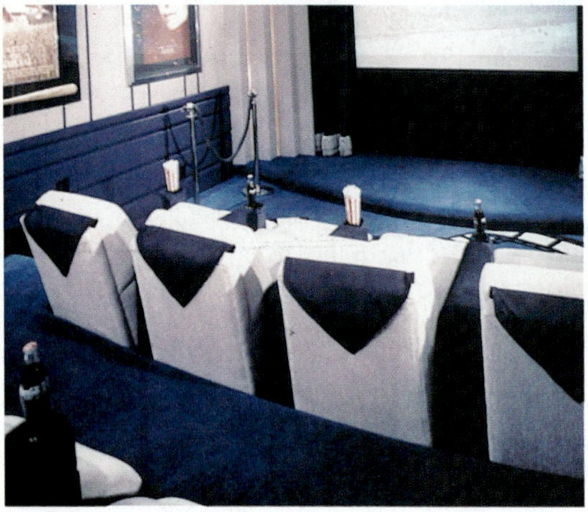

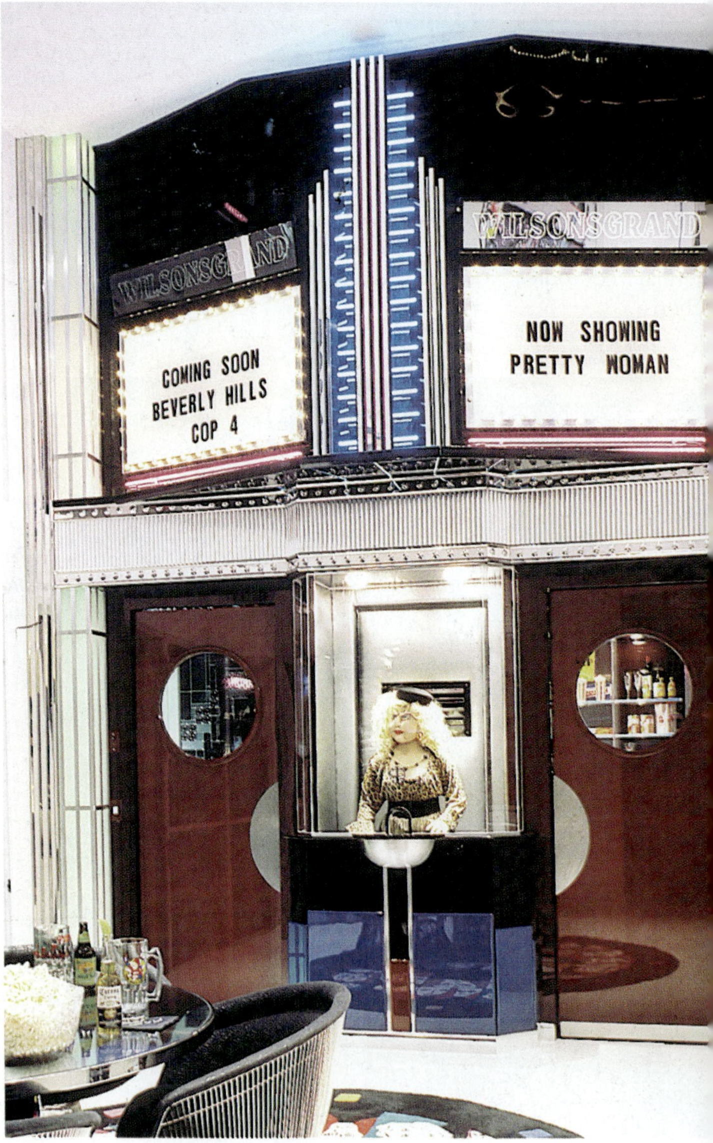

Figure 13.14 *Specialty Design, Technology. This elaborate home theatre includes neon lights, a marquee, and a concession stand. The interior of the theatre includes an oversized movie screen, comfortable theatre seats, and speakers that surround the viewer. (Designer: Stevenson Design Group. Photograph by Robert Brantley.)*

ble 13.2 lists them in order of importance based on the sur-
y results. Some of the more prominent trends from the
oject and other professional sources are discussed below.

ore info online @

p://www.greenwayconsulting.com/press.htm Design Futures
uncil

p://www.di.net *DesignIntelligence* website

nvironmental Conservation

e need for environmental conservation has surfaced not ly in interior design practice, but also as a relevant national d global issue involving industry, manufacturing, and ed- ation. This trend, which began with the environmental ovement of the 1960s, is still evolving. According to a 1994 nes Mirror-Roper study, approximately 42 percent of the nerican population donate their time or money to envi- nmental causes.

As noted throughout this text, many manufacturers in the sign industry also recognized this trend and are now pro- cing sustainable design products. Websites and periodicals e dedicated to green products and green design. A true stainable product mimics nature. All designs in nature are sed on recycling; nothing is wasted. True green products e not only environmentally friendly, they also provide for e sustainability of the natural environment. Manufacturers d inventors are wise to follow in this direction; designers, representatives of end users, are wise to specify these een products.

Dennis Weaver, actor, humanitarian, and environmental- , has developed an interesting approach in response to this nd by forming the Institute of Ecolonomics. "Ecolonom- ." is a blend of the words *ecology* and *economics* in recog- ion of human dependence on both a healthy environment d a healthy economy. The institute advocates the use of sponsible business practices—including design—to clean the environment. In Weaver's words, "When we realize can make a buck cleaning up the environment, it will be ne." As demonstration of his commitment to the environ- ent, Weaver resides in an Earthship—a building made from ed tires, aluminum cans, and sustainable materials. (See stainable Design: Solar Architecture and the Earthship").

Table 13.2 *Survey Results*

Environmental Conservation: Interior designers are likely to become increasingly responsible for ecological impacts of design decisions.

Accountability: Reliable performance standards and quantifiable measures of user satisfaction must demonstrate that interior design is a tangible benefit to clients.

Profession Gains Respect: The interior design profession is maturing as it deals with licensing, increasing codes and regulations, adjusting to an electronic age, and dealing with economic shifts. As a result, the profession will be more respected by the public.

Teams of Specialists: Teams of knowledgeable design specialists and experts with different backgrounds are likely to be required for future design projects.

Expand Studio Education: Studio teaching must change to emphasize broad-based general knowledge and critical thinking skills to solve complex problems of people and place.

Sharing Cost of High-Tech Education: Technology has increased costs and time required for undergraduate education. These costs need to be shared by industry, practice, and educational institutions.

Client Participation: Clients and design experts will work more closely and accommodation of clients' needs and desires will be the priority.

Preserve Cultural-Social Diversity: Interior designers are likely to become increasingly responsible for the cultural and social implications of design decisions.

Global Resource Competition: Design firms and companies are likely to face increasing competition from foreign companies for global markets and resources.

Graduate Education Gains Significance: In response to the rapid proliferation of new knowledge, graduate education gains importance.

Customization of Products: Industry will use large database systems so designers may work more directly with a manufacturer to specify a customized product.

Culturally Diverse Designers: Interior designers with cross-cultural language skills and international travel experiences will be in high demand.

For statistical analysis of these results, see FIDER, or *IDEC Conference Proceedings,* March 1996, pp. 15–20.

countability

other relevant trend in the future of the profession is the ed to be accountable. Interior design professional organi- tions must work together to demonstrate the tangible ben- ts of interior design.

Kerwin Kettler, in *ASID Professional Designer,* surveyed 0 business owners and their opinions about productivity. nety percent believe productivity could be increased by provements in office design. The top four factors influ- cing productivity included access, comfort, privacy, and xibility. As designers work with commercial clients, a pre- ninary productivity analysis could be performed. The results of this analysis could be used as a baseline to measure productivity levels at the end of the design process. Designers must be able to document the benefit of their services to clients, particularly commercial clients. Research and programming analysis need to establish productivity baselines to document the quantifiable benefits of a quality interior environment.

FIDER is also conducting a research project called *Strategic Stories.* The stories are gathered from case studies of interior design projects. The interior design process and results are reviewed using a productivity and personal analysis of the client, the designer, the architects, and the end user.

SUSTAINABLEDESIGN

Solar Architecture and the Earthship

As discussed in Chapter 5, passive and active solar designs and earth-sheltered designs create living environments that require less energy to run and produce less waste. A cutting-edge design utilizing these principles, while incorporating waste materials as buildings blocks, is the Earthship.

The ecological consequences of the construction industry are well explored and documented. Old growth forests are vanishing forever. Generating electricity leaves nuclear waste and gasses that lead to acid rain. Sewage and chemicals contaminate the groundwater necessary for all life to survive. The environment cannot indefinitely support the current methods of construction and their many hidden costs.

Michael Reynolds, the architect behind the Earthship philosophy and design, noted the direction of these wasteful construction methods over thirty years ago. He also noted the inordinate amount of time and effort that is required to obtain the "American dream" of home ownership. The average wage earner works thirty years to pay off the debt of the home, in addition to paying monthly bills to utility companies. Reynolds searched for a better solution to this seemingly endless cycle of bills and waste. His goals were far reaching:

- Develop construction methods that would reuse existing waste products as building blocks for construction.
- Design a building that would create its own energy and treat its own waste.
- Develop construction methods that can be executed with little training.
- Make the design affordable.

The major structural building component of the Earthship is recycled automobile tires filled with compacted earth to form a 3′-0″ thick rammed earth brick enclosed in steel-belted rubber. The massive "brick" walls, and the method of incorporating them into the earth, create living spaces that retain a constant temperature. Thus, with natural ventilation systems built in, an Earthship will heat itself in the winter and cool itself in the summer without the use of fossil or nuclear fuels.

Earthships produce their own electricity through a photovoltaic power system; they also collect their own water from a unique metal roof, silt catch, and cistern system, and deal with their own sewage through food-producing greenhouse technology that allows contained-flush toilets.

Earthships have been designed and developed with an emphasis on global availability of all aspects of their construction. They exist now in Bolivia, Australia, Mexico, Japan, Canada, and all over the United States. Earthships are comparable in cost to typical frame construction; however, they are much more durable, better insulated, and have no utility bills.

The buildings look like Spanish adobe structures and can be designed in single or multifloor units (see Figures SD13.1–SD13.2).

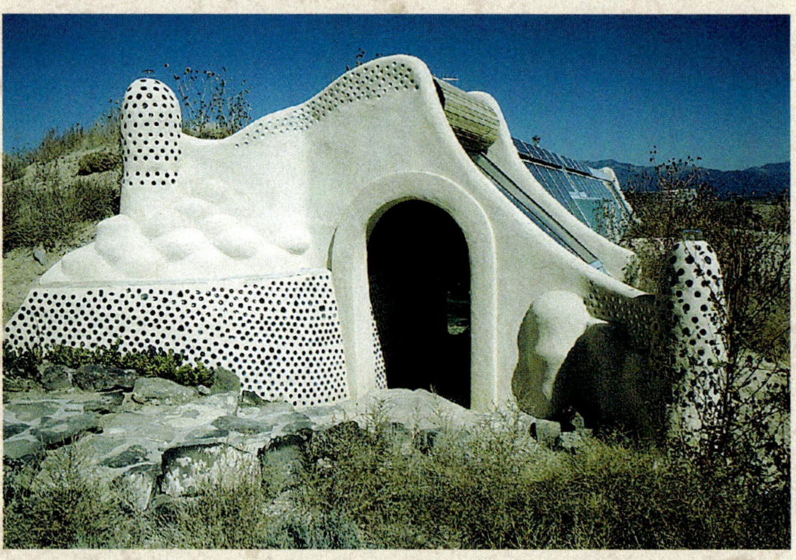

Figure SD13.1 *The exterior of an Earthship with glass sloping to the south. Facades can be customized utilizing various-sized tires, shaped retaining walls, and whimsical accoutrements. (Architect: Michael E. Reynolds.)*

SUSTAINABLEDESIGN

Solar Architecture and the Earthship—cont'd

Interior walls, which can be painted or left in their natural color, are formed out of stacked aluminum cans. Walls can be pierced with clear or colored glass and formed in a variety of shapes. Figure I.3 illustrates a completed Earthship called the Suncatcher.

More info online @

http://www.earthship.org/ Earthship website

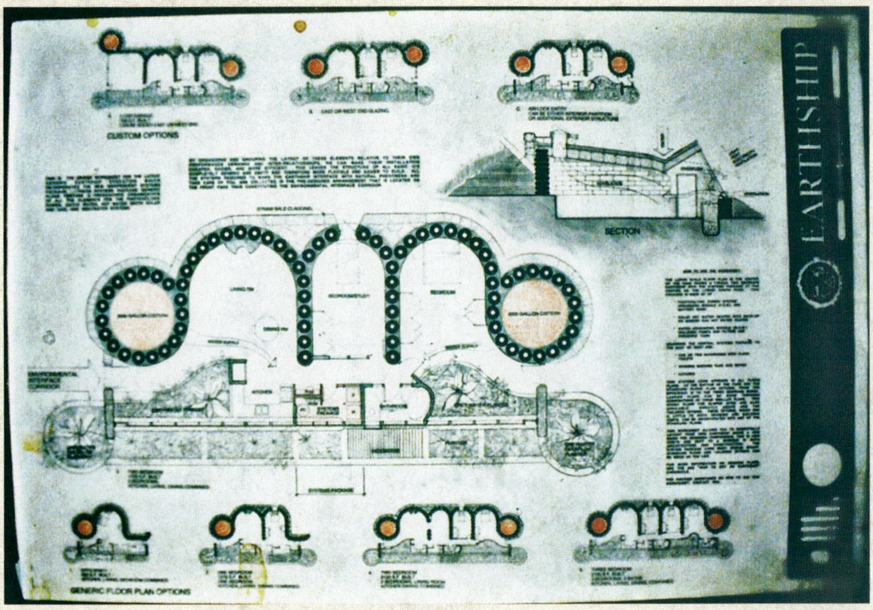

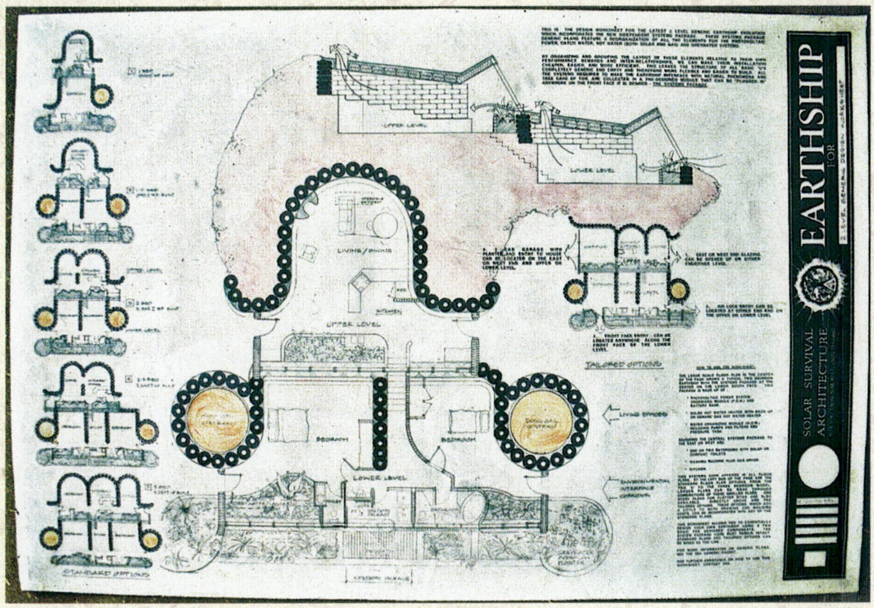

Figure SD13.2 *Rooms in Earthship are based on U-shaped modules grouped side by side or on two levels that can be added or deleted as needed. The sections through the designs illustrate construction and airflow. (Architect: Michael E. Reynolds.)*

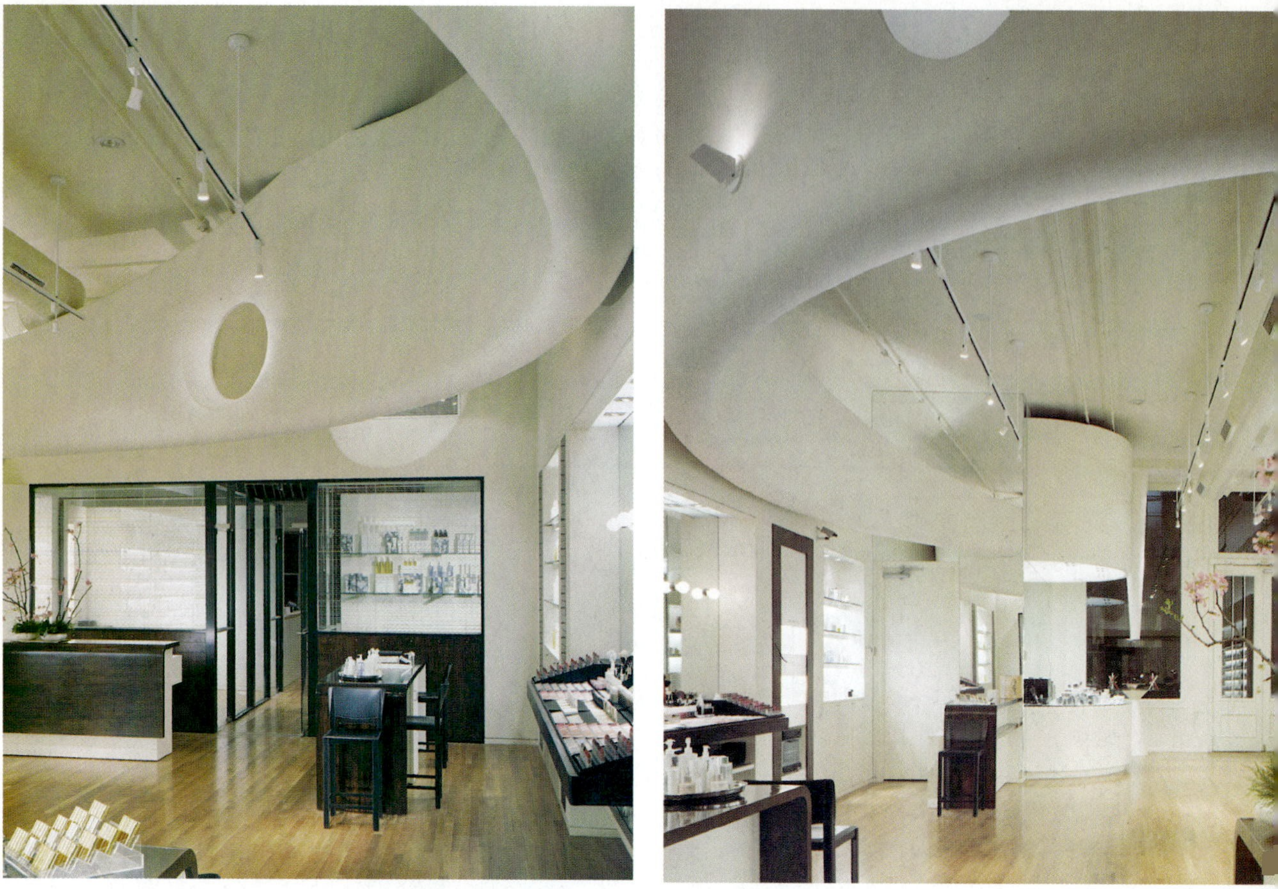

Figure 13.15 *Retail Design. Form defines the character of this sweeping cosmetics showroom. The designer was charged with creating an interior environment that did not feel like a tunnel in this 24′W × 100′L × 14′H space. Undulating gypsumboard soffits draw clients into the retail establishment, adding interest and the appearance of width. (Designer: Yoshinari Matsuyama. Photographs by Paul Warchol.)*

Profession Gains Respect

As the profession engages in environmentally sustainable practices and develops quantifiable standards of accountability, respect for the profession will grow. According to White and Dickson in the *Journal of Interior Design,* sociologists have found that professions mature based on the development of their educational requirements and legal recognition. In the past thirty years the interior design profession has sought to define educational programs through FIDER and establish a basic competency level through NCIDQ. The continuing registration and licensing efforts, coupled with the ongoing development of an advanced research database, will enhance the profession's image and credibility.

Another key factor in establishing credibility (and thereby developing respect for the profession) is to ensure that the various voices of the professional design organizations blend as one to work with the public and represent the profession's goals, ideals, and visions. In the late 1980s and early '90s a move called the "Unified Voice" sought to establish a single organization. The move met with some success as three professional organizations merged to form IIDA. In the fall of 2001, ASID and IIDA jointly announced that they were pu suing a merger into one professional organization. Althou the merger did not happen, ongoing efforts to share info mation and establish joint events continue, particularly at t local level. Perhaps future leadership and grassroots effo will allow a truly unified voice to emerge.

An additional move to strengthen the profession revolv around the need to establish the profession's body of know edge, or research base. At the IIDA Design Research Summ delegates considered the following six key issues:

1. Although an abundance of interior design research exists, it is difficult to access quickly.
2. Design professionals need to collaborate more with ea other and with experts from related fields.
3. Academics and practitioners reside in different cultures and this communication issue must be addressed.
4. Unlike other professions such as engineering and medicine, interior design practitioners, the industry, an school administrators do not yet appreciate the need fo graduate education and research to broaden the intellectual foundation of the profession.

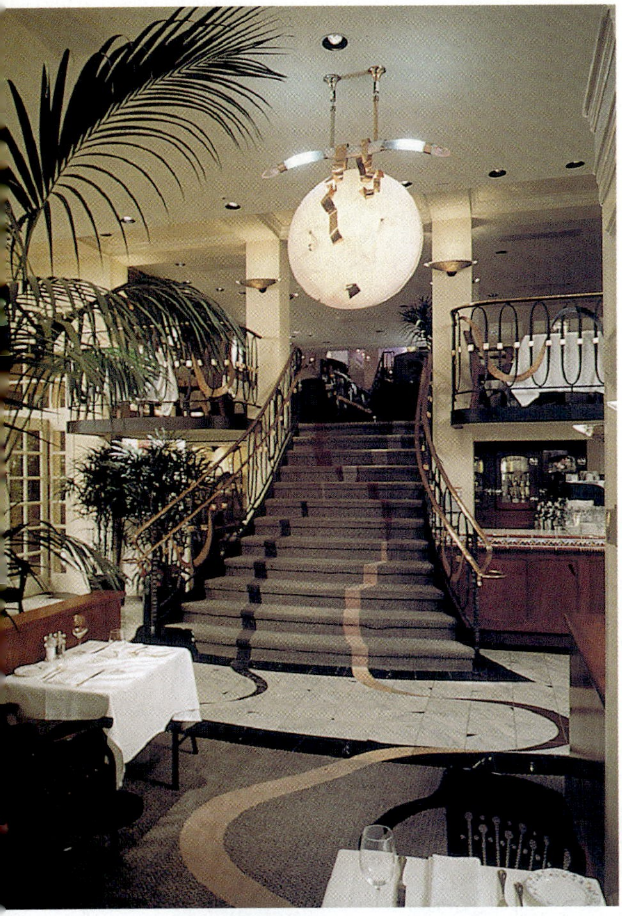

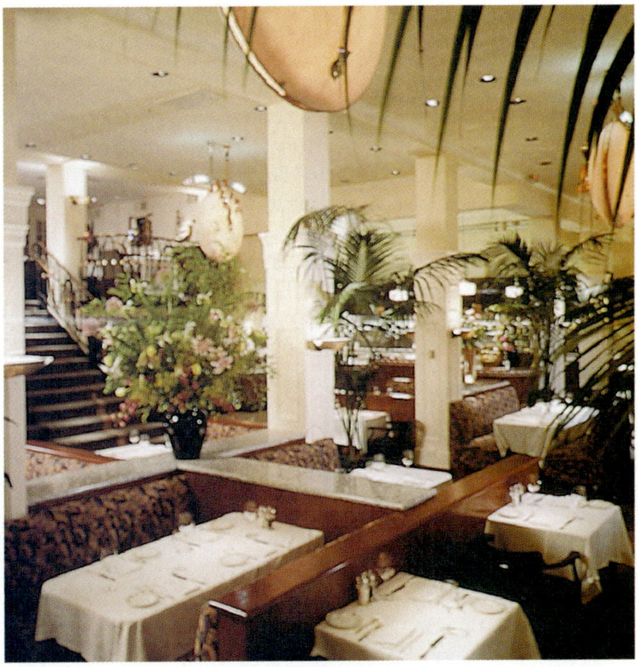

Figure 13.16 *Restaurant Design. A playful intertwining of ribbons and grids defines the relaxed yet refined character of this main dining room. Imaginative light fixtures combine with architectural lighting to pinpoint tabletop displays. Live plants and cut flower arrangements bring human scale and natural warmth to the interior. (Designer: Kuleto Consulting and Design. Photographs by Cesar Rubio. Courtesy of Kimpton Group.)*

Increased sponsorship and funding are imperative to building and maintaining a strong and relevant body of knowledge for the design profession.

The design profession must consider and define ethical boundaries in regard to interior design research.

ccording to Neal Frankel, IIDA, the connection between ractitioners and researchers will continue to grow, creating n expanded body of knowledge.

ASID has partnered with the University of Minnesota's in- rior design department to develop a website of summaries f interior design research projects. FIDER, in a Future Vi- ons conference, ranked interior design research as its num- er one concern for the future of the profession. FIDER also ecently raised its requirements so that by the year 2010, only achelor level programs or higher are eligible to receive DER accreditation.

ore info online @

tp://www.egroups.com/group/DesignResearch

eams of Specialists

he breadth and depth of the design professions will con- nue to require the use of teams of specialists. Teams will nsist of members with advanced degrees or members who e involved in continuing education and research into un- arted areas; cooperation among allied professionals will be essential. Already ASID and IIDA have developed forums that focus on specialty areas of residential, hospitality, retail, health care, and commercial design, as well as facility planning, historic preservation, education, and research.

Technology and the Human Factor

Global developments have surfaced in the areas of communication and computer technology, as well as in the understanding of human physical and cultural diversity. These two topics initially may appear to work against each other; however, in many cases it is the technology that is opening doors (both literally and figuratively) to human design issues.

Due to technological advances products are more readily customized, and design education has progressed to include teaching advanced computer skills. New knowledge made available by technology will expand the need for graduate education. Advances in telecommunications will enhance designers' understanding of cultural and social diversity and increase the demand for culturally diverse designers. According to Gary Wheeler, FASID, designers deal with the "human factor and the human spirit. We possess a profound responsibility to change the future."

Technology is a significant factor in achieving the sensitive adaptation of the human environment. The blending of technology to assist in the understanding of human needs will greatly affect the field of interior design.

Summary

The progression of steps to becoming a professional interior designer include education, experience, and examination. Once established as a professional, the designer continues his or her education through advanced coursework and participation in professional organizations. The successful professional designer knows that the diverse nature of design, both as a science and as an art, also requires an advanced knowledge of business skills and ethical behavior.

The future of interior design will see the maturation of a young profession eager to provide for a multicultural community. Designers will work in specialized fields with allied design professionals in teams that encourage the sustainab use of products, materials, and space. Designers will active search for universal design solutions that enhance the qua ity of life in all interior environments.

Chief Oren R. Lyons, traditional Faithkeeper of the Tur Clan, speaking at the 20th Congress of the Internation Council of Societies of Industrial Design, said,

> Each generation raises its intellectuals, heroes, and lea ers. . . . We must raise leaders of vision who think and make decisions in the long term. . . . Think positive, be courageous, be generous, share your wealth. Divest fo the future.

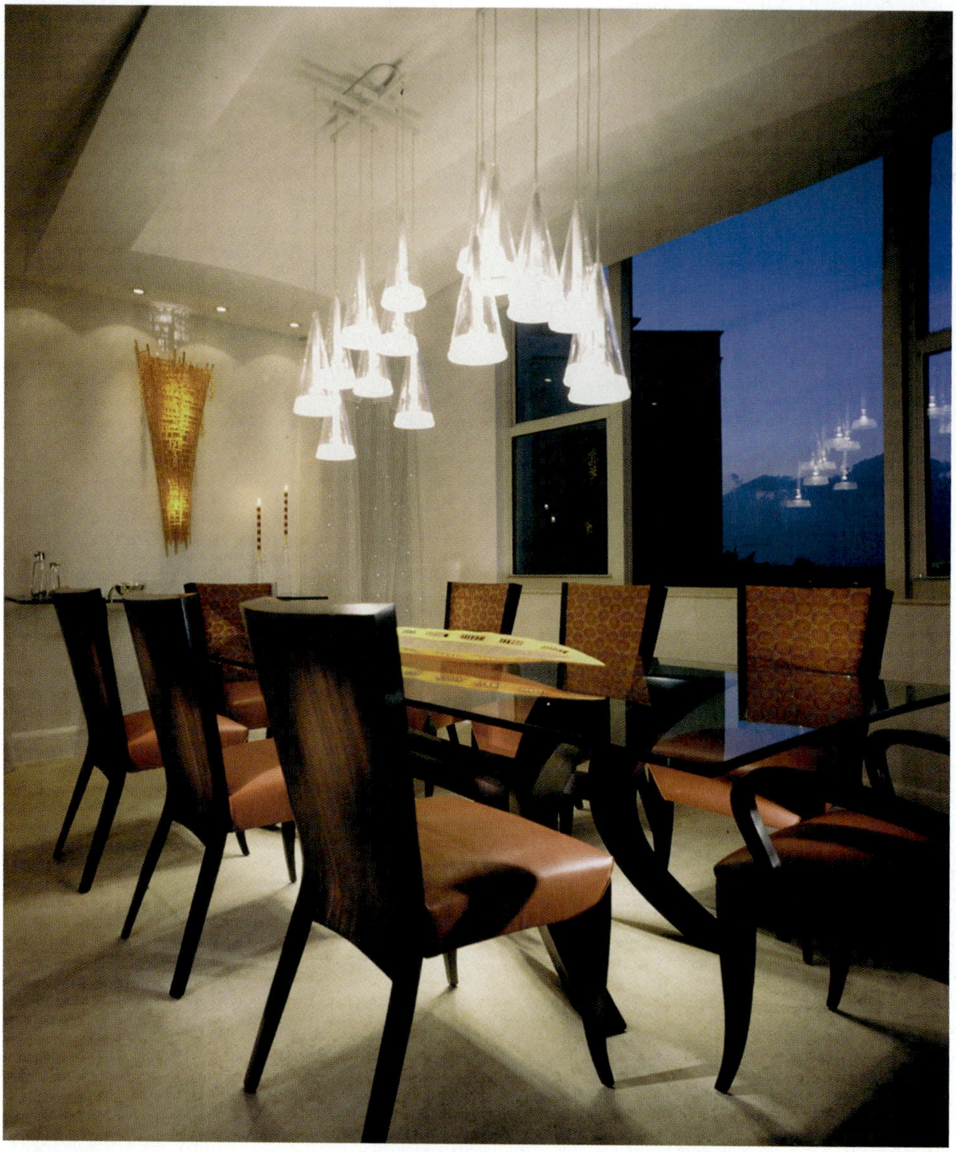

Figure 13.17 *Lighting Design. In this contemporary interior, emphasis has been placed on interior lighting. The focal point chandelier is suspended from a custom-designed frame. Recessed downlighting highlights the artwork, and lights hidden from view create a silhouette of the art on the ceiling. (Designer: Charles Greenwood, IIDA, of Greenwood Design Group, Inc. Photograph © Robert Thien.)*

Appendix A

Residential Programming Questionnaire

RESIDENTIAL PROGRAMMING QUESTIONNAIRE

I General Information **Date**

Client Name

Address

Home Phone Work Phone

Occupation(s)

II Family Members

Name	**Age**	**Universal Concerns**

III Family Members' Hobbies and Activities

Activity	**Family Member(s)**	**Where does activity take place?**
Computer		
Television		
Stereo		
Sewing		
Crafts		
Instruments		
Model Building		
Reading		
Other		

IV Room Requirements

Living Room

Entertainment Yes _____ No _____ How Many? _____ How Often? _____

Dining Room

Formal/Casual/Both (circle one)

Number of people maximum ____

Comments ____

Breakfast Room

Number of people maximum _____

Comments ____

Family Room

Activities

Bedrooms

#	Who	Requirements
1		
2		
3		
4		
5		

Baths

1		
2		
3		
4		

Other Rooms

Rooms	Requirements
Laundry	
Kitchen	
Office	
Workshop	
Garage	
Playroom	
Study	
Music Room	

V Design Preferences

Colors	
Mood	
Budget	
Time Frame	
Reuse Items	(if yes, see furniture inventory sheet)
Other	

VI Other Information & Comments

VII Business Information

Travel Directions

Fee Basis

Appendix B

Furniture Inventory Sheet

FURNITURE INVENTORY SHEET

Item #	Description	Size W × D × H	Style	Comments

Appendix C

Typical Set of Residential Construction Drawings

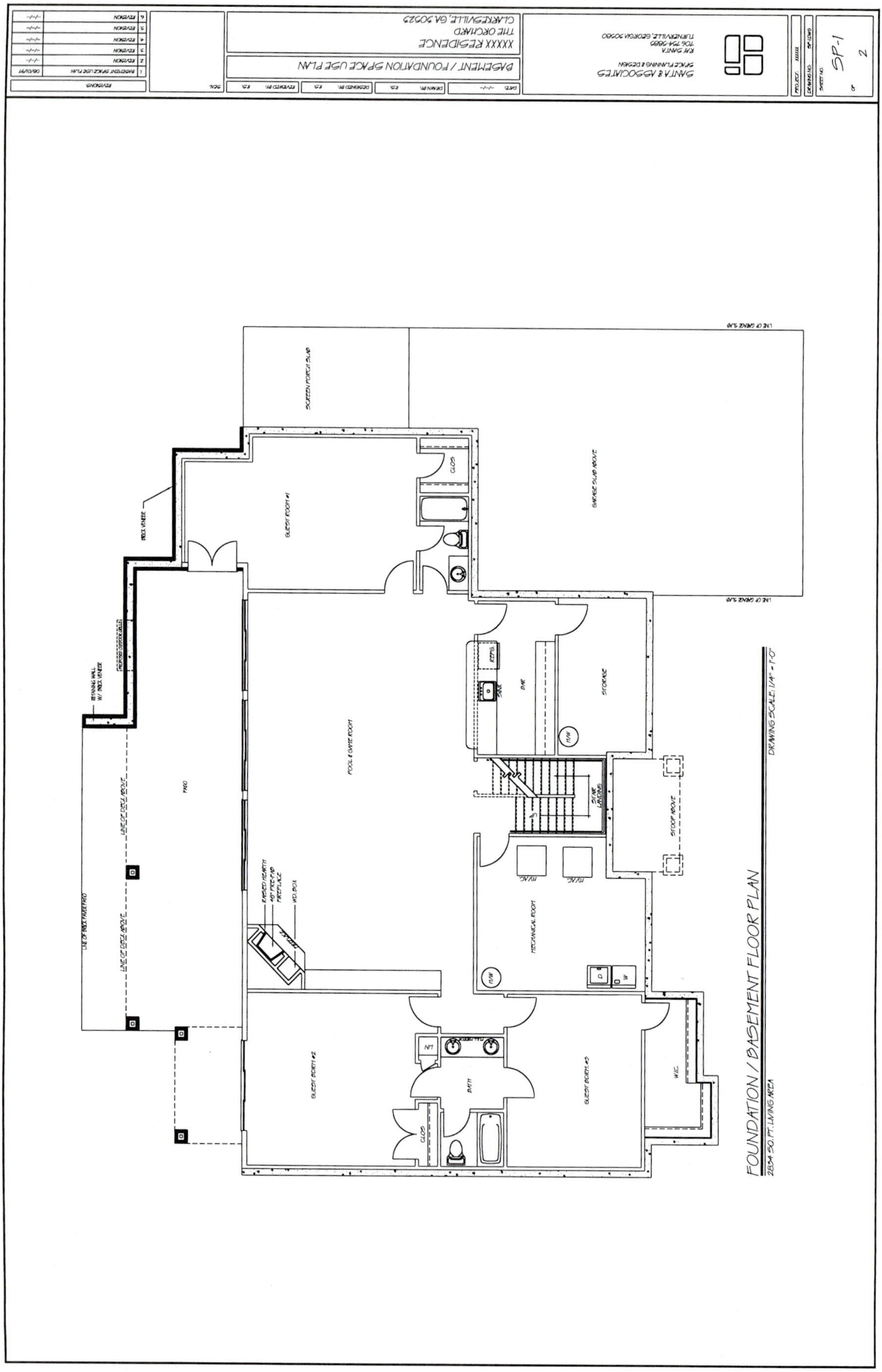

FOUNDATION / BASEMENT FLOOR PLAN
2834 SQ. FT. LIVING AREA
BASEMENT / FOUNDATION SPACE USE PLAN
XXXXX RESIDENCE
THE ORCHARD
CLARKESVILLE, GA 30523
SANTA & ASSOCIATES
SP-1

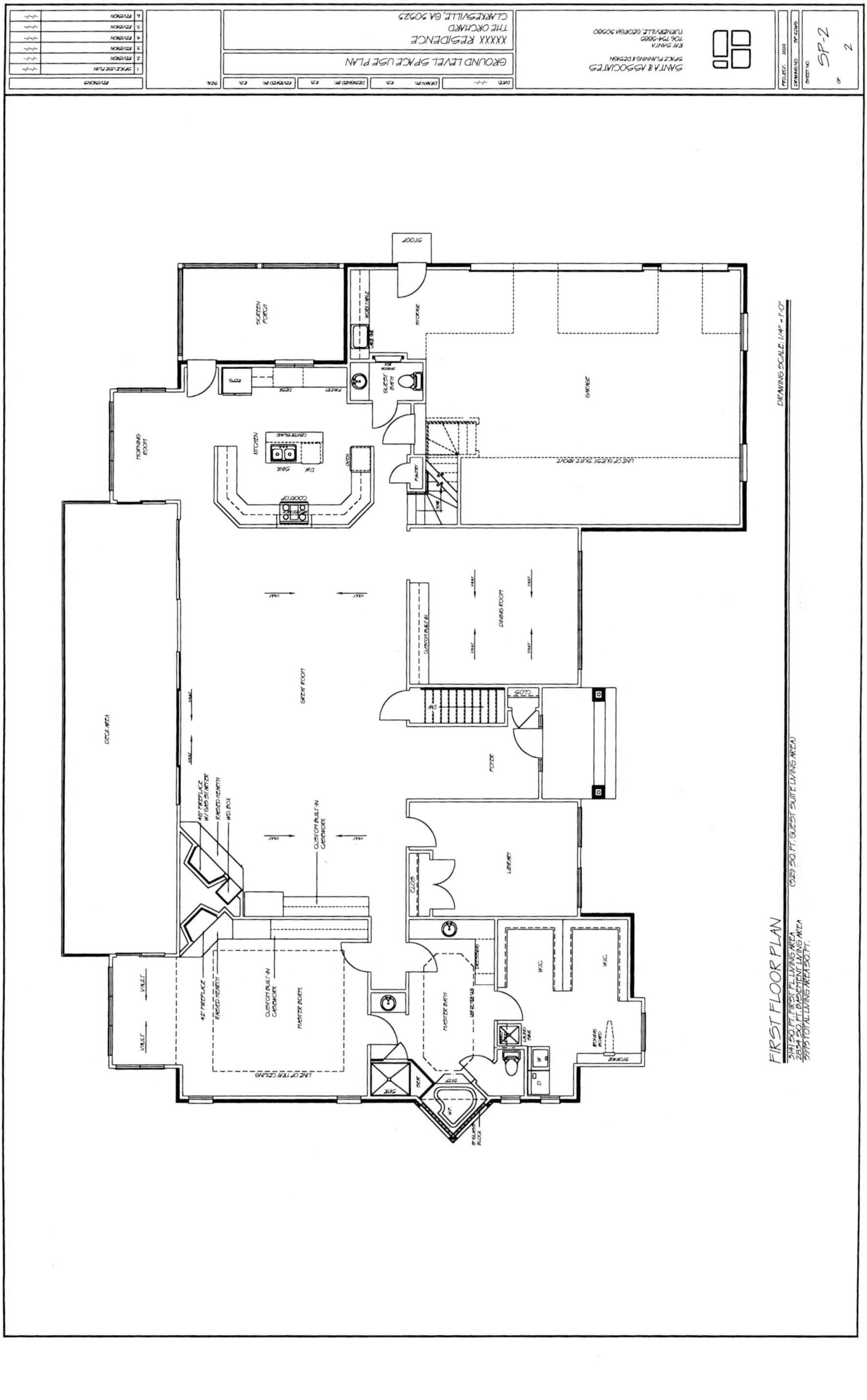

Figure C.2 *First floor space use plan. (Courtesy of Santa & Associates.)*

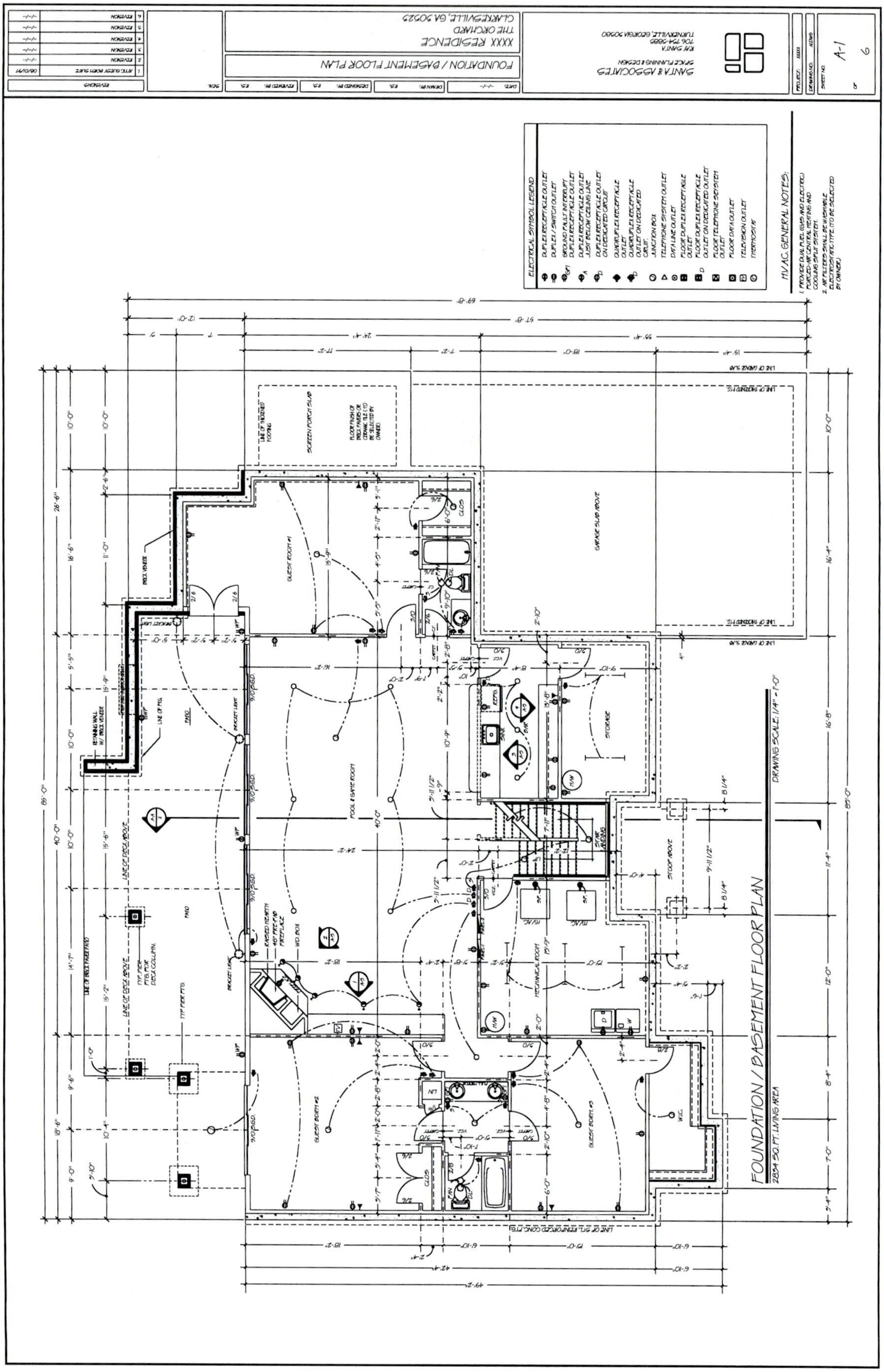
FOUNDATION / BASEMENT FLOOR PLAN
2834 SQ. FT. LIVING AREA
DRAWING SCALE: 1/4" = 1'-0"
ELECTRICAL SYMBOL LEGEND
H.V.A.C. GENERAL NOTES:
XXXX RESIDENCE
THE ORCHARD
CLARKESVILLE, GA 30523
SANTA B ASSOCIATES
A-1
6

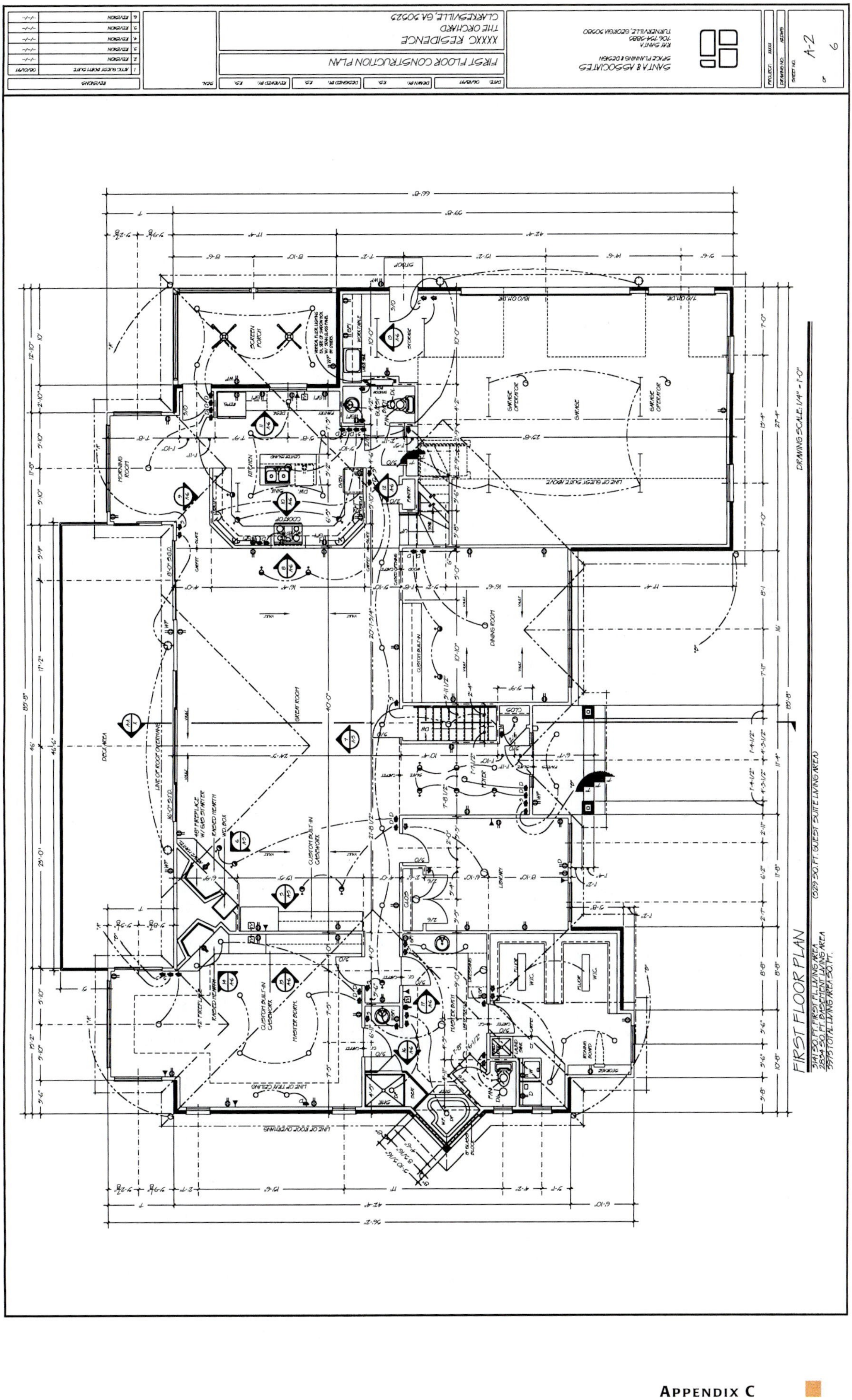

Figure C.4 *First floor construction plan. (Courtesy of Santa & Associates.)*

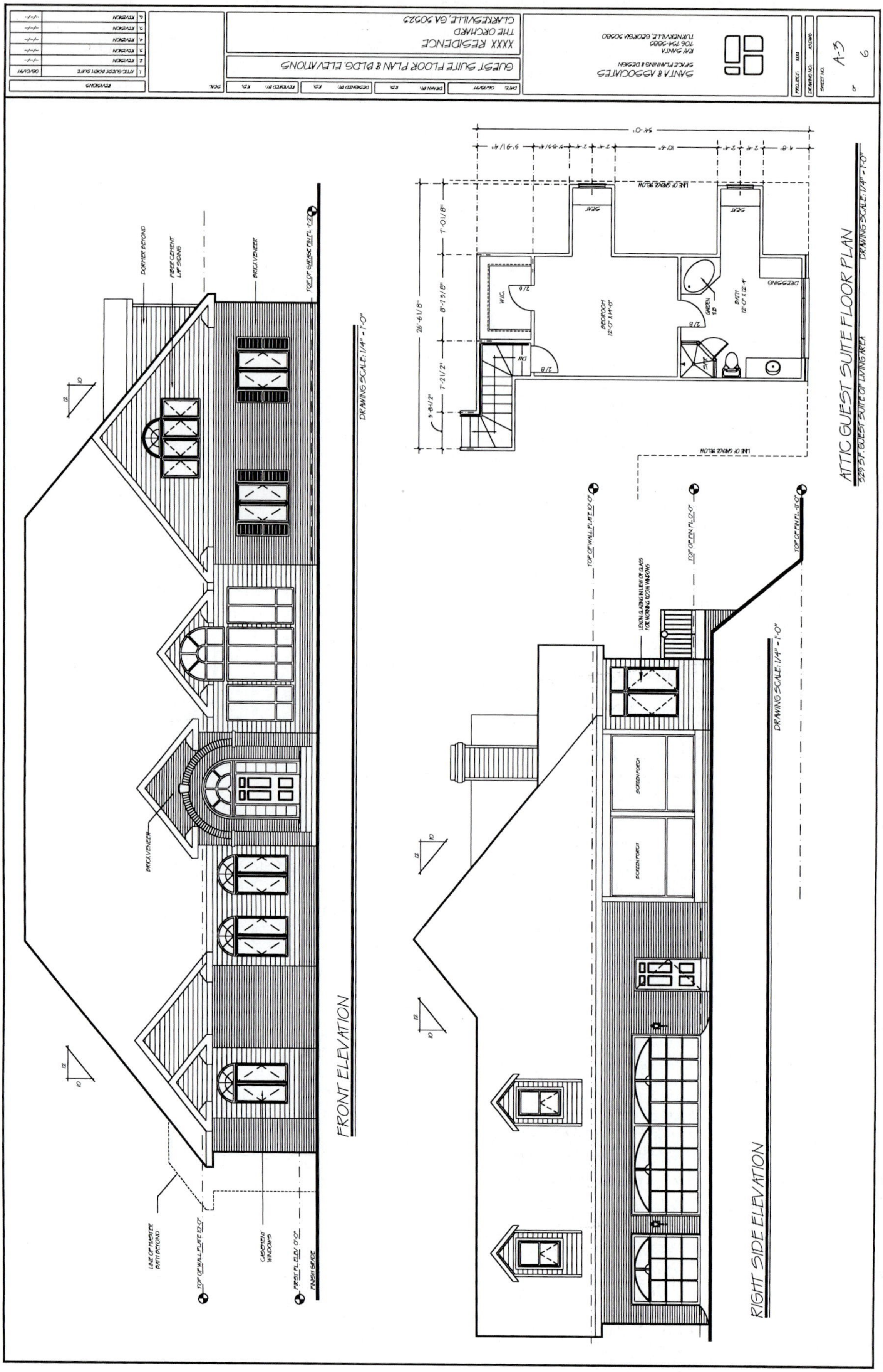
FRONT ELEVATION
RIGHT SIDE ELEVATION
ATTIC GUEST SUITE FLOOR PLAN
DRAWING SCALE: 1/4" = 1'-0"
GUEST SUITE FLOOR PLAN & BLDG. ELEVATIONS
XXXX RESIDENCE
THE ORCHARD
CLARKESVILLE, GA 30523
SANTA & ASSOCIATES
A-3

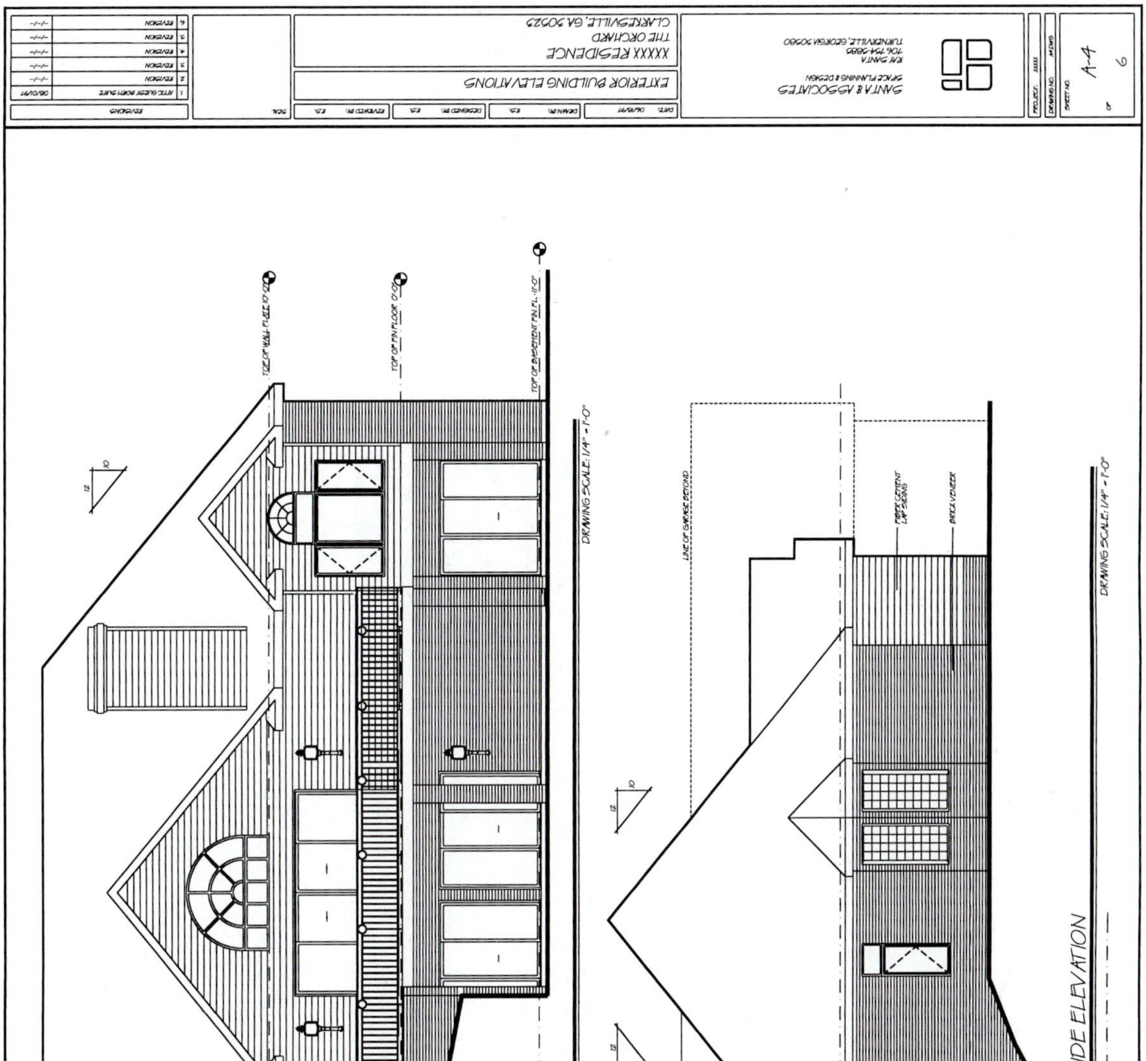

Figure C.6 *Exterior elevations. (Courtesy of Santa & Associates.)*

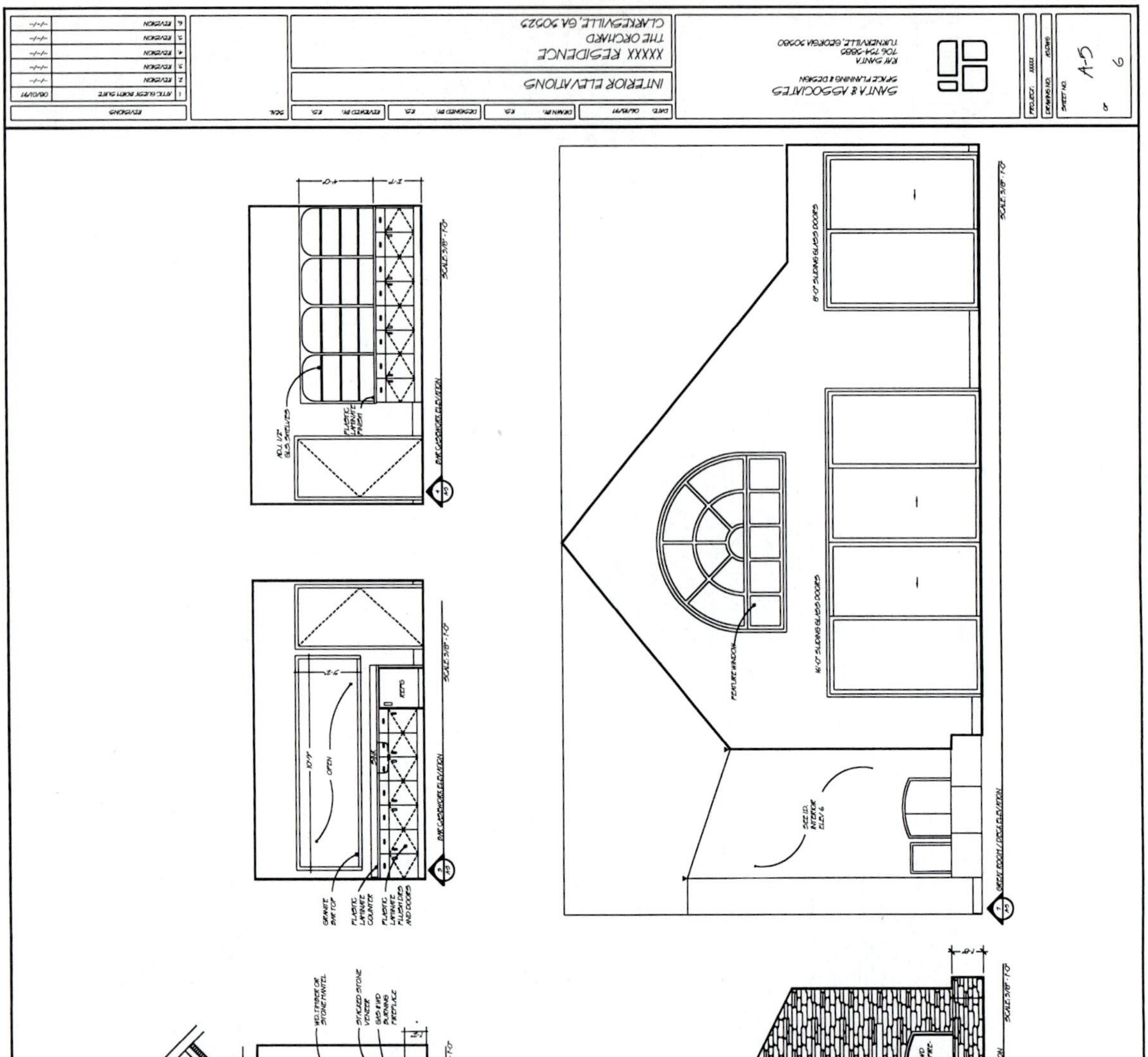

SANTA & ASSOCIATES
SPACE PLANNING & DESIGN
INTERIOR ELEVATIONS
XXXXX RESIDENCE
THE ORCHARD
A-5

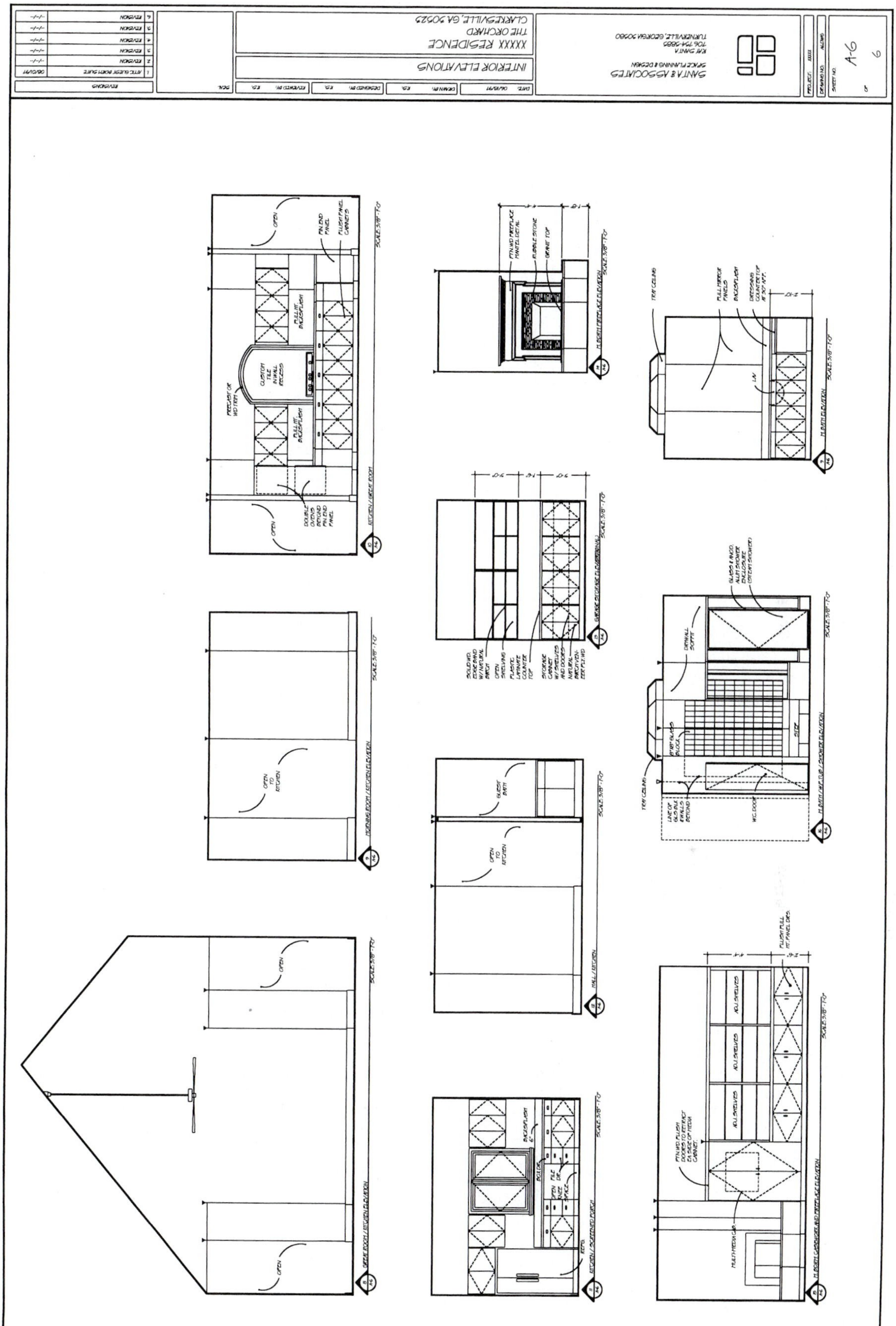

Figure C.8 *Interior elevations. (Courtesy of Santa & Associates.)*

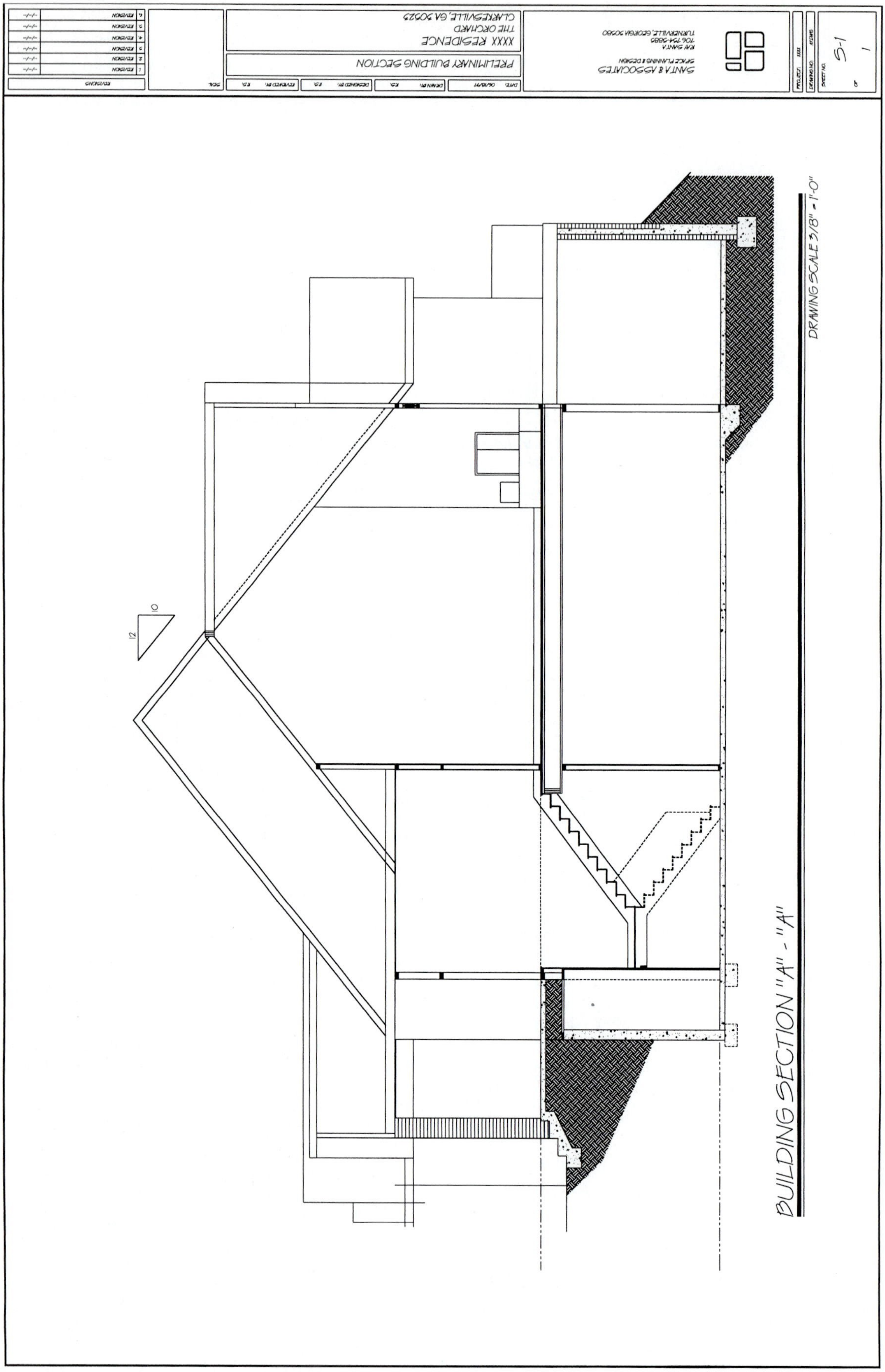
PRELIMINARY BUILDING SECTION
XXXX RESIDENCE
THE ORCHARD
CLARKESVILLE, GA 30523
SANTA & ASSOCIATES
SPACE PLANNING & DESIGN
KAY SANTA
706 754-5885
TURNERVILLE, GEORGIA 30580
S-1
12
10
BUILDING SECTION "A" - "A"
DRAWING SCALE 3/8" = 1'-0"

eferences

xts and Internet Resources

essibility, Building Codes, and Universal Design (Also see code ok references in Chapter 4)

erican National Standard for Buildings and Facilities—Providing Accessibility and Usability for Physically Handicapped People. A11.1–1986. Washington, DC: U.S. Department of Housing and Urban Development, 1986.

erican National Standard Specifications for Making Buildings and Facilities Accessible to and Usable by Physically Handicapped People. ANSI A117.1–1980. New York: American National Standards Institute, 1980.

rmon, Sharon Koomen, and Katherine E. Kennon. *The Codes Guidebook for Interiors*. 2d ed. New York: Wiley, 2001.

brock, Cynthia A., and James Evan Terry. *Beautiful Universal Design: A Visual Guide*. New York: Wiley, 1999.

nimum Guidelines and Requirements for Accessible Design. Washington, DC: U.S. Architectural & Transportation Barriers Compliance Board, 1982.

PA 101® Life Safety Code® 1991. Quincy, MA: National Fire Protection Association, 1991.

rry, Lawrence G., Michael A. Jawer, John T. Murdoch, and James C. Dinegar. *ADA Compliance Guidebook: A Checklist for Your Building*. Washington, DC: BOMA, 1992.

lkoff, W. M. L., James S. Brady, and Laura W. Abed. *Practicing Universal Design: An Interpretation of the ADA*. New York: Wiley, 1997.

p://www.access-board.gov/adaag/html/adaag.htm ADA Guide.

p://www.ansi.org/ American National Standards Institute.

p://www.bocai.org/ Building Official Code Administration International.

p://www.ed.gov/offices/OSERS/NIDRR/About/ ADA assistance.

p://www.hud.gov/offices/hsg/ Fair Housing Administration.

p://www.icbo.org/ International Conference of Building Officials.

p://www.intlcode.org/ International Code Council.

p://www.nfpa.org/Home/index.asp National Fire Protection Association.

p://www.osha.gov/ Occupational Safety and Health Administration.

p://www.sbcci.org/ Southern Building Code Congress International.

p://www.usdoj.gov/crt/ada/adahom1.htm ADA Homepage.

Business Profession

Coleman, Cindy (ed.). *Interior Design Handbook of Professional Practice*. New York: McGraw-Hill, 2001.

Farren, Carol E. *Planning and Managing Interior Projects*. Kingston, MA: R. S. Means, 1988.

Knackstedt, Mary V. *The Interior Design Business Handbook: A Complete Guide to Profitability*. 3d ed. New York: Wiley, 2002.

Loebelson, Andrew. *How to Profit in Contract Design*. New York: Van Nostrand Reinhold, 1983.

Morgan, Jim. *Marketing for the Small Design Firm*. New York: Whitney Library of Design/Watson-Guptill Publications, 1984.

Murphy, Dennis Grant. *The Business Management of Interior Design*. North Hollywood, CA: Stratford House Publishing Company, 1988.

Piotrowski, Christine. *Interior Design Management: A Handbook for Owners and Managers*. New York: Van Nostrand Reinhold, 1992.

———. *Professional Practice for Interior Designers*. 3d ed. New York: Wiley, 2002.

Rose, Stuart W. *Achieving Excellence in Your Design Practice*. New York: Whitney Library of Design/Watson-Guptill Publications, 1987.

Siegel, Harry, and Alan Siegel. *A Guide to Business Principles and Practices for Interior Designers*. Rev. ed. New York: Whitney Library of Design, 1982.

Stasiowski, Frank, and David Burstein. *Project Management for the Design Professional*. New York: Whitney Library of Design/Watson-Guptill Publications, 1982.

Thompson, Jo Ann Asher (ed.). *ASID Professional Practice Manual*. New York: Whitney Library of Design, 1992.

Veitch, Ronald, et al. *Professional Practice*. Winnipeg, Canada: Peguis, 1990.

http://asla.org/ American Society of Landscape Architects.

http://www.agc.org/ Association of General Contractors of America.

http://www.aia.org American Society of Architects.

http://www.aiga.org/ American Institute of Graphic Designers.

http://www.asce.org/ American Society of Civil Engineers.

http://www.ashrae.org/ American Society of Heating, Refrigeration and Air-Conditioning Engineers.

http://www.asid.org American Society of Interior Designers.

http://www.asid.org/design_basics/working_with_designer/how_services.asp ASID article on how designers charge for their services.

http://www.fider.org/ Foundation for Interior Design Education Research.
http://www.icograda.org/web/home/index.html International Council of Graphic Designers.
http://www.iida.org International Interior Design Association.
http://www.interiordesigncanada.org/english-site/idc-home.html Interior Designers of Canada.
http://www.nawic.org/ National Association of Women in Construction.
http://www.ncidq.org National Council for Interior Design Qualifications.

Color

Birren, Faber. *Color and Human Response*. New York: Van Nostrand Reinhold, 1984.
Holtzschue, Linda. *Understanding Color: An Introduction for Designers*. 2d ed. New York: Wiley, 2001.
Hope, Augustine, and Margaret Walch. *The Color Compendium*. New York: Van Nostrand Reinhold, 1990.
Kaufman, Donald. *Color: Color Palettes for Painted Rooms*. New York: Clarkson Potter, 1992.
Ladau, Robert F., Brent K. Smith, and Jennifer Place. *Color in Interior Design and Architecture*. New York: Van Nostrand Reinhold, 1989.
Leibrock, Cynthia A. *Design Details for Health: Making the Most of Interior Design's Healing Potential*. New York: Wiley, 1999.
Mahnke, Frank H. *Color, Environment, and Human Response: The Beneficial Use of Color in the Architectural Environment*. New York: Wiley, 1996.
Miller, Mary C. *Color for Interior Architecture*. New York: Wiley, 1997.
Ostwald, Wilhelm. *The Color Primer*. New York: Van Nostrand Reinhold, 1969.
Sharpe, Deborah T. *The Psychology of Color and Design*. Chicago: Nelson-Hall, 1975.
Verity, Enid. *Color Observed*. New York: Van Nostrand Reinhold, 1982.
http://www.colorassociation.com/splash.html Color Association of the United States.
http://www.colormarketing.org/ Color Marketing Group.
http://www.colormatters.com This is a creative and fun hobby website.
http://www.internationalcolourauthority.com/ International Colour Authority.
http://www.sherwin-williams.com/DIY/interior/colorselect/confidence/dwc4.asp Sherwin Williams Color Wheel with terminology.

Fundamentals and Theory

Abercrombie, Stanley. *A Philosophy of Interior Design*. New York: Harper & Row, 1990.
Barnard, Malcolm. *Approaches to Understanding Visual Culture*. New York: Palgrave, 2001.
Bevlin, Marjorie Elliott. *Design Through Discovery*. New York: Holt, Rinehart & Winston, 1985.
Carpenter, James M. *Visual Art: A Critical Introduction*. New York: Harcourt Brace Jovanovich, 1982.
Cheatham, Frank R., Jane Hart Cheatham, and Sheryl A. Haler. *Design Concepts and Applications*. Englewood Cliffs, NJ: Prentice Hall, 1983.
Ching, Francis D. K. *Architecture: Space, Form, and Order*. New York: Van Nostrand Reinhold, 1980.
De Sausmarez, Maurice. *Basic Design: The Dynamics of Vis Form*. New York: Van Nostrand Reinhold, 1983.
Dondis, Donis A. *A Primer of Visual Literacy*. Boston: MIT Pr 1973.
Johnson, Paul-Alan. *The Theory of Architecture*. New York: ley, 1994.
Kleeman, Walter B. *The Challenge of Interior Design*. New Yo Van Nostrand Reinhold, 1981.
Lauer, David A., and Stephen Pentak. *Design Basics*. 4th ed. F Worth, TX: Harcourt Brace College Publishers, 1995.
Malnar, Joy Monice, and Frank Vodvarka. *The Interior Dim sion: A Theoretical Approach to Enclosed Space*. New Yo Van Nostrand Reinhold, 1992.
Ocvirk, Otto G., Robert E. Stinson, Philip R. Wigg, Robert Bone, and David L. Cayton. *Art Fundamentals: Theor Practice*. 8th ed. New York: McGraw-Hill, 1998.
Pena, William. *Problem Seeking*. Washington, DC: AIA Press, 19
Rodemann, Patricia A. *Patterns in Interior Environments*. N York: Wiley, 1999.
Rybczynski, Witold. *Home: A Short History of an Idea*. N York: Penguin Books, 1987.
Zelanski, Paul, and Mary Pat Fisher. *Shaping Space*. Fort Wo TX: Harcourt Brace College Publishers, 1995.
http://mitpress2.mit.edu/e-journals/Leonardo/isast/articles/behrens.html Art, Design and Gestalt Theory by Behrens.
http://www.digitalarchitectures.com/gmean.htm Digital Arc tectures, Inc., Golden Section information.
http://www.ivla.org/ International Visual Literacy Associatio
http://www.ivla.org/news/rdocs/vlbib/ International Visual eracy Association Bibliography.
http://www.math.vt.edu/people/gao/math/godensection/index.html Information on the Golden Section and Fibona numbers.
http://www.mcs.surrey.ac.uk/Personal/R.Knott/Fibonacci/fibInArt.html Information on the Golden Section a Fibonacci numbers.
http://www.usask.ca/education/coursework/skaalid/theory/gestalt/similar.htm Information on Gestalt.

Furniture and Accessories

Aronson, Joseph. *The Encyclopedia of Furniture*. 3d ed. N York: Crown, 1965.
Battersby, Martin, et al. *History of Furniture*. New York: Morro 1976.
Boger, Louise Ade. *The Complete Guide to Furniture Sty* Prospect Heights, IL: Waveland Press, 1997.
Boyce, Charles. *Dictionary of Furniture*. New York: Roundta Press, 1985.
Butler, Joseph T. *Field Guide to American Antique Furnitu* New York: Henry Holt and Company, 1985.
Crochet, Treena M., and David Vleck. *Designer's Guide to Fur ture Styles*. Upper Saddle River, NJ: Pearson Educatio Prentice Hall, 1999.
Deasy, C. M., and Thomas E. Lasswell. *Designing Places for P ple*. New York: Whitney Library of Design, 1985.
Emery, Marc. *Furniture by Architects*. New York: Harry Abrams, 1983.
Fitzgerald, Oscar P. *Three Centuries of American Furniture*. glewood Cliffs, NJ: Prentice Hall, 1982.
Furuta, Tok. *Interior Landscaping*. Reston, VA: Reston Pub. C 1983.

andy, Charles D., and Susan Zimmermann-Stidham. *Contemporary Classics: Furniture of the Masters*. New York: McGraw-Hill, 1981.
arner, Philippe. *Twentieth-Century Furniture*. New York: Van Nostrand Reinhold, 1980.
abegger, Jerryll, and Joseph H. Osman. *Sourcebook of Modern Furniture*. 2d ed. New York: Norton, 1996.
anks, David A. *Innovative Furniture in America from 1800 to the Present*. New York: Horizon, 1981.
ewin, Leonard Bruce. *Shopping for Furniture: A Consumer's Guide*. Fresno, CA: Linden, 1999.
ıcie-Smith, Edward. *Furniture: A Concise History*. London: Thames & Hudson, 1985.
ackay, James. *Turn-of-the-Century Antiques: An Encyclopedia*. New York: Dutton, 1974.
ang, Karl. *History of Modern Furniture*. New York: Harry N. Abrams, 1979.
eadmore, Clement. *The Modern Chair*. New York: Van Nostrand Reinhold, 1975.
ussell, Frank, Philippe Garner, and John Read. *A Century of Chair Design*. New York: Rizzoli International, 1980.
impson, Miriam. *Modern Furniture Classics*. New York: Whitney Library of Design, 1987.
atson, Sir Francis. *The History of Furniture*. London: Orbio, 1982.
tp://interiordec.about.com/cs/upholstery/ General information on upholstery furniture.
tp://www.finefurnitureintl.com *Fine Furniture International* magazine.
tp://www.gocohens.com/hwtobuy/upholstery.html Guides to Residential Upholstery Furniture Construction.
tp://www.guild.com/ Excellent source for fine one-of-a-kind art.
tp://www.rosefurniture.com/yellowpage/upholsteryvalue.html Guides to Residential Upholstery Furniture Construction.
ttp://www.upholsterysupply.com/yardage.htm Chart of approximate yardage quantities for upholstered goods.

eneral

llen, Edward, and Joseph Iano. *The Architect's Studio Companion*. New York: Wiley, 1989.
all, Victoria Kloss. *The Art of Interior Design*. 2d ed. New York: Wiley, 1982.
allast, David Kent. *Architecture, Design, and Construction Word Finder*. Englewood Cliffs, NJ: Prentice Hall, 1991.
———. *Interior Design Reference Manual*. 2d ed. Belmont, CA: Professional Publications, 2002.
hing, Francis D. K. *Interior Design Illustrated*. New York: Van Nostrand Reinhold, 1987.
eChiara, Joseph, Julius Panero, and Martin Zelnik. *Time-Saver Standards for Interior Design and Space Planning*. New York: McGraw-Hill, 1991.
izik, A. Allen. *Concise Encyclopedia of Interior Design*. 2d ed. New York: Van Nostrand Reinhold, 1988.
aulkner, Ray, Sarah Faulkner, and LuAnn Nissen. *Inside Today's Home*. 5th ed. New York: Holt, Rinehart & Winston, 1986.
riedmann, Arnold, John F. Pile, and Forrest Wilson. *Interior Design: An Introduction to Architectural Interiors*. 3d ed. New York: Elsevier, 1982.
uthrie, Pat. *The Interior Designer's Portable Handbook*. New York: McGraw-Hill, 2000.
ilmer, Rosemary, and W. Otie Kilmer. *Designing Interiors*. Fort Worth, TX: Harcourt Brace Jovanovich College Publishers, 1992.
National Council for Interior Design Qualification. *NCIDQ Examination Guide*. New York: National Council for Interior Design Qualification, 1989.
Nielson, Karla J., and David A. Taylor. *Interiors: An Introduction*. 2d ed. Madison, WI: Brown & Benchmark, 1994.
Nissen, LuAnn, Ray Faulkner, and Sarah Faulkner. *Inside Today's Home*. 6th ed. Fort Worth, TX: Harcourt Brace College Publishers, 1994.
Pile, John. *Dictionary of 20th-Century Design*. New York: Facts on File, 1990.
———. *Interior Design*. 2d ed. Englewood Cliffs, NJ: Prentice Hall; New York: Harry N. Abrams, 1995.
Ramsey, Charles George, and Harold Reeve Sleeper. *Architectural Graphic Standards*. 8th ed. New York: Wiley, 1988.
Reznikoff, S. C. *Interior Graphic and Design Standards*. New York: Whitney Library of Design, 1986.
Russell, Beverly. *Architecture and Design*. New York: Harry N. Abrams, 1989.
Tate, Allen. *The Making of Interiors: An Introduction*. New York: Harper & Row, 1987.

Historic Preservation

Debaigts, Jacques. *Interiors for Old Houses*. New York: Van Nostrand Reinhold, 1973.
Duerksen, Christopher J. (ed.). *A Handbook on Historic Preservation Law*. Washington, DC: The Conservation Foundation and The National Center for Preservation Law, 1983.
Gottfried, Herbert, and Jan Jennings. *American Vernacular Design: 1870–1940*. Ames, IA: Iowa State University Press, 1988.
Guidelines for Local Surveys: A Basis for Preservation Planning. Washington, DC: National Register of Historic Places, 1985.
Hiss, Tony. *The Experience of Place*. New York: Vintage Books, 1990.
Maddex, Diane (ed.). *All About Old Buildings*. Washington, DC: The Preservation Press, 1985.
Murtagh, William J. *Keeping Time: The History & Theory of Preservation in America*. Rev. ed. New York: Wiley, 1997.
Respectful Rehabilitation: Answers to Your Questions about Old Buildings. Washington, DC: The Preservation Press, 1982.
Shopsin, William C. *Restoring Old Buildings for Contemporary Uses*. New York: Whitney Library of Design, 1986.
Stipe, Robert E., and Antoinette J. Lee (eds.). *The American Mosaic: Preserving a Nation's Heritage*. Washington, DC: United States Committee of the International Council on Monuments and Sites, 1987.
Tyler, Norman. *Historic Preservation: An Introduction to Its History, Principles, and Practice*. New York: Norton, 1999.
Vale, Thomas R., and Geraldine R. Vale. *U.S. 40 Today: Thirty Years of Landscape Change in America*. Madison, WI: University of Wisconsin Press, 1983.
http://www.nationaltrust.org National Preservation Conference.

History

Anscombe, Isabelle. *Arts and Crafts Style*. New York: Rizzoli, 1991.
Ball, Victoria Kloss. *Architecture and Interior Design: A Basic History Through the Seventeenth Century*. New York: Wiley, 1980.
———. *Architecture and Interior Design: Europe and America from the Colonial Era to Today*. New York: Wiley, 1980.
Blakemore, Robbie G. *History of Interior Design Furniture*. New York: Van Nostrand Reinhold, 1997.

Blumenson, John J.-G. *Identifying American Architecture*. New York: W. W. Norton, 1981.

Brown, Erica. *Sixty Years of Interior Design*. New York: Viking Press, 1982.

Bush, Donald J. *The Streamlined Decade*. New York: George Braziller, 1975.

Clark, Robert Judson (ed.). *Arts and Crafts Movement in America, 1876–1916*. Princeton, NJ: Princeton University Press, 1972.

Curtis, William J. R. *Modern Architecture Since 1900*. 3d ed. Upper Saddle River, NJ: Prentice Hall, 1996.

de la Croix, Horst, Richard G. Tansey, and Diane Kirkpatrick. *Art Through the Ages*. 9th ed. Fort Worth, TX: Harcourt Brace Jovanovich College Publishers, 1991.

Fehrman, Cherie, and Kenneth Fehrman. *Post-War Interior Design, 1945–1960*. New York: Van Nostrand Reinhold, 1986.

Ferebee, Ann. *A History of Design from the Victorian Era to the Present*. New York: Van Nostrand Reinhold, 1970.

Foley, Mary Mix. *The American House*. New York: Harper & Row, 1980.

Garner, Philippe. *Contemporary Decorative Arts*. New York: Facts on File, 1980.

Gaynor, Elizabeth. *Scandinavia Living Design*. New York: Stewart, Tabori & Chang, 1987.

Gowans, Alan. *Styles and Types of North American Architecture*. New York: Harper Collins, 1992.

Hicks, David. *Style and Design*. Boston: Little, Brown, 1987.

Hitchcock, Henry-Russell, and Philip Johnson. *The International Style*. (1932, reprint). New York: Norton, 1966.

Horn, Richard. *Memphis: Objects, Furniture, and Patterns*. Philadelphia: Rushing Press, 1985.

Itten, Johannes. *Design and Form: The Basic Course at the Bauhaus*. New York: Van Nostrand Reinhold, 1964.

Jaffe, Hans L. C. *De Stijl*. New York: Harry N. Abrams, 1967.

Janson, H. W. *History of Art*. 2 vols. 5th ed. Englewood Cliffs, NJ: Prentice Hall; New York: Harry N. Abrams, 1995.

Jones, Frederic H. *Concise Dictionary of Architectural and Design History*. Los Altos, CA: Crisp Publications, 1992.

Jordan, R. Furneaux. *A Concise History of Western Architecture*. London: Thames & Hudson, 1969.

Klein, Dan. *Art Deco*. New York: Crown, 1974.

Kostof, Spiro. *History of Architecture*. New York: Oxford University Press, 1985.

Kron, Joan, and Suzanne Slesin. *High Tech: The Industrial Style and Source Book for the Home*. New York: Clarkson N. Potter, 1978.

Maass, John. *The Victorian Home in America*. New York: Hawthorn, 1972.

Massey, Anne. *Interior Design of the 20th Century*. New York: Thames and Hudson, 1990.

Mather, Christine, and Sharon Woods. *Santa Fe Style*. New York: Rizzoli International, 1986.

McAlester, Virginia, and Lee McAlester. *A Field Guide to American Houses*. New York: Alfred A. Knopf, 1984.

McFadden, David. *Scandinavian Modern Design*. New York: Harry N. Abrams, 1982.

Naylor, Gillian. *The Bauhaus*. New York: Dutton, 1968.

Pevsner, Nikolaus. *Pioneers of Modern Design from William Morris to Walter Gropius*. 2d ed. New York: Museum of Modern Art, 1975.

Pierson, William H., Jr. *American Buildings and Their Architects: The Colonial and Neoclassical Styles*. New York: Doubleday, 1970.

Pile, John. *A History of Interior Design*. New York: Wiley, 200

Radice, Barbara. *Memphis*. New York: Rizzoli Internationa 1984.

Sharp, Denis. *Showcase of Interior Design—Pacific Editio* Grand Rapids, MI: Vitae, 1992.

———. *Twentieth Century Architecture*. New York: Facts c File, 1991.

Smith, C. Ray. *A History of Interior Design in 20th Century Ame ica*. New York: Harper & Row, 1987.

Smith, S. Jane. *Elsie de Wolfe: A Life in the High Style*. New Yor Atheneum, 1982.

Tate, Allen, and C. Ray Smith. *Interior Design in the 20th Ce tury*. New York: Harper & Row, 1986.

Trachtenberg, Marvin, and Isabelle Hyman. *Architecture fro Prehistory to Post-Modernism*. New York: Harry N. Abram 1986.

Warren, Geoffrey. *Art Nouveau Style*. London: Octopus, 1972.

Whiffen, Marcus, and Frederick Koeper. *American Architectu 1607–1976*. 2 vols. Cambridge, MA: The MIT Press, 1983.

Whiton, Sherrill, and Stanley Abercrombie. *Interior Design Decoration*. 5th ed. Upper Saddle River, NJ: Prentic Hall/Pearson, 2002.

Wright, Frank Lloyd. *The Natural House*. New York: Bramha House, 1954.

http://www.dezignare.com/library.html Comprehensive site f all facets of design, this link specifically related to history.

http://www.greatbuildings.com/ General website of worldwi buildings.

http://www.washington.edu/ark2/ University of Washingto database of over 5000 buildings worldwide.

Lighting

Burton, Jack L. *Fundamentals of Interior Lighting, Volume On* Upper Saddle River, NJ: Pearson Education/Prentice Ha 1999.

Design Criteria for Lighting Interior Living Spaces. New York: I luminating Engineering Society of North America, 1980.

Gardner, Carl, and Barry Hannaford. *Lighting Design: An Intr ductory Guide for Professionals*. New York: Wiley, 1993.

General Electric. *The Light Book*. Cleveland, OH: Nela Park, 198

Gordon, Gary. *Interior Lighting for Designers*. 4th ed. New Yor Wiley, 2002.

Grosslight, Jane. *Light: Effective Use of Daylight and Electr Lighting in Residential and Commercial Projects*. Englewoo Cliffs, NJ: Prentice Hall, 1984.

Jankowski, Wanda. *Designing with Light*. Glen Cove, NY: P. B. (International, 1992.

Jones, Frederic H. *Architectural Lighting Design*. Los Altos, C Crisp Publications, 1989.

Karlen, Mark, and James R. Benya. *Lighting Design Basics: De sign Methods for Architects*. New York: Wiley, 2002.

Kaufmann, John E. *IES Lighting Handbook Reference Volum* New York: Illuminating Engineering Society of North Ame ica (IESNA), 1981.

Lightolier. *The Light Book*. Jersey City, NJ: Lightolier, 1981.

Michel, Lou. *Light: The Shape of Space*. New York: Van Nostran Reinhold, 1996.

Moore, Fuller. *Concepts and Practice of Architectural Dayligh ing*. New York: Van Nostrand Reinhold, 1985.

Nuckolls, James L. *Interior Lighting for Environmental Design ers*. 2d ed. New York: Wiley, 1983.

Robbins, C. C. *Daylighting Design and Analysis*. New York: Va Nostrand Reinhold, 1986.

ooney, William F. *Practical Guide to Home Lighting*. New York: Van Nostrand Reinhold, 1980.
mith, Fran Kellogg, and Fred J. Bertolone. *Bringing Interiors to Light*. New York: Whitney Library of Design, 1986.
orcar, Prafulla C. *Architectural Lighting for Commercial Interiors*. New York: Wiley-Interscience, 1987.
teffy, Gary R. *Architectural Lighting Design*. 2d ed. New York: Wiley, 2001.
ttp://iald.org/index.htm International Association of Lighting Designers.
ttp://iesna.org/ Illuminating Engineers Society of North America.
ttp://lightforum.com/architecturallighting/about_us/site_map.jsp Lighting information published by *Architectural Lighting* magazine.
ttp://ncqlp.org/ International Council of Qualifications for Lighting Professions.
ttp://www.lrc.rpi.edu/ Lighting Research Center for universities published by Rensselaer Polytechnic Institute.
ttp://www.schorsch.com/ International website of lighting information. Includes a glossary.

laterials (Floors, Walls, Window Treatments, Etc.)

Commercial & Residential Wallcoverings Reference Manual, Created for Design Schools. Chicago: Wallcoverings Association, 1997.
onran, Terence. *New House Book*. New York: Random House, Villard Books, 1985.
———. *The Bed and Bath Book*. New York: Crown, 1978.
———. *The House Book*. New York: Crown, 1976.
iland, Murray L. *Oriental Rugs: A Comprehensive Study*. Greenwich, CT: New York Graphic Society, 1973.
Iall, William R. *Contract Interior Finishes: A Handbook of Materials, Products, and Applications*. New York: Whitney Library of Design, 1993.
acobson, Charles W. *Check Points on How to Buy Oriental Rugs*. Rutland, VT: Charles E. Tuttle, 1969.
ahlenberg, Mary Hunt, and Anthony Berlant. *Navajo Blanket*. New York: Praeger, 1972.
opp, Joel, and Kate Kopp. *American Hooked and Sewn Rugs*. New York: Dutton, 1975.
Jeal, Mary. *Custom Draperies in Interior Design*. New York: Elsevier, 1982.
Jielson, Karla J. *Window Treatments*. New York: Van Nostrand Reinhold, 1990.
adford, Penny. *Designer's Guide to Surfaces and Finishes*. New York: Watson-Guptill, 1984.
eznikoff, S. C. *Specifications for Commercial Interiors*. Rev. ed. New York: Whitney Library of Design, 1989.
iggs, J. Rosemary. *Materials and Components of Interior Architecture*. 5th ed. Upper Saddle River, NJ: Prentice Hall, 1999.
upp, William, and Arnold Friedmann. *Construction Materials for Interior Design*. New York: Whitney Library of Design/ Watson-Guptill Publications, 1989.
Vrey, Lady Caroline. *Complete Book of Curtains and Draperies*. London: Ebury/Random Century, 1991.
ttp://benjaminmoore.com/index.asp Benjamin Moore Home page.
ttp://hardwoodfloorsmag.com/ *Magazine of the National Wood Flooring Association*.
ttp://lafiber.com/ Carpet and Textile Recycling Plant.
ttp://mathforum.org/geometry/rugs/ Information and images on Oriental Rugs.
http://vinylinfo.org/index.html The Vinyl Institute.
http://www.afpf.com/carpetwhypoly.html Alliance for Polyurethane Foam Padding.
http://www.armstrong.com/commceilingsna/glossary.html Armstrong commercial ceilings glossary.
http://www.awinet.org/ Architectural Woodwork Institute.
http://www.blonderwall.com/history.htm Timeline of Wallpaper history.
http://www.carpetcushion.org/ Carpet Cushion Council.
http://www.carpetinfo.co.uk/pages/aboutpp/construc.htm Carpet Construction information from the United Kingdom.
http://www.carpetinfo.co.uk/pages/aboutpp/history.htm History of Carpet-timeline from United Kingdom.
http://www.carpetinfo.co.uk/pages/intro.htm Carpet Information from the United Kingdom.
http://www.carpetrecovery.org/ Carpet America Recovery Effort (CARE).
http://www.carpet-rug.com Carpet and Rug Institute.
http://www.carpet-rug.com/drill_down_2.cfm?page=3&sub=2 Carpet and Rug Institute's site on fiber and construction.
http://www.ctdahome.org/ Ceramic Tile Distributors Association.
http://www.dicknsons.com/glossary.htm Glossary on floor covering terms.
http://www.dwcdesignet.com/DWC/ *Drapery and Window Coverings Magazine*.
http://www.dwcinternational.com/ Drapery and Window Coverings International Directory.
http://www.epa.gov/OSWRCRA/non-hw/procure/products/carpcush.htm EPA's guidelines on Carpet Cushions.
http://www.ianr.unl.edu/pubs/homefurnish/g1222.htm Articles on carpet construction, care, and selection. Adapted by Shirley M. Niemeyer, Extension Specialist, Interior Design/Home Furnishings.
http://www.ianr.unl.edu/pubs/homefurnish/g1316.htm Articles on carpet construction, care, and selection. Adapted by Shirley M. Niemeyer, Extension Specialist, Interior Design/Home Furnishings.
http://www.maplefloor.org/ Maple Flooring Manufacturers Association.
http://www.nofma.org/ National Oak Flooring Manufacturers Association.
http://www.oria.org/ Oriental Rug Importers Association.
http://www.ppg.com/ppgaf/school.htm Pittsburgh Paint, online paint school.
http://www.sherwin-williams.com/diy/interior/ Sherwin Williams Do it Yourself information.
http://www.tile-assn.com/ National Tile Contractors Association.
http://www.virginiagalleries.com/wood-recog.htm Images of types of wood.
http://www.wallpaperinstaller.com/index.html Wallpaper installation information and terminology.
http://www.wcaa.org/ Window Coverings Association of America.
http://www.wmmpa.com/ Wood Moulding & Millwork Producers Association. Many links to other sites.
http://www.woodfloors.org/ National Wood Flooring Association.
http://www2.cr.nps.gov/tps/briefs/brief40.htm National Park Service, Historic Preservation Brief on Restoring Ceramic Tile.

Space Planning/Human Scale

Hall, Edward T. *The Hidden Dimension*. Garden City, NJ: Doubleday, 1969.

Harrigan, J. E. *Human Factors Research: Methods & Applications for Architects & Interior Designers*. New York: Elsevier Dutton, 1987.

Henry Dreyfuss Associates. *The Measure of Man and Woman: Human Factors in Design*. Rev. ed. New York: Wiley, 2002.

Karlen, Mark. *Space Planning Basics*. New York: Van Nostrand Reinhold, 1993.

Laseau, Paul. *Graphic Problem Solving for Architects & Designers*. 2d ed. New York: Van Nostrand Reinhold, 1986.

Niels, Diffrient. *Humanscale Four-Five-Six*. Cambridge, MA: MIT Press, 1981.

———. *Humanscale One-Two-Three*. Cambridge, MA: MIT Press, 1974.

———. *Humanscale Seven-Eight-Nine*. Cambridge, MA: MIT Press, 1981.

Panero, Julius, and Martin Zelnick. *Human Dimensions and Interior Space*. New York: Whitney Library of Design, 1979.

Papanek, Victor. *Design for Human Scale*. New York: Van Nostrand Reinhold, 1983.

Preiser, Wolfgang. *Post-Occupancy Evaluation*. New York: Van Nostrand Reinhold, 1988.

———. *Programming the Built Environment*. New York: Van Nostrand Reinhold, 1985.

Scott-Webber, Lennie. *Programming: A Problem-Solving Approach for Users of Interior Spaces*. Houston: Dame Publications, 1998.

Temple, Nancy. *Interior Design Workbook*. New York: Van Nostrand Reinhold, 1993.

http://www.adaptiveenvironments.org/about/index.php Nonprofit organization on adaptive environments.

http://www.arthritis.org/resources/Home_Life/design.asp Arthritis Foundation information on barrier-free design.

http://www.dezignare.com/newsletter/ergonomics.html General information on Universal and Barrier-Free Design and Terms.

http://www.usdoj.gov/crt/ada/adahom1.htm Americans with Disabilities Act site.

Specialty Design

Baraban, Regina S., and Joseph F. Durocher. *Successful Restaurant Design*. 2d ed, New York: Wiley, 2001.

Barr, Wilma, and Charles Broudy. *Designing to Sell: A Complete Guide to Retail Store Planning and Design*. New York: McGraw-Hill, 1985.

Boykin, Paula Jo. *Hotel Guestroom Design*. Dubuque, IA: Kendall/Hunt Publishing, 1991.

Bush-Brown, Albert. *Hospitable Design for Healthcare and Senior Communities*. New York: Van Nostrand Reinhold, 1992.

Gosling, David, and Barry Maitland. *Design and Planning of Retail Systems*. New York: Whitney Library of Design, 1976.

Howell, Sandra C. *Designing for Aging: Patterns of Use*. Cambridge, MA: MIT Press, 1987.

Jones, Lynn M. *The Design of National Park Visitor Centers: The Relationships Between Buildings and Their Sites*. Athens, GA: University of Georgia, 1990.

Logrippo, Ro. *In My World: Designing Living & Learning Environments for the Young*. New York: Wiley, 1995.

Malkin, Jain. *Hospital Interior Architecture: Creating Healing Environments*. New York: Van Nostrand Reinhold, 1992.

———. *Medical and Dental Space Planning: A Comprehensive Guide to Design, Equipment, and Clinical Procedures*. New York: Wiley, 2002.

Mazzurco, Philip. *Bath Design*. New York: Whitney Library c Design, 1986.

Mount, Charles Morris. *Residential Interiors*. Glen Cove, NY: I B. C. International, 1992.

Novak, Adolph. *Store Planning and Design*. New York: Lebha Friedman, 1977.

Pile, John. *Open Office Planning: A Handbook for Interior De signers and Architects*. New York: Whitney Library of Design Watson-Guptill Publications, 1986.

Piotrowski, Christine. *Open Office Planning: A Handbook for In terior Designers and Architects*. New York: Whitney Librar of Design, 1986.

Raschko, Bettyann. *Housing Interiors for the Disabled and El derly*. New York: Van Nostrand Reinhold, 1982.

Russell, Beverly. *The Interiors Book of Shops and Restaurants* New York: Watson-Guptill, 1981.

Weinhold, Virginia. *Interior Finish Materials for Health Care Fa cilities*. Springfield, IL: Charles C Thomas, 1988.

Weishar, Joseph. *Design for Effective Selling Space*. New York McGraw-Hill, 1992.

http://www.kitchen-bath.com/kitchenandbath/ideas/index.jsp Kitchen and bath website published by *Kitchen and Bath Business Magazine*. Includes glossary and basic guideline for design.

http://www.nkba.org/ National Kitchen & Bath Association site

http://www.notsobighouse.com/ Not So Big House website.

Sustainable Design

Coles, Elizabeth A. *Designing Green Interiors: Green Concept Teaching Manual*. Indianapolis, IN: Purdue School of Engineering and Technology, 1999.

Hawkseed Group. *The Passive Solar House Book*. New York Rand McNally, 1980.

Lichtenwalter, Rachel. *Green Eggs and Spam: Could You, Woul You, Should You, Use These Materials?* [Brochure]. Atlanta GA: Author, 2002.

Pilatowicz, Grazyna. *Eco-Interiors*. New York: Wiley, 1995.

Reynolds, Michael. *EARTHSHIP Vol. I—How to Build Your Own* Taos, NM: Solar Survival Press, 1990.

———. *EARTHSHIP Vol. II—Systems and Components*. Taos NM: Solar Survival Press, 1990.

———. *EARTHSHIP Vol. III—Evolution Beyond Economics* Taos, NM: Solar Survival Press, 1993.

Wright, David. *Natural Solar Architecture: The Passive Sola Primer*. 3d ed. New York: Van Nostrand Reinhold, 1984.

Zeiher, Laura C. *The Ecology of Architecture*. New York: Whitne Library of Design, 1996.

http://southface.org/ Southface Energy Institute.

http://www.ases.org American Solar Energy Society.

http://www.carpet-rug.com/ Carpet and Rug Institute.

http://www.certifiedwood.org/ Certified Forest Products Counci

http://www.earthship.org/ Earthship website.

http://www.eeba.org/default.htm Energy and Environmenta Building Association.

http://www.energybuilder.com/greenbld.htm Green Buildin Guide.

http://www.envirosense.org The Envirosense Consortium, nonprofit organization that address IAQ.

http://www.epa.gov/iaq/atozindex.html EPA Indoor Air Qualit Index.

http://www.epa.gov/oar/oaqps/peg_caa/pegcaain.html EPA' Clean Air Act in "Plain English."

p://www.forestworld.com/ Sustainable Forest Products Resource.
p://www.hardwoodcouncil.com/ The Hardwoods Council.
p://www.ises.org/ises.nsf!Open International Solar Energy Society.
p://www.isf-sw.org/ Institute for Sustainable Forestry.
p://www.rmi.org/ Rocky Mountain Institute.
p://www.sbicouncil.org/ Sustainable Buildings Industry Council.
p://www.seia.org/ Solar Energy Industries Association.
p://www.tropicalforestfoundation.org/ Tropical Forest Foundation.
p://www.woodcom.com/woodcom/afpa/afpabp02.html Principles of Sustainable Forests by the American Forest and Paper Association.

hnical Data (Construction)

en, Edward, and Rob Thallon. *Fundamentals of Residential Construction*. New York: Wiley, 2002.
derson, L. O. *How to Build a Wood-Frame House*. New York: Dover Publications, 1973.
llast, David Kent. *Interior Construction & Detailing for Designers and Architects*. Belmont, CA: Professional Publications, 1998.
——. *Practical Guide to Computer Applications for Architecture and Design*. Englewood Cliffs, NJ: Prentice Hall, 1986.
ggeli, Corky. *Building Systems for Interior Designers*. New York: Wiley, 2002.
owning, Hugh C. *The Principles of Architectural Drafting*. New York: Whitney Library of Design, 1996.
ing, Francis D. K. *Building Construction Illustrated*. 3d ed. New York: Wiley, 2002.
e Encyclopedia of Wood. New York: Sterling, 1989.
nn, John E., A. Segil, and G. Steffy. *Architectural Interior Systems*. 2d ed. New York: Van Nostrand Reinhold, 1988.
af, Don. *Basic Building Data*. 3d ed. New York: Van Nostrand Reinhold, 1985.
th, Mark W. *Understanding Construction Drawings*. Albany, NY: Delmar Publishers, 1983.
door Air Quality Programs: A Two-Part Program Package for the Design Professions. Washington, DC: American Society of Interior Designers, 1994.
nes, Frederic H. *Interior Architecture Drafting and Perspective*. Menlo Park, CA: Crisp Publications, 1986.
cklighter, Clois E., Ronald J. Baird, and Joan C. Kicklighter. *Architecture: Residential Drawing and Design*. South Holland, IL: The Goodheart-Wilcox Company, 1990.
cklighter, Clois E., and Joan C. Kicklighter. *Residential Interiors*. South Holland, IL: Goodheart-Wilcox, 1986.
mit, Louis Gary. *Technical Drawing and Design*. Minneapolis/St. Paul: West Publishing Company, 1994.
bing, Ralph W. *Architectural Working Drawings*. 4th ed. New York: Wiley, 1999.
ller, Edward J., and James G. Fausett. *Architectural Drawing and Light Construction*. Englewood Cliffs, NJ: Prentice Hall, 1993.
ith, R. C. *Materials of Construction*. 3d ed. New York: McGraw-Hill, 1979.
ebler, Wendy. *Architectural Detailing in Contract Interiors*. New York: Whitney Library of Design/Watson-Guptill Publications, 1988.
Stein, Ben M., Frederick H. Reynolds, and William McGuiness. *Mechanical and Electrical Equipment for Building*. New York: Wiley, 1986.
Veitch, Ronald M. *Detailing Fundamentals for Interior Design*. Winnipeg, Canada: Peguis, 1994.
Wakita, Dr. Osamu A., and Richard M. Linde. *The Professional Practice of Architectural Working Drawings*. 3d ed. New York: Wiley, 2002.
Wakita, Osamu A., and Richard M. Linde. *The Professional Practice of Architectural Detailing*. 3d ed. New York: Wiley, 1999.
Wallach, Paul I., and Donald E. Helper. *Reading Construction Drawings*. New York: McGraw-Hill, 1979.
http://www.awinet.org/ American Woodworking Institute.
http://www.b4ubuild.com/ General residential building site.
http://www.ballandball-us.com/commondoorconstructionterms.html Door construction terms.
http://www.bernards.co.uk/door_furniture_period_styles_faq.htm Historic Decorative Door hardware.
http://www.constructionworknews.com/field-manual/index2.html Site containing construction symbols and terminology.
http://www.efficientwindows.org/ Energy-efficient window site.
http://www.hearthed.com/ Hearth Education Foundation.
http://www.homebuildingmanual.com/Glossary.htm Glossary of building construction terms.
http://www.hometime.com/projects/howto/windoor/pc3wdgl.htm Residential glossary of door and window terms.
http://www.hpba.org/consumer/2/Glossary/index.shtml Hearth, Patio, and Barbecue Association, glossary of terms.
http://www.jsc.nasa.gov/bu2/resources.html Cost-estimating resources.
http://www.kcma.org/ Kitchen Cabinet Manufacturers Association.
http://www.kraftmaid.com/Main/DoorConstr.htm Images of cabinet construction.
http://www.maconline.org/tech/design/fireplace2.html Energy-efficient fireplace design guide provided by the Masonry Design Council.
http://www.nahb.com/ National Association of Homebuilders.
http://www.nahbrc.org National Association of Homebuilders Research Center.
http://www.onlinetools.com/cwd/vinylcut.html Cut section of a window and glossary of window terms.
http://www.pella.com/learn/glossary/ Pella's glossary of terms for doors and windows.
http://www.sandkuhl.com/html/default_plan_design.html Design and plans for masonry fireplace construction.
http://www.selectmillwork.com/doors/ Images of door styles.
http://www.solve-chimney-problems.co.uk/pages/section6.html Glossary of fireplace terms.
http://www.sweets.com/ Construction resources guide from *Sweets Catalog*.

Textiles

Corbman, Bernard P. *Fiber to Fabric*. New York: McGraw-Hill, 1983.
Jackman, Dianne R., and Mary K. Dixon. *The Guide to Textiles for Interior Designers*. 2d ed. Winnipeg, Canada: Peguis, 1988.
Joseph, Marjory L. *Essentials of Textiles*. 3d ed. New York: Holt, Rinehart & Winston, 1984.
Kadolph, Sara J., and Anna L. Langford. *Textiles*. 8th ed. Upper Saddle River, NJ: Merrill/Prentice Hall, 1998.

Larsen, Jack Lenor, and Jeanne Weeks. *Fabrics for Interiors*. New York: Van Nostrand Reinhold, 1975.
Lyle, Dorothy Siegert. *Modern Textiles*. New York: John Wiley, 1983.
Tortora, Phyllis G., and Billie J. Collier. *Understanding Textiles*. 5th ed. Upper Saddle River, NJ: Merrill/Prentice Hall, 1997.
Yates, Marypaul. *Fabrics: A Guide for Interior Designers and Architects*. New York: Norton, 2001.
Yeager, Jan I. *Textiles for Residential and Commercial Interiors*. 2d ed. New York: Fairchild, 2000.
http://info.cas.org/STNEWS/OCTOBER98/textiles.html Information on textile history.
http://textilesociety.org/about.htm Textile Society of America.
http://www.contract-textiles.com/ Association for Contract Textiles.
http://www.fabriclink.com/ Educational resource on fabrics.
http://www.fibersource.com/ Educational link to fiber sources.
http://www.interlog.com/~gwhite/ttt/tttintro.html Information on textile history with links to many sites.
http://www.nsf.gov/nstw/teach/nstw1996/nice/chart.htm Chart of fabric characteristics.
http://www.ntcresearch.org/ National Textile Research-Links to current articles.
http://www.rosefurniture.com/howdo/fabric.htm Fabric Upholstery Guide for Residential Use.
http://www.surfacedesign.org/ Surface Design Association.

Visual Communications

Burde, Ernest. *Design Presentation Techniques*. New York: McGraw-Hill, 1992.
Ching, Francis D. K. *Architectural Graphics*. 4th ed. New York: Wiley, 2003.
Cooper, Douglas. *Drawing and Perceiving: Life Drawing for Students of Architecture and Design*. 3d ed. New York: Wiley, 2000.
Dong, Wei. *Color Rendering: A Guide for Interior Designers and Architects*. New York: McGraw-Hill, 1997.
Doyle, Michael E. *Color Drawing*. New York: Wiley Reinhold, 1999.
Evans, Larry. *Illustration Guide, Vol. Two*. New York: Van Nostrand Reinhold, 1988.
Gerds, Donald A. *Markers: Interiors, Exteriors, Product Design*. Santa Monica, CA: DAG Design, 1983.
Koenig, Peter A. *Design Graphics: Drawing Techniques for Design Professionals*. Upper Saddle River, NJ: Pearson Education/Prentice Hall, 2000.
Laseau, Paul. *Graphic Thinking for Architects & Designers*. 3d ed. New York: Wiley, 2001.
McGarry, Richard, and Greg Madsen. *Marker Magic: The Rendering Problem Solver for Designers*. New York: Van Nostrand Reinhold, 1993.
Porter, Tom, and Sue Goodman. *Manual of Graphic Techniques 2*. New York: Charles Scribner's Sons, 1982.
Walker, Theodore D. *Perspective Sketches II*. West Lafayette, IN: P. D. A. Publishers, 1975.
———. *Plan Graphics*. West Lafayette, IN: P. D. A. Publishe[rs,] 1975.
Wang, Thomas C. *Plan and Section Drawing*. New York: V[an] Nostrand Reinhold, 1979.

Selected Periodicals, Trade Journals, Produc[t] Publications, and Professional Journals

Abitare
American Craft
American Homestyle & Gardening
Architectural Digest
Architectural Lighting
Architectural Record
Art and Antiques
Atlanta Homes & Lifestyles
Audio/Video Interiors
Conference Proceedings—Interior Design Educators Council
Contract Design
Design Solutions
The Designer Magazine
Domus
Elle Decor
EnvironDesign Journal
Facilities Design and Management
Fine Furniture International
Florida Design
Home
Home Building
Hospitality Design
Interior Design
Interiors
Interiors & Sources
Journal of Interior Design
Kitchen and Bath Business
Lighting Dimensions
Luxury Kitchen and Bath
Metropolis
Metropolitan Home
National Trust for Historic Preservation
Old House Journal
On Design
Professional Builder
Progressive Architecture
Southern Accents
Traditional Home
Veranda
Western Interiors and Design

Current catalogs and brochures are published by and ava[il]able from major manufacturers of fabrics, wallpaper, wall pa[n]eling, hard floor coverings, carpets, and furniture.

Glossary

lso see pages 297 through 299 for textile terms.

bacus Small slab found on top of the capital of a column.

bstract A type of decorative design, modified so that the subject may not be recognizable.

canthus leaves A stylized design motif inspired by the acanthus plant and especially favored by the ancient Greeks and Romans.

ccent lighting Lighting used to focus and/or emphasize particular objects or features.

ccessible Unobstructive passage into and throughout a structure making it negotiable for wheelchair users and others with physical limitations.

chromatic Hues "without color"; specifically, gray, black, and white.

coustics In design, the study of sound, including its properties and successful adaptation in a human environment.

ctive solar energy system Mechanical systems particularly designed to collect and distribute solar heat.

daptation The modification of an item to make it fit more perfectly under conditions of its current environment. In furniture design, indicates that only some elements of the original have been adapted to the present design.

daptive reuse Historical structures redesigned for a current use.

dditive color Mixing or adding primary hues through the use of either dyes and pigments or lighting.

dobe brick A brick of sun-dried earth and straw; most often used in the Southwest adobe-style dwelling.

.F.F. Above finished floor.

fterimage When the human eye focuses on a strong hue, the eye becomes saturated with that hue and an afterimage of that hue's complement can be seen when the eye focuses on a neutral surface.

ir-exchange unit A unit that allows fresh outside air to be drawn into a structure and discharges stale air. Contributes to a "healthy environment."

isle A hallway that runs parallel to the nave of a church and is separated from it by an arcade.

mbient lighting A term interchangeable with general lighting; lighting that provides overall illumination.

mp (or ampere) The measurement of electrical current in a particular circuit.

nalogous colors Hues adjacent on the color wheel.

nodize The application of a protective oxide covering on metal.

nthemion A radiating stylized honeysuckle flower motif used by the ancient Greeks and in Neoclassic design.

nthropometrics The science of measuring the dimensions and proportions of the human body in various activities.

Antique A work of art, piece of furniture, or decorative object made at a much earlier period than the present, often at least 100 years old.

Apron The horizontal section beneath a table top, chair seat, chest of drawers, or window sill.

Apse A semicircular or polygonal recess at the end of a church plan.

Arabesque A leaf-and-scroll pattern with stems rising from a root or other motif branching in spiral form; usually in a vertical panel.

Arcade A series of adjoining arches with their supporting columns on piers.

Architectural lighting Permanently wired and architecturally fixed luminaires.

Architrave A horizontal member located above the column and capital in classical architecture.

Armoire The French term for a tall cupboard or wardrobe with doors.

Artesonado Ornately carved wood; usually used in Hispanic styles.

Ashlar Square or rectangular blocks of stone masonry used in the construction of a building.

ASID American Society of Interior Designers.

Asymmetrical balance Balance created by grouping objects or furnishings to give a sense of equilibrium.

Baffle A mechanism for deflecting light or directing it to reduce glare.

Balance Placing objects or furnishings in a symmetrical, asymmetrical, or radial approach to create a sense of equilibrium.

Balcony A projecting platform from the exterior or interior wall of a structure, enclosed by a railing.

Ballast An electrical transformer that converts current necessary for fluorescent lighting.

Balloon-frame construction A type of construction employing a simple, economical skeletal frame. Used most often for small wood houses with closely placed supportive elements with spaces in between for wiring, plumbing, and insulation.

Baluster A turned, upright support of a rail, as in the railing of a staircase.

Balustrade A row of balusters topped by a rail.

Banister A handrail.

Banquette Architecturally built-in seating units used in restaurants and sometimes in residential design.

Barrel vault An arched roof known since 4000 B.C. and perfected by the ancient Romans.

Barrier-free design Designs where no physical obstacles prevent access for wheelchair users to various facilities throughout a space.

Base molding Moldings near or at the bottom of the wall along the floor's edge.

Bas-relief A type of decoration in which the design is slightly raised from the surface or background.

Batik A process of decorating fabric by wax coating the parts not to be dyed. After the fabric is dyed, the wax is removed.

Batten A long strip of wood covering the joint between two larger wood strips.

Bay window An angled window that projects outward from the wall surface.

Bead-and-reel A convex classical Greek molding, with disks singly or in pairs, alternating with oblong beads.

Beam A horizontal timber or metal bar supported on vertical posts, used to support a roof or ceiling.

Bell gambrel A type of gambrel roof where the lower section splays outward to give the roof a "bell-shaped" appearance.

Beltcourse See *stringcourse.*

Belvedere See *cupola.*

Bentwood A process of bending narrow strips of wood into various artistic forms; developed primarily by Austrian designer Michael Thonet during the latter half of the nineteenth century.

Bergère A French armchair featuring a wood frame with upholstered arm panels, seat, and back.

Berm A mound of soil. In solar design, placed against a building to add insulating qualities.

Bevel The edge of any flat surface that has been cut at a slant to the main surface.

Bidet A water-cleansing fixture.

Biodegradable The ability of a material to decompose naturally.

Biotechnology The use of new advancements in engineering and technology in product design and the environment.

Blocking In construction, rough lumber is placed in a hidden location to support a joint or future object.

Blocking diagram A visual drawing that groups individuals, departments, or spaces into block. Used in conceptual design.

Blueprint A photographic print, formerly white lines on a bright blue ground, used for copying architectural plans. The standard today is blue lines on a white ground.

Board-and-batten construction Construction employing wide upright boards placed side by side with joints covered by battens.

Boiserie A French word generally used to designate elaborate carved wood paneling.

Bolection molding A projecting molding with a rounded edge.

Bonnet roof A type of French hipped roof with a bottom that covers a surrounding porch. The shape resembles a bonnet.

Bow window A semicurved window that projects outward from the wall surface.

Breakfront A large cabinet or bookcase with a center section projecting beyond the flanking end sections.

Brewster color theory Another term for the standard color wheel theory based on the three primary colors of blue, red, and yellow. May also be called the *Prang* or Palette system.

Broadloom Carpet woven in 27-inch to 18-foot widths. Most commonly used in 12-foot widths.

Bubble diagram A visual drawing indicating individuals, departments, or spaces with bubbles. Used in conceptual design.

Buffet A cabinet for holding dining room accessories and from which food may be served.

Bullnose A 180-degree rounded wooden edge on a table, step, or cabinet top.

Burl A strong irregularity in the wood grain providing an inte esting design and color; often used for veneering in furnitur

Burnish To make shiny or lustrous by rubbing.

Butt joint An expensive joint where two flush edges a joined by glue, screws, or other means.

Buttress A supportive structure first used on the Gothic cath dral that splays from a wall to make it stable.

Cabriole leg A furniture leg support designed in the form a conventionalized animal leg with knee, ankle, and foot cr ating a double curve or *S* shape.

CAD (CADD) Computer-aided design (and drafting).

Calendering A finishing process for fabrics; the textile pressed between rollers.

Candela In lighting, the unit of measure for the intensity light in a given direction directly from the lamp.

Caning Flexible rattan or cane woven in open mesh for cha backs, seats, and other furniture members.

Canister A small box or case for holding tea, coffee, flour, sa or sugar.

Cantilever A projecting beam or furniture member supporte at one end only.

Capital The top treatment of a column. In classical Gree architecture, the capitals were Doric, Ionic, or Corinthian in styl

Captain's walk A balustraded observation platform built atc the roof of a coastal dwelling, providing an unobstructe view of the sea; also called a widow's walk.

Caryatid The human form used as a structural support.

Casement window A window hinged on one side only, a lowing it to swing inward or outward.

Casepiece A general term applied to furniture storage piece that have no upholstered components.

Cathedral In ceiling design, the vertical area formed by pitched roof.

Cella The interior space (or cell) of an ancient Greek or Roma temple, especially copied during the Greek Revival period.

Chair rail The decorative trim horizontally positioned about 3′-0″ above the floor.

Chaise longue A French term for a lounge chair (with or witl out arms) with an extended seat providing leg support for th occupant.

Chandelier A lighting fixture suspended from the ceiling wit branches to support candles or electric lamps.

Chase A concealed channel in a wall that carries HVAC, ele trical, or plumbing lines from floor to floor.

Chateau A castle or large country house in France.

Chevron A repeating *V* shape or zigzag motif consisting of d agonal bars meeting at a point.

Chimneypiece The architectural design that sheathes the fir box and flue.

Chinoiserie (shinwá zor ee) (French) Refers to Chinese la quered designs, which were popularly employed during th eighteenth century on European furniture.

Chroma The purity or saturation of a color. Also calle *intensity.*

Circulation The traffic patterns of occupants within an inte rior space, particularly important when planning rooms, stai ways, hallways, etc.

Clapboard A horizontal overlapping of thin wood board used for the exterior sheathing of structures; popularly en ployed for seventeenth- and eighteenth-century colonia style homes.

assic A term generally applied to design of timeless quality that transcends changes in taste and fashion.

assical A term relating to the arts of ancient Greece or Rome.

earance The planning of space required by building codes to clear combustible heating units such as fireplaces, stoves, or furnaces. Also, adequate clearance space between furnishings for the convenience of users.

erestory Windows placed at the top of a structure's wall allowing extra light.

ub foot A club-shaped or rounded foot on a cabriole leg, especially associated with Queen Anne furniture.

uster planning A method of arranging concentrated dwelling units, usually low-rise and either separate or attached, to take advantage of communal open spaces.

de Federal, state, or local laws applied to the design of buildings in relation to safety and health standards.

ffered ceiling Ornamental sunken panels between beams employed for a flat, vaulted, or domed ceiling providing a three-dimensional effect.

lonnade Columns arranged in a straight or curved row, often supporting an entablature.

lonnette A miniature colonnade used for decoration.

lor rendering index A measurement in graph form of a lamp's color spectrum.

lumned chimney (clustered chimney) A cluster or arrangement of a number of chimneys together.

O.M. Customer's own material. The customer purchases fabric for a job from another source.

mmode A French term referring to a low chest supported on legs with drawers.

mplementary colors Contrasting colors based on the opposite colors of the color wheel. Various combinations of cool and warm colors.

mputer network Computer terminals within an office that are connected by cables, permitting access to the same data.

ncept The basic beliefs that define the solution to a project. May include physical elements or design directions such as historical styles, but also extends to abstract thoughts and feelings.

nceptual design The phase of the design process in which designers formulate preliminary broad-based concepts. May be called *schematic design*.

ndominium A multiunit structure, such as an apartment house, in which each unit is individually owned. Maintenance and services are paid for by the residents as a group.

nsole table A table designed to be fixed on a wall; sometimes supported by two front legs.

nstruction drawings Drawings that indicate how to build something.

ntemporary style Living or occurring at the same period of time. In furniture, the term commonly refers to a modified type of modern or updated traditional design. Some styles are considered classic.

ntract administration A phase of design where the designer administers the contracts completed in construction documentation.

ntract documentation A design phase where the designer documents the design decisions approved by the client in previous design phases.

rbel A bracket or projection from a wall used to support a molding or beam.

Corinthian The most ornate of the three Greek orders, characterized by its capital of small volutes (spiral, scroll-shaped ornaments) and acanthus leaves.

Cornice A horizontal and projecting member that crowns an architectural composition; a molding on a wall near the ceiling or under the eaves of the roof. Cornice board is a molding used with drapery instead of a valance.

Coromandel screen A large freestanding paneled lacquered screen with incised designs, made in China but originally imported from the Coromandel Coast of India.

Corridor Term used for a hallway, generally in a public building.

Coved ceiling A ceiling that meets the wall by means of a concave curve rather than a right angle.

Credenza A long, table-height cupboard with drawers and doors. Popular during the Italian Renaissance; today, a low storage unit with doors and often drawers, usually placed behind a desk.

Critical path A timetable or schedule used to determine the processes needed to complete a construction project.

Crown lintel An architectural detail used above windows, particularly in the late eighteenth and early nineteenth centuries. The lintel, often called a jack-arch lintel, features a crown-shaped keystone.

Crown molding The uppermost molding, usually joining the wall and ceiling.

Cruciform A cross-shaped form.

Crystal The finest quality of lead glass.

Cupola A small structure built on top of a roof for a lookout or to provide interior lighting; commonly used in Georgian, Federal, and Victorian structures.

Cyma curve A double curve formed by the union of a concave and convex line.

Dado The lower part of an interior wall when treated in a different manner from the wall above; usually defined by a molding called a dado cap or chair railing.

Daub A sticky or heavy mud or plaster infill between half-timber construction work with wattle.

Day-bed An extended type of couch or chair that can be used as a bed.

Decibel Unit by which sound is measured.

Design The planned arrangement of basic elements and principles that work together to create an image, object, or environment.

Design concept statement A statement outlining the goals and needs of the end users for a specific design project.

Design development A phase of design that involves specific selections of FF&E and illustrated 3-D designs.

Design process A progression of steps involving the analysis and synthesis of the design solution.

Direct lighting See *downlighting*.

Distressed Refers to a surface treatment for antique reproductions when the furniture is intentionally damaged to provide an aged appearance.

Doric Pertaining to the simplest of the three orders of ancient Greek architecture.

Dormer A window in a small gablelike projection built out from a sloping roof.

Double glazing A process of hermetically sealing two sheets of glass together with air trapped between. Provides efficient insulation against heat and cold.

Double-hung window A window divided into two sections, one lowering from the top and the other rising from the bottom. Each section is called a sash.
Dovetail joint A type of wood joint used in furniture construction consisting of two slotted fan-shaped pieces that interlock.
Dowel A round wood peg. Often used for furniture joinery, the peg is inserted into a cavity of the same size.
Dower chest A chest to hold items for a prospective bride. In early Pennsylvania it took on distinctive characteristics.
Downlighting Recessed or ceiling-mounted architectural lighting with lamps that direct the light downward. Sometimes called *direct lighting*. Downlights produce general lighting.
Dresden Fine porcelain made in Meissen, near Dresden, Germany. Established 1710–1720, the factory produced some of the most famous china in Europe.
Drop-leaf table A table with one or two hinged members that can drop to the sides or be supported to provide a larger tabletop surface.
Drywall A type of wallboard applied to studs. May also be called sheetrock, plasterboard, or gypsumboard.
Dutch door A single-hinged door divided horizontally so each section can be opened independently.
Ears Small squares or rectangles outlined with moldings. Found on the edges of some chimneypieces, doors, or other architectural details.
Eave A protecting lower edge of a roof which overhangs the walls of a building.
Eclecticism Mixing furnishings or borrowing styles from various sources and periods with an eye to compatibility.
Efficacy In lighting, measures the efficiency of a lamp.
Egg-and-dart A classical Greek molding consisting of ovoid (egg-shaped) forms alternating with dartlike designs.
Egress The direct route to exit a building. Commonly used in life safety/fire codes.
Elements of design The "tools" used by the designer to create an environment and achieve the goals or principles of design. The elements are space, line, shape and mass, texture, color, light, and pattern.
Elevation Two-dimensional drawings of walls.
Ell A wing or extension placed at a right angle to the structure.
Elliptical fanlight A fan-shaped window that tops doorways or other windows.
End user The client or the client's client; the person who ultimately uses the interior space.
Entablature The upper part of a wall, usually supported by columns or pilasters and in classical orders consisting of the architrave, friezé, and cornice.
Ergonomics The study of human beings and their responses to various working conditions and environments.
Escutcheon In hardware, refers to a shaped plate for a keyhole or a metal fitting to which a handle or knob is attached.
Etagere A series of shelves supported by vertical supports; used chiefly for display.
Eyeball In lighting, a ceiling-mounted or recessed fixture with a pivoting spherical lamp that can be maneuvered to direct the light where desired.
Fabrics Fibers and yarns made into cloth.
Facade Refers to the exterior front of a building, either decorative or structural.
Fanlight See *elliptical fanlight*.
Fascia The vertical portion of the eave.
Fauteuil (fau tool) The French term for an open armchair.
Faux finish A "false" impression of a natural material. For e ample, to finish a surface so it looks like wood, marble, granite.
Fenestration The placement, type, and design of windo and other openings found on a building or wall.
Festoon A carved, molded, or painted classical ornament re resenting a decorative chain, swag, or strip.
FF&E Furniture, finishes, and equipment.
Fiber A natural or synthetic substance processed into a thre or yarn of continuous length.
Fiberglass Glass fibers used for fabric or molded for furnitu furniture parts, or skylights.
FIDER Foundation for Interior Design Education Research.
Filament A threadlike conductor (as of carbon or metal) th is rendered incandescent (brilliant) by the passage of an ele tric current.
Finial An upright ornament that forms the upper extremity an architectural detail, a piece of furniture, or an accessor
Fish-scale shingles Small pointed or rounded shingles th provide decorative interest on the exterior of the Que Anne Victorian house.
Fixture In lighting, the physical structure that supports t lamp and other necessary and decorative accoutrements.
Flemish gable A gable composed of graceful curves or ste An architectural detail especially used by the Dutch settle
Fluorescent lighting Artificial light produced when gaseous mixture of mercury and argon, sealed within a gl tube that is lined with a fluorescent coating, is activated an electrical current.
Fluting Parallel concave grooves commonly used on t shafts of columns.
Foil Anything that serves, by contrast of color, pattern, textu or other elements, to adorn or set off another thing to a vantage; also, a wallpaper with the appearance of a th sheet of metal; a background.
Footcandle An international unit of light measurement. It the illumination at a 1-ft. distance from the light of one ca dle falling onto a 1-ft. square surface. The intensity of ligh calculated in footcandles.
Footings Structural foundation of a building.
Footlambert In lighting, the unit of measure for reflected lig
French doors Single-hinged doors of paned glass, sometim paired; a walk-through window that swings either inward outward.
Fresco The art of painting on moist lime plaster with wat based pigments.
Fretwork Interlaced ornamental work either perforated or c in low relief, usually in geometric patterns; also, tracery glazed doors and windows.
Friezé The horizontal decorative section found between t architrave and the cornice in classical architecture.
Fusuma screen A sliding movable screen used in Japane houses as a partition to define space.
Gable The triangular-shaped end portion of a building form by a pitched roof.
Galerie A term for a covered porch found on the French hon
Gallery A miniature railing placed along the edge of a tab top or shelf.
Gambrel roof A roof made from two lengths of lumber, t upper one being flatter and the lower one a steeper slope
Generic In textile use, a term pertaining to the characterist of a particular type or class of fibers.

eodesic dome A dome of interlocking polygons held together by a self-supporting network of rods and covered with a variety of materials; usually a plastic membrane or glass.

ingerbread Lacy architectural detail.

lass block Hollow glass forms in a variety of sizes and textures used in building construction to emit light.

lazing (paint treatment) A type of painted surface treatment achieved by applying layers of colored transparent paint to produce a striated effect.

lazing (windows) Placement of window glass in an architectural opening.

olden mean The division of a line somewhere between $\frac{1}{2}$ and $\frac{1}{3}$ its length.

olden rectangle Rectangle with width to length proportion of 2:3.

olden section The division of a line or form in such a way that the ratio of the smaller portion to the larger is the same as that of the larger portion to the whole. Sometimes called the golden ratio.

radation A type of rhythm produced by the succession of the size of an object from large to small or of a color from dark to light.

rain Refers to the vertical configurations or textural (coarse or fine) features of wood.

ray goods or greige Woven fabrics that have not been dyed, treated, or changed from their natural state.

reen design Interiors and products designed to be environmentally friendly and sustainable.

rotesques Decorative architectural treatment incorporating fanciful human/animal forms.

rout A mortar (generally of cement) used to set tiles or fill in cavities.

alf-timber construction Construction of timber frame, with the spaces filled with masonry or lath and plaster.

and or handle The feel of an object or drape of a fabric.

ardware Metal fittings used for furniture such as keyholes, drawer, and cupboard pulls.

eader In construction, the structural member over a door, window, or other opening that transfers the weight to the side supports.

ID High-intensity discharge lighting.

ieroglyphics Inscriptions on walls, some telling pictorial stories.

ighboy A tall chest of drawers supported on tall legs and divided horizontally into two sections; particularly popular during the Georgian period.

ip roof A roof with sloping ends and sloping sides.

ue The distinct name of a color such as blue, orange, or yellow. One of the three dimensions of color in the Munsell color system.

utch An informal chest or cabinet common to many countries, which came to America from England. The type most commonly used has bottom doors and open upper shelves.

VAC Heating, ventilating, and air-conditioning systems.

AQ Indoor Air Quality.

DC Interior Designers of Canada.

DEC Interior Design Educators Council.

IDA International Interior Design Association.

kebana The Japanese term for the art of arranging flowers according to precise rules.

Incandescent lamps Light produced by heating a filament sealed in a light bulb.

Indigenous Inherent; native to or living naturally in an environment.

Indirect lighting See *uplighting*.

Ingress A term referring to the entrance into a building.

Inlay Pieces of stone, wood, shell, metal, or ivory arranged in a design composition and set into another piece of wood or other material for a decorative effect.

Intensity A dimension of color that denotes the dullness or brightness of a hue. Also referred to as *chroma*.

Ionic The Greek order designated by the spiral volutes of its capital.

Jack-arch lintel See *crown lintel*.

Jacquard A special loom designed by Joseph-Marie Jacquard to produce intricate weaves. Weaves produced on the loom, such as damasks and tapestries, are called Jacquard weaves.

Jalousie window A window made of narrow horizontal and adjustable glass louvers that control ventilation and light.

Jamb The vertical side sections of a window or door.

Jetty The overhang produced when a second floor of a building extends over the first.

Kelvin A measurement of a light's temperature.

Ladderback A term describing a chair with a back composed of horizontal slats resembling a ladder.

Lambrequin An ornamental window treatment, usually in the form of a wooden frame across the top and down the sides of the window, either painted or covered with fabric.

Laminate The binding of layers of materials together. In paneling, several layers are laid alternately across the grain for strength and durability. For decorative purposes, a thin layer of fine wood (veneer) is glued to the surface of the base wood; a process also used for plastics.

Lamp The light source (bulb or tube) of artificial lighting.

Lath Thin strips of wood or a metal mesh attached to the structural frame of a building to support plaster, tile, reinforced concrete, or other material.

Lathe A machine used to turn wood or metal into various shapes.

Latillas Crude sticks laid between the vigas (pole beams) in the Southwest adobe-style home.

Law of chromatic distribution The large areas should be covered in the most neutralized colors of the scheme. As the areas reduce in size, the chromatic intensity may be proportionally increased.

Life-cycle costing Analysis of a product's total costs from conception through disposal.

Light emitting diode lamp or LED's Light produced without a heated filament. Strands of light are typically grouped together in interior applications. Used for accent lighting.

Linenfold A Gothic decorative detail depicting a stylized folded linen fabric.

Lintel The horizontal beam or component that spans the area between openings such as columns, windows, and doors.

Louver A slatted panel (usually wood) for controlling the flow of air and the radiation of light; most often used as a window treatment.

Lowboy A low chest of drawers supported on legs; particularly associated with the Georgian style.

Lumen A measure of the flow of light produced by one lamp.

Luminaire A complete light fixture including the lamp and all supportive elements.

Mansard roof A roof having two slopes on all sides, the lower one steeper than the upper one. The roof usually conceals a second or third floor.
Mantel The shelf that projects from a chimneypiece.
Marbleizing A painted surface treatment that imitates the texture of polished marble.
Marlborough leg A square straight leg with a square foot most often associated with Chippendale furniture.
Marquetry A decorative inlay design glued into furniture and floors employing a variety of woods or other materials.
Masonry Construction materials of stone, bricks, tiles, blocks, or other material joined with mortar.
Matrix A diagram indicating adjacencies between individuals, departments, or spaces.
Matte A dull finish.
Metamerism The effect of various types of light in changing the appearance of a color.
Metope In classic architecture, the square panels between the triglyphs found on the entablature of the Doric order.
Miter Joining two members of material at a 45-degree angle to form a corner.
Modern style A new art form that breaks all ties with previous design forms and styles.
Modillion An ornamental bracket (usually console shaped) that often supports a cornice or soffit.
Modular Constructed with standardized units or modules.
Module One in a series of standardized units to be integrated together, such as building construction units or a set of furniture.
Molding An architectural wood strip, usually decorative, that projects from the ceiling or wall surface; may also be of metal, plaster, or plastic.
Monochromatic A color scheme that uses one color with varying value and chroma.
Monotone A color scheme that uses one color of very low chroma, neutralized.
Mordant Any substance that serves to produce a fixed color in a textile fiber, leather, or other similar material.
Mortise and tenon A type of joint used in furniture construction with a projecting tenon that fits into the mortise or cavity.
Mosaic A floor or wall decoration made up of small pieces of stone or glass arranged in a design.
Mottle A dripped or irregular color.
Mullion A vertical member dividing glazed doors, windows, or bookcases.
Munsell color theory A color theory based on three dimensions of color: hue, value, and chroma. Each color has a number notation.
Muntin A horizontal bar dividing the panes of a window, door, or bookcase. The term is often used interchangeably with mullion.
Nap A fuzzy surface found on fabrics composed of short fibers or hairs.
Nave The principal section of a church, usually flanked by the aisles and extending from the entrance to the altar or chancel.
NCIDQ National Council for Interior Design Qualification.
Newel post The main post at the foot of a stairway.
Niche A shallow recess in an exterior or interior wall; usually with a rounded head.
Nogging The brickwork (or infill) found between half-timbe construction.
Nonarchitectural lighting Any type of luminaire that i portable.
Nosing The projecting edge at the top of a stair's riser.
Open office planning A large office space where division are made by modular furnishings to create workstations.
Orders of architecture In classical Grecian architecture: th Doric, Ionic, and Corinthian styles of columns.
Organic design or architecture Modern architectural ap proach put forth by Frank Lloyd Wright. The house shoul "grow out of the land."
Orientation Placement or arrangement of various element such as buildings, windows, rooms, or furnishings in relatio to points on the compass or other elements.
Ormolu mount A decorative treatment usually applied to fu niture; made from copper and zinc alloy to look like gold Common in French design.
Ostwald color theory A color theory based on the yellow red, blue, and green and the amount of black and whit added to a hue.
Ottoman A general term for a large upholstered footstool.
Palladian window A window consisting of three vertic parts with the central section higher than the flanking one and surmounted by a fanlight.
Panic hardware In commercial design, hardware on a doc that opens when pushed against.
PAR lamp Reflective parabolic aluminized reflector lamp.
Parapet A low wall or protective railing at the edge of a roc or platform.
Parquetry A mosaic of wood laid in geometric patterns.
Parti Usually an abstract or geometric sketch that helps to for the basis of a design concept. The shape or forms of the par are reflected in characteristics of the interior environment.
Passive solar energy system A system of collecting, storing and distributing solar heat by employing elements of th structure.
Paterae Oval or round decorative details, particularly use during the Neoclassic era.
Patina A mellow surface often developed with age.
Patio A courtyard.
Pavilion A part of a building projecting from the main structure
Pedestal A support at the base of a column; any base or foun dation on which to display an art object.
Pediment A triangular architectural structure above a portico window, or door.
Pembroke table A small table with one drawer and drop leave
Pendant An object suspended from above.
Pendant chandelier A light suspended from the ceiling wit a single fixture.
Pent roof A small projected eave found above the first story
Period style A term used to designate a single item or a con plete interior including the architectural background, furni ture, and decorative arts prevalent in a specific country or a particular time in history.
Peristyle A series of columns surrounding a structure. Also, garden surrounded by columns at the back of an ancient Ro man house.
Piece dyeing Color is added to a fabric after it is woven.
Pier A rectangular pillar devoid of detail.

aster An upright rectangular or circular projection or partial column fixed to a wall, architecturally treated as a column.
ched roof A sloping roof, either a low or high pitch.
n A drawn arrangement of elements in a structure indicating walls, rooms, spaces, and so forth shown looking down at the floor.
num Area between the ceiling of one level and the floor of the next. Usually conceals mechanical, electrical, and plumbing systems.
wood A process of laminating layers of wood with alternating grain direction. Usually the top layer or veneer is of a finer quality; used for furniture and paneling.
E Postoccupancy evaluation.
rtfolio A flexible case used by designers containing renderings, pictures, and other design-related projects.
rtico A projection from the main structure of a building over the front entrance, supported by columns and often capped by a pediment.
ng color wheel Another term for the standard color wheel.
fabricated (prefab) Mass-produced in standardized modules or parts for later assembly at the factory or building site.
nciples of design The goals of a design composition consisting of scale, proportion, balance, rhythm, emphasis, and harmony.
ogramming The information-gathering phase of the design process.
oxemics A study of spatial needs of humans relating to personal and cultural aspects.
eblo One of the Native American tribes of New Mexico; a Native American village built in the form of apartment houses.
nch list A final list indicating all items still to be completed on a construction or design project.
oin A solid material at the corner of a building distinguished from the adjoining surface by material, color, size, or projection.
bbeted A type of joint where one edge has a groove cut the entire width to accommodate a straight edge piece.
dial balance Balance created from a central point.
gging and rag rolling A wall surface treatment where paint is partially wiped or rolled off with a rag.
il The horizontal member of a door frame or panel.
nch style Also known as a California ranch or rambler home; a ground-hugging single-level plan with a low-pitched overhanging roof supported by posts.
ndom plank Wood planks laid in a manner disregarding the width of individual boards.
eding A small convex molding, the reverse of fluting; used on columns, pilasters, and furniture.
flected ceiling plan Commercial design lighting plan in a set of construction drawings. May include HVAC and sprinkler information.
plica An accurate reproduction.
poussé Relief work done on metal, created by hammering the material on the reverse side.
production A precise duplication of an historic style; a replica.
silience The ability of a particular material to give or spring back when pressed.
ythm Elements in a room that assist the eye in moving easily from one area to another.

Riser The upright member between two stair treads.
Sash The framework (in a window or door) in which the glass is set. It may constitute a movable part.
Schematic design See *conceptual design.*
Sconce A lighting fixture secured to the wall.
Scope of services The tasks that designers will perform in order to complete a specific client's job; used when describing the responsibilities of the designer in a business contract.
Section A cut-through view of a building, interior wall, cabinet, or other interior component.
Shade A color that has been darkened by adding black; a low value.
Shed In ceiling design, the area formed by one wall extended higher than the opposite wall, also called a lean-to.
Shibui (shih BOO ee) Japanese approach to beauty; appreciation of serenity, not ostentation.
Shoji A basic element of a Japanese house, made of panes of rice paper and wooden mullions and used as an exterior window. Shoji panels are also employed as wall partitions and freestanding screens.
Sick building syndrome An unhealthy environment with stale or polluted air.
Sidelight A vertical window placed beside a door.
Sillplate Construction member that secures the floor to the foundation.
Simultaneous contrast When a hue, value, or chroma is perceived as different as a result of being viewed beside or on a different colored background.
Soffit A lower section of a ceiling; area underneath this section.
Solution dyeing Color is added to the fiber in its liquid state.
Space planning The process of determining square footage requirements and then manipulating the spaces into an appropriate arrangement to meet the client's needs. May involve the use of a matrix, bubble, blocking, and stacking diagrams, and furniture plans.
Specifications or spec book Written directions indicating appropriate means to produce or purchase furniture, furnishings, and equipment.
Spinneret A device (similar to a showerhead in appearance) through which liquid viscose is forced to form manufactured fibers.
Stacking diagram A chart or graph indicating on which floors individuals, departments, or spaces will be placed. Used in conceptual design.
Standard milled items Items of various kinds (e.g., doors, door frames, windows, window frames, and mantels) made in standard sizes in large quantities in the factory, thus making the cost much less than for custom-made items.
Stepped gable A gable in which the sides ascend to the peak in steps.
Stile The vertical or upright supportive frame for a door.
Stock dyeing Color is added to fibers before they are processed into yarns.
Stretcher The horizontal supportive crosspiece spanning the area between the legs of a chair or table.
Stringcourse A narrow horizontal band placed on the exterior of the Georgian house between the first and the second floors.
Stucco A type of plaster surface treatment used on exterior or interior walls.

Subtractive color Color that is visible to the eye via the reflection of wavelength not absorbed by an object.

Sustainable design Designs incorporating energy conscious and environmentally friendly elements and products.

Swag A festoon of flowers or fruit. May also refer to a gathering of fabric at the top of a window, gently draped over each end.

Symmetrical balance Balance is created by objects arranged equally on either side of an imaginary line.

Synthetic Something artificial simulating the genuine piece.

Systems furniture Flexible type of component furniture that can be arranged and rearranged to accommodate various needs for workstations.

Tambour The front of a piece of furniture made with strips of wood attached to fabric and adjusted on a track, allowing it to open and close.

Task lighting Lighting designed for specific types of work or tasks.

Tatami mat A soft straw mat, approximately 3 ft. by 6 ft. by 1 in., which is the basic element of the Japanese house and serves as a unit of measurement, determining the size and proportion of all spaces. The dark lines of its binding form an overall grid pattern, according to which rooms are sized.

Templates Small patterns of furniture (either to cut or trace) used as guides in planning rooms.

Terrace Usually refers to a relatively level paved area adjoining a building.

Textile A general term used to describe a fiber, yarn, or fabric.

Tint A color that is lightened by adding white; a high value.

Tokonoma A sacred recessed niche or alcove in the Japanese house.

Tone A neutralized hue produced by adding gray or the color's complement.

Tongue-and-groove joint The rib on one edge of a board is made to fit into a corresponding groove in the edge of another board to make a flush joint.

Torchère A tall floor lamp with a design that casts light in an upward direction. Particularly popular for Art Deco and Post-Modern styles.

Trabeated construction Post and lintel design for structural support; developed by the Egyptians.

Tracery Decorative carved stone or wood openwork; associated with Gothic design.

Traffic lanes In design, refers to the walkways or passages.

Transept The lateral arms (across the nave) of cruciform churches.

Transom Small window above a door or window.

Tray In ceiling design, the area that extends vertically above the lower ceiling. Usually a 6″–18″ rise.

Tread The horizontal section of a stair.

Trompe l'oeil French expression meaning "to fool the eye"; a term applied to two-dimensional decoration showing a three-dimensional drawing or effect.

Truss system A triangular construction system for structu support; developed by the Greeks.

Tryglyph Greek for "thrice grooved." On a Doric friezé, t blocks that alternate with the metopes.

Tudor arch A low or flattened elliptical arch.

Turning See *lathe.*

Universal design Spaces and furnishings created to meet t needs of individuals regardless of age and ability.

Uplighting Suspended or wall-mounted lighting with lam that direct the light up. Sometimes called *indirect lighting*

Valance A short decorative fabric treatment at the top of window that conceals drapery, curtains, and often lighting

Value The lightness or darkness of a color, on a scale fro white to black.

Vaulted In ceiling design, the area formed beneath the arch

Veneer Thin sheets of wood or other material (usually of fi quality) used as a top surface over other more ordinary m terials such as particleboard.

Veranda An open galley or portico (usually roofed) attach to the exterior of a building.

Vernacular Reference to the distinguishing attributes or qu ities of a certain culture.

Vigas The large exposed pole beams that support the roof the Southwest adobe structure.

Villa (Italian) A large residential structure.

Visual communications The drawings, plans, and presen tion materials designers create to visually explain the desi to the client prior to implementation.

Visual literacy The effective application of design eleme and principles coupled with an understanding of pattern, dering, and visual perception.

Volume The area that occupies any space including the wid depth, and height.

Volute The spiral-shaped decoration that tops the capital the Ionic column.

Wainscoting Wood paneling that extends partway to the ce ing, associated with the medieval-style interior.

Wall-washer In lighting, a ceiling-mounted or recessed fixtu with a lens that focuses the light on the wall or object.

Warp Vertical or lengthwise threads in a woven fabric.

Wattle Interlacing twigs that function as infilling for timb framed structures. Wattle and daub often work together.

Weft Horizontal threads in a woven fabric, also called filli threads.

Working drawings See *construction drawings.*

Wrought iron Ornamental iron that has been worked int decorative shape or design.

Yarn Twisted or assembled fibers that produce cloth.

Yarn dyeing Color is added to yarns before they are wov into fabrics.

Zapata A carved decorative supportive bracket found on t Southwest adobe house.

ndex

G

H

I

N

O

P